ROMANTICISM
AN ANTHOLOGY

EDITED BY
DUNCAN WU

BLACKWELL
Oxford UK & Cambridge USA

First published 1994

Reprinted 1995, 1996 (twice)

Blackwell Publishers Ltd
108 Cowley Road
Oxford OX4 1JF, UK

Blackwell Publishers Inc.
238 Main Street
Cambridge, Massachusetts 02142, USA

British Library Cataloguing in Publication Data
A CIP catalogue record for this book is available from the British Library

Library of Congress Cataloging in Publication Data
Romanticism : an anthology/edited by Duncan Wu
p. cm. - (Blackwell anthologies)
Includes bibliographical references (p.) and index
ISBN 0-631-19195-X - ISBN 0-631-19196-8 (pbk.)
1. English literature - 19th century. 2. English literature - 18th
century. 3. Romanticism - Great Britain. I. Wu. Duncan
II Series.
PR1139.R66   1994   94-7570
820.8'0145 - dc20   CIP

Cover illustration: John Martin, *Manfred on the Jungfrau*, 1837, water-colour and
body colour, 38.4 x 57.5 cm, reproduced by kind permission of Birmingham
Museum and Art Gallery

Typeset in 9.5 x 11 pt Garamond by Pure Tech Corporation, Pondicherry, India
Printed in Great Britain by T.J. Press Ltd, Padstow, Cornwall

This book is printed on acid-free paper

Contents

Introduction

I

The last three decades have been eventful ones for Romanticists. Years of scholarly and critical activity have led to a drastic revision of the literary canon, proving its power to renew itself. This anthology aims to bring the fruits of this work to students of the period.

The revolution in Romantic studies has been led by scholars: returning to manuscripts and early printed sources, they have produced editions more accurate and more consistent than any published previously. In certain cases they have added, often considerably, to the range of works ascribed to particular authors. For instance, most readers of Wordsworth have until recently had to rely on the revised texts edited by the poet himself for his final lifetime edition of 1849–50. Many completed poems, or versions of poems, were never formally published by him, and were known only to his family and close friends. The textual history of *The Prelude*, now regarded as among his finest achievements in verse, has been particularly hazardous. A much-revised fourteen-book version of the poem was published only after his death, in a text embodying numerous alterations by his literary executors (exemplifying the argument that the acts of publication, and even composition, are collaborative). Only after Ernest de Selincourt's 1926 Clarendon edition made the thirteen-book poem available for the first time did it begin to attract serious critical attention, more than a century after it was written. The breakthrough in Wordsworth scholarship came in 1975 with the publication of the first volume in the Cornell Wordsworth Series, under the general editorship of Stephen M. Parrish. Beginning with a detailed bibliographical breakdown of the poet's manuscripts and printed works, the series makes available reading texts of scores of hitherto unknown poems or early versions, many of which are just as good as those published by Wordsworth. Readers can now consult a multiplicity of versions and works unknown to earlier readers.[1]

---

[1] This has stimulated valuable debate about the place of the author's intentions; contributions include Stephen M. Parrish, 'The Whig Interpretation of Literature', *Text*, 4 (1988), 343–50; Jack Stillinger,

In a similar manner, the Collected Coleridge Series initiated by Kathleen Coburn, also still in progress, has enlarged the Coleridge canon; it is now possible to consult printed texts of the poet's lectures, notebooks, and annotations to the books he read. J. C. C. Mays's forthcoming synoptic edition of the poetry will enable readers to see, for the first time, the numerous layers of revision beneath the received texts.[2] Donald H. Reiman and the scholars working with him are in the process of completing an exhaustive bibliographical survey of Shelley's manuscripts and printed works preparatory to the first comprehensive edition of his poetry and prose. And within the last twenty years Jack Stillinger, G. E. Bentley, Jr., and Jerome J. McGann, have published new editions of the works of Keats, Blake, and Byron, that will remain the critical standard for years to come.

The revival in the fortunes of John Clare is symptomatic of recent developments. Clare has published a good deal more since the early 1970s than during his lifetime,[3] culminating in 1989 and 1984 respectively with the appearance of his *Early Poems* and *Later Poems*, both edited by Eric Robinson and David Powell. A complete edition of Clare's prose and poetry has yet to appear.

Readers are now in possession of more information about the evolution of literary works than ever, bringing us closer to the bibliographical details and politics of their publication. We may now compare different versions of the same poem, or discuss the implications of manuscript drafts, many of which have been published in facsimile. And we are better informed than ever about authors' involvement in the publishing process; their collaboration with amanuenses, editors, publishers, and printers; and critical responses to their work.

But the advances made by textual critics account only in part for the renewed importance of Romantic studies. The last three decades have seen an explosion of critical activity in the field, traceable through such 'landmark' works of criticism as Harold Bloom's *The Visionary Company* (1961), Geoffrey Hartman's *Wordsworth's Poetry, 1787–1814* (1964), M. H. Abrams's *Natural Supernaturalism* (1971), and Jerome J. McGann's *The Romantic Ideology* (1983). Generations of commentators have reacted to the insights offered by these writers, sometimes consolidating their findings, sometimes generating alternative schools of thought. This is hardly the place for a survey of Romantic criticism over the last thirty years, but it is worth pointing out that it has become increasingly diverse and prolific, and shows no sign of slowing down. This process of renewal comes down in part to the amorphous nature of Romanticism itself – which can be explained, in turn, by the fact that it is largely the invention of critics themselves. In 1798, not even Wordsworth and Coleridge saw themselves as beginning a literary movement, and as late as 1816 Byron believed that Classical and Romantic 'were not subjects of Classification in England'.[4] Even now, the relation of Byron himself to those categories remains problematic. In fact, Romanticism is subject to

---

'Textual Primitivism and the Editing of Wordsworth', *Studies in Romanticism*, 28 (1989), 3–28; Duncan Wu, 'Editing Intentions', *Essays in Criticism*, 41 (1991), 1–10; and Zachary Leader, 'Wordsworth, Revision, and Personal Identity', *English Literary History*, 60 (1993), 651–83.

[2] See J. C. C. Mays, 'Reflections on Having Edited Coleridge's Poems', in *Romantic Revisions*, ed. Keith

Hanley and Robert Brinkley (Cambridge, 1992), pp. 136–53.

[3] For a detailed account see Greg Crossan's interim report, 'John Clare's Poetry: An Examination of the Textual Accuracy of Some Recent Editions', *Studies in Romanticism*, 24 (1985), 581–98.

[4] Byron's rejected Dedication to *Marino Faliero* (1820).

redefinition partly because the authors included here never perceived themselves as advocates of a common cause in quite the same way as, say, the Imagists or the Pre-Raphaelite Brotherhood. Agreement may be found among some of them at certain times, but no manifesto could embrace such diverse productions as *Urizen, The Prelude, Don Juan, Prometheus Unbound,* and *Kubla Khan.*

This built-in susceptibility to the perceiving eye of the critic is one of the strengths of the subject. Over the years, the boundaries of the accepted canon have been pushed back to reveal fugitive or hitherto undiscovered Romanticisms. For instance, one writer has observed that 'The age of English Romanticism is an age of revolutions'.[5] The revolution debate, which was initiated by Richard Price and inspired Burke, Paine, Wollstonecraft, and Godwin, was a formative influence on Wordsworth and Coleridge, and in turn shaped the thinking of the generation that followed them. Besides the renewed interest in the political content of literary works, this has encouraged an interest in the circumstances of their publication. One effect of this has been to highlight the various forms in which literary works appeared – including the pamphlet, the broadside (the form in which Hannah More published her Cheap Repository Tracts), newspapers, and periodicals. Many of the contributors to these were women, and only in the last ten years have critics begun to revalue the work of such writers as Felicia Dorothea Hemans, Letitia Elizabeth Landon, Caroline Norton, Lady Caroline Lamb, and Anna Laetitia Barbauld. The bibliographical terrain surrounding this important area has been mapped out by J. R. de J. Jackson.[6]

In their various ways, these developments are driven by a preoccupation with issues, an important one being that of race. A triumph of the age was the abolition of slavery in 1807, after a long and arduous fight led by Wilberforce and Clarkson. Recent critics have examined how concerns about slavery and racial attitudes influenced writers including Cowper, Coleridge, Southey, Ann Yearsley, Mrs Barbauld, and Thomas Campbell, as well as Lamb and De Quincey. At the same time critics have explored how the literature of the eighteenth century fed into Romanticism, and how Romantic writers affected the work of the Victorians who followed them.

II

If critics create their own versions of Romanticism, so too do anthologists. While aware of the extent to which personal taste has governed my selection, I have given priority to the needs of contemporary readers. To ascertain what these are, I sought the views and advice of many teachers of the subject before finalizing the contents. It is my hope that the student or general reader coming fresh to the subject will need no other primary text. Complete works have been preferred to extracts; in particular, the book is dominated by Wordsworth's *Thirteen-Book Prelude.* Wordsworth was a central literary personality, and was perceived as such by second-generation Romantics. Although this poem was unknown to most of his contemporaries, it influenced Coleridge and De Quincey, and is now regarded as one of his finest achievements. The present text has been newly edited from the original manuscripts for this volume. Readers are not

---

[5] Jonathan Wordsworth, Michael C. Jaye, and Robert Woof, *William Wordsworth and the Age of English Romanticism* (New Brunswick, N. J., 1987), p. 1.

[6] See his bibliography *Romantic Poetry by Women* (Oxford, 1993).

restricted to highlights (as they are in comparable anthologies), but have access to the entire work, with all its fluctuations of tone, mood, and rhythm. Complete texts of some other long poems are also included: namely, Blake's *The Marriage of Heaven and Hell* and *The Book of Urizen*, Byron's *Manfred* and *Don Juan* (Dedication and Canto I), Shelley's *Prometheus Unbound*, *The Mask of Anarchy* and *Adonais*, and Keats's *Hyperion* and *The Fall of Hyperion*. Coleridge's poetry is more comprehensively selected than in other anthologies of this kind. Besides different versions of 'The Ancient Mariner' and 'Dejection: An Ode', it includes all the 'conversation poems', early printed texts of 'Kubla Khan' and 'Christabel', much of the 1802 poetry, including 'The Picture' and 'Chamouny; the Hour Before Sunrise. A Hymn', as well as the complete text of 'On Donne's First Poem', which until now has been known only as two separate works, 'Ne Plus Ultra' and 'Limbo'.[7] Two important volumes of the period are presented in full and in sequence, so as to preserve their integrity as distinct titles: Blake's *Songs of Innocence and Experience* and Wordsworth's and Coleridge's *Lyrical Ballads* (1798).

Women Romantics are represented, ranging from such writers of sensibility as Charlotte Smith and Helen Maria Williams to early Victorians like Elizabeth Barrett. Besides selections from the work of Mary Tighe, Mrs Hemans, and Letitia Landon, it includes most of Dorothy Wordsworth's poems from her Commonplace Book, newly edited for this volume, and a complete text of Lady Caroline Lamb's neglected response to Byron, *A New Canto* [of *Don Juan*] (1819), which, as one recent critic has noted, 'fizzes with verbal inventiveness'.[8] Lamb's success in both emulating Byron's world-weary narrative voice and subverting it has gone unrecognized, partly because her poem has seldom been reprinted since its first appearance. The major participants in the Revolution debate are present here, along with letter-writers, diarists, broadside balladeers, painters, and reviewers.

Essays are generally included in full. This volume contains complete texts of Lamb's 'Imperfect Sympathies' and 'Witches, and Other Night-Fears', Hazlitt's 'On Gusto', 'My First Acquaintance with Poets', and 'Mr Coleridge', Leigh Hunt's 'A Now, Descriptive of a Hot Day', and De Quincey's 'On the Knocking at the Gate in Macbeth'. For obvious reasons I have been able to provide only excerpts from the longer prose works. Although I have drawn the line at fiction – the anthologist prepared to extract from *Frankenstein* and *Mansfield Park* needs nerves stronger than mine – I have included non-fiction by novelists: Edgeworth and Scott reflect on their craft, and Mary Shelley is represented by poetry and editorial work.

There are numerous connections between the various items, some picked up in footnotes – although readers will enjoy discovering for themselves those which are not. Shelley, for instance, was not alone in writing an elegy on Keats: Taylor's 'Sonnet on the Death of the Poet J. Keats' and Hood's 'Ode: Autumn' and 'Sonnet Written in Keats' Endymion' appear below. Poems addressed to the youthful Coleridge constitute a similar sub-genre and include Anna Laetitia Barbauld's 'To Mr Coleridge', Mary Robinson's 'Mrs Robinson to the Poet Coleridge', and Thelwall's 'Lines Written at

---

[7] The detachment of 'Limbo' and 'Ne Plus Ultra' from each other, and indeed from the poem of which they are both part, 'On Donne's First Poem', has been deplored by, among others, Frederick Burwick, 'Coleridge's "Limbo" and "Ne Plus Ultra":

The Multeity of Intertextuality', *Romanticism Past and Present*, 9 (1985), 35–45.
[8] *The Feminist Companion to Literature in English*, ed. Virginia Blain, Patricia Clements, and Isobel Grundy (London, 1990), p. 624.

Bridgwater in Somersetshire, on 27 July 1797, during a Long Excursion in Quest of a Peaceful Retreat'. The image of the flowing river, which runs through Wordsworth's *Thirteen-Book Prelude*, may be traced to Coleridge's 'To the River Otter', Bowles's 'To the River Itchin, near Winton', and Warton's 'To the River Lodon'.

That image befits the evolving discourse between the writers here represented – how indebted, for instance, Letitia Landon felt to Wordsworth, and how Elizabeth Barrett felt moved to respond to Landon's elegy on Hemans's death. Important critical responses are to be found here, including Lockhart's strictures on Keats, Jeffrey's on Wordsworth, and Southey's review of *Lyrical Ballads* (1798). Even those working against the tide, such as Landor and Crabbe, have their place. And readers may see how Elizabeth Barrett, John Stuart Mill, and Tennyson look back to the central currents of Romantic thought, while at the same time casting forward to a mood and tone uniquely Victorian.

This anthology tells the story of one of the richest periods in literary history, from its eighteenth-century beginnings to the point at which younger writers transformed it into something distinct. In doing so, it seeks to reflect both the renewal that has taken place in the canon and recent shifts in emphasis that have occurred in critical writing about the period.

Editorial Principles

This edition is designed for the use of students and the general reader, and editorial procedures have been formulated with this in mind. It also adopts the policy recommended by Coleridge on New Year's Day 1834, widely accepted as the basis for most contemporary scholarly editions: 'After all you can say, I think the chronological order is the best for arranging a poet's works. All your divisions are in particular instances inadequate, and they destroy the interest which arises from watching the progress, maturity and even the decay of Genius.'[1] This anthology is arranged chronologically, in that authors are introduced successively by date of birth. Works are placed in order of composition, where known; when not known, by date of publication. As a rule, they are presented in their earliest completed recoverable form, whether it be early printed source or manuscript.

Except for poems in dialect or in which archaic effects were deliberately sought, texts have been modernized: punctuation and orthography have been normalized, pervasive initial capitals and italics removed, and contractions expanded except when of metrical significance. Although the accidental features of late eighteenth- and early nineteenth-century printed texts do have their own intrinsic interest, it should be noted that most poets were happy to leave such matters to the printer or to collaborators of various sorts.[2] From this it follows that, where the capitalization employed throughout a work is both clearly attributable to the author and consistently applied, it should be allowed to stand – as in the case of Shelley's *Adonais*. The punctuation applied by writers to their own works is a different matter, as it is frequently misleading to the modern reader.

A number of texts are edited from manuscripts for this anthology (see pp. xxxv–xxxvii). In this case, in order to produce a clean reading text, deletions and overwritings are accepted only if made at the time of drafting; alternative readings are accepted only if accompanied by deletion of the earlier reading; errors in transcription and other scribal

---

[1] *Table Talk*, i. 453.

[2] The numerous errors in *Lyrical Ballads* (1800) were due in part to Wordsworth's reliance on Humphry Davy, whom he had not met, as punctuator and proof-reader.

errors are silently corrected, except in cases where some explanation is necessary for a full understanding of the text; and gaps in manuscripts are filled, where possible, from related sources.

There is, perhaps inevitably, an exception to this policy: John Clare, who famously told his publisher, John Taylor, that 'grammer in learning is like Tyranny in government'.[3] In editing the poet's manuscripts, Eric Robinson, his longest-serving textual critic, has consistently defended the practice of transcribing 'exactly what Clare wrote' without standardizing his spelling, punctuation, or grammar. And John Barrell has written persuasively on the significance of the fact that although Clare could punctuate, he deliberately chose not to, as he saw it as 'an imprisonment of the words of the poem, an imposition on them of a sort of *military* discipline'.[4] This procedure may at times appear over-cautious and even pedantic, especially when it leads to the reproduction of scribal errors, but it has governed most contemporary editions of Clare's work, and it would be inappropriate to challenge it here. In this exceptional case I have therefore followed other editors in reproducing the punctuation, capitalization, and grammar of the manuscripts of Clare and his copyists. ('To Elia', which derives from a printed source, is edited according to the standards applied to other printed sources in this volume.)

Limitations of space make it impossible to provide a selection of Romantic translations, as was originally planned; it would have included translations from Goethe, Rousseau, Bürger, Volney, Roland, and Louvet, to name a few. However, many of these authors' works are available in modern editions, and facsimile reprints of some Romantic translations have been published in recent years.

Dates of composition, where they can be verified, are indicated at the head of each work, alongside details of publication. Headnotes are provided for each author, each of which is designed to outline the importance of the works selected. For reasons of space it is not possible, and would not necessarily be appropriate, to provide author biographies or critical interpretations of the works selected. By the same token, my annotations are generally restricted to supplying information necessary to an understanding of the text, glossing obscure or archaic words, noting significant allusions and borrowings, and on rare occasions referring the reader to secondary material such as short articles or notes of a scholarly nature.

---

[3] *The Letters of John Clare*, ed. Mark Storey (Oxford, 1985), p. 231.

[4] *Poetry, Language and Politics* (Manchester, 1988), p. 120.

Acknowledgements

Work on this volume began with consultation of numerous colleagues, who offered kind advice on the anthology they wished to see. For that and for help of various kinds it is a pleasure to thank Jonathan Bate, Shahin Bekhradnia, Drummond Bone, Geoffrey Brackett, Richard W. Clancey, David Fairer, Richard Gravil, Jack Haeger, Keith Hanley, Anthony Harding, Brooke Hopkins, M. C. Howatson, Kenneth Johnston, Grevel Lindop, Jerome J. McGann, Philip Martin, Michael O'Neill, Roy Park, Janice Patten, Tom Paulin, Cecilia Powell, Roger Robinson, Nicholas Roe, the late William Ruddick, Charles Rzepka, William S. Smith, Jane Stabler, David Stewart, Tim Trengove-Jones, J. R. Watson, Mary Wedd, Pamela Woof, and Jonathan Wordsworth. I wish also to thank the advisers consulted by Blackwell for their comments and advice. I have received generous assistance from librarians in London, Oxford, and Grasmere; in particular, I thank B. C. Barker-Benfield and the staff of the Bodleian Library, Oxford; Elaine Scoble of the library of St Catherine's College, Oxford; the staff of the English Faculty Library, Oxford; Deborah Hedgecock of the Guildhall Library, London; and Jeff Cowton of the Wordsworth Library, Grasmere. It has been my good fortune to have been a Fellow of St Catherine's College, Oxford, during work on this book, and among friends and colleagues there, I acknowledge the generous help of Richard Parish, J. Ch. Simopoulos, and J. B. McLaughlin. Nicola Trott was my collaborator at an early stage of work on this anthology, when she played a crucial part in formulating its aims and procedures and in seeking advice from colleagues. My work has been expedited by the rapid and accurate typing of Pat Wallace; James Price of Woodstock Books kindly provided me with early printed texts of a number of the works included here; and Andrew McNeillie, my editor, offered enthusiastic and helpful counsel throughout. For a retreat in the Cotswolds where much of the editing was completed during the summer of 1993, and for help of many kinds, I thank Caroline Cochrane.

This book was produced during my tenure of a British Academy postdoctoral Fellowship; I am deeply grateful to the Academy for its kind support.

The editor and publishers wish to thank the following for permission to quote material in copyright:

Curtis Brown on behalf of Eric Robinson for material from John Clare, *The Shepherd's Calendar*, eds. Eric Robinson and Geoffrey Summerfield, Oxford University Press, 1964; and *John Clare*, eds. Eric Robinson and David Powell, The Oxford Authors, Oxford University Press, 1984. Copyright © 1964 and 1984 Eric Robinson; Harvard University Press for material from John Keats, *The Letters of John Keats*, ed. Hyder Edward Rollins, Vols. I & II. Copyright © 1958 by the President and Fellows of Harvard College; The Houghton Library, Harvard University, for material from texts of John Keats MS transcripts; and manuscript material by Mary Shelley, MS Eng 822, 2r-2v and Percy Bysshe Shelley, MS Eng 258.3, 2r-3r; The London Borough of Camden from the Collections at Keats House, Hampstead the John Keats holograph texts, 'On Sitting Down to Read King Lear Once Again' and 'Bright Star, would I were steadfast as thou art'; John Murray Publishers Ltd. for material from Lord Byron's letters from Byron's Letters and Journals, ed. Leslie Marchand; Oxford University Press for material from William Blake, *The Letters of William Blake*, ed. Geoffrey Keynes, 3rd edition, Clarendon Press, 1980; Robert Burns, *The Letters of Robert Burns*, edited by J. De Lancey Ferguson, 2nd edition, ed. G. Ross Roy, Vols. I & II Clarendon Press, 1985; Dorothy Wordsworth, *The Grasmere Journals*, ed. Pamela Woof, Clarendon Press, 1991; Samuel Taylor Coleridge, *The Letters of Samuel Taylor Coleridge*, ed. Earl Leslie Griggs, Vols. I–VI, Clarendon Press, 1956–71; George Gordon Byron, 6th Baron Byron, *The Complete Poetical Works of Lord Byron*, ed. Jerome J. McGann and Barry Weller, Vols. I–VII, Clarendon Press, 1980–93; and Percy Bysshe Shelley, *The Letters of Percy Bysshe Shelley*, ed. Frederick L. Jones, Vols. I & II, Clarendon Press, 1964; Routledge for material from Samuel Taylor Coleridge, *Table Talk*, ed. Carl Woodring, Vols I & II, 1990; Suffolk Record Society for material from John Constable, *John Constable's Correspondence*, Vol. 6, ed. R. B. Beckett, 1968; The Bodleian Library, Oxford, for material from MS texts of John Clare, George Dyer, Mary Shelley and Percy Bysshe Shelley; The Wordsworth Trust, Grasmere, for material from MS texts of Samuel Taylor Coleridge, Dorothy Wordsworth and William Wordsworth; The British Library, for material from MS texts of Samuel Taylor Coleridge and John Thelwall; Lord Abinger, for material from MS texts of Mary Shelley.

Every effort has been made to trace all the copyright holders, but if any have been inadvertently overlooked the publishers will be pleased to make the necessary arrangement at the first opportunity.

Inventory of Manuscripts

Texts in this volume were edited from the following manuscripts:

JOHN CLARE

'Sonnet' ('Ere I had known the world and understood'): copy-text is Clare's letter to Taylor and Hessey of 18 July 1822 (Bodleian Library, MS Montagu d.4, 97r), which served as press copy for the printed text published that Sept.

SAMUEL TAYLOR COLERIDGE

'To William Wordsworth': fair copy in Coleridge's hand at the Wordsworth Library, MS 14/7.

'On Donne's First Poem': draft in Coleridge's hand, BL Add. MS 47515, 145v–147v, 149r. The later, revised readings of the draft have been preferred, even where there are no crossings-out.

Letter to William Wordsworth, 30 May 1815, Wordsworth Library, MS 14/9.

GEORGE DYER

'In deep distress, I cried to God': from Dyer's fair copy notebook bearing the title 'The Blind Man's Legacy, 1836', Bodleian Library, MS Eng. poet. c.21, pp. 73–4. Hitherto unpublished.

LEIGH HUNT

'To Hampstead': copy-text from *The Examiner* (14 May 1815); draft of the poem in Hunt's hand at Bodleian Library, MS Eng. poet. e.38, 46v.

JOHN KEATS

'On Sitting Down to Read King Lear Once Again': edited from Keats's fair copy holograph in his 1808 facsimile of Shakespeare's first folio, Keats House, Hampstead.

'Sonnet' ('When I have fears that I may cease to be'): edited from Charles Brown's fair copy, MS transcript at Harvard, 20r.

'La Belle Dame Sans Merci: A Ballad': edited from Charles Brown's fair copy, MS transcript at Harvard, 7r.

'Ode on Indolence': edited from Charles Brown's fair copy, MS transcript at Harvard, 112r.

'The Fall of Hyperion': from Richard Woodhouse's fair copy, MS transcript at Harvard, 165r–181r.

'Bright star, would I were steadfast as thou art': edited from Keats's fair copy holograph on a blank page of the 1806 *Poetical Works* of William Shakespeare at Keats House, Hampstead.

MARY SHELLEY

Journals: 28 May 1817, Bodleian Library, Abinger Deposit, Dep. d.311(2), 52v–53r; 15 May 1824, Bodleian Library, Abinger Deposit, Dep. d.311(4), 38v–39r.

'On Reading Wordsworth's Lines on Peele Castle': fair copy in Mary Shelley's hand, Bodleian Library, Abinger Deposit, Dep. c.516/12.

'A Dirge': edited from Mary Shelley's press copy, now at Harvard, fMS Eng. 822, 2r–2v. Collated with the printed text in *The Keepsake* (1831), p. 35.

'Oh listen while I sing to thee': fair copy in Mary Shelley's hand, Bodleian Library, MS Shelley adds. c.5, 111r. Hitherto unpublished.

PERCY BYSSHE SHELLEY

'Hymn to Intellectual Beauty': copy-text from *The Examiner* no. 473 (19 Jan. 1817), as corrected by Shelley, Harvard MS Eng. 258.3, 2r–3r.

'Lines to Lord Byron': from fair copy, MS facsimile, Sotheby's sale catalogue, 15 Dec. 1931, Lot 713. The MS, the present whereabouts of which is unknown, may have been a leaf of Bodleian Library MS Shelley adds e.17.

'On Love': copy-text is Shelley's draft at Bodleian Library, MS Shelley adds. e.11, pp. 1–9.

'England in 1819': copy-text is Shelley's fair copy at Bodleian Library, MS Shelley adds. e.12, p. 182, entered Dec. 1819.

'Prometheus Unbound': copy-text is the flawed printed text of 1820 corrected and emended from Shelley's fair copy, Bodleian Library, MSS Shelley e.1, e.2, and e.3. Where Mary Shelley's edition of 1839 returns to the readings of the MSS, the MSS readings have been preferred over those of 1820. Errors and emendations introduced by hands other than Shelley's have been corrected from the MSS; and where the MSS provide clearer or more trustworthy readings, they have been given priority over printed sources. Shelley's capitals have been regularized, and the primary authority for punctuation is 1820, corrected by reference to the MSS.

'The Mask of Anarchy': text from Mary Shelley's press copy, corrected by Percy Bysshe Shelley, complete by 23 Sept. 1819, Library of Congress, MMC 1399.

'Defence of Poetry': first extract from Mary Shelley's press copy, corrected by Percy Bysshe Shelley, Mar. 1821, Bodleian Library, MS Shelley e.6; second extract from Shelley's fair copy, Bodleian Library, MS Shelley adds. c.4, ff. 221v–230r, 232r–241r.

JOHN THELWALL

Letter to S. T. Coleridge, 10 May 1796: BL MS Add. 35,344, f. 183. Hitherto unpublished.

DOROTHY WORDSWORTH

Poems edited from her Commonplace Book, Wordsworth Library, MS 120:
'A Sketch': 19r.

'A Cottage in Grasmere Vale': 19r–20r.
'After-recollection': 20r.
'A winter's ramble': 20v–21r.
'Floating Island': 29v–30r.
'Thoughts': 30v–31r.
'When shall I tread': 51r.

WILLIAM WORDSWORTH

'Dear native brooks': draft in Dorothy Wordsworth's hand, Wordsworth Library, MS 38, 14r.

Prospectus to 'The Recluse': fair copy in Wordsworth's hand, Wordsworth Library, MS 45, 2r–4r. Gaps in the MS filled from Wordsworth Library MS 59.

'These chairs they have no words to utter': draft at Wordsworth Library, MS 41, 17v.

'The Thirteen-Book Prelude': fair copies, Wordsworth Library, MSS 52, 53. Like Mark L. Reed, I present an AB-Stage text, designed to reveal the 'poet's latest preference' for his work as it stood at the end of composition in early 1806. Gaps are filled from draft MSS.

Abbreviations

EHC	*The Poetical Works of Samuel Taylor Coleridge*, ed. E. H. Coleridge (2 vols, Oxford, 1912)
FN	*The Fenwick Notes of William Wordsworth*, ed. Jared Curtis (London, 1993)
Griggs	*The Collected Letters of Samuel Taylor Coleridge*, ed. E. L. Griggs (6 vols, Oxford, 1956–71)
Jones	*The Letters of Percy Bysshe Shelley*, ed. F. L. Jones (2 vols, Oxford, 1964)
Lucas	*The Letters of Charles and Mary Lamb*, ed. E. V. Lucas (3 vols, London, 1935)
LY	*The Letters of William and Dorothy Wordsworth: The Later Years 1821–53*, ed. Ernest de Selincourt, rev. Alan G. Hill (4 vols, Oxford, 1978–88)
Marchand	*Byron's Letters and Journals*, ed. Leslie A. Marchand (12 vols, London, 1973–82)
Marrs	*The Letters of Charles and Mary Anne Lamb*, ed. Edwin W. Marrs, Jr. (3 vols, Ithaca, NY, 1975–8)
Medwin	Thomas Medwin, *Conversations of Lord Byron* (London, 1824)
Morley	*The Correspondence of Crabb Robinson with the Wordsworth Circle*, ed. Edith J. Morley (2 vols, Oxford, 1927)
MY	*The Letters of William and Dorothy Wordsworth: The Middle Years 1806–20*, ed. Ernest de Selincourt, rev. Mary Moorman and Alan G. Hill (2 vols, Oxford, 1969–70)
N&Q	*Notes and Queries*
Notebooks	*The Notebooks of Samuel Taylor Coleridge*, ed. Kathleen Coburn et al. (5 vols, New York, 1957–)
Owen and Smyser	*The Prose Works of William Wordsworth*, ed. W. J. B. Owen and Jane Worthington Smyser (3 vols, Oxford, 1974)

SC   *Shelley and his Circle 1773–1822*, ed. K. N. Cameron and
                                D. H. Reiman (8 vols, Cambridge, Mass., 1961–86)

Table Talk   S. T. Coleridge, *Table Talk*, ed. Carl Woodring (2 vols,
                                London, 1990)

The Brownings' Correspondence *The Brownings' Correspondence*, ed. Philip Kelley, Ronald
                                Hudson, and Scott Lewis (9 vols, Winfield, Kan.,
                                1984–91)

WPW   *The Poetical Works of William Wordsworth*, ed. Ernest de
                                Selincourt and Helen Darbishire (5 vols, Oxford,
                                1940–9)

Richard Price   (1723–91)

Political theorist, Unitarian minister, mathematician, and insurance expert, who preached his Discourse *as a sermon on 4 November 1789, at a meeting of the radical Society for Commemorating the Revolution (of 1688) in Great Britain. It sparked off a vigorous pamphlet debate involving Burke, Paine, Wollstonecraft, and Godwin, which was followed by Wordsworth, who in* The Thirteen-Book Prelude *recalls having read 'the master pamphlets of the day' (ix. 97). At the time Price was writing, the storming of the Bastille (14 July) was still news; less than a month before he spoke, 20,000 soldiers had stormed Versailles, and escorted the King and Queen to Paris in what many saw as one of the most sinister events in the Revolution so far. The Reign of Terror was still several years away.*

From A Discourse on the Love of our Country (1789)

ON REPRESENTATION (PP. 40–2)

When the representation is fair and equal, and at the same time vested with such powers as our House of Commons possesses, a kingdom may be said to govern itself, and consequently to possess true liberty. When the representation is partial, a kingdom possesses liberty only partially; and if extremely partial, it only gives a *semblance* of liberty. But if not only extremely partial, but corruptly chosen, and under corrupt influence after being chosen, it becomes a *nuisance*, and produces the worst of all forms of government: a government by corruption, a government carried on and supported by spreading venality and profligacy through a kingdom.

May heaven preserve this kingdom from a calamity so dreadful! It is the point of depravity to which abuses under such a government as ours naturally tend, and the last stage of national unhappiness. We are at present, I hope, at a great distance from it. But it cannot be pretended that there are no advances towards it, or that there is no reason for apprehension and alarm.

The inadequateness of our representation has been long a subject of complaint. This is, in truth, our fundamental grievance, and I do not think that anything is much more our duty (as men who love their country and are grateful for the Revolution)[1] than to unite our zeal in endeavouring to get it redressed. At the time of the American war, associations were formed for this purpose in London and other parts of the kingdom, and our present Minister himself has, since that war, directed to it an effort which made him a favourite with many of us.[2] But all attention to it seems now lost, and the probability is that this inattention will continue and that nothing will be done towards gaining for us this essential blessing till some great calamity again alarms our fears, or till some great abuse of power again provokes our resentment – or perhaps till the acquisition of a pure and equal representation by other countries (while we are mocked with the shadow)[3] kindles our shame.

ON REPRESENTATION

[1] The Glorious Revolution of 1688, which the Re- volution Society was established to commemorate.
[2] In the early 1780s William Pitt the Younger ad- vocated peace with the American colonies, economic reform, and reform of parliamentary representation.

Such organizations as the Constitutional Society (es- tablished 1780) lobbied for parliamentary reform.
[3] 'A representation chosen principally by the Treas- ury, and a few thousands of the dregs of the people, who are generally paid for their votes' (Price's foot- note).

PROSPECTS FOR REFORM (PP. 49–51)

What an eventful period is this! I am thankful that I have lived to it, and I could almost say, 'Lord, now lettest thou thy servant depart in peace, for mine eyes have seen thy salvation.'[1] I have lived to see a diffusion of knowledge which has undermined superstition and error; I have lived to see the rights of men better understood than ever, and nations panting for liberty which seemed to have lost the idea of it. I have lived to see *thirty millions* of people, indignant and resolute, spurning at slavery, and demanding liberty with an irresistible voice, their King led in triumph, and an arbitrary monarch surrendering himself to his subjects.[2]

After sharing in the benefits of one revolution, I have been spared to be a witness to two other revolutions, both glorious.[3] And now, methinks, I see the ardour for liberty catching and spreading; a general amendment beginning in human affairs; the dominion of kings changed for the dominion of laws, and the dominion of priests giving way to the dominion of reason and conscience.

Be encouraged, all ye friends of freedom, and writers in its defence! The times are auspicious. Your labours have not been in vain. Behold kingdoms admonished by you, starting from sleep, breaking their fetters, and claiming justice from their oppressors! Behold the light you have struck out, after setting America free, reflected to France and there kindled into a blaze that lays despotism in ashes, and warms and illuminates Europe!

Tremble all ye oppressors of the world! Take warning all ye supporters of slavish governments and slavish hierarchies! Call no more (absurdly and wickedly) reformation, innovation. You cannot now hold the world in darkness. Struggle no longer against increasing light and liberality. Restore to mankind their rights, and consent to the correction of abuses, before they and you are destroyed together.

Thomas Warton   (1728–90)

Professor of Poetry at Oxford, poet laureate (from 1785), and man of letters; 'To the Lodon' was probably his best-known work (read by Wordsworth during his boyhood), and it began the series of poems to 'native streams', including Bowles's 'To the Itchin' (p. 143), Coleridge's 'To the River Otter' (p. 504), and Wordsworth's 'Dear native brooks, your ways have I pursued' (p. 274–5).

From Poems (1777)

SONNET IX. TO THE RIVER LODON

Ah! what a weary race my feet have run
Since first I trod thy banks with alders crowned,

PROSPECTS FOR REFORM
[1]   Luke 2: 29–30.
[2]   On 5–6 Oct. 1789, less than a month before Price's *Discourse* was written, 20,000 men of the National Guard marched from Paris to Versailles under La Fayette, stormed the palace, and escorted the King and Queen back to the capital.

[3]   Price sees himself as a beneficiary of the Glorious Revolution of 1688, which ousted the Catholic James II and brought the Protestant William of Orange to the English throne; he witnessed the American Revolution, which resulted in independence from Britain in 1776, and the French.

And thought my way was all through fairy ground
Beneath thy azure sky and golden sun,
Where first my muse to lisp her notes begun.   5
While pensive memory traces back the round
Which fills the varied interval between,
Much pleasure, more of sorrow, marks the scene.
Sweet native stream, those skies and suns so pure
No more return to cheer my evening road;   10
Yet still one joy remains – that not obscure,
Nor useless, all my vacant days have flowed,
From youth's gay dawn to manhood's prime mature,
Nor with the muse's laurel unbestowed.

Edmund Burke   (1729–97)

Burke's Philosophical Enquiry into the Sublime and Beautiful *(1757) shaped the way in which the romantics interpreted the literature of the past and formulated their own aims; the section on obscurity, with its remarks on Milton's description of Death from* Paradise Lost, *underlines its literary significance.*

Prior to 1790, Burke was known as a reformer, an advocate of the American cause and of emancipation in Ireland; he was also a friend and correspondent of Thomas Paine. However, the fall of the Bastille in July 1789 and the storming of Versailles in October, led him to fear anarchy. Price's Discourse *(1789) inspired his enduring defence of conservativism, the* Reflections *(1790).*

From A Philosophical Enquiry into the Origins of our Ideas of the Sublime and Beautiful (1757)

ON OBSCURITY

To make anything very terrible, obscurity seems in general to be necessary. When we know the full extent of any danger, when we can accustom our eyes to it, a great deal of the apprehension vanishes. Everyone will be sensible of this who considers how greatly night adds to our dread in all cases of danger, and how much the notions of ghosts and goblins (of which none can form clear ideas) affect minds, which give credit to the popular tales concerning such sorts of beings.

Those despotic governments which are founded on the passions of men – and principally upon the passion of fear – keep their chief as much as may be from the public eye. The policy has been the same in many cases of religion; almost all the heathen temples were dark. Even in the barbarous temples of the Americans[1] at this day, they keep their idol in a dark part of the hut, which is consecrated to his worship. For this purpose too the druids performed all their ceremonies in the bosom of the darkest woods, and in the shade of the oldest and most spreading oaks.

ON OBSCURITY
[1]   *the Americans* i.e. the American Indians.

No person seems better to have understood the secret of heightening, or of setting terrible things (if I may use the expression) in their strongest light by the force of a judicious obscurity, than Milton. His description of Death in the second Book is admirably studied; it is astonishing with what a gloomy pomp, with what a significant and expressive uncertainty of strokes and colouring he has finished the portrait of the king of terrors.

> The other shape
> (If shape it might be called) that shape had none
> Distinguishable in member, joint, or limb;
> Or substance might be called that shadow seemed,
> For each seemed either. Black he stood as night,
> Fierce as ten furies, terrible as hell,
> And shook a deadly dart. What seemed his head
> The likeness of a kingly crown had on.
> *(Paradise Lost*, ii. 666–73)

In this description all is dark, uncertain, confused, terrible and sublime to the last degree.

From Reflections on the Revolution in France (1790)

ON ENGLISHNESS (PP. 127–30)

I almost venture to affirm that not one in a hundred amongst us participates in the 'triumph' of the Revolution Society. If the King and Queen of France and their children were to fall into our hands by the chance of war in the most acrimonious of all hostilities (I deprecate such an event, I deprecate such hostility), they would be treated with another sort of triumphal entry into London. We formerly have had a king of France in that situation; you have read how he was treated by the victor in the field, and in what manner he was afterwards received in England. Four hundred years have gone over us, but I believe we are not materially changed since that period.[1]

Thanks to our sullen resistance to innovation, thanks to the cold sluggishness of our national character, we still bear the stamp of our forefathers. We have not (as I conceive) lost the generosity and dignity of thinking of the fourteenth century, nor as yet have we subtilized[2] ourselves into savages.[3] We are not the converts of Rousseau; we are not the disciples of Voltaire; Helvetius has made no progress amongst us.[4] Atheists are not our preachers; madmen are not our lawgivers. We know that *we* have made no discoveries, and we think that no discoveries are to be made in morality – nor many in the great principles of government, nor in the ideas of liberty which were understood long before we were born, altogether as well as they will be after the grave has heaped its mould upon our presumption, and the silent tomb shall have imposed its law on our pert loquacity.[5]

ON ENGLISHNESS
[1]   John II of France was captured by the Black Prince at the Battle of Poitiers in 1356, and died in captivity in London in 1364.
[2]   *subtilized* refined (an ironic usage).

[3]   *savages* according to Rousseau's ideal of the noble savage, the state of nature is exalted above society.
[4]   The thoughts of Rousseau, Voltaire, and Helvetius inspired the French Revolution.
[5]   *pert loquacity* impudent talk.

In England we have not yet been completely embowelled of our natural entrails; we still feel within us, and we cherish and cultivate, those inbred sentiments which are the faithful guardians, the active monitors[6] of our duty, the true supporters of all liberal and manly[7] morals. We have not been drawn and trussed[8] in order that we may be filled, like stuffed birds in a museum, with chaff and rags and paltry blurred shreds of paper about the rights of man. We preserve the whole of our feelings still native and entire, unsophisticated by pedantry and infidelity. We have real hearts of flesh and blood beating in our bosoms. We fear God. We look up with awe to kings, with affection to parliaments, with duty to magistrates, with reverence to priests, and with respect to nobility. Why? Because when such ideas are brought before our minds, it is *natural* to be so affected; because all other feelings are false and spurious, and tend to corrupt our minds, to vitiate our primary morals, to render us unfit for rational liberty, and (by teaching us a servile, licentious, and abandoned insolence) to be our low sport for a few holidays, to make us perfectly fit for, and justly deserving of slavery, through the whole course of our lives.

You see, sir,[9] that in this enlightened age I am bold enough to confess that we are generally men of untaught feelings, that instead of casting away all our old prejudices, we cherish them to a very considerable degree and, to take more shame to ourselves, we cherish them because they *are* prejudices. And the longer they have lasted, and the more generally they have prevailed, the more we cherish them.

We are afraid to put men to live and trade each on his own private stock of reason,[10] because we suspect that this stock in each man is small, and that the individuals would do better to avail themselves of the general bank and capital of nations and of ages. Many of our men of speculation, instead of exploding general prejudices, employ their sagacity to discover the latent wisdom which prevails in them. If they find what they seek (and they seldom fail), they think it more wise to continue the prejudice, with the reason involved, than to cast away the coat of prejudice, and to leave nothing but the naked reason – because prejudice, with its reason, has a motive to give action to that reason, and an affection which will give it permanence. Prejudice is of ready application in the emergency; it previously engages the mind in a steady course of wisdom and virtue, and does not leave the man hesitating in the moment of decision – sceptical, puzzled and unresolved. Prejudice renders a man's virtue his habit, and not a series of unconnected acts. Through just prejudice, his duty becomes a part of his nature.

SOCIETY IS A CONTRACT (PP. 143–7)

Society is indeed a contract.[1] Subordinate contracts for objects of mere occasional interest may be dissolved at pleasure, but the state ought not to be considered as nothing better than a partnership agreement in a trade of pepper and coffee, calico or tobacco, or some other such low concern, to be taken up for a little temporary interest, and to be dissolved by the fancy of the parties. It is to be looked on with other reverence because it is not a partnership in things subservient only to the gross animal existence of a temporary and perishable nature.

---

[6] *monitors* reminders.
[7] *manly* humane.
[8] *drawn and trussed* after disembowelling (drawing) a bird, its wings were pinned to its sides with skewers (trussing).
[9] *sir* Richard Price.

[10] *reason* leading radicals placed their faith in the redeeming power of reason.
SOCIETY IS A CONTRACT
[1] Burke offers a conservative variation on Rousseau's *Contrat Social* (1762).

It is a partnership in all science, a partnership in all art, a partnership in every virtue and in all perfection. As the ends of such a partnership cannot be obtained in many generations, it becomes a partnership not only between those who are living, but between those who are living, those who are dead, and those who are to be born. Each contract of each particular state is but a clause in the great primeval contract of eternal society, linking the lower with the higher natures, connecting the visible and invisible world according to a fixed compact sanctioned by the inviolable oath which holds all physical and all moral natures each in their appointed place. This law is not subject to the will of those who, by an obligation above them and infinitely superior, are bound to submit their will to that law. The municipal corporations of that universal kingdom[2] are not morally at liberty at their pleasure, and on their speculations of a contingent improvement wholly to separate and tear asunder the bands of their subordinate community, and to dissolve it into an unsocial, uncivil, unconnected chaos of elementary principles.

It is the first and supreme necessity only, a necessity that is not chosen but chooses, a necessity paramount to deliberation, that admits no discussion and demands no evidence, which alone can justify a resort to anarchy. This necessity is no exception to the rule because this necessity itself is a part too of that moral and physical disposition of things to which man must be obedient by consent or force. But if that which is only submission to necessity should be made the object of choice, the law is broken, nature is disobeyed, and the rebellious are outlawed, cast forth, and exiled from this world of reason, and order, and peace, and virtue, and fruitful penitence, into the antagonist world of madness, discord, vice, confusion, and unavailing sorrow.

These, my dear sir, are, were, and I think long will be the sentiments of not the least learned and reflecting part of this kingdom. They who are included in this description form their opinions on such grounds as such persons ought to form them; the less enquiring receive them from an authority which those whom providence dooms to live on trust need not be ashamed to rely on. These two sorts of men move in the same direction, though in a different place. They both move with the order of the universe. They all know or feel this great ancient truth: 'Quod illi principi et praepotenti Deo qui omnem hunc mundum regit, nihil eorum quae quidem fiant in terris acceptius quam concilia et caetus hominum jure sociati quae civitates appellantur.'[3] They take this tenet of the head and heart not from the great name which it immediately bears, nor from the greater from whence it is derived, but from that which alone can give true weight and sanction to any learned opinion: the common nature and common relation of men.

Persuaded that all things ought to be done with reference, and referring all to the point of reference to which all should be directed,[4] they think themselves bound (not only as individuals in the sanctuary of the heart, or as congregated in that personal capacity) to renew the memory of their high origin and caste; but also in their corporate character to perform their national homage to the institutor and author and protector of civil society, without which civil society man could not by any possibility arrive at the perfection of which his nature is capable, nor even make a remote and faint approach to it.

---

[2] i.e. the various states that compose the universal society of the human race.
[3] 'To the great and all-powerful God who rules this entire universe, nothing is more pleasing than the unions and gatherings of men bound together by laws that are called states' (Cicero, *Dream of Scipio*, III: 5 (13)).
[4] i.e. God.

They conceive that He who gave our nature to be perfected by our virtue willed also the necessary means of its perfection. He willed therefore the state; He willed its connection with the source and original archetype of all perfection. They who are convinced of this His will (which is the law of laws and the sovereign of sovereigns) cannot think it reprehensible that this our corporate fealty and homage, that this our recognition of a signiory paramount[5] (I had almost said this oblation[6] of the state itself), as a worthy offering on the high altar of universal praise, should be performed as all public solemn acts are performed – in buildings, in music, in decoration, in speech, in the dignity of persons, according to the customs of mankind, taught by their nature; that is, with modest splendour, with unassuming state, with mild majesty and sober pomp.

For those purposes they think some part of the wealth of the country is as usefully employed as it can be, in fomenting[7] the luxury of individuals. It is the public ornament; it is the public consolation; it nourishes the public hope. The poorest man finds his own importance and dignity in it, whilst the wealth and pride of individuals at every moment makes the man of humble rank and fortune sensible of his inferiority, and degrades and vilifies his condition. It is for the man in humble life – and to raise his nature, and to put him in mind of a state[8] in which the privileges of opulence will cease, when he will be equal by nature, and may be more than equal by virtue – that this portion of the general wealth of his country is employed and sanctified.

I assure you I do not aim at singularity.[9] I give you opinions which have been accepted amongst us from very early times to this moment, with a continued and general approbation, and which indeed are so worked into my mind that I am unable to distinguish what I have learned from others from the results of my own meditation.

William Cowper   (1731–1800)

His popular blank verse poem The Task *(1785) exercised a strong influence on the romantics, not least because of its ruminative, relatively informal style. In particular, his influence can be found in the work of Coleridge, who praised Cowper's 'divine chit-chat' (Marrs, i. 78); compare with the last of the* Task *extracts Coleridge's 'Frost at Midnight' (pp. 516–18). Cowper's portrait of Crazy Kate inspired other accounts of female solitaries, including Southey's 'Hannah' (pp. 603–4) and Margaret in Wordsworth's* The Ruined Cottage.

From The Task (1785)

CRAZY KATE (BOOK I)

There often wanders one whom better days
Saw better clad, in cloak of satin trimmed
With lace, and hat with splendid ribbon bound.

535

---

[5] *signiory paramount* executive authority.
[6] *oblation* devotional offering.
[7] *fomenting* encouraging.

[8] *a state* i.e. heaven.
[9] *singularity* eccentricity.

A serving-maid was she, and fell in love
With one who left her, went to sea, and died.
Her fancy followed him through foaming waves
To distant shores, and she would sit and weep   540
At what a sailor suffers; fancy too
(Delusive most where warmest wishes are)
Would oft anticipate his glad return
And dream of transports she was not to know.
She heard the doleful tidings of his death   545
And never smiled again. And now she roams
The dreary waste; there spends the livelong day,
And there, unless when Charity forbids,[1]
The livelong night. A tattered apron hides,
Worn as a cloak, and hardly hides a gown   550
More tattered still; and both but ill conceal
A bosom heaved with never-ceasing sighs.
She begs an idle pin of all she meets,
And hoards them in her sleeve, but needful food,
Though pressed with hunger oft, or comelier clothes,   555
Though pinched with cold, asks never. Kate is crazed.

ON SLAVERY (BOOK II)

Oh for a lodge in some vast wilderness,
Some boundless contiguity of shade,
Where rumour of oppression and deceit,
Of unsuccessful or successful war
Might never reach me more! My ear is pained,   5
My soul is sick with ev'ry day's report
Of wrong and outrage with which earth is filled.
There is no flesh in man's obdurate heart –
It does not feel for man. The nat'ral bond
Of brotherhood is fevered as the flax   10
That falls asunder at the touch of fire.
He finds his fellow guilty of a skin
Not coloured like his own, and having pow'r
T'inforce the wrong, for such a worthy cause
Dooms and devotes[1] him as his lawful prey.   15
Lands intersected by a narrow frith
Abhor each other. Mountains interposed
Make enemies of nations who had else
Like kindred drops been mingled into one.
Thus man devotes his brother, and destroys;   20
And worse than all, and most to be deplored

CRAZY KATE
[1] Charity (in the form of a householder) might give
Kate shelter for the night.

ON SLAVERY
[1] *devotes* condemns.

As human nature's broadest, foulest blot,
Chains him, and tasks him, and exacts his sweat
With stripes that Mercy with a bleeding heart
Weeps when she sees inflicted on a beast.   25
    Then what is man? And what man seeing this,
And having human feelings, does not blush
And hang his head to think himself a man?
I would not have a slave to till my ground,
To carry me, to fan me while I sleep   30
And tremble when I wake, for all the wealth
That sinews bought and sold have ever earned.
No; dear as freedom is, and in my heart's
Just estimation prized above all price,
I had much rather be myself the slave   35
And wear the bonds, than fasten them on him.
We have no slaves at home – then why abroad?
And they themselves, once ferried o'er the wave
That parts us, are emancipate and loosed.
Slaves cannot breathe in England; if their lungs   40
Receive our air, that moment they are free,
They touch our country and their shackles fall.
That's noble, and bespeaks a nation proud
And jealous of the blessing.[2] Spread it then,
And let it circulate through ev'ry vein   45
Of all your Empire, that where Britain's power
Is felt, mankind may feel her mercy too.

THE WINTER EVENING (BOOK IV)

Just when our drawing-rooms begin to blaze
With lights by clear reflection multiplied
From many a mirror (in which he of Gath,
Goliath, might have seen his giant bulk   270
Whole without stooping, tow'ring crest and all),
My pleasures too begin. But me perhaps
The glowing hearth may satisfy awhile
With faint illumination that uplifts
The shadow to the ceiling, there by fits   275
Dancing uncouthly to the quiv'ring flame.
    Not undelightful is an hour to me
So spent in parlour twilight; such a gloom
Suits well the thoughtful or unthinking mind,
The mind contemplative, with some new theme   280
Pregnant, or indisposed alike to all.
Laugh ye, who boast your more mercurial pow'rs

---

[2] Any slave who set foot in the British Isles became immediately free – a ruling made in 1772 in the celebrated case of the Negro Somerset.

That never feel a stupor, know no pause
Nor need one. I am conscious, and confess
Fearless, a soul that does not always think.   285
Me oft has fancy ludicrous and wild
Soothed with a waking dream of houses, tow'rs,
Trees, churches, and strange visages expressed
In the red cinders, while with poring eye
I gazed, myself creating what I saw.   290
Nor less amused have I quiescent watched
The sooty films that play upon the bars –
Pendulous, and foreboding in the view
Of superstition, prophesying still,
Though still deceived, some stranger's near approach.   295
    'Tis thus the understanding takes repose
In indolent vacuity of thought,
And sleeps and is refrshed. Meanwhile the face
Conceals the mood lethargic with a mask
Of deep deliberation, as the man   300
Were tasked to his full strength, absorbed and lost.
Thus oft reclined at ease, I lose an hour
At evening, till at length the freezing blast
That sweeps the bolted shutter, summons home
The recollected powers and, snapping short   305
The glassy threads with which the fancy weaves
Her brittle toys, restores me to myself.
How calm is my recess, and how the frost
Raging abroad, and the rough wind, endear
The silence and the warmth enjoyed within.   310
    I saw the woods and fields at close of day,
A variegated show; the meadows green
Though faded, and the lands where lately waved
The golden harvest, of a mellow brown,
Upturned so lately by the forceful share.¹   315
I saw far off the weedy fallows² smile
With verdure not unprofitable, grazed
By flocks fast-feeding and selecting each
His fav'rite herb; while all the leafless groves
That skirt th' horizon wore a sable hue   320
Scarce noticed in the kindred dusk of eve.
Tomorrow brings a change, a total change
Which even now – though silently performed
And slowly, and by most unfelt – the face
Of universal nature undergoes.   325
    Fast falls a fleecy show'r. The downy flakes
Descending, and with never-ceasing lapse

THE WINTER EVENING   ² *weedy fallows* fields lying fallow, full of weeds.
¹ *share* ploughshare.

Softly alighting upon all below,
Assimilate all objects. Earth receives
Gladly the thick'ning mantle, and the green   330
And tender blade that feared the chilling blast
Escapes unhurt beneath so warm a veil.

From Works, ed. Robert Southey (15 vols., 1835–7) x 10

SWEET MEAT HAS SOUR SAUCE, OR THE SLAVE-TRADER IN THE DUMPS
(COMPOSED 1788)

A trader I am to the African shore,
But since that my trading is like to be o'er,
I'll sing you a song that you ne'er heard before,
          Which nobody can deny, deny,
          Which nobody can deny.   5

When I first heard the news it gave me a shock,
Much like what they call an electrical knock,
And now I am going to sell off my stock,
          Which nobody can deny.

'Tis a curious assortment of dainty regales,   10
To tickle the Negroes with when the ship sails –
Fine chains for the neck, and a cat with nine tails,
          Which nobody can deny.

Here's supple-jack plenty, and store of rattan[1]
That will wind itself round the sides of a man   15
As close as a hoop round a bucket or can,
          Which nobody can deny.

Here's padlocks and bolts, and screws for the thumbs
That squeeze them so lovingly till the blood comes;
They sweeten the temper like comfits or plums,   20
          Which nobody can deny.

When a Negro his head from his victuals withdraws
And clenches his teeth and thrusts out his paws,
Here's a notable engine to open his jaws,
          Which nobody can deny.   25

Thus going to market, we kindly prepare
A pretty black cargo of African ware,

SWEET MEAT HAS SOUR SAUCE, OR THE SLAVE-TRADER IN
THE DUMPS
[1] Canes, switches, and ropes were made out of
supple-jack and rattan.

For what they must meet with when they get there,
        Which nobody can deny.

'Twould do your heart good to see 'em below   30
Lie flat on their backs all the way as we go,
Like sprats on a gridiron, scores in a row,
        Which nobody can deny.

But ah! if in vain I have studied an art
So gainful to me, all boasting apart   35
I think it will break my compassionate heart,
        Which nobody can deny.

For oh, how it enters my soul like an awl!
This pity, which some people self-pity call,
Is sure the most heart-piercing pity of all,   40
        Which nobody can deny.

So this is my song, as I told you before;
Come buy off my stock, for I must no more
Carry Caesars and Pompeys to sugar-cane shore,
        Which nobody can deny, deny,   45
        Which nobody can deny.

Thomas Paine   (1737–1809)

Paine's impassioned pamphlet in support of the American War of Independence, Common Sense
*(1776), was enormously popular, selling 120,000 copies within three months of publication. It
gained him a reputation as a determined republican, well established by the time he published*
The Rights of Man *(1791–2), the most effective of the numerous responses to Burke's* Reflections.
This sold 200,000 copies in 1791–3, many in cheap editions designed for working people.

From Common Sense (1776)

OF THE ORIGIN AND DESIGN OF GOVERNMENT IN GENERAL (PP. 1–2)

Some writers have so confounded society with government as to leave little or no
distinction between them – whereas they are not only different, but have different
origins. Society is produced by our wants, and government by our wickedness; the
former promotes our happiness positively by uniting our affections, the latter negative-
ly by restraining our vices. The one encourages intercourse, the other creates distinctions. The first is a patron, the last a punisher.

Society in every state is a blessing, but government even in its best state is but a necessary
evil – in its worst state an intolerable one. For when we suffer, or are exposed to the same
miseries by a government which we expect in a country without government, our calamity
is heightened by reflecting that we furnish the means by which we suffer.

Government, like dress, is the badge of lost innocence; the palaces of kings are built on the ruins of the bowers of paradise.[1] For were the impulses of conscience clear, uniform, and irresistibly obeyed, man would need no other lawgiver. But that not being the case, he finds it necessary to surrender up a part of his property to furnish means for the protection of the rest – and this he is induced to do by the same prudence which in every other case advises him out of two evils to choose the least. Wherefore, security being the true design and end of government, it unanswerably follows that whatever form thereof appears most likely to ensure it to us, with the least expense and greatest benefit, is preferable to all others.

From The Rights of Man, Part I (1791)

FREEDOM OF POSTERITY (PP. 8–10)

The English Parliament of 1688 did a certain thing which, for themselves and their constituents, they had a right to do, and which it appeared right should be done.[1] But, in addition to this right (which they possessed by delegation), they set up another right by assumption: that of binding and controlling posterity to the end of time. The case, therefore, divides itself into two parts – the right which they possessed by delegation, and the right which they set up by assumption. The first is admitted, but with respect to the second I reply:

There never did, there never will, and there never can exist a parliament, or any description of men, or any generation of men, in any country, possessed of the right or the power of binding and controlling posterity to the 'end of time', or of commanding for ever how the world shall be governed, or who shall govern it. And therefore all such clauses, acts or declarations by which the makers of them attempt to do what they have neither the right nor the power to do – nor the power to execute – are in themselves null and void. Every age and generation must be as free to act for itself, in all cases, as the ages and generations which preceded it.

The vanity and presumption of governing beyond the grave is the most ridiculous and insolent of all tyrannies. Man has no property in man, neither has any generation a property in the generations which are to follow. The parliament or the people of 1688, or of any other period, had no more right to dispose of the people of the present day, or to bind or to control them *in any shape whatever*, than the parliament or the people of the present day have to dispose of, bind or control those who are to live a hundred or a thousand years hence. Every generation is and must be competent to all the purposes which its occasions require. It is the living, and not the dead, that are to be accommodated. When man ceases to be, his power and his wants cease with him, and having no longer any participation in the concerns of this world, he has no longer any authority in directing who shall be its governors, or how its government shall be organized, or how administered.

OF THE ORIGIN AND DESIGN OF GOVERNMENT IN
GENERAL
[1] An idea that derives from Rousseau's concept of the noble savage, outlined in his *Discourse on Inequality*.

FREEDOM OF POSTERITY
[1] i.e. replace the Catholic James II with the Protestant William of Orange.

ON REVOLUTION (PP. 156–9)

When we survey the wretched condition of man under the monarchical and hereditary systems of government, dragged from his home by one power, or driven by another, and impoverished by taxes more than by enemies, it becomes evident that those systems are bad, and that a general revolution in the principle and construction of governments is necessary.

What is government more than the management of the affairs of a nation? It is not, and from its nature cannot be, the property of any particular man or family, but of the whole community at whose expense it is supported. And though by force or contrivance it has been usurped into an inheritance, the usurpation cannot alter the right of things. Sovereignty, as a matter of right, appertains to the nation only, and not to any individual; and a nation has at all times an inherent indefeasible[1] right to abolish any form of government it finds inconvenient, and establish such as accords with its interest, disposition and happiness. The romantic[2] and barbarous distinction of men into kings and subjects, though it may suit the condition of courtiers, cannot that of citizens – and is exploded by the principle upon which governments are now founded. Every citizen is a member of the sovereignty, and as such can acknowledge no personal subjection, and his obedience can be only to the laws.

When men think of what government is, they must necessarily suppose it to possess a knowledge of all the objects and matters upon which its authority is to be exercised. In this view of government, the republican system as established by America and France operates to embrace the whole of a nation, and the knowledge necessary to the interest of all the parts is to be found in the centre, which the parts by representation form. But the old governments are on a construction that excludes knowledge as well as happiness – government by monks who know nothing of the world beyond the walls of a convent is as consistent as government by kings.

What were formerly called revolutions were little more than a change of persons or an alteration of local circumstances. They rose and fell like things of course,[3] and had nothing in their existence or their fate that could influence beyond the spot that produced them. But what we now see in the world, from the revolutions of America and France, are a renovation of the natural order of things, a system of principles as universal as truth and the existence of man, and combining moral with political happiness and national prosperity.

I. Men are born and always continue free and equal in respect of their rights. Civil distinctions, therefore, can be founded only on public utility.

II. The end of all political associations is the preservation of the natural and imprescriptible rights of man; and these rights are liberty, property, security, and resistance of oppression.

III. The nation is essentially the source of all sovereignty; nor can any individual or any body of men be entitled to any authority which is not expressly derived from it.

In these principles there is nothing to throw a nation into confusion by inflaming ambition. They are calculated to call forth wisdom and abilities, and to exercise them for the public

---

ON REVOLUTION
[1] *indefeasible* undeniable.

[2] *romantic* impractical.

[3] *of course* i.e. of succession, over a course of time.

good, and not for the emolument or aggrandizement of particular descriptions of men or families. Monarchical sovereignty – the enemy of mankind and the source of misery – is abolished, and sovereignty itself is restored to its natural and original place: the nation. Were this the case throughout Europe, the cause of wars would be taken away.

From The Rights of Man, Part II (1792)
REPUBLICANISM (PP. 22–3, 24)

What is called a republic is not any particular form of government. It is wholly characteristical of the purport, matter or object for which government ought to be instituted, and on which it is to be employed: 'res-publica' (the public affairs, or the public good – or, literally translated, the public thing). It is a word of a good original,[1] referring to what ought to be the character and business of government, and in this sense it is naturally opposed to the word 'monarchy', which has a base original signification – it means arbitrary power in an individual person, in the exercise of which *himself* (and not the 'res-publica') is the object.

Every government that does not act on the principle of a republic – or, in other words, that does not make the res-publica its whole and sole object – is not a good government. Republican government is no other than government established and conducted for the interest of the public, as well individually as collectively. It is not necessarily connected with any particular form, but it most naturally associates with the representative form, as being best calculated to secure the end for which a nation is at the expense of supporting it.

Various forms of government have affected to style themselves a republic. Poland calls itself a republic, which is an hereditary aristocracy with what is called an elective monarchy. Holland calls itself a republic, which is chiefly aristocratical with an hereditary stadtholder-ship.[2] But the government of America, which is wholly on the system of representation, is the only real republic in character and in practice that now exists. Its government has no other object than the public business of the nation, and therefore it is properly a republic; and the Americans have taken care that *this* and no other shall always be the object of their government, by their rejecting everything hereditary, and establishing government on the system of representation only.... What Athens was in miniature, America will be in magnitude: the one was the wonder of the ancient world, the other is becoming the admiration, the model of the present. It is the easiest of all the forms of government to be understood, and the most eligible in practice – and excludes at once the ignorance and insecurity of the hereditary mode, and the inconvenience of the simple democracy.

Anna Seward (1742–1809)

The 'swan of Lichfield' (as she was known) was a luminary of Lichfield intellectual circles and an associate of Erasmus Darwin, Thomas Day, and William Hayley. Her reputation as a poet and novelist was established with the famous Elegy on Captain Cook *(1780) and* Louisa, *a*

REPUBLICANISM
[1] *original* referent, thing.

[2] *stadtholdership* magistrate-general (abolished 1802).

Poetical Novel *(1784)*. *The sonnet published here looks forward to Wordsworth's address to a different River Derwent in* Thirteen-Book Prelude, *i. 272ff.*

From Sonnets (1799)

SONNET VII

By Derwent's rapid stream as oft I strayed
    With infancy's light step and glances wild,
    And saw vast rocks on steepy mountains piled
    Frown o'er th' umbrageous glen, or pleased surveyed
The cloudy moonshine in the shadowy glade,   5
    Romantic nature to th' enthusiast child
    Grew dearer far than when serene she smiled
    In uncontrasted loveliness arrayed.
But oh! in every scene, with sacred sway
    Her graces fire me; from the bloom that spreads   10
    Resplendent in the lucid morn of May,
To the green light the little glow-worm sheds
    On mossy banks when midnight glooms prevail,
    And softest silence broods o'er all the dale.

Mary Alcock   (c.1742–98)

Alcock's ironic 'Instructions' was written in 1792, and is a valuable reflection of the anxiety felt by many that the Revolution in France might spread to England and the ideals advocated by Paine be implemented there.

From Poems (1799)

INSTRUCTIONS, SUPPOSED TO BE WRITTEN IN PARIS, FOR THE MOB IN ENGLAND

Of liberty, reform, and rights I sing –
Freedom I mean, without or church or king;
Freedom to seize and keep whate'er I can,
And boldly claim my right – The Rights of Man!
Such is the blessed liberty in vogue,   5
The envied liberty to be a rogue,
The right to pay no taxes, tithes or dues,
The liberty to do whate'er I choose;
The right to take by violence and strife
My neighbour's goods, and (if I please) his life;   10
The liberty to raise a mob or riot
(For spoil and plunder ne'er were got by quiet);
The right to level and reform the great;

The liberty to overturn the state;
The right to break through all the nation's laws   15
And boldly dare to take rebellion's cause:
Let all be equal, every man my brother –
Why have one property and not another?
Why suffer titles to give awe and fear?
There shall not long remain one British peer –   20
Nor shall the criminal appalled stand
Before the mighty judges of the land;
Nor judge nor jury shall there longer be,
Nor any jail, but ev'ry pris'ner free;
All law abolished, and with sword in hand   25
We'll seize the property of all the land.
Then hail to liberty, reform and riot! –
Adieu contentment, safety, peace and quiet!

Anna Laetitia Barbauld (1743–1825)

Unitarian poet and woman of letters, Barbauld gained immediate recognition with the publication of her Poems *(1773), from which 'A Summer Evening's Meditation' is drawn – a poem which exercised a formative influence on both Wordsworth and Coleridge. Although written c.1795, 'The Rights of Woman' was not published until 1825 – posthumously, when her niece Lucy Aikin edited her* Works. *Barbauld composed her 'Epistle to William Wilberforce' after Wilberforce's first bill urging the abolition of slavery, proposed on 18 April 1791, was defeated. Wilberforce (1759–1833) tried again in April 1792, and although that bill was passed by the House of Commons, it was thrown out by the Lords in 1793; this is the struggle recalled by Wordsworth in* Thirteen-Book Prelude, x. *201–10. Slavery was outlawed finally in February 1807. Barbauld's poem to the young Coleridge was probably written in the wake of their meeting in Bristol, August 1797, though it was not published until two years later; it is distinguished by her early recognition of his talents and by her shrewd warning against the 'metaphysic lore' which preoccupied him in later years.*

From Poems (1773)

A SUMMER EVENING'S MEDITATION

One sun by day, by night ten thousand shine
    (Young, *Night Thoughts*, ix. 748)

'Tis passed! – the sultry tyrant of the south
Has spent his short-lived rage. More grateful hours
Move silent on; the skies no more repel
The dazzled sight, but with mild maiden beams
Of tempered light invite the cherished eye   5
To wander o'er their sphere, where, hung aloft,
Dian's bright crescent, like a silver bow

New-strung in heaven, lifts high its beamy horns
Impatient for the night, and seems to push
Her brother down the sky. Fair Venus shines   10
Even in the eye of day – with sweetest beam
Propitious shines, and shakes a trembling flood
Of softened radiance from her dewy locks.
The shadows spread apace, while meekened Eve,
Her cheek yet warm with blushes, slow retires   15
Through the Hesperian gardens of the west,[1]
And shuts the gates of day.
                                    'Tis now the hour
When Contemplation from her sunless haunts
(The cool damp grotto or the lonely depth
Of unpierced woods, where, wrapped in solid shade,   20
She mused away the gaudy hours of noon
And fed on thoughts unripened by the sun)[2]
Moves forward, and with radiant finger points
To yon blue concave swelled by breath divine,
Where, one by one, the living eyes of heaven   25
Awake, quick kindling o'er the face of ether
One boundless blaze – ten thousand trembling fires
And dancing lustres – where th' unsteady eye,
Restless and dazzled, wanders unconfined
O'er all this field of glories: spacious field,   30
And worthy of the Master! – He whose hand
With hieroglyphics older than the Nile
Inscribed the mystic tablet[3] hung on high
To public gaze, and said, 'Adore, oh man,
The finger of thy God!' From what pure wells   35
Of milky light, what soft o'erflowing urn
Are all these lamps so filled – these friendly lamps
For ever streaming o'er the azure deep
To point our path and light us to our home?
How soft they slide along their lucid spheres,   40
And, silent as the foot of time, fulfil
Their destined courses! Nature's self is hushed
And, but a scattered leaf which rustles through
The thick-wove foliage, not a sound is heard
To break the midnight air – though the raised ear,   45
Intensely listening, drinks in every breath.
How deep the silence, yet how loud the praise!
But are they silent all? or is there not

A SUMMER EVENING'S MEDITATION
[1] In Greek myth, the daughters of Hesperus (the
Evening Star) guarded the garden in which golden
apples grew on the Isles of the Blessed, at the western
extremity of the earth.

[2] Cf. Wordsworth, 'These Chairs They Have no
Words to Utter', 13: 'I have thoughts that are fed by
the sun'.
[3] *the mystic tablet* on which were written the Ten
Commandments.

A tongue in every star that talks with man
And woos him to be wise – nor woos in vain?   50
    This dead of midnight is the noon of thought,
And wisdom mounts her zenith with the stars.
At this still hour the self-collected soul
Turns inward, and beholds a stranger there
Of high descent, and more than mortal rank: 55
An embryo God, a spark of fire divine
Which must burn on for ages, when the sun
(Fair transitory creature of a day!)
Has closed his golden eye and, wrapped in shades,
Forgets his wonted journey through the east.   60
    Ye citadels of light and seats of gods!
Perhaps my future home from whence the soul,
Revolving periods past, may oft look back
With recollected tenderness on all
The various busy scenes she left below,   65
Its deep-laid projects and its strange events,
As on some fond and doting tale that soothed
Her infant hours. Oh be it lawful now
To tread the hallowed circle of your courts,
And with mute wonder and delighted awe   70
Approach your burning confines!
                              Seized in thought,
On fancy's wild and roving wing I sail,
From the green borders of the peopled earth
And the pale moon, her duteous fair attendant;
From solitary Mars; from the vast orb   75
Of Jupiter, whose huge gigantic bulk
Dances in either like the lightest leaf;
To the dim verge, the suburbs of the system[4]
Where cheerless Saturn midst her wat'ry moons,
Girt with a lucid zone, majestic sits   80
In gloomy grandeur, like an exiled queen
Amongst her weeping handmaids. Fearless thence
I launch into the trackless deeps of space
Where, burning round, ten thousand suns appear
Of elder beam, which ask no leave to shine   85
Of our terrestrial star, nor borrow light
From the proud regent of our scanty day –
Sons of the morning, first-born of creation,
And only less than Him who marks their track
And guides their fiery wheels. Here must I stop,   90
Or is there aught beyond? What hand unseen
Impels me onward through the glowing orbs

---

[4] *suburbs of the system* outskirts of the solar system.

Of habitable nature far remote,
To the dread confines of eternal night,
To solitudes of vast unpeopled space,   95
The deserts of creation, wide and wild,
Where embryo systems and unkindled suns
Sleep in the womb of chaos?
                              Fancy droops,
And thought astonished stops her bold career;
But oh, thou mighty mind, whose powerful word   100
Said, 'Thus let all things be', and thus they were –
Where shall I seek thy presence? How unblamed
Invoke thy dread perfection?
Have the broad eyelids of the morn beheld thee,
Or does the beamy shoulder of Orion   105
Support thy throne? Oh, look with pity down
On erring, guilty man – not in thy names
Of terror clad; not with those thunders armed
That conscious Sinai felt, when fear appalled
The scattered tribes: Thou hast a gentler voice   110
That whispers comfort to the swelling heart
Abashed, yet longing to behold her maker.
    But now my soul, unused to stretch her powers
In flight so daring, drops her weary wing
And seeks again the known accustomed spot   115
Dressed up with sun and shade, and lawns and streams,
A mansion fair and spacious for its guest,
And full replete with wonders. Let me here,
Content and grateful, wait th' appointed time
And ripen for the skies: the hour will come   120
When all these splendours bursting on my sight
Shall stand unveiled, and to my ravished sense
Unlock the glories of the world unknown.

From Poems (1792)

EPISTLE TO WILLIAM WILBERFORCE, ESQ., ON THE REJECTION OF THE BILL FOR ABOLISHING THE SLAVE TRADE

Cease, Wilberforce, to urge thy generous aim –
Thy country knows the sin and stands the shame!
The preacher, poet, senator, in vain
Has rattled in her sight the Negro's chain,
With his deep groans assailed her startled ear   5
And rent the veil that hid his constant tear,
Forced her averted eyes his stripes to scan,
Beneath the bloody scourge laid bare the man,
Claimed pity's tear, urged conscience's strong control
And flashed conviction on her shrinking soul.   10

The muse, too soon awaked, with ready tongue
At mercy's shrine applausive paeans rung,
And freedom's eager sons in vain foretold
A new astrean[1] reign, an age of gold!
She knows and she persists – still Afric bleeds;   15
Unchecked, the human traffic still proceeds;
She stamps her infamy to future time
And on her hardened forehead seals the crime.
    In vain, to thy white standard gathering round,
Wit, worth, and parts and eloquence are found;   20
In vain to push to birth thy great design
Contending chiefs and hostile virtues join;
All from conflicting ranks, of power possessed
To rouse, to melt, or to inform the breast.
Where seasoned tools of avarice prevail,   25
A nation's eloquence, combined, must fail.
Each flimsy sophistry by turns they try –
The plausive argument, the daring lie,
The artful gloss that moral sense confounds,
Th' acknowledged thirst of gain that honour wounds,   30
(Bane of ingenuous minds!) th' unfeeling sneer
Which sudden turns to stone the falling tear.
They search assiduous with inverted skill
For forms of wrong, and precedents of ill;
With impious mockery wrest the sacred page,   35
And glean up crimes from each remoter age;
Wrung nature's tortures, shuddering, while you tell,
From scoffing fiends bursts forth the laugh of hell;
In Britain's senate, misery's pangs give birth
To jests unseemly, and to horrid mirth –   40
Forbear! thy virtues but provoke our doom
And swell th' account of vengeance yet to come.
For (not unmarked in Heaven's impartial plan)
Shall man, proud worm, contemn his fellow man?
And injured Afric, by herself redressed,   45
Darts her own serpents at her tyrant's breast.
Each vice, to minds depraved by bondage known,
With sure contagion fastens on his own;
In sickly languors melts his nerveless frame,
And blows to rage impetuous passion's flame;   50
Fermenting swift, the fiery venom gains
The milky innocence of infant veins;
There swells the stubborn will, damps learning's fire,
The whirlwind wakes of uncontrolled desire,
Sears the young heart to images of woe   55

EPISTLE TO WILBERFORCE
[1]   *astrean* starry, cosmic.

And blasts the buds of virtue as they blow.
  Lo! where reclined, pale beauty courts the breeze,
Diffused on sofas of voluptuous ease;
With anxious awe, her menial train around
Catch her faint whispers of half-uttered sound.   60
See her, in monstrous fellowship, unite
At once the Scythian and the Sybarite;[2]
Blending repugnant vices, misallied,
Which frugal nature purposed to divide;
See her, with indolence to fierceness joined,   65
Of body delicate, infirm of mind,
With languid tones imperious mandates urge,
With arm recumbent wield the household scourge,
And with unruffled mien, and placid sounds,
Contriving torture and inflicting wounds.   70
  Nor in their palmy walks and spicy groves
The form benign of rural pleasure roves;
No milkmaid's song or hum of village talk
Soothes the lone poet in his evening walk;
No willing arm the flail unwearied plies   75
Where the mixed sounds of cheerful labour rise;
No blooming maids and frolic swains are seen
To pay gay homage to their harvest queen;
No heart-expanding scenes their eyes must prove[3]
Of thriving industry and faithful love: 80
But shrieks and yells disturb the balmy air,
Dumb sullen looks of woe announce despair
And angry eyes through dusky features glare.
Far from the sounding lash the muses fly
And sensual riot drowns each finer joy.   85
  Nor less from the gay east on essenced wings,
Breathing unnamed perfumes, contagion springs;
The soft luxurious plague alike pervades
The marble palaces and rural shades;
Hence thronged Augusta builds her rosy bowers   90
And decks in summer wreaths her smoky towers;
And hence in summer bow'rs art's costly hand
Pours courtly splendours o'er the dazzled land.
The manners melt, one undistinguished blaze
O'erwhelms the sober pomp of elder days;   95
Corruption follows with gigantic stride
And scarce vouchsafes his shameless front to hide;
The spreading leprosy taints ev'ry part,
Infects each limb, and sickens at the heart.
Simplicity! most dear of rural maids,   100

---

[2] *the Scythian and the Sybarite* the pagan and the   [3] *prove* experience, witness.
sensualist.

Weeping resigns her violated shades;
Stern independence from his glebe⁴ retires
And anxious freedom eyes her drooping fires;
By foreign wealth are British morals changed,
And Afric's sons, and India's, smile avenged.   105
    For you whose tempered ardour long has borne
Untired the labour, and unmoved the scorn,
In virtue's fasti⁵ be inscribed your fame,
And uttered yours with Howard's honoured name.⁶
Friends of the friendless – hail, ye generous band   110
Whose efforts yet arrest Heaven's lifted hand,
Around whose steady brows in union bright
The civic wreath and Christian's palm unite!
Your merit stands, no greater and no less,
Without or with the varnish of success;   115
But seek no more to break a nation's fall,
For ye have saved yourselves, and that is all.
Succeeding times your struggles, and their fate,
With mingled shame and triumph shall relate,
While faithful history in her various page,   120
Marking the features of this motley age,
To shed a glory, and to fix a stain,
Tells how you strove, and that you strove in vain.

From Works (1825)

THE RIGHTS OF WOMAN (COMPOSED *C*.1795)

Yes, injured woman – rise, assert thy right!
Woman! too long degraded, scorned, oppressed;
Oh born to rule in partial law's despite,
Resume thy native empire o'er the breast!

Go forth arrayed in panoply divine,   5
That angel pureness which admits no stain;
Go bid proud man his boasted rule resign
And kiss the golden sceptre of thy reign.

Go gird thyself with grace, collect thy store
Of bright artillery glancing from afar –   10
Soft melting tones thy thundering cannon's roar,
Blushes and fears thy magazine of war.

Thy rights are empire: urge no meaner claim –
Felt, not defined, and, if debated, lost;

---

⁴ *glebe* field.
⁵ *fasti* calendar, annals.

⁶ John Howard (1726–90), prison reformer and philanthropist.

Like sacred mysteries which, withheld from fame,   15
Shunning discussion, are revered the most.

Try all that wit and art suggest to bend
Of thy imperial foe the stubborn knee;
Make treacherous man thy subject, not thy friend –
Thou mayst command, but never canst be free.   20

Awe the licentious and restrain the rude;
Soften the sullen, clear the cloudy brow;
Be more than princes' gifts, thy favours sued –
She hazards all, who will the least allow.

But hope not, courted idol of mankind,   25
On this proud eminence secure to stay;
Subduing and subdued, thou soon shalt find
Thy coldness soften, and thy pride give way.

Then, then, abandon each ambitious thought,
Conquest or rule thy heart shall feebly move,   30
In Nature's school, by her soft maxims taught
That separate rights are lost in mutual love.

From Monthly Magazine, 7 (1799) 231–2

TO MR COLERIDGE (COMPOSED *C.*1797)

Midway the hill of science, after steep
And rugged paths that tire the unpractised feet,
A grove extends, in tangled mazes wrought,
And filled with strange enchantment: dubious shapes
Flit through dim glades, and lure the eager foot   5
Of youthful ardour to eternal chase;
Dreams hang on every leaf; unearthly forms
Glide through the gloom, and mystic visions swim
Before the cheated sense. Athwart the mists,
Far into vacant space, huge shadows stretch   10
And seem realities; while things of life,
Obvious to sight and touch, all glowing round,
Fade to the hue of shadows. Scruples here,
With filmy net, most like the autumnal webs
Of floating gossamer, arrest the foot   15
Of generous enterprise, and palsy[1] hope
And fair ambition with the chilling touch
Of sickly hesitation and blank fear.

TO MR COLERIDGE
[1] *palsy* paralyse.

Nor seldom Indolence these lawns among
Fixes her turf-built seat, and wears the garb   20
Of deep philosophy, and museful sits
In dreamy twilight of the vacant mind,
Soothed by the whispering shade – for soothing soft
The shades, and vistas lengthening into air
With moonbeam rainbows tinted. Here each mind   25
Of finer mould,[2] acute and delicate,
In its high progress to eternal truth
Rests for a space in fairy bowers entranced,
And loves the softened light and tender gloom,
And, pampered with most unsubstantial food,   30
Looks down indignant on the grosser world
And matter's cumbrous shapings.
                                        Youth beloved
Of science, of the muse beloved: not here,
Not in the maze of metaphysic lore
Build thou thy place of resting! Lightly tread   35
The dangerous ground, on noble aims intent;
And be this Circe[3] of the studious cell
Enjoyed but still subservient. Active scenes
Shall soon with healthful spirit brace thy mind,
And fair exertion, for bright fame sustained,   40
For friends, for country, chase each spleen-fed fog
That blots the wide creation:
Now heaven conduct thee with a parent's love!

Hannah More (1745–1833)

*Poet, dramatist, moralist, and educationalist – and, perhaps surprisingly, among the most
financially successful writers of her time, having made £30,000 by 1825. One of her most popular
ventures was the series of 'Cheap Repository Tracts', two million of which were sold as broadsides,
1795–8. 'The Sorrows of Yamba', though not by More, is presented here as typical of the series
and its radical, proselytizing aims. In 'Sensibility', More popularized the ideology espoused by
the intellectual women known as Blue Stockings, which influenced Charlotte Smith and Helen
Maria Williams. Wollstonecraft's* Vindication of the Rights of Woman *(1792) attacked
the cult of sensibility in favour of 'the rational woman'.*

---

[2] *mould* nature, model.
[3] *Circe* Greek enchantress who changed all who
drank her cup into swine.

From Sacred Dramas (1782)

SENSIBILITY: A POETICAL EPISTLE TO THE HON. MRS BOSCAWEN
(EXTRACT)

Sweet Sensibility, thou soothing pow'r   240
Who shed'st thy blessings on the natal hour
Like fairy favours! Art can never seize,
Nor affectation catch, thy pow'r to please;
Thy subtle essence still eludes the chains
Of definition, and defeats her pains.   245
Sweet Sensibility, thou keen delight!
Thou hasty moral, sudden sense of right,
Thou untaught goddess, virtue's precious seed,
Thou sweet precursor of the gen'rous deed!
Beauty's quick relish, reason's radiant morn   250
Which dawns soft light before reflection's born!
To those who know thee not, no words can paint,
And those who know thee, know all words are faint!
'Tis not to mourn because a sparrow dies,
To rave in artificial ecstasies;   255
'Tis not to melt in tender Otway's fires;
'Tis not to faint when injured Shore expires;
'Tis not because the ready eye o'erflows
At Clementina's or Clarissa's woes.[1]
    Forgive, oh Richardson, nor think I mean   260
With cold contempt to blast thy peerless scene;
If some faint love of virtue glow in me,
Pure spirit, I first caught that flame from thee!
    While soft compassion silently relieves,
Loquacious Feeling hints how much she gives,   265
Laments how oft her wounded heart has bled
And boasts of many a tear she never shed.
    As words are but th' external marks to tell
The fair ideas in the mind that dwell,
And only are of things the outward sign,   270
And not the things themselves they but define,
So exclamations, tender tones, fond tears,
And all the graceful drapery Pity wears –
These are not Pity's self, they but express
Her inward sufferings by their pictured dress;   275
And these fair marks (reluctant I relate),

TO SENSIBILITY
[1] More refers to Catullus's poem in which Lesbia
mourns her dead sparrow, Thomas Otway's *Venice
Preserved* (1682), Nicholas Rowe's tragedy *Jane Shore*
(1714), Richardson's *Sir Charles Grandison* (1754), the
heroine of which is called Clementina Porretta, and
Clarissa (1747–8).

These lovely symbols may be counterfeit.
   Celestial Pity! why must I deplore
Thy sacred image stamped on basest ore?
There are, who fill with brilliant plaints the page   280
If a poor linnet meet the gunner's rage;
There are, who for a dying fawn display
The tend'rest anguish in the sweetest lay;
Who for a wounded animal deplore
As if friend, parent, country were no more;   285
Who boast quick rapture trembling in their eye
If from the spider's snare they save a fly;
Whose well-sung sorrows every breast inflame,
And break all hearts but his from whom they came –
Yet, scorning life's dull duties to attend,   290
Will persecute a wife or wrong a friend;
Alive to every woe by fiction dressed,
The innocent he wronged, the wretch distressed
May plead in vain – their sufferings come not near,
Or he relieves them cheaply with a tear.   295

The Sorrows of Yamba, or the Negro Woman's Lamentation (c.1795) (published by Hannah More as a Cheap Repository broadside, but not written by her)

'In St. Lucie's distant isle
   Still with Afric's love I burn,
Parted many a thousand mile
   Never, never to return.

Come, kind death, and give me rest!   5
   Yamba has no friend but thee;
Thou canst ease my throbbing breast,
   Thou canst set the prisoner free.

Down my cheeks the tears are dripping,
   Broken is my heart with grief,   10
Mangled my poor flesh with whipping;
   Come, kind death, and bring relief!

Born on Afric's golden coast,
   Once I was as blessed as you;
Parents tender I could boast,   15
   Husband dear, and children too.

Whity man he came from far,
   Sailing o'er the briny flood,

Who, with help of British tar,
  Buys up human flesh and blood.   20

With the baby at my breast
  (Other two were sleeping by),
In my hut I sat at rest
  With no thought of danger nigh.

From the bush at eventide   25
  Rushed the fierce man-stealing crew,
Seized the children by my side,
  Seized the wretched Yamba too.

Then for love of filthy gold,
  Straight they bore me to the sea,   30
Crammed me down a slave-ship's hold
  Where were hundreds stowed like me.

Naked on the platform lying,
  Now we cross the tumbling wave –
Shrieking, sickening, fainting, dying,   35
  Dead of shame for Britons brave.

At the savage Captain's beck
  Now like brutes they make us prance;
Smack the cat about the deck,
  And in scorn they bid us dance.   40

I in groaning passed the night,
  And did roll my aching head:
At the break of morning light
  My poor child was cold and dead.

Happy, happy, there she lies!   45
  Thou shalt feel the lash no more;
Thus full many a Negro dies
  Ere we reach the destined shore.

Driven like cattle to a fair,
  See they sell us, young and old;   50
Child from mother too they tear,
  All for love of filthy gold.

I was sold to massa hard –
  Some have massas kind and good;
And again my back was scarred,   55
  Bad and stinted was my food.

Poor and wounded, faint and sick,
  All exposed to burning sky,
Massa bids me grass to pick,
  And I now am near to die.   60

What and if to death he send me,
  Savage murder though it be?
British laws shall ne'er befriend me;
  They protect not slaves like me!'

Mourning thus my wretched state   65
  (Ne'er may I forget the day),
Once in dusk of evening late,
  Far from home I dared to stray –

Dared, alas, with impious haste
  Tow'rds the roaring sea to fly;   70
Death itself I longed to taste,
  Longed to cast me in and die.

There I met upon the strand
  English missionary good;
He had Bible book in hand   75
  Which poor me no understood.

Then he led me to his cot,
  Soothed and pitied all my woe,
Told me 'twas the Christian's lot
  Much to suffer here below.   80

Told me then of God's dear Son
  (Strange and wondrous is the story),
What sad wrong to him was done
  Though he was the Lord of Glory.

Told me too, like one who knew him   85
  (Can such love as this be true?),
How he died for them that slew him,
  Died for wretched Yamba too.

Freely he his mercy proffered
  And to sinners he was sent,   90
E'en to massa pardons offered –
  Oh, if massa would repent!

Wicked deed full many a time
  Sinful Yamba too hath done,

But she wails to God her crime;   95
  But she trusts his only Son.

Oh ye slaves whom massas beat,
  Ye are stained with guilt within;
As ye hope for mercy sweet,
  So forgive your massas' sin.   100

And with grief when sinking low,
  Mark the road that Yamba trod,
Think how all her pain and woe
  Brought the captive home to God.

Now let Yamba too adore   105
  Gracious Heaven's mysterious plan;
Now I'll count thy mercies o'er
  Flowing through the guilt of man.

Now I'll bless my cruel capture
  (Hence I've known a Saviour's name),   110
Till my grief is turned to rapture
  And I half forget the blame.

But though here a convert rare
  Thanks her God for grace divine,
Let not man the glory share –   115
  Sinner, still the guilt is thine.

Duly now baptized am I
  By good missionary man;
Lord my nature purify
  As no outward water can!   120

All my former thoughts abhorred,
  Teach me now to pray and praise;
Joy and glory in my Lord,
  Trust and serve him all my days.

But though death this hour may find me,   125
  Still with Afric's love I burn
(There I've left a spouse behind me),
  Still to native land I turn.

And when Yamba sinks in death,
  This my latest prayer shall be   130
While I yield my parting breath:
  'Oh that Afric might be free!'

Cease, ye British sons of murder!
  Cease from forging Afric's chain;
Mock your Saviour's name no further,   135
  Cease your savage lust of gain.

Ye that boast ye 'rule the waves',
  Bid no slave-ship soil the sea;
Ye that 'Never will be slaves',
  Bid poor Afric's land be free.   140

Where ye gave to war its birth,
  Where your traders fixed their den,
There go publish 'Peace on earth',
  Go proclaim 'Goodwill to men.'

Where ye once have carried slaughter,   145
  Vice and slavery and sin,
Seized on husband, wife and daughter,
  Let the gospel enter in.

Thus where Yamba's native home,
  Humble hut of rushes stood –   150
Oh! if there should chance to roam
  Some dear missionary good,

Thou in Afric's distant land
  Still shalt see the man I love,
Join him to the Christian band,   155
  Guide his soul to realms above.

There no fiend again shall sever
  Those whom God hath joined and blessed;
There they dwell with Him for ever,
  There 'the weary are at rest'.[1]   160

Charlotte Smith   (1749–1806)

Poet and novelist, whose Elegiac Sonnets *(1784) gained immense critical acclaim during the
last years of the eighteenth century, Wordsworth including himself among the subscribers to
the 5th edn, 1789. Other admirers of her work include Coleridge and Leigh Hunt.*

THE SORROWS OF YAMBA
[1] Job 3: 17.

From Elegiac Sonnets (1784)

SONNET V. TO THE SOUTH DOWNS[1]

Ah, hills beloved! – where once, an happy child,
   Your beechen shades, 'your turf, your flowers among',[2]
I wove your bluebells into garlands wild
   And woke your echoes with my artless song.
Ah, hills beloved! your turf, your flowers remain;   5
   But can they peace to this sad breast restore,
For one poor moment soothe the sense of pain
   And teach a breaking heart to throb no more?
And you, Aruna, in the vale below,
   As to the sea your limpid waves you bear,   10
Can you one kind Lethean[3] cup bestow
   To drink a long oblivion to my care?
Ah no! when all, e'en hope's last ray, is gone,
There's no oblivion – but in death alone!

From Elegiac Sonnets (1786)

SONNET XXXII. TO MELANCHOLY. WRITTEN ON THE BANKS OF THE ARUN, OCTOBER 1785

When latest autumn spreads her evening veil,
   And the grey mists from these dim waves arise,
   I love to listen to the hollow sighs
Through the half-leafless wood that breathes the gale;
For at such hours the shadowy phantom pale   5
   Oft seems to fleet before the poet's eyes –
   Strange sounds are heard, and mournful melodies
As of night-wanderers who their woes bewail!
Here by his native stream at such an hour
   Pity's own Otway[1] I methinks could meet,   10
   And hear his deep sighs swell the saddened wind.
Oh Melancholy, such thy magic power
   That to the soul these dreams are often sweet,
   And soothe the pensive visionary mind!

TO THE SOUTH DOWNS
[1] Smith apparently composed this important sonnet in Woolbeding, on the South Downs, in West Sussex, which is served by the River Rother, a tributary of the River Arun.
[2] In a note Smith acknowledges an allusion to Gray, 'Ode on a Distant Prospect of Eton College', 8.

[3] Lethe is the river of forgetfulness in Hades, where souls drank and forgot their previous existence.
TO MELANCHOLY
[1] Thomas Otway (1652–85), dramatist, grew up in Woolbeding, where Smith also lived.

George Crabbe (1754–1832)

'Crabbe's the man,' Byron told John Murray in 1817 (Marchand, v. 266). One reason for Byron's admiration was Crabbe's mastery of the post-Popean manner so popular towards the end of the eighteenth century. That quality, which brought him success during his lifetime, helps explain his comparative unpopularity today. All the same, Crabbe's style should not hinder our appreciation of his imaginative genius, seen at its most striking in 'Peter Grimes', a complete text of which appears below. 'Peter Grimes' deserves to be compared with Coleridge's 'The Ancient Mariner' for its psychological insight, particularly in its handling of guilt. It is best known today through Benjamin Britten's opera (1945).

From The Borough (1810)

LETTER XXII: THE POOR OF THE BOROUGH

PETER GRIMES[1]

Old Peter Grimes made fishing his employ;
His wife he cabined with him and his boy,
And seemed that life laborious to enjoy:
To town came quiet Peter with his fish,
And had of all a civil word and wish.   5
He left his trade upon the Sabbath-day
And took young Peter in his hand to pray;
But soon the stubborn boy from care broke loose –
At first refused, then added his abuse.
His father's love he scorned, his power defied,   10
But being drunk, wept sorely when he died.
   Yes, then he wept, and to his mind there came
Much of his conduct, and he felt the shame!
How he had oft the good old man reviled,
And never paid the duty of a child;   15
How when the father in his Bible read,
He in contempt and anger left the shed:
'It is the Word of life!', the parent cried –
'This is the life itself!' the boy replied;
And while old Peter in amazement stood,   20
Gave the hot spirit to his boiling blood:
How he, with oath and furious speech, began
To prove his freedom and assert the man;
And when the parent checked his impious rage

PETER GRIMES
[1] 'The original of Peter Grimes was an old fisherman of Aldeburgh while Mr Crabbe was practising there as a surgeon. He had a succession of apprentices from London, and a certain sum with each. As the boys all disappeared under circumstances of strong suspicion, the man was warned that if another followed in like manner he should certainly be charged with murder' (note in 1834 edn of Crabbe's *Works*).

How he had cursed the tyranny of age –   25
Nay, once had dealt the sacrilegious[2] blow
On his bare head and laid his parent low!
The father groaned – 'If thou art old', said he,
'And hast a son, thou wilt remember me:
Thy mother left me in an happy time,   30
Thou kill'dst not her – Heav'n spares the double crime.'
On an inn settle[3] in his maudlin grief,
This he revolved and drank for his relief.
    Now lived the youth in freedom, but debarred
From constant pleasure, and he thought it hard –   35
Hard that he could not every wish obey,
But must awhile relinquish ale and play –
Hard that he could not to his cards attend,
But must acquire the money he would spend.
With greedy eye he looked on all he saw,   40
He knew not justice, and he laughed at law;
On all he marked, he stretched his ready hand –
He fished by water and he filched by land.
Oft in the night has Peter dropped his oar,
Fled from his boat and sought for prey on shore;   45
Oft up the hedgerow glided, on his back
Bearing the orchard's produce in a sack,
Or farmyard load tugged fiercely from the stack.
And as these wrongs to greater numbers rose,
The more he looked on all men as his foes.   50
    He built a mud-walled hovel where he kept
His various wealth, and there he oft-times slept;
But no success could please his cruel soul –
He wished for one to trouble and control;
He wanted some obedient boy to stand   55
And bear the blow of his outrageous hand,
And hoped to find in some propitious hour
A feeling creature subject to his power.
Peter had heard there were in London then
(Still have they being?) workhouse-clearing men   60
Who, undisturbed by feelings just or kind,
Would parish-boys to needy tradesmen bind.
They in their want a trifling sum would take,
And toiling slaves of piteous orphans make.[4]
    Such Peter sought, and when a lad was found,   65
The sum was dealt him and the slave was bound.

---

[2] *sacrilegious* because he was disobeying the Fifth
Commandment.
[3] *settle* bench.
[4] In order to reduce the poor-rate in London, it was
customary towards the end of the eighteenth century
to farm out children of paupers to 'masters' in other
parishes, who would be given about £5 in return for
maintaining them and teaching them a trade.

Some few in town observed in Peter's trap
A boy, with jacket blue and woollen cap;
But none enquired how Peter used the rope,
Or what the bruise that made the stripling stoop;   70
None could the ridges on his back behold,
None sought him shiv'ring in the winter's cold,
None put the question, 'Peter, dost thou give
The boy his food? — What, man? The lad must live!
Consider, Peter, let the child have bread,   75
He'll serve thee better if he's stroked and fed.'
None reasoned thus — and some, on hearing cries,
Said calmly, 'Grimes is at his exercise.'
    Pinned,⁵ beaten, cold, pinched, threatened and abused,
His efforts punished and his food refused,   80
Awake tormented, soon aroused from sleep,
Struck if he wept, and yet compelled to weep,
The trembling boy dropped down and strove to pray,
Received a blow and trembling turned away,
Or sobbed and hid his piteous face, while he,   85
The savage master, grinned in horrid glee!
He'd now the power he ever loved to show,
A feeling being subject to his blow.
    Thus lived the lad in hunger, peril, pain,
His tears despised, his supplications vain;   90
Compelled by fear to lie, by need to steal,
His bed uneasy and unblessed his meal.
For three sad years the boy his tortures bore,
And then his pains and trials were no more.
    'How died he, Peter?' — when the people said,   95
He growled, 'I found him lifeless in his bed';
Then tried for softer tone, and sighed, 'Poor Sam is dead.'
Yet murmurs were there and some questions asked —
How he was fed, how punished and how tasked?
Much they suspected but they little proved,   100
And Peter passed untroubled and unmoved.
    Another boy with equal ease was found,
The money granted and the victim bound;
And what his fate? One night it chanced he fell
From the boat's mast and perished in her well   105
Where fish were living kept, and where the boy
(So reasoned men) could not himself destroy.
'Yes, so it was!', said Peter, 'in his play;
For he was idle both by night and day!
He climbed the main mast and then fell below' —   110
Then showed his corpse and pointed to the blow.

---

⁵ *Pinned* pinned down by force.

What said the Jury? They were long in doubt,
But sturdy Peter faced the matter out.
So they dismissed him, saying at the time,
'Keep fast your hatchway when you've boys who climb.'   115
This hit the conscience, and he coloured more
Than for the closest questions put before.
Thus all his fears the verdict set aside,
And at the slave-shop Peter still applied.
   Then came a boy, of manners soft and mild –   120
Our seamen's wives with grief beheld the child;
All thought (though poor themselves) that he was one
Of gentle blood, some noble sinner's son
Who had, belike, deceived some humble maid
Whom he had first seduced and then betrayed.   125
However this, he seemed a gracious lad,
In grief submissive and with patience sad.
Passive he laboured, till his slender frame
Bent with his loads, and he at length was lame;
Strange that a frame so weak could bear so long   130
The grossest insult and the foulest wrong.
But there were causes – in the town they gave
Fire, food and comfort to the gentle slave;
And though stern Peter, with a cruel hand
And knotted rope, enforced the rude command,   135
Yet he considered what he'd lately felt,
And his vile blows with selfish pity dealt.
   One day such draughts the cruel fisher made,
He could not vend them in his borough trade
But sailed for London mart: the boy was ill,   140
But ever humbled to his master's will.
And on the river, where they smoothly sailed,
He strove with terror and awhile prevailed;
But new to danger on the angry sea,
He clung affrighted to his master's knee;   145
The boat grew leaky and the wind was strong,
Rough was the passage and the time was long;
His liquor failed, and Peter's wrath arose ...
No more is known – the rest we must suppose
Or learn of Peter. 'Peter', says he, 'spied   150
The stripling's danger and for harbour tried;
Meantime the fish and then th' apprentice died.'
   The pitying women raised a clamour round,
And weeping said, 'Thou hast thy 'prentice drowned!'
Now the stern man was summoned to the hall,   155
To tell his tale before the burghers all:
He gave th' account, professed the lad he loved,
And kept his brazen features all unmoved.
The Mayor himself with tone severe replied,

'Henceforth with thee shall never boy abide;   160
Hire thee a freeman whom thou durst not beat,
But who, in thy despite, will sleep and eat.
Free thou art now! – again shouldst thou appear,
Thou'lt find thy sentence, like thy soul, severe.'
    Alas for Peter! not an helping hand,   165
So was he hated, could he now command;
Alone he rowed his boat, alone he cast
His nets beside, or made his anchor fast;
To hold a rope or hear a curse was none –
He toiled and railed, he groaned and swore alone.   170
Thus by himself compelled to live each day,
To wait for certain hours the tide's delay;
At the same times the same dull views to see,
The bounding marsh-bank and the blighted tree;
The water only, when the tides were high,   175
When low, the mud half-covered and half-dry;
The sunburnt tar that blisters on the planks,
And bankside stakes in their uneven ranks;
Heaps of entangled weeds that slowly float
As the tide rolls by the impeded boat.   180
    When tides were neap, and in the sultry day,
Through the tall bounding mud-banks made their way,[6]
Which on each side rose swelling, and below
The dark warm flood ran silently and slow;
There anchoring, Peter chose from man to hide,   185
There hang his head, and view the lazy tide
In its hot slimy channel slowly glide –
Where the small eels that left the deeper way
For the warm shore, within the shallows play;
Where gaping mussels, left upon the mud,   190
Slope their slow passage to the fallen flood.
Here dull and hopeless he'd lie down and trace
How sidelong crabs had scrawled their crooked race,
Or sadly listen to the tuneless cry
Of fishing gull or clanging golden-eye;[7]   195
What time the seabirds to the marsh would come,
And the loud bittern, from the bullrush home,
Gave from the salt-ditch side the bellowing boom.
He nursed the feelings these dull scenes produce,
And loved to stop beside the opening sluice,   200
Where the small stream, confined in narrow bound,
Ran with a dull, unvaried, sad'ning sound –
Where all presented to the eye or ear

---

[6] When the tide is neap, the high-water level is at its lowest point, leaving a larger area of mud exposed than at other times.

[7] *golden-eye* a sea duck.

Oppressed the soul with misery, grief and fear.
　　Besides these objects there were places three   205
Which Peter seemed with certain dread to see;
When he drew near them he would turn from each,
And loudly whistle till he passed the reach.[8]
　　A change of scene to him brought no relief:
In town, 'twas plain, men took him for a thief;   210
The sailors' wives would stop him in the street
And say, 'Now, Peter, thou'st no boy to beat!'
Infants at play, when they perceived him, ran,
Warning each other, 'That's the wicked man!'
He growled an oath, and in an angry tone   215
Cursed the whole place and wished to be alone.
Alone he was, the same dull scenes in view,
And still more gloomy in his sight they grew.
Though man he hated, yet employed alone
At bootless labour, he would swear and groan,   220
Cursing the shoals that glided by the spot,
And gulls that caught them when his arts could not.
　　Cold nervous tremblings shook his sturdy frame,
And strange disease (he couldn't say the name);
Wild were his dreams, and oft he rose in fright,   225
Waked by his view of horrors in the night –
Horrors that would the sternest minds amaze,
Horrors that demons might be proud to raise.
And though he felt forsaken, grieved at heart
To think he lived from all mankind apart,   230
Yet if a man approached, in terrors he would start.
　　A winter passed since Peter saw the town,
And summer lodgers were again come down;
These, idly curious, with their glasses spied
The ships in bay as anchored for the tide –   235
The river's craft, the bustle of the quay,
And sea-port views which landmen love to see.
One, up the river, had a man and boat
Seen day by day – now anchored, now afloat.
Fisher he seemed, yet used no net nor hook;   240
Of sea fowl swimming by no heed he took,
But on the gliding waves still fixed his lazy look.
At certain stations he would view the stream
As if he stood bewildered in a dream,
Or that some power had chained him for a time   245
To feel a curse or meditate on crime.
　　This known, some curious, some in pity went,
And others questioned, 'Wretch, dost thou repent?'

---

[8]   *reach* portion of the river between two bends.

He heard, he trembled, and in fear resigned
His boat: new terror filled his restless mind.   250
Furious he grew and up the country ran,
And there they seized him – a distempered man.
Him we received, and to a parish bed,
Followed and cursed, the groaning man was led.
Here when they saw him whom they used to shun –   255
A lost lone man, so harassed and undone –
Our gentle females (ever prompt to feel)
Perceived compassion on their anger steal;
His crimes they couldn't from their memories blot,
But they were grieved and trembled at his lot.   260
A priest too came to whom his words are told,
And all the signs they shuddered to behold.
    'Look, look!' they cried, 'his limbs with horror shake,
And as he grinds his teeth, what noise they make!
How glare his angry eyes, and yet he's not awake!   265
See what cold drops upon his forehead stand,
And how he clenches that broad bony hand!'
The priest attending found he spoke at times
As one alluding to his fears and crimes:
'It was the fall', he muttered, 'I can show   270
The manner how – I never struck a blow!'
And then aloud, 'Unhand me, free my chain!
On oath, he fell – it struck him to the brain!
Why ask my father? That old man will swear
Against my life – besides he wasn't there!   275
What, all agreed? Am I to die today?
My Lord, in mercy, give me time to pray!'
    Then as they watched him, calmer he became,
And grew so weak he couldn't move his frame,
But murmuring spake, while they could see and hear   280
The start of terror and the groan of fear;
See the large dew-beads on his forehead rise
And the cold death-drop glaze his sunken eyes.
Nor yet he died, but with unwonted force
Seemed with some fancied being to discourse.   285
He knew not us, or with accustomed art
He hid the knowledge, yet exposed his heart;
'Twas part confession and the rest defence –
A madman's tale, with gleams of waking sense.
    'I'll tell you all', he said, 'the very day   290
When the old man first placed them in my way –
My father's spirit (he who always tried
To give me trouble when he lived and died)!
When he was gone, he could not be content
To see my days in painful labour spent,   295
But would appoint his meetings, and he made

Me watch at these, and so neglect my trade.
  'Twas one hot noon – all silent, still, serene;
No living being had I lately seen.
I paddled up and down and dipped my net   300
But (such his pleasure) I could nothing get;
A father's pleasure! – when his toil was done,
To plague and torture thus an only son.
And so I sat and looked upon the stream,
How it ran on – and felt as in a dream: 305
But dream it was not. No – I fixed my eyes
On the midstream and saw the spirits rise:
I saw my father on the water stand
And hold a thin pale boy in either hand,
And there they glided ghastly on the top   310
Of the salt flood, and never touched a drop.
I would have struck them, but they knew th' intent,
And smiled upon the oar, and down they went.
  Now from that day, whenever I began
To dip my net, there stood the hard old man,   315
He and those boys. I humbled me and prayed
They would be gone – they heeded not but stayed.
Nor could I turn, nor would the boat go by,
But gazing on the spirits, there was I;
They bade me leap to death, but I was loath to die.   320
And every day, as sure as day arose,
Would these three spirits meet me ere the close:
To hear and mark them daily was my doom,
And "Come", they said with weak sad voices, "come!"
To row away with all my strength I tried,   325
But there were they, hard by me in the tide,
The three unbodied forms – and "Come", still "come!" they cried.
  Fathers should pity, but this old man shook
His hoary locks and froze me by a look.
Thrice, when I struck them, through the water came   330
An hollow groan that weakened all my frame.
"Father," said I, "have mercy!" He replied
I know not what – the angry spirit lied:
"Didst thou not draw thy knife?" said he. 'Twas true,
But I had pity and my arm withdrew;   335
He cried for mercy, which I kindly gave,
But he has no compassion in his grave.
  There were three places where they ever rose –
The whole long river has not such as those –
Places accursed where, if a man remain,   340
He'll see the things which strike him to the brain.
And there they made me on my paddle lean
And look at them for hours – accursed scene!
When they would glide to that smooth eddy space,

Then bid me leap and join them in the place;   345
And at my groans each little villain sprite
Enjoyed my pains and vanished in delight.
   In one fierce summer day, when my poor brain
Was burning hot, and cruel was my pain,
Then came this father-foe, and there he stood   350
With his two boys again upon the flood.
There was more mischief in their eyes, more glee
In their pale faces when they glared at me.
Still did they force me on the oar to rest,
And when they saw me fainting and oppressed,   355
He with his hand (the old man) scooped the flood,
And there came flame about him mixed with blood;
He bade me stoop and look upon the place,
Then flung the hot red liquor in my face –
Burning it blazed, and then I roared for pain –   360
I thought the demons would have turned my brain!
   Still there they stood, and forced me to behold
A place of horrors – they cannot be told:
Where the flood opened, there I heard the shriek
Of tortured guilt no earthly tongue can speak.   365
"All days alike for ever!" did they say,
"And unremitted torments every day!"
Yes, so they said . . .' But here he ceased and gazed
On all around, affrightened and amazed;
And still he tried to speak and looked in dread   370
Of frightened females gathering round his bed,
Then dropped exhausted and appeared at rest,
Till the strong foe the vital powers possessed.
Then with an inward, broken voice he cried,
'Again they come!' and muttered as he died.   375

George Dyer (1755–1841)

Dyer's Complaints of the Poor People of England *was among the numerous responses to
Burke's* Reflections, *but, unlike many of the other radicals, Dyer writes as a representative of
the oppressed. 'The Injustice of the Law' is an example of the* Complaints *at its best; beginning
with an outline of the situation, Dyer finally allows his indignation to boil over in a statement
of 'broad English'. Although he became best known as a scholar and man of letters, Dyer was
also the author of a moving confessional lyric: 'In Deep Distress', inspired by depression at his
failing sight, and published here for the first time, apparently draws on the prime confessional
poem of the age, Coleridge's 'Dejection: An Ode' (pp. 560–4).*

From The Complaints of the Poor People of England (1793)

THE INJUSTICE OF THE LAW (PP. 55–8)

The air and the water, and the creatures that live in them, are the common gifts of providence. And till a man has, by his own industry, acquired some right in what nature has left common, they are as much one man's as another's. How far society has a right to appropriate what nature has left common, I shall not stop to enquire. God has never said, the squire may shoot a partridge or a pheasant, but the labourer shall not. Or that Sir Robert may draw the fish out of the river, and that his poor tenant shall be imprisoned for the same action.

I do but just mention these among the many laws that oppress the poor, and not to insist that these are unjust – which, however, they certainly are. I affirm in general that the more injustice there is in the laws, the greater is the necessity for their being known, that a poor man may not be caught in a trap by his ignorance.

Considering the present complicated system of our laws, and the vast number of causes (the consequence of such a system) that are tried in our courts of law, frequent circumlocutions and the use of many technical expressions are useful for the profession and cannot be avoided. But this is only admitting that the smaller evil is tolerable that qualifies the greater. The greater evil should be removed.

I know it will be said that poor men need not be so ignorant of these laws as I seem to intimate. And I acknowledge that as the squire and lord of the manor are taught by our laws to consider the birds and the fish as their property, they are likely to let the poor man know who is master. And as they have time and money to procure the acts of parliament, and see occasion, may have them written out plain and get them pasted up in the village. This, however, is accidental; it may or it may not happen. But in a thousand instances in which the interest of the poor is concerned, it is literally true that a poor man has neither time nor money to know what our laws have made (in many instances unjustly) his duty, or to ascertain his just rights. In this country the consumption of time and money necessary to know what is law is more than poor men can afford to lose. And, after all, perhaps they may get ensnared, for if they should be able to spell out an act of parliament, they may probably get tricked by some dirty lawyer – if not directly to get money, in compliance at least with the wishes of some great person, and through fear of doing justice to a poor man.

Several poor men are now lingering in prison, when the men who have thrown them in are the criminals. But ignorance was the lot of the poor man, and their prosecutors and lawyers were, in broad English, KNOWING RASCALS.

'In Deep Distress, I Cried to God' (edited from MS)

In deep distress, I cried to God,
To God I cried, and told my grief;
He heard, and in my time of need
His goodness sent the wished relief.[1]

IN DEEP DISTRESS
[1]   Coleridge uses the grief/relief rhyme in 'Dejection: An Ode', 22–3.

But still I mourned, for though relieved,   5
I felt my heart of secret sin,
And though relieved from foes without,
I felt a lurking foe within.

Body and mind, by night and day,
Pressed on me with their baneful powers;   10
My frailties had disturbed my days,
And frightful dreams my midnight hours.

And when in sleep my eyelids close,
Short is the sweet repose of sleep;
I wake, but ah! I wake in vain –   15
Alas, I only wake to weep.

My voice grows faint, my spirits droop,[2]
And all of life within me dies;
I strive to utter my complaint,
But I can only breathe in sighs.   20

Oh for that grace to sinners given,
That grace so ample, rich and free!
Shall that which is vouchsafed to all
Be, oh my God, denied to me?

Ah no! thy deeds of ancient times,   25
Thy works of love, unfold my will;
Thou art, Jehovah, still the same,
The same benignant Being still.

Thy firm decree is nature's law,
And worlds move as thy hand directs;   30
No eye can pierce the wondrous cause,
But all perceive the vast effects.

In heaven and earth, through seas and skies,
In all we see or feel or hear,
Each has a voice that speaks to man,   35
Each speaks a God for ever near.

The seas, as by thy presence ruled,
Over the mountain-tops aspire,
Or troubled, as if seeing thee,
Into their inmost caves retire.   40

---

[2] *my spirits droop* compare both Milton, 'Samson
Agonistes', 594: 'my genial spirits droop', and Coleridge, 'Dejection: An Ode', 40.

William Godwin (1756–1836)

In a mood of extreme optimism, the radical Godwin envisaged a society in which institutions would wither away thanks to a progressive moral improvement in humanity, which he believed would come about through the influence of Reason. Ultimately, he suggested, all would be made morally perfect. Published February 1793, within weeks of the execution of Louis XVI, Political Justice became a rallying point for embattled radicalism in England; among its early readers was Wordsworth, who discusses his flirtation and disillusionment with Godwinism in Thirteen-Book Prelude, *x. 805–904. Coleridge was always sceptical of Godwin, in large part because of his atheism. Nevertheless, the two men became friends during the later 1790s, and Coleridge advised him on revisions to the 3rd edn of* Political Justice *(1798).*

The extracts below come from the 1st edn, which was the most influential. 'On Property' provides Godwin's most concise account of the world he would ideally like to live in; 'Love of Justice' outlines his belief that humanity is motivated by an innate sense of moral good; 'On Marriage' observes that marriage is a branch of the property system, and suggests that in a rational society propagation would be motivated not by lust but 'by the dictates of reason and duty'.

From Political Justice (2 vols., 1793)

ON PROPERTY (II 806–7)

Accumulated property treads the powers of thought in the dust, extinguishes the sparks of genius, and reduces the great mass of mankind to be immersed in sordid cares – beside depriving the rich (as we have already said) of the most salubrious and effectual motives to activity.

If superfluity were banished, the necessity for the greater part of the manual industry of mankind would be superseded, and the rest (being amicably shared among all the active and vigorous members of the community) would be burdensome to none. Every man would have a frugal yet wholesome diet; every man would go forth to that moderate exercise of his corporal functions that would give hilarity to the spirits – none would be made torpid with fatigue, but all would have leisure to cultivate the kindly and philanthropical[1] affections of the soul, and to let loose his faculties in the search of intellectual improvement.

What a contrast does this scene present us with the present state of human society, where the peasant and the labourer work till their understandings are benumbed with toil, their sinews contracted and made callous by being forever on the stretch, and their bodies invaded with infirmities and surrendered to an untimely grave! What is the fruit of this disproportioned and unceasing toil? At evening they return to a family, famished with hunger, exposed half-naked to the inclemencies of the sky, hardly sheltered, and denied the slenderest instruction (unless in a few instances, where it is dispensed by the hands of ostentatious charity, and the first lesson communicated is unprincipled servility). All this while their rich neighbour – but we visited him before.

ON PROPERTY
[1] *philanthropical* benevolent.

LOVE OF JUSTICE (II 808)

All men love justice. All men are conscious that man is a being of one common nature, and feel the propriety of the treatment they receive from one another being measured by a common standard. Every man is desirous of assisting another, whether we should choose to ascribe this to an instinct implanted in his nature which renders this conduct a source of personal gratification, or to his perception of the reasonableness of such assistance. So necessary a part is this of the constitution of mind, that no man perpetrates any action, however criminal, without having first invented some sophistry, some palliation, by which he proves to himself that it is best to be done.

Hence it appears that offence, the invasion of one man upon the security of another, is a thought alien to mind, and which nothing could have reconciled to us but the sharp sting of necessity. To consider merely the present order of human society, it is evident that the first offence must have been his who began a monopoly, and took advantage of the weakness of his neighbours to secure certain exclusive privileges to himself. The man on the other hand who determined to put an end to this monopoly, and who peremptorily demanded what was superfluous to the possessor and would be of extreme benefit to himself, appeared to his own mind to be merely avenging the violated laws of justice. Were it not for the plausibleness of this apology, it is to be presumed that there would be no such thing as crime in the world.

ON MARRIAGE (II 849–52)

It is absurd to expect that the inclinations and wishes of two human beings should coincide through any long period of time. To oblige them to act and to live together is to subject them to some inevitable portion of thwarting, bickering, and unhappiness. This cannot be otherwise so long as man has failed to reach the standard of absolute perfection. The supposition that I must have a companion for life is the result of a complication of vices. It is the dictate of cowardice, and not of fortitude. It flows from the desire of being loved and esteemed for something that is not desert.[1]

But the evil of marriage as it is practised in European countries lies deeper than this. The habit is for a thoughtless and romantic youth of each sex to come together, to see each other for a few times and under circumstances full of delusion, and then to vow to each other eternal attachment.

What is the consequence of this? In almost every instance they find themselves deceived. They are reduced to make the best of an irretrievable mistake. They are presented with the strongest imaginable temptation to become the dupes of falsehood. They are led to conceive it their wisest policy to shut their eyes upon realities, happy if by any perversion of intellect they can persuade themselves that they were right in their first crude opinion of their companion. The institution of marriage is a system of fraud – and men who carefully mislead their judgements in the daily affair of their life must always have a crippled judgement in every other concern.

We ought to dismiss our mistake as soon as it is detected, but we are taught to cherish it. We ought to be incessant in our search after virtue and worth, but we are taught to check our enquiry and shut our eyes upon the most attractive and admirable

---

ON MARRIAGE
[1] *desert* deserving.

objects. Marriage is law, and the worst of all laws. Whatever our understandings may tell us of the person from whose connection we should derive the greatest improvement – of the worth of one woman and the demerits of another – we are obliged to consider what is law, and not what is justice.

Add to this that marriage is an affair of property, and the worst of all properties. So long as two human beings are forbidden by positive institution to follow the dictates of their own mind, prejudice is alive and vigorous. So long as I seek to engross one woman to myself, and to prohibit my neighbour from proving his superior desert and reaping the fruits of it, I am guilty of the most odious of all monopolies. Over this imaginary prize men watch with perpetual jealousy, and one man will find his desires and his capacity to circumvent as much excited, as the other is excited to traverse his projects and frustrate his hopes. As long as this state of society continues, philanthropy will be crossed and checked in a thousand ways, and the still augmenting stream of abuse will continue to flow.

The abolition of marriage will be attended with no evils. We are apt to represent it to ourselves as the harbinger of brutal lust and depravity. But it really happens (in this as in other cases) that the positive laws which are made to restrain our vices, irritate and multiply them – not to say that the same sentiments of justice and happiness which in a state of equal property would destroy the relish for luxury, would decrease our inordinate appetites of every kind, and lead us universally to prefer the pleasures of intellect to the pleasures of sense.

The intercourse of the sexes will in such a state fall under the same system as any other species of friendship. Exclusively of all groundless and obstinate attachments, it will be impossible for me to live in the world without finding one man of a worth superior to that of any other whom I have an opportunity of observing. To this man I shall feel a kindness in exact proportion to my apprehension of his worth. The case will be precisely the same with respect to the female sex. I shall assiduously cultivate the intercourse of that woman whose accomplishments shall strike me in the most powerful manner. 'But it may happen that other men will feel for her the same preference that I do': this will create no difficulty. We may all enjoy her conversation, and we shall all be wise enough to consider the sensual intercourse as a very trivial object. This, like every other affair in which two persons are concerned, must be regulated in each successive instance by the unforced consent of either party.

It is a mark of the extreme depravity of our present habits that we are inclined to suppose the sensual intercourse any wise material to the advantages arising from the purest affection. Reasonable men now eat and drink not from the love of pleasure, but because eating and drinking are essential to our healthful existence. Reasonable men then will propagate their species not because a certain sensible pleasure is annexed to this action, but because it is right the species should be propagated. And the manner in which they exercise this function will be regulated by the dictates of reason and duty.

Ann Yearsley (1756–1806)

Yearsley worked as a milkmaid near Bristol until Hannah More arranged for the publication of her poetry and tried to set her up as a schoolmistress. Her keen sense of injustice is evident in A Poem on the Inhumanity of the Slave Trade *(1788); the extract reproduced here describes the fate of a slave, Luco, when he is captured, separated from his beloved Incilanda, and put to work on a sugar plantation.*

From A Poem on the Inhumanity of the Slave Trade (1788)

Luco is borne around the neighb'ring isles,
Losing the knowledge of his native shore
Amid the pathless wave, destined to plant 215
The sweet luxuriant cane. He strives to please,
Nor once complains, but greatly smothers grief.
His hands are blistered, and his feet are worn,
Till ev'ry stroke dealt by his mattock[1] gives
Keen agony to life; while from his breast 220
The sigh arises, burdened with the name
Of Incilanda. Time inures the youth,
His limbs grow nervous, strained by willing toil;
And resignation, or a calm despair
(Most useful either) lulls him to repose. 225
   A Christian renegade – that from his soul
Abjures the tenets of our schools, nor dreads
A future punishment, nor hopes for mercy –
Had fled from England to avoid those laws
Which must have made his life a retribution 230
To violated justice, and had gained,
By fawning guile, the confidence (ill-placed)
Of Luco's master. O'er the slave he stands
With knotted whip, lest fainting nature shun
The task too arduous, while his cruel soul 235
Unnat'ral, ever feeds with gross delight
Upon his suff'rings. Many slaves there were,
But none who could suppress the sigh, and bend
So quietly as Luco. Long he bore
The stripes that from his manly bosom drew 240
The sanguine stream (too little prized). At length
Hope fled his soul, giving her struggles o'er,
And he resolved to die. The sun had reached
His zenith; pausing faintly, Luco stood
Leaning upon his hoe, while mem'ry brought, 245
In piteous imag'ry, his aged father,
His poor fond mother, and his faithful maid.
The mental group in wildest motion set
Fruitless imagination: fury, grief,
Alternate shame, the sense of insult – all 250

POEM ON THE INHUMANITY OF THE SLAVE TRADE
[1] *mattock* tool for loosening hard ground.

Conspire to aid the inward storm. Yet words
Were no relief, he stood in silent woe.
    Gorgon, remorseless Christian, saw the slave
Stand musing mid the ranks and, stealing soft
Behind the studious Luco, struck his cheek   255
With a too-heavy whip that reached his eye,
Making it dark for ever. Luco turned
In strongest agony, and with his hoe
Struck the rude Christian on the forehead. Pride,
With hateful malice, seize on Gorgon's soul,   260
By nature fierce; while Luco sought the beach
And plunged beneath the wave. But near him lay
A planter's barge, whose seamen grasped his hair,
Dragging to life a wretch who wished to die.
    Rumour now spreads the tale, while Gorgon's breath   265
Envenomed, aids her blast: imputed crimes
Oppose the plea of Luco, till he scorns
Even a just defence and stands prepared.
The planters, conscious that to fear alone
They owe their cruel pow'r, resolve to blend   270
New torment with the pangs of death, and hold
Their victims high in dreadful view, to fright
The wretched number left. Luco is chained
To a huge tree, his fellow slaves are ranged
To share the horrid sight. Fuel is placed   275
In an increasing train some paces back
To kindle slowly, and approach the youth
With more than native terror. See, it burns!
He gazes on the growing flame, and calls
For 'water, water!' The small boon's denied.   280
E'en Christians throng each other to behold
The different alterations of his face
As the hot death approaches. (Oh shame, shame
Upon the followers of Jesus! Shame
On him that dares avow a God!) He writhes,   285
While down his breast glide the unpitied tears,
And in their sockets strain their scorched balls.
'Burn, burn me quick! I cannot die!' he cries,
'Bring fire more close!' The planters heed him not,
But still prolonging Luco's torture, threat   290
Their trembling slaves around. His lips are dry,
His senses seem to quiver ere they quit
His frame for ever, rallying strong, then driv'n
From the tremendous conflict.
                       Sight no more
Is Luco's, his parched tongue is ever mute.   295
Yet in his soul his Incilanda stays
Till both escape together. Turn, my muse,

From this sad scene; lead Bristol's milder soul[2]
To where the solitary spirit roves
Wrapped in the robe of innocence, to shades   300
Where pity breathing in the gale dissolves
The mind, when fancy paints such real woe.

William Blake   (1757–1827)

'Blake is a real name, I assure you – and a most extraordinary man, if he be still living' (Lucas, ii. 424). Blake was indeed still alive but, by the time Lamb made this remark to Bernard Barton in 1824, living in poverty and obscurity. During his lifetime, his work enjoyed only a limited circulation (partly because each copy of his books was hand-printed and hand-illuminated), and it was only in the late nineteenth century that Alexander Gilchrist's biography (1863) brought about a revival of interest in him.

The Book of Thel concerns the place of sexual experience in life, and introduces a number of preoccupations: a parallel world, a fall from grace, and sexual initiation. The fact that Blake varied the order of his Songs of Innocence and of Experience, sometimes placing some of the former ('The Schoolboy' and 'The Voice of the Ancient Bard', e.g.) among the latter, suggests that he regarded the two groupings as less in opposition than as companions to each other. Early admirers of the Songs included Wordsworth and Lamb. With its claim that the imagination reveals a higher, spiritual reality ('If the doors of perception were cleansed, everything would appear to man as it is: infinite'), The Marriage of Heaven and Hell might be argued to be the first truly romantic work. For Blake, the imagination is both creative and perceptive, and instrumental in the fulfilment of his revolutionary aims. Visions of the Daughters of Albion extends the concerns of Thel in a plea for tolerance in sexual politics and an attack on the imperialistic, chauvinistic attitudes of the time. Underlying these works is the nagging question: why did God permit the Fall? Blake attempts an answer in The Book of Urizen, which contains the kernel of the mythology developed in Jerusalem and Milton and recapitulated in detail in The Four Zoas.

All Religions Are One (composed c.1788)

The voice of one crying in the wilderness.
The Argument. As the true method of knowledge is experiment, the true faculty of knowing must be the faculty which experiences: this faculty I treat of.

Principle 1. That the poetic genius is the true man, and that the body or outward form of man is derived from the poetic genius. Likewise that the forms of all things are derived from their genius which, by the ancients, was called an angel and spirit and demon.

Principle 2. As all men are alike in outward form, so (and with the same infinite variety) all are alike in the poetic genius.

Principle 3. No man can think, write or speak from his heart, but he must intend truth. Thus all sects of philosophy are from the poetic genius adapted to the weaknesses of every individual.

---

[2]   Many slave-traders operated from Bristol.

Principle 4. As none by travelling over known lands can find out the unknown, so, from already acquired knowledge, man could not acquire more. Therefore an universal poetic genius exists.

Principle 5. The religions of all nations are derived from each nation's different reception of the poetic genius, which is everywhere called the spirit of prophecy.

Principle 6. The Jewish and Christian Testaments are an original derivation from the poetic genius. This is necessary from the confined nature of bodily sensation.

Principle 7. As all men are alike (though infinitely various), so all religions and, as all similars, have one source.

The true man is the source, he being the poetic genius.

There is no natural religion (a)

The Argument. Man has no notion of moral fitness but from education. Naturally he is only a natural organ subject to sense.

I Man cannot naturally perceive but through his natural or bodily organs.

II Man by his reasoning power can only compare and judge of what he has already perceived.

III From a perception of only three senses or three elements none could deduce a fourth or fifth.

IV None could have other than natural or organic thoughts if he had none but organic perceptions.

V Man's desires are limited by his perceptions; none can desire what he has not perceived.

VI The desires and perceptions of man, untaught by anything but organs of sense, must be limited to objects of sense.

There is no natural religion (b)

I Man's perceptions are not bounded by organs of perception. He perceives more than sense (though ever so acute) can discover.

II Reason, or the ratio of all we have already known, is not the same that it shall be when we know more.

III [*missing*]

IV The bounded is loathed by its possessor. The same dull round, even of a universe, would soon become a mill with complicated wheels.

V If the many become the same as the few when possessed, 'More, more!' is the cry of a mistaken soul; less than all cannot satisfy man.

VI If any could desire what he is incapable of possessing, despair must be his eternal lot.

VII The desire of man being infinite, the possession is infinite, and himself infinite.

Conclusion. If it were not for the poetic or prophetic character, the philosophic and experimental would soon be at the ratio of all things, and stand still, unable to do other than repeat the same dull round over again.

Application. He who sees the infinite in all things, sees God. He who sees the ratio only, sees himself only.

Therefore God becomes as we are, that we may be as He is.

The Book of Thel (1789)

Thel's Motto

Does the eagle know what is in the pit
Or wilt thou go ask the mole?
Can wisdom be put in a silver rod
Or love in a golden bowl?

Thel

I

The daughters of Mne Seraphim led round their sunny flocks,
All but the youngest; she in paleness sought the secret air,
To fade away like morning beauty from her mortal day.
Down by the river of Adona her soft voice is heard,
And thus her gentle lamentation falls like morning dew: 5
   'Oh life of this our spring, why fades the lotus of the water?
Why fade these children of the spring, born but to smile and fall?
Ah, Thel is like a wat'ry bow and like a parting cloud,
Like a reflection in a glass, like shadows in the water,
Like dreams of infants, like a smile upon an infant's face,   10
Like the dove's voice, like transient day, like music in the air.
Ah, gentle may I lay me down, and gentle rest my head;
And gentle sleep the sleep of death, and gentle hear the voice
Of him that walketh in the garden in the evening time.'
   The lily of the valley[1] breathing in the humble grass   15
Answered the lovely maid and said, 'I am a wat'ry weed,
And I am very small, and love to dwell in lowly vales –
So weak, the gilded butterfly scarce perches on my head.
Yet I am visited from heaven, and he that smiles on all
Walks in the valley, and each morn over me spreads his hand   20
Saying, "Rejoice, thou humble grass, thou new-born lily flower,
Thou gentle maid of silent valleys, and of modest brooks;
For thou shalt be clothed in light, and fed with morning manna
Till summer's heat melts thee beside the fountains and the springs
To flourish in eternal vales!" Then why should Thel complain?   25
Why should the mistress of the vales of Har utter a sigh?'
She ceased and smiled in tears, then sat down in her silver shrine.
   Thel answered: 'Oh thou little virgin of the peaceful valley,
Giving to those that cannot crave – the voiceless, the o'ertired;
Thy breath doth nourish the innocent lamb, he smells thy milky garments,   30
He crops thy flowers while thou sittest smiling in his face,

THE BOOK OF THEL
[1] *lily of the valley* flower of innocence, symbol of
Thel's virginity.

Wiping his mild and meekin² mouth from all contagious taints.
Thy wine doth purify the golden honey; thy perfume,
Which thou dost scatter on every little blade of grass that springs,
Revives the milked cow, and tames the fire-breathing steed.   35
But Thel is like a faint cloud kindled at the rising sun:
I vanish from my pearly throne, and who shall find my place?'
    'Queen of the vales', the lily answered, 'ask the tender cloud³
And it shall tell thee why it glitters in the morning sky,
And why it scatters its bright beauty through the humid air: 40
Descend, oh little cloud, and hover before the eyes of Thel.'
    The cloud descended, and the lily bowed her modest head
And went to mind her numerous charge among the verdant grass.

II

'Oh little cloud', the virgin said, 'I charge thee tell to me
Why thou complainest not when in one hour thou fade away;   45
Then we shall seek thee but not find. Ah, Thel is like to thee:
I pass away – yet I complain, and no one hears my voice.
    The cloud then showed his golden head and his bright form emerged,
Hovering and glittering on the air before the face of Thel.
'Oh virgin, know'st thou not our steeds drink of the golden springs   50
Where Luvah⁴ doth renew his horses? Look'st thou on my youth,
And fearest thou because I vanish and am seen no more?
Nothing remains. Oh maid, I tell thee, when I pass away,
It is to tenfold life – to love, to peace, and raptures holy;
Unseen descending, weigh my light wings upon balmy flowers,   55
And court the fair-eyed dew to take me to her shining tent:
The weeping virgin trembling kneels before the risen sun
Till we arise linked in a golden band, and never part,
But walk united, bearing food to all our tender flowers.'
    'Dost thou, oh little cloud? I fear that I am not like thee;   60
For I walk through the vales of Har and smell the sweetest flowers,
But I feed not the little flowers; I hear the warbling birds,
But I feed not the warbling birds – they fly and seek their food.
But Thel delights in these no more because I fade away,
And all shall say, "Without a use this shining woman lived –   65
Or did she only live to be at death the food of worms?"'
    The cloud reclined upon his airy throne and answered thus:
'Then if thou art the food of worms, oh virgin of the skies,
How great thy use, how great thy blessing! Everything that lives
Lives not alone, nor for itself. Fear not, and I will call   70
The weak worm from its lowly bed, and thou shalt hear its voice.

---

² *meekin* meek.
³ *the tender cloud* the male principle.

⁴ *Luvah* god of desire; one of Blake's Four Zoas (the
four principles which rule human life).

Come forth, worm of the silent valley, to thy pensive queen!'
 The helpless worm arose and sat upon the lily's leaf,
And the bright cloud sailed on to find his partner in the vale.

III

Then Thel, astonished, viewed the worm upon its dewy bed. 75
'Art thou a worm? Image of weakness, art thou but a worm?
I see thee like an infant wrapped in the lily's leaf;
Ah, weep not, little voice, thou canst not speak but thou canst weep.
Is this a worm? I see thee lay helpless and naked – weeping
And none to answer, none to cherish thee with mother's smiles.' 80
 The clod of clay heard the worm's voice⁵ and raised her pitying head:
She bowed over the weeping infant, and her life exhaled
In milky fondness; then on Thel she fixed her humble eyes.
'Oh, beauty of the vales of Har, we live not for ourselves!
Thou seest me the meanest thing, and so I am indeed; 85
My bosom of itself is cold, and of itself is dark,
But he that loves the lowly pours his oil upon my head
And kisses me, and binds his nuptial bands around my breast,
And says, "Thou mother of my children, I have loved thee,
And I have given thee a crown that none can take away." 90
But how this is, sweet maid, I know not and I cannot know;
I ponder and I cannot ponder – yet I live and love.'
 The daughter of beauty wiped her pitying tears with her white veil
And said, 'Alas, I knew not this, and therefore did I weep.
That God would love a worm, I knew, and punish the evil foot 95
That, wilful, bruised its helpless form. But that he cherished it
With milk and oil, I never knew. And therefore did I weep,
And I complained in the mild air because I fade away,
And lay me down in thy cold bed, and leave my shining lot.'
 'Queen of the vales', the matron clay answered, 'I heard thy sighs, 100
And all thy moans flew o'er my roof, but I have called them down.
Wilt thou, oh Queen, enter my house? 'Tis given thee to enter
And to return. Fear nothing; enter with thy virgin feet.'

IV

The eternal gate's terrific porter lifted the northern bar;
Thel entered in and saw the secrets of the land unknown. 105
She saw the couches of the dead, and where the fibrous roots
Of every heart on earth infixes deep its restless twists –
A land of sorrows and of tears where never smile was seen.

---

⁵ The worm and the clod are the baby and its
mother.

She wandered in the land of clouds through valleys dark, list'ning
Dolours and lamentations; waiting oft beside a dewy grave   110
She stood in silence, list'ning to the voices of the ground,
Till to her own grave-plot she came, and there she sat down
And heard this voice of sorrow breathed from the hollow pit:
  'Why cannot the ear be closed to its own destruction,
Or the glist'ning eye, to the poison of a smile?   115
Why are eyelids stored with arrows ready drawn
Where a thousand fighting men in ambush lie,
Or an eye of gifts and graces, show'ring fruits and coined gold?
Why a tongue impressed with honey from every wind?
Why an ear, a whirlpool fierce to draw creations in?   120
Why a nostril wide inhaling terror, trembling and affright?
Why a tender curb upon the youthful burning boy?
Why a little curtain of flesh on the bed of our desire?'
  The virgin started from her seat, and with a shriek
Fled back unhindered till she came into the vales of Har.   125

Songs of Innocence and of Experience (1789–94)

Songs of Innocence (1789)

INTRODUCTION

Piping down the valleys wild,
Piping songs of pleasant glee,
On a cloud I saw a child
And he laughing said to me:

'Pipe a song about a lamb!'   5
So I piped with a merry cheer;
'Piper, pipe that song again!'
So I piped – he wept to hear.

'Drop thy pipe, thy happy pipe,
Sing thy songs of happy cheer!'
So I sung the same again   10
While he wept with joy to hear.

'Piper, sit thee down and write
In a book, that all may read.'
So he vanished from my sight   15
And I plucked a hollow reed.

And I made a rural pen,
And I stained the water clear,
And I wrote my happy songs
Every child may joy to hear.   20

THE SHEPHERD

How sweet is the shepherd's sweet lot!
From the morn to the evening he strays;
He shall follow his sheep all the day
And his tongue shall be filled with praise.

For he hears the lamb's innocent call,   5
And he hears the ewe's tender reply;
He is watchful while they are in peace,
For they know when their shepherd is nigh.

THE ECHOING GREEN

The sun does arise
And make happy the skies;
The merry bells ring
To welcome the spring;
The skylark and thrush,   5
The birds of the bush,
Sing louder around
To the bells' cheerful sound,
While our sports shall be seen
On the echoing green.   10

Old John with white hair
Does laugh away care,
Sitting under the oak
Among the old folk.
They laugh at our play   15
And soon they all say,
'Such, such were the joys
When we all, girls and boys,
In our youth-time were seen
On the echoing green.'   20

Till the little ones weary
No more can be merry,
The sun does descend
And our sports have an end;
Round the laps of their mothers,   25
Many sisters and brothers
Like birds in their nest
Are ready for rest,
And sport no more seen
On the darkening green.   30

THE LAMB

Little lamb, who made thee?
Dost thou know who made thee?
Gave thee life and bid thee feed
By the stream and o'er the mead;
Gave thee clothing of delight –   5
Softest clothing, woolly, bright;
Gave thee such a tender voice,
Making all the vales rejoice?
Little lamb, who made thee?
Dost thou know who made thee?   10

Little lamb, I'll tell thee,
Little lamb, I'll tell thee;
He is called by thy name,
For he calls himself a lamb;
He is meek and he is mild,   15
He became a little child:
I a child and thou a lamb,
We are called by his name.
Little lamb, God bless thee,
Little lamb, God bless thee.   20

THE LITTLE BLACK BOY

My mother bore me in the southern wild
And I am black, but oh, my soul is white!
White as an angel is the English child,
But I am black, as if bereaved of light.

My mother taught me underneath a tree,   5
And sitting down before the heat of day,
She took me on her lap and kissed me,
And pointing to the east began to say,

'Look on the rising sun: there God does live,
And gives his light, and gives his heat away;   10
And flowers and trees and beasts and men receive
Comfort in morning, joy in the noon-day.

And we are put on earth a little space
That we may learn to bear the beams of love;
And these black bodies and this sunburnt face   15
Is but a cloud, and like a shady grove.

For when our souls have learned the heat to bear
The cloud will vanish; we shall hear his voice

Saying, "Come out from the grove, my love and care,
And round my golden tent like lambs rejoice!"'   20

Thus did my mother say, and kissed me;
And thus I say to little English boy,
When I from black and he from white cloud free,
And round the tent of God like lambs we joy,

I'll shade him from the heat, till he can bear   25
To lean in joy upon our Father's knee;
And then I'll stand and stroke his silver hair,
And be like him, and he will then love me.

THE BLOSSOM

Merry merry sparrow
Under leaves so green!
A happy blossom
Sees you swift as arrow;
Seek your cradle narrow   5
Near my bosom.

Pretty pretty robin
Under leaves so green!
A happy blossom
Hears you sobbing, sobbing,   10
Pretty pretty robin,
Near my bosom.

THE CHIMNEY SWEEPER

When my mother died I was very young,
And my father sold me while yet my tongue
Could scarcely cry 'weep weep weep weep!'
So your chimneys I sweep, and in soot I sleep.

There's little Tom Dacre, who cried when his head,   5
That curled like a lamb's back, was shaved; so I said,
'Hush, Tom! Never mind it, for when your head's bare
You know that the soot cannot spoil your white hair.'

And so he was quiet, and that very night,
As Tom was a-sleeping, he had such a sight!   10
That thousands of sweepers – Dick, Joe, Ned and Jack,
Were all of them locked up in coffins of black.

And by came an angel who had a bright key,
And he opened the coffins and set them all free;

Then down a green plain leaping, laughing they run   15
And wash in a river, and shine in the sun.

Then naked and white, all their bags left behind,
They rise upon clouds and sport in the wind;
And the angel told Tom, if he'd be a good boy,
He'd have God for his father and never want joy.   20

And so Tom awoke, and we rose in the dark,
And got with our bags and our brushes to work;
Though the morning was cold, Tom was happy and warm –
So if all do their duty, they need not fear harm.

THE LITTLE BOY LOST

'Father, father, where are you going?
Oh do not walk so fast!
Speak, father, speak to your little boy
Or else I shall be lost.'

The night was dark, no father was there,   5
The child was wet with dew;
The mire was deep, and the child did weep,
And away the vapour flew.

THE LITTLE BOY FOUND

The little boy lost in the lonely fen,
Led by the wand'ring light,[1]
Began to cry; but God, ever nigh,
Appeared like his father in white.

He kissed the child, and by the hand led,   5
And to his mother brought,
Who in sorrow pale, through the lonely dale
Her little boy weeping sought.

LAUGHING SONG

When the green woods laugh with the voice of joy,
And the dimpling stream runs laughing by;
When the air does laugh with our merry wit,
And the green hill laughs with the noise of it;

When the meadows laugh with lively green,   5
And the grasshopper laughs in the merry scene;
When Mary and Susan and Emily
With their sweet round mouths sing, 'Ha, ha, he!'

THE LITTLE BOY FOUND
[1]   *the wand'ring light* will-o'-the-wisp.

When the painted birds laugh in the shade,
Where our table with cherries and nuts is spread,　　　　　10
Come live and be merry, and join with me
To sing the sweet chorus of 'Ha, ha, he!'

A CRADLE SONG

Sweet dreams, form a shade
O'er my lovely infant's head;
Sweet dreams of pleasant streams
By happy, silent, moony beams.

Sweet sleep, with soft down　　　　　5
Weave thy brows an infant crown;
Sweet sleep, angel mild,
Hover o'er my happy child.

Sweet smiles in the night
Hover over my delight;　　　　　10
Sweet smiles, mother's smiles,
All the livelong night beguiles.

Sweet moans, dovelike sighs,
Chase not slumber from thy eyes;
Sweet moans, sweeter smiles,　　　　　15
All the dovelike moans beguiles.

Sleep, sleep, happy child,
All creation slept and smiled;
Sleep, sleep, happy sleep,
While o'er thee thy mother weep.　　　　　20

Sweet babe, in thy face
Holy image I can trace;
Sweet babe, once like thee,
Thy maker lay and wept for me,

Wept for me, for thee, for all,　　　　　25
When he was an infant small;
Thou his image ever see,
Heavenly face that smiles on thee —

Smiles on thee, on me, on all,
Who became an infant small:　　　　　30
Infant smiles are his own smiles;
Heaven and earth to peace beguiles.

THE DIVINE IMAGE

To mercy, pity, peace and love
All pray in their distress;
And to these virtues of delight
Return their thankfulness.

For mercy, pity, peace and love   5
Is God our Father dear;
And mercy, pity, peace and love
Is man, his child and care.

For mercy has a human heart,
Pity, a human face,   10
And love, the human form divine,
And peace, the human dress.

Then every man of every clime
That prays in his distress,
Prays to the human form divine –   15
Love, mercy, pity, peace.

And all must love the human form
In heathen, Turk, or Jew;
Where mercy, love and pity dwell
There God is dwelling too.   20

HOLY THURSDAY

'Twas on a Holy Thursday, their innocent faces clean,
The children walking two and two in red and blue and green,
Grey-headed beadles walked before, with wands as white as snow,
Till into the high dome of Paul's they like Thames' waters flow.[1]

Oh what a multitude they seemed, these flowers of London town!   5
Seated in companies they sit, with radiance all their own;
The hum of multitudes was there, but multitudes of lambs –
Thousands of little boys and girls raising their innocent hands.

Now like a mighty wind they raise to heaven the voice of song,
Or like harmonious thunderings the seats of heaven among;   10
Beneath them sit the aged men, wise guardians of the poor;
Then cherish pity, lest you drive an angel from your door.

HOLY THURSDAY
[1] Blake describes the service for all the charity schools in London held in St Paul's Cathedral, usually on the first Thursday in May, from 1782 onwards.

NIGHT

The sun descending in the west,
The evening star does shine;
The birds are silent in their nest
And I must seek for mine.
The moon like a flower 5
In heaven's high bower,
With silent delight
Sits and smiles on the night.

Farewell, green fields and happy groves,
Where flocks have took delight; 10
Where lambs have nibbled, silent moves
The feet of angels bright;
Unseen they pour blessing
And joy without ceasing
On each bud and blossom 15
And each sleeping bosom.

They look in every thoughtless nest
Where birds are covered warm,
They visit caves of every beast
To keep them all from harm. 20
If they see any weeping
That should have been sleeping,
They pour sleep on their head
And sit down by their bed.

When wolves and tigers howl for prey 25
They pitying stand and weep,
Seeking to drive their thirst away
And keep them from the sheep;
But if they rush dreadful,
The angels most heedful 30
Receive each mild spirit,
New worlds to inherit.

And there the lion's ruddy eyes
Shall flow with tears of gold,
And pitying the tender cries, 35
And walking round the fold,
Saying, 'Wrath, by his meekness,
And by his health, sickness
Is driven away
From our immortal day. 40

And now beside thee, bleating lamb,
I can lie down and sleep,

Or think on him who bore thy name,
Graze after thee and weep.
For, washed in life's river,   45
My bright mane for ever
Shall shine like the gold
As I guard o'er the fold.'

SPRING

Sound the flute!
Now it's mute.
Birds delight
Day and night;
Nightingale   5
In the dale,
Lark in sky,
Merrily
Merrily, merrily, to welcome in the year.

Little boy   10
Full of joy;
Little girl
Sweet and small;
Cock does crow,
So do you;   15
Merry voice,
Infant noise –
Merrily, merrily, to welcome in the year.

Little lamb
Here I am,   20
Come and lick
My white neck!
Let me pull
Your soft wool,
Let me kiss   25
Your soft face;
Merrily, merrily, we welcome in the year.

NURSE'S SONG

When the voices of children are heard on the green
And laughing is heard on the hill,
My heart is at rest within my breast
And everything else is still.

'Then come home, my children, the sun is gone down   5
And the dews of night arise;

Come, come, leave off play, and let us away
Till the morning appears in the skies.'

'No, no! Let us play, for it is yet day   10
And we cannot go to sleep;
Besides, in the sky, the little birds fly
And the hills are all covered with sheep.'

'Well, well, go and play till the light fades away
And then go home to bed.'
The little ones leaped and shouted and laughed   15
And all the hills echoed.

INFANT JOY

'I have no name,
I am but two days old.'
What shall I call thee?
'I happy am,
Joy is my name.'   5
Sweet joy befall thee!

Pretty joy!
Sweet joy but two days old,
Sweet joy I call thee;
Thou dost smile,   10
I sing the while,
Sweet joy befall thee!

A DREAM

Once a dream did weave a shade
O'er my angel-guarded bed,
That an emmet[1] lost its way
Where on grass methought I lay.

Troubled, wildered, and forlorn,   5
Dark, benighted, travel-worn,
Over many a tangled spray,
All heart-broke I heard her say,

'Oh my children! Do they cry?
Do they hear their father sigh?   10
Now they look abroad to see;
Now return and weep for me.'

A DREAM
[1] *emmet* ant.

Pitying, I dropped a tear;
But I saw a glow-worm near
Who replied, 'What wailing wight
Calls the watchman of the night?

I am set to light the ground
While the beetle goes his round;
Follow now the beetle's hum –
Little wanderer, hie thee home.'

ON ANOTHER'S SORROW

Can I see another's woe
And not be in sorrow too?
Can I see another's grief
And not seek for kind relief?

Can I see a falling tear
And not feel my sorrow's share?
Can a father see his child
Weep, nor be with sorrow filled?

Can a mother sit and hear
An infant groan, an infant fear?
No, no! never can it be!
Never, never can it be!

And can He who smiles on all,
Hear the wren with sorrows small,
Hear the small bird's grief and care,
Hear the woes that infants bear –

And not sit beside the nest
Pouring pity in their breast?
And not sit the cradle near
Weeping tear on infant's tear?

And not sit both night and day
Wiping all our tears away?
Oh no! never can it be!
Never, never can it be!

He doth give his joy to all,
He becomes an infant small;
He becomes a man of woe,
He doth feel the sorrow too.

Think not thou canst sigh a sigh
And thy maker is not by;

Think not thou canst weep a tear
And thy maker is not near.

Oh! he gives to us his joy
That our grief he may destroy;
Till our grief is fled and gone   35
He doth sit by us and moan.

Songs of Experience (1794)

INTRODUCTION

Hear the voice of the bard!
Who present, past and future sees;
Whose ears have heard
The Holy Word
That walked among the ancient trees   5

Calling the lapsed soul,
And weeping in the evening dew;
That might control
The starry pole,
And fallen, fallen light renew!   10

'Oh Earth, oh Earth, return!
Arise from out the dewy grass;
Night is worn,
And the morn
Rises from the slumberous mass.   15

Turn away no more!
Why wilt thou turn away?
The starry floor,
The wat'ry shore,
Is giv'n thee till the break of day.'   20

EARTH'S ANSWER

Earth raised up her head
From the darkness, dread and drear;
Her light fled,
Stony dread!
And her locks covered with grey despair.   5

'Prisoned on wat'ry shore,
Starry Jealousy does keep my den;
Cold and hoar,
Weeping o'er,
I hear the father of the ancient men.   10

Selfish father of men!
Cruel, jealous, selfish fear!
Can delight
Chained in night
The virgins of youth and morning bear?   15

Does spring hide its joy
When buds and blossoms grow?
Does the sower
Sow by night,
Or the ploughman in darkness plough?   20

Break this heavy chain
That does freeze my bones around! –
Selfish, vain,
Eternal bane!
That free love with bondage bound.'   25

THE CLOD AND THE PEBBLE

'Love seeketh not itself to please,
Nor for itself hath any care;
But for another gives its ease
And builds a heaven in hell's despair.'

So sung a little clod of clay   5
Trodden with the cattle's feet,
But a pebble of the brook
Warbled out these metres meet:

'Love seeketh only self to please,
To bind another to its delight;   10
Joys in another's loss of ease,
And builds a hell in heaven's despite.'

HOLY THURSDAY

Is this a holy thing to see
In a rich and fruitful land?
Babes reduced to misery,
Fed with cold and usurous hand?

Is that trembling cry a song?   5
Can it be a song of joy?
And so many children poor?
It is a land of poverty!

And their sun does never shine,
And their fields are bleak and bare,   10

And their ways are filled with thorns –
It is eternal winter there.

For where'er the sun does shine
And where'er the rain does fall,
Babe can never hunger there,   15
Nor poverty the mind appal.

THE LITTLE GIRL LOST

In futurity
I prophetic see
That the earth from sleep
(Grave the sentence deep)

Shall arise and seek   5
For her maker meek,
And the desert wild
Become a garden mild.

In the southern clime,
Where the summer's prime   10
Never fades away,
Lovely Lyca lay.

Seven summers old
Lovely Lyca told;
She had wandered long   15
Hearing wild birds' song.

'Sweet sleep, come to me
Underneath this tree;
Do father, mother weep? –
Where can Lyca sleep?   20

Lost in desert wild
Is your little child;
How can Lyca sleep
If her mother weep?

If her heart does ache   25
Then let Lyca wake;
If my mother sleep
Lyca shall not weep.

Frowning, frowning night,
O'er this desert bright,   30
Let thy moon arise
While I close my eyes.'

Sleeping Lyca lay
While the beasts of prey,
Come from caverns deep,   35
Viewed the maid asleep.

The kingly lion stood
And the virgin viewed,
Then he gambolled round
O'er the hallowed ground.   40

Leopards, tigers play
Round her as she lay,
While the lion old
Bowed his mane of gold

And her bosom lick,   45
And upon her neck
From his eyes of flame
Ruby tears there came;

While the lioness
Loosed her slender dress,   50
And naked they conveyed
To caves the sleeping maid.

THE LITTLE GIRL FOUND

All the night in woe
Lyca's parents go;
Over valleys deep,
While the deserts weep.

Tired and woe-begone,   5
Hoarse with making moan,
Arm in arm seven days
They traced the desert ways.

Seven nights they sleep
Among shadows deep,   10
And dream they see their child
Starved in desert wild.

Pale through pathless ways
The fancied image strays –
Famished, weeping, weak,   15
With hollow piteous shriek.

Rising from unrest,
The trembling woman pressed

With feet of weary woe;
She could no further go.   20

In his arms he bore
Her, armed with sorrow sore;
Till before their way
A couching lion lay.

Turning back was vain;   25
Soon his heavy mane
Bore them to the ground:
Then he stalked around

Smelling to his prey.
But their fears allay   30
When he licks their hands,
And silent by them stands.

They look upon his eyes
Filled with deep surprise,
And wondering behold   35
A spirit armed in gold.

On his head a crown,
On his shoulders down
Flowed his golden hair;
Gone was all their care.   40

'Follow me', he said,
'Weep not for the maid;
In my palace deep
Lyca lies asleep.'

Then they followed   45
Where the vision led,
And saw their sleeping child
Among tigers wild.

To this day they dwell
In a lonely dell;   50
Nor fear the wolvish howl,
Nor the lion's growl.

THE CHIMNEY SWEEPER

A little black thing among the snow,
Crying 'weep weep' in notes of woe;
'Where are thy father and mother, say?'
'They are both gone up to the church to pray.

Because I was happy upon the heath   5
And smiled among the winter's snow,
They clothed me in the clothes of death,
And taught me to sing the notes of woe.

And because I am happy and dance and sing,
They think they have done me no injury,   10
And are gone to praise God and his priest and king,
Who make up a heaven of our misery.'

NURSE'S SONG

When the voices of children are heard on the green
And whisp'rings are in the dale,
The days of my youth rise fresh in my mind,
My face turns green and pale.

Then come home, my children, the sun is gone down,   5
And the dews of night arise;
Your spring and your day are wasted in play,
And your winter and night in disguise.

THE SICK ROSE

Oh rose, thou art sick;
The invisible worm
That flies in the night
In the howling storm

Has found out thy bed   5
Of crimson joy,
And his dark secret love
Does thy life destroy.

THE FLY

Little fly,
Thy summer's play
My thoughtless hand
Has brushed away.

Am not I   5
A fly like thee?
Or art not thou
A man like me?

For I dance
And drink and sing   10
Till some blind hand
Shall brush my wing.

If thought is life
And strength and breath,
And the want   15
Of thought is death,

Then am I
A happy fly,
If I live
Or if I die.   20

THE ANGEL

I dreamt a dream! What can it mean?
And that I was a maiden queen
Guarded by an angel mild:
Witless woe was ne'er beguiled!

And I wept both night and day,   5
And he wiped my tears away,
And I wept both day and night,
And hid from him my heart's delight.

So he took his wings and fled,
Then the morn blushed rosy red;   10
I dried my tears, and armed my fears
With ten thousand shields and spears.

Soon my angel came again:
I was armed, he came in vain –
For the time of youth was fled,   15
And grey hairs were on my head

THE TIGER

Tiger, tiger, burning bright
In the forests of the night,
What immortal hand or eye
Could frame thy fearful symmetry?

In what distant deeps or skies   5
Burnt the fire of thine eyes?
On what wings dare he aspire?
What the hand dare seize the fire?

And what shoulder and what art
Could twist the sinews of thy heart?   10
And when thy heart began to beat,
What dread hand and what dread feet?

What the hammer? What the chain?
In what furnace was thy brain?
What the anvil? What dread grasp   15
Dare its deadly terrors clasp?

When the stars threw down their spears
And watered heaven with their tears,
Did he smile his work to see?
Did he who made the lamb make thee?   20

Tiger, tiger, burning bright
In the forests of the night,
What immortal hand or eye
Dare frame thy fearful symmetry?

MY PRETTY ROSE-TREE

A flower was offered to me,
Such a flower as May never bore;
But I said, 'I've a pretty rose-tree',
And I passed the sweet flower o'er.

Then I went to my pretty rose-tree   5
To tend her by day and by night;
But my rose turned away with jealousy
And her thorns were my only delight.

AH, SUNFLOWER!

Ah, sunflower! weary of time,
Who countest the steps of the sun,
Seeking after that sweet golden clime
Where the traveller's journey is done;

Where the youth pined away with desire,   5
And the pale virgin shrouded in snow,
Arise from their graves and aspire
Where my sunflower wishes to go.

THE LILY

The modest rose puts forth a thorn,
The humble sheep a threat'ning horn;
While the lily white shall in love delight,
Nor a thorn nor a threat stain her beauty bright.

THE GARDEN OF LOVE

I went to the Garden of Love
And saw what I never had seen:

A chapel was built in the midst
Where I used to play on the green.

And the gates of this chapel were shut,   5
And 'Thou shalt not' writ over the door;
So I turned to the Garden of Love
That so many sweet flowers bore,

And I saw it was filled with graves
And tombstones where flowers should be;   10
And priests in black gowns were walking their rounds,
And binding with briars my joys and desires.

THE LITTLE VAGABOND

Dear mother, dear mother, the church is cold
But the alehouse is healthy and pleasant and warm;
Besides I can tell where I am used well –
Such usage in heaven will never do well.

But if at the church they would give us some ale,   5
And a pleasant fire our souls to regale,
We'd sing and we'd pray all the livelong day,
Nor ever once wish from the church to stray.

Then the parson might preach and drink and sing,
And we'd be as happy as birds in the spring;   10
And modest Dame Lurch, who is always at church,
Would not have bandy¹ children nor fasting nor birch.

And God, like a father rejoicing to see
His children as pleasant and happy as he,
Would have no more quarrel with the devil or the barrel,   15
But kiss him and give him both drink and apparel.

LONDON

I wander through each chartered¹ street
Near where the chartered Thames does flow,
And mark in every face I meet
Marks of weakness, marks of woe.

In every cry of every man,   5
In every infant's cry of fear,
In every voice, in every ban,
The mind-forged manacles I hear.

THE LITTLE VAGABOND
¹ *bandy* bandy legs are a symptom of rickets, caused
by a vitamin D deficiency.

LONDON
¹ *chartered* mapped, but also owned by corporations
(by the terms of a charter).

How the chimney-sweeper's cry
Every black'ning church appals,   10
And the hapless soldier's sigh
Runs in blood down palace walls.

But most through midnight streets I hear
How the youthful harlot's curse
Blasts the new born infant's tear,   15
And blights with plagues the marriage hearse.

THE HUMAN ABSTRACT

Pity would be no more
If we did not make somebody poor;
And mercy no more could be,
If all were as happy as we.

And mutual fear brings peace   5
Till the selfish loves increase;
Then Cruelty knits a snare
And spreads his baits with care.

He sits down with holy fears
And waters the ground with tears;   10
Then humility takes its root
Underneath his foot.

Soon spreads the dismal shade
Of mystery over his head,
And the caterpillar and fly   15
Feed on the mystery.

And it bears the fruit of deceit,
Ruddy and sweet to eat;
And the raven his nest has made
In its thickest shade.   20

The gods of the earth and sea
Sought through nature to find this tree,
But their search was all in vain –
There grows one in the human brain.

INFANT SORROW

My mother groaned, my father wept!
Into the dangerous world I leapt:
Helpless, naked, piping loud
Like a fiend hid in a cloud.

Struggling in my father's hands,   5
Striving against my swaddling bands,
Bound and weary I thought best
To sulk upon my mother's breast.

A POISON TREE

I was angry with my friend;
I told my wrath, my wrath did end.
I was angry with my foe;
I told it not, my wrath did grow.

And I watered it in fears,   5
Night and morning with my tears;
And I sunned it with smiles,
And with soft deceitful wiles.

And it grew both day and night
Till it bore an apple bright;   10
And my foe beheld it shine,
And he knew that it was mine.

And into my garden stole
When the night had veiled the pole –
In the morning glad I see   15
My foe outstretched beneath the tree.

A LITTLE BOY LOST

'Nought loves another as itself,
Nor venerates another so,
Nor is it possible to thought
A greater than itself to know.

And, father, how can I love you   5
Or any of my brothers more?
I love you like the little bird
That picks up crumbs around the door.'

The priest sat by and heard the child,
In trembling zeal he seized his hair;   10
He led him by his little coat
And all admired the priestly care.

And standing on the altar high,
'Lo, what a fiend is here!' said he,
'One who sets reason up for judge   15
Of our most holy mystery.'

The weeping child could not be heard,
The weeping parents wept in vain;
They stripped him to his little shirt
And bound him in an iron chain,   20

And burned him in a holy place
Where many had been burned before.
The weeping parents wept in vain –
Are such things done on Albion's shore?

A LITTLE GIRL LOST

Children of the future age
Reading this indignant page,
Know that in a former time
Love, sweet love, was thought a crime.

In the age of gold,   5
Free from winter's cold,
Youth and maiden bright
To the holy light,
Naked in the sunny beams delight.

Once a youthful pair   10
Filled with softest care
Met in garden bright
Where the holy light
Had just removed the curtains of the night.

There in rising day   15
On the grass they play;
Parents were afar,
Strangers came not near,
And the maiden soon forgot her fear.

Tired with kisses sweet,   20
They agree to meet
When the silent sleep
Waves o'er heavens deep,
And the weary tired wanderers weep.

To her father white   25
Came the maiden bright,
But his loving look,
Like the holy book
All her tender limbs with terror shook.

'Ona, pale and weak,   30
To thy father speak! –

Oh, the trembling fear!
Oh, the dismal care
That shakes the blossoms of my hoary hair!'

TO TIRZAH

Whate'er is born of mortal birth
Must be consumed with the earth
To rise from generation free;
Then what have I to do with thee?

The sexes sprung from shame and pride –   5
Blowed in the morn, in evening died;
But mercy changed death into sleep –
The sexes rose to work and weep.

Thou mother of my mortal part,
With cruelty didst mould my heart   10
And with false self-deceiving tears
Didst bind my nostrils, eyes and ears;

Didst close my tongue in senseless clay
And me to mortal life betray:
The death of Jesus set me free –   15
Then what have I to do with thee?

THE SCHOOLBOY

I love to rise in a summer morn
When the birds sing on every tree;
The distant huntsman winds his horn,
And the skylark sings with me –
Oh, what sweet company!   5

But to go to school in a summer morn,
Oh, it drives all joy away;
Under a cruel eye outworn,
The little ones spend the day
In sighing and dismay.   10

Ah! then at times I drooping sit
And spend many an anxious hour;
Nor in my book can I take delight,
Nor sit in learning's bower,
Worn through with the dreary shower.   15

How can the bird that is born for joy
Sit in a cage and sing?
How can a child, when fears annoy,

But droop his tender wing
And forget his youthful spring?   20

Oh, father and mother, if buds are nipped
And blossoms blown away,
And if the tender plants are stripped
Of their joy in the springing day
By sorrow and care's dismay,   25

How shall the summer arise in joy
Or the summer fruits appear?
Or how shall we gather what griefs destroy,
Or bless the mellowing year
When the blasts of winter appear?   30

THE VOICE OF THE ANCIENT BARD

Youth of delight, come hither
And see the opening morn –
Image of truth new-born;
Doubt is fled, and clouds of reason,
Dark disputes and artful teasing.   5
Folly is an endless maze,
Tangled roots perplex her ways –
How many have fallen there!
They stumble all night over bones of the dead,
And feel they know not what but care,   10
And wish to lead others, when they should be led.

A DIVINE IMAGE[1]

Cruelty has a human heart
And jealousy a human face;
Terror the human form divine,
And secrecy the human dress.

The human dress is forged iron,   5
The human form a fiery forge,
The human face a furnace sealed,
The human heart its hungry gorge.

THE DIVINE IMAGE
[1]   This poem is known to us only through a print
made after Blake's death.

The Marriage of Heaven and Hell (1790)

The Argument
Rintrah[1] roars and shakes his fires in the burdened air;
Hungry clouds swag on the deep.

Once meek, and in a perilous path,
The just man kept his course along
The vale of death;   5
Roses are planted where thorns grow,
And on the barren heath
Sing the honey bees.

Then the perilous path was planted;
And a river, and a spring   10
On every cliff and tomb;
And on the bleached bones
Red clay brought forth.

Till the villain left the paths of ease
To walk in perilous paths, and drive   15
The just man into barren climes.

Now the sneaking serpent walks
In mild humility
And the just man rages in the wilds
Where lions roam.   20

Rintrah roars and shakes his fires in the burdened air;
Hungry clouds swag on the deep.

As a new heaven is begun, and it is now thirty-three years since its advent, the eternal
hell revives. And lo! Swedenborg[2] is the angel sitting at the tomb; his writings are the
linen clothes folded up. Now is the dominion of Edom[3] and the return of Adam into
paradise (see Isaiah 34 and 35).[4]

Without contraries is no progression. Attraction and repulsion, reason and energy,
love and hate, are necessary to human existence.

From these contraries spring what the religious call good and evil. Good is the
passive that obeys reason. Evil is the active springing from energy.

Good is heaven; evil is hell.

THE MARRIAGE OF HEAVEN AND HELL.
[1] *Rintrah* the just wrath of the prophet.
[2] Emanuel Swedenborg (1688–1772), Swedish mystic whose works prophesying the end of the world Blake read and admired; 'Marriage' contains tributes to, as well as parodies of, his writings.

[3] *Edom* Esau; his dominion is a time of anarchy and revolution.
[4] Isa. 34 and 35 concern the end of the world and the Last Judgement.

The Voice of the Devil
All Bibles or sacred codes have been the causes of the following errors:

1. That man has two real existing principles, viz. a body and a soul.
2. That energy, called evil, is alone from the body, and that reason, called good, is alone from the soul.
3. That God will torment man in eternity for following his energies.

But the following contraries to these are true:

1. Man has no body distinct from his soul, for that called body is a portion of soul discerned by the five senses (the chief inlets of soul in this age).
2. Energy is the only life and is from the body, and reason is the bound or outward circumference of energy.
3. Energy is eternal delight.

Those who restrain desire do so because theirs is weak enough to be restrained; and the restrainer (or reason) usurps its place and governs the unwilling.

And, being restrained, it by degrees becomes passive, till it is only the shadow of desire.

The history of this is written in *Paradise Lost*, and the governor (or reason) is called Messiah.

And the original archangel, or possessor of the command of the heavenly host, is called the Devil, or Satan, and his children are called Sin and Death.

But in the Book of Job, Milton's Messiah is called Satan.

For this history has been adopted by both parties.

It indeed appeared to Reason as if Desire was cast out. But the Devil's account is that the Messiah fell, and formed a heaven of what he stole from the abyss.

This is shown in the gospel, where he prays to the Father to send the comforter, or Desire, that Reason may have ideas to build on, the Jehovah of the Bible being no other than he who dwells in flaming fire.

Know that after Christ's death he became Jehovah.

But in Milton the Father is destiny, the Son a ratio of the five senses, and the Holy Ghost vacuum!

Note: The reason Milton wrote in fetters when he wrote of angels and God, and at liberty when of devils and hell, is because he was a true poet and of the Devil's party without knowing it.

A Memorable Fancy
As I was walking among the fires of hell, delighted with the enjoyments of genius (which to angels look like torment and insanity), I collected some of their proverbs, thinking that as the sayings used in a nation mark its character, so the proverbs of hell show the nature of infernal wisdom better than any description of buildings or garments.

When I came home, on the abyss of the five senses, where a flat-sided steep frowns over the present world, I saw a mighty devil folded in black clouds, hovering on the sides of the rock. With corroding fires he wrote the following sentence, now perceived by the minds of men, and read by them on earth:

> How do you know but ev'ry bird that cuts the airy way
> Is an immense world of delight, closed by your senses five?

Proverbs of Hell

In seed-time learn, in harvest teach, in winter enjoy.

Drive your cart and your plough over the bones of the dead.

The road of excess leads to the palace of wisdom.

Prudence is a rich ugly old maid courted by Incapacity.

He who desires but acts not breeds pestilence.

The cut worm forgives the plough.

Dip him in the river who loves water.

A fool sees not the same tree that a wise man sees.

He whose face gives no light shall never become a star.

Eternity is in love with the productions of time.

The busy bee has no time for sorrow.

The hours of folly are measured by the clock, but of wisdom no clock can measure.

All wholesome food is caught without a net or a trap.

Bring out number, weight and measure in a year of dearth.

No bird soars too high, if he soars with his own wings.

A dead body revenges not injuries.

The most sublime act is to set another before you.

If the fool would persist in his folly he would become wise.

Folly is the cloak of knavery.

Shame is pride's cloak.

Prisons are built with stones of Law, brothels with bricks of Religion.

The pride of the peacock is the glory of God.

The lust of the goat is the bounty of God.

The wrath of the lion is the wisdom of God.

The nakedness of woman is the work of God.

Excess of sorrow laughs; excess of joy weeps.

The roaring of lions, the howling of wolves, the raging of the stormy sea, and the destructive sword, are portions of eternity too great for the eye of man.

The fox condemns the trap, not himself.

Joys impregnate; sorrows bring forth.

Let man wear the fell[5] of the lion, woman the fleece of the sheep.

The bird a nest, the spider a web, man friendship.

The selfish smiling fool and the sullen frowning fool shall be both thought wise, that they may be a rod.

What is now proved, was once only imagined.

The rat, the mouse, the fox, the rabbit, watch the roots; the lion, the tiger, the horse, the elephant, watch the fruits.

The cistern contains; the fountain overflows.

One thought fills immensity.

Always be ready to speak your mind, and a base man will avoid you.

Everything possible to be believed is an image of truth.

The eagle never lost so much time as when he submitted to learn of the crow.

The fox provides for himself, but God provides for the lion.

Think in the morning, act in the noon, eat in the evening, sleep in the night.

---

[5] *fell* skin.

He who has suffered you to impose on him knows you.

As the plough follows words, so God rewards prayers.

The tigers of wrath are wiser than the horses of instruction.

Expect poison from the standing water.

You never know what is enough, unless you know what is more than enough.

Listen to the fool's reproach! It is a kingly title!

The eyes of fire, the nostrils of air, the mouth of water, the beard of earth.

The weak in courage is strong in cunning.

The apple tree never asks the beech how he shall grow; nor the lion, the horse how he shall take his prey.

The thankful receiver bears a plentiful harvest.

If others had not been foolish we should be so.

The soul of sweet delight can never be defiled.

When thou seest an eagle, thou seest a portion of genius – lift up thy head!

As the caterpillar chooses the fairest leaves to lay her eggs on, so the priest lays his curse on the fairest joys.

To create a little flower is the labour of ages.

'Damn!' braces; 'Bless!' relaxes.

The best wine is the oldest, the best water the newest.

Prayers plough not; praises reap not.

Joys laugh not; sorrows weep not.

The head sublime, the heart pathos, the genitals beauty, the hands and feet proportion.

As the air to a bird, or the sea to a fish, so is contempt to the contemptible.

The crow wished everything was black; the owl, that everything was white.

Exuberance is beauty.

If the lion was advised by the fox, he would be cunning.

Improvement makes straight roads, but the crooked roads without improvement are roads of genius.

Sooner murder an infant in its cradle than nurse unacted desires.

Where man is not, nature is barren.

Truth can never be told so as to be understood, and not be believed.

   Enough! Or too much!

The ancient poets animated all sensible objects with gods or geniuses, calling them by the names and adorning them with the properties of woods, rivers, mountains, lakes, cities, nations, and whatever their enlarged and numerous senses could perceive.

   And particularly they studied the genius of each city and country, placing it under its mental deity.

   Till a system was formed, which some took advantage of, and enslaved the vulgar by attempting to realize or abstract the mental deities from their objects: thus began priesthood.

   Choosing forms of worship from poetic tales.

   And at length they pronounced that the gods had ordered such things.

   Thus men forgot that all deities reside in the human breast.

A Memorable Fancy

The prophets Isaiah and Ezekiel dined with me, and I asked them how they dared so roundly to assert that God spake to them, and whether they did not think at the time that they would be misunderstood, and so be the cause of imposition?

Isaiah answered, 'I saw no God, nor heard any, in a finite organical perception. But my senses discovered the infinite in everything, and, as I was then persuaded, and remain confirmed, that the voice of honest indignation is the voice of God, I cared not for consequences, but wrote.'

Then I asked, 'Does a firm persuasion that a thing is so, make it so?'

He replied, 'All poets believe that it does, and in ages of imagination this firm persuasion removed mountains; but many are not capable of a firm persuasion of anything.'

Then Ezekiel said, 'The philosophy of the east taught the first principles of human perception. Some nations held one principle for the origin and some another. We of Israel taught that the poetic genius (as you now call it) was the first principle and all the others merely derivative, which was the cause of our despising the priests and philosophers of other countries, and prophesying that all gods would at last be proved to originate in ours and to be the tributaries of the poetic genius. It was this that our great poet King David desired so fervently, and invokes so pathetic'ly, saying by this he conquers enemies and governs kingdoms. And we so loved our God that we cursed in his name all the deities of surrounding nations, and asserted that they had rebelled. From these opinions the vulgar came to think that all nations would at last be subject to the Jews.

'This', said he, 'like all firm persuasions, is come to pass, for all nations believe the Jews' code and worship the Jews' God, and what greater subjection can be?'

I heard this with some wonder, and must confess my own conviction. After dinner I asked Isaiah to favour the world with his lost works; he said none of equal value was lost. Ezekiel said the same of his.

I also asked Isaiah what made him go naked and barefoot three years. He answered, 'The same that made our friend, Diogenes the Grecian.'[6]

I then asked Ezekiel why he ate dung, and lay so long on his right and left side.[7] He answered, 'The desire of raising other men into a perception of the infinite. This the North American tribes practise, and is he honest who resists his genius or conscience only for the sake of present ease or gratification?'

The ancient tradition that the world will be consumed in fire at the end of six thousand years is true, as I have heard from hell.[8]

For the cherub with his flaming sword is hereby commanded to leave his guard at the tree of life; and when he does, the whole creation will be consumed and appear infinite and holy, whereas it now appears finite and corrupt.

This will come to pass by an improvement of sensual enjoyment.

But first the notion that man has a body distinct from his soul is to be expunged. This I shall do by printing in the infernal method, by corrosives which in hell are salutary and medicinal, melting apparent surfaces away, and displaying the infinite which was hid.[9]

---

[6] *Diogenes the Grecian* philosopher known for contempt of physical luxury and belief in a simple life-style.
[7] Ezekiel lay 390 days on his left side, 40 on his right.

[8] It was widely believed, at the end of the eighteenth century, that the 6,000-year life span of the world was about to end.
[9] Blake's printing technique involved the use of acid.

If the doors of perception were cleansed, everything would appear to man as it is: infinite.

For man has closed himself up till he sees all things through narrow chinks of his cavern.

A Memorable Fancy

I was in a printing-house in hell and saw the method in which knowledge is transmitted from generation to generation.

In the first chamber was a dragon-man, clearing away the rubbish from a cave's mouth; within, a number of dragons were hollowing the cave.

In the second chamber was a viper folding round the rock and the cave, and others adorning it with gold, silver, and precious stones.

In the third chamber was an eagle with wings and feathers of air – he caused the inside of the cave to be infinite; around were numbers of eagle-like men, who built palaces in the immense cliffs.

In the fourth chamber were lions of flaming fire, raging around and melting the metals into living fluids.

In the fifth chamber were unnamed forms which cast the metals into the expanse.

There they were received by men who occupied the sixth chamber, and took the forms of books and were arranged in libraries.

The giants who formed this world into its sensual existence and now seem to live in it in chains are, in truth, the causes of its life and the sources of all activity. But the chains are the cunning of weak and tame minds, which have power to resist energy. According to the proverb, the weak in courage is strong in cunning.

Thus one portion of being is the prolific; the other, the devouring. To the devourer it seems as if the producer was in his chains, but it is not so: he only takes portions of existence and fancies that the whole.

But the prolific would cease to be prolific unless the devourer, as a sea, received the excess of his delights.

Some will say, 'Is not God alone the prolific?' I answer, 'God only acts and is in existing beings or men.'

These two classes of men are always upon earth, and they should be enemies; whoever tries to reconcile them seeks to destroy existence.

Religion is an endeavour to reconcile the two.

Note: Jesus Christ did not wish to unite, but to separate them (as in the parable of sheep and goats), and he says, 'I came not to send peace, but a sword.'[10]

Messiah or Satan or Tempter was formerly thought to be one of the antediluvians who are our energies.

A Memorable Fancy

An angel came to me and said, 'Oh, pitiable foolish young man! Oh, horrible! Oh, dreadful state! Consider the hot burning dungeon thou art preparing for thyself to all eternity, to which thou art going in such career.'

I said, 'Perhaps you will be willing to show me my eternal lot, and we will contemplate together upon it and see whether your lot or mine is most desirable.'

---

[10]   Matt. 10: 34.

So he took me through a stable, and through a church, and down into the church-vault, at the end of which was a mill. Through the mill we went, and came to a cave. Down the winding cavern we groped our tedious way, till a void, boundless as a nether sky, appeared beneath us, and we held by the roots of trees and hung over this immensity. But I said, 'If you please, we will commit ourselves to this void, and see whether providence is here also; if you will not, I will.' But he answered, 'Do not presume, oh young man; but as we here remain, behold thy lot which will soon appear when the darkness passes away.'

So I remained with him, sitting in the twisted root of an oak. He was suspended in a fungus which hung with the head downward into the deep.

By degrees we beheld the infinite abyss, fiery as the smoke of a burning city; beneath us, at an immense distance, was the sun, black but shining; round it were fiery tracks on which revolved vast spiders, crawling after their prey, which flew, or rather swum, in the infinite deep, in the most terrific shapes of animals sprung from corruption. And the air was full of them, and seemed composed of them. These are devils, and are called Powers of the Air. I now asked my companion which was my eternal lot. He said, 'Between the black and white spiders.'

But now, from between the black and white spiders, a cloud and fire burst and rolled through the deep, black'ning all beneath so that the nether deep grew black as a sea, and rolled with a terrible noise. Beneath us was nothing now to be seen but a black tempest, till, looking east between the clouds and the waves, we saw a cataract of blood mixed with fire; and, not many stones' throw from us, appeared and sunk again the scaly fold of a monstrous serpent. At last, to the east, distant about three degrees, appeared a fiery crest above the waves. Slowly it reared, like a ridge of golden rocks, till we discovered two globes of crimson fire from which the sea fled away in clouds of smoke. And now we saw it was the head of Leviathan.[11] His forehead was divided into streaks of green and purple, like those on a tiger's forehead; soon we saw his mouth and red gills hang just above the raging foam, tinging the black deep with beams of blood, advancing toward us with all the fury of a spiritual existence.

My friend the angel climbed up from his station into the mill; I remained alone, and then this appearance was no more, but I found myself sitting on a pleasant bank beside a river by moonlight, hearing a harper who sung to the harp. And his theme was, 'The man who never alters his opinion is like standing water, and breeds reptiles of the mind.'

But I arose and sought for the mill, and there I found my angel, who, surprised, asked me how I escaped.

I answered, 'All that we saw was owing to your metaphysics. For when you ran away, I found myself on a bank by moonlight hearing a harper. But now we have seen my eternal lot, shall I show you yours?' He laughed at my proposal, but I by force suddenly caught him in my arms, and flew westerly through the night, till we were elevated above the earth's shadow. Then I flung myself with him directly into the body of the sun; here I clothed myself in white, and, taking in my hand Swedenborg's volumes, sunk from the glorious clime, and passed all the planets till we came to Saturn. Here I stayed to rest, and then leaped into the void between Saturn and the fixed stars.[12]

---

[11] *Leviathan* huge sea-dragon, though by association with Thomas Hobbes's *Leviathan* (1651) it also symbolizes a system of natural morality.

[12] i.e. into the outermost point of the universe.

'Here', said I, 'is your lot – in this space (if space it may be called).' Soon we saw the stable and the church, and I took him to the altar, and opened the Bible, and lo! it was a deep pit, into which I descended, driving the angel before me. Soon we saw seven houses of brick. One we entered; in it were a number of monkeys, baboons, and all of that species, chained by the middle, grinning and snatching at one another, but withheld by the shortness of their chains. However, I saw that they sometimes grew numerous, and then the weak were caught by the strong, and, with a grinning aspect, first coupled with, and then devoured, by plucking off first one limb and then another, till the body was left a helpless trunk. This, after grinning and kissing it with seeming fondness, they devoured too. And here and there I saw one savourily picking the flesh off of his own tail. As the stench terribly annoyed us both, we went into the mill, and I in my hand brought the skeleton of a body, which in the mill was Aristotle's *Analytics*.[13]

So the angel said, 'Thy fantasy has imposed upon me and thou oughtest to be ashamed.'

I answered, 'We impose on one another, and it is but lost time to converse with you whose works are only analytics.'

Opposition is true friendship.

I have always found that angels have the vanity to speak of themselves as the only wise; this they do with a confident insolence sprouting from systematic reasoning.

Thus Swedenborg boasts that what he writes is new, though it is only the contents or index of already published books.

A man carried a monkey about for a show, and, because he was a little wiser than the monkey, grew vain, and conceived himself as much wiser than seven men. It is so with Swedenborg: he shows the folly of churches and exposes hypocrites, till he imagines that all are religious, and himself the single one on earth that ever broke a net.

Now hear a plain fact: Swedenborg has not written one new truth. Now hear another: he has written all the old falsehoods.

And now hear the reason: he conversed with angels, who are all religious, and conversed not with devils, who all hate religion, for he was incapable through his conceited notions.

Thus Swedenborg's writings are a recapitulation of all superficial opinions, and an analysis of the more sublime – but no further.

Have now another plain fact: any man of mechanical talents may, from the writings of Paracelsus or Jacob Behmen,[14] produce ten thousand volumes of equal value with Swedenborg's – and, from those of Dante or Shakespeare, an infinite number.

But when he has done this, let him not say that he knows better than his master, for he only holds a candle in sunshine.

A Memorable Fancy

Once I saw a devil in a flame of fire, who arose before an angel that sat on a cloud, and the devil uttered these words:

---

[13] Aristotle wrote 2 vols of *Analytics*, which symbolize an inhuman rationality.

[14] Theophrastus Bombastus von Hohenheim, known as Paracelsus (1493–1541), and Jacob Boehme, or Behmen (1575–1624), both mystics.

'The worship of God is honouring his gifts in other men, each according to his genius, and loving the greatest men best. Those who envy or calumniate great men hate God, for there is no other God.'

The angel hearing this became almost blue; but, mastering himself, he grew yellow, and, at last, white, pink and smiling. And then replied:

'Thou idolater! Is not God one? And is not he visible in Jesus Christ? And has not Jesus Christ given his sanction to the law of ten commandments, and are not all other men fools, sinners, and nothings?'

The devil answered, 'Bray a fool in a mortar with wheat, yet shall not his folly be beaten out of him. If Jesus Christ is the greatest man, you ought to love him in the greatest degree; now hear how he has given his sanction to the law of ten commandments. Did he not mock at the Sabbath, and so mock the Sabbath's God? Murder those who were murdered because of him? Turn away the law from the woman taken in adultery? Steal the labour of others to support him? Bear false witness when he omitted making a defence before Pilate? Covet when he prayed for his disciples, and when he bid them shake off the dust of their feet against such as refused to lodge them? I tell you, no virtue can exist without breaking these ten commandments: Jesus was all virtue, and acted from impulse – not from rules.'

When he had so spoken, I beheld the angel who stretched out his arms embracing the flame of fire, and he was consumed and arose as Elijah.

Note: This angel, who is now become a devil, is my particular friend. We often read the Bible together in its infernal or diabolical sense, which the world shall have if they behave well.

I have also the Bible of hell, which the world shall have whether they will or no.

One law for the lion and ox is oppression.

A Song of Liberty

1. The Eternal Female groaned![15] It was heard over all the earth:
2. Albion's coast is sick, silent; the American meadows faint!
3. Shadows of prophecy shiver along by the lakes and the rivers, and mutter across the ocean! France, rend down thy dungeon![16]
4. Golden Spain, burst the barriers of old Rome!
5. Cast thy keys, oh Rome, into the deep, down falling, even to eternity down falling,
6. And weep!
7. In her trembling hands, she took the new-born terror howling;
8. On those infinite mountains of light now barred out by the Atlantic sea, the new-born fire stood before the starry king!
9. Flagged[17] with grey-browed snows and thunderous visages, the jealous wings waved over the deep.
10 The speary hand burned aloft, unbuckled was the shield, forth went the hand of jealousy among the flaming hair, and hurled the new-born wonder through the starry night.
11. The fire, the fire, is falling!

[15] This momentous birth heralds an apocalypse.
[16] The Bastille was torn down in 1789.
[17] flagged covered.

12. Look up! Look up! Oh, citizen of London, enlarge thy countenance! Oh Jew, leave counting gold, return to thy oil and wine! Oh African, black African! (Go, winged thought, widen his forehead.)
13. The fiery limbs, the flaming hair, shot like the sinking sun into the western sea.
14. Waked from his eternal sleep, the hoary element roaring fled away;
15. Down rushed, beating his wings in vain, the jealous king; his grey-browed counsellors, thunderous warriors, curled veterans, among helms and shields and chariots, horses, elephants, banners, castles, slings and rocks,
16. Falling, rushing, ruining! – buried in the ruins, on Urthona's[18] dens.
17. All night beneath the ruins; then, their sullen flames faded, emerge round the gloomy king.
18. With thunder and fire, leading his starry hosts through the waste wilderness, he promulgates his ten commands, glancing his beamy eyelids over the deep in dark dismay,
19. Where the son of fire in his eastern cloud, while the morning plumes her golden breast,
20. Spurning the clouds written with curses, stamps the stony law[19] to dust, loosing the eternal horses from the dens of night, crying,

'Empire is no more! And now the lion and wolf shall cease.'

Chorus

Let the priests of the raven of dawn no longer, in deadly black, with hoarse note, curse the sons of joy; nor his accepted brethren (whom, tyrant, he calls free) lay the bound or build the roof; nor pale religious lechery call that virginity that wishes but acts not.
    For everything that lives is holy.

Visions of the Daughters of Albion (1793)

The eye sees more than the heart knows.

The Argument
I loved Theotormon[1]
And I was not ashamed;
I trembled in my virgin fears
And I hid in Leutha's vale!

I plucked Leutha's flower,[2]   5
And I rose up from the vale;
But the terrible thunders tore
My virgin mantle in twain.

---

[18] Urthona is the creative, imaginative principle.
[19] The Ten Commandments were written on tablets of stone.

VISIONS OF THE DAUGHTERS OF ALBION
[1] *Theotormon* Blake's coinage; the speaker at this point is Oothoon, who represents thwarted love.

[2] Symbolic of an attempt to acquire sexual experience. Leutha symbolizes sex under law, or the sense of guilt or sin.

Visions

Enslaved, the Daughters of Albion weep: a trembling lamentation
Upon their mountains, in their valleys, sighs toward America.[3]   10
For the soft soul of America, Oothoon wandered in woe
Along the vales of Leutha seeking flowers to comfort her;
And thus she spoke to the bright marigold of Leutha's vale:
    'Art thou a flower? Art thou a nymph? I see thee now a flower,
Now a nymph! I dare not pluck thee from thy dewy bed!'   15
    The golden nymph replied, 'Pluck thou my flower, Oothoon the mild;
Another flower shall spring, because the soul of sweet delight
Can never pass away.' She ceased and closed her golden shrine.
    Then Oothoon plucked the flower, saying, 'I pluck thee from thy bed,
Sweet flower, and put thee here to glow between my breasts;   20
And thus I turn my face to where my whole soul seeks.'
Over the waves she went in winged exulting swift delight,
And over Theotormon's reign took her impetuous course.
    Bromion rent her with his thunders.[4] On his stormy bed
Lay the faint maid, and soon her woes appalled his thunders hoarse.   25
Bromion spoke: 'Behold this harlot here on Bromion's bed,
And let the jealous dolphins sport around the lovely maid.[5]
Thy soft American plains are mine, and mine thy north and south.
Stamped with my signet are the swarthy children of the sun –
They are obedient, they resist not, they obey the scourge;   30
Their daughters worship terrors and obey the violent.
Now thou may'st marry Bromion's harlot, and protect the child
Of Bromion's rage that Oothoon shall put forth in nine moons' time.'
    Then storms rent Theotormon's limbs; he rolled his waves around
And folded his black jealous waters round the adulterate pair.   35
Bound back to back in Bromion's caves, terror and meekness dwell.
At entrance Theotormon sits wearing the threshold hard
With secret tears;[6] beneath him sound like waves on a desert shore
The voice of slaves beneath the sun, and children bought with money
That shiver in religious caves beneath the burning fires   40
Of lust, that belch incessant from the summits of the earth.
Oothoon weeps not – she cannot weep! Her tears are locked up
But she can howl incessant writhing her soft snowy limbs,
And calling Theotormon's eagles to prey upon her flesh.
    'I call with holy voice, kings of the sounding air!   45
Rend away this defiled bosom that I may reflect
The image of Theotormon on my pure transparent breast.'
The eagles at her call descend and rend their bleeding prey:
Theotormon severely smiles – her soul reflects the smile

---

[3] *America* a country of liberation and revolution.
[4] On her way to her beloved Theotormon, Oothoon is raped by Bromion. Bromion also embodies the cruelty of slave-owners (lines 29–30).

[5] The jealous dolphins represent the feelings of Theotormon, whom Bromion is addressing.
[6] Oothoon and Bromion are bound back to back in Theotormon's cave, while he guards its entrance.

As the clear spring mudded with feet of beasts grows pure and smiles.   50
    The Daughters of Albion hear her woes, and echo back her sighs:
'Why does my Theotormon sit weeping upon the threshold,
And Oothoon hovers by his side, persuading him in vain?
I cry, "Arise, oh Theotormon, for the village dog
Barks at the breaking day; the nightingale has done lamenting.   55
The lark does rustle in the ripe corn, and the eagle returns
From nightly prey, and lifts his golden beak to the pure east,
Shaking the dust from his immortal pinions to awake
The sun that sleeps too long. Arise, my Theotormon, I am pure
Because the night is gone that closed me in its deadly black."   60
They told me that the night and day were all that I could see;
They told me that I had five senses to enclose me up,
And they enclosed my infinite brain into a narrow circle,
And sunk my heart into the abyss, a red round globe, hot burning,
Till all from life I was obliterated and erased.   65
Instead of morn arises a bright shadow like an eye
In the eastern cloud; instead of night, a sickly charnel house,
That Theotormon hears me not! To him the night and morn
Are both alike: a night of sighs, a morning of fresh tears –
And none but Bromion can hear my lamentations.   70
    With what sense is it that the chicken shuns the ravenous hawk?
With what sense does the tame pigeon measure out the expanse?
With what sense does the bee form cells? Have not the mouse and frog
Eyes and ears and sense of touch? Yet are their habitations
And their pursuits as different as their forms and as their joys.   75
Ask the wild ass why he refuses burdens; and the meek camel
Why he loves man – is it because of eye, ear, mouth or skin
Or breathing nostrils? No, for these the wolf and tiger have.
Ask the blind worm the secrets of the grave, and why her spires
Love to curl round the bones of death; and ask the rav'nous snake   80
Where she gets poison; and the winged eagle why he loves the sun –
And then tell me the thoughts of man that have been hid of old.
    Silent I hover all the night, and all day could be silent
If Theotormon once would turn his loved eyes upon me.
How can I be defiled when I reflect thy image pure?   85
Sweetest the fruit that the worm feeds on, and the soul preyed on by woe,
The new-washed lamb tinged with the village smoke, and the bright swan
By the red earth of our immortal river! I bathe my wings
And I am white and pure to hover round Theotormon's breast.'
    Then Theotormon broke his silence, and he answered: 90
'Tell me what is the night or day to one o'erflowed with woe?
Tell me what is a thought, and of what substance is it made?
Tell me what is a joy, and in what gardens do joys grow?
And in what rivers swim the sorrows, and upon what mountains
Wave shadows of discontent? And in what houses dwell the wretched   95
Drunken with woe forgotten, and shut up from cold despair?
Tell me where dwell the thoughts forgotten till thou call them forth?

Tell me where dwell the joys of old, and where the ancient loves?
And when will they renew again, and the night of oblivion past?
That I might traverse times and spaces far remote, and bring   100
Comforts into a present sorrow and a night of pain.
Where goest thou, oh thought? To what remote land is thy flight?
If thou returnest to the present moment of affliction
Wilt thou bring comforts on thy wings, and dews and honey and balm?
Or poison from the desert wilds, from the eyes of the envier?'   105
    Then Bromion said (and shook the cavern with his lamentation),
'Thou knowest that the ancient trees seen by thine eyes have fruit,
But knowest thou that trees and fruits flourish upon the earth
To gratify senses unknown? Trees, beasts and birds unknown?
Unknown, not unperceived, spread in the infinite microscope,   110
In places yet unvisited by the voyager, and in worlds
Over another kind of seas, and in atmospheres unknown.
Ah, are there other wars, beside the wars of sword and fire?
And are there other sorrows, beside the sorrows of poverty?
And are there other joys, beside the joys of riches and ease?   115
And is there not one law for both the lion and the ox?
And is there not eternal fire, and eternal chains
To bind the phantoms of existence from eternal life?'
    Then Oothoon waited silent all the day and all the night,
But when the morn arose, her lamentation renewed –   120
The Daughters of Albion hear her woes, and echo back her sighs.
'Oh Urizen,[7] creator of men, mistaken demon of heaven!
Thy joys are tears, thy labour vain – to form men to thine image.
How can one joy absorb another? Are not different joys
Holy, eternal, infinite? And each joy is a love!   125
Does not the great mouth laugh at a gift, and the narrow eyelids mock
At the labour that is above payment? And wilt thou take the ape
For thy counsellor? Or the dog, for a schoolmaster to thy children?
Does he who contemns poverty, and he who turns with abhorrence
From usury, feel the same passion? Or are they moved alike?   130
How can the giver of gifts experience the delights of the merchant?
How the industrious citizen the pains of the husbandman?
How different far the fat-fed hireling with hollow drum
Who buys whole cornfields into wastes, and sings upon the heath –
How different their eye and ear![8] How different the world to them!   135
With what sense does the parson claim the labour of the farmer?[9]
What are his nets and gins and traps, and how does he surround him
With cold floods of abstraction, and with forests of solitude,
To build him castles and high spires where kings and priests may dwell?
Till she who burns with youth, and knows no fixed lot, is bound   140
In spells of law to one she loathes. And must she drag the chain

---

7 Urizen ('your reason') is the creator of the fallen, fragmented world.

8 Expenditure of harvests and men on war is associated with enclosure and agricultural decline.

9 A reference to tithes.

Of life in weary lust? Must chilling murderous thoughts obscure
The clear heaven of her eternal spring? – to bear the wintry rage
Of a harsh terror, driv'n to madness, bound to hold a rod
Over her shrinking shoulders all the day, and all the night   145
To turn the wheel of false desire? – and longings that wake her womb
To the abhorred birth of cherubs in the human form
That live a pestilence and die a meteor, and are no more?
Till the child dwell with one he hates, and do the deed he loathes,
And the impure scourge force his seed into its unripe birth   150
Ere yet his eyelids can behold the arrows of the day.
    Does the whale worship at thy footsteps as the hungry dog?
Or does he scent the mountain prey because his nostrils wide
Draw in the ocean? Does his eye discern the flying cloud
As the raven's eye? Or does he measure the expanse like the vulture? 155
Does the still spider view the cliffs where eagles hide their young?
Or does the fly rejoice because the harvest is brought in?
Does not the eagle scorn the earth and despise the treasures beneath?
But the mole knoweth what is there, and the worm shall tell it thee.
Does not the worm erect a pillar in the mouldering churchyard,   160
And a palace of eternity in the jaws of the hungry grave?
Over his porch these words are written: "Take thy bliss, oh man,
And sweet shall be thy taste, and sweet thy infant joys renew!"
    Infancy – fearless, lustful, happy! – nestling for delight
In laps of pleasure. Innocence! – honest, open, seeking   165
The vigorous joys of morning light, open to virgin bliss –
Who taught thee modesty, subtle modesty, child of night and sleep?
When thou awakest, wilt thou dissemble all thy secret joys
Or wert thou not awake when all this mystery was disclosed?
Then com'st thou forth a modest virgin knowing to dissemble   170
With nets found under thy night pillow, to catch virgin joy,
And brand it with the name of whore, and sell it in the night
In silence, ev'n without a whisper, and in seeming sleep.
Religious dreams and holy vespers light thy smoky fires;
Once were thy fires lighted by the eyes of honest morn.   175
And does my Theotormon seek this hypocrite modesty,
This knowing, artful, secret, fearful, cautious, trembling hypocrite?
Then is Oothoon a whore indeed, and all the virgin joys
Of life are harlots, and Theotormon is a sick man's dream,
And Oothoon is the crafty slave of selfish holiness.   180
    But Oothoon is not so: a virgin filled with virgin fancies,
Open to joy and to delight wherever beauty appears.
If in the morning sun I find it, there my eyes are fixed
In happy copulation; if in evening mild, wearied with work,
Sit on a bank and draw the pleasures of this free-born joy.   185
    The moment of desire! The moment of desire! The virgin
That pines for man shall awaken her womb to enormous joys
In the secret shadows of her chamber; the youth shut up from
The lustful joy shall forget to generate, and create an amorous image

In the shadows of his curtains and in the folds of his silent pillow.   190
Are not these the places of religion? The rewards of continence?
The self-enjoyings of self-denial? Why dost thou seek religion?
Is it because acts are not lovely that thou seekest solitude
Where the horrible darkness is impressed with reflections of desire?
    Father of jealousy,[10] be thou accursed from the earth!   195
Why hast thou taught my Theotormon this accursed thing?
Till beauty fades from off my shoulders, darkened and cast out,
A solitary shadow wailing on the margin of nonentity.
    I cry, "Love! Love! Love! Happy, happy Love! Free as the mountain wind!"
Can that be love, that drinks another as a sponge drinks water?   200
That clouds with jealousy his nights, with weepings all the day?
To spin a web of age around him, grey and hoary, dark,
Till his eyes sicken at the fruit that hangs before his sight?
Such is self-love that envies all! – a creeping skeleton
With lamp-like eyes, watching around the frozen marriage bed.   205
    But silken nets and traps of adamant will Oothoon spread,
And catch for thee girls of mild silver, or of furious gold;
I'll lie beside thee on a bank and view their wanton play
In lovely copulation, bliss on bliss, with Theotormon;
Red as the rosy morning, lustful as the first-born beam,   210
Oothoon shall view his dear delight, nor e'er with jealous cloud
Come in the heaven of generous love, nor selfish blightings bring.
    Does the sun walk in glorious raiment on the secret floor
Where the cold miser spreads his gold? Or does the bright cloud drop
On his stone threshold? Does his eye behold the beam that brings   215
Expansion to the eye of pity? Or will he bind himself
Beside the ox to thy hard furrow? Does not that mild beam blot
The bat, the owl, the glowing tiger, and the king of night?
The sea-fowl takes the wintry blast for a cov'ring to her limbs
And the wild snake the pestilence to adorn him with gems and gold;   220
And trees and birds and beasts and men behold their eternal joy.
Arise, you little glancing wings, and sing your infant joy!
Arise and drink your bliss, for everything that lives is holy!'
    Thus every morning wails Oothoon, but Theotormon sits
Upon the margined ocean, conversing with shadows dire.   225
    The Daughters of Albion hear her woes, and echo back her sighs.

The Book of Urizen (1794)

Preludium to the Book of Urizen

Of the primeval priest's assumed power,
When Eternals spurned back his religion

---

[10]   i.e. Urizen.

And gave him a place in the north –
Obscure, shadowy, void, solitary.[1]

Eternals, I hear your call gladly –   5
Dictate swift-winged words, and fear not
To unfold your dark visions of torment!

Chapter I
1. Lo, a shadow of horror is risen
In eternity – unknown, unprolific,
Self-closed, all-repelling! What demon   10
Hath formed this abominable void,
This soul-shudd'ring vacuum? Some said
'It is Urizen'. But unknown, abstracted,
Brooding secret, the dark power hid.

2. Times on times he divided, and measured   15
Space by space in his ninefold darkness,[2]
Unseen, unknown; changes appeared
In his desolate mountains, rifted furious
By the black winds of perturbation.

3. For he strove in battles dire,   20
In unseen conflictions, with shapes
Bred from his forsaken wilderness,
Of beast, bird, fish, serpent and element,
Combustion, blast, vapour and cloud.

4. Dark, revolving in silent activity,   25
Unseen in tormenting passions,
An activity unknown and horrible;
A self-contemplating shadow
In enormous labours occupied.

5. But Eternals beheld his vast forests.   30
Age on ages he lay, closed, unknown,
Brooding, shut in the deep; all avoid
The petrific[3] abominable chaos.

6. His cold horrors silent, dark Urizen
Prepared: his ten thousands of thunders   35
Ranged in gloomed array stretch out across

THE BOOK OF URIZEN
[1] Blake imitates the usual opening to an epic poem
(e.g. 'Of arms and the man I sing ...'). Urizen, the
primeval priest, will be exiled by the Eternals, the unfallen gods who are powerless to stop his creative acts.

[2] Milton's Satan lay for nine days in the abyss of
hell.
[3] Miltonic coinage, meaning 'stony'.

The dread world, and the rolling of wheels,
As of swelling seas, sound in his clouds,
In his hills of stored snows, in his mountains
Of hail and ice; voices of terror   40
Are heard, like thunders of autumn,
When the cloud blazes over the harvests.

Chapter II
1. Earth was not, nor globes of attraction.[4]
The will of the Immortal expanded
Or contracted his all-flexible senses.   45
Death was not, but eternal life sprung.

2. The sound of a trumpet! The heavens
Awoke, and vast clouds of blood rolled
Round the dim rocks of Urizen (so named
That solitary one in immensity).   50

3. Shrill the trumpet, and myriads of eternity
Muster around the bleak deserts,
Now filled with clouds, darkness, and waters
That rolled perplexed, lab'ring, and uttered
Words articulate, bursting in thunders   55
That rolled on the tops of his mountains.

4. 'From the depths of dark solitude, from
The eternal abode in my holiness
Hidden, set apart in my stern counsels,
Reserved for the days of futurity,   60
I have sought for a joy without pain,
For a solid without fluctuation.
Why will you die, oh Eternals?
Why live in unquenchable burnings?

5. First I fought with the fire, consumed   65
Inwards, into a deep world within,
A void immense, wild, dark and deep,
Where nothing was: nature's wide womb.
And self-balanced, stretched o'er the void,
I alone (even I!) the winds merciless   70
Bound. But condensing, in torrents
They fall and fall; strong, I repelled
The vast waves, and arose on the waters,
A wide world of solid obstruction.

---

[4] *globes of attraction* solar systems; planets held
together by gravity.

6. Here alone I, in books formed of metals,   75
Have written the secrets of wisdom,
The secrets of dark contemplation,
By fightings and conflicts dire
With terrible monsters sin-bred,
Which the bosoms of all inhabit,   80
Seven deadly sins of the soul.

7. Lo! I unfold my darkness. And on
This rock place with strong hand the book
Of eternal brass, written in my solitude:

8. Laws of peace, of love, of unity,   85
Of pity, compassion, forgiveness.
Let each choose one habitation,
His ancient infinite mansion.
One command, one joy, one desire,
One curse, one weight, one measure   90
One king, one God, one law.'

Chapter III
1. The voice ended. They saw his pale visage
Emerge from the darkness, his hand
On the rock of eternity unclasping
The book of brass. Rage seized the strong,   95

2. Rage, fury, intense indignation,
In cataracts of fire, blood and gall,
In whirlwinds of sulphurous smoke
And enormous forms of energy;
All the seven deadly sins of the soul   100
In living creations appeared
In the flames of eternal fury.

3. Sund'ring, dark'ning, thund'ring!
Rent away with a terrible crash,
Eternity rolled wide apart,   105
Wide asunder rolling,
Mountainous, all around
Departing, departing, departing,
Leaving ruinous fragments of life,
Hanging frowning cliffs, and all between   110
An ocean of voidness unfathomable.

4. The roaring fires ran o'er the heav'ns
In whirlwinds and cataracts of blood,
And o'er the dark deserts of Urizen
Fires pour through the void on all sides   115
On Urizen's self-begotten armies.

5. But no light from the fires: all was darkness
In the flames of eternal fury.

6. In fierce anguish and quenchless flames
To the deserts and rocks he ran raging   120
To hide, but he could not; combining,
He dug mountains and hills in vast strength,
He piled them in incessant labour,
In howlings and pangs and fierce madness;
Long periods in burning fires labouring   125
Till hoary and age-broke and aged,
In despair and the shadows of death.

7. And a roof, vast, petrific, around,
On all sides he framed, like a womb
Where thousands of rivers in veins   130
Of blood pour down the mountains to cool
The eternal fires beating without
From Eternals; and, like a black globe
Viewed by sons of eternity, standing
On the shore of the infinite ocean,   135
Like a human heart struggling and beating,
The vast world of Urizen appeared.

8. And Los,[5] round the dark globe of Urizen,
Kept watch for Eternals, to confine
The obscure separation alone;   140
For eternity stood wide apart,
As the stars are apart from the earth.

9. Los wept, howling around the dark demon
And cursing his lot; for in anguish
Urizen was rent from his side –   145
And a fathomless void for his feet,
And intense fires for his dwelling.

10. But Urizen laid in a stony sleep
Unorganized, rent from eternity.

11. The Eternals said, 'What is this? Death.   150
Urizen is a clod of clay!'

12. Los howled in a dismal stupor,
Groaning, gnashing, groaning,
Till the wrenching apart was healed.

---

[5] *Los* the imagination, now separated from Urizen.

13. But the wrenching of Urizen healed not;   155
Cold, featureless, flesh or clay,
Rifted with direful changes,
He lay in a dreamless night

14. Till Los roused his fires, affrighted
At the formless unmeasurable death.   160

Chapter IVa
1. Los, smitten with astonishment,
Frightened at the hurtling bones,

2. And at the surging, sulphureous,
Perturbed Immortal, mad-raging

3. In whirlwinds and pitch and nitre   165
Round the furious limbs of Los;

4. And Los formed nets and gins,
And threw the nets round about.

5. He watched in shudd'ring fear
The dark changes, and bound every change   170
With rivets of iron and brass.

6. And these were the changes of Urizen:

Chapter IVb
1. Ages on ages rolled over him!
In stony sleep ages rolled over him!
Like a dark waste stretching, changeable,   175
By earthquakes riv'n, belching sullen fires,
On ages rolled ages in ghastly
Sick torment; around him in whirlwinds
Of darkness, the Eternal Prophet[6] howled,
Beating still on his rivets of iron,   180
Pouring sodor[7] of iron, dividing
The horrible night into watches.

2. And Urizen (so his eternal name)
His prolific delight obscured more and more
In dark secrecy, hiding in surging   185
Sulphureous fluid his fantasies.
The Eternal Prophet heaved the dark bellows
And turned restless the tongs, and the hammer

---

[6]   *the Eternal Prophet* Los.   [7]   *sodor* solder.

Incessant beat, forging chains new and new,
Numb'ring with links, hours, days, and years.   190

3. The Eternal Mind bounded began to roll
Eddies of wrath ceaseless, round and round,
And the sulphureous foam surging thick
Settled – a lake, bright and shining clear,
White as the snow on the mountains cold.   195

4. Forgetfulness, dumbness, necessity!
In chains of the mind locked up
Like fetters of ice shrinking together,
Disorganized, rent from eternity.
Los beat on his fetters of iron,   200
And heated his furnaces, and poured
Iron sodor and sodor of brass.

5. Restless turned the Immortal enchained,
Heaving dolorous, anguished, unbearable,
Till a roof, shaggy, wild, enclosed   205
In an orb his fountain of thought.

6. In a horrible dreamful slumber
Like the linked infernal chain,
A vast spine writhed in torment
Upon the winds, shooting pained   210
Ribs, like a bending cavern,
And bones of solidness froze
Over all his nerves of joy.
And a first age passed over
And a state of dismal woe.   215

7. From the caverns of his jointed spine
Down sunk with fright a red
Round globe, hot burning, deep
Deep down into the abyss,
Panting, conglobing, trembling,   220
Shooting out ten thousand branches
Around his solid bones.
And a second age passed over
And a state of dismal woe.

8. In harrowing fear rolling round   225
His nervous brain shot branches
Round the branches of his heart
On high into two little orbs;
And fixed in two little caves
Hiding carefully from the wind,   230

His eyes beheld the deep.
And a third age passed over
And a state of dismal woe.

9. The pangs of hope began,
In heavy pain, striving, struggling;   235
Two ears in close volutions
From beneath his orbs of vision
Shot spiring out and petrified
As they grew. And a fourth age passed
And a state of dismal woe.   240

10. In ghastly torment sick,
Hanging upon the wind,
Two nostrils bent down to the deep.
And a fifth age passed over
And a state of dismal woe.   245

11. In ghastly torment sick,
Within his ribs bloated round,
A craving hungry cavern;
Thence arose his channelled throat,
And like a red flame a tongue   250
Of thirst and of hunger appeared.
And a sixth age passed over
And a state of dismal woe.

12. Enraged and stifled with torment,
He threw his right arm to the north,   255
His left arm to the south,
Shooting out in anguish deep;
And his feet stamped the nether abyss
In trembling and howling and dismay.
And a seventh age passed over   260
And a state of dismal woe.

Chapter V
1. In terrors Los shrunk from his task –
His great hammer fell from his hand;
His fires beheld and, sickening,
Hid their strong limbs in smoke.   265
For with noises, ruinous, loud,
With hurtlings and clashings and groans,
The Immortal endured his chains
Though bound in a deadly sleep.

2. All the myriads of eternity,   270
All the wisdom and joy of life,

Roll like a sea around him,
Except what his little orbs
Of sight by degrees unfold.

3. And now his eternal life,   275
Like a dream, was obliterated.

4. Shudd'ring, the Eternal Prophet smote
With a stroke, from his north to south region.
The bellows and hammer are silent now,
A nerveless silence; his prophetic voice   280
Seized; a cold solitude and dark void
The Eternal Prophet and Urizen closed.

5. Ages on ages rolled over them,
Cut off from life and light, frozen
Into horrible forms of deformity.   285
Los suffered his fires to decay,
Then he looked back with anxious desire.
But the space undivided by existence
Struck horror into his soul.

6. Los wept, obscured with mourning;   290
His bosom earthquaked with sighs;
He saw Urizen, deadly black,
In his chains bound, and pity began,

7. In anguish dividing and dividing
(For pity divides the soul),[8]   295
In pangs, eternity on eternity,
Life in cataracts poured down his cliffs.
The void shrunk the lymph into nerves
Wand'ring wide on the bosom of night,
And left a round globe of blood   300
Trembling upon the void.
Thus the Eternal Prophet was divided
Before the death-image of Urizen;
For in changeable clouds and darkness
In a winterly night beneath,   305
The abyss of Los stretched immense.
And now seen, now obscured, to the eyes
Of Eternals the visions remote
Of the dark separation appeared.
As glasses discover worlds   310
In the endless abyss of space,

[8] Pity is a divisive - and therefore unfavourable – quality for Blake, since it is allied to fear and selfishness. It leads Los to split into two parts, a fallen Los (or Adam) and Enitharmon (or Eve).

So the expanding eyes of Immortals
Beheld the dark visions of Los,
And the globe of life-blood trembling.

8. The globe of life-blood trembled   315
Branching out into roots,
Fibrous, writhing upon the winds,
Fibres of blood, milk, and tears,
In pangs, eternity on eternity.
At length, in tears and cries embodied,   320
A female form, trembling and pale,
Waves before his deathy face.

9. All eternity shuddered at sight
Of the first female now separate,
Pale as a cloud of snow,   325
Waving before the face of Los.

10. Wonder, awe, fear, astonishment,
Petrify the eternal myriads
At the first female form now separate.
They called her Pity, and fled.   330

11. 'Spread a tent, with strong curtains around them;
Let cords and stakes bind in the void,
That Eternals may no more behold them!'

12. They began to weave curtains of darkness;
They erected large pillars round the void   335
With golden hooks fastened in the pillars.
With infinite labour the Eternals
A woof wove, and called it 'science'.

Chapter VI
1. But Los saw the female and pitied;
He embraced her, she wept, she refused.   340
In perverse and cruel delight
She fled from his arms, yet he followed.

2. Eternity shuddered when they saw
Man begetting his likeness
On his own divided image.   345

3. A time passed over, the Eternals
Began to erect the tent –
When Enitharmon sick
Felt a worm within her womb.

4. Yet helpless it lay like a worm 350
In the trembling womb,
To be moulded into existence.

5. All day the worm lay on her bosom,
All night within her womb
The worm lay till it grew to a serpent, 355
With dolorous hissings and poisons
Round Enitharmon's loins folding.

6. Coiled within Enitharmon's womb,
The serpent grew, casting its scales;
With sharp pangs the hissings began 360
To change to a grating cry;
Many sorrows and dismal throes,
Many forms of fish, bird and beast,
Brought forth an infant form
Where was a worm before. 365

7. The Eternals their tent finished,
Alarmed with these gloomy visions,
When Enitharmon groaning
Produced a man-child to the light.

8. A shriek ran through eternity, 370
And a paralytic stroke
At the birth of the human shadow.

9. Delving earth in his resistless way,
Howling, the child with fierce flames
Issued from Enitharmon. 375

10. The Eternals closed the tent.
They beat down the stakes, the cords
Stretched for a work of eternity.
No more Los beheld eternity.

11. In his hands he seized the infant, 380
He bathed him in springs of sorrow,
He gave him to Enitharmon.

Chapter VII
1. They named the child Orc; he grew
Fed with milk of Enitharmon.

2. Los awoke her – oh sorrow and pain! 385
A tight'ning girdle grew
Around his bosom. In sobbings

He burst the girdle in twain,
But still another girdle
Oppressed his bosom. In sobbings   390
Again he burst it. Again
Another girdle succeeds;
The girdle was formed by day,
By night was burst in twain.

3. These, falling down on the rock   395
Into an iron chain,
In each other link by link locked.

4. They took Orc to the top of a mountain –
Oh how Enitharmon wept!
They chained his young limbs to the rock   400
With the chain of jealousy,
Beneath Urizen's deathful shadow.

5. The dead heard the voice of the child
And began to awake from sleep;
All things heard the voice of the child   405
And began to awake to life.

6. And Urizen craving with hunger,
Stung with the odours of nature,
Explored his dens around.

7. He formed a line and a plummet   410
To divide the abyss beneath.
He formed a dividing rule;

8. He formed scales to weigh;
He formed massy weights;
He formed a brazen quadrant;   415
He formed golden compasses
And began to explore the abyss,
And he planted a garden of fruits.

9. But Los encircled Enitharmon
With fires of prophecy   420
From the sight of Urizen and Orc.

10. And she bore an enormous race.

Chapter VIII
1. Urizen explored his dens –
Mountain, moor and wilderness,
With a globe of fire lighting his journey,   425

A fearful journey, annoyed
By cruel enormities, forms
Of life on his forsaken mountains.

2. And his world teemed vast enormities,
Fright'ning, faithless, fawning.   430
Portions of life, similitudes
Of a foot, or a hand, or a head,
Or a heart, or an eye, they swam, mischievous
Dread terrors, delighting in blood.

3. Most Urizen sickened to see   435
His eternal creations appear –
Sons and daughters of sorrow on mountains
Weeping, wailing! First Thiriel appeared,
Astonished at his own existence
Like a man from a cloud born; and Utha,   440
From the waters emerging, laments;
Grodna rent the deep earth howling
Amazed, his heavens immense cracks
Like the ground parched with heat; then Fuzon
Flamed out! – first begotten, last born.[9]   445
All his eternal sons in like manner,
His daughters from green herbs and cattle,
From monsters and worms of the pit.

4. He, in darkness closed, viewed all his race
And his soul sickened! He cursed   450
Both sons and daughters, for he saw
That no flesh nor spirit could keep
His iron laws one moment.

5. For he saw that life lived upon death;
The ox in the slaughterhouse moans,   455
The dog at the wintry door.
And he wept, and he called it 'pity',
And his tears flowed down on the winds.

6. Cold he wandered on high, over their cities
In weeping and pain and woe!   460
And wherever he wandered in sorrows
Upon the aged heavens
A cold shadow followed behind him
Like a spider's web – moist, cold, and dim,
Drawing out from his sorrowing soul   465

---

[9] Thiriel, Utha, Grodna, and Fuzon correspond to
the four elements.

The dungeon-like heaven dividing,
Wherever the footsteps of Urizen
Walked over the cities in sorrow.

7. Till a web dark and cold, throughout all
The tormented element stretched   470
From the sorrows of Urizen's soul;
And the web is a female in embryo.
None could break the web, no wings of fire,

8. So twisted the cords, and so knotted
The meshes, twisted like to the human brain.   475

9. And all called it 'the net of religion'.

Chapter IX
1. Then the inhabitants of those cities
Felt their nerves change into marrow,
And hardening bones began
In swift diseases and torments,   480
In throbbings and shootings and grindings
Through all the coasts; till, weakened,
The senses inward rushed, shrinking,
Beneath the dark net of infection;

2. Till the shrunken eyes, clouded over,   485
Discerned not the woven hypocrisy.
But the streaky slime in their heavens,
Brought together by narrowing perceptions,
Appeared transparent air; for their eyes
Grew small like the eyes of a man,   490
And in reptile forms, shrinking together,
Of seven feet stature they remained.

3. Six days they shrunk up from existence,
And on the seventh day they rested;
And they blessed the seventh day, in sick hope,   495
And forgot their eternal life.

4. And their thirty cities divided
In form of a human heart;
No more could they rise at will
In the infinite void, but, bound down   500
To earth by their narrowing perceptions,
They lived a period of years,
Then left a noisome body
To the jaws of devouring darkness.

5. And their children wept, and built   505
    Tombs in the desolate places,
    And formed laws of prudence, and called them
    The eternal laws of God.

6. And the thirty cities remained,
    Surrounded by salt floods, now called   510
    Africa; its name was then Egypt.

7. The remaining sons of Urizen
    Beheld their brethren shrink together
    Beneath the net of Urizen;
    Persuasion was in vain,   515
    For the ears of the inhabitants
    Were withered and deafened and cold,
    And their eyes could not discern
    Their brethren of other cities.

8. So Fuzon called all together   520
    The remaining children of Urizen,
    And they left the pendulous earth;
    They called it Egypt, and left it.

9. And the salt ocean rolled englobed.

From Letter to Revd Dr Trusler, 23 August 1799

Reverend Sir,
    I really am sorry that you are fall'n out with the spiritual world, especially if I should
have to answer for it. I feel very sorry that your ideas and mine on moral painting
differ so much as to have made you angry with my method of study. If I am wrong,
I am wrong in good company. I had hoped your plan comprehended all species of
this art, and especially that you would not regret that species which gives existence
to every other – namely, visions of eternity. You say that I want somebody to
elucidate my ideas, but you ought to know that what is grand is necessarily obscure
to weak men. That which can be made explicit to the idiot is not worth my care.
The wisest of the ancients considered what is not too explicit as the fittest for
instruction because it rouses the faculties to act – I name Moses, Solomon, Aesop,
Homer, Plato. . . .
    I have therefore proved your reasonings ill-proportioned, which you can never prove
my figures to be. They are those of Michelangelo, Raphael, and the antique, and of the
best living models. I perceive that your eye is perverted by caricature prints, which
ought not to abound so much as they do. Fun I love, but too much fun is, of all things,
the most loathsome. Mirth is better than fun, and happiness is better than mirth. I feel
that a man may be happy in this world. And I know that this world is a world of
imagination and vision. I see everything I paint in this world, but everybody does not

see alike. To the eyes of a miser, a guinea[1] is more beautiful than the sun, and a bag worn with the use of money has more beautiful proportions than a vine filled with grapes. The tree which moves some to tears of joy is, in the eyes of others, only a green thing that stands in the way. Some see nature all ridicule and deformity (and by these I shall not regulate my proportions), and some scarce see nature at all. But to the eyes of the man of imagination, nature is imagination itself. As a man is, so he sees; as the eye is formed, such are its powers.

You certainly mistake when you say that the visions of fancy are not be found in this world. To me, this world is all one continued vision of fancy or imagination, and I feel flattered when I am told so. What is it sets Homer, Virgil, and Milton in so high a rank of art? Why is the Bible more entertaining and instructive than any other book? Is it not because they are addressed to the imagination (which is spiritual sensation), and but mediately to the understanding or reason? Such is true painting, and such was alone valued by the Greeks and the best modern artists. Consider what Lord Bacon says: 'Sense sends over to imagination before reason have judged, and reason sends over to imagination before the decree can be acted' (see *Advancement of Learning*, Part 2, p. 47, of 1st edn).

But I am happy to find a great majority of fellow mortals who can elucidate my visions – and particularly they have been elucidated by children, who have taken a greater delight in contemplating my pictures than I even hoped. Neither youth nor childhood is folly or incapacity; some children are fools and so are some old men. But there is a vast majority on the side of imagination or spiritual sensation ...

From The Pickering Manuscript (composed 1800–4)

THE MENTAL TRAVELLER

I travelled through a land of men,
A land of men and women too,
And heard and saw such dreadful things
As cold earth-wanderers never knew.

For there the babe is born in joy   5
That was begotten in dire woe;
Just as we reap in joy the fruit
Which we in bitter tears did sow.

And, if the babe is born a boy,
He's given to a woman old   10
Who nails him down upon a rock,
Catches his shrieks in cups of gold.

She binds iron thorns around his head,
She pierces both his hands and feet,

FROM LETTER TO THE REVD DR TRUSLER
[1] *guinea* gold coin worth 21*s.*, not coined since 1813.

She cuts his heart out at his side 15
To make it feel both cold and heat.

Her fingers number every nerve
Just as a miser counts his gold,
She lives upon his shrieks and cries,
And she grows young as he grows old. 20

Till he becomes a bleeding youth
And she becomes a virgin bright;
Then he rends up his manacles
And binds her down for his delight.

He plants himself in all her nerves 25
Just as a husbandman¹ his mould,
And she becomes his dwelling-place,
And garden fruitful seventy-fold.

An aged shadow soon he fades,
Wand'ring round an earthly cot, 30
Full filled all with gems and gold
Which he by industry had got.

And these are the gems of the human soul,
The rubies and pearls of a lovesick eye,
The countless gold of the aching heart, 35
The martyr's groan and the lover's sigh.

They are his meat, they are his drink;
He feeds the beggar and the poor,
And the wayfaring traveller –
Forever open is his door. 40

His grief is their eternal joy;
They make the roofs and walls to ring,
Till from the fire on the hearth
A little female babe does spring.

And she is all of solid fire, 45
And gems and gold, that none his hand
Dares stretch to touch her baby form
Or wrap her in his swaddling-band.

But she comes to the man she loves,
If young or old, or rich or poor. 50

THE MENTAL TRAVELLER
¹ *husbandman* farmer.

They soon drive out the aged host –
A beggar at another's door.

He wanders weeping far away
Until some other take him in;
Oft blind and age-bent, sore distressed,   55
Until he can a maiden win.

And to allay his freezing age
The poor man takes her in his arms;
The cottage fades before his sight,
The garden and its lovely charms;   60

The guests are scattered through the land.
For the eye altering, alters all;
The senses roll themselves in fear
And the flat earth becomes a ball;

The stars, sun, moon – all shrink away,   65
A desert vast without a bound;
And nothing left to eat or drink,
And a dark desert all around.

The honey of her infant lips,
The bread and wine of her sweet smile,   70
The wild game² of her roving eye
Does him to infancy beguile.

For as he eats and drinks he grows
Younger and younger every day,
And on the desert wild they both   75
Wander in terror and dismay.

Like the wild stag she flees away,
Her fear plants many a thicket wild;
While he pursues her night and day,
By various arts of love beguiled,   80

By various arts of love and hate;
Till the wide desert planted o'er
With labyrinths of wayward love,
Where roams the lion, wolf, and boar;

Till he becomes a wayward babe   85
And she a weeping woman old.
Then many a lover wanders here;
The sun and stars are nearer rolled;

---

² *game* sport.

The trees bring forth sweet ecstasy
To all who in the desert roam –   90
Till many a city there is built,
And many a pleasant shepherd's home.

But when they find the frowning babe,
Terror strikes through the region wide;
They cry, 'The babe, the babe is born!'   95
And flee away on every side.

For who dare touch the frowning form –
His arm is withered to its root;
Lions, boars, wolves, all howling flee
And every tree does shed its fruit.   100

And none can touch that frowning form
Except it be a woman old;
She nails him down upon the rock
And all is done as I have told.

THE CRYSTAL CABINET

The maiden caught me in the wild
Where I was dancing merrily,
She put me into her cabinet
And locked me up with a golden key.

This cabinet is formed of gold   5
And pearl and crystal, shining bright,
And within it opens into a world
And a little lovely moony night.

Another England there I saw,
Another London with its Tower,   10
Another Thames and other hills
And another pleasant Surrey bower,

Another maiden like herself,
Translucent, lovely, shining clear –
Threefold each in the other closed: 15
Oh, what a pleasant trembling fear!

Oh, what a smile, a threefold smile
Filled me that like a flame I burned;
I bent to kiss the lovely maid
And found a threefold kiss returned.   20

I strove to seize the inmost form
With ardour fierce and hands of flame,

But burst the crystal cabinet
And like a weeping babe became –

A weeping babe upon the wild   25
And weeping woman, pale, reclined.
And in the outward air again
I filled with woes the passing wind.

From The Four Zoas (composed 1803–7)

ENION'S LAMENTATION (FROM 'NIGHT THE SECOND', PP. 35–6)

I am made to sow the thistle for wheat, the nettle for a nourishing dainty.   390
I have planted a false oath in the earth; it has brought forth a poison tree.
I have chosen the serpent for a counsellor, and the dog
For a schoolmaster to my children.[1]
I have blotted out from light and living the dove and nightingale.
And I have caused the earthworm to beg from door to door.   395
I have taught the thief a secret path into the house of the just.
I have taught pale artifice to spread his nets upon the morning.
My heavens are brass, my earth is iron, my moon a clod of clay,
My sun a pestilence burning at noon and a vapour of death in night.
    What is the price of experience? Do men buy it for a song?   400
Or wisdom for a dance in the street? No, it is bought with the price
Of all that a man hath – his house, his wife, his children.
Wisdom is sold in the desolate market where none come to buy,
And in the withered field where the farmer ploughs for bread in vain.
    It is an easy thing to triumph in the summer's sun   405
And in the vintage, and to sing on the wagon loaded with corn.
It is an easy thing to talk of patience to the afflicted,
To speak the laws of prudence to the houseless wanderer,
To listen to the hungry raven's cry in wintry season
When the red blood is filled with wine and with the marrow of lambs.   410
    It is an easy thing to laugh at wrathful elements,
To hear the dog howl at the wintry door, the ox in the slaughterhouse moan;[2]
To see a god on every wind and a blessing on every blast;
To hear sounds of love in the thunderstorm that destroys our enemy's house;
To rejoice in the blight that covers his field, and the sickness that cuts   415
    off his children,
While our olive and vine sing and laugh round our door, and our children
    bring fruits and flowers.
Then the groan and the dolour are quite forgotten, and the slave grinding
    at the mill,
And the captive in chains, and the poor in the prison, and the soldier in the
    field,
When the shattered bone hath laid him groaning among the happier dead.

ENION'S LAMENTATION   [2] Cf. *Urizen*, 455–6.
[1] Cf. *Visions of the Daughters of Albion*, 127–8.

It is an easy thing to rejoice in the tents of prosperity;   420
Thus could I sing and thus rejoice – but it is not so with me.

REVIVAL OF THE ETERNAL MAN (FROM 'NIGHT THE NINTH', PP. 133–5)

When morning dawned, the Eternals rose to labour at the vintage.
Beneath they saw their sons and daughters wondering inconceivable
At the dark myriads in shadows in the worlds beneath.   640
    The morning dawned, Urizen rose, and in his hand the flail
Sounds, on the floor heard terrible by all beneath the heavens;
Dismal loud redounding, the nether floor shakes with the sound,
And all nations were threshed out, and the stars threshed from their husks.
    Then Tharmas[1] took the winnowing fan, the winnowing wind furious   645
Above, veered round by the violent whirlwind driven west and south,
Tossed the nations like chaff into the seas of Tharmas.[2]
'Oh Mystery[3] fierce!' Tharmas cries, 'Behold thy end is come!
Art thou she that made the nations drunk with the cup of religion?
Go down, ye kings and councillors and giant warriors,   650
Go down into the depths, go down and hide yourselves beneath!
Go down with horse and chariots and trumpets of hoarse war!'
    Lo! how the pomp of Mystery goes down into the caves:
Her great men howl and throw the dust and rend their hoary hair;
Her delicate women and children shriek upon the bitter wind,   655
Spoiled of their beauty, their hair rent, and their skin shrivelled up.
Lo! darkness covers the long pomp of banners on the wind,
And black horses and armed men and miserable bound captives.
Where shall the graves receive them all, and where shall be their place?
And who shall mourn for Mystery, who never loosed her captives?   660
    Let the slave grinding at the mill run out into the field;
Let him look up into the heavens and laugh in the bright air;
Let the enchained soul shut up in darkness and in sighing,
Whose face has never seen a smile in thirty weary years,
Rise and look out! – his chains are loose, his dungeon doors are open.   665
And let his wife and children return from the oppressor's scourge:
They look behind at every step and believe it is a dream.
    Are these the slaves that groaned along the streets of Mystery?
Where are your bonds and task-masters? Are these the prisoners?
Where are your chains? Where are your tears? Why do you look around.   670
If you are thirsty, there is the river; go bathe your parched limbs:
The good of all the land is before you, for Mystery is no more!
    Then all the slaves from every earth in the wide universe
Sing a new song, drowning confusion in its happy notes,
While the flail of Urizen sounded loud and the winnowing wind of Tharmas   675
So loud, so clear in the wide heavens! And the song that they sung was this,

---

REVIVAL OF THE ETERNAL MAN
[1] In Blake's scheme, Tharmas represents the senses.
Here, he is one of the forces of liberation.

[2] The process of threshing and winnowing is apocalyptic.
[3] *Mystery* the devious goddess of false religion, who
has misled humanity.

Composed by an African black from the little earth of Sotha:
'Aha! Aha! How came I here, so soon in my sweet native land?
How came I here? Methinks I am as I was in my youth,
When in my father's house I sat, and heard his cheering voice.   680
Methinks I see his flocks and herds, and feel my limbs renewed –
And lo! my brethren in their tents, and their little ones around them!'
   The song arose to the golden feast: the Eternal Man rejoiced.

From Milton (composed 1803–8)

'AND DID THOSE FEET IN ANCIENT TIME'

> And did those feet in ancient time
> Walk upon England's mountains green?
> And was the holy lamb of God
> On England's pleasant pastures seen?
>
> And did the countenance divine   5
> Shine forth upon our clouded hills?
> And was Jerusalem builded here,
> Among these dark Satanic mills?
>
> Bring me my bow of burning gold!
> Bring me my arrows of desire!   10
> Bring me my spear – oh clouds unfold!
> Bring me my chariot of fire!¹
>
> I will not cease from mental fight
> Nor shall my sword sleep in my hand,
> Till we have built Jerusalem   15
> In England's green and pleasant land.

Mary Robinson   (1758–1800)

'She is a woman of undoubted genius,' Coleridge remarked of Mary Robinson in 1800; 'I never knew a human being with so full a mind – bad, good, and indifferent, I grant you – but full and overflowing' (Griggs, i. 562). By the time she made Coleridge's acquaintance, Robinson was at the end of a fruitful career as one of the foremost novelists and poets of her time. Prior to that, during the late 1770s, she had won fame as an actress, particularly as Perdita in A Winter's Tale. *During one of her performances in this role during the 1779–80 season, she came to the attention of the Prince of Wales (the future George IV), whose mistress she subsequently became. He left her within a year. Her novels included* Hubert de Sevrac *(1796) and* Walsingham *(1797), both known to Wordsworth and Coleridge; her acquaintance with Coleridge came about when he paid tribute to her talents in* The Morning Post, *to which she was also*

'AND DID THOSE FEET IN ANCIENT TIME'
¹ A reference to the chariot of fire that carried
Elijah to heaven.

a contributor. He regarded 'The Haunted Beach', which appeared in her Lyrical Tales *(1800),
as 'a poem of fascinating metre' (Griggs, i. 575), and it is one of her finest. She was one of the
earliest readers of 'Kubla Khan', having been sent a manuscript copy in 1800, which inspired
one of her last works, 'Mrs Robinson to the Poet Coleridge'.*

From Lyrical Tales (1800)

THE HAUNTED BEACH

Upon a lonely desert beach
   Where the white foam was scattered,
A little shed upreared its head,
   Though lofty barks were shattered.
The seaweeds gath'ring near the door   5
   A sombre path displayed,
And all around, the deaf'ning roar
Re-echoed on the chalky shore,
   By the green billows made.

Above, a jutting cliff was seen   10
   Where sea-birds hovered, craving,
And all around the crags were bound
   With weeds, forever waving;
And here and there, a cavern wide
   Its shad'wy jaws displayed,   15
And near the sands, at ebb of tide,
A shivered mast was seen to ride
   Where the green billows strayed.

And often, while the moaning wind
   Stole o'er the summer ocean,   20
The moonlight scene was all serene,
   The waters scarce in motion;
Then while the smoothly slanting sand
   The tall cliff wrapped in shade,
The fisherman beheld a band   25
Of spectres gliding hand in hand,
   Where the green billows played.

And pale their faces were as snow,
   And sullenly they wandered;
And to the skies, with hollow eyes,   30
   They looked, as though they pondered.
And sometimes from their hammock shroud
   They dismal howlings made;
And while the blast blew strong and loud
The clear moon marked the ghastly crowd   35
   Where the green billows played.

And then above the haunted hut,
  The curlews, screaming, hovered;
And the low door, with furious roar,
  The frothy breakers covered.   40
For in the fisherman's lone shed
  A murdered man was laid,
With ten wide gashes on his head;
And deep was made his sandy bed
  Where the green billows played.   45

A shipwrecked mariner was he,
  Doomed from his home to sever,
Who swore to be, through wind and sea,
  Firm and undaunted ever;
And when the wave resistless rolled,   50
  About his arm he made
A packet rich of Spanish gold,
And, like a British sailor bold,
  Plunged where the billows played.

The spectre band, his messmates brave,   55
  Sunk in the yawning ocean,
While to the mast he lashed him fast
  And braved the storm's commotion.
The winter moon upon the sand
  A silv'ry carpet made,   60
And marked the sailor reach the land,
And marked his murd'rer wash his hand,
  Where the green billows played.

And since that hour the fisherman
  Has toiled and toiled in vain;   65
For all the night, the moony light
  Gleams on the spectred main.
And when the skies are veiled in gloom,
  The murd'rer's liquid way
Bounds o'er the deeply yawning tomb,   70
And flashing fires the sands illume
  Where the green billows play.

Full thirty years his task has been,
  Day after day more weary;
For Heaven designed his guilty mind   75
  Should feed on prospects dreary.
Bound by a strong and mystic chain,
  He has not pow'r to stray,
But destined mis'ry to sustain,
He wastes, in solitude and pain,   80
  A loathsome life away.

From Memoirs of the Late Mrs Robinson (4 vols., 1801)

MY FIRST ENCOUNTER WITH THE PRINCE OF WALES (II 36–7, 38–9)

The play of 'The Winter's Tale' was this season commanded by their Majesties. I never had performed before the Royal family, and the first character in which I was destined to appear was that of Perdita. I had frequently played the part, both with the Hermione of Mrs Hartley and of Miss Farren, but I felt a strange degree of alarm when I found my name announced to perform it before the Royal family.

In the green room I was rallied on the occasion, and Mr Smith (whose gentlemanly manners and enlightened conversation rendered him an ornament to the profession), who performed the part of Leontes, laughingly exclaimed, 'By Jove, Mrs Robinson, you will make a conquest of the Prince, for tonight you look handsomer than ever.' I smiled at the unmerited compliment, and little foresaw the vast variety of events that would arise from that night's exhibition! ... I hurried through the first scene – not without much embarrassment, owing to the fixed attention with which the Prince of Wales honoured me. Indeed, some flattering remarks which were made by his Royal Highness met my ear as I stood near his box, and I was overwhelmed with confusion.

The Prince's particular attention was observed by everyone, and I was again rallied at the end of the play. On the last curtsy, the Royal family condescendingly returned a bow to the performers, but, just as the curtain was falling, my eyes met those of the Prince of Wales. And, with a look that I *never shall forget*, he gently inclined his head a second time: I felt the compliment, and blushed my gratitude.

MRS ROBINSON TO THE POET COLERIDGE (COMPOSED OCTOBER 1800)

Rapt in the visionary theme,
  Spirit divine, with thee I'll wander,
Where the blue, wavy, lucid stream
  Mid forest glooms shall slow meander!
With thee I'll trace the circling bounds   5
  Of thy new paradise, extended,
And listen to the varying sounds
  Of winds and foamy torrents blended!

Now by the source, which lab'ring heaves
  The mystic fountain, bubbling, panting,   10
While gossamer its network weaves
  Adown the blue lawn, slanting –
I'll mark thy 'sunny dome' and view
Thy 'caves of ice',[1] thy fields of dew,
Thy ever-blooming mead, whose flow'r   15
Waves to the cold breath of the moonlight hour!
Or, when the day-star,[2] peering bright
On the grey wing of parting night;

MRS ROBINSON TO THE POET COLERIDGE   [2] *day-star* Morning Star.
[1] 'Kubla Khan', 36.

While more than vegetating pow'r
Throbs, grateful to the burning hour,   20
As summer's whispered sighs unfold
Her million million buds of gold! –
Then will I climb the breezy bounds
   Of thy new paradise, extended,
And listen to the distant sounds   25
   Of winds and foamy torrents blended!

Spirit divine, with thee I'll trace
Imagination's boundless space!
With thee, beneath thy 'sunny dome'
   I'll listen to the minstrel's lay   30
Hymning the gradual close of day;
In 'caves of ice' enchanted roam,
Where on the glitt'ring entrance plays
The moon's beam with its silv'ry rays;
Or when the glassy stream   35
   That through the deep dell flows,
Flashes the noon's hot beam –
   The noon's hot beam that midway shows
Thy flaming temple, studded o'er
With all Peruvia's lustrous store!   40
There will I trace the circling bounds
   Of thy new paradise, extended,
And listen to the awful sounds
   Of winds and foamy torrents blended.

And now I'll pause to catch the moan   45
   Of distant breezes, cavern-pent;
Now, ere the twilight tints are flown,
   Purpling the landscape far and wide,
   On the dark promontory's side
I'll gather wild-flow'rs, dew-besprent,   50
And weave a crown for thee,
Genius of heav'n-taught poesy!
While, op'ning to my wond'ring eyes,
Thou bid'st a new creation rise,
I'll raptured trace the circling bounds   55
   Of thy rich paradise, extended,
And listen to the varying sounds
   Of winds and foamy torrents blended.

And now, with lofty tones inviting,
Thy nymph, her dulcimer swift-smiting,   60
Shall wake me in ecstatic measures
Far, far removed from mortal pleasures,
In cadence rich, in cadence strong,

Proving the wondrous witcheries of song!
I hear her voice – thy 'sunny dome', 65
Thy 'caves of ice' aloud repeat –
Vibrations, madd'ning sweet,
Calling the visionary wand'rer home!
She sings of thee, oh favoured child
Of minstrelsy, sublimely wild! – 70
Of thee whose soul can feel the tone
Which gives to airy dreams a magic all thy own!

Robert Burns (1759–96)

Burns's first volume, Poems, Chiefly in the Scottish Dialect *(1786), was an overnight success, which won him popularity with all the major romantics, from Wordsworth to Byron; the selection given here is designed to indicate his range and influence. 'Epistle to J. Lapraik, an Old Scotch Bard' shows Burns's colloquial, lyric style at its most engaging; his advocacy of 'nature's fire' reveals a poetic creed that would strongly influence* Lyrical Ballads. *'To a Mouse' (one of Dorothy Wordsworth's favourite poems) underlines Burns's sympathy with the natural world. 'Man was Made to Mourn' is a precursor of Wordsworth's 'The Last of the Flock' and 'Simon Lee', the old man at its centre anticipating such characters as Wordsworth's leech-gatherer. 'Tam o' Shanter' may be Burns's most important single work, remarkable for the skill of its storytelling and its energy; as Wordsworth put it, 'Who but some impenetrable dunce, or narrow-minded puritan in works of art, ever read without delight the picture which he has drawn of the convivial exaltation of the rustic adventurer, Tam o' Shanter?' (Owen and Smyser, iii. 124).*

From Poems, Chiefly in the Scottish Dialect (1786)

EPISTLE TO J. LAPRAIK, AN OLD SCOTCH BARD, 1 APRIL 1785[1]

While briers an' woodbines budding green,
An' paitricks[2] scraichan loud at e'en,
And morning poossie[3] whiddan seen,
Inspire my muse,
This freedom, in an *unknown* frien', 5
I pray excuse.

On Fasteneen[4] we had a rockin,[5]
To ca' the crack[6] and weave our stockin;
And there was muckle fun and jokin,

EPISTLE TO JOHN LAPRAIK
[1] John Lapraik (1727–1807) was a farmer from Dalfram, near Muirkirk. While imprisoned for debt in 1785 he addressed a song to his wife. 'When I Upon thy Bosom Lean'. Burns's admiring *Epistle* led to its publication in Lapraik's *Poems on Several Occasions* (1788).

[2] *paitricks* partridges.
[3] *poossie* hare.
[4] *Fasteneen* Shrove Tuesday evening.
[5] *rockin* spinning party.
[6] *crack* conversation, news.

Ye need na doubt;   10
At length we had a hearty yokin,[7]
   At sang about.

There was ae sang[8] amang the rest,
Aboon them a' it pleased me best,
That some kind husband had addressed   15
   To some sweet wife:
It thirled the heart-strings through the breast,
   A' to the life.

I've scarce heard aught described[9] sae weel
What gen'rous, manly bosoms feel;   20
Thought I, 'Can this be Pope or Steele
   Or Beattie's wark?'
They tald me 'twas an odd kind chiel[10]
   About Muirkirk.

It pat me fidgean-fain[11] to hear't,   25
An' sae about him there I spier't;[12]
Then a' that kent him round declared
   He had ingine.[13]
That nane excelled it, few cam near't,
   It was sae fine   30

That set him to a pint of ale,
An' either douse[14] or merry tale,
Or rhymes an' sangs he'd made himsel,
   Or witty catches –
'Tween Inverness and Tiviotdale   35
   He had few matches.

Then up I gat, an swoor an aith,
Though I should pawn my pleugh an' graith,[15]
Or die a cadger pownie's[16] death
   At some dyke-back,   40
A pint an' gill I'd gie them baith
   To hear your crack.

But first an' foremost, I should tell,
Amaist as soon as I could spell,
I to the crambo-jingle[17] fell,   45

---

[7] *yokin* contest.
[8] *ae sang* Lapraik's 'When I Upon thy Bosom Lean'.
[9] *aught described* anything that described.
[10] *chiel* man.
[11] *fidgean-fain* fidgeting with eagerness.
[12] *spier't* asked about him.
[13] *ingine* poetic genius.
[14] *douse* sweet.
[15] *pleugh an' graith* plough and tackle.
[16] *cadger pownie* pony belonging to a hawker.
[17] *crambo-jingle* rhyming songs.

> Though rude an' rough,
Yet crooning to a body's sel
> Does weel eneugh.

I am nae poet, in a sense,
But just a rhymer like by chance,   50
An' hae to learning nae pretence –
> Yet what the matter?
Whene'er my muse does on me glance,
> I jingle at her.

Your critic-folk may cock their nose   55
And say, 'How can you e'er propose
You wha ken hardly verse frae prose,
> To mak a sang?'
But by your leaves, my learned foes,
> Ye're maybe wrang.   60

What's a' your jargon o' your schools,
Your Latin names for horns an' stools?
If honest nature made you fools,
> What sairs your Grammars?
Ye'd better taen up spades and shools   65
> Or knappin-hammers.[18]

A set o' dull, conceited hashes
Confuse their brains in College classes!
They gang in stirks[19] and come out asses –
> Plain truth to speak;   70
An' syne they think to climb Parnassus [20]
> By dint o' Greek!

Gie me ae spark o' nature's fire,
That's a' the learning I desire;
Then, though I drudge through dub an' mire   75
> At pleugh or cart,
My muse, though hamely in attire,
> May touch the heart.

Oh for a spunk o' Allan's glee,
Or Ferguson's, the bauld an' slee,   80
Or bright Lapraik's, my friend to be,
> If I can hit it![21]

---

[18] *shools* shovels. *knappin-hammers* hammers for breaking stones or flints.
[19] *stirks* young bullocks, idiots.
[20] *Parnassus* mountain of Greek myth, sacred to the Muses.

[21] Allan Ramsay (1686–1758), Scottish poet; Robert Ferguson (1750–74), whose *Poems* (Edinburgh, 1773) strongly influenced Burns.

That would be lear[22] eneugh for me,
        If I could get it.

Now sir, if ye hae friends enow,   85
Though real friends I b'lieve are few,
Yet, if your catalogue be fow,
        I'se no insist;
But gif ye want ae friend that's true,
        I'm on your list.   90

I winna blaw about mysel,
As ill I like my fauts to tell;
But friends an' folk that wish me well,
        They sometimes roose[23] me –
Though I maun own as monie still   95
        As far abuse me.

There's ae wee faut they whiles lay to me:
I like the lasses (Gude forgie me!);
For monie a plack[24] they wheedle frae me,
        At dance or fair –   100
Maybe some ither thing they gie me
        They weel can spare.

But Mauchline Race or Mauchline Fair,
I should be proud to meet you there;
We'se gie ae night's discharge to care   105
        If we forgather,
An' hae a swap o' rhymin-ware
        Wi' ane anither.

The four-gill chap, we'se gar him clatter,
An' kirs'n him wi' reekin water;   110
Syne we'll sit down an' tak our whitter
        To cheer our heart;
An' faith, we'se be acquainted better
        Before we part.

Awa ye selfish, warly race,   115
Wha think that havins, sense an' grace,
Ev'n love an' friendship should give place
        To 'catch-the-plack'!
I dinna like to see your face,
        Nor hear your crack.   120

---

[22] *lear* learning.
[23] *roose* praise.

[24] *plack* coin.

But ye whom social pleasure charms,
Whose hearts the tide of kindness warms,
Who hold your being on the terms,
    'Each aid the others' –
Come to my bowl, come to my arms,   125
    My friends, my brothers!

But to conclude my lang epistle,
As my auld pen's worn to the gristle;
Twa lines frae you wad gar me fissle,²⁵
    Who am, most fervent,   130
While I can either sing or whistle,
    Your friend and servant.

TO A MOUSE, ON TURNING HER UP IN HER NEST, WITH THE PLOUGH, NOVEMBER 1785

Wee, sleeket,¹ cowran, tim'rous beastie,
Oh what a panic's in thy breastie!
Thou need na start awa sae hasty
    Wi' bickering brattle!
I wad be laith to rin an' chase thee   5
    Wi' murd'ring pattle!²

I'm truly sorry man's dominion
Has broken nature's social union,
An' justifies that ill opinion
    Which makes thee startle   10
At me, thy poor earth-born companion
    An' fellow mortal!

I doubt na, whyles, but thou may thieve;
What then? Poor beastie, thou maun live!
A daimen-icker in a thrave³   15
    'S a sma' request:
I'll get a blessin wi' the lave,⁴
    An' never miss't!

Thy wee-bit housie, too, in ruin!
It's silly wa's⁵ the win's are strewin!
An' naething, now, to big⁶ a new ane   20
    O' foggage⁷ green!

---

²⁵ *gar me fissle* make me fidget (with excitement).
TO A MOUSE
¹ *sleeket* smooth, sleek.
² *pattle* plough-staff.
³ *A daimen-icker* the occasional ear of corn. *thrave* two stooks of corn.
⁴ *lave* rest, remainder.
⁵ *silly wa's* helpless walls.
⁶ *big* build.
⁷ *foggage* long grass.

An' bleak December's winds ensuin,
   Baith snell[8] an' keen!

Thou saw the fields laid bare an' wast,   25
An' weary winter comin fast,
An' cozie here, beneath the blast,
   Thou thought to dwell;
Till crash! the cruel coulter passed
   Out through thy cell.   30

That wee-bit heap o' leaves an' stibble
Has cost thee monie a weary nibble!
Now thou's turned out, for a' thy trouble,
   But house or hald,
To thole[9] the winter's sleety dribble,   35
   An' cranreuch[10] cauld!

But mousie, thou art no thy-lane[11]
In proving foresight may be vain:
The best-laid schemes o' mice an' men
   Gang aft agley,[12]   40
An' lea'e us nought but grief an' pain
   For promised joy!

Still, thou art blessed compared wi' me!
The present only toucheth thee:
But och! I backward cast my e'e
   On prospects drear!   45
An' forward, though I canna see,
   I guess an' fear!

MAN WAS MADE TO MOURN, A DIRGE

I

When chill November's surly blast
 Made fields and forests bare,
One ev'ning, as I wand'red forth
 Along the banks of Aire,
I spied a man whose aged step   5
 Seemed weary, worn with care;
His face was furrowed o'er with years
 And hoary was his hair.

---

8 *snell* sharp, severe.   11 *thy-lane* on your own.
9 *thole* endure.   12 *agley* awry.
10 *cranreuch* hoar-frost.

II

'Young stranger, whither wand'rest thou?'
   Began the rev'rend sage,   10
'Does thirst of wealth thy step constrain,
   Or youthful pleasure's rage?
Or haply, pressed with cares and woes,
   Too soon thou hast began
To wander forth, with me to mourn   15
   The miseries of man.

III

The sun that overhangs yon moors,
   Out-spreading far and wide,
Where hundreds labour to support
   A haughty lordling's pride;   20
I've seen yon weary winter sun
   Twice forty times return,
And ev'ry time has added proofs
   That man was made to mourn.

IV

Oh man, while in thy early years,   25
   How prodigal of time!
Misspending all thy precious hours,
   Thy glorious, youthful prime!
Alternate follies take the sway,
   Licentious passions burn,   30
Which tenfold force gives nature's law
That man was made to mourn.

V

Look not alone on youthful prime
   Or manhood's active might;
Man then is useful to his kind,   35
   Supported is his right:
But see him on the edge of life,
   With cares and sorrows worn,
Then age and want (oh, ill-matched pair!)
   Show man was made to mourn   40

VI

A few seem favourites of fate,
   In pleasure's lap caressed;
Yet think not all the rich and great
   Are likewise truly blessed.
But oh! what crowds in ev'ry land,   45
   All wretched and forlorn,
Through weary life this lesson learn –
   That man was made to mourn!

VII

Many and sharp the num'rous ills
   Enwoven with our frame!   50
More pointed still we make ourselves
   Regret, remorse and shame!
And man, whose heav'n-erected face
   The smiles of love adorn,
Man's inhumanity to man   55
   Makes countless thousands mourn!

VIII

See yonder poor, o'erlaboured wight,
   So abject, mean and vile,
Who begs a brother of the earth
   To give him leave to toil;   60
And see his lordly fellow-worm
   The poor petition spurn –
Unmindful, though a weeping wife
   And helpless offspring mourn.

IX

If I'm designed yon lordling's slave,   65
   By nature's law designed,
Why was an independent wish
   E'er planted in my mind?
If not, why am I subject to
   His cruelty or scorn?   70
Or why has man the will and pow'r
   To make his fellow mourn?

X

Yet let not this too much, my son,
  Disturb thy youthful breast;
This partial view of humankind   75
  Is surely not the last!
The poor, oppressed, honest man
  Had never, sure, been born,
Had there not been some recompense
  To comfort those that mourn!   80

XI

Oh death – the poor man's dearest friend,
  The kindest and the best!
Welcome the hour, my aged limbs
  Are laid with thee at rest!
The great, the wealthy, fear thy blow,   85
  From pomp and pleasure torn;
But oh, a blessed relief for those
  That weary-laden mourn!'

From Francis Grose, The Antiquities of Scotland (1791)
ii 199–201

TAM O' SHANTER. A TALE (COMPOSED LATE 1790)

When chapman billies[1] leave the street,
And drouthy[2] neebors, neebors meet,
As market-days are wearing late,
And folk begin to tak the gate;[3]
While we sit bowsing at the nappy,[4]   5
And gettin fou, and unco[5] happy,
We think na on the lang Scots miles,[6]
The waters, mosses, slaps[7] and styles
That lie between us and our hame,
Where sits our sulky sullen dame,   10
Gathering her brows like gathering storm,
Nursing her wrath to keep it warm.
  This truth fand honest Tam o' Shanter,
As he frae Ayr ae night did canter

TAM O' SHANTER
[1] *chapman billies* pedlars.
[2] *drouthy* thirsty.
[3] *gate* road.

[4] *nappy* ale.
[5] *fou and unco* full and mighty.
[6] The Scottish mile was longer than the English.
[7] *slaps* bogs.

(Auld Ayr, whom ne'er a town surpasses 15
For honest men and bonnie lasses).
　Oh Tam, hadst thou but been sae wise
As taen thy ain wife Kate's advice!
She tauld thee weel, thou was a skellum,[8]
A bletherin, blusterin, drunken blellum;[9] 20
That frae November till October,
Ae market-day thou was na sober;
That ilka melder[10] wi' the miller,
Thou sat as long as thou had siller;[11]
That every naig was ca'd a shoe on, 25
The smith and thee gat roarin fou[12] on;
That at the L——d's house, even on Sunday,
Thou drank wi' Kirkton Jean till Monday.
She prophesied that late or soon,
Thou wad be found deep drowned in Doon;[13] 30
Or catched wi' warlocks in the mirk,
By Alloway's auld haunted kirk.
　Ah, gentle dames, it gars me greet,[14]
To think how mony counsels sweet,
How mony lengthened sage advices, 35
The husband frae the wife despises!
　But to our tale: ae market-night
Tam had got planted[15] unco right,
Fast by an ingle bleezing[16] finely,
Wi' reamin swats[17] that drank divinely; 40
And at his elbow, souter[18] Johnie,
His ancient, trusty, drouthy crony –
Tam lo'ed him like a vera brither,
They had been fou for weeks tegither.
The night drave on wi' sangs and clatter, 45
And ay the ale was growing better;
The landlady and Tam grew gracious
With favours secret, sweet and precious;
The souter tauld his queerest stories,
The landlord's laugh was ready chorus; 50
The storm without might rair and rustle,
Tam did na mind the storm a whistle.
　Care, mad to see a man sae happy,
E'en drowned himsel amang the nappy;
As bees flee hame wi' lades o' treasure, 55

---

[8] *skellum* good-for-nothing.
[9] *blellum* chatterer.
[10] *melder* meal-grinding.
[11] *siller* silver.
[12] *fou* drunk.
[13] The River Doon runs through Ayrshire, to the sea beyond Burns's birthplace at Alloway.
[14] *gars me greet* makes me weep.
[15] *planted* settled.
[16] *an ingle bleezing* a fire blazing.
[17] *reamin swats* foaming new ale.
[18] *souter* cobbler.

The minutes winged their way wi' pleasure –
Kings may be blessed, but Tam was glorious,
O'er a' the ills o' life victorious!
But pleasures are like poppies spread:
You seize the flower, its bloom is shed;   60
Or like the snow-falls in the river,
A moment white, then melts for ever;
Or like the borealis race[19]
That flit ere you can point their place;
Or like the rainbow's lovely form,   65
Evanishing amid the storm.
Nae man can tether time or tide,
The hour approaches Tam maun ride;
That hour, o' night's black arch the keystane,
That dreary hour he mounts his beast in;   70
And sic a night he taks the road in,
As ne'er poor sinner was abroad in.
The wind blew as 'twad blawn its last,
The rattling showers rose on the blast,
The speedy gleams the darkness swallowed,   75
Loud, deep and lang, the thunder bellowed:
That night, a child might understand,
The Deil had business on his hand.
Weel mounted on his grey mare, Meg
(A better never lifted leg),   80
Tam skelpit[20] on through dub and mire,
Despising wind and rain and fire,
Whyles holding fast his gude blue bonnet,
Whyles crooning o'er an auld Scots sonnet,
Whyles glowring round wi' prudent cares   85
Lest bogles[21] catch him unawares:
Kirk Alloway[22] was drawing nigh,
Whare ghaists and houlets nightly cry.
By this time he was cross the ford
Where in the snaw the chapman smoored,   90
And past the birks and meikle stane
Where drunken Charlie brak's neck-bane;
And through the whins and by the cairn
Where hunters fand the murdered bairn;
And near the tree aboon the well   95
Whare Mungo's mither hanged hersel.
Before him, Doon pours all his floods;
The doubling storm roars through the woods;
The lightnings flash from pole to pole;

---

[19] *borealis race* the aurora borealis, an electrical
phenomenon in the sky in the Northern hemisphere.
[20] *skelpit* hurried.
[21] *bogles* spectres.
[22] Alloway Church.

Near and more near, the thunders roll: 100
When, glimmering through groaning trees,
Kirk Alloway seemed in a bleeze –
Through ilka bore the beams were glancing,
And loud resounded mirth and dancing.
    Inspiring, bold John Barleycorn,[23]   105
What dangers thou canst make us scorn!
Wi' tippeny,[24] we fear nae evil;
Wi' usquabae,[25] we'll face the Devil!
The swats sae reamed in Tammie's noddle,
Fair play, he cared na deils a boddle.   110
But Maggie stood right sair astonished
Till, by the heel and hand admonished,
She ventured forward on the light,
And, wow, Tam saw an unco sight!
Warlocks and witches in a dance,   115
Nae cotillon brent new frae France,
But hornpipes, jigs, strathspeys and reels
Put life and mettle in their heels.
A winnock-bunker in the east,[26]
There sat auld Nick in shape o' beast: 120
A towzie tyke,[27] black, grim and large –
To gie them music was his charge.
He screwed the pipes and gart them skirl[28]
Till roof and rafters a' did dirl!
Coffins stood round like open presses   125
That shawed the dead in their last dresses,
And by some devilish cantraip slight
Each in its cauld hand held a light
By which heroic Tam was able
To note upon the haly table   130
A murderer's banes in gibbet airns;
Twa span-lang, wee, unchirstened bairns;
A thief new-cutted frae a rape,
Wi' his last gasp his gab did gape;
Five tomahawks, wi' blood red-rusted;   135
Five scymitars, wi' murder crusted;
A garter which a babe had strangled;
A knife a father's throat had mangled,
Whom his ain son of life bereft,
The grey hairs yet stak to the heft;   140
Wi' mair of horrible and awefu',

---

[23] *John Barleycorn* malt whisky.
[24] *tippeny* ale.
[25] *usquabae* whisky.
[26] *A winnock-bunker in the east* a bunker beneath the small east window, at the far end of the church.

[27] *towzie tyke* shaggy dog.
[28] He turned ('screwed') the drones on the bagpipes and made them squeal ('skirl').

That even to name wad be unlawfu':
Three lawyers' tongues turned inside out,
Wi' lies seamed like a beggar's clout;
Three priests' hearts, rotten, black as muck,   145
Lay stinking, vile, in every neuk.[29]
   As Tammie glow'r'd, amazed and curious,
The mirth and fun grew fast and furious.
The piper loud and louder blew;
The dancers quick and quicker flew —   150
They reeled, they set, they crossed, they cleekit,
Till ilka carlin swat and reekit[30]
And coost her duddies[31] on the wark,
And linket[32] at it in her sark.[33]
   Now Tam, oh Tam! had thae been queans[34]   155
A' plump and strappin in their teens,
Their sarks, instead o' creeshie flainen,
Been snaw-white seventeen-hunder linen[35] —
Thir breeks o' mine, my only pair,
That ance were plush, o' gude blue hair,   160
I wad hae gien them off my hurdies[36]
For ae blink o' the bonie burdies!
But withered beldams, auld and droll,
Rigwoodie[37] hags wad spean a foal,
Loupin and flingin on a crumock —   165
I wonder did na turn thy stomach.
   But Tam kend what was what fu' brawlie,
There was ae winsome wench and walie[38]
That night enlisted in the core
(Lang after kend on Carrick shore,   170
For mony a beast to dead she shot
And perished mony a bonnie boat,
And shook baith meikle corn and bear,
And kept the countryside in fear);
Her cutty sark o' Paisley harn,[39]   175
That while a lassie she had worn,
In longitude though sorely scanty,
It was her best, and she was vauntie.[40]
Ah, little thought thy reverend graunie,

---

[29] Lines 143–6 were removed from later versions of the poem.
[30] They whirled round in the reel, faced their partners, passed across the circle of the dance, linked arms, and turned, till every witch sweated and steamed.
[31] *duddies* clothes.
[32] *linket* tripped.
[33] *sark* shirt.
[34] *queans* young girls.
[35] ... had their shirts, instead of being filthy flannels, been quality linen ...
[36] *hurdies* buttocks.
[37] *Rigwoodie* ancient
[38] *ae winsome wench and walie* one choice, handsome wench.
[39] Her shortened undershirt was made of 'harn' (coarse linen).
[40] *vauntie* proud.

That sark she coft[41] for her wee Nannie,   180
Wi' twa pund Scots ('twas a' her riches)
Should ever graced a dance o' witches!
    But here my muse her wing maun cour
(Sic flights are far beyond her power)
To sing how Nannie lap and flang –   185
A souple jad she was, and strang –
And how Tam stood, like ane bewitched,
And thought his very een enriched;
Even Satan glow'r'd and fidged fu' fain,
And hotched, and blew wi' might and main;   190
Till first ae caper – syne anither –
Tam lost his reason a' thegither
And roars out, 'Weel done, Cutty Sark!'
And in an instant all was dark:
And scarcely had he Maggie rallied,   195
When out the hellish legion sallied.
    As bees bizz out wi' angry fyke
When plundering herds assail their byke;[42]
As open pussie's[43] mortal foes,
When, pop! she starts before their nose;   200
As eager rins the market-croud,
When 'Catch the thief!' resounds aloud;
So Maggie rins, the witches follow,
Wi' mony an eldritch[44] shout and hollo.
    Ah, Tam! Ah, Tam! thou'll get thy fairin!   205
In hell they'll roast thee like a herrin!
In vain thy Kate awaits thy comin,
Kate soon will be a woefu' woman!!!
Now do thy speedy utmost, Meg,
And win the keystane o' the brig;[45]   210
There at them thou thy tail may toss –
A running stream they dare na cross!
    But ere the keystane she could make,
The fient a tail she had to shake;
For Nannie, far before the rest,   215
Hard upon noble Maggy pressed,
And flew at Tam with furious ettle –
But little kend she Maggy's mettle!
Ae spring brought off her master hale,
But left behind her ain grey tail: 220

---

[41] *coft* bought.
[42] *byke* hive.
[43] *pussie's* hare's.
[44] *eldritch* ghostly.
[45] *the keystane o' the brig* the keystone of the bridge. 'It is a well-known fact that witches, or any evil spirits, have no power to follow a poor wight any farther than the middle of the next running stream. It may be proper likewise to mention to the benighted traveller, that when he falls in with "bogles", whatever danger may be in his going forward, there is much more hazard in turning back' (Burns's note).

The carlin claught her by the rump
And left poor Maggy scarce a stump.
  Now wha this tale o' truth shall read,
Ilk man and mother's son, take heed:
Whene'er to drink you are inclined,   225
Or cutty sarks rin in your mind –
Think, ye may buy the joys o'er dear,
Remember Tam o' Shanter's mare!

Song (composed by November 1793, published 1796, edited from MS)

Oh my love's like the red, red rose,
  That's newly sprung in June;
My love's like the melody
  That's sweetly played in tune.

As fair art thou, my bonny lass,   5
  So deep in love am I;
And I can love thee still, my dear,
  Till a' the seas gang dry.

Till a' the seas gang dry, my dear,
  And the rocks melt wi' the sun;   10
I will love thee still, my dear,
  While the sands o' life shall run.

And fare thee weel, my only love,
  Oh fare thee weel awhile!
And I will come again, my love,   15
  Though 'twere ten thousand mile.

Mary Wollstonecraft   (1759–97)

Prolific woman of letters, moral writer, and novelist. A Vindication of the Rights of Men *was published anonymously, 29 November 1790, within a month of Burke's* Reflections, *to which it was the first major response. In the extract below Wollstonecraft deplores the poverty and oppression that led to the French Revolution, and criticizes Burke's tendency to resort to pure rhetoric. Her most important work is* A Vindication of the Rights of Woman (1792), *which argues that true political freedom implies equality of the sexes.*

From A Vindication of the Rights of Men (1790)

ON POVERTY (PP. 141–5)

In this great city[1] that proudly rears its head and boasts of its population and commerce, how much misery lurks in pestilential corners, whilst idle mendicants assail, on every side, the man who hates to encourage impostors, or repress, with angry frown, the plaints of the poor! How many mechanics, by a flux of trade or fashion, lose their employment – whom misfortunes (not to be warded off) lead to the idleness that vitiates their character and renders them afterwards averse to honest labour! Where is the eye that marks these evils, more gigantic than any of the infringements of property which you piously deprecate? Are these remediless evils? And is the human heart satisfied in turning the poor over to another world to receive the blessings this could afford?

If society was regulated on a more enlarged plan; if man was contented to be the friend of man, and did not seek to bury the sympathies of humanity in the servile appellation of master; if, turning his eyes from ideal regions of taste and elegance, he laboured to give the earth he inhabited all the beauty it is capable of receiving, and was ever on the watch to shed abroad all the happiness which human nature can enjoy – he who, respecting the rights of men, wishes to convince or persuade society that this is true happiness and dignity, is not the cruel oppressor of the poor, nor a short-sighted philosopher – *he* fears God and loves his fellow-creatures. Behold the whole duty of man! The citizen who acts differently is a sophisticated being.

Surveying civilized life, and seeing with undazzled eye the polished vices of the rich, their insincerity, want of natural affections, with all the specious train that luxury introduces, I have turned impatiently to the poor to look for man undebauched by riches or power. But alas, what did I see? A being scarcely above the brutes over which it tyrannized – a broken spirit, worn-out body, and all those gross vices which the example of the rich, rudely copied, could produce. Envy built a wall of separation that made the poor hate, whilst they bent to their superiors who, on their part, stepped aside to avoid the loathsome sight of human misery.

What were the outrages of a day[2] to these continual miseries? Let those sorrows hide their diminished head before the tremendous mountain of woe that thus defaces our globe! Man preys on man – and you[3] mourn for the idle tapestry that decorated a gothic pile, and the dronish bell that summoned the fat priest to prayer. You mourn for the empty pageant of a name, when slavery flaps her wing, and the sick heart retires to die in lonely wilds far from the abodes of man. Did the pangs you felt for insulted nobility, the anguish that rent your heart when the gorgeous robes were torn off the idol human weakness had set up, deserve to be compared with the long-drawn sigh of melancholy reflection, when misery and vice thus seem to haunt our steps, and swim on the top of every cheering prospect? Why is our fancy to be appalled by terrific perspectives of a hell beyond the grave? Hell stalks abroad: the lash resounds on the slave's naked sides, and the sick wretch, who can no longer earn the sour bread of unremitting labour, steals to a ditch to bid the world a long goodnight – or, neglected in some ostentatious hospital, breathes its last amidst the laugh of mercenary attendants.

ON POVERTY
[1] London.
[2] On 6 Oct. 1789 the people marched on the palace of Versailles, and conducted the King and Queen back to Paris.
[3] *you* Edmund Burke.

Such misery demands more than tears. I pause to recollect myself, and smother the contempt I feel rising for your rhetorical flourishes and infantine sensibility.

From A Vindication of the Rights of Woman (1792)

ON THE LACK OF LEARNING (PP. 40–2)

Many are the causes that, in the present corrupt state of society, contribute to enslave women by cramping their understandings and sharpening their senses. One, perhaps, that silently does more mischief than all the rest, is their disregard of order.

To do everything in an orderly manner is a most important precept which women who, generally speaking, receive only a disorderly kind of education, seldom attend to with that degree of exactness that men, who from their infancy are broken into method, observe. This negligent kind of guesswork (for what other epithet can be used to point out the random exertions of a sort of instinctive common sense never brought to the test of reason?) prevents their generalizing matters of fact, so they do today what they did yesterday, merely because they did it yesterday.

This contempt of the understanding in early life has more baneful consequences than is commonly supposed, for the little knowledge which women of strong minds attain is, from various circumstances, of a more desultory kind than the knowledge of men, and it is acquired more by sheer observations on real life than from comparing what has been individually observed with the results of experience generalized by speculation. Led by their dependent situation and domestic employments more into society, what they learn is rather by snatches; and as learning is with them, in general, only a secondary thing, they do not pursue any one branch with that persevering ardour necessary to give vigour to the faculties and clearness to the judgement.

In the present state of society, a little learning is required to support the character of a gentleman, and boys are obliged to submit to a few years of discipline. But in the education of women, the cultivation of the understanding is always subordinate to the acquirement of some corporeal accomplishment. Even while enervated by confinement and false notions of modesty, the body is prevented from attaining that grace and beauty which relaxed half-formed limbs never exhibit. Besides, in youth their faculties are not brought forward by emulation, and having no serious scientific study, if they have natural sagacity it is turned too soon on life and manners. They dwell on effects and modifications without tracing them back to causes, and complicated rules to adjust behaviour are a weak substitute for simple principles.

As a proof that education gives this appearance of weakness to females, we may instance the example of military men, who are, like them, sent into the world before their minds have been stored with knowledge or fortified by principles. The consequences are similar: soldiers acquire a little superficial knowledge snatched from the muddy current of conversation; and, from continually mixing with society, they gain what is termed a knowledge of the world; and this acquaintance with manners and customs has frequently been confounded with a knowledge of the human heart.

But can the crude fruit of casual observation, never brought to the test of judgement, formed by comparing speculation and experience, deserve such a distinction? Soldiers, as well as women, practise the minor virtues with punctilious politeness. Where is then the sexual difference, when the education has been the same? All the difference that I can discern arises from the superior advantage of liberty, which enables the former to see more of life.

A REVOLUTION IN FEMALE MANNERS (PP. 92–3)

Let not men then in the pride of power use the same arguments that tyrannic kings and venal ministers have used, and fallaciously assert that woman ought to be subjected because she has always been so. But when man, governed by reasonable laws, enjoys his natural freedom, let him despise woman if she do not share it with him – and, till that glorious period arrives, in descanting on the folly of the sex, let him not overlook his own.

Women, it is true, obtaining power by unjust means by practising or fostering vice, evidently lose the rank which reason would assign them, and they become either abject slaves or capricious tyrants. They lose all simplicity, all dignity of mind, in acquiring power, and act as men are observed to act when they have been exalted by the same means.

It is time to effect a revolution in female manners, time to restore to them their lost dignity, and make them (as a part of the human species) labour, by reforming themselves, to reform the world. It is time to separate unchangeable morals from local manners. If men be demi-gods, why let us serve them! And if the dignity of the female soul be as disputable as that of animals; if their reason does not afford sufficient light to direct their conduct whilst unerring instinct is denied, they are surely of all creatures the most miserable, and, bent beneath the iron hand of destiny, must submit to be a fair defect in creation. But to justify the ways of providence respecting them, by pointing out some irrefragable reason for thus making such a large portion of mankind accountable and not accountable, would puzzle the subtlest casuist.

ON STATE EDUCATION (PP. 386–90)

When, therefore, I call women slaves, I mean in a political and civil sense, for indirectly they obtain too much power, and are debased by their exertions to obtain illicit sway.

Let an enlightened nation[1] then try what effect reason would have to bring them back to nature and their duty; and allowing them to share the advantages of education and government with man, see whether they will become better, as they grow wiser and become free. They cannot be injured by the experiment, for it is not in the power of man to render them more insignificant than they are at present.

To render this practicable, day-schools for particular ages should be established by government in which boys and girls might be educated together. The school for the younger children, from five to nine years of age, ought to be absolutely free and open to all classes. A sufficient number of masters should also be chosen by a select committee in each parish, to whom any complaint of negligence, etc., might be made, if signed by six of the children's parents.

Ushers[2] would then be unnecessary, for I believe experience will ever prove that this kind of subordinate authority is particularly injurious to the morals of youth. What, indeed, can tend to deprave the character more than outward submission and inward contempt? Yet how can boys be expected to treat an usher with respect, when the

---

ON STATE EDUCATION

[1] 'France' (Wollstonecraft's note).

[2] *Ushers* assistant masters.

master seems to consider him in the light of a servant, and almost to countenance the ridicule which becomes the chief amusement of the boys during the play hours?

But nothing of this kind could occur in an elementary day-school, where boys and girls, the rich and poor, should meet together. And to prevent any of the distinctions of vanity, they should be dressed alike, and all obliged to submit to the same discipline, or leave the school. The schoolroom ought to be surrounded by a large piece of ground in which the children might be usefully exercised, for at this age they should not be confined to any sedentary employment for more than an hour at a time. But these relaxations might all be rendered a part of elementary education, for many things improve and amuse the senses when introduced as a kind of show, to the principles of which, drily laid down, children would turn a deaf ear – for instance, botany, mechanics, and astronomy. Reading, writing, arithmetic, natural history and some simple experiments in natural philosophy might fill up the day, but these pursuits should never encroach on gymnastic plays in the open air. The elements of religion, history, the history of man, and politics, might also be taught by conversations in the socratic form.

After the age of nine, girls and boys intended for domestic employments or mechanical trades ought to be removed to other schools, and receive instruction in some measure appropriated to the destination of each individual, the two sexes being still together in the morning. But in the afternoon, the girls should attend a school where plain-work, mantua-making, millinery, etc., would be their employment.

The young people of superior abilities or fortune might now be taught, in another school, the dead and living languages, the elements of science, and continue the study of history and politics on a more extensive scale, which would not exclude polite literature.

'Girls and boys still together?' I hear some readers ask. Yes. And I should not fear any other consequence than that some early attachment might take place – which, whilst it had the best effect on the moral character of the young people, might not perfectly agree with the views of the parents (for it will be a long time, I fear, before the world is so enlightened that parents, only anxious to render their children virtuous, will let them choose companions for life themselves).

Besides, this would be a sure way to promote early marriages, and from early marriages the most salutary physical and moral effects naturally flow. What a different character does a married citizen assume from the selfish coxcomb who lives but for himself, and who is often afraid to marry lest he should not be able to live in a certain style. Great emergencies excepted, which would rarely occur in a society of which equality was the basis, a man can only be prepared to discharge the duties of public life by the habitual practice of those inferior ones which form the man.

In this plan of education the constitution of boys would not be ruined by the early debaucheries which now make men so selfish, nor girls rendered weak and vain by indolence and frivolous pursuits. But I presuppose that such a degree of equality should be established between the sexes as would shut out gallantry and coquetry, yet allow friendship and love to temper the heart for the discharge of higher duties.

From Letters Written during a Short Residence in Sweden, Norway, and Denmark (1796)

ON CAPITAL PUNISHMENT (PP. 207–8)

Business having obliged me to go a few miles out of town this morning, I was surprised at meeting a crowd of people of every description – and enquiring the cause of a servant who spoke French, I was informed that a man had been executed two hours before, and the body afterwards burnt.

I could not help looking with horror around; the fields lost their verdure, and I turned with disgust from the well-dressed women who were returning with their children from this sight. What a spectacle for humanity! The seeing such a flock of idle gazers plunged me into a train of reflections on the pernicious effects produced by false notions of justice. And I am persuaded that till capital punishments be entirely abolished, executions ought to have every appearance of horror given to them, instead of being (as they are now) a scene of amusement for the gaping crowd, where sympathy is quickly effaced by curiosity.

I have always been of opinion that the allowing actors to die in the presence of the audience has an immoral tendency – but trifling when compared with the ferocity acquired by viewing the reality as a show. For it seems to me that in all countries the common people go to executions to see how the poor wretch plays his part, rather than to commiserate his fate, much less to think of the breach of morality which has brought him to such a deplorable end. Consequently executions, far from being useful examples to the survivors, have, I am persuaded, a quite contrary effect, by hardening the heart they ought to terrify. Besides, the fear of an ignominious death, I believe, never deterred anyone from the commission of a crime – because, in committing it, the mind is roused to activity about present circumstances. It is a game at hazard, at which all expect the turn of the die in their own favour, never reflecting on the chance of ruin till it comes.

NORWEGIAN MORALS (PP. 213–14)

Love here seems to corrupt the morals, without polishing the manners, by banishing confidence and truth – the charm as well as cement of domestic life. A gentleman who has resided in this city some time assures me that he could not find language to give me an idea of the gross debaucheries into which the lower order of people fall; and the promiscuous amours of the men of the middling class with their female servants debases both beyond measure, weakening every species of family affection.

I have everywhere been struck by one characteristic difference in the conduct of the two sexes: women, in general, are seduced by their superiors, and men jilted by their inferiors. Rank and manners awe the one, and cunning and wantonness subjugate the other, ambition creeping into the woman's passion, and tyranny giving force to the man's – for most men treat their mistresses as kings do their favourites: *ergo* is not man then the tyrant of the creation?

Still harping on the same subject, you will exclaim. How can I avoid it, when most of the struggles of an eventful life have been occasioned by the oppressed state of my sex? We reason deeply, when we forcibly feel.

Helen Maria Williams (1762–1827)

Williams became famous during the 1780s for her poems, among the best of which is her 'Sonnet to Twilight'. Her Letters *written in France applies the philosophy of sensibility to the French Revolution. Events were unfolding as she wrote, and it was still possible for radicals to feel optimistic. In particular, her thoughts 'On Revolution' are typical of the apologies for its violence, and may be compared with Mackintosh's thoughts on the same subject (pp. 157–8). A few years later, she witnessed the Terror at first hand, having been imprisoned by Robespierre. Her* Letters *containing a Sketch of the Politics of France registers her disillusionment, one of its most effective passages being her account of Madame Roland.*

From Poems (1786)

SONNET TO TWILIGHT

Meek twilight! soften the declining day
   And bring the hour my pensive spirit loves,
When, o'er the mountain slow descends the ray
   That gives to silence the deserted groves.
Ah, let the happy court the morning still, 5
   When, in her blooming loveliness arrayed,
She bids fresh beauty light the vale or hill,
   And rapture warble in the vocal shade.
Sweet is the odour of the morning's flower,
   And rich in melody her accents rise; 10
Yet dearer to my soul the shadowy hour
   At which her blossoms close, her music dies –
For then, while languid nature droops her head,
She wakes the tear 'tis luxury to shed.

From Letters Written in France in the Summer of 1790 (1790)

A VISIT TO THE BASTILLE (PP. 22–4, 29–30)

Before I suffered my friends at Paris to conduct me through the usual routine of convents, churches and palaces, I requested to visit the Bastille, feeling a much stronger desire to contemplate the ruins of that building than the most perfect edifices of Paris. When we got into the carriage, our French servant called to the coachman, with an air of triumph, 'A la Bastille – mais nous n'y resterons pas.'[1]

We drove under that porch which so many wretches have entered never to repass, and alighting from the carriage descended with difficulty into the dungeons, which

---

A VISIT TO THE BASTILLE
[1] 'To the Bastille – but we shall not remain there'
(Williams's translation).

were too low to admit of our standing upright, and so dark that we were obliged at noonday to visit them with the light of a candle. We saw the hooks of those chains by which the prisoners were fastened round the neck to the walls of their cells – many of which, being below the level of the water, are in a constant state of humidity; and a noxious vapour issued from them, which more than once extinguished the candle, and was so insufferable that it required a strong spirit of curiosity to tempt one to enter. Good God! – and to these regions of horror were human creatures dragged at the caprice of despotic power. What a melancholy consideration, that

> Man, proud man,
> Dressed in a little brief authority,
> Plays such fantastic tricks before high heaven
> As make the angels weep.
> (*Measure for Measure*, II. ii. 117–20)

There appears to be a greater number of these dungeons than one could have imagined the hard heart of tyranny itself would contrive, for, since the destruction of the building, many subterraneous cells have been discovered underneath a piece of ground which was enclosed within the walls of the Bastille, but which seemed a bank of solid earth before the horrid secrets of this prison-house were disclosed. Some skeletons were found in these recesses with irons still fastened on their decaying bones.

After having visited the Bastille, we may indeed be surprised that a nation so enlightened as the French submitted so long to the oppressions of their government. But we must cease to wonder that their indignant spirits at length shook off the galling yoke. . . .

When the Bastille was taken, and the old man of whom you have no doubt heard, and who had been confined in a dungeon thirty-five years, was brought into daylight, which had not for so long a space of time visited his eyes, he staggered, shook his white beard, and cried faintly, 'Messieurs, vous m'avez rendu un grand service, rendez m'en un autre, tuez moi! Je ne fais pas où aller.' 'Allons, allons,' the crowd answered with one voice, 'La nation te nourrira.'[2]

As the heroes of the Bastille passed along the streets after its surrender, the citizens stood at the doors of their houses loaded with wine, brandy, and other refreshments which they offered to these deliverers of their country. But they unanimously refused to taste any strong liquors, considering the great work they had undertaken as not yet accomplished, and being determined to watch the whole night, in case of any surprise.

ON REVOLUTION (PP. 80–2)

As we came out of La Maison de Ville, we were shown, immediately opposite, the far-famed lantern at which, for want of a gallows, the first victims of popular fury were sacrificed. I own that the sight of La Lanterne chilled the blood within my veins. At that moment, for the first time, I lamented the revolution, and, forgetting the imprudence or the guilt of those unfortunate men, could only reflect with horror on the dreadful expiation they had made. I painted in my imagination the agonies of their

---

[2] 'Gentlemen, you have rendered me one great service; render me another: kill me, for I know not where to go.' 'Come along, come along, the nation will provide for you' (Williams's translation).

families and friends, nor could I for a considerable time chase these gloomy images from my thoughts.

It is forever to be regretted that so dark a shade of ferocious revenge was thrown across the glories of the revolution. But alas! Where do the records of history point out a revolution unstained by some actions of barbarity? When do the passions of human nature rise to that pitch which produces great events, without wandering into some irregularities? If the French Revolution should cost no farther bloodshed, it must be allowed, notwithstanding a few shocking instances of public vengeance, that the liberty of twenty-four millions of people will have been purchased at a far cheaper rate than could ever have been expected from the former experience of the world.

RETROSPECT FROM ENGLAND (PP. 217–21)

Every visitor brings me intelligence from France full of dismay and horror. I hear of nothing but crimes, assassinations, torture and death. I am told that every day witnesses a conspiracy, that every town is the scene of a massacre, that every street is blackened with a gallows, and every highway deluged with blood. I hear these things, and repeat to myself: Is this the picture of France? Are these the images of that universal joy which called tears into my eyes and made my heart throb with sympathy? To me, the land which these mighty magicians have suddenly covered with darkness where, waving their evil wand, they have reared the dismal scaffold, have clotted the knife of the assassin with gore, have called forth the shriek of despair and the agony of torture – to me, this land of desolation appeared dressed in additional beauty beneath the genial smile of liberty. The woods seemed to cast a more refreshing shade, and the lawns to wear a brighter verdure, while the carols of freedom burst from the cottage of the peasant, and the voice of joy resounded on the hill and in the valley.

Must I be told that my mind is perverted, that I am become dead to all sensations of sympathy, because I do not weep with those who have lost a part of their superfluities, rather than rejoice that the oppressed are protected, that the wronged are redressed, that the captive is set at liberty, and that the poor have bread? Did the universal parent of the human race implant the feelings of pity in the heart, that they should be confined to the artificial wants of vanity, the ideal deprivations of greatness; that they should be fixed beneath the dome of the palace, or locked within the gate of the chateau; without extending one commiserating sigh to the wretched hamlet, as if its famished inhabitants, though not ennobled by man, did not bear, at least, the ensigns of nobility stamped on our nature by God?

Must I hear the charming societies in which I found all the elegant graces of the most polished manners, all the amiable urbanity of liberal and cultivated minds, compared with the most rude, ferocious, and barbarous levellers that ever existed? Really, some of my English acquaintance (whatever objections they may have to republican principles) do, in their discussions of French politics, adopt a most free and republican style of censure. Nothing can be more democratical than their mode of expression, or display a more levelling spirit, than their unqualified contempt of *all* the leaders of the revolution.

It is not my intention to shiver lances in every society I enter, in the cause of the National Assembly. Yet I cannot help remarking that, since the Assembly does not presume to set itself up as an example to this country, we seem to have very little right to be furiously angry, because they think proper to try another system of government themselves. Why should they not be suffered to make an experiment in politics? I have always been told that the improvement of every science depends upon experiment. But I now hear that, instead of their new attempt to form the great machine of society upon a simple principle of general amity upon the Federation of its members, they ought to have repaired the feudal wheels and springs by which their ancestors directed its movements.

Yet if mankind had always observed this retrograde motion, it would surely have led them to few acquisitions in virtue or in knowledge, and we might even have been worshipping the idols of paganism at this moment. To forbid, under the pains and penalties of reproach, all attempts of the human mind to advance to greater perfection, seems to be proscribing every art and science. And we cannot much wonder that the French, having received so small a legacy of public happiness from their forefathers, and being sensible of the poverty of their own patrimony, should try new methods of transmitting a richer inheritance to their posterity.

From Letters Containing a Sketch of the Politics of France (1795)

MADAME ROLAND (PP. 195–7, 200–1)

At this period one of the most accomplished women that France has produced perished on the scaffold. This lady was Madame Roland, the wife of the late minister. On the 31st of May he had fled from his persecutors, and his wife who remained was carried to prison. The wits observed on this occasion that the body of Roland was missing, but that he had left his soul behind.

Madame Roland was indeed possessed of the most distinguished talents and a mind highly cultivated by the study of literature. I had been acquainted with her since I first came to France, and had always observed in her conversation the most ardent attachment to liberty and the most enlarged sentiments of philanthropy – sentiments which she developed with an eloquence peculiar to herself, with a flow and power of expression which gave new graces and new energy to the French language. With these extraordinary endowments of mind she united all the warmth of a feeling heart and all the charms of the most elegant manners. She was tall and well-shaped, her air was dignified, and although more than thirty-five years of age she was still handsome. Her countenance had an expression of uncommon sweetness, and her full dark eyes beamed with the brightest rays of intelligence.

I visited her in the prison of St. Pelagie, where her soul, superior to circumstances, retained its accustomed serenity, and she conversed with the same animated cheerfulness in her little cell as she used to do in the hotel of the minister. She had provided herself with a few books, and I found her reading Plutarch. She told me she expected to die, and the look of placid resignation with which she spoke of it convinced me that she was prepared to meet death with a firmness worthy of her exalted character....

When more than one person is led at the same time to execution, since they can suffer only in succession, those who are reserved to the last are condemned to feel multiplied deaths at the sound of the falling instrument and the sight of the bloody scaffold. To be the first victim was therefore considered as a privilege, and had been allowed to Madame Roland as a woman. But when she observed the dismay of her companion, she said to him, 'Allez le premier: que je vous épargne au moins la douleur de voir couler mon sang."¹ She then turned to the executioner and begged that this sad indulgence might be granted to her fellow sufferer. The executioner told her that he had received orders that she should perish first.

'But you cannot, I am sure', said she with a smile, 'refuse the last request of a lady.' The executioner complied with her demand. When she mounted the scaffold and was tied to the fatal plank, she lifted up her eyes to the statue of Liberty near which the guillotine was placed, and exclaimed, 'Ah Liberté, comme on t'a jouée!'² The next moment she perished. But her name will be recorded in the annals of history as one of those illustrious women whose superior attainments seem fitted to exalt her sex in the scale of being.

William Lisle Bowles (1762–1850)

Bowles combined the tender melancholy found in the sonnets of his Oxford tutor, Thomas Warton, with a sophisticated sense of the picturesque and sublime, fashionable during the late eighteenth century. His sonnet to the Itchin looks back to Warton's 'To the River Lodon' (see pp. 2–3), and forward to Coleridge's 'To the River Otter' (p. 504). Coleridge and Wordsworth were highly enthusiastic readers of Bowles when his Fourteen Sonnets were first published.

From Fourteen Sonnets (1789)

SONNET VIII. TO THE RIVER ITCHIN, NEAR WINTON

Itchin, when I behold thy banks again,
Thy crumbling margin, and thy silver breast
On which the self-same tints still seem to rest,
Why feels my heart the shiv'ring sense of pain?
Is it that many a summer's day has passed   5
Since in life's morn I carolled on thy side?
Is it that oft since then my heart has sighed
As youth, and hope's delusive gleams, flew fast?
Is it that those who circled on thy shore,
Companions of my youth, now meet no more?   10
Whate'er the cause, upon thy banks I bend
Sorrowing, yet feel such solace at my heart,
As at the meeting of some long-lost friend
From whom, in happier hours, we wept to part.

MADAME ROLAND
¹ 'Go first; let me at least spare you the pain of seeing my blood shed' (Williams's translation).

² 'Ah Liberty, how hast thou been sported with!' (Williams's translation); apparently the source of Wordsworth, *Thirteen-Book Prelude*, x. 352–4.

Joanna Baillie   (1762–1851)

Baillie's most important works were her plays, admired by Wordsworth, Coleridge, Southey, Scott, Edgeworth, and Barbauld. Her 'Introductory Discourse' of 1798 argued for a drama faithful to 'passion that is permanent in its nature', just as Wordsworth's Preface to Lyrical Ballads *was to justify the concern with 'low and rustic life' through the claim that 'in that situation the passions of men are incorporated with the beautiful and permanent forms of nature' (p. 252).*

From A Series of Plays (1798)

ON PASSION (FROM 'INTRODUCTORY DISCOURSE') (PP. 38–9)

But the last part of the task which I have mentioned as peculiarly belonging to tragedy – unveiling the human mind under the dominion of those strong and fixed passions which, seemingly unprovoked by outward circumstances, will from small beginnings brood within the breast till all the better dispositions, all the fair gifts of nature, are borne down before them – her poets in general have entirely neglected, and even her first and greatest have but imperfectly attempted. They have made use of the passions to mark their several characters and animate their scenes, rather than to open to our view the nature and portraitures of those great disturbers of the human breast with whom we are all, more or less, called upon to contend.

With their strong and obvious features, therefore, they have been presented to us stripped almost entirely of those less obtrusive (but not less discriminating) traits which mark them in their actual operation. To trace them in their rise and progress in the heart seems but rarely to have been the object of any dramatist. We commonly find the characters of a tragedy affected by the passions in a transient, loose, unconnected manner. Or, if they are represented as under the permanent influence of the more powerful ones, they are generally introduced to our notice in the very height of their fury, when all that timidity, irresolution, distrust, and a thousand delicate traits which make the infancy of every great passion more interesting perhaps than its full-blown strength, are fled. The impassioned character is generally brought into view under those irresistible attacks of their power which it is impossible to repel, whilst those gradual steps that led him into this state (in some of which a stand might have been made against the foe) are left entirely in the shade.

These passions that may be suddenly excited and are of short duration, as anger, fear, and oftentimes jealousy, may in this manner be fully represented. But those great masters of the soul (ambition, hatred, love – every passion that is permanent in its nature and varied in progress), if represented to us but in one stage of its course, is represented imperfectly.

It is a characteristic of the more powerful passions that they will increase and nourish themselves on very slender aliment: it is from within that they are chiefly supplied with what they feed on, and it is in contending with opposite passions and affections of the mind that we least discover their strength – not with events. But in tragedy it is events more frequently than opposite affections which are opposed to them, and those often of such force and magnitude that the passions themselves are almost obscured by the splendour and importance of the transactions to which they are attached.

John Thelwall   (1764–1834)

Thelwall was one of the most important radical agitators and pamphleteers of the 1790s. 'The Old Peasant', a precursor of the protagonists of Wordsworth's 'Simon Lee' and 'The Last of the Flock' (pp. 202–4, 216–18), shows how well Thelwall understood the plight of working people. In November 1794 he was among the defendants at the Treason Trials (the penalty for which was hanging, drawing, and quartering – all the defendants were acquitted), and during that period composed his Poems Written in Close Confinement. *When in December 1795 Pitt introduced the two Gagging Acts, designed to silence opposition to an increasingly repressive administration, Thelwall warned in The* Tribune *that such measures would give rise to even worse problems for the government. In the last issue of* The Tribune, *he published his moving 'Civic Oration', announcing his decision to retire from politics. His letter of 10 May 1796 provides a shrewd assessment of Coleridge's ornate poetic manner, which Coleridge subsequently curbed; indeed, Thelwall's own 'Lines Written at Bridgwater' (written after his stay at Nether Stowey, 17–27 July 1797, when he met the Wordsworths) and 'To the Infant Hampden' embody many of the principles underlying Coleridge's mature conversation poems and Wordsworth's* Lyrical Ballads.

From The Peripatetic (1793)

THE OLD PEASANT (iii 137–41)

'Detested villains! Proud parochial tyrants! And are these violators of all that endears society the objects who are to monopolize your generosity, while the oppressed mechanic groans in our streets unpitied, and the aged and infirm, whose strength has been exhausted in the labours most important to the community, feel the oppressions of want and sorrow accumulated to the infirmities of years, and apply for relief in vain? How different, my Wentworth – oh, how different were the appearance, the sentiments, and the fate of the honest unfortunate peasant whom (bending with age, and propping his feeble steps upon his hoe) we met upon Ewell common on a late excursion! Do you not see him again in fancy? Does not the tear start again into your eye as he lifts his hat in humble obeisance from his hairless forehead as we approach him? Unmerited complacency! Why was that obeisance paid to us? For aught you knew, poor victim, we might have been in the number of your oppressors, and that distinction of appearance which claimed your reverence might have entitled us to your execration. But the bruised reed turns not upon its destroyer, but bends beneath the foot that tramples it; else what proud gentility! In this insolence of thy oppression, what must be thy instant fate? Poor old man! At such a time of life to be doomed to wander from place to place for employment, and be doomed to wander in vain! To be repulsed from every door on account of those infirmities which former toils and former sorrows had brought upon thee, and to have thy appeals for charity retorted by the unfeeling malevolence of that upstart opulence which, in thy better days, had crouched to thee for obligations!'

'Your lamentation is interesting', said Ambulator, 'but you forget that here are two of us unacquainted with the story it alludes to.'

'It is short and simple, but it is not therefore the less pathetic. My wife', said he, with a mixed expression of anguish and resignation, 'is out of her distresses. Heaven has taken her from her sorrows. I have but one to care for – but that is *one too much*. Times go very hard, particularly with us who are grown old and slow. I have wandered from place to place, and though I am willing to work for less wages, nobody will employ a feeble old man now there are so many young ones out of other works, who are glad to go into the fields. I have applied to the parish here, for I was an inhabitant about five and twenty years ago, and lived in a better way. I had a little farm, and a few cows, and two or three sheep of my own, till my landlord turned me out that he might make three or four joining farms into one. So as I could not afford to take a large farm, I was obliged to sell my stock and go into another country. The churchwarden as is now, who is grown so proud and lives so grand, was a poor man then, and owed me seven pounds. But as it is so long since, I find I can't demand it. And when I asked him for relief, and told him the times were very hard, he told me he had nothing for me, and that if times were hard, I must live hard. And so shut the door in my face. I would have asked him else, what we were to do when times are so hard that we cannot live at all? Everything is very dear, there is no work to be had, and I am too old to go a-soldiering. Beside, why should we poor folks go and help the rich to fight against the poor?'

Perhaps, with some, this concluding sentiment may destroy all the compassion excited by his tale. But oh! that I had a voice like thunder, to shout the solemn truth in the ears of all the poor in Europe, that the kings and nobles of the earth might be reduced to the sole option of fighting their own battle, or restoring peace!

From Poems Written in Close Confinement in the Tower and Newgate upon a Charge of Treason (1795)

STANZAS ON HEARING FOR CERTAINTY THAT WE WERE TO BE TRIED FOR HIGH TREASON (COMPOSED 28 SEPTEMBER 1794)

Short is perhaps our date of life,[1]
But let us while we live be gay –
To those be thought and anxious care
Who build upon the distant day.

Though in our cup tyrannic power   5
Would dash the bitter dregs of fear,
We'll gaily quaff the mantling draught,
While patriot toasts the fancy cheer.

Sings not the seaman, tempest-tossed,
When surges wash the riven shroud –   10
Scorning the threat'ning voice of fate,
That pipes in rocking winds aloud?

Yes, he can take his cheerful glass,
And toast his mistress in the storm,

STANZAS ON HEARING FOR CERTAINTY THAT WE WERE TO BE TRIED FOR HIGH TREASON

[1] Thelwall was acquitted. The penalty for Treason was hanging, drawing, and quartering.

While duty and remembered joys 15
By turns his honest bosom warm.

And shall not we, in storms of state,
At base oppression's fury laugh,
And while the vital spirits flow,
To freedom fill, and fearless quaff? 20

Short is perhaps our date of life,
But let us while we live be gay –
To those be thought and anxious care
Who build upon the distant day.

(*Tower,* 28 September 1794)

From The Tribune (1795)

DANGEROUS TENDENCY OF THE ATTEMPT TO SUPPRESS POLITICAL
DISCUSSION (PUBLISHED 21 MARCH 1795) (I 25–6)

While prudent and moderate measures leave the door open to peaceful investigation, men of talents and moral character step forward into the field of politics, and never fail to take the lead in popular meetings and associations, for which nature seems to have intended them.

While this continues, all is peaceful and rational enquiry, and the people, though bold, are orderly. Nor even when persecution inflames their passions, are they easily provoked to actual intemperance. But when words are construed into treason, and men can no longer unbosom themselves to their friends at a tavern, or associate together for the diffusion of political information, but at the peril of their lives, the benevolent and moderate part of mankind retire from the scene of action, to brood, with prophetic anxiety, over the melancholy prospect.[1]

Enquiry is thus, it is true, in some degree suppressed, and the counsellors of these overbearing measures are apt to congratulate themselves on their supposed success. But the calm is more dreadful than the hurricane they pretended to apprehend. In the ferment of half-smothered indignation, feelings of a more gloomy complexion are generated, and characters of a very different stamp are called into action.

Men who have neither genius nor benevolence succeed those who had both, and, with no other stimulus than fury, and no other talent than hypocrisy and intrigue, embark in projects which every friend of humanity must abhor – and which, while the free, open, and manly character of the species was yet uncrushed by the detestable system of persecuting opinions, never could have entered the imagination.

Whoever will consult the page of history will find that in every country on the earth where liberty has been alternately indulged and trampled, this has been but too uniformly the progress of the human mind.

DANGEROUS TENDENCY OF THE ATTEMPT TO SUPPRESS
POLITICAL DISCUSSION
[1] Thelwall writes in anticipation of the Gagging
Acts of Dec. 1795, which banned 'seditious meetings'
and aimed to ensure the 'safety of his majesty's person'.

Let us ask then this serious question: is it possible for any person to be a more dangerous enemy to the peace and personal safety of the sovereign, than he who advises the persecution of opinion and the suppression of peaceable associations?

CIVIC ORATION ON THE ANNIVERSARY OF THE ACQUITTAL OF THE LECTURER [5 DECEMBER] BEING A VINDICATION OF THE PRINCIPLES, AND A REVIEW OF THE CONDUCT THAT PLACED HIM AT THE BAR OF THE OLD BAILEY. DELIVERED WEDNESDAY 9 DECEMBER 1795. (EXTRACT) (III 257–60)

I was born near this place. My residence can be traced with ease during every part of my life, and if there had been any disgraceful particulars in my history, the industrious malice of faction need not have been confined to general abuses. There have been times in which poverty and misfortune frowned upon my youth, and in which I had to struggle with the bitterest disadvantages to which an independent spirit could be subjected; when without a profession (for I could not eat the bread of legal peculation), I had to support an aged mother and a brother robbed of every faculty of reason.

Yet upon all these embarrassments, when a debating society and a magazine brought me together but about £50 or £60 a year, I look back with the proud consciousness of never having stooped even to a mean action. Search then, probe me to the quick, and if you can find one stain upon my character, think me in reality a plunderer and an assassin. But if you cannot, what will you think of a profligate administration, with more vices upon their heads than I have words to speak them? What will you think of their assassins, and the black epithets and calumnies with which they have so incessantly pursued me? ...

When our beloved associates – when those men of mind and virtue, whose names I will cherish with veneration so long as 'memory holds her seat'[1] – when Gerrald, Margarot, Muir, Palmer and Skirving[2] were doomed to Botany Bay without having violated one law or principle of our constitution, it was natural (though it was not wise) for men who revered their talents and their virtues to indulge the British vice of intemperance – for it is a British vice, and we are too apt to be proud of it. It was natural that under such circumstances, our blood should boil, and that we should say angry things, and pass vapouring, intemperate resolutions. But the minister knew that the 'very head and jut of our offending went but to this – no further!'[3]

What, then, is that administration, which wishes to hang every man who makes use of an intemperate word against them?

But they have been disappointed – and what do they now attempt? They attempt to pass laws which will make all those things treason which they endeavoured to make treason before without any law whatever.

The minister introduces Two Bills.[4] What are they? Bills that subject a man to all the penalties of High Treason who shall publish, or even write, *without publishing*, any

CIVIC ORATION ON THE ANNIVERSARY OF THE ACQUITTAL OF THE LECTURER [5 DECEMBER] BEING A VINDICATION OF THE PRINCIPLES, AND A REVIEW OF THE CONDUCT THAT PLACED HIM AT THE BAR OF THE OLD BAILEY. DELIVERED WEDNESDAY 9 DECEMBER 1795.
[1]   *Hamlet*, I. v. 96.
[2]   Gerrald, Margarot, and Skirving were arrested at a reform meeting in Edinburgh, Dec. 1793, and sen-

tenced in 1794 to 14 years' transportation. Muir and Palmer, two other Scottish reformers, had been sentenced in Aug.–Sept. 1793 to 14 and 7 years' transportation.
[3]   *Othello*, I. iii. 80–1.
[4]   The two Bills were introduced in Nov. 1795 and became law on 18 Dec.

dissertation which approves any form of government but the existing government of the country. . . .

I cannot be ignorant that these acts are made in a very considerable degree with a view to my destruction. I know also that the time will come when – in consequence of the persecutions I have endured, and the temper (permit me to say) with which I have faced those persecutions – I may be an instrument of some service to the liberties and happiness of my country. I shall not therefore give the minister an opportunity to destroy me upon any trifling contest. I have here maintained myself in decency, and cleared away the encumbrances which former persecutions had brought upon me. With something less than £100 in my pocket I shall retire from this place, for the cultivation of my mind, and, carrying the consciousness of my own integrity into retirement, maintain myself by the labours of my pen.

Having been so long seeking for my country, and having endured so much persecution in that search, I think I shall not be accused either of selfishness or pusillanimity, when I say that I shall now wait till my country seeks for me, and that when my country does seek for me, she shall find me ready for my post, whatever may be the difficulty or the danger.

From A Letter from John Thelwall to Samuel Taylor Coleridge, 10 May 1796 (edited from MS)

Of your favourite poem I fear I shall speak in terms that will disappoint you. There are passages most undoubtedly in the *Religious Musings* of very great merit, and perhaps there is near half of the poem that no poet in our language need have been ashamed to own. But this praise belongs almost exclusively to those parts that are not at all religious. As for the generality of those passages which are most so, they are certainly anything in the world rather than poetry (unless indeed the mere glowing rapidity of the blank verse may entitle them to that distinction).

They are the very acme of abstruse, metaphysical, mystical rant, and all ranting abstraction, metaphysics and mysticism are wider from true poetry than the equator from the poles. The whole poem also is infected with inflation and turgidity. . . . 'a vision *shadowy* of truth', '*wormy* grave', and a heap of like instances might be selected worthy of Blackmore[1] himself. ('Ye petrify th' *imbrothelled atheist's* heart' is one of those illiberal and unfounded calumnies with which Christian meekness never yet disdained to supply the want of argument – but this by the way.) '*Lovely* was the *death* of him whose life was love' is certainly enough to make any man sick whose taste has not been corrupted by the licentious (I mean 'pious') nonsense of the conventicle.

You may, if you please, 'lay the flattering unction to your soul' that my irreligious principles dictate the severity of this criticism, and, though it may strengthen you in the suspicion, I must confess that your religious verses approach much nearer to poetry than those of Milton on the same subject. In short, while I was yet a Christian, and a

---

From A LETTER FROM JOHN THELWALL TO SAMUEL TAYLOR COLERIDGE

[1] Sir Richard Blackmore (1654–1729), author of indifferent epics including *Creation: A Philosophical Poem* (1712).

very zealous one (i.e. when I was about your age), I became thoroughly convinced that Christian poetry was very vile stuff – that religion was a subject which none but a rank infidel could handle poetically.

Before I wipe the gall from my pen, I must notice an affectation of the Della Crusca[2] school which blurs almost every one of your poems – I mean the frequent accent upon the adjectives and weak words.... 'For chiefly in the oppressed *good* man's face' etc.

Having dwelt thus largely upon the defects, I shall proceed to prove my qualifications to set up for a critic by running very slightly over the numerous beauties with which it abounds. 'The *thought-benighted sceptic*' is very happy, as is also 'Mists dim-floating of idolatry – misshaped the omnipresent sin'. (The word 'Split' appears to me ill-chosen and unpoetical.) The whole passage 'Thus from the elect'... (ll. 102–18), though not quite free either from mysticism or turgidity, is upon the whole very grand and very poetical. Lines 133–5 and 138–44 are also equally fine in sentiment, conception and expression. And though '*connatural* mind', '*tortuous* folds', '*savagery* of holy zeal', 'at his mouth *im*breathe', and '*fiendish* deeds', offend me not a little as being affected and pedantic (and therefore of course unpoetical), yet the whole passage, lines 181–255, delights me very much. The satire is dignified, the poetry sublime and ardent. Of the ensuing paragraph, 'In the primeval age' etc., the first and third lines are bad; but the ensuing passage consisting of 144 lines beginning with 'soon imagination conjured up a host of new desires', and ending at line 364 breathes a rapture and energy of mind seldom to be met with among modern bards. I must however in sincerity add that, according to my judgement, all that follows hangs like a dead weight upon the poem.

From Poems Written Chiefly in Retirement (1801)

LINES WRITTEN AT BRIDGWATER IN SOMERSETSHIRE, ON 27 JULY 1797, DURING A LONG EXCURSION IN QUEST OF A PEACEFUL RETREAT (EXTRACT)

> Ah, let me, far in some sequestered dell,   85
> Build my low cot! Most happy might it prove,
> My Samuel,[1] near to thine, that I might oft
> Share thy sweet converse, best-beloved of friends,
> Long-loved ere known – for kindred sympathies
> Linked (though far distant) our congenial souls!   90
> Ah! 'twould be sweet, beneath the neighb'ring thatch,
> In philosophic amity to dwell,
> Inditing moral verse, or tale, or theme,
> Gay or instructive. And it would be sweet,
> With kindly interchange of mutual aid,   95
> To delve our little garden plots, the while

---

[2] The Della Cruscans of the late eighteenth century advocated an affected, ornamented sentimentality, and are probably in Wordsworth's mind when he mentions the 'gaudiness and inane phraseology of many modern writers' in the Advertisement to *Lyrical Ballads* (1798), p. 166 below.

EXTRACT FROM LINES WRITTEN AT BRIDGWATER (COMPOSED 27 JULY 1797)
[1] Coleridge.

Sweet converse flowed, suspending oft the arm
And half-driven spade, while, eager, one propounds,
And listens one, weighing each pregnant word,
And pondering fit reply that may untwist   100
The knotty point – perchance of import high –
Of moral truth, of causes infinite
(Creating power, or uncreated worlds
Eternal and uncaused!), or whatsoe'er
Of metaphysic or of ethic lore   105
The mind with curious subtlety[2] pursues,
Agreeing or dissenting – sweet alike,
When wisdom, and not victory, the end.
    And 'twould be sweet, my Samuel (ah, most sweet!),
To see our little infants[3] stretch their limbs   110
In gambols unrestrained, and early learn
Practical love, and – wisdom's noblest lore –
Fraternal kindliness, while rosiest health
Bloomed on their sunburnt cheeks. And 'twould be sweet
(When what to toil was due, to study what,   115
And literary effort, had been paid)[4]
Alternate in each other's bower to sit,
In summer's genial season. Or, when bleak,
The wintry blast had stripped the leafy shade,
Around the blazing hearth, social and gay,   120
To share our frugal viands, and the bowl
Sparkling with home-brewed beverage – by our sides
Thy Sara and my Susan,[5] and, perchance,
Alfoxden's musing tenant, and the maid
Of ardent eye who with fraternal love   125
Sweetens his solitude.[6] With these should join
Arcadian pool, swain of a happier age
When Wisdom and Refinement loved to dwell
With rustic Plainness, and the pastoral vale
Was vocal to the melodies of verse,   130
Echoing sweet minstrelsy.
                     With such, my friend –
With such, how pleasant to unbend awhile,
Winging the idle hour with song or tale,
Pun or quaint joke or converse, such as fits
Minds gay, but innocent. And we would laugh   135
(Unless, perchance, pity's more kindly tear

---

[2] *The mind with curious subtlety*, perhaps the source of Coleridge's phrase 'the self-watching subtilizing mind' ('Frost at Midnight', 27).

[3] *our little infants* Hartley Coleridge (b. 1796) and Algernon Sydney Thelwall (b. 1795).

[4] ... when we had fully laboured, studied, and written ...

[5] Sara Fricker married Coleridge, 4 Oct. 1795; Susan Vellum married Thelwall, 27 July 1791.

[6] William and Dorothy Wordsworth, who had just moved into Alfoxden House in Holford, close to Coleridge's village of Nether Stowey.

Check the obstreperous mirth) at such who waste
Life's precious hours in the delusive chase
Of wealth and worldly gewgaws, and contend
For honours emptier than the hollow voice   140
That rings in echo's cave, and which, like that,
Exists but in the babbling of a world
Creating its own wonder. Wiselier we
To intellectual joys will thus devote
Our fleeting years, mingling Arcadian sports   145
With healthful industry. Oh, it would be
A golden age revived!

TO THE INFANT HAMPDEN. WRITTEN DURING A SLEEPLESS NIGHT. DERBY, OCTOBER 1797

Sweet babe, that on thy mother's guardian breast
Slumberest, unheedful of the autumnal blast
That rocks our lowly dwelling, nor dost dream
Of woes, or cares, or persecuting rage,
Or rending passions, or the pangs that wait   5
On ill-requited services – sleep on,
Sleep, and be happy! 'Tis the sole relief
This anxious mind can hope from the dire pangs
Of deep corroding wrong, that thou, my babe,
And the sweet twain (the firstlings of my love!)   10
As yet are blessed; and that my heart's best pride,
Who, with maternal fondness, pillows thee
Beside thy life's warm fountain, is not quite
Hopeless or joyless, but with matron cares
And calm domestic virtues can avert   15
The melancholy fiend, and in your smiles
Read nameless consolations.
                              Ah, sleep on,
As yet unconscious of the patriot's name
Or of a patriot's sorrows, of the cares
For which thy name-sire bled.[1] And, more unblessed,   20
Thy natural father in his native land
Wanders an exile, and of all that land
Can find no spot his home. Ill-omened babe,
Conceived in tempests, and in tempests born –
What destiny awaits thee? Reekless[2] thou.   25
Oh, blessed inapprehension – let it last!
Sleep on, my babe, now while the rocking wind
Pipes mournful, length'ning my nocturnal plaint

TO THE INFANT HAMPDEN. WRITTEN DURING A SLEEPLESS
NIGHT. DERBY, OCTOBER 1797.
[1] Hampden Thelwall was named after John Hampden (1594–1643), leader of the Long Parliament,
famous for his historic refusal in 1636 to pay the
ship-money exacted by Charles I, mortally wounded
at Chalgrove Field, near Oxford.
[2] *Reekless* unknowing.

With troubled symphony! Ah, sleep secure,
And may thy dream of life be ne'er disturbed   30
With visions such as mar thy father's peace –
Visions (ah, that they were but such indeed!)
That show this world a wilderness of wrongs,
A waste of troubled waters, whelming floods
Of tyrannous injustice canopied   35
With clouds dark-louring, whence the pelting storms
Of cold unkindness the rough torrents swell
On every side resistless. There my ark,
The scanty remnant of my deluged joys,
Floats anchorless, while through the dreary round,   40
Fluttering on anxious pinion, the tired foot
Of persecuted virtue cannot find
One spray on which to rest, or scarce one leaf
To cheer with promise of subsiding woe.

Mary Anne Lamb (1764–1847)

Despite her mental instability (see p. 614), Mary Lamb lived happily, for much of her life, with her brother, and was a favourite among his friends, including Landor (see pp. 630–1), Hazlitt, Leigh Hunt, Hood, Procter, and the Wordsworths. Her lines on the loss of Captain John Wordsworth demonstrate how deeply felt her verse can be; 'The Two Boys', with its powerful message, was published at the end of her brother's essay, 'Detached Thoughts on Books and Reading', July 1822.

From Letter from Mary Anne Lamb to Dorothy Wordsworth, 7 May 1805

My dear Miss Wordsworth,

I thank you, my kind friend, for your most comfortable letter. Till I saw your own handwriting, I could not persuade myself that I should do well to write to you, though I have often attempted it, but I always left off dissatisfied with what I had written, and feeling that I was doing an improper thing to intrude upon your sorrow.[1] I wished to tell you that you would one day feel the kind of peaceful state of mind, and sweet memory of the dead which you so happily describe as now almost begun. But I felt that it was improper and most grating to the feelings of the afflicted, to say to them that the memory of their affliction would in time become a constant part not only of their 'dream, but of their most wakeful sense of happiness'.[2] That you would see every

---

From LETTER FROM MARY ANNE LAMB TO DOROTHY WORDSWORTH, 7 MAY 1805
[1]   The Wordsworths were devastated by the death of their brother John Wordsworth, drowned at sea 5

Feb. 1805 – a loss that inspired Wordsworth's 'Elegiac Stanzas' (pp. 474–6).
[2]   Quoted, apparently, from Dorothy Wordsworth's 'most comfortable' letter to Mary Lamb, which has not survived.

object with and through your lost brother, and that that would at last become a real and everlasting source of comfort to you, I felt, and well knew, from my own experience in sorrow; but till you yourself began to feel this I did not dare tell you so. But I send you some poor lines which I wrote under this conviction of mind, and before I heard Coleridge was returning home.[3] I will transcribe them now before I finish my letter, lest a false shame prevent me then, for I know they are much worse than they ought to be. Written as they were with strong feeling and on such a subject, every line seems to me to be borrowed, but I had no better way of expressing my thoughts, and I never have the power of altering or amending anything I have once laid aside with dissatisfaction.

> Why is he wandering o'er the sea?
> Coleridge should now with Wordsworth be.
> By slow degrees he'd steal away
> Their woe, and gently bring a ray
> (So happily he'd time relief)   5
> Of comfort from their very grief;
> He'd tell them that their brother dead,
> When years have passed o'er their head,
> Will be remembered with such holy,
> True, and perfect melancholy,   10
> That ever this lost brother John
> Will be their heart's companion.
> His voice they'll always hear, his face they'll always see;
> There's nought in life so sweet as such a memory.

From London Magazine, 6 (1822) 36

THE TWO BOYS

> I saw a boy with eager eye
> Open a book upon a stall,
> And read as he'd devour it all;
> Which, when the stall-man did espy,
> Soon to the boy I heard him call,   5
> 'You, sir, you never buy a book,
> Therefore in one you shall not look!'
> The boy passed slowly on, and with a sigh
> He wished he never had been taught to read,
> Then of the old churl's books he should have had no need.   10
>
> Of sufferings the poor have many,
> Which never can the rich annoy.
> I soon perceived another boy —

---

[3] On 2 Apr. 1805, Dorothy told Mrs Thomas Clarkson that Coleridge had written to Southey in February that he intended returning to England in March. Dorothy presumably passed this information on to Mary Lamb in her 'most comfortable' letter.

Who looked as if he'd not had any
Food, for that day at least – enjoy   15
The sight of cold meat in a tavern larder.
This boy's case, then thought I, is surely harder;
Thus hungry, longing thus without a penny,
Beholding choice of dainty-dressed meat –
No wonder if he wish he ne'er had learned to eat.   20

From The Keepsake for 1829 (1828)

WHAT IS LOVE? (SIGNED 'M.L.') (P. 237)

Love is the passion which endureth,
Which neither time nor absence cureth;
Which nought of earthly change can sever:
Love is the light which shines for ever.

What cold and selfish breasts deem madness   5
Lives in its depths of joy and sadness;
In hearts, on lips, of flame it burneth –
One is its world, to *one* it turneth.

Its chain of gold – what hand can break it?
Its deathless hold – what force can shake it?   10
Mere passion aught of earth may sever,
But *souls* that love, love on for ever.

Ann Radcliffe (1764–1823)

Radcliffe was one of the most successful Gothic novelists of the eighteenth century. The verse contained in her novels was sufficiently popular to be collected and published as Poems *(1815). Her* Journey Made in the Summer of 1794 *provides a dramatic account of the Lake District, which coloured the landscapes described in her fiction.*

From The Mysteries of Udolpho (4 vols., 1794)

RONDEAU (II 59–60)

Soft as yon silver ray that sleeps
Upon the ocean's trembling tide;
Soft as the air that lightly sweeps
Yon sail, that swells in stately pride;

Soft as the surge's stealing note   5
That dies along the distant shores,

Or warbled strain that sinks remote –
So soft the sigh my bosom pours!

True as the wave to Cynthia's ray,
True as the vessel to the breeze,   10
True as the soul to music's sway
Or music to Venetian seas;

Soft as yon silver beams that sleep
Upon the ocean's trembling breast;
So soft, so true, fond love shall weep,   15
So soft, so true, with thee shall rest.

From A Journey Made in the Summer of 1794 (1795)
THE ROAD TO EMONT (PP. 407–8)

Soon after, the road brought us to the brows of Emont, a narrow well-wooded vale, the river from which it takes its name meandering through it from Ullswater among pastures and pleasure-grounds, to meet the Lowther near Brougham castle. Penrith and its castle and beacon look up the vale from the north, and the astonishing fells of Ullswater close upon it in the south, while Delemain, the house and beautiful grounds of Mr Hassel; Hutton St John, a venerable old mansion; and the single tower called Dacre Castle adorn the valley.

But who can pause to admire the elegancies of art, when surrounded by the wonders of nature? The approach to this sublime lake along the heights of Emont is exquisitely interesting, for the road (being shrouded by woods) allows the eye only partial glimpses of the gigantic shapes that are assembled in the distance and, awakening high expectation, leaves the imagination thus elevated to paint the 'forms of things unseen'. Thus it was when we caught a first view of the dark broken tops of the fells that rise round Ullswater, of size and shape most huge, bold, and awful, overspread with a blue mysterious tint that seemed almost supernatural, though according in gloom and sublimity with the severe features it involved.

THE JAWS OF BORROWDALE (P. 465)

Dark rocks yawn at its entrance, terrific as the wildness of a maniac, and disclose a narrow pass running up between mountains of granite that are shook into almost every possible form of horror. All above resembles the accumulations of an earthquake – splintered, shivered, piled, amassed. Huge cliffs have rolled down into the glen below, where, however, is still a miniature of the sweetest pastoral beauty on the banks of the river Derwent. But description cannot paint either the wildness of the mountains, or the pastoral and sylvan peace and softness that wind at their base.

GRASMERE (P. 470)

Beyond Dunmail Raise, one of the grand passes from Cumberland into Westmorland, Helm Crag rears its crest, a strange fantastic summit – round, yet jagged and splintered like the wheel of a watermill – overlooking Grasmere, which soon after opened below. A green spreading circle of mountains embosoms this small lake and, beyond, a wider range rises in amphitheatre, whose rocky tops are rounded and scalloped, yet are great, wild, irregular, and were then overspread with a tint of faint purple. The softest verdure margins the water and mingles with corn enclosures and woods that wave up the hills, but scarcely a cottage anywhere appears, except at the northern end of the lake, where the village of Grasmere and its very neat white church stand among trees near the shore, with Helm Crag and a multitude of fells rising over it and beyond each other in the perspective.

James Mackintosh (1765–1832)

With Vindiciae Gallicae *Mackintosh produced one of the most effective replies to Burke's* Reflections *– which makes it all the more ironic that, under Burke's influence, he recanted in his lectures of 1799, declaring that he did 'abhor, abjure, and forever renounce' his former allegiance to the revolutionary cause. Wordsworth and Coleridge were deeply shocked by this change of heart. Wordsworth mentions it at* Thirteen-Book Prelude, *ii. 450–6, and in a letter to Godwin of May 1800 Coleridge referred to 'the great dung-fly Mackintosh' (Griggs, i. 588); see also Lamb's 'On Mackintosh', p. 616 below.*

From Vindiciae Gallicae (1791)

POPULAR EXCESSES WHICH ATTENDED THE REVOLUTION (PP. 162–4)

That no great revolutions can be accomplished without excesses and miseries at which humanity revolts is a truth which cannot be denied.

This unfortunately is true, in a peculiar manner, of those revolutions which, like that of France, are strictly *popular*. Where the people are led by a faction, its leaders find no difficulty in the re-establishment of that order which must be the object of their wishes, because it is the sole security of their power. But when a general movement of the popular mind levels a despotism with the ground, it is far less easy to restrain excess. There is more resentment to satiate, and less authority to control. The passion which produced an effect so tremendous is too violent to subside in a moment into serenity and submission. The spirit of revolt breaks out with fatal violence after its object is destroyed, and turns against the order of freedom those arms by which it had subdued the strength of tyranny. The attempt to punish the spirit that actuates a people, if it were just, would be vain, and if it were possible would be cruel. They are too many to be punished in a view of justice, and too strong to be punished in a view of policy. The ostentation of vigour would in such a case prove the display of impotence, and the rigour of justice conduct to the cruelty of extirpation.

No remedy is therefore left but the progress of instruction, the force of persuasion, the mild authority of opinion. These remedies, though infallible, are of slow operation, and in the interval which elapses before a calm succeeds the boisterous moments of a revolution, it is vain to expect that a people inured to barbarism by their oppressors, and which has ages of oppression to avenge, will be punctiliously generous in their triumph, nicely discriminative in their vengeance, or cautiously mild in their mode of retaliation: 'they will break their chains on the heads of their oppressors'.[1]

Robert Bloomfield   (1766–1823)

'What Wordsworth and I have seen of The Farmer's Boy *(only a few short extracts) pleased us very much,' Coleridge wrote, 17 September 1800 (Griggs, i. 623). They were among the first readers of this Suffolk farm-labourer and cobbler turned poet, and were apparently impressed by the close observation of the natural world evident throughout his poem, which described the life of Giles, an orphan peasant, during the agricultural year. The poem was a success, and sold 26,000 copies in less than three years.*

From The Farmer's Boy (1800)

SPRING (extract)

Neglected now the early daisy lies,
Nor thou, pale primrose, bloom'st the only prize;   270
Advancing spring profusely spreads abroad
Flow'rs of all hues, with sweetest fragrance stored.
Where'er she treads, love gladdens every plain,
Delight on tiptoe bears her lucid train,
Sweet hope with conscious brow before her flies,   275
Anticipating wealth from summer skies.
All nature feels her renovating sway,
The sheep-fed pasture, and the meadow gay,
And trees and shrubs, no longer budding seen,
Display the new-grown branch of lighter green.   280
On airy downs the shepherd idling lies,
And sees tomorrow in the marbled skies;
Here then, my soul, thy darling theme pursue,
For every day was Giles a shepherd too.
    Small was his charge – no wilds had they to roam,   285
But bright enclosures circling round their home.
Nor yellow-blossomed furze, nor stubborn thorn
(The heath's rough produce) had their fleeces torn;
Yet ever roving, ever seeking thee,
Enchanting spirit, dear variety!   290
Oh happy tenants, prisoners of a day,
Released to ease, to pleasure, and to play!
Indulged through every field by turns to range,

POPULAR EXCESSES WHICH ATTENDED THE REVOLUTION
[1]   'The eloquent expression of Mr Curran in the
Parliament of Ireland, respecting the Revolution'
(Mackintosh's note).

And taste them all in one continual change –
For though luxuriant their grassy food,   295
Sheep long confined but loathe the present good;
Instinctively they haunt the homeward gate,
And starve and pine with plenty at their feet.
   Loosed from the winding lane, a joyful throng,
See, o'er yon pasture how they pour along!   300
Giles round their boundaries takes his usual stroll,
Sees every pass secured, and fences whole –
High fences, proud to charm the gazing eye,
Where many a nestling first assays to fly;
Where blows the woodbine, faintly streaked with red,   305
And rests on every bough its tender head;
Round the young ash its twining branches meet,
Or crown the hawthorn with its odours sweet.
Say, ye that know, ye who have felt and seen
Spring's morning smiles, and soul-enliv'ning green,   310
Say, did you give the thrilling transport way?
Did your eye brighten, when young lambs at play
Leaped o'er your path with animated pride,
Or gazed in merry clusters by your side?
Ye who can smile (to wisdom no disgrace)   315
At the arch meaning of a kitten's face,
If spotless innocence and infant mirth
Excites to praise, or gives reflection birth;
In shades like these pursue your fav'rite joy,
Midst nature's revels, sports that never cloy.   320
A few begin a short but vigorous race,
And indolence abashed soon flies the place;
Thus challenged forth, see thither one by one,
From every side assembling playmates run.
A thousand wily antics mark their stay,   325
A starting crowd impatient of delay;
Like the fond dove from fearful prison freed,
Each seems to say, 'Come, let us try our speed!'
Away they scour, impetuous, ardent, strong,
The green turf trembling as they bound along;   330
Adown the slope, then up the hillock climb,
Where every molehill is a bed of thyme;
There panting stop, yet scarcely can refrain –
A bird, a leaf, will set them off again!
Or if a gale with strength unusual blow,   335
Scatt'ring the wild-brier roses into snow,
Their little limbs increasing efforts try,
Like the torn flower the fair assemblage fly.
   Ah, fallen rose, sad emblem of their doom;
Frail as thyself, they perish while they bloom!   340
Though unoffending innocence may plead,

Though frantic ewes may mourn the savage deed,
Their shepherd comes, a messenger of blood,
And drives them bleating from their sports and food.
Care loads his brow, and pity wrings his heart,   345
For lo, the murd'ring butcher with his cart
Demands the firstlings of his flock to die,
And makes a sport of life and liberty!
His gay companions Giles beholds no more –
Closed are their eyes, their fleeces drenched in gore;   350
Nor can compassion, with her softest notes,
Withhold the knife that plunges through their throats.
   Down, indignation! Hence, ideas foul!
Away the shocking image from my soul!
Let kindlier visitants attend my way   355
Beneath approaching summer's fervid ray;
Nor thankless glooms obtrude, nor cares annoy,
Whilst the sweet theme is universal joy.

SUMMER (EXTRACT)

Now ere sweet summer bids its long adieu,
And winds blow keen where late the blossom grew,
The bustling day and jovial night must come,
The long accustomed feast of harvest-home.[1]   290
No blood-stained victory in story bright
Can give the philosophic mind delight;
No triumph please whilst rage and death destroy –
Reflection sickens at the monstrous joy.
And where the joy, if rightly understood,   295
Like cheerful praise for universal good?
The soul nor check nor doubtful anguish knows,
But free and pure the grateful current flows.
   Behold the sound oak table's massy frame
Bestride the kitchen floor! The careful dame   300
And gen'rous host invite their friends around,
While all that cleared the crop or tilled the ground
Are guests by right of custom, old and young.
And many a neighbouring yeoman[2] join the throng
With artisans that lent their dextrous aid   305
When o'er each field the flaming sunbeams played.
   Yet plenty reigns and, from her boundless hoard
(Though not one jelly trembles on the board),
Supplies the feast with all that sense can crave,
With all that made our great forefathers brave   310

SUMMER
[1] harvest-home party to celebrate the successful homing of the corn.

[2] yeoman servant in a noble household; Bloomfield celebrates a time when the servants of lords mixed with peasants.

Ere the cloyed palate countless flavours tried,
And cooks had nature's judgement set aside.
With thanks to Heaven, and tales of rustic lore,
The mansion echoes when the banquet's o'er.
A wider circle spreads, and smiles abound,   315
As quick the frothing horn³ performs its round
(Care's mortal foe), that sprightly joys imparts
To cheer the frame and elevate their hearts.
Here, fresh and brown, the hazel's produce lies
In tempting heaps; and peals of laughter rise,   320
And crackling music with the frequent song,
Unheeded bear the midnight hour along.
    Here once a year distinction low'rs its crest –
The master, servant and the merry guest
Are equal all, and round the happy ring   325
The reaper's eyes exulting glances fling
And, warmed with gratitude, he quits his place
With sunburnt hands and ale-enlivened face,
Refills the jug his honoured host to tend,
To serve at once the master and the friend,   330
Proud thus to meet his smiles, to share his tale,
His nuts, his conversation, and his ale.
    Such were the days, of days long past I sing,
When pride gave place to mirth without a sting;
Ere tyrant customs strength sufficient bore   335
To violate the feelings of the poor,
To leave them distanced in the mad'ning race
Where'er refinement shows its hated face –
Nor causeless hated: 'tis the peasant's curse
That hourly makes his wretched station worse,   340
Destroys life's intercourse, the social plan
That rank to rank cements, as man to man.
Wealth flows around him, fashion lordly reigns;
Yet poverty is his, and mental pains.

Maria Edgeworth   (1767–1849)

Edgeworth's Letters for Literary Ladies *made an important contribution to the debate on women's intellectual emancipation. In 'Letter IV', below, she describes the plight of women who wished to separate from their husbands during the eighteenth century. Like Wollstonecraft, she regards education as the key to women's freedom. She was best known as a novelist, and her letter to Mrs Stark of 6 September 1834 gives a useful insight into her working methods.*

---

³ *frothing horn* animal horn hollowed out and filled
with ale.

From Letters for Literary Ladies (1795)

LETTER IV: CAROLINE TO LADY V., UPON HER INTENDED SEPARATION FROM HER HUSBAND (EXTRACT) (PP. 44–51)

From domestic uneasiness a man has a thousand resources: in middling life, the tavern; in high life, the gaming-table suspends the anxiety of thought. Dissipation, ambition, business, the occupation of a profession, change of place, change of company, afford him agreeable and honourable relief from domestic chagrin. If his home become tiresome, he leaves it; if his wife become disagreeable to him, he leaves her, and in leaving her loses *only* a wife.

But what resource has a woman? Precluded from all the occupations common to the other sex, she loses even those peculiar to her own. She has no remedy from the company of a man she dislikes but a separation – and this remedy, desperate as it is, is allowed only to a certain class of women in society, to those whose fortune affords them the means of subsistence, and whose friends have secured to them a separate maintenance. A peeress then, probably, can leave her husband if she wish it; a peasant's wife cannot. She depends upon the character and privileges of a wife for actual subsistence. Her domestic care, if not her affection, is secured to her husband, and it is just that it should. He sacrifices his liberty, his labour, his ingenuity, his time, for the support and protection of his wife. And in proportion to his protection is his power.

In higher life, where the sacrifices of both parties in the original union are more equal, the evils of a separation are more nearly balanced. But even here, the wife, who has hazarded least, suffers the most by the dissolution of the partnership. She loses a great part of her fortune, and of the conveniences and luxuries of life. She loses her home, her rank in society. She loses both the repellent and the attractive power of a mistress of a family: 'Her occupation is gone.'[1] She becomes a wanderer through life. Whilst her youth and beauty last, she may enjoy that species of delirium caused by public admiration, fortunate if habit does not destroy the power of this charm before the season of its duration expire.

It was said to be the wish of a celebrated modern beauty 'that she might not survive her nine and twentieth birthday'. I have often heard this wish quoted from its extravagance, but I always admired it for its good sense. The lady foresaw the inevitable doom of her declining years. Her apprehensions for the future embittered even her enjoyment of the present, and she had resolution enough to offer to take a 'bond of fate', to sacrifice one half of her life to secure the pleasure of the other.

But dear Lady V., probably this wish was made at some distance from the destined period of its accomplishment. On the eve of her nine-and-twentieth birthday, the lady perhaps might have felt inclined to retract her prayer. At least we should provide for the cowardice which might seize the female mind at such an instant. Even the most wretched life has power to attach us. None can be more wretched than the old age of a dissipated beauty – unless, Lady V., it be that of a woman who, to all her evils, has the addition of remorse for having abjured her duties and abandoned her family. Such is the situation of a woman who separates from her husband. Reduced to go the same

---

[1] *Othello*, III. iii. 357.

insipid round of public amusements – yet more restrained than an unmarried beauty in youth, yet more miserable in age – the superiority of her genius and the sensibility of her heart become her greatest evils. She, indeed, must pray for indifference. Avoided by all her family connections, hated and despised where she might have been loved and respected, solitary in the midst of society, she feels herself deserted at the time of life when she most wants social comfort and assistance.

Dear Julia, whilst it is yet in your power, secure to yourself a happier fate, retire to the bosom of your own family; prepare for yourself a new society; perform the duties, and you shall soon enjoy the pleasures of domestic life; educate your children (whilst they are young, it shall be your occupation; as they grow up, it shall be your glory). Let me anticipate your future success, when they shall appear such as you can make them, when the world shall ask, 'Who educated these amiable young women? Who formed their character? Who cultivated the talents of this promising young man? Why does this whole family live together so perfectly united?'

With one voice, dear Julia, your children shall name their mother: she who in the bloom of youth checked herself in the career of dissipation, and turned all the ability and energy of her mind to their education.

From The Life and Letters of Maria Edgeworth, ed. Augustus J. C. Hare (2 vols., 1894)

LETTER FROM MARIA EDGEWORTH TO MRS STARK, 6 SEPTEMBER 1834 (EXTRACT) (II 250–1)

I have seldom or ever drawn any one character – certainly not any ridiculous or faulty character – from any individual. Wherever, in writing, a real character rose to my view, from memory or resemblance, it has always been hurtful to me, because, to avoid that resemblance, I was tempted by cowardice or compelled by conscience to throw in differences, which often ended in making my character inconsistent, unreal.

At the hazard of talking too much of myself (which people usually do when once they begin), I must tell my penetrating critic exactly the facts, as far as I know them, about my habits of composition. He will at least see, by my throwing open my mind thus, that he has not made me afraid of him, but has won my confidence, and made me look for his future sympathy and assistance.

I have no 'vast magazine of a commonplace book'. In my whole life, since I began to write (which is now, I am concerned to state, upwards of forty years), I have had only about half a dozen little notebooks, strangely and irregularly kept, sometimes with only words of reference to some book or fact I could not bring accurately to mind. At first I was much urged by my father to note down remarkable traits of character or incidents which he thought might be introduced in stories, and he often blamed that idleness or laziness (as he thought it in me) which resisted his urgency. But I was averse to noting down because I was conscious that it did better for me to keep the things in my head, if they suited my purpose – and if they did not, they would only encumber me. I knew that, when I wrote down, I put the thing out of my care, out of my head, and that (though it might be put by very safe) I should not know where to look for it, that the labour of looking over a notebook would never do when I was in the warmth and pleasure of inventing, that I should never recollect the facts or ideas at the right time if I did not put them up in my own way in my own head. That is, if I felt with hope or pleasure 'that thought or that fact will be useful to me in such a character or story of which I have now a first idea, the same fact or thought would recur, I knew, when I wanted it, in right order for invention'.

In short (as Colonel Stewart guessed), the process of combination, generalization, invention, was carried on always in my head best. Wherever I brought in, bodily unaltered, as I have sometimes done, facts from real life, or sayings, or recorded observations of my own, I have almost always found them objected to by good critics as unsuited to the character, or in some way *de trop*. Sometimes, when the first idea of a character was taken from life from some original, and the characteristic facts noted down, or even noted only in my head, I have found it necessary entirely to alter these, not only from propriety, to avoid individual resemblance, but from the sense that the character would be only an exception to general feeling and experience – not a rule.

Amelia Opie   (1769–1853)

Friend of Godwin, Wollstonecraft, and Coleridge, Opie was a prolific novelist and poet. Her treatment of the subject of Aeolus's harp might be compared with Coleridge's less formal The Eolian Harp.

From Poems (1808)

STANZAS WRITTEN UNDER AEOLUS' HARP

Come ye, whose hearts the tyrant sorrows wound,
Come ye, whose breasts the tyrant passions tear,
And seek this harp in whose still varying sound
Each woe its own appropriate plaint may hear.

Solemn and slow yon murmuring cadence rolls   5
Till on the attentive ear it dies away;
To your fond griefs responsive – ye, whose souls
O'er loved lost friends regret's sad tribute pay.

But hark, in regular progression move
Yon silver sounds, and mingle as they fall!   10
Do they not wake thy trembling nerves, oh love,
And into warmer life thy feelings call?

Again it speaks, but, shrill and swift, the tones
In wild disorder strike upon the ear!
Pale frenzy listens, kindred wildness owns   15
And starts – appalled the well-known sounds to hear.

Lo, e'en the gay, the giddy and the vain
In deep delight these vocal wires attend,

Silent and breathless watch the varying strain,
And pleased the vacant toils of mirth suspend. 20

So when the lute on Memnon's statue hung
At day's first rising strains melodious poured
Untouched by mortal hands, the gathering throng
In silent wonder listened and adored.

But the wild cadence of these trembling strings 25
The enchantress Fancy with most rapture hears;
At the sweet sound to grasp her wand she springs,
And lo, her band of airy shapes appears!

She (rapt enthusiast) thinks the melting strains
A choir of angels breathe, in bright array 30
Bearing on radiant clouds to yon blue plains
A soul just parted from its silent clay.

And oft at eve her wild creative eye
Sees to the gale their silken pinions stream,
While in the quivering trees soft zephyrs sigh, 35
And through the leaves disclose the moon's pale beam.

Oh, breathing instrument, be ever near
While to the pensive muse my vows I pay;
Thy softest call the inmost soul can hear,
Thy faintest breath can Fancy's pinions play. 40

And when art's laboured strains my feelings tire,
To seek thy simple music shall be mine;
I'll strive to win its graces to my lyre,
And make my plaintive lays enchant like thine.

William Wordsworth (1770–1850)

Publications include Lyrical Ballads *(1798, 1800, 1802, 1805);* Poems in Two Volumes *(1807);* The Excursion *(1814); and the first collected edition of his poems (1815). One of his most important works,* The Prelude, *remained unpublished until his death in 1850. The selection given here includes* Lyrical Ballads *(1798) and the complete text of* The Thirteen-Book Prelude.

Lyrical Ballads, *published anonymously in 1798, contains works by both Wordsworth and Coleridge. In order not to compromise its integrity, its contents are presented here in the order in which they were first published, with brief notes giving authorship details — not available, of course, to the volume's first readers. These poems should be read in the light of the important* Preface, *presented here in the 1802 text with its important additions. The 'Prospectus' to Wordsworth's never completed epic poem* The Recluse *is a vitally important statement of faith, and informs our reading of all his work. It was published, in revised form, in the Preface to* The Excursion *(1814), and is presented here in its earliest recoverable form, edited from a manuscript draft dating probably from 1800. 'To Toussaint L'Ouverture', '1 September 1802', and 'London 1802' show how effectively Wordsworth could discuss political issues in verse. The* Thirteen-Book Prelude *was completed in early 1806. Although a very much revised text, in fourteen books, was published posthumously in 1850, this version of the poem remained unavailable until 1926.*

Lyrical Ballads (1798)
ADVERTISEMENT (BY WORDSWORTH, COMPOSED JULY 1798)[1]

It is the honourable characteristic of poetry that its materials are to be found in every subject which can interest the human mind. The evidence of this fact is to be sought not in the writings of critics, but in those of poets themselves.

The majority of the following poems are to be considered as experiments. They were written chiefly with a view to ascertain how far the language of conversation in the middle and lower classes of society is adapted to the purposes of poetic pleasure.

Readers accustomed to the gaudiness and inane phraseology of many modern writers, if they persist in reading this book to its conclusion, will perhaps frequently have to struggle with feelings of strangeness and awkwardness: they will look round for poetry, and will be induced to enquire by what species of courtesy these attempts can be permitted to assume that title. It is desirable that such readers, for their own sakes, should not suffer the solitary word 'poetry' (a word of very disputed meaning) to stand in the way of their gratification, but that while they are perusing this book, they should ask themselves if it contains a natural delineation of human passions, human characters, and human incidents; and, if the answer be favourable to the author's wishes, that they should consent to be pleased in spite of that most dreadful enemy to our pleasures: our own pre-established codes of decision.

Readers of superior judgement may disapprove of the style in which many of these pieces are executed. It must be expected that many lines and phrases will not exactly suit their taste. It will perhaps appear to them that, wishing to avoid the prevalent fault of the day, the author has sometimes descended too low, and that many of his expressions are too familiar, and not of sufficient dignity. It is apprehended that the more conversant the reader is with our elder writers, and with those in modern times who have been the most successful in painting manners and passions,[2] the fewer complaints of this kind will he have to make.

An accurate taste in poetry and in all the other arts, Sir Joshua Reynolds has observed, is an acquired talent which can only be produced by severe thought, and a long continued intercourse with the best models of composition. This is mentioned not with so ridiculous a purpose as to prevent the most inexperienced reader from judging for himself, but merely to temper the rashness of decision, and to suggest that if poetry be a subject on which much time has not been bestowed, the judgement may be erroneous, and that in many cases it necessarily will be so.

ADVERTISEMENT
[1] Though by Wordsworth, the 'Advertisement' and its ideas would have been worked out with Coleridge; see p. 251, n. 4.

[2] Wordsworth probably has in mind Milton and Shakespeare ('elder writers') and Burns and Cowper ('those in modern times').

The tale of 'Goody Blake and Harry Gill' is founded on a well-authenticated fact which happened in Warwickshire. Of the other poems in the collection, it may be proper to say that they are either absolute inventions of the author or facts which took place within his personal observation or that of his friends.

The poem of 'The Thorn', as the reader will soon discover, is not supposed to be spoken in the author's own person: the character of the loquacious narrator will sufficiently show itself in the course of the story. 'The Rime of the Ancyent Marinere' was professedly written in imitation of the style, as well as of the spirit, of the elder poets. But with a few exceptions, the author believes that the language adopted in it has been equally intelligible for these three last centuries. The lines entitled 'Expostulation and Reply', and those which follow, arose out of conversation with a friend[3] who was somewhat unreasonably attached to modern books of moral philosophy.

THE RIME OF THE ANCYENT MARINERE, IN SEVEN PARTS
(BY COLERIDGE, COMPOSED NOVEMBER 1797-MARCH 1798)[1]

Argument
How a ship, having passed the line,[2] was driven by storms to the cold country towards the South Pole, and how from thence she made her course to the tropical latitude of the great Pacific Ocean; and of the strange things that befell, and in what manner the ancyent marinere came back to his own country.

I

It is an ancyent marinere,
    And he stoppeth one of three:
'By thy long grey beard and thy glittering eye
    Now wherefore stoppest me?

The bridegroom's doors are opened wide,   5
    And I am next of kin;
The guests are met, the feast is set –
    Mayst hear the merry din.'

But still he holds the wedding-guest:
    'There was a ship', quoth he –   10
'Nay, if thou'st got a laughsome tale,
    Marinere, come with me!'

He holds him with his skinny hand,
    Quoth he, 'There was a ship –'
'Now get thee hence, thou grey-beard loon,   15
    Or my staff shall make thee skip!'

---

[3] *a friend* William Hazlitt.
THE ANCIENT MARINER
[1] For circumstances of composition see Fenwick Note to 'We are Seven', pp. 481–2 below. Coleridge published a substantially revised version of this poem in *Sibylline Leaves* (1817), which may be found at pp. 578–95, below.
[2] *line* equator.

He holds him with his glittering eye –
  The wedding-guest stood still,
And listens like a three years' child:
  The marinere hath his will.[3]   20

The wedding-guest sat on a stone,
  He cannot choose but hear;
And thus spake on that ancyent man,
  The bright-eyed marinere:

'The ship was cheered, the harbour cleared,   25
  Merrily did we drop
Below the kirk, below the hill,
  Below the lighthouse top.

The sun came up upon the left,
  Out of the sea came he;   30
And he shone bright, and on the right
  Went down into the sea.

Higher and higher every day,
  Till over the mast at noon –'
The wedding-guest here beat his breast,   35
  For he heard the loud bassoon.

The bride hath paced into the hall,
  Red as a rose is she;
Nodding their heads before her goes
  The merry minstrelsy.   40

The wedding-guest he beat his breast,
  Yet he cannot choose but hear;
And thus spake on that ancyent man,
  The bright-eyed marinere.

'Listen, stranger! Storm and wind,   45
  A wind and tempest strong!
For days and weeks it played us freaks –
  Like chaff we drove along.

Listen, stranger! Mist and snow,
  And it grew wondrous cauld: 50
And ice mast-high came floating by
  As green as emerauld.

---

[3] Lines 19–20 were by Wordsworth; see p. 482
below.

And through the drifts the snowy clifts[4]
    Did send a dismal sheen;
Ne shapes of men ne beasts we ken –   55
    The ice was all between.

The ice was here, the ice was there,
    The ice was all around;
It cracked and growled, and roared and howled
    Like noises of a swound.[5]   60

At length did cross an albatross,
    Thorough the fog it came;
And an it were a Christian soul,
    We hailed it in God's name.

The marineres gave it biscuit-worms,[6]   65
    And round and round it flew:
The ice did split with a thunder-fit;
    The helmsman steered us through.

And a good south wind sprung up behind,
    The albatross did follow;
And every day, for food or play,   70
    Came to the marineres' hollo!

In mist or cloud, on mast or shroud,
    It perched for vespers[7] nine,
Whiles all the night, through fogsmoke white,   75
    Glimmered the white moonshine.'

'God save thee, ancyent marinere,
    From the fiends that plague thee thus!
Why look'st thou so?' 'With my crossbow
    I shot the albatross.[8]   80

II

The sun came up upon the right,
    Out of the sea came he;
And broad as a weft[9] upon the left
    Went down into the sea.

---

[4] *drifts* floating ice. *clifts* clefts.
[5] *swound* swoon.
[6] This detail was removed from later versions of the poem.
[7] *vespers* evenings.

[8] No explanation for the action is given; it was suggested by Wordsworth after reading Shelvocke's *Voyages* (1726).
[9] *weft* signal-flag.

And the good south wind still blew behind,   85
   But no sweet bird did follow,
Ne any day for food or play
   Came to the marineres' hollo!

And I had done an hellish thing
   And it would work 'em woe: 90
For all averred I had killed the bird
   That made the breeze to blow.

Ne dim ne red, like God's own head
   The glorious sun uprist:
Then all averred I had killed the bird   95
   That brought the fog and mist.
"'Twas right", said they, "such birds to slay,
   That bring the fog and mist."

The breezes[10] blew, the white foam flew,
   The furrow followed free: 100
We were the first that ever burst
   Into that silent sea.

Down dropt the breeze, the sails dropt down,
   'Twas sad as sad could be,
And we did speak only to break   105
   The silence of the sea.

All in a hot and copper sky
   The bloody sun at noon
Right up above the mast did stand,
   No bigger than the moon   110

Day after day, day after day,
   We stuck, ne breath ne motion,
As idle as a painted ship
   Upon a painted ocean.

Water, water, everywhere,   115
   And all the boards did shrink;
Water, water, everywhere,
   Ne any drop to drink.

The very deeps did rot: oh Christ,
   That ever this should be!   120
Yea, slimy things did crawl with legs
   Upon the slimy sea.

---

[10] *breezes* trade winds.

About, about, in reel and rout
    The death-fires danced at night;
The water, like a witch's oils,   125
    Burnt green and blue and white.

And some in dreams assured were
    Of the spirit that plagued us so;
Nine fathom deep he had followed us
    From the land of mist and snow.   130

And every tongue, through utter drouth,[11]
    Was withered at the root;
We could not speak, no more than if
    We had been choked with soot.

Ah wel-a-day! what evil looks   135
    Had I from old and young!
Instead of the cross the albatross
    About my neck was hung.

III

I saw a something in the sky
    No bigger than my fist;   140
At first it seemed a little speck
    And then it seemed a mist;
It moved and moved, and took at last
    A certain shape, I wist.

A speck, a mist, a shape, I wist!   145
    And still it nered and nered:
And an it dodged a water-sprite,
    It plunged and tacked and veered.

With throat unslaked, with black lips baked,
    Ne could we laugh, ne wail;   150
Then while through drouth all dumb they stood,
I bit my arm, and sucked the blood,
    And cried, "A sail! A sail!"

With throat unslaked, with black lips baked,
    Agape they heard me call: 155
Gramercy![12] they for joy did grin
And all at once their breath drew in
    As they were drinking all.

---

[11] *drouth* dryness.   [12] *Gramercy!* Mercy on us!

She doth not tack from side to side
    Hither to work us weal;   160
Withouten wind, withouten tide
    She steddies with upright keel.

The western wave was all a-flame,
    The day was well nigh done!
Almost upon the western wave   165
    Rested the broad bright sun;
When that strange shape drove suddenly
    Betwixt us and the sun.

And strait the sun was flecked with bars
    (Heaven's Mother send us grace!)   170
As if through a dungeon-grate he peered
    With broad and burning face.

Alas! thought I, and my heart beat loud,
    How fast she neres and neres!
Are those *her* sails that glance in the sun   175
    Like restless gossameres?

Are these *her* naked ribs, which flecked
    The sun that did behind them peer?
And are these two all, all the crew,
    That woman and her fleshless pheere?[13]   180

His bones were black with many a crack,
    All black and bare, I ween;
Jet black and bare, save where with rust
Of mouldy damps and charnel crust
    They're patched with purple and green.   185

Her lips are red, *her* looks are free,
    Her locks are yellow as gold;
Her skin is as white as leprosy,
And she is far liker death than he,
    Her flesh makes the still air cold.   190

The naked hulk alongside came,
    And the twain were playing dice;
"The game is done! I've won! I've won!"
    Quoth she, and whistled thrice.

A gust of wind sterte up behind   195
    And whistled through his bones;

---

[13] *pheere* companion.

Through the holes of his eyes and the hole of his mouth
  Half-whistles and half-groans.

With never a whisper in the sea
  Off darts the spectre-ship;   200
While clombe above the eastern bar
The horned moon, with one bright star
  Almost atween the tips.

One after one by the horned moon
  (Listen, oh stranger, to me!)   205
Each turned his face with a ghastly pang
  And cursed me with his ee.

Four times fifty living men,
  With never a sigh or groan,
With heavy thump, a lifeless lump,   210
  They dropped down one by one.

Their souls did from their bodies fly,
  They fled to bliss or woe,
And every soul, it passed me by
  Like the whiz of my crossbow.'   215

IV

'I fear thee, ancyent marinere,
  I fear thy skinny hand;
And thou art long and lank and brown
  As is the ribbed sea-sand.

I fear thee and thy glittering eye,   220
  And thy skinny hand so brown –'
'Fear not, fear not, thou wedding-guest,
  This body dropt not down.

Alone, alone, all all alone,
  Alone on the wide wide sea;   225
And Christ would take no pity on
  My soul in agony.

The many men so beautiful,
  And they all dead did lie!
And a million million slimy things   230
  Lived on – and so did I.

I looked upon the rotting sea
  And drew my eyes away;

I looked upon the eldritch[14] deck,
　And there the dead men lay.

I looked to heaven and tried to pray   235
　But or ever a prayer had gusht,
A wicked whisper came and made
　My heart as dry as dust.

I closed my lids and kept them close   240
　Till the balls like pulses beat;
For the sky and the sea, and the sea and the sky
Lay like a load on my weary eye,
　And the dead were at my feet.

The cold sweat melted from their limbs,   245
　Ne rot, ne reek did they;
The look with which they looked on me
　Had never passed away.

An orphan's curse would drag to hell
　A spirit from on high;   250
But oh! more horrible than that
　Is the curse in a dead man's eye!
Seven days, seven nights, I saw that curse
　And yet I could not die.

The moving moon went up the sky   255
　And nowhere did abide;
Softly she was going up
　And a star or two beside;

Her beams bemocked the sultry main
　Like morning frosts yspread;   260
But where the ship's huge shadow lay
The charmed water burnt alway
　A still and awful red.

Beyond the shadow of the ship
　I watched the water-snakes;   265
They moved in tracks of shining white,
And when they reared, the elfish light
　Fell off in hoary flakes.

Within the shadow of the ship
　I watched their rich attire: 270

---

[14] *eldritch* ghostly.

Blue, glossy green, and velvet black,
They coiled and swam, and every track
   Was a flash of golden fire.

Oh happy living things! no tongue
   Their beauty might declare: 275
A spring of love gusht from my heart
   And I blessed them unaware!
Sure my kind saint took pity on me,
   And I blessed them unaware.

The self-same moment I could pray,   280
   And from my neck so free
The albatross fell off and sank
   Like lead into the sea.

V

Oh sleep, it is a gentle thing
   Beloved from pole to pole!   285
To Mary Queen the praise be yeven;
She sent the gentle sleep from heaven
   That slid into my soul.

The silly[15] buckets on the deck
   That had so long remained,   290
I dreamt that they were filled with dew
   And when I awoke it rained.

My lips were wet, my throat was cold,
   My garments all were dank;
Sure I had drunken in my dreams   295
   And still my body drank.

I moved and could not feel my limbs,
   I was so light, almost
I thought that I had died in sleep
   And was a blessed ghost.   300

The roaring wind – it roared far off,
   It did not come anear;
But with its sound it shook the sails
   That were so thin and sere.

The upper air bursts into life   305
And a hundred fire-flags sheen,

---

[15] *silly* helpless, innocent.

To and fro they are hurried about;
And to and fro, and in and out
The stars dance on between.[16]

The coming wind doth roar more loud, 310
The sails do sigh like sedge;
The rain pours down from one black cloud,
And the moon is at its edge.

Hark, hark! The thick black cloud is cleft
And the moon is at its side; 315
Like waters shot from some high crag,
The lightning falls with never a jag,
A river steep and wide.

The strong wind reached the ship, it roared
And dropped down like a stone! 320
Beneath the lightning and the moon
The dead men gave a groan.

They groaned, they stirred, they all uprose,
Ne spake, ne moved their eyes;
It had been strange, even in a dream, 325
To have seen those dead men rise.

The helmsman steered, the ship moved on,
Yet never a breeze up-blew;
The marineres all 'gan work the ropes
Where they were wont to do; 330
They raised their limbs like lifeless tools –
We were a ghastly crew.

The body of my brother's son
Stood by me, knee to knee;
The body and I pulled at one rope 335
But he said nought to me –
And I quaked to think of my own voice,
How frightful it would be!

The daylight dawned, they dropped their arms
And clustered round the mast; 340
Sweet sounds rose slowly through their mouths
And from their bodies passed.

---

[16] The aurora borealis, which recurs in Wordsworth's 'The Complaint of a Forsaken Indian Woman'.

Around, around, flew each sweet sound
 Then darted to the sun;
Slowly the sounds came back again,   345
 Now mixed, now one by one.

Sometimes a-dropping from the sky
 I heard the lavrock[17] sing;
Sometimes all little birds that are,
How they seemed to fill the sea and air   350
 With their sweet jargoning!

And now 'twas like all instruments,
 Now like a lonely flute,
And now it is an angel's song
 That makes the heavens be mute.   355

It ceased, yet still the sails made on
 A pleasant noise till noon,
A noise like of a hidden brook
 In the leafy month of June,
That to the sleeping woods all night   360
 Singeth a quiet tune –

Listen, oh listen, thou wedding-guest!'
 'Marinere, thou hast thy will!
For that which comes out of thine eye doth make
 My body and soul to be still.'   365

'Never sadder tale was told
 To a man of woman born;
Sadder and wiser thou wedding-guest
 Thou'lt rise tomorrow morn!

Never sadder tale was heard   370
 By a man of woman born;
The marineres all returned to work
 As silent as beforne.

The marineres all 'gan pull the ropes,
 But look at me they n'old;[18]   375
Thought I, I am as thin as air –
 They cannot me behold.

Till noon we silently sailed on,
 Yet never a breeze did breathe;

---

[17] *lavrock* lark.   [18] *n'old* would not.

Slowly and smoothly went the ship,   380
  Moved onward from beneath.

Under the keel nine fathom deep,
  From the land of mist and snow,
The spirit slid, and it was he
  That made the ship to go.   385
The sails at noon left off their tune
  And the ship stood still also.

The sun right up above the mast
  Had fixed her to the ocean;
But in a minute she 'gan stir   390
  With a short uneasy motion –
Backwards and forwards half her length,
  With a short uneasy motion.

Then like a pawing horse let go,
  She made a sudden bound;   395
It flung the blood into my head,
  And I fell into a swound.

How long in that same fit I lay,
  I have not to declare;
But ere my living life returned,   400
I heard and in my soul discerned
  Two voices in the air.

"Is it he?" quoth one, "Is this the man?
  By him who died on cross,
With his cruel bow he laid full low   405
  The harmless albatross.

The spirit who bideth by himself
  In the land of mist and snow,
He loved the bird that loved the man
  Who shot him with his bow."   410

The other was a softer voice,
  As soft as honey-dew;
Quoth he, "The man hath penance done
  And penance more will do."'

VI

FIRST VOICE

But tell me, tell me! speak again,   415
  Thy soft response renewing –

What makes that ship drive on so fast?
    What is the ocean doing?

SECOND VOICE

Still as a slave before his lord,
    The ocean hath no blast;   420
His great bright eye most silently
    Up to the moon is cast —

If he may know which way to go,
    For she guides him smooth or grim.
See, brother, see — how graciously   425
    She looketh down on him!

FIRST VOICE

But why drives on that ship so fast
    Withouten wave or wind?

SECOND VOICE

The air is cut away before
    And closes from behind
                                                430

Fly, brother, fly! more high, more high,
    Or we shall be belated;
For slow and slow that ship will go
    When the marinere's trance is abated.

'I woke, and we were sailing on
    As in a gentle weather;   435
'Twas night, calm night, the moon was high —
    The dead men stood together.

All stood together on the deck,
    For a charnel-dungeon fitter;
All fixed on me their stony eyes   440
    That in the moon did glitter.

The pang, the curse, with which they died
    Had never passed away;
I could not draw my een from theirs
    Ne turn them up to pray.   445

And in its time the spell was snapt
    And I could move my een;
I looked far forth but little saw
    Of what might else be seen —
                                                450

Like one that on a lonely road
    Doth walk in fear and dread,

And having once turned round walks on
    And turns no more his head,
Because he knows a frightful fiend   455
    Doth close behind him tread.

But soon there breathed a wind on me,
    Ne sound ne motion made;
Its path was not upon the sea,
    In ripple or in shade.   460

It raised my hair, it fanned my cheek,
    Like a meadow-gale of spring –
It mingled strangely with my fears,
    Yet it felt like a welcoming.

Swiftly, swiftly flew the ship,   465
    Yet she sailed softly too;
Sweetly, sweetly blew the breeze –
    On me alone it blew.

Oh dream of joy! Is this indeed
    The lighthouse top I see?   470
Is this the hill? Is this the kirk?
    Is this mine own countrée?

We drifted o'er the harbour-bar,[19]
    And I with sobs did pray,
"Oh let me be awake, my God!   475
    Or let me sleep alway!"

The harbour-bay was clear as glass,
    So smoothly it was strewn!
And on the bay the moonlight lay
    And the shadow of the moon.   480

The moonlight bay was white all o'er
    Till rising from the same,
Full many shapes that shadows were
    Like as of torches came.

A little distance from the prow   485
    Those dark red shadows were;
But soon I saw that my own flesh
    Was red as in a glare.

I turned my head in fear and dread
    And by the holy rood,   490

---

[19] *bar* bank of silt across the mouth of the harbour.

The bodies had advanced, and now
   Before the mast they stood.

They lifted up their stiff right arms,
   They held them strait and tight;
And each right arm burnt like a torch,   495
   A torch that's borne upright.
Their stony eyeballs glittered on
   In the red and smoky light.

I prayed and turned my head away
   Forth looking as before;   500
There was no breeze upon the bay,
   No wave against the shore.

The rock shone bright, the kirk no less
   That stands above the rock;
The moonlight steeped in silentness   505
   The steady weathercock.

And the bay was white with silent light,
   Till rising from the same
Full many shapes that shadows were
   In crimson colours came.   510

A little distance from the prow
   Those crimson shadows were;
I turned my eyes upon the deck –
   Oh Christ! what saw I there?

Each corse lay flat, lifeless and flat,   515
   And by the holy rood
A man all light, a seraph-man
   On every corse there stood.

This seraph-band, each waved his hand –
   It was a heavenly sight!   520
They stood as signals to the land,
   Each one a lovely light;

This seraph-band, each waved his hand,
   No voice did they impart –
No voice, but oh! the silence sank   525
   Like music on my heart.

Eftsones[20] I heard the dash of oars,
   I heard the pilot's cheer;

---

[20] *Eftsones* again.

My head was turned perforce away
  And I saw a boat appear.   530

Then vanished all the lovely lights,
  The bodies rose anew;
With silent pace each to his place
  Came back the ghastly crew.
The wind that shade nor motion made,   535
  On me alone it blew.

The pilot and the pilot's boy,
  I heard them coming fast –
Dear Lord in heaven! it was a joy
  The dead men could not blast.   540

I saw a third, I heard his voice –
  It is the hermit good!
He singeth loud his godly hymns
  That he makes in the wood.
He'll shrieve[21] my soul, he'll wash away   545
  The albatross' blood.

VII

This hermit good lives in that wood
  Which slopes down to the sea;
How loudly his sweet voice he rears!
He loves to talk with marineres   550
  That come from a far countrée.

He kneels at morn, and noon and eve,
  He hath a cushion plump;
It is the moss that wholly hides
  The rotted old oak-stump   555

The skiff-boat nered, I heard them talk:
  "Why, this is strange, I trow!
Where are those lights so many and fair,
  That signal made but now?"

"Strange, by my faith!" the hermit said,   560
  "And they answered not our cheer!
The planks look warped, and see those sails,
  How thin they are and sere!
I never saw aught like to them
  Unless perchance it were.   565

---

[21]   *shrieve* to hear the confession of, absolve.

The skeletons of leaves that lag
  My forest brook along,
When the ivy-tod[22] is heavy with snow
And the owlet whoops to the wolf below
  That eats the she-wolf ˙ young."   570

"Dear Lord! it has a fiendish look",
  The pilot made reply,
"I am a-feared." "Push on, push on!"
  Said the hermit cheerily.

The boat came closer to the ship   575
  But I ne spake ne stirred;
The boat came close beneath the ship
  And strait a sound was heard!

Under the water it rumbled on,
  Still louder and more dread;   580
It reached the ship, it split the bay –
  The ship went down like lead.

Stunned by that loud and dreadful sound
  Which sky and ocean smote,
Like one that hath been seven days drowned,   585
  My body lay afloat;
But swift as dreams, myself I found
  Within the pilot's boat.

Upon the whirl where sank the ship
  The boat spun round and round,   590
And all was still, save that the hill
  Was telling of the sound.

I moved my lips – the pilot shrieked
  And fell down in a fit;
The holy hermit raised his eyes   595
  And prayed where he did sit.

I took the oars; the pilot's boy,
  Who now doth crazy go,
Laughed loud and long, and all the while
  His eyes went to and fro: 600
"Ha! ha!" quoth he, "full plain I see
  The Devil knows how to row."

And now all in my own countrée
  I stood on the firm land!

---

[22] *ivy-tod* ivy bush.

The hermit stepped forth from the boat,   605
  And scarcely he could stand.

"Oh shrieve me, shrieve me, holy man!"
  The hermit crossed his brow.
"Say quick", quoth he, "I bid thee say
  What manner man art thou?"   610

Forthwith this frame of mine was wrenched
  With a woeful agony,
Which forced me to begin my tale –
  And then it left me free.

Since then, at an uncertain hour,   615
  Now oft-times and now fewer,
That anguish comes and makes me tell
  My ghastly aventure.

I pass, like night, from land to land,
  I have strange power of speech;   620
The moment that his face I see
I know the man that must hear me –
  To him my tale I teach.

What loud uproar bursts from that door!
  The wedding-guests are there   625
But in the garden bower the bride
  And bridemaids singing are;
And hark, the little vesper bell
  Which biddeth me to prayer.

Oh wedding-guest! this soul hath been   630
  Alone on a wide wide sea;
So lonely 'twas, that God himself
  Scarce seemed there to be.

Oh sweeter than the marriage-feast,
  'Tis sweeter far to me   635
To walk together to the kirk
  With a goodly company!

To walk together to the kirk
  And all together pray,
While each to his great Father bends,
Old men, and babes, and loving friends,   640
  And youths and maidens gay.

Farewell, farewell! but this I tell
  To thee, thou wedding-guest!

He prayeth well who loveth well   645
   Both man and bird and beast.

He prayeth best who loveth best
   All things both great and small,
For the dear God who loveth us,
   He made and loveth all.'   650

The marinere, whose eye is bright,
   Whose beard with age is hoar,
Is gone; and now the wedding-guest
   Turned from the bridegroom's door.

He went like one that hath been stunned   655
   And is of sense forlorn:
A sadder and a wiser man
   He rose the morrow morn.

THE FOSTER-MOTHER'S TALE: A DRAMATIC FRAGMENT (BY COLERIDGE, EXTRACTED FROM OSORIO, COMPOSED 1797)

Foster-Mother. I never saw the man whom you describe.
Maria. 'Tis strange! He spake of you familiarly
As mine and Albert's common foster-mother.
Foster-Mother. Now blessings on the man, whoe'er he be,
That joined your names with mine! Oh my sweet lady,   5
As often as I think of those dear times
When you two little ones would stand at eve
On each side of my chair, and make me learn
All you had learnt in the day; and how to talk
In gentle phrase, then bid me sing to you –   10
'Tis more like heaven to come than what *has* been!
Maria. Oh my dear mother! This strange man has left me
Troubled with wilder fancies than the moon
Breeds in the lovesick maid who gazes at it,
Till, lost in inward vision, with wet eye   15
She gazes idly! But that entrance, Mother!
Foster-Mother. Can no one hear? It is a perilous tale.
Maria. No one.
Foster-Mother. My husband's father told it me,
Poor old Leoni! (Angels rest his soul!)
He was a woodman, and could fell and saw   20
With lusty arm. You know that huge round beam
Which props the hanging wall of the old chapel?
Beneath that tree, while yet it was a tree,
He found a baby wrapped in mosses lined
With thistle-beards and such small locks of wool   25
As hang on brambles. Well, he brought him home

And reared him at the then Lord Velez's cost.
And so the babe grew up a pretty boy –
A pretty boy, but most unteachable,
And never learnt a prayer, nor told a bead,   30
But knew the names of birds, and mocked their notes,
And whistled as he were a bird himself.
And all the autumn 'twas his only play
To get the seeds of wild-flowers, and to plant them
With earth and water on the stumps of trees.   35
A friar who gathered simples[1] in the wood,
A grey-haired man, he loved this little boy,
The boy loved him. And when the friar taught him,
He soon could write with the pen, and from that time
Lived chiefly at the convent or the castle.   40
So he became a very learned youth.
    But oh, poor wretch – he read, and read, and read,
Till his brain turned! And ere his twentieth year
He had unlawful thoughts of many things,
And though he prayed, he never loved to pray   45
With holy men, nor in a holy place.
But yet his speech – it was so soft and sweet,
The late Lord Velez ne'er was wearied with him.
And once, as by the north side of the chapel
They stood together, chained in deep discourse,   50
The earth heaved under them with such a groan
That the wall tottered, and had well-nigh fallen
Right on their heads. My Lord was sorely frightened;
A fever seized him, and he made confession
Of all the heretical and lawless talk   55
Which brought this judgement: so the youth was seized
And cast into that hole. My husband's father
Sobbed like a child – it almost broke his heart.
And once as he was working in the cellar,
He heard a voice distinctly: 'twas the youth's,   60
Who sung a doleful song about green fields,
How sweet it were on lake or wild savannah
To hunt for food and be a naked man,
And wander up and down at liberty.
He always doted on the youth and now   65
His love grew desperate; and, defying death,
He made that cunning entrance I described –
And the young man escaped.
Maria.   'Tis a sweet tale,
Such as would lull a listening child to sleep,

THE FOSTER-MOTHER'S TALE
[1] *simples* medicinal herbs.

His rosy face besoiled with unwiped tears.   70
And what became of him?
Foster-Mother.   He went on shipboard
With those bold voyagers who made discovery
Of golden lands. Leoni's younger brother
Went likewise, and when he returned to Spain,
He told Leoni that the poor mad youth,   75
Soon after they arrived in that new world,
In spite of his dissuasion, seized a boat,
And all alone set sail by silent moonlight
Up a great river, great as any sea,
And ne'er was heard of more. But 'tis supposed   80
He lived and died among the savage men.

LINES LEFT UPON A SEAT IN A YEW-TREE WHICH STANDS NEAR THE
LAKE OF ESTHWAITE, ON A DESOLATE PART OF THE SHORE, YET
COMMANDING A BEAUTIFUL PROSPECT (BY WORDSWORTH, COMPOSED
BETWEEN FEBRUARY AND JULY 1797)

Nay, traveller, rest! This lonely yew-tree stands
Far from all human dwelling. What if here
No sparkling rivulet spread the verdant herb?
What if these barren boughs the bee not loves?
Yet, if the wind breathe soft, the curling waves   5
That break against the shore shall lull thy mind,
By one soft impulse saved from vacancy.
                        Who he was
That piled these stones, and with the mossy sod
First covered o'er, and taught this aged tree,   10
Now wild, to bend its arms in circling shade,
I well remember. He was one who owned
No common soul. In youth by genius nursed,
And big with lofty views, he to the world
Went forth, pure in his heart, against the taint   15
Of dissolute tongues, 'gainst jealousy and hate
And scorn, against all enemies prepared –
All but neglect. And so his spirit damped
At once, with rash disdain he turned away,
And with the food of pride sustained his soul   20
In solitude. Stranger, these gloomy boughs
Had charms for him – and here he loved to sit,
His only visitants a straggling sheep,
The stonechat or the glancing sandpiper;
And on these barren rocks, with juniper   25
And heath and thistle thinly sprinkled o'er,
Fixing his downward eye, he many an hour
A morbid pleasure nourished, tracing here
An emblem of his own unfruitful life.

And lifting up his head, he then would gaze   30
On the more distant scene – how lovely 'tis
Thou seest – and he would gaze till it became
Far lovelier, and his heart could not sustain
The beauty still more beauteous. Nor, that time,
Would he forget those beings to whose minds,   35
Warm from the labours of benevolence,
The world, and man himself, appeared a scene
Of kindred loveliness: then he would sigh
With mournful joy, to think that others felt
What he must never feel. And so, lost man,   40
On visionary views would fancy feed,
Till his eye streamed with tears. In this deep vale
He died, this seat his only monument.
    If thou be one whose heart the holy forms
Of young imagination have kept pure,   45
Stranger, henceforth be warned – and know that pride,
Howe'er disguised in its own majesty,
Is littleness; that he who feels contempt
For any living thing hath faculties
Which he has never used; that thought with him   50
Is in its infancy. The man whose eye
Is ever on himself doth look on one
The least of nature's works – one who might move
The wise man to that scorn which wisdom holds
Unlawful ever. Oh be wiser thou!   55
Instructed that true knowledge leads to love,
True dignity abides with him alone
Who, in the silent hour of inward thought,
Can still suspect, and still revere himself,
In lowliness of heart.   60

THE NIGHTINGALE; A CONVERSATIONAL POEM, WRITTEN IN APRIL 1798 (BY COLERIDGE)

No cloud, no relic of the sunken day
Distinguishes the west, no long thin slip
Of sullen light, no obscure trembling hues.
Come, we will rest on this old mossy bridge.
You see the glimmer of the stream beneath   5
But hear no murmuring: it flows silently
O'er its soft bed of verdure. All is still,
A balmy night, and though the stars be dim
Yet let us think upon the vernal showers
That gladden the green earth, and we shall find   10
A pleasure in the dimness of the stars.
And hark, the nightingale begins its song –

'Most musical, most melancholy' bird!¹
A melancholy bird? Oh idle thought!
In nature there is nothing melancholy.   15
    But some night-wandering man whose heart was pierced
With the remembrance of a grievous wrong
Or slow distemper or neglected love
(And so, poor wretch, filled all things with himself
And made all gentle sounds tell back the tale   20
Of his own sorrows) – he, and such as he,
First named these notes a melancholy strain,
And many a poet echoes the conceit –
Poet who hath been building up the rhyme
When he had better far have stretched his limbs   25
Beside a brook in mossy forest-dell
By sun or moonlight, to the influxes
Of shapes and sounds and shifting elements
Surrendering his whole spirit, of his song
And of his fame forgetful! So his fame   30
Should share in nature's immortality
(A venerable thing!), and so his song
Should make all nature lovelier, and itself
Be loved, like nature! But 'twill not be so;
And youths and maidens most poetical   35
Who lose the deep'ning twilights of the spring
In ballrooms and hot theatres, they still,
Full of meek sympathy, must heave their sighs
O'er Philomela's pity-pleading strains.
    My friend, and my friend's sister,² we have learnt   40
A different lore; we may not thus profane
Nature's sweet voices always full of love
And joyance! 'Tis the merry nightingale
That crowds and hurries and precipitates
With fast thick warble his delicious notes,   45
As he were fearful that an April night
Would be too short for him to utter forth
His love-chant, and disburden his full soul
Of all its music! And I know a grove
Of large extent, hard by a castle huge   50
Which the great lord inhabits not – and so
This grove is wild with tangling underwood,
And the trim walks are broken up, and grass,

THE NIGHTINGALE
¹ Milton, *Il Penseroso*, 62. 'This passage in Milton possesses an excellence far superior to that of mere description: it is spoken in the character of the melancholy man, and has therefore a *dramatic* propriety. The author makes this remark to rescue him-self from the charge of having alluded with levity to a line in Milton – a charge than which none could be more painful to him, except perhaps that of having ridiculed his Bible' (note by Coleridge, 1798).
² William and Dorothy Wordsworth.

Thin grass and king-cups grow within the paths.
But never elsewhere in one place I knew   55
So many nightingales. And far and near
In wood and thicket over the wide grove,
They answer and provoke each other's songs
With skirmish and capricious passagings,
And murmurs musical and swift jug jug   60
And one low piping sound more sweet than all,
Stirring the air with such an harmony,
That should you close your eyes, you might almost
Forget it was not day. On moonlight bushes
Whose dewy leafits are but half-disclosed,   65
You may perchance behold them on the twigs,
Their bright, bright eyes, their eyes both bright and full,
Glist'ning, while many a glow-worm in the shade
Lights up her love-torch.[3]
                         A most gentle maid
Who dwelleth in her hospitable home   70
Hard by the castle, and at latest eve
(Even like a lady vowed and dedicate
To something more than nature in the grove)
Glides through the pathways. She knows all their notes,
That gentle maid, and oft, a moment's space,   75
What time the moon was lost behind a cloud,
Hath heard a pause of silence; till the moon
Emerging hath awakened earth and sky
With one sensation, and those wakeful birds
Have all burst forth in choral minstrelsy,   80
As if one quick and sudden gale had swept
An hundred airy harps![4] And she hath watched
Many a nightingale perch giddily
On blos'my twig still swinging from the breeze,
And to that motion tune his wanton song,   85
Like tipsy joy that reels with tossing head.
    Farewell, oh warbler, till tomorrow eve!
And you, my friends – farewell, a short farewell!
We have been loitering long and pleasantly,
And now for our dear homes. That strain again!   90
Full fain it would delay me! My dear babe[5]
Who, capable of no articulate sound,
Mars all things with his imitative lisp –
How he would place his hand beside his ear,

---

[3] Technically correct; the female glow-worm emits a green light to attract males.

[4] airy harps i.e. aeolian harps.

[5] Hartley Coleridge. In a notebook entry for 1797, Coleridge describes how Hartley 'fell down and hurt himself. I caught him up crying and screaming, and ran out of doors with him. The moon caught his eye, he ceased crying immediately, and his eyes and the tears in them – how they glittered in the moonlight!' (Notebooks, i. 219).

His little hand, the small forefinger up, 95
And bid us listen! And I deem it wise
To make him nature's playmate. He knows well
The evening star; and once, when he awoke
In most distressful mood (some inward pain
Had made up that strange thing, an infant's dream) 100
I hurried with him to our orchard-plot
And he beholds the moon, and hushed at once
Suspends his sobs and laughs most silently,
While his fair eyes that swam with undropped tears
Did glitter in the yellow moonbeam! Well, 105
It is a father's tale. But if that Heaven
Should give me life, his childhood shall grow up
Familiar with these songs, that with the night
He may associate joy. Once more farewell,
Sweet nightingale! Once more, my friends, farewell! 110

THE FEMALE VAGRANT (BY WORDSWORTH, DERIVED FROM 'SALISBURY PLAIN', PROBABLY COMPOSED BETWEEN LATE JULY AND SEPTEMBER 1793)

'By Derwent's side my father's cottage stood',
The woman thus her artless story told,
'One field, a flock, and what the neighbouring flood
Supplied, to him were more than mines of gold.
Light was my sleep, my days in transport rolled; 5
With thoughtless joy I stretched along the shore
My father's nets, or watched (when from the fold
High o'er the cliffs I led my fleecy store),
A dizzy depth below, his boat and twinkling oar.

My father was a good and pious man, 10
An honest man by honest parents bred,
And I believe that, soon as I began
To lisp, he made me kneel beside my bed,
And in his hearing there my prayers I said;
And afterwards, by my good father taught, 15
I read, and loved the books in which I read –
For books in every neighbouring house I sought,
And nothing to my mind a sweeter pleasure brought.

Can I forget what charms did once adorn
My garden, stored with peas and mint and thyme, 20
And rose and lily for the Sabbath morn?
The Sabbath bells, and their delightful chime;
The gambols and wild freaks at shearing time;
My hen's rich nest through long grass scarce espied;
The cowslip-gathering at May's dewy prime; 25
The swans that, when I sought the waterside,
From far to meet me came, spreading their snowy pride.

The staff I yet remember, which upbore
The bending body of my active sire;
His seat beneath the honeyed sycamore   30
When the bees hummed, and chair by winter fire;
When market-morning came, the neat attire
With which, though bent on haste, myself I decked;
My watchful dog, whose starts of furious ire
When stranger passed, so often I have checked;   35
The redbreast known for years, which at my casement pecked.

The suns of twenty summers danced along –
Ah, little marked, how fast they rolled away!
Then rose a mansion proud our woods among,
And cottage after cottage owned its sway;   40
No joy to see a neighbouring house, or stray
Through pastures not his own, the master took.
My father dared his greedy wish gainsay:
He loved his old hereditary nook,
And ill could I the thought of such sad parting brook.   45

But when he had refused the proffered gold,
To cruel injuries he became a prey –
Sore traversed in whate'er he bought and sold.
His troubles grew upon him day by day
Till all his substance fell into decay: 50
His little range of water was denied,[1]
All but the bed where his old body lay,
All, all was seized, and weeping side by side
We sought a home where we uninjured might abide.

Can I forget that miserable hour   55
When from the last hilltop my sire surveyed,
Peering above the trees, the steeple tower
That on his marriage-day sweet music made?
Till then he hoped his bones might there be laid
Close by my mother in their native bowers.   60
Bidding me trust in God, he stood and prayed;
I could not pray – through tears that fell in showers
Glimmered our dear loved home: alas, no longer ours!

There was a youth whom I had loved so long,
That when I loved him not I cannot say.   65
Mid the green mountains many and many a song

THE FEMALE VAGRANT
[1] 'Several of the lakes in the north of England are let out to different fishermen, in parcels marked out by imaginary lines drawn from rock to rock' (note by Wordsworth, 1798).

We two had sung like little birds in May.
When we began to tire of childish play
We seemed still more and more to prize each other:
We talked of marriage and our marriage-day,   70
And I in truth did love him like a brother,
For never could I hope to meet with such another.

His father said that to a distant town
He must repair to ply the artist's trade:
What tears of bitter grief till then unknown!   75
What tender vows our last sad kiss delayed!
To him we turned – we had no other aid.
Like one revived, upon his neck I wept,
And her whom he had loved in joy, he said
He well could love in grief: his faith he kept,   80
And in a quiet home once more my father slept.

Four years each day with daily bread was blessed,
By constant toil and constant prayer supplied.
Three lovely infants lay upon my breast,
And often, viewing their sweet smiles, I sighed   85
And knew not why. My happy father died
When sad distress reduced the children's meal –
Thrice happy, that from him the grave did hide
The empty loom, cold hearth and silent wheel,
And tears that flowed for ills which patience could not heal. 90

'Twas a hard change, an evil time was come:
We had no hope, and no relief could gain.
But soon with proud parade, the noisy drum
Beat round to sweep the streets of want and pain.
My husband's arms now only served to strain   95
Me and his children hungering in his view.
In such dismay my prayers and tears were vain;
To join those miserable men he flew,
And now to the sea-coast, with numbers more we drew.

There foul neglect for months and months we bore,   100
Nor yet the crowded fleet its anchor stirred.
Green fields before us and our native shore,
By fever, from polluted air incurred,
Ravage was made for which no knell was heard.
Fondly we wished and wished away, nor knew   105
Mid that long sickness, and those hopes deferred,
That happier days we never more must view.
The parting signal streamed, at last the land withdrew,

But from delay the summer calms were passed.
On as we drove, the equinoctial[2] deep   110
Ran mountains high before the howling blast.
We gazed with terror on the gloomy sleep
Of them that perished in the whirlwind's sweep,
Untaught that soon such anguish must ensue,
Our hopes such harvest of affliction reap,   115
That we the mercy of the waves should rue.
We reached the western world,[3] a poor devoted[4] crew.

Oh dreadful price of being to resign
All that is dear *in* being: better far
In want's most lonely cave till death to pine,   120
Unseen, unheard, unwatched by any star;
Or, in the streets and walks where proud men are,
Better our dying bodies to obtrude,
Than dog-like, wading at the heels of war,
Protract a cursed existence with the brood   125
That lap (their very nourishment) their brother's blood.

The pains and plagues that on our heads came down –
Disease and famine, agony and fear,
In wood or wilderness, in camp or town –
It would thy brain unsettle even to hear.   130
All perished; all, in one remorseless year,
Husband and children! One by one, by sword
And ravenous plague, all perished. Every tear
Dried up, despairing, desolate, on board
A British ship I waked, as from a trance restored.   135

Peaceful as some immeasurable plain
By the first beams of dawning light impressed,
In the calm sunshine slept the glittering main.
The very ocean has its hour of rest
That comes not to the human mourner's breast   140
Remote from man and storms of mortal care,
A heavenly silence did the waves invest;
I looked and looked along the silent air,
Until it seemed to bring a joy to my despair.

Ah, how unlike those late terrific sleeps!   145
And groans, that rage of racking famine spoke,

---

[2]   *equinoctial* equatorial.
[3]   *the western world* America, where the female vagrant's husband was to fight in the War of Independence on the British side. Wordsworth later
recalled that 'All that relates to her sufferings as a
soldier's wife in America, and her condition of mind

during her voyage home, were faithfully taken from
the report made to me of her own case by a friend
who had been subjected to the same trials and
affected in the same way' (*FN*, 62).
[4]   *devoted* doomed.

Where looks inhuman dwelt on festering heaps!
The breathing pestilence that rose like smoke!
The shriek that from the distant battle broke!
The mine's dire earthquake, and the pallid host   150
Driven by the bomb's incessant thunderstroke
To loathsome vaults where heartsick anguish tossed,
Hope died, and fear itself in agony was lost!

Yet does that burst of woe congeal my frame
When the dark streets appeared to heave and gape,   155
While like a sea the storming army came,
And Fire from hell reared his gigantic shape,
And Murder, by the ghastly gleam, and Rape
Seized their joint prey – the mother and the child!
But from these crazing thoughts, my brain, escape!   160
For weeks the balmy air breathed soft and mild,
And on the gliding vessel heaven and ocean smiled.

Some mighty gulf of separation passed,
I seemed transported to another world:
A thought resigned with pain, when from the mast   165
The impatient mariner the sail unfurled,
And, whistling, called the wind that hardly curled
The silent sea. From the sweet thoughts of home
And from all hope I was forever hurled.
For me, farthest from earthly port to roam   170
Was best, could I but shun the spot where man might come.

And oft, robbed of my perfect mind, I thought
At last my feet a resting-place had found.
Here will I weep in peace (so fancy wrought),
Roaming the illimitable waters round;   175
Here watch, of every human friend disowned,
All day, my ready tomb the ocean flood,
To break my dream the vessel reached its bound,
And homeless near a thousand homes I stood,
And near a thousand tables pined, and wanted food.   180

By grief enfeebled was I turned adrift,
Helpless as sailor cast on desert rock;
Nor morsel to my mouth that day did lift,
Nor dared my hand at any door to knock.
I lay where, with his drowsy mates, the cock   185
From the cross timber of an outhouse⁵ hung.
How dismal tolled that night the city clock!

---

⁵ *outhouse* barn.

At morn my sick heart-hunger scarcely stung,
Nor to the beggar's language could I frame my tongue.

So passed another day, and so the third.   190
Then did I try (in vain) the crowd's resort;
In deep despair by frightful wishes stirred,
Near the seaside I reached a ruined fort.
There pains which nature could no more support,
With blindness linked, did on my vitals fall;   195
Dizzy my brain, with interruption short
Of hideous sense. I sunk, nor step could crawl,
And thence was borne away to neighbouring hospital.

Recovery came with food. But still my brain
Was weak, nor of the past had memory.   200
I heard my neighbours in their beds complain
Of many things which never troubled me:
Of feet still bustling round with busy glee,
Of looks where common kindness had no part,
Of service done with careless cruelty,   205
Fretting the fever round the languid heart,
And groans which, as they said, would make a dead man start.

These things just served to stir the torpid sense,
Nor pain nor pity in my bosom raised;
Memory, though slow, returned with strength; and thence   210
Dismissed, again on open day I gazed
At houses, men and common light, amazed.
The lanes I sought and, as the sun retired,
Came where beneath the trees a faggot blazed.
The wild brood saw me weep, my fate enquired,   215
And gave me food and rest – more welcome, more desired.

My heart is touched to think that men like these,
The rude earth's tenants, were my first relief.
How kindly did they paint their vagrant ease!
And their long holiday that feared not grief –   220
For all belonged to all, and each was chief.
No plough their sinews strained; on grating road
No wain they drove; and yet the yellow sheaf
In every vale for their delight was stowed:
For them in nature's meads the milky udder flowed.   225

Semblance, with straw and panniered ass, they made
Of potters wandering on from door to door.
But life of happier sort to me portrayed,
And other joys my fancy to allure:
The bagpipe dinning on the midnight moor   230

In barn uplighted, and companions boon
Well-met from far with revelry secure
In depth of forest glade, when jocund June
Rolled fast along the sky his warm and genial moon.

But ill it suited me, in journey dark   235
O'er moor and mountain, midnight theft to hatch;
To charm the surly housedog's faithful bark,
Or hang on tiptoe at the lifted latch.
The gloomy lantern and the dim blue match,
The black disguise, the warning whistle shrill,   240
And ear still busy on its nightly watch,
Were not for me, brought up in nothing ill.
Besides, on griefs so fresh my thoughts were brooding still.

What could I do, unaided and unblessed?
Poor father, gone was every friend of thine!   245
And kindred of dead husband are at best
Small help, and after marriage such as mine,
With little kindness would to me incline.
Ill was I then for toil or service fit:
With tears whose course no effort could confine,   250
By highway-side forgetful would I sit
Whole hours, my idle arms in moping sorrow knit.

I lived upon the mercy of the fields,
And oft of cruelty the sky accused;
On hazard, or what general bounty yields –   255
Now coldly given, now utterly refused.
The fields I for my bed have often used.
But what afflicts my peace with keenest ruth[6]
Is that I have my inner self abused,
Foregone the home delight of constant truth   260
And clear and open soul, so prized in fearless youth.

Three years a wanderer, often have I viewed,
In tears, the sun towards that country tend
Where my poor heart lost all its fortitude.
And now across this moor my steps I bend –   265
Oh tell me whither, for no earthly friend
Have I!' She ceased and, weeping, turned away,
As if because her tale was at an end.
She wept because she had no more to say
Of that perpetual weight which on her spirit lay.   270

---

[6] *ruth* remorse.

Goody Blake and Harry Gill: A True Story (by Wordsworth, composed 7–13 March 1798)

Oh what's the matter? What's the matter?
What is't that ails young Harry Gill,
That evermore his teeth they chatter,
Chatter, chatter, chatter still?
Of waistcoats Harry has no lack,   5
Good duffle grey, and flannel fine;
He has a blanket on his back,
And coats enough to smother nine.

In March, December, and in July,
'Tis all the same with Harry Gill;   10
The neighbours tell, and tell you truly,
His teeth they chatter, chatter still.
At night, at morning, and at noon,
'Tis all the same with Harry Gill;
Beneath the sun, beneath the moon,   15
His teeth they chatter, chatter still.

Young Harry was a lusty drover,
And who so stout of limb as he?
His cheeks were red as ruddy clover,
His voice was like the voice of three.   20
Auld Goody Blake was old and poor,
Ill fed she was, and thinly clad;
And any man who passed her door
Might see how poor a hut she had.

All day she spun in her poor dwelling,   25
And then her three hours' work at night –
Alas, 'twas hardly worth the telling,
It would not pay for candle-light.
This woman dwelt in Dorsetshire,
Her hut was on a cold hillside,   30
And in that country coals are dear,
For they come far by wind and tide.

By the same fire to boil their pottage,
Two poor old dames (as I have known)
Will often live in one small cottage,   35
But she, poor woman, dwelt alone.
'Twas well enough when summer came,
The long, warm, lightsome summer day;
Then at her door the canty[1] dame
Would sit, as any linnet gay.   40

Goody Blake and Harry Gill
[1] *canty* cheerful.

But when the ice our streams did fetter,
Oh, then how her old bones would shake!
You would have said, if you had met her,
'Twas a hard time for Goody Blake.
Her evenings then were dull and dead —   45
Sad case it was, as you may think,
For very cold to go to bed,
And then for cold not sleep a wink.

Oh joy for her, whene'er in winter
The winds at night had made a rout,   50
And scattered many a lusty splinter,
And many a rotten bough about.
Yet never had she, well or sick
(As every man who knew her says),
A pile beforehand, wood or stick   55
Enough to warm her for three days.

Now when the frost was past enduring
And made her poor old bones to ache,
Could anything be more alluring
Than an old hedge to Goody Blake?   60
And now and then, it must be said,
When her old bones were cold and chill,
She left her fire or left her bed
To seek the hedge of Harry Gill.

Now Harry he had long suspected   65
This trespass of old Goody Blake,
And vowed that she should be detected,
And he on her would vengeance take.
And oft from his warm fire he'd go,
And to the fields his road would take,   70
And there at night, in frost and snow,
He watched to seize old Goody Blake.

And once, behind a rick of barley,
Thus looking out did Harry stand;
The moon was full and shining clearly,   75
And crisp with frost the stubble-land.
He hears a noise, he's all awake —
Again? On tiptoe down the hill
He softly creeps: 'tis Goody Blake,
She's at the hedge of Harry Gill.

        80

Right glad was he when he beheld her:
Stick after stick did Goody pull.
He stood behind a bush of elder

Till she had filled her apron full.
When with her load she turned about,   85
The by-road back again to take,
He started forward with a shout
And sprang upon poor Goody Blake.

And fiercely by the arm he took her,
And by the arm he held her fast,   90
And fiercely by the arm he shook her,
And cried, 'I've caught you then at last!'
Then Goody, who had nothing said,
Her bundle from her lap let fall,
And kneeling on the sticks she prayed   95
To God that is the judge of all.

She prayed, her withered hand uprearing,
While Harry held her by the arm:
'God, who art never out of hearing –
Oh may he never more be warm!'   100
The cold, cold moon above her head,
Thus on her knees did Goody pray,
Young Harry heard what she had said,
And icy cold he turned away.

He went complaining all the morrow   105
That he was cold and very chill;
His face was gloom, his heart was sorrow –
Alas that day for Harry Gill!
That day he wore a riding-coat
But not a whit the warmer he;   110
Another was on Thursday brought,
And ere the Sabbath he had three.

'Twas all in vain, a useless matter,
And blankets were about him pinned;
Yet still his jaws and teeth they clatter   115
Like a loose casement in the wind.
And Harry's flesh it fell away,
And all who see him say 'tis plain
That, live as long as live he may,
He never will be warm again.   120

No word to any man he utters,
Abed or up, to young or old,
But ever to himself he mutters,
'Poor Harry Gill is very cold.'
Abed or up, by night or day,   125
His teeth they chatter, chatter still:

Now think, ye farmers all, I pray,
Of Goody Blake and Harry Gill.

LINES WRITTEN AT A SMALL DISTANCE FROM MY HOUSE, AND SENT
BY MY LITTLE BOY TO THE PERSON TO WHOM THEY ARE ADDRESSED
(BY WORDSWORTH, COMPOSED 1–9 MARCH 1798)

It is the first mild day of March;
Each minute sweeter than before,
The redbreast sings from the tall larch
That stands beside our door.

There is a blessing in the air   5
Which seems a sense of joy to yield
To the bare trees and mountains bare,
And grass in the green field.

My sister, 'tis a wish of mine
Now that our morning meal is done –   10
Make haste, your morning task resign,
Come forth and feel the sun!

Edward will come with you – and pray
Put on with speed your woodland dress,
And bring no book, for this one day   15
We'll give to idleness.

No joyless forms shall regulate
Our living calendar;
We from today, my friend, will date
The opening of the year.   20

Love, now an universal birth,
From heart to heart is stealing,
From earth to man, from man to earth –
It is the hour of feeling.

One moment now may give us more   25
Than fifty years of reason;
Our minds shall drink at every pore
The spirit of the season.

Some silent laws our hearts may make
Which they shall long obey;   30
We for the year to come may take
Our temper from today.

And from the blessed power that rolls
About, below, above,

We'll frame the measure of our souls –   35
They shall be tuned to love.

Then come, my sister, come, I pray,
With speed put on your woodland dress;
And bring no book, for this one day
We'll give to idleness.   40

SIMON LEE, THE OLD HUNTSMAN, WITH AN INCIDENT IN WHICH HE WAS CONCERNED (BY WORDSWORTH, COMPOSED BETWEEN MARCH AND 16 MAY 1798)

In the sweet shire of Cardigan
Not far from pleasant Ivor Hall,
An old man dwells, a little man,
I've heard he once was tall.
Of years he has upon his back,   5
No doubt, a burden weighty;
He says he is three score and ten,
But others say he's eighty.

A long blue livery-coat has he
That's fair behind and fair before;   10
Yet meet him where you will, you see
At once that he is poor.
Full five and twenty years he lived
A running huntsman merry,
And though he has but one eye left,   15
His cheek is like a cherry.

No man like him the horn could sound,
And no man was so full of glee;
To say the least, four counties round
Had heard of Simon Lee.   20
His master's dead, and no one now
Dwells in the Hall of Ivor,
Men, dogs, and horses – all are dead;
He is the sole survivor.

His hunting feats have him bereft   25
Of his right eye, as you may see;
And then, what limbs those feats have left
To poor old Simon Lee!
He has no son, he has no child;
His wife, an aged woman,   30
Lives with him near the waterfall,
Upon the village common.

And he is lean and he is sick,
His little body's half awry,
His ankles they are swoln and thick,   35
His legs are thin and dry.
When he was young he little knew
Of husbandry or tillage,
And now he's forced to work, though weak –
The weakest in the village.   40

He all the country could outrun,
Could leave both man and horse behind;
And often, ere the race was done,
He reeled and was stone-blind.
And still there's something in the world   45
At which his heart rejoices,
For when the chiming hounds are out
He dearly loves their voices!

Old Ruth works out of doors with him
And does what Simon cannot do;   50
For she, not over-stout of limb,
Is stouter of the two.
And though you with your utmost skill
From labour could not wean them,
Alas, 'tis very little, all   55
Which they can do between them!

Beside their moss-grown hut of clay
Not twenty paces from the door,
A scrap of land they have, but they
Are poorest of the poor.   60
This scrap of land he from the heath
Enclosed when he was stronger,
But what avails the land to them
Which they can till no longer?

Few months of life has he in store   65
As he to you will tell,
For still, the more he works, the more
His poor old ankles swell.
My gentle reader, I perceive
How patiently you've waited,   70
And I'm afraid that you expect
Some tale will be related.

Oh reader, had you in your mind
Such stores as silent thought can bring –

Oh gentle reader, you would find   75
A tale in every thing.
What more I have to say is short,
I hope you'll kindly take it;
It is no tale, but, should you think,
Perhaps a tale you'll make it.   80

One summer day I chanced to see
This old man doing all he could
About the root of an old tree,
A stump of rotten wood.
The mattock tottered in his hand;   85
So vain was his endeavour,
That at the root of the old tree
He might have worked forever.

'You're overtasked, good Simon Lee,
Give me your tool', to him I said;   90
And at the word, right gladly he
Received my proffered aid.
I struck, and with a single blow
The tangled root I severed,
At which the poor old man so long   95
And vainly had endeavoured.

The tears into his eyes were brought,
And thanks and praises seemed to run
So fast out of his heart, I thought
They never would have done   100
I've heard of hearts unkind, kind deeds
With coldness still returning;
Alas, the gratitude of men
Has oft'ner left me mourning.

ANECDOTE FOR FATHERS, SHOWING HOW THE ART OF LYING MAY BE TAUGHT (BY WORDSWORTH, COMPOSED BETWEEN APRIL AND 16 MAY 1798)

I have a boy of five years old,
His face is fair and fresh to see,
His limbs are cast in beauty's mould,
And dearly he loves me.

One morn we strolled on our dry walk,   5
Our quiet house all full in view,
And held such intermitted talk
As we are wont to do.

My thoughts on former pleasures ran;
I thought of Kilve's[1] delightful shore –   10
My pleasant home when spring began
A long long year before.

A day it was when I could bear
To think, and think, and think again;
With so much happiness to spare   15
I could not feel a pain.

My boy was by my side, so slim
And graceful in his rustic dress!
And oftentimes I talked to him
In very idleness.   20

The young lambs ran a pretty race,
The morning sun shone bright and warm;
'Kilve', said I, 'was a pleasant place,
And so is Liswyn farm.

My little boy, which like you more?'   25
I said and took him by the arm,
'Our home by Kilve's delightful shore,
Or here at Liswyn farm?

And tell me, had you rather be
(I said and held him by the arm)   30
At Kilve's smooth shore by the green sea
Or here at Liswyn farm?'

In careless mood he looked at me
While still I held him by the arm
And said, 'At Kilve I'd rather be   35
Than here at Liswyn farm.'

'Now, little Edward, say why so,
My little Edward, tell me why.'
'I cannot tell, I do not know.'
'Why this is strange!' said I.   40

'For here are woods and green hills warm;
There surely must some reason be
Why you would change sweet Liswyn farm
For Kilve by the green sea.'

ANECDOTE FOR FATHERS
[1] *Kilve* a village on the Bristol Channel, a mile from
Wordsworth's residence at Alfoxden.

At this, my boy, so fair and slim,   45
Hung down his head, nor made reply,
And five times did I say to him,
'Why? Edward, tell me why?'

His head he raised; there was in sight –
It caught his eye, he saw it plain –   50
Upon the house-top, glittering bright,
A broad and gilded vane.

Then did the boy his tongue unlock
And thus to me he made reply;
'At Kilve there was no weathercock,   55
And that's the reason why.'

Oh dearest, dearest boy! my heart
For better lore would seldom yearn,
Could I but teach the hundredth part
Of what from thee I learn   60

WE ARE SEVEN (BY WORDSWORTH, COMPOSED BETWEEN MARCH AND
16 MAY 1798)

A simple child, dear brother Jim,
That lightly draws its breath,
And feels its life in every limb –
What should it know of death?

I met a little cottage girl,   5
She was eight years old, she said;
Her hair was thick with many a curl
That clustered round her head.

She had a rustic woodland air
And she was wildly clad;   10
Her eyes were fair, and very fair –
Her beauty made me glad.

'Sisters and brothers, little maid,
How many may you be?'
'How many? Seven in all,' she said,   15
And wondering looked at me.

'And where are they, I pray you tell?'
She answered, 'Seven are we,
And two of us at Conway dwell,
And two are gone to sea.   20

Two of us in the churchyard lie
(My sister and my brother),

And in the churchyard cottage I
Dwell near them with my mother.'

'You say that two at Conway dwell   25
And two are gone to sea,
Yet you are seven – I pray you tell,
Sweet maid, how this may be?'

Then did the little maid reply,
'Seven boys and girls are we;   30
Two of us in the churchyard lie
Beneath the churchyard tree.'

'You run about, my little maid,
Your limbs they are alive;
If two are in the churchyard laid,   35
Then ye are only five.'

'Their graves are green, they may be seen,'
The little maid replied,
'Twelve steps or more from my mother's door,
And they are side by side.   40

My stockings there I often knit,
My kerchief there I hem,
And there upon the ground I sit,
I sit and sing to them.

And often after sunset, sir,   45
When it is light and fair,
I take my little porringer[1]
And eat my supper there.

The first that died was little Jane,
In bed she moaning lay,   50
Till God released her of her pain
And then she went away.

So in the churchyard she was laid
And all the summer dry,
Together round her grave we played,   55
My brother John and I.

And when the ground was white with snow,
And I could run and slide,

WE ARE SEVEN
[1] *porringer* bowl.

My brother John was forced to go,
And he lies by her side.'   60

'How many are you then', said I,
'If they two are in heaven?'
The little maiden did reply,
'Oh master, we are seven!'

'But they are dead – those two are dead!   65
Their spirits are in heaven!'
'Twas throwing words away, for still
The little maid would have her will
And said, 'Nay, we are seven!'

LINES WRITTEN IN EARLY SPRING (BY WORDSWORTH, COMPOSED BETWEEN MARCH AND 16 MAY 1798)

I heard a thousand blended notes
While in a grove I sat reclined
In that sweet mood when pleasant thoughts
Bring sad thoughts to the mind.

To her fair works did nature link   5
The human soul that through me ran,
And much it grieved my heart to think
What man has made of man.

Through primrose-tufts, in that sweet bower,
The periwinkle trailed its wreaths;   10
And 'tis my faith that every flower
Enjoys the air it breathes.

The birds around me hopped and played,
Their thoughts I cannot measure,
But the least motion which they made –   15
It seemed a thrill of pleasure.

The budding twigs spread out their fan
To catch the breezy air;
And I must think, do all I can,
That there was pleasure there.   20

If I these thoughts may not prevent,
If such be of my creed the plan,
Have I not reason to lament
What man has made of man?

THE THORN (BY WORDSWORTH, COMPOSED BETWEEN 19 MARCH AND 20 APRIL 1798)[1]

I

There is a thorn, it looks so old,
In truth you'd find it hard to say
How it could ever have been young,
It looks so old and grey.
Not higher than a two years' child,   5
It stands erect, this aged thorn;
No leaves it has, no thorny points –
It is a mass of knotted joints,
A wretched thing forlorn.
It stands erect and, like a stone,   10
With lichens it is overgrown.

II

Like rock or stone, it is o'ergrown
With lichens to the very top,
And hung with heavy tufts of moss,
A melancholy crop;   15
Up from the earth these mosses creep,
And this poor thorn they clasp it round
So close, you'd say that they were bent
With plain and manifest intent
To drag it to the ground –   20
And all had joined in one endeavour
To bury this poor thorn for ever.

III

High on a mountain's highest ridge
Where oft the stormy winter gale
Cuts like a scythe, while through the clouds   25
It sweeps from vale to vale;
Not five yards from the mountain path
This thorn you on your left espy,

THE THORN
[1] In *Fenwick Notes*, Wordsworth recalled that the poem 'arose out of my observing, on the ridge of Quantock Hill, on a stormy day, a thorn which I had often passed in calm and bright weather without noticing it. I said to myself, "Cannot I by some invention do as much to make this thorn permanently an impressive object as the storm has made it to my eyes at this moment?" I began the poem accordingly, and composed it with great rapidity' (*FN*, 14). See also the 'Note to "The Thorn"' (1800), pp. 248–50 below.

And to the left, three yards beyond,
You see a little muddy pond   30
Of water, never dry.
I've measured it from side to side;
'Tis three feet long and two feet wide.

IV

And close beside this aged thorn
There is a fresh and lovely sight,   35
A beauteous heap, a hill of moss,
Just half a foot in height.
All lovely colours there you see,
All colours that were ever seen,
And mossy network too is there,   40
As if by hand of lady fair
The work had woven been,
And cups, the darlings of the eye,
So deep is their vermilion dye.

V

Ah me, what lovely tints are there   45
Of olive-green and scarlet bright!
In spikes, in branches, and in stars,
Green, red, and pearly white.
This heap of earth o'ergrown with moss,
Which close beside the thorn you see,   50
So fresh in all its beauteous dyes,
Is like an infant's grave in size,
As like as like can be;
But never, never, anywhere
An infant's grave was half so fair.   55

VI

Now would you see this aged thorn,
This pond and beauteous hill of moss,
You must take care and choose your time
The mountain when to cross.
For oft there sits, between the heap   60
That's like an infant's grave in size
And that same pond of which I spoke,
A woman in a scarlet cloak,
And to herself she cries,

'Oh misery! Oh misery!   65
Oh woe is me! Oh misery!'

VII

At all times of the day and night
This wretched woman thither goes,
And she is known to every star
And every wind that blows;   70
And there beside the thorn she sits
When the blue daylight's in the skies,
And when the whirlwind's on the hill,
Or frosty air is keen and still,
And to herself she cries,   75
'Oh misery! Oh misery!
Oh woe is me! Oh misery!'

VIII

'Now wherefore thus, by day and night,
In rain, in tempest, and in snow,
Thus to the dreary mountain-top   80
Does this poor woman go?
And why sits she beside the thorn
When the blue daylight's in the sky,
Or when the whirlwind's on the hill,
Or frosty air is keen and still,   85
And wherefore does she cry?
Oh wherefore, wherefore, tell me why
Does she repeat that doleful cry?'

IX

I cannot tell, I wish I could;
For the true reason no one knows.   90
But if you'd gladly view the spot,
The spot to which she goes —
The heap that's like an infant's grave,
The pond, and thorn so old and grey —
Pass by her door ('tis seldom shut),   95
And if you see her in her hut,
Then to the spot away!
I never heard of such as dare
Approach the spot when she is there.

X

'But wherefore to the mountain-top   100
Can this unhappy woman go,
Whatever star is in the skies,
Whatever wind may blow?'
Nay rack your brain, 'tis all in vain –
I'll tell you everything I know;   105
But to the thorn, and to the pond
Which is a little step beyond,
I wish that you would go.
Perhaps when you are at the place
You something of her tale may trace.   110

XI

I'll give you the best help I can:
Before you up the mountain go,
Up to the dreary mountain-top,
I'll tell you all I know.
'Tis now some two and twenty years   115
Since she (her name is Martha Ray)
Gave with a maiden's true goodwill
Her company to Stephen Hill,
And she was blithe and gay,
And she was happy, happy still   120
Whene'er she thought of Stephen Hill.

XII

And they had fixed the wedding-day,
The morning that must wed them both,
But Stephen to another maid
Had sworn another oath,
And with this other maid to church   125
Unthinking Stephen went –
Poor Martha! On that woeful day
A cruel, cruel fire, they say,
Into her bones was sent: 130
It dried her body like a cinder
And almost turned her brain to tinder.

XIII

They say full six months after this,
While yet the summer leaves were green,

She to the mountain-top would go, 135
And there was often seen;
'Tis said a child was in her womb,
As now to any eye was plain –
She was with child and she was mad,
Yet often she was sober-sad 140
From her exceeding pain.
Oh me! Ten thousand times I'd rather
That he had died, that cruel father!

XIV

Sad case for such a brain to hold
Communion with a stirring child! 145
Sad case (as you may think) for one
Who had a brain so wild!
Last Christmas when we talked of this,
Old Farmer Simpson did maintain
That in her womb the infant wrought 150
About its mother's heart, and brought
Her senses back again;
And when at last her time drew near,
Her looks were calm, her senses clear.

XV

No more I know – I wish I did, 155
And I would tell it all to you.
For what became of this poor child
There's none that ever knew;
And if a child was born or no,
There's no one that could ever tell; 160
And if 'twas born alive or dead,
There's no one knows, as I have said.
But some remember well
That Martha Ray about this time
Would up the mountain often climb. 165

XVI

And all that winter, when at night
The wind blew from the mountain-peak,
'Twas worth your while, though in the dark,
The churchyard path to seek:
For many a time and oft were heard 170
Cries coming from the mountain-head.

Some plainly living voices were,
And others, I've heard many swear,
Were voices of the dead.
I cannot think, whate'er they say,   175
They had to do with Martha Ray.

XVII

But that she goes to this old thorn,
The thorn which I've described to you,
And there sits in a scarlet cloak,
I will be sworn is true.   180
For one day with my telescope,
To view the ocean wide and bright,
When to this country first I came,
Ere I had heard of Martha's name,
I climbed the mountain's height,   185
A storm came on, and I could see
No object higher than my knee.

XVIII

'Twas mist and rain, and storm and rain,
No screen, no fence could I discover;
And then the wind – in faith, it was   190
A wind full ten times over!
I looked around, I thought I saw
A jutting crag, and off I ran
Head-foremost through the driving rain,
The shelter of the crag to gain;   195
And, as I am a man,
Instead of jutting crag, I found
A woman seated on the ground.

XIX

I did not speak – I saw her face,
Her face it was enough for me,   200
I turned about and heard her cry,
'Oh misery! Oh misery!'
And there she sits, until the moon
Through half the clear blue sky will go,
And when the little breezes make   205
The waters of the pond to shake,
As all the country know,

She shudders and you hear her cry,
'Oh misery! Oh misery!'

XX

'But what's the thorn? And what's the pond?   210
And what's the hill of moss to her?
And what's the creeping breeze that comes
The little pond to stir?'
I cannot tell, but some will say
She hanged her baby on the tree;   215
Some say she drowned it in the pond
Which is a little step beyond;
But all and each agree
The little babe was buried there,
Beneath that hill of moss so fair.   220

XXI

I've heard the scarlet moss is red
With drops of that poor infant's blood –
But kill a new-born infant thus?
I do not think she could.
Some say, if to the pond you go,   225
And fix on it a steady view,
The shadow of a babe you trace,
A baby and a baby's face,
And that it looks at you;
Whene'er you look on it, 'tis plain   230
The baby looks at you again.

XXII

And some had sworn an oath that she
Should be to public justice brought,
And for the little infant's bones
With spades they would have sought.   235
But then the beauteous hill of moss
Before their eyes began to stir,
And for full fifty yards around,
The grass it shook upon the ground.
But all do still aver   240
The little babe is buried there,
Beneath that hill of moss so fair.

XXIII

I cannot tell how this may be,
But plain it is, the thorn is bound
With heavy tufts of moss that strive   245
To drag it to the ground.
And this I know, full many a time
When she was on the mountain high,
By day, and in the silent night,
When all the stars shone clear and bright,   250
That I have heard her cry,
'Oh misery! Oh misery!
Oh woe is me! Oh misery!'

THE LAST OF THE FLOCK (BY WORDSWORTH, COMPOSED BETWEEN MARCH AND 16 MAY 1798)

In distant countries I have been,
And yet I have not often seen
A healthy man, a man full grown,
Weep in the public roads alone.
But such a one on English ground   5
And in the broad highway, I met;
Along the broad highway he came,
His cheeks with tears were wet.
Sturdy he seemed, though he was sad,
And in his arms a lamb he had.   10

He saw me and he turned aside
As if he wished himself to hide;
Then with his coat he made essay
To wipe those briny tears away.
I followed him, and said, 'My friend,   15
What ails you? Wherefore weep you so?'
'Shame on me, sir! This lusty lamb,
He makes my tears to flow;
Today I fetched him from the rock –
He is the last of all my flock.   20

When I was young, a single man,
And after youthful follies ran,
Though little given to care and thought,
Yet so it was a ewe I bought;
And other sheep from her I raised,   25
As healthy sheep as you might see.
And then I married, and was rich
As I could wish to be;

Of sheep I numbered a full score,
And every year increased my store.   30

Year after year my stock it grew,
And from this one, this single ewe,
Full fifty comely sheep I raised –
As sweet a flock as ever grazed!
Upon the mountain did they feed,   35
They throve, and we at home did thrive.
This lusty lamb of all my store
Is all that is alive;
And now I care not if we die
And perish all of poverty.   40

Ten children, sir, had I to feed –
Hard labour in a time of need!
My pride was tamed, and in our grief
I of the parish asked relief.
They said I was a wealthy man;   45
My sheep upon the mountain fed
And it was fit that thence I took
Whereof to buy us bread.
"Do this. How can we give to you",
They cried, "what to the poor is due?"   50

I sold a sheep as they had said,
And bought my little children bread,
And they were healthy with their food;
For me it never did me good.
A woeful time it was for me   55
To see the end of all my gains,
The pretty flock which I had reared
With all my care and pains,
To see it melt like snow away!
For me it was a woeful day.   60

Another still, and still another!
A little lamb and then its mother!
It was a vein that never stopped,
Like blood-drops from my heart they dropped
Till thirty were not left alive;   65
They dwindled, dwindled, one by one,
And I may say that many a time
I wished they all were gone:
They dwindled one by one away –
For me it was a woeful day.   70

To wicked deeds I was inclined,
And wicked fancies crossed my mind,

And every man I chanced to see,
I thought he knew some ill of me.
No peace, no comfort could I find,   75
No ease, within doors or without,
And crazily, and wearily,
I went my work about.
Oft-times I thought to run away;
For me it was a woeful day.   80

Sir, 'twas a precious flock to me,
As dear as my own children be;
For daily with my growing store
I loved my children more and more.
Alas, it was an evil time,   85
God cursed me in my sore distress;
I prayed, yet every day I thought
I loved my children less;
And every week, and every day
My flock, it seemed to melt away.   90

They dwindled, sir, sad sight to see,
From ten to five, from five to three –
A lamb, a wether, and a ewe;
And then at last, from three to two.
And of my fifty, yesterday   95
I had but only one,
And here it lies upon my arm –
Alas, and I have none!
Today I fetched it from the rock;
It is the last of all my flock.'   100

THE DUNGEON (BY COLERIDGE, EXTRACTED FROM OSORIO, COMPOSED 1797)

And this place our forefathers made for man!
This is the process of our love and wisdom
To each poor brother who offends against us;
Most innocent, perhaps – and what if guilty?
Is this the only cure, merciful God?   5
Each pore and natural outlet shrivelled up
By ignorance and parching poverty,
His energies roll back upon his heart
And stagnate and corrupt; till, changed to poison,
They break out on him like a loathsome plague-spot.   10
Then we call in our pampered mountebanks
And this is their best cure: uncomforted
And friendless solitude, groaning and tears
And savage faces at the clanking hour,
Seen through the steams and vapour of his dungeon,   15

By the lamp's dismal twilight. So he lies
Circled with evil, till his very soul
Unmoulds its essence, hopelessly deformed
By sights of ever more deformity!
   With other ministrations, thou, oh nature, 20
Healest thy wandering and distempered child:
Thou pourest on him thy soft influences,
Thy sunny hues, fair forms, and breathing sweets,
Thy melodies of woods, and winds, and waters,
Till he relent, and can no more endure 25
To be a jarring and a dissonant thing
Amid this general dance and minstrelsy;
But, bursting into tears, wins back his way,
His angry spirit healed and harmonized
By the benignant touch of love and beauty. 30

THE MAD MOTHER (BY WORDSWORTH, COMPOSED BETWEEN MARCH AND 16 MAY 1798)

Her eyes are wild, her head is bare,
The sun has burnt her coal-black hair,
Her eyebrows have a rusty stain,
And she came far from over the main.
She has a baby on her arm, 5
Or else she were alone;
And underneath the haystack warm,
And on the greenwood stone,
She talked and sung the woods among –
And it was in the English tongue.[1] 10

'Sweet babe, they say that I am mad,
But nay, my heart is far too glad;
And I am happy when I sing
Full many a sad and doleful thing.
Then, lovely baby, do not fear! 15
I pray thee, have no fear of me,
But safe as in a cradle, here
My lovely baby, thou shalt be;
To thee I know too much I owe,
I cannot work thee any woe. 20

A fire was once within my brain,
And in my head a dull, dull pain;

THE MAD MOTHER
[1] On 24 Sept. 1836, Wordsworth told John Kenyon that this line 'shows her either to be of these islands, or a North American. On the latter supposition, while the distance removes her from us, the fact of her speaking our language brings us at once into close sympathy with her' (*LY*, iii. 293).

And fiendish faces – one, two, three,
Hung at my breasts, and pulled at me.
But then there came a sight of joy,   25
It came at once to do me good;
I waked and saw my little boy,
My little boy of flesh and blood –
Oh joy for me that sight to see!
For he was here, and only he.   30

Suck, little babe, oh suck again!
It cools my blood, it cools my brain;
Thy lips I feel them, baby, they
Draw from my heart the pain away.
Oh, press me with thy little hand,   35
It loosens something at my chest;
About that tight and deadly band
I feel thy little fingers pressed.
The breeze I see is in the tree,
It comes to cool my babe and me.   40

Oh love me, love me, little boy!
Thou art thy mother's only joy;
And do not dread the waves below,
When o'er the sea-rock's edge we go.
The high crag cannot work me harm,   45
Nor leaping torrents when they howl;
The babe I carry on my arm,
He saves for me my precious soul.
Then happy lie, for blessed am I –
Without me my sweet babe would die.   50

Then do not fear, my boy, for thee
Bold as a lion I will be;
And I will always be thy guide
Through hollow snows and rivers wide.
I'll build an Indian bower; I know   55
The leaves that make the softest bed;
And if from me thou wilt not go,
But still be true till I am dead –
My pretty thing, then thou shalt sing,
As merry as the birds in spring.   60

Thy father cares not for my breast;
'Tis thine, sweet baby, there to rest,
'Tis all thine own! And if its hue
Be changed, that was so fair to view,
'Tis fair enough for thee, my dove!   65
My beauty, little child, is flown;

But thou wilt live with me in love –
And what if my poor cheek be brown?
'Tis well for me; thou canst not see
How pale and wan it else would be.   70

Dread not their taunts, my little life!
I am thy father's wedded wife,
And underneath the spreading tree
We two will live in honesty.
If his sweet boy he could forsake,   75
With me he never would have stayed;
From him no harm my babe can take,
But he, poor man, is wretched made;
And every day we two will pray
For him that's gone and far away.   80

I'll teach my boy the sweetest things,
I'll teach him how the owlet sings.
My little babe, thy lips are still,
And thou hast almost sucked thy fill.
Where art thou gone, my own dear child?   85
What wicked looks are those I see?
Alas, alas! that look so wild,
It never, never came from me;
If thou art mad, my pretty lad,
Then I must be forever sad.   90

Oh smile on me, my little lamb,
For I thy own dear mother am.
My love for thee has well been tried;
I've sought thy father far and wide.
I know the poisons of the shade,   95
I know the earth-nuts fit for food;
Then, pretty dear, be not afraid –
We'll find thy father in the wood.
Now laugh and be gay, to the woods away,
And there, my babe, we'll live for aye.'   100

THE IDIOT BOY (BY WORDSWORTH, COMPOSED BETWEEN MARCH AND 16 MAY 1798)

'Tis eight o'clock, a clear March night,
The moon is up, the sky is blue,
The owlet in the moonlight air –
He shouts from nobody knows where,
He lengthens out his lonely shout: 5
Halloo, halloo! A long halloo!

Why bustle thus about your door?
What means this bustle, Betty Foy?
Why are you in this mighty fret?
And why on horseback have you set   10
Him whom you love, your idiot boy?

Beneath the moon that shines so bright,
Till she is tired, let Betty Foy
With girt¹ and stirrup fiddle-faddle;
But wherefore set upon a saddle   15
Him whom she loves, her idiot boy?

There's scarce a soul that's out of bed –
Good Betty, put him down again!
His lips with joy they burr at you,
But, Betty, what has he to do   20
With stirrup, saddle, or with rein?

The world will say 'tis very idle –
Bethink you of the time of night?
There's not a mother – no not one,
But when she hears what you have done,   25
Oh Betty, she'll be in a fright!

But Betty's bent on her intent,
For her good neighbour, Susan Gale
(Old Susan, she who dwells alone)
Is sick and makes a piteous moan   30
As if her very life would fail.

There's not a house within a mile,
No hand to help them in distress,
Old Susan lies abed in pain,
And sorely puzzled are the twain,   35
For what she ails they cannot guess.

And Betty's husband's at the wood
Where by the week he doth abide,
A woodman in the distant vale;
There's none to help poor Susan Gale –   40
What must be done? What will betide?

And Betty from the lane has fetched
Her pony that is mild and good
Whether he be in joy or pain,

THE IDIOT BOY
¹ *girt* saddle-girth.

Feeding at will along the lane,   45
Or bringing faggots from the wood.

And he is all in travelling trim,
And by the moonlight, Betty Foy
Has up upon the saddle set
(The like was never heard of yet)   50
Him whom she loves, her idiot boy.

And he must post without delay
Across the bridge that's in the dale,
And by the church and o'er the down
To bring a Doctor from the town,   55
Or she will die, old Susan Gale.

There is no need of boot or spur,
There is no need of whip or wand,
For Johnny has his holly-bough,
And with a hurly-burly now   60
He shakes the green bough in his hand.

And Betty o'er and o'er has told
The boy who is her best delight
Both what to follow, what to shun,
What do, and what to leave undone,   65
How turn to left, and how to right,

And Betty's most especial charge
Was, 'Johnny, Johnny! Mind that you
Come home again, nor stop at all,
Come home again whate'er befall –   70
My Johnny do, I pray you do.'

To this did Johnny answer make
Both with his head and with his hand,
And proudly shook the bridle too,
And then! his words were not a few,   75
Which Betty well could understand.

And now that Johnny is just going,
Though Betty's in a mighty flurry,
She gently pats the pony's side
On which her idiot boy must ride,   80
And seems no longer in a hurry.

But when the pony moved his legs –
Oh then for the poor idiot boy!
For joy he cannot hold the bridle,

For joy his head and heels are idle,   85
He's idle all for very joy.

And while the pony moves his legs,
In Johnny's left hand you may see
The green bough's motionless and dead;
The moon that shines above his head   90
Is not more still and mute than he.

His heart it was so full of glee
That till full fifty yards were gone
He quite forgot his holly whip
And all his skill in horsemanship –   95
Oh happy, happy, happy John!

And Betty's standing at the door,
And Betty's face with joy o'erflows,
Proud of herself and proud of him,
She sees him in his travelling trim;   100
How quietly her Johnny goes!

The silence of her idiot boy –
What hopes it sends to Betty's heart!
He's at the guide-post,[2] he turns right,
She watches till he's out of sight,   105
And Betty will not then depart.

Burr, burr, now Johnny's lips they burr
As loud as any mill or near it;
Meek as a lamb the pony moves,
And Johnny makes the noise he loves,   110
And Betty listens, glad to hear it.

Away she hies to Susan Gale,
And Johnny's in a merry tune;
The owlets hoot, the owlets curr,
And Johnny's lips they burr, burr, burr,   115
And on he goes beneath the moon.

His steed and he right well agree,
For of this pony there's a rumour
That should he lose his eyes and ears,
And should he live a thousand years,   120
He never will be out of humour.

But then he is a horse that thinks!
And when he thinks his pace is slack;

---

[2]   *guide-post* sign-post.

Now, though he knows poor Johnny well,
Yet for his life he cannot tell   125
What he has got upon his back.

So through the moonlight lanes they go
And far into the moonlight dale,
And by the church and o'er the down
To bring a Doctor from the town   130
To comfort poor old Susan Gale.

And Betty, now at Susan's side,
Is in the middle of her story,
What comfort Johnny soon will bring,
With many a most diverting thing   135
Of Johnny's wit and Johnny's glory.

And Betty's still at Susan's side —
By this time she's not quite so flurried;
Demure with porringer and plate
She sits, as if in Susan's fate   140
Her life and soul were buried.

But Betty (poor good woman!), she —
You plainly in her face may read it —
Could lend out of that moment's store
Five years of happiness or more   145
To any that might need it.

But yet I guess that now and then
With Betty all was not so well,
And to the road she turns her ears,
And thence full many a sound she hears,   150
Which she to Susan will not tell.

Poor Susan moans, poor Susan groans;
'As sure as there's a moon in heaven',
Cries Betty, 'he'll be back again —
They'll both be here, 'tis almost ten;   155
They'll both be here before eleven.'

Poor Susan moans, poor Susan groans,
The clock gives warning for eleven —
'Tis on the stroke. 'If Johnny's near',
Quoth Betty, 'he will soon be here,   160
As sure as there's a moon in heaven.'

The clock is on the stroke of twelve
And Johnny is not yet in sight;

The moon's in heaven, as Betty sees,
But Betty is not quite at ease –   165
And Susan has a dreadful night.

And Betty, half an hour ago,
On Johnny vile reflections cast;
'A little idle sauntering thing!'
With other names, an endless string,   170
But now that time is gone and past.

And Betty's drooping at the heart,
That happy time all past and gone;
'How can it be he is so late?
The Doctor, he has made him wait –   175
Susan, they'll both be here anon!'

And Susan's growing worse and worse,
And Betty's in a sad quandary,
And then there's nobody to say
If she must go or she must stay –   180
She's in a sad quandary.

The clock is on the stroke of one,
But neither Doctor nor his guide
Appear along the moonlight road;
There's neither horse nor man abroad,   185
And Betty's still at Susan's side.

And Susan, she begins to fear
Of sad mischances not a few;
That Johnny may perhaps be drowned,
Or lost perhaps, and never found –   190
Which they must both forever rue.

She prefaced half a hint of this
With, 'God forbid it should be true!'
At the first word that Susan said,
Cried Betty, rising from the bed,   195
'Susan, I'd gladly stay with you;

I must be gone, I must away.
Consider, Johnny's but half-wise;
Susan, we must take care of him,
If he is hurt in life or limb –'   200
'Oh God forbid!' poor Susan cries.

'What can I do?' says Betty, going,
'What can I do to ease your pain?

Good Susan tell me, and I'll stay;
I fear you're in a dreadful way,   205
But I shall soon be back again.'

'Good Betty go, good Betty go,
There's nothing that can ease my pain.'
Then off she hies, but with a prayer
That God poor Susan's life would spare   210
Till she comes back again.

So through the moonlight lane she goes
And far into the moonlight dale;
And how she ran and how she walked
And all that to herself she talked   215
Would surely be a tedious tale.

In high and low, above, below,
In great and small, in round and square,
In tree and tower was Johnny seen,
In bush and brake, in black and green,   220
'Twas Johnny, Johnny, everywhere.

She's past the bridge that's in the dale,
And now the thought torments her sore –
Johnny perhaps his horse forsook
To hunt the moon that's in the brook,   225
And never will be heard of more.

And now she's high upon the down,
Alone amid a prospect wide;
There's neither Johnny nor his horse
Among the fern or in the gorse;   230
There's neither Doctor nor his guide.

'Oh saints! What is become of him?
Perhaps he's climbed into an oak
Where he will stay till he is dead;
Or sadly he has been misled   235
And joined the wandering gipsy-folk;

Or him that wicked pony's carried
To the dark cave, the goblin's hall;
Or in the castle he's pursuing,
Among the ghosts, his own undoing,   240
Or playing with the waterfall.'

At poor old Susan then she railed,
While to the town she posts away;

'If Susan had not been so ill,
Alas! I should have had him still,   245
My Johnny, till my dying day.'

Poor Betty, in this sad distemper,
The Doctor's self would hardly spare;
Unworthy things she talked, and wild –
Even he, of cattle³ the most mild,   250
The pony had his share.

And now she's got into the town
And to the Doctor's door she hies;
'Tis silence all on every side –
The town so long, the town so wide   255
Is silent as the skies.

And now she's at the Doctor's door,
She lifts the knocker – rap, rap, rap!
The Doctor at the casement shows
His glimmering eyes that peep and doze,   260
And one hand rubs his old nightcap.

'Oh Doctor, Doctor! Where's my Johnny?'
'I'm here, what is't you want with me?'
'Oh sir, you know I'm Betty Foy
And I have lost my poor dear boy –   265
You know him, him you often see;

He's not so wise as some folks be.'
'The devil take his wisdom!' said
The Doctor, looking somewhat grim,
'What, woman, should I know of him?'   270
And grumbling, he went back to bed.

'Oh woe is me! Oh woe is me!
Here will I die, here will I die;
I thought to find my Johnny here,
But he is neither far nor near –   275
Oh what a wretched mother I!'

She stops, she stands, she looks about,
Which way to turn she cannot tell.
Poor Betty, it would ease her pain
If she had heart to knock again;   280
The clock strikes three – a dismal knell!

---

³ *cattle* animals.

Then up along the town she hies,
No wonder if her senses fail,
This piteous news so much it shocked her
She quite forgot to send the Doctor   285
To comfort poor old Susan Gale.

And now she's high upon the down
And she can see a mile of road;
'Oh cruel! I'm almost threescore;
Such night as this was ne'er before,   290
There's not a single soul abroad.'

She listens, but she cannot hear
The foot of horse, the voice of man;
The streams with softest sound are flowing,
The grass you almost hear it growing,   295
You hear it now if e'er you can.

The owlets through the long blue night
Are shouting to each other still,
Fond lovers, yet not quite hob-nob,
They lengthen out the tremulous sob   300
That echoes far from hill to hill.

Poor Betty now has lost all hope,
Her thoughts are bent on deadly sin;
A green-grown pond she just has passed
And from the brink she hurries fast   305
Lest she should drown herself therein.

And now she sits her down and weeps,
Such tears she never shed before;
'Oh dear, dear pony! My sweet joy!
Oh carry back my idiot boy   310
And we will ne'er o'erload thee more.'

A thought is come into her head;
'The pony he is mild and good
And we have always used him well;
Perhaps he's gone along the dell   315
And carried Johnny to the wood.'

Then up she springs as if on wings –
She thinks no more of deadly sin;
If Betty fifty ponds should see,
The last of all her thoughts would be   320
To drown herself therein.

Oh reader, now that I might tell
What Johnny and his horse are doing,
What they've been doing all this time –
Oh could I put it into rhyme,   325
A most delightful tale pursuing!

Perhaps (and no unlikely thought)
He with his pony now doth roam
The cliffs and peaks so high that are,
To lay his hands upon a star   330
And in his pocket bring it home.

Perhaps he's turned himself about,
His face unto his horse's tail,
And still and mute, in wonder lost,
All like a silent horseman-ghost   335
He travels on along the vale.

And now, perhaps, he's hunting sheep,
A fierce and dreadful hunter he!
Yon valley that's so trim and green,
In five months' time, should he be seen,   340
A desert wilderness will be.

Perhaps, with head and heels on fire,
And like the very soul of evil,
He's galloping away, away,
And so he'll gallop on for aye,   345
The bane of all that dread the devil.

I to the muses have been bound
These fourteen years by strong indentures;[4]
Oh gentle muses, let me tell
But half of what to him befell,   350
For sure he met with strange adventures.

Oh gentle muses, is this kind?
Why will ye thus my suit repel?
Why of your further aid bereave me?
And can ye thus unfriended leave me,   355
Ye muses, whom I love so well?

Who's yon, that, near the waterfall
Which thunders down with headlong force,
Beneath the moon, yet shining fair,

---

[4]   *indentures* contract by which apprentice is bound to   apprenticeship to the muse of poetry, by his reckon-
a master who will teach him a trade. Wordsworth's   ing, began in 1784, when he was 14.

As careless as if nothing were,   360
Sits upright on a feeding horse?

Unto his horse that's feeding free
He seems, I think, the rein to give;
Of moon or stars he takes no heed,
Of such we in romances read –   365
'Tis Johnny, Johnny, as I live!

And that's the very pony too!
Where is she, where is Betty Foy?
She hardly can sustain her fears;
The roaring waterfall she hears,   370
And cannot find her idiot boy.

Your pony's worth his weight in gold,
Then calm your terrors, Betty Foy!
She's coming from among the trees,
And now, all full in view, she sees   375
Him whom she loves, her idiot boy,

And Betty sees the pony too.
Why stand you thus, good Betty Foy?
It is no goblin, 'tis no ghost –
'Tis he whom you so long have lost,   380
He whom you love, your idiot boy.

She looks again, her arms are up,
She screams, she cannot move for joy;
She darts as with a torrent's force,
She almost has o'erturned the horse,   385
And fast she holds her idiot boy.

And Johnny burrs and laughs aloud –
Whether in cunning or in joy
I cannot tell; but while he laughs,
Betty a drunken pleasure quaffs   390
To hear again her idiot boy.

And now she's at the pony's tail,
And now she's at the pony's head,
On that side now, and now on this,
And almost stifled with her bliss,   395
A few sad tears does Betty shed.

She kisses o'er and o'er again
Him whom she loves, her idiot boy;
She's happy here, she's happy there,

She is uneasy everywhere;   400
Her limbs are all alive with joy.

She pats the pony, where or when
She knows not, happy Betty Foy!
The little pony glad may be,
But he is milder far than she,   405
You hardly can perceive his joy.

'Oh Johnny, never mind the Doctor;
You've done your best, and that is all.'
She took the reins when this was said,
And gently turned the pony's head   410
From the loud waterfall.

By this the stars were almost gone,
The moon was setting on the hill
So pale you scarcely looked at her;
The little birds began to stir,   415
Though yet their tongues were still.

The pony, Betty, and her boy,
Wind slowly through the woody dale;
And who is she, betimes abroad,
That hobbles up the steep rough road?   420
Who is it but old Susan Gale?

Long Susan lay deep lost in thought
And many dreadful fears beset her,
Both for her messenger and nurse;
And as her mind grew worse and worse,   425
Her body it grew better.

She turned, she tossed herself in bed,
On all sides doubts and terrors met her,
Point after point did she discuss,
And while her mind was fighting thus,   430
Her body still grew better.

'Alas, what is become of them?
These fears can never be endured –
I'll to the wood.' The word scarce said,
Did Susan rise up from her bed,   435
As if by magic cured.

Away she posts up hill and down,
And to the wood at length is come,
She spies her friends, she shouts a greeting –

Oh me, it is a merry meeting   440
As ever was in Christendom!

The owls have hardly sung their last
While our four travellers homeward wend;
The owls have hooted all night long,
And with the owls began my song,   445
And with the owls must end.

For while they all were travelling home,
Cried Betty, 'Tell us Johnny, do,
Where all this long night you have been,
What you have heard, what you have seen –   450
And Johnny, mind you tell us true.'

Now Johnny all night long had heard
The owls in tuneful concert strive;
No doubt too he the moon had seen,
For in the moonlight he had been   455
From eight o'clock till five.

And thus to Betty's question he
Made answer like a traveller bold
(His very words I give to you):
'The cocks did crow to-whoo, to-whoo,   460
And the sun did shine so cold.'
Thus answered Johnny in his glory,
And that was all his travel's story.

LINES WRITTEN NEAR RICHMOND, UPON THE THAMES, AT EVENING (BY
WORDSWORTH, DERIVED FROM A SONNET WRITTEN IN 1788, COMPLETE
IN THIS FORM BY 29 MARCH 1797)

How rich the wave in front, impressed
With evening twilight's summer hues,
While, facing thus the crimson west,
The boat her silent path pursues!
And see how dark the backward stream,   5
A little moment past, so smiling!
And still, perhaps, with faithless gleam,
Some other loiterer beguiling.

Such views the youthful bard allure,
But heedless of the following gloom,   10
He deems their colours shall endure
Till peace go with him to the tomb.
And let him nurse his fond deceit,
And what if he must die in sorrow?

Who would not cherish dreams so sweet,   15
Though grief and pain may come tomorrow?

Glide gently, thus forever glide,
Oh Thames! that other bards may see
As lovely visions by thy side
As now, fair river; come to me!   20
Oh glide, fair stream, forever so;
Thy quiet soul on all bestowing,
Till all our minds forever flow,
As thy deep waters now are flowing.

Vain thought! Yet be as now thou art,   25
That in thy waters may be seen
The image of a poet's heart,
How bright, how solemn, how serene!
Such heart did once the poet[1] bless
Who, pouring here a *later* ditty,   30
Could find no refuge from distress
But in the milder grief of pity.

Remembrance! as we glide along,
For him suspend the dashing oar,[2]
And pray that never child of song   35
May kno his freezing sorrows more.
How calm, how still! the only sound
The dripping of the oar suspended!
The evening darkness gathers round
By virtue's holiest powers attended.   40

EXPOSTULATION AND REPLY (BY WORDSWORTH, COMPOSED PROBABLY 23 MAY 1798)

'Why, William,[1] on that old grey stone,
Thus for the length of half a day,
Why, William, sit you thus alone
And dream your time away?

Where are your books that light bequeathed   5
To beings else forlorn and blind?

LINES WRITTEN NEAR RICHMOND
[1] 'Collins' "Ode on the Death of Thomson" – the last written, I believe, of the poems which were published during his lifetime. This Ode is also alluded to in the next stanza' (Wordsworth's note). James Thomson (1700–48), poet and author of *The Seasons*, was buried in Richmond Church. Wordsworth was a lifelong admirer of both poets.

[2] Cf. Collins, 'Ode on the Death of Mr Thomson', 13–16.
EXPOSTULATION AND REPLY
[1] See Advertisement to *Lyrical Ballads* (1798) above, for Wordsworth's explanation of the poem. See Hazlitt's recollection, p. 653.

Up, up, and drink the spirit breathed
From dead men to their kind!

You look round on your mother earth
As if she for no purpose bore you;   10
As if you were her first-born birth,
And none had lived before you!'

One morning thus, by Esthwaite lake,
When life was sweet I knew not why,
To me my good friend Matthew spake,   15
And thus I made reply.

'The eye it cannot choose but see,
We cannot bid the ear be still;
Our bodies feel where'er they be,
Against or with our will.   20

Nor less I deem that there are powers
Which of themselves our minds impress,
That we can feed this mind of ours
In a wise passiveness.

Think you, mid all this mighty sum   25
Of things forever speaking,
That nothing of itself will come,
But we must still be seeking?

Then ask not wherefore, here, alone,
Conversing as I may,   30
I sit upon this old grey stone
And dream my time away.'

THE TABLES TURNED: AN EVENING SCENE, ON THE SAME SUBJECT (BY WORDSWORTH, COMPOSED PROBABLY 23 MAY 1798)

Up, up, my friend, and clear your looks!
Why all this toil and trouble?
Up, up, my friend, and quit your books,
Or surely you'll grow double!

The sun above the mountain's head   5
A freshening lustre mellow
Through all the long green fields has spread,
His first sweet evening yellow.

Books! 'tis a dull and endless strife;
Come hear the woodland linnet –   10

How sweet his music! On my life,
There's more of wisdom in it.

And hark, how blithe the throstle sings!
And he is no mean preacher;
Come forth into the light of things,   15
Let nature be your teacher.

She has a world of ready wealth,
Our minds and hearts to bless –
Spontaneous wisdom breathed by health,
Truth breathed by cheerfulness.   20

One impulse from a vernal wood
May teach you more of man,
Of moral evil and of good
Than all the sages can.

Sweet is the lore which nature brings,   25
Our meddling intellect
Misshapes the beauteous forms of things –
We murder to dissect.

Enough of science and of art,
Close up these barren leaves;   30
Come forth, and bring with you a heart
That watches and receives.

OLD MAN TRAVELLING; ANIMAL TRANQUILLITY AND DECAY, A SKETCH
(BY WORDSWORTH, COMPOSED BY JUNE 1797)

The little hedgerow birds
That peck along the road, regard him not.
He travels on, and in his face, his step,
His gait, is one expression; every limb,
His look and bending figure, all bespeak   5
A man who does not move with pain, but moves
With thought. He is insensibly subdued
To settled quiet; he is one by whom
All effort seems forgotten, one to whom
Long patience has such mild composure given,   10
That patience now doth seem a thing of which
He hath no need. He is by nature led
To peace so perfect that the young behold
With envy what the old man hardly feels.
    I asked him whither he was bound, and what   15
The object of his journey; he replied:
'Sir, I am going many miles to take

A last leave of my son, a mariner,
Who from a sea-fight has been brought to Falmouth,
And there is dying in an hospital.'"   20

THE COMPLAINT OF A FORSAKEN INDIAN WOMAN (BY WORDSWORTH, COMPOSED BETWEEN EARLY MARCH AND 16 MAY 1798)

When a Northern Indian, from sickness, is unable to continue his journey with his companions, he is left behind, covered over with deer-skins, and is supplied with water, food, and fuel, if the situation of the place will afford it. He is informed of the track which his companions intend to pursue, and, if he is unable to follow or overtake them, he perishes alone in the desert (unless he should have the good fortune to fall in with some other tribes of Indians). It is unnecessary to add that the females are equally, or still more, exposed to the same fate; see that very interesting work, Hearne's Journey from Hudson's Bay to the Northern Ocean. *When the Northern Lights (as the same writer informs us) vary their position in the air, they make a rustling and a crackling noise. This circumstance is alluded to in the first stanza of the following poem.*

Before I see another day
Oh let my body die away!
In sleep I heard the northern gleams,¹
The stars they were among my dreams;
In sleep did I behold the skies,   5
I saw the crackling flashes drive,
And yet they are upon my eyes,
And yet I am alive.
Before I see another day
Oh let my body die away!   10

My fire is dead – it knew no pain,
Yet is it dead, and I remain.
All stiff with ice the ashes lie,
And they are dead, and I will die.
When I was well, I wished to live,   15
For clothes, for warmth, for food and fire;
But they to me no joy can give,
No pleasure now, and no desire.
Then here contented will I lie,
Alone I cannot fear to die.   20

Alas, you might have dragged me on
Another day, a single one!
Too soon despair o'er me prevailed,
Too soon my heartless spirit failed;

OLD MAN TRAVELLING
¹ Lines 15–20 were removed from texts of the poem published after 1815.

THE COMPLAINT OF A FORSAKEN INDIAN WOMAN
¹ *northern gleams* northern lights, or aurora borealis.

When you were gone my limbs were stronger –   25
And oh, how grievously I rue
That afterwards, a little longer,
My friends, I did not follow you!
For strong and without pain I lay,
My friends, when you were gone away.   30

My child, they gave thee to another,
A woman who was not thy mother;
When from my arms my babe they took,
On me how strangely did he look!
Through his whole body something ran,   35
A most strange something did I see –
As if he strove to be a man,
That he might pull the sledge for me.
And then he stretched his arms, how wild!
Oh mercy, like a little child!   40

My little joy! My little pride!
In two days more I must have died.
Then do not weep and grieve for me;
I feel I must have died with thee.
Oh wind, that o'er my head art flying   45
The way my friends their course did bend,
I should not feel the pain of dying
Could I with thee a message send.
Too soon, my friends, you went away,
For I had many things to say.   50

I'll follow you across the snow,
You travel heavily and slow;
In spite of all my weary pain,
I'll look upon your tents again.
My fire is dead, and snowy white   55
The water which beside it stood;
The wolf has come to me tonight
And he has stolen away my food.
Forever left alone am I,
Then wherefore should I fear to die?   60

My journey will be shortly run,
I shall not see another sun,
I cannot lift my limbs to know
If they have any life or no.
My poor forsaken child, if I   65
For once could have thee close to me,
With happy heart I then would die
And my last thoughts would happy be.

> I feel my body die away,
> I shall not see another day. 70

THE CONVICT (BY WORDSWORTH, COMPOSED BETWEEN 21 MARCH AND OCTOBER 1796)

The glory of evening was spread through the west –
    On the slope of a mountain I stood;
While the joy that precedes the calm season of rest
    Rang loud through the meadow and wood.

'And must we then part from a dwelling so fair?' 5
    In the pain of my spirit I said,
And with a deep sadness I turned to repair
    To the cell where the convict is laid.

The thick-ribbed walls that o'ershadow the gate
    Resound, and the dungeons unfold; 10
I pause, and at length through the glimmering grate
    That outcast of pity behold.

His black-matted head on his shoulder is bent,
    And deep is the sigh of his breath,
And with steadfast dejection his eyes are intent 15
    On the fetters that link him to death.

'Tis sorrow enough on that visage to gaze,
    That body dismissed from his care;
Yet my fancy has pierced to his heart, and portrays
    More terrible images there. 20

His bones are consumed and his life-blood is dried,
    With wishes the past to undo;
And his crime, through the pains that o'erwhelm him, descried,
    Still blackens and grows on his view.

When from the dark synod[1] or blood-reeking field, 25
    To his chamber the monarch is led,
All soothers of sense their soft virtue shall yield,
    And quietness pillow his head.

But if grief, self-consumed, in oblivion would doze,
    And conscience her tortures appease, 30
Mid tumult and uproar this man must repose
    In the comfortless vault of disease.

THE CONVICT
[1]   synod council, government.

When his fetters at night have so pressed on his limbs
    That the weight can no longer be borne,
If, while a half-slumber his memory bedims,   35
    The wretch on his pallet should turn;

While the jail-mastiff howls at the dull-clanking chain,
    From the roots of his hair there shall start
A thousand sharp punctures of cold-sweating pain,
    And terror shall leap at his heart.   40

But now he half-raises his deep-sunken eye
    And the motion unsettles a tear;
The silence of sorrow it seems to supply,
    And asks of me why I am here.

'Poor victim! No idle intruder has stood   45
    With o'erweening complacence our state to compare –
But one whose first wish is the wish to be good
    Is come as a brother thy sorrows to share.

At thy name, though compassion her nature resign,
    Though in virtue's proud mouth thy report be a stain,   50
My care, if the arm of the mighty were mine,
    Would plant thee where yet thou might'st blossom again.'[2]

LINES WRITTEN A FEW MILES ABOVE TINTERN ABBEY, ON REVISITING THE BANKS OF THE WYE DURING A TOUR, 13 JULY 1798 (BY WORDSWORTH, COMPOSED 10–13 JULY 1798)

Five years have passed; five summers, with the length
Of five long winters![1] And again I hear
These waters, rolling from their mountain springs
With a sweet inland murmur.[2] Once again
Do I behold these steep and lofty cliffs,   5
Which on a wild secluded scene impress
Thoughts of more deep seclusion, and connect
The landscape with the quiet of the sky.[3]
The day is come when I again repose
Here, under this dark sycamore, and view   10
These plots of cottage-ground, these orchard-tufts,
Which, at this season, with their unripe fruits,

---

[2] Wordsworth pleads for the humane transportation of convicts.

TINTERN ABBEY

[1] Wordsworth's first visit to the Wye was in Aug. 1793; he returned 10–13 July 1798.

[2] 'The river is not affected by the tides a few miles above Tintern' (Wordsworth's note).

[3] William Gilpin, *Observations on the River Wye* (1782): 'Many of the furnaces on the banks of the river consume charcoal which is manufactured on the spot, and the smoke (which is frequently seen issuing from the sides of the hills, and spreading its thin veil over a part of them) beautifully breaks their lines, and unites them with the sky' (p. 12).

Among the woods and copses lose themselves,
Nor, with their green and simple hue, disturb
The wild green landscape. Once again I see   15
These hedgerows – hardly hedgerows, little lines
Of sportive wood run wild; these pastoral farms
Green to the very door; and wreaths of smoke
Sent up in silence from among the trees,
With some uncertain notice, as might seem,   20
Of vagrant dwellers in the houseless woods,
Or of some hermit's cave, where by his fire
The hermit sits alone.
                              Though absent long,
These forms of beauty have not been to me
As is a landscape to a blind man's eye;   25
But oft, in lonely rooms, and mid the din
Of towns and cities, I have owed to them,
In hours of weariness, sensations sweet,
Felt in the blood, and felt along the heart,
And passing even into my purer mind   30
With tranquil restoration; feelings too
Of unremembered pleasure – such, perhaps,
As may have had no trivial influence
On that best portion of a good man's life,
His little, nameless, unremembered acts   35
Of kindness and of love. Nor less, I trust,
To them I may have owed another gift,
Of aspect more sublime; that blessed mood
In which the burden of the mystery,
In which the heavy and the weary weight   40
Of all this unintelligible world
Is lightened – that serene and blessed mood
In which the affections gently lead us on
Until the breath of this corporeal frame
And even the motion of our human blood   45
Almost suspended, we are laid asleep
In body, and become a living soul;
While with an eye made quiet by the power
Of harmony, and the deep power of joy,
We see into the life of things.   50
                                    If this
Be but a vain belief – yet oh, how oft
In darkness, and amid the many shapes
Of joyless daylight, when the fretful stir
Unprofitable, and the fever of the world,
Have hung upon the beatings of my heart,   55
How oft, in spirit, have I turned to thee
Oh sylvan Wye! Thou wanderer through the woods,
How often has my spirit turned to thee!

And now, with gleams of half-extinguished thought,
With many recognitions dim and faint   60
And somewhat of a sad perplexity,
The picture of the mind revives again;
While here I stand, not only with the sense
Of present pleasure, but with pleasing thoughts
That in this moment there is life and food   65
For future years. And so I dare to hope,
Though changed, no doubt, from what I was when first
I came among these hills, when like a roe
I bounded o'er the mountains by the sides
Of the deep rivers and the lonely streams   70
Wherever nature led, more like a man
Flying from something that he dreads than one
Who sought the thing he loved. For nature then
(The coarser pleasures of my boyish days
And their glad animal movements all gone by)   75
To me was all in all.
             I cannot paint
What then I was. The sounding cataract
Haunted me like a passion; the tall rock,
The mountain, and the deep and gloomy wood,
Their colours and their forms, were then to me   80
An appetite, a feeling and a love
That had no need of a remoter charm
By thought supplied, or any interest
Unborrowed from the eye. That time is past,
And all its aching joys are now no more,   85
And all its dizzy raptures. Not for this
Faint I, nor mourn, nor murmur; other gifts
Have followed – for such loss, I would believe,
Abundant recompense. For I have learned
To look on nature not as in the hour   90
Of thoughtless youth, but hearing oftentimes
The still sad music of humanity,
Not harsh nor grating, though of ample power
To chasten and subdue. And I have felt
A presence that disturbs me with the joy   95
Of elevated thoughts, a sense sublime
Of something far more deeply interfused,
Whose dwelling is the light of setting suns,
And the round ocean, and the living air,
And the blue sky, and in the mind of man –   100
A motion and a spirit that impels
All thinking things, all objects of all thought,
And rolls through all things. Therefore am I still
A lover of the meadows and the woods
And mountains, and of all that we behold   105

From this green earth, of all the mighty world
Of eye and ear (both what they half-create[4]
And what perceive) – well-pleased to recognize
In nature and the language of the sense,
The anchor of my purest thoughts, the nurse,   110
The guide, the guardian of my heart, and soul
Of all my moral being.
                                   Nor, perchance,
If I were not thus taught, should I the more
Suffer my genial spirits to decay;
For thou art with me, here, upon the banks   115
Of this fair river – thou, my dearest friend,
My dear, dear friend, and in thy voice I catch
The language of my former heart, and read
My former pleasures in the shooting lights
Of thy wild eyes. Oh, yet a little while   120
May I behold in thee what I was once,
My dear, dear sister! And this prayer I make,
Knowing that nature never did betray
The heart that loved her; 'tis her privilege,
Through all the years of this our life, to lead   125
From joy to joy, for she can so inform
The mind that is within us, so impress
With quietness and beauty, and so feed
With lofty thoughts, that neither evil tongues,[5]
Rash judgements, nor the sneers of selfish men,   130
Nor greetings where no kindness is, nor all
The dreary intercourse of daily life,
Shall e'er prevail against us, or disturb
Our cheerful faith that all which we behold
Is full of blessings. Therefore let the moon   135
Shine on thee in thy solitary walk,
And let the misty mountain-winds be free
To blow against thee. And in after-years,
When these wild ecstasies shall be matured
Into a sober pleasure, when thy mind   140
Shall be a mansion for all lovely forms,
Thy memory be as a dwelling-place
For all sweet sounds and harmonies – oh then
If solitude, or fear, or pain, or grief
Should be thy portion, with what healing thoughts   145
Of tender joy wilt thou remember me,
And these my exhortations! Nor perchance,
If I should be where I no more can hear

---

[4] Wordsworth notes a borrowing from Young,   [5] *evil tongues* Paradise Lost, vii. 26.
Night Thoughts, vi. 424: 'And half-create the wondrous
world they [the senses] see'.

Thy voice, nor catch from thy wild eyes these gleams
Of past existence, wilt thou then forget 150
That on the banks of this delightful stream
We stood together; and that I, so long
A worshipper of nature, hither came
Unwearied in that service — rather say
With warmer love, oh with far deeper zeal 155
Of holier love! Nor wilt thou then forget
That, after many wanderings, many years
Of absence, these steep woods and lofty cliffs
And this green pastoral landscape, were to me
More dear, both for themselves, and for thy sake. 160

From Lyrical Ballads (2nd ed., 2 vols., 1800)

STRANGE FITS OF PASSION I HAVE KNOWN (COMPOSED BETWEEN 6 OCTOBER AND 28 DECEMBER 1798)[1]

Strange fits of passion I have known,
And I will dare to tell,
But in the lover's ear alone,
What once to me befell.

When she I loved was strong and gay 5
And like a rose in June,
I to her cottage bent my way
Beneath the evening moon.

Upon the moon I fixed my eye,
All over the wide lea; 10
My horse trudged on, and we drew nigh
Those paths so dear to me.

And now we reached the orchard-plot,
And as we climbed the hill,
Towards the roof of Lucy's cot 15
The moon descended still.

In one of those sweet dreams I slept,
Kind nature's gentlest boon!
And all the while my eyes I kept
On the descending moon. 20

My horse moved on; hoof after hoof
He raised and never stopped:

STRANGE FITS OF PASSION I HAVE KNOWN
[1] For Coleridge on the Lucy poems, see his letter to
Poole, 6 Apr. 1799, p. 526.

When down behind the cottage roof
At once the planet dropped.

What fond and wayward thoughts will slide   25
Into a lover's head;
'Oh mercy!' to myself I cried,
'If Lucy should be dead!'

SONG (COMPOSED BETWEEN 6 OCTOBER AND 28 DECEMBER 1798)

She dwelt among th' untrodden ways
    Beside the springs of Dove,
A maid whom there were none to praise
    And very few to love.

A violet by a mossy stone   5
    Half-hidden from the eye!
Fair as a star when only one
    Is shining in the sky!

She *lived* unknown, and few could know
    When Lucy ceased to be;   10
But she is in her grave, and oh!
    The difference to me.

A SLUMBER DID MY SPIRIT SEAL (COMPOSED BETWEEN 6 OCTOBER AND 28 DECEMBER 1798)

A slumber did my spirit seal,
    I had no human fears;
She seemed a thing that could not feel
    The touch of earthly years.

No motion has she now, no force;   5
    She neither hears nor sees;
Rolled round in earth's diurnal course
    With rocks and stones and trees!

THREE YEARS SHE GREW IN SUN AND SHOWER (COMPOSED BETWEEN 6 OCTOBER AND 28 DECEMBER 1798)

Three years she grew in sun and shower,
Then Nature said, 'A lovelier flower
On earth was never sown;
This child I to myself will take,
She shall be mine, and I will make   5
A lady of my own.

Myself will to my darling be
Both law and impulse, and with me

The girl in rock and plain,
In earth and heaven, in glade and bower,   10
Shall feel an overseeing power
To kindle or restrain.

She shall be sportive as the fawn
That wild with glee across the lawn
Or up the mountain springs,   15
And hers shall be the breathing balm
And hers the silence and the calm
Of mute insensate things.

The floating clouds their state shall lend
To her, for her the willow bend,   20
Nor shall she fail to see
Even in the motions of the storm
A beauty that shall mould her form
By silent sympathy.

The stars of midnight shall be dear   25
To her, and she shall lean her ear
In many a secret place
Where rivulets dance their wayward round,
And beauty born of murmuring sound
Shall pass into her face.   30

And vital feelings of delight
Shall rear her form to stately height,
Her virgin bosom swell,
Such thoughts to Lucy I will give
While she and I together live   35
Here in this happy dell.'

Thus Nature spake – the work was done –
How soon my Lucy's race was run!
She died and left to me
This heath, this calm and quiet scene,   40
The memory of what has been,
And never more will be.

Prospectus to 'The Recluse' (composed probably spring 1800; edited from MS)

On man, on nature, and on human life,
Thinking in solitude, from time to time
I find sweet passions traversing my soul
Like music; unto these, where'er I may,
I would give utterance in numerous verse.   5

Of truth, of grandeur, beauty, love, and hope,
Of joy in various commonalty spread,
Of th' individual mind that keeps its own
Inviolate retirement, and consists
With being limitless – the one great life –   10
I sing: fit audience let me find, though few.
    'Fit audience find, though few!' Thus prayed the bard,
Holiest of men.[1] Urania,[2] I shall need
Thy guidance, or a greater muse (if such
Descend to earth, or dwell in highest heaven),   15
For I must tread on shadowy ground, must sink
Deep, and ascend aloft, and breathe in worlds
To which the heaven of heavens[3] is but a veil.
All strength, all terror, single, or in bands,
That ever was put forth by personal forms –   20
Jehovah with his thunder, and the choir
Of shouting angels, and th' empyreal thrones –
I pass them unalarmed. The darkest pit
Of the profoundest hell, night, chaos, death,
Nor aught of blinder vacancy scooped out   25
By help of dreams, can breed such fear and awe
As fall upon me often when I look
Into my soul, into the soul of man –
My haunt, and the main region of my song.
    Beauty, whose living home is the green earth,   30
Surpassing far what hath by special craft
Of delicate poets been culled forth and shaped
From earth's materials, waits upon my steps,
Pitches her tents before me as I move,
My hourly neighbour. Paradise and groves   35
Elysian, blessed islands in the deep
Of choice seclusion – wherefore need they be
A history, or but a dream, when minds
Once wedded to this outward frame of things
In love, finds these the growth of common day?   40
    Such pleasant haunts foregoing, if my song
Must turn elsewhere, and travel near the tribes
And fellowships of man, and see ill sights
Of passions ravenous from each other's rage,
Insult and injury, and wrong and strife;   45
Must hear humanity in fields and groves
Pipe solitary anguish; or must hang
Brooding above the fierce confederate[4] storm

PROSPECTUS TO 'THE RECLUSE'
[1] *Paradise Lost*, vii. 31.
[2] Urania, Muse of astronomy, is invoked by Milton,
Paradise Lost, Book vii.
[3] Ibid., vii. 553.
[4] *confederate* leagued, allied.

Of sorrow, barricadoed[5] evermore
Within the walls of cities, to these sounds   50
Let me find meaning more akin to that
Which to God's ear they carry, that even these
Hearing, I be not heartless or forlorn.
    Come thou, prophetic spirit, soul of man,
Thou human soul of the wide earth, that hast   55
Thy metropolitan temple in the hearts
Of mighty poets, unto me vouchsafe
Thy foresight, teach me to discern, and part
Inherent things from casual, what is fixed
From fleeting, that my soul may live, and be   60
Even as a light hung up in heaven to cheer
The world in times to come. And if with this
I mingle humbler matter – with the thing
Contemplated describe the mind and man
Contemplating, and who he was, and what   65
The transitory being that beheld
This vision, when and where and how he lived
With all his little realities of life
(In part a fellow-citizen, in part
An outlaw, and a borderer of his age) –   70
Be not this labour useless.
               Oh great God!
To less than thee I cannot make this prayer;
Innocent mighty spirit, let my life
Express the image of a better time,
Desires more wise and simpler manners, nurse   75
My heart in genuine freedom, all pure thoughts
Be with me and uphold me to the end.

From Lyrical Ballads (2nd ed., 2 vols., 1800)

Note to 'The Thorn' (composed late September 1800) (i 211–14)

This poem ought to have been preceded by an introductory poem which I have been
prevented from writing by never having felt myself in a mood when it was probable
that I should write it well.

    The character which I have here introduced speaking is sufficiently common. The
reader will perhaps have a general notion of it if he has ever known a man (a captain
of a small trading vessel, for example)[1] who, being past the middle age of life, had
retired upon an annuity or small independent income to some village or country town
of which he was not a native, or in which he had not been accustomed to live. Such

---

5 Cf. *Paradise Lost*, viii. 241.
Note to 'The Thorn'
1 The telescope at line 181 of the poem supports
this suggestion.

men, having little to do, become credulous and talkative from indolence. And from the same cause (and other predisposing causes by which it is probable that such men may have been affected) they are prone to superstition. On which account it appeared to me proper to select a character like this to exhibit some of the general laws by which superstition acts upon the mind. Superstitious men are almost always men of slow faculties and deep feelings. Their minds are not loose but adhesive.[2] They have a reasonable share of imagination, by which word I mean the faculty which produces impressive effects out of simple elements. But they are utterly destitute of fancy – the power by which pleasure and surprise are excited by sudden varieties of situation and by accumulated imagery.

It was my wish in this poem to show the manner in which such men cleave to the same ideas, and to follow the turns of passion (always different, yet not palpably different) by which their conversation is swayed. I had two objects to attain: first, to represent a picture which should not be unimpressive, yet consistent with the character that should describe it; secondly (while I adhered to the style in which such persons describe), to take care that words – which in their minds are impregnated with passion – should likewise convey passion to readers who are not accustomed to sympathize with men feeling in that manner, or using such language. It seemed to me that this might be done by calling in the assistance of lyrical and rapid metre. It was necessary that the poem, to be natural, should in reality move slowly. Yet I hoped that by the aid of the metre, to those who should at all enter into the spirit of the poem, it would appear to move quickly. (The reader will have the kindness to excuse this note, as I am sensible that an introductory poem is necessary to give this poem its full effect.)

Upon this occasion I will request permission to add a few words closely connected with 'The Thorn', and many other poems in these volumes. There is a numerous class of readers who imagine that the same words cannot be repeated without tautology. This is a great error. Virtual tautology is much oftener produced by using different words when the meaning is exactly the same. Words – a poet's words more particularly – ought to be weighed in the balance of feeling, and not measured by the space which they occupy upon paper. For the reader cannot be too often reminded that poetry is passion: it is the history or science of feelings. Now every man must know that an attempt is rarely made to communicate impassioned feelings without something of an accompanying consciousness of the inadequateness of our own powers, or the deficiencies of language. During such efforts there will be a craving in the mind, and as long as it is unsatisfied the speaker will cling to the same words, or words of the same character.

There are also various other reasons why repetition and apparent tautology are frequently beauties of the highest kind. Among the chief of these reasons is the interest which the mind attaches to words not only as symbols of the passion, but as *things*, active and efficient, which are of themselves part of the passion. And further, from a spirit of fondness, exultation, and gratitude, the mind luxuriates in the repetition of words which appear successfully to communicate its feelings.

The truth of these remarks might be shown by innumerable passages from the Bible, and from the impassioned poetry of every nation.

---

[2] *adhesive* persevering, obsessive.

Awake, awake, Deborah! Awake, awake, utter a song! Arise, Barak, and lead thy captivity captive, thou son of Abinoam!

At her feet he bowed, he fell, he lay down. At her feet he bowed, he fell. Where he bowed, there he fell down dead.

Why is his chariot so long in coming? Why tarry the wheels of his chariot?
(Judges 5: 12, 27, and part of 28; see also the whole of that tumultuous and wonderful poem)

From Poems in Two Volumes (1807)

I TRAVELLED AMONG UNKNOWN MEN (COMPOSED *C.*29 APRIL 1801)

I travelled among unknown men
In lands beyond the sea;
Nor, England, did I know till then
What love I bore to thee.

'Tis past, that melancholy dream!   5
Nor will I quit thy shore
A second time, for still I seem
To love thee more and more.

Among thy mountains did I feel
The joy of my desire;   10
And she I cherished turned her wheel
Beside an English fire.

Thy mornings showed, thy nights concealed
The bowers where Lucy played;
And thine is, too, the last green field   15
Which Lucy's eyes surveyed!

From Lyrical Ballads (2 vols., 1802)

PREFACE[1]

The first volume of these poems has already been submitted to general perusal. It was published as an experiment which, I hoped, might be of some use to ascertain how far, by fitting to metrical arrangement a selection of the real language[2] of men in a state of vivid sensation, that sort of pleasure and that quantity of pleasure may be imparted which a poet may rationally endeavour to impart.

PREFACE
[1] Though first published in 1800, the Preface was revised and expanded for the 1802 edn of *Lyrical Ballads*. This second version is presented here, with its important additions; it was complete in this form by 6 Apr. 1802. It was written at Coleridge's insistence,

and drew on ideas conceived or gathered by Coleridge; as Coleridge told Southey in a letter of 29 July 1802, 'Wordsworth's Preface is half a child of my own brain' (Griggs, ii. 830).
[2] *language* idiom, way of speaking.

I had formed no very inaccurate estimate of the probable effect of those poems. I flattered myself that they who should be pleased with them would read them with more than common pleasure, and on the other hand, I was well aware that by those who should dislike them they would be read with more than common dislike. The result has differed from my expectation in this only: that I have pleased a greater number than I ventured to hope I should please.

For the sake of variety, and from a consciousness of my own weakness, I was induced to request the assistance of a friend who furnished me with the poems of 'The Ancient Mariner', 'The Foster Mother's Tale', 'The Nightingale' and the poem entitled 'Love'.[3] I should not however have requested this assistance had I not believed that the poems of my friend would in a great measure have the same tendency as my own, and that though there would be found a difference, there would be found no discordance in the colours of our style, as our opinions on the subject of poetry do almost entirely coincide.

Several of my friends are anxious for the success of these poems from a belief that, if the views with which they were composed were indeed realised, a class of poetry would be produced well adapted to interest mankind permanently, and not unimportant in the multiplicity and in the quality of its moral relations. And on this account they have advised me to prefix a systematic defence of the theory upon which the poems were written.[4]

But I was unwilling to undertake the task because I knew that on this occasion the reader would look coldly upon my arguments, since I might be suspected of having been principally influenced by the selfish and foolish hope of reasoning him into an approbation of these particular poems. And I was still more unwilling to undertake the task because adequately to display my opinions, and fully to enforce my arguments, would require a space wholly disproportionate to the nature of a preface. For to treat the subject with the clearness and coherence of which I believe it susceptible, it would be necessary to give a full account of the present state of the public taste in this country, and to determine how far this taste is healthy or depraved – which again could not be determined without pointing out in what manner language and the human mind act and react on each other, and without retracing the revolutions not of literature alone but likewise of society itself. I have therefore altogether declined to enter regularly upon this defence, yet I am sensible that there would be some impropriety in abruptly obtruding upon the public, without a few words of introduction, poems so materially different from those upon which general approbation is at present bestowed.

It is supposed that by the act of writing in verse, an author makes a formal engagement that he will gratify certain known habits of association, that he not only thus apprises the reader that certain classes of ideas and expressions will be found in his book, but that others will be carefully excluded. This exponent or symbol held forth by metrical language must in different eras of literature have excited very different expectations – for example, in the age of Catullus, Terence, and Lucretius, and that of Statius or Claudian; and, in our own country, in the age of Shakespeare and Beaumont and Fletcher, and that of Donne and Cowley, or Dryden, or Pope.

---

[3] Coleridge's 'Love' was added to *Lyrical Ballads* (1800).
[4] Years later, Wordsworth recalled: 'I never cared a straw about the theory. And the Preface was written at the request of Coleridge, out of sheer good nature.

I recollect the very spot, a deserted quarry in the vale of Grasmere, where he pressed the thing upon me. And but for that it would never have been thought of' (BL, Add. MS 41325, 111v).

I will not take upon me to determine the exact import of the promise which, by the act of writing in verse, an author in the present day makes to his reader, but I am certain it will appear to many persons that I have not fulfilled the terms of an engagement thus voluntarily contracted. They who have been accustomed to the gaudiness and inane phraseology of many modern writers, if they persist in reading this book to its conclusion, will no doubt frequently have to struggle with feelings of strangeness and awkwardness. They will look round for poetry and will be induced to enquire by what species of courtesy these attempts can be permitted to assume that title. I hope, therefore, the reader will not censure me if I attempt to state what I have proposed to myself to perform, and also (as far as the limits of a preface will permit) to explain some of the chief reasons which have determined me in the choice of my purpose, that at least he may be spared any unpleasant feeling of disappointment, and that I myself may be protected from the most dishonourable accusation which can be brought against an author – namely, that of an indolence which prevents him from endeavouring to ascertain what is his duty, or, when his duty is ascertained, prevents him from performing it.

The principal object, then, which I proposed to myself in these poems, was to choose incidents and situations from common life, and to relate or describe them throughout, as far as was possible, in a selection of language really used by men, and at the same time to throw over them a certain colouring of imagination, whereby ordinary things should be presented to the mind in an unusual way. And further, and above all, to make these incidents and situations interesting by tracing in them (truly, though not ostentatiously) the primary laws of our nature, chiefly as far as regards the manner in which we associate ideas in a state of excitement.

Low and rustic life was generally chosen because in that condition the essential passions of the heart find a better soil in which they can attain their maturity, are less under restraint, and speak a plainer and more emphatic language; because in that condition of life our elementary feelings coexist in a state of greater simplicity, and consequently may be more accurately contemplated and more forcibly communicated; because the manners of rural life germinate from those elementary feelings, and (from the necessary character of rural occupations) are more easily comprehended and are more durable; and, lastly, because in that condition the passions of men are incorporated with the beautiful and permanent forms of nature.

The language, too, of these men is adopted (purified indeed from what appear to be its real defects – from all lasting and rational causes of dislike or disgust) because such men hourly communicate with the best objects from which the best part of language is originally derived, and because, from their rank in society and the sameness and narrow circle of their intercourse being less under the influence of social vanity, they convey their feelings and notions in simple and unelaborated expressions. Accordingly, such a language, arising out of repeated experience and regular feelings, is a more permanent and a far more philosophical language than that which is frequently substituted for it by poets who think that they are conferring honour upon themselves and their art, in proportion as they separate themselves from the sympathies of men and indulge in arbitrary and capricious habits of expression, in order to furnish food for fickle tastes and fickle appetites of their own creation.[5]

---

[5] 'It is worthwhile here to observe that the affecting parts of Chaucer are almost always expressed in language pure and universally intelligible even to this day' (Wordsworth's note).

I cannot, however, be insensible to the present outcry against the triviality and meanness both of thought and language which some of my contemporaries have occasionally introduced into their metrical compositions. And I acknowledge that this defect, where it exists, is more dishonourable to the writer's own character than false refinement or arbitrary innovation (though I should contend at the same time that it is far less pernicious in the sum of its consequences).

From such verses the poems in these volumes will be found distinguished at least by one mark of difference – that each of them has a worthy purpose. Not that I mean to say that I always began to write with a distinct purpose formally conceived, but I believe that my habits of meditation have so formed my feelings, as that my descriptions of such objects as strongly excite those feelings will be found to carry along with them a purpose. If in this opinion I am mistaken, I can have little right to the name of a poet; for all good poetry is the spontaneous overflow of powerful feelings. But though this be true, poems to which any value can be attached were never produced on any variety of subjects but by a man who, being possessed of more than usual organic[6] sensibility, had also thought long and deeply. For our continued influxes of feeling are modified and directed by our thoughts, which are indeed the representatives of all our past feelings. And, as by contemplating the relation of these general representatives to each other we discover what is really important to men, so, by the repetition and continuance of this act, our feelings will be connected with important subjects. Till at length (if we be originally possessed of much sensibility) such habits of mind will be produced that, by obeying blindly and mechanically the impulses of those habits, we shall describe objects and utter sentiments of such a nature, and in such connection with each other, that the understanding of the being to whom we address ourselves – if he be in a healthful state of association – must necessarily be in some degree enlightened, and his affections ameliorated.

I have said that each of these poems has a purpose. I have also informed my reader what this purpose will be found principally to be; namely, to illustrate the manner in which our feelings and ideas are associated in a state of excitement. But (speaking in language somewhat more appropriate) it is to follow the fluxes and refluxes of the mind when agitated by the great and simple affections of our nature. This object I have endeavoured in these short essays to attain by various means: by tracing the maternal passion through many of its more subtle windings (as in the poems of 'The Idiot Boy' and 'The Mad Mother'); by accompanying the last struggles of a human being at the approach of death, cleaving in solitude to life and society (as in the poem of the forsaken Indian); by showing, as in the stanzas entitled 'We are Seven', the perplexity and obscurity which in childhood attend our notion of death – or rather our utter inability to admit that notion; or by displaying the strength of fraternal or (to speak more philosophically) of moral attachment when early associated with the great and beautiful objects of nature (as in 'The Brothers'); or, as in the incident of 'Simon Lee', by placing my reader in the way of receiving from ordinary moral sensations another and more salutary impression than we are accustomed to receive from them.

It has also been part of my general purpose to attempt to sketch characters under the influence of less impassioned feelings (as in 'The Two April Mornings', 'The Fountain', the 'Old Man Travelling', 'The Two Thieves', etc.); characters of which the

---

[6] *organic* innate, inherent.

elements are simple, belonging rather to nature than to manners, such as exist now and will probably always exist, and which from their constitution may be distinctly and profitably contemplated.

I will not abuse the indulgence of my reader by dwelling longer upon this subject, but it is proper that I should mention one other circumstance which distinguishes these poems from the popular poetry of the day. It is this – that the feeling therein developed gives importance to the action and situation, and not the action and situation to the feeling. My meaning will be rendered perfectly intelligible by referring my reader to the poems entitled 'Poor Susan' and 'The Childless Father' (particularly to the last stanza of the latter poem).

I will not suffer a sense of false modesty to prevent me from asserting that I point my reader's attention to this mark of distinction far less for the sake of these particular poems than from the general importance of the subject. The subject is indeed important! For the human mind is capable of being excited without the application of gross and violent stimulants, and he must have a very faint perception of its beauty and dignity who does not know this, and who does not further know that one being is elevated above another in proportion as he possesses this capability.

It has therefore appeared to me that to endeavour to produce or enlarge this capability is one of the best services in which (at any period) a writer can be engaged – but this service, excellent at all times, is especially so at the present day. For a multitude of causes, unknown to former times, are now acting with a combined force to blunt the discriminating powers of the mind and, unfitting it for all voluntary exertion, to reduce it to a state of almost savage torpor. The most effective of these causes are the great national events[7] which are daily taking place, and the increasing accumulation of men in cities, where the uniformity of their occupations produces a craving for extraordinary incident, which the rapid communication[8] of intelligence hourly gratifies. To this tendency of life and manners the literature and theatrical exhibitions of the country have conformed themselves. The invaluable works of our elder writers (I had almost said the works of Shakespeare and Milton) are driven into neglect by frantic novels, sickly and stupid German tragedies, and deluges of idle and extravagant stories in verse.[9]

When I think upon this degrading thirst after outrageous stimulation, I am almost ashamed to have spoken of the feeble effort with which I have endeavoured to counteract it. And, reflecting upon the magnitude of the general evil, I should be oppressed with no dishonourable melancholy had I not a deep impression of certain inherent and indestructible qualities of the human mind (and likewise of certain powers in the great and permanent objects that act upon it which are equally inherent and indestructible), and did I not further add to this impression a belief that the time is approaching when the evil will be systematically opposed by men of greater powers and with far more distinguished success.

Having dwelt thus long on the subjects and aim of these poems, I shall request the reader's permission to apprise him of a few circumstances relating to their style, in order (among other reasons) that I may not be censured for not having performed what I never attempted. The reader will find that personifications of abstract ideas rarely occur in these volumes, and I hope are utterly rejected as an ordinary device to elevate

---

[7] *national events* Britain had been at war with France since 1793.
[8] *rapid communication* the telegraph and the stage-coach.
[9] Gothic novels and plays by sentimental writers like Kotzebue were popular at this time.

the style and raise it above prose. I have proposed to myself to imitate – and as far as is possible, to adopt – the very language of men, and assuredly such personifications do not make any natural or regular part of that language. They are, indeed, a figure of speech occasionally prompted by passion (and I have made use of them as such), but I have endeavoured utterly to reject them as a mechanical device of style or as a family language which writers in metre seem to lay claim to by prescription. I have wished to keep my reader in the company of flesh and blood, persuaded that by so doing I shall interest him. I am, however, well aware that others who pursue a different track may interest him likewise. I do not interfere with their claim; I only wish to prefer a different claim of my own.

There will also be found in these volumes little of what is usually called poetic diction: I have taken as much pains to avoid it as others ordinarily take to produce it. This I have done for the reason already alleged – to bring my language near to the language of men, and, further, because the pleasure which I have proposed to myself to impart is of a kind very different from that which is supposed by many persons to be the proper object of poetry. I do not know how, without being culpably particular, I can give my reader a more exact notion of the style in which I wished these poems to be written than by informing him that I have at all times endeavoured to look steadily at my subject. Consequently, I hope that there is in these poems little falsehood of description, and that my ideas are expressed in language fitted to their respective importance.

Something I must have gained by this practice, as it is friendly to one property of all good poetry – namely, good sense. But it has necessarily cut me off from a large portion of phrases and figures of speech which, from father to son, have long been regarded as the common inheritance of poets. I have also thought it expedient to restrict myself still further, having abstained from the use of many expressions in themselves proper and beautiful, but which have been foolishly repeated by bad poets till such feelings of disgust are connected with them as it is scarcely possible by any art of association to overpower.

If in a poem there should be found a series of lines (or even a single line) in which the language, though naturally arranged and according to the strict laws of metre, does not differ from that of prose, there is a numerous class of critics who, when they stumble upon these 'prosaisms' (as they call them), imagine that they have made a notable discovery and exult over the poet as over a man ignorant of his own profession. Now these men would establish a canon of criticism which the reader will conclude he must utterly reject if he wishes to be pleased with these volumes. And it would be a most easy task to prove to him that not only the language of a large portion of every good poem, even of the most elevated character, must necessarily (except with reference to the metre) in no respect differ from that of good prose, but likewise that some of the most interesting parts of the best poems will be found to be strictly the language of prose, when prose is well-written.

The truth of this assertion might be demonstrated by innumerable passages from almost all the poetical writings – even of Milton himself. I have not space for much quotation, but to illustrate the subject in a general manner I will here adduce a short composition of Gray, who was at the head of those who, by their reasonings, have attempted to widen the space of separation betwixt prose and metrical composition, and was, more than any other man, curiously elaborate in the structure of his own poetic diction.

SONNET ON THE DEATH OF RICHARD WEST

In vain to me the smiling mornings shine,
And reddening Phoebus lifts his golden fire;
The birds in vain their amorous descant join,
Or cheerful fields resume their green attire.
These ears, alas, for other notes repine;
A different object do these eyes require –
My lonely anguish melts no heart but mine
And in my breast the imperfect joys expire.
Yet morning smiles the busy race to cheer
And new-born pleasure brings to happier men,
The fields to all their wonted tribute bear,
To warm their little loves the birds complain.
I fruitless mourn to him that cannot hear,
And weep the more because I weep in vain.

It will easily be perceived that the only part of this sonnet which is of any value is the
lines printed in italics. It is equally obvious that, except in the rhyme and in the use of
the single word 'fruitless' for 'fruitlessly' (which is so far a defect), the language of these
lines does in no respect differ from that of prose.

By the foregoing quotation I have shown that the language of prose may yet be well
adapted to poetry, and I have previously asserted that a large portion of the language
of every good poem can in no respect differ from that of good prose. I will go further.
I do not doubt that it may be safely affirmed that there neither is, nor can be, any
essential difference between the language of prose and metrical composition. We are
fond of tracing the resemblance between poetry and painting, and accordingly we call
them sisters – but where shall we find bonds of connection sufficiently strict to typify
the affinity betwixt metrical and prose composition? They both speak by and to the
same organs; the bodies in which both of them are clothed may be said to be of the
same substance; their affections are kindred, and almost identical (not necessarily
differing even in degree). Poetry[10] sheds no tears 'such as angels weep',[11] but natural and
human tears. She can boast of no celestial ichor[12] that distinguishes her vital juices from
those of prose – the same human blood circulates through the veins of them both.

If it be affirmed that rhyme and metrical arrangement of themselves constitute a
distinction which overturns what I have been saying on the strict affinity of metrical
language with that of prose, and paves the way for other artificial distinctions which
the mind voluntarily admits, I answer that the language of such poetry as I am
recommending is, as far as is possible, a selection of the language really spoken by men;
that this selection, wherever it is made with true taste and feeling, will of itself form a
distinction far greater than would at first be imagined, and will entirely separate the

---

[10] 'I here use the word "poetry" (though against my
own judgement) as opposed to the word "prose", and
synonymous with metrical composition. But much
confusion has been introduced into criticism by this
contradistinction of poetry and prose, instead of the
more philosophical one of poetry and matter of fact,
or science. The only strict antithesis to prose is metre
– nor is this, in truth, a strict antithesis, because lines
and passages of metre so naturally occur in writing
prose, that it would be scarcely possible to avoid
them, even were it desirable' (Wordsworth's note).

[11] *Paradise Lost*, i. 620.

[12] *ichor* the divine fluid said to flow like blood
through the veins of the gods.

composition from the vulgarity and meanness of ordinary life; and if metre be superadded thereto, I believe that a dissimilitude will be produced altogether sufficient for the gratification of a rational mind.

What other distinction would we have? Whence is it to come? And where is it to exist? Not, surely, where the poet speaks through the mouths of his characters – it cannot be necessary here, either for elevation of style or any of its supposed ornaments. For if the poet's subject be judiciously chosen, it will naturally, and upon fit occasion, lead him to passions the language of which (if selected truly and judiciously) must necessarily be dignified and variegated, and alive with metaphors and figures. I forbear to speak of an incongruity which would shock the intelligent reader, should the poet interweave any foreign splendour of his own with that which the passion naturally suggests; it is sufficient to say that such addition is unnecessary. And surely it is more probable that those passages, which with propriety abound with metaphors and figures, will have their due effect if, upon other occasions where the passions are of a milder character, the style also be subdued and temperate.

But as the pleasure which I hope to give by the poems I now present to the reader must depend entirely on just notions upon this subject and, as it is in itself of the highest importance to our taste and moral feelings, I cannot content myself with these detached remarks. And if, in what I am about to say, it shall appear to some that my labour is unnecessary, and that I am like a man fighting a battle without enemies, I would remind such persons that whatever may be the language outwardly holden by men, a practical faith in the opinions which I am wishing to establish is almost unknown. If my conclusions are admitted and carried as far as they must be carried if admitted at all, our judgements concerning the works of the greatest poets both ancient and modern will be far different from what they are at present – both when we praise and when we censure – and our moral feelings influencing and influenced by these judgements will, I believe, be corrected and purified.

Taking up the subject, then, upon general grounds, I ask what is meant by the word poet? What is a poet? To whom does he address himself? And what language is to be expected from him? He is a man speaking to men – a man (it is true) endued with more lively sensibility, more enthusiasm and tenderness, who has a greater knowledge of human nature, and a more comprehensive soul, than are supposed to be common among mankind; a man pleased with his own passions and volitions, and who rejoices more than other men in the spirit of life that is in him, delighting to contemplate similar volitions and passions as manifested in the goings-on of the universe, and habitually impelled to create them where he does not find them.

To these qualities he has added a disposition to be affected more than other men by absent things as if they were present, an ability of conjuring up in himself passions which are indeed far from being the same as those produced by real events, yet (especially in those parts of the general sympathy which are pleasing and delightful) do more nearly resemble the passions produced by real events than anything which, from the motions of their own minds merely, other men are accustomed to feel in themselves – whence, and from practice, he has acquired a greater readiness and power in expressing what he thinks and feels, and especially those thoughts and feelings which, by his own choice, or from the structure of his own mind, arise in him without immediate external excitement.

But whatever portion of this faculty we may suppose even the greatest poet to possess, there cannot be a doubt but that the language which it will suggest to him must in liveliness and truth fall far short of that which is uttered by men in real life under the actual pressure of those passions – certain shadows of which the poet thus produces, or feels to be produced, in himself.

However exalted a notion we would wish to cherish of the character of a poet, it is obvious that, while he describes and imitates passions, his situation is altogether slavish and mechanical compared with the freedom and power of real and substantial action and suffering. So that it will be the wish of the poet to bring his feelings near to those of the persons whose feelings he describes – nay, for short spaces of time perhaps, to let himself slip into an entire delusion, and even confound and identify his own feelings with theirs, modifying only the language which is thus suggested to him by a consideration that he describes for a particular purpose: that of giving pleasure. Here, then, he will apply the principle on which I have so much insisted – namely, that of selection. On this he will depend for removing what would otherwise be painful or disgusting in the passion; he will feel that there is no necessity to trick out or elevate nature.[13] And the more industriously he applies this principle, the deeper will be his faith that no words which his fancy or imagination can suggest will be compared with those which are the emanations of reality and truth.

But it may be said (by those who do not object to the general spirit of these remarks) that, as it is impossible for the poet to produce upon all occasions language as exquisitely fitted for the passion as that which the real passion itself suggests, it is proper that he should consider himself as in the situation of a translator who deems himself justified when he substitutes excellences of another kind for those which are unattainable by him, and endeavours occasionally to surpass his original in order to make some amends for the general inferiority to which he feels that he must submit. But this would be to encourage idleness and unmanly despair. Further, it is the language of men who speak of what they do not understand; who talk of poetry as of a matter of amusement and idle pleasure; who will converse with us as gravely about a *taste* for poetry (as they express it) as if it were a thing as indifferent as a taste for rope-dancing, or frontiniac[14] or sherry.

Aristotle, I have been told, hath said that poetry is the most philosophic of all writing. It is so. Its object is truth, not individual and local, but general and operative; not standing upon external testimony, but carried alive into the heart by passion – truth which is its own testimony, which gives strength and divinity to the tribunal to which it appeals, and receives them from the same tribunal.

Poetry is the image of man and nature. The obstacles which stand in the way of the fidelity of the biographer and historian (and of their consequent utility) are incalculably greater than those which are to be encountered by the poet who has an adequate notion of the dignity of his art. The poet writes under one restriction only – namely, that of the necessity of giving immediate pleasure to a human being possessed of that information which may be expected from him not as a lawyer, a physician, a mariner, an astronomer, or a natural philosopher, but as a man. Except this one restriction, there is no object standing between the poet and the image of things; between this, and the biographer and historian, there are a thousand.

Nor let this necessity of producing immediate pleasure be considered as a degradation of the poet's art; it is far otherwise. It is an acknowledgement of the beauty of the

---

[13] *nature* natural utterance.   [14] *frontiniac* muscat wine from Frontignan, France.

universe, an acknowledgement the more sincere because it is not formal, but indirect; it is a task light and easy to him who looks at the world in the spirit of love. Further, it is a homage paid to the native and naked dignity of man, to the grand elementary principle of pleasure by which he knows, and feels, and lives, and moves.

We have no sympathy but what is propagated by pleasure. I would not be misunderstood – but wherever we sympathize with pain it will be found that the sympathy is produced and carried on by subtle combinations with pleasure. We have no knowledge – that is, no general principles drawn from the contemplation of particular facts, but what has been built up by pleasure, and exists in us by pleasure alone. The man of science, the chemist and mathematician, whatever difficulties and disgusts they may have had to struggle with, know and feel this. However painful may be the objects with which the anatomist's knowledge is connected, he feels that his knowledge is pleasure – and where he has no pleasure he has no knowledge.

What then does the poet? He considers man and the objects that surround him as acting and reacting upon each other so as to produce an infinite complexity of pain and pleasure. He considers man in his own nature and in his ordinary life as contemplating this with a certain quantity of immediate knowledge, with certain convictions, intuitions, and deductions which by habit become of the nature of intuitions. He considers him as looking upon this complex scene of ideas and sensations, and finding everywhere objects that immediately excite in him sympathies which (from the necessities of his nature) are accompanied by an overbalance of enjoyment.

To this knowledge which all men carry about with them, and to these sympathies in which, without any other discipline than that of our daily life, we are fitted to take delight, the poet principally directs his attention. He considers man and nature as essentially adapted to each other, and the mind of man as naturally the mirror of the fairest and most interesting qualities of nature.

And thus the poet, prompted by this feeling of pleasure which accompanies him through the whole course of his studies, converses with general nature with affections akin to those which, through labour and length of time, the man of science has raised up in himself by conversing with those particular parts of nature which are the objects of his studies. The knowledge both of the poet and the man of science is pleasure. But the knowledge of the one cleaves to us as a necessary part of our existence, our natural and unalienable inheritance; the other is a personal and individual acquisition, slow to come to us, and by no habitual and direct sympathy connecting us with our fellow-beings.

The man of science seeks truth as a remote and unknown benefactor; he cherishes and loves it in his solitude. The poet, singing a song in which all human beings join with him, rejoices in the presence of truth as our visible friend and hourly companion. Poetry is the breath and finer spirit of all knowledge; it is the impassioned expression which is in the countenance of all science. Emphatically may it be said of the poet, as Shakespeare hath said of man, that he 'looks before and after'.[15] He is the rock of defence of human nature, an upholder and preserver, carrying everywhere with him relationship and love. In spite of difference of soil and climate, of language and manners, of laws and customs; in spite of things silently gone out of mind and things

---

[15] *Hamlet*, IV. iv. 37.

violently destroyed, the poet binds together by passion and knowledge the vast empire of human society as it is spread over the whole earth and over all time.

The objects of the poet's thoughts are everywhere. Though the eyes and senses of man are, it is true, his favourite guides, yet he will follow wheresoever he can find an atmosphere of sensation in which to move his wings. Poetry is the first and last of all knowledge; it is as immortal as the heart of man. If the labours of men of science should ever create any material revolution (direct or indirect) in our condition, and in the impressions which we habitually receive, the poet will sleep then no more than at present but he will be ready to follow the steps of the man of science, not only in those general indirect effects, but he will be at his side, carrying sensation into the midst of the objects of the science itself. The remotest discoveries of the chemist, the botanist, or mineralogist, will be as proper objects of the poet's art as any upon which it can be employed, if the time should ever come when these things shall be familiar to us, and the relations under which they are contemplated by the followers of these respective sciences shall be manifestly and palpably material to us as enjoying and suffering beings. If the time should ever come when what is now called science (thus familiarized to men) shall be ready to put on, as it were, a form of flesh and blood, the poet will lend his divine spirit to aid the transfiguration, and will welcome the being thus produced as a dear and genuine inmate of the household of man. It is not then to be supposed that anyone who holds that sublime notion of poetry which I have attempted to convey will break in upon the sanctity and truth of his pictures by transitory and accidental ornaments, and endeavour to excite admiration of himself by arts, the necessity of which must manifestly depend upon the assumed meanness of his subject.

What I have thus far said applies to poetry in general, but especially to those parts of composition where the poet speaks through the mouths of his characters. And upon this point it appears to have such weight that I will conclude there are few persons of good sense who would not allow that the dramatic parts of composition are defective in proportion as they deviate from the real language of nature, and are coloured by a diction of the poet's own, either peculiar to him as an individual poet or belonging simply to poets in general — to a body of men who, from the circumstance of their compositions being in metre, it is expected will employ a particular language.

It is not, then, in the dramatic parts of composition that we look for this distinction of language, but still it may be proper and necessary where the poet speaks to us in his own person and character. To this I answer by referring my reader to the description which I have before given of a poet. Among the qualities which I have enumerated as principally conducing to form a poet, is implied nothing differing in kind from other men, but only in degree. The sum of what I have there said is that the poet is chiefly distinguished from other men by a greater promptness to think and feel without immediate external excitement, and a greater power in expressing such thoughts and feelings as are produced in him in that manner.

But these passions and thoughts and feelings are the general passions and thoughts and feelings of men. And with what are they connected? Undoubtedly with our moral sentiments and animal sensations, and with the causes which excite these; with the operations of the elements, and the appearances of the visible universe; with storm and sunshine, with the revolutions of the seasons, with cold and heat, with loss of friends and kindred, with injuries and resentments, gratitude and hope, with fear and sorrow. These and the like are the sensations and objects which the poet describes, as they are the sensations of other men and the objects which interest them.

The poet thinks and feels in the spirit of the passions of men. How, then, can his language differ in any material degree from that of all other men who feel vividly and see clearly? It might be *proved* that it is impossible. But supposing that this were not the case: the poet might then be allowed to use a peculiar language when expressing his feelings for his own gratification, or that of men like himself. But poets do not write for poets alone, but for men. Unless therefore we are advocates for that admiration which depends upon ignorance, and that pleasure which arises from hearing what we do not understand, the poet must descend from this supposed height, and in order to excite rational sympathy, he must express himself as other men express themselves. To this it may be added that, while he is only selecting from the real language of men or (which amounts to the same thing) composing accurately in the spirit of such selection, he is treading upon safe ground, and we know what we are to expect from him. Our feelings are the same with respect to metre for (as it may be proper to remind the reader) the distinction of metre is regular and uniform, and not like that which is produced by what is usually called poetic diction – arbitrary, and subject to infinite caprices upon which no calculation whatever can be made. In the one case, the reader is utterly at the mercy of the poet respecting what imagery or diction he may choose to connect with the passion; whereas in the other, the metre obeys certain laws to which the poet and reader both willingly submit because they are certain, and because no interference is made by them with the passion but such as the concurring testimony of ages has shown to heighten and improve the pleasure which coexists with it.

It will now be proper to answer an obvious question – namely, why, professing these opinions, have I written in verse? To this, in addition to such answer as is included in what I have already said, I reply in the first place, because (however I may have restricted myself) there is still left open to me what confessedly constitutes the most valuable object of all writing, whether in prose or verse: the great and universal passions of men, the most general and interesting of their occupations, and the entire world of nature from which I am at liberty to supply myself with endless combinations of forms and imagery.

Now supposing for a moment that whatever is interesting in these objects may be as vividly described in prose; why am I to be condemned if to such description I have endeavoured to superadd the charm which, by the consent of all nations, is acknowledged to exist in metrical language? To this (by such as are unconvinced by what I have already said) it may be answered that a very small part of the pleasure given by poetry depends upon the metre, and that it is injudicious to write in metre unless it be accompanied with the other artificial distinctions of style with which metre is usually accompanied – and that by such deviation, more will be lost from the shock which will be thereby given to the reader's associations, than will be counterbalanced by any pleasure which he can derive from the general power of numbers.

In answer to those who still contend for the necessity of accompanying metre with certain appropriate colours of style in order to the accomplishment of its appropriate end, and who also, in my opinion, greatly underrate the power of metre in itself, it might perhaps (as far as relates to these poems) have been almost sufficient to observe that poems are extant, written upon more humble subjects, and in a more naked and simple style than I have aimed at – which poems have continued to give pleasure from generation to generation. Now if nakedness and simplicity be a defect, the fact here mentioned affords a strong presumption that poems somewhat less naked and simple are capable of affording pleasure at the present day, and what I wished chiefly to attempt at present was to justify myself for having written under the impression of this belief.

But I might point out various causes why, when the style is manly, and the subject of some importance, words metrically arranged will long continue to impart such a pleasure to mankind as he who is sensible of the extent of that pleasure will be desirous to impart. The end of poetry is to produce excitement in coexistence with an overbalance of pleasure. Now, by the supposition, excitement is an unusual and irregular state of the mind; ideas and feelings do not in that state succeed each other in accustomed order. But if the words by which this excitement is produced are in themselves powerful, or the images and feelings have an undue proportion of pain connected with them, there is some danger that the excitement may be carried beyond its proper bounds. Now the co-presence of something regular, something to which the mind has been accustomed in various moods and in a less excited state, cannot but have great efficacy in tempering and restraining the passion by an intertexture of ordinary feeling, and of feeling not strictly and necessarily connected with the passion. This is unquestionably true, and hence (though the opinion will at first appear paradoxical from the tendency of metre to divest language in a certain degree of its reality, and thus to throw a sort of half-consciousness of unsubstantial existence over the whole composition) there can be little doubt but that more pathetic situations and sentiments – that is, those which have a greater proportion of pain connected with them – may be endured in metrical composition, especially in rhyme, than in prose. The metre of the old ballads is very artless, yet they contain many passages which would illustrate this opinion – and I hope, if the following poems be attentively perused, similar instances will be found in them.

This opinion may be further illustrated by appealing to the reader's own experience of the reluctance with which he comes to the re-perusal of the distressful parts of *Clarissa Harlowe* or *The Gamester*,[16] while Shakespeare's writings in the most pathetic scenes never act upon us as pathetic beyond the bounds of pleasure – an effect which, in a much greater degree than might at first be imagined, is to be ascribed to small, but continual and regular, impulses of pleasurable surprise from the metrical arrangement. On the other hand (what it must be allowed will much more frequently happen), if the poet's words should be incommensurate with the passion, and inadequate to raise the reader to a height of desirable excitement, then (unless the poet's choice of his metre has been grossly injudicious) in the feelings of pleasure which the reader has been accustomed to connect with metre in general, and in the feeling (whether cheerful or melancholy) which he has been accustomed to connect with that particular movement of metre, there will be found something which will greatly contribute to impart passion to the words, and to effect the complex end which the poet proposes to himself.

If I had undertaken a systematic defence of the theory upon which these poems are written, it would have been my duty to develop the various causes upon which the pleasure received from metrical language depends. Among the chief of these causes is to be reckoned a principle which must be well-known to those who have made any of

---

[16] Samuel Richardson, *Clarissa* (1747–8), and Edward Moore, *The Gamester* (1753), popular tragic prose works.

the arts the object of accurate reflection: I mean the pleasure which the mind derives from the perception of similitude in dissimilitude. This principle is the great spring of the activity of our minds, and their chief feeder. From this principle the direction of the sexual appetite, and all the passions connected with it, take their origin. It is the life of our ordinary conversation, and upon the accuracy with which similitude in dissimilitude and dissimilitude in similitude are perceived, depend our taste and our moral feelings. It would not have been a useless employment to have applied this principle to the consideration of metre, and to have shown that metre is hence enabled to afford much pleasure, and to have pointed out in what manner that pleasure is produced. But my limits will not permit me to enter upon this subject, and I must content myself with a general summary.

I have said that poetry is the spontaneous overflow of powerful feelings; it takes its origin from emotion recollected in tranquillity. The emotion is contemplated till, by a species of reaction, the tranquillity gradually disappears, and an emotion kindred to that which was before the subject of contemplation is gradually produced, and does itself actually exist in the mind. In this mood successful composition generally begins, and in a mood similar to this it is carried on. But the emotion (of whatever kind and in whatever degree) from various causes is qualified by various pleasures, so that in describing any passions whatsoever which are voluntarily described, the mind will upon the whole be in a state of enjoyment. Now, if nature be thus cautious in preserving in a state of enjoyment a being thus employed, the poet ought to profit by the lesson thus held forth to him, and ought especially to take care that, whatever passions he communicates to his reader, those passions (if his reader's mind be sound and vigorous) should always be accompanied with an overbalance of pleasure.

Now, the music of harmonious metrical language, the sense of difficulty overcome, and the blind association of pleasure which has been previously received from works of rhyme or metre of the same or similar construction, an indistinct perception perpetually renewed of language closely resembling that of real life (and yet, in the circumstance of metre, differing from it so widely) – all these imperceptibly make up a complex feeling of delight, which is of the most important use in tempering the painful feeling which will always be found intermingled with powerful descriptions of the deeper passions. This effect is always produced in pathetic and impassioned poetry, while, in lighter compositions, the ease and gracefulness with which the poet manages his numbers are themselves confessedly a principal source of the gratification of the reader.

I might perhaps include all which it is necessary to say upon this subject by affirming what few persons will deny – that, of two descriptions, either of passions, manners, or characters, each of them equally well-executed, the one in prose and the other in verse, the verse will be read a hundred times where the prose is read once. We see that Pope, by the power of verse alone, has contrived to render the plainest common sense interesting, and even frequently to invest it with the appearance of passion. In consequence of these convictions I related in metre the tale of 'Goody Blake and Harry Gill', which is one of the rudest of this collection. I wished to draw attention to the truth that the power of the human imagination is sufficient to produce such changes even in our physical nature as might almost appear miraculous. The truth is an important one; the fact (for it is a fact) is a valuable illustration of it. And I have the satisfaction of knowing that it has been communicated to many hundreds of people who would never have heard of it had it not been narrated as a ballad, and in a more impressive metre than is usual in ballads.

Having thus explained a few of my reasons why I have written in verse and why I have chosen subjects from common life, and endeavoured to bring my language near to the real language of men – if I have been too minute in pleading my own cause, I have at the same time been treating a subject of general interest. And it is for this reason that I request the reader's permission to add a few words with reference solely to these particular poems, and to some defects which will probably be found in them. I am sensible that my associations must have sometimes been particular instead of general, and that, consequently – giving to things a false importance, sometimes from diseased impulses – I may have written upon unworthy subjects. But I am less apprehensive on this account, than that my language may frequently have suffered from those arbitrary connections of feelings and ideas with particular words and phrases from which no man can altogether protect himself. Hence I have no doubt that in some instances, feelings even of the ludicrous may be given to my readers by expressions which appeared to me tender and pathetic.

Such faulty expressions, were I convinced they were faulty at present, and that they must necessarily continue to be so, I would willingly take all reasonable pains to correct. But it is dangerous to make these alterations on the simple authority of a few individuals, or even of certain classes of men. For where the understanding of an author is not convinced, or his feelings altered, this cannot be done without great injury to himself, for his own feelings are his stay and support – and if he sets them aside in one instance, he may be induced to repeat this act till his mind loses all confidence in itself, and becomes utterly debilitated.

To this it may be added that the reader ought never to forget that he is himself exposed to the same errors as the poet – and perhaps in a much greater degree. For there can be no presumption in saying that it is not probable he will be so well acquainted with the various stages of meaning through which words have passed, or with the fickleness or stability of the relations of particular ideas to each other – and above all, since he is so much less interested in the subject, he may decide lightly and carelessly.

Long as I have detained my reader, I hope he will permit me to caution him against a mode of false criticism which has been applied to poetry in which the language closely resembles that of life and nature. Such verses have been triumphed over in parodies of which Dr Johnson's stanza is a fair specimen.

> I put my hat upon my head
> And walked into the Strand,
> And there I met another man
> Whose hat was in his hand.

Immediately under these lines I will place one of the most justly admired stanzas of 'The Babes in the Wood'.

> These pretty babes with hand in hand
> Went wandering up and down,
> But never more they saw the man
> Approaching from the town.

In both these stanzas the words, and the order of the words, in no respect differ from the most unimpassioned conversation. There are words in both (for example, 'the

Strand' and 'the town') connected with none but the most familiar ideas. Yet the one stanza we admit as admirable, and the other as a fair example of the superlatively contemptible. Whence arises this difference? Not from the metre, not from the language, not from the order of the words – but the *matter* expressed in Dr Johnson's stanza is contemptible. The proper method of treating trivial and simple verses (to which Dr Johnson's stanza would be a fair parallelism) is not to say, 'This is a bad kind of poetry', or 'This is not poetry', but 'This wants sense. It is neither interesting in itself, nor can lead to anything interesting. The images neither originate in that sane state of feeling which arises out of thought, nor can excite thought or feeling in the reader.' This is the only sensible manner of dealing with such verses. Why trouble yourself about the species till you have previously decided upon the genus? Why take pains to prove that an ape is not a Newton when it is self-evident that he is not a man?

I have one request to make of my reader, which is, that in judging these poems he would decide by his own feelings genuinely, and not by reflection upon what will probably be the judgement of others. How common is it to hear a person say, 'I myself do not object to this style of composition, or this or that expression, but to such and such classes of people it will appear mean or ludicrous.' This mode of criticism, so destructive of all sound unadulterated judgement, is almost universal. I have therefore to request that the reader would abide independently by his own feelings, and that if he finds himself affected he would not suffer such conjectures to interfere with his pleasure.

If an author by any single composition has impressed us with respect for his talents, it is useful to consider this as affording a presumption that, on other occasions where we have been displeased, he nevertheless may not have written ill or absurdly. And further, to give him so much credit for this one composition as may induce us to review what has displeased us with more care than we should otherwise have bestowed upon it. This is not only an act of justice but, in our decisions upon poetry especially, may conduce in a high degree to the improvement of our own taste. For an *accurate* taste in poetry, and in all the other arts (as Sir Joshua Reynolds has observed) is an *acquired* talent which can only be produced by thought and a long continued intercourse with the best models of composition. This is mentioned not with so ridiculous a purpose as to prevent the most inexperienced reader from judging for himself (I have already said that I wish him to judge for himself), but merely to temper the rashness of decision, and to suggest that if poetry be a subject on which much time has not been bestowed, the judgement may be erroneous, and that in many cases it necessarily will be so.

I know that nothing would have so effectually contributed to further the end which I have in view, as to have shown of what kind the pleasure is, and how that pleasure is produced which is confessedly produced by metrical composition essentially different from that which I have here endeavoured to recommend. For the reader will say that he has been pleased by such composition, and what can I do more for him?

The power of any art is limited, and he will suspect that, if I propose to furnish him with new friends, it is only upon condition of his abandoning his old friends. Besides, as I have said, the reader is himself conscious of the pleasure which he has received from such composition – composition to which he has peculiarly attached the endearing name of poetry – and all men feel an habitual gratitude and something of an honourable bigotry for the objects which have long continued to please them. We not only wish to be pleased, but to be pleased in that particular way in which we have been accustomed to be pleased.

There is a host of arguments in these feelings, and I should be the less able to combat them successfully, as I am willing to allow that, in order entirely to enjoy the poetry which I am recommending, it would be necessary to give up much of what is ordinarily enjoyed. But would my limits have permitted me to point out how this pleasure is produced, I might have removed many obstacles and assisted my reader in perceiving that the powers of language are not so limited as he may suppose, and that it is possible that poetry may give other enjoyments, of a purer, more lasting, and more exquisite nature. This part of my subject I have not altogether neglected, but it has been less my present aim to prove that the interest excited by some other kinds of poetry is less vivid and less worthy of the nobler powers of the mind, than to offer reasons for presuming that, if the object which I have proposed to myself were adequately attained, a species of poetry would be produced which is genuine poetry, in its nature well adapted to interest mankind permanently, and likewise important in the multiplicity and quality of its moral relations.

From what has been said, and from a perusal of the poems, the reader will be able clearly to perceive the object which I have proposed to myself. He will determine how far I have attained this object and (what is a much more important question) whether it be worth attaining. And upon the decision of these two questions will rest my claim to the approbation of the public.

APPENDIX (COMPOSED EARLY 1802)

As perhaps I have no right to expect from a reader of an introduction to a volume of poems that attentive perusal without which it is impossible, imperfectly as I have been compelled to express my meaning, that what I have said in the preface should throughout be fully understood, I am the more anxious to give an exact notion of the sense in which I use the phrase 'poetic diction'. And for this purpose I will here add a few words concerning the origin of the phraseology which I have condemned under that name.

The earliest poets of all nations generally wrote from passion excited by real events. They wrote naturally, and as men. Feeling powerfully as they did, their language was daring and figurative. In succeeding times, poets and men ambitious of the fame of poets, perceiving the influence of such language and desirous of producing the same effect without having the same animating passion, set themselves to a mechanical adoption of those figures of speech, and made use of them, sometimes with propriety, but much more frequently applied them to feelings and ideas with which they had no natural connection whatsoever. A language was thus insensibly produced, differing materially from the real language of men *in any situation*.

The reader or hearer of this distorted language found himself in a perturbed and unusual state of mind; when affected by the genuine language of passion he had been in a perturbed and unusual state of mind also. In both cases he was willing that his common judgement and understanding should be laid asleep, and he had no instinctive and infallible perception of the true to make him reject the false; the one served as a passport for the other. The agitation and confusion of mind were in both cases delightful, and no wonder if he confounded the one with the other, and believed them both to be produced by the same, or similar, causes. Besides, the poet spake to him in the character of a man to be looked up to, a man of genius and authority.

Thus, and from a variety of other causes, this distorted language was received with admiration, and poets (it is probable) who had before contented themselves for the most part with misapplying only expressions which at first had been dictated by real passion, carried the abuse still further, and introduced phrases composed apparently in the spirit of the original figurative language of passion, yet altogether of their own invention, and distinguished by various degrees of wanton deviation from good sense and nature.

It is indeed true that the language of the earliest poets was felt to differ materially from ordinary language because it was the language of extraordinary occasions – but it was really spoken by men, language which the poet himself had uttered when he had been affected by the events which he described, or which he had heard uttered by those around him. To this language it is probable that metre of some sort or other was early superadded. This separated the genuine language of poetry still further from common life, so that whoever read or heard the poems of these earliest poets felt himself moved in a way in which he had not been accustomed to be moved in real life, and by causes manifestly different from those which acted upon him in real life. This was the great temptation to all the corruptions which have followed. Under the protection of this feeling, succeeding poets constructed a phraseology which had one thing, it is true, in common with the genuine language of poetry – namely, that it was not heard in ordinary conversation, that it was unusual. But the first poets, as I have said, spake a language which, though unusual, was still the language of men. This circumstance, however, was disregarded by their successors. They found that they could please by easier means. They became proud of a language which they themselves had invented, and which was uttered only by themselves. And, with the spirit of a fraternity, they arrogated it to themselves as their own. In process of time metre became a symbol or promise of this unusual language, and whoever took upon him to write in metre, according as he possessed more or less of true poetic genius, introduced less or more of this adulterated phraseology into his compositions, and the true and the false became so inseparably interwoven that the taste of men was gradually perverted, and this language was received as a natural language – and at length, by the influence of books upon men, did to a certain degree really become so. Abuses of this kind were imported from one nation to another, and with the progress of refinement this diction became daily more and more corrupt, thrusting out of sight the plain humanities of nature by a motley masquerade of tricks, quaintnesses, hieroglyphics, and enigmas.

It would be highly interesting to point out the causes of the pleasure given by this extravagant and absurd language, but this is not the place. It depends upon a great variety of causes, but upon none perhaps more than its influence in impressing a notion of the peculiarity and exaltation of the poet's character, and in flattering the reader's self-love by bringing him nearer to a sympathy with that character – an effect which is accomplished by unsettling ordinary habits of thinking, and thus assisting the reader to approach to that perturbed and dizzy state of mind in which, if he does not find himself, he imagines that he is balked of a peculiar enjoyment which poetry can and ought to bestow.

The sonnet which I have quoted from Gray in the preface, except the lines printed in italics, consists of little else but this diction, though not of the worst kind – and indeed, if I may be permitted to say so, it is far too common in the best writers, both ancient and modern. Perhaps I can in no way, by positive example, more easily give my reader a notion of what I mean by the phrase 'poetic diction' than by referring him to a comparison between the metrical paraphrases which we have of passages in the Old and New Testament, and those passages as they exist in our common translation; see Pope's 'Messiah' throughout; Prior's 'Did sweeter sounds adorn my flowing

tongue', etc., etc.; 'Though I speak with the tongues of men and of angels', etc., etc;
see 1 Corinthians 13.

By way of immediate example, take the following of Dr Johnson:

> Turn on the prudent ant thy heedless eyes,
> Observe her labours, sluggard, and be wise!
> No stern command, no monitory voice
> Prescribes her duties, or directs her choice;
> Yet, timely provident, she hastes away
> To snatch the blessings of a plenteous day.
> When fruitful summer loads the teeming plain,
> She crops the harvest and she stores the grain.
> How long shall sloth usurp thy useless hours,
> Unnerve thy vigour, and enchain thy powers?
> While artful shades thy downy couch enclose,
> And soft solicitation courts repose,
> Amidst the drowsy charms of dull delight
> Year chases year with unremitted flight;
> Till want now following, fraudulent and slow,
> Shall spring to seize thee, like an ambushed foe.
>
> *(The Ant)*

From this hubbub of words pass to the original: 'Go to the ant, thou sluggard, consider
her ways and be wise – which having no guide, overseer, or ruler, provideth her meat
in the summer, and gathereth her food in the harvest. How long wilt thou sleep, oh
sluggard? When wilt thou arise out of thy sleep? Yet a little sleep, a little slumber, a
little folding of the hands to sleep. So shall thy poverty come as one that travaileth,
and thy want as an armed man' (Proverbs 6).

One more quotation and I have done. It is from Cowper's 'Verses Supposed to be
Written by Alexander Selkirk'.

> Religion – what treasure untold
> Resides in that heavenly word!
> More precious than silver and gold
> Or all that this earth can afford.
> But the sound of the church-going bell
> These valleys and rocks never heard,
> Ne'er sighed at the sound of a knell,
> Or smiled when a sabbath appeared.
>
> Ye winds that have made me your sport,
> Convey to this desolate shore
> Some cordial endearing report
> Of a land I must visit no more.
> My friends, do they now and then send
> A wish or a thought after me?
> Oh tell me I yet have a friend,
> Though a friend I am never to see.

I have quoted this passage as an instance of three different styles of composition. The first four lines are poorly expressed. Some critics would call the language prosaic; the fact is it would be bad prose – so bad that it is scarcely worse in metre. The epithet 'church-going' applied to a bell (and that by so chaste a writer as Cowper) is an instance of the strange abuses which poets have introduced into their language till they and their readers take them as matters of course, if they do not single them out expressly as objects of admiration. The two lines 'Ne'er sighed at the sound', etc., are in my opinion an instance of the language of passion wrested from its proper use, and, from the mere circumstance of the composition being in metre, applied upon an occasion that does not justify such violent expressions – and I should condemn the passage (though perhaps few readers will agree with me) as vicious poetic diction.

The last stanza is throughout admirably expressed. It would be equally good whether in prose or verse, except that the reader has an exquisite pleasure in seeing such natural language so naturally connected with metre. The beauty of this stanza tempts me here to add a sentiment which ought to be the pervading spirit of a system, detached parts of which have been imperfectly explained in the preface – namely, that in proportion as ideas and feelings are valuable, whether the composition be in prose or in verse, they require and exact one and the same language.

From Poems in Two Volumes (1807)

THE RAINBOW (COMPOSED PROBABLY 26 MARCH 1802)

My heart leaps up when I behold
A rainbow in the sky;
So was it when my life began,
So is it now I am a man,
So be it when I shall grow old   5
Or let me die!
The child is father of the man,
And I could wish my days to be
Bound each to each by natural piety.

'These Chairs they have no Words to Utter' (composed *c.*22 April 1802; edited from MS)[1]

These chairs they have no words to utter,
No fire is in the grate to stir or flutter,
The ceiling and floor are mute as a stone,
My chamber is hushed and still,
And I am alone,   5
Happy and alone.

'THESE CHAIRS THEY HAVE NO WORDS TO UTTER'
[1] These two poems should be read in the light of Dorothy Wordsworth's journal entry of 29 Apr. 1802, p. 497 below.

Oh, who would be afraid of life,
The passion, the sorrow, and the strife,
When he may lie
Sheltered so easily —   10
May lie in peace on his bed,
Happy as they who are dead?

Half an hour afterwards

I have thoughts that are fed by the sun;
The things which I see
Are welcome to me,   15
Welcome every one;
I do not wish to lie
Dead, dead,
Dead, without any company.
Here alone on my bed,   20
With thoughts that are fed by the sun
And hopes that are welcome every one,
Happy am I.

Oh life, there is about thee
A deep delicious peace;   25
I would not be without thee —
Stay, oh stay!
Yet be thou ever as now,
Sweetness and breath with the quiet of death,
Peace, peace, peace   30

From Poems in Two Volumes (1807)

RESOLUTION AND INDEPENDENCE (COMPOSED PROBABLY 3 MAY–4 JULY 1802)

There was a roaring in the wind all night,
The rain came heavily and fell in floods;
But now the sun is rising calm and bright,
The birds are singing in the distant woods;
Over his own sweet voice the stock-dove broods,   5
The jay makes answer as the magpie chatters,
And all the air is filled with pleasant noise of waters.

All things that love the sun are out of doors,
The sky rejoices in the morning's birth,
The grass is bright with raindrops, on the moors   10
The hare is running races in her mirth
And with her feet she from the plashy earth
Raises a mist which, glittering in the sun,
Runs with her all the way, wherever she doth run.

I was a traveller then upon the moor;[1]   15
I saw the hare that raced about with joy;
I heard the woods and distant waters roar,
Or heard them not, as happy as a boy –
The pleasant season did my heart employ.
My old remembrances went from me wholly,   20
And all the ways of men, so vain and melancholy.

But as it sometimes chanceth, from the might
Of joy in minds that can no farther go,
As high as we have mounted in delight
In our dejection do we sink as low –   25
To me that morning did it happen so,
And fears and fancies thick upon me came,
Dim sadness, and blind thoughts I knew not nor could name.

I heard the skylark singing in the sky,[2]
And I bethought me of the playful hare;   30
Even such a happy child of earth am I,
Even as these blissful creatures do I fare;
Far from the world I walk, and from all care.
But there may come another day to me –
Solitude, pain of heart, distress, and poverty.   35

My whole life I have lived in pleasant thought
As if life's business were a summer mood,
As if all needful things would come unsought
To genial faith, still rich in genial good;
But how can he expect that others should   40
Build for him, sow for him, and at his call
Love him, who for himself will take no heed at all?

I thought of Chatterton, the marvellous boy,
The sleepless soul that perished in its pride;
Of him who walked in glory and in joy   45
Behind his plough upon the mountainside.[3]
By our own spirits are we deified;
We poets in our youth begin in gladness,
But thereof comes in the end despondency and madness.

Now whether it were by peculiar grace,   50
A leading from above, a something given,

RESOLUTION AND INDEPENDENCE
[1] In *Fenwick Notes*, Wordsworth recalls: 'This old
man I met a few hundred yards from my cottage at
Town End, Grasmere, and the account of him is
taken from his own mouth' (*FN*, 14). The encounter
is described by Dorothy Wordsworth, p. 496.
[2] Cf. 'The Ancient Mariner' (1798), 348.

[3] During his short life, Thomas Chatterton (1752–
70) composed a number of forged medieval poems
supposedly by a fifteenth-century poet called Thomas
Rowley; 'him' in line 45 is Burns. Wordsworth read
both Chatterton and Burns in early youth, and admired
their work throughout his life.

Yet it befell that, in this lonely place,
When up and down my fancy thus was driven,
And I with these untoward thoughts had striven,
I saw a man before me unawares –   55
The oldest man he seemed that ever wore grey hairs.

My course I stopped as soon as I espied
The old man in that naked wilderness;
Close by a pond, upon the further side,
He stood alone. A minute's space I guess   60
I watched him, he continuing motionless.
To the pool's further margin then I drew,
He being all the while before me full in view.

As a huge stone is sometimes seen to lie
Couched on the bald top of an eminence,   65
Wonder to all who do the same espy
By what means it could thither come, and whence;
So that it seems a thing endued with sense,
Like a sea-beast crawled forth, which on a shelf
Of rock or sand reposeth, there to sun itself –   70

Such seemed this man, not all alive nor dead,
Nor all asleep, in his extreme old age.
His body was bent double, feet and head
Coming together in their pilgrimage,
As if some dire constraint of pain, or rage   75
Of sickness felt by him in times long past,
A more than human weight upon his frame had cast.

Himself he propped, his body, limbs, and face,
Upon a long grey staff of shaven wood;
And still as I drew near with gentle pace,   80
Beside the little pond or moorish flood,
Motionless as a cloud the old man stood
That heareth not the loud winds when they call,
And moveth altogether, if it move at all.[4]

At length, himself unsettling, he the pond   85
Stirred with his staff, and fixedly did look
Upon the muddy water, which he conned[5]
As if he had been reading in a book.
And now such freedom as I could I took,
And drawing to his side, to him did say,   90
'This morning gives us promise of a glorious day.'

---

[4] See Wordsworth's Preface of 1815, pp. 478–9   [5] *conned* studied.
below.

A gentle answer did the old man make
In courteous speech which forth he slowly drew,
And him with further words I thus bespake,
'What kind of work is that which you pursue?   95
This is a lonesome place for one like you.'
He answered me with pleasure and surprise,
And there was, while he spake, a fire about his eyes.

His words came feebly, from a feeble chest,
Yet each in solemn order followed each,   100
With something of a lofty utterance dressed,
Choice word and measured phrase, above the reach
Of ordinary men – a stately speech
Such as grave livers do in Scotland use,
Religious men, who give to God and man their dues.   105

He told me that he to this pond had come
To gather leeches, being old and poor –
Employment hazardous and wearisome!
And he had many hardships to endure;
From pond to pond he roamed, from moor to moor,   110
Housing, with God's good help, by choice or chance;
And in this way he gained an honest maintenance.

The old man still stood talking by my side,
But now his voice to me was like a stream
Scarce heard, nor word from word could I divide;   115
And the whole body of the man did seem
Like one whom I had met with in a dream,
Or like a man from some far region sent
To give me human strength, and strong admonishment.

My former thoughts returned: the fear that kills,   120
The hope that is unwilling to be fed,
Cold, pain, and labour, and all fleshly ills,
And mighty poets in their misery dead.
And now, not knowing what the old man had said,
My question eagerly did I renew,   125
'How is it that you live, and what is it you do?'

He with a smile did then his words repeat,
And said that gathering leeches far and wide
He travelled, stirring thus about his feet
The waters of the ponds where they abide.   130
'Once I could meet with them on every side
But they have dwindled long by slow decay;
Yet still I persevere, and find them where I may.'

While he was talking thus, the lonely place,
The old man's shape and speech, all troubled me;   135
In my mind's eye I seemed to see him pace
About the weary moors continually,
Wandering about alone and silently.
While I these thoughts within myself pursued,
He, having made a pause, the same discourse renewed.   140

And soon with this he other matter blended,
Cheerfully uttered, with demeanour kind,
But stately in the main; and when he ended,
I could have laughed myself to scorn to find
In that decrepit man so firm a mind.   145
'God', said I, 'be my help and stay secure;
I'll think of the leech-gatherer on the lonely moor.'

THE WORLD IS TOO MUCH WITH US (COMPOSED BETWEEN 21 MAY 1802 AND 6 MARCH 1804)

The world is too much with us; late and soon,
Getting and spending, we lay waste our powers:
Little we see in nature that is ours;
We have given our hearts away – a sordid boon!
This sea that bares her bosom to the moon,   5
The winds that will be howling at all hours
And are up-gathered now like sleeping flowers –
For this, for everything, we are out of tune,
It moves us not. Great God! I'd rather be
A pagan suckled in a creed outworn;   10
So might I, standing on this pleasant lea,
Have glimpses that would make me less forlorn;
Have sight of Proteus coming from the sea;
Or hear old Triton blow his wreathed horn.

DEAR NATIVE BROOKS, YOUR WAYS I HAVE PURSUED (COMPOSED BETWEEN 21 MAY AND 25 DECEMBER 1802; EDITED FROM MS)

Dear native brooks,[1] your ways I have pursued
How fondly! whether ye delight, in screen
Of shady trees to rest yourselves unseen,
Or, from your lofty dwellings scarcely viewed
But by the mountain eagle, your bold brood   5
Pure as the morning, angry, boisterous, keen,
Green as sea water, foaming white and green,
Comes roaring like a joyous multitude –
Nor have I been your follower in vain;

DEAR NATIVE BROOKS, YOUR WAYS I HAVE PURSUED
[1] Borrowed from Coleridge, 'To the River Otter', 1.

For not to speak of life and its first joys 10
Bound to your goings by a tender chain
Of flowers and delicate dreams that entertain
Loose minds when men are growing out of boys,
My manly heart has owed to your rough noise
Triumph and thoughts no bondage can restrain 15

From Poems in Two Volumes (1807)

To Toussaint L'Ouverture (composed August 1802)

Toussaint, the most unhappy man of men![1]
Whether the rural milkmaid by her cow
Sing in thy hearing, or thou liest now
Alone in some deep dungeon's earless den –
Oh miserable chieftain, where and when 5
Wilt thou find patience? Yet die not! Do thou
Wear rather in thy bonds a cheerful brow;
Though fallen thyself, never to rise again,
Live, and take comfort. Thou hast left behind
Powers that will work for thee – air, earth, and skies; 10
There's not a breathing of the common wind
That will forget thee; thou hast great allies;
Thy friends are exultations, agonies,
And love, and man's unconquerable mind.

1 September 1802 (composed 29 August–1 September 1802)[1]

We had a fellow-passenger who came
From Calais with us, gaudy in array –
A Negro woman, like a lady gay,
Yet silent as a woman fearing blame;
Dejected, meek – yea, pitiably tame 5
She sat, from notice turning not away,
But on our proffered kindness still did lay
A weight of languid speech, or at the same
Was silent, motionless in eyes and face.
She was a Negro woman driv'n from France, 10
Rejected like all others of that race,
Not one of whom may now find footing there;
This the poor outcast did to us declare,
Nor murmured at the unfeeling ordinance.

To Toussaint L'Ouverture
[1] François Dominique Toussaint l'Ouverture (b. 1743), son of a Negro slave, became governor of San Domingo (Haiti) in 1801. He was imprisoned in Paris, June 1802, having resisted Napoleon's decision to reintroduce slavery, and died in prison Apr. 1803.

1 September 1802
[1] Composed during Wordsworth's brief visit to France during the Treaty of Amiens, 1802. In 1827, he added a headnote: 'Among the capricious acts of tyranny that disgraced these times was the chasing of all Negroes from France by decree of the government. We had a fellow-passenger who was one of the expelled.'

COMPOSED UPON WESTMINSTER BRIDGE, 3 SEPTEMBER 1802
(COMPOSED 31 JULY–3 SEPTEMBER 1802)

Earth has not any thing to show more fair:
Dull would he be of soul who could pass by
A sight so touching in its majesty.
This city now doth like a garment wear
The beauty of the morning – silent, bare,   5
Ships, towers, domes, theatres, and temples lie
Open unto the fields, and to the sky,
All bright and glittering in the smokeless air.
Never did sun more beautifully steep
In his first splendour valley, rock, or hill;   10
Ne'er saw I, never felt, a calm so deep.
The river glideth at his own sweet will –
Dear God! the very houses seem asleep;
And all that mighty heart is lying still.

LONDON 1802 (COMPOSED SEPTEMBER 1802)

Milton, thou shouldst be living at this hour,
England hath need of thee! She is a fen
Of stagnant waters. Altar, sword, and pen,
Fireside, the heroic wealth of hall and bower,
Have forfeited their ancient English dower   5
Of inward happiness. We are selfish men;
Oh raise us up, return to us again,
And give us manners, virtue, freedom, power!
Thy soul was like a star and dwelt apart;
Thou hadst a voice whose sound was like the sea,   10
Pure as the naked heavens, majestic, free –
So didst thou travel on life's common way,
In cheerful godliness, and yet thy heart
The lowliest duties on itself did lay.

ODE (COMPOSED 27 MARCH 1802–MARCH 1804)[1]

There was a time when meadow, grove, and stream,
The earth, and every common sight,
          To me did seem
          Apparelled in celestial light,
The glory and the freshness of a dream.   5
It is not now as it has been of yore;
          Turn wheresoe'er I may

ODE
[1] From 1815 onwards this poem was published as 'Ode. Intimations of Immortality from Recollections of Early Childhood'. The first four stanzas were composed in 1802, and the remainder in 1804. See the Fenwick Note to this poem, pp. 480–1, and Mill's reading of it, pp. 1108–9.

By night or day
The things which I have seen I now can see no more.

The rainbow comes and goes   10
And lovely is the rose,
The moon doth with delight
Look round her when the heavens are bare;
Waters on a starry night
Are beautiful and fair;   15
The sunshine is a glorious birth;
But yet I know, where'er I go,
That there hath passed away a glory from the earth.

Now while the birds thus sing a joyous song,
And while the young lambs bound   20
As to the tabor's sound,
To me alone there came a thought of grief;
A timely utterance[2] gave that thought relief
And I again am strong.
The cataracts blow their trumpets from the steep –   25
No more shall grief of mine the season wrong;
I hear the echoes through the mountains throng,
The winds come to me from the fields of sleep
And all the earth is gay;
Land and sea   30
Give themselves up to jollity,
And with the heart of May
Doth every beast keep holiday.
Thou child of joy
Shout round me, let me hear thy shouts, thou happy shepherd-boy!   35

Ye blessed creatures, I have heard the call
Ye to each other make; I see
The heavens laugh with you in your jubilee;
My heart is at your festival,
My head hath its coronal –   40
The fullness of your bliss, I feel, I feel it all.
Oh evil day! if I were sullen
While the earth herself is adorning
This sweet May morning,
And the children are pulling   45
On every side
In a thousand valleys far and wide
Fresh flowers, while the sun shines warm
And the babe leaps up on his mother's arm –

---

[2] *A timely utterance* probably 'The Rainbow'.

I hear, I hear, with joy I hear!   50
    But there's a tree, of many one,
A single field which I have looked upon,
Both of them speak of something that is gone;
        The pansy at my feet
        Doth the same tale repeat: 55
Whither is fled the visionary gleam?
Where is it now, the glory and the dream?

Our birth is but a sleep and a forgetting.
The soul that rises with us, our life's star,
        Hath had elsewhere its setting   60
        And cometh from afar.
        Not in entire forgetfulness,
        And not in utter nakedness,
But trailing clouds of glory do we come
        From God, who is our home.   65
Heaven lies about us in our infancy!
Shades of the prison-house begin to close
        Upon the growing boy,
But he beholds the light and whence it flows,
        He sees it in his joy;   70
The youth who daily farther from the east
    Must travel, still is nature's priest,
        And by the vision splendid
        Is on his way attended:
At length the man perceives it die away   75
And fade into the light of common day.

Earth fills her lap with pleasures of her own;
Yearnings she hath in her own natural kind,
And even with something of a mother's mind
        And no unworthy aim,   80
    The homely nurse doth all she can
To make her foster-child, her inmate man,
    Forget the glories he hath known
And that imperial palace whence he came.

Behold the child³ among his new-born blisses,   85
A four years' darling of a pigmy size!
See where mid work of his own hand he lies,
Fretted by sallies of his mother's kisses
With light upon him from his father's eyes!
See at his feet some little plan or chart,   90
Some fragment from his dream of human life

---

³ Hartley Coleridge.

Shaped by himself with newly-learned art –
  A wedding or a festival,
  A mourning or a funeral;
    And this hath now his heart, 95
  And unto this he frames his song.
    Then will he fit his tongue
To dialogues of business, love, or strife;
  But it will not be long
  Ere this be thrown aside, 100
  And with new joy and pride
The little actor cons another part,
Filling from time to time his 'humorous stage'[4]
With all the persons down to palsied Age
That life brings with her in her equipage – 105
  As if his whole vocation
  Were endless imitation.

Thou whose exterior semblance doth belie
  Thy soul's immensity;
Thou best philosopher who yet dost keep 110
Thy heritage; thou eye among the blind
That, deaf and silent, read'st the eternal deep,
Haunted forever by the eternal mind;
  Mighty prophet! Seer blessed!
  On whom those truths do rest 115
Which we are toiling all our lives to find;
Thou, over whom thy immortality
Broods like the day, a master o'er a slave,
A presence which is not to be put by,
  To whom the grave 120
Is but a lonely bed without the sense or sight
  Of day or the warm light,
A place of thought where we in waiting lie;[5]
Thou little child, yet glorious in the might
Of untamed pleasures, on thy being's height – 125
Why with such earnest pains dost thou provoke
The years to bring the inevitable yoke,
Thus blindly with thy blessedness at strife?
Full soon thy soul shall have her earthly freight,
And custom lie upon thee with a weight 130
Heavy as frost, and deep almost as life.

  Oh joy! that in our embers
  Is something that doth live,

---

[4] *humorous* fanciful. Samuel Daniel, *Musophilus*, dedicatory sonnet to Fulke Greville, I.

[5] See Dorothy Wordsworth's journal, p. 497 below. Lines 121–4 were cut from versions of the poem after 1815.

That nature yet remembers
What was so fugitive!   135
The thought of our past years in me doth breed
Perpetual benedictions, not indeed
For that which is most worthy to be blessed –
Delight and liberty, the simple creed
Of childhood, whether fluttering or at rest,   140
With new-born hope forever in his breast –
        Not for these I raise
        The song of thanks and praise;
    But for those obstinate questionings
    Of sense and outward things,   145
    Fallings from us, vanishings,[6]
    Blank misgivings of a creature
Moving about in worlds not realized,
High instincts before which our mortal nature
Did tremble like a guilty thing surprised;[7]   150
    But for those first affections,
    Those shadowy recollections
        Which, be they what they may,
Are yet the fountain-light of all our day,
Are yet a master-light of all our seeing;   155
        Uphold us, cherish us, and make
Our noisy years seem moments in the being
Of the eternal silence – truths that wake
        To perish never,
Which neither listlessness nor mad endeavour,   160
        Nor man nor boy,
Nor all that is at enmity with joy
Can utterly abolish or destroy!
    Hence, in a season of calm weather,
        Though inland far we be,   165
Our souls have sight of that immortal sea
        Which brought us hither,
        Can in a moment travel thither
And see the children sport upon the shore,
And hear the mighty waters rolling evermore.   170

    Then sing, ye birds; sing, sing a joyous song!
        And let the young lambs bound
        As to the tabor's sound!
    We in thought will join your throng,
        Ye that pipe and ye that play,   175

---

[6] Late in life, Wordsworth is reported to have said, 'There was a time in my life when I had to push against something that resisted, to be sure that there was anything outside me. I was sure of my own mind; everything else fell away and vanished into thought' (*WPW*, iv. 467); see also Fenwick Note to this poem, pp. 480–1 below.
[7] Cf. *Hamlet*, I. i. 148–9.

   Ye that through your hearts today
   Feel the gladness of the May!
What though the radiance which was once so bright
Be now for ever taken from my sight?
  Though nothing can bring back the hour   180
Of splendour in the grass, of glory in the flower,
   We will grieve not, rather find
   Strength in what remains behind,
   In the primal sympathy
   Which having been must ever be,   185
   In the soothing thoughts that spring
   Out of human suffering,
   In the faith that looks through death,
In years that bring the philosophic mind.

And oh, ye fountains, meadows, hills and groves,   190
Think not of any severing of our loves!
Yet in my heart of hearts I feel your might;
I only have relinquished one delight
To live beneath your more habitual sway.
I love the brooks which down their channels fret   195
Even more than when I tripped lightly as they;
The innocent brightness of a new-born day
   Is lovely yet;
The clouds that gather round the setting sun
Do take a sober colouring from an eye   200
That hath kept watch o'er man's mortality;
Another race hath been, and other palms are won.
Thanks to the human heart by which we live,
Thanks to its tenderness, its joys and fears,
To me the meanest flower that blows can give   205
Thoughts that do often lie too deep for tears.

DAFFODILS (COMPOSED MARCH 1804–APRIL 1807)[1]

   I wandered lonely as a cloud
   That floats on high o'er vales and hills,
   When all at once I saw a crowd
   A host of dancing daffodils;
   Along the lake, beneath the trees,   5
   Ten thousand dancing in the breeze.[2]

DAFFODILS
[1] For the incident that inspired this poem see Dorothy Wordsworth's journal, pp. 496–7 below.
[2] At this point in 1815 Wordsworth added an extra stanza:

Continuous as the stars that shine
And twinkle on the milky way,
They stretched in never-ending line
Along the margin of a bay –
Ten thousand saw I at a glance,
Tossing their heads in sprightly dance.

The waves beside them danced, but they
Outdid the sparkling waves in glee;
A poet could not but be gay
In such a laughing company.   10
I gazed, and gazed, but little thought
What wealth the show to me had brought –

For oft when on my couch I lie
In vacant or in pensive mood,
They flash upon that inward eye   15
Which is the bliss of solitude,
And then my heart with pleasure fills,
And dances with the daffodils.

STEPPING WESTWARD (COMPOSED 3 JUNE 1805)

*While my fellow-traveller and I were walking by the side of Loch Ketterine one fine evening
after sunset, in our road to a hut where, in the course of our tour, we had been hospitably
entertained some weeks before, we met in one of the loneliest parts of that solitary region two
well-dressed women, one of whom said to us by way of greeting, 'What you are stepping
westward?'*

'What you are stepping westward?' 'Yea.'
'Twould be a wildish destiny
If we, who thus together roam
In a strange land, and far from home,
Were in this place the guests of Chance –   5
Yet who would stop, or fear to advance,
Though home or shelter he had none,
With such a sky to lead him on?

The dewy ground was dark and cold;
Behind, all gloomy to behold;   10
And stepping westward seemed to be
A kind of *heavenly* destiny.
I liked the greeting – 'twas a sound
Of something without place or bound,
And seemed to give me spiritual right   15
To travel through that region bright.

The voice was soft, and she who spake
Was walking by her native lake;
The salutation had to me
The very sound of courtesy: 20
Its power was felt, and while my eye
Was fixed upon the glowing sky,
The echo of the voice enwrought
A human sweetness with the thought

Of travelling through the world that lay 25
Before me in my endless way.

THE SOLITARY REAPER (COMPOSED 5 NOVEMBER 1805)

Behold her, single in the field,
Yon solitary highland lass!
Reaping and singing by herself –
Stop here, or gently pass!
Alone she cuts, and binds the grain, 5
And sings a melancholy strain;
Oh listen! for the vale profound
Is overflowing with the sound.

No nightingale did ever chaunt
So sweetly to reposing bands 10
Of travellers in some shady haunt
Among Arabian sands;
No sweeter voice was ever heard
In springtime from the cuckoo-bird,
Breaking the silence of the seas 15
Among the farthest Hebrides.

Will no one tell me what she sings?
Perhaps the plaintive numbers flow
For old, unhappy, far-off things
And battles long ago; 20
Or is it some more humble lay,
Familiar matter of today?
Some natural sorrow, loss, or pain
That has been, and may be again?

Whate'er the theme, the maiden sang 25
As if her song could have no ending;
I saw her singing at her work
And o'er the sickle bending;
I listened till I had my fill,
And as I mounted up the hill, 30
The music in my heart I bore
Long after it was heard no more.[1]

THE SOLITARY REAPER
[1] Suggested partly by a passage in Thomas Wilkinson, *Tours to the British Mountains* (1824), which Wordsworth read in MS: 'Passed a female who was reaping alone. She sung in Erse as she bended over her sickle – the sweetest human voice I ever heard. Her strains were tenderly melancholy, and felt delicious, long after they were heard no more' (p. 12).

The Thirteen-Book Prelude (composed 1799–1806; edited from MS)

Book One
Introduction – Childhood and School-Time

Oh there is blessing in this gentle breeze
That blows from the green fields and from the clouds
And from the sky – it beats against my cheek,
And seems half-conscious of the joy it gives.
Oh welcome messenger, oh welcome friend!   5
A captive greets thee, coming from a house
Of bondage, from yon city's walls[1] set free,
A prison where he hath been long immured.
Now I am free, enfranchised and at large,
May fix my habitation where I will.   10
What dwelling shall receive me? In what vale
Shall be my harbour? Underneath what grove
Shall I take up my home, and what sweet stream
Shall with its murmurs lull me to my rest?
The earth is all before me: with a heart   15
Joyous, nor scared at its own liberty,
I look about, and should the guide I choose
Be nothing better than a wandering cloud,
I cannot miss my way. I breathe again;
Trances of thought and mountings of the mind   20
Come fast upon me. It is shaken off –
As by miraculous gift 'tis shaken off,
That burden of my own unnatural self,
The heavy weight of many a weary day
Not mine, and such as were not made for me.   25
Long months of peace (if such bold word accord
With any promises of human life),
Long months of ease and undisturbed delight
Are mine in prospect – whither shall I turn?
By road or pathway, or through open field,   30
Or shall a twig or any floating thing
Upon the river, point me out my course?
    Enough that I am free, for months to come
May dedicate myself to chosen tasks,
May quit the tiresome sea and dwell on shore –   35
If not a settler on the soil, at least
To drink wild water, and to pluck green herbs,

BOOK ONE
[1] *yon city's walls* partly London, partly Goslar (in
which Wordsworth had spent the preceding winter).

And gather fruits fresh from their native tree.
Nay more: if I may trust myself, this hour
Hath brought a gift that consecrates my joy,   40
For I, methought, while the sweet breath of heaven
Was blowing on my body, felt within
A corresponding mild creative breeze,
A vital breeze which travelled gently on
O'er things which it had made, and is become   45
A tempest, a redundant energy
Vexing its own creation. 'Tis a power
That does not come unrecognized, a storm
Which, breaking up a long-continued frost,
Brings with it vernal promises, the hope   50
Of active days, of dignity and thought,
Of prowess in an honourable field,
Pure passions, virtue, knowledge, and delight,
The holy life of music and of verse.
    Thus far, oh friend,[2] did I, not used to make   55
A present joy the matter of my song,
Pour out that day my soul in measured strains,
Even in the very words which I have here
Recorded. To the open fields I told
A prophecy; poetic numbers came   60
Spontaneously, and clothed in priestly robe
My spirit, thus singled out, as it might seem,
For holy services – great hopes were mine!
My own voice cheered me, and, far more, the mind's
Internal echo of the imperfect sound.   65
To both I listened, drawing from them both
A cheerful confidence in things to come.
    Whereat, being not unwilling now to give
A respite to this passion, I paced on
Gently, with careless steps, and came erelong   70
To a green shady place where down I sat
Beneath a tree, slackening my thoughts by choice
And settling into gentler happiness.
'Twas autumn, and a calm and placid day
With warmth as much as needed from a sun   75
Two hours declined towards the west, a day
With silver clouds and sunshine on the grass,
And, in the sheltered grove where I was couched,
A perfect stillness. On the ground I lay
Passing through many thoughts, yet mainly such   80
As to myself pertained. I made a choice
Of one sweet vale whither my steps should turn,

---

[2] Coleridge.

And saw, methought, the very house³ and fields
Present before my eyes. Nor did I fail
To add meanwhile assurance of some work   85
Of glory,⁴ there forthwith to be begun –
Perhaps too there performed. Thus long I lay
Cheered by the genial pillow of the earth
Beneath my head, soothed by a sense of touch
From the warm ground, that balanced me (else lost   90
Entirely), seeing nought, nought hearing, save
When here and there, about the grove of oaks
Where was my bed, an acorn from the trees
Fell audibly and with a startling sound.

   Thus occupied in mind, I lingered here   95
Contented, nor rose up until the sun
Had almost touched the horizon; bidding then
A farewell to the city left behind,
Even on the strong temptation of that hour
And with its chance equipment, I resolved   100
To journey towards the vale which I had chosen.
It was a splendid evening, and my soul
Did once again make trial of her strength
Restored to her afresh – nor did she want
Eolian visitations. But the harp   105
Was soon defrauded, and the banded host
Of harmony dispersed in straggling sounds;
And lastly, utter silence. 'Be it so,
It is an injury', said I, 'to this day
To think of anything but present joy.'   110
So, like a peasant, I pursued my road
Beneath the evening sun, nor had one wish
Again to bend the sabbath of that time
To a servile yoke. What need of many words?
A pleasant loitering journey, through two days   115
Continued, brought me to my hermitage.
   I spare to speak, my friend, of what ensued:
The admiration and the love, the life
In common things, the endless store of things
Rare (or at least so seeming) every day   120
Found all about me in one neighbourhood,
The self-congratulation, the complete
Composure, and the happiness entire.
But speedily a longing in me rose
To brace myself to some determined aim,   125
Reading or thinking, either to lay up
New stores, or rescue from decay the old

---

³ Dove Cottage.

⁴ *some work / Of glory* Wordsworth's projected, but
never to be completed, epic poem, *The Recluse.*

By timely interference. I had hopes
Still higher: that with a frame of outward life
I might endue, might fix in a visible home   130
Some portion of those phantoms of conceit
That had been floating loose about so long,
And to such beings temperately deal forth
The many feelings that oppressed my heart.
But I have been discouraged; gleams of light   135
Flash often from the east, then disappear
And mock me with a sky that ripens not
Into a steady morning. If my mind,
Remembering the sweet promise of the past,
Would gladly grapple with some noble theme,   140
Vain is her wish; where'er she turns she finds
Impediments from day to day renewed.
     And now it would content me to yield up
Those lofty hopes awhile, for present gifts
Of humbler industry. But oh dear friend,   145
The poet, gentle creature as he is,
Hath, like the lover, his unruly times,
His fits when he is neither sick nor well,
Though no distress be near him but his own
Unmanageable thoughts. The mind itself,   150
The meditative mind (best pleased perhaps
While she, as duteous as the mother dove,
Sits brooding), lives not always to that end,
But hath less quiet instincts, goadings-on
That drive her as in trouble through the groves.   155
With me is now such passion, which I blame
No otherwise than as it lasts too long.
     When, as becomes a man who would prepare
For such a glorious work, I through myself
Make rigorous inquisition, the report   160
Is often cheering, for I neither seem
To lack that first great gift – the vital soul,
Nor general truths which are themselves a sort
Of elements and agents, under-powers,
Subordinate helpers of the living mind.   165
Nor am I naked in external things –
Forms, images – nor numerous other aids
Of less regard, though won perhaps with toil
And needful to build up a poet's praise.
Time, place, and manners, these I seek, and these   170
I find in plenteous store, but nowhere such
As may be singled out with steady choice –
No little band of yet remembered names
Whom I, in perfect confidence, might hope
To summon back from lonesome banishment   175

And make them inmates in the hearts of men
Now living, or to live in times to come.
   Sometimes, mistaking vainly (as I fear)
Proud spring-tide swellings for a regular sea,
I settle on some British theme, some old   180
Romantic tale by Milton left unsung;
More often, resting at some gentle place
Within the groves of chivalry, I pipe
Among the shepherds, with reposing knights
Sit by a fountain-side and hear their tales.   185
Sometimes, more sternly moved, I would relate
How vanquished Mithridates northward passed
And, hidden in the cloud of years, became
That Odin, father of a race by whom
Perished the Roman Empire;[5] how the friends   190
And followers of Sertorius,[6] out of Spain
Flying, found shelter in the Fortunate Isles,
And left their usages, their arts and laws,
To disappear by a slow gradual death,
To dwindle and to perish one by one   195
Starved in those narrow bounds – but not the soul
Of liberty, which fifteen hundred years
Survived and, when the European came
With skill and power that could not be withstood,
Did, like a pestilence, maintain its hold   200
And wasted down by glorious death that race
Of natural heroes. Or I would record
How in tyrannic times some unknown man,
Unheard-of in the chronicles of kings,
Suffered in silence for the love of truth;   205
How that one Frenchman,[7] through continued force
Of meditation on the inhuman deeds
Of the first conquerors of the Indian Isles,
Went single in his ministry across
The ocean – not to comfort the oppressed,   210
But, like a thirsty wind, to roam about,
Withering the oppressor; how Gustavus found
Help at his need in Dalecarlia's mines;[8]
How Wallace[9] fought for Scotland, left the name
Of Wallace to be found like a wild-flower   215

---

[5] Mithridates (131–63 BC), King of Pontus, defeated by Pompey in 66 BC, and associated by a number of historians with Odin, who led his tribe north to Sweden, in the hope of taking revenge on the Romans.

[6] Sertorius, Roman general (c.112–72 BC), who ruled Spain. After his assassination his followers fled to the Canary Islands.

[7] 'Dominique de Gourges, a French gentlemen who went in 1568 to Florida to avenge the massacre of the French by the Spaniards there' (*Prelude* note, 1850).

[8] Gustavus I of Sweden (1496–1560) agitated among the miners of Dalecarlia, liberating his country from Danish rule in 1521–3.

[9] William Wallace (?1272–?1305), Scottish general and patriot.

All over his dear country, left the deeds
Of Wallace, like a family of ghosts,
To people the steep rocks and river banks,
Her natural sanctuaries, with a local soul
Of independence and stern liberty. 220
Sometimes it suits me better to shape out
Some tale from my own heart, more near akin
To my own passions and habitual thoughts,
Some variegated story, in the main
Lofty, with interchange of gentler things. 225
But deadening admonitions will succeed,
And the whole beauteous fabric seems to lack
Foundation, and withal appears throughout
Shadowy and unsubstantial.
                Then, last wish,
My last and favourite aspiration – then 230
I yearn towards some philosophic song[10]
Of truth that cherishes our daily life;
With meditations passionate from deep
Recesses in man's heart, immortal verse
Thoughtfully fitted to the Orphean lyre. 235
But from this awful burden I full soon
Take refuge, and beguile myself with trust
That mellower years will bring a riper mind
And clearer insight. Thus from day to day
I live, a mockery of the brotherhood 240
Of vice and virtue, with no skill to part
Vague longing that is bred by want of power
From paramount impulse not to be withstood;
A timorous capacity from prudence;
From circumspection, infinite delay. 245
Humility and modest awe themselves
Betray me, serving often for a cloak
To a more subtle selfishness, that now
Doth lock my functions up in blank reserve,
Now dupes me by an over-anxious eye 250
That with a false activity beats off
Simplicity and self-presented truth.
Ah! better far than this to stray about
Voluptuously through fields and rural walks
And ask no record of the hours given up 255
To vacant musing, unreproved neglect
Of all things, and deliberate holiday;
Far better never to have heard the name
Of zeal and just ambition, than to live

---

[10] *some philosophic song The Recluse*, Wordsworth's projected epic poem.

Thus baffled by a mind that every hour   260
Turns recreant to her task, takes heart again,
Then feels immediately some hollow thought
Hang like an interdict upon her hopes.
This is my lot; for either still I find
Some imperfection in the chosen theme,   265
Or see of absolute accomplishment
Much wanting – so much wanting in myself
That I recoil and droop, and seek repose
In indolence from vain perplexity,
Unprofitably travelling towards the grave   270
Like a false steward who hath much received
And renders nothing back.[11]
                        Was it for this
That one,[12] the fairest of all rivers, loved
To blend his murmurs with my nurse's song,
And from his alder shades and rocky falls,   275
And from his fords and shallows, sent a voice
That flowed along my dreams? For this didst thou,
Oh Derwent, travelling over the green plains
Near my sweet birthplace, didst thou, beauteous stream,
Make ceaseless music through the night and day   280
Which with its steady cadence tempering
Our human waywardness, composed my thoughts
To more than infant softness, giving me
Among the fretful dwellings of mankind
A knowledge, a dim earnest of the calm   285
Which nature breathes among the hills and groves?
    When, having left his mountains, to the towers[13]
Of Cockermouth that beauteous river came,
Behind my father's house he passed, close by,
Along the margin of our terrace-walk –   290
He was a playmate whom we dearly loved.
Oh many a time have I, a five years' child,
A naked boy, in one delightful rill,
A little mill-race severed from his stream,
Made one long bathing of a summer's day,   295
Basked in the sun, and plunged and basked again
Alternate all a summer's day, or coursed
Over the sandy fields, leaping through groves
Of yellow grunsel; or, when crag and hill,
The woods, and distant Skiddaw's lofty height,[14]   300
Were bronzed with a deep radiance, stood alone

---

[11] Cf. Matt. 25: 14–30.
[12] one The River Derwent, which flows behind the house in Cockermouth in which Wordsworth was brought up.
[13] towers of Cockermouth castle.
[14] Skiddaw oldest and fourth-highest peak in the Lake District (3,053 ft), nine miles due east of Cockermouth.

Beneath the sky, as if I had been born
On Indian plains and from my mother's hut
Had run abroad in wantonness to sport,
A naked savage in the thunder shower.   305
    Fair seed-time had my soul, and I grew up
Fostered alike by beauty and by fear,
Much favoured in my birthplace, and no less
In that beloved vale[15] to which erelong
I was transplanted. Well I call to mind   310
('Twas at an early age, ere I had seen
Nine summers) when upon the mountain-slope
The frost and breath of frosty wind had snapped
The last autumnal crocus, 'twas my joy
To wander half the night among the cliffs,   315
And the smooth hollows where the woodcocks ran
Along the open turf. In thought and wish
That time, my shoulder all with springes hung,
I was a fell destroyer. On the heights,
Scudding away from snare to snare, I plied   320
My anxious visitation – hurrying on,
Still hurrying, hurrying onward; moon and stars
Were shining o'er my head; I was alone,
And seemed to be a trouble to the peace
That was among them. Sometimes it befell   325
In these night-wanderings, that a strong desire
O'erpowered my better reason, and the bird
Which was the captive of another's toils
Became my prey; and when the deed was done
I heard among the solitary hills   330
Low breathings coming after me, and sounds
Of undistinguishable motion, steps
Almost as silent as the turf they trod.
    Nor less in springtime, when on southern banks
The shining sun had from his knot of leaves   335
Decoyed the primrose flower, and when the vales
And woods were warm, was I a plunderer then
In the high places, on the lonesome peaks
Where'er among the mountains and the winds
The mother-bird had built her lodge. Though mean   340
My object and inglorious, yet the end
Was not ignoble. Oh, when I have hung
Above the raven's nest,[16] by knots of grass
And half-inch fissures in the slippery rock
But ill sustained, and almost (as it seemed)   345

---

[15] *that beloved vale* of Esthwaite, southern part of the Lake District; site of Hawkshead Grammar School, which Wordsworth attended 1779–87.

[16] *the raven's nest* Hawkshead schoolboys descended cliff-faces on ropes in order to destroy ravens' nests; the ravens preyed on lambs.

Suspended by the blast which blew amain,
Shouldering the naked crag – oh, at that time
While on the perilous ridge I hung alone,
With what strange utterance did the loud dry wind
Blow through my ears! The sky seemed not a sky   350
Of earth, and with what motion moved the clouds!
     The mind of man is framed even like the breath
And harmony of music; there is a dark
Invisible workmanship that reconciles
Discordant elements, and makes them move   355
In one society. Ah me! that all
The terrors, all the early miseries,
Regrets, vexations, lassitudes, that all
The thoughts and feelings which have been infused
Into my mind, should ever have made up   360
The calm existence that is mine when I
Am worthy of myself. Praise to the end –
Thanks likewise for the means! But I believe
That nature, oftentimes, when she would frame
A favoured being, from his earliest dawn   365
Of infancy doth open out the clouds
As at the touch of lightning, seeking him
With gentlest visitation; not the less,
Though haply aiming at the self-same end,
Does it delight her sometimes to employ   370
Severer interventions, ministry
More palpable – and so she dealt with me.
     One evening (surely I was led by her)
I went alone into a shepherd's boat,
A skiff that to a willow-tree was tied   375
Within a rocky cave, its usual home.
'Twas by the shores of Patterdale,[17] a vale
Wherein I was a stranger, thither come
A schoolboy-traveller at the holidays.
Forth rambled from the village inn alone   380
No sooner had I sight of this small skiff,
Discovered thus by unexpected chance,
Than I unloosed her tether and embarked.
The moon was up, the lake was shining clear
Among the hoary mountains; from the shore   385
I pushed, and struck the oars, and struck again
In cadence, and my little boat moved on
Even like a man who walks with stately step
Though bent on speed. It was an act of stealth
And troubled pleasure; nor without the voice   390

---

[17] *Patterdale* the western side of Ullswater, in the
north-east Lake District.

Of mountain-echoes did my boat move on,
Leaving behind her still on either side
Small circles glittering idly in the moon
Until they melted all into one track
Of sparkling light.
          A rocky steep uprose   395
Above the cavern of the willow-tree,
And now, as suited one who proudly rowed
With his best skill, I fixed a steady view
Upon the top of that same craggy ridge,
The bound of the horizon, for behind   400
Was nothing but the stars and the grey sky.
She was an elfin pinnace; lustily
I dipped my oars into the silent lake,
And as I rose upon the stroke my boat
Went heaving through the water like a swan –   405
When, from behind that craggy steep (till then
The bound of the horizon), a huge cliff,[18]
As if with voluntary power instinct,
Upreared its head. I struck and struck again,
And growing still in stature, the huge cliff   410
Rose up between me and the stars, and still,
With measured motion, like a living thing
Strode after me. With trembling hands I turned
And through the silent water stole my way
Back to the cavern of the willow-tree.   415
There in her mooring-place I left my bark,
And through the meadows homeward went with grave
And serious thoughts; and after I had seen
That spectacle, for many days my brain
Worked with a dim and undetermined sense   420
Of unknown modes of being. In my thoughts
There was a darkness – call it solitude
Or blank desertion; no familiar shapes
Of hourly objects, images of trees,
Of sea or sky, no colours of green fields,   425
But huge and mighty forms that do not live
Like living men moved slowly through my mind
By day, and were the trouble of my dreams.
   Wisdom and spirit of the universe,
Thou soul that art the eternity of thought,   430
That givest to forms and images a breath
And everlasting motion! – not in vain,
By day or star-light thus from my first dawn

---

[18] *a huge cliff* Glenridding Dodd, the stepped-back summit of which causes its peak to make a sudden, delayed appearance above the 'craggy steep' of Sty-barrow Crag as one rows out from the shores of Patterdale (Grevel Lindop, *A Literary Guide to the Lake District* (1993), pp. 317–18).

Of childhood didst thou intertwine for me
The passions that build up our human soul,   435
Not with the mean and vulgar works of man,
But with high objects, with enduring things,
With life and nature, purifying thus
The elements of feeling and of thought,
And sanctifying by such discipline   440
Both pain and fear, until we recognize
A grandeur in the beatings of the heart.
Nor was this fellowship vouchsafed to me
With stinted kindness. In November days
When vapours rolling down the valleys made   445
A lonely scene more lonesome, among woods
At noon, and mid the calm of summer nights
When by the margin of the trembling lake
Beneath the gloomy hills I homeward went
In solitude, such intercourse was mine –   450
'Twas mine among the fields both day and night,
And by the waters all the summer long.
      And in the frosty season, when the sun
Was set, and visible for many a mile,
The cottage windows through the twilight blazed,   455
I heeded not the summons; happy time
It was indeed for all of us – to me
It was a time of rapture. Clear and loud
The village clock tolled six; I wheeled about,
Proud and exulting like an untired horse   460
That cares not for its home. All shod with steel
We hissed along the polished ice in games
Confederate, imitative of the chase
And woodland pleasures – the resounding horn,
The pack loud bellowing, and the hunted hare.   465
So through the darkness and the cold we flew,
And not a voice was idle. With the din,
Meanwhile, the precipices rang aloud,
The leafless trees and every icy crag
Tinkled like iron, while the distant hills   470
Into the tumult sent an alien sound
Of melancholy, not unnoticed – while the stars
Eastward were sparkling clear, and in the west
The orange sky of evening died away.
      Not seldom from the uproar I retired   475
Into a silent bay, or sportively
Glanced sideway, leaving the tumultuous throng,
To cut across the image of a star
That gleamed upon the ice. And oftentimes,
When we had given our bodies to the wind,   480
And all the shadowy banks on either side

Came sweeping through the darkness, spinning still
The rapid line of motion – then at once
Have I, reclining back upon my heels,
Stopped short: yet still the solitary cliffs   485
Wheeled by me, even as if the earth had rolled
With visible motion her diurnal round;
Behind me did they stretch in solemn train
Feebler and feebler, and I stood and watched
Till all was tranquil as a dreamless sleep.   490
   Ye presences of nature, in the sky
Or on the earth! Ye visions of the hills
And souls of lonely places, can I think
A vulgar hope was yours when ye employed
Such ministry – when ye through many a year   495
Haunting me thus among my boyish sports,
On caves and trees, upon the woods and hills,
Impressed upon all forms the characters
Of danger or desire, and thus did make
The surface of the universal earth   500
With triumph and delight, and hope and fear,
Work like a sea?
            Not uselessly employed,
I might pursue this theme through every change
Of exercise and play to which the year
Did summon us in its delightful round.   505
We were a noisy crew; the sun in heaven
Beheld not vales more beautiful than ours,
Nor saw a race in happiness and joy
More worthy of the fields where they were sown.
I would record with no reluctant voice   510
The woods of autumn and their hazel-bowers
With milk-white clusters hung, the rod and line
(True symbol of the foolishness of hope)
Which with its strong enchantment led us on
By rocks and pools shut out from every star   515
All the green summer, to forlorn cascades
Among the windings of the mountain brooks.
Unfading recollections! – at this hour
The heart is almost mine with which I felt
From some hill-top on sunny afternoons   520
The kite high up among the fleecy clouds
Pull at its rein like an impatient courser,
Or, from the meadows sent on gusty days,
Beheld her breast the wind, then suddenly
Dashed headlong, and rejected by the storm.   525
   Ye lowly cottages in which we dwelt,
A ministration of your own was yours,
A sanctity, a safeguard, and a love.

Can I forget you, being as ye were
So beautiful among the pleasant fields   530
In which ye stood? Or can I here forget
The plain and seemly countenance with which
Ye dealt out your plain comforts? Yet had ye
Delights and exultations of your own:
Eager and never weary we pursued   535
Our home amusements by the warm peat-fire
At evening, when with pencil and with slate
(In square divisions parcelled out, and all
With crosses and with cyphers scribbled o'er)[19]
We schemed and puzzled, head opposed to head,   540
In strife too humble to be named in verse;
Or round the naked table, snow-white deal,
Cherry or maple, sat in close array,
And to the combat, loo or whist, led on
A thick-ribbed army – not (as in the world)   545
Neglected and ungratefully thrown by
Even for the very service they had wrought,
But husbanded through many a long campaign.
Uncouth assemblage was it, where no few
Had changed their functions – some, plebeian cards   550
Which fate, beyond the promise of their birth,
Had glorified, and called to represent
The persons of departed potentates.
Oh with what echoes on the board they fell!
Ironic diamonds – clubs, hearts, diamonds, spades,   555
A congregation piteously akin!
Cheap matter did they give to boyish wit,
Those sooty knaves, precipitated down
With scoffs and taunts, like Vulcan out of heaven;
The paramount ace, a moon in her eclipse;   560
Queens gleaming through their splendour's last decay,
And monarchs surly at the wrongs sustained
By royal visages. Meanwhile abroad
The heavy rain was falling, or the frost
Raged bitterly with keen and silent tooth,   565
And, interrupting the impassioned game,
From Esthwaite's neighbouring lake the splitting ice,
While it sank down towards the water, sent
Among the meadows and the hills its long
And dismal yellings, like the noise of wolves   570
When they are howling round the Bothnic main.[20]
      Nor, sedulous as I have been to trace
How nature by extrinsic passion first
Peopled my mind with beauteous forms or grand

---

[19] Tick-tack-toe, or noughts and crosses.   [20] *Bothnic main* northern area of the Baltic Sea.

And made me love them, may I well forget 575
How other pleasures have been mine, and joys
Of subtler origin – how I have felt,
Not seldom, even in that tempestuous time,
Those hallowed and pure motions of the sense
Which seem in their simplicity to own 580
An intellectual charm, that calm delight
Which (if I err not) surely must belong
To those first-born affinities that fit
Our new existence to existing things,
And in our dawn of being constitute 585
The bond of union betwixt life and joy.
   Yes, I remember when the changeful earth
And twice five seasons on my mind had stamped
The faces of the moving year; even then,
A child, I held unconscious intercourse 590
With the eternal beauty, drinking in
A pure organic pleasure from the lines
Of curling mist, or from the level plain
Of waters coloured by the steady clouds.
   The sands of Westmorland, the creeks and bays 595
Of Cumbria's rocky limits, they can tell
How when the sea threw off his evening shade
And to the shepherd's hut beneath the crags
Did send sweet notice of the rising moon,
How I have stood, to fancies such as these 600
(Engrafted in the tenderness of thought)
A stranger, linking with the spectacle
No conscious memory of a kindred sight,
And bringing with me no peculiar sense
Of quietness or peace – yet I have stood, 605
Even while mine eye has moved o'er three long leagues
Of shining water, gathering as it seemed
Through every hair-breadth of that field of light
New pleasure like a bee among the flowers.
   Thus often in those fits of vulgar joy 610
Which through all seasons on a child's pursuits
Are prompt attendants, mid that giddy bliss
Which like a tempest works along the blood
And is forgotten – even then I felt
Gleams like the flashing of a shield. The earth 615
And common face of nature spake to me
Rememberable things – sometimes, 'tis true,
By chance collisions and quaint accidents
(Like those ill-sorted unions, work supposed
Of evil-minded fairies), yet not vain 620
Nor profitless if haply they impressed
Collateral objects and appearances,

Albeit lifeless then and doomed to sleep
Until maturer seasons called them forth
To impregnate and to elevate the mind.   625
And if the vulgar joy by its own weight
Wearied itself out of the memory,
The scenes which were a witness of that joy
Remained in their substantial lineaments
Depicted on the brain, and to the eye   630
Were visible, a daily sight. And thus,
By the impressive discipline of fear,
By pleasure, and repeated happiness
(So frequently repeated), and by force
Of obscure feelings representative   635
Of joys that were forgotten, these same scenes
So beauteous and majestic in themselves,
Though yet the day was distant, did at length
Become habitually dear, and all
Their hues and forms were by invisible links   640
Allied to the affections.
                         I began
My story early, feeling (as I fear)
The weakness of a human love for days
Disowned by memory, ere the birth of spring
Planting my snowdrops among winter snows.   645
Nor will it seem to thee, my friend so prompt
In sympathy, that I have lengthened out
With fond and feeble tongue a tedious tale.
Meanwhile my hope has been that I might fetch
Invigorating thoughts from former years,   650
Might fix the wavering balance of my mind,
And haply meet reproaches too whose power
May spur me on, in manhood now mature,
To honourable toil.[21] Yet should these hopes
Be vain, and thus should neither I be taught   655
To understand myself, nor thou to know
With better knowledge how the heart was framed
Of him thou lovest, need I dread from thee
Harsh judgements if I am so loath to quit
Those recollected hours that have the charm   660
Of visionary things, and lovely forms
And sweet sensations that throw back our life
And almost make our infancy itself
A visible scene on which the sun is shining?
    One end hereby at least hath been attained: 665
My mind hath been revived; and if this mood

---

[21] *honourable toil* composition of *The Recluse*, which
Coleridge wanted Wordsworth to complete.

Desert me not, I will forthwith bring down
Through later years the story of my life.
The road lies plain before me; 'tis a theme
Single and of determined bounds, and hence   670
I choose it rather at this time, than work
Of ampler or more varied argument.

Book Two
School-Time (continued)

Thus far, oh friend, have we, though leaving much
Unvisited, endeavoured to retrace
My life through its first years, and measured back
The way I travelled when I first began
To love the woods and fields. The passion yet   5
Was in its birth, sustained (as might befall)
By nourishment that came unsought; for still
From week to week, from month to month, we lived
A round of tumult. Duly were our games
Prolonged in summer till the daylight failed.   10
No chair remained before the doors; the bench
And threshold steps were empty; fast asleep
The labourer, and the old man who had sat
A later lingerer – yet the revelry
Continued, and the loud uproar! At last,   15
When all the ground was dark, and the huge clouds
Were edged with twinkling stars, to bed we went,
With weary joints and with a beating mind.
   Ah! is there one who ever has been young
And needs a monitory voice to tame   20
The pride of virtue and of intellect?
And is there one, the wisest and the best
Of all mankind, who does not sometimes wish
For things which cannot be, who would not give,
If so he might, to duty and to truth   25
The eagerness of infantine desire?
A tranquillizing spirit presses now
On my corporeal frame, so wide appears
The vacancy between me and those days
Which yet have such self-presence in my mind   30
That sometimes, when I think of them I seem
Two consciousnesses – conscious of myself
And of some other being. A grey stone
Of native rock, left midway in the square
Of our small market-village,¹ was the home   35

And centre of these joys; and when, returned
After long absence,[2] thither I repaired,
I found that it was split, and gone to build
A smart assembly-room that perked and flared
With wash and rough-cast, elbowing the ground   40
Which had been ours. But let the fiddle scream
And be ye happy! Yet, my friends, I know
That more than one of you will think with me
Of those soft starry nights, and that old dame
From whom the stone was named, who there had sat   45
And watched her table with its huckster's wares,
Assiduous through the length of sixty years.
We ran a boisterous race: the year span round
With giddy motion. But the time approached
That brought with it a regular desire   50
For calmer pleasures, when the beauteous forms
Of nature were collaterally attached
To every scheme of holiday delight
And every boyish sport – less grateful else,
And languidly pursued.
　　　　　　　When summer came   55
It was the pastime of our afternoons
To beat along the plain of Windermere
With rival oars, and the selected bourne
Was now an island musical with birds
That sang for ever; now a sister isle   60
Beneath the oak's umbrageous covert, sown
With lilies-of-the-valley, like a field;
And now a third small island where remained
An old stone table and a mouldered cave –
A hermit's history. In such a race,   65
So ended, disappointment could be none,
Uneasiness, or pain, or jealousy;
We rested in the shade, all pleased alike,
Conquered and conqueror. Thus the pride of strength
And the vainglory of superior skill   70
Were interfused with objects which subdued
And tempered them, and gradually produced
A quiet independence of the heart.
And to my friend who knows me, I may add,
Unapprehensive of reproof, that hence   75
Ensued a diffidence and modesty,
And I was taught to feel (perhaps too much)
The self-sufficing power of solitude.
　　No delicate viands sapped our bodily strength:

[2] Wordsworth returned to Hawkshead, with his
brother John and Coleridge, c.2 Nov. 1799.

More than we wished we knew the blessing then   80
Of vigorous hunger, for our daily meals
Were frugal, Sabine fare;[3] and then, exclude
A little weekly stipend, and we lived
Through three divisions of the quartered year
In penniless poverty. But now, to school   85
Returned from the half-yearly holidays,
We came with purses more profusely filled,
Allowance which abundantly sufficed
To gratify the palate with repasts
More costly than the dame of whom I spake,   90
That ancient woman, and her board, supplied.
Hence inroads into distant vales, and long
Excursions far away among the hills,
Hence rustic dinners on the cool green ground,
Or in the woods, or near a riverside,   95
Or by some shady fountain – while soft airs
Among the leaves were stirring, and the sun
Unfelt shone sweetly round us in our joy.
    Nor is my aim neglected if I tell
How twice in the long length of those half-years   100
We from our funds perhaps with bolder hand
Drew largely – anxious for one day, at least,
To feel the motion of the galloping steed.
And with the good old innkeeper, in truth,
On such occasion sometimes we employed   105
Sly subterfuge, for the intended bound
Of the day's journey was too distant far
For any cautious man: a structure famed
Beyond its neighbourhood – the antique walls
Of that large Abbey[4] which within the Vale   110
Of Nightshade, to St Mary's honour built,
Stands yet, a mouldering pile with fractured arch,
Belfry, and images, and living trees,
A holy scene! Along the smooth green turf
Our horses grazed. To more than inland peace   115
Left by the sea wind passing overhead
(Though wind of roughest temper) trees and towers
May in that valley oftentimes be seen,
Both silent and both motionless alike;
Such is the shelter that is there, and such   120
The safeguard for repose and quietness.
    Our steeds remounted and the summons given,
With whip and spur we by the chantry flew
In uncouth race, and left the cross-legged knight,

<hr>

[3] Horace wrote of his frugal existence on his Sabine   [4] Furness Abbey, near Barrow-in-Furness.
farm.

And the stone abbot,[5] and that single wren   125
Which one day sang so sweetly in the nave
Of the old church that though from recent showers
The earth was comfortless, and, touched by faint
Internal breezes – sobbings of the place
And respirations – from the roofless walls   130
The shuddering ivy dripped large drops, yet still
So sweetly mid the gloom the invisible bird
Sang to itself that there I could have made
My dwelling-place, and lived forever there
To hear such music. Through the walls we flew   135
And down the valley, and, a circuit made
In wantonness of heart, through rough and smooth
We scampered homeward. Oh, ye rocks and streams,
And that still spirit of the evening air!
Even in this joyous time I sometimes felt   140
Your presence, when with slackened step we breathed[6]
Along the sides of the steep hills, or when,
Lighted by gleams of moonlight from the sea,
We beat with thundering hoofs the level sand.

    Upon the eastern shore of Windermere   145
Above the crescent of a pleasant bay,
There was an inn[7] – no homely-featured shed,
Brother of the surrounding cottages,
But 'twas a splendid place, the door beset
With chaises, grooms, and liveries, and within   150
Decanters, glasses, and the blood-red wine.
In ancient times, or ere the Hall[8] was built
On the large island, had this dwelling been
More worthy of a poet's love, a hut
Proud of its one bright fire and sycamore shade.   155
But though the rhymes were gone which once inscribed
The threshold, and large golden characters
On the blue-frosted signboard had usurped
The place of the old lion, in contempt
And mockery of the rustic painter's hand,   160
Yet to this hour the spot to me is dear
With all its foolish pomp. The garden lay
Upon a slope surmounted by the plain
Of a small bowling-green; beneath us stood
A grove, with gleams of water through the trees   165
And over the tree-tops – nor did we want
Refreshment, strawberries and mellow cream.
And there, through half an afternoon, we played

---

[5] *the cross-legged knight, / And the stone abbot* memorial statues.

[6] *breathed* the horses got their breath back.

[7] The White Lion, Bowness (now gone).

[8] *the Hall* the Curwen mansion on Belle Isle, built in the early 1780s.

On the smooth platform, and the shouts we sent
Made all the mountains ring. But ere the fall　　　　　　170
Of night, when in our pinnace we returned
Over the dusky lake, and to the beach
Of some small island steered our course, with one,[9]
The minstrel of our troop, and left him there,
And rowed off gently while he blew his flute　　　　　　175
Alone upon the rock, oh then the calm
And dead still water lay upon my mind
Even with a weight of pleasure, and the sky,
Never before so beautiful, sank down
Into my heart, and held me like a dream.　　　　　　180
　　Thus daily were my sympathies enlarged,
And thus the common range of visible things
Grew dear to me. Already I began
To love the sun – a boy I loved the sun
Not as I since have loved him (as a pledge　　　　　　185
And surety of our earthly life, a light
Which while we view we feel we are alive),
But for this cause: that I had seen him lay
His beauty on the morning hills, had seen
The western mountain touch his setting orb　　　　　　190
In many a thoughtless hour, when from excess
Of happiness my blood appeared to flow
With its own pleasure, and I breathed with joy.
And from like feelings, humble though intense
(To patriotic and domestic love　　　　　　195
Analogous), the moon to me was dear:
For I would dream away my purposes,
Standing to look upon her while she hung
Midway between the hills, as if she knew
No other region, but belonged to thee –　　　　　　200
Yea, appertained by a peculiar right
To thee and thy grey huts, my darling vale!
　　Those incidental charms which first attached
My heart to rural objects day by day
Grew weaker, and I hasten on to tell　　　　　　205
How nature – intervenient till this time,
And secondary – now at length was sought
For her own sake. But who shall parcel out
His intellect by geometric rules,
Split like a province into round and square?　　　　　　210
Who knows the individual hour in which
His habits were first sown, even as a seed?
Who that shall point as with a wand, and say,

---

[9] *one* Robert Greenwood, later Senior Fellow of
Trinity College, Cambridge.

'This portion of the river of my mind
Came from yon fountain'? Thou, my friend, art one   215
More deeply read in thy own thoughts; to thee
Science appears but what in truth she is –
Not as our glory and our absolute boast,
But as a succedaneum[10] and a prop
To our infirmity. Thou art no slave   220
Of that false secondary power by which
In weakness we create distinctions, then
Deem that our puny boundaries are things
Which we perceive, and not which we have made.
To thee, unblinded by these outward shows,   225
The unity of all has been revealed;[11]
And thou wilt doubt with me, less aptly skilled
Than many are to class the cabinet
Of their sensations, and in voluble phrase
Run through the history and birth of each   230
As of a single independent thing.
Hard task to analyse a soul, in which
Not only general habits and desires,
But each most obvious and particular thought –
Not in a mystical and idle sense,   235
But in the words of reason deeply weighed –
Hath no beginning.
                    Blessed the infant babe
(For with my best conjectures I would trace
The progress of our being) – blessed the babe
Nursed in his mother's arms, the babe who sleeps   240
Upon his mother's breast, who, when his soul
Claims manifest kindred with an earthly soul,
Doth gather passion from his mother's eye!
Such feelings pass into his torpid life
Like an awakening breeze, and hence his mind,   245
Even in the first trial of its powers,
Is prompt and watchful, eager to combine
In one appearance all the elements
And parts of the same object, else detached
And loath to coalesce. Thus day by day   250
Subjected to the discipline of love,
His organs and recipient faculties
Are quickened, are more vigorous; his mind spreads,
Tenacious of the forms which it receives.
In one beloved presence – nay and more;   255
In that most apprehensive habitude

---

[10] *succedaneum* remedy.
[11] *The unity of all has been revealed* Coleridge was a
Unitarian (one who rejects the doctrine of the Trinity
in favour of the belief that God is one person).

And those sensations which have been derived
From this beloved presence, there exists
A virtue which irradiates and exalts
All objects through all intercourse of sense.   260
No outcast he, bewildered and depressed:
Along his infant veins are interfused
The gravitation and the filial bond
Of nature that connect him with the world.
Emphatically such a being lives   265
An inmate of this *active* universe.
From nature largely he receives, nor so
Is satisfied, but largely gives again –
For feeling has to him imparted strength;
And, powerful in all sentiments of grief,   270
Of exultation, fear, and joy, his mind,
Even as an agent of the one great mind,[12]
Creates, creator and receiver both,[13]
Working but in alliance with the works
Which it beholds. Such, verily, is the first   275
Poetic spirit of our human life,
By uniform control of after-years
In most abated and suppressed, in some
Through every change of growth or of decay
Pre-eminent till death.   280
               From early days,
Beginning not long after that first time
In which, a babe, by intercourse of touch,
I held mute dialogues with my mother's heart,
I have endeavoured to display the means
Whereby the infant sensibility,   285
Great birthright of our being, was in me
Augmented and sustained. Yet is a path
More difficult before me, and I fear
That in its broken windings we shall need
The chamois' sinews and the eagle's wing.   290
For now a trouble came into my mind
From unknown causes: I was left alone,
Seeking the visible world, nor knowing why.
The props of my affections were removed,
And yet the building stood, as if sustained   295
By its own spirit. All that I beheld
Was dear to me, and from this cause it came:
That now to nature's finer influxes
My mind lay open to that more exact
And intimate communion which our hearts   300

---

[12]   *one great mind* God.   [13]   *creator and receiver both* the child's mind is both creative and perceptive.

Maintain with the minuter properties
Of objects which already are beloved,
And of those only.
                    Many are the joys
Of youth, but oh what happiness to live
When every hour brings palpable access   305
Of knowledge, when all knowledge is delight,
And sorrow is not there! The seasons came,
And every season to my notice brought
A store of transitory qualities
Which, but for this most watchful power of love,   310
Had been neglected – left a register
Of permanent relations, else unknown.
Hence life, and change, and beauty, solitude
More active even than 'best society',[14]
Society made sweet as solitude   315
By silent inobtrusive sympathies,
And gentle agitations of the mind
From manifold distinctions (difference
Perceived in things where to the common eye
No difference is) – and hence, from the same source, 320
Sublimer joy. For I would walk alone
In storm and tempest, or in starlight nights
Beneath the quiet heavens, and at that time
Have felt whate'er there is of power in sound
To breathe an elevated mood, by form   325
Or image unprofaned. And I would stand
Beneath some rock, listening to sounds that are
The ghostly language of the ancient earth
Or make their dim abode in distant winds:
Thence did I drink the visionary power.   330
I deem not profitless those fleeting moods
Of shadowy exultation – not for this,
That they are kindred to our purer mind
And intellectual life, but that the soul,
Remembering how she felt, but what she felt   335
Remembering not, retains an obscure sense
Of possible sublimity, to which
With growing faculties she doth aspire,
With faculties still growing, feeling still
That whatsoever point they gain they still   340
Have something to pursue.
                         And not alone
In grandeur and in tumult, but no less
In tranquil scenes, that universal power

---

[14] *Paradise Lost*, ix. 249, Adam in Eden: 'For solitude
sometimes is best society'.

And fitness in the latent qualities
And essences of things, by which the mind   345
Is moved with feelings of delight, to me
Came strengthened with a superadded soul,
A virtue not its own. My morning walks
Were early; oft before the hours of school[15]
I travelled round our little lake, five miles   350
Of pleasant wandering – happy time more dear
For this, that one was by my side, a friend[16]
Then passionately loved. With heart how full
Will he peruse these lines, this page (perhaps
A blank to other men), for many years   355
Have since flowed in between us, and, our minds
Both silent to each other, at this time
We live as if those hours had never been.
Nor seldom did I lift our cottage latch
Far earlier, and before the vernal thrush   360
Was audible, among the hills I sat
Alone upon some jutting eminence
At the first hour of morning, when the vale
Lay quiet in an utter solitude.
How shall I trace the history, where seek   365
The origin of what I then have felt?
Oft in those moments such a holy calm
Did overspread my soul, that I forgot
That I had bodily eyes, and what I saw
Appeared like something in myself – a dream,   370
A prospect in my mind.
                        'Twere long to tell
What spring and autumn, what the winter snows,
And what the summer shade, what day and night,
The evening and the morning, what my dreams
And what my waking thoughts supplied to nurse   375
That spirit of religious love in which
I walked with nature. But let this at least
Be not forgotten – that I still retained
My first creative sensibility,
That by the regular action of the world   380
My soul was unsubdued. A plastic[17] power
Abode with me, a forming hand, at times
Rebellious, acting in a devious mood,
A local spirit of its own, at war
With general tendency, but for the most   385
Subservient strictly to the external things
With which it communed. An auxiliar light

[15] School began at 6 or 6.30 in summer, and at 7 in winter.
[16] John Fleming, another Hawkshead schoolboy.
[17] *plastic* shaping, creative.

Came from my mind, which on the setting sun
Bestowed new splendour; the melodious birds,
The gentle breezes, fountains that ran on   390
Murmuring so sweetly in themselves, obeyed
A like dominion, and the midnight storm
Grew darker in the presence of my eye.
Hence my obeisance, my devotion hence,
And hence my transport!
                                Nor should this perchance   395
Pass unrecorded, that I still had loved
The exercise and produce of a toil
Than analytic industry to me
More pleasing, and whose character I deem
Is more poetic, as resembling more   400
Creative agency – I mean to speak
Of that interminable building reared
By observation of affinities
In objects where no brotherhood exists
To common minds. My seventeenth year was come,   405
And, whether from this habit rooted now
So deeply in my mind, or from excess
Of the great social principle of life
Coercing all things into sympathy,
To unorganic natures I transferred   410
My own enjoyments, or, the power of truth
Coming in revelation, I conversed
With things that really are, I at this time
Saw blessings spread around me like a sea.
Thus did my days pass on, and now at length   415
From nature and her overflowing soul
I had received so much that all my thoughts
Were steeped in feeling.
                                I was only then
Contented when with bliss ineffable
I felt the sentiment of being spread   420
O'er all that moves, and all that seemeth still,
O'er all that, lost beyond the reach of thought
And human knowledge, to the human eye
Invisible, yet liveth to the heart;
O'er all that leaps and runs, and shouts and sings,   425
Or beats the gladsome air; o'er all that glides
Beneath the wave, yea in the wave itself
And mighty depth of waters. Wonder not
If such my transports were, for in all things
I saw one life,[18] and felt that it was joy.   430

---

[18] *one life* Wordsworth was a pantheist, briefly, in
spring and summer 1798 – some 11 years after the
period described here.

One song they sang, and it was audible –
Most audible then when the fleshly ear,
O'ercome by grosser prelude of that strain,
Forgot its functions and slept undisturbed.
    If this be error, and another faith   435
Find easier access to the pious mind,
Yet were I grossly destitute of all
Those human sentiments which make this earth
So dear, if I should fail with grateful voice
To speak of you, ye mountains and ye lakes   440
And sounding cataracts, ye mists and winds
That dwell among the hills where I was born.
If in my youth I have been pure in heart,
If, mingling with the world, I am content
With my own modest pleasures, and have lived   445
With God and nature communing, removed
From little enmities and low desires,
The gift is yours; if in these times of fear,
This melancholy waste of hopes o'erthrown,
If, mid indifference and apathy   450
And wicked exultation, when good men[19]
On every side fall off, we know not how,
To selfishness, disguised in gentle names
Of peace and quiet and domestic love,
Yet mingled not unwillingly with sneers   455
On visionary minds – if in this time
Of dereliction and dismay I yet
Despair not of our nature, but retain
A more than Roman confidence, a faith
That fails not, in all sorrow my support,   460
The blessing of my life, the gift is yours,
Ye mountains! – thine, oh nature! Thou hast fed
My lofty speculations, and in thee,
For this uneasy heart of ours, I find
A never-failing principle of joy   465
And purest passion.
                    Thou, my friend, wert reared
In the great city, mid far other scenes,[20]
But we by different roads at length have gained
The self-same bourne. And for this cause to thee
I speak unapprehensive of contempt,   470

[19] *good men* James Mackintosh, apologist for the Revolution in *Vindiciae Gallicae* (1791), who renounced his radicalism in 1799, when these lines were composed, is probably in Wordsworth's mind. See also Lamb, 'On Mackintosh', p. 616, and Coleridge, *Notebooks*, i. 947.

[20] *Thou, my friend ... other scenes* compare Coleridge's address to his son, Hartley, in 'Frost at Midnight', 55–7: 'thou shalt learn far other lore / And in far other scenes! For I was reared / In the great city ...'

The insinuated scoff of coward tongues,
And all that silent language which so oft
In conversation betwixt man and man
Blots from the human countenance all trace
Of beauty and of love. For thou hast sought   475
The truth in solitude, and thou art one,
The most intense of nature's worshippers,
In many things my brother, chiefly here
In this my deep devotion.
                         Fare thee well!
Health and the quiet of a healthful mind   480
Attend thee, seeking oft the haunts of men,
And yet more often living with thyself,
And for thyself. So haply shall thy days
Be many, and a blessing to mankind.

Book Three
Residence at Cambridge

It was a dreary morning[1] when the chaise
Rolled over the flat plains of Huntingdon
And through the open windows first I saw
The long-backed chapel of King's College rear
His pinnacles above the dusky groves.   5
Soon afterwards, we espied upon the road
A student clothed in gown and tasselled cap;
He passed – nor was I master of my eyes
Till he was left a hundred yards behind.
The place, as we approached, seemed more and more   10
To have an eddy's force, and sucked us in
More eagerly at every step we took.
Onward we drove beneath the castle; down
By Magdalene Bridge we went and crossed the Cam,
And at the Hoop we landed, famous inn!   15
    My spirit was up, my thoughts were full of hope;
Some friends I had – acquaintances who there
Seemed friends – poor simple schoolboys, now hung round
With honour and importance. In a world
Of welcome faces up and down I roved;   20
Questions, directions, counsel and advice,
Flowed in upon me from all sides. Fresh day
Of pride and pleasure! – to myself I seemed
A man of business and expense, and went

BOOK THREE
[1] *It was a dreary morning* probably that of 30 Oct.
1787; Wordsworth was formally admitted to St John's
College, Cambridge, on 6 Nov.

From shop to shop about my own affairs,   25
To tutors or to tailors as befell,
From street to street with loose and careless heart.
   I was the dreamer, they the dream; I roamed
Delighted through the motley spectacle –
Gowns (grave or gaudy), doctors, students, streets,   30
Lamps, gateways, flocks of churches, courts and towers:
Strange transformation for a mountain youth,
A northern villager!
           As if by word
Of magic or some fairy's power, at once
Behold me rich in moneys, and attired   35
In splendid clothes, with hose of silk, and hair
Glittering like rimy trees when frost is keen[2]
(My lordly dressing-gown, I pass it by,
With other signs of manhood which supplied
The lack of beard). The weeks went roundly on   40
With invitations, suppers, wine and fruit,
Smooth housekeeping within, and all without
Liberal, and suiting gentleman's array!
   The Evangelist St John my patron was:
Three gloomy courts are his, and in the first   45
Was my abiding-place, a nook obscure.
Right underneath, the College kitchens made
A humming sound, less tuneable than bees
But hardly less industrious, with shrill notes
Of sharp command and scolding intermixed.   50
Near me was Trinity's loquacious clock
Who never let the quarters, night or day,
Slip by him unproclaimed, and told the hours
Twice over with a male and female voice.
Her pealing organ was my neighbour too,   55
And from my bedroom I in moonlight nights
Could see right opposite, a few yards off,
The antechapel where the statue stood
Of Newton with his prism and silent face.
   Of College labours, of the lecturer's room   60
(All studded round, as thick as chairs could stand,
With loyal students faithful to their books,
Half-and-half idlers, hardy recusants,[3]
And honest dunces), of important days –
Examinations, when the man was weighed   65
As in the balance – of excessive hopes,
Tremblings withal and commendable fears,
Small jealousies and triumphs good or bad,

---

[2] Wordsworth powdered his hair, as was the   [3] *recusants* rebels.
fashion.

I make short mention. Things they were which then
I did not love, nor do I love them now: 70
Such glory was but little sought by me
And little won. But it is right to say
That even so early, from the first crude days
Of settling-time in this my new abode,
Not seldom I had melancholy thoughts   75
From personal and family regards
(Wishing to hope without a hope), some fears
About my future worldly maintenance,
And, more than all, a strangeness in my mind,
A feeling that I was not for that hour,   80
Nor for that place. But wherefore be cast down?
Why should I grieve? I was a chosen son.
For hither I had come with holy powers
And faculties (whether to work or feel)
To apprehend all passions and all moods   85
Which time and place and season do impress
Upon the visible universe, and work
Like changes there by force of my own mind.
I was a freeman – in the purest sense
Was free – and to majestic ends was strong.   90
I do not speak of learning, moral truth
Or understanding; 'twas enough for me
To know that I was otherwise endowed.
    When the first glitter of the show was passed,
And the first dazzle of the taper-light,   95
As if with a rebound my mind returned
Into its former self. Oft did I leave
My comrades, and the crowd, buildings and groves,
And walked along the fields, the level fields,
With heaven's blue concave reared above my head   100
And now it was that, through such change entire
And this first absence from those shapes sublime
Wherewith I had been conversant, my mind
Seemed busier in itself than heretofore –
At least I more directly recognized   105
My powers and habits. Let me dare to speak
A higher language, say that now I felt
The strength and consolation which were mine.
As if awakened, summoned, roused, constrained,
I looked for universal things, perused   110
The common countenance of earth and heaven,
And, turning the mind in upon itself,
Pored, watched, expected, listened, spread my thoughts
And spread them with a wider creeping – felt
Incumbences more awful, visitings   115
Of the upholder, of the tranquil soul

Which underneath all passion lives secure,
A steadfast life. But peace; it is enough
To notice that I was ascending now
To such community with highest truth.   120
    A track pursuing not untrod before,
From deep analogies by thought supplied
Or consciousnesses not to be subdued,
To every natural form – rock, fruit or flower,
Even the loose stones that cover the highway –   125
I gave a moral life; I saw them feel,
Or linked them to some feeling. The great mass
Lay bedded in a quickening soul, and all
That I beheld respired with inward meaning.
Thus much for the one presence, and the life   130
Of the great whole; suffice it here to add
That whatsoe'er of terror or of love
Or beauty, nature's daily face put on
From transitory passion, unto this
I was as wakeful even as waters are   135
To the sky's motion, in a kindred sense
Of passion was obedient as a lute
That waits upon the touches of the wind.
So was it with me in my solitude;
So, often among multitudes of men.   140
Unknown, unthought of, yet I was most rich,
I had a world about me – 'twas my own,
I made it; for it only lived to me
And to the God who looked into my mind.
    Such sympathies would sometimes show themselves   145
By outward gestures and by visible looks –
Some called it madness; such indeed it was,
If childlike fruitfulness in passing joy,
If steady moods of thoughtfulness matured
To inspiration, sort with such a name;   150
If prophecy be madness; if things viewed
By poets of old time, and higher up
By the first men, earth's first inhabitants,
May in these tutored days no more be seen
With undisordered sight. But leaving this,   155
It was no madness; for I had an eye
Which in my strongest workings evermore
Was looking for the shades of difference
As they lie hid in all exterior forms,
Near or remote, minute or vast – an eye   160
Which from a stone, a tree, a withered leaf,
To the broad ocean and the azure heavens
Spangled with kindred multitudes of stars,
Could find no surface where its power might sleep,

Which spake perpetual logic to my soul,   165
And by an unrelenting agency
Did bind my feelings even as in a chain.
  And here, oh friend, have I retraced my life
Up to an eminence, and told a tale
Of matters which not falsely I may call   170
The glory of my youth. Of genius, power,
Creation and divinity itself
I have been speaking, for my theme has been
What passed within me. Not of outward things
Done visibly for other minds – words, signs,   175
Symbols or actions – but of my own heart
Have I been speaking, and my youthful mind.
Oh heavens! how awful is the might of souls,
And what they do within themselves while yet
The yoke of earth is new to them, the world   180
Nothing but a wild field where they were sown.
This is in truth heroic argument[4]
And genuine prowess, which I wished to touch
With hand however weak, but in the main
It lies far hidden from the reach of words.   185
Points have we all of us within our souls
Where all stand single; this I feel, and make
Breathings for incommunicable powers.
Yet each man is a memory to himself,
And therefore, now that I must quit this theme,   190
I am not heartless, for there's not a man
That lives who hath not had his godlike hours,
And knows not what majestic sway we have
As natural beings in the strength of nature.
  Enough – for now into a populous plain   195
We must descend. A traveller I am,
And all my tale is of myself; even so,
So be it, if the pure in heart delight
To follow me, and thou, oh honoured friend,
Who in my thoughts art ever at my side,   200
Uphold as heretofore my fainting steps.
  It hath been told already how my sight
Was dazzled by the novel show, and how
Erelong I did into myself return:
So did it seem, and so in truth it was –   205
Yet this was but short-lived; thereafter came
Observance less devout. I had made a change
In climate, and my nature's outward coat
Changed also, slowly and insensibly.

---

[4]   *heroic argument* at *Paradise Lost*, ix. 14, Milton claims   heroic' than the epics of Homer and Virgil; Word-
his theme ('argument') to be 'Not less but more   sworth places himself in this great tradition.

To the deep quiet and majestic thoughts   210
Of loneliness succeeded empty noise
And superficial pastimes, now and then
Forced labour, and more frequently forced hopes;
And, worse than all, a treasonable growth
Of indecisive judgements that impaired   215
And shook the mind's simplicity. And yet
This was a gladsome time. Could I behold
(Who, less insensible than sodden clay
On a sea-river's bed at ebb of tide,
Could have beheld) with undelighted heart   220
So many happy youths, so wide and fair
A congregation in its budding-time
Of health, and hope, and beauty, all at once
So many diverse samples of the growth
Of life's sweet season? – could have seen unmoved   225
That miscellaneous garland of wild-flowers
Upon the matron temples of a place
So famous through the world? To me at least
It was a goodly prospect, for, through youth,
Though I had been trained up to stand unpropped,   230
And independent musings pleased me so
That spells seemed on me when I was alone,
Yet could I only cleave to solitude
In lonesome places. If a throng was near,
That way I leaned by nature, for my heart   235
Was social, and loved idleness and joy.
     Not seeking those who might participate
My deeper pleasures (nay, I had not once,
Though not unused to mutter lonesome songs,
Even with myself divided such delight,   240
Or looked that way for aught that might be clothed
In human language), easily I passed
From the remembrances of better things,
And slipped into the weekday works of youth,
Unburdened, unalarmed, and unprofaned.   245
Caverns there were within my mind which sun
Could never penetrate, yet did there not
Want store of leafy arbours where the light
Might enter in at will. Companionships,
Friendships, acquaintances, were welcome all;   250
We sauntered, played, we rioted, we talked
Unprofitable talk at morning hours,
Drifted about along the streets and walks,
Read lazily in lazy books, went forth
To gallop through the country in blind zeal   255
Of senseless horsemanship, or on the breast
Of Cam sailed boisterously, and let the stars

Come out, perhaps without one quiet thought.
    Such was the tenor of the opening act
In this new life. Imagination slept,   260
And yet not utterly: I could not print
Ground where the grass had yielded to the steps
Of generations of illustrious men
Unmoved. I could not always lightly pass
Through the same gateways, sleep where they had slept,   265
Wake where they waked, range that enclosure old,
That garden of great intellects, undisturbed.
Place also by the side of this dark sense
Of nobler feeling, that those spiritual men,
Even the great Newton's own ethereal self,   270
Seemed humbled in these precincts, thence to be
The more beloved – invested here with tasks
Of life's plain business, as a daily garb
(Dictators at the plough),[5] a change that left
All genuine admiration unimpaired.   275
    Beside the pleasant mills of Trumpington
I laughed with Chaucer;[6] in the hawthorn-shade
Heard him, while birds were warbling, tell his tales
Of amorous passion. And that gentle bard
Chosen by the muses for their page of state,   280
Sweet Spenser, moving through his clouded heaven
With the moon's beauty, and the moon's soft pace:
I called him brother, Englishman, and friend!
Yea, our blind poet,[7] who in his later day
Stood almost single, uttering odious truth –   285
Darkness before, and danger's voice behind:
Soul awful (if the earth hath ever lodged
An awful soul), I seemed to see him here
Familiarly, and in his scholar's dress
Bounding before me, yet a stripling youth –   290
A boy, no better, with his rosy cheeks
Angelical, keen eye, courageous look,
And conscious step of purity and pride.
    Among the band of my compeers was one,
My class-fellow at school, whose chance it was   295
To lodge in the apartments which had been,
Time out of mind, honoured by Milton's name –
The very shell reputed of the abode
Which he had tenanted. Oh temperate bard!
One afternoon, the first time I set foot   300
In this thy innocent nest and oratory,
Seated with others in a festive ring

---

[5] Cincinnatus was at the plough when summoned to
be dictator of Rome in 458 BC.

[6] *The Reeve's Tale* is set in Trumpington.
[7] *our blind poet* Milton.

Of commonplace convention, I to thee
Poured out libations, to thy memory drank,
Within my private thoughts, till my brain reeled, 305
Never so clouded by the fumes of wine
Before that hour or since. Thence forth I ran
From that assembly, through a length of streets
Ran ostrich-like,[8] to reach our chapel door
In not a desperate or opprobrious time, 310
Albeit long after the importunate bell
Had stopped, with wearisome Cassandra[9] voice
No longer haunting the dark winter night
(Call back, oh friend, a moment to thy mind,
The place itself and fashion of the rites). 315
Upshouldering in a dislocated lump
With shallow ostentatious carelessness
My surplice, gloried in and yet despised,
I clove in pride through the inferior throng
Of the plain burghers, who in audience stood 320
On the last skirts of their permitted ground,
Beneath the pealing organ. Empty thoughts!
I am ashamed of them; and that great bard,
And thou, oh friend, who in thy ample mind
Hast stationed me for reverence and love, 325
Ye will forgive the weakness of that hour,
In some of its unworthy vanities
Brother of many more.
                    In this mixed sort
The months passed on, remissly, not given up
To wilful alienation from the right, 330
Or walks of open scandal, but in vague
And loose indifference, easy likings, aims
Of a low pitch – duty and zeal dismissed,
Yet nature, or a happy course of things,
Not doing in their stead the needful work. 335
The memory languidly revolved, the heart
Reposed in noontide rest, the inner pulse
Of contemplation almost failed to beat.
Rotted as by a charm, my life became
A floating island,[10] an amphibious thing, 340
Unsound, of spongy texture, yet withal
Not wanting a fair face of water-weeds
And pleasant flowers. The thirst of living praise,
A reverence for the glorious dead, the sight

---

[8] *ostrich-like* Wordsworth's gown is hitched up so that he can run.
[9] *Cassandra* predicted the fall of Troy but was ignored.

[10] *floating island* There were floating islands at Derwentwater and Esthwaite (Owen and Smyser, ii. 184, 333).

Of those long vistas, catacombs in which   345
Perennial minds lie visibly entombed,
Have often stirred the heart of youth, and bred
A fervent love of rigorous discipline.
Alas! such high commotion touched not me.
No look was in these walls to put to shame   350
My easy spirits, and discountenance
Their light composure, far less to instil
A calm resolve of mind, firmly addressed
To puissant efforts. Nor was this the blame
Of others, but my own; I should in truth,   355
As far as doth concern my single self,
Misdeem most widely, lodging it elsewhere.
For I, bred up in nature's lap, was even
As a spoiled child, and (rambling like the wind,
As I had done in daily intercourse   360
With those delicious rivers, solemn heights
And mountains, ranging like a fowl of the air)
I was ill-tutored for captivity –
To quit my pleasure, and from month to month
Take up a station calmly on the perch   365
Of sedentary peace. Those lovely forms
Had also left less space within my mind,
Which, wrought upon instinctively, had found
A freshness in those objects of its love,
A winning power beyond all other power.   370
Not that I slighted books (that were to lack
All sense), but other passions had been mine
More fervent, making me less prompt perhaps
To indoor study than was wise or well
Or suited to my years.
                Yet I could shape   375
The image of a place which, soothed and lulled
As I had been, trained up in paradise
Among sweet garlands and delightful sounds,
Accustomed in my loneliness to walk
With nature magisterially – yet I,   380
Methinks, could shape the image of a place
Which with its aspect should have bent me down
To instantaneous service, should at once
Have made me pay to science and to arts
And written lore (acknowledged my liege-lord)   385
A homage frankly offered up, like that
Which I had paid to nature. Toil and pains
In this recess which I have bodied forth
Should spread from heart to heart; and stately groves,
Majestic edifices, should not want   390
A corresponding dignity within.

The congregating temper which pervades
Our unripe years, not wasted, should be made
To minister to works of high attempt,
Which the enthusiast would perform with love.   395
Youth should be awed, possessed, as with a sense
Religious, of what holy joy there is
In knowledge, if it be sincerely sought
For its own sake – in glory, and in praise,
If but by labour won, and to endure.   400
The passing day should learn to put aside
Her trappings here, should strip them off, abashed
Before antiquity and steadfast truth
And strong book-mindedness; and over all
Should be a healthy, sound simplicity,   405
A seemly plainness – name it as you will,
Republican, or pious.
                    If these thoughts
Be a gratuitous emblazonry
That does but mock this recreant age, at least
Let folly and false-seeming (we might say)   410
Be free to affect whatever formal gait
Of moral or scholastic discipline
Shall raise them highest in their own esteem –
Let them parade among the schools at will,
But spare the house of God. Was ever known   415
The witless shepherd who would drive his flock
With serious repetition to a pool
Of which 'tis plain to sight they never taste?
A weight must surely hang on days begun
And ended with worst mockery; be wise,   420
Ye Presidents and Deans, and to your bells
Give seasonable rest, for 'tis a sound
Hollow as ever vexed the tranquil air,
And your officious doings bring disgrace
On the plain steeples of our English Church   425
Whose worship mid remotest village trees
Suffers for this. Even science[11] too, at hand
In daily sight of such irreverence,
Is smitten thence with an unnatural taint,
Loses her just authority, falls beneath   430
Collateral suspicion else unknown.
This obvious truth did not escape me then,
Unthinking as I was, and I confess
That, having in my native hills given loose
To a schoolboy's dreaming, I had raised a pile   435

---

[11] *science* knowledge.

Upon the basis of the coming time,
Which now before me melted fast away –
Which could not live, scarcely had life enough
To mock the builder.
                              Oh, what joy it were
To see a sanctuary for our country's youth   440
With such a spirit in it as might be
Protection for itself, a virgin grove[12]
Primeval in its purity and depth,
Where, though the shades were filled with cheerfulness,
Nor indigent of songs warbled from crowds   445
In under-coverts, yet the countenance
Of the whole place should wear a stamp of awe –
A habitation sober and demure
For ruminating creatures, a domain
For quiet things to wander in, a haunt   450
In which the heron might delight to feed
By the shy rivers, and the pelican
Upon the cypress-spire in lonely thought
Might sit and sun himself. Alas, alas!
In vain for such solemnity we look.   455
Our eyes are crossed by butterflies, our ears
Hear chattering popinjays; the inner heart
Is trivial, and the impresses without
Are of a gaudy region.
                              Different sight
Those venerable doctors saw of old,   460
When all who dwelt within these famous walls
Led in abstemiousness a studious life,
When, in forlorn and naked chambers cooped
And crowded, o'er their ponderous books they sat,
Like caterpillars eating out their way   465
In silence, or with keen devouring noise
Not to be tracked or fathered. Princes then
At matins froze, and couched at curfew-time,
Trained up through piety and zeal to prize
Spare diet, patient labour, and plain weeds.   470
Oh seat of arts, renowned throughout the world,
Far different service in those homely days
The nurslings of the muses underwent
From their first childhood – in that glorious time
When learning, like a stranger come from far,   475
Sounding through Christian lands her trumpet, roused
The peasant and the king; when boys and youths,

---

[12]   Wordsworth's source for the grove and most of
its denizens is William Bartram's *Travels through North
and South Carolina* (Philadelphia, 1791).

The growth of ragged villages and huts,
Forsook their homes, and (errant in the quest
Of patron, famous school or friendly nook 480
Where, pensioned, they in shelter might sit down)
From town to town and through wide-scattered realms
Journeyed with their huge folios in their hands,
And often, starting from some covert place,
Saluted the chance-comer on the road 485
Crying, 'An obolus, a penny give
To a poor scholar';[13] when illustrious men,
Lovers of truth by penury constrained –
Bucer, Erasmus, or Melancthon[14] – read
Before the doors and windows of their cells 490
By moonshine, through mere lack of taper-light.
   But peace to vain regrets! We see but darkly[15]
Even when we look behind us, and best things
Are not so pure by nature that they needs
Must keep to all (as fondly all believe) 495
Their highest promise. If the mariner,
When at reluctant distance he hath passed
Some fair enticing island, did but know
What fate might have been his, could he have brought
His bark to land upon the wished-for spot, 500
Good cause full often would he have to bless
The belt of churlish surf that scared him thence,
Or haste of the inexorable wind.
For me, I grieve not; happy is the man
Who only misses what I missed, who falls 505
No lower than I fell.
           I did not love
(As hath been noticed heretofore) the guise
Of our scholastic studies, could have wished
The river to have had an ampler range
And freer pace. But this I tax not; far, 510
Far more I grieved to see among the band
Of those who in the field of contest stood
As combatants, passions that did to me
Seem low and mean – from ignorance of mine,
In part, and want of just forbearance, yet 515
My wiser mind grieves now for what I saw.
Willingly did I part from these, and turn
Out of their track to travel with the shoal
Of more unthinking natures, easy minds
And pillowy, and not wanting love that makes 520
The day pass lightly on – when foresight sleeps,

---

[13] The cry of Belisarius, a disgraced Byzantine general.   [14] Distinguished sixteenth-century scholars.   [15] Wordsworth here alludes to 1 Cor. 13: 12.

And wisdom and the pledges interchanged
With our own inner being are forgot.
　To books, our daily fare prescribed, I turned
With sickly appetite, and when I went   525
At other times in quest of my own food
I chased not steadily the manly deer,
But laid me down to any casual feast
Of wildwood honey, or, with truant eyes
Unruly, peeped about for vagrant fruit.   530
And as for what pertains to human life,
The deeper passions working round me here
(Whether of envy, jealousy, pride, shame,
Ambition, emulation, fear, or hope,
Or those of dissolute pleasure) were by me   535
Unshared, and only now and then observed –
So little was their hold upon my being,
As outward things that might administer
To knowledge or instruction. Hushed, meanwhile,
Was the under-soul, locked up in such a calm   540
That not a leaf of the great nature stirred.
　Yet was this deep vacation not given up
To utter waste. Hitherto I had stood
In my own mind remote from human life –
At least from what we commonly so name –   545
Even as a shepherd on a promontory
Who, lacking occupation, looks far forth
Into the endless sea, and rather makes
Than finds what he beholds. And sure it is
That this first transit from the smooth delights   550
And wild outlandish walks of simple youth
To something that resembled an approach
Towards mortal business (to a privileged world
Within a world, a midway residence
With all its intervenient imagery)   555
Did better suit my visionary mind
(Far better than to have been bolted forth,
Thrust out abruptly into fortune's way
Among the conflicts of substantial life),
By a more just gradation did lead on   560
To higher things, more naturally matured
For permanent possession, better fruits,
Whether of truth or virtue, to ensue.
　In playful zest of fancy did we note
(How could we less?) the manners and the ways   565
Of those who in the livery were arrayed
Of good or evil fame, of those with whom
By frame of academic discipline
Perforce we were connected, men whose sway

And whose authority of office served   570
To set our minds on edge, and did no more.
Nor wanted we rich pastime of this kind,
Found everywhere but chiefly in the ring
Of the grave elders – men unscoured, grotesque
In character, tricked out like aged trees   575
Which through the lapse of their infirmity
Give ready place to any random seed
That chooses to be reared upon their trunks.
　　Here on my view, confronting as it were
Those shepherd swains whom I had lately left,   580
Did flash a different image of old age
(How different!), yet both withal alike
A book of rudiments for the unpractised sight –
Objects embossed, and which with sedulous care
Nature holds up before the eye of youth   585
In her great school, with further view perhaps
To enter early on her tender scheme
Of teaching comprehension with delight
And mingling playful with pathetic thoughts.
　　The surfaces of artificial life   590
And manners finely spun, the delicate race
Of colours, lurking, gleaming up and down
Through that state arras woven with silk and gold,
This wily interchange of snaky hues,
Willingly and unwillingly revealed –   595
I had not learned to watch; and at this time,
Perhaps, had such been in my daily sight
I might have been indifferent thereto
As hermits are to tales of distant things.
Hence for these rarities elaborate   600
Having no relish yet, I was content
With the more homely produce rudely piled
In this our coarser warehouse. At this day
I smile in many a mountain solitude
At passages and fragments that remain   605
Of that inferior exhibition, played
By wooden images, a theatre
For wake or fair. And oftentimes do flit
Remembrances before me of old men,
Old humorists who have been long in their graves,   610
And having almost in my mind put off
Their human names, have into phantoms passed
Of texture midway betwixt life and books.
　　I play the loiterer; 'tis enough to note
That here in dwarf proportions were expressed   615
The limbs of the great world – its goings-on
Collaterally portrayed as in mock fight,

A tournament of blows, some hardly dealt
Though short of mortal combat – and whate'er
Might of this pageant be supposed to hit   620
A simple rustic's notice (this way less,
More that way) was not wasted upon me.
And yet this spectacle may well demand
A more substantial name, no mimic show –
Itself a living part of a live whole,   625
A creek of the vast sea. For all degrees
And shapes of spurious fame and short-lived praise
Here sat in state, and, fed with daily alms,
Retainers won away from solid good.
And here was Labour, his own bond-slave; Hope,   630
That never set the pains against the prize;
Idleness, halting with his weary clog,
And poor misguided Shame, and witless Fear,
And simple Pleasure, foraging for Death;
Honour misplaced, and Dignity astray;   635
Feuds, factions, flatteries, enmity, and guile;
Murmuring Submission and bald Government
(The idol weak as the idolator),
And Decency and Custom starving Truth,
And blind Authority beating with his staff   640
The child that might have led him; Emptiness
Followed as of good omen, and meek Worth
Left to itself, unheard-of and unknown.
    Of these and other kindred notices
I cannot say what portion is in truth   645
The naked recollection of that time,
And what may rather have been called to life
By after-meditation. But delight
That, in an easy temper lulled asleep,
Is still with innocence its own reward –   650
This surely was not wanting. Carelessly
I gazed, roving as through a cabinet
Or wide museum (thronged with fishes, gems,
Birds, crocodiles, shells) where little can be seen
Well understood, or naturally endeared,   655
Yet still does every step bring something forth
That quickens, pleases, stings; and here and there
A casual rarity is singled out
And has its brief perusal, then gives way
To others, all supplanted in their turn.   660
Meanwhile amid this gaudy congress, framed
Of things by nature most unneighbourly,
The head turns round and cannot right itself,
And though an aching and a barren sense
Of gay confusion still be uppermost,   665

With few wise longings and but little love,
Yet something to the memory sticks at last
Whence profit may be drawn in times to come.
   Thus in submissive idleness, my friend,
The labouring time of autumn, winter, spring,   670
Nine months, rolled pleasingly away; the tenth
Returned me to my native hills again.

Book Four
Summer Vacation

A pleasant sight it was when, having clomb
The Heights of Kendal, and that dreary moor
Was crossed, at length as from a rampart's edge
I overlooked the bed of Windermere.[1]
I bounded down the hill, shouting amain   5
A lusty summons to the farther shore
For the old ferryman, and when he came
I did not step into the well-known boat
Without a cordial welcome. Thence right forth
I took my way, now drawing towards home,   10
To that sweet valley[2] where I had been reared;
'Twas but a short hour's walk ere, veering round,
I saw the snow-white church upon its hill
Sit like a thronèd lady, sending out
A gracious look all over its domain.   15
Glad greetings had I, and some tears perhaps,
From my old dame,[3] so motherly and good,
While she perused me with a parent's pride.
The thoughts of gratitude shall fall like dew
Upon thy grave, good creature! While my heart   20
Can beat I never will forget thy name.
Heaven's blessing be upon thee where thou liest
After thy innocent and busy stir
In narrow cares, thy little daily growth
Of calm enjoyments; after eighty years,   25
And more than eighty, of untroubled life –
Childless, yet by the strangers to thy blood
Honoured with little less than filial love.
Great joy was mine to see thee once again,
Thee and thy dwelling, and a throng of things   30
About its narrow precincts, all beloved
And many of them seeming yet my own!

BOOK FOUR
[1] Wordsworth returned to Hawkshead, scene of his schooldays, at the beginning of the Cambridge summer vacation of 1788.

[2] *that sweet valley* the Vale of Esthwaite.
[3] Ann Tyson, Wordsworth's landlady at Hawkshead, who died in 1796, aged 83.

Why should I speak of what a thousand hearts
Have felt, and every man alive can guess?
The rooms, the court, the garden, were not left   35
Long unsaluted, and the spreading pine
And broad stone table underneath its boughs
(Our summer seat in many a festive hour),
And that unruly child of mountain birth,
The froward brook, which, soon as he was boxed   40
Within our garden, found himself at once,
As if by trick insidious and unkind,
Stripped of his voice and left to dimple down
Without an effort and without a will –
A channel paved by the hand of man.   45
I looked at him and smiled, and smiled again,
And in the press of twenty thousand thoughts,
'Ha', quoth I, 'pretty prisoner, are you there!'
And now, reviewing soberly that hour,
I marvel that a fancy did not flash   50
Upon me, and a strong desire, straightway
(At sight of such an emblem that showed forth
So aptly my late course of even days
And all their smooth enthralment) to pen down
A satire on myself. My aged dame   55
Was with me, at my side; she guided me,
I willing – nay, nay, wishing to be led.
The face of every neighbour whom I met
Was as a volume to me: some I hailed
Far off, upon the road or at their work,   60
Unceremonious greetings interchanged
With half the length of a long field between.
Among my schoolfellows I scattered round
A salutation that was more constrained,
Though earnest – doubtless with a little pride,   65
But with more shame, for my habiliments,
The transformation, and the gay attire.
    Delighted did I take my place again
At our domestic table, and, dear friend,
Relating simply as my wish hath been   70
A poet's history, can I leave untold
The joy with which I laid me down at night
In my accustomed bed? – more welcome now
Perhaps than if it had been more desired
Or been more often thought of with regret;   75
That bed whence I had heard the roaring wind
And clamorous rain; that bed where I so oft
Had lain awake on breezy nights to watch
The moon in splendour couched among the leaves
Of a tall ash that near our cottage stood,   80

Had watched her with fixed eyes, while to and fro
In the dark summit of the moving tree
She rocked with every impulse of the wind.
    Among the faces which it pleased me well
To see again was one by ancient right   85
Our inmate, a rough terrier of the hills,
By birth and call of nature pre-ordained
To hunt the badger and unearth the fox
Among the impervious crags, but having been
From youth our own adopted, he had passed   90
Into a gentler service. And when first
The boyish spirit flagged, and day by day
Along my veins I kindled with the stir,
The fermentation, and the vernal heat
Of poesy, affecting private shades   95
Like a sick lover, then this dog was used
To watch me, an attendant and a friend,
Obsequious to my steps early and late –
Though often of such dilatory walk
Tired, and uneasy at the halts I made.   100
A hundred times when in these wanderings
I have been busy with the toil of verse
(Great pains and little progress), and at once
Some fair enchanting image in my mind
Rose up full-formed, like Venus from the sea,   105
Have I sprung forth towards him and let loose
My hand upon his back with stormy joy,
Caressing him again and yet again.
And when in the public roads at eventide
I sauntered, like a river murmuring   110
And talking to itself, at such a season
It was his custom to jog on before;
But duly, whensoever he had met
A passenger approaching, would he turn
To give me timely notice, and straightway,   115
Punctual to such admonishment, I hushed
My voice, composed my gait, and shaped myself
To give and take a greeting that might save
My name from piteous rumours such as wait
On men suspected to be crazed in brain.   120
    Those walks well worthy to be prized and loved –
Regretted, that word too was on my tongue,
But they were richly laden with all good
And cannot be remembered but with thanks
And gratitude and perfect joy of heart –   125
Those walks did now like a returning spring
Come back on me again. When first I made
Once more the circuit of our little lake,

If ever happiness hath lodged with man
That day consummate happiness was mine,   130
Wide-spreading, steady, calm, contemplative.
The sun was set, or setting, when I left
Our cottage-door, and evening soon brought on
A sober hour – not winning or serene
(For cold and raw the air was, and untuned),   135
But as a face we love is sweetest then
When sorrow damps it, or, whatever look
It chance to wear is sweetest if the heart
Have fullness in itself: even so with me
It fared that evening. Gently did my soul   140
Put off her veil, and self-transmuted stood
Naked as in the presence of her God.
As on I walked, a comfort seemed to touch
A heart that had not been disconsolate;
Strength came where weakness was not known to be,   145
At least not felt; and restoration came,
Like an intruder knocking at the door
Of unacknowledged weariness.
                          I took
The balance in my hand and weighed myself.
I saw but little, and thereat was pleased;   150
Little did I remember, and even this
Still pleased me more. But I had hopes and peace
And swellings of the spirits, was rapt and soothed,
Conversed with promises, had glimmering views
How life pervades the undecaying mind;   155
How the immortal soul with godlike power
Informs, creates, and thaws the deepest sleep
That time can lay upon her; how, on earth,
Man, if he do but live within the light
Of high endeavours, daily spreads abroad   160
His being with a strength that cannot fail.
Nor was there want of milder thoughts – of love,
Of innocence and holiday repose,
And more than pastoral quiet in the heart
Of amplest projects, and a peaceful end   165
At last, or glorious, by endurance won.
Thus musing, in a wood I sat me down
Alone, continuing there to muse; meanwhile
The mountain-heights were slowly overspread
With darkness, and before a rippling breeze   170
The long lake lengthened out its hoary line.
And in the sheltered coppice where I sat,
Around me from among the hazel leaves
(Now here, now there, stirred by the straggling wind)
Came intermittingly a breath-like sound,   175

A respiration short and quick, which oft –
Yea, might I say, again and yet again –
Mistaking for the panting of my dog,
The off and on companion of my walk,
I turned my head to look if he were there.   180
   A freshness also found I at this time
In human life – the life I mean of those
Whose occupations really I loved.
The prospect often touched me with surprise,
Crowded and full and changed, as seemed to me,   185
Even as a garden in the heat of spring
After an eight-days' absence. For (to omit
The things which were the same and yet appeared
So different) amid this solitude,
The little vale where was my chief abode,   190
'Twas not indifferent to a youthful mind
To note perhaps some sheltered seat in which
An old man had been used to sun himself,
Now empty; pale-faced babes whom I had left
In arms, known children of the neighbourhood,   195
Now rosy prattlers tottering up and down;
And growing girls whose beauty, filched away
With all its pleasant promises, was gone
To deck some slighted playmate's homely cheek.
   Yes, I had something of another eye,   200
And often looking round was moved to smiles
Such as a delicate work of humour breeds.
I read, without design, the opinions, thoughts
Of those plain-living people, in a sense
Of love and knowledge; with another eye   205
I saw the quiet woodman in the woods,
The shepherd on the hills. With new delight
(This chiefly) did I view my grey-haired dame,
Saw her go forth to church or other work
Of state, equipped in monumental trim: 210
Short velvet cloak, her bonnet of the like,
A mantle such as Spanish cavaliers
Wore in old time. Her smooth domestic life,
Affectionate without uneasiness,
Her talk, her business, pleased me; and no less   215
Her clear though shallow stream of piety
That ran on sabbath days a fresher course.
With thoughts unfelt till now, I saw her read
Her Bible on the Sunday afternoons,
And loved the book when she had dropped asleep,   220
And made of it a pillow for her head.
   Nor less do I remember to have felt
Distinctly manifested at this time

A dawning, even as of another sense:
A human-heartedness about my love   225
For objects – hitherto the gladsome air
Of my own private being and no more,
Which I had loved even as a blessed spirit
Or angel if he were to dwell on earth
Might love, in individual happiness.   230
But now there opened on me other thoughts
Of change, congratulation and regret –
A new-born feeling. It spread far and wide:
The trees, the mountains shared it, and the brooks,
The stars of heaven (now seen in their old haunts),   235
White Sirius glittering o'er the southern crags,
Orion with his belt, and those fair Seven
(Acquaintances of every little child),
And Jupiter, my own beloved star.[4]
Whatever shadings of mortality   240
Had fallen upon these objects heretofore
Were different in kind. Not tender; strong,
Deep, gloomy were they, and severe, the scatterings
Of childhood – and moreover had given way
In later youth to beauty, and to love   245
Enthusiastic, to delight and joy.
    As one who hangs down-bending from the side
Of a slow-moving boat upon the breast
Of a still water, solacing himself
With such discoveries as his eye can make   250
Beneath him in the bottom of the deeps,
Sees many beauteous sights (weeds, fishes, flowers,
Grots, pebbles, roots of trees) and fancies more,
Yet often is perplexed and cannot part
The shadow from the substance – rocks and sky,   255
Mountains and clouds, from that which is indeed
The region, and the things which there abide
In their true dwelling; now is crossed by gleam
Of his own image, by a sunbeam now,
And motions that are sent he knows not whence,   260
Impediments that make his task more sweet:
Such pleasant office have we long pursued
Incumbent o'er the surface of past time
With like success. Nor have we often looked
On more alluring shows (to me, at least),   265
More soft, or less ambiguously descried,
Than those which now we have been passing by,
And where we still are lingering.

---

[4] Jupiter was dominant at the time of Wordsworth's
birth, 7 Apr. 1770.

Yet, in spite
Of all these new employments of the mind,
There was an inner falling-off. I loved,   270
Loved deeply, all that I had loved before –
More deeply even than ever; but a swarm
Of heady thoughts jostling each other, gawds
And feast and dance and public revelry
And sports and games (less pleasing in themselves,   275
Than as they were a badge glossy and fresh
Of manliness and freedom), these did now
Seduce me from the firm habitual quest
Of feeding pleasures, from that eager zeal,
Those yearnings which had every day been mine   280
(A wild, unworldly-minded youth, given up
To nature and to books, or, at the most,
From time to time, by inclination shipped
One among many in societies
That were, or seemed, as simple as myself).   285
But now was come a change. It would demand
Some skill, and longer time than may be spared,
To paint even to myself these vanities,
And how they wrought. But sure it is that now
Contagious air did oft environ me,   290
Unknown among these haunts in former days.
The very garments that I wore appeared
To prey upon my strength, and stopped the course
And quiet stream of self-forgetfulness.
Something there was about me that perplexed   295
The authentic sight of reason, pressed too closely
On that religious dignity of mind
That is the very faculty of truth –
Which wanting (either from the very first
A function never lighted up, or else   300
Extinguished), man, a creature great and good,
Seems but a pageant plaything with vile claws,
And this great frame of breathing elements
A senseless idol.
                          This vague heartless chase
Of trivial pleasures was a poor exchange   305
For books and nature at that early age.
'Tis true some casual knowledge might be gained
Of character or life; but at that time,
Of manners put to school I took small note,
And all my deeper passions lay elsewhere.   310
Far better had it been to exalt the mind
By solitary study, to uphold
Intense desire by thought and quietness –
And yet, in chastisement of these regrets,

The memory of one particular hour   315
Doth here rise up against me.
                                    In a throng,
A festal company of maids and youths,
Old men and matrons staid – promiscuous rout,
A medley of all tempers – I had passed
The night in dancing, gaiety, and mirth,   320
With din of instruments and shuffling feet
And glancing forms and tapers glittering
And unaimed prattle flying up and down,
Spirits upon the stretch, and here and there
Slight shocks of young love-liking interspersed   325
That mounted up like joy into the head
And tingled through the veins. Ere we retired,
The cock had crowed, the sky was bright with day;
Two miles I had to walk along the fields
Before I reached my home. Magnificent   330
The morning was, a memorable pomp,
More glorious than I ever had beheld.
The sea was laughing at a distance; all
The solid mountains were as bright as clouds,
Grain-tinctured,⁵ drenched in empyrean light;   335
And in the meadows and the lower grounds
Was all the sweetness of a common dawn –
Dews, vapours, and the melody of birds,
And labourers going forth into the fields.
Ah, need I say, dear friend, that to the brim   340
My heart was full? I made no vows, but vows
Were then made for me: bond unknown to me
Was given that I should be, else sinning greatly,
A dedicated spirit. On I walked
In blessedness, which even yet remains.   345
    Strange rendezvous my mind was at that time,
A parti-coloured show of grave and gay,
Solid and light, short-sighted and profound –
Of inconsiderate habits and sedate,
Consorting in one mansion unreproved.   350
I knew the worth of that which I possessed,
Though slighted and misused. Besides in truth
That summer, swarming as it did with thoughts
Transient and loose, yet wanted not a store
Of primitive hours, when – by these hindrances   355
Unthwarted – I experienced in myself
Conformity as just as that of old
To the end and written spirit of God's works,

---

⁵ *grain* scarlet.

Whether held forth in nature or in man.
   From many wanderings that have left behind   360
Remembrances not lifeless, I will here
Single out one, then pass to other themes.
A favourite pleasure hath it been with me
From time of earliest youth to walk alone
Along the public way, when, for the night   365
Deserted, in its silence it assumes
A character of deeper quietness
Than pathless solitudes. At such an hour
Once, ere these summer months were passed away,
I slowly mounted up a steep ascent   370
Where the road's watery surface, to the ridge
Of that sharp rising, glittered in the moon,
And seemed before my eyes another stream
Creeping with silent lapse to join the brook
That murmured in the valley.
                    On I went   375
Tranquil, receiving in my own despite
Amusement, as I slowly passed along,
From such near objects as from time to time
Perforce intruded on the listless sense
Quiescent and disposed to sympathy,   380
With an exhausted mind worn out by toil
And all unworthy of the deeper joy
Which waits on distant prospect – cliff or sea,
The dark blue vault and universe of stars.
Thus did I steal along that silent road,   385
My body from the stillness drinking in
A restoration like the calm of sleep,
But sweeter far. Above, before, behind,
Around me, all was peace and solitude:
I looked not round, nor did the solitude   390
Speak to my eye, but it was heard and felt.
Oh happy state, what beauteous pictures now
Rose in harmonious imagery! They rose
As from some distant region of my soul
And came along like dreams; yet such as left   395
Obscurely mingled with their passing forms
A consciousness of animal delight,
A self-possession felt in every pause
And every gentle movement of my frame.
   While thus I wandered, step by step led on,   400
It chanced a sudden turning of the road
Presented to my view an uncouth shape,
So near that, slipping back into the shade
Of a thick hawthorn, I could mark him well,
Myself unseen. He was of stature tall,   405

A foot above man's common measure tall,
Stiff in his form, and upright, lank and lean –
A man more meagre, as it seemed to me,
Was never seen abroad by night or day.
His arms were long, and bare his hands; his mouth   410
Showed ghastly in the moonlight; from behind,
A milestone propped him, and his figure seemed
Half sitting and half standing. I could mark
That he was clad in military garb,
Though faded yet entire. He was alone,   415
Had no attendant, neither dog, nor staff,
Nor knapsack; in his very dress appeared
A desolation, a simplicity
That seemed akin to solitude. Long time
Did I peruse him with a mingled sense   420
Of fear and sorrow. From his lips meanwhile
There issued murmuring sounds, as if of pain
Or of uneasy thought; yet still his form
Kept the same steadiness, and at his feet
His shadow lay, and moved not. In a glen   425
Hard by, a village stood, whose roofs and doors
Were visible among the scattered trees,
Scarce distant from the spot an arrow's flight.
I wished to see him move, but he remained
Fixed to his place, and still from time to time   430
Sent forth a murmuring voice of dead complaint,
Groans scarcely audible.
                          Without self-blame
I had not thus prolonged my watch; and now,
Subduing my heart's specious cowardice,
I left the shady nook where I had stood   435
And hailed him. Slowly from his resting-place
He rose, and with a lean and wasted arm
In measured gesture lifted to his head
Returned my salutation, then resumed
His station as before. And when erelong   440
I asked his history, he in reply
Was neither slow nor eager, but unmoved
And with a quiet uncomplaining voice,
A stately air of mild indifference,
He told in simple words a soldier's tale –   445
That in the tropic islands he had served,
Whence he had landed scarcely ten days past;
That on his landing he had been dismissed,
And now was travelling to his native home.
At this I turned and looked towards the village,   450
But all were gone to rest, the fires all out,
And every silent window to the moon

Shone with a yellow glitter. 'No one there',
Said I, 'is waking; we must measure back
The way which we have come. Behind yon wood   455
A labourer dwells, and (take it on my word)
He will not murmur should we break his rest,
And with a ready heart will give you food
And lodging for the night.' At this he stooped
And from the ground took up an oaken staff   460
By me yet unobserved – a traveller's staff
Which I suppose from his slack hand had dropped,
And lain till now neglected in the grass.
   Towards the cottage without more delay
We shaped our course. As it appeared to me   465
He travelled without pain, and I beheld
With ill-suppressed astonishment his tall
And ghastly figure moving at my side;
Nor, while we journeyed thus, could I forbear
To question him of what he had endured   470
From hardship, battle, or the pestilence.
He all the while was in demeanour calm,
Concise in answer. Solemn and sublime
He might have seemed, but that in all he said
There was a strange half-absence, and a tone   475
Of weakness and indifference, as of one
Remembering the importance of his theme
But feeling it no longer. We advanced
Slowly, and ere we to the wood were come
Discourse had ceased. Together on we passed   480
In silence through the shades gloomy and dark;
Then, turning up along an open field,
We gained the cottage. At the door I knocked,
Calling aloud, 'My friend, here is a man
By sickness overcome. Beneath your roof   485
This night let him find rest, and give him food,
If food he need, for he is faint and tired.'
Assured that now my comrade would repose
In comfort, I entreated that henceforth
He would not linger in the public ways   490
But ask for timely furtherance, and help
Such as his state required. At this reproof,
With the same ghastly mildness in his look,
He said, 'My trust is in the God of Heaven,
And in the eye of him that passes me.'   495
   The cottage door was speedily unlocked,
And now the soldier touched his hat again
With his lean hand, and in a voice that seemed
To speak with a reviving interest
Till then unfelt, he thanked me; I returned   500

The blessing of the poor unhappy man,
And so we parted. Back I cast a look,
And lingered near the door a little space,
Then sought with quiet heart my distant home.

Book Five
Books

Even in the steadiest mood of reason, when
All sorrow for thy transitory pains
Goes out, it grieves me for thy state, oh man
(Though paramount creature) and thy race, while ye
Shall sojourn on this planet – not for woes   5
Which thou endurest (that weight, albeit huge,
I charm away), but for those palms achieved
Through length of time, by study and hard thought,
The honours of thy high endowments. There
My sadness finds its fuel.   10
                   Hitherto
In progress through this verse, my mind hath looked
Upon the speaking face of earth and heaven
As her prime teacher, intercourse with man
Established by the sovereign intellect
Who through that bodily image hath diffused   15
A soul divine which we participate,
A deathless spirit. Thou also, man, hast wrought,
For commerce of thy nature with itself,
Things worthy of unconquerable life;
And yet we feel, we cannot choose but feel   20
That these must perish. Tremblings of the heart
It gives to think that the immortal being
No more shall need such garments; and yet man,
As long as he shall be the child of earth,
Might almost 'weep to have'[1] what he may lose,   25
Nor be himself extinguished, but survive
Abject, depressed, forlorn, disconsolate.
A thought is with me sometimes, and I say:
'Should earth by inward throes be wrenched throughout,
Or fire be sent from far to wither all   30
Her pleasant habitations, and dry up
Old ocean in his bed, left singed and bare,
Yet would the living presence still subsist
Victorious, and composure would ensue,
And kindlings like the morning – presage sure   35
(Though slow perhaps) of a returning day.

Book Five
[1] Wordsworth alludes to Shakespeare's Sonnet 64.

But all the meditations of mankind,
Yea, all the adamantine holds of truth
By reason built, or passion (which itself
Is highest reason in a soul sublime),   40
The consecrated works of bard and sage,
Sensuous or intellectual, wrought by men,
Twin labourers and heirs of the same hopes –
Where would they be? Oh, why hath not the mind
Some element to stamp her image on   45
In nature somewhat nearer to her own?
Why, gifted with such powers to send abroad
Her spirit, must it lodge in shrines so frail?'
    One day, when in the hearing of a friend[2]
I had given utterance to thoughts like these,   50
He answered with a smile that in plain truth
'Twas going far to seek disquietude;
But on the front of his reproof confessed
That he at sundry seasons had himself
Yielded to kindred hauntings – and forthwith   55
Added that once upon a summer's noon
While he was sitting in a rocky cave
By the sea-side (perusing, as it chanced,
The famous history of the errant knight
Recorded by Cervantes),[3] these same thoughts   60
Came to him, and to height unusual rose
While listlessly he sat, and, having closed
The book, had turned his eyes towards the sea.
On poetry and geometric truth
(The knowledge that endures), upon these two   65
And their high privilege of lasting life
Exempt from all internal injury,
He mused; upon these chiefly – and at length,
His senses yielding to the sultry air,
Sleep seized him and he passed into a dream.[4]   70
    He saw before him an Arabian waste,
A desert, and he fancied that himself
Was sitting there in the wide wilderness
Alone upon the sands. Distress of mind
Was growing in him when, behold, at once   75
To his great joy a man was at his side,
Upon a dromedary mounted high!
He seemed an Arab of the bedouin tribes;
A lance he bore, and underneath one arm
A stone, and in the opposite hand a shell   80
Of a surpassing brightness. Much rejoiced

[2] Probably Coleridge.
[3] *Don Quixote.*
[4] Wordsworth's account is based on a dream described by Descartes.

The dreaming man that he should have a guide
To lead him through the desert, and he thought –
While questioning himself what this strange freight
Which the newcomer carried through the waste   85
Could mean – the Arab told him that the stone
(To give it in the language of the dream)
Was Euclid's *Elements*.⁵ '"And this", said he,
"This other", pointing to the shell, "this book,
Is something of more worth." And at the word   90
The stranger', said my friend continuing,
'Stretched forth the shell towards me, with command
That I should hold it to my ear. I did so,
And heard that instant in an unknown tongue,
Which yet I understood, articulate sounds,   95
A loud prophetic blast of harmony,
An ode in passion uttered, which foretold
Destruction to the children of the earth
By deluge now at hand.'
           No sooner ceased
The song, but with calm look the Arab said   100
That all was true, that it was even so
As had been spoken, and that he himself
Was going then to bury those two books –
The one that held acquaintance with the stars
And wedded man to man by purest bond   105
Of nature, undisturbed by space or time;
The other that was a god – yea, many gods,
Had voices more than all the winds, and was
A joy, a consolation, and a hope.
My friend continued, 'Strange as it may seem   110
I wondered not, although I plainly saw
The one to be a stone, the other a shell,
Nor doubted once but that they both were books,
Having a perfect faith in all that passed.
   A wish was now engendered in my fear   115
To cleave unto this man, and I begged leave
To share his errand with him. On he passed
Not heeding me; I followed, and took note
That he looked often backward with wild look,
Grasping his twofold treasure to his side.   120
Upon a dromedary, lance in rest
He rode, I keeping pace with him; and now
I fancied that he was the very knight
Whose tale Cervantes tells, yet not the knight,
But was an Arab of the desert too –   125

---

⁵ *Euclid* Greek mathematician of third century BC.

Of these was neither, and was both at once.
His countenance meanwhile grew more disturbed,
And, looking backwards when he looked, I saw
A glittering light, and asked him whence it came.
"It is", said he, "the waters of the deep   130
Gathering upon us." Quickening then his pace,
He left me. I called after him aloud;
He heeded not, but with his twofold charge
Beneath his arm, before me, full in view,
I saw him riding o'er the desert sands   135
With the fleet waters of the drowning world
In chase of him. Whereat I waked in terror,
And saw the sea before me, and the book
In which I had been reading at my side.'

   Full often, taking from the world of sleep   140
This Arab phantom which my friend beheld,
This semi-Quixote, I to him have given
A substance, fancied him a living man,
A gentle dweller in the desert, crazed
By love and feeling and internal thought   145
Protracted among endless solitudes –
Have shaped him, in the oppression of his brain,
Wandering upon this quest, and thus equipped.
And I have scarcely pitied him, have felt
A reverence for a being thus employed,   150
And thought that in the blind and awful lair
Of such a madness, reason did lie couched.
Enow[6] there are on earth to take in charge
Their wives, their children, and their virgin loves,
Or whatsoever else the heart holds dear –   155
Enow to think of these; yea, will I say,
In sober contemplation of the approach
Of such great overthrow, made manifest
By certain evidence, that I methinks
Could share that maniac's anxiousness, could go   160
Upon like errand. Oftentimes, at least,
Me hath such deep entrancement half possessed
When I have held a volume in my hand
(Poor earthly casket of immortal verse) –
Shakespeare or Milton, labourers divine!   165
   Mighty indeed, supreme must be the power
Of living nature, which could thus so long
Detain me from the best of other thoughts!
Even in the lisping time of infancy
And later down in prattling childhood, even   170

---

[6] *Enow* enough.

While I was travelling back among those days,
How could I ever play an ingrate's part?
Once more should I have made those bowers resound,
And intermingled strains of thankfulness
With their own thoughtless melodies. At least   175
It might have well beseemed me to repeat
Some simply-fashioned tale, to tell again,
In slender accents of sweet verse, some tale
That did bewitch me then and soothes me now.
Oh friend, oh poet, brother of my soul!   180
Think not that I could ever pass along
Untouched by these remembrances – no, no,
But I was hurried forward by a stream
And could not stop. Yet wherefore should I speak?
Why call upon a few weak words to say   185
What is already written in the hearts
Of all that breathe – what in the path of all
Drops daily from the tongue of every child
Wherever man is found? The trickling tear
Upon the cheek of listening infancy   190
Tells it, and the insuperable look
That drinks as if it never could be full.
    That portion of my story I shall leave
There registered. Whatever else there be
Of power or pleasure, sown or fostered thus,   195
Peculiar to myself, let that remain
Where it lies hidden in its endless home
Among the depths of time. And yet it seems
That here, in memory of all books which lay
Their sure foundations in the heart of man   200
(Whether by native prose, or numerous[7] verse),
That in the name of all inspired souls,
From Homer the great thunderer, from the voice
Which roars along the bed of Jewish song,
And that, more varied and elaborate,   205
Those trumpet-tones of harmony that shake
Our shores in England – from those loftiest notes
Down to the low and wren-like warblings made
For cottagers and spinners at the wheel,
And weary travellers when they rest themselves   210
By the highways and hedges: ballad tunes,
Food for the hungry ears of little ones
And of old men who have survived their joy –
It seemeth, in behalf of these, the works,
And of the men who framed them (whether known,   215

---

[7] *numerous* i.e. metrical.

Or sleeping nameless in their scattered graves),
That I should here assert their rights, attest
Their honours, and should once for all pronounce
Their benediction, speak of them as powers
For ever to be hallowed – only less,   220
For what we may become and what we need,
Than nature's self, which is the breath of God.
   Rarely and with reluctance would I stoop
To transitory themes, yet I rejoice –
And, by these thoughts admonished, must speak out   225
Thanksgivings from my heart – that I was reared
Safe from an evil which these days have laid
Upon the children of the land, a pest[8]
That might have dried me up, body and soul.
This verse is dedicate to nature's self,   230
And things that teach as nature teaches; then
Oh where had been the man, the poet? where,
Where had we been, we two, beloved friend,
If we, in lieu of wandering as we did,
Through heights and hollows and by-spots of tales   235
Rich with indigenous produce (open ground
Of fancy, happy pastures ranged at will),
Had been attended, followed, watched and noosed,
Each in his several melancholy walk
Stringed like a poor man's heifer at its feed,   240
Led through the lanes in forlorn servitude –
Or rather, like a stalled ox shut out
From touch of growing grass, that may not taste
A flower till it have yielded up its sweets,
A prelibation to the mower's scythe.   245
   Behold the parent hen amid her brood –
Though fledged and feathered, and well-pleased to part
And straggle from her presence, still a brood,
And she herself from the maternal bond
Still undischarged. Yet doth she little more   250
Than move with them in tenderness and love,
A centre of the circle which they make;
And now and then, alike from need of theirs
And call of her own natural appetites,
She scratches, ransacks up the earth for food   255
Which they partake at pleasure. Early died
My honoured mother, she who was the heart
And hinge of all our learnings and our loves;
She left us destitute, and, as we might,
Trooping together.

---

[8] *pest* the proliferation of educational theories at the
end of the eighteenth century.

                    Little suits it me   260
To break upon the sabbath of her rest
With any thought that looks at others' blame,
Nor would I praise her but in perfect love.
Hence am I checked, but I will boldly say
In gratitude, and for the sake of truth,   265
Unheard by her, that she (not falsely taught,
Fetching her goodness rather from times past
Than shaping novelties from those to come)
Had no presumption, no such jealousy,
Nor did by habit of her thoughts mistrust   270
Our nature, but had virtual faith that He
Who fills the mother's breasts with innocent milk
Doth also for our nobler part provide,
Under His great correction and control,
As innocent instincts, and as innocent food.   275
This was her creed, and therefore she was pure
From feverish dread of error and mishap
And evil (overweeningly so called),
Was not puffed up by false unnatural hopes,
Nor selfish with unnecessary cares,   280
Nor with impatience from the season asked
More than its timely produce – rather loved
The hours for what they are, than from regards
Glanced on their promises in restless pride.
Such was she; not from faculties more strong   285
Than others have, but from the times perhaps
And spot in which she lived, and through a grace
Of modest meekness, simple-mindedness,
A heart that found benignity and hope,
Being itself benign.
                    My drift hath scarcely,   290
I fear, been obvious, for I have recoiled
From showing as it is the monster birth
Engendered by these too industrious times.
Let few words paint it: 'tis a child – no child,
But a dwarf man – in knowledge, virtue, skill,   295
In what he is not and in what he is,
The noontide shadow of a man complete;
A worshipper of worldly seemliness,
Not quarrelsome (for that were far beneath
His dignity), with gifts he bubbles o'er   300
As generous as a fountain. Selfishness
May not come near him, gluttony or pride;
The wandering beggars propagate his name,
Dumb creatures find him tender as a nun.
Yet deem him not for this a naked dish   305
Of goodness merely, he is garnished out:

Arch are his notices, and nice his sense
Of the ridiculous; deceit and guile,
Meanness and falsehood he detects, can treat
With apt and graceful laughter, nor is blind   310
To the broad follies of the licensed world;
Though shrewd, yet innocent himself withal,
And can read lectures upon innocence.
 He is fenced round – nay armed, for aught we know,
In panoply complete; and fear itself,   315
Natural or supernatural alike,
Unless it leap upon him in a dream,
Touches him not. Briefly, the moral part
Is perfect, and in learning and in books
He is a prodigy. His discourse moves slow,   320
Massy and ponderous as a prison door,
Tremendously embossed with terms of art;
Rank growth of propositions overruns
The stripling's brain; the path in which he treads
Is choked with grammars; cushion of divine   325
Was never such a type of thought profound
As is the pillow where he rests his head.
The ensigns of the empire which he holds,
The globe and sceptre of his royalties,
Are telescopes and crucibles and maps.   330
Ships he can guide across the pathless sea,
And tell you all their cunning; he can read
The inside of the earth, and spell the stars;
He knows the policies of foreign lands,
Can string you names of districts, cities, towns   335
The whole world over, tight as beads of dew
Upon a gossamer thread! He sifts, he weighs,
Takes nothing upon trust: his teachers stare,
The country people pray for God's good grace
And tremble at his deep experiments.   340
All things are put to question. He must live
Knowing that he grows wiser every day
Or else not live at all – and seeing too
Each little drop of wisdom as it falls
Into the dimpling cistern of his heart.   345
Meanwhile old Grandame Earth is grieved to find
The playthings which her love designed for him
Unthought of: in their woodland beds the flowers
Weep, and the riversides are all forlorn.
 Now this is hollow, 'tis a life of lies   350
From the beginning, and in lies must end.
Forth bring him to the air of common sense,
And, fresh and showy as it is, the corpse
Slips from us into powder. Vanity,

That is his soul, there lives he, and there moves –   355
It is the soul of everything he seeks;
That gone, nothing is left which he can love.
Nay, if a thought of purer birth should rise
To carry him towards a better clime,
Some busy helper still is on the watch   360
To drive him back, and pound him like a stray
Within the pinfold of his own conceit,
Which is his home, his natural dwelling-place.
Oh, give us once again the wishing-cap
Of Fortunatus, and the invisible coat   365
Of Jack the giant-killer, Robin Hood,
And Sabra in the forest with St George!⁹
The child whose love is here at least doth reap
One precious gain – that he forgets himself.
      These mighty workmen of our later age   370
Who with a broad highway have overbridged
The froward chaos of futurity,
Tamed to their bidding; they who have the art
To manage books, and things, and make them work
Gently on infant minds as does the sun   375
Upon a flower – the tutors of our youth,
The guides, the wardens of our faculties
And stewards of our labour, watchful men
And skilful in the usury of time,
Sages who in their prescience would control   380
All accidents, and to the very road
Which they have fashioned would confine us down
Like engines – when will they be taught
That in the unreasoning progress of the world
A wiser spirit is at work for us,   385
A better eye than theirs, most prodigal
Of blessings and most studious of our good,
Even in what seem our most unfruitful hours?
      There was a boy, ye knew him well, ye cliffs
And islands of Winander!¹⁰ Many a time   390
At evening, when the stars had just begun
To move along the edges of the hills,
Rising or setting, would he stand alone
Beneath the trees or by the glimmering lake,
And there, with fingers interwoven, both hands   395
Pressed closely palm to palm and to his mouth
Uplifted, he as through an instrument

---

⁹ Fortunatus's hat transported him wherever he
wished; Jack's coat made him invisible when fighting
the giant; St George married Sabra, daughter of the
King of Egypt, after rescuing her from a dragon.

¹⁰ *Winander* Windermere. For De Quincey's comments on lines 389–422, first published as an independent poem, 'There Was a Boy', in *Lyrical Ballads*
(1800), see pp. 686–8 below.

Blew mimic hootings to the silent owls
That they might answer him. And they would shout
Across the watery vale, and shout again   400
Responsive to his call, with quivering peals
And long halloos, and screams, and echoes loud
Redoubled and redoubled – concourse wild
Of mirth and jocund din! And when it chanced
That pauses of deep silence mocked his skill,   405
Then sometimes in that silence while he hung
Listening, a gentle shock of mild surprise
Has carried far into his heart the voice
Of mountain torrents; or the visible scene
Would enter unawares into his mind   410
With all its solemn imagery, its rocks,
Its woods, and that uncertain heaven, received
Into the bosom of the steady lake.
    This boy was taken from his mates, and died
In childhood ere he was full ten years old.   415
Fair are the woods, and beauteous is the spot,
The vale where he was born. The churchyard hangs
Upon a slope above the village school,
And there, along that bank, when I have passed
At evening, I believe that oftentimes   420
A full half-hour together I have stood
Mute, looking at the grave in which he lies.
    Even now, methinks, I have before my sight
That self-same village church; I see her sit
(The throned lady spoken of erewhile)   425
On her green hill, forgetful of this boy
Who slumbers at her feet – forgetful too
Of all her silent neighbourhood of graves,
And listening only to the gladsome sounds
That, from the rural school ascending, play   430
Beneath her and about her. May she long
Behold a race of young ones like to those
With whom I herded! (easily indeed
We might have fed upon a fatter soil
Of arts and letters, but be that forgiven) –   435
A race of real children, not too wise,
Too learned, or too good, but wanton, fresh,
And bandied up and down by love and hate;
Fierce, moody, patient, venturous, modest, shy,
Mad at their sports like withered leaves in winds;   440
Though doing wrong and suffering, and full oft
Bending beneath our life's mysterious weight
Of pain and fear, yet still in happiness
Not yielding to the happiest upon earth.
Simplicity in habit, truth in speech,   445

Be these the daily strengtheners of their minds;
May books and nature be their early joy,
And knowledge rightly honoured with that name –
Knowledge not purchased with the loss of power!
   Well do I call to mind the very week   450
When I was first entrusted to the care
Of that sweet valley – when its paths, its shores
And brooks, were like a dream of novelty
To my half-infant thoughts; that very week,
While I was roving up and down alone   455
Seeking I knew not what, I chanced to cross
One of those open fields which, shaped like ears,
Make green peninsulas on Esthwaite's Lake.
Twilight was coming on, yet through the gloom
I saw distinctly on the opposite shore   460
A heap of garments – left, as I supposed,
By one who there was bathing. Long I watched,
But no one owned them; meanwhile the calm lake
Grew dark with all the shadows on its breast,
And now and then a fish up-leaping snapped   465
The breathless stillness. The succeeding day
(Those unclaimed garments telling a plain tale)
Went there a company, and in their boat
Sounded with grappling-irons and long poles.
At length, the dead man,[11] mid that beauteous scene   470
Of trees and hills and water, bolt upright
Rose with his ghastly face – a spectre-shape
Of terror even. And yet no vulgar fear,
Young as I was (a child not nine years old),
Possessed me, for my inner eye had seen   475
Such sights before, among the shining streams
Of fairyland, the forests of romance.
Thence came a spirit hallowing what I saw
With decoration and ideal grace,
A dignity, a smoothness, like the works   480
Of Grecian art and purest poesy.
   I had a precious treasure at that time,
A little yellow canvas-covered book,
A slender abstract of the *Arabian Tales*;[12]
And when I learned, as now I first did learn   485
From my companions in this new abode,
That this dear prize of mine was but a block
Hewn from a mighty quarry – in a word,
That there were four large volumes, laden all
With kindred matter – 'twas in truth to me   490

---

[11] *the dead man* Joseph Jackson, drowned on Es-   [12] A selection from *The Arabian Nights*.
thwaite, 18 June 1779.

A promise scarcely earthly. Instantly
I made a league, a covenant with a friend
Of my own age, that we should lay aside
The moneys we possessed, and hoard up more,
Till our joint savings had amassed enough   495
To make this book our own. Through several months
Religiously did we preserve that vow,
And spite of all temptation hoarded up
And hoarded up; but firmness failed at length,
Nor were we ever masters of our wish.   500
    And afterwards, when to my father's house
Returning at the holidays I found
That golden store of books which I had left
Open to my enjoyment once again,
What heart was mine! Full often through the course   505
Of those glad respites in the summertime,
When armed with rod and line we went abroad
For a whole day together, I have lain
Down by thy side, oh Derwent, murmuring stream,
On the hot stones and in the glaring sun,   510
And there have read, devouring as I read,
Defrauding the day's glory, desperate! –
Till, with a sudden bound of smart reproach
Such as an idler deals with in his shame,
I to my sport betook myself again.   515
    A gracious spirit o'er this earth presides,
And o'er the heart of man: invisibly
It comes, directing those to works of love
Who care not, know not, think not what they do.
The tales that charm away the wakeful night   520
In Araby, romances, legends penned
For solace by the light of monkish lamps;
Fictions for ladies, of their love, devised
By youthful squires; adventures endless, spun
By the dismantled warrior in old age   525
Out of the bowels of those very thoughts
In which his youth did first extravagate –
These spread like day, and something in the shape
Of these will live till man shall be no more.
Dumb yearnings, hidden appetites, are ours,   530
And they must have their food. Our childhood sits,
Our simple childhood sits upon a throne
That hath more power than all the elements.
I guess not what this tells of being past,
Nor what it augurs of the life to come,   535
But so it is. And in that dubious hour,
That twilight when we first begin to see
This dawning earth, to recognize, expect,

And, in the long probation that ensues
(The time of trial, ere we learn to live   540
In reconcilement with our stinted powers),
To endure this state of meagre vassalage,
Unwilling to forego, confess, submit,
Uneasy and unsettled – yoke-fellows
To custom, mettlesome, and not yet tamed   545
And humbled down – oh then we feel, we feel,
We know, when we have friends! Ye dreamers, then –
Forgers of lawless tales! – we bless you then
(Impostors, drivellers, dotards, as the ape
Philosophy will call you), then we feel   550
With what, and how great might ye are in league,
Who make our wish, our power, our thought a deed,
An empire, a possession; ye whom time
And seasons serve – all faculties – to whom
Earth crouches, the elements are potter's clay,   555
Space like a heaven filled up with northern lights,
Here, nowhere, there, and everywhere at once.
    It might demand a more impassioned strain[13]
To tell of later pleasures linked to these,
A tract of the same isthmus which we cross   560
In progress from our native continent
To earth and human life. I mean to speak
Of that delightful time of growing youth
When cravings for the marvellous relent,
And we begin to love what we have seen;   565
And sober truth, experience, sympathy
Take stronger hold of us, and words themselves
Move us with conscious pleasure.
                              I am sad
At thought of raptures now for ever flown;
Even unto tears I sometimes could be sad   570
To think of, to read over, many a page,
Poems withal of name – which at that time
Did never fail to entrance me, and are now
Dead in my eyes as is a theatre
Fresh emptied of spectators. Thirteen years,   575
Or haply less, I might have seen when first
My ears began to open to the charm
Of words in tuneful order, found them sweet
For their own sakes – a passion and a power;
And phrases pleased me, chosen for delight,   580
For pomp, or love.
                    Oft in the public roads,

---

[13] Such as *The Recluse*.

Yet unfrequented, while the morning light
Was yellowing the hilltops, with that dear friend[14]
(The same whom I have mentioned heretofore)
I went abroad, and for the better part   585
Of two delightful hours we strolled along
By the still borders of the misty lake
Repeating favourite verses with one voice,
Or conning more, as happy as the birds
That round us chanted. Well might we be glad,   590
Lifted above the ground by airy fancies
More bright than madness or the dreams of wine.
And though full oft the objects of our love
Were false, and in their splendour overwrought,
Yet surely at such time no vulgar power   595
Was working in us, nothing less in truth
Than that most noble attribute of man
(Though yet untutored and inordinate) –
That wish for something loftier, more adorned
Than is the common aspect, daily garb,   600
Of human life. What wonder then if sounds
Of exultation echoed through the groves?
For images, and sentiments, and words,
And everything with which we had to do
In that delicious world of poesy,   605
Kept holiday, a never-ending show
With music, incense, festival, and flowers!
   Here must I pause: this only will I add,
From heart-experience and in humblest sense
Of modesty, that he who in his youth,   610
A wanderer among the woods and fields,
With living nature hath been intimate,
Not only in that raw unpractised time
Is stirred to ecstasy, as others are,
By glittering verse, but he doth furthermore,   615
In measure only dealt out to himself,
Receive enduring touches of deep joy
From the great nature that exists in works
Of mighty poets. Visionary power
Attends upon the motions of the winds   620
Embodied in the mystery of words;
There darkness makes abode, and all the host
Of shadowy things do work their changes there,
As in a mansion like their proper home.
Even forms and substances are circumfused   625
By that transparent veil with light divine,

---

[14] *that dear friend* John Fleming.

And through the turnings intricate of verse
Present themselves as objects recognized
In flashes, and with a glory scarce their own.
   Thus far a scanty record is deduced   630
Of what I owed to books in early life;
Their later influence yet remains untold,
But as this work was taking in my thoughts
Proportions that seemed larger than had first
Been meditated, I was indisposed   635
To any further progress at a time
When these acknowledgements were left unpaid.

Book Six
Cambridge and the Alps

The leaves were yellow when to Furness Fells,[1]
The haunt of shepherds, and to cottage life
I bade adieu, and, one among the flock
Who by that season are convened, like birds
Trooping together at the fowler's lure,   5
Went back to Granta's[2] cloisters – not so fond
Or eager, though as gay and undepressed
In spirit, as when I thence had taken flight
A few short months before. I turned my face
Without repining from the mountain pomp   10
Of autumn, and its beauty (entered in
With calmer lakes and louder streams); and you,
Frank-hearted maids of rocky Cumberland,
You and your not unwelcome days of mirth
I quitted, and your nights of revelry,   15
And in my own unlovely cell sat down
In lightsome mood. Such privilege has youth,
That cannot take long leave of pleasant thoughts.
   We need not linger o'er the ensuing time,
But let me add at once that now, the bonds   20
Of indolent and vague society
Relaxing in their hold, I lived henceforth
More to myself, read more, reflected more,
Felt more, and settled daily into habits
More promising. Two winters may be passed   25
Without a separate notice;[3] many books
Were read in process of this time – devoured,
Tasted or skimmed, or studiously perused –
Yet with no settled plan. I was detached

BOOK SIX
[1] *Furness Fells* mountainous area, south-west Lake District.
[2] Granta is a name for Cambridge, deriving from the river of that name.
[3] 1788–90.

Internally from academic cares, 30
From every hope of prowess and reward,
And wished to be a lodger in that house
Of letters, and no more – and should have been
Even such, but for some personal concerns
That hung about me in my own despite 35
Perpetually, no heavy weight, but still
A baffling and a hindrance, a control
Which made the thought of planning for myself
A course of independent study seem
An act of disobedience towards them 40
Who loved me, proud rebellion and unkind.
This bastard virtue – rather let it have
A name it more deserves, this cowardice –
Gave treacherous sanction to that over-love
Of freedom planted in me from the very first, 45
And indolence, by force of which I turned
From regulations even of my own,
As from restraints and bonds. And who can tell,
Who knows what thus may have been gained, both then
And at a later season, or preserved – 50
What love of nature, what original strength
Of contemplation, what intuitive truths
The deepest and the best, and what research
Unbiased, unbewildered, and unawed?
   The poet's soul was with me at that time, 55
Sweet meditations, the still overflow
Of happiness and truth. A thousand hopes
Were mine, a thousand tender dreams of which
No few have since been realized, and some
Do yet remain, hopes for my future life. 60
Four years and thirty, told this very week,[4]
Have I been now a sojourner on earth,
And yet the morning gladness is not gone
Which then was in my mind. Those were the days
Which also first encouraged me to trust 65
With firmness (hitherto but lightly touched
With such a daring thought), that I might leave
Some monument behind me which pure hearts
Should reverence. The instinctive humbleness,
Upheld even by the very name and thought 70
Of printed books and authorship, began
To melt away; and further, the dread awe
Of mighty names was softened down and seemed
Approachable, admitting fellowship

---

[4] The week of 7 Apr. 1804.

Of modest sympathy. Such aspect now,   75
Though not familiarly, my mind put on:
I loved and I enjoyed, that was my chief
And ruling business, happy in the strength
And loveliness of imagery and thought.
   All winter long, whenever free to take   80
My choice, did I at nights frequent our groves
And tributary walks – the last, and oft
The only one, who had been lingering there
Through hours of silence till the porter's bell,
A punctual follower on the stroke of nine,   85
Rang with its blunt unceremonious voice,
Inexorable summons![5] Lofty elms
Inviting shades of opportune recess
Did give composure to a neighbourhood
Unpeaceful in itself. A single tree   90
There was (no doubt yet standing there), an ash
With sinuous trunk, boughs exquisitely wreathed.
Up from the ground and almost to the top
The trunk and master-branches everywhere
Were green with ivy, and the lightsome twigs   95
And outer spray profusely tipped with seeds
That hung in yellow tassels and festoons,
Moving or still – a favourite trimmed out
By winter for himself, as if in pride,
And with outlandish grace. Oft have I stood   100
Foot-bound uplooking at this lovely tree
Beneath a frosty moon. The hemisphere
Of magic fiction, verse of mine perhaps
May never tread; but scarcely Spenser's self
Could have more tranquil visions in his youth,   105
More bright appearances could scarcely see
Of human forms and superhuman powers
Than I beheld, standing on winter nights
Alone beneath this fairy work of earth.
   'Twould be a waste of labour to detail   110
The rambling studies of a truant youth,
Which further may be easily divined –
What, and what kind they were. My inner knowledge
(This barely will I note) was oft in depth
And delicacy like another mind   115
Sequestered from my outward taste in books.
And yet the books which then I loved the most
Are dearest to me now; for, being versed
In living nature, I had there a guide

---

[5] The porter's bell indicated that the college gates
were closing.

Which opened frequently my eyes, else shut,   120
A standard which was usefully applied,
Even when unconsciously, to other things
Which less I understood. In general terms
I was a better judge of thoughts than words,
Misled as to these latter, not alone   125
By common inexperience of youth
But by the trade in classic niceties
(Delusion to young scholars incident,
And old ones also), by that overprized
And dangerous craft of picking phrases out   130
From languages that want the living voice
To make of them a nature to the heart,
To tell us what is passion, what is truth,
What reason, what simplicity and sense.[6]
    Yet must I not entirely overlook   135
The pleasure gathered from the elements
Of geometric science. I had stepped
In these enquiries but a little way,
No farther than the threshold (with regret
Sincere I mention this), but there I found   140
Enough to exalt, to cheer me, and compose.
With Indian awe and wonder, ignorance
Which even was cherished, did I meditate
Upon the alliance of those simple, pure
Proportions and relations with the frame   145
And laws of nature – how they could become
Herein a leader to the human mind –
And made endeavours frequent to detect
The process by dark guesses of my own.
Yet from this source more frequently I drew   150
A pleasure calm and deeper, a still sense
Of permanent and universal sway
And paramount endowment in the mind,
An image not unworthy of the one
Surpassing life which – out of space and time,   155
Nor touched by welterings of passion – is,
And hath the name of, God. Transcendent peace
And silence did await upon these thoughts
That were a frequent comfort to my youth.
    And as I have read of one by shipwreck thrown   160
With fellow-sufferers whom the waves had spared
Upon a region uninhabited,
An island of the deep, who, having brought
To land a single volume and no more,

---

[6] Wordsworth is critical of the practice of composing Latin verses using phrases from classical authors.

A treatise of geometry, was used,   165
Although of food and clothing destitute
And beyond common wretchedness depressed,
To part from company and take this book
(Then first a self-taught pupil in those truths)
To spots remote and corners of the isle   170
By the seaside, and draw his diagrams
With a long stick upon the sand, and thus
Did oft beguile his sorrow and almost
Forget his feeling:[7] even so (if things
Producing like effect, from outward cause   175
So different, may rightly be compared),
So was it with me then, and so will be
With poets ever. Mighty is the charm
Of those abstractions to a mind beset
With images, and haunted by itself,   180
And specially delightful unto me
Was that clear synthesis built up aloft
So gracefully, even then when it appeared
No more than as a plaything, or a toy
Embodied to the sense – not what it is   185
In verity, an independent world
Created out of pure intelligence.
    Such dispositions then were mine, almost
Through grace of heaven and inborn tenderness.
And not to leave the picture of that time   190
Imperfect, with these habits I must rank
A melancholy (from humours of the blood
In part, and partly taken up) that loved
A pensive sky, sad days, and piping winds,
The twilight more than dawn, autumn than spring –   195
A treasured and luxurious gloom, of choice
And inclination mainly, and the mere
Redundancy of youth's contentedness.
Add unto this a multitude of hours
Pilfered away by what the bard who sang   200
Of the enchanter Indolence hath called
'Good-natured lounging', and behold a map
Of my collegiate life – far less intense
Than duty called for, or, without regard
To duty, might have sprung up of itself   205
By change of accidents, or even (to speak
Without unkindness) in another place.
    In summer among distant nooks I roved –
Dovedale,[8] or Yorkshire dales, or through by-tracts

[7] Based on John Newton's *Authentic Narrative* (1764).   [8] *Dovedale* picturesque beauty spot on border of Derbyshire and Staffordshire.

Of my own native region – and was blessed   210
Between those sundry wanderings with a joy
Above all joys, that seemed another morn
Risen on mid-noon: the presence, friend, I mean
Of that sole sister, she who hath been long
Thy treasure also, thy true friend and mine,   215
Now after separation desolate
Restored to me[9] – such absence that she seemed
A gift then first bestowed. The gentle banks
Of Emont, hitherto unnamed in song,
And that monastic castle,[10] on a flat   220
Low-standing by the margin of the stream,
A mansion not unvisited of old
By Sidney, where, in sight of our Helvellyn,
Some snatches he might pen, for aught we know,
Of his *Arcadia*, by fraternal love   225
Inspired[11] – that river and that mouldering dome
Have seen us sit in many a summer hour,
My sister and myself, when, having climbed
In danger through some window's open space,
We looked abroad, or on the turret's head   230
Lay listening to the wild-flowers and the grass
As they gave out their whispers to the wind.
    Another maid there was[12] who also breathed
A gladness o'er that season, then to me
By her exulting outside look of youth   235
And placid under-countenance first endeared –
That other spirit, Coleridge, who is now
So near to us, that meek confiding heart
So reverenced by us both. O'er paths and fields
In all that neighbourhood, through narrow lanes   240
Of eglantine, and through the shady woods,
And o'er the Border Beacon[13] and the waste
Of naked pools and common crags that lay
Exposed on the bare fell, was scattered love,
A spirit of pleasure, and youth's golden gleam.   245
Oh friend, we had not seen thee at that time,
And yet a power is on me and a strong
Confusion, and I seem to plant thee there!
Far art thou wandered now in search of health

---

[9] After their mother's death, Dorothy stayed with relatives. She was reunited with Wordsworth in summer 1787.
[10] Brougham Castle, beside the River Emont near Penrith. Local historians mistakenly believed it to have been visited by Sidney.

[11] Sidney wrote *Arcadia* for his sister, the Countess of Pembroke.
[12] Mary Hutchinson, whom William had known since childhood, and married 4 Oct. 1802; see Dorothy's account of the marriage, pp. 497–8 below.
[13] The Border Beacon overlooks Penrith.

And milder breezes, melancholy lot![14]   250
But thou art with us, with us in the past,
The present, with us in the times to come.
There is no grief, no sorrow, no despair,
No languor, no dejection, no dismay,
No absence scarcely can there be, for those   255
Who love as we do. Speed thee well! Divide
Thy pleasure with us; thy returning strength,
Receive it daily as a joy of ours;
Share with us thy fresh spirits, whether gift
Of gales Etesian,[15] or of loving thoughts.   260
    I too have been a wanderer, but alas,
How different is the fate of different men
Though twins almost in genius and in mind!
Unknown unto each other – yea, and breathing
As if in different elements – we were framed   265
To bend at last to the same discipline,
Predestined, if two beings ever were,
To seek the same delights, and have one health,
One happiness. Throughout this narrative,
Else sooner ended, I have known full well   270
For whom I thus record the birth and growth
Of gentleness, simplicity, and truth,
And joyous loves that hallow innocent days
Of peace and self-command. Of rivers, fields,
And groves, I speak to thee, my friend – to thee   275
Who, yet a liveried schoolboy in the depths
Of the huge city,[16] on the leaded roof
Of that wide edifice, thy home and school,
Wast used to lie and gaze upon the clouds
Moving in heaven, or haply, tired of this,   280
To shut thine eyes and by internal light
See trees, and meadows, and thy native stream,[17]
Far distant, thus beheld from year to year
Of thy long exile. Nor could I forget
In this late portion of my argument   285
That scarcely had I finally resigned
My rights among those academic bowers
When thou wert thither guided. From the heart
Of London, and from cloisters there, thou camest,
And didst sit down in temperance and peace,   290
A rigorous student.[18] What a stormy course

---

[14] Coleridge sailed for Malta aboard the Speedwell (note the pun in line 256) on 9 Apr. 1804.
[15] gales Etesian northwesterly Mediterranean winds.
[16] Coleridge was at Christ's Hospital, City of London, 1782–9.
[17] The River Otter; Coleridge was born at Ottery St Mary, Devon.
[18] Coleridge matriculated at Cambridge, Oct. 1791. He left without a degree in Nov./Dec. 1794 after a wretched three years.

Then followed! Oh, it is a pang that calls
For utterance, to think how small a change
Of circumstances might to thee have spared
A world of pain, ripened ten thousand hopes   295
For ever withered.
          Through this retrospect
Of my own college life I still have had
Thy after-sojourn in the self-same place
Present before my eyes; I have played with times
(I speak of private business of the thought)   300
And accidents as children do with cards,
Or as a man who when his house is built,
A frame locked up in wood and stone, doth still
In impotence of mind by his fireside
Rebuild it to his liking. I have thought   305
Of thee, thy learning, gorgeous eloquence,
And all the strength and plumage of thy youth,
Thy subtle speculations, toils abstruse
Among the schoolmen,[19] and Platonic forms
Of wild ideal pageantry, shaped out   310
From things well-matched or ill, and words for things –
The self-created sustenance of a mind
Debarred from nature's living images,
Compelled to be a life unto itself,
And unrelentingly possessed by thirst   315
Of greatness, love, and beauty. Not alone,
Ah, surely not in singleness of heart,
Should I have seen the light of evening fade
Upon the silent Cam, if we had met
Even at that early time. I needs must hope,   320
Must feel, must trust, that my maturer age
And temperature less willing to be moved,
My calmer habits and more steady voice,
Would with an influence benign have soothed
Or chased away the airy wretchedness   325
That battened on thy youth. But thou hast trod,
In watchful meditation thou hast trod
A march of glory, which doth put to shame
These vain regrets; health suffers in thee, else
Such grief for thee would be the weakest thought   330
That ever harboured in the breast of man.
  A passing word erewhile did lightly touch
On wanderings of my own, and now to these
My poem leads me with an easier mind.
The employments of three winters when I wore   335

---

[19] *schoolmen* medieval scholastic philosophers.

A student's gown have been already told,
Or shadowed forth as far as there is need;
When the third summer brought its liberty,
A fellow student and myself (he too
A mountaineer) together sallied forth   340
And, staff in hand, on foot pursued our way
Towards the distant Alps.[20] An open slight
Of college cares and study was the scheme,
Nor entertained without concern for those
To whom my worldly interests were dear.   345
But nature then was sovereign in my heart,
And mighty forms seizing a youthful fancy
Had given a charter to irregular hopes.
In any age, without an impulse sent
From work of nations and their goings-on,   350
I should have been possessed by like desire;
But 'twas a time when Europe was rejoiced,
France standing on the top of golden hours,
And human nature seeming born again.
   Bound, as I said, to the Alps, it was our lot   355
To land at Calais on the very eve
Of that great federal day;[21] and there we saw,
In a mean city and among a few,
How bright a face is worn when joy of one
Is joy of tens of millions. Southward thence   360
We took our way, direct through hamlets, towns,
Gaudy with relics of that festival,
Flowers left to wither on triumphal arcs,
And window-garlands. On the public roads –
And once, three days successively, through paths   365
By which our toilsome journey was abridged –
Among sequestered villages we walked,
And found benevolence and blessedness
Spread like a fragrance everywhere, like spring
That leaves no corner of the land untouched.   370
Where elms for many and many a league in files
With their thin umbrage, on the stately roads
Of that great kingdom, rustled o'er our heads
For ever near us as we paced along,
'Twas sweet at such a time (with such delights   375
On every side, in prime of youthful strength)
To feed a poet's tender melancholy
And fond conceit of sadness, to the noise

---

[20] On his last Cambridge long vacation, 1790,
Wordsworth and his student friend Robert Jones
walked through France, Switzerland, Italy, Germany,
and the Netherlands.

[21] *that great federal day* 14 July 1790, first anniversary
of the fall of the Bastille.

And gentle undulation which they made.
Unhoused beneath the evening star we saw   380
Dances of liberty, and in late hours
Of darkness, dances in the open air.
   Among the vine-clad hills of Burgundy,
Upon the bosom of the gentle Saône,
We glided forward with the flowing stream;   385
Swift Rhône, thou wert the wings on which we cut
Between thy lofty rocks! Enchanting show
Those woods and farms and orchards did present,
And single cottages and lurking towns –
Reach after reach, procession without end   390
Of deep and stately vales. A lonely pair
Of Englishmen we were, and sailed along
Clustered together with a merry crowd
Of those emancipated, with a host
Of travellers, chiefly delegates returning   395
From the great spousals newly solemnized
At their chief city, in the sight of heaven.
Like bees they swarmed, gaudy and gay as bees;
Some vapoured in the unruliness of joy,
And flourished with their swords as if to fight   400
The saucy air. In this blithe company
We landed, took with them our evening meal,
Guests welcome almost as the angels were
To Abraham of old. The supper done,
With flowing cups elate and happy thoughts   405
We rose at signal given, and formed a ring
And hand in hand danced round and round the board.
All hearts were open, every tongue was loud
With amity and glee; we bore a name
Honoured in France, the name of Englishmen,   410
And hospitably did they give us hail
As their forerunners in a glorious course[22] –
And round and round the board they danced again!
   With this same throng our voyage we pursued
At early dawn. The monastery bells   415
Made a sweet jingling in our youthful ears;
The rapid river, flowing without noise,
And every spire we saw among the rocks,
Spake with a sense of peace – at intervals
Touching the heart amid the boisterous crew   420
With which we were environed. Having parted
From this glad rout, the Convent of Chartreuse
Received us two days afterwards, and there

---

[22] the Glorious Revolution of 1688.

We rested in an awful solitude;[23]
Thence onward to the country of the Swiss.   425
    'Tis not my present purpose to retrace
That variegated journey step by step;
A march it was of military speed,
And earth did change her images and forms
Before us, fast as clouds are changed in heaven.   430
Day after day, up early and down late,
From vale to vale, from hill to hill we went,
From province on to province did we pass,
Keen hunters in a chase of fourteen weeks,
Eager as birds of prey, or as a ship   435
Upon the stretch when winds are blowing fair.
Sweet coverts did we cross of pastoral life,
Enticing valleys – greeted them and left
Too soon, while yet the very flash and gleam
Of salutation were not passed away.   440
Oh sorrow for the youth who could have seen
Unchastened, unsubdued, unawed, unraised
To patriarchal dignity of mind
And pure simplicity of wish and will,
Those sanctified abodes of peaceful man!   445
My heart leaped up when first I did look down
On that which was first seen of those deep haunts,
A green recess, an aboriginal vale
Quiet, and lorded over and possessed
By naked huts, wood-built, and sown like tents   450
Or Indian cabins over the fresh lawns
And by the riverside.
                    That day we first
Beheld the summit of Mont Blanc, and grieved
To have a soulless image on the eye
Which had usurped upon a living thought   455
That never more could be. The wondrous Vale
Of Chamouny did on the following dawn,
With its dumb cataracts and streams of ice,
A motionless array of mighty waves,
Five rivers broad and vast, make rich amends,   460
And reconciled us to realities.
There small birds warble from the leafy trees,
The eagle soareth in the element;
There doth the reaper bind the yellow sheaf,
The maiden spread the haycock in the sun,   465
While winter like a tamed lion walks,

---

[23] The monastery of the Grande Chartreuse stands in a valley high up in the awe-inspiring ('awful') solitude of the Alps; for further discussion see my article, 'The Grande Chartreuse and the Development of Wordsworth's *Recluse*', *Charles Lamb Bulletin*, NS 71 (1990), 235–46.

Descending from the mountain to make sport
Among the cottages by beds of flowers.
   Whate'er in this wide circuit we beheld
Or heard was fitted to our unripe state   470
Of intellect and heart. By simple strains
Of feeling, the pure breath of real life,
We were not left untouched. With such a book
Before our eyes we could not choose but read
A frequent lesson of sound tenderness,   475
The universal reason of mankind,
The truth of young and old. Nor, side by side
Pacing, two brother pilgrims, or alone
Each with his humour, could we fail to abound
(Craft this which hath been hinted at before)   480
In dreams and fictions pensively composed,
Dejection taken up for pleasure's sake,
And gilded sympathies. The willow wreath,
Even among those solitudes sublime,
And sober posies of funereal flowers   485
Culled from the gardens of the Lady Sorrow,
Did sweeten many a meditative hour.
   Yet still in me, mingling with these delights,
Was something of stern mood, an under-thirst
Of vigour never utterly asleep.   490
Far different dejection once was mine,
A deep and genuine sadness then I felt,
The circumstances I will here relate
Even as they were. Upturning with a band
Of travellers, from the Valais we had clomb   495
Along the road that leads to Italy;
A length of hours, making of these our guides
Did we advance, and having reached an inn
Among the mountains, we together ate
Our noon's repast, from which the travellers rose   500
Leaving us at the board. Erelong we followed,
Descending by the beaten road that led
Right to a rivulet's edge, and there broke off.
The only track now visible was one
Upon the further side, right opposite,   505
And up a lofty mountain. This we took
After a little scruple and short pause,
And climbed with eagerness – though not, at length
Without surprise and some anxiety
On finding that we did not overtake   510
Our comrades gone before. By fortunate chance,
While every moment now increased our doubts,
A peasant met us, and from him we learned
That to the place which had perplexed us first

We must descend, and there should find the road   515
Which in the stony channel of the stream
Lay a few steps, and then along its banks –
And further, that thenceforward all our course
Was downwards with the current of that stream.
Hard of belief, we questioned him again,   520
And all the answers which the man returned
To our enquiries, in their sense and substance,
Translated by the feelings which we had,
Ended in this – that we had crossed the Alps.
   Imagination! lifting up itself   525
Before the eye and progress of my song
Like an unfathered vapour; here that power,
In all the might of its endowments, came
Athwart me. I was lost as in a cloud,
Halted without a struggle to break through,   530
And now, recovering, to my soul I say,
'I recognize thy glory.' In such strength
Of usurpation, in such visitings
Of awful promise, when the light of sense
Goes out in flashes that have shown to us   535
The invisible world, doth greatness make abode,
There harbours whether we be young or old.
Our destiny, our nature, and our home,
Is with infinitude, and only there –
With hope it is, hope that can never die,   540
Effort, and expectation, and desire,
And something evermore about to be.
The mind beneath such banners militant
Thinks not of spoils or trophies, nor of aught
That may attest its prowess, blessed in thoughts   545
That are their own perfection and reward –
Strong in itself, and in the access of joy
Which hides it like the overflowing Nile.
   The dull and heavy slackening which ensued
Upon those tidings by the peasant given   550
Was soon dislodged. Downwards we hurried fast,
And entered with the road which we had missed
Into a narrow chasm. The brook and road
Were fellow-travellers in this gloomy pass,
And with them did we journey several hours   555
At a slow step. The immeasurable height
Of woods decaying, never to be decayed,
The stationary blasts of waterfalls,
And everywhere along the hollow rent
Winds thwarting winds, bewildered and forlorn,   560
The torrents shooting from the clear blue sky,
The rocks that muttered close upon our ears,

Black drizzling crags that spake by the wayside
As if a voice were in them, the sick sight
And giddy prospect of the raving stream, 565
The unfettered clouds and region of the heavens,
Tumult and peace, the darkness and the light,
Were all like workings of one mind, the features
Of the same face, blossoms upon one tree,
Characters of the great Apocalypse, 570
The types and symbols of eternity,
Of first, and last, and midst, and without end.[24]
   That night our lodging was an Alpine house,
An inn or hospital (as they are named)
Standing in that same valley by itself 575
And close upon the confluence of two streams –
A dreary mansion, large beyond all need,
With high and spacious rooms, deafened and stunned
By noise of waters, making innocent sleep
Lie melancholy among weary bones. 580
   Uprisen betimes, our journey we renewed
Led by the stream, ere noonday magnified
Into a lordly river, broad and deep,
Dimpling along in silent majesty
With mountains for its neighbours, and in view 585
Of distant mountains and their snowy tops –
And thus proceeding to Locarno's Lake,[25]
Fit resting-place for such a visitant.
Locarno, spreading out in width like heaven,
And Como – thou, a treasure by the earth 590
Kept to itself, a darling bosomed up
In Abyssinian privacy; I spake
Of thee, thy chestnut woods, and garden plots
Of Indian corn tended by dark-eyed maids,
Thy lofty steeps, and pathways roofed with vines 595
Winding from house to house, from town to town
(Sole link that binds them to each other), walks,
League after league, and cloistral avenues
Where silence is, if music be not there:
While yet a youth undisciplined in verse, 600
Through fond ambition of my heart I told
Your praises,[26] nor can I approach you now
Ungreeted by a more melodious song,
Where tones of learned art and nature mixed
May frame enduring language. Like a breeze 605
Or sunbeam over your domain I passed

---

[24] Cf. Milton's description of God: 'Him first, Him last, Him midst, and without end' (*Paradise Lost*, v. 165).

[25] *Locarno's Lake* Lake Maggiore.
[26] In *Descriptive Sketches*, published 1793.

In motion without pause; but ye have left
Your beauty with me, an impassioned sight
Of colours and of forms, whose power is sweet
And gracious, almost (might I dare to say?)   610
As virtue is, or goodness – sweet as love,
Or the remembrance of a noble deed,
Or gentlest visitations of pure thought
When God, the giver of all joy, is thanked
Religiously in silent blessedness –   615
Sweet as this last itself, for such it is.
   Through those delightful pathways we advanced
Two days, and still in presence of the Lake,
Which winding up among the Alps now changed
Slowly its lovely countenance and put on   620
A sterner character. The second night,
In eagerness, and by report misled
Of those Italian clocks that speak the time
In fashion different from ours,[27] we rose
By moonshine, doubting not that day was near   625
And that meanwhile, coasting the water's edge
As hitherto, and with as plain a track
To be our guide, we might behold the scene
In its most deep repose. We left the town
Of Gravedona with this hope, but soon   630
Were lost, bewildered among woods immense
Where, having wandered for a while, we stopped
And on a rock sat down to wait for day.
An open place it was and overlooked
From high the sullen water underneath   635
On which a dull red image of the moon
Lay bedded, changing oftentimes its form
Like an uneasy snake. Long time we sat,
For scarcely more than one hour of the night
(Such was our error) had been gone when we   640
Renewed our journey. On the rock we lay
And wished to sleep but could not for the stings
Of insects which with noise like that of noon
Filled all the woods. The cry of unknown birds,
The mountains (more by darkness visible   645
And their own size, than any outward light),
The breathless wilderness of clouds, the clock
That told with unintelligible voice
The widely-parted hours, the noise of streams
And sometimes rustling motions nigh at hand   650
Which did not leave us free from personal fear,

[27] Bells sounded for each of the hours that had passed, as well as for each of the quarters. The four bells at 1:45 a.m. could therefore be mistaken for 4:00 a.m.

And lastly the withdrawing moon, that set
Before us while she yet was high in heaven –
These were our food; and such a summer night
Did to that pair of golden days succeed,   655
With now and then a doze and snatch of sleep
On Como's banks, the same delicious lake.
    But here I must break off, and quit at once
(Though loath) the record of these wanderings,
A theme which may seduce me else beyond   660
All reasonable bounds. Let this alone
Be mentioned as a parting word: that not
In hollow exultation, dealing forth
Hyperboles of praise comparative,
Not rich one moment to be poor for ever,   665
Not prostrate, overborne, as if the mind
Itself were nothing, a mean pensioner
On outward forms, did we in presence stand
Of that magnificent region. On the front
Of this whole song is written that my heart   670
Must in such temple needs have offered up
A different worship. Finally whate'er
I saw, or heard, or felt, was but a stream
That flowed into a kindred stream, a gale
That helped me forwards; did administer   675
To grandeur and to tenderness – to the one
Directly, but to tender thoughts by means
Less often instantaneous in effect;
Conducted me to these along a path
Which in the main was more circuitous.   680
    Oh, most beloved friend, a glorious time,
A happy time that was! Triumphant looks
Were then the common language of all eyes:
As if awaked from sleep, the nations hailed
Their great expectancy; the fife of war   685
Was then a spirit-stirring sound indeed,
A blackbird's whistle in a vernal grove.
We left the Swiss exulting in the fate
Of their near neighbours, and, when shortening fast
Our pilgrimage, nor distant far from home,   690
We crossed the Brabant armies[28] on the fret
For battle in the cause of liberty.
A stripling, scarcely of the household then
Of social life, I looked upon these things
As from a distance – heard, and saw, and felt,   695

---

[28] *Brabant armies* armies of the short-lived Belgian
republic, suppressed by Leopold II, Emperor of
Austria, Dec. 1790.

Was touched, but with no intimate concern;
I seemed to move among them as a bird
Moves through the air, or as a fish pursues
Its business in its proper element.
I needed not that joy, I did not need   700
Such help: the ever-living universe
And independent spirit of pure youth
Were with me at that season, and delight
Was in all places spread around my steps,
As constant as the grass upon the fields.   705

Book Seven
Residence in London

Five years are vanished since I first poured out,
Saluted by that animating breeze
Which met me issuing from the city's walls –
A glad preamble[1] to this verse. I sang
Aloud in dithyrambic[2] fervour, deep   5
But short-lived transport, like a torrent sent
Out of the bowels of a bursting cloud
Down Scafell or Blencathra's rugged sides,[3]
A waterspout from heaven. But 'twas not long
Ere the interrupted stream broke forth once more   10
And flowed awhile in strength, then stopped for years –
Not heard again until a little space
Before last primrose-time. Beloved friend,
The assurances then given unto myself
Which did beguile me of some heavy thoughts   15
At thy departure to a foreign land
Have failed, for slowly doth this work advance.
Through the whole summer have I been at rest,
Partly from voluntary holiday
And part through outward hindrance. But I heard   20
After the hour of sunset yester-even,
Sitting within doors betwixt light and dark,
A voice that stirred me. 'Twas a little band,
A choir of redbreasts gathered somewhere near
My threshold, minstrels from the distant woods   25
And dells, sent in by winter to bespeak
For the old man a welcome, to announce
With preparation artful and benign
(Yea, the most gentle music of the year)
That their rough lord had left the surly north   30

BOOK SEVEN
[1] Writing in early Oct. 1804, Wordsworth refers to
the composition of Book I, lines 1–54, in early 1800.

[2] *dithyrambic* fervent.
[3] Scafell and Blencathra are mountains in Cumbria.

And hath begun his journey.
                    A delight
At this unthought-of greeting unawares
Smote me, a sweetness of the coming time,
And, listening, I half whispered, 'We will be,
Ye heartsome choristers, ye and I will be   35
Brethren, and in the hearing of bleak winds
Will chant together.' And thereafter, walking
By later twilight on the hills, I saw
A glow-worm from beneath a dusky shade
Or canopy of yet unwithered fern   40
Clear-shining, like a hermit's taper seen
Through a thick forest. Silence touched me here
No less than sound had done before: the child
Of summer, lingering, shining by itself,
The voiceless worm on the unfrequented hills   45
Seemed sent on the same errand with the choir
Of winter that had warbled at my door,
And the whole year seemed tenderness and love.

The last night's genial feeling overflowed
Upon this morning, and my favourite grove,   50
Now tossing its dark boughs in sun and wind,
Spreads through me a commotion like its own,
Something that fits me for the poet's task,
Which we will now resume with cheerful hope,
Nor checked by aught of tamer argument   55
That lies before us, needful to be told.

Returned from that excursion, soon I bade
Farewell for ever to the private bowers
Of gowned students[4] – quitted these, no more
To enter them – and pitched my vagrant tent,   60
A casual dweller and at large, among
The unfenced regions of society.
Yet undetermined to what plan of life
I should adhere, and seeming thence to have
A little space of intermediate time   65
Loose and at full command, to London first
I turned, if not in calmness, nevertheless
In no disturbance of excessive hope –
At ease from all ambition personal,
Frugal as there was need, and though self-willed,   70
Yet temperate and reserved, and wholly free
From dangerous passions. 'Twas at least two years
Before this season when I first beheld
That mighty place, a transient visitant,

---

[4] Wordsworth took his degree Jan. 1791.

And now it pleased me my abode to fix   75
Single in the wide waste. To have a house
It was enough (what matter for a home?)
That owned me, living cheerfully abroad
With fancy on the stir from day to day
And all my young affections out of doors.   80
   There was a time when whatsoe'er is feigned
Of airy palaces and gardens built
By genii of romance, or hath in grave
Authentic history been set forth of Rome,
Alcairo, Babylon or Persepolis,[5]   85
Or given upon report by pilgrim friars
Of golden cities ten months' journey deep
Among Tartarian wilds, fell short, far short
Of that which I in simpleness believed
And thought of London – held me by a chain   90
Less strong of wonder and obscure delight.
I know not that herein I shot beyond
The common mark of childhood, but I well
Remember that among our flock of boys
Was one, a cripple from the birth, whom chance   95
Summoned from school to London – fortunate
And envied traveller! And when he returned
After short absence, and I first set eyes
Upon his person, verily (though strange
The thing may seem) I was not wholly free   100
From disappointment to behold the same
Appearance, the same body, not to find
Some change, some beams of glory brought away
From that new region. Much I questioned him,
And every word he uttered on my ears   105
Fell flatter than a caged parrot's note
That answers unexpectedly awry
And mocks the prompter's listening. Marvellous things
My fancy had shaped forth, of sights and shows,
Processions, equipages, lords and dukes,   110
The King, and the King's palace, and, not last
Or least (Heaven bless him!), the renowned Lord Mayor –
Dreams hardly less intense than those which wrought
A change of purpose in young Whittington
When he in friendlessness, a drooping boy,   115
Sat on a stone and heard the bells speak out
Articulate music.[6] Above all, one thought
Baffled my understanding: how men lived

---

[5] *Alcairo* ancient city of Memphis, near present-day
Cairo; Persepolis was the capital of the Persian Empire, sacked by Alexander the Great in 331 BC.

[6] About to leave London, Dick Whittington is said
to have heard the bells of St Mary-le-Bow call 'Turn
again Whittington, Lord Mayor of London'.

Even next door neighbours (as we say) yet still
Strangers, and knowing not each other's names.   120
    Oh wondrous power of words, how sweet they are
According to the meaning which they bring!
Vauxhall and Ranelagh![7] I then had heard
Of your green groves and wilderness of lamps,
Your gorgeous ladies, fairy cataracts   125
And pageant fireworks. Nor must we forget
Those other wonders, different in kind
Though scarcely less illustrious in degree:
The river proudly bridged, the giddy top
And Whispering Gallery of St Paul's, the tombs   130
Of Westminster, the Giants of Guildhall,[8]
Bedlam and the two figures at its gates,[9]
Streets without end and churches numberless,
Statues with flowery gardens in vast squares,
The Monument and Armoury of the Tower.[10]   135
    These fond imaginations of themselves
Had long before given way in season due,
Leaving a throng of others in their stead;
And now I looked upon the real scene,
Familiarly perused it day by day   140
With keen and lively pleasure, even there
Where disappointment was the strongest, pleased
Through courteous self-submission, as a tax
Paid to the object by prescriptive right –
A thing that ought to be.
                        Shall I give way,   145
Copying the impression of the memory
(Though things remembered idly do half seem
The work of fancy) – shall I, as the mood
Inclines me, here describe for pastime's sake
Some portion of that motley imagery,   150
A vivid pleasure of my youth, and now,
Among the lonely places that I love,
A frequent daydream for my riper mind?
And first, the look and aspect of the place,
The broad highway appearance as it strikes   155
On strangers of all ages;[11] the quick dance
Of colours, lights, and forms; the Babel din;
The endless stream of men and moving things;
From hour to hour the illimitable walk

<hr/>

7 *Vauxhall and Ranelagh* pleasure-gardens in Lambeth
and Chelsea.
8 The carved wooden figures of Gog and Magog.
9 The Bethlehem mental hospital was adorned by
two statues carved by Caius Gabriel Cibber.

10 The Monument commemorates the great fire
of London, 1666; the Armoury is in the Tower of
London.
11 Lines 154–243 are probably inspired by Lamb's
letter to Wordsworth, pp. 615–16.

Still among streets with clouds and sky above;   160
The wealth, the bustle and the eagerness;
The glittering chariots with their pampered steeds;
Stalls, barrows, porters; midway in the street
The scavenger, that begs with hat in hand;
The labouring hackney coaches, the rash speed   165
Of coaches travelling far, whirled on with horn
Loud blowing, and the sturdy drayman's team
Ascending from some alley of the Thames
And striking right across the crowded Strand
Till the fore-horse veer round with punctual skill: 170
Here, there and everywhere a weary throng,
The comers and the goers face to face,
Face after face; the string of dazzling wares,
Shop after shop, with symbols, blazoned names,
And all the tradesman's honours overhead –   175
Here, fronts of houses, like a title-page,
With letters huge inscribed from top to toe;
Stationed above the door like guardian saints –
There, allegoric shapes, female or male,
Or physiognomies of real men,   180
Land-warriors, kings, or admirals of the sea,
Boyle, Shakespeare, Newton, or the attractive head
Of some Scotch doctor, famous in his day.[12]
    Meanwhile the roar continues, till at length,
Escaped as from an enemy, we turn   185
Abruptly into some sequestered nook,
Still as a sheltered place when winds blow loud.
At leisure, thence, through tracts of thin resort
And sights and sounds that come at intervals,
We take our way. A raree-show[13] is here   190
With children gathered round; another street
Presents a company of dancing dogs,
Or dromedary with an antic pair
Of monkeys on his back, a minstrel band
Of Savoyards, or, single and alone,   195
An English ballad-singer. Private courts
Gloomy as coffins, and unsightly lanes
Thrilled by some female vendor's scream (belike
The very shrillest of all London cries),
May then entangle us awhile,   200
Conducted through those labyrinths unawares
To privileged regions and inviolate,
Where from their airy lodges studious lawyers

---

[12] Robert Boyle (1627–91) was a chemist; the   [13] raree-show peep-show.
Scotch doctor is probably James Graham (1745–94),
whose Temple of Health opened in 1779.

Look out on waters, walks, and gardens green.
    Thence back into the throng, until we reach,   205
Following the tide that slackens by degrees,
Some half-frequented scene where wider streets
Bring straggling breezes of suburban air.
Here files of ballads dangle from dead walls,
Advertisements of giant-size from high   210
Press forward in all colours on the sight:
These bold in conscious merit; lower down
That – fronted with a most imposing word –
Is peradventure one in masquerade.
As on the broadening causeway we advance,   215
Behold a face turned up towards us, strong
In lineaments, and red with over-toil.[14]
'Tis one perhaps already met elsewhere,
A travelling cripple, by the trunk cut short
And stumping with his arms. In sailor's garb   220
Another lies at length beside a range
Of written characters with chalk inscribed
Upon the smooth flat stones. The nurse is here,
The bachelor that loves to sun himself,
The military idler, and the dame   225
That field-ward takes her walk in decency.
    Now homeward through the thickening hubbub, where
See, among less distinguishable shapes,
The Italian, with his frame of images
Upon his head, with basket at his waist   230
The Jew, the stately and slow-moving Turk
With freight of slippers piled beneath his arm.
Briefly we find (if tired of random sights,
And haply to that search our thoughts should turn)
Among the crowd, conspicuous less or more   235
As we proceed, all specimens of man
Through all the colours which the sun bestows,
And every character of form and face:
The Swede, the Russian; from the genial south,
The Frenchman and the Spaniard; from remote   240
America, the hunter-Indian; Moors,
Malays, Lascars,[15] the Tartar and Chinese,
And Negro ladies in white muslin gowns.
    At leisure let us view from day to day,
As they present themselves, the spectacles   245
Within doors: troops of wild beasts, birds and beasts
Of every nature, from all climes convened,
And, next to these, those mimic sights that ape

---

[14] Samuel Horsey, 'King of the Beggars'.   [15] *Lascars* East Indians.

The absolute presence of reality,
Expressing, as in mirror, sea and land   250
And what earth is, and what she hath to show.
I do not here allude to subtlest craft
By means refined attaining purest ends,
But imitations fondly made in plain
Confession of man's weakness and his loves.   255
Whether the painter – fashioning a work
To nature's circumambient scenery,
And with his greedy pencil taking in
A whole horizon on all sides[16] – with power
Like that of angels or commissioned spirits   260
Plant us upon some lofty pinnacle,
Or in a ship on waters (with a world
Of life, and lifelike mockery, to east,
To west, beneath, behind us, and before),
Or more mechanic artist represent   265
By scale exact, in model, wood or clay,
From shading colours also borrowing help,
Some miniature of famous spots and things
Domestic or the boast of foreign realms:
The Firth of Forth, and Edinburgh throned   270
On crags – fit empress of that mountain land!
St Peter's Church, or (more aspiring aim),
In microscopic vision, Rome itself;
Or else perhaps some rural haunt, the Falls
Of Tivoli, and high upon that steep   275
The Temple of the Sibyl[17] – every tree
Through all the landscape, tuft, stone, scratch minute,
And every cottage lurking in the rocks –
All that the traveller sees when he is there.
    Add to these exhibitions mute and still   280
Others of wider scope, where living men,
Music, and shifting pantomimic scenes,
Together joined their multifarious aid
To heighten the allurement. Need I fear
To mention by its name (as in degree   285
Lowest of these and humblest in attempt,
Yet richly graced with honours of its own)
Half-rural Sadler's Wells?[18] Though at this time
Intolerant, as is the way of youth
Unless itself be pleased, I more than once   290

---

[16] Thomas Girtin's 'Eidometropolis', a panoramic view of London, was 9 ft high and 216 ft in circumference. Other such depictions of the London skyline are discussed by Philip Shaw, ' "Mimic Sights": A note on Panorama and Other Indoor Displays in Book 7 of *The Prelude*', N&Q, 40 (1993), 462–4.

[17] The Temple of the Sibyl is at Tivoli, near Rome.

[18] *Sadler's Wells* popular theatre in Islington.

Here took my seat, and maugre[19] frequent fits
Of irksomeness, with ample recompense
Saw singers, rope-dancers, giants and dwarfs,
Clowns, conjurors, posture-masters,[20] harlequins,
Amid the uproar of the rabblement   295
Perform their feats. Nor was it mean delight
To watch crude nature work in untaught minds,
To note the laws and progress of belief
(Though obstinate on this way, yet on that
How willingly we travel, and how far!),   300
To have, for instance, brought upon the scene
The champion, Jack the giant-killer – lo!
He dons his coat of darkness, on the stage
Walks, and achieves his wonders, from the eye
Of living mortal safe as is the moon   305
'Hid in her vacant interlunar cave'.
Delusion bold! (and faith must needs be coy)
How is it wrought? His garb is black, the word
'Invisible' flames forth upon his chest!
    Nor was it unamusing here to view   310
Those samples as of ancient comedy
And Thespian times, dramas of living men
And recent things yet warm with life: a sea-fight,
Shipwreck, or some domestic incident
The fame of which is scattered through the land –   315
Such as of late this daring brotherhood
Set forth (too holy theme for such a place,
And doubtless treated with irreverence,
Albeit with their very best of skill):
I mean, oh distant friend, a story drawn   320
From our own ground, *The Maid of Buttermere*,[21]
And how the spoiler came, 'a bold bad man',
To God unfaithful, children, wife, and home,
And wooed the artless daughter of the hills,
And wedded her, in cruel mockery   325
Of love and marriage bonds. Oh friend, I speak
With tender recollection of that time
When first we saw the maiden, then a name
By us unheard of; in her cottage-inn
Were welcomed and attended on by her,   330
Both stricken with one feeling of delight,
An admiration of her modest mien
And carriage, marked by unexampled grace.

---

[19] *maugre* despite.
[20] *posture-masters* contortionists.
[21] Charles Dibdin's Lakeland drama, *Edward and Susan, or The Beauty of Buttermere*, was based on the true story of John Hatfield, who bigamously married Mary Robinson of Buttermere. Charles and Mary Lamb saw it in July 1803, and described it to Dorothy Wordsworth (Marrs, ii. 117).

Not unfamiliarly we since that time
Have seen her, her discretion have observed,   335
Her just opinions, female modesty,
Her patience, and retiredness of mind,
Unsoiled by commendation and the excess
Of public notice. This memorial verse
Comes from the poet's heart, and is her due –   340
For we were nursed (as almost might be said)
On the same mountains; children at one time,
Must haply often on the self-same day
Have from our several dwellings gone abroad
To gather daffodils on Coker's stream.[22]   345
   These last words uttered, to my argument
I was returning, when – with sundry forms
Mingled, that in the way which I must tread
Before me stand – thy image rose again,
Mary of Buttermere! She lives in peace   350
Upon the spot where she was born and reared;
Without contamination does she live
In quietness, without anxiety.
Beside the mountain chapel sleeps in earth
Her new-born infant, fearless as a lamb   355
That thither comes from some unsheltered place
To rest beneath the little rock-like pile
When storms are blowing. Happy are they both,
Mother and child! These feelings, in themselves
Trite, do yet scarcely seem so when I think   360
Of those ingenuous moments of our youth
Ere yet by use we have learnt to slight the crimes
And sorrows of the world. Those days are now
My theme, and, mid the numerous scenes which they
Have left behind them, foremost I am crossed   365
Here by remembrance of two figures: one
A rosy babe who, for a twelvemonth's space
Perhaps, had been of age to deal about
Articulate prattle – child as beautiful
As ever sat upon a mother's knee!   370
The other was the parent of that babe,
But on the mother's cheek the tints were false,
A painted bloom.
          'Twas at a theatre
That I beheld this pair; the boy had been
The pride and pleasure of all lookers-on   375
In whatsoever place, but seemed in this
A sort of alien scattered[23] from the clouds.

---

[22] The River Cocker flows from Buttermere to
Wordsworth's birthplace, Cockermouth.

[23] *scattered* dropped.

Of lusty vigour, more than infantine,
He was in limbs; in face a cottage rose
Just three parts blown – a cottage-child, but ne'er   380
Saw I, by cottage or elsewhere, a babe
By nature's gifts so honoured. Upon a board
Whence an attendant of the theatre
Served out refreshments, had this child been placed,
And there he sat, environed with a ring   385
Of chance spectators, chiefly dissolute men
And shameless women – treated and caressed,
Ate, drank, and with the fruit and glasses played,
While oaths, indecent speech, and ribaldry
Were rife about him as are songs of birds   390
In springtime after showers. The mother too
Was present, but of her I know no more
Than hath been said, and scarcely at this time
Do I remember her. But I behold
The lovely boy as I beheld him then   395
Among the wretched and the falsely gay,
Like one of those who walked with hair unsinged
Amid the fiery furnace.[24] He hath since
Appeared to me oft-times as if embalmed
By nature, through some special privilege   400
Stopped at the growth he had – destined to live,
To be, to have been, come and go, a child
And nothing more, no partner in the years
That bear us forward to distress and guilt,
Pain and abasement: beauty in such excess   405
Adorned him in that miserable place.
So have I thought of him a thousand times,
And seldom otherwise. But he perhaps,
Mary, may now have lived till he could look
With envy on thy nameless babe that sleeps   410
Beside the mountain-chapel undisturbed.
    It was but little more than three short years
Before the season which I speak of now
When first, a traveller from our pastoral hills
Southward two hundred miles I had advanced[25]   415
And for the first time in my life did hear
The voice of woman utter blasphemy –
Saw woman as she is to open shame
Abandoned, and the pride of public vice.
Full surely, from the bottom of my heart   420
I shuddered. But the pain was almost lost,
Absorbed and buried in the immensity

[24] Shadrach, Meshach, and Abednego; see Dan. 3: 27.   [25] Wordsworth went south to Cambridge, Oct. 1787.

Of the effect: a barrier seemed at once
Thrown in, that from humanity divorced
The human form, splitting the race of man   425
In twain, yet leaving the same outward shape.
Distress of mind ensued upon this sight
And ardent meditation. Afterwards
A milder sadness on such spectacles
Attended – thought, commiseration, grief   430
For the individual, and the overthrow
Of her soul's beauty: farther at that time
Than this I was but seldom led. In truth
The sorrow of the passion stopped me here.

   I quit this painful theme; enough is said   435
To show what thoughts must often have been mine
At theatres, which then were my delight –
A yearning made more strong by obstacles
Which slender funds imposed. Life then was new,
The senses easily pleased. The lustres,[26] lights,   440
The carving and the gilding, paint and glare,
And all the mean upholstery of the place,
Wanted not animation in my sight:
Far less the living figures on the stage,
Solemn or gay – whether some beauteous dame   445
Advanced in radiance through a deep recess
Of thick-entangled forest, like the moon
Opening the clouds; or sovereign king, announced
With flourishing trumpets, came in full-blown state
Of the world's greatness, winding round with train   450
Of courtiers, banners, and a length of guards,
Or captive led in abject weeds and jingling
His slender manacles; or romping girl
Bounced, leapt, and pawed the air; or mumbling sire,
A scarecrow pattern of old age patched up   455
Of all the tatters of infirmity,
All loosely put together, hobbled in,
Stumping upon a cane with which he smites,
From time to time, the solid boards, and makes them
Prate somewhat loudly of the whereabout   460
Of one so overloaded with his years.
But what of this? The laugh, the grin, grimace,
And all the antics and buffoonery,
The least of them not lost, were all received
With charitable pleasure. Through the night,   465
Between the show, and many-headed mass
Of the spectators, and each little nook

---

26 *lustres* chandeliers.

That had its fray or brawl, how eagerly
And with what flashes (as it were) the mind
Turned this way, that way – sportive and alert,   470
And watchful as a kitten when at play
While winds are blowing round her, among grass
And rustling leaves. Enchanting age and sweet –
Romantic almost, looked at through a space
(How small!) of intervening years. For then,   475
Though surely no mean progress had been made
In meditations holy and sublime,
Yet something of a girlish childlike gloss
Of novelty survived for scenes like these –
Pleasure that had been handed down from times   480
When, at a country playhouse, having caught
In summer through the fractured wall, a glimpse
Of daylight, at the thought of where I was
I gladdened more than if I had beheld
Before me some bright cavern of romance,   485
Or than we do when on our beds we lie
At night, in warmth, when rains are beating hard.
    The matter which detains me now will seem
To many neither dignified enough
Nor arduous, and is doubtless in itself   490
Humble and low; yet not to be despised
By those who have observed the curious props
By which the perishable hours of life
Rest on each other, and the world of thought
Exists and is sustained. More lofty themes,   495
Such as at least do wear a prouder face,
Might here be spoken of, but when I think
Of these, I feel the imaginative power
Languish within me. Even then it slept
When, wrought upon by tragic sufferings,   500
The heart was full; amid my sobs and tears
It slept even in the season of my youth.
For though I was most passionately moved,
And yielded to the changes of the scene
With most obsequious feeling, yet all this   505
Passed not beyond the suburbs of the mind.
If aught there were of real grandeur here
'Twas only then when gross realities,
The incarnation of the spirits that moved
Amid the poet's beauteous world – called forth   510
With that distinctness which a contrast gives,
Or opposition – made me recognize,
As by a glimpse, the things which I had shaped
And yet not shaped, had seen and scarcely seen,
Had felt, and thought of in my solitude.   515

    Pass we from entertainments that are such
Professedly, to others titled higher,
Yet (in the estimate of youth at least)
More near akin to these than names imply –
I mean the brawls of lawyers in their courts   520
Before the ermined judge, or that great stage
Where senators, tongue-favoured men, perform,
Admired and envied. Oh, the beating heart
When one among the prime of these rose up,
One of whose name from childhood we had heard   525
Familiarly,[27] a household term like those,
The Bedfords, Gloucesters, Salisburys of old
Which the fifth Harry talks of. Silence! Hush!
This is no trifler, no short-flighted wit,
Nor stammerer of a minute, painfully   530
Delivered. No, the orator hath yoked
The hours, like young Aurora,[28] to his car –
Oh presence of delight, can patience e'er
Grow weary of attending on a track
That kindles with such glory? Marvellous!   535
The enchantment spreads and rises – all are rapt,
Astonished; like a hero in romance
He winds away his never-ending horn.
Words follow words, sense seems to follow sense –
What memory and what logic! till the strain,   540
Transcendent, superhuman as it is,
Grows tedious even in a young man's ear.
    These are grave follies; other public shows
The capital city teems with, of a kind
More light – and where but in the holy church?   545
There have I seen a comely bachelor,
Fresh from a toilette of two hours, ascend
The pulpit, with seraphic glance look up,
And, in a tone elaborately low
Beginning, lead his voice through many a maze   550
A minuet course, and, winding up his mouth
From time to time into an orifice
Most delicate, a lurking eyelet, small
And only not invisible, again
Open it out, diffusing thence a smile   555
Of rapt irradiation, exquisite.
Meanwhile the Evangelists, Isaiah, Job,
Moses, and he who penned, the other day,
The Death of Abel, Shakespeare, Doctor Young,

---

[27] William Pitt the Younger (1759–1806), Prime   [28] Goddess of dawn.
Minister 1783–1801, 1804–6.

And Ossian (doubt not, 'tis the naked truth) 560
Summoned from streamy Morven[29] – each and all
Must in their turn lend ornament and flowers
To entwine the crook of eloquence with which
This pretty shepherd, pride of all the plains,
Leads up and down his captivated flock. 565
    I glance but at a few conspicuous marks,
Leaving ten thousand others that do each –
In hall or court, conventicle or shop,
In public room or private, park or street –
With fondness reared on his own pedestal, 570
Look out for admiration. Folly, vice,
Extravagance in gesture, mien and dress,
And all the strife of singularity
(Lies to the ear, and lies to every sense) –
Of these, and of the living shapes they wear, 575
There is no end. Such candidates for regard,
Although well-pleased to be where they were found,
I did not hunt after or greatly prize,
Nor made unto myself a secret boast
Of reading them with quick and curious eye; 580
But as a common produce – things that are
Today, tomorrow will be – took of them
Such willing note as, on some errand bound
Of pleasure or of love, some traveller might
(Among a thousand other images) 585
Of sea-shells that bestud the sandy beach,
Or daisies swarming through the fields in June.
    But foolishness and madness in parade,
Though most at home in this their dear domain,
Are scattered everywhere, no rarities 590
Even to the rudest novice of the schools.
Oh friend, one feeling was there which belonged
To this great city by exclusive right:
How often in the overflowing streets
Have I gone forwards with the crowd, and said 595
Unto myself, 'The face of everyone
That passes by me is a mystery!'
Thus have I looked, nor ceased to look, oppressed
By thoughts of what and whither, when and how,
Until the shapes before my eyes became 600
A second-sight procession such as glides
Over still mountains, or appears in dreams,

---

[29] The preacher borrows from popular works of the late eighteenth century: Salomon Gessner's *Death of Abel* (1758), Young's *Night Thoughts*, and James Mac- pherson's *Fingal* and *Temora* (1762–3). Macpherson set his works in north-west Scotland (Morven) and attributed them to the Celtic poet Ossian.

And all the ballast of familiar life –
The present and the past, hope, fear, all stays,
All laws, of acting, thinking, speaking man –
Went from me, neither knowing me, nor known.
And once, far travelled in such mood, beyond
The reach of common indications, lost
Amid the moving pageant, 'twas my chance
Abruptly to be smitten with the view
Of a blind beggar who, with upright face,
Stood propped against a wall, upon his chest
Wearing a written paper to explain
The story of the man and who he was.
My mind did at this spectacle turn round
As with the might of waters, and it seemed
To me that in this label was a type
Or emblem of the utmost that we know
Both of ourselves and of the universe;
And, on the shape of this unmoving man,
His fixed face and sightless eyes, I looked
As if admonished from another world.
　Though reared upon the base of outward things,
These chiefly are such structures as the mind
Builds for itself. Scenes different there are,
Full-formed, which take, with small internal help,
Possession of the faculties: the peace
Of night, for instance, the solemnity
Of nature's intermediate hours of rest
When the great tide of human life stands still,
The business of the day to come unborn,
Of that gone by locked up as in the grave;
The calmness, beauty, of the spectacle,
Sky, stillness, moonshine, empty streets, and sounds
Unfrequent as in deserts; at late hours
Of winter evenings, when unwholesome rains
Are falling hard, with people yet astir,
The feeble salutation from the voice
Of some unhappy woman now and then
Heard as we pass, when no one looks about,
Nothing is listened to. But these I fear
Are falsely catalogued – things that are, are not,
Even as we give them welcome, or assist,
Are prompt or are remiss. What say you then
To times when half the city shall break out
Full of one passion – vengeance, rage, or fear –
To executions, to a street on fire,
Mobs, riots, or rejoicings? From those sights
Take one, an annual festival, the Fair
Holden where martyrs suffered in past time,

605
610
615
620
625
630
635
640
645
650

And named of St Bartholomew.[30] There see
A work that's finished to our hands, that lays
(If any spectacle on earth can do)
The whole creative powers of man asleep!
For once the muse's help will we implore,   655
And she shall lodge us, wafted on her wings,
Above the press and danger of the crowd,
Upon some showman's platform: what a hell
For eyes and ears! What anarchy and din
Barbarian and infernal! 'Tis a dream   660
Monstrous in colour, motion, shape, sight, sound!
Below, the open space, through every nook
Of the wide area, twinkles, is alive
With heads; the midway region and above
Is thronged with staring pictures and huge scrolls,   665
Dumb proclamations of the prodigies!
And chattering monkeys dangling from their poles,
And children whirling in their roundabouts;
With those that stretch the neck and strain the eyes,
And crack the voice in rivalship (the crowd   670
Inviting); with buffoons against buffoons
Grimacing, writhing, screaming; him who grinds
The hurdy-gurdy, at the fiddle weaves,
Rattles the salt-box, thumps the kettle-drum,
And him who at the trumpet puffs his cheeks;   675
The silver-collared Negro with his timbrel,
Equestrians, tumblers, women, girls and boys,
Blue-breeched, pink-vested, and with towering plumes.
All moveables of wonder, from all parts
Are here: albinos, painted Indians, dwarfs,   680
The horse of knowledge and the learned pig,[31]
The stone-eater, the man that swallows fire,
Giants, ventriloquists, the invisible girl,
The bust that speaks and moves its goggling eyes,
The waxwork,[32] clockwork, all the marvellous craft   685
Of modern Merlins, wild beasts, puppet-shows,
All out-o'-the-way, far-fetched, perverted things,
All freaks of nature, all Promethean[33] thoughts
Of man – his dullness, madness, and their feats –
All jumbled up together to make up   690
This parliament of monsters. Tents and booths
Meanwhile, as if the whole were one vast mill,

---

[30] Four-day fair, held at Smithfield, where Protestant martyrs were burned in Queen Mary's reign (1553–8). William and Dorothy Wordsworth visited it with Charles Lamb, Sept. 1802.
[31] Animals exhibited at Bartholomew Fair were said to be capable of reading, counting, and playing cards, among other things.
[32] *waxwork* Madame Tussaud brought her collection of effigies to London in 1802.
[33] innovative.

Are vomiting, receiving, on all sides,
Men, women, three years' children, babes in arms.
    Oh blank confusion! and a type not false   695
Of what the mighty city is itself
To all except a straggler here and there –
To the whole swarm of its inhabitants –
An undistinguishable world to men,
The slaves unrespited of low pursuits   700
Living amid the same perpetual flow
Of trivial objects, melted and reduced
To one identity by differences
That have no law, no meaning, and no end –
Oppression under which even highest minds   705
Must labour, whence the strongest are not free!
But though the picture weary out the eye,
By nature an unmanageable sight,
It is not wholly so to him who looks
In steadiness, who hath among least things   710
An under-sense of greatest, sees the parts
As parts, but with a feeling of the whole.
This (of all acquisitions first) awaits
On sundry and most widely different modes
Of education; nor with least delight   715
On that through which I passed. Attention comes,
And comprehensiveness and memory,
From early converse with the works of God
Among all regions, chiefly where appear
Most obviously simplicity and power.   720
By influence habitual to the mind
The mountain's outline and its steady form
Gives a pure grandeur, and its presence shapes
The measure and the prospect of the soul
To majesty. Such virtue have the forms   725
Perennial of the ancient hills; nor less
The changeful language of their countenances
Gives movement to the thoughts, and multitude,
With order and relation. This (if still
As hitherto with freedom I may speak,   730
And the same perfect openness of mind –
Not violating any just restraint,
As I would hope, of real modesty),
This did I feel in that vast receptacle.
The spirit of nature was upon me here;   735
The soul of beauty and enduring life
Was present as a habit, and diffused –
Through meagre lines and colours, and the press
Of self-destroying, transitory things –
Composure and ennobling harmony.   740

Book Eight
Retrospect. Love of Nature leading to Love of Mankind.

What sounds are those, Helvellyn, which are heard
Up to thy summit, through the depth of air
Ascending, as if distance had the power
To make the sounds more audible?[1] What crowd
Is yon, assembled in the gay green field?   5
Crowd seems it, solitary hill, to thee,
Though but a little family of men
(Twice twenty) with their children and their wives,
And here and there a stranger interspersed.
It is a summer festival, a fair   10
Such as – on this side now, and now on that,
Repeated through his tributary vales –
Helvellyn in the silence of his rest
Sees annually, if storms be not abroad
And mists have left him an unshrouded head.   15
Delightful day it is for all who dwell
In this secluded glen, and eagerly
They give it welcome.
                    Long ere heat of noon,
Behold the cattle are driven down; the sheep
That have for traffic been culled out are penned   20
In cotes that stand together on the plain
Ranged side by side; the chaffering is begun.
The heifer lows, uneasy at the voice
Of a new master; bleat the flocks aloud.
Booths are there none: a stall or two is here,   25
A lame man or a blind (the one to beg,
The other to make music); hither too
From far, with basket slung upon her arm
Of hawker's wares – books, pictures, combs and pins –
Some aged woman finds her way again,   30
Year after year a punctual visitant;
The showman with his freight upon his back,
And once perchance in lapse of many years
Prouder itinerant, mountebank,[2] or he
Whose wonders in a covered wain lie hid.   35
But one is here, the loveliest of them all,
Some sweet lass of the valley, looking out
For gains – and who that sees her would not buy?
Fruits of her father's orchard, apples, pears
(On that day only to such office stooping),   40

BOOK EIGHT
[1] Helvellyn looks down on Grasmere's annual fair,
3,118 ft below.

[2] *mountebank* quack doctor.

She carries in her basket, and walks round
Among the crowd, half pleased with, half ashamed
Of her new calling, blushing restlessly.
The children now are rich, the old man now
Is generous; so gaiety prevails   45
Which all partake of, young and old. Immense
Is the recess, the circumambient world
Magnificent, by which they are embraced.
They move about upon the soft green field;
How little they, they and their doings, seem,   50
Their herds and flocks about them, they themselves,
And all which they can further or obstruct –
Through utter weakness pitiably dear
As tender infants are – and yet how great!
For all things serve them: them the morning light   55
Loves as it glistens on the silent rocks;
And them the silent rocks, which now from high
Look down upon them; the reposing clouds,
The lurking brooks from their invisible haunts;
And old Helvellyn, conscious of the stir;   60
And the blue sky that roofs their calm abode.
    With deep devotion, nature, did I feel
In that great city what I owed to thee:
High thoughts of God and man, and love of man,
Triumphant over all those loathsome sights   65
Of wretchedness and vice – a watchful eye,
Which, with the outside of our human life
Not satisfied, must read the inner mind.
For I already had been taught to love
My fellow beings, to such habits trained   70
Among the woods and mountains, where I found
In thee a gracious guide to lead me forth
Beyond the bosom of my family,
My friends and youthful playmates. 'Twas thy power
That raised the first complacency[3] in me   75
And noticeable kindliness of heart,
Love human to the creature in himself
As he appeared, a stranger in my path,
Before my eyes a brother of this world –
Thou first didst with those motions of delight   80
Inspire me.
              I remember, far from home
Once having strayed, while yet a very child,
I saw a sight – and with what joy and love!
It was a day of exhalations spread

---

[3] *complacency* pleasure.

Upon the mountains, mists and steam-like fogs   85
Redounding[4] everywhere, not vehement
But calm and mild, gentle and beautiful,
With gleams of sunshine on the eyelet spots
And loopholes of the hills – wherever seen,
Hidden by quiet process, and as soon   90
Unfolded, to be huddled up again.
Along a narrow valley and profound
I journeyed, when, aloft above my head,
Emerging from the silvery vapours, lo!
A shepherd and his dog, in open day.   95
Girt round with mists they stood and looked about
From that enclosure small, inhabitants
Of an aerial island floating on,
As seemed, with that abode in which they were,
A little pendant area of grey rocks   100
By the soft wind breathed forward. With delight
As bland almost, one evening I beheld,
And at as early age (the spectacle
Is common, but by me was then first seen),
A shepherd in the bottom of a vale,   105
Towards the centre standing, who with voice,
And hand waved to and fro as need required,
Gave signal to his dog, thus teaching him
To chase along the mazes of steep crags
The flock he could not see. And so the brute   110
(Dear creature!) with a man's intelligence
Advancing, or retreating on his steps,
Through every pervious strait to right or left
Thridded a way unbaffled, while the flock
Fled upwards from the terror of his bark   115
Through rocks and seams of turf with liquid gold
Irradiate – that deep farewell light by which
The setting sun proclaims the love he bears
To mountain regions.
              Beauteous the domain
Where to the sense of beauty first my heart   120
Was opened, tract more exquisitely fair
Than is that paradise of ten thousand trees,
Or Gehol's famous gardens,[5] in a clime
Chosen from widest empire, for delight
Of the Tartarian dynasty composed   125
Beyond that mighty wall, not fabulous
(China's stupendous mound!),[6] by patient skill

---

4   *Redounding* overflowing.   6   The Great Wall of China.
5   This description is drawn from John Barrow,
Travels in China (1804).

Of myriads, and boon nature's lavish help:
Scene linked to scene, an ever-growing change,
Soft, grand, or gay, with palaces and domes   130
Of pleasure spangled over, shady dells
For eastern monasteries, sunny mounds
With temples crested, bridges, gondolas,
Rocks, dens, and groves of foliage taught to melt
Into each other their obsequious hues –   135
Going and gone again, in subtle chase
Too fine to be pursued – or standing forth
In no discordant opposition, strong
And gorgeous as the colours side by side
Bedded among the plumes of tropic birds;   140
And mountains over all, embracing all,
And all the landscape endlessly enriched
With waters running, falling, or asleep.
  But lovelier far than this, the paradise
Where I was reared; in nature's primitive gifts   145
Favoured no less, and more to every sense
Delicious, seeing that the sun and sky,
The elements, and seasons in their change,
Do find their dearest fellow-labourer there
The heart of man – a district on all sides   150
The fragrance breathing of humanity:
Man free, man working for himself, with choice
Of time, and place, and object; by his wants,
His comforts, native occupations, cares,
Conducted on to individual ends   155
Or social, and still followed by a train
Unwooed, unthought of even – simplicity,
And beauty, and inevitable grace.
Yea, doubtless, at an age when but a glimpse
Of those resplendent gardens, with their frame   160
Imperial, and elaborate ornaments,
Would to a child be transport over-great,
When but a half-hour's roam through such a place
Would leave behind a dance of images
That shall break in upon his sleep for weeks,   165
Even then the common haunts of the green earth,
With the ordinary human interests
Which they embosom (all without regard
As both may seem) are fastening on the heart
Insensibly, each with the other's help,   170
So that we love, not knowing that we love,
And feel, not knowing whence our feeling comes.
  Such league have these two principles of joy
In our affections. I have singled out
Some moments, the earliest that I could, in which   175

Their several currents, blended into one –
Weak yet, and gathering imperceptibly –
Flowed in by gushes. My first human love,
As hath been mentioned, did incline to those
Whose occupations and concerns were most   180
Illustrated by nature and adorned,
And shepherds were the men who pleased me first:
Not such as in Arcadian fastnesses
Sequestered handed down among themselves
(So ancient poets sing) the golden age;   185
Nor such – a second race, allied to these –
As Shakespeare in the Wood of Arden placed
Where Phoebe sighed for the false Ganymede,
Or there where Florizel and Perdita
Together danced, Queen of the feast and King;   190
Nor such as Spenser fabled.[7] True it is
That I had heard (what he perhaps had seen)
Of maids at sunrise bringing in from far
Their maybush,[8] and along the streets in flocks
Parading with a song of taunting rhymes   195
Aimed at the laggards slumbering within doors –
Had also heard, from those who yet remembered,
Tales of the maypole dance, and flowers that decked
The posts and the kirk-pillars, and of youths,
That each one with his maid at break of day   200
By annual custom issued forth in troops
To drink the waters of some favourite well,
And hang it round with garlands.
                  This, alas,
Was but a dream: the times had scattered all
These lighter graces, and the rural ways   205
And manners which it was my chance to see
In childhood were severe and unadorned,
The unluxuriant produce of a life
Intent on little but substantial needs,
Yet beautiful; and beauty that was felt.   210
But images of danger and distress
And suffering, these took deepest hold of me:
Man suffering among awful powers and forms.
Of this I heard and saw enough to make
The imagination restless, nor was free   215
Myself from frequent perils. Nor were tales
Wanting, the tragedies of former times,

---

[7] Writers idealize country folk; Wordsworth ques-
tions the authenticity of the Arcadias of Shakespeare's
As You Like It and *A Winter's Tale* and Spenser's *The
Shepherd's Calendar.*

[8] *maybush* hawthorn.

Or hazards and escapes, which in my walks
I carried with me among crags and woods
And mountains; and of these may here be told   220
One, as recorded by my household dame.[9]
   At the first falling of autumnal snow,
A shepherd and his son one day went forth
(Thus did the matron's tale begin) to seek
A straggler of their flock. They both had ranged   225
Upon this service the preceding day
All over their own pastures and beyond,
And now at sunrise sallying out again
Renewed their search, begun where from Dove Crag –
Ill home for bird so gentle – they looked down   230
On Deepdale Head and Brothers Water,[10] named
From those two brothers that were drowned therein.
Thence northward, having passed by Arthur's Seat
To Fairfield's highest summit, on the right
Leaving St Sunday's Pike, to Grisedale Tarn   235
They shot, and over that cloud-loving hill,
Seat Sandal (a fond lover of the clouds);
Thence up Helvellyn, a superior mount
With prospect underneath of Striding Edge
And Grisedale's houseless vale, along the brink   240
Of Russet Cove and those two other coves,
Huge skeletons of crags, which from the trunk
Of old Helvellyn spread their arms abroad
And make a stormy harbour for the winds.
Far went those shepherds in their devious quest,   245
From mountain ridges peeping as they passed
Down into every glen; at length the boy
Said, 'Father, with your leave I will go back
And range the ground which we have searched before.'
So speaking, southward down the hill the lad   250
Sprang like a gust of wind, crying aloud,
'I know where I shall find him.'
                       'For take note',
Said here my grey-haired dame, 'that though the storm
Drive one of these poor creatures miles and miles,
If he can crawl he will return again   255
To his own hills, the spots where when a lamb
He learnt to pasture at his mother's side.'
After so long a labour, suddenly
Bethinking him of this, the boy
Pursued his way towards a brook whose course   260
Was through that unfenced tract of mountain-ground

---

[9] *my household dame* Ann Tyson, Wordsworth's land-lady at Hawkshead.

[10] Wordsworth refers to the range of mountains and valleys to the east and north-east of Grasmere.

Which to his father's little farm belonged,
The home and ancient birthright of their flock.
Down the deep channel of the stream he went,
Prying through every nook; meanwhile the rain   265
Began to fall upon the mountain-tops –
Thick storm and heavy which for three hours' space
Abated not – and all that time the boy
Was busy in his search, until at length
He spied the sheep upon a plot of grass,   270
An island in the brook. It was a place
Remote and deep, piled round with rocks where foot
Of man or beast was seldom used to tread;
But now, when everywhere the summer grass
Had failed, this one adventurer, hunger-pressed,   275
Had left his fellows and made his way alone
To the green plot of pasture in the brook.
Before the boy knew well what he had seen
He leapt upon the island with proud heart
And with a prophet's joy. Immediately   280
The sheep sprang forward to the further shore
And was borne headlong by the roaring flood.
At this the boy looked round him, and his heart
Fainted with fear. Thrice did he turn his face
To either brink, nor could he summon up   285
The courage that was needful to leap back
Cross the tempestuous torrent. So he stood,
A prisoner on the island, not without
More than one thought of death and his last hour.
    Meanwhile the father had returned alone   290
To his own house; and now at the approach
Of evening he went forth to meet his son,
Conjecturing vainly for what cause the boy
Had stayed so long. The shepherd took his way
Up his own mountain-grounds, where as he walked   295
Along the steep that overhung the brook
He seemed to hear a voice, which was again
Repeated, like the whistling of a kite.[11]
At this, not knowing why (as oftentimes
Long afterwards he has been heard to say),   300
Down to the brook he went, and tracked its course
Upwards among the o'erhanging rocks; nor thus
Had he gone far ere he espied the boy
Where on that little plot of ground he stood
Right in the middle of the roaring stream,   305
Now stronger every moment and more fierce.

---

[11] *Kite* large fork-tailed hawk, now an endangered
species in the British Isles.

The sight was such as no one could have seen
Without distress and fear. The shepherd heard
The outcry of his son, he stretched his staff
Towards him, bade him leap – which word scarce said,   310
The boy was safe within his father's arms.

   Smooth life had flock and shepherd in old time,
Long springs and tepid winters on the banks
Of delicate Galesus, and no less
Those scattered along Adria's myrtle shores;   315
Smooth life the herdsman, and his snow-white herd,
To triumphs and to sacrificial rites
Devoted, on the inviolable stream
Of rich Clitumnus; and the goatherd lived
As sweetly underneath the pleasant brows   320
Of cool Lucretilis, where the pipe was heard
Of Pan, the invisible god, thrilling the rocks
With tutelary music, from all harm
The fold protecting.[12] I myself (mature
In manhood then) have seen a pastoral tract   325
Like one of these, where fancy might run wild,
Though under skies less generous and serene;
Yet there, as for herself, had nature framed
A pleasure-ground, diffused a fair expanse
Of level pasture, islanded with groves   330
And banked with woody risings – but the plain
Endless, here opening widely out, and there
Shut up in lesser lakes or beds of lawn
And intricate recesses, creek or bay
Sheltered within a shelter, where at large   335
The shepherd strays, a rolling hut his home.
Thither he comes with springtime, there abides
All summer, and at sunrise ye may hear
His flute or flageolet resounding far.
There's not a nook or hold of that vast space,   340
Nor strait where passage is, but it shall have
In turn its visitant, telling there his hours
In unlaborious pleasure, with no task
More toilsome than to carve a beechen bowl
For spring or fountain, which the traveller finds   345
When through the region he pursues at will
His devious course.
           A glimpse of such sweet life
I saw when, from the melancholy walls
Of Goslar, once imperial, I renewed

---

[12]   The Rivers Galesus and Clitumnus, both in Cala-
bria, are mentioned by Virgil and Horace; Lucretilis
was a hill near Horace's farm.

My daily walk along that cheerful plain 350
Which, reaching to her gates, spreads east and west
And northwards from beneath the mountainous verge
Of the Hercynian forest.[13] Yet, hail to you,
Your rocks and precipices! – ye that seize
The heart with firmer grasp, your snows and streams 355
Ungovernable, and your terrifying winds
That howled so dismally when I have been
Companionless among your solitudes.
There 'tis the shepherd's task the winter long
To wait upon the storms: of their approach 360
Sagacious, from the height he drives his flock
Down into sheltering coves, and feeds them there
Through the hard time, long as the storm is locked
(So do they phrase it), bearing from the stalls
A toilsome burden up the craggy ways 365
To strew it on the snow. And when the spring
Looks out, and all the mountains dance with lambs,
He through the enclosures won from the steep waste,
And through the lower heights, hath gone his rounds;
And when the flock with warmer weather climbs 370
Higher and higher, him his office leads
To range among them, through the hills dispersed,
And watch their goings – whatsoever track
Each wanderer chooses for itself – a work
That lasts the summer through. He quits his home 375
At dayspring, and no sooner doth the sun
Begin to strike him with a fire-like heat
Than he lies down upon some shining place
And breakfasts with his dog. When he hath stayed
(As for the most he doth) beyond his time, 380
He springs up with a bound, and then away! –
Ascending fast with his long pole in hand,
Or winding in and out among the crags.
   What need to follow him through what he does
Or sees in his day's march? He feels himself, 385
In those vast regions where his service is,
A freeman, wedded to his life of hope
And hazard, and hard labour interchanged
With that majestic indolence so dear
To native man. A rambling schoolboy, thus 390
Have I beheld him; without knowing why,
Have felt his presence in his own domain
As of a lord and master, or a power

[13] Wordsworth and Dorothy spent the winter of
1798–9 at Goslar, near the Hartz ('Hercynian') mountains.

Or genius – under nature, under God
Presiding – and severest solitude   395
Seemed more commanding oft when he was there.
Seeking the raven's nest, and suddenly
Surprised with vapours, or on rainy days
When I have angled up the lonely brooks,
Mine eyes have glanced upon him few steps off,   400
In size a giant, stalking through the fog,
His sheep like Greenland bears. At other times,
When round some shady promontory turning,
His form hath flashed upon me, glorified
By the deep radiance of the setting sun;   405
Or him have I descried in distant sky,
A solitary object and sublime,
Above all height, like an aerial cross
As it is stationed on some spiry rock
Of the Chartreuse, for worship.   410
                      Thus was man
Ennobled outwardly before mine eyes,
And thus my heart at first was introduced
To an unconscious love and reverence
Of human nature; hence the human form
To me was like an index of delight,   415
Of grace and honour, power and worthiness.
Meanwhile this creature (spiritual almost
As those of books, but more exalted far,
Far more of an imaginative form)
Was not a Corin of the groves, who lives   420
For his own fancies, or to dance by the hour
In coronal, with Phyllis in the midst,[14]
But, for the purposes of kind, a man
With the most common – husband, father – learned,
Could teach, admonish, suffered with the rest   425
From vice and folly, wretchedness and fear.
Of this I little saw, cared less for it,
But something must have felt.
                      Call ye these appearances
Which I beheld of shepherds in my youth,
This sanctity of nature given to man,   430
A shadow, a delusion – ye who are fed
By the dead letter, not the spirit of things,[15]
Whose truth is not a motion or a shape
Instinct with vital functions, but a block
Or waxen image which yourselves have made   435
And ye adore! But blessed be the God

---

[14] *Corin . . . Phyllis* stock pastoral names. *In coronal* In
a ring.

[15] Lines 432–7 condense a number of biblical allusions, to 2 Cor. 3: 6, Lev. 26: 1, and Isa. 44: 9–20.

Of nature and of man that this was so,
That men did at the first present themselves
Before my untaught eyes thus purified,
Removed, and at a distance that was fit.   440
And so we all of us in some degree
Are led to knowledge – whencesoever led,
And howsoever; were it otherwise,
And we found evil fast as we find good
In our first years (or think that it is found),   445
How could the innocent heart bear up and live?
But doubly fortunate my lot: not here
Alone, that something of a better life
Perhaps was round me than it is the privilege
Of most to move in, but that first I looked   450
At man through objects that were great and fair,
First communed with him by their help. And thus
Was founded a sure safeguard and defence
Against the weight of meanness, selfish cares,
Coarse manners, vulgar passions, that beat in   455
On all sides from the ordinary world
In which we traffic. Starting from this point
I had my face towards the truth, began
With an advantage, furnished with that kind
Of prepossession without which the soul   460
Receives no knowledge that can bring forth good –
No genuine insight ever comes to her –
Happy in this, that I with nature walked,
Not having a too early intercourse
With the deformities of crowded life,   465
And those ensuing laughters and contempts
Self-pleasing, which if we would wish to think
With admiration and respect of man
Will not permit us, but pursue the mind
That to devotion willingly would be raised,   470
Into the temple and the temple's heart.
    Yet do not deem, my friend, though thus I speak
Of man as having taken in my mind
A place thus early which might almost seem
Pre-eminent, that this was really so.   475
Nature herself was at this unripe time
But secondary to my own pursuits
And animal activities, and all
Their trivial pleasures; and long afterwards
When those had died away, and nature did   480
For her own sake become my joy, even then
(And upwards through late youth, until not less
Than three-and-twenty summers had been told)
Was man in my affections and regards

Subordinate to her, her awful forms   485
And viewless[16] agencies: a passion she,
A rapture often, and immediate joy
Ever at hand; he distant, but a grace
Occasional, an accidental thought,
His hour being not yet come. Far less had then   490
The inferior creatures, beast or bird, attuned
My spirit to that gentleness of love,
Won from me those minute obeisances
Of tenderness which I may number now
With my first blessings. Nevertheless on these   495
The light of beauty did not fall in vain,
Or grandeur circumfuse them to no end.
    Why should I speak of tillers of the soil? –
The ploughman and his team; or men and boys
In festive summer busy with the rake,   500
Old men and ruddy maids and little ones
All out together, and in sun and shade
Dispersed among the hay-grounds alder-fringed;
The quarryman, far heard, that blasts the rocks;
The fishermen in pairs, the one to row   505
And one to drop the net, plying their trade
'Mid tossing lakes and tumbling boats'[17] and winds
Whistling; the miner (melancholy man!)
That works by taper-light while all the hills
Are shining with the glory of the day.   510
    But when that first poetic faculty
Of plain imagination and severe –
No longer a mute influence of the soul,
An element of the nature's inner self –
Began to have some promptings to put on   515
A visible shape, and to the works of art,
The notions and the images of books,
Did knowingly conform itself (by these
Inflamed, and proud of that her new delight),
There came among those shapes of human life   520
A wilfulness of fancy and conceit
Which gave them new importance to the mind –
And nature and her objects beautified
These fictions as (in some sort) in their turn
They burnished her. From touch of this new power   525
Nothing was safe: the elder-tree that grew
Beside the well-known charnel-house had then
A dismal look, the yew-tree had its ghost
That took its station there for ornament.

---

[16] *viewless* invisible.
[17] Wordsworth alludes to 'I'll never love thee more'

by James Graham, first Marquis of Montrose (1612–50).

Then common death was none, common mishap, 530
But matter for this humour everywhere —
The tragic, super-tragic, else left short.
Then, if a widow, staggering with the blow
Of her distress, was known to have made her way
To the cold grave in which her husband slept, 535
One night, or haply more than one, through pain
Or half-insensate impotence of mind,
The fact was caught at greedily, and there
She was a visitant the whole year through,
Wetting the turf with never-ending tears, 540
And all the storms of heaven must beat on her!
    Through wild obliquities could I pursue
Among all objects of the fields and groves
These cravings; when the foxglove, one by one,
Upwards through every stage of its tall stem 545
Had shed its bells, and stood by the wayside
Dismantled, with a single one perhaps
Left at the ladder's top, with which the plant
Appeared to stoop — as slender blades of grass
Tipped with a bead of rain or dew — behold! 550
If such a sight were seen, would fancy bring
Some vagrant thither with her babes and seat her
Upon the turf beneath the stately flower
Drooping in sympathy, and making so
A melancholy crest above the head 555
Of the lorn creature while her little ones
(All unconcerned with her unhappy plight)
Were sporting with the purple cups that lay
Scattered upon the ground.
                            There was a copse,
An upright bank of wood and woody rock 560
That opposite our rural dwelling stood,
In which a sparkling patch of diamond light
Was in bright weather duly to be seen
On summer afternoons, within the wood
At the same place. 'Twas doubtless nothing more 565
Than a black rock, which, wet with constant springs,
Glistered far seen from out its lurking-place
As soon as ever the declining sun
Had smitten it. Beside our cottage hearth
Sitting with open door, a hundred times 570
Upon this lustre have I gazed, that seemed
To have some meaning which I could not find —
And now it was a burnished shield, I fancied,
Suspended over a knight's tomb, who lay
Inglorious, buried in the dusky wood; 575
An entrance now into some magic cave

Or palace for a fairy of the rock.
Nor would I, though not certain whence the cause
Of the effulgence, thither have repaired
Without a precious bribe, and day by day   580
And month by month I saw the spectacle,
Nor ever once have visited the spot
Unto this hour.
          Thus sometimes were the shapes
Of wilful fancy grafted upon feelings
Of the imagination, and they rose   585
In worth accordingly. My present theme
Is to retrace the way that led me on
Through nature to the love of humankind;
Nor could I with such object overlook
The influence of this power which turned itself   590
Instinctively to human passions, things
Least understood – of this adulterate power –
For so it may be called, and without wrong,
When with that first compared. Yet in the midst
Of these vagaries, with an eye so rich   595
As mine was, through the chance (on me not wasted)
Of having been brought up in such a grand
And lovely region, I had forms distinct
To steady me. These thoughts did oft revolve
About some centre palpable, which at once   600
Incited them to motion, and controlled;
And whatsoever shape the fit might take,
And whencesoever it might come, I still
At all times had a real solid world
Of images about me – did not pine   605
As one in cities bred might do (as thou,
Beloved friend, hast told me that thou didst,
Great spirit as thou art), in endless dreams
Of sickliness, disjoining, joining, things
Without the light of knowledge. Where the harm   610
If, when the woodman languished with disease
From sleeping night by night among the woods
Within his sod-built cabin, Indian-wise,
I called the pangs of disappointed love
And all the long etcetera of such thought   615
To help him to his grave? Meanwhile the man,
If not already from the woods retired
To die at home, was haply (as I knew)
Pining alone among the gentle airs,
Birds, running streams, and hills so beautiful   620
On golden evenings, while the charcoal-pile
Breathed up its smoke, an image of his ghost
Or spirit that was soon to take its flight.

There came a time of greater dignity
Which had been gradually prepared, and now   625
Rushed in as if on wings – the time in which
The pulse of being everywhere was felt;
When all the several frames of things, like stars
Through every magnitude distinguishable,
Were half confounded in each other's blaze,   630
One galaxy of life and joy. Then rose
Man, inwardly contemplated, and present
In my own being, to a loftier height,
As of all visible natures, crown, and first
In capability of feeling what   635
Was to be felt – in being rapt away
By the divine effect of power and love –
As, more than anything we know, instinct
With godhead, and by reason and by will
Acknowledging dependency sublime.   640
    Erelong, transported hence as in a dream,
I found myself begirt with temporal shapes
Of vice and folly thrust upon my view,
Objects of sport, and ridicule, and scorn,
Manners and characters discriminate,   645
And little busy passions that eclipsed,
As well they might, the impersonated thought,
The idea, or abstraction of the kind.
An idler among academic bowers,
Such was my new condition (as at large   650
Hath been set forth), yet here the vulgar light
Of present, actual, superficial life,
Gleaming through colouring of other times,
Old usages and local privilege,
Thereby was softened, almost solemnized,   655
And rendered apt and pleasing to the view.
This notwithstanding, being brought more near
As I was now to guilt and wretchedness,
I trembled, thought of human life at times
With an indefinite terror and dismay –   660
Such as the storms and angry elements
Had bred in me, but gloomier far, a dim
Analogy to uproar and misrule,
Disquiet, danger, and obscurity.
    It might be told – but wherefore speak of things   665
Common to all? – that, seeing, I essayed
To give relief, began to deem myself
A moral agent (judging between good
And evil, not as for the mind's delight
But for her safety), one who was to *act*,   670
As sometimes to the best of my weak means

I did, by human sympathy impelled –
And, through dislike and most offensive pain
Was to the truth conducted; of this faith
Never forsaken, that by acting well,   675
And understanding, I should learn to love
The end of life and everything we know.
    Preceptress stern, that didst instruct me next –
London, to thee I willingly return!
Erewhile my verse played only with the flowers   680
Enwrought upon thy mantle, satisfied
With this amusement, and a simple look
Of childlike inquisition now and then
Cast upwards on thine eye to puzzle out
Some inner meanings which might harbour there.   685
Yet did I not give way to this light mood
Wholly beguiled, as one incapable
Of higher things, and ignorant that high things
Were round me. Never shall I forget the hour,
The moment rather say, when, having thridded   690
The labyrinth of suburban villages,
At length I did unto myself first seem
To enter the great city. On the roof
Of an itinerant vehicle I sat,
With vulgar men about me, vulgar forms   695
Of houses, pavement, streets, of men and things,
Mean shapes on every side, but at the time
When to myself it fairly might be said
(The very moment that I seemed to know)
'The threshold now is overpassed' – great God!   700
That aught external to the living mind
Should have such mighty sway, yet so it was.
A weight of ages did at once descend
Upon my heart – no thought embodied, no
Distinct remembrances, but weight and power,   705
Power growing with the weight. Alas, I feel
That I am trifling; 'twas a moment's pause,
All that took place within me came and went
As in a moment, and I only now
Remember that it was a thing divine.   710
    As when a traveller hath from open day
With torches passed into some vault of earth,
The Grotto of Antiparos or the Den
Of Yordas among Craven's mountain tracts;[18]
He looks and sees the cavern spread and grow,   715

---

[18] Antiparos is an Aegean island; the Den of Yordas is a limestone cave near Ingleton in West Yorkshire, visited by Wordsworth and his brother John in May 1800. Wu and Trott identify 'Three Sources for Wordsworth's *Prelude* Cave', *N&Q*, 38 (1991), 298–9.

Widening itself on all sides, sees, or thinks
He sees,[19] erelong the roof above his head,
Which instantly unsettles and recedes –
Substance and shadow, light and darkness, all
Commingled, making up a canopy   720
Of shapes and forms and tendencies to shape
That shift and vanish, change and interchange
Like spectres, ferment quiet and sublime
Which after a short space works less and less,
Till, every effort, every motion gone,   725
The scene before him lies in perfect view,
Exposed and lifeless as a written book.
But let him pause awhile and look again
And a new quickening shall succeed, at first
Beginning timidly, then creeping fast   730
Through all which he beholds. The senseless mass,
In its projections, wrinkles, cavities,
Through all its surface, with all colours streaming
Like a magician's airy pageant, parts,
Unites, embodying everywhere some pressure   735
Or image, recognized or new, some type
Or picture of the world; forests and lakes,
Ships, rivers, towers, the warrior clad in mail,
The prancing steed, the pilgrim with his staff,
The mitred bishop and the throned king –   740
A spectacle to which there is no end.
   No otherwise had I at first been moved
With such a swell of feeling, followed soon
By a blank sense of greatness passed away –
And afterwards continued to be moved –   745
In presence of that vast metropolis,
The fountain of my country's destiny
And of the destiny of earth itself;
That great emporium, chronicle at once
And burial-place of passions, and their home   750
Imperial and chief living residence.
   With strong sensations teeming as it did
Of past and present, such a place must needs
Have pleased me in those times. I sought not then
Knowledge, but craved for power – and power I found   755
In all things. Nothing had a circumscribed
And narrow influence, but all objects, being
Themselves capacious, also found in me
Capaciousness and amplitude of mind:

[19] *sees, or thinks / He sees* from Virgil, *Aeneid*, vi. 454:
'aut videt, aut vidisse putat', subsequently borrowed
by Milton, *Paradise Lost*, i. 783–4.

Such is the strength and glory of our youth.   760
The human nature unto which I felt
That I belonged, and which I loved and reverenced,
Was not a punctual presence,[20] but a spirit
Living in time and space, and far diffused –
In this my joy, in this my dignity   765
Consisted. The external universe,
By striking upon what is found within,
Had given me this conception, with the help
Of books and what they picture and record.
    'Tis true, the history of my native land,   770
With those of Greece compared and popular[21] Rome
(Events not lovely nor magnanimous,
But harsh and unaffecting in themselves
And in our high-wrought modern narratives
Stripped of their harmonizing soul, the life   775
Of manners and familiar incidents)
Had never much delighted me. And less
Than other minds I had been used to owe
The pleasure which I found in place or thing
To extrinsic transitory accidents,   780
To records or traditions; but a sense
Of what had been here done, and suffered here
Through ages – and was doing, suffering, still –
Weighed with me, could support the test of thought,
Was like the enduring majesty and power   785
Of independent nature. And not seldom
Even individual remembrances,
By working on the shapes before my eyes,
Became like vital functions of the soul;
And out of what had been, what was, the place   790
Was thronged with impregnations, like those wilds
In which my early feelings had been nursed,
And naked valleys full of caverns, rocks,
And audible seclusions, dashing lakes,
Echoes and waterfalls, and pointed crags   795
That into music touch the passing wind.
    Thus here imagination also found
An element that pleased her, tried her strength
Among new objects – simplified, arranged,
Impregnated my knowledge, made it live –   800
And the result was elevating thoughts
Of human nature. Neither guilt nor vice,
Debasement of the body or the mind,
Nor all the misery forced upon my sight

---

[20] *punctual* restricted to one place.   [21] *popular* republican, ruled by the people.

(Which was not lightly passed, but often scanned 805
Most feelingly) could overthrow my trust
In what we may become, induce belief
That I was ignorant, had been falsely taught,
A solitary, who with vain conceits
Had been inspired, and walked about in dreams. 810
When from that rueful prospect, overcast
And in eclipse, my meditations turned,
Lo! everything that was indeed divine
Retained its purity inviolate
And unencroached upon – nay, seemed brighter far 815
For this deep shade in counterview, this gloom
Of opposition, such as showed itself
To the eyes of Adam (yet in Paradise
Though fallen from bliss) when 'in the east he saw
Darkness ere day's mid course, and morning light 820
More orient in the western cloud, that drew
O'er the blue firmament a radiant white,
Descending slow with something heavenly fraught.'[22]
    Add also that among the multitudes
Of that great city oftentimes was seen 825
Affectingly set forth – more than elsewhere
Is possible – the unity of man,
One spirit over ignorance and vice
Predominant: in good and evil hearts
One sense for moral judgements, as one eye 830
For the sun's light. When strongly breathed upon
By this sensation (whencesoe'er it comes,
Of union or communion), doth the soul
Rejoice as in her highest joy; for there,
There chiefly, hath she feeling whence she is, 835
And passing through all nature rests with God.
    And is not, too, that vast abiding-place
Of human creatures, turn where'er we may,
Profusely sown with individual sights
Of courage, and integrity, and truth 840
And tenderness, which, here set off by foil,
Appears more touching? In the tender scenes
Chiefly was my delight, and one of these
Never will be forgotten. 'Twas a man
Whom I saw sitting in an open square 845
Close to the iron paling that fenced in
The spacious grass-plot; on the corner-stone
Of the low wall in which the pales were fixed
Sat this one man, and with a sickly babe

---

[22] *Paradise Lost*, xi. 203–7.

Upon his knee, whom he had thither brought   850
For sunshine, and to breathe the fresher air.
Of those who passed, and me who looked at him,
He took no note; but in his brawny arms
(The artificer was to the elbow bare,
And from his work this moment had been stolen)   855
He held the child, and, bending over it
As if he were afraid both of the sun
And of the air which he had come to seek,
He eyed it with unutterable love.

    Thus from a very early age, oh friend   860
My thoughts had been attracted more and more
By slow gradations towards humankind
And to the good and ill of human life.
Nature had led me on, and now I seemed
To travel independent of her help   865
As if I had forgotten her; but no,
My fellow beings still were unto me
Far less than she was. Though the scale of love
Were filling fast, 'twas light as yet, compared
With that in which her mighty objects lay.   870

Book Nine
Residence in France

As oftentimes a river (it might seem)
Yielding in part to old remembrances,
Part swayed by fear to tread an onward road
That leads direct to the devouring sea,
Turns and will measure back his course – far back,   5
Towards the very regions which he crossed
In his first outset – so have we long time
Made motions retrograde, in like pursuit
Detained. But now we start afresh: I feel
An impulse to precipitate my verse.   10
Fair greetings to this shapeless eagerness,
Whene'er it comes, needful in work so long,
Thrice needful to the argument which now
Awaits us – oh, how much unlike the past! –
One which, though bright the promise, will be found,   15
Ere far we shall advance, ungenial, hard
To treat of, and forbidding in itself.

    Free as a colt at pasture on the hills
I ranged at large through the metropolis,
Month after month. Obscurely did I live,   20
Not courting the society of men
By literature, or elegance, or rank
Distinguished – in the midst of things, it seemed,

Looking as from a distance on the world
That moved about me. Yet insensibly   25
False preconceptions were corrected thus
And errors of the fancy rectified
(Alike with reference to men and things),
And sometimes from each quarter were poured in
Novel imaginations and profound.   30
A year thus spent,[1] this field (with small regret
Save only for the bookstalls in the streets,
Wild produce, hedgerow fruit, on all sides hung
To tempt the sauntering traveller aside)
I quitted, and betook myself to France,   35
Led thither chiefly by a personal wish
To speak the language more familiarly,
With which intent I chose for my abode
A city on the borders of the Loire.[2]
    Through Paris lay my readiest path, and there   40
I sojourned a few days and visited
In haste each spot of old and recent fame –
The latter chiefly – from the Field of Mars
Down to the suburbs of St Anthony,
And from Mont Martyr southward to the Dome   45
Of Genevieve.[3] In both her clamorous halls
(The National Synod and the Jacobins[4])
I saw the revolutionary power
Toss like a ship at anchor, rocked by storms;
The arcades I traversed in the Palace huge   50
Of Orleans,[5] coasted round and round the line
Of tavern, brothel, gaming-house and shop,
Great rendezvous of worst and best, the walk
Of all who had a purpose, or had not.
I stared, and listened with a stranger's ears   55
To hawkers and haranguers (hubbub wild!)[6]
And hissing factionists with ardent eyes,
In knots, or pairs, or single – ant-like swarms
Of builders and subverters, every face
That hope or apprehension could put on –   60
Joy, anger and vexation, in the midst
Of gaiety and dissolute idleness.
    Where silent zephyrs sported with the dust

BOOK NINE
[1] In fact, Wordsworth spent only Jan.–May in London during 1791.
[2] Orléans, which he reached 6 Dec. 1791; Wordsworth moved to Blois in early 1792.
[3] Wordsworth visited places connected with the Revolution: the Champs de Mars, scene of the Festival of Federation; the Faubourg St-Antoine, a working-class area near the Bastille; Montmartre, Revolutionary meeting-place; and the Pantheon (church of St Geneviève), where Rousseau, Voltaire, and Mirabeau were buried.
[4] The National Assembly and the Jacobin Club.
[5] Shops lined the courtyard of the Palais Royal.
[6] Cf. Paradise Lost, ii. 951.

Of the Bastille I sat in the open sun,
And from the rubbish gathered up a stone   65
And pocketed the relic in the guise
Of an enthusiast; yet, in honest truth,
Though not without some strong incumbences
And glad (could living man be otherwise?),
I looked for something which I could not find,   70
Affecting more emotion than I felt.
For 'tis most certain that the utmost force
Of all these various objects which may show
The temper of my mind as then it was
Seemed less to recompense the traveller's pains –   75
Less moved me, gave me less delight – than did
A single picture merely, hunted out
Among other sights: the 'Magdalene' of Le Brun,[7]
A beauty exquisitely wrought, fair face
And rueful, with its ever-flowing tears.   80
    But hence to my more permanent residence[8]
I hasten. There, by novelties in speech,
Domestic manners, customs, gestures, looks,
And all the attire of ordinary life,
Attention was at first engrossed, and thus   85
Amused and satisfied I scarcely felt
The shock of these concussions, unconcerned,
Tranquil almost, and careless as a flower
Glassed in a greenhouse – or a parlour-shrub
When every bush and tree, the country through,   90
Is shaking to the roots – indifference this
Which may seem strange, but I was unprepared
With needful knowledge, had abruptly passed
Into a theatre of which the stage
Was busy with an action far advanced.   95
Like others I had read, and eagerly
Sometimes, the master pamphlets of the day,[9]
Nor wanted such half-insight as grew wild
Upon that meagre soil, helped out by talk
And public news; but having never chanced   100
To see a regular chronicle which might show
(If any such indeed existed then)
Whence the main organs of the public power
Had sprung – their transmigrations, when and how
Accomplished – giving thus unto events   105
A form and body, all things were to me
Loose and disjointed, and the affections left

---

[7] Charles Le Brun's portrait of Mary Magdalene is
now at the Louvre.
[8] Orléans.

[9] e.g. Burke, *Reflections on the Revolution in France*;
Paine, *The Rights of Man*.

Without a vital interest. At that time,
Moreover, the first storm was overblown,
And the strong hand of outward violence   110
Locked up in quiet. For myself (I fear
Now in connection with so great a theme
To speak, as I must be compelled to do,
Of one so unimportant), a short time
I loitered, and frequented night by night   115
Routs, card-tables, the formal haunts of men
Whom in the city privilege of birth
Sequestered from the rest, societies
Where, through punctilios of elegance
And deeper causes, all discourse alike   120
Of good and evil in the time was shunned
With studious care. But 'twas not long ere this
Proved tedious, and I gradually withdrew
Into a noisier world, and thus did soon
Become a patriot – and my heart was all   125
Given to the people, and my love was theirs.
   A knot of military officers
That to a regiment appertained which then
Was stationed in the city[10] were the chief
Of my associates; some of these wore swords   130
Which had been seasoned in the wars, and all
Were men well-born – at least laid claim to such
Distinction, as the chivalry of France.
In age and temper differing, they had yet
One spirit ruling in them all, alike   135
(Save only one, hereafter to be named)
Were bent upon undoing what was done.
This was their rest, and only hope; therewith
No fear had they of bad becoming worse,
For worst to them was come – nor would have stirred,   140
Or deemed it worth a moment's while to stir,
In anything, save only as the act
Looked thitherward. One, reckoning by years,
Was in the prime of manhood, and erewhile
He had sat lord in many tender hearts,   145
Though heedless of such honours now, and changed:
His temper was quite mastered by the times,
And they had blighted him, had eat away
The beauty of his person, doing wrong
Alike to body and to mind. His port,   150
Which once had been erect and open, now
Was stooping and contracted, and a face,

---

[10] *the city* Wordsworth is now talking about Blois.

By nature lovely in itself, expressed
As much as any that was ever seen
A ravage out of season, made by thoughts   155
Unhealthy and vexatious. At the hour,
The most important of each day, in which
The public news was read, the fever came,
A punctual visitant, to shake this man,
Disarmed his voice and fanned his yellow cheek   160
Into a thousand colours. While he read,
Or mused, his sword was haunted by his touch
Continually, like an uneasy place
In his own body.
    'Twas in truth an hour
Of universal ferment. Mildest men   165
Were agitated, and commotions, strife
Of passion and opinion, filled the walls
Of peaceful houses with unquiet sounds.
The soil of common life was at that time
Too hot to tread upon! Oft said I then,   170
And not then only, 'What a mockery this
Of history, the past and that to come!
Now do I feel how I have been deceived,
Reading of nations and their works in faith –
Faith given to vanity and emptiness;   175
Oh, laughter for the page that would reflect
To future times the face of what now is!'
The land all swarmed with passion, like a plain
Devoured by locusts – Carra, Gorsas[11] – add
A hundred other names forgotten now,   180
Nor to be heard of more. Yet were they powers
Like earthquakes, shocks repeated day by day,
And felt through every nook of town and field.
  The men already spoken of as chief
Of my associates were prepared for flight   185
To augment the band of emigrants in arms
Upon the borders of the Rhine, and leagued
With foreign foes[12] mustered for instant war.
This was their undisguised intent, and they
Were waiting with the whole of their desires   190
The moment to depart.
    An Englishman,
Born in a land the name of which appeared
To license some unruliness of mind –
A stranger, with youth's further privilege,

---

[11] *Carra, Gorsas* influential Revolutionary journalists,
deputies of the National Assembly, and members
of the Girondin group with whom Beaupuy and
Wordsworth were in sympathy; both guillotined Oct.
1793.
[12] *foreign foes* Austria and Prussia.

And that indulgence which a half-learnt speech   195
Wins from the courteous – I, who had been else
Shunned and not tolerated, freely lived
With these defenders of the Crown, and talked,
And heard their notions; nor did they disdain
The wish to bring me over to their cause.   200
But though untaught by thinking or by books
To reason well of polity or law,
And nice distinctions – then on every tongue –
Of natural rights and civil; and to acts
Of nations and their passing interests   205
(I speak comparing these with other things)
Almost indifferent – even the historian's tale
Prizing but little otherwise than I prized
Tales of the poets; as it made my heart
Beat high and filled my fancy with fair forms,   210
Old heroes and their sufferings and their deeds –
Yet in the regal sceptre, and the pomp
Of orders and degrees, I nothing found
Then, or had ever even in crudest youth,
That dazzled me; but rather what my soul   215
Mourned for, or loathed, beholding that the best
Ruled not, and feeling that they ought to rule.
   For, born in a poor district (and which yet
Retaineth more of ancient homeliness,
Manners erect, and frank simplicity,   220
Than any other nook of English land),
It was my fortune scarcely to have seen
Through the whole tenor of my schoolday time
The face of one, who, whether boy or man,
Was vested with attention or respect   225
Through claims of wealth or blood. Nor was it least
Of many debts which afterwards I owed
To Cambridge and an academic life
That something there was holden up to view
Of a republic, where all stood thus far   230
Upon equal ground, that they were brothers all
In honour, as of one community –
Scholars and gentlemen – where, furthermore,
Distinction lay open to all that came,
And wealth and titles were in less esteem   235
Than talents and successful industry.
Add unto this, subservience from the first
To God and nature's single sovereignty
(Familiar presences of awful power),
And fellowship with venerable books   240
To sanction the proud workings of the soul
And mountain liberty. It could not be

But that one tutored thus, who had been formed
To thought and moral feeling in the way
This story hath described, should look with awe   245
Upon the faculties of man, receive
Gladly the highest promises, and hail
As best the government of equal rights
And individual worth. And hence, oh friend,
If at the first great outbreak I rejoiced   250
Less than might well befit my youth, the cause
In part lay here, that unto me the events
Seemed nothing out of nature's certain course,
A gift that rather had come late than soon.
No wonder then if advocates like these   255
Whom I have mentioned, at this riper day
Were impotent to make my hopes put on
The shape of theirs, my understanding bend
In honour to their honour. Zeal, which yet
Had slumbered, now in opposition burst   260
Forth like a polar summer: every word
They uttered was a dart by counter-winds
Blown back upon themselves. Their reason seemed
Confusion-stricken by a higher power
Than human understanding, their discourse   265
Maimed, spiritless – and, in their weakness strong,
I triumphed.
                Meantime day by day the roads,
While I consorted with these royalists,
Were crowded with the bravest youth of France
And all the promptest of her spirits, linked   270
In gallant soldiership, and posting on
To meet the war upon her frontier bounds.
Yet at this very moment do tears start
Into mine eyes (I do not say I weep –
I wept not then – but tears have dimmed my sight)   275
In memory of the farewells of that time,
Domestic severings, female fortitude
At dearest separation, patriot love
And self-devotion, and terrestrial hope
Encouraged with a martyr's confidence.   280
Even files of strangers merely, seen but once
And for a moment, men from far with sound
Of music, martial tunes, and banners spread,
Entering the city – here and there a face
Or person singled out among the rest,   285
Yet still a stranger and beloved as such –
Even by these passing spectacles my heart
Was oftentimes uplifted, and they seemed
Like arguments from heaven that 'twas a cause

Good, and which no one could stand up against   290
Who was not lost, abandoned, selfish, proud,
Mean, miserable, wilfully depraved,
Hater perverse of equity and truth.
   Among that band of officers was one,
Already hinted at, of other mould[13] –   295
A patriot, thence rejected by the rest,
And with an oriental loathing spurned
As of a different caste. A meeker man
Than this lived never, or a more benign,
Meek though enthusiastic to the height   300
Of highest expectation. Injuries
Made him more gracious, and his nature then
Did breathe its sweetness out most sensibly,
As aromatic flowers on Alpine turf
When foot hath crushed them. He through the events   305
Of that great change wandered in perfect faith
As through a book, an old romance or tale
Of fairy, or some dream of actions wrought
Behind the summer clouds. By birth he ranked
With the most noble, but unto the poor   310
Among mankind he was in service bound
As by some tie invisible, oaths professed
To a religious order. Man he loved
As man, and to the mean and the obscure,
And all the homely in their homely works,   315
Transferred a courtesy which had no air
Of condescension, but did rather seem
A passion and a gallantry, like that
Which he, a soldier, in his idler day
Had paid to woman. Somewhat vain he was,   320
Or seemed so; yet it was not vanity
But fondness, and a kind of radiant joy
That covered him about when he was bent
On works of love or freedom, or revolved
Complacently the progress of a cause   325
Whereof he was a part – yet this was meek
And placid, and took nothing from the man
That was delightful. Oft in solitude
With him did I discourse about the end
Of civil government, and its wisest forms,   330
Of ancient prejudice and chartered rights,
Allegiance, faith, and laws by time matured,
Custom and habit, novelty and change –
Of self-respect and virtue in the few

---

[13] Michel Beaupuy (1755–96). *mould* model.

For patrimonial honour set apart,   335
And ignorance in the labouring multitude.
For he, an upright man and tolerant,
Balanced these contemplations in his mind;
And I, who at that time was scarcely dipped
Into the turmoil, had a sounder judgement   340
Than afterwards, carried about me yet
With less alloy to its integrity
The experience of past ages, as (through help
Of books and common life) it finds its way
To youthful minds, by objects over-near   345
Not pressed upon, nor dazzled or misled
By struggling with the crowd for present ends.
    But though not deaf and obstinate to find
Error without apology on the side
Of those who were against us, more delight   350
We took (and let this freely be confessed)
In painting to ourselves the miseries
Of royal courts, and that voluptuous life
Unfeeling where the man who is of soul
The meanest thrives the most, where dignity,   355
True personal dignity, abideth not –
A light and cruel world, cut off from all
The natural inlets of just sentiment,
From lowly sympathy and chastening truth –
When good and evil never have the name,   360
That which they ought to have, but wrong prevails,
And vice at home. We added dearest themes:
Man and his noble nature (as it is
The gift of God and lies in his own power),
His blind desires and steady faculties   365
Capable of clear truth – the one to break
Bondage, the other to build liberty
On firm foundations, making social life
(Through knowledge spreading and imperishable)
As just in regulation and as pure,   370
As individual in the wise and good.
    We summoned up the honourable deeds
Of ancient story, thought of each bright spot
That could be found in all recorded time
Of truth preserved and error passed away;   375
Of single spirits that catch the flame from Heaven,
And how the multitude of men will feed
And fan each other – thought of sects, how keen
They are to put the appropriate nature on,
Triumphant over every obstacle   380
Of custom, language, country, love and hate,
And what they do and suffer for their creed,

How far they travel, and how long endure;
How quickly mighty nations have been formed
From least beginnings; how, together locked   385
By new opinions, scattered tribes have made
One body, spreading wide as clouds in heaven.
To aspirations then of our own minds
Did we appeal, and, finally, beheld
A living confirmation of the whole   390
Before us in a people risen up
Fresh as the morning star. Elate we looked
Upon their virtues, saw in rudest men
Self-sacrifice the firmest, generous love
And continence of mind, and sense of right   395
Uppermost in the midst of fiercest strife.
    Oh sweet it is in academic groves –
Or such retirement, friend, as we have known
Among the mountains, by our Rotha's stream,
Greta, or Derwent,[14] or some nameless rill –   400
To ruminate, with interchange of talk,
On rational liberty and hope in man,
Justice and peace! But far more sweet such toil
(Toil, say I, for it leads to thoughts abstruse)
If nature then be standing on the brink   405
Of some great trial, and we hear the voice
Of one devoted, one whom circumstance
Hath called upon to embody his deep sense
In action, give it outwardly a shape,
And that of benediction to the world.   410
Then doubt is not, and truth is more than truth –
A hope it is and a desire, a creed
Of zeal (by an authority divine
Sanctioned), of danger, difficulty, or death.
Such conversation, under Attic shades,   415
Did Dion hold with Plato, ripened thus
For a deliverer's glorious task, and such
He (on that ministry already bound)
Held with Eudemus and Timonides
Surrounded by adventurers in arms,   420
When those two vessels, with their daring freight
For the Sicilian tyrant's overthrow,
Sailed from Zacynthus – philosophic war
Led by philosophers.[15] With harder fate,
Though like ambition, such was he, oh friend,   425
Of whom I speak. So Beaupuy – let the name

---

[14] *Rotha's stream, / Greta, or Derwent* Lake District rivers.
[15] Dion, Eudemus, and Timonides sailed from the Ionian island of Zante (Zacynthus), in an effort to liberate Sicily from the tyranny of Dionysius the Younger, 357 BC.

Stand near the worthiest of antiquity –
Fashioned his life; and many a long discourse,
With like persuasion honoured, we maintained,
He on his part accoutred for the worst.   430
He perished fighting (in supreme command,
Upon the borders of the unhappy Loire)
For liberty against deluded men,
His fellow countrymen, and yet most blessed
In this, that he the fate of later times   435
Lived not to see, nor what we now behold
Who have as ardent hearts as he had then.[16]
    Along that very Loire, with festivals
Resounding at all hours, and innocent yet
Of civil slaughter, was our frequent walk;   440
Or in wide forests of the neighbourhood,
High woods and over-arched, with open space
On every side, and footing many a mile,
Inwoven roots and moss smooth as the sea,
A solemn region. Often in such place   445
From earnest dialogues I slipped in thought
And let remembrance steal to other times,
When hermits, from their sheds and caves forth-strayed,
Walked by themselves, so met in shades like these.
And if a devious traveller was heard   450
Approaching from a distance, as might chance,
With speed and echoes loud of trampling hoofs
From the hard floor reverberated, then
It was Angelica thundering through the woods
Upon her palfrey, or that gentler maid   455
Erminia, fugitive as fair as she.[17]
Sometimes I saw, methought, a pair of knights
Joust underneath the trees, that as in storm
Did rock above their heads; anon the din
Of boisterous merriment and music's roar,   460
With sudden proclamation burst from haunt
Of satyrs in some viewless glade, with dance
Rejoicing o'er a female in the midst,
A mortal beauty, their unhappy thrall.
The width of those huge forests, unto me   465
A novel scene, did often in this way
Master my fancy while I wandered on
With that revered companion. And sometimes,
When to a convent in a meadow green

---

[16] Beaupuy died not in the civil war of the Vendée but in a battle beside the River Eltz in Germany, 19 Oct. 1796; see Roe, 'Wordsworth's Account of Beaupuy's Death', N&Q, 32 (1985), 337.

[17] Angelica and Erminia, heroines of Ariosto's *Orlando Furioso* and Tasso's *Gerusalemme Liberata*, which Wordsworth read at Cambridge.

By a brookside we came – a roofless pile,   470
And not by reverential touch of time
Dismantled, but by violence abrupt –
In spite of those heart-bracing colloquies,
In spite of real fervour, and of that
Less genuine and wrought up within myself,   475
I could not but bewail a wrong so harsh,
And for the matin-bell (to sound no more)
Grieved, and the evening taper, and the cross
High on the topmost pinnacle – a sign
Admonitory, by the traveller   480
First seen above the woods.
             And when my friend
Pointed upon occasion to the site
Of Romorantin,[18] home of ancient kings;
To the imperial edifice of Blois;
Or to that rural castle, name now slipped   485
From my remembrance (where a lady lodged,
By the first Francis wooed, and, bound to him
In chains of mutual passion, from the tower,
As a tradition of the country tells,
Practised to commune with her royal knight   490
By cressets and love-beacons, intercourse
'Twixt her high-seated residence and his
Far off at Chambord[19] on the plain beneath) –
Even here, though less than with the peaceful house
Religious, mid these frequent monuments   495
Of kings, their vices or their better deeds,
Imagination, potent to inflame
At times with virtuous wrath and noble scorn,
Did also often mitigate the force
Of civic prejudice, the bigotry   500
(So call it) of a youthful patriot's mind;
And on these spots with many gleams I looked
Of chivalrous delight. Yet not the less,
Hatred of absolute rule, where will of one
Is law for all, and of that barren pride   505
In those who, by immunities unjust,
Betwixt the sovereign and the people stand
(His helpers and not theirs), laid stronger hold
Daily upon me – mixed with pity too
And love, for where hope is, there love will be   510
For the abject multitude.
              And when we chanced
One day to meet a hunger-bitten girl,
Who crept along, fitting her languid self

---

[18] Town near Blois.   [19] Château built by Francis I near Blois.

Unto a heifer's motion, by a cord
Tied to her arm, and picking thus from the lane   515
Its sustenance, while the girl with her two hands
Was busy knitting in a heartless mood
Of solitude – and at the sight my friend
In agitation said ''Tis against that
Which we are fighting', I with him believed   520
Devoutly that a spirit was abroad
Which could not be withstood; that poverty,
At least like this, would in a little time
Be found no more; that we should see the earth
Unthwarted in her wish to recompense   525
The industrious and the lowly child of toil,
All institutes for ever blotted out
That legalized exclusion, empty pomp
Abolished, sensual state and cruel power,
Whether by edict of the one or few;   530
And finally, as sum and crown of all,
Should see the people having a strong hand
In making their own laws, whence better days
To all mankind.
                    But, these things set apart,
Was not the single confidence enough   535
To animate the mind that ever turned
A thought to human welfare? – that henceforth
Captivity by mandate without law
Should cease, and open accusation lead
To sentence in the hearing of the world,   540
And open punishment – if not the air
Be free to breathe in, and the heart of man
Dread nothing. Having touched this argument
I shall not (as my purpose was) take note
Of other matters which detained us oft   545
In thought or conversation – public acts,
And public persons, and the emotions wrought
Within our minds by the ever-varying wind
Of record and report which day by day
Swept over us – but I will here instead   550
Draw from obscurity a tragic tale,
Not in its spirit singular indeed
But haply worth memorial, as I heard
The events related by my patriot friend
And others who had borne a part therein.   555
      Oh, happy time of youthful lovers! – thus
My story may begin.[20] Oh balmy time

---

[20] Although various sources have been suggested, the 'story' owes much to Wordsworth's thwarted relationship with Annette Vallon, by whom he had a child, Anne-Caroline Wordsworth, in Dec. 1792.

In which a love-knot on a lady's brow
Is fairer than the fairest star in heaven!
To such inheritance of blessedness   560
Young Vaudracour was brought by years that had
A little overstepped his stripling prime.
A town of small repute in the heart of France
Was the youth's birthplace; there he vowed his love
To Julia, a bright maid, from parents sprung   565
Not mean in their condition, but with rights
Unhonoured of nobility – and hence
The father of the young man, who had place
Among that order, spurned the very thought
Of such alliance. From their cradles up,   570
With but a step between their several homes,
The pair had thriven together year by year,
Friends, playmates, twins in pleasure – after strife
And petty quarrels had grown fond again –
Each other's advocate, each other's help,   575
Nor ever happy if they were apart.
A basis this for deep and solid love,
And endless constancy, and placid truth;
But – whatsoever of such treasures might,
Beneath the outside of their youth, have lain   580
Reserved for mellower years – his present mind
Was under fascination: he beheld
A vision, and he loved the thing he saw.
   Arabian fiction never filled the world
With half the wonders that were wrought for him.   585
Earth lived in one great presence of the spring,
Life turned the meanest of her implements
Before his eyes to price above all gold,
The house she dwelt in was a sainted shrine,
Her chamber-window did surpass in glory   590
The portals of the east, all paradise
Could by the simple opening of a door
Let itself in upon him. Pathways, walks,
Swarmed with enchantment, till his spirits sunk
Beneath the burden, over-blessed for life.   595
This state was theirs, till – whether through effect
Of some delirious hour, or that the youth,
Seeing so many bars betwixt himself
And the dear haven where he wished to be
In honourable wedlock with his love,   600
Without a certain knowledge of his own
Was inwardly prepared to turn aside
From law and custom, and entrust himself
To nature for a happy end of all
(And thus abated of that pure reserve   605

Congenial to his loyal heart, with which
It would have pleased him to attend the steps
Of maiden so divinely beautiful),
I know not – but reluctantly must add
That Julia, yet without the name of wife,   610
Carried about her for a secret grief
The promise of a mother.
                           To conceal
The threatened shame the parents of the maid
Found means to hurry her away by night
And unforewarned, that in a distant town   615
She might remain shrouded in privacy
Until the babe was born. When morning came
The lover, thus bereft, stung with his loss
And all uncertain whither he should turn,
Chafed like a wild beast in the toils. At length,   620
Following as his suspicions led, he found
(Oh joy!) sure traces of the fugitives,
Pursued them to the town where they had stopped,
And lastly to the very house itself
Which had been chosen for the maid's retreat.   625
The sequel may be easily divined:
Walks backwards, forwards, morning, noon and night
(When decency and caution would allow),
And Julia, who, whenever to herself
She happened to be left a moment's space   630
Was busy at her casement, as a swallow
About its nest, erelong did thus espy
Her lover; thence a stolen interview
By night accomplished, with a ladder's help.
    I pass the raptures of the pair; such theme   635
Hath by a hundred poets been set forth
In more delightful verse than skill of mine
Could fashion – chiefly by that darling Bard
Who told of Juliet and her Romeo,
And of the lark's note heard before its time,   640
And of the streaks that laced the severing clouds
In the unrelenting east.[21] 'Tis mine to tread
The humbler province of plain history,
And, without choice of circumstance, submissively
Relate what I have heard. The lovers came   645
To this resolve (with which they parted, pleased
And confident): that Vaudracour should hie
Back to his father's house, and there employ

---

[21] Wordsworth alludes to *Romeo and Juliet*, III. v.
1–8.

Means aptest to obtain a sum of gold –
A final portion even, if that might be;   650
Which done, together they could then take flight
To some remote and solitary place
Where they might live with no one to behold
Their happiness, or to disturb their love.
   Immediately, and with this mission charged,   655
Home to his father's house did he return
And there remained a time without hint given
Of his design; but if a word were dropped
Touching the matter of his passion, still
In hearing of his father, Vaudracour   660
Persisted openly that nothing less
Than death should make him yield up hope to be
A blessed husband of the maid he loved.
   Incensed at such obduracy and slight
Of exhortations and remonstrances,   665
The father threw out threats that by a mandate
Bearing the private signet of the state
He should be baffled of his mad intent –
And that should cure him. From this time the youth
Conceived a terror, and by night or day   670
Stirred nowhere without arms. Soon afterwards
His parents to their country seat withdrew
Upon some feigned occasion, and the son
Was left with one attendant in the house.
Retiring to his chamber for the night,   675
While he was entering at the door, attempts
Were made to seize him by three armed men,
The instruments of ruffian power. The youth,
In the first impulse of his rage, laid one
Dead at his feet, and to the second gave   680
A perilous wound – which done, at sight
Of the dead man, he peacefully resigned
His person to the law, was lodged in prison,
And wore the fetters of a criminal.
   Through three weeks' space (by means which love devised)   685
The maid in her seclusion had received
Tidings of Vaudracour, and how he sped
Upon his enterprise. Thereafter came
A silence: half a circle did the moon
Complete, and then a whole, and still the same   690
Silence. A thousand thousand fears and hopes
Stirred in her mind – thoughts waking, thoughts of sleep,
Entangled in each other – and at last
Self-slaughter seemed her only resting-place:
So did she fare in her uncertainty.   695
   At length, by interference of a friend

(One who had sway at court), the youth regained
His liberty, on promise to sit down
Quietly in his father's house, nor take
One step to reunite himself with her   700
Of whom his parents disapproved – hard law,
To which he gave consent only because
His freedom else could nowise be procured.
Back to his father's house he went, remained
Eight days, and then his resolution failed.   705
He fled to Julia, and the words with which
He greeted her were these: 'All right is gone,
Gone from me; thou no longer now art mine,
I thine. A murderer, Julia, cannot love
An innocent woman. I behold thy face,   710
I see thee, and my misery is complete!'
She could not give him answer; afterwards
She coupled with his father's name some words
Of vehement indignation, but the youth
Checked her, nor would he hear of this; for thought   715
Unfilial, or unkind, had never once
Found harbour in his breast. The lovers, thus
United once again, together lived
For a few days, which were to Vaudracour
Days of dejection, sorrow and remorse   720
For that ill deed of violence which his hand
Had hastily committed; for the youth
Was of a loyal spirit, a conscience nice,
And over-tender for the trial which
His fate had called him to. The father's mind,   725
Meanwhile, remained unchanged, and Vaudracour
Learned that a mandate had been newly issued
To arrest him on the spot. Oh, pain it was
To part! He could not – and he lingered still
To the last moment of his time, and then   730
(At dead of night with snow upon the ground)
He left the city, and in villages
The most sequestered of the neighbourhood
Lay hidden for the space of several days,
Until, the horseman bringing back report   735
That he was nowhere to be found, the search
Was ended. Back returned the ill-fated youth,
And from the house where Julia lodged (to which
He now found open ingress, having gained
The affection of the family, who loved him   740
Both for his own, and for the maiden's sake)
One night retiring, he was seized.
                              But here

A portion of the tale may well be left
In silence, though my memory could add
Much how the youth (and in short space of time)   745
Was traversed from without; much, too, of thoughts
By which he was employed in solitude
Under privation and restraint, and what
Through dark and shapeless fear of things to come,
And what through strong compunction for the past   750
He suffered, breaking down in heart and mind.
Such grace (if grace it were) had been vouchsafed –
Or such effect had through the father's want
Of power, or through his negligence, ensued –
That Vaudracour was suffered to remain,   755
Though under guard and without liberty,
In the same city with the unhappy maid
From whom he was divided. So they fared,
Objects of general concern, till, moved
With pity for their wrongs, the magistrate   760
(The same who had placed the youth in custody)
By application to the minister
Obtained his liberty upon condition
That to his father's house he should return.

He left his prison almost on the eve   765
Of Julia's travail. She had likewise been
(As from the time indeed, when she had first
Been brought for secrecy to this abode),
Though treated with consoling tenderness,
Herself a prisoner – a dejected one,   770
Filled with a lover's and a woman's fears –
And whensoe'er the mistress of the house
Entered the room for the last time at night,
And Julia with a low and plaintive voice
Said, 'You are coming then to lock me up',   775
The housewife when these words (always the same)
Were by her captive languidly pronounced
Could never hear them uttered without tears.
A day or two before her childbed time
Was Vaudracour restored to her, and soon   780
As he might be permitted to return
Into her chamber after the child's birth,
The master of the family begged that all
The household might be summoned, doubting not
But that they might receive impressions then   785
Friendly to human kindness. Vaudracour
(This heard I from one present at the time)
Held up the new-born infant in his arms
And kissed, and blessed, and covered it with tears,

Uttering a prayer that he might never be   790
As wretched as his father. Then he gave
The child to her who bore it, and she too
Repeated the same prayer – took it again
And, muttering something faintly afterwards,
He gave the infant to the standers-by,   795
And wept in silence upon Julia's neck.
   Two months did he continue in the house,
And often yielded up himself to plans
Of future happiness. 'You shall return,
Julia', said he, 'and to your father's house   800
Go with your child. You have been wretched, yet
It is a town where both of us were born;
None will reproach you, for our loves are known.
With ornaments the prettiest you shall dress
Your boy as soon as he can run about,   805
And when he thus is at his play my father
Will see him from the window, and the child
Will by his beauty move his grandsire's heart,
So that it will be softened, and our loves
End happily, as they began.' These gleams   810
Appeared but seldom; oftener he was seen
Propping a pale and melancholy face
Upon the mother's bosom, resting thus
His head upon one breast, while from the other
The babe was drawing in its quiet food.   815
At other times, when he in silence long
And fixedly had looked upon her face,
He would exclaim, 'Julia, how much thine eyes
Have cost me!' During daytime when the child
Lay in its cradle, by its side he sat,   820
Not quitting it an instant. The whole town
In his unmerited misfortunes now
Took part, and if he either at the door
Or window for a moment with his child
Appeared, immediately the street was thronged;   825
While others, frequently without reserve,
Passed and repassed before the house to steal
A look at him.
              Oft at this time he wrote
Requesting, since he knew that the consent
Of Julia's parents never could be gained   830
To a clandestine marriage, that his father
Would from the birthright of an eldest son
Exclude him, giving but (when this was done)
A sanction to his nuptials. Vain request,
To which no answer was returned. And now   835
From her own home the mother of his love

Arrived to apprise the daughter of her fixed
And last resolve – that, since all hope to move
The old man's heart proved vain, she must retire
Into a convent, and be there immured.   840
Julia was thunderstricken by these words,
And she insisted on a mother's rights
To take her child along with her – a grant
Impossible, as she at last perceived.
The persons of the house no sooner heard   845
Of this decision upon Julia's fate
Than everyone was overwhelmed with grief,
Nor could they frame a manner soft enough
To impart the tidings to the youth. But great
Was their astonishment when they beheld him   850
Receive the news in calm despondency,
Composed and silent, without outward sign
Of even the least emotion. Seeing this,
When Julia scattered some upbraiding words
Upon his slackness, he thereto returned   855
No answer, only took the mother's hand
(Who loved him scarcely less than her own child)
And kissed it, without seeming to be pressed
By any pain that 'twas the hand of one
Whose errand was to part him from his love   860
For ever.
        In the city he remained
A season after Julia had retired
And in the convent taken up her home,
To the end that he might place his infant babe
With a fit nurse; which done, beneath the roof   865
Where now his little one was lodged, he passed
The day entire, and scarcely could at length
Tear himself from the cradle to return
Home to his father's house – in which he dwelt
Awhile, and then came back that he might see   870
Whether the babe had gained sufficient strength
To bear removal. He quitted this same town
For the last time, attendant by the side
Of a close-chair – a litter or sedan –
In which the child was carried. To a hill   875
Which rose at a league's distance from the town
The family of the house where he had lodged
Attended him, and from him parted there,
Watching below until he disappeared
On the hilltop. His eyes he scarcely took,   880
Through all that journey, from the chair in which
The babe was carried; and at every inn
Or place at which they halted or reposed,

Laid him upon his knees, nor would permit
The hands of any but himself to dress   885
The infant or undress. By one of those
Who bore the chair, these facts, at his return,
Were told, and in relating them he wept.
   This was the manner in which Vaudracour
Departed with his infant, and thus reached   890
His father's house, where to the innocent child
Admittance was denied. The young man spake
No word of indignation or reproof,
But of his father begged (a last request)
That a retreat might be assigned to him,   895
A house where in the country he might dwell
With such allowance as his wants required –
And the more lonely that the mansion was
'Twould be more welcome. To a lodge that stood
Deep in a forest, with leave given, at the age   900
Of four and twenty summers he retired;
And thither took with him his infant babe,
And one domestic for their common needs,
An aged woman. It consoled him here
To attend upon the orphan and perform   905
The office of a nurse to his young child,
Which, after a short time, by some mistake
Or indiscretion of the father, died.
The tale I follow to its last recess
Of suffering or of peace, I know not which;   910
Theirs be the blame who caused the woe, not mine.
   From that time forth he never uttered word
To any living. An inhabitant
Of that same town in which the pair had left
So lively a remembrance of their griefs,   915
By chance of business coming within reach
Of his retirement, to the spot repaired
With the intent to visit him; he reached
The house and only found the matron there,
Who told him that his pains were thrown away,   920
For that her master never uttered word
To living soul – not even to her. Behold,
While they were speaking, Vaudracour approached,
But, seeing someone there, just as his hand
Was stretched towards the garden gate, he shrunk,   925
And like a shadow glided out of view.
Shocked at his savage outside, from the place
The visitor retired.
          Thus lived the youth,
Cut off from all intelligence with man,
And shunning even the light of common day.   930

Nor could the voice of freedom, which through France
Soon afterwards resounded, public hope,
Or personal memory of his own deep wrongs,
Rouse him; but in those solitary shades
His days he wasted, an imbecile mind.   935

Book Ten
Residence in France and French Revolution

It was a beautiful and silent day
That overspread the countenance of earth,
Then fading, withunusual quietness,
When from the Loire I parted,[1] and through scenes
Of vineyard, orchard, meadow-ground and tilth,   5
Calm waters, gleams of sun, and breathless trees,
Towards the fierce metropolis turned my steps
Their homeward way to England.[2] From his throne
The King had fallen;[3] the congregated host –
Dire cloud, upon the front of which was written   10
The tender mercies of the dismal wind
That bore it – on the plains of liberty
Had burst innocuously.[4] Say more, the swarm
That came elate and jocund, like a band
Of eastern hunters, to enfold in ring   15
Narrowing itself by moments, and reduce
To the last punctual spot of their despair
A race of victims (so they deemed), themselves
Had shrunk from sight of their own task, and fled
In terror. Desolation and dismay   20
Remained for them whose fancies had grown rank
With evil expectations: confidence
And perfect triumph to the better cause.
    The state – as if to stamp the final seal
On her security, and to the world   25
Show what she was, a high and fearless soul;
Or rather in a spirit of thanks to those
Who had stirred up her slackening faculties
To a new transition – had assumed with joy
The body and the venerable name   30
Of a republic.[5] Lamentable crimes,
'Tis true, had gone before this hour, the work

BOOK TEN
[1] Wordsworth left Orléans (and Annette Vallon) late Oct. 1792, arriving in Paris 29 Oct. He left for London during the next five or six weeks.
[2] Perhaps a reference to the storming of the Tuileries, 10 Aug., and the September massacres.

[3] Louis XVI was imprisoned 10 Aug. 1792.
[4] The Austrian and Prussian forces were repelled by the French at Valmy, 20 Sept.
[5] 22 Sept. 1792.

Of massacre, in which the senseless sword
Was prayed to as a judge;[6] but these were past,
Earth free from them for ever, as was thought –   35
Ephemeral monsters to be seen but once,
Things that could only show themselves and die.
    This was the time in which, inflamed with hope,
To Paris I returned. Again I ranged,
More eagerly than I had done before,   40
Through the wide city, and in progress passed
The prison where the unhappy monarch lay,
Associate with his children and his wife
In bondage, and the palace, lately stormed
With roar of cannon and a numerous host.[7]   45
I crossed (a black and empty area then)
The Square of the Carousel, few weeks back
Heaped up with dead and dying – upon these
And other sights looking as doth a man
Upon a volume whose contents he knows   50
Are memorable but from him locked up,
Being written in a tongue he cannot read,
So that he questions the mute leaves with pain
And half upbraids their silence. But that night
When on my bed I lay, I was most moved   55
And felt most deeply in what world I was.
My room was high and lonely, near the roof
Of a large mansion or hotel, a spot
That would have pleased me in more quiet times,[8]
Nor was it wholly without pleasure then.   60
With unextinguished taper I kept watch,
Reading at intervals. The fear gone by
Pressed on me almost like a fear to come.
I thought of those September Massacres
Divided from me by a little month,   65
And felt and touched them, a substantial dread
(The rest was conjured up from tragic fictions
And mournful calendars of true history,
Remembrances and dim admonishments):
'The horse is taught his manage, and the wind   70
Of heaven wheels round and treads in his own steps;
Year follows year, the tide returns again,

[6] News of the fall of Verdun to Brunswick's invading army triggered four days of mob violence, 2–6
Sept., in which about half the inmates in the prisons
of Paris were executed after summary trials.
[7] Louis XVI and his family were imprisoned at the
Temple until their executions. On 10 Aug. 1792, a
month before Wordsworth's arrival, the Paris mob
stormed the Tuileries. Around 1,200 people were

killed, many of whose bodies were burned in the
Place du Carousel.
[8] MacGillivray, 'Wordsworth and J.-P. Brissot', *TLS*,
29 Jan. 1931, 79, identifies this as the period during
which Wordsworth roomed in the house of the
Girondin leader, Jean Pierre Brissot, 1 Rue Grétry.

Day follows day, all things have second birth;
The earthquake is not satisfied at once.'
And in such way I wrought upon myself   75
Until I seemed to hear a voice that cried
To the whole city, 'Sleep no more!'[9] To this
Add comments of a calmer mind, from which
I could not gather full security,
But at the best it seemed a place of fear   80
Unfit for the repose of night,
Defenceless as a wood where tigers roam.

   Betimes next morning to the Palace Walk
Of Orleans I repaired, and entering there
Was greeted, among diverse other notes,   85
By voices of the hawkers in the crowd
Bawling, 'Denunciation of the crimes
Of Maximilian Robespierre!' The speech
Which in their hands they carried was the same
Which had been recently pronounced, the day   90
When Robespierre (well knowing for what mark
Some words of indirect reproof had been
Intended) rose in hardihood, and dared
The man who had an ill surmise of him
To bring his charge in openness. Whereat,   95
When a dead pause ensued and no one stirred,
In silence of all present, from his seat
Louvet walked singly through the avenue
And took his station in the tribune, saying,
'I, Robespierre, accuse thee!'[10] 'Tis well known   100
What was the issue of that charge, and how
Louvet was left alone without support
Of his irresolute friends. But these are things
Of which I speak only as they were storm
Or sunshine to my individual mind,   105
No further.
      Let me then relate that now,
In some sort seeing with my proper eyes
That liberty, and life, and death, would soon
To the remotest corners of the land
Lie in the arbitrement of those who ruled   110
The capital city (what was struggled for,
And by what combatants victory must be won;
The indecision on their part[11] whose aim
Seemed best, and the straightforward path of those
Who in attack or in defence alike   115

---

[9] Wordsworth alludes to *Macbeth*, II. ii. 32.   [11] *their part* i.e. that of the moderate Girondins.
[10] Louvet accused Robespierre of dictatorship 29
Oct. 1792.

Were strong through their impiety), greatly I
Was agitated. Yea, I could almost
Have prayed that throughout earth upon all souls
Worthy of liberty, upon every soul
Matured to live in plainness and in truth, 120
The gift of tongues might fall, and men arrive
From the four quarters of the winds to do
For France what without help she could not do –
A work of honour. Think not that to this
I added work of safety: from such thought, 125
And the least fear about the end of things,
I was as far as angels are from guilt.
   Yet did I grieve, nor only grieved, but thought
Of opposition and of remedies;
An insignificant stranger and obscure, 130
Mean as I was, and little graced with powers
Of eloquence even in my native speech,
And all unfit for tumult and intrigue,
Yet would I willingly have taken up
A service at this time for cause so great, 135
However dangerous. Inly I revolved
How much the destiny of man had still
Hung upon single persons – that there was,
Transcendent to all local patrimony,
One nature, as there is one sun in heaven; 140
That objects, even as they are great, thereby
Do come within the reach of humblest eyes;
That man was only weak through his mistrust
And want of hope, where evidence divine
Proclaimed to him that hope should be most sure; 145
That, with desires heroic and firm sense,
A spirit thoroughly faithful to itself,
Unquenchable, unsleeping, undismayed,
Was as an instinct among men, a stream
That gathered up each petty straggling rill 150
And vein of water, glad to be rolled on
In safe obedience; that a mind whose rest
Was where it ought to be, in self-restraint,
In circumspection and simplicity,
Fell rarely in entire discomfiture 155
Below its aim, or met with from without
A treachery that defeated it, or foiled.
   On the other side, I called to mind those truths
Which are the commonplaces of the schools,
A theme for boys, too trite even to be felt, 160
Yet, with a revelation's liveliness
In all their comprehensive bearings known
And visible to philosophers of old,

Men who (to business of the world untrained)
Lived in the shade – and to Harmodius known   165
And his compeer Aristogiton; known
To Brutus[12] – that tyrannic power is weak,
Hath neither gratitude, nor faith, nor love,
Nor the support of good or evil men
To trust in; that the Godhead which is ours   170
Can never utterly be charmed or stilled;
That nothing hath a natural right to last
But equity and reason; that all else
Meets foes irreconcilable, and at best
Doth live but by variety of disease.   175
   Well might my wishes be intense, my thoughts
Strong and perturbed, not doubting at that time –
Creed which ten shameful years have not annulled –
But that the virtue of one paramount mind
Would have abashed those impious crests, have quelled   180
Outrage and bloody power, and, in despite
Of what the people were through ignorance
And immaturity (and in the teeth
Of desperate opposition from without),
Have cleared a passage for just government   185
And left a solid birthright to the state,
Redeemed according to example given
By ancient lawgivers.
                        In this frame of mind
Reluctantly to England I returned,
Compelled by nothing less than absolute want   190
Of funds for my support; else[13] (well assured
That I both was and must be of small worth,
No better than an alien in the land[14])
I doubtless should have made a common cause
With some who perished, haply perished too –   195
A poor mistaken and bewildered offering,
Should to the breast of nature have gone back
With all my resolutions, all my hopes,
A poet only to myself, to men
Useless, and even, beloved friend, a soul   200
To thee unknown.
                  When to my native land
(After a whole year's absence) I returned,
I found the air yet busy with the stir
Of a contention which had been raised up
Against the traffickers in Negro blood,   205

---

[12] Harmodius and Aristogiton attempted to liberate Athens from the tyrants Hippias and Hipparchus, 514 BC; Brutus helped assassinate Julius Caesar.

[13] *else* otherwise, i.e. 'if I hadn't returned to England'.
[14] *the land* France.

An effort which, though baffled, nevertheless
Had called back old forgotten principles
Dismissed from service, had diffused some truths
And more of virtuous feeling through the heart
Of the English people.[15] And no few of those   210
So numerous (little less in verity
Than a whole nation crying with one voice)
Who had been crossed in this their just intent
And righteous hope, thereby were well prepared
To let that journey sleep awhile, and join   215
Whatever other caravan appeared
To travel forward towards liberty
With more success. For me that strife had ne'er
Fastened on my affections, nor did now
Its unsuccessful issue much excite   220
My sorrow, having laid this faith to heart:
That if France prospered good men would not long
Pay fruitless worship to humanity,
And this most rotten branch of human shame
(Object, as seemed, of a superfluous pains)   225
Would fall together with its parent tree.
    Such was my then belief – that there was one,
And only one, solicitude for all.
And now the strength of Britain was put forth
In league with the confederated host;[16]   230
Not in my single self alone I found,
But in the minds of all ingenuous youth,
Change and subversion from this hour. No shock
Given to my moral nature had I known
Down to that very moment – neither lapse   235
Nor turn of sentiment that might be named
A revolution, save at this one time.
All else was progress on the self-same path
On which, with a diversity of pace,
I had been travelling: this a stride at once   240
Into another region. True it is,
'Twas not concealed with what ungracious eyes
Our native rulers from the very first
Had looked upon regenerated France,
Nor had I doubted that this day would come;   245
But in such contemplation I had thought
Of general interests only, beyond this
Had never once foretasted the event.

---

[15] A bill seeking to abolish slavery was proposed on 18 Apr. 1791, but defeated. Another was proposed in Apr. 1792, but though passed by the House of Commons, was thrown out by the Lords in 1793.

[16] France declared war on England and Holland, 1 Feb. 1793.

Now had I other business, for I felt
The ravage of this most unnatural strife   250
In my own heart; there lay it like a weight
At enmity with all the tenderest springs
Of my enjoyments. I who with the breeze
Had played, a green leaf on the blessed tree
Of my beloved country (nor had wished   255
For happier fortune than to wither there),
Now from my pleasant station was cut off
And tossed about in whirlwinds. I rejoiced,
Yes, afterwards (truth painful to record)
Exulted in the triumph of my soul   260
When Englishmen by thousands were o'erthrown,
Left without glory on the field, or driven,
Brave hearts, to shameful flight. It was a grief —
Grief call it not, 'twas anything but that —
A conflict of sensations without name,   265
Of which he only who may love the sight
Of a village steeple as I do can judge,
When in the congregation bending all
To their great Father, prayers were offered up
Or praises for our country's victories,   270
And, mid the simple worshippers perchance
I only, like an uninvited guest
Whom no one owned, sat silent — shall I add,
Fed on the day of vengeance yet to come.
    Oh, much have they to account for who could tear   275
By violence, at one decisive rent,
From the best youth in England their dear pride,
Their joy in England. This, too, at a time
In which worst losses easily might wear
The best of names, when patriotic love   280
Did of itself in modesty give way,
Like the precursor when the Deity
Is come whose harbinger he is — a time
In which apostasy from ancient faith
Seemed but conversion to a higher creed —   285
Withal a season dangerous and wild,
A time in which Experience would have plucked
Flowers out of any hedge to make thereof
A chaplet in contempt of his grey locks.
    Ere yet the fleet of Britain had gone forth   290
On this unworthy service whereunto
The unhappy counsel of a few weak men
Had doomed it, I beheld the vessels lie,
A brood of gallant creatures — on the deep,
I saw them in their rest — a sojourner   295
Through a whole month of calm and glassy days

In that delightful island[17] which protects
Their place of convocation. There I heard
Each evening, walking by the still seashore,
A monitory sound which never failed,   300
The sunset cannon. When the orb went down
In the tranquillity of nature came
That voice (ill requiem!) seldom heard by me
Without a spirit overcast, a deep
Imagination, thought of woes to come,   305
And sorrow for mankind, and pain of heart.
    In France the men who for their desperate ends
Had plucked up mercy by the roots were glad
Of this new enemy. Tyrants, strong before
In devilish pleas, were ten times stronger now;[18]   310
And thus beset with foes on every side,
The goaded land waxed mad; the crimes of few
Spread into madness of the many; blasts
From hell came sanctified like airs from heaven.
The sternness of the just, the faith of those   315
Who doubted not that providence had times
Of anger and of vengeance, theirs who throned
The human understanding paramount
And made of that their god,[19] the hopes of those
Who were content to barter short-lived pangs   320
For a paradise of ages, the blind rage
Of insolent tempers, the light vanity
Of intermeddlers, steady purposes
Of the suspicious, slips of the indiscreet,
And all the accidents of life, were pressed   325
Into one service, busy with one work.
The Senate was heart-stricken, not a voice
Uplifted, none to oppose or mitigate.
    Domestic carnage now filled all the year
With feast-days: the old man from the chimney-nook,   330
The maiden from the bosom of her love,
The mother from the cradle of her babe,
The warrior from the field – all perished.
Friends, enemies, of all parties, ages, ranks,
Head after head, and never heads enough   335
For those who bade them fall. They found their joy,
They made it, ever thirsty, as a child
(If light desires of innocent little ones
May with such heinous appetites be matched)

[17] The Isle of Wight, where Wordsworth spent late June–early Aug. 1793.
[18] Robespierre came to power in July 1793; the Reign of Terror began in Oct. and lasted until July 1794.
[19] The Cathedral of Notre Dame in Paris was reconsecrated 10 Nov. 1793 as the Temple of Reason.

Having a toy, a windmill, though the air 340
Do of itself blow fresh and makes the vane
Spin in his eyesight, he is not content,
But with the plaything at arm's length he sets
His front against the blast, and runs amain
To make it whirl the faster.
     In the depth 345
Of these enormities even thinking minds
Forgot at seasons whence they had their being,
Forgot that such a sound was ever heard
As liberty upon earth; yet all beneath
Her innocent authority was wrought, 350
Nor could have been, without her blessed name.
The illustrious wife of Roland, in the hour
Of her composure, felt that agony
And gave it vent in her last words.[20] Oh friend,
It was a lamentable time for man, 355
Whether a hope had e'er been his or not –
A woeful time for them whose hopes did still
Outlast the shock; most woeful for those few
(They had the deepest feeling of the grief)
Who still were flattered, and had trust in man. 360
Meanwhile, the invaders fared as they deserved;
The herculean commonwealth had put forth her arms
And throttled with an infant godhead's might
The snakes about her cradle[21] – that was well
And as it should be, yet no cure for those 365
Whose souls were sick with pain of what would be
Hereafter brought in charge against mankind.
  Most melancholy at that time, oh friend,
Were my day-thoughts, my dreams were miserable.
Through months, through years, long after the last beat 370
Of those atrocities (I speak bare truth,
As if to thee alone in private talk),
I scarcely had one night of quiet sleep,
Such ghastly visions had I of despair
And tyranny, and implements of death, 375
And long orations which in dreams I pleaded
Before unjust tribunals, with a voice
Labouring, a brain confounded, and a sense
Of treachery and desertion in the place
The holiest that I knew of – my own soul. 380
  When I began at first in early youth
To yield myself to nature, when that strong
And holy passion overcame me first,

---

[20] 'Ah Liberté, comme on t'a jouée!'; see p. 143 above.   [21] While in his cradle, the infant Hercules strangled two snakes sent to kill him.

Neither the day nor night, evening or morn,
Were free from the oppression. But, great God, 385
Who send'st thyself into this breathing world
Through nature and through every kind of life,
And mak'st man what he is — creature divine,
In single or in social eminence
Above all these raised infinite ascents 390
When reason, which enables him to be,
Is not sequestered — what a change is here!
How different ritual for this after-worship,
What countenance to promote this second love!
That first was service but to things which lie 395
At rest within the bosom of thy will;
Therefore to serve was high beatitude,
The tumult was a gladness, and the fear
Ennobling, venerable — sleep secure,
And waking thoughts more rich than happiest dreams. 400
    But as the ancient prophets were inflamed,
Nor wanted consolations of their own
And majesty of mind when they denounced
On towns and cities, wallowing in the abyss
Of their offences, punishment to come; 405
Or saw like other men, with bodily eyes,
Before them in some desolated place
The consummation of the wrath of Heaven;
So did some portions of that spirit fall
On me, to uphold me through those evil times, 410
And in their rage and dog-day heat I found
Something to glory in, as just and fit
And in the order of sublimest laws.
And even if that were not, amid the awe
Of unintelligible chastisement 415
I felt a kind of sympathy with power —
Motions raised up within me nevertheless
Which had relationship to highest things.
Wild blasts of music thus did find their way
Into the midst of terrible events, 420
So that worst tempests might be listened to.
Then was the truth received into my heart
That under heaviest sorrow earth can bring,
Griefs bitterest of ourselves or of our kind,
If from the affliction somewhere do not grow 425
Honour which could not else have been — a faith,
An elevation, and a sanctity —
If new strength be not given or old restored,
The blame is ours, not nature's. When a taunt
Was taken up by scoffers in their pride, 430
Saying, 'Behold the harvest which we reap

From popular government and equality!'
I saw that it was neither these nor aught
Of wild belief engrafted on their names
By false philosophy that caused the woe,   435
But that it was a reservoir of guilt
And ignorance filled up from age to age
That could no longer hold its loathsome charge,
But burst and spread in deluge through the land.

    And as the desert hath green spots, the sea   440
Small islands in the midst of stormy waves,
So that disastrous period did not want
Such sprinklings of all human excellence
As were a joy to hear of. Yet (nor less
For those bright spots, those fair examples given   445
Of fortitude and energy and love,
And human nature faithful to itself
Under worst trials) was I impelled to think
Of the glad time when first I traversed France,
A youthful pilgrim – above all remembered   450
That day when through an arch that spanned the street,
A rainbow made of garish ornaments
(Triumphal pomp for liberty confirmed),
We walked, a pair of weary travellers,
Along the town of Arras,[22] place from which   455
Issued that Robespierre who afterwards
Wielded the sceptre of the atheist crew.
When the calamity spread far and wide,
And this same city, which had even appeared
To outrun the rest in exultation, groaned   460
Under the vengeance of her cruel son,
As Lear reproached the winds, I could almost
Have quarrelled with that blameless spectacle
For being yet an image in my mind
To mock me under such a strange reverse.   465
    Oh friend, few happier moments have been mine
Through my whole life than that when first I heard
That this foul tribe of Moloch[23] was o'erthrown
And their chief regent levelled with the dust.
The day was one which haply may deserve   470
A separate chronicle. Having gone abroad
From a small village[24] where I tarried then,
To the same far-secluded privacy
I was returning. Over the smooth sands
Of Leven's ample estuary lay   475

---

[22] Wordsworth and Jones spent the night of 16 July 1790 at Arras.
[23] Cf. *Paradise Lost*, i. 392–3.
[24] Rampside, south-west coast of the Lake District, Aug.–Sept. 1794.

My journey, and beneath a genial sun,
With distant prospect among gleams of sky
And clouds, and intermingled mountain-tops,
In one inseparable glory clad –
Creatures of one ethereal substance met   480
In consistory, like a diadem
Or crown of burning seraphs as they sit
In the empyrean. Underneath this show
Lay, as I knew, the nest of pastoral vales
Among whose happy fields I had grown up   485
From childhood. On the fulgent spectacle,
Which neither changed, nor stirred, nor passed away,
I gazed, and with a fancy more alive
On this account – that I had chanced to find
That morning, ranging through the churchyard graves   490
Of Cartmel's rural town, the place in which
An honoured teacher of my youth was laid.[25]
While we were schoolboys he had died among us,
And was borne hither, as I knew, to rest
With his own family. A plain stone, inscribed   495
With name, date, office, pointed out the spot,
To which a slip of verses was subjoined
(By his desire, as afterwards I learnt),
A fragment from the *Elegy* of Gray.
A week, or little less, before his death,   500
He had said to me, 'My head will soon lie low.'
And when I saw the turf that covered him
After the lapse of full eight years, those words,
With sound of voice, and countenance of the man,
Came back upon me, so that some few tears   505
Fell from me in my own despite. And now,
Thus travelling smoothly o'er the level sands,
I thought with pleasure of the verses graven
Upon his tombstone, saying to myself,
'He loved the poets, and if now alive   510
Would have loved me, as one not destitute
Of promise, nor belying the kind hope
Which he had formed when I at his command
Began to spin, at first, my toilsome song.'
      Without me and within, as I advanced,   515
All that I saw, or felt, or communed with,
Was gentleness and peace. Upon a small
And rocky island near, a fragment stood
(Itself like a sea-rock) of what had been
A Romish chapel, where in ancient times   520

---

[25]   William Taylor (1754–86), headmaster of Hawkshead Grammar School, buried at Cartmel Priory.

Masses were said at the hour which suited those
Who crossed the sands with ebb of morning tide.
Not far from this still ruin all the plain
Was spotted with a variegated crowd
Of coaches, wains, and travellers, horse and foot,   525
Wading beneath the conduct of their guide
In loose procession through the shallow stream
Of inland water; the great sea meanwhile
Was at safe distance, far retired. I paused,
Unwilling to proceed, the scene appeared   530
So gay and cheerful, when – a traveller
Chancing to pass – I carelessly enquired
If any news were stirring. He replied
In the familiar language of the day
That Robespierre was dead.[26] Nor was a doubt,   535
On further question, left within my mind
But that the tidings were substantial truth –
That he and his supporters all were fallen.
   Great was my glee of spirit, great my joy
In vengeance, and eternal justice, thus   540
Made manifest. 'Come now, ye golden times',
Said I, forth-breathing on those open sands
A hymn of triumph, 'as the morning comes
Out of the bosom of the night, come ye!
Thus far our trust is verified: behold,   545
They who with clumsy desperation brought
Rivers of blood, and preached that nothing else
Could cleanse the Augean stable,[27] by the might
Of their own helper[28] have been swept away!
Their madness is declared and visible –   550
Elsewhere will safety now be sought, and earth
March firmly towards righteousness and peace.'
Then schemes I framed more calmly: when and how
The madding factions might be tranquillized,
And – though through hardships manifold and long –   555
The mighty renovation would proceed.
Thus, interrupted by uneasy bursts
Of exultation, I pursued my way
Along that very shore which I had skimmed
In former times, when (spurring from the Vale   560
Of Nightshade, and St Mary's mouldering fane
And the stone abbot) after circuit made
In wantonness of heart, a joyous crew

---

[26] Robespierre was executed 28 July 1794; news
reached London 16 Aug.
[27] Hercules cleaned King Augeus's stable by diverting the rivers Alpheus and Peneus through it.
[28] The guillotine.

Of schoolboys hastening to their distant home
Along the margin of the moonlight sea,   565
We beat with thundering hoofs the level sand.
   From this time forth in France, as is well known,
Authority put on a milder face,
Yet everything was wanting that might give
Courage to those who looked for good by light   570
Of rational experience – good I mean
At hand, and in the spirit of past aims.
The same belief I, nevertheless, retained:
The language of the Senate, and the acts
And public measures of the Government,   575
Though both of heartless omen, had not power
To daunt me. In the people was my trust
And in the virtues which mine eyes had seen,
And to the ultimate repose of things
I looked with unabated confidence.   580
I knew that wound external could not take
Life from the young Republic – that new foes
Would only follow in the path of shame
Their brethren, and her triumphs be in the end
Great, universal, irresistible.   585
This faith (which was an object in my mind
Of passionate intuition) had effect
Not small in dazzling me; for thus through zeal,
Such victory I confounded in my thoughts
With one far higher and more difficult –   590
Triumphs of unambitious peace at home
And noiseless fortitude. Beholding still
Resistance strong as heretofore, I thought
That what was in degree the same was likewise
The same in quality, that as the worse   595
Of the two spirits then at strife remained
Untired, the better surely would preserve
The heart that first had roused him – never dreamt
That transmigration could be undergone,
A fall of being suffered, and of hope,   600
By creature that appeared to have received
Entire conviction what a great ascent
Had been accomplished, what high faculties
It had been called to.
                              Youth maintains, I knew,
In all conditions of society   605
Communion more direct and intimate
With nature and the inner strength she has,
And hence, oft-times, no less with reason too,
Than age or manhood even. To nature then
Power had reverted: habit, custom, law,   610

Had left an interregnum's open space
For her to stir about in uncontrolled.
The warmest judgements and the most untaught
Found in events which every day brought forth
Enough to sanction them, and far, far more   615
To shake the authority of canons drawn
From ordinary practice. I could see
How Babel-like the employment was of those
Who, by the recent deluge stupefied,
With their whole souls went culling from the day   620
Its petty promises, to build a tower
For their own safety – laughed at gravest heads
Who, watching in their hate of France for signs
Of her disasters, if the stream of rumour
Brought with it one green branch, conceited thence   625
That not a single tree was left alive
In all her forests. How could I believe
That wisdom could, in any shape, come near
Men clinging to delusions so insane?
And thus, experience proving that no few   630
Of my opinions had been just, I took
Like credit to myself where less was due,
And thought that other notions were as sound –
Yea, could not but be right – because I saw
That foolish men opposed them.
                  To a strain   635
More animated I might here give way,
And tell (since juvenile errors are my theme)
What in those days through Britain was performed
To turn all judgements out of their right course;
But this is passion over-near ourselves,   640
Reality too close and too intense,
And mingled up with something, in my mind,
Of scorn and condemnation personal
That would profane the sanctity of verse.
Our shepherds – this say merely – at that time   645
Thirsted to make the guardian crook of law
A tool of murder. They who ruled the state
(Though with such awful proof before their eyes
That he who would sow death, reaps death, or worse,
And can reap nothing better) child-like longed   650
To imitate, not wise enough to avoid.
Giants in their impiety alone,
But in their weapons and their warfare base
As vermin working out of reach, they leagued
Their strength perfidiously, to undermine   655
Justice and make an end of liberty.
   But from these bitter truths I must return

To my own history. It hath been told
That I was led to take an eager part
In arguments of civil polity   660
Abruptly, and indeed before my time.
I had approached, like other youth, the shield
Of human nature from the golden side,
And would have fought even to the death to attest
The quality of the metal which I saw.   665
What there is best in individual man,
Of wise in passion and sublime in power,
What there is strong and pure in household love,
Benevolent in small societies
And great in large ones also when called forth   670
By great occasions – these were things of which
I something knew, yet even these (themselves
Felt deeply) were not thoroughly understood
By reason. Nay, far from it: they were yet
(As cause was given me afterwards to learn)   675
Not proof against the injuries of the day –
Lodged only at the sanctuary's door,
Not safe within its bosom. Thus prepared,
And with such general insight into evil,
And of the bounds which sever it from good,   680
As books and common intercourse with life
Must needs have given (to the noviciate mind,
When the world travels in a beaten road,
Guide faithful as is needed), I began
To think with fervour upon management   685
Of nations, what it is and ought to be,
And how their worth depended on their laws
And on the constitution of the state.
    Oh pleasant exercise of hope and joy –
For great were the auxiliars which then stood   690
Upon our side, we who were strong in love!
Bliss was it in that dawn to be alive,
But to be young was very heaven! Oh times,
In which the meagre, stale, forbidding ways
Of custom, law, and statute, took at once   695
The attraction of a country in romance –
When reason seemed the most to assert her rights
When most intent on making of herself
A prime enchanter to assist the work
Which then was going forwards in her name!   700
Not favoured spots alone, but the whole earth
The beauty wore of promise, that which sets
(To take an image which was felt, no doubt,
Among the bowers of paradise itself)
The budding rose above the rose full-blown.   705

What temper at the prospect did not wake
To happiness unthought of? The inert
Were roused, and lively natures rapt away.
They who had fed their childhood upon dreams,
The playfellows of fancy who had made   710
All powers of swiftness, subtlety, and strength
Their ministers, used to stir in lordly wise
Among the grandest objects of the sense
And deal with whatsoever they found there
As if they had within some lurking right   715
To wield it; they too, who of gentle mood
Had watched all gentle motions, and to these
Had fitted their own thoughts (schemers more mild,
And in the region of their peaceful selves),
Did now find helpers to their hearts' desire,   720
And stuff at hand, plastic as they could wish,
Were called upon to exercise their skill
Not in Utopia (subterraneous fields,
Or some secreted island, heaven knows where)
But in the very world which is the world   725
Of all of us, the place on which in the end
We find our happiness, or not at all.
      Why should I not confess that earth was then
To me what an inheritance new-fallen
Seems, when the first time visited, to one   730
Who thither comes to find in it his home?
He walks about and looks upon the place
With cordial transport, moulds it and remoulds,
And is half pleased with things that are amiss,
'Twill be such joy to see them disappear.   735
An active partisan, I thus convoked
From every object pleasant circumstance
To suit my ends. I moved among mankind
With genial feelings still predominant,
When erring, erring on the better part   740
And in the kinder spirit; placable,
Indulgent oft-times to the worst desires
(As on one side, not uninformed that men
See as it hath been taught them, and that time
Gives rights to error; on the other hand,   745
That throwing off oppression must be work
As well of license as of liberty);
And above all – for this was more than all –
Not caring if the wind did now and then
Blow keen upon an eminence that gave   750
Prospect so large into futurity; happy,
In brief a child of nature as at first,
Diffusing only those affections wider

That from the cradle had grown up with me,
And losing, in no other way than light   755
Is lost in light, the weak in the more strong.
   In the main outline, such it might be said
Was my condition, till with open war
Britain opposed the liberties of France.
This threw me first out of the pale of love,   760
Soured and corrupted upwards to the source
My sentiments (was not, as hitherto,
A swallowing up of lesser things in great,
But change of them into their opposites),
And thus a way was opened for mistakes   765
And false conclusions of the intellect,
As gross in their degree, and in their kind
Far, far more dangerous. What had been a pride
Was now a shame. My likings and my loves
Ran in new channels, leaving old ones dry,   770
And thus a blow, which in maturer age
Would but have touched the judgement, struck more deep
Into sensations near the heart. Meantime,
As from the first, wild theories were afloat,
Unto the subtleties of which at least   775
I had but lent a careless ear, assured
Of this, that time would soon set all things right,
Prove that the multitude had been oppressed,
And would be so no more.
                But when events
Brought less encouragement, and unto these   780
The immediate proof of principles no more
Could be entrusted (while the events themselves,
Worn out in greatness and in novelty,
Less occupied the mind, and sentiments
Could through my understanding's natural growth   785
No longer justify themselves through faith
Of inward consciousness and hope that laid
Its hand upon its object), evidence
Safer, of universal application, such
As could not be impeached, was sought elsewhere.   790
   And now, become oppressors in their turn,
Frenchmen had changed a war of self-defence
For one of conquest, losing sight of all
Which they had struggled for — and mounted up,
Openly in the view of earth and heaven,   795
The scale of liberty. I read her doom,
Vexed inly somewhat, it is true, and sore,
But not dismayed, nor taking to the shame
Of a false prophet; but, roused up, I stuck
More firmly to old tenets, and to prove   800

Their temper strained them more. And thus in heat
Of contest did opinions every day
Grow into consequence, till round my mind
They clung, as if they were the life of it.

    This was the time when all things tended fast   805
To depravation; the philosophy
That promised to abstract the hopes of man
Out of his feelings, to be fixed thenceforth
For ever in a purer element
Found ready welcome.[29] Tempting region that   810
For zeal to enter and refresh herself,
Where passions had the privilege to work,
And never hear the sound of their own names!
But (speaking more in charity) the dream
Was flattering to the young ingenuous mind   815
Pleased with extremes, and not the least with that
Which makes the human reason's naked self
The object of its fervour. What delight!
How glorious, in self-knowledge and self-rule,
To look through all the frailties of the world!   820
And, with a resolute mastery shaking off
The accidents of nature, time and place,
That make up the weak being of the past,
Build social freedom on its only basis,
The freedom of the individual mind,   825
Which (to the blind restraint of general laws
Superior) magisterially adopts
One guide, the light of circumstances, flashed
Upon an independent intellect.

    For, howsoe'er unsettled, never once   830
Had I thought ill of humankind, or been
Indifferent to its welfare. But, inflamed
With thirst of a secure intelligence,
And sick of other passion, I pursued
A higher nature, wished that man should start   835
Out of the worm-like state in which he is,
And spread abroad the wings of liberty,
Lord of himself in undisturbed delight –
A noble aspiration, yet I feel
The aspiration, but with other thoughts   840
And happier. For I was perplexed, and sought
To accomplish the transition by such means
As did not lie in nature – sacrificed
The exactness of a comprehensive mind
To scrupulous and microscopic views   845

---

[29]   William Godwin's *Political Justice* (1793) proclaimed
the power of reason at the expense of emotion.

That furnished out materials for a work
Of false imagination, placed beyond
The limits of experience and of truth.
   Enough, no doubt, the advocates themselves
Of ancient institutions had performed   850
To bring disgrace upon their very names –
Disgrace, of which custom, and written law,
And sundry moral sentiments, as props
And emanations of these institutes,
Too justly bore a part. A veil had been   855
Uplifted – why deceive ourselves? 'Twas so,
'Twas even so, and sorrow for the man
Who either had not eyes wherewith to see,
Or, seeing, hath forgotten. Let this pass;
Suffice it that a shock had then been given   860
To old opinions, and the minds of all men
Had felt it – that my mind was both let loose,
Let loose and goaded. After what hath been
Already said of patriotic love,
And hinted at in other sentiments,   865
We need not linger long upon this theme.
This only may be said, that from the first
Having two natures in me (joy the one,
The other melancholy), and withal
A happy man, and therefore bold to look   870
On painful things – slow, somewhat, too, and stern
In temperament – I took the knife in hand
And, stopping not at parts less sensitive,
Endeavoured with my best of skill to probe
The living body of society   875
Even to the heart. I pushed without remorse
My speculations forward – yea, set foot
On nature's holiest places.
                  Time may come
When some dramatic story may afford
Shapes livelier to convey to thee, my friend,   880
What then I learned, or think I learned, of truth,
And the errors into which I was betrayed
By present objects, and by reasonings false
From the beginning, inasmuch as drawn
Out of a heart which had been turned aside   885
From nature by external accidents,
And which was thus confounded more and more,
Misguiding and misguided. Thus I fared,
Dragging all passions, notions, shapes of faith,
Like culprits to the bar; suspiciously   890
Calling the mind to establish in plain day
Her titles and her honours; now believing,

Now disbelieving; endlessly perplexed
With impulse, motive, right and wrong, the ground
Of moral obligation, what the rule   895
And what the sanction – till, demanding proof,
And seeking it in everything, I lost
All feeling of conviction, and (in fine)
Sick, wearied out with contrarieties,
Yielded up moral questions in despair,   900
And for my future studies, as the sole
Employment of the enquiring faculty,
Turned towards mathematics, and their clear
And solid evidence.
                    Ah, then it was
That thou, most precious friend, about this time   905
First known to me,[30] didst lend a living help
To regulate my soul. And then it was
That the beloved woman[31] in whose sight
Those days were passed (now speaking in a voice
Of sudden admonition, like a brook   910
That does but cross a lonely road; and now
Seen, heard and felt, and caught at every turn,
Companion never lost through many a league)
Maintained for me a saving intercourse
With my true self. For, though impaired and changed   915
Much, as it seemed, I was no further changed
Than as a clouded, not a waning moon.
She, in the midst of all, preserved me still
A poet, made me seek beneath that name
My office upon earth, and nowhere else.   920
And lastly Nature's self, by human love
Assisted, through the weary labyrinth
Conducted me again to open day,
Revived the feelings of my earlier life,
Gave me that strength and knowledge full of peace,   925
Enlarged and never more to be disturbed,
Which through the steps of our degeneracy,
All degradation of this age, hath still
Upheld me, and upholds me at this day
In the catastrophe (for so they dream,   930
And nothing less) when finally to close
And rivet up the gains of France, a Pope
Is summoned in to crown an Emperor[32] –
This last opprobrium, when we see the dog

[30] In fact Wordsworth met Coleridge six months earlier, in Sept. 1795.
[31] Dorothy Wordsworth lived with her brother at Racedown Lodge in Dorset from Sept. 1795.
[32] Napoleon summoned Pope Pius VII to his imperial coronation, 2 Dec. 1804.

Returning to his vomit; when the sun   935
That rose in splendour, was alive, and moved
In exultation among living clouds,
Hath put his function and his glory off,
And, turned into a gewgaw, a machine,
Sets like an opera phantom.
                        Thus, oh friend,   940
Through times of honour and through times of shame
Have I descended, tracing faithfully
The workings of a youthful mind beneath
The breath of great events – its hopes no less
Than universal, and its boundless love –   945
A story destined for thy ear, who now
Among the basest and the lowest fallen
Of all the race of men dost make abode,
Where Etna looketh down on Syracuse,
The city of Timoleon.[33] Living God,   950
How are the mighty prostrated! They first,
They first of all that breathe, should have awaked
When the great voice was heard out of the tombs
Of ancient heroes. If for France I have grieved,
Who in the judgement of no few hath been   955
A trifler only in her proudest day –
Have been distressed to think of what she once
Promised, now is – a far more sober cause
Thine eyes must see of sorrow in a land
Strewed with the wreck of loftiest years, a land   960
Glorious indeed, substantially renowned
Of simple virtue once and manly praise,
Now without one memorial hope; not even
A hope to be deferred, for that would serve
To cheer the heart in such entire decay.   965
    But indignation works where hope is not,
And thou, oh friend, wilt be refreshed. There is
One great society alone on earth:
The noble living and the noble dead.
Thy consolation shall be there, and time   970
And nature shall before thee spread in store
Imperishable thoughts, the place itself
Be conscious of thy presence, and the dull
Sirocco air of its degeneracy
Turn as though mov'st into a healthful breeze   975
To cherish and invigorate thy frame.
    Thine be those motions strong and sanative,

---

[33] Timoleon drove the tyrannical Dionysus the
Younger from Syracuse in 343 BC; Etna is 45 miles
north of Syracuse.

A ladder for thy spirit to reascend
To health and joy and pure contentedness;
To me the grief confined, that thou art gone 980
From this last spot of earth where freedom now
Stands single in her only sanctuary[34] —
A lonely wanderer art gone, by pain
Compelled and sickness, at this latter day,
This heavy time of change for all mankind. 985
I feel for thee, must utter what I feel:
The sympathies erewhile in part discharged
Gather afresh, and will have vent again.
My own delights do scarcely seem to me
My own delights; the lordly Alps themselves 990
(Those rosy peaks, from which the morning looks
Abroad on many nations) are not now,
Since thy migration and departure, friend,
The gladsome image in my memory
Which they were used to be. To kindred scenes 995
On errand (at a time how different!)
Thou takest thy way, carrying a heart more ripe
For all divine enjoyment, with the soul
Which nature gives to poets, now by thought
Matured and in the summer of its strength. 1000
Oh, wrap him in your shades, ye giant woods
On Etna's side! And thou, oh flowery vale
Of Enna, is there not some nook of thine
From the first playtime of the infant earth
Kept sacred to restorative delight? 1005
    Child of the mountains, among shepherds reared,
Even from my earliest schoolday time I loved
To dream of Sicily, and now a strong
And vital promise wafted from that land
Comes o'er my heart! There's not a single name 1010
Of note belonging to that honoured isle,
Philosopher or bard, Empedocles
Or Archimedes, deep and tranquil soul,
That is not like a comfort to my grief.[35]
And, oh Theocritus,[36] so far have some 1015
Prevailed among the powers of heaven and earth
By force of graces which were theirs, that they
Have had (as thou reportest) miracles
Wrought for them in old time. Yea, not unmoved,
When thinking of my own beloved friend, 1020

---

[34] Britain was Napoleon's sole opponent by late 1804.
[35] Empedocles was a philosopher and poet who threw himself into Etna; Archimedes was a Syracusan mathematician.
[36] Theocritus, a Syracuse-born pastoral poet, described Comates' fate, *Idyll*, vii. 78–83.

I hear thee tell how bees with honey fed
Divine Comates, by his tyrant lord
Within a chest imprisoned impiously –
How with their honey from the fields they came
And fed him there, alive, from month to month,   1025
Because the goatherd, blessed man, had lips
Wet with the muse's nectar.
                   Thus I soothe
The pensive moments by this calm fireside,
And find a thousand fancied images
That cheer the thoughts of those I love, and mine.   1030
Our prayers have been accepted: thou wilt stand
Not as an exile but a visitant
On Etna's top; by pastoral Arethuse[37]
(Or if that fountain be indeed no more,
Then near some other spring, which by the name   1035
Though gratulatest,[38] willingly deceived)
Shalt linger as a gladsome votary,
And not a captive pining for his home.

Book Eleven
Imagination, how Impaired and Restored.

Long time hath man's unhappiness and guilt
Detained us: with what dismal sights beset
For the outward view, and inwardly oppressed
With sorrow, disappointment, vexing thoughts,
Confusion of the judgement, zeal decayed,   5
And lastly, utter loss of hope itself
And things to hope for. Not with these began
Our song, and not with these our song must end.
Ye motions of delight that through the fields
Stir gently, breezes and soft airs that breathe   10
The breath of paradise, and find your way
To the recesses of the soul! Ye brooks
Muttering along the stones, a busy noise
By day, a quiet one in silent night;
And you, ye groves, whose ministry it is   15
To interpose the covert of your shades
Even as a sleep, betwixt the heart of man
And the uneasy world – 'twixt man himself
Not seldom, and his own unquiet heart –
Oh, that I had a music and a voice   20
Harmonious as your own, that I might tell

---

[37] Arethusa, spring near Syracuse, which Wordsworth would have known from Virgil, *Eclogue*, x. 1,
and Milton, *Lycidas*, 85.

[38] *gratulatest* greet.

What ye have done for me. The morning shines,
Nor heedeth man's perverseness; spring returns –
I saw the spring return when I was dead
To deeper hope, yet had I joy for her   25
And welcomed her benevolence, rejoiced
In common with the children of her love,
Plants, insects, beast in field, and bird in bower.
So neither were complacency, nor peace,
Nor tender yearnings, wanting for my good   30
Through those distracted times;[1] in nature still
Glorying, I found a counterpoise in her
Which, when the spirit of evil was at height,
Maintained for me a secret happiness.
Her I resorted to, and loved so much   35
I seemed to love as much as heretofore –
And yet this passion, fervent as it was,
Had suffered change; how could there fail to be
Some change, if merely hence, that years of life
Were going on, and with them loss or gain   40
Inevitable, sure alternative?
    This history, my friend, hath chiefly told
Of intellectual power, from stage to stage
Advancing, hand in hand with love and joy,
And of imagination teaching truth,   45
Until that natural graciousness of mind
Gave way to over-pressure of the times
And their disastrous issues. What availed,
When spells forbade the voyager to land,
The fragrance which did ever and anon   50
Give notice of the shore, from arbours breathed
Of blessed sentiment and fearless love?
What did such sweet remembrances avail –
Perfidious then, as seemed – what served they then?
My business was upon the barren seas,   55
My errand was to sail to other coasts.
Shall I avow that I had hope to see,
I mean that future times would surely see
The man to come parted as by a gulf
From him who had been, that I could no more   60
Trust the elevation which had made me one
With the great family that here and there
Is scattered through the abyss of ages past
(Sage, patriot, lover, hero), for it seemed
That their best virtues were not free from taint   65

BOOK ELEVEN
[1] *distracted times* a reminder of the crisis described at
the end of Book X.

Of something false and weak, which could not stand
The open eye of reason. Then I said,
'Go to the poets, they will speak to thee
More perfectly of purer creatures (yet
If reason be nobility in man,   70
Can aught be more ignoble than the man
Whom they describe?), would fasten if they may
Upon our love by sympathies of truth?'
   Thus strangely did I war against myself –
A bigot to a new idolatry   75
Did like a monk who hath forsworn the world
Zealously labour to cut off my heart
From all the sources of her former strength,
And, as by simple waving of a wand
The wizard instantaneously dissolves   80
Palace or grove, even so did I unsoul
As readily by syllogistic words
(Some charm of logic ever within reach)
Those mysteries of passion which have made,
And shall continue evermore to make   85
(In spite of all that reason hath performed
And shall perform to exalt and to refine)
One brotherhood of all the human race
Through all the habitations of past years
And those to come. And hence an emptiness   90
Fell on the historian's page, and even on that
Of poets, pregnant with more absolute truth –
The works of both withered in my esteem.
Their sentence was, I thought, pronounced; their rights
Seemed mortal, and their empire passed away.   95
   What then remained in such eclipse, what light
To guide or cheer? The laws of things which lie
Beyond the reach of human will or power,
The life of nature, by the God of love
Inspired (celestial presence ever pure) –   100
These left, the soul of youth must needs be rich,
Whatever else be lost; and these were mine,
Not a deaf echo merely of the thought
(Bewildered recollections, solitary)
But living sounds. Yet in despite of this –   105
This feeling, which howe'er impaired or damped,
Yet having been once born can never die –
'Tis true that earth with all her appanage[2]
Of elements and organs, storm and sunshine,
With its pure forms and colours, pomp of clouds,   110

---

[2] *appanage* endowment.

Rivers and mountains, objects among which
It might be thought that no dislike or blame,
No sense of weakness or infirmity
Or aught amiss could possibly have come,
Yea, even the visible universe was scanned   115
With something of a kindred spirit, fell
Beneath the domination of a taste
Less elevated, which did in my mind
With its more noble influence interfere,
Its animation and its deeper sway.   120
   There comes (if need be now to speak of this
After such long detail of our mistakes),
There comes a time when reason – not the grand
And simple reason, but that humbler power
Which carries on its no inglorious work   125
By logic and minute analysis –
Is of all idols that which pleases most
The growing mind. A trifler would he be
Who on the obvious benefits should dwell
That rise out of this process; but to speak   130
Of all the narrow estimates of things
Which hence originate were a worthy theme
For philosophic verse.³ Suffice it here
To hint that danger cannot but attend
Upon a function rather proud to be   135
The enemy of falsehood, than the friend
Of truth – to sit in judgement, than to feel.
   Oh soul of nature, excellent and fair! –
That didst rejoice with me, with whom I too
Rejoiced through early youth, before the winds   140
And powerful waters, and in lights and shades
That marched and counter-marched about the hills
In glorious apparition – now all eye
And now all ear, but ever with the heart
Employed, and the majestic intellect;   145
Oh soul of nature, that dost overflow
With passion and with life, what feeble men
Walk on this earth, how feeble have I been
When thou wert in thy strength! Nor this through stroke
Of human suffering such as justifies   150
Remissness and inaptitude of mind,
But through presumption; even in pleasure pleased
Unworthily, disliking here, and there
Liking, by rules of mimic art transferred
To things above all art. But more – for this,   155

---

³ *philosophic verse The Recluse.*

Although a strong infection of the age,[4]
Was never much my habit – giving way
To a comparison of scene with scene,
Bent overmuch on superficial things,
Pampering myself with meagre novelties   160
Of colour and proportion, to the moods
Of time or season, to the moral power,
The affections, and the spirit of the place
Less sensible. Nor only did the love
Of sitting thus in judgement interrupt   165
My deeper feelings, but another cause,
More subtle and less easily explained,
That almost seems inherent to the creature –
Sensuous and intellectual as he is,
A twofold frame of body and of mind   170
The state to which I now allude was one
In which the eye was master of the heart,
When that which is in every stage of life
The most despotic of our senses gained
Such strength in me as often held my mind   175
In absolute dominion.
                              Gladly here,
Entering upon abstruser argument,
Would I endeavour to unfold the means
Which nature studiously employs to thwart
This tyranny, summons all the senses each   180
To counteract the other (and themselves),
And makes them all, and the objects with which all
Are conversant, subservient in their turn
To the great ends of liberty and power.
But this is matter for another song[5]   185
Here only let me add that my delights,
Such as they were, were sought insatiably,
Though 'twas a transport of the outward sense,
Not of the mind – vivid but not profound –
Yet was I often greedy in the chase   190
And roamed from hill to hill, from rock to rock,
Still craving combinations of new forms,
New pleasure, wider empire for the sight,
Proud of its own endowments, and rejoiced
To lay the inner faculties asleep   195
    Amid the turns and counter-turns, the strife
And various trials of our complex being
As we grow up, such thraldom of that sense

---

[4] The fashionable cult of the picturesque, which   [5] *another song* another reference to *The Recluse*.
stemmed from Burke's *Sublime and Beautiful*.

Seems hard to shun. And yet I knew a maid[6]
Who, young as I was then, conversed with things   200
In higher style. From appetites like these
She, gentle visitant, as well she might,
Was wholly free. Far less did critic rules
Or barren intermeddling subtleties
Perplex her mind, but (wise as women are   205
When genial circumstance hath favoured them)
She welcomed what was given, and craved no more.
Whatever scene was present to her eyes,
That was the best, to that she was attuned
Through her humility and lowliness   210
And through a perfect happiness of soul,
Whose variegated feelings were in this
Sisters, that they were each some new delight.
For she was nature's inmate: her the birds
And every flower she met with, could they but   215
Have known her, would have loved. Methought such depth
Of sweetness did her presence breathe around
That all the trees, and all the silent hills,
And everything she looked on, should have had
An intimation how she bore herself   220
Towards them and to all creatures. God delights
In such a being, for her common thoughts
Are piety, her life is blessedness.
    Even like this maid, before I was called forth
From the retirement of my native hills   225
I loved whate'er I saw – nor lightly loved,
But fervently – did never dream of aught
More grand, more fair, more exquisitely framed,
Than those few nooks to which my happy feet
Were limited. I had not at that time   230
Lived long enough, nor in the least survived
The first diviner influence of this world
As it appears to unaccustomed eyes.
I worshipped then among the depths of things
As my soul bade me; could I then take part   235
In aught but admiration, or be pleased
With anything but humbleness and love?
I felt, and nothing else; I did not judge –
I never thought of judging – with the gift
Of all this glory filled and satisfied   240
And afterwards, when through the gorgeous Alps
Roaming, I carried with me the same heart.
In truth, this degradation, howsoe'er

---

[6]   *a maid* Mary Hutchinson, whom he married 4 Oct.
1802.

Induced – effect (in whatsoe'er degree)
Of custom, that prepares such wantonness   245
As makes the greatest things give way to least,
Of any other cause which hath been named,
Or, lastly, aggravated by the times
Which with their passionate sounds might often make
The milder minstrelsies of rural scenes   250
Inaudible – was transient. I had felt
Too forcibly, too early in my life,
Visitings of imaginative power
For this to last: I shook the habit off
Entirely and for ever, and again   255
In nature's presence stood, as I stand now,
A sensitive, and a creative soul.
    There are in our existence spots of time
Which with distinct pre-eminence retain
A renovating[7] virtue, whence, depressed   260
By false opinion and contentious thought,
Or aught of heavier or more deadly weight
In trivial occupations and the round
Of ordinary intercourse, our minds
Are nourished and invisibly repaired –   265
A virtue by which pleasure is enhanced,
That penetrates, enables us to mount
When high, more high, and lifts us up when fallen.
This efficacious spirit chiefly lurks
Among those passages of life in which   270
We have had deepest feeling that the mind
Is lord and master, and that outward sense
Is but the obedient servant of her will.
Such moments, worthy of all gratitude,
Are scattered everywhere, taking their date   275
From our first childhood – in our childhood even
Perhaps are most conspicuous. Life with me,
As far as memory can look back, is full
Of this beneficent influence.
                                    At a time
When scarcely (I was then not six years old)   280
My hand could hold a bridle, with proud hopes
I mounted, and we rode towards the hills.
We were a pair of horsemen: honest James
Was with me, my encourager and guide.[8]
We had not travelled long ere some mischance   285
Disjoined me from my comrade, and, through fear

---

[7]   In earlier MS versions of the poem, Wordsworth
has 'fructifying' and 'vivifying'.
[8]   Wordsworth, probably aged 5, was staying with his

maternal grandparents, the Cooksons of Penrith, who
seem to have been James's employers.

Dismounting, down the rough and stony moor
I led my horse, and, stumbling on, at length
Came to a bottom where in former times
A murderer had been hung in iron chains[9]   290
The gibbet-mast was mouldered down, the bones
And iron case were gone; but on the turf
Hard by, soon after that fell deed was wrought,
Some unknown hand had carved the murderer's name.
The monumental writing was engraven   295
In times long past, and still from year to year
By superstition of the neighbourhood
The grass is cleared away, and to this hour
The letters are all fresh and visible.
Faltering, and ignorant where I was, at length   300
I chanced to espy those characters inscribed
On the green sod. Forthwith I left the spot
And reascending the bare common saw
A naked pool that lay beneath the hills,
The beacon on the summit, and, more near   305
A girl who bore a pitcher on her head
And seemed with difficult steps to force her way
Against the blowing wind. It was in truth
An ordinary sight, but I should need
Colours and words that are unknown to man   310
To paint the visionary dreariness
Which, while I looked all round for my lost guide,
Did at that time invest the naked pool,
The beacon on the lonely eminence,
The woman and her garments vexed and tossed   315
By the strong wind.
                      When, in a blessed season
With those two dear ones[10] – to my heart so dear –
When in the blessed time of early love
Long afterwards,[11] I roamed about
In daily presence of this very scene   320
Upon the naked pool and dreary crags,
And on the melancholy beacon, fell
The spirit of pleasure and youth's golden gleam –
And think ye not with radiance more divine
From these remembrances, and from the power   325
They left behind? So feeling comes in aid
Of feeling, and diversity of strength

---

9   The 'bottom' was Cowdrake Quarry, east of Penrith,
where Thomas Nicholson had been hanged for the
murder of Thomas Parker, 18 Nov. 1767. The letters
cut into the turf were 'TPM' – Thomas Parker
Murdered.

10   Dorothy Wordsworth and Mary Hutchinson.
11   Wordsworth looks back to summer 1787, just
before he went up to Cambridge.

Attends us, if but once we have been strong.
Oh, mystery of man, from what a depth
Proceed thy honours! I am lost, but see   330
In simple childhood something of the base
On which thy greatness stands – but this I feel:
That from thyself it is that thou must give,
Else never canst receive. The days gone by
Come back upon me from the dawn almost   335
Of life; the hiding-places of my power
Seem open; I approach, and then they close.
I see by glimpses now, when age comes on
May scarcely see at all; and I would give
While yet we may (as far as words can give)   340
A substance and a life to what I feel:
I would enshrine the spirit of the past
For future restoration. Yet another
Of these to me affecting incidents,
With which we will conclude.
                     One Christmas-time   345
The day before the holidays began,
Feverish, and tired, and restless, I went forth
Into the fields, impatient for the sight
Of those two horses which should bear us home,
My brothers and myself. There was a crag   350
An eminence, which from the meeting-point
Of two highways ascending, overlooked
At least a long half-mile of those two roads,
By each of which the expected steeds might come,
The choice uncertain. Thither I repaired   355
Up to the highest summit. 'Twas a day
Stormy, and rough, and wild, and on the grass
I sat half sheltered by a naked wall.
Upon my right hand was a single sheep,
A whistling hawthorn on my left, and there   360
With those companions at my side, I watched,
Straining my eyes intensely, as the mist
Gave intermitting prospect of the wood
And plain beneath. Ere I to school returned
That dreary time, ere I had been ten days   365
A dweller in my father's house, he died,[12]
And I and my two brothers (orphans then)
Followed his body to the grave. The event,
With all the sorrow which it brought, appeared
A chastisement; and when I called to mind   370
That day so lately past, when from the crag

---

[12] John Wordsworth Sr died 30 Dec. 1783. Richard
and John accompanied Wordsworth to the funeral.

I looked in such anxiety of hope,
With trite reflections of morality,
Yet in the deepest passion, I bowed low
To God, who thus corrected my desires   375
And afterwards the wind and sleety rain
And all the business of the elements,
The single sheep, and the one blasted tree,
And the bleak music of that old stone wall,
The noise of wood and water, and the mist   380
Which on the line of each of those two roads
Advanced in such indisputable shapes –
All these were spectacles and sounds to which
I often would repair, and thence would drink
As at a fountain. And I do not doubt   385
That in this later time, when storm and rain
Beat on my roof at midnight, or by day
When I am in the woods, unknown to me
The workings of my spirit thence are brought.

    Thou wilt not languish here, oh friend, for whom   390
I travel in these dim uncertain ways;
Thou wilt assist me as a pilgrim gone
In quest of highest truth. Behold me then
Once more in nature's presence, thus restored
Or otherwise, and strengthened once again   395
(With memory left of what had been escaped)
To habits of devoutest sympathy.

Book Twelve
Same Subject Continued

From nature doth emotion come, and moods
Of calmness equally are nature's gift –
This is her glory. These two attributes
Are sister horns that constitute her strength;
This twofold influence is the sun and shower   5
Of all her bounties, both in origin
And end alike benignant. Hence it is
That genius, which exists by interchange
Of peace and excitation, finds in her
His best and purest friend – from her receives   10
That energy by which he seeks the truth
(Is roused, aspires, grasps, struggles, wishes, craves),
From her, that happy stillness of the mind
Which fits him to receive it when unsought.

    Such benefit may souls of humblest frame   15
Partake of, each in their degree: 'tis mine
To speak of what myself have known and felt.
Sweet task! – for words find easy way, inspired

By gratitude and confidence in truth.
Long time in search of knowledge desperate   20
I was benighted heart and mind, but now
On all sides day began to reappear,
And it was proved indeed that not in vain
I had been taught to reverence a power
That is the very quality and shape   25
And image of right reason, that matures
Her processes by steady laws; gives birth
To no impatient or fallacious hopes,
No heat of passion or excessive zeal,
No vain conceits; provokes to no quick turns   30
Of self-applauding intellect, but lifts
The being into magnanimity;
Holds up before the mind, intoxicate
With present objects and the busy dance
Of things that pass away, a temperate show   35
Of objects that endure; and by this course
Disposes her, when over-fondly set
On leaving her encumbrances behind,
To seek in man (and in the frame of life,
Social and individual) what there is   40
Desirable, affecting, good or fair,
Of kindred permanence – the gifts divine
And universal, pervading grace
That hath been, is, and shall be. Above all
Did nature bring again that wiser mood,   45
More deeply re-established in my soul,
Which – seeing little worthy or sublime
In what we blazon with the pompous names
Of power and action – early tutored me
To look with feelings of fraternal love   50
Upon those unassuming things that hold
A silent station in this beauteous world.
    Thus moderated, thus composed, I found
Once more in man an object of delight,
Of pure imagination, and of love;   55
And, as the horizon of my mind enlarged,
Again I took the intellectual eye
For my instructor, studious more to see
Great truths, than touch and handle little ones.
Knowledge was given accordingly: my trust   60
Was firmer in the feelings which had stood
The test of such a trial, clearer far
My sense of what was excellent and right;
The promise of the present time retired
Into its true proportion; sanguine schemes,   65
Ambitious virtues, pleased me less – I sought

For good in the familiar face of life,
And built thereon my hopes of good to come.
   With settling judgements now of what would last
And what would disappear; prepared to find   70
Ambition, folly, madness, in the men
Who thrust themselves upon this passive world
As rulers of the world (to see in these,
Even when the public welfare is their aim,
Plans without thought, or bottomed on false thought   75
And false philosophy); having brought to test
Of solid life and true result the books
Of modern statists, and thereby perceived
The utter hollowness of what we name
The wealth of nations,[1] where alone that wealth   80
Is lodged, and how increased; and having gained
A more judicious knowledge of what makes
The dignity of individual man –
Of man, no composition of the thought,
Abstraction, shadow, image, but the man   85
Of whom we read, the man whom we behold
With our own eyes – I could not but enquire,
Not with less interest than heretofore
But greater, though in a spirit more subdued,
Why is this glorious creature to be found   90
One only in ten thousand? What one is,
Why may not many be? What bars are thrown
By nature in the way of such a hope?
Our animal wants and the necessities
Which they impose, are these the obstacle?   95
If not, then others vanish into air.
   Such meditations bred an anxious wish
To ascertain how much of real worth,
And genuine knowledge, and true power of mind,
Did at this day exist in those who lived   100
By bodily labour – labour far exceeding
Their due proportion – under all the weight
Of that injustice which upon ourselves
By composition of society
Ourselves entail. To frame such estimate   105
I chiefly looked (what need to look beyond?)
Among the natural abodes of men,
Fields with their rural works; recalled to mind
My earliest notices, with these compared
The observations of my later youth   110

BOOK TWELVE
[1] The 'statists' are political and economic theorists such as Adam Smith, to whose *Inquiry into the Nature and Causes of the Wealth of Nations* (1776) Wordsworth alludes.

Continued downwards to that very day.
   For time had never been in which the throes
And mighty hopes of nations, and the stir
And tumult of the world, to me could yield
(How far soe'er transported and possessed)   115
Full measure of content; but still I craved
An intermixture of distinct regards
And truths of individual sympathy
Nearer ourselves. Such often might be gleaned
From that great city, else it must have been   120
A heart-depressing wilderness indeed —
Full soon to me a wearisome abode —
But much was wanting; therefore did I turn
To you, ye pathways and ye lonely roads,
Sought you, enriched with everything I prized,   125
With human kindness and with nature's joy.
   Oh, next to one dear state of bliss vouchsafed,
Alas, to few in this untoward world —
The bliss of walking daily in life's prime
Through field or forest with the maid we love   130
While yet our hearts are young, while yet we breathe
Nothing but happiness, living in some place
(Deep vale, or anywhere, the home of both)
From which it would be misery to stir;
Oh, next to such enjoyment of our youth,   135
In my esteem, next to such dear delight,
Was that of wandering on from day to day
Where I could meditate in peace, and find
The knowledge which I loved, and teach the sound
Of poet's music to strange fields and groves;   140
Converse with men, where if we meet a face
We almost meet a friend, on naked moors
With long long ways before, by cottage bench,
Or well-spring where the weary traveller rests.
   Few sights more please me than a public road;   145
'Tis my delight! Such object hath had power
O'er my imagination since the dawn
Of childhood, when its disappearing line
Seen daily afar off, on one bare steep
Beyond the limits which my feet had trod,   150
Was like a guide into eternity,[2]
At least to things unknown and without bound.
Even something of the grandeur which invests
The mariner who sails the roaring sea

---

[2] From the terrace of the Wordsworth house in
Cockermouth, the young poet would have seen the
road to the village of Isel over Watch Hill.

Through storm and darkness, early in my mind   155
Surrounded too the wanderers of the earth –
Grandeur as much, and loveliness far more.
Awed have I been by strolling bedlamites;[3]
From many other uncouth vagrants (passed
In fear) have walked with quicker step – but why   160
Take note of this? When I began to enquire,
To watch and question those I met, and held
Familiar talk with them, the lonely roads
Were schools to me in which I daily read
With most delight the passions of mankind,   165
There saw into the depth of human souls –
Souls that appear to have no depth at all
To vulgar eyes. And now, convinced at heart
How little that to which alone we give
The name of education, hath to do   170
With real feeling and just sense; how vain
A correspondence with the talking world
Proves to the most – and called to make good search
If man's estate, by doom of nature yoked
With toil, is therefore yoked with ignorance,   175
If virtue be indeed so hard to rear,
And intellectual strength so rare a boon –
I prized such walks still more. For there I found
Hope to my hope, and to my pleasure peace
And steadiness, and healing and repose   180
To every angry passion. There I heard,
From mouths of lowly men and of obscure,
A tale of honour – sounds in unison
With loftiest promises of good and fair.

    There are who think that strong affections, love   185
Known by whatever name, is falsely deemed
A gift (to use a term which they would use)
Of vulgar nature; that its growth requires
Retirement, leisure, language purified
By manners thoughtful and elaborate;   190
That whoso feels such passion in excess
Must live within the very light and air
Of elegances that are made by man.
True is it, where oppression worse than death
Salutes the being at his birth, where grace   195
Of culture hath been utterly unknown,
And labour in excess and poverty
From day to day preoccupy the ground
Of the affections, and to nature's self

---

[3] *bedlamites* madmen.

Oppose a deeper nature – there indeed 200
Love cannot be. Nor does it easily thrive
In cities, where the human heart is sick,
And the eye feeds it not, and cannot feed.
Thus far, no further, is that inference good.
   Yes, in those wanderings deeply did I feel 205
How we mislead each other, above all
How books mislead us, looking for their fame
To judgements of the wealthy few who see
By artificial lights; how they debase
The many for the pleasure of those few, 210
Effeminately level down the truth
To certain general notions for the sake
Of being understood at once (or else
Through want of better knowledge in the men
Who frame them), flattering thus our self-conceit 215
With pictures that ambitiously set forth
The differences, the outside marks by which
Society has parted man from man,
Neglectful of the universal heart.
   Here, calling up to mind what then I saw, 220
A youthful traveller, and see daily now
Before me in my rural neighbourhood –
Here might I pause, and bend in reverence
To nature and the power of human minds,
To men as they are men within themselves. 225
How oft high service is performed within
When all the external man is rude in show:
Not like a temple rich with pomp and gold,
But a mere mountain chapel such as shields
Its simple worshippers from sun and shower. 230
'Of these', said I, 'shall be my song; of these,
If future years mature me for the task,
Will I record the praises, making verse
Deal boldly with substantial things – in truth
And sanctity of passion speak of these, 235
That justice may be done, obeisance paid
Where it is due. Thus haply shall I teach,
Inspire – through unadulterated ears
Pour rapture, tenderness and hope; my theme
No other than the very heart of man 240
As found among the best of those who live
Not unexalted by religious hope,
Nor uninformed by books (good books, though few)
In nature's presence. Thence may I select
Sorrow that is not sorrow but delight, 245
And miserable love that is not pain
To hear of, for the glory that redounds

Therefrom to humankind and what we are.
  Be mine to follow with no timid step
Where knowledge leads me: it shall be my pride   250
That I have dared to tread this holy ground
Speaking no dream, but things oracular,
Matter not lightly to be heard by those
Who to the letter of the outward promise
Do read the invisible soul – by men adroit   255
In speech, and for communion with the world
Accomplished – minds whose faculties are then
Most active when they are most eloquent,
And elevated most when most admired.
Men may be found of other mould than these   260
Who are their own upholders, to themselves
Encouragement, and energy, and will,
Expressing liveliest thoughts in lively words
As native passion dictates. Others too
There are among the walks of homely life   265
Still higher, men for contemplation framed,
Shy, and unpractised in the strife of phrase,
Meek men, whose very souls perhaps would sink
Beneath them, summoned to such intercourse.
Theirs is the language of the heavens, the power,   270
The thought, the image, and the silent joy.
Words are but under-agents in their souls;
When they are grasping with their greatest strength,
They do not breathe among them.[4] This I speak
In gratitude to God, who feeds our hearts   275
For his own service – knoweth, loveth us
When we are unregarded by the world.
  Also about this time did I receive
Convictions still more strong than heretofore
Not only that the inner frame is good   280
And graciously composed, but that, no less,
Nature through all conditions hath a power
To consecrate (if we have eyes to see)
The outside of her creatures, and to breathe
Grandeur upon the very humblest face   285
Of human life. I felt that the array
Of outward circumstance and visible form
Is to the pleasure of the human mind
What passion makes it; that, meanwhile,[5] the forms
Of nature have a passion in themselves   290
That intermingles with those works of man
To which she summons him (although the works

---

[4] *them* i.e. words; 'silent poets' transcend language.   [5] *meanwhile* i.e. on the other hand.

Be mean, have nothing lofty of their own),
And that the genius of the poet hence
May boldly take his way among mankind   295
Wherever nature leads – that he hath stood
By nature's side among the men of old,
And so shall stand for ever. Dearest friend,
Forgive me if I say that I – (who long
Had harboured reverentially a thought   300
That poets, even as prophets, each with each
Connected in a mighty scheme of truth,
Have each for his peculiar dower a sense
By which he is enabled to perceive
Something unseen before) forgive me, friend,   305
If I, the meanest of this band – had hope
That unto me had also been vouchsafed
An influx, that in some sort I possessed
A privilege, and that a work of mine,
Proceeding from the depth of untaught things,   310
Enduring and creative, might become
A power like one of nature's.
                              To such mood
Once above all, a traveller at that time
Upon the Plain of Sarum, was I raised:[6]
There on the pastoral downs without a track   315
To guide me, or along the bare white roads
Lengthening in solitude their dreary line,
While through those vestiges of ancient times
I ranged, and by the solitude o'ercome,
I had a reverie and saw the past,   320
Saw multitudes of men, and here and there
A single Briton in his wolfskin vest,
With shield and stone-axe, stride across the wold;
The voice of spears was heard, the rattling spear
Shaken by arms of mighty bone, in strength   325
Long mouldered, of barbaric majesty.
I called upon the darkness, and it took –
A midnight darkness seemed to come and take
All objects from my sight; and lo, again
The desert visible by dismal flames!   330
It is the sacrificial altar fed
With living men – how deep the groans! – the voice
Of those in the gigantic wicker thrills
Throughout the region far and near, pervades
The monumental hillocks, and the pomp   335
Is for both worlds, the living and the dead.

---

[6] Upset by his inability to return to Annette Vallon   crossed Salisbury Plain in the summer of 1793, in a
in France (due to the outbreak of war), Wordsworth   mood that gave rise to visions of Druid sacrifice.

At other moments (for through that wide waste
Three summer days I roamed), when 'twas my chance
To have before me on the downy plain
Lines, circles, mounts, a mystery of shapes   340
Such as in many quarters yet survive,
With intricate profusion figuring o'er
The untilled ground – the work, as some divine,
Of infant science, imitative forms
By which the Druids covertly expressed   345
Their knowledge of the heavens, and imaged forth
The constellations – I was gently charmed,
Albeit with an antiquarian's dream,
And saw the bearded teachers, with white wands
Uplifted, pointing to the starry sky   350
Alternately, and plain below, while breath
Of music seemed to guide them, and the waste
Was cheered with stillness and a pleasant sound.

    This for the past, and things that may be viewed
Or fancied in the obscurities of time.   355
Nor is it, friend, unknown to thee; at least,
Thyself delighted, thou for my delight
Hast said (perusing some imperfect verse
Which in that lonesome journey was composed[7])
That also I must then have exercised   360
Upon the vulgar forms of present things
And actual world of our familiar days
A higher power – have caught from them a tone,
An image, and a character, by books
Not hitherto reflected. Call we this   365
But a persuasion taken up by thee
In friendship? Yet the mind is to herself
Witness and judge, and I remember well
That in life's everyday appearances
I seemed about this period to have sight   370
Of a new world – a world, too, that was fit
To be transmitted, and made visible
To other eyes, as having for its base
That whence our dignity originates,
That which both gives it being, and maintains   375
A balance, an ennobling interchange
Of action from within and from without:
The excellence, pure spirit, and best power,
Both of the object seen, and eye that sees.

---

[7] Coleridge read Wordsworth's *Adventures on Salisbury Plain* in 1795–6, which drew on the experience Wordsworth has just described.

Book Thirteen
Conclusion

In one of these excursions, travelling then
Through Wales on foot and with a youthful friend,[1]
I left Beddgelert's huts at couching-time
And westward took my way to see the sun
Rise from the top of Snowdon. Having reached   5
The cottage at the mountain's foot, we there
Roused up the shepherd who by ancient right
Of office is the stranger's usual guide,
And after short refreshment sallied forth.

   It was a summer's night, a close warm night,   10
Wan, dull and glaring,[2] with a dripping mist
Low-hung and thick that covered all the sky,
Half threatening storm and rain; but on we went
Unchecked, being full of heart and having faith
In our tried pilot. Little could we see,   15
Hemmed round on every side with fog and damp,
And, after ordinary travellers' chat
With our conductor, silently we sunk
Each into commerce with his private thoughts.
Thus did we breast the ascent, and by myself   20
Was nothing either seen or heard the while
Which took me from my musings, save that once
The shepherd's cur did to his own great joy
Unearth a hedgehog in the mountain crags
Round which he made a barking turbulent.   25
This small adventure (for even such it seemed
In that wild place and at the dead of night)
Being over and forgotten, on we wound
In silence as before.
                            With forehead bent
Earthward, as if in opposition set   30
Against an enemy, I panted up
With eager pace, and no less eager thoughts.
Thus might we wear perhaps an hour away,
Ascending at loose distance each from each,
And I, as chanced, the foremost of the band –   35
When at my feet the ground appeared to brighten,
And with a step or two seemed brighter still;
Nor had I time to ask the cause of this,
For instantly a light upon the turf

Book Thirteen   [2] *glaring* clammy.
[1] Wordsworth's walking tour of North Wales with
Robert Jones took place in summer 1791. Their
ascent of Snowdon began from Beddgelert.

Fell like a flash. I looked about, and lo!   40
The moon stood naked in the heavens at height
Immense above my head, and on the shore
I found myself of a huge sea of mist,
Which meek and silent rested at my feet.
A hundred hills their dusky backs upheaved   45
All over this still ocean; and beyond,
Far, far beyond, the vapours shot themselves
In headlands, tongues, and promontory shapes,
Into the sea – the real sea, that seemed
To dwindle and give up its majesty,   50
Usurped upon as far as sight could reach.
Meanwhile, the moon looked down upon this show
In single glory, and we stood, the mist
Touching our very feet. And from the shore
At distance not the third part of a mile   55
Was a blue chasm, a fracture in the vapour,
A deep and gloomy breathing-place through which
Mounted the roar of waters, torrents, streams
Innumerable, roaring with one voice.
The universal spectacle throughout   60
Was shaped for admiration and delight,
Grand in itself alone, but in that breach
Through which the homeless voice of waters rose,
That dark deep thoroughfare, had nature lodged
The soul, the imagination of the whole.   65
  A meditation rose in me that night
Upon the lonely mountain when the scene
Had passed away, and it appeared to me
The perfect image of a mighty mind,
Of one that feeds upon infinity,   70
That is exalted by an under-presence,
The sense of God, or whatsoe'er is dim
Or vast in its own being. Above all,
One function of such mind had nature there
Exhibited by putting forth, in midst   75
Of circumstance most awful and sublime:
That domination which she oftentimes
Exerts upon the outward face of things,
So moulds them, and endues, abstracts, combines,
Or by abrupt and unhabitual influence   80
Doth make one object so impress itself
Upon all others, and pervade them so,
That even the grossest minds must see and hear
And cannot choose but feel.
                           The power which these
Acknowledge when thus moved, which nature thus   85
Thrusts forth upon the senses, is the express

Resemblance, in the fullness of its strength
Made visible, a genuine counterpart
And brother, of the glorious faculty
Which higher minds bear with them as their own.   90
This is the very spirit in which they deal
With all the objects of the universe;
They from their native selves can send abroad
Like transformation, for themselves create
A like existence, and, whene'er it is   95
Created for them, catch it by an instinct.
Them the enduring and the transient both
Serve to exalt. They build up greatest things
From least suggestions, ever on the watch,
Willing to work and to be wrought upon.   100
They need not extraordinary calls
To rouse them: in a world of life they live,
By sensible impressions not enthralled,
But quickened, roused, and made thereby more fit
To hold communion with the invisible world.   105
Such minds are truly from the Deity
For they are Powers, and hence the highest bliss
That can be known is theirs – the consciousness
Of whom they are, habitually infused
Through every image and through every thought,   110
And all impressions. Hence religion, faith,
And endless occupation for the soul,
Whether discursive or intuitive;[3]
Hence sovereignty within and peace at will,
Emotion which best foresight need not fear,   115
Most worthy then of trust when most intense;
Hence cheerfulness in every act of life;
Hence truth in moral judgements and delight
That fails not in the external universe.
　　Oh, who is he that hath his whole life long   120
Preserved, enlarged, this freedom in himself? –
For this alone is genuine liberty.
Witness, ye solitudes where I received
My earliest visitations, careless then
Of what was given me, and where now I roam   125
A meditative, oft a suffering, man,
And yet I trust with undiminished powers –
Witness, whatever falls my better mind,
Revolving with the accidents of life,
May have sustained, that howsoe'er misled,   130
I never, in the quest of right and wrong,

---

[3] This distinction recalls *Paradise Lost*, v. 487–90.

Did tamper with myself from private aims;
Nor was in any of my hopes the dupe
Of selfish passions; nor did wilfully
Yield ever to mean cares and low pursuits,   135
But rather did with jealousy shrink back
From every combination that might aid
The tendency, too potent in itself,
Of habit to enslave the mind – I mean
Oppress it by the laws of vulgar sense   140
And substitute a universe of death,
The falsest of all worlds, in place of that
Which is divine and true.
              To fear and love
(To love as first and chief, for there fear ends)
Be this ascribed, to early intercourse   145
In presence of sublime and lovely forms
With the adverse principles of pain and joy –
Evil as one is rashly named by those
Who know not what they say. From love (for here
Do we begin and end) all grandeur comes,   150
All truth and beauty – from pervading love;
That gone, we are as dust. Behold the fields
In balmy springtime full of rising flowers
And happy creatures! See that pair, the lamb
And the lamb's mother, and their tender ways   155
Shall touch thee to the heart. In some green bower
Rest, and be not alone, but have thou there
The one who is thy choice of all the world –
There linger, lulled and lost, and rapt away –
Be happy to thy fill! Thou call'st this love,   160
And so it is, but there is higher love
Than this, a love that comes into the heart
With awe and a diffusive sentiment;
Thy love is human merely – this proceeds
More from the brooding soul, and is divine.   165
   This love more intellectual cannot be
Without imagination, which in truth
Is but another name for absolute strength
And clearest insight, amplitude of mind
And reason in her most exalted mood.   170
This faculty hath been the moving soul
Of our long labour: we have traced the stream
From darkness and the very place of birth
In its blind cavern, whence is faintly heard
The sound of waters; followed it to light   175
And open day, accompanied its course
Among the ways of nature; afterwards
Lost sight of it bewildered and engulfed,

Then given it greeting as it rose once more
With strength, reflecting in its solemn breast   180
The works of man and face of human life;
And lastly, from its progress have we drawn
The feeling of life endless, the great thought
By which we live, infinity and God.
   Imagination having been our theme,   185
So also hath that intellectual love,
For they are each in each, and cannot stand
Dividually. Here must thou be, oh man,
Strength to thyself – no helper hast thou here;
Here keepest thou thy individual state.   190
No other can divide with thee this work,
No secondary hand can intervene
To fashion this ability. 'Tis thine,
The prime and vital principle is thine
In the recesses of thy nature, far   195
From any reach of outward fellowship,
Else 'tis not thine at all. But joy to him,
Oh, joy to him who here hath sown, hath laid
Here the foundations of his future years! –
For all that friendship, all that love can do,   200
All that a darling countenance can look
Or dear voice utter, to complete the man,
Perfect him (made imperfect in himself),
All shall be his. And he whose soul hath risen
Up to the height of feeling intellect   205
Shall want no humbler tenderness, his heart
Be tender as a nursing mother's heart;
Of female softness shall his life be full,
Of little loves and delicate desires,
Mild interests and gentlest sympathies.   210
   Child of my parents, sister of my soul,
Elsewhere have strains of gratitude been breathed
To thee for all the early tenderness
Which I from thee imbibed. And true it is
That later seasons owed to thee no less;   215
For, spite of thy sweet influence and the touch
Of other kindred hands that opened out
The springs of tender thought in infancy,
And spite of all which singly I had watched
Of elegance, and each minuter charm   220
In nature and in life, still to the last,
Even to the very going-out of youth,
The period which our story now hath reached –
I too exclusively esteemed that love,
And sought that beauty, which (as Milton sings)   225
Hath terror in it. Thou didst soften down

This over-sternness; but for thee, sweet friend,
My soul, too reckless of mild grace, had been
Far longer what by nature it was framed –
Longer retained its countenance severe –   230
A rock with torrents roaring, with the clouds
Familiar, and a favourite of the stars;
But thou didst plant its crevices with flowers,
Hang it with shrubs that twinkle in the breeze,
And teach the little birds to build their nests   235
And warble in its chambers. At a time
When nature, destined to remain so long
Foremost in my affections, had fallen back
Into a second place, well pleased to be
A handmaid to a nobler than herself;   240
When every day brought with it some new sense
Of exquisite regard for common things,
And all the earth was budding with these gifts
Of more refined humanity – thy breath,
Dear sister, was a kind of gentler spring   245
That went before my steps.
                                   With such a theme,
Coleridge, with this my argument, of thee
Shall I be silent? Oh most loving soul,
Placed on this earth to love and understand,
And from thy presence shed the light of love,   250
Shall I be mute, ere thou be spoken of?
Thy gentle spirit to my heart of hearts
Did also find its way; and thus the life
Of all things and the mighty unity
In all which we behold, and feel, and are,   255
Admitted more habitually a mild
Interposition, and closelier gathering thoughts
Of man and his concerns, such as become
A human creature, be he who he may,
Poet, or destined to an humbler name.   260
And so the deep enthusiastic joy,
The rapture of the hallelujah sent
From all that breathes and is, was chastened, stemmed,
And balanced by a reason which indeed
Is reason, duty and pathetic truth –   265
And God and man divided, as they ought,
Between them the great system of the world
Where man is sphered, and which God animates.
   And now, oh friend, this history is brought
To its appointed close. The discipline   270
And consummation of the poet's mind,
In everything that stood most prominent,
Have faithfully been pictured. We have reached

The time (which was our object from the first)
When we may – not presumptuously, I hope –   275
Suppose my powers so far confirmed, and such
My knowledge, as to make me capable
Of building up a work that should endure.
Yet much hath been omitted, as need was –
Of books how much! – and even of the other wealth   280
Which is collected among woods and fields,
Far more. For nature's secondary grace,
That outward illustrtation which is hers,
Hath hitherto been barely touched upon:
The charm more superficial, and yet sweet,   285
Which from her works finds way, contemplated
As they hold forth a genuine counterpart
And softening mirror of the moral world.
    Yes, having tracked the main essential power,
Imagination, up her way sublime,   290
In turn might fancy also be pursued
Through all her transmigrations, till she too
Was purified, had learned to ply her craft
By judgement steadied. Then might we return
And in the rivers and the groves behold   295
Another face, might hear them from all sides
Calling upon the more instructed mind
To link their images – with subtle skill
Sometimes, and by elaborate research –
With forms and definite appearances   300
Of human life, presenting them sometimes
To the involuntary sympathy
Of our internal being, satisfied
And soothed with a conception of delight
Where meditation cannot come, which thought   305
Could never heighten.
                    Above all, how much
Still nearer to ourselves is overlooked
In human nature and that marvellous world
As studied first in my own heart, and then
In life among the passions of mankind   310
And qualities commixed and modified
By the infinite varieties and shades
Of individual character. Herein
It was for me (this justice bids me say)
No useless preparation to have been   315
The pupil of a public school,[4] and forced
In hardy independence to stand up

---

[4] Hawkshead Grammar School was open to all –
hence 'public'.

Among conflicting passions and the shock
Of various tempers – to endure and note
What was not understood, though known to be –   320
Among the mysteries of love and hate,
Honour and shame, looking to right and left,
Unchecked by innocence too delicate
And moral notions too intolerant,
Sympathies too contracted. Hence, when called   325
To take a station among men, the step
Was easier, the transition more secure,
More profitable also; for the mind
Learns from such timely exercise to keep
In wholesome separation the two natures: 330
The one that feels, the other that observes.
    Let one word more of personal circumstance –
Not needless, as it seems – be added here.
Since I withdrew unwillingly from France
The story hath demanded less regard   335
To time and place; and where I lived, and how,
Hath been no longer scrupulously marked.
Three years, until a permanent abode
Received me with that sister of my heart
Who ought by rights the dearest to have been   340
Conspicuous through this biographic verse –
Star seldom utterly concealed from view –
I led an undomestic wanderer's life.
In London chiefly was my home, and thence
Excursively, as personal friendships, chance   345
Or inclination led, or slender means
Gave leave, I roamed about from place to place,
Tarrying in pleasant nooks, wherever found,
Through England or through Wales.[5] A youth (he bore
The name of Calvert – it shall live if words   350
Of mine can give it life) without respect
To prejudice or custom, having hope
That I had some endowments by which good
Might be promoted, in his last decay
From his own family withdrawing part   355
Of no redundant patrimony, did
By a bequest sufficient for my needs
Enable me to pause for choice, and walk
At large and unrestrained, nor damped too soon
By mortal cares.[6] Himself no poet, yet   360
Far less a common spirit of the world,
He deemed that my pursuits and labours lay

---

[5] Robert Jones, Wordsworth's Cambridge friend, was Welsh.

[6] Raisley Calvert died of consumption in 1795, aged 22, leaving Wordsworth £900.

Apart from all that leads to wealth – or even
Perhaps to necessary maintenance,
Without some hazard to the finer sense –   365
He cleared a passage for me, and the stream
Flowed in the bent of nature.
                                        Having now
Told what best merits mention, further pains
Our present labour seems not to require,
And I have other tasks.[7] Call back to mind   370
The mood in which this poem was begun,
Oh friend – the termination of my course
Is nearer now, much nearer, yet even then
In that distraction and intense desire
I said unto the life which I had lived,   375
'Where art thou? Hear I not a voice from thee
Which 'tis reproach to hear?' Anon I rose
As if on wings, and saw beneath me stretched
Vast prospect of the world which I had been
And was; and hence this song, which like a lark   380
I have protracted, in the unwearied heavens
Singing, and often with more plaintive voice
Attempered to the sorrows of the earth –
Yet centring all in love, and in the end
All gratulant if rightly understood.   385
    Whether to me shall be allotted life,
And with life power to accomplish aught of worth
Sufficient to excuse me in men's sight
For having given this record of myself,
Is all uncertain. But, beloved friend,   390
When looking back thou seest, in clearer view
Than any sweetest sight of yesterday,
That summer when on Quantock's grassy hills
Far ranging, and among the sylvan coombs,
Thou in delicious words, with happy heart,   395
Didst speak the vision of that ancient man,
The bright-eyed Mariner, and rueful woes
Didst utter of the Lady Christabel,
And I, associate in such labour, walked
Murmuring of him who (joyous hap!) was found   400
After the perils of his moonlight ride
Near the loud waterfall, or her who sat
In misery near the miserable thorn –
When thou dost to that summer turn thy thoughts
And hast before thee all which then we were,   405
To thee, in memory of that happiness,

---

[7] Wordsworth was anxious to write *The Recluse*.

It will be known – by thee at least, my friend,
Felt – that the history of a poet's mind
Is labour not unworthy of regard:
To thee the work shall justify itself.[8]   410
    The last and later portions of this gift
Which I for thee design, have been prepared
In times which have from those wherein we first
Together wantoned in wild poesy
Differed thus far: that they have been, oh friend,   415
Times of much sorrow, of a private grief[9]
Keen and enduring, which the frame of mind
That in this meditative history
Hath been described, more deeply makes me feel –
Yet likewise hath enabled me to bear   420
More firmly; and a comfort now, a hope,
One of the dearest which this life can give,
Is mine: that thou art near, and wilt be soon
Restored to us in renovated health,
When, after the first mingling of our tears,   425
'Mong other consolations, we may find
Some pleasure from this offering of my love.
    Oh yet a few short years of useful life
And all will be complete, thy race be run,
Thy monument of glory will be raised!   430
Then, though (too weak to tread the ways of truth)
This age fall back to old idolatry,
Though men return to servitude as fast
As the tide ebbs, to ignominy and shame
By nations sink together, we shall still   435
Find solace in the knowledge which we have,
Blessed with true happiness if we may be
United helpers forward of a day
Of firmer trust, joint labourers in a work
(Should Providence such grace to us vouchsafe)   440
Of their redemption, surely yet to come.
Prophets of nature, we to them will speak
A lasting inspiration, sanctified
By reason and by truth. What we have loved
Others will love, and we may teach them how –   445
Instruct them how the mind of man becomes
A thousand times more beautiful than the earth
On which he dwells, above this frame of things

---

8 The Quantocks are above Alfoxden, where the
Wordsworths resided in 1797–8. During that time Coleridge composed, among other things, 'The Ancient
Mariner' and 'Christabel', Part I, while Wordsworth's
achievements included 'The Idiot Boy' and 'The Thorn'.

9 Wordsworth's younger brother John, Captain of
the *Earl of Abergavenny*, was drowned off the Dorset
coast, 5 Feb. 1805.

(Which, mid all revolutions in the hopes
And fears of men, doth still remain unchanged)   450
In beauty exalted, as it is itself
Of substance and of fabric more divine.

From Poems in Two Volumes (1807)

ELEGIAC STANZAS, SUGGESTED BY A PICTURE OF PEELE CASTLE IN A STORM, PAINTED BY SIR GEORGE BEAUMONT (COMPOSED BETWEEN 20 MAY AND 27 JUNE 1806)

I was thy neighbour once, thou rugged pile![1]
Four summer weeks I dwelt in sight of thee;
I saw thee every day, and all the while
Thy form was sleeping on a glassy sea.

So pure the sky, so quiet was the air!   5
So like, so very like, was day to day!
Whene'er I looked, thy image still was there –
It trembled, but it never passed away.

How perfect was the calm; it seemed no sleep,
No mood which season takes away, or brings;   10
I could have fancied that the mighty deep
Was even the gentlest of all gentle things.

Ah *then*, if mine had been the painter's hand
To express what then I saw, and add the gleam,
The light that never was, on sea or land,   15
The consecration, and the poet's dream,

I would have planted thee, thou hoary pile,
Amid a world how different from this!
Beside a sea that could not cease to smile,
On tranquil land, beneath a sky of bliss;   20

Thou shouldst have seemed a treasure-house, a mine
Of peaceful years, a chronicle of heaven –
Of all the sunbeams that did ever shine
The very sweetest had to thee been given.

ELEGIAC STANZAS, SUGGESTED BY A PICTURE OF
PEELE CASTLE IN A STORM, PAINTED BY SIR GEORGE
BEAUMONT
[1] Peele Castle is in northern Lancashire, on a promontory opposite Rampside, where Wordsworth
lived during the summer of 1794.

A picture had it been of lasting ease, 25
Elysian quiet, without toil or strife;
No motion but the moving tide, a breeze,
Or merely silent nature's breathing life.

Such, in the fond delusion of my heart,
Such picture would I at that time have made; 30
And seen the soul of truth in every part –
A faith, a trust that could not be betrayed.

So once it would have been – 'tis so no more;
I have submitted to a new control:
A power is gone, which nothing can restore – 35
A deep distress hath humanized my soul.

Not for a moment could I now behold
A smiling sea and be what I have been;
The feeling of my loss will ne'er be old –
This, which I know, I speak with mind serene. 40

Then, Beaumont, friend! who would have been the friend,
If he had lived, of him[2] whom I deplore,
This work of thine[3] I blame not, but commend;
This sea in anger, and that dismal shore.

Oh 'tis a passionate work! – yet wise and well, 45
Well-chosen is the spirit that is here;
That hulk which labours in the deadly swell,
This rueful sky, this pageantry of fear!

And this huge castle, standing here sublime,
I love to see the look with which it braves, 50
Cased in the unfeeling armour of old time,
The lightning, the fierce wind, and trampling waves.

Farewell, farewell the heart that lives alone,
Housed in a dream, at distance from the kind![4]
Such happiness, wherever it be known, 55
Is to be pitied, for 'tis surely blind.

But welcome fortitude, and patient cheer,
And frequent sights of what is to be borne!

---

[2] Wordsworth's brother John was drowned at sea in the wreck of the *Earl of Abergavenny*, 5 Feb. 1805. The news inspired Mary Lamb to write her own poem, pp. 153–4, and a reading of Wordsworth's lines led Mary Shelley to compose an elegy for her drowned husband, pp. 1083.

[3] Sir George Beaumont's 'A Storm: Peele Castle' was exhibited at the Royal Academy, 2 May 1806, where Wordsworth probably saw it.
[4] *kind* humankind.

Such sights, or worse, as are before me here –
Not without hope we suffer and we mourn.[5]   60

A COMPLAINT (COMPOSED BETWEEN 30 OCTOBER 1806 AND APRIL 1807)

There is a change – and I am poor;[1]
Your love hath been, nor long ago,
A fountain at my fond heart's door
Whose only business was to flow –
And flow it did, not taking heed   5
Of its own bounty, or my need.

What happy moments did I count!
Blessed was I then all bliss above!
Now, for this consecrated fount
Of murmuring, sparkling, living love,   10
What have I? Shall I dare to tell?
A comfortless and hidden well.

A well of love – it may be deep –
I trust it is, and never dry;
What matter if the waters sleep   15
In silence and obscurity?
Such change, and at the very door
Of my fond heart, hath made me poor.

From Poems (1815)

PREFACE (EXTRACT) (PP. xx-xxviii)

Imagination (in the sense of the word as giving title to a class of the following poems[1]) has no reference to images that are merely a faithful copy existing in the mind of certain external objects, but is a word of higher import, denoting operations of the mind upon those objects, and processes of creation or of composition governed by certain fixed laws. I proceed to illustrate my meaning by instances.

A parrot *hangs* from the wires of his cage by his beak or by his claws, or a monkey from the bough of a tree by his paws or his tail: each creature does so literally and actually. In the first *Eclogue* of Virgil, the shepherd, thinking of the time when he is to take leave of his farm, thus addresses his goats:

---

[5] Wilson notes that this line echoes the Book of Common Prayer's 'Order for the Burial of the Dead': 'Oh merciful God ... who also hath taught us, by his holy Apostle St Paul, not to be sorry, as men without hope, for them that sleep in him' ('An Echo of St Paul and Words of Consolation in Wordsworth's "Elegiac Stanzas"', *RES*, 43 (1992), 75–80).

A COMPLAINT
[1] In the Fenwick Note Wordsworth recorded that this poem was 'suggested by a change in the manners of a friend', Coleridge (*FN*, 9).
PREFACE (1815)
[1] In *Poems* (1815) Wordsworth divided his collected works into 'classes' or categories, one of which was 'Imagination'.

Non ego vos posthac viridi projectus in antro
Dumosa *pendere* procul de rupe videbo ...
(Virgil, *Eclogues*, i. 76–7)

... half way up
Hangs one who gathers samphire
(*King Lear*, IV. vi. 15–16)

is the well-known expression of Shakespeare, delineating an ordinary image upon the cliffs of Dover. In these two instances is a slight exertion of the faculty which I denominate imagination, in the use of one word. Neither the goats nor the samphire-gatherer do literally hang (as does the parrot or the monkey), but, presenting to the senses something of such an appearance, the mind in its activity, for its own gratification, contemplates them as hanging.

As when far off at sea a fleet descried
Hangs in the clouds, by equinoxial winds
Close sailing from Bengala or the Isles
Of Ternate or Tydore, whence merchants bring
Their spicy drugs; they on the trading flood
Through the wide Ethiopian to the Cape
Ply, stemming nightly toward the pole – so seemed
Far off the flying fiend.
(*Paradise Lost*, ii. 636–43)

Here is the full strength of the imagination involved in the word *hangs* and exerted upon the whole image. First the fleet (an aggregate of many ships) is represented as one mighty person whose track, we know and feel, is upon the waters; but taking advantage of its appearance to the senses, the poet dares to represent it as *hanging in the clouds*, both for the gratification of the mind in contemplating the image itself, and in reference to the motion and appearance of the sublime object to which it is compared.

From images of sight we will pass to those of sound: 'Over his own sweet voice the stock-dove *broods* ... ' (*Resolution and Independence*, 5). Of the same bird:

His voice was *buried* among trees,
Yet to be come at by the breeze ...
(*Oh nightingale*, 13–14)

Oh cuckoo! shall I call thee *bird*
Or but a wandering *voice*?
(*To the Cuckoo*, 3–4)

The stock-dove is said to *coo*, a sound well imitating the note of the bird. But by the intervention of the metaphor *broods*, the affections are called in by the imagination to assist in marking the manner in which the bird reiterates and prolongs her soft note, as if herself delighting to listen to it, and participating of a still and quiet satisfaction like that which may be supposed inseparable from the continuous process of incubation.

'His voice was buried among trees': a metaphor expressing the love of seclusion by which this bird is marked, and characterizing its note as not partaking of the shrill and the piercing, and therefore more easily deadened by the intervening shade – yet a note so peculiar, and withal so pleasing, that the breeze, gifted with that love of the sound which the poet feels, penetrates the shade in which it is entombed, and conveys it to the ear of the listener.

> ... shall I call thee bird
> Or but a wandering voice?

This concise interrogation characterizes the seeming ubiquity of the voice of the cuckoo, and dispossesses the creature almost of a corporeal existence – the imagination being tempted to this exertion of her power by a consciousness in the memory that the cuckoo is almost perpetually heard throughout the season of spring, but seldom becomes an object of sight.

Thus far of images independent of each other, and immediately endowed by the mind with properties that do not inhere in them, upon an incitement from properties and qualities the existence of which is inherent and obvious. These processes of imagination are carried on either by conferring additional properties upon an object, or abstracting from it some of those which it actually possesses, and thus enabling it to react upon the mind which hath performed the process, like a new existence.

I pass from the imagination acting upon an individual image to a consideration of the same faculty employed upon images in a conjunction by which they modify each other. The reader has already had a fine instance before him in the passage quoted from Virgil, where the apparently perilous situation of the goat hanging upon the shaggy precipice is contrasted with that of the shepherd contemplating it from the seclusion of the cavern in which he lies stretched at ease and in security. Take these images separately, and how unaffecting the picture compared with that produced by their being thus connected with, and opposed to, each other!

> As a huge stone is sometimes seen to lie
> Couched on the bald top of an eminence,
> Wonder to all who do the same espy
> By what means it could thither come, and whence;
> So that it seems a thing endued with sense,
> Like a sea-beast crawled forth, which on a shelf
> Of rock or sand reposeth, there to sun himself –
>
> Such seemed this man, not all alive nor dead,
> Nor all asleep, in his extreme old age....
> Motionless as a cloud the old man stood
> That heareth not the loud winds when they call
> And moveth altogether, if it move at all.
>   (*Resolution and Independence*, 64–72, 82–4)

In these images, the conferring, the abstracting, and the modifying powers of the imagination, immediately and mediately acting, are all brought into conjunction. The stone is endowed with something of the power of life to approximate it to the sea-beast, and the sea-beast stripped of some of its vital qualities to assimilate it to the stone – which intermediate image is thus treated for the purpose of bringing the original image (that of the stone) to a nearer resemblance to the figure and condition of the aged man, who is divested of so much of the indications of life and motion as to bring him to the point where the two objects unite and coalesce in just comparison. After what has been said, the image of the cloud need not be commented upon.

Thus far of an endowing or modifying power. But the imagination also shapes and *creates* – and how? By innumerable processes, and in none does it more delight than in that of consolidating numbers into unity, and dissolving and separating unity into number – alternations proceeding from, and governed by, a sublime consciousness of the soul in her own mighty and almost divine powers. Recur to the passage already cited from Milton. When the compact fleet, as one person, has been introduced 'sailing from Bengala', 'they' (i.e. the 'merchants' representing the fleet resolved into a multitude of ships) 'Ply' their voyage towards the extremities of the earth; 'so' (referring to the word 'As' in the commencement) 'seemed the flying fiend' – the image of his person acting to recombine the multitude of ships into one body, the point from which the comparison set out.

'So seemed': and to whom 'seemed'? To the heavenly muse who dictates the poem, to the eye of the poet's mind, and to that of the reader, present at one moment in the wide Ethiopian, and the next in the solitudes, then first broken in upon, of the infernal regions!

From The Newcastle Journal, 4 (5 December 1835), no. 188

EXTEMPORE EFFUSION, UPON READING, IN THE NEWCASTLE JOURNAL, THE NOTICE OF THE DEATH OF THE POET, JAMES HOGG (COMPOSED *C.*30 NOVEMBER 1835)

When first, descending from the moorlands,
I saw the stream of Yarrow glide
Along a bare and open valley,
The Ettrick Shepherd[1] was my guide;

When last along its banks I wandered   5
Through groves that had begun to shed
Their golden leaves upon the pathways,
My steps the Border Minstrel[2] led.

The mighty Minstrel breathes no longer,
Mid mouldering ruins low he lies;   10
And death upon the braes of Yarrow
Has closed the Shepherd-poet's eyes.

Nor has the rolling year twice measured,
From sign to sign, his steadfast course,

EXTEMPORE EFFUSION UPON THE DEATH OF JAMES HOGG   [2] Sir Walter Scott, d. 21 Sept. 1832.
[1] James Hogg, d. 21 Nov. 1835.

Since every mortal power of Coleridge   15
Was frozen at its marvellous source;[3]

The rapt one of the godlike forehead,
The heaven-eyed creature sleeps in earth;
And Lamb, the frolic and the gentle,
Has vanished from his lonely hearth.[4]   20

Like clouds that rake the mountain-summits,
Or waves that own no curbing hand,
How fast has brother followed brother
From sunshine to the sunless land!

Yet I, whose lids from infant slumbers   25
Were earlier raised, remain to hear
A timid voice that asks in whispers,
'Who next will drop and disappear?'

Our haughty life is crowned with darkness,
Like London with its own black wreath,   30
On which with thee, oh Crabbe,[5] forth-looking
I gazed from Hampstead's breezy heath;

As if but yesterday departed,
Thou too art gone before – yet why
For ripe fruit seasonably gathered   35
Should frail survivors heave a sigh?[6]

No more of old romantic sorrows
For slaughtered youth and love-lorn maid;
With sharper grief is Yarrow smitten,
And Ettrick mourns with her their Shepherd dead!   40

From The Fenwick Notes (dictated 1843)

ON THE 'ODE' (EXTRACT)

Nothing was more difficult for me in childhood than to admit the notion of death as
a state applicable to my own being. I have said elsewhere: 'A simple child ... that
lightly draws its breath, / And feels its life in every limb – / What should it know of
death?' ('We are Seven', 1–4). But it was not so much from [excess][1] of animal vivacity

---

[3] Samuel Taylor Coleridge, d. 25 July 1834.
[4] Charles Lamb, d. 27 Dec. 1834.
[5] George Crabbe, d. 3 Feb. 1832.
[6] When Wordsworth collected this poem in 1837,
he added a stanza at this point lamenting Felicia
Hemans, who died 16 May 1835:

Mourn rather for that holy spirit,
Sweet as the spring, as ocean deep;
For her who, ere her summer faded,
Has sunk into a breathless sleep.

ODE
[1] *excess* editorial conjecture, necessary to fill a gap
left in the MS.

that *my* difficulty came, as from a sense of the indomitableness of the spirit within me. I used to brood over the stories of Enoch and Elijah, and almost to persuade myself that, whatever might become of others, I should be translated in something of the same way to heaven.

With a feeling congenial to this, I was often unable to think of external things as having external existence, and I communed with all that I saw as something not apart from, but inherent in, my own immaterial nature. Many times while going to school have I grasped at a wall or tree to recall myself from this abyss of idealism to the reality. At that time I was afraid of such processes. In later periods of life I have deplored (as we have all reason to do) a subjugation of an opposite character, and have rejoiced over the remembrances, as is expressed in the lines, 'obstinate questionings', etc. To that dreamlike vividness and splendour which invest objects of sight in childhood, everyone (I believe, if he would look back) could bear testimony, and I need not dwell upon it here.

But having in the poem regarded it as presumptive evidence of a prior state of existence, I think it right to protest against a conclusion which has given pain to some good and pious persons that I meant to inculcate such a belief. It is far too shadowy a notion to be recommended to faith as more than an element in our instincts of immortality. But let us bear in mind that, though the idea is not advanced in revelation, there is nothing there to contradict it, and the fall of man presents an analogy in its favour. Accordingly, a pre-existent state has entered into the popular creeds of many nations, and among all persons acquainted with classic literature is known as an ingredient in Platonic philosophy.

Archimedes said that he could move the world if he had a point whereon to rest his machine. Who has not felt the same aspirations as regards the world of his own mind? Having to wield some of its elements when I was impelled to write this poem on the immortality of the soul, I took hold of the notion of pre-existence as having sufficient foundation in humanity for authorizing me to make for my purpose the best use of it I could as a poet.

ON 'WE ARE SEVEN' (EXTRACT)

In reference to this poem, I will here mention one of the most remarkable facts in my own poetic history and that of Mr Coleridge.

In the spring of the year 1798,[1] he, my sister and myself started from Alfoxden, pretty late in the afternoon, with a view to visit Lynton and the Valley of Stones near it. And as our united funds were very small, we agreed to defray the expense of the tour by writing a poem to be sent to the new *Monthly Magazine* set up by Phillips the bookseller, and edited by Dr Aikin.[2] Accordingly we set off and proceeded along the Quantock Hills towards Watchet, and in the course of this walk was planned the poem of 'The Ancient Mariner', founded on a dream (as Mr Coleridge said) of his friend Mr Cruikshank.[3] Much the greatest part of the story was Mr Coleridge's invention, but

---

On 'WE ARE SEVEN'
[1] The walking tour took place not in spring 1798 but in mid-Nov. 1797.
[2] The *Monthly Magazine*, an influential radical periodical founded in 1796 by Richard Phillips and edited by Dr John Aikin (1747–1822), brother of Mrs Barbauld.

[3] John Cruikshank, land agent to Lord Egmont at Nether Stowey and Coleridge's neighbour there. He was the brother of Ellen Cruikshank, the 'most gentle maid' of Coleridge's 'The Nightingale', 69.

certain parts I myself suggested; for example, some crime was to be committed which should bring upon the Old Navigator (as Coleridge afterwards delighted to call him) the spectral persecution, as a consequence of that crime and his own wanderings.

I had been reading in Shelvocke's *Voyages*[4] a day or two before, that while doubling Cape Horn they frequently saw albatrosses – in that latitude the largest sort of seafowl, some extending their wings 12 or 13 feet. 'Suppose', I said, 'you represent him as having killed one of these birds on entering the South Sea, and that the tutelary spirits of these regions take upon them to avenge the crime?' The incident was thought fit for the purpose, and adopted accordingly. I also suggested the navigation of the ship by the dead men, but do not recollect that I had anything more to do with the scheme of the poem.

The gloss with which it was subsequently accompanied was not thought of by either of us at the time – at least, not a hint of it was given to me – and I have no doubt it was a gratuitous afterthought.[5] We began the composition together on that (to me) memorable evening; I furnished two or three lines at the beginning of the poem, in particular:

> And listened like a three years' child:
> The mariner had his will.

These trifling contributions all but one (which Mr Coleridge has with unnecessary scrupulosity recorded[6]) slipped out of his mind – as they well might. As we endeavoured to proceed conjointly (I speak of the same evening), our respective manners proved so widely different that it would have been quite presumptuous in me to do anything but separate from an undertaking upon which I could only have been a clog.

Sir Walter Scott   (1771–1832)

Scott was one of the most prolific and popular poets and novelists of the age; contemporary critical opinion has come to regard the 'Waverley' novels as his masterpiece. Byron liked them so much that he claimed, in 1821, to have read each one 50 times (Marchand, viii. 13), and in 1812 he told Scott that even the Prince Regent 'preferred you to every bard past and present' (ibid., ii. 182). The poems presented here offer a taste of Scott's verse, some of which was contained in the novels, and the extract from his diary provides valuable insight into his technique.

---

[4]   George Shelvocke, *Voyage Round the World, by the Way of the Great South Sea* (1726); the passage to which Wordsworth refers may be found on pp. 72–3.
[5]   The 1817 text of 'The Ancient Mariner', carries a series of marginal glosses; see pp. 578–95.

[6]   See note to the 1817 text of 'The Ancient Mariner' 227, p. 585.

From The Lay of the Last Minstrel (1805)

CALEDONIA (FROM CANTO SIX)

I

Breathes there the man, with soul so dead,
Who never to himself hath said,
   'This is my own, my native land!' –
Whose heart hath ne'er within him burned
As home his footsteps he hath turned   5
   From wandering on a foreign strand?
If such there breathe, go mark him well;
For him no minstrel raptures swell;
High though his titles, proud his name,
Boundless his wealth as wish can claim;   10
Despite those titles, power and pelf,[1]
The wretch, concentred all in self,
Living, shall forfeit fair renown,
And, doubly dying, shall go down
To the vile dust from whence he sprung,   15
Unwept, unhonoured, and unsung.

II

Oh Caledonia, stern and wild,
Meet nurse for a poetic child!
Land of brown heath and shaggy wood,
Land of the mountain and the flood,   20
Land of my sires! What mortal hand
Can e'er untie the filial band
That knits me to thy rugged strand?
Still as I view each well-known scene,
Think what is now, and what hath been,   25
Seems as, to me, of all bereft,
Sole friends, thy woods and streams were left;
And thus I love them better still,
Even in extremity of ill.
By Yarrow's stream still let me stray,   30
Though none should guide my feeble way;
Still feel the breeze down Ettrick break
Although it chill my withered cheek;
Though there, forgotten and alone,
The bard may draw his parting groan.   35

CALEDONIA
[1] *pelf* booty, plunder.

From Marmion (1808)

LOCHINVAR (FROM CANTO FIVE)

Oh, young Lochinvar is come out of the west,
Through all the wide Border[1] his steed was the best;
And save his good broadsword he weapons had none,
He rode all unarmed, and he rode all alone.
So faithful in love, so dauntless in war,   5
There never was knight like the young Lochinvar.

He stayed not for brake and he stopped not for stone,
He swam the Esk river where ford there was none;
But ere he alighted at Netherby gate,
The bride had consented, the gallant came late: 10
For a laggard in love and a dastard in war
Was to wed the fair Ellen of brave Lochinvar.

So boldly he entered the Netherby Hall
Among bridesmen and kinsmen and brothers and all;
Then spoke the bride's father, his hand on his sword   15
(For the poor craven bridegroom said never a word),
'Oh come ye in peace here, or come ye in war,
Or to dance at our bridal, young Lord Lochinvar?'

'I long wooed your daughter, my suit you denied;
Love swells like the Solway but ebbs like its tide.   20
And now am I come, with this lost love of mine
To lead but one measure, drink one cup of wine.
There are maidens in Scotland more lovely by far
That would gladly be bride to the young Lochinvar.'

The bride kissed the goblet; the knight took it up,   25
He quaffed off the wine and he threw down the cup.
She looked down to blush and she looked up to sigh
With a smile on her lips and a tear in her eye.
He took her soft hand ere her mother could bar,
'Now tread we a measure!' said young Lochinvar.   30

So stately his form and so lovely her face
That never a hall such a galliard[2] did grace;
While her mother did fret and her father did fume
And the bridegroom stood dangling his bonnet and plume,
And the bride-maidens whispered, ''Twere better by far   35
To have matched our fair cousin with young Lochinvar.'

LOCHINVAR
[1] *Border* the region on either side of the English and
Scottish border.

[2] *galliard* quick, lively dance in triple time.

One touch to her hand and one word in her ear;
When they reached the hall-door, and the charger stood near –
So light to the croupe[3] the fair lady he swung,
So light to the saddle before her he sprung!   40
'She is won! We are gone over bank, bush, and scaur![4]
They'll have fleet steeds that follow,' quoth young Lochinvar.

There was mounting 'mong Graemes of the Netherby clan;
Forsters, Fenwicks, and Musgraves, they rode and they ran;
There was racing and chasing on Cannobie Lee   45
But the lost bride of Netherby ne'er did they see.
So daring in love and so dauntless in war,
Have ye e'er heard of gallant like young Lochinvar?

From Tales of My Landlord (1819); *The Bride of Lammermoor*

LUCY ASHTON'S SONG

Look not thou on beauty's charming,
Sit thou still when kings are arming,
Taste not when the wine-cup glistens,
Speak not when the people listens,
Stop thine ear against the singer,
From the red gold keep thy finger;
Vacant heart, and hand, and eye,
Easy live and quiet die.

From J. G. Lockhart, Memoirs of the Life of Scott (1837–8)

SCOTT'S DIARY: 12 FEBRUARY 1826

Having ended the second volume of *Woodstock* last night, I had to begin the third this morning.[1] Now I have not the slightest idea how the story is to be wound up to a catastrophe. I am just in the same case as I used to be when I lost myself in former days in some country to which I was a stranger. I always pushed for the pleasantest route, and either found or made it the nearest. It is the same in writing. I never could lay down a plan – or, having laid it down, I never could adhere to it. The action of composition always extended some passages, and abridged or omitted others; and personages were rendered important or insignificant, not according to their agency in the original conception of the piece, but according to the success (or otherwise) with which I was able to bring them out. I only tried to make that which I was actually writing diverting and interesting, leaving the rest to fate.

---

3 *croupe* hind end of the saddle.
4 *scaur* ridge of a hill.

SCOTT'S DIARY
1 Scott's novel *Woodstock* was published in 3 vols in 1826.

I have been often amused with the critics distinguishing some passages as particularly laboured, when the pen passed over the whole as fast as it could move, and the eye never again saw them, except in proof. Verse I write twice, and sometimes three times over. This hab nab[2] at a venture is a perilous style, I grant, but I cannot help it. When I strain my mind to ideas which are purely imaginative (for argument is a different thing), it seems to me that the sun leaves the landscape – that I think away the whole vivacity of my original conception, and that the results are cold, tame and spiritless. It is the difference between a written oration and one bursting from the unpremeditated exertions of the speaker which have always something of the air of enthusiasm and inspiration. I would not have young authors imitate my carelessness, however.

James Hogg (1770–1835)

The self-styled 'Ettrick Shepherd' (as he was known) was one of the finest storytellers of the age, both in verse and in prose. His most important novel is The Private Memoirs and Confessions of a Justified Sinner *(1824); 'The Witch of Fife', from* The Queen's Wake *(which made his reputation as a poet), is one of his finest poems, and was one of Wordsworth's favourites (MY, ii. 169). Hogg's prominence in literary circles led to his appearance as a character in* Noctes Ambrosianae, *the humourous conversations serialized in* Blackwood's Edinburgh Magazine; *see pp. 673–5 below.*

From The Queen's Wake (1813)

THE WITCH OF FIFE

'Quhare haif ye been, ye ill womyne,
　　These three lang nightis fra hame?
Quhat garris[1] the sweit drap fra yer brow,
　　Like clotis of the saut sea faem?

It fearis me muckil ye haif seen　　　　　　　　　　5
　　Quhat good man never knew;
It fearis me muckil ye haif been
　　Quhare the grey cock never crew.

But the spell may crack and the brydel breck,
　　Then sherpe yer werde will be;　　　　　　　　10
Ye had better sleipe in yer bed at hame
　　Wi yer deire littil bairnis and me.'

'Sit dune, sit dune, my leile auld man,
　　Sit dune and listin to me;

---

[2] *hab nab* hit or miss.

THE WITCH OF FIFE
[1] *garris* makes.

I'll gar the hayre stand on yer crown   15
   And the cauld sweit blind yer e'e.

But tell nae wordis, my gude auld man,
   Tell never word again;
Or deire shall be yer courtisye,
   And driche and sair yer pain.   20

The first leet-night,[2] quhan the new moon set,
   Quhan all was douffe[3] and mirk,
We saddled ouir naigis wi the moon-fern leif
   And rode fra Kilmerrin kirk.

Some horses ware of the brume-cow[4] framit   25
   And some of the greine bay tree,
But mine was made of ane humloke schaw,[5]
   And a stout stallion was he.

We raide the tod[6] doune on the hill,
   The martin on the law,[7]   30
And we huntyd the hoolet[8] out of brethe,
   And forcit him doune to fa.'

'Quhat guid was that, ye ill womyn?
   Quhat guid was that to thee?
Ye wald better haif bein in yer bed at hame   35
   Wi yer deire littil bairnis and me.'

'And ay we raide and se merrily we raide
   Throw the merkist gloffis[9] of the night,
And we swam the floode and we darnit the woode
   Till we cam to the Lommond height.   40

And quhen we cam to the Lommond height,
   Se lythlye we lychtid doune;
And we drank fra the hornis that never grew,
   The beer that was never browin.

Than up there rase ane wee wee man,   45
   Franethe[10] the moss-grey stane;
His fece was wan like the collifloure,
   For he nouthir had blude nor bane.

---

[2] *leet-night* chosen night.
[3] *douffe* dull.
[4] *brume-cow* broom.
[5] *ane humloke schaw* a small piece of hemlock wood.
[6] *tod* fox.

[7] *law* hill.
[8] *hoolet* owl.
[9] *gloffis* fears.
[10] *Franethe* from beneath.

He set ane reid-pipe till his muthe
  And he playit se bonnilye,   50
Till the grey curlew and the black-cock flew
  To listen his melodye.

It rang se sweet through the green Lommond
  That the nycht-winde lowner[11] blew,
And it soupit[12] alang the Loch Leven   55
  And wakinit the white seamew.

It rang se sweet through the grein Lommond,
  Se sweitly butt and se shill,
That the wezilis laup out of their mouldy holis
  And dancit on the mydnycht hill.   60

The corby-craw[13] cam gledgin[14] near,
  The ern[15] gede veeryng bye,
And the troutis laup[16] out of the Leven Louch,
  Charmit with the melodye.

And ay we dancit on the green Lommond   65
  Till the dawn on the ocean grew –
Ne wonder I was a weary wycht
  Quhan I cam hame to you!'

'Quhat guid, quhat guid, my weird weird wyfe,
  Quhat guid was that to thee?   70
Ye wald better haif bein in yer bed at hame
  Wi yer deire littil bairnis and me.'

'The second nychte quhan the new moon set,
  O'er the roaryng sea we flew;
The cockle-shell our trusty bark,   75
  Our sailis of the grein sea-rue.[17]

And the bauls windis blew, and the fire flauchtis[18] flew,
  And the sea ran to the skie;
And the thunner it growlit and the sea-dogs[19] howlit
  As we gaed scouryng bye.   80

And ay we mountit the sea-green hillis,
  Quhill we brushit thro' the cludis of the hevin;

---

[11] *lowner* more gently.
[12] *soupit* swept.
[13] *corby-craw* carrion crow.
[14] *gledgin* looking slyly at.
[15] *ern* eagle.
[16] *laup* leaped.
[17] *sea-rue* shrub that grows on sea shores.
[18] *flauchtis* flies.
[19] *sea-dogs* seals.

Than sousit[20] dounright like the stern-shot light,
    Fra the liftis[21] blue casement driven.

But our taickil stood and our bark was good,   85
    And se pang[22] was our pearily[23] prowe;
Quhan we culdna speil[24] the brow of the wavis,
    We needilit them throu belowe.

As fast as the hail, as fast as the gale,
    As fast as the midnycht leme,[25]   90
We borit the breiste of the burstyng swale,[26]
    Or fluffit i' the flotyng faem.

And quhan to the Norraway shore we wan,
    We muntyd our steedis of the wynd,
And we splashit the floode, and we darnit the woode,   95
    And we left the shouir behynde.

Fleet is the roe on the green Lommond
    And swift is the couryng grew;[27]
The reindeir dun[28] can eithly[29] run
    Quhan the houndis and the hornis pursue.   100

But nowther the roe nor the reindeir dun,
    The hinde nor the couryng grew,
Culde fly owr muntaine, muir and dale,
    As owr braw[30] steedis they flew.

The dales war deep, and the Doffrinis steep,[31]   105
    And we rase to the skyis ee-bree;
Quhite, quhite was ouir rode, that was never trode,
    Owr the snawis of eternity!

And quhan we cam to the Lapland lone[32]
    The fairies war all in array,   110
For all the genii of the north
    War keepyng their holeday.

The warlock men and the weerd wemyng
    And the fays of the wood and the steep,

---

[20] *sousit* fell.
[21] *liftis* sky's.
[22] *pang* strong.
[23] *pearily* tiny.
[24] *speil* climb.
[25] *leme* gleam.
[26] *swale* swelling wave.

[27] *the couryng grew* the cowering greyhound.
[28] *dun* brown.
[29] *eithly* easily.
[30] *braw* handsome.
[31] *the Doffrinis steep* the Dovre Fjeld mountain range, Norway.
[32] *lone* common.

And the phantom hunteris all war there,   115
    And the mermaidis of the deep.

And they washit us all with the witch-water
    Distillit fra the moorland dew,
Quhill our beauty blumit like the Lapland rose,
    That wylde in the foreste grew.'   120

'Ye lee, ye lee, ye ill womyne,
    Se loud as I heir ye lee!
For the warst-faurd[33] wyfe on the shoris of Fife
    Is cumlye comparet wi thee.'

'Then the mermaidis sang and the woodlandis rang,   125
    Se sweetly swellit the quire;
On every cliff a herpe they hang,
    On every tree a lyre.

And ay they sang and the woodlandis rang,
    And we drank and we drank se deep;   130
Then soft in the armis of the warlock men,
    We laid us dune to sleep.'

'Away, away, ye ill womyne,
    An ill deide met ye dee!
Quhan ye hae pruvit se false to yer God   135
    Ye can never pruve trew to me.'

'And there we lernit fra the fairy foke
    And fra our master true,
The wordis that can beire us throu the air,
    And lokkis and baris undo.   140

Last nycht we met at Maisry's cot,
    Richt weil the wordis we knew;
And we set a foot on the black cruik-shell,[34]
    And out at the lum[35] we flew.

And we flew owr hill and we flew owr dale   145
    And we flew owr firth and sea,
Until we cam to merry Carlisle
    Quhar we lightit on the lea.

We gaed to the vault beyound the towir
    Quhar we enterit free as ayr;   150

---

[33] *warst-faurd* least favoured.   [35] *lum* chimney-top.
[34] *cruik-shell* hook for hanging a pot over a fire.

And we drank and we drank of the bishopis wine
    Quhill we culde drynk ne mair.'

'Gin[36] that be trew, my gude auld wyfe,
    Whilk thou hast tauld to me,
Betide my death, betide my lyfe,   155
    I'll beire thee companye.

Neist tyme ye gaung to merry Carlisle
    To drynk of the blude-reid wine –
Beshrew my heart, I'll fly with thee,
    If the diel shulde fly behynde.'   160

'Ah, littil do ye ken, my silly auld man,
    The daingeris we maun dree;[37]
Last nichte we drank of the bishopis wyne
    Quhill near near taen war we.

Afore we wan to the sandy ford   165
    The gorcockis[38] nichering flew;
The lofty crest of Ettrick Pen[39]
    Was wavit about with blew,
And flichtering throu the air we fand
    The chill chill mornyng dew.   170

As we flew owr the hillis of Braid,[40]
    The sun rase fair and clear;
There gurly[41] James and his baronis braw
    War out to hunt the deere.

Their bowis they drew, their arrowis flew,   175
    And peircit the ayr with speede,
Quhill purpil fell the mornyng dew
    With witch-blude rank and reide.

Littil do ye ken, my silly auld man,
    The dangeris we maun dree;   180
Ne wonder I am a weary wycht
    Quhan I come hame to thee.'

'But tell me the *word*, my gude auld wyfe,
    Come tell it me speedilye;

---

[36] *Gin* If.
[37] *dree* endure.
[38] *gorcockis* moorcocks.
[39] Ettrick Pen, a mountain in the Scottish Borders
near Moffat.
[40] The Braid Hills south of Edinburgh.
[41] *gurly James* deceitful James IV, King of Scotland
(1488–1513).

For I lang to drink of the gude reide wyne,   185
   And to wyng the ayr with thee.

Yer hellish horse I wilna ryde,
   Nor sail the seas in the wynd;
But I can flee as well as thee
   And I'll drynk quhill ye be blynd.'   190

'O fy! O fy! my leil auld man,
   That word I darena tell;
It wald turn this warld all upside down,
   And make it warse than hell,

For all the lasses in the land   195
   Wald munt the wynd and fly;
And the men wald doff their doublets syde
   And after them wald ply.'

But the auld gudeman was ane cunnyng auld man,
   And ane cunnyng auld man was he;   200
And he watchit and he watchit for mony a night
   The witches' flychte to see.

Ane nychte he darnit[42] in Maisry's cot,
   The fearless haggs came in;
And he heard the word of awsome weird,
   And he saw their deedis of synn.   205

Then ane by ane they said that word
   As fast to the fire they drew,
Then set a foot on the black cruik-shell
   And out at the lum they flew.   210

The auld gude-man cam fra his hole
   With feire and muckil dreide,
But yet he culdna think to rue,
   For the wyne came in his head.

He set his foot in the black cruik-shell   215
   With ane fixit and ane wawlyng[43] ee,
And he said the word that I darena say
   And out at the lum flew he.

The witches skalit the moonbeam pale,
   Deep groanit the trembling wynde;   220

---

[42] *darnit* hid.   [43] *wawlyng* wildly gazing.

But they never wist till our auld gudeman
    Was hoveryng them behynde.

They flew to the vaultis of merry Carlisle
    Quhair they enterit free as ayr,
And they drank and they drank of the byshopis wyne   225
    Quhill they culde drynk ne mair.

The auld gudeman he grew se crouse,[44]
    He dancit on the mouldy ground,
And he sang the bonniest sangis of Fife,
    And he tuzzlit the kerlyngs[45] round.   230

And ay he percit the tither butt,
    And he suckit and he suckit se lang,
Quhill his een they closit, and his voice grew low,
    And his tongue wold hardly gang.

The kerlyngs drank of the bishopis wyne   235
    Quhill they scentit the mornyng wynde,
Then clove again the yeilding ayr
    And left the auld man behynde.

And ay he slepit on the damp damp floor,
    He slepit and he snorit amain;   240
He never dremit he was far fra hame,
    Or that the auld wyvis war gane.

And ay he slepit on the damp damp floor
    Quhill past the midday highte,
Quhan wakenit by five rough Englishmen   245
    That trailit him to the lychte.

'Now quha are ye, ye silly auld man,
    That sleepis se sound and se weil?
Or how gat ye into the bishopis vault
    Throu lokkis and barris of steel?'   250

The auld gudeman he tryit to speak
    But ane word he culdna fynde;
He tryit to think but his head whirlit round,
    And ane thing he culdna mynde;
'I cam fra Fife', the auld man cryit,   255
    'And I cam on the midnycht wynde.'

---

[44] *crouse* cheerful.
[45] *he tuzzlit the kerlyngs* he roughly hugged the old women.

They nickit the auld man and they prickit[46] the auld man,
　　And they yerkit his limbis with twine,
Quhill the reid blude ran in his hose and shoon,
　　But some cryit it was wyne.　　　　　　　　　　　　　260

They lickit the auld man and they prickit the auld man,
　　And they tyit him till ane stone;
And they set ane bele-fire[47] him about,
　　And they burnit him skin and bone.

Now wae be to the puir auld man　　　　　　　　　　265
　　That ever he saw the day!
And wae be to all the ill wemyng
　　That lead puir men astray!

Let never ane auld man after this
　　To lawless greide inclyne;　　　　　　　　　　　　270
Let never an auld man after this
　　Rin post to the diel for wyne.

Barbara Hoole　(1770–1844)

Prolific poet and novelist, known mainly for her novel The Clergyman's Widow *(1812), which sold 17,000 copies. 'Cumberland Rocks' was published in 1805, and shows her to be a poet of sensibility.*

From Poems (1805)

CUMBERLAND ROCKS

Scenes of magnificence! your powerful charms
That burst stupendous on mine aching sight,
Now thrill the trembling vein with wild alarms,
Now wrap th' exulting soul in high delight!

From Alpine mountains gush the maddening streams　　5
That sweep with snow-tipped wave the verdant vale,
Catch with pellucid drops light's quivering beams,
The gay foam sparkling in the gusty gale;

While on the hoary rock, whose rugged breast
Hath braved the pelting storms of many a year,　　10
Eve's brilliant sunbeams sink in lovely rest
And tinge the purple clouds that linger near.

---

[46] *nickit ... prickit* hit ... cut.　　　　　[47] *bele-fire* large fire.

Sweet scenes of wonder, scenes of beauty – cease!
Ye charm the eye, but can your powers impart
The long-lost vision of returning peace,   15
The long-lost raptures of a widowed heart?

Ah no! in vain your mighty rocks arise,
Your soft streams murmur in the pensive ear;
Like them my drooping heart more deeply sighs,
Like them dissolves in many an anxious tear.   20

Dorothy Wordsworth (1771–1855)

Although space permits the inclusion of only a small number of entries, Dorothy Wordsworth's journals have in recent years, particularly through the work of such scholars as Pamela Woof, become increasingly studied in their own right, for their detailed observations of the natural world and sensitivity to the hardships of the poor. Dorothy was also an accomplished poet, and some of her best verses are included here, all of them edited from her Commonplace Book at the Wordsworth Library, Grasmere.

From The Grasmere Journals

Wednesday 3 September 1800.   Coleridge, William and John[1] went from home to go upon Helvellyn with Mr Simpson. They set out after breakfast. I accompanied them up near the blacksmith's – a fine, coolish morning. I ironed till half past three, now very hot. I then went to a funeral at John Dawson's[2] – about ten men and four women. Bread, cheese and ale; they talked sensibly and cheerfully about common things. The dead person, 56 years of age, buried by the parish; the coffin was neatly lettered and painted black and covered with a decent cloth. They set the corpse down at the door and, while we stood within the threshold, the men with their hats off sang with decent and solemn countenances a verse of a funeral psalm. The corpse was then borne down the hill and they sang till they had got past the Town End.

I was affected to tears while we stood in the house, the coffin lying before me. There were no near kindred, no children. When we got out of the dark house, the sun was shining and the prospect looked so divinely beautiful as I never saw it. It seemed more sacred than I had ever seen it, and yet more allied to human life. The green fields, neighbours of the churchyard, were green as possible and, with the brightness of the sunshine, looked quite gay. I thought she was going to a quiet spot and I could not help weeping very much.

When we came to the bridge, they began to sing again and stopped during four lines before they entered the churchyard. The priest met us – he did not look as a man ought

---

THE GRASMERE JOURNALS 3 SEPTEMBER 1800.
[1] John Wordsworth (1773–1805), brother of William and Dorothy, a sea-captain, visited Dove Cottage, Jan.–Sept. 1800.

[2] John Dawson's farm was on the Rydal road at the top of the hill behind Dove Cottage. The funeral was that of a pauper, Susan Shacklock.

to do on such an occasion (I had seen him half-drunk the day before in a pothouse[3]). Before we came with the corpse one of the company observed he wondered what sort of cue[4] 'our parson would be in'? N.B. It was the day after the fair. I had not finished ironing till 7 o'clock. The wind was now high and I did not walk. Writing my journal now at 8 o'clock. William and John came home at 10 o'clock.

Friday 3 October 1800 (extract)   When William and I returned from accompanying Jones, we met an old man almost double.[1] He had on a coat thrown over his shoulders above his waistcoat and coat. Under this he carried a bundle and had an apron on and a nightcap. His face was interesting. He had dark eyes and a long nose (John, who afterwards met him at Wythburn, took him for a Jew). He was of Scotch parents but had been born in the army. He had had a wife, 'and a good woman, and it pleased God to bless us with ten children'; all these were dead but one of whom he had not heard for many years, a sailor. His trade was to gather leeches, but now leeches are scarce and he had not strength for it. He lived by begging and was making his way to Carlisle where he should buy a few godly books to sell. He said leeches were very scarce partly owing to this dry season, but many years they have been scarce. He supposed it owing to their being much sought after, that they did not breed fast, and were of slow growth. Leeches were formerly 2s. 6d. per 100; they are now 30s. He had been hurt in driving a cart: his leg broke, his body driven over, his skull fractured. He felt no pain till he recovered from his first insensibility; it was then 'late in the evening, when the light was just going away'.

Thursday 15 April 1802.[1]   It was a threatening misty morning, but mild. We set off after dinner from Eusemere; Mrs Clarkson went a short way with us but turned back. The wind was furious and we thought we must have returned. We first rested in the large boathouse, then under a furze-bush opposite Mr Clarkson's; saw the plough going in the field. The wind seized our breath, the lake was rough. There was a boat by itself floating in the middle of the bay below Water Millock; we rested again in the Water Millock lane. The hawthorns are black and green, the birches here and there greenish but there is yet more of purple to be seen on the twigs. We got over into a field to avoid some cows – people working, a few primroses by the roadside, woodsorrel flowers, the anemone, scentless violets, strawberries, and that starry yellow flower which Mrs Clarkson calls pilewort.[2]

When we were in the woods beyond Gowbarrow Park we saw a few daffodils close to the waterside. We fancied that the lake had floated the seeds ashore and that the little colony had so sprung up. But as we went along there were more and yet more, and at last, under the boughs of the trees, we saw that there was a long belt of them along the shore, about the breadth of a country turnpike road. I never saw daffodils so beautiful. They grew among the mossy stones, about and about them; some rested their heads upon these stones as on a pillow for weariness, and the rest tossed and reeled and danced, and seemed as if they verily laughed with the wind that blew upon

---

[3] *pothouse* ale-house, tavern.
[4] *cue* humour, disposition.
3 OCTOBER 1800
[1] This entry was written a week after the encounter had taken place; it is a source for Wordsworth's

'Resolution and Independence', composed 18 months later.
15 APRIL 1802
[1] This entry is a source for Wordsworth's 'Daffodils'.
[2] *pilewort* the lesser celandine.

them over the lake. They looked so gay – ever-glancing, ever-changing. This wind blew directly over the lake to them. There was, here and there, a little knot, and a few stragglers a few yards higher up – but they were so few as not to disturb the simplicity and unity and life of that one busy highway. We rested again and again.

The bays were stormy, and we heard the waves at different distances and in the middle of the water like the sea. Rain came on; we were wet when we reached Luff's but we called in. Luckily all was cheerless and gloomy, so we faced the storm – we *must* have been wet if we had waited; put on dry clothes at Dobson's. I was very kindly treated by a young woman, the landlady looked sour but it is her way. She gave us a goodish supper, excellent ham and potatoes. We paid 7s. when we came away. William was sitting by a bright fire when I came downstairs; he soon made his way to the library piled up in a corner of the window. He brought out a volume of Enfield's *Speaker*, another miscellany, and an odd volume of Congreve's plays. We had a glass of warm rum and water; we enjoyed ourselves and wished for Mary. It rained and blew when we went to bed. N.B. Deer in Gowbarrow Park like to skeletons.

Thursday 29 April 1802   A beautiful morning. The sun shone and all was pleasant. We sent off our parcel to Coleridge by the wagon. Mr Simpson heard the cuckoo today. Before we went out, after I had written down 'The Tinker', which William finished this morning, Luff called. He was very lame, limped into the kitchen (he came on a little pony).

We then went to John's Grove, sat a while at first. Afterwards William lay and I lay in the trench under the fence – he with his eyes shut and listening to the waterfalls and the birds. There was no one waterfall above another – it was a sound of waters in the air, the voice of the air. William heard me breathing and rustling now and then, but we both lay still and unseen by one another. He thought that it would be as sweet thus to lie so in the grave, to hear the *peaceful* sounds of the earth and just to know that one's dear friends were near.[1] The lake was still; there was a boat out. Silver How reflected with delicate purple and yellowish hues as I have seen [in] spar. Lambs on the island and running races together by the half-dozen in the round field near us. The copses green*ish*, hawthorn green.

Came home to dinner, then went to Mr Simpson. We rested a long time under a wall. Sheep and lambs were in the field – cottages smoking. As I lay down on the grass, I observed the glittering silver line on the ridges of the backs of the sheep, owing to their situation respecting the sun, which made them look beautiful but with something of strangeness, like animals of another kind – as if belonging to a more splendid world. Met old Mr Simpson at the door; Mrs Simpson poorly. I got mullens and pansies. I was sick and ill and obliged to come home soon. We went to bed immediately – I slept upstairs. The air coldish where it was felt somewhat frosty.

4 October 1802   On Monday 4 October 1802, my brother William was married to Mary Hutchinson. I slept a good deal of the night and rose fresh and well in the morning. At a little after 8 o'clock I saw them go down the avenue towards the church.[1] William

---

29 APRIL 1802
[1]   These remarks provide a context for 'These chairs they have no words to utter', composed a week before, pp. 269–70 above.

4 OCTOBER 1802
[1]   Wordsworth was married at Brompton Church, a mile or so down the road from Gallow Hill, where he was staying with the Hutchinson family.

had parted from me upstairs. I gave him the wedding ring – with how deep a blessing! I took it from my forefinger where I had worn it the whole of the night before; he slipped it again onto my finger and blessed me fervently.

When they were absent, my dear little Sara[2] prepared the breakfast. I kept myself as quiet as I could, but when I saw the two men running up the walk, coming to tell us it was over, I could stand it no longer and threw myself on the bed where I lay in stillness, neither hearing or seeing anything till Sara came upstairs to me and said, 'They are coming'. This forced me from the bed where I lay, and I moved I knew not how straightforward, faster than my strength could carry me, till I met my beloved William and fell upon his bosom. He and John Hutchinson led me to the house and there I stayed to welcome my dear Mary. As soon as we had breakfasted we departed. It rained when we set off. Poor Mary was much agitated when she parted from her brothers and sisters and her home.

A Cottage in Grasmere Vale (composed c.1805)

Peaceful our valley, fair and green,
And beautiful her cottages,
Each in its nook, its sheltered hold,
Or guarded by its tuft of trees –

Many and beautiful they are,   5
But there is *one* that I love best,
A lowly shed in truth it is,
A brother of the rest.

Yet when I sit on rock or hill,
Down looking on the valley fair,   10
That cottage with its clustering trees
Summons my heart – it settles there.

Others there are whose small domain
Of fertile fields and hedgerows green
Might more entice a wanderer's mind   15
To wish that *there* his home had been.

Such wish be his! I blame him not,
My fancy is unfettered, wild!
I love that house because it is
The very mountains' child.   20

Fields hath it of its own, green fields,
But they are craggy, steep and bare;
Their fence is of the mountain stone
And moss and lichen flourish there.

---

[2]   Sara Hutchinson.

And when the storm comes from the north   25
It lingers near that pastoral spot,
And piping through the mossy walls,
It seems delighted with its lot.

And let it take its own delight,
And let it range the pastures bare;   30
Until it reach that group of trees
It may not enter there.

A green unfading grove it is,
Skirted with many a lesser tree –
Hazel and holly, beech and oak –   35
A bright and flourishing company!

Precious the shelter of those trees,
They screen the cottage that I love;
The sunshine pierces to the roof
And the tall pine-trees tower above.   40

After-recollection at Sight of the Same Cottage

When first I saw that dear abode
It was a lovely winter's day;
After a night of perilous storm
The west wind ruled with gentle sway –

A day so mild it might have been   5
The first day of the gladsome spring;
The robins warbled, and I heard
One solitary throstle sing.

A Winter's Ramble in Grasmere Vale

A stranger, Grasmere, in thy vale,
All faces then to me unknown,
I left my sole companion-friend
To wander out alone.

Lured by a little winding path,   5
Quickly I left the public road,
A smooth and tempting path it was,
By sheep and shepherds trod.

Eastward, towards the lofty hills
That pathway led me on   10

Until I reached a stately rock
With velvet moss o'ergrown.

With russet oak and tufts of fern
Its top was richly garlanded,
Its sides adorned with eglantine   15
Bedropped with hips of glossy red.

There, too, in many a sheltered chink
The foxglove's broad leaves flourished fair,
And silver birch whose purple twigs
Bend to the softest breathing air.   20

Beneath that rock my course I stayed,
And, looking to its summit high,
'Thou wear'st', said I, 'a splendid garb –
Here winter keeps his revelry.

Full long a dweller on the plains,   25
I grieved when summer days were gone;
No more I'll grieve, for winter here
Hath pleasure-gardens of his own.

What need of flowers? The splendid moss
Is gayer than an April mead –   30
More rich its hues of varied green,
Orange, and gold, and glowing red.'

Beside that gay and lovely rock
There came with merry voice
A foaming streamlet glancing by –   35
It seemed to say, 'Rejoice!'

My youthful wishes all fulfilled,
Wishes matured by thoughtful choice,
I stood an inmate of this vale –
How *could* I but rejoice?   40

A Sketch (composed by 1826)

There is one cottage in our dale,
In naught distinguished from the rest,
Save by a tuft of flourishing trees,
The shelter of that little nest.

The public road through Grasmere vale   5
Winds close beside that cottage small,

And there 'tis hidden by the trees
That overhang the orchard wall.

You lose it there – its serpent line
Is lost in that close household grove;   10
A moment lost – and then it mounts
The craggy hills above.

Floating Island at Hawkshead: An Incident in the Schemes of Nature (composed during the 1820s)[1]

Harmonious powers with nature work
On sky, earth, river, lake and sea;
Sunshine and storm, whirlwind and breeze,
All in one duteous task agree.

Once did I see a slip of earth   5
By throbbing waves long undermined,
Loosed from its hold – *how* no one knew,
But all might see it float, obedient to the wind;

Might see it from the verdant shore
Dissevered float upon the lake,   10
Float with its crest of trees adorned
On which the warbling birds their pastime take.

Food, shelter, safety, there they find;
There berries ripen, flowerets bloom;
There insects live their lives and die –   15
A peopled *world* it is, in size a tiny room.

And thus through many seasons' space
This little island may survive,
But nature (though we mark her not)
Will take away, may cease to give.   20

Perchance when you are wandering forth
Upon some vacant sunny day
Without an object, hope, or fear,
Thither your eyes may turn – the isle is passed away.

Buried beneath the glittering lake,   25
Its place no longer to be found,

FLOATING ISLAND AT HAWKSHEAD: AN INCIDENT IN THE
SCHEMES OF NATURE
[1] As Wordsworth mentions in his *Guide through the District of the Lakes* (1835), 'on one of the pools near the lake of Esthwaite may sometimes be seen a mossy islet, with trees upon it, shifting about before the wind' (Owen and Smyser, ii. 184).

Yet the lost fragments shall remain
To fertilize some other ground.

Thoughts on my Sickbed (composed *c*.1831)

And has the remnant of my life
Been pilfered of this sunny spring?
And have its own prelusive sounds
Touched in my heart no echoing string?

Ah, say not so! The hidden life,   5
Couchant within this feeble frame,
Hath been enriched by kindred gifts
That undesired, unsought-for, came

With joyful heart in youthful days,
When fresh each season in its round   10
I welcomed the earliest celandine
Glittering upon the mossy ground.

With busy eyes I pierced the lane
In quest of known and unknown things;
The primrose a lamp on its fortress rock,   15
The silent butterfly spreading its wings,

The violet betrayed by its noiseless breath,
The daffodil dancing in the breeze,
The carolling thrush on his naked perch,
Towering above the budding trees.   20

Our cottage-hearth no longer our home,
Companions of nature were we;
The stirring, the still, the loquacious, the mute –
To all we gave our sympathy.

Yet never in those careless days   25
When springtime in rock, field, or bower
Was but a fountain of earthly hope
A promise of fruits and the *splendid* flower –

No! – then I never felt a bliss
That might with *that* compare,   30
Which, piercing to my couch of rest,
Came on the vernal air.

When loving friends an offering brought,
The first flowers of the year,

Culled from the precincts of our home,   35
From nooks to memory dear,

With some sad thoughts the work was done,
Unprompted and unbidden,
But joy it brought to my *hidden* life,
To consciousness no longer hidden.   40

I felt a power unfelt before,
Controlling weakness, languor, pain;
It bore me to the terrace-walk,
I trod the hills again.

No prisoner in this lonely room,   45
I *saw* the green banks of the Wye,
Recalling thy prophetic words –
Bard, brother, friend from infancy!

No need of motion or of strength
Or even the breathing air,   50
I thought of nature's loveliest scenes,
And with memory I was there.

When Shall I Tread Your Garden Path (composed 11 November 1835)

When shall I tread your garden path
Or climb your sheltering hill?
When shall I wander, free as air,
And track the foaming rill?

A prisoner on my pillowed couch,   5
Five years in feebleness I've lain –
Oh shall I e'er with vigorous step
Travel the hills again?

Samuel Taylor Coleridge (1772–1834)

Besides 'The Ancient Mariner', 'Kubla Khan', and 'Christabel', the reader will find all of Coleridge's 'conversation' poems below. In addition, there are complete texts of the 'Letter to Sara Hutchinson', 'The Day-Dream', and 'To William Wordsworth', edited from manuscript. Among his early works, 'To the River Otter' extends the tradition of the nativity sonnet in a manner that anticipates Wordsworth's spots of time (Thirteen-Book Prelude, xi. 258ff.). In 'The Eolian Harp', Coleridge hopes that humanity might be spiritually awakened and harmonized by a pantheistic perception of God. 'Religious Musings' is important as a manifesto for the convictions that later influenced Wordsworth; Lamb regarded the lines selected from it as 'without rival in the whole compass of my poetical reading' (Marrs, i. 95). 'Frost at Midnight' develops the manner of the 'conversation' poem under the influence of Cowper's 'The Winter's Evening', from The Task *(pp. 9–11), to produce a work of intense self-analysis. 'France: An Ode', with which it was published in 1798, was written to protest against the French invasion of republican Switzerland in January. As the year wore on, fears that France might attempt to invade England grew, leading Coleridge to compose 'Fears in Solitude' in April. This selection also presents the best of Coleridge's 1802 poetry, including 'Chamouny; the Hour Before Sunrise. A Hymn' (which inspired Shelley's 'Mont Blanc'), 'The Picture', and the* Morning Post *text of 'Dejection: An Ode'. The poems usually published as 'Limbo' and 'Ne Plus Ultra' are presented here as part of 'On Donne's First Poem', which is how they appear in the manuscript from which they were first edited.*

From Sonnets from Various Authors (1796)

SONNET V. TO THE RIVER OTTER (COMPOSED *C.*1793)[1]

Dear native brook, wild streamlet of the west!
  How many various-fated years have passed,
    What blissful and what anguished hours, since last
I skimmed the smooth thin stone along thy breast,
    Numbering its light leaps! Yet so deep impressed   5
    Sink the sweet scenes of childhood, that mine eyes
  I never shut amid the sunny blaze,
    But straight with all their tints thy waters rise,
Thy crossing plank, thy margin's willowy maze,
    And bedded sand that, veined with various dyes,   10
Gleamed through thy bright transparence to the gaze!
    Visions of childhood, oft have ye beguiled
Lone manhood's cares, yet waking fondest sighs –
  Ah, that once more I were a careless child!

From Letter from S. T. Coleridge to George Dyer, 10 March 1795

There is one sentence in your last letter which affected me greatly: 'I feel a degree of languor, etc. etc., and, by seeing and frequently feeling much illiberality, acquire something of misanthropy'! It is melancholy to think that the best of us are liable to be shaped and coloured by surrounding objects – and a demonstrative proof that man was not made to live in great cities![1] Almost all the physical evil in the world depends on the existence of moral evil, and the long-continued contemplation of the latter does not tend to meliorate the human heart. The pleasures which we receive from rural

---

TO THE RIVER OTTER
[1] Coleridge was born at Ottery St Mary in Devon on the River Otter.

From LETTER FROM S. T. COLERIDGE TO GEORGE DYER, 10 March 1795
[1] Dyer lived in London.

beauties are of little consequence compared with the moral effect of these pleasures; beholding constantly the best possible, we at last become ourselves the best possible.[2] In the country, all around us smile good and beauty, and the images of this divine καλοκἀγαθόυ[3] are miniatured on the mind of the beholder as a landscape on a convex mirror.[4] Thomson, in that most lovely poem, *The Castle of Indolence*, says,

> I care not, Fortune, what you me deny –
> You cannot rob me of free nature's grace!
> You cannot shut the windows of the sky
> Through which the morning shows her dewy face;
> You cannot bar my constant feet to rove
> Through wood and vale by living stream at eve ...
>
> (ii. 19–24)

Alas, alas! She *can* deny us all this, and can force us, fettered and handcuffed by our dependencies and wants, to *wish* and *wish* away the bitter little of life in the felon-crowded dungeon of a great city!

God love you, my very dear sir! I would that we could form a pantisocracy[5] in England and that you could be one of us! The finely-fibred heart that, like the statue of Memnon,[6] trembles into melody on the sunbeam touch of benevolence, is most easily jarred into the dissonance of misanthropy. But you will never suffer your feelings to be benumbed by the torpedo touch of that fiend – I know you, and know that you will drink of every mourner's sorrows even while your own cup is trembling over its brink!

From Poems on Various Subjects (1796)

THE EOLIAN HARP (PUBLISHED AS *EFFUSION XXXV. COMPOSED 20 AUGUST 1795, AT CLEVEDON, SOMERSETSHIRE*)

> My pensive Sara,[1] thy soft cheek reclined
> Thus on mine arm, most soothing sweet it is
> To sit beside our cot, our cot o'ergrown
> With white-flowered jasmine and the broad-leaved myrtle
> (Meet emblems they of innocence and love),   5
> And watch the clouds that late were rich with light
> Slow-sad'ning round, and mark the star of eve
> Serenely brilliant (such should wisdom be)
> Shine opposite! How exquisite the scents
> Snatched from yon bean-field! And the world *so* hushed!   10
> The stilly murmur of the distant sea

[2] The principle that love of nature leads to moral improvement was to be one of the main tenets of Wordsworth's projected epic, *The Recluse*.

[3] Nobility and beauty.

[4] Coleridge has in mind the Claude Lorraine Glass, a dark or coloured hand-mirror, used by tourists of the day to concentrate the features of a landscape in subdued tones.

[5] *pantisocracy* Coleridge and Southey wished to go to America and set up an ideal society in which everyone was equal and all possessions were shared.

[6] The statue of Memnon at Thebes in Egypt was said to give forth a musical sound when touched by the dawn.

THE EOLIAN HARP

[1] Coleridge married Sara Fricker, to whom this poem is addressed, 4 Oct. 1795, and they honeymooned at Clevedon in Somerset.

Tells us of silence. And that simplest lute
Placed lengthways in the clasping casement – hark
How by the desultory breeze caressed![2]
Like some coy maid half-yielding to her lover,   15
It pours such sweet upbraidings as must needs
Tempt to repeat the wrong. And now its strings
Boldlier swept, the long sequacious notes
Over delicious surges sink and rise,
Such a soft floating witchery of sound   20
As twilight elfins make when they at eve
Voyage on gentle gales from fairyland,
Where melodies round honey-dropping flowers
Footless and wild, like birds of paradise,
Nor pause nor perch, hov'ring on untamed wing.   25
   And thus, my love, as on the midway slope
Of yonder hill I stretch my limbs at noon,
Whilst through my half-closed eyelids I behold
The sunbeams dance, like diamonds, on the main,
And tranquil muse upon tranquillity,   30
Full many a thought uncalled and undetained,
And many idle flitting fantasies
Traverse my indolent and passive brain –
As wild and various as the random gales
That swell or flutter on this subject lute!   35
And what if all of animated nature
Be but organic harps diversely framed,
That tremble into thought, as o'er them sweeps,
Plastic and vast, one intellectual breeze,
At once the soul of each, and God of all?[3]   40
   But thy more serious eye a mild reproof
Darts, oh beloved woman![4] – nor such thoughts
Dim and unhallowed dost thou not reject,
And biddest me walk humbly with my God.
Meek daughter in the family of Christ,   45
Well hast thou said and holily dispraised
These shapings of the unregenerate mind,

---

[2] The aeolian harp is a stringed instrument placed in front of an open window so as to catch the breeze.
[3] A major pantheist declaration: 'And what if all living things are like individual harps, unified in a spiritual ("intellectual") apprehension of the one God?' An early MS of the poem contains a more detailed and explicit version of lines 36–40:

And what if all of animated life
Be but as instruments diversely framed,
That tremble into thought, while through them breathes
One infinite and intellectual breeze,
And all in diff'rent heights so aptly hung

That murmurs indistinct and bursts sublime,
Shrill discords and most soothing melodies,
Harmonious from Creation's vast consent?
Thus God would be the universal soul,
Mechanized matter as th' organic harps
And each one's tunes be that which each calls 'I'.

[4] Referring to these lines, Lamb told Coleridge that he and his sister enjoyed the 'pleasing picture of Mrs C checking your wild wanderings, which we were so fond of hearing you indulge when among us. It has endeared us more than anything to your good lady, and your own self-reproof that follows delighted us' (Marrs, i. 12).

Bubbles that glitter as they rise and break
On vain philosophy's aye-babbling spring.
For never guiltless may I speak of Him,   50
Th' INCOMPREHENSIBLE! save when with awe
I praise him, and with faith that inly *feels* –
Who with his saving mercies healed me,
A sinful and most miserable man
Wildered and dark, and gave me to possess   55
Peace, and this cot, and thee, heart-honoured maid!

Religious Musings (extract) (composed 1794–6)

There is one Mind, one omnipresent Mind
Omnific. His most holy name is LOVE –   120
Truth of subliming import! with the which
Who feeds and saturates his constant soul,
He from his small particular orbit flies
With blessed outstarting![1] From himself he flies,
Stands in the sun, and with no partial gaze   125
Views all creation, and he loves it all
And blesses it, and calls it very good![2]
This is indeed to dwell with the Most High –
Cherubs and rapture-trembling seraphim
Can press no nearer to th' Almighty's throne.   130
But that we roam unconscious, or with hearts
Unfeeling of our universal Sire,
And that in his vast family no Cain
Injures uninjured (in her best-aimed blow
Victorious murder a blind suicide[3]),   135
Haply for this some younger angel now
Looks down on human nature – and behold!
A sea of blood bestrewed with wrecks where mad
Embattling interests on each other rush
With unhelmed rage!
                        'Tis the sublime of man,   140
Our noontide majesty, to know ourselves
Parts and proportions of one wondrous whole;
This fraternizes[4] man, this constitutes
Our charities and bearings – but 'tis God
Diffused through all that doth make all one whole.   145

RELIGIOUS MUSINGS
[1] Those who recognize the 'one omnipresent Mind' (of which we all partake) may 'outstart' (transcend) themselves.
[2] Cf. Gen. 1: 31. Transcendence of the self leading to love of nature may be found in most of Coleridge's poems, e.g. 'The Ancient Mariner' (1798), 269–79, 'This Lime-Tree Bower my Prison', 44ff.

[3] Because we are united in a common humanity, a well-aimed blow hurts the murderer as much as the victim.
[4] *fraternizes* 'fraternité' was one of the ideals of the French Revolution. Coleridge believes mankind to be united because we are capable of perceiving the shared existence of God.

This the worst superstition: Him except,
Aught to desire,[5] supreme reality,
The plenitude and permanence of bliss!
Oh fiends of superstition! – not that oft
Your pitiless rites have floated with man's blood   150
The skull-piled temple, not for this shall wrath
Thunder against you from the Holy One!
But (whether ye th' unclimbing bigot mock
With secondary gods, or if more pleased
Ye petrify th' imbrothelled atheist's heart[6] –   155
The atheist your worst slave) I o'er some plain
Peopled with death, and to the silent sun
Steaming with tyrant-murdered multitudes,
Or where mid groans and shrieks loud-laughing trade[7]
More hideous packs his bales of living anguish –   160
I will raise up a mourning, oh ye fiends,
And curse your spells that film the eye of faith:
Hiding the present God, whose presence lost,
The moral world's cohesion, we become
An anarchy of spirits! Toy-bewitched,   165
Made blind by lusts, disherited of soul
No common centre man, no common sire
Knoweth! A sordid solitary thing,
Mid countless brethren with a lonely heart,
Through courts and cities the smooth savage roams   170
Feeling himself, his own low self the whole,
When he by sacred sympathy might make
The whole one self! Self, that no alien knows!
Self, far diffused as fancy's wing can travel!
Self, spreading still, oblivious of its own,   175
Yet all of all possessing! This is faith!
This the Messiah's destined victory!

From Poems (1797)

REFLECTIONS ON HAVING LEFT A PLACE OF RETIREMENT (FIRST
PUBLISHED AS *REFLECTIONS ON ENTERING INTO ACTIVE LIFE. A POEM
WHICH AFFECTS NOT TO BE POETRY*; COMPOSED C.FEB. 1796)

Sermoni propriora.
(Horace, *Satires*, I. iv. 42)

Low was our pretty cot; our tallest rose
Peeped at the chamber-window. We could hear

---

[5]   The worst superstition is to desire anything but Him.   [7]   *trade* the slave-trade.
[6]   *th' imbrothelled atheist's heart* for Thelwall's view of
this phrase, see p. 149 above.

At silent noon, and eve, and early morn,
The sea's faint murmur. In the open air
Our myrtles blossomed, and across the porch 5
Thick jasmines twined; the little landscape round
Was green and woody and refreshed the eye.
It was a spot which you might aptly call
The Valley of Seclusion. Once I saw
(Hallowing his sabbath-day by quietness) 10
A wealthy son of commerce saunter by,
Bristowa's[1] citizen; methought it calmed
His thirst of idle gold, and made him muse
With wiser feelings – for he paused and looked
With a pleased sadness, and gazed all around, 15
Then eyed our cottage, and gazed round again,
And sighed, and said it was a blessed place.
And we *were* blessed. Oft with patient ear,
Long-listening to the viewless skylark's note
(Viewless, or haply for a moment seen 20
Gleaming on sunny wing), in whispered tones
I've said to my beloved, 'Such, sweet girl,
The inobtrusive song of happiness,
Unearthly minstrelsy – then only heard
When the soul seeks to hear, when all is hushed 25
And the heart listens!'
⠀⠀⠀⠀⠀⠀⠀⠀⠀But the time when first
From that low dell, steep up the stony mount
I climbed with perilous toil and reached the top –
Oh, what a goodly scene! *Here* the bleak mount,
The bare bleak mountain speckled thin with sheep; 30
Grey clouds, that shadowing spot the sunny fields;
And river, now with bushy rocks o'erbrowed,
Now winding bright and full with naked banks;
And seats, and lawns, the abbey and the wood,
And cots, and hamlets, and faint city-spire; 35
The channel *there*, the islands and white sails,
Dim coasts, and cloudlike hills, and shoreless ocean –
It seemed like Omnipresence! God, methought,
Had built him there a temple: the whole world
Seemed *imaged* in its vast circumference.[2] 40
No wish profaned my overwhelmed heart –
Blessed hour! It was a luxury – to be!
⠀⠀Ah, quiet dell, dear cot, and mount sublime!
I was constrained to quit you. Was it right,

REFLECTIONS ON HAVING LEFT A PLACE OF RETIREMENT
[1] Bristol's.
[2] This is the first poem by either Coleridge or
Wordsworth to present the ascent of a mountain as a

meeting with divine forces; compare the ascent of
Snowdon, *Prelude*, Book XIII.

While my unnumbered brethren toiled and bled,   45
That I should dream away the trusted hours
On rose-leaf beds, pamp'ring the coward heart
With feelings all too delicate for use?
Sweet is the tear that from some Howard's[3] eye
Drops on the cheek of one he lifts from earth;   50
And he that works me good with unmoved face
Does it but half – he chills me while he aids –
My benefactor, not my brother man.
Yet even this, this cold beneficence
Seizes my praise, when I reflect on those   55
(The sluggard pity's vision-weaving tribe!)
Who sigh for wretchedness, yet shun the wretched,
Nursing in some delicious solitude
Their slothful loves and dainty sympathies!
I therefore go and join head, heart and hand,   60
Active and firm, to fight the bloodless fight[4]
Of Science, Freedom, and the Truth in Christ.
    Yet oft when after honourable toil
Rests the tired mind, and waking loves to dream,
My spirit shall revisit thee, dear cot!   65
Thy jasmine and thy window-peeping rose,
And myrtles fearless of the mild sea-air;
And I shall sigh fond wishes, sweet abode!
Ah, had none greater, and that all had such!
It might be so, but the time is not yet: 70
Speed it, oh Father! Let thy Kingdom come!

From Letter from S. T. Coleridge to John Thelwall, 19 November 1796

Your portrait of yourself interested me. As to me, my face, unless when animated by immediate eloquence, expresses great sloth and great (indeed almost idiotic) good nature. 'Tis a mere carcass of a face – fat, flabby, and expressive chiefly of inexpression. Yet I am told that my eyes, eyebrows, and forehead are physiognomically good, but of this the deponent knoweth not. As to my shape, 'tis a good shape enough if measured – but my gait is awkward, and the walk and the whole man indicates *indolence capable of energies*. I am, and ever have been, a great reader, and have read almost everything – a library-cormorant. I am deep in all out of the way books, whether of the monkish times or of the puritanical era. I have read and digested most of the historical writers but I do not *like* history. Metaphysics and poetry and 'facts of mind' (i.e. accounts of all the strange phantasms that ever possessed your philosophy-dreamers from Thoth the Egyptian to Taylor[1] the English pagan) are my darling studies.

---

[3] John Howard (1726–90), prison reformer and philanthropist.
[4] The 'bloodless fight' turned out to be the editing of *The Watchman*, Coleridge's proselytizing journal.

From LETTER FROM S. T. COLERIDGE TO JOHN THELWALL, 19 NOVEMBER 1796
[1] Thomas Taylor (1758–1835), classical scholar and neoplatonist.

In short, I seldom read except to amuse myself, and I am almost always reading. Of useful knowledge, I am a so-so chemist, and I love chemistry. All else is blank, but I *will* be (please God) an horticulturist and a farmer. I compose very little and I absolutely hate composition. Such is my dislike that even a sense of duty is sometimes too weak to overpower it.

I cannot breathe through my nose, so my mouth, with sensual thick lips, is almost always open. In conversation I am impassioned, and oppose what I deem error with an eagerness which is often mistaken for personal asperity – but I am ever so swallowed up in the *thing*, that I perfectly forget my opponent. Such am I.

From The Annual Anthology (1800)

THIS LIME-TREE BOWER MY PRISON, A POEM ADDRESSED TO CHARLES LAMB OF THE INDIA HOUSE, LONDON (COMPOSED JULY 1797)

Advertisement
In the June of 1797, some long-expected friends paid a visit to the author's cottage; and on the morning of their arrival, he met with an accident which disabled him from walking during the whole time of their stay. One evening, when they had left him for a few hours, he composed the following lines in the garden bower.

> Well, they are gone, and here must I remain,
> This lime-tree bower my prison! I have lost
> Such beauties and such feelings, as had been
> Most sweet to have remembered, even when age
> Had dimmed mine eyes to blindness! They, meanwhile,   5
> My friends, whom I may never meet again,
> On springy heath, along the hilltop edge,
> Wander in gladness, and wind down, perchance,
> To that still roaring dell of which I told;
> The roaring dell, o'erwooded, narrow, deep,   10
> And only speckled by the midday sun;
> Where its slim trunk the ash from rock to rock
> Flings arching like a bridge; that branchless ash,
> Unsunned and damp, whose few poor yellow leaves
> Ne'er tremble in the gale, yet tremble still,   15
> Fanned by the waterfall! And there my friends
> Behold the dark green file of long lank weeds,[1]
> That all at once (a most fantastic sight!)
> Still nod and drip beneath the dripping edge
> Of the dim clay-stone.
>   Now my friends emerge   20
> Beneath the wide wide heaven – and view again

THIS LIME-TREE BOWER MY PRISON, A POEM ADDRESSED TO CHARLES LAMB OF THE INDIA HOUSE, LONDON
[1] *of long lank weeds* 'The Asplenium scolopendrium, called in some countries the Adder's tongue, in others the Hart's tongue; but Withering gives the Adder's tongue, as the trivial name of the Ophioalossum only' (Coleridge's note).

The many-steepled tract magnificent
Of hilly fields and meadows, and the sea,
With some fair bark, perhaps, which lightly touches
The slip of smooth clear blue betwixt two isles   25
Of purple shadow! Yes, they wander on
In gladness all; but thou, methinks, most glad,
My gentle-hearted Charles![2] For thou hadst pined
And hungered after nature many a year
In the great city pent, winning thy way,   30
With sad yet patient soul, through evil and pain
And strange calamity![3] Ah, slowly sink
Behind the western ridge, thou glorious sun!
Shine in the slant beams of the sinking orb,
Ye purple heath-flowers! Richlier burn, ye clouds!   35
Live in the yellow light, ye distant groves!
And kindle, thou blue ocean! So my friend,
Struck with deep joy, may stand, as I have stood,
Silent with swimming sense; yea, gazing round
On the wide landscape, gaze till all doth seem   40
Less gross than bodily, a living thing
Which *acts* upon the mind – and with such hues
As clothe the Almighty Spirit, when he makes
Spirits perceive His presence.[4]
                              A delight
Comes sudden on my heart, and I am glad   45
As I myself were there! Nor in this bower,
This little lime-tree bower, have I not marked
Much that has soothed me. Pale beneath the blaze
Hung the transparent foliage; and I watched
Some broad and sunny leaf, and loved to see   50
The shadow of the leaf and stem above
Dappling its sunshine! And that walnut tree
Was richly tinged, and a deep radiance lay
Full on the ancient ivy which *usurps*
Those fronting elms, and now with blackest mass   55
Makes their dark branches gleam a lighter hue
Through the late twilight; and though now the bat
Wheels silent by, and not a swallow twitters,
Yet still the solitary humble-bee

---

[2]   *My gentle-hearted Charles* 'For God's sake', Lamb wrote to Coleridge, when the poem was published in 1800, 'don't make me ridiculous any more by terming me gentle-hearted in print, or do it in better verses.... the meaning of "gentle" is equivocal at best, and almost always means "poor-spirited"' (Marrs, i. 217–18).
[3]   In Sept. 1796 Lamb's sister Mary murdered her mother in a fit of insanity; see p. 614 below. Lamb had been working in East India House in London since 1792.
[4]   In the version of this poem sent in a letter to Southey in July 1797, Coleridge placed a note at this point, reading, 'You remember, I am a Berkeleian' (Griggs, i. 335). George Berkeley, Bishop of Cloyne (1685–1753), denied the existence of the material world in favour of an invisible world created by God, perceptible by human beings in moments of heightened vision.

Sings in the bean-flower! Henceforth I shall know   60
That nature ne'er deserts the wise and pure –
No scene so narrow but may well employ
Each faculty of sense, and keep the heart
Awake to love and beauty! And sometimes
'Tis well to be bereaved of promised good,   65
That we may lift the soul, and contemplate
With lively joy the joys we cannot share.
My gentle-hearted Charles! when the last rook
Beat its straight path along the dusky air
Homewards, I blessed it, deeming its black wing   70
(Now a dim speck, now vanishing in the light)
Had crossed the mighty orb's dilated glory
While thou stoodst gazing; or, when all was still,
Flew creaking o'er thy head, and had a charm
For thee, my gentle-hearted Charles! to whom   75
No sound is dissonant which tells of Life.

From Letter from S. T. Coleridge to John Thelwall, 14 October 1797

I can at times feel strongly the beauties you describe – in themselves and for themselves. But more frequently all things appear little – all the knowledge that can be acquired, child's play; the universe itself, what but an immense heap of *little* things? I can contemplate nothing but parts, and parts are all little! My mind feels as if it ached to behold and know something *great*, something *one* and *indivisible* – and it is only in the faith of this that rocks or waterfalls, mountains or caverns, give me the sense of sublimity or majesty! But in this faith *all things* counterfeit infinity! 'Struck with the deepest calm of joy', I stand

> Silent, with swimming sense, and gazing round
> On the wide landscape, gaze till all doth seem
> Less gross than bodily, a living thing
> Which acts upon the mind, and with such hues
> As clothe th' Almighty Spirit, when he makes
> Spirits perceive his presence!
>   ('This Lime-Tree Bower my Prison', 39–44)

From Letter from S. T. Coleridge to Thomas Poole, 16 October 1797

I read every book that came in my way without distinction. And my father was fond of me, and used to take me on his knee, and hold long conversations with me. I remember that at eight years old I walked with him one winter evening from a farmer's house a mile from Ottery, and he told me the names of the stars, and how Jupiter was a thousand times larger than our world, and that the other twinkling stars were suns that had worlds rolling round them. And when I came home, he showed me how they rolled round. I heard him with a profound delight and admiration, but without the least mixture of wonder or incredulity. For, from my early reading of fairy tales and genii etc. etc., my mind had been habituated *to the Vast* – and I never regarded my senses in any way as the criteria of my belief. I regulated all my creeds by my conceptions – not by my sight, even at that age.

Should children be permitted to read romances, and relations of giants and magicians and genii? I know all that has been said against it, but I have formed my faith in the affirmative. I know no other way of giving the mind a love of 'the Great' and 'the Whole'. Those who have been led to the same truths step by step through the constant testimony of their senses, seem to me to want a sense which I possess: they contemplate nothing but *parts*, and all parts are necessarily little. And the universe to them is but a mass of *little things*. It is true that the mind *may* become credulous and prone to superstition by the former method – but are not the experimentalists[1] credulous even to madness in believing any absurdity rather than believe the grandest truths, if they have not the testimony of their own senses in their favour? I have known some who have been *rationally* educated, as it is styled. They were marked by a microscopic acuteness, but when they looked at great things, all became a blank and they saw nothing – and denied (very illogically) that anything could be seen, and uniformly put the negation of a power for the possession of a power, and called the want of imagination 'judgement', and the never being moved to rapture 'philosophy'!

From Christabel; Kubla Khan: A Vision; The Pains of Sleep (1816)

KUBLA KHAN (COMPOSED EARLY NOVEMBER 1797)

In Xanadu did Kubla Khan
A stately pleasure-dome decree,
Where Alph, the sacred river, ran
Through caverns measureless to man
  Down to a sunless sea.   5
So twice five miles of fertile ground
With walls and towers were girdled round;
And here were gardens bright with sinuous rills
Where blossomed many an incense-bearing tree;
And here were forests ancient as the hills,   10
And folding sunny spots of greenery.

But oh, that deep romantic chasm which slanted
Down the green hill athwart a cedarn cover!
A savage place, as holy and enchanted
As e'er beneath a waning moon was haunted   15

From LETTER FROM S. T. COLERIDGE TO THOMAS POOLE, 16 OCTOBER 1797
[1] The experimentalists adhered to empirical doctrines.

By woman wailing for her demon-lover!
And from this chasm, with ceaseless turmoil seething,
As if this earth in fast thick pants were breathing,
A mighty fountain momently was forced
Amid whose swift half-intermitted burst   20
Huge fragments vaulted like rebounding hail,
Or chaffy grain beneath the thresher's flail!
And mid these dancing rocks at once and ever,
It flung up momently the sacred river.
Five miles meandering with a mazy motion   25
Through wood and dale the sacred river ran,
Then reached the caverns measureless to man
And sank in tumult to a lifeless ocean.
And mid this tumult Kubla heard from far
Ancestral voices prophesying war!   30

    The shadow of the dome of pleasure
    Floated midway on the waves,
    Where was heard the mingled measure
    From the fountain and the caves;
It was a miracle of rare device,   35
A sunny pleasure-dome with caves of ice!

    A damsel with a dulcimer
    In a vision once I saw:
    It was an Abyssinian maid
    And on her dulcimer she played,   40
    Singing of Mount Abora.
    Could I revive within me
    Her symphony and song,
    To such a deep delight 'twould win me
That with music loud and long,   45
I would build that dome in air,
That sunny dome, those caves of ice!
And all who heard should see them there,
And all should cry, 'Beware, beware!
His flashing eyes, his floating hair!   50
Weave a circle round him thrice,
And close your eyes with holy dread –
For he on honey-dew hath fed
And drank the milk of paradise.'

From Fears in Solitude, Written in 1798 during the Alarms of an Invasion; to which are Added France: An Ode; and Frost at Midnight (1798)

FROST AT MIDNIGHT (COMPOSED FEBRUARY 1798)

The frost performs its secret ministry
Unhelped by any wind. The owlet's cry
Came loud – and hark, again! loud as before.
The inmates of my cottage, all at rest,
Have left me to that solitude which suits   5
Abstruser musings, save that at my side
My cradled infant[1] slumbers peacefully.
'Tis calm indeed! – so calm that it disturbs
And vexes meditation with its strange
And extreme silentness. Sea, hill, and wood,   10
This populous village! Sea, and hill, and wood,
With all the numberless goings-on of life,
Inaudible as dreams! The thin blue flame
Lies on my low-burnt fire, and quivers not;
Only that film[2] which fluttered on the grate   15
Still flutters there, the sole unquiet thing.
Methinks its motion in this hush of nature
Gives it dim sympathies with me who live,
Making it a companionable form
With which I can hold commune. Idle thought!   20
But still the living spirit in our frame
That loves not to behold a lifeless thing,
Transfuses into all its own delights
Its own volition – sometimes with deep faith
And sometimes with fantastic playfulness.   25
   Ah me! amused by no such curious toys
Of the self-watching subtilizing[3] mind,
How often in my early schoolboy days,
With most believing superstitious wish
Presageful have I gazed upon the bars,   30
To watch the *stranger* there! – and oft belike,
With unclosed lids, already had I dreamt
Of my sweet birthplace, and the old church-tower
Whose bells, the poor man's only music, rang
From morn to evening all the hot fair-day,   35
So sweetly that they stirred and haunted me
With a wild pleasure, falling on mine ear

FROST AT MIDNIGHT
[1] Hartley Coleridge.
[2] 'In all parts of the kingdom these films are called "strangers", and supposed to portend the arrival of some absent friend' (Coleridge's note).
[3] *subtilizing* given to subtle reasoning.

Most like articulate sounds of things to come!
So gazed I till the soothing things I dreamt
Lulled me to sleep, and sleep prolonged my dreams!   40
And so I brooded all the following morn,
Awed by the stern preceptor's face, mine eye
Fixed with mock study on my swimming book;
Save if the door half-opened, and I snatched
A hasty glance, and still my heart leaped up,   45
For still I hoped to see the *stranger's* face –
Townsman, or aunt, or sister more beloved,
My playmate when we both were clothed alike![4]
      Dear babe, that sleepest cradled by my side,
Whose gentle breathings heard in this dead calm   50
Fill up the interspersed vacancies
And momentary pauses of the thought;
My babe so beautiful, it fills my heart
With tender gladness thus to look at thee,
And think that thou shalt learn far other lore   55
And in far other scenes! For I was reared
In the great city, pent mid cloisters dim,[5]
And saw nought lovely but the sky and stars.
But *thou*, my babe, shalt wander like a breeze
By lakes and sandy shores, beneath the crags   60
Of ancient mountain, and beneath the clouds
Which image in their bulk both lakes and shores
And mountain crags;[6] so shalt thou see and hear
The lovely shapes and sounds intelligible
Of that eternal language which thy God   65
Utters, who from eternity doth teach
Himself in all, and all things in himself.
Great universal teacher! He shall mould
Thy spirit, and by giving make it ask.
      Therefore all seasons shall be sweet to thee,   70
Whether the summer clothe the general earth
With greenness, or the redbreasts sit and sing
Betwixt the tufts of snow on the bare branch
Of mossy apple-tree, while all the thatch
Smokes in the sun-thaw; whether the eave-drops fall   75
Heard only in the trances of the blast,
Or whether the secret ministry of cold
Shall hang them up in silent icicles,

---

[4] Until well into the nineteenth century, boys and girls were dressed in frocks until, between the ages of three and seven, boys were 'breeched'.

[5] Coleridge was at Christ's Hospital in the City of London, where he was a contemporary of Charles Lamb; see Lamb's essay, 'Christ's Hospital Five and Thirty Years Ago'.

[6] Coleridge had not actually seen the Lake District in Feb. 1798, when these lines were written; the Cumbrian lakes do not have 'sandy shores'. Presumably he was extrapolating descriptions given him by Wordsworth.

Quietly shining to the quiet moon;
Like those, my babe, which ere tomorrow's warmth 80
Have capped their sharp keen points with pendulous drops,
Will catch thine eye, and with their novelty
Suspend thy little soul; then make thee shout
And stretch and flutter from thy mother's arms,
As thou would'st fly for very eagerness.[7]

FRANCE: AN ODE (COMPOSED FEBRUARY 1798)

I

Ye clouds, that far above me float and pause,
Whose pathless march no mortal may control!
Ye ocean waves, that, wheresoe'er ye roll,
Yield homage only to eternal laws!
Ye woods, that listen to the night-bird's singing, 5
Midway the smooth and perilous steep reclined;
Save when your own imperious branches swinging
Have made a solemn music of the wind!
Where, like a man beloved of God,
Through glooms which never woodman trod, 10
How oft, pursuing fancies holy,
My moonlight way o'er flow'ring weeds I wound,
Inspired beyond the guess of folly
By each rude shape, and wild unconquerable sound!
Oh ye loud waves, and oh ye forests high, 15
And oh ye clouds, that far above me soared!
Thou rising sun! Thou blue rejoicing sky!
Yea, every thing that is and will be free,
Bear witness for me wheresoe'er ye be,
With what deep worship I have still adored 20
The spirit of divinest liberty.

II

When France in wrath her giant limbs upreared,
And with that oath which smote earth, air, and sea,
Stamped her strong foot and said she would be free,
Bear witness for me, how I hoped and feared![1] 25
With what a joy, my lofty gratulation
Unawed, I sung amid a slavish band;
And when to whelm the disenchanted nation,

---

[7] Lines 80–5 were removed from subsequent versions of the poem. For Hartley's sensitivity to natural things, see Coleridge's notebook entry, p. 190 above.

FRANCE: AN ODE
[1] Coleridge recalls his earlier support for the French Revolution.

Like fiends embattled by a wizard's wand,
The monarchs marched in evil day, 30
And Britain joined the dire array[2] –
Though dear her shores, and circling ocean,
Though many friendships, many youthful loves
Had swoln the patriot emotion,
And flung a magic light o'er all her hills and groves; 35
Yet still my voice unaltered sang defeat
To all that braved the tyrant-quelling lance,
And shame too long delayed, and vain retreat!
For ne'er, oh Liberty! with partial aim
I dimmed thy light, or damped thy holy flame; 40
But blessed the paeans of delivered France,
And hung my head, and wept at Britain's name!

III

'And what', I said, 'though blasphemy's loud scream
With that sweet music of deliv'rance strove;
Though all the fierce and drunken passions wove 45
A dance more wild than ever maniac's dream;
Ye storms, that round the dawning east assembled,
The sun was rising, though ye hid his light!'
And when to soothe my soul, that hoped and trembled,
The dissonance ceased, and all seemed calm and bright; 50
When France, her front deep-scarred and gory,
Concealed with clust'ring wreaths of glory;
When insupportably advancing,
Her arm made mock'ry of the warrior's ramp,
While, timid looks of fury glancing, 55
Domestic treason, crushed beneath her fatal stamp,
Writhed like a wounded dragon in his gore –
Then I reproached my fears that would not flee,
'And soon', I said, 'shall wisdom teach her lore
In the low huts of them that toil and groan! 60
And conqu'ring by her happiness alone,
Shall France compel the nations to be free,
Till love and joy look round, and call the earth their own!'

IV

Forgive me, Freedom! Oh forgive these dreams!
I hear thy voice, I hear thy loud lament, 65

---

[2] France and Britain were at war from Feb. 1793.

From bleak Helvetia's[3] icy caverns sent –
I hear thy groans upon her bloodstained streams!
Heroes, that for your peaceful country perished,
And ye, that fleeing spot the mountain snows
With bleeding wounds – forgive me, that I cherished   70
One thought that ever blessed your cruel foes!
To scatter rage and trait'rous guilt
Where Peace her jealous home had built;
A patriot race to disinherit
Of all that made their stormy wilds so dear,   75
And with inexpiable spirit
To taint the bloodless freedom of the mountaineer.
Oh France! that mockest heav'n, adult'rous, blind,
And patriot only in pernicious toils!
Are these thy boasts, champion of humankind?   80
To mix with kings in the low lust of sway,[4]
Yell in the hunt, and share the murd'rous prey;
T' insult the shrine of liberty with spoils
From freemen torn; to tempt and to betray!

V

The sensual and the dark rebel in vain,   85
Slaves by their own compulsion! In mad game
They burst their manacles, and wear the name
Of freedom graven on a heavier chain!
Oh Liberty! with profitless endeavour
Have I pursued thee many a weary hour: 90
But thou nor swellst the victor's strain, nor ever
Didst breathe thy soul in forms of human pow'r.
Alike from all, howe'er they praise thee
(Nor pray'r, nor boastful name delays thee),
Alike from priesthood's harpy minions   95
And factious blasphemy's obscener slaves,
Thou speedest on thy subtle pinions,
To live amid the winds, and move upon the waves!
And then I felt thee on the sea-cliff's verge,
Whose pines, scarce travelled by the breeze above,   100
Had made one murmur with the distant surge!
Yes, while I stood and gazed, my temples bare,
And shot my being through earth, sea, and air,
Possessing all things with intensest love,
Oh Liberty, my spirit felt thee there!   105

---

[3] *Helvetia* Switzerland.   [4] *sway* power.

FEARS IN SOLITUDE. WRITTEN APRIL 1798, DURING THE ALARMS OF AN
INVASION (COMPOSED 20 APRIL 1798)

A green and silent spot amid the hills!
A small and silent dell! O'er stiller place
No singing skylark ever poised himself!
The hills are heathy, save that swelling slope
Which hath a gay and gorgeous covering on,   5
All golden with the never bloomless furze,
Which now blooms most profusely; but the dell,
Bathed by the mist, is fresh and delicate
As vernal cornfield, or the unripe flax,
When through its half-transparent stalks, at eve,   10
The level sunshine glimmers with green light.
Oh 'tis a quiet spirit-healing nook,
Which all, methinks, would love – but chiefly he,
The humble man, who in his youthful years
Knew just so much of folly as had made   15
His early manhood more securely wise;
Here he might lie on fern or withered heath,
While from the singing lark (that sings unseen –
The minstrelsy which solitude loves best),
And from the sun, and from the breezy air,   20
Sweet influences trembled o'er his frame;
And he with many feelings, many thoughts,
Made up a meditative joy, and found
Religious meanings in the forms of nature!
And so, his senses gradually wrapped   25
In a half-sleep, he dreams of better worlds,
And dreaming hears thee still, oh singing lark!
That singest like an angel in the clouds.
    My God! it is a melancholy thing
For such a man, who would full fain preserve   30
His soul in calmness, yet perforce must feel
For all his human brethren; oh my God,
It is indeed a melancholy thing,
And weighs upon the heart, that he must think
What uproar and what strife may now be stirring   35
This way or that way o'er these silent hills –
Invasion,¹ and the thunder and the shout,
And all the crash of onset; fear and rage
And undetermined conflict – even now,
Ev'n now, perchance, and in his native isle,   40

FEARS IN SOLITUDE. WRITTEN APRIL 1798, DURING THE
ALARMS OF AN INVASION
¹ In Apr. 1798 it was widely believed that the
French were about to invade England.

Carnage and screams beneath this blessed sun!
We have offended, oh my countrymen!
We have offended very grievously,
And have been tyrannous. From east to west
A groan of accusation pierces heaven!   45
The wretched plead against us, multitudes
Countless and vehement, the sons of God,
Our brethren! Like a cloud that travels on,
Steamed up from Cairo's swamps of pestilence,
Ev'n so, my countrymen, have we gone forth   50
And borne to distant tribes slavery and pangs –
And, deadlier far, our vices, whose deep taint
With slow perdition murders the whole man,
His body and his soul! Meanwhile, at home,
We have been drinking with a riotous thirst   55
Pollutions from the brimming cup of wealth –
A selfish, lewd, effeminated race,
Contemptuous of all honourable rule,
Yet bartering freedom, and the poor man's life,
For gold, as at a market! The sweet words   60
Of Christian promise (words that even yet
Might stem destruction, were they wisely preached)
Are muttered o'er by men, whose tones proclaim
How flat and wearisome they feel their trade.
Rank scoffers some, but most too indolent   65
To deem them falsehoods, or to *know* their truth.
Oh blasphemous! the book of life is made
A superstitious instrument on which
We gabble o'er the oaths we mean to break,
For all must swear – all, and in every place,   70
College and wharf, council and justice-court,
All, all must swear, the briber and the bribed,
Merchant and lawyer, senator and priest,
The rich, the poor, the old man, and the young,
All, all make up one scheme of perjury,   75
That faith doth reel; the very name of God
Sounds like a juggler's charm; and bold with joy,
Forth from his dark and lonely hiding-place
(Portentous sight!), the owlet Atheism,
Sailing on obscene wings athwart the noon,   80
Drops his blue-fringed lids, and holds them close,
And, hooting at the glorious sun in heaven,
Cries out, 'Where is it?'
                              Thankless too for peace
(Peace long preserved by fleets and perilous seas),
Secure from actual warfare, we have loved   85
To swell the war-whoop, passionate for war!
Alas! for ages ignorant of all

Its ghastlier workings (famine or blue plague,
Battle, or siege, or flight through wintry snows),
We, this whole people, have been clamorous   90
For war and bloodshed, animating sports,
The which we pay for, as a thing to talk of,
Spectators and not combatants! No guess
Anticipative of a wrong unfelt,
No speculation on contingency,   95
However dim and vague, too vague and dim
To yield a justifying cause – and forth
(Stuffed out with big preamble, holy names,
And adjurations of the God in heaven)
We send our mandates for the certain death   100
Of thousands and ten thousands! Boys and girls,
And women that would groan to see a child
Pull off an insect's leg – all read of war,
The best amusement for our morning meal!
The poor wretch, who has learnt his only prayers   105
From curses, who knows scarcely words enough
To ask a blessing of his heavenly Father,
Becomes a fluent phraseman, absolute
And technical in victories and defeats,
And all our dainty terms for fratricide,   110
Terms which we trundle smoothly o'er our tongues
Like mere abstractions, empty sounds to which
We join no feeling and attach no form,
As if the soldier died without a wound;
As if the fibres of this godlike frame   115
Were gored without a pang; as if the wretch,
Who fell in battle doing bloody deeds,
Passed off to heaven, *translated* and not killed;
As though he had no wife to pine for him,
No God to judge him! Therefore evil days   120
Are coming on us, oh my countrymen!
And what if all-avenging Providence,
Strong and retributive, should make us know
The meaning of our words, force us to feel
The desolation and the agony   125
Of our fierce doings?
                          Spare us yet awhile,
Father and God! Oh spare us yet awhile!
Oh let not English women drag their flight
Fainting beneath the burden of their babes,
Of the sweet infants, that but yesterday   130
Laughed at the breast! Sons, brothers, husbands, all
Who ever gazed with fondness on the forms
Which grew up with you round the same fireside,
And all who ever heard the sabbath bells

Without the infidel's scorn, make yourselves pure!   135
Stand forth! Be men! Repel an impious foe,
Impious and false, a light yet cruel race
That laugh away all virtue, mingling mirth
With deeds of murder; and still promising
Freedom, themselves too sensual to be free,   140
Poison life's amities, and cheat the heart
Of Faith and quiet Hope, and all that soothes
And all that lifts the spirit! Stand we forth;
Render them back upon th' insulted ocean,
And let them toss as idly on its waves   145
As the vile seaweeds which some mountain blast
Swept from our shores! And oh! may we return
Not with a drunken triumph, but with fear,
Repenting of the wrongs with which we stung
So fierce a foe to frenzy!
                         I have told,   150
Oh Britons! Oh my brethren! I have told
Most bitter truth, but without bitterness.
Nor deem my zeal or factious or mistimed;
For never can true courage dwell with them
Who, playing tricks with conscience, dare not look   155
At their own vices. We have been too long
Dupes of a deep delusion! Some, belike,
Groaning with restless enmity, expect
All change from change of constituted power –
As if a government had been a robe   160
On which our vice and wretchedness were tagged
Like fancy-points and fringes, with the robe
Pulled off at pleasure. Fondly these attach
A radical causation to a few
Poor drudges of chastising Providence,   165
Who borrow all their hues and qualities
From our own folly and rank wickedness,
Which gave them birth, and nurse them. Others, meanwhile,
Dote with a mad idolatry; and all
Who will not fall before their images   170
And yield them worship, they are enemies
Ev'n of their country! Such have I been deemed.
But oh dear Britain! Oh my mother isle!
Needs must thou prove a name most dear and holy
To me, a son, a brother, and a friend,   175
A husband and a father who revere
All bonds of natural love, and find them all
Within the limits of thy rocky shores.
Oh native Britain! Oh my mother isle!
How shouldst thou prove aught else but dear and holy   180
To me, who from thy lakes and mountain hills,

Thy clouds, thy quiet dales, thy rocks, and seas,
Have drunk in all my intellectual life,
All sweet sensations, all ennobling thoughts,
All adoration of the God in nature, 185
All lovely and all honourable things,
Whatever makes this mortal spirit feel
The joy and greatness of its future being?
There lives nor form nor feeling in my soul
Unborrowed from my country! Oh divine 190
And beauteous island, thou hast been my sole
And most magnificent temple, in the which
I walk with awe, and sing my stately songs,
Loving the God that made me!
                     May my fears,
My filial fears, be vain! and may the vaunts 195
And menace of the vengeful enemy
Pass like the gust that roared and died away
In the distant tree, which heard, and only heard;
In this low dell bowed not the delicate grass.
But now the gentle dew-fall sends abroad 200
The fruitlike perfume of the golden furze;
The light has left the summit of the hill,
Though still a sunny gleam lies beautiful
On the long-ivied beacon. Now farewell,
Farewell awhile, oh soft and silent spot! 205
On the green sheep-track, up the heathy hill,
Homeward I wind my way; and lo! recalled
From bodings, that have well-nigh wearied me,
I find myself upon the brow, and pause
Startled! And after lonely sojourning 210
In such a quiet and surrounded scene,
This burst of prospect, here the shadowy main,
Dim-tinted, there the mighty majesty
Of that huge amphitheatre of rich
And elmy fields, seems like society 215
Conversing with the mind, and giving it
A livelier impulse, and a dance of thought;
And now, beloved Stowey, I behold
Thy church-tower, and (methinks) the four huge elms
Clust'ring, which mark the mansion of my friend;[2] 220
And close behind them, hidden from my view,
Is my own lowly cottage, where my babe
And my babe's mother dwell in peace! With light
And quickened footsteps thitherward I tend,
Remem'bring thee, oh green and silent dell! 225

---

[2] Alfoxden House, where the Wordsworths were
resident.

And grateful that by nature's quietness
And solitary musings all my heart
Is softened, and made worthy to indulge
Love, and the thoughts that yearn for humankind.

From Letter from S. T. Coleridge to Thomas Poole, 6 April 1799

My baby has not lived in vain![1] This life has been to him what it is to all of us – education and development! Fling yourself forward into your immortality only a few thousand years, and how small will not the difference between one year old and sixty years appear! Consciousness! It is no otherwise necessary to our conceptions of future continuance than as connecting the *present link* of our being with the one *immediately* preceding it – and *that* degree of consciousness, *that* small portion of *memory*, it would not only be arrogant, but in the highest degree absurd, to deny even to a much younger infant.

'Tis a strange assertion that the essence of identity lies in *recollective* consciousness; 'twere scarcely less ridiculous to affirm that the 8 miles from Stowey to Bridgwater consist in the 8 milestones. Death in a doting old age falls upon my feelings ever as a more hopeless phenomenon than death in infancy – but *nothing* is hopeless.

What if the vital force which I sent from my arm into the stone, as I flung it in the air and skimmed it upon the water – what if even that did not perish? It was *Life*! It was a particle of *Being*! It was *Power*! – and *how could* it perish? *Life, Power, Being*! – organization may be and probably *is* their *effect*; their *cause* it *cannot* be! I have indulged very curious fancies concerning that force, that *swarm* of motive powers which I sent out of my body into that stone – and which, one by one, left the untractable or already possessed mass, and – but the German ocean lies between us. It is all too far to send you such fancies as these! Grief indeed,

> Doth love to dally with fantastic thoughts,
> And smiling, like a sickly moralist,
> Finds some resemblance to her own concerns
> In the straws of chance, and things inanimate!
> (Coleridge, *Osorio*, V. i. 11–14)

But I cannot truly say that I grieve. I am perplexed, I am sad – and a little thing, a very trifle, would make me weep. But for the death of the baby I have *not* wept! Oh, this strange, strange, strange scene-shifter, death! – that giddies one with insecurity, and so unsubstantiates the living things that one has grasped and handled! Some months ago Wordsworth transmitted to me a most sublime epitaph;[2] whether it had any reality, I cannot say. Most probably, in some gloomier moment he had fancied the moment in which his sister might die.

From LETTER FROM S. T. COLERIDGE TO THOMAS POOLE, 6 APRIL 1799
[1] Coleridge's son, Berkeley (b. 14 May 1798), died 10 Feb. 1799 during his father's stay in Germany. At first the news was kept from Coleridge, but later Poole thought it better to let him know. This letter is Coleridge's first written response to the news, from Göttingen. Berkeley's death seems to have been a catalyst for the Infant Babe passage in *Thirteen-Book Prelude*, ii. 237–80.
[2] 'A Slumber did my Spirit Seal'.

From The Annual Anthology (1800)

LINES WRITTEN IN THE ALBUM AT ELBINGERODE, IN THE HARTZ FOREST (COMPOSED BY 17 MAY 1799)[1]

I stood on Brocken's sovran height,[2] and saw
Woods crowding upon woods, hills over hills,
A *surging* scene, and only limited
By the blue distance. Heavily my way
Homeward I dragged through fir-groves evermore, 5
Where bright green moss heaves in sepulchral forms,
Speckled with sunshine; and, but seldom heard,
The sweet bird's song became an hollow sound;
And the breeze murmuring indivisibly
Preserved its solemn murmur most distinct 10
From many a note of many a waterfall,
And the brook's chatter, mid whose islet stones
The dingy kidling with its tinkling bell
Leapt frolicsome, or old romantic goat
Sat, his white beard slow-waving. I moved on 15
In low and languid mood,[3] for I had found
That grandest scenes have but imperfect charms,
Where the sight vainly wanders, nor beholds
One spot with which the heart associates
Holy remembrances of friend or child, 20
Or gentle maid, our first and early love,
Or father, or the venerable name
Of our adored country!
                            Oh thou Queen,
Thou delegated deity of earth,
Oh dear, dear, England! How my longing eye 25
Turned westward, shaping in the steady clouds
Thy sand and high white cliffs! Oh native land,
Filled with the thought of thee, this heart was proud,
Yea, mine eye swam with tears, that all the view

LINES WRITTEN IN THE ALBUM AT ELBINGERODE, IN THE HARTZ FOREST
[1] Coleridge sent this poem in a letter to his wife, 17 May 1799, with the introduction: 'At the inn they brought us an Album, or Stammbuch, requesting that we would write our names and something or other as a remembrance that we had been there. I wrote the following lines, which I send to you not that they possess a grain of merit as poetry, but because they contain a true account of my journey from the Brocken to Elbinrode' (Griggs, i. 504).
[2] Coleridge notes that the Great Brocken is 'the highest mountain in the Hartz, and indeed in north Germany'.

[3] *In low and languid mood* Coleridge glosses this with a quotation from Southey:

When I have gazed
From some high eminence on goodly vales,
And cots and villages embowered below,
The thought would rise that all to me was strange
Amid the scenes so fair, nor one small spot
Where my tired mind might rest, and call it 'home'.
Southey's *Hymn to the Penates*

From sovran Brocken, woods and woody hills,   30
Floated away like a departing dream,
Feeble and dim! Stranger, these impulses
Blame thou not lightly, nor will I profane
With hasty judgement or injurious doubt
That man's sublimer spirit, who can feel   35
That God is everywhere! – the God who framed
Mankind to be one mighty family,
Himself our Father, and the world our home.

From Christabel; Kubla Khan: A Vision; The Pains of Sleep (1816)

CHRISTABEL (PART I COMPOSED *C.*FEBRUARY 1798; PART II COMPOSED SEPTEMBER–OCTOBER 1800; CONCLUSION TO PART II COMPOSED *C.*1801)

Part I

'Tis the middle of night by the castle clock,
And the owls have awakened the crowing cock;
Tu—whit! Tu—whoo!
And hark, again! the crowing cock,
How drowsily it crew.   5

Sir Leoline, the Baron rich,
Hath a toothless mastiff bitch;
From her kennel beneath the rock
She makes answer to the clock –
Four for the quarters and twelve for the hour,   10
Ever and aye, moonshine or shower,
Sixteen short howls not over loud;
Some say she sees my lady's shroud.

Is the night chilly and dark?
The night is chilly, but not dark –   15
The thin grey cloud is spread on high,
It covers but not hides the sky.
The moon is behind, and at the full,
And yet she looks both small and dull;
The night is chill, the cloud is grey –   20
'Tis a month before the month of May
And the spring comes slowly up this way.

The lovely lady, Christabel,
Whom her father loves so well,
What makes her in the wood so late,   25
A furlong from the castle gate?
She had dreams all yesternight
Of her own betrothed knight –

Dreams that made her moan and leap
As on her bed she lay in sleep;   30
And she in the midnight wood will pray
For the weal[1] of her lover that's far away.

She stole along, she nothing spoke,
The breezes they were still also;
And nought was green upon the oak   35
But moss and rarest mistletoe;
She kneels beneath the huge oak tree
And in silence prayeth she.

The lady leaps up suddenly,
The lovely lady, Christabel!   40
It moaned as near as near can be,
But what it is, she cannot tell:
On the other side it seems to be
Of the huge, broad-breasted, old oak tree.

The night is chill, the forest bare —   45
Is it the wind that moaneth bleak?
There is not wind enough in the air
To move away the ringlet curl
From the lovely lady's cheek;
There is not wind enough to twirl   50
The one red leaf, the last of its clan,
That dances as often as dance it can,
Hanging so light and hanging so high
On the topmost twig that looks up at the sky.

Hush, beating heart of Christabel!   55
Jesu Maria, shield her well!
She folded her arms beneath her cloak
And stole to the other side of the oak:
      What sees she there?

There she sees a damsel bright   60
Dressed in a silken robe of white;
Her neck, her feet, her arms were bare,
And the jewels disordered in her hair.
I guess 'twas frightful there to see
A lady so richly clad as she —   65
Beautiful exceedingly!

'Mary mother, save me now!'
Said Christabel, 'And who art thou?'

CHRISTABEL
[1] *weal* welfare.

The lady strange made answer meet
And her voice was faint and sweet.
'Have pity on my sore distress,
I scarce can speak for weariness!'
'Stretch forth thy hand, and have no fear',
Said Christabel, 'How cam'st thou here?'
And the lady whose voice was faint and sweet
Did thus pursue her answer meet:

'My sire is of a noble line,
And my name is Geraldine.
Five warriors seized me yestermorn –
Me, even me, a maid forlorn;
They choked my cries with force and fright
And tied me on a palfrey white.
The palfrey was as fleet as wind,
And they rode furiously behind.
They spurred amain, their steeds were white,
And once we crossed the shade of night.
As sure as Heaven shall rescue me,
I have no thought what men they be;
Nor do I know how long it is
(For I have lain in fits, I wis)
Since one, the tallest of the five,
Took me from the palfrey's back,
A weary woman scarce alive.
Some muttered words his comrades spoke,
He placed me underneath this oak,
He swore they would return with haste;
Whither they went I cannot tell –
I thought I heard, some minutes past,
Sounds as of a castle-bell.
Stretch forth thy hand (thus ended she)
And help a wretched maid to flee.'

Then Christabel stretched forth her hand
And comforted fair Geraldine,
Saying that she should command
The service of Sir Leoline,
And straight be convoyed, free from thrall,
Back to her noble father's hall.

So up she rose and forth they passed
With hurrying steps, yet nothing fast;
Her lucky stars the lady blessed,
And Christabel, she sweetly said,
'All our household are at rest,
Each one sleeping in his bed.

70

75

80

85

90

95

100

105

110

Sir Leoline is weak in health
And may not well awakened be,   115
So to my room we'll creep in stealth
And you tonight must sleep with me.'

They crossed the moat, and Christabel
Took the key that fitted well –
A little door she opened straight   120
All in the middle of the gate,
The gate that was ironed within and without
Where an army in battle array had marched out.

The lady sank, belike through pain,
And Christabel with might and main   125
Lifted her up, a weary weight,
Over the threshold of the gate;
Then the lady rose again
And moved as she were not in pain.

So free from danger, free from fear,   130
They crossed the court – right glad they were.
And Christabel devoutly cried
To the lady by her side,
'Praise we the Virgin all divine
Who hath rescued thee from thy distress!'   135
'Alas, alas,' said Geraldine,
'I cannot speak for weariness.'
So free from danger, free from fear,
They crossed the court – right glad they were.

Outside her kennel, the mastiff old   140
Lay fast asleep in moonshine cold.
The mastiff old did not awake,
Yet she an angry moan did make.
And what can ail the mastiff bitch?
Never till now she uttered yell   145
Beneath the eye of Christabel.
Perhaps it is the owlet's scritch,
For what can ail the mastiff bitch?

They passed the hall that echoes still,
Pass as lightly as you will.   150
The brands were flat, the brands were dying,
Amid their own white ashes lying;
But when the lady passed, there came
A tongue of light, a fit of flame,
And Christabel saw the lady's eye,   155
And nothing else saw she thereby

Save the boss of the shield of Sir Leoline tall
Which hung in a murky old nitch[2] in the wall.
'Oh softly tread,' said Christabel,
'My father seldom sleepeth well.'   160

Sweet Christabel, her feet she bares
And they are creeping up the stairs,
Now in glimmer and now in gloom,
And now they pass the Baron's room,
As still as death with stifled breath;   165
And now have reached her chamber door,
And now with eager feet press down
The rushes of her chamber floor.

The moon shines dim in the open air
And not a moonbeam enters here.   170
But they without its light can see
The chamber carved so curiously,
Carved with figures strange and sweet
All made out of the carver's brain
For a lady's chamber meet;   175
The lamp with twofold silver chain
Is fastened to an angel's feet.

The silver lamp burns dead and dim,
But Christabel the lamp will trim.
She trimmed the lamp and made it bright   180
And left it swinging to and fro,
While Geraldine in wretched plight
Sank down upon the floor below.

'Oh weary lady Geraldine,
I pray you, drink this cordial wine.   185
It is a wine of virtuous powers –
My mother made it of wild-flowers.'

'And will your mother pity me,
Who am a maiden most forlorn?'
Christabel answered, 'Woe is me!   190
She died the hour that I was born.
I have heard the grey-haired friar tell
How on her deathbed she did say
That she should hear the castle bell
Strike twelve upon my wedding day.   195
Oh mother dear, that thou wert here!'
'I would', said Geraldine, 'she were.'

---

[2]   nitch niche.

But soon with altered voice said she,
'Off, wandering mother! Peak and pine!
I have power to bid thee flee.'   200
Alas, what ails poor Geraldine?
Why stares she with unsettled eye?
Can she the bodiless dead espy?
And why with hollow voice cries she,
'Off, woman, off! this hour is mine –   205
Though thou her guardian spirit be,
Off, woman, off! – 'tis given to me'?

Then Christabel knelt by the lady's side,
And raised to heaven her eyes so blue;
'Alas!' said she, 'this ghastly ride –   210
Dear lady, it hath wildered³ you!'
The lady wiped her moist cold brow,
And faintly said, ''Tis over now!'

Again the wild-flower wine she drank;
Her fair large eyes 'gan glitter bright,   215
And from the floor whereon she sank,
The lofty lady stood upright:
She was most beautiful to see,
Like a lady of a far countrée.

And thus the lofty lady spake: 220
'All they who live in the upper sky
Do love you, holy Christabel!
And you love them, and for their sake,
And for the good which me befell,
Even I, in my degree will try,   225
Fair maiden, to requite you well.
But now unrobe yourself, for I
Must pray, ere yet in bed I lie.'

Quoth Christabel, 'So let it be!'
And as the lady bade, did she.   230
Her gentle limbs did she undress,
And lay down in her loveliness.

But through her brain, of weal and woe
So many thoughts moved to and fro
That vain it were her lids to close;   235
So halfway from the bed she rose,
And on her elbow did recline
To look at the lady Geraldine.

---

³ *wildered* perplexed, bewildered.

Beneath the lamp the lady bowed
And slowly rolled her eyes around;   240
Then drawing in her breath aloud
Like one that shuddered, she unbound
The cincture[4] from beneath her breast:
Her silken robe and inner vest
Dropped to her feet, and full in view,   245
Behold! her bosom and half her side —
A sight to dream of, not to tell!
And she is to sleep by Christabel.[5]

She took two paces and a stride,
And lay down by the maiden's side;   250
And in her arms the maid she took,
        Ah wel-a-day!
And with low voice and doleful look
        These words did say:
'In the touch of this bosom there worketh a spell   255
Which is lord of thy utterance, Christabel!
Thou knowest tonight, and wilt know tomorrow,
This mark of my shame, this seal of my sorrow;
        But vainly thou warrest,
            For this is alone in   260
        Thy power to declare,
            That in the dim forest
            Thou heard'st a low moaning,
And found'st a bright lady surpassingly fair,
And didst bring her home with thee in love and in charity,   265
To shield her and shelter her from the damp air.'

The Conclusion to Part I
It was a lovely sight to see
The lady Christabel, when she
Was praying at the old oak tree.
        Amid the jagged shadows   270
        Of mossy leafless boughs,
        Kneeling in the moonlight
        To make her gentle vows;
Her slender palms together pressed,
Heaving sometimes on her breast;   275
Her face resigned to bliss or bale,
Her face — oh call it fair, not pale!
And both blue eyes more bright than clear,
Each about to have a tear.

---

4 *cincture* belt.
5 The MS text of 1800, in the *Christabel* notebook
at the Wordsworth Library, Grasmere, is slightly
more explicit:

Behold! her bosom and half her side
Are lean and old and foul of hue —
A sight to dream of, not to tell,
And she is to sleep with Christabel.

With open eyes (ah woe is me!) 280
Asleep, and dreaming fearfully,
Fearfully dreaming, yet I wis,
Dreaming that alone, which is –
Oh sorrow and shame! Can this be she,
The lady who knelt at the old oak tree? 285
And lo! the worker of these harms
That holds the maiden in her arms,
Seems to slumber still and mild,
As a mother with her child.

A star hath set, a star hath risen, 290
Oh Geraldine, since arms of thine
Have been the lovely lady's prison!
Oh Geraldine, one hour was thine –
Thou'st had thy will! By tairn and rill
The night-birds all that hour were still; 295
But now they are jubilant anew,
From cliff and tower, tu-whoo! tu-whoo!
Tu-whoo! tu-whoo! from wood and fell!

And see! the lady Christabel
Gathers herself from out her trance; 300
Her limbs relax, her countenance
Grows sad and soft; the smooth thin lids
Close o'er her eyes, and tears she sheds –
Large tears that leave the lashes bright;
And oft the while she seems to smile 305
As infants at a sudden light!

Yea she doth smile and she doth weep
Like a youthful hermitess
Beauteous in a wilderness,
Who praying always, prays in sleep. 310
And if she move unquietly,
Perchance 'tis but the blood so free
Comes back and tingles in her feet.
No doubt she hath a vision sweet:
What if her guardian spirit 'twere? 315
What if she knew her mother near?
But this she knows – in joys and woes,
That saints will aid if men will call,
For the blue sky bends over all.

Part II
'Each matin bell', the Baron saith, 320
'Knells us back to a world of death.'
These words Sir Leoline first said

When he rose and found his lady dead;
These words Sir Leoline will say
Many a morn to his dying day.   325
And hence the custom and law began
That still at dawn the sacristan[6]
Who duly pulls the heavy bell
Five and forty beads must tell
Between each stroke – a warning knell   330
Which not a soul can choose but hear
From Bratha Head to Windermere.[7]

Saith Bracy the bard, 'So let it knell!
And let the drowsy sacristan
Still count as slowly as he can!   335
There is no lack of such, I ween,
As well fill up the space between.
In Langdale Pike and Witch's Lair
And Dungeon Ghyll[8] (so foully rent),
With ropes of rock and bells of air   340
Three sinful sextons' ghosts are pent,
Who all give back, one after t'other,
The death-note to their living brother;
And oft too, by the knell offended,
Just as their one! – two! – three! is ended,   345
The Devil mocks the doleful tale
With a merry peal from Borrowdale.[9]

The air is still – through mist and cloud
That merry peal comes ringing loud;
And Geraldine shakes off her dread   350
And rises lightly from the bed,
Puts on her silken vestments white
And tricks her hair in lovely plight,[10]
And nothing doubting of her spell
Awakens the lady Christabel.   355
'Sleep you, sweet lady Christabel?
I trust that you have rested well.'

And Christabel awoke and spied
The same who lay down by her side –
Oh rather say, the same whom she   360
Raised up beneath the old oak tree!
Nay, fairer yet, and yet more fair,

---

[6] *sacristan* sexton of a parish church.
[7] i.e. the length of Langdale, through which the
River Brathay runs until it reaches Windermere. Sir
Leoline's castle is presumably in Langdale.

[8] High ascents in Langdale.
[9] Borrowdale is to the north-west of Langdale.
[10] *plight* fashion.

For she belike hath drunken deep
Of all the blessedness of sleep!
And while she spake, her looks, her air   365
Such gentle thankfulness declare,
That (so it seemed) her girded vests
Grew tight beneath her heaving breasts.
'Sure I have sinned!' said Christabel,
'Now heaven be praised if all be well!'   370
And in low faltering tones, yet sweet,
Did she the lofty lady greet
With such perplexity of mind
As dreams too lively leave behind.

So quickly she rose, and quickly arrayed   375
Her maiden limbs, and having prayed
That He who on the cross did groan
Might wash away her sins unknown,
She forthwith led fair Geraldine
To meet her sire, Sir Leoline.   380

The lovely maid and the lady tall
Are pacing both into the hall,
And pacing on through page and groom,
Enter the Baron's presence room.

The Baron rose, and while he pressed   385
His gentle daughter to his breast,
With cheerful wonder in his eyes
The lady Geraldine espies,
And gave such welcome to the same,
As might beseem so bright a dame!   390

But when he heard the lady's tale,
And when she told her father's name,
Why waxed Sir Leoline so pale,
Murmuring o'er the name again –
Lord Roland de Vaux of Tryermaine?   395

Alas, they had been friends in youth,
But whispering tongues can poison truth,
And constancy lives in realms above;
And life is thorny, and youth is vain,
And to be wroth with one we love   400
Doth work like madness in the brain.
And thus it chanced, as I divine,
With Roland and Sir Leoline;
Each spake words of high disdain
And insult to his heart's best brother –   405

They parted, ne'er to meet again!
But never either found another
To free the hollow heart from paining;
They stood aloof, the scars remaining
Like cliffs which had been rent asunder.   410
A dreary sea now flows between,
But neither heat, nor frost, nor thunder
Shall wholly do away, I ween,
The marks of that which once hath been.

Sir Leoline a moment's space   415
Stood gazing on the damsel's face,
And the youthful Lord of Tryermaine
Came back upon his heart again.

Oh then the Baron forgot his age,
His noble heart swelled high with rage;   420
He swore by the wounds in Jesu's side
He would proclaim it far and wide
With trump and solemn heraldry,
That they who thus had wronged the dame
Were base as spotted infamy!   425
'And if they dare deny the same,
My herald shall appoint a week,
And let the recreant traitors seek
My tournay court[11] – that there and then
I may dislodge their reptile souls   430
From the bodies and forms of men!'
He spake – his eye in lightning rolls,
For the lady was ruthlessly seized, and he kenned
In the beautiful lady the child of his friend.

And now the tears were on his face,   435
And fondly in his arms he took
Fair Geraldine, who met th' embrace,
Prolonging it with joyous look,
Which when she viewed, a vision fell
Upon the soul of Christabel –   440
The vision of fear, the touch and pain!
She shrunk and shuddered, and saw again
(Ah woe is me! Was it for thee,
Thou gentle maid, such sights to see?) –
Again she saw that bosom old,   445
Again she felt that bosom cold,
And drew in her breath with a hissing sound.

---

[11] The sheriff's county court usually met twice a
year.

Whereat the knight turned wildly round,
And nothing saw but his own sweet maid
With eyes upraised, as one that prayed. 450

The touch, the sight, had passed away,
And in its stead that vision blessed,
Which comforted her after rest,
While in the lady's arms she lay,
Had put a rapture in her breast, 455
And on her lips and o'er her eyes
Spread smiles like light!
               With new surprise,
'What ails then my beloved child?'
The Baron said. His daughter mild
Made answer, 'All will yet be well!' 460
I ween she had no power to tell
Aught else, so mighty was the spell.
Yet he who saw this Geraldine
Had deemed her sure a thing divine,
Such sorrow with such grace she blended, 465
As if she feared she had offended
Sweet Christabel, that gentle maid!
And with such lowly tones she prayed
She might be sent without delay
Home to her father's mansion.
                   'Nay, 470
Nay, by my soul!' said Leoline.
'Ho! Bracy the bard, the charge be thine!
Go thou with music sweet and loud,
And take two steeds with trappings proud,
And take the youth whom thou lov'st best 475
To bear thy harp and learn thy song,
And clothe you both in solemn vest,
And over the mountains haste along,
Lest wand'ring folk that are abroad
Detain you on the valley road. 480

And when he has crossed the Irthing flood,
My merry bard, he hastes, he hastes
Up Knorren Moor, through Halegarth Wood,
And reaches soon that castle good
Which stands and threatens Scotland's wastes. 485

Bard Bracy! Bard Bracy! Your horses are fleet,
Ye must ride up the hall, your music so sweet,
More loud than your horses' echoing feet!
And loud and loud to Lord Roland call,
"Thy daughter is safe in Langdale hall! 490

Thy beautiful daughter is safe and free —
Sir Leoline greets thee thus through me.
He bids thee come without delay
With all thy numerous array,
And take thy lovely daughter home;   495
And he will meet thee on the way
With all his numerous array,
White with their panting palfreys' foam!"
And, by mine honour, I will say
That I repent me of the day   500
When I spake words of fierce disdain
To Roland de Vaux of Tryermaine!
For since that evil hour hath flown,
Many a summer's sun have shone;
Yet ne'er found I a friend again   505
Like Roland de Vaux of Tryermaine.'

The lady fell and clasped his knees,
Her face upraised, her eyes o'erflowing;
And Bracy replied, with faltering voice,
His gracious hail on all bestowing: 510
'Thy words, thou sire of Christabel,
Are sweeter than my harp can tell;
Yet might I gain a boon of thee,
This day my journey should not be,
So strange a dream hath come to me,   515
That I had vowed with music loud
To clear yon wood from thing unblessed,
Warned by a vision in my rest!
For in my sleep I saw that dove,
That gentle bird whom thou dost love,   520
And call'st by thy own daughter's name —
Sir Leoline! I saw the same
Fluttering and uttering fearful moan
Among the green herbs in the forest alone;
Which when I saw, and when I heard,   525
I wondered what might ail the bird,
For nothing near it could I see
Save the grass and green herbs underneath the old tree.

And in my dream methought I went
To search out what might there be found,   530
And what the sweet bird's trouble meant
That thus lay fluttering on the ground.
I went, and peered, and could descry
No cause for her distressful cry;
But yet for her dear lady's sake   535
I stooped, methought the dove to take,

When lo! I saw a bright green snake
Coiled around its wings and neck.
Green as the herbs on which it couched,
Close by the dove's its head it crouched,   540
And with the dove it heaves and stirs,
Swelling its neck as she swelled hers!
I woke – it was the midnight hour,
The clock was echoing in the tower;
But though my slumber was gone by,   545
This dream it would not pass away –
It seems to live upon my eye!
And thence I vowed this self-same day,
With music strong and saintly song,
To wander through the forest bare   550
Lest aught unholy loiter there.'

Thus Bracy said. The Baron the while,
Half-listening, heard him with a smile,
Then turned to Lady Geraldine,
His eyes made up of wonder and love;   555
And said, in courtly accents fine,
'Sweet maid, Lord Roland's beauteous dove,
With arms more strong than harp or song,
Thy sire and I will crush the snake!'
He kissed her forehead as he spake,   560
And Geraldine, in maiden wise,
Casting down her large bright eyes,
With blushing cheek and courtesy fine
She turned her from Sir Leoline,
Softly gathering up her train   565
That o'er her right arm fell again,
And folded her arms across her chest,
And couched her head upon her breast,
And looked askance at Christabel –
Jesu Maria, shield her well!   570

A snake's small eye blinks dull and shy,
And the lady's eyes they shrunk in her head,
Each shrunk up to a serpent's eye;
And with somewhat of malice and more of dread
At Christabel she looked askance!   575
One moment and the sight was fled;
But Christabel, in dizzy trance,
Stumbling on the unsteady ground,
Shuddered aloud with a hissing sound;
And Geraldine again turned round   580
And like a thing that sought relief,
Full of wonder and full of grief,

She rolled her large bright eyes divine
Wildly on Sir Leoline.

The maid, alas, her thoughts are gone,   585
She nothing sees, no sight but one!
The maid, devoid of guile and sin,
I know not how, in fearful wise
So deeply had she drunken in
That look, those shrunken serpent eyes,   590
That all her features were resigned
To this sole image in her mind,
And passively did imitate
That look of dull and treacherous hate.
And thus she stood in dizzy trance,   595
Still picturing that look askance
With forced unconscious sympathy
Full before her father's view —
As far as such a look could be,
In eyes so innocent and blue!   600

But when the trance was o'er, the maid
Paused awhile and inly prayed,
Then falling at her father's feet,
'By my mother's soul do I entreat
That thou this woman send away!'   605
She said — and more she could not say,
For what she knew she could not tell,
O'er-mastered by the mighty spell.

Why is thy cheek so wan and wild,
Sir Leoline? Thy only child   610
Lies at thy feet, thy joy, thy pride,
So fair, so innocent, so mild —
The same for whom thy lady died!
Oh by the pangs of her dear mother,
Think thou no evil of thy child!   615
For her and thee, and for no other
She prayed the moment ere she died,
Prayed that the babe for whom she died
Might prove her dear lord's joy and pride!
    That prayer her deadly pangs beguiled,   620
        Sir Leoline!
    And would'st thou wrong thy only child,
        Her child and thine?
Within the Baron's heart and brain,
If thoughts like these had any share,   625
They only swelled his rage and pain
And did but work confusion there;

His heart was cleft with pain and rage,
His cheeks they quivered, his eyes were wild –
Dishonoured thus in his old age, 630
Dishonoured by his only child,
And all his hospitality
To th' insulted daughter of his friend
By more than woman's jealousy
Brought thus to a disgraceful end. 635
He rolled his eye with stern regard
Upon the gentle minstrel bard,
And said in tones abrupt, austere,
'Why, Bracy, dost thou loiter here?
I bade thee hence!' The bard obeyed; 640
And, turning from his own sweet maid,
The aged knight, Sir Leoline,
Led forth the lady Geraldine.

The Conclusion to Part the Second
A little child, a limber elf,
Singing, dancing to itself, 645
A fairy thing with red round cheeks
That always finds and never seeks,
Makes such a vision to the sight
As fills a father's eyes with light,
And pleasures flow in so thick and fast 650
Upon his heart, that he at last
Must needs express his love's excess
With words of unmeant bitterness.
Perhaps 'tis pretty to force together
Thoughts so all unlike each other, 655
To mutter and mock a broken charm,
To dally with wrong that does no harm.
Perhaps 'tis tender too and pretty
At each wild word to feel within
A sweet recoil of love and pity. 660
And what if, in a world of sin
(Oh sorrow and shame should this be true!),
Such giddiness of heart and brain
Comes seldom save from rage and pain,
So talks as it's most used to do. 665

Letter to Sara Hutchinson, 4 April 1802. Sunday Evening. (edited from MS)[1]

1

Well! if the bard was weather-wise who made
The dear old ballad of Sir Patrick Spence,
This night, so tranquil now, will not go hence
Unroused by winds that ply a busier trade
Than that which moulds yon clouds in lazy flakes,   5
Or the dull sobbing draught that drones and rakes
Upon the strings of this Eolian lute,
Which better far were mute.
For lo! the new moon, winter-bright,
And all suffused with phantom light   10
(With swimming phantom light o'erspread,
But rimmed and circled with a silver thread);
I see the old moon in her lap, foretelling
The coming-on of rain and squally blast.
Ah Sara! that the gust ev'n now were swelling,   15
And the slant night-shower driving loud and fast.

2

A grief without a pang – void, dark, and drear;
A stifling, drowsy, unimpassioned grief
That finds no natural outlet, no relief
In word, or sigh, or tear –   20
This, Sara, well thou know'st,
Is that sore evil which I dread the most
And oft'nest suffer in this heartless mood,
To other thoughts by yonder throstle wooed,
That pipes within the larch-tree not unseen   25
(The larch which pushes out in tassels green
Its bundled leafits), wooed to mild delights
By all the tender sounds and gentle sights
Of this sweet primrose-month – and *vainly* wooed,
Oh dearest Sara, in this heartless mood.   30

LETTER TO SARA HUTCHINSON
[1]   The MS from which the present text is taken is the earliest of the poem in this form. Though called 'The Cornell Manuscript', it is retained at the Wordsworth Library, Grasmere.

3

All this long eve so balmy and serene,
Have I been gazing on the western sky
And its peculiar tint of yellow-green;
And still I gaze, and with how blank an eye!
And those thin clouds above, in flakes and bars,   35
That give away their motion to the stars,
Those stars that glide behind them and between,
Now sparkling, now bedimmed, but always seen;
Yon crescent moon, as fixed as if it grew
In its own cloudless, starless lake of blue –   40
A boat becalmed! Dear William's sky canoe![2]
I see them all, so excellently fair;
I *see*, not *feel*, how beautiful they are!

4

My genial spirits fail,[3]
And what can these avail   45
To lift the smoth'ring weight from off my breast?
It were a vain endeavour,
Though I should gaze forever
On that green light that lingers in the west:
I may not hope from outward forms to win   50
The passion and the life, whose fountains are within;
These lifeless shapes, around, below, above –
Oh dearest Sara, what can they impart?
Even when the gentle thought that thou, my love,
Art gazing now like me   55
And see'st the heaven I see –
Sweet thought it is, yet feebly stirs my heart! –

5

Feebly, oh feebly! Yet
(I well remember it)
In my first dawn of youth, that fancy stole   60
With many gentle yearnings on my soul.
At eve, sky-gazing in 'ecstatic fit'[4]
(Alas, far-cloistered in a city school,[5]

---

[2] *Dear William's sky canoe* as featured in the Prologue to Wordsworth's *Peter Bell* (1798, published 1819).
[3] An echo of Milton, 'Samson Agonistes', 594: 'my genial spirits droop'.
[4] Milton, 'The Passion', 42.
[5] Christ's Hospital in the City of London; compare 'Frost at Midnight', 57.

The sky was all I knew of beautiful),
At the barred window often did I sit,   65
And often on the leaded school-roof lay,
    And to myself would say,
'There does not live the man so stripped of good affections
As not to love to see a maiden's quiet eyes
Upraised and linking on sweet dreams by dim connections   70
To moon, or evening star, or glorious western skies!'
While yet a boy, this thought would so pursue me,
That often it became a kind of vision to me.

6

Sweet thought, and dear of old
To hearts of finer mould –   75
Ten thousand times by friends and lovers blessed!
    I spake with rash despair,
    And ere I was aware,
The weight was somewhat lifted from my breast!
Dear Sara! in the weather-fended wood,   80
Thy loved haunt where the stock-doves coo at noon,
    I guess that thou hast stood
And watched yon crescent and that ghost-like moon;
    And yet far rather, in my present mood,
I would that thou'dst been sitting all this while   85
Upon the sod-built seat of camomile,[6]
And though thy robin may have ceased to sing,
Yet needs for *my* sake must thou love to hear
    The beehive murmuring near –
That ever-busy and most quiet thing   90
Which I have heard at midnight murmuring.

7

    I feel my spirit moved:
    And wheresoe'er thou be,
    Oh sister, oh beloved!
Thy dear mild eyes that see   95
The very heaven *I* see –
There is a prayer in them, it is for *me*!
And I, dear Sara, *I* am blessing *thee*!

[6] 'Sara's seat' was built by Coleridge and the Wordsworths in the garden of Dove Cottage, 10 Oct. 1801.

8

It was as calm as this, the happy night
When Mary, thou and I together were,   100
The low decaying fire our only light,
And listened to the stillness of the air!
Oh, that affectionate and blameless maid,
Dear Mary, on her lap my head she laid –
    Her hand was on my brow   105
    Even as my own is now,
And on my cheek I felt thy eyelash play.
Such joy I had that I may truly say
My spirit was awe-stricken with the excess
And trance-like depth of its brief happiness.   110

9

Ah fair remembrances, that so revive
My heart, and fill it with a living power –
Where were they, Sara? Or did I not strive
To win them to me on the fretting hour
Then when I wrote thee that complaining scroll,   115
Which even to bodily sickness bruised thy soul?
And yet thou blam'st thyself alone, and yet
    Forbidd'st me all regret.

10

And must I not *regret* that I distressed
Thee, best beloved, who lovest me the best?   120
My better mind had fled I know not whither,
For oh! was this an absent friend's employ,
To send from far both pain and sorrow thither,
Where still his blessings should have called down joy?
I read thy guileless letter o'er again,   125
I hear thee of thy blameless self complain,
And only this I learn – and this, alas, I know –
That thou art weak and pale with sickness, grief, and pain,
And *I – I* made thee so!

11

Oh, *for my own sake*, I regret *perforce*   130
Whatever turns *thee*, Sara, from the course
Of calm well-being and a heart at rest.

When thou and, with thee, those whom thou lov'st best
Shall dwell together in one quiet home,
One home the sure *abiding* home of all,   135
I too will crown me with a coronal;[7]
Nor shall this heart in idle wishes roam
    Morbidly soft!
No, let me trust that I shall wear away
In no inglorious toils the manly day;   140
And only now and then, and not too oft,
Some dear and memorable eve shall bless,
Dreaming of all your love and happiness.

12

Be happy, and I need thee not in sight!
Peace in thy heart, and quiet in thy dwelling,   145
Health in thy limbs, and in thy eyes the light
Of love, and hope, and honourable feeling;
Where'er I am, I needs must be content –
Not near thee, haply shall be more content!
To all things I prefer the permanent.[8]   150
And better seems it for a heart like mine
Always to *know*, than sometimes to *behold*
    Their happiness and thine:
For change doth trouble me with pangs untold!
To see thee, hear thee, feel thee, then to part –   155
    Oh, it weighs down the heart!
To visit those I love, as I love *thee*,
Mary, William, and dear Dorothy,
It is but a temptation to repine!
The transientness is poison in the wine,   160
Eats out the pith of joy, makes all joy hollow,
All pleasure a dim dream of pain to follow!
My own peculiar lot, my household life,
It is (and will remain) indifference or strife;
While ye are well and happy, 'twould but wrong you   165
If I should fondly yearn to be among you –
Wherefore, oh wherefore, should I wish to be
A withered branch upon a blossoming tree?

13

But (let me say it, for I vainly strive
To beat away the thought) – but if thou pined,   170

---

[7] An allusion to Wordsworth's 'Ode', 40.
[8] Compare Wordsworth's reference to the 'beautiful

and permanent forms of nature', Preface to *Lyrical
Ballads*, p. 252.

Whate'er the cause, in body or in mind,
I were the miserablest man alive
To know it and be absent! Thy delights
Far off or near, alike shall I partake –
But oh! to mourn for thee, and to forsake   175
All power, all hope of giving comfort to thee;
To know that thou art weak and worn with pain
And not to hear thee, Sara, not to view thee,
    Not sit beside thy bed,
    Not press thy aching head,   180
    Not bring thee health again,
    At least to hope, to try
By this voice which thou lov'st, and by this earnest eye –

14

Nay, wherefore did I let it haunt my mind,
    This dark distressful dream?   185
I turn from it and listen to the wind
Which long has howled unnoticed; what a scream
Of agony, by torture lengthened out,
That lute sent forth! Oh, thou wild storm without!
Or crag, or tairn, or lightning-blasted tree,   190
Or pine-grove whither woodman never clomb,
Or lonely house long held the witches' home,
Methinks were fitter instruments for thee,
Mad lutanist, that in this month of showers,
Of dark-brown gardens and of peeping flowers,   195
Mak'st devil's yule, with worse than wintry song,
The blooms and buds and timorous leaves among!
Thou actor, perfect in all tragic sounds,
Thou mighty poet, even to frenzy bold,
    What tell'st thou now about?   200
'Tis of a rushing of an host in rout,
And many groans from men with smarting wounds,
That groan at once from smart, and shudder with the cold!
But hush, there is a break of deepest silence –
Again! But that dread sound, as of a rushing crowd,   205
And groans and tremulous shuddering – all are over.
And it has other sounds, and all less deep, less loud;
    A tale of less affright,
    And tempered with delight,
As William's self had made the tender lay!   210
    'Tis of a little child
    Upon a heathy wild[9]

---

[9] Coleridge has in mind Wordsworth's 'Lucy Gray'.

Not far from home, but it has lost its way,
And now moans low in utter grief and fear,
And now screams loud, and hopes to make its mother hear!　　　215

15

'Tis midnight, and small thought have I of sleep;
Full seldom may my friend such vigils keep –
Oh breathe she softly in her gentle sleep!
Cover her, gentle sleep, with wings of healing,
And be this tempest but a mountain birth;　　　220
May all the stars hang bright above her dwelling,
Silent, as though they watched the sleeping earth,
Like elder sisters with love-twinkling eyes!
Healthful and light, my darling, may'st thou rise,
And of the same good tidings to me send –　　　225
For oh, beloved friend,
I am not the buoyant thing I was of yore,
When like an own child, I to joy belonged;
For others mourning oft, myself oft sorely wronged,
Yet bearing all things then as if I nothing bore.　　　230

16

Ere I was wedded, though my path was rough,
The joy within me dallied with distress,
And all misfortunes were but as the stuff
Whence fancy made me dreams of happiness;
For hope grew round me like the climbing vine,　　　235
And leaves and fruitage not my own, seemed mine!
But now ill tidings bow me down to earth,
Nor care I that they rob me of my mirth;
　　　But oh! each visitation
Suspends what nature gave me at my birth –　　　240
My shaping spirit of imagination!
I speak not now of those habitual ills
That wear out life, when two unequal minds
Meet in one house, and two discordant wills –
　　　This leaves me where it finds,　　　245
Past cure and past complaint, a fate austere
Too fixed and hopeless to partake of fear!

17

But thou, *dear* Sara – dear indeed thou art,
My comforter, a heart within my heart! –

Thou and the few we love (though few ye be)   250
Make up a world of hopes and fears for me;
And when affliction or distempering pain
Or wayward chance befall you, I complain.
Not that I mourn – oh friends most dear, most true,
    Methinks to weep with you   255
Were better far than to rejoice alone –
But that my coarse domestic life[10] has known
No griefs but such as dull and deaden me,
No habits of heart-nursing sympathy,
No mutual mild enjoyments of its own,   260
No hopes of its own vintage – none, oh none! –
Whence, when I mourn for you, my heart must borrow
Fair forms and living motions for its sorrow.
For not to think of what I needs must feel,
But to be still and patient all I can,   265
And haply by abstruse research to steal
From my own nature all the natural man –
This was my sole resource, my wisest plan;
And that which suits a part infects the whole,
And now is almost grown the temper of my soul.   270

18

My little children[11] are a joy, a love,
    A good gift from above!
But what is bliss that ever calls up woe,
    And makes it doubly keen,
Compelling me to feel what well I know –   275
What a most blessed lot mine *might* have been?
Those little angel children (woe is me!),
There have been hours when, feeling how they bind
And pluck out the wing-feathers of my mind,
Turning my error to necessity,   280
I have half-wished they never had been born.
That, seldom; but sad thought they always bring,
And, like the poet's nightingale, I sing
My love-song with my breast against a thorn.

19

With no unthankful spirit I confess   285
This clinging grief, too, in its turn awakes

---

[10] A reference to Coleridge's marriage, the failure of
which would lead him to leave his family with Southey in Keswick.

[11] Hartley (born 19 Sept. 1796); Sara would be born
23 Dec. 1802.

That love and father's joy – but oh! it makes
The love the greater, and the joy far less.
These mountains too, these vales, these woods, these lakes,
Scenes full of beauty and of loftiness   290
Where all my life I fondly hope to live –
I were sunk low indeed, did they *no* solace give.
But oft I seem to feel, and evermore to fear,
They are not to me now the things which once they were.[12]

20

Oh Sara, we receive but what we give,   295
And in *our* life alone does nature live;
Ours is her wedding-garment, ours her shroud!
And would we aught behold of higher worth
Than that inanimate cold world allowed
To the poor loveless, ever-anxious crowd –   300
Ah! from the soul itself must issue forth
A light, a glory, and a luminous cloud
        Enveloping the earth!
And from the soul itself must there be sent
A sweet and potent voice, of its own birth,   305
Of all sweet sounds the life and element.
Oh pure of heart! thou need'st not ask of me
What this strange music in the soul may be,
What and wherein it doth exist,
This light, this glory, this fair luminous mist,   310
This beautiful and beauty-making power!
Joy, innocent Sara! Joy that ne'er was given
Save to the pure and in their purest hour,
Joy, Sara, is the spirit and the power
That, wedding nature to us, gives in dower   315
        A new earth and new heaven
Undreamt of by the sensual and the proud!
Joy is that sweet voice, joy that luminous cloud –
        We, we ourselves rejoice!
And thence flows all that charms or ear or sight,   320
All melodies the echoes of that voice,
All colours a suffusion from that light.
Sister and friend of my devoutest choice;
Thou being innocent and full of love,
And nested with the darlings of thy love;   325
And feeling in thy soul, heart, lips, and arms
Even what the conjugal and mother dove
That borrows genial warmth from these she warms

---

[12] A reworking of Wordsworth, 'Ode', 9.

Feels in her thrilled wings, blessedly outspread;
Thou, freed awhile from cares and human dread   330
By the immenseness of the good and fair
    Which thou seest everywhere –
Thus, thus would'st thou rejoice!
To thee would all things *live* from pole to pole,
Their life the eddying of thy living soul.   335
Oh dear! Oh innocent! Oh full of love!
Sara, thou friend of my devoutest choice,
As dear as light and impulse from above –
So may'st thou ever, evermore rejoice!

The Day-Dream (composed by 31 July 1802; published in *Morning Post*, 19 October 1802; edited from MS)

I

If thou wert here, these tears were tears of light!
But from as sweet a day-dream did I start
As ever made these eyes grow idly bright;
And though I weep, yet still about the heart
A dear and playful tenderness doth linger,   5
Touching my heart as with a baby's finger.

2

My mouth half-open like a witless man,
I saw the couch, I saw the quiet room,
The heaving shadows and the firelight gloom;
And on my lips I know not what there ran –   10
On my unmoving lips a subtle feeling;
I know not what, but had the same been stealing

3

Upon a sleeping mother's lips, I guess
It would have made the loving mother dream
That she was softly stooping down to kiss   15
Her babe, that something more than babe did seem –
An obscure presence of its darling father,
Yet still its own sweet baby self far rather!

4

Across my chest there lived a weight so warm
As if some bird had taken shelter there;   20

And lo, upon the couch, a woman's form!
Thine, Sara, thine! Oh joy, if thine it were!
I gazed with anxious hope, and feared to stir it –
A deeper trance ne'er rapt a yearning spirit!

5

And now, when I seemed *sure* my love to see,   25
Her very self in her own quiet home,
There came an elfish laugh, and wakened me!
'Twas Hartley, who behind my chair had clomb,
And with his bright eyes at my face was peeping;
I blessed him, tried to laugh – and fell a-weeping.   30

From Morning Post, no. 10,584 (6 September 1802)

THE PICTURE; OR, THE LOVER'S RESOLUTION

Through weeds and thorns, and matted underwood
I force my way; now climb, and now descend
O'er rocks, or bare or mossy, with blind foot
Crushing the purple whorts; while oft unseen,
Hurrying along the drifted forest leaves,   5
The scared snake rustles. Onward still I toil,
I know not, ask not whither. A new joy
Lovely as light, sudden as summer gust
And gladsome as the first-born of the spring,
Beckons me on, or follows from behind,   10
Playmate or guide.[1] The master-passion quelled,
I feel that I am free. With dun-red bark
The fir-trees and th' unfrequent slender oak
Forth from this tangle wild of bush and brake
Soar up, and form a melancholy vault   15
High o'er me, murm'ring like a distant sea.
No myrtle-walks are here! These are no groves
For love to dwell in; the low stumps would gore
His dainty feet; the briar and the thorn
Make his plumes haggard; till, like wounded bird,   20
Easily caught, the dusky dryads,
With prickles sharper than his darts, would mock
His little godship, making him perforce
Creep through a thorn-bush on yon hedgehog's back.

THE PICTURE; OR, THE LOVER'S RESOLUTION
[1]   Lines 7–11 recall Wordsworth's search for a guide
in the Glad Preamble (composed early 1800), *Thirteen-
Book Prelude*, i. 1–54.

This is my hour of triumph! I can now 25
With my own fancies play the merry fool,
And laugh away worse folly, being free.
Here will I seat myself beside this old,
Hollow, and woody oak, which ivy-twine
Clothes, as with network; here will couch my limbs 30
Close by this river, in this silent shade,
As safe and sacred from the step of man
As an invisible world – unheard, unseen,
And list'ning only to the pebbly stream
That murmurs with a dead yet bell-like sound 35
Tinkling, or bees, that in the neighb'ring trunk
Make honey-hoards. This breeze that visits me
Was never Love's accomplice, never raised
The tendril ringlets from the maiden's brow,
And the blue, delicate veins above her cheek; 40
Ne'er played the wanton, never half-disclosed
The maiden's snowy bosom, scatt'ring thence
Eye-poisons for some love-distempered youth,
Who ne'er, henceforth, may see an aspen-grove
Shiver in sunshine, but his feeble heart 45
Shall flow away like a dissolving thing.
Sweet breeze! thou only, if I guess aright,
Liftest the feathers of the robin's breast,
Who swells his little breast, so full of song,
Singing above me on the mountain ash. 50
And thou too, desert stream! No pool of thine,
Though clear as lake in latest summer eve,
Did e'er reflect the stately virgin's robe,
The face, the form divine, her downcast look
Contemplative, her cheek upon her palm 55
Supported; the white arm and elbow rest
On the bare branch of half-uprooted tree,
That leans towards its mirror! He, meanwhile,
Who from her count'nance turned, or looked by stealth
(For fear is true love's cruel nurse), he now, 60
With steadfast gaze and unoffending eye,
Worships the wat'ry idol, dreaming hopes
Delicious to the soul, but fleeting, vain,
Ev'n as that phantom-world on which he gazed!
She, sportive tyrant, with her left hand plucks 65
The heads of tall flow'rs that behind her grow –
Lychnis, and willow-herb, and foxglove-bells;
And suddenly, as one that toys with time,
Scatters them on the pool! Then all the charm
Is broken – all that phantom world so fair 70
Vanishes, and a thousand circlets spread,
And each misshape the other. Stay awhile,

Poor youth, who scarcely dar'st lift up thine eyes –
The stream will soon renew its smoothness, soon
The visions will return! And lo, he stays,   75
And soon the fragments dim of lovely forms
Come trembling back, unite, and now once more
The pool becomes a mirror;[2] and behold
Each wild-flow'r on the marge inverted there,
And there the half-uprooted tree – but where,   80
Oh where the virgin's snowy arm, that leaned
On its bare branch? He turns, and she is gone!
Homeward she steals through many a woodland maze
Which he shall seek in vain. Ill-fated youth,
Go, day by day, and waste thy manly prime   85
In mad love-gazing on the vacant brook,
Till sickly thoughts bewitch thine eyes, and thou
Behold'st her shadow still abiding there,
The naiad of the mirror!
               Not to thee,
Oh wild and desert stream, belongs this tale.   90
Gloomy and dark art thou; the crowded firs
Tow'r from thy shores, and stretch across thy bed,
Making thee doleful as a cavern well!
Save when the shy kingfishers build their nest
On thy steep banks, no loves hast thou, wild stream!   95
This be my chosen haunt – emancipate
From passion's dreams, a freeman, and alone,
I rise and trace its devious course. Oh lead,
Lead me to deeper shades, to lonelier glooms.
Lo! stealing through the canopy of firs,   100
How fair the sunshine spots that mossy rock,
Isle of the river, whose disparted waters
Dart off asunder with an angry sound,
How soon to reunite! They meet, they join
In deep embrace, and open to the sun   105
Lie calm and smooth. Such the delicious hour
Of deep enjoyment, foll'wing love's brief quarrels!
And hark, the noise of a near waterfall!
I come out into light – I find myself
Beneath a weeping birch (most beautiful   110
Of forest trees, the lady of the woods)
Hard by the brink of a tall weedy rock
That overbrows the cataract. How bursts
The landscape on my sight! Two crescent hills
Fold in behind each other, and so make   115
A circular vale, and landlocked, as might seem,

---

[2]   Lines 69–78 are quoted by Coleridge in the introduction to the printed text of *Kubla Khan* (1816), p. 578.

With brook and bridge, and grey-stone cottages,
Half hid by rocks and fruit-trees. Beneath my feet
The whortle-berries are bedewed with spray,
Dashed upwards by the furious waterfall.   120
How solemnly the pendent ivy mass
Swings in its winnow! All the air is calm,
The smoke from cottage chimneys, tinged with light,
Rises in columns; from this house alone
Close by the waterfall, the column slants   125
And feels its ceaseless breeze. But what is this?
That cottage, with its slanting chimney smoke,
And close beside its porch a sleeping child,
His dear head pillowed on a sleeping dog,
One arm between its forelegs, and the hand   130
Holds loosely its small handful of wild-flow'rs,
Unfilletted, and of unequal lengths –
A curious picture, with a master's haste
Sketched on a strip of pinky-silver skin
Peeled from the birchen bark! Divinest maid –   135
Yon bark her canvas, and these purple berries
Her pencil! See, the juice is scarcely dried
On the fine skin! She has been newly here,
And lo! Yon patch of heath has been her couch –
The pressure still remains! Oh blessed couch,   140
For this may'st thou flow'r early, and the sun
Slanting, at eve rest bright, and linger long
Upon thy purple bells! Oh Isabel,
Daughter of genius, stateliest of our maids,
More beautiful than whom Alcaeus wooed,   145
The Lesbian woman of immortal song,[3]
Oh child of genius, stately, beautiful,
And full of love to all, save only one,
And not ungentle ev'n to me! My heart,
Why beats it thus? Through yonder coppice-wood   150
Needs must the pathway turn, that leads away
On to her father's house. She is alone!
The night draws on – such ways are hard to hit –
And fit it is, I should restore this sketch,
Dropped unawares, no doubt. Why should I yearn   155
To keep the relic? 'Twill but idly feed
The passion that consumes me. Let me haste!
This picture in my hand, which she has left;
She cannot blame me, that I followed her,
And I may be her guide the long wood through!   160

---

[3] Sappho, as in Wordsworth's 'Alcaeus to Sappho',
published in *Morning Post* 2 Oct. 1800 (see Griggs,
i. 629).

From Morning Post, no. 10,589 (11 September 1802)

CHAMOUNY; THE HOUR BEFORE SUNRISE. A HYMN (COMPOSED NOT BEFORE 26 AUGUST 1802[1])

Chamouny is one of the highest mountain valleys of the Barony of Faucigny in the Savoy Alps, and exhibits a kind of fairy world in which the wildest appearances (I had almost said horrors) of nature alternate with the softest and most beautiful. The chain of Mont Blanc is its boundary, and, besides the Arvè, it is filled with sounds from the Arveiron, which rushes from the melted glaciers like a giant mad with joy from a dungeon, and forms other torrents of snow-water, having their rise in the glaciers which slope down into the valley. The beautiful gentiana major, *or greater gentian, with blossoms of the brightest blue, grows in large companies a few steps from the never-melted ice of the glaciers. I thought it an affecting emblem of the boldness of human hope, venturing near, and, as it were, leaning over, the brink of the grave. Indeed, the whole vale, its every light, its every sound, must needs impress every mind not utterly callous with the thought, Who would be, who could be an atheist in this valley of wonders? If any readers of* The Morning Post *have visited this vale in their journeys among the Alps, I am confident that they will not find the sentiments and feelings expressed, or attempted to be expressed, in the following poem, extravagant.*

Hast thou a charm to stay the morning star
In his steep course? So long he seems to pause
On thy bald awful head, oh Chamouny!
The Arvè and Arveiron at thy base
Rave ceaselessly; but thou, dread mountain form,   5
Risest from forth thy silent sea of pines
How silently! Around thee and above,
Deep is the sky, and black – transpicuous,[2] deep,
An ebon mass. Methinks thou piercest it
As with a wedge! But when I look again,   10
It seems thy own calm home, thy crystal shrine,
Thy habitation from eternity.
Oh dread and silent form! I gazed upon thee
Till thou, still present to my bodily eye,
Didst vanish from my thought. Entranced in pray'r,   15
I worshipped the Invisible alone.
Yet thou, meantime, wast working on my soul,
E'en like some deep enchanting melody,
So sweet, we know not we are list'ning to it.

CHAMOUNY; THE HOUR BEFORE SUNRISE. A HYMN
[1] On 10 Sept. 1802 Coleridge told William Sotheby that he composed this poem 'when I was on Scafell. I involuntarily poured forth a hymn in the manner of the Psalms, though afterwards I thought the ideas etc. disproportionate to our humble mountains, and, accidentally lighting on a short note in some Swiss poems concerning the Vale of Chamouni and its mountains, I transferred myself thither, in the spirit, and adapted my former feelings to these grander external objects' (Griggs, ii. 864–5). However, Griggs notes that the poem could not have been composed until after 26 Aug. 1802 – three weeks after Coleridge's ascent of Scafell. The poem which inspired him is Frederika Brun's 'Chamouny beym Sonnenaufgange', reprinted EHC, ii. 1131; see Griggs, ii. 865n.
[2] As at *Paradise Lost*, viii. 141, the air is 'transpicuous' (transparent).

But I awake, and with a busier mind   20
And active will self-conscious, offer now,
Not, as before, involuntary pray'r
And passive adoration.
                   Hand and voice,
Awake, awake! And thou, my heart, awake!
Awake, ye rocks! Ye forest pines, awake!   25
Green fields and icy cliffs, all join my hymn!
And thou, oh silent mountain, sole and bare,
Oh blacker than the darkness, all the night,
And visited all night by troops of stars,
Or when they climb the sky, or when they sink;   30
Companion of the morning star at dawn,
Thyself earth's rosy star, and of the dawn
Co-herald! Wake, oh wake, and utter praise!
Who sank thy sunless pillars deep in earth?
Who filled thy countenance with rosy light?   35
Who made thee father of perpetual streams?
And you, ye five wild torrents, fiercely glad,
Who called you forth from night and utter death,
From darkness let you loose, and icy dens,
Down those precipitous, black, jagged rocks   40
For ever shattered, and the same for ever?
Who gave you your invulnerable life,
Your strength, your speed, your fury, and your joy,
Unceasing thunder, and eternal foam?
And who commanded (and the silence came),   45
'Here shall the billows stiffen, and have rest'?
   Ye ice-falls! Ye that from yon dizzy heights
Adown enormous ravines steeply slope –
Torrents, methinks, that heard a mighty voice,
And stopped at once amid their maddest plunge!   50
Motionless torrents! Silent cataracts!
Who made you glorious as the gates of heav'n
Beneath the keen full moon? Who bade the sun
Clothe you with rainbows? Who with lovely flow'rs
Of living blue spread garlands at your feet?   55
'God, God!' the torrents, like a shout of nations,
Utter. The ice-plain bursts, and answers 'God!'
'God!' sing the meadow-streams with gladsome voice,
And pine-groves, with their soft and soul-like sound!
The silent snow-mass, loos'ning, thunders 'God!'   60
Ye dreadless flow'rs that fringe th' eternal frost!
Ye wild goats bounding by the eagle's nest!
Ye eagles, playmates of the mountain blast!
Ye lightnings, the dread arrows of the clouds!
Ye signs and wonders of the element   65
Utter forth 'God!' and fill the hills with praise!

And thou, oh silent form, alone and bare,
Whom, as I lift again my head bowed low
In adoration, I again behold,
And to thy summit upward from thy base   70
Sweep slowly with dim eyes suffused by tears,
Awake, thou mountain form! Rise like a cloud!
Rise like a cloud of incense from the earth!
Thou kingly spirit throned among the hills,
Thou dread ambassador from earth to heav'n –   75
Great hierarch, tell thou the silent sky,
And tell the stars, and tell the rising sun,
Earth with her thousand voices calls on God!

From Morning Post, no. 10,608 (4 October 1802)

DEJECTION: AN ODE, WRITTEN 4 APRIL 1802[1]

Late, late yestreen I saw the new moon
With the old moon in her arms;
And I fear, I fear, my master dear,
We shall have a deadly storm.
(Ballad of Sir Patrick Spence)

I

Well! if the bard was weather-wise who made
  The grand old ballad of Sir Patrick Spence,
  This night, so tranquil now, will not go hence
Unroused by winds that ply a busier trade
Than those which mould yon clouds in lazy flakes,   5
Or this dull sobbing draught that drones and rakes
Upon the strings of this Œolian lute,
Which better far were mute.
For lo! the new moon, winter-bright,
And overspread with phantom light   10
(With swimming phantom light o'erspread,
But rimmed and circled by a silver thread);
I see the old moon in her lap, foretelling
  The coming-on of rain and squally blast.
And oh, that even now the gust were swelling,   15
  And the slant night-show'r driving loud and fast.
Those sounds which oft have raised me while they awed
And sent my soul abroad,

DEJECTION: AN ODE
[1] This is the text of the poem as first published in
Morning Post, 4 Oct. 1802, as a sort of gift to
Wordsworth, whose wedding-day it was. It next appeared in *Sibylline Leaves* (1817), revised.

Might now perhaps their wonted impulse give,
Might startle this dull pain, and make it move and live! 20

II

A grief without a pang – void, dark, and drear;
   A stifled, drowsy, unimpassioned grief
   Which finds no nat'ral outlet, no relief
In word, or sigh, or tear –
Oh Edmund![2] in this wan and heartless mood, 25
To other thoughts by yonder throstle wooed
All this long eve so balmy and serene,
   Have I been gazing on the western sky
And its peculiar tint of yellow-green;
   And still I gaze, and with how blank an eye! 30
And those thin clouds above, in flakes and bars,
That give away their motion to the stars,
Those stars that glide behind them or between,
Now sparkling, now bedimmed, but always seen;
Yon crescent moon, as fixed as if it grew 35
In its own cloudless, starless lake of blue –
A boat becalmed! A lovely sky-canoe![3]
I see them all, so excellently fair;
I *see*, not *feel*, how beautiful they are!

III

   My genial spirits fail,[4] 40
   And what can these avail
To lift the smoth'ring weight from off my breast?
   It were a vain endeavour,
   Though I should gaze forever
On that green light that lingers in the west: 45
I may not hope from outward forms to win
The passion and the life, whose fountains are within!

IV

Oh Edmund, we receive but what we give,
And in *our* life alone does nature live;

---

[2] There are four addressees in successive versions of
this poem: (i) Sara Hutchinson in 'Letter to Sara
Hutchinson', presented above; (ii) Wordsworth (letters to William Sotheby, July 1802, and Sir George
Beaumont, Aug. 1803); (iii) 'Edmund' (in the version
presented here); (iv) 'Lady' (*Sibylline Leaves* (1817)).

[3] This reference to the Prologue of Wordsworth's
Peter Bell would not have been understood by most
of the readers of *Morning Post* since the poem was
unpublished, and would remain so until 1819.
[4] An echo of Milton, 'Samson Agonistes', 594: 'my
genial spirits droop'.

Ours is her wedding-garment, ours her shroud!   50
And would we aught behold of higher worth
Than that inanimate cold world allowed
To the poor loveless ever-anxious crowd –
Ah! from the soul itself must issue forth
A light, a glory, a fair luminous cloud   55
Enveloping the earth!
And from the soul itself must there be sent
A sweet and potent voice, of its own birth,
Of all sweet sounds the life and element.
Oh pure of heart! thou need'st not ask of me   60
What this strong music in the soul may be,
What and wherein it doth exist,
This light, this glory, this fair luminous mist,
This beautiful and beauty-making pow'r!
Joy, virtuous Edmund! Joy that ne'er was given   65
Save to the pure and in their purest hour,
Joy, Edmund, is the spirit and the pow'r
Which, wedding nature to us, gives in dow'r
    A new earth and new heaven
Undreamed of by the sensual and the proud!   70
Joy is the sweet voice, Joy the luminous cloud –
    We, we ourselves rejoice!
And thence flows all that charms or ear or sight,[5]
All melodies the echoes of that voice,
All colours a suffusion from that light.   75

                                   V

Yes, dearest Edmund, yes!
    There was a time when, though my path was rough,
    This joy within me dallied with distress,
And all misfortunes were but as the stuff
        Whence fancy made me dreams of happiness;   80
For hope grew round me like the twining vine,
And fruits and foliage not my own, seemed mine!
But now afflictions bow me down to earth,
Nor care I that they rob me of my mirth;
    But oh! each visitation   85
Suspends what nature gave me at my birth –
    My shaping spirit of imagination!

[The sixth and seventh stanzas omitted.[6]]

---

[5] *sight* other versions of the poem give 'sight',   [6] There is no textual evidence to support the claim
suggesting that 'light', the reading of the *Morning Post*   of this note.
text at this point, is an error.

VIII

Oh, wherefore did I let it haunt my mind,
    This dark distressful dream?
I turn from it and listen to the wind   90
    Which long has raved unnoticed; what a scream
Of agony, by torture lengthened out,
That lute sent forth! Oh wind, that rav'st without!
    Bare crag, or mountain tairn,[7] or blasted tree,
Or pine-grove whither woodman never clomb,   95
Or lonely house long held the witches' home,
    Methinks were fitter instruments for thee,
Mad lutanist, who in this month of show'rs,
Of dark-brown gardens and of peeping flow'rs,
Mak'st devil's yule, with worse than wintry song,   100
The blossoms, buds, and tim'rous leaves among!
    Thou actor, perfect in all tragic sounds,
        Thou mighty poet, ev'n to frenzy bold,
What tell'st thou now about?
'Tis of the rushing of an host in rout,   105
    With many groans of men with smarting wounds –
        At once they groan with pain, and shudder with the cold!
But hush, there is a pause of deepest silence!
    And all that noise, as of a rushing crowd,
        With groans and tremulous shudderings – all is over.   110
It tells another tale, with sounds less deep and loud,
      A tale of less affright
      And tempered with delight,
As Edmund's self had framed the tender lay –
    'Tis of a little child   115
      Upon a lonesome wild[8]
Not far from home, but she has lost her way,
And now moans low in utter grief and fear,
And now screams loud, and hopes to make her mother *hear!*

IX

'Tis midnight, and small thoughts have I of sleep;   120
Full seldom may my friend such vigils keep!
Visit him, gentle sleep, with wings of healing,
    And may this storm be but a mountain birth;

---

[7] 'Tairn: a small lake, generally (if not always) applied to the lakes up in the mountains, and which are the feeders of those in the valleys. This address to the wind will not appear extravagant to those who have heard it at night in a mountainous country' (Coleridge's note).

[8] Coleridge has in mind Wordsworth's 'Lucy Gray'.

May all the stars hang bright above his dwelling,
  Silent, as though they *watched* the sleeping earth!   125
    With light heart may he rise,
    Gay fancy, cheerful eyes,
And sing his lofty song, and teach me to rejoice!
Oh Edmund, friend of my devoutest choice,
Oh, raised from anxious dread and busy care,   130
By the immenseness of the good and fair
Which thou see'st ev'rywhere[9] –
Joy lifts thy spirit, joy attunes thy voice,
To thee do all things live from pole to pole,
Their life the eddying of thy living soul!   135
Oh simple spirit, guided from above;
Oh lofty poet, full of light and love;
Brother and friend of my devoutest choice,
Thus may'st thou ever, evermore rejoice!

From Morning Post, no. 10,614 (11 October 1802)

SPOTS IN THE SUN[1]

My father confessor is strict and holy,
'Mi fili', still he cries, 'peccare noli.'[2]
And yet how oft I find the pious man
At Annette's door, the lovely courtesan!
Her soul's deformity the good man wins,   5
And not her charms – he comes to hear her sins!
Good father, I would fain not do thee wrong,
But ah! I fear that they who oft and long
Stand gazing at the sun, to count each spot,
Must sometimes find the sun itself too hot.   10

From Christabel; Kubla Khan: A Vision; The Pains of Sleep (1816)

THE PAINS OF SLEEP (COMPOSED BY 10 SEPTEMBER 1803)

Ere on my bed my limbs I lay,
It hath not been my use to pray
With moving lips or bended knees;
But silently, by slow degrees,
My spirit I to love compose,   5
In humble trust mine eyelids close
With reverential resignation;

---

[9] Lines 128–32 were removed from subsequent texts.
SPOTS IN THE SUN
[1] Like Wordsworth's 'A Complaint', this poem
arose out of the strains that had crept into the relationship between Coleridge and Wordsworth.
[2] 'Sin not, my son.'

No wish conceived, no thought expressed!
Only a *sense* of supplication,
A sense o'er all my soul impressed   10
That I am weak, yet not unblessed –
Since in me, round me, everywhere,
Eternal strength and wisdom are.

But yesternight I prayed aloud
In anguish and in agony,   15
Upstarting from the fiendish crowd
Of shapes and thoughts that tortured me;
A lurid light, a trampling throng,
Sense of intolerable wrong,
And whom I scorned, those only strong!   20
Thirst of revenge, the powerless will
Still baffled, and yet burning still!
Desire with loathing strangely mixed,
On wild or hateful objects fixed.
Fantastic passions! Mad'ning brawl!   25
And shame and terror over all!
Deeds to be hid which were not hid,
Which all confused I could not know,
Whether I suffered or I did –
For all seemed guilt, remorse or woe,   30
My own or others, still the same
Life-stifling fear, soul-stifling shame!
So two nights passed: the night's dismay
Saddened and stunned the coming day.
Sleep, the wide blessing, seemed to me   35
Distemper's worst calamity.
The third night when my own loud scream
Had waked me from the fiendish dream,
O'ercome with sufferings strange and wild,
I wept as I had been a child –   40
And having thus by tears subdued
My anguish to a milder mood,
Such punishments, I said, were due
To natures deepliest stained with sin:
For aye entempesting anew   45
Th' unfathomable hell within,
The horror of their deeds to view,
To know and loathe, yet wish and do!
Such griefs with such men well agree,
But wherefore, wherefore fall on me?   50
To be beloved is all I need,
And whom I love, I love indeed.

566 SAMUEL TAYLOR COLERIDGE

From Letter from S. T. Coleridge to Thomas Poole, 14 October 1803[1]

Wordsworth is in good health, and all his family. He has one large boy, christened John. He has made a beginning to his *Recluse*.[2] He was here on Sunday last. His wife's sister, who is on a visit at Grasmere, was in a bad hysterical way, and he rode in to consult our excellent medical men.[3] I now see very little of Wordsworth. My own health makes it inconvenient and unfit for me to go thither one third as often, as I used to do – and Wordsworth's indolence, etc., keeps him at home. Indeed, were I an irritable man (and an unthinking one), I should probably have considered myself as having been very unkindly used by him in this respect, for I was at one time confined for two months, and he never came in to see me – me, who had ever paid such unremitting attentions to him!

But we must take the good and the ill together – and by seriously and habitually reflecting on our own faults and endeavouring to amend them, we shall then find little difficulty in confining our attention (as far as it acts on our friends' characters) to their good qualities. Indeed, I owe it to truth and justice, as well as to myself, to say that the concern which I have felt in this instance (and one or two other more *crying* instances) of self-involution in Wordsworth, has been almost wholly a feeling of friendly regret and disinterested apprehension. I saw him more and more benetted in hypochondriacal fancies, living wholly among *devotees*, having every the minutest thing, almost his very eating and drinking, done for him by his sister or wife – and I trembled lest a film should rise and thicken on his moral eye.

The habit too of writing such a multitude of small poems was in this instance hurtful to him – such things as that sonnet of his in Monday's *Morning Post* about Simonides and the ghost.[4] I rejoice, therefore, with a deep and true joy, that he has at length yielded to my urgent and repeated (almost unremitting) requests and remonstrances, and will go on with *The Recluse* exclusively – a great work in which he will sail on an open ocean and a steady wind, unfretted by short tacks, reefing and hauling and disentangling the ropes; great work necessarily comprehending his attention and feelings within the circle of great objects and elevated conceptions. This is his natural element. The having been out of it has been his disease; to return into it is the specific remedy – both remedy and health. It is what food is to famine.

I have seen enough positively to give me feelings of hostility towards the plan of several of the poems in the *Lyrical Ballads*, and I really consider it as a misfortune that

From LETTER FROM S. T. COLERIDGE TO THOMAS POOLE, 14 October 1803
[1] This important letter, written from Greta Hall, Keswick, where Coleridge's family were now living with Southey, indicates something of the strain that had crept into the relationship with Wordsworth. Cf. Wordsworth's 'A Complaint', p. 476 above.
[2] *The Recluse* was the epic poem planned in 1798 which, Coleridge and Wordsworth believed, would help precipitate the millennium (Christ's 1000-year rule on earth predicted in the Bible). Wordsworth managed to compose only fragments, including the 'Prospectus', pp. 246–8, above.

[3] Joanna Hutchinson suffered a 'hysteric and fainting fit' at Dove Cottage on the evening of 7 Oct. 1803. Wordsworth rode to Keswick to consult Mr Edmondson about it the next day, meeting Southey and Coleridge on 9 Oct. before returning to Grasmere that evening.
[4] 'I find it written of Simonides', composed by 7 Oct. 1803, published in *Morning Post*, 10 Oct. 1803. Coleridge may also have had in mind some of the poems which were to appear in *Poems in Two Volumes* (1807).

Wordsworth ever deserted his former mountain-track to wander in lanes and alleys – though in the event it may prove to have been a great benefit to him. He will steer, I trust, the middle course.

To William Wordsworth. Lines Composed, for the Greater Part, on the Night on which he Finished the Recitation of his Poem in Thirteen Books, Concerning the Growth and History of his own Mind, January 1807, Coleorton, near Ashby-de-la-Zouch (composed January 1807; first published 1817; edited from MS)

Oh friend! Oh teacher! God's great gift to me!
Into my heart have I received that lay
More than historic, that prophetic lay
Wherein (high theme by thee first sung aright)
Of the foundations and the building up   5
Of thy own spirit, thou hast loved to tell
What may be told, to th' understanding mind
Revealable; and what within the mind
May rise enkindled. Theme as hard as high!
Of smiles spontaneous, and mysterious fear   10
(The first-born they of reason, and twin-birth);
Of tides obedient to external force,
And currents self-determined, as might seem,
Or by interior power; of moments awful,
Now in thy hidden life, and now abroad,   15
Mid festive crowds, *thy* brows too garlanded,
A brother of the feast; of fancies fair,
Hyblaean[1] murmurs of poetic thought,
Industrious in its joy, by lilied streams
Native or outland, lakes and famous hills!   20
Of more than fancy – of the hope of man
Amid the tremor of a realm aglow,
Where France in all her towns lay vibrating,
Ev'n as a bark becalmed on sultry seas
Beneath the voice from heaven, the bursting crash   25
Of heaven's immediate thunder, when no cloud
Is visible, or shadow on the main!
Ah, soon night rolled on night, and every cloud
Opened its eye of fire; and hope aloft
Now fluttered, and now tossed upon the storm   30
Floating! Of hope afflicted, and struck down,
Thence summoned homeward – homeward to thy heart,

To William Wordsworth
[1] *Hyblaean* honeyed.

Oft from the watchtower of man's absolute self,
With light unwaning on her eyes, to look
Far on – herself a glory to behold,   35
The angel of the vision! Then (last strain!)
Of duty, chosen laws controlling² choice,
Virtue and love! An Orphic tale indeed,
A tale divine of high and passionate thoughts
To their own music chaunted!
                          Ah great bard!   40
Ere yet that last swell dying awed the air,
With steadfast ken I viewed thee in the choir
Of ever-enduring men. The truly great
Have all one age, and from one visible space
Shed influence; for they, both power and act,   45
Are permanent, and time is now with them,
Save as it worketh for them, they in it.
Nor less a sacred roll, than those of old,
And to be placed, as they, with gradual fame
Among the archives of mankind, thy work   50
Makes audible a linked song of truth,
Of truth profound a sweet continuous song
Not learnt but native, her own natural notes!
Dear shall it be to every human heart,
To me how more than dearest! Me, on whom   55
Comfort from thee and utterance of thy love
Came with such heights and depths of harmony
Such sense of wings uplifting, that the storm
Scattered and whirled me, till my thoughts became
A bodily tumult! And thy faithful hopes,   60
Thy hopes of me, dear friend, by me unfelt
Were troublous to me, almost as a voice
Familiar once and more than musical
To one cast forth, whose hope had seemed to die,
A wanderer with a worn-out heart,   65
Mid strangers pining with untended wounds!
    Oh friend, too well thou know'st, of what sad years
The long suppression had benumbed my soul,
That even as life returns upon the drowned,
Th' unusual joy awoke a throng of pains –   70
Keen pangs of *love*, awakening, as a babe,
Turbulent, with an outcry in the heart;
And fears self-willed, that shunned the eye of hope,
And hope, that would not know itself from fear;
Sense of passed youth, and manhood come in vain;   75
And genius given, and knowledge won in vain;

---

² 'Impelling? Directing?' (Coleridge's note).

And all, which I had culled in wood-walks wild,
And all, which patient toil had reared, and all
Commune with thee had opened out, but flowers
Strewed on my corse, and borne upon my bier,   80
In the same coffin, for the self-same grave!
   That way no more! And ill beseems it me,
Who came a welcomer in herald's guise,
Singing of glory and futurity,
To wander back on such unhealthful road   85
Plucking the poisons of self-harm! And ill
Such intertwine beseems triumphal wreaths
Strewed before thy advancing! Thou too, friend!
Oh injure not the memory of that hour
Of thy communion with my nobler mind   90
By pity or grief, already felt too long!
Nor let my words import more blame than needs.
The tumult rose and ceased; for peace is nigh
Where wisdom's voice has found a list'ning heart.
Amid the howl of more than wintry storms,   95
The halcyon hears the voice of vernal hours,
Already on the wing!
               Eve following eve,[3]
Dear tranquil time, when the sweet sense of home
Becomes most sweet! hours for their own sake hailed,
And more desired, more precious, for thy song!   100
In silence list'ning, like a devout child,
My soul lay passive, by thy various strain
Driven as in surges now, beneath the stars,
With momentary stars of my own birth,
Fair constellated foam still darting off   105
Into the darkness! – now a tranquil sea
Outspread and bright, yet swelling to the moon!
   And when, oh friend, my comforter, my guide,
Strong in thyself and powerful to give strength,
Thy long-sustained lay finally closed,   110
And thy deep voice had ceased (yet thou thyself
Wert still before mine eyes, and round us both
That happy vision of beloved faces,
All whom I deepliest love, in one room all!),
Scarce conscious and yet conscious of its close,   115
I sat, my being blended in one thought
(Thought was it? Or aspiration? Or resolve?)
Absorbed, yet hanging still upon the sound:
And when I rose, I found myself in prayer!

---

[3] The evenings when Wordsworth recited The
Thirteen-Book Prelude to Coleridge.

On Donne's First Poem (composed *c.*2 May 1811; edited from MS)[1]

Be proud as Spaniards! Leap for pride, ye fleas!
Henceforth in nature's minim[2] world grandees,
In Phoebus' archives registered are ye –
And this your patent of nobility.
No skipjacks[3] now, nor civiller skip-johns,   5
Dread Anthropophagi![4] Specks of living bronze,
I hail you one and all, sans pros or cons,
Descendants from a noble race of dons.

What though that great ancestral flea be gone,
Immortal with immortalizing Donne –   10
His earthly spots bleached off as Papists gloze
In purgatory fire on Bardolph's nose?
For skimming in the wake, it mocked the care
Of the old boat-god for his farthing fare,
Though Irus' ghost[5] he ne'er frowned blacker on,   15
The skin and skin-pent druggist crossed the Acheron,
Styx and with Puriphlegethon Cocytus[6]
(The very names, methinks, might thither fright us);
Unchanged it crossed, and shall keep in ghost-light
Of lank half-nothings his, the thinnest sprite,   20
The sole true something – this in limbo den:
It frightens ghosts as ghosts here frighten men.
Thence crossed unseized, and shall, some fated hour,
Be pulverized by Demogorgon's power,
And given as poison to annihilate souls –   25
Even now it shrinks them! They shrink in, as moles
(Nature's mute monks, live mandrakes of the ground)
Creep back from light, then listen for its sound –
See but to dread, and dread they know not why –
The natural alien of their negative eye.   30

'Tis a strange place, this limbo! Not a place,
Yet name it so – where time and weary space
Fettered from flight, with nightmare sense of fleeing,
Strive for their last crepuscular half-being;

ON DONNE'S FIRST POEM
[1] Parts of this poem have previously appeared in print as 'Limbo' and 'Ne Plus Ultra'. In fact, the latter both derive from this larger work; for a detailed account, see *Notebooks*, iii. 4073n. This poem was inspired by a reading of Donne's *Poems* (1669), which Coleridge annotated 2 May 1811. 'The Flea' is the first poem in the volume.

[2] *minim* smallest.
[3] *skipjacks* hoppers, jumpers.
[4] Cf. *Othello*, I. iii. 143–4: 'the cannibals that each other eat, / The Anthropophagi'.
[5] *Irus* the voracious beggar of Ithaca, in the *Odyssey*.
[6] Acheron, Styx, Phlegethon, and Cocytus are rivers of hell.

Lank space, and scytheless Time with branny hands, 35
Barren and soundless as the measuring sands,
Marked but by flit of shades – unmeaning they
As moonlight on the dial of the day.
But that is lovely – looks like human time,
An old man with a steady look sublime, 40
That stops his earthly task to watch the skies;
But he is blind – a statue hath such eyes –
Yet having moonward turned his face by chance,
Gazes the orb with moonlike countenance,
With scant white hairs, with foretop bald and high, 45
He gazes still, his eyeless face all eye,
As 'twere an organ full of silent sight,
His whole face seemeth to rejoice in light.
Lip touching lip – all moveless, bust and limb,
He seems to gaze at that which seems to gaze on him! 50

No such sweet sights doth limbo den immure,
Walled round and made a spirit-jail secure,
By the mere horror of blank nought-at-all,
Whose circumambience doth these ghosts enthrall.
A lurid thought is growthless dull privation, 55
Yet that is but a purgatory curse;
Hell knows a fear far worse –
A fear, a future fate: 'tis positive negation!

     Sole Positive of Night!
       Antipathist of light! 60
Fate's only essence! Primal scorpion rod!
  The one permitted opposite of God!
    Condensed blackness, and abysmal storm
     Compacted to one sceptre
      Arms the grasp enorm – 65
       The Intercepter!
The substance, that still casts the shadow, death!
    The dragon foul and fell!
     The unrevealable
    And hidden one, whose breath 70
Gives wind and fuel to the fires of hell!
     Ah sole despair
Of both th' eternities in heaven!
Sole interdict of all-bedewing prayer,
     The All-compassionate! 75
Save to the lampads seven[7]
Revealed to none of all th' angelic state,

---

[7] *the lampads seven* the seven lamps of fire burning
before the throne of God (Rev. 4: 5).

Save to the lampads seven
That watch the throne of heaven!

From Letter from S. T. Coleridge to William Wordsworth, 30 May 1815[1]

What did my criticism amount to, reduced to its full and naked sense? This: that, *comparatively* with the former poem, *The Excursion*, as far as it was new to me, had disappointed my expectations; that the excellences were so many and of so high a class, that it was impossible to attribute the inferiority (if any such really existed) to any flagging of the writer's own genius; and that I conjectured that it might have been occasioned by the influence of self-established convictions having given to certain thoughts and expressions a depth and force which they had not for readers in general. In order, therefore, to explain the disappointment, I must recall to your mind what my expectations were; and as these again were founded on the supposition that (in whatever order it might be published) the poem on the growth of your own mind was as the ground-plat and the roots out of which *The Recluse* was to have sprung up as the tree. As far as the same sap in both, I expected them doubtless to have formed one complete whole, but in matter, form, and product to be different, each not only a distinct but a different work. In the first I had found 'themes by thee first sung aright':

Of smiles spontaneous, and mysterious fears
(The first-born they of reason, and twin-birth);
Of tides obedient to external force,
And currents self-determined, as might seem,
Or by some central breath; of moments awful,
Now in thy inner life, and now abroad,
When power streamed from thee, and thy soul received
The light reflected as a light bestowed!
Of fancies fair, and milder hours of youth,
Hyblaean murmurs of poetic thought,
Industrious in its joy, in vales and glens
Native or outland, lakes and famous hills!
Or on the lonely high-road, when the stars
Were rising, or by secret mountain streams,
The guides and the companions of thy way;
Of more than fancy – of the social sense
Distending wide, and man beloved as man,
Where France in all her towns lay vibrating,
Ev'n as a bark becalmed beneath the burst
Of heaven's immediate thunder, when no cloud

From LETTER FROM S. T. COLERIDGE TO WILLIAM WORDS-
WORTH, 30 May 1815
[1] This important letter, which Coleridge wrote to Wordsworth to explain his disappointment with *The Excursion* (1814), outlines what he had hoped Wordsworth would achieve in *The Recluse* (of which *The* Excursion was part), though the reader should bear in mind that it was written 17 years after *The Recluse* was originally formulated, and that Coleridge's response may be coloured by his quarrel with Wordsworth in 1810. Another account of 'The Recluse' may be found on pp. 595–6 below.

Is visible, or shadow on the main!
For thou wert there, thy own brows garlanded
Amid the tremor of a realm aglow,
Amid a mighty nation jubilant,
When from the general heart of humankind
Hope sprang forth, like a full-born deity!
Of that dear hope afflicted, and amazed,
So homeward summoned! Thenceforth calm and sure
From the dread watchtower of man's absolute self,
With light unwaning on her eyes, to look
Far on – herself a glory to behold,
The angel of the vision! Then (last strain!)
Of duty, chosen laws controlling choice,
Action and joy! *An Orphic song indeed,*
A song divine of high and passionate truths
To their own music chaunted!

Indeed through the whole of that poem με Αὔρα τις εἰσέπνευσε μυστικωτάτη.[2] *This* I considered as *The Excursion,* and the second as *The Recluse* I had (from what I had at different times gathered from your conversation on the plan) anticipated as commencing with you set down and settled in an abiding home, and that with the description of that home you were to begin a *Philosophical Poem,* the result and fruits of a spirit so framed and so disciplined, as had been told in the former.

Whatever in Lucretius[3] is poetry is not philosophical; whatever is philosophical is not poetry – and in the very pride of confident hope I looked forward to *The Recluse* as the *first* and *only* true philosophical poem in existence. Of course, I expected the colours, music, imaginative life, and passion of *poetry,* but the matter and arrangement of *philosophy* – not doubting from the advantages of the subject that the totality of a system was not only capable of being harmonized with, but even calculated to aid, the unity (beginning, middle, and end) of a *poem.* Thus, whatever the length of the work might be, still it was a *determinate* length.

Of the subjects announced each would have its own appointed place and, excluding repetitions, each would relieve and rise in interest above the other. I supposed you first to have meditated the faculties of man in the abstract; in their correspondence with his sphere of action – and first, in the feeling, touch, and taste, then in the eye, and last in the ear; to have laid a solid and immovable foundation for the edifice by removing the sandy sophisms of Locke and the mechanic dogmatists;[4] and demonstrating that the senses were living growths and developments of the mind and spirit in a much juster as well as higher sense than the mind can be said to be formed by the senses. Next I understood that you would take the human race in the concrete, have exploded the absurd notion of Pope's *Essay on Man,*[5] Darwin,[6] and all the countless

[2] 'a certain most mystical breeze blew into me' (Aristophanes, *The Frogs,* 313–14).

[3] Lucretius, *De Rerum Natura,* philosophical poem in 6 books.

[4] John Locke (1632–1704), author of the *Essay concerning Human Understanding* (1690); other 'dogmatists' probably include Isaac Newton (1642–1727) and Francis Bacon (1561–1626).

[5] *Essay on Man* (1732–4), a philosophical poem, part of a larger work never completed by Pope, in which he seeks to vindicate the ways of God to man and prove that the universe is the best of all possible schemes.

[6] Erasmus Darwin (1731–1802), grandfather of Charles Darwin, author of *The Botanic Garden* (1789–91) and *Zoönomia* (1794–6).

believers (even, strange to say, among Christians) of man's having progressed from an orang-utan state – so contrary to all history, to all religion, nay, to all possibility; to have affirmed a fall, in some sense, as a fact the possibility of which cannot be understood from the nature of the will, but the reality of which is attested by experience and conscience; fallen men contemplated in the different ages of the world, and in the different states – savage – barbarous – civilized – the lonely cot or borderer's wigwam – the village – the manufacturing town – sea-port – city – universities – and, not disguising the sore evils under which the whole creation groans, to point out, however, a manifest scheme of redemption from this slavery, of reconciliation from this enmity with nature (What are the obstacles? The Antichrist that must be and already is); and to conclude by a grand didactic swell on the necessary identity of a true philosophy with true religion, agreeing in the results and differing only as the analytic and synthetic process, as discursive from intuitive, the former chiefly useful as perfecting the latter.

In short, the necessity of a general revolution in the modes of developing and disciplining the human mind by the substitution of life and intelligence (considered in its different powers, from the plant up to that state in which the difference of degree becomes a new kind – man, self-consciousness – but yet not by essential opposition), for the philosophy of mechanism which in everything that is needworthy of the human intellect strikes *death*, and cheats itself by mistaking clear images for distinct conceptions, and which idly demands conceptions where intuitions alone are possible or adequate to the majesty of the truth. In short, facts elevated into theory, theory into laws, and laws into living and intelligent powers – true idealism necessarily perfecting itself in realism, and realism refining itself into idealism.

From Biographia Literaria, ed. Henry Nelson and Sara Coleridge (1847)

CHAPTER 13 (EXTRACT)[1] (I. 297–8)

The imagination then I consider either as primary or secondary. The primary imagination I hold to be the living power and prime agent of all human perception, and as a repetition in the finite mind of the eternal act of creation in the infinite I AM. The secondary imagination I consider as an echo of the former, coexisting with the conscious will, yet still as identical with the primary in the *kind* of its agency, and differing only in *degree*, and in the *mode* of its operation. It dissolves, diffuses, dissipates, in order to recreate; or, where this process is rendered impossible, yet still at all events it struggles to idealize and to unify. It is essentially *vital*, even as all objects (*as* objects) are essentially fixed and dead.

Fancy, on the contrary, has no other counters to play with but fixities and definites. The fancy is indeed no other than a mode of memory emancipated from the order of time and space – while it is blended with, and modified by, that empirical phenomenon of the will which we express by the word 'choice'. But equally with the ordinary memory the fancy must receive all its materials ready-made from the law of association.

CHAPTER 13
[1] Coleridge's famous definition of imagination has produced differing interpretations. Unlike Words-worth, Coleridge insisted that fancy involved a different process from the imagination.

CHAPTER 14 (EXTRACTS)[1] (II. 1–9, 13–14)

During the first year that Mr Wordsworth and I were neighbours,[2] our conversations turned frequently on the two cardinal points of poetry: the power of exciting the sympathy of the reader by a faithful adherence to the truth of nature, and the power of giving the interest of novelty by the modifying colours of imagination. The sudden charm which accidents of light and shade, which moonlight or sunset diffused over a known and familiar landscape, appeared to represent the practicability of combining both. These are the poetry of nature.

The thought suggested itself (to which of us I do not recollect) that a series of poems might be composed of two sorts. In the one, the incidents and agents were to be (in part at least) supernatural – and the excellence aimed at was to consist in the interesting of the affections by the dramatic truth of such emotions as would naturally accompany such situations, supposing them real. And real in this sense they have been to every human being who, from whatever source of delusion, has at any time believed himself under supernatural agency. For the second class, subjects were to be chosen from ordinary life. The characters and incidents were to be such as will be found in every village and its vicinity, where there is a meditative and feeling mind to seek after them or to notice them when they present themselves.

In this idea originated the plan of the *Lyrical Ballads*, in which it was agreed that my endeavours should be directed to persons and characters supernatural, or at least romantic – yet so as to transfer, from our inward nature, a human interest and a semblance of truth sufficient to procure for these shadows of imagination that willing suspension of disbelief for the moment, which constitutes poetic faith. Mr Wordsworth, on the other hand, was to propose to himself as his object, to give the charm of novelty to things of every day, and to excite a feeling analogous to the supernatural, by awakening the mind's attention to the lethargy of custom, and directing it to the loveliness and the wonders of the world before us – an inexhaustible treasure but for which, in consequence of the film of familiarity and selfish solicitude, we have eyes yet see not, ears that hear not, and hearts that neither feel nor understand.

With this view I wrote 'The Ancient Mariner', and was preparing (among other poems) 'The Dark Ladie' and the 'Christabel', in which I should have more nearly realised my ideal than I had done in my first attempt. But Mr Wordsworth's industry had proved so much more successful, and the number of his poems so much greater, that my compositions, instead of forming a balance, appeared rather an interpolation of heterogeneous matter. Mr Wordsworth added two or three poems written in his own character, in the impassioned, lofty, and sustained diction which is characteristic of his genius. In this form the *Lyrical Ballads* were published, and were presented by him, as an 'experiment'[3] whether subjects, which from their nature rejected the usual ornaments and extra-colloquial style of poems in general, might not be so managed in the

---

CHAPTER 14
[1] This account given by Coleridge of the evolution of *Lyrical Ballads* is important, but fictionalizes in retrospect; it differs markedly from that later given by Wordsworth (see pp. 481–2, above). The facts may be found in the Introduction to *Lyrical Ballads, and Other Poems, 1797–1800*, ed. James Butler and Karen Green (Ithaca, N.Y., 1992), pp. 3–12.

[2] July 1797–July 1798, when Wordsworth was at Alfoxden and Coleridge at Nether Stowey.
[3] *experiment* see the Advertisement to *Lyrical Ballads* (1798), p. 166 above. See also his remarks to Hazlitt, p. 652 below.

language of ordinary life as to produce the pleasurable interest which it is the peculiar business of poetry to impart.

To the second edition he added a Preface of considerable length in which (notwithstanding some passages of apparently a contrary import) he was understood to contend for the extension of this style to poetry of all kinds, and to reject as vicious and indefensible all phrases and forms of speech that were not included in what he – unfortunately, I think, adopting an equivocal expression – called the language of *real* life.[4] From this Preface, prefixed to poems in which it was impossible to deny the presence of original genius (however mistaken its direction might be deemed), arose the whole long-continued controversy. For, from the conjunction of perceived power with supposed heresy, I explain the inveteracy and (in some instances, I grieve to say) the acrimonious passions with which the controversy has been conducted by the assailants.[5]

Had Mr Wordsworth's poems been the silly, the childish things which they were for a long time described as being; had they been really distinguished from the compositions of other poets merely by meanness of language and inanity of thought; had they indeed contained nothing more than what is found in the parodies and pretended imitations of them – they must have sunk at once, a dead weight, into the slough of oblivion, and have dragged the Preface along with them. But year after year increased the number of Mr Wordsworth's admirers. They were found, too, not in the lower classes of the reading public, but chiefly among young men of strong sensibility and meditative minds, and their admiration (inflamed perhaps in some degree by opposition) was distinguished by its intensity – I might almost say, by its religious fervour.

These facts, and the intellectual energy of the author (which was more or less consciously felt, where it was outwardly and even boisterously denied), meeting with sentiments of aversion to his opinions, and of alarm at their consequences, produced an eddy of criticism which would of itself have borne up the poems by the violence with which it whirled them round and round.

With many parts of this Preface in the sense attributed to them and which the words undoubtedly seem to authorize, I never concurred – but on the contrary objected to them as erroneous in principle, and as contradictory (in appearance at least) both to other parts of the same Preface, and to the author's own practice in the greater part of the poems themselves. Mr Wordsworth in his recent collection[6] has, I find, degraded this prefatory disquisition to the end of his second volume, to be read or not at the reader's choice. But he has not (as far as I can discover) announced any change in his poetic creed. At all events, considering it as the source of a controversy in which I have been honoured more than I deserve by the frequent conjunction of my name with his, I think it expedient to declare once for all, in what points I coincide with the opinions supported in that Preface, and in what points I altogether differer....

'What is poetry?' is so nearly the same question with 'what is a poet?' that the answer to the one is involved in the solution of the other. For it is a distinction resulting from the poetic genius itself, which sustains and modifies the images, thoughts, and emotions

---

[4] Coleridge's account of the Preface is not strictly accurate; Wordsworth referred to the 'real language of men', see p. 252 above.

[5] Coleridge refers to the criticism Wordsworth received particularly from the *Edinburgh Review*, culminat-

ing with Jeffrey's review of *The Excursion*, see pp. 599–601 below.

[6] *Poems* (1815).

of the poet's own mind. The poet, described in ideal perfection, brings the whole soul of man into activity, with the subordination of its faculties to each other, according to their relative worth and dignity. He diffuses a tone and spirit of unity that blends and (as it were) *fuses* each into each by that synthetic and magical power to which I would exclusively appropriate the name of imagination. This power, first put in action by the will and understanding, and retained under their irremissive, though gentle and unnoticed, control (*laxis effertur habenis*[7]), reveals itself in the balance or reconcilement of opposite or discordant qualities; of sameness with difference; of the general with the concrete; the idea with the image; the individual with the representative; the sense of novelty and freshness, with old and familiar objects; a more than usual state of emotion, with more than usual order; judgement ever awake and steady self-possession, with enthusiasm and feeling profound or vehement – and, while it blends and harmonizes the natural and the artificial, still subordinates art to nature; the manner to the matter; and our admiration of the poet to our sympathy with the poetry.

From Christabel; Kubla Khan: A Vision; The Pains of Sleep (1816)

OF THE FRAGMENT OF 'KUBLA KHAN'[1] (PP. 51–4)

The following fragment is here published at the request of a poet of great and deserved celebrity,[2] and as far as the author's own opinions are concerned, rather as a psychological curiosity than on the ground of any supposed *poetic* merits.

   In the summer of the year 1797,[3] the author, then in ill health, had retired to a lonely farmhouse between Porlock and Lynton on the Exmoor confines of Somerset and Devonshire. In consequence of a slight indisposition, an anodyne had been prescribed,[4] from the effects of which he fell asleep in his chair at the moment that he was reading the following sentence, or words of the same substance, in *Purchas's Pilgrimage*: 'Here the Khan Kubla commanded a palace to be built, and a stately garden thereunto. And thus ten miles of fertile ground were enclosed with a wall.'[5]

   The author continued for about three hours in a profound sleep (at least of the external senses) during which time he has the most vivid confidence that he could not have composed less than from two to three hundred lines – if that indeed can be called composition in which all the images rose up before him as *things*, with a parallel production of the correspondent expressions, without any sensation or consciousness of effort. On awaking he appeared to himself to have a distinct recollection of the whole, and taking his pen, ink, and paper, instantly and eagerly wrote down the lines

---

[7] 'carried on with slackened reins' (Petrarch, *Epistola Barbato Sulmonensi*, 39); see *Notebooks*, iii. 4178 and n.
OF THE FRAGMENT OF 'KUBLA KHAN'
[1] This short essay was prefaced to 'Kubla Khan' on its first publication in 1816.
[2] Lord Byron, who described it as 'a fine wild poem' (Marchand, v. 108). 'Kubla Khan' and 'Christabel' circulated in MS in literary circles for years before they were formally published. Other early readers included Charles Lamb, Sir Walter Scott, and Mrs Robinson (see p. 115 above).

[3] The correct date is early Nov. 1797.
[4] Opium was generally used for the treatment of dysentery at this time.
[5] 'In Xaindu did Cublai Can build a stately pallace, encompassing sixteene miles of plaine ground with a wall, wherein are fertile meddowes, pleasant springs, delightfull streames, and all sorts of beasts of chase and game, and in the middest thereof a sumptuous house of pleasure, which may be removed from place to place' (Samuel Purchas, *Purchas his Pilgrimage* [1613], p. 350).

that are here preserved. At this moment he was unfortunately called out by a person on business from Porlock and detained by him above an hour, and on his return to his room, found to his no small surprise and mortification that though he still retained some vague and dim recollection of the general purpose of the vision, yet, with the exception of some eight or ten scattered lines and images, all the rest had passed away like the images on the surface of a stream into which a stone has been cast – but, alas! without the after-restoration of the latter:

> Then all the charm
> Is broken – all that phantom-world so fair
> Vanishes, and a thousand circlets spread,
> And each misshapes the other. Stay awhile,
> Poor youth, who scarcely dar'st lift up thine eyes –
> The stream will soon renew its smoothness, soon
> The visions will return! And lo, he stays,
> And soon the fragments dim of lovely forms
> Come trembling back, unite, and now once more
> The pool becomes a mirror.
>
> (Coleridge, *The Picture*, 69–78)

Yet from the still-surviving recollections in his mind, the author has frequently purposed to finish for himself what had been originally, as it were, given to him. Σαμερον αδιον ασω,[6] but the tomorrow is yet to come.

From Sibylline Leaves (1817)

THE RIME OF THE ANCIENT MARINER. IN SEVEN PARTS.

Facile credo, plures esse Naturas invisibiles quam visibiles in rerum universitate. Sed horum omnium familiam quis nobis enarrabit? et gradus et cognationes et discrimina et singulorum munera? Quid agunt? quae loca habitant? Harum rerum notitiam semper ambivit ingenium humanum, nunquam attigit. Juvat, interea, non diffiteor, quandoque in animo, tanquam in Tabulâ, majoris et melioris mundi imaginem contemplari: ne mens assuefacta hodierniae vitae minutiis se contrahat nimis, et tota subsidat in pusillas cogitationes. Sed veritati interea invigilandum est, modusque servandus, ut certa ab incertis, diem a nocte, dist-inguamus.[1]

(Thomas Burnet, *Archaeologiae Philosophicae* (London, 1692), pp. 68–9)

---

[6] 'Today I shall sing more sweetly', adapted by Coleridge from Theocritus, *Idyll*, i. 145.

THE RIME OF THE ANCIENT MARINER
[1] This adaptation from Burnet may be translated: 'I can easily believe that there are more invisible than visible beings in the universe. But who will describe to us their families, ranks, affinities, differences, and functions? What do they do? Where do they live? The human mind has always sought knowledge of these things, but has never attained it. I admit that it is good sometimes to contemplate in thought, as in a picture, the image of a greater and better world; otherwise the mind, used to the minor concerns of daily life, may contract itself too much, and concentrate entirely on trivia. But meanwhile we must be vigilant for truth and moderation, that we may distinguish certainty from doubt, day from night.' Coleridge entered Burnet's remarks in his notebook, 1801 or 1802; see *Notebooks*, i. 1000H and n.

Part the First

An ancient
mariner meeteth
three gallants
bidden to a
wedding-feast,
and detaineth one.

It is an ancient mariner,
And he stoppeth one of three:
'By thy long grey beard and glittering eye
Now wherefore stopp'st thou me?

The bridegroom's doors are opened wide,   5
And I am next of kin;
The guests are met, the feast is set –
Mayst hear the merry din.'

He holds him with his skinny hand,
'There was a ship', quoth he;   10
'Hold off! Unhand me, grey-beard loon!'
Eftsoons his hand dropped he.

The
wedding-guest is
spellbound by the
eye of the old
seafaring man,
and constrained
to hear his tale.

He holds him with his glittering eye –
The wedding-guest stood still,
And listens like a three years' child: 15
The mariner hath his will.

The wedding-guest sat on a stone,
He cannot choose but hear;
And thus spake on that ancient man,
The bright-eyed mariner: 20

'The ship was cheered, the harbour cleared,
Merrily did we drop
Below the kirk, below the hill,
Below the lighthouse top.

The mariner tells
how the ship
sailed southward
with a good wind
and fair weather
till it reached the
line.

The sun came up upon the left,   25
Out of the sea came he;
And he shone bright, and on the right
Went down into the sea.

Higher and higher every day,
Till over the mast at noon –'   30
The wedding-guest here beat his breast,
For he heard the loud bassoon.

The
wedding-guest
heareth the bridal
music; but the
mariner
continueth his
tale.

The bride hath paced into the hall,
Red as a rose is she;
Nodding their heads before her goes   35
The merry minstrelsy.

The wedding-guest he beat his breast,
Yet he cannot choose but hear;

And thus spake on that ancient man,
The bright-eyed mariner. 40

The ship drawn by a storm toward the south pole.

'And now the storm-blast came, and he
Was tyrannous and strong;
He struck with his o'ertaking wings,
And chased us south along.

With sloping masts and dipping prow, 45
As who pursued with yell and blow
Still treads the shadow of his foe
And forward bends his head,
The ship drove fast, loud roared the blast,
And southward aye we fled. 50

And now there came both mist and snow,
And it grew wondrous cold:
And ice mast-high came floating by
As green as emerald.

The land of ice, and of fearful sounds, where no living thing was to be seen.

And through the drifts the snowy clift[2] 55
Did send a dismal sheen;
Nor shapes of men nor beasts we ken –
The ice was all between.

The ice was here, the ice was there,
The ice was all around; 60
It cracked and growled, and roared and howled
Like noises in a swound.[3]

Till a great sea-bird, called the albatross, came through the snow-fog, and was received with great joy and hospitality.

At length did cross an albatross,
Thorough the fog it came;
As if it had been a Christian soul, 65
We hailed it in God's name.

It ate the food it ne'er had eat,
And round and round it flew:
The ice did split with a thunder-fit;
The helmsman steered us through. 70

And lo! the albatross proveth a bird of good omen, and followeth the ship as it returned northward, through fog and floating ice.

And a good south wind sprung up behind,
The albatross did follow;
And every day, for food or play,
Came to the mariners' hollo!

---

[2] *drifts* floating ice. *clift* cleft.   [3] *swound* swoon.

In mist or cloud, on mast or shroud,   75
It perched for vespers[4] nine,
Whiles all the night, through fogsmoke white,
Glimmered the white moonshine.'

The ancient mariner inhospitably killeth the pious bird of good omen.

'God save thee, ancient mariner,
From the fiends that plague thee thus!   80
Why look'st thou so?' 'With my crossbow
I shot the albatross.

Part the Second
The sun now rose upon the right,
Out of the sea came he;
Still hid in mist, and on the left   85
Went down into the sea.

And the good south wind still blew behind,
But no sweet bird did follow,
Nor any day for food or play
Came to the mariners' hollo!   90

His shipmates cry out against the ancient mariner, for killing the bird of good luck.

And I had done an hellish thing
And it would work 'em woe:
For all averred I had killed the bird
That made the breeze to blow.
"Ah wretch!" said they, "the bird to slay   95
That made the breeze to blow!"

But when the fog cleared off, they justify the same – and thus make themselves accomplices in the crime.

Nor dim nor red, like God's own head
The glorious sun uprist:
Then all averred I had killed the bird
That brought the fog and mist.   100
"'Twas right", said they, "such birds to slay,
That bring the fog and mist."

The fair breeze continues; the ship enters the Pacific Ocean and sails northward, even till it reaches the Line. The ship hath been suddenly becalmed.

The fair breeze blew, the white foam flew,
The furrow[5] streamed off free:
We were the first that ever burst   105
Into that silent sea.

Down dropped the breeze, the sails dropped down,
'Twas sad as sad could be,
And we did speak only to break
The silence of the sea.   110

---

4 *vespers* evenings.
5 'In the former edition the line was "The furrow followed free". But I had not been long on board a ship before I perceived that this was the image as seen by a spectator from the shore, or from another vessel. From the ship itself the wake appears like a brook flowing off from the stern' (Coleridge's note).

582 SAMUEL TAYLOR COLERIDGE

All in a hot and copper sky
The bloody sun at noon
Right up above the mast did stand,
No bigger than the moon.

Day after day, day after day,   115
We stuck, nor breath nor motion,
As idle as a painted ship
Upon a painted ocean.

And the albatross
begins to be avenged.

Water, water, everywhere,
And all the boards did shrink;   120
Water, water, everywhere,
Nor any drop to drink.

The very deeps did rot: oh Christ,
That ever this should be!
Yea, slimy things did crawl with legs   125
Upon the slimy sea.

A spirit had followed
them; one of the
invisible inhabitants of
this planet, neither
departed souls nor
angels; concerning
whom the learned Jew,
Josephus, and the
Platonic
Constantinopolitan,
Michael Psellus, may be
consulted. They are very
numerous, and there is
no climate or element
without one or more.

About, about, in reel and rout
The death-fires danced at night;
The water, like a witch's oils,
Burnt green and blue and white.   130

And some in dreams assured were
Of the spirit that plagued us so;
Nine fathom deep he had followed us
From the land of mist and snow.

And every tongue, through utter drought,   135
Was withered at the root;
We could not speak, no more than if
We had been choked with soot.

The shipmates in their
sore distress would fain
throw the whole guilt
on the ancient mariner:
in sign whereof they
hang the dead sea-bird
round his neck.

Ah wel-a-day! what evil looks
Had I from old and young!   140
Instead of the cross the albatross
About my neck was hung.

Part the Third
There passed a weary time. Each throat
Was parched, and glazed each eye.
A weary time! a weary time!   145
How glazed each weary eye!

The ancient mariner
beholdeth a sign in the
element afar off.

When looking westward, I beheld
A something in the sky.

At first it seemed a little speck
And then it seemed a mist;   150
It moved and moved, and took at last
A certain shape, I wist.

A speck, a mist, a shape, I wist!
And still it neared and neared:
And as if it dodged a water-sprite,   155
It plunged and tacked and veered.

At its nearer approach, it seemeth him to be a ship; and at a dear ransom he freeth his speech from the bonds of thirst.

With throat unslaked, with black lips baked,
We could nor laugh nor wail;
Through utter drought all dumb we stood!
I bit my arm, I sucked the blood,   160
And cried, "A sail! A sail!"

With throat unslaked, with black lips baked,
Agape they heard me call:

A flash of joy.

Gramercy!⁶ they for joy did grin
And all at once their breath drew in   165
As they were drinking all.

And horror follows. For can it be a *ship* that comes onward without wind or tide?

"See, see!" I cried, "She tacks no more,
Hither to work us weal;
Without a breeze, without a tide,
She steadies with upright keel."   170

The western wave was all a-flame,
The day was well nigh done!
Almost upon the western wave
Rested the broad bright sun;
When that strange shape drove suddenly   175
Betwixt us and the sun.

It seemeth him but the skeleton of a ship.

And straight the sun was flecked with bars
(Heaven's Mother send us grace!),
As if through a dungeon-grate he peered
With broad and burning face.   180

Alas! thought I, and my heart beat loud,
How fast she nears and nears!
Are those *her* sails that glance in the sun
Like restless gossameres?

And its ribs are seen as bars on the face of the setting sun.

Are those *her* ribs through which the sun   185
Did peer, as through a grate?

⁶ *Gramercy!* mercy on us!

The spectre-woman
and her death-mate,
and no other on
board the skeleton
ship.

And is that woman all her crew?
Is that a Death? And are there two?
Is Death that woman's mate?

Her lips were red, *her* looks were free,   190
Her locks were yellow as gold;
Her skin was as white as leprosy,
The nightmare Life-in-Death was she
Who thicks man's blood with cold.

Like vessel, like
crew!

Death and
Life-in-Death have
diced for the ship's
crew, and she (the
latter) winneth the
ancient mariner.

The naked hulk alongside came,   195
And the twain were casting dice;
"The game is done! I've won! I've won!"
Quoth she, and whistles thrice.

The sun's rim dips, the stars rush out,
At one stride comes the dark;   200
With far-heard whisper, o'er the sea,
Off shot the spectre-bark.

We listened and looked sideways up!
Fear at my heart, as at a cup,
My life-blood seemed to sip!   205
The stars were dim, and thick the night,
The steersman's face by his lamp gleamed white;
From the sails the dews did drip —

At the rising of the
moon,

Till clomb above the eastern bar
The horned moon, with one bright star   210
Within the nether tip.

One after another,

One after one, by the star-dogged moon
Too quick for groan or sigh,
Each turned his face with a ghastly pang
And cursed me with his eye.   215

His shipmates drop
down dead;

Four times fifty living men
(And I heard nor sigh nor groan)
With heavy thump, a lifeless lump,
They dropped down one by one.

But Life-in-Death
begins her work on
the ancient mariner.

The souls did from their bodies fly,   220
They fled to bliss or woe!
And every soul, it passed me by
Like the whiz of my crossbow.'

Part the Fourth

The wedding-guest feareth that
a spirit is talking to him;

'I fear thee, ancient mariner,
I fear thy skinny hand;   225

And thou art long and lank and brown
As is the ribbed sea-sand.[7]

I fear thee and thy glittering eye,
And thy skinny hand so brown –'

But the ancient
mariner assureth
him of his bodily
life, and proceedeth
to relate his horrible
penance.
'Fear not, fear not, thou wedding-guest,
This body dropped not down.   230

Alone, alone, all all alone,
Alone on a wide wide sea;
And never a saint took pity on
My soul in agony.   235

He despiseth the
creatures of the
calm,
The many men so beautiful,
And they all dead did lie!
And a thousand thousand slimy things
Lived on – and so did I.

And envieth that
they should live, and
so many lie dead.
I looked upon the rotting sea   240
And drew my eyes away;
I looked upon the rotting deck,
And there the dead men lay.

I looked to heaven and tried to pray
But or ever a prayer had gushed,   245
A wicked whisper came and made
My heart as dry as dust.

I closed my lids and kept them close
And the balls like pulses beat;
For the sky and the sea, and the sea and the sky   250
Lay like a load on my weary eye,
And the dead were at my feet.

But the curse liveth
for him in the eye of
the dead men.
The cold sweat melted from their limbs,
Nor rot nor reek did they;
The look with which they looked on me   255
Had never passed away.

An orphan's curse would drag to hell
A spirit from on high;
But oh! more horrible than that
Is the curse in a dead man's eye!   260
Seven days, seven nights, I saw that curse
And yet I could not die.

---

7   'For the last two lines of this stanza I am indebted to Mr Wordsworth. It was on a delightful walk from Nether Stowey to Dulverton, with him and his sister, in the autumn of 1797, that this poem was planned and in part composed' (Coleridge's note).

In his loneliness and fixedness, he yearneth towards the journeying moon, and the stars that still sojourn, yet still move onward; and everywhere the blue sky belongs to them, and is their appointed rest, and their native country, and their own natural homes, which they enter unannounced, as lords that are certainly expected, and yet there is a silent joy at their arrival. By the light of the moon he beholdeth God's creatures of the great calm.	The moving moon went up the sky And nowhere did abide; Softly she was going up And a star or two beside; 265 Her beams bemocked the sultry main Like April hoar-frost spread; But where the ship's huge shadow lay The charmed water burnt alway 270 A still and awful red. Beyond the shadow of the ship I watched the water-snakes; They moved in tracks of shining white, And when they reared, the elfish light 275 Fell off in hoary flakes. Within the shadow of the ship I watched their rich attire: Blue, glossy green, and velvet black, They coiled and swam, and every track 280 Was a flash of golden fire.
Their beauty and their happiness. He blesseth them in his heart.	Oh happy living things! no tongue Their beauty might declare: A spring of love gushed from my heart And I blessed them unaware! 285 Sure my kind saint took pity on me, And I blessed them unaware.
The spell begins to break.	The self-same moment I could pray, And from my neck so free The albatross fell off and sank 290 Like lead into the sea.
	Part the Fifth Oh sleep, it is a gentle thing Beloved from pole to pole! To Mary Queen the praise be given; She sent the gentle sleep from heaven 295 That slid into my soul.
By grace of the holy Mother, the ancient mariner is refreshed with rain.	The silly[8] buckets on the deck That had so long remained, I dreamt that they were filled with dew And when I awoke it rained. 300

---

[8]   *silly* helpless, innocent.

My lips were wet, my throat was cold,
My garments all were dank;
Sure I had drunken in my dreams
And still my body drank.

I moved and could not feel my limbs,   305
I was so light, almost
I thought that I had died in sleep
And was a blessed ghost.

He heareth sounds,   And soon I heard a roaring wind,
and seeth strange   It did not come anear;   310
sights and   But with its sound it shook the sails
commotions in the   That were so thin and sere.
sky and the element.

The upper air bursts into life
And a hundred fire-flags sheen,
To and fro they were hurried about;   315
And to and fro, and in and out
The wan stars danced between.

And the coming wind did roar more loud,
And the sails did sigh like sedge;
And the rain poured down from one black cloud,   320
The moon was at its edge.

The thick black cloud was cleft, and still
The moon was at its side;
Like waters shot from some high crag,
The lightning fell with never a jag,   325
A river steep and wide.

The bodies of the   The loud wind never reached the ship,
ship's crew are   Yet now the ship moved on!
inspirited, and the   Beneath the lightning and the moon
ship moves on;   The dead men gave a groan.   330

They groaned, they stirred, they all uprose,
Nor spake, nor moved their eyes;
It had been strange, even in a dream,
To have seen those dead men rise.

The helmsman steered, the ship moved on,   335
Yet never a breeze up-blew;
The mariners all 'gan work the ropes
Where they were wont to do;
They raised their limbs like lifeless tools –
We were a ghastly crew.   340

The body of my brother's son
Stood by me, knee to knee;
The body and I pulled at one rope
But he said nought to me.'

But not by the souls of the men, nor by daemons of earth or middle air, but by a blessed troop of angelic spirits, sent down by the invocation of the guardian saint.

'I fear thee, ancient mariner!'   345
'Be calm, thou wedding-guest!
'Twas not those souls that fled in pain,
Which to their corses came again,
But a troop of spirits blessed;

For when it dawned, they dropped their arms   350
And clustered round the mast;
Sweet sounds rose slowly through their mouths
And from their bodies passed.

Around, around, flew each sweet sound
Then darted to the sun;   355
Slowly the sounds came back again,
Now mixed, now one by one.

Sometimes a-dropping from the sky
I heard the skylark sing;
Sometimes all little birds that are,   360
How they seemed to fill the sea and air
With their sweet jargoning!

And now 'twas like all instruments,
Now like a lonely flute,
And now it is an angel's song   365
That makes the heavens be mute.

It ceased, yet still the sails made on
A pleasant noise till noon,
A noise like of a hidden brook
In the leafy month of June,   370
That to the sleeping woods all night
Singeth a quiet tune.

Till noon we quietly sailed on,
Yet never a breeze did breathe;
Slowly and smoothly went the ship,   375
Moved onward from beneath.

The lonesome spirit from the South Pole carries on the ship as far as the line, in

Under the keel nine fathom deep,
From the land of mist and snow,
The spirit slid, and it was he
That made the ship to go.   380

obedience to the angelic
troop, but still requireth
vengeance.

The sails at noon left off their tune
And the ship stood still also.

The sun right up above the mast
Had fixed her to the ocean;
But in a minute she 'gan stir   385
With a short uneasy motion –
Backwards and forwards half her length,
With a short uneasy motion.

Then like a pawing horse let go,
She made a sudden bound;   390
It flung the blood into my head,
And I fell down in a swound.

The Polar Spirit's
fellow-daemons, the
invisible inhabitants of
the element, take part in
his wrong; and two of
them relate, one to the
other, that penance long
and heavy for the ancient
mariner hath been
accorded to the Polar
Spirit, who returneth
southward.

How long in that same fit I lay,
I have not to declare;
But ere my living life returned,   395
I heard and in my soul discerned
Two voices in the air.

"Is it he?" quoth one, "Is this the man?
By him who died on cross,
With his cruel bow he laid full low   400
The harmless albatross.

The spirit who bideth by himself
In the land of mist and snow,
He loved the bird that loved the man
Who shot him with his bow."   405

The other was a softer voice,
As soft as honey-dew;
Quoth he, "The man hath penance done
And penance more will do."'

Part the Sixth

FIRST VOICE

But tell me, tell me! speak again,   410
Thy soft response renewing –
What makes that ship drive on so fast?
What is the ocean doing?

SECOND VOICE

Still as a slave before his lord,
The ocean hath no blast;   415
His great bright eye most silently
Up to the moon is cast –

If he may know which way to go,
For she guides him smooth or grim.
See, brother, see – how graciously   420
She looketh down on him!

                    FIRST VOICE

The mariner hath   But why drives on that ship so fast
been cast into a   Without or wave or wind?
trance; for the angelic   SECOND VOICE
power causeth the
vessel to drive   The air is cut away before
northward, faster than   And closes from behind.
human life could
endure.   425

                          Fly, brother, fly! more high, more high,
                          Or we shall be belated;
                          For slow and slow that ship will go
                          When the mariner's trance is abated.

The supernatural   'I woke, and we were sailing on   430
motion is retarded;   As in a gentle weather;
the mariner awakes,   'Twas night, calm night, the moon was high –
and his penance   The dead men stood together.
begins anew.

                          All stood together on the deck,
                          For a charnel-dungeon fitter;
                          All fixed on me their stony eyes   435
                          That in the moon did glitter.

                          The pang, the curse, with which they died
                          Had never passed away;
                          I could not draw my eyes from theirs   440
                          Nor turn them up to pray.

The curse is finally   And now this spell was snapped; once more
expiated.   I viewed the ocean green,
                          And looked far forth, yet little saw
                          Of what had else been seen –   445

                          Like one that on a lonesome road
                          Doth walk in fear and dread,
                          And having once turned round walks on
                          And turns no more his head,
                          Because he knows a frightful fiend   450
                          Doth close behind him tread.

                          But soon there breathed a wind on me,
                          Nor sound nor motion made;
                          Its path was not upon the sea,
                          In ripple or in shade.   455

It raised my hair, it fanned my cheek,
Like a meadow-gale of spring –
It mingled strangely with my fears,
Yet it felt like a welcoming.

Swiftly, swiftly flew the ship,   460
Yet she sailed softly too;
Sweetly, sweetly blew the breeze –
On me alone it blew.

And the ancient mariner beholdeth his native country.

Oh dream of joy! Is this indeed
The lighthouse top I see?   465
Is this the hill? Is this the kirk?
Is this mine own countree?

We drifted o'er the harbour-bar,[9]
And I with sobs did pray,
"Oh let me be awake, my God!   470
Or let me sleep alway!"

The harbour-bay was clear as glass,
So smoothly it was strewn!
And on the bay the moonlight lay
And the shadow of the moon.   475

The rock shone bright, the kirk no less
That stands above the rock;
The moonlight steeped in silentness
The steady weathercock.

The angelic spirits leave the dead bodies,

And the bay was white with silent light,   480
Till rising from the same,
Full many shapes that shadows were
In crimson colours came.

And appear in their own forms of light.

A little distance from the prow
Those crimson shadows were;   485
I turned my eyes upon the deck –
Oh Christ! What saw I there!

Each corse lay flat, lifeless and flat,
And by the holy rood,
A man all light, a seraph-man   490
On every corse there stood.

9 *harbour-bar* bank of silt across the mouth of the
harbour.

This seraph-band, each waved his hand –
It was a heavenly sight!
They stood as signals to the land,
Each one a lovely light; 495

This seraph-band, each waved his hand,
No voice did they impart –
No voice, but oh! the silence sank
Like music on my heart.

But soon I heard the dash of oars, 500
I heard the pilot's cheer;
My head was turned perforce away
And I saw a boat appear.

The pilot and the pilot's boy,
I heard them coming fast – 505
Dear Lord in heaven! it was a joy
The dead men could not blast.

I saw a third, I heard his voice –
It is the hermit good!
He singeth loud his godly hymns 510
That he makes in the wood.
He'll shrieve[10] my soul, he'll wash away
The albatross' blood.

Part the Seventh

This hermit of the wood   This hermit good lives in that wood
Which slopes down to the sea; 515
How loudly his sweet voice he rears!
He loves to talk with mariners
That come from a far countree.

He kneels at morn, and noon and eve,
He hath a cushion plump; 520
It is the moss that wholly hides
The rotted old oak-stump.

The skiff-boat neared, I heard them talk:
"Why, this is strange, I trow!
Where are those lights so many and fair, 525
That signal made but now?"

Approacheth the ship   "Strange, by my faith!" the hermit said,
with wonder.   "And they answered not our cheer!

---

[10] *shrieve* to hear the confession of, absolve.

The planks look warped, and see those sails,
How thin they are and sere!   530
I never saw aught like to them
Unless perchance it were

The skeletons of leaves that lag
My forest brook along,
When the ivy-tod[11] is heavy with snow   535
And the owlet whoops to the wolf below
That eats the she-wolf's young."

"Dear Lord! it hath a fiendish look,"
The pilot made reply,
"I am a-feared." "Push on, push on!"   540
Said the hermit cheerily.

The boat came closer to the ship
But I nor spake nor stirred;
The boat came close beneath the ship
And straight a sound was heard!   545

The ship suddenly sinketh.

Under the water it rumbled on,
Still louder and more dread;
It reached the ship, it split the bay –
The ship went down like lead.

The ancient mariner is saved in the pilot's boat.

Stunned by that loud and dreadful sound   550
Which sky and ocean smote,
Like one that hath been seven days drowned,
My body lay afloat;
But swift as dreams, myself I found
Within the pilot's boat.   555

Upon the whirl where sank the ship
The boat spun round and round,
And all was still, save that the hill
Was telling of the sound.

I moved my lips – the pilot shrieked   560
And fell down in a fit;
The holy hermit raised his eyes
And prayed where he did sit.

I took the oars; the pilot's boy,
Who now doth crazy go,   565

---

[11] *ivy-tod* ivy-bush.

Laughed loud and long, and all the while
His eyes went to and fro:
"Ha! ha!" quoth he, "full plain I see
The Devil knows how to row."

And now all in my own countree   570
I stood on the firm land!
The hermit stepped forth from the boat,
And scarcely he could stand.

The ancient mariner
earnestly entreateth the
hermit to shrieve him;
and the penance of life
falls on him.

"Oh shrieve me, shrieve me, holy man!"
The hermit crossed his brow.   575
"Say quick", quoth he, "I bid thee say
What manner of man art thou?"

Forthwith this frame of mine was wrenched
With a woeful agony,
Which forced me to begin my tale –   580
And then it left me free.

And ever and anon
throughout his future
life an agony
constraineth him to
travel from land to
land,

Since then, at an uncertain hour,
That agony returns,
And till my ghastly tale is told,
This heart within me burns.   585

I pass, like night, from land to land,
I have strange power of speech;
The moment that his face I see,
I know the man that must hear me –
To him my tale I teach.   590

What loud uproar bursts from that door!
The wedding-guests are there;
But in the garden bower the bride
And bridemaids singing are;
And hark, the little vesper bell   595
Which biddeth me to prayer.

Oh wedding-guest! this soul hath been
Alone on a wide wide sea;
So lonely 'twas, that God himself
Scarce seemed there to be.   600

Oh sweeter than the marriage-feast,
'Tis sweeter far to me
To walk together to the kirk
With a goodly company!

To walk together to the kirk   605
And all together pray,
While each to his great Father bends,
Old men, and babes, and loving friends,
And youths and maidens gay.

And to teach by his own   Farewell, farewell! but this I tell   610
example love and   To thee, thou wedding-guest!
reverence to all things that He prayeth well who loveth well
God made and loveth.   Both man and bird and beast.

He prayeth best who loveth best
All things both great and small,   615
For the dear God who loveth us,
He made and loveth all.'

The mariner, whose eye is bright,
Whose beard with age is hoar,
Is gone; and now the wedding-guest   620
Turned from the bridegroom's door.

He went like one that hath been stunned
And is of sense forlorn:
A sadder and a wiser man
He rose the morrow morn.   625

From Table Talk (edited from MS)

ON 'THE ANCIENT MARINER' (DICTATED 30 MAY 1830)

The fault of 'The Ancient Mariner' consists in making the moral sentiment too apparent and bringing it in too much as a principle or cause in a work of such pure imagination.

THE TRUE WAY FOR A POET (DICTATED 19 SEPTEMBER 1830)

Southey picked nature's pockets as a poet, instead of borrowing from her. He went out and took some particular image, for example a water-insect – and then exactly copied its make, colours and motions. This he put in a poem. The true way for a poet is to examine nature, but write from your recollection, and trust more to your imagination than your memory.

ON 'THE RECLUSE' (DICTATED 21 JULY 1832)

Wordsworth should have first published his Thirteen Books on the growth of an individual mind,[1] far superior to any part of *The Excursion*. Then the plan suggested and

---

ON 'THE RECLUSE' (dictated 21 July 1832)
[1] *Thirteen-Book Prelude.*

laid out by me was that he should assume the station of a man in repose, whose mind was made up, and so prepared to deliver upon authority a system of philosophy. He was to treat man as man – a subject of eye, ear, touch, taste, in contact with external nature, informing the senses from the mind and not compounding a mind out of the senses; then the pastoral and other states, assuming a satiric or Juvenalian spirit as he approached the high civilization of cities and towns; and then opening a melancholy picture of the present state of degeneracy and vice; thence revealing the necessity for and proof of the whole state of man and society being subject to and illustrative of a redemptive process in operation, showing how this idea reconciled all the anomalies, and how it promised future glory and restoration. Something of this sort I suggested, and it was agreed on. It is what in substance I have been all my life doing in my system of philosophy.

Wordsworth spoilt many of his best poems by abandoning the contemplative position, which is alone fitted for him, and introducing the object in a dramatic way. This is seen in 'The Leech-Gatherer'[2] and 'Ruth'. Wordsworth had more materials for the great philosophic poet than any man I ever knew or (as I think) has existed in this country for a long time – but he was utterly unfitted for the epic or narrative style. His mental-internal action is always so excessively disproportionate to the actual business that the latter either goes to sleep or becomes ridiculous.[3] In his reasoning you will find no progression: it eddies, it comes round and round again, perhaps with a wider circle, but it is repetition still.

KEATS (DICTATED 11 AUGUST 1832)

A loose, not well-dressed youth, met Mr Green and me in Mansfield Lane.[1] Green knew him and spoke. It was Keats. He was introduced to me, and stayed a minute or so. After he had gone a little, he came back and said, 'Let me carry away the memory, Coleridge, of having pressed your hand.' There is death in *his* hand, said I to Green when he was gone. Yet this was before the consumption showed itself.

Mary Tighe (1772–1810)

After studying Latin with her husband, Tighe wrote Psyche *in 1801–3, a six-canto allegory in Spenserian stanzas. Though first published in 1805, it gained popularity only after publication of its 3rd edition, in 1811, by which time its author had died of consumption. In her Preface, Tighe defends her choice of an erotic subject, declaring that 'I have only pictured innocent love, such love as the purest bosom might confess' (pp. x–xi). All the same, its sensuous language is one of its most noticeable features, and probably for that reason it profoundly influenced Keats. Tighe is the subject of one of Mrs Hemans's most important elegies (pp. 989–91).*

---

[2] i.e. 'Resolution and Independence'.
[3] Coleridge here echoes the point made by Jeffrey in his review of *The Excursion*, when he notes that its incidents are 'few and trifling', p. 601 below.

KEATS (dictated 11 August 1832)
[1] Keats's account of this meeting may be found on p. 1051; it took place probably on 11 Apr. 1819. Joseph Henry Green (1791–1863) was Coleridge's literary executor, and had been Keats's demonstrator at Guy's Hospital.

The extract below comes from the beginning of Psyche. *Jealous of Psyche's superior beauty,
Cytherea has sent Cupid to make her fall in love with 'some base wretch to foul disgrace allied'.
Cupid finds Psyche sleeping in Pleasure's garden, where two fountains are playing – one the
fountain of jealousy and shame, the other of desire and pleasure.*

From Psyche, with Other Poems, 3rd edition (1811)

PSYCHE; OR THE LEGEND OF LOVE (EXTRACT)

Here Cupid tempers his unerring darts,
And in the fount of bliss delights to play;   200
Here mingles balmy sighs and pleasing smarts,
And here the honeyed draught will oft allay[1]
With that black poison's all-polluting sway,
For wretched man. Hither, as Venus willed,
For Psyche's punishment he bent his way;   205
From either stream his amber vase he filled –
For her were meant the drops which grief alone distilled.

His quiver, sparkling bright with gems and gold,
From his fair plumed shoulder graceful hung,
And from its top in brilliant cords enrolled   210
Each little vase resplendently was slung;
Still as he flew, around him sportive clung
His frolic train of winged zephyrs light,
Wafting the fragrance which his tresses flung,
While odours dropped from every ringlet bright,   215
And from his blue eyes beamed ineffable delight.

Wrapped in a cloud unseen by mortal eye,[2]
He sought the chamber of the royal maid –
There, lulled by careless soft security,
Of the impending mischief nought afraid,   220
Upon her purple couch was Psyche laid,
Her radiant eyes a downy slumber sealed;
In light transparent veil alone arrayed,
Her bosom's opening charms were half-revealed,
And scarce the lucid folds her polished limbs concealed.   225

A placid smile plays o'er each roseate lip –
Sweet severed lips, while thus your pearls disclose,
That slumbering thus unconscious she may sip
The cruel presage of her future woes!
Lightly, as fall the dews upon the rose,   230

PSYCHE; OR THE LEGEND OF LOVE (extract)   [2] Cf. the sylphs in Pope's *The Rape of the Lock*, ii. 61:
[1] *allay* mix.   'too fine for mortal sight'.

Upon the coral gates of that sweet cell
The fatal drops he pours – nor yet he knows,
Nor, though a god, can he presaging tell
How he himself shall mourn the ills of that sad spell!

Nor yet content, he from his quiver drew,   235
Sharpened with skill divine, a shining dart;
No need had he for bow, since thus too true
His hand might wound her all-exposed heart;
Yet her fair side he touched with gentlest art,
And half-relenting on her beauties gazed: 240
Just then awaking with a sudden start
Her opening eye in humid lustre blazed –
Unseen he still remained, enchanted and amazed.

The dart which in his hand now trembling stood,
As o'er the couch he bent with ravished eye,   245
Drew with its daring point celestial blood
From his smooth neck's unblemished ivory;
Heedless of this, but with a pitying sigh
(The evil done now anxious to repair),
He shed in haste the balmy drops of joy   250
O'er all the silky ringlets of her hair,
Then stretched his plumes divine, and breathed celestial air.

Unhappy Psyche! Soon the latent wound
The fading roses of her cheek confess;
Her eyes' bright beams, in swimming sorrows drowned,   255
Sparkle no more with life and happiness,
Her parent's fond exulting heart to bless;
She shuns adoring crowds, and seeks to hide
The pining sorrows which her soul oppress,
Till to her mother's tears no more denied,   260
The secret grief she owns, for which she lingering sighed.

A dream of mingled terror and delight
Still heavy hangs upon her troubled soul,
An angry form still swims before her sight,
And still the vengeful thunders seem to roll;   265
Still crushed to earth she feels the stern control
Of Venus unrelenting, unappeased.
The dream returns, she feels the fancied dole;
Once more the furies on her heart have seized,
But still she views the youth who all her sufferings eased. 270

Of wondrous beauty did the vision seem,
And in the freshest prime of youthful years;
Such at the close of her distressful dream

A graceful champion to her eyes appears;
Her loved deliverer from her foes and fears   275
She seems in grateful transport still to press,
Still his soft voice sounds in her ravished ears;
Dissolved in fondest tears of tenderness
His form she oft invokes her waking eyes to bless.

Nor was it quite a dream, for as she woke,   280
Ere heavenly mists concealed him from her eye,
One sudden transitory view she took
Of Love's most radiant bright divinity –
From the fair image never can she fly,
As still consumed with vain desire she pines;   285
While her fond parents heave the anxious sigh,
And to avert her fate seek holy shrines
The threatened ills to learn by auguries and signs.

Francis, Lord Jeffrey (1773–1850)

Despite his reputation for severity, Jeffrey wrote appreciatively of Crabbe, Scott, Byron, and, surprisingly, Keats. Like Byron, he regarded the Preface to Lyrical Ballads *as an attack on Pope and his imitators, and set out, in a series of deeply unsympathetic reviews of the three very different poets he lumped together as the 'Lake School' (Wordsworth, Coleridge, Southey), to demolish its central theses. For him, Wordsworth's* White Doe of Rylstone *(1815) was 'the very worst poem we ever saw imprinted in a quarto volume' (Edinburgh Review, 25 (1815) 355), but his most notorious attack remains that on* The Excursion, *which he opposes on the grounds of plainness of diction, lowly subject-matter, and bogus metaphysics. His portrayal of Wordsworth as a self-obsessed mystic stuck, and helped depress his popularity for years. In private, Wordsworth remarked that he held the review 'in entire contempt, and therefore shall not pollute my fingers with the touch of it' (MY, ii. 190). It is ironic that in later years Jeffrey told Henry Crabb Robinson, '"I was always among Wordsworth's admirers." I answered him rudely enough (but I did not wish to be civil), "You had an odd way of showing it"' (Morley, ii. 838).*

From Edinburgh Review, 24 (1814) 1–30

REVIEW OF WILLIAM WORDSWORTH, 'THE EXCURSION' (EXTRACTS)

This will never do. It bears, no doubt, the stamp of the author's heart and fancy – but unfortunately not half so visibly as that of his peculiar system. His former poems were intended to recommend that system, and to bespeak favour for it by their individual merit, but this, we suspect, must be recommended by the system, and can only expect to succeed where it has been previously established. It is longer, weaker, and tamer, than any of Mr Wordsworth's other productions, with less boldness of originality, and less even of that extreme simplicity and lowliness of tone which wavered so prettily, in the *Lyrical Ballads*, between silliness and pathos. We have imitations of Cowper and even of Milton here, engrafted on the natural drawl of the Lakers – and all diluted into harmony by that profuse and irrepressible wordiness which deluges all the blank verse of this school of poetry, and lubricates and weakens the whole structure of their style.

Though it fairly fills four hundred and twenty good quarto pages, without note, vignette, or any sort of extraneous assistance, it is stated in the title (with something of an imprudent candour) to be but 'a portion' of a larger work,[1] and in the preface – where an attempt is rather unsuccessfully made to explain the whole design – it is still more rashly disclosed that it is but 'a part of the second part of a *long* and laborious work' which is to consist of three parts!

What Mr Wordsworth's ideas of length are, we have no means of accurately judging, but we cannot help suspecting that they are liberal to a degree that will alarm the weakness of most modern readers. As far as we can gather from the preface, the entire poem – or one of them (for we really are not sure whether there is to be one or two) – is of a biographical nature, and is to contain the history of the author's mind and of the origin and progress of his poetical powers up to the period when they were sufficiently matured to qualify him for the great work on which he has been so long employed. Now the quarto before us contains an account of one of his youthful rambles in the vales of Cumberland, and occupies precisely the period of three days; so that, by the use of a very powerful calculus,[2] some estimate may be formed of the probable extent of the entire biography.

This small specimen, however, and the statements with which it is prefaced, have been sufficient to set our minds at rest in one particular. The case of Mr Wordsworth, we perceive, is now manifestly hopeless, and we give him up as altogether incurable, and beyond the power of criticism. We cannot indeed altogether omit taking precautions now and then against the spreading of the malady – but for himself, though we shall watch the progress of his symptoms as a matter of professional curiosity and instruction, we really think it right not to harass him any longer with nauseous remedies, but rather to throw in cordials and lenitives, and wait in patience for the natural termination of the disorder. In order to justify this desertion of our patient, however, it is proper to state why we despair of the success of a more active practice. . . .

The volume before us, if we were to describe it very shortly, we should characterize as a tissue of moral and devotional ravings in which innumerable changes are rung upon a few very simple and familiar ideas – but with such an accompaniment of long words, long sentences, and unwieldy phrases, and such a hubbub of strained raptures and fantastical sublimities, that it is often extremely difficult for the most skilful and attentive student to obtain a glimpse of the author's meaning, and altogether impossible for an ordinary reader to conjecture what he is about.

Moral and religious enthusiasm, though undoubtedly poetical emotions, are at the same time but dangerous inspirers of poetry, nothing being so apt to run into interminable dullness or mellifluous extravagance, without giving the unfortunate author the slightest intimation of his danger. His laudable zeal for the efficacy of his preachments, he very naturally mistakes for the ardour of poetical inspiration – and, while dealing out the high words and glowing phrases which are so readily supplied by themes of this description, can scarcely avoid believing that he is eminently original

---

REVIEW OF WILLIAM WORDSWORTH, 'THE EXCURSION'   [2] *calculus* computation.
[1] *The Recluse.*

and impressive. All sorts of commonplace notions and expressions are sanctified in his eyes by the sublime ends for which they are employed, and the mystical verbiage of the Methodist pulpit is repeated till the speaker entertains no doubt that he is the elected organ of divine truth and persuasion. But if such be the common hazards of seeking inspiration from those potent fountains, it may easily be conceived what chance Mr Wordsworth had of escaping their enchantment, with his natural propensities to wordiness, and his unlucky habit of debasing pathos with vulgarity.[3] The fact accordingly is that in this production he is more obscure than a Pindaric poet of the seventeenth century, and more verbose 'than even himself of yore', while the wilfulness with which he persists in choosing his examples of intellectual dignity and tenderness exclusively from the lowest ranks of society will be sufficiently apparent from the circumstance of his having thought fit to make his chief prolocutor in this poetical dialogue, and chief advocate of providence and virtue, *an old Scotch pedlar*, retired indeed from business, but still rambling about in his former haunts, and gossiping among his old customers without his pack on his shoulders. The other persons of the drama are a retired military chaplain, who has grown half an atheist and half a misanthrope; the wife of an unprosperous weaver; a servant girl with her infant; a parish pauper, and one or two other personages of equal rank and dignity.

The character of the work is decidedly didactic, and more than nine-tenths of it are occupied with a species of dialogue, or rather a series of long sermons or harangues which pass between the pedlar, the author, the old chaplain, and a worthy vicar who entertains the whole party at dinner on the last day of their excursion. The incidents which occur in the course of it are as few and trifling as can be imagined – and those which the different speakers narrate in the course of their discourses, are introduced rather to illustrate their arguments or opinions than for any interest they are supposed to possess of their own. The doctrine which the work is intended to enforce, we are by no means certain that we have discovered. In so far as we can collect, however, it seems to be neither more nor less than the old familiar one that a firm belief in the providence of a wise and beneficent Being must be our great stay and support[4] under all afflictions and perplexities upon earth, and that there are indications of his power and goodness in all the aspects of the visible universe, whether living or inanimate – every part of which should therefore be regarded with love and reverence, as exponents of those great attributes. We can testify, at least, that these salutary and important truths are inculcated at far greater length, and with more repetitions, than in any ten volumes of sermons that we ever perused. It is also maintained, with equal conciseness and originality, that there is frequently much good sense, as well as much enjoyment, in the humbler conditions of life; and that, in spite of great vices and abuses, there is a reasonable allowance both of happiness and goodness in society at large. If there be any deeper or more recondite doctrines in Mr Wordsworth's book, we must confess that they have escaped us – and, convinced as we are of the truth and soundness of those to which we have alluded, we cannot help thinking that they might have been better enforced with less parade and prolixity. His effusions on what may be called the physiognomy of external nature, or its moral and theological expression, are eminently fantastic, obscure, and affected.

---

[3] *vulgarity* coarseness (i.e. of his characters).   [4] An echo of 'Resolution and Independence', 146.

Robert Southey (1774–1843)

On the basis of Joan of Arc, *Lamb declared, 'I expect Southey one day to rival Milton. I
already deem him equal to Cowper, and superior to all living poets besides' (Marrs, i. 16). Lamb
must have recognized the influence of Coleridge, evident in* Natural Religion, *in which Joan,
questioned by doctors of divinity about her faith, gives an account of her upbringing which
culminates in a pantheist declaration. In September 1797, Coleridge told Southey that 'Hannah'
'is to me the most affecting of all your little pieces' (Griggs, i. 345); while reflecting the influence
of Cowper's 'Crazy Kate' (pp. 7–8 above), it is also one of his most Wordsworthian. In these
respects it is, however, untypical. Several months before, Coleridge had expressed his fear that Southey
depended 'too much on story and event in his poems, to the neglect of those lofty imaginings that
are peculiar to, and definitive of, the poet' (Griggs, i. 320) – and a comparison of 'The Idiot'
with 'The Idiot Boy' shows that his fears were well-grounded. Southey's review of* Lyrical Ballads
*(1798) gives a foretaste of the kind of criticism Wordsworth was later to receive from Jeffrey,
drawing attention to the lowliness of his subject-matter and to the claims of the Advertisement.*

From Joan of Arc (1796)

NATURAL RELIGION (BOOK III)

In forest shade my infant years trained up   355
Knew not devotion's forms. The chaunted mass,
The silver altar and religious robe,
The mystic wafer and the hallowed cup,
Gods priest-created, are to me unknown.
Beneath no high-arched roof I bowed in prayer,   360
No solemn light by storied pane disguised,
No trophied pillars and no imaged cross
Waked my young mind to artificial awe
To fear the God I only learnt to love.
I saw th' eternal energy pervade   365
The boundless range of nature, with the sun
Pour life and radiance from his flamy path,
And on the lowliest flowret in the field
The kindly dew-drops shed; all nature's voice
Proclaimed the all-good Parent – nor myself   370
Deemed I by him neglected. This good Power
My more than father taught my youth to know,
Knowing to love, and loving to adore.
At earliest morn to him my grateful heart
Poured forth th' unstudied prayer that spake my thanks   375
For mercies oft vouchsafed, and humbly asked
Protection yet to come. Each flower that bloomed
Expanding in the new-born spring called forth
The soul of full devotion. Every morn
My soaring spirit glorified the God   380

Of light, and every evening thanked the Power
Preserving through the day. For sins confessed
To holy priest and absolution given,
I knew them not – for, ignorant of sin,
Why should I seek forgiveness? Of the points   385
Abstruse of nice religion, and the bounds
Subtle and narrow which confine the path
Of orthodox belief, my artless creed
Knew nought. 'Twas nature taught my early youth
Religion; nature bade me see the God   390
Confessed in all that lives, and moves, and is.

From Monthly Magazine, 4 (1797) 287

HANNAH, A PLAINTIVE TALE (COMPOSED BY 15 SEPTEMBER 1797)

The coffin, as I crossed the common lane,
Came sudden on my view;[1] it was not here
A sight of every day, as in the streets
Of the great city – and we paused and asked
Who to the grave was going. It was one,   5
A village girl; they told us she had borne
An eighteen months' strange illness, pined away
With such slow wasting as had made the hour
Of death most welcome. To the house of mirth
We held our way and, with that idle talk   10
That passes o'er the mind and is forgot,
We wore away the hour. But it was eve
When homewardly I went, and in the air
Was that cool freshness, that discolouring shade
That makes the eye turn inward. Then I heard,   15
Over the vale, the heavy toll of death
Sound slow, and questioned of the dead again.
    It was a very plain and simple tale.
She bore, unhusbanded, a mother's name,
And he who should have cherished her, far off   20
Sailed on the seas, self-exiled from his home,
For he was poor. Left thus, a wretched one,
Scorn made a mock of her, and evil tongues
Were busy with her name. She had one ill
Heavier: neglect, forgetfulness from him   25
Whom she had loved so dearly. Once he wrote,

HANNAH
[1] When 'Hannah' was published, revised, in *Poems*
(1799), Southey noted: 'It is proper to remark that the
story related in this Eclogue is strictly true. I met the
funeral, and learnt the circumstances, in a village in
Hampshire. The indifference of the child was mentioned to me; indeed, no addition whatever has been
made to the story. I should have thought it wrong to
have weakened the effect of a faithful narrative by
adding anything' (p. 202).

But only once that drop of comfort came,
To mingle with her cup of wretchedness;
And when his parents had some tidings from him
There was no mention of poor Hannah there;   30
Or 'twas the cold enquiry, bitterer
Than silence. So she pined and pined away,
And for herself and baby toiled and toiled,
Till she sunk with very weakness; her old mother
Omitted no kind office, and she worked   35
Most hard, and with hard working barely earned
Enough to make life struggle. Thus she lay
On the sickbed of poverty, so worn
That she could make no effort to express
Affection for her infant – and the child   40
Whose lisping love perhaps had solaced her,
With strangest infantine ingratitude,
Shunned her as one indifferent. She was past
That anguish, for she felt her hour draw on,
And 'twas her only comfort now to think   50
Upon the grave. 'Poor girl!' her mother said,
'Thou hast suffered much.' 'Aye mother; there is none
Can tell what I have suffered', she replied,
'But I shall soon be where the weary rest.'
And she did rest her soon, for it pleased God   55
To take her to his mercy.

From Morning Post, no. 9198 (30 June 1798)
THE IDIOT[1]

The circumstance related in the following ballad happened some years since in Herefordshire.

It had pleased God to form poor Ned
    A thing of idiot mind,
Yet to the poor unreas'ning man
    God had not been unkind;

Old Sarah loved her helpless child   5
    Whom helplessness made dear,
And life was happiness to him
    Who had no hope nor fear.

THE IDIOT
[1]   This poem was first attributed to Southey by B. R.
McElderry Jr., 'Southey, and Wordsworth's "The
Idiot Boy"', *N&Q*, 200 (1955), 490–1.

She knew his wants, she understood
    Each half-artic'late call,   10
And he was ev'rything to her
    And she to him was all.

And so for many a year they dwelt
    Nor knew a wish beside,
But age at length on Sarah came,   15
    And she fell sick and died.

He tried in vain to waken her,
    And called her o'er and o'er;
They told him she was dead – the sound
    To him no import bore.   20

They closed her eyes and shrouded her,
    And he stood wond'ring by;
And when they bore her to the grave
    He followed silently.

They laid her in the narrow house,[2]   25
    They sung the fun'ral stave,
But when the fun'ral train dispersed
    He loitered by the grave.

The rabble boys who used to jeer
    Whene'er they saw poor Ned   30
Now stood and watched him at the grave,
    And not a word they said.

They came and went and came again
    Till night at last came on,
And still he loitered by the grave   35
    Till all to rest were gone.

And when he found himself alone
    He swift removed the clay,
And raised the coffin up in haste
    And bore it swift away.   40

And when he reached his hut he laid
    The coffin on the floor,
And with the eagerness of joy
    He barred the cottage door.

And out he took his mother's corpse   45
    And placed it in her chair,

---

[2] *narrow house* grave.

And then he heaped the hearth and blew
  The kindling fire with care.

He placed his mother in her chair
  And in her wonted place,   50
And blew the kindling fire that shone
  Reflected on her face.

And pausing now, her hand would feel,
  And now her face behold –
'Why, mother, do you look so pale   55
  And why are you so cold?'

It had pleased God from the poor wretch
  His only friend to call,
But God was kind to him and soon
  In death restored him all.[3]   60

From Critical Review, 24 (1798) 197–204

REVIEW OF WILLIAM WORDSWORTH AND S. T. COLERIDGE, 'LYRICAL BALLADS'

The majority of these poems, we are informed in the Advertisement, are to be considered as 'experiments': 'They were written chiefly with a view to ascertain how far the language of conversation in the middle and lower classes of society is adapted to the purposes of poetic pleasure.'

  Of these 'experimental' poems, the most important is 'The Idiot Boy', the story of which is simply this: Betty Foy's neighbour Susan Gale is indisposed, and no one can be conveniently sent for the doctor but Betty's idiot boy. She therefore puts him upon her pony at eight o'clock in the evening, gives him proper directions, and returns to take care of her sick neighbour. Johnny is expected with the doctor by eleven, but the clock strikes eleven, and twelve, and one, without the appearance either of Johnny or the doctor. Betty's restless fears become insupportable and she now leaves her friend to look for her idiot son. She goes to the doctor's house but hears nothing of Johnny. About five o'clock, however, she finds him sitting quietly upon his feeding pony. As they go home they meet old Susan, whose apprehensions have cured her, and brought her out to seek them. And they all return merrily together. Upon this subject the author has written nearly five hundred lines. With what spirit the story is told, our extract will evince. [Southey quotes *Idiot Boy*, 322–401.]

---

[3] When 'The Idiot' was published in *Sarah Farley's Bristol Journal*, 21 July 1798, two new stanzas were substituted for the last stanza of this text:

But, hapless boy, he now found out
  His efforts were in vain,

Sarah would warmth again ne'er feel,
  Her eyes ne'er ope again.

Heaven pitying, saw the wretch had lost
  The only friend it gave;
Then shortly had his lifeless limbs
  Conveyed to Sarah's grave.

No tale less deserved the labour that appears to have been bestowed upon this. It resembles a Flemish picture in the worthlessness of its design and the excellence of its execution. From Flemish artists we are satisfied with such pieces; who would not have lamented if Correggio or Raphael had wasted their talents in painting Dutch boors or the humours of a Flemish wake?

The other ballads of this kind are as bald in story, and are not so highly embellished in narration. With that which is entitled 'The Thorn' we were altogether displeased. The Advertisement says it is not told in the person of the author, but in that of some 'loquacious narrator'. The author should have recollected that he who personates tiresome loquacity becomes tiresome himself. The story of a man who suffers the perpetual pain of cold because an old woman prayed that he never might be warm is perhaps a good story for a ballad because it is a well-known tale – but is the author certain that it is 'well-authenticated'? And does not such an assertion promote the popular superstition of witchcraft?

In a very different style of poetry is 'The Rime of the Ancyent Marinere' – a ballad (says the Advertisement) 'professedly written in imitation of the *style*, as well as of the spirit, of the elder poets.' We are tolerably conversant with the early English poets and can discover no resemblance whatever, except in antiquated spelling and a few obsolete words. This piece appears to us perfectly original in style as well as in story. Many of the stanzas are laboriously beautiful, but in connection they are absurd or unintelligible. Our readers may exercise their ingenuity in attempting to unriddle what follows. [Southey quotes 'Ancient Mariner', 301–22.] We do not sufficiently understand the story to analyze it. It is a Dutch attempt at German sublimity. Genius has here been employed in producing a poem of little merit.

With pleasure we turn to the serious pieces, the better part of the volume. 'The Foster-Mother's Tale' is in the best style of dramatic narrative; 'The Dungeon' and the 'Lines upon the Yew-Tree Seat' are beautiful. The tale of 'The Female Vagrant' is written in the stanza, not the style, of Spenser. We extract a part of this poem. [Southey quotes 'Female Vagrant' 91–180.] Admirable as this poem is, the author seems to discover still superior powers in the 'Lines written near Tintern Abbey'. On reading this production it is impossible not to lament that he should ever have condescended to write such pieces as 'The Last of the Flock', 'The Convict', and most of the ballads. In the whole range of English poetry, we scarcely recollect anything superior to a part of the following passage. [Southey quotes 'Tintern Abbey', 65–111.]

The 'experiment', we think, has failed, not because the language of conversation is little adapted to 'the purposes of poetic pleasure', but because it has been tried upon uninteresting subjects. Yet every piece discovers genius, and, ill as the author has frequently employed his talents, they certainly rank him with the best of living poets.

From Poems (1799)

THE SAILOR WHO HAD SERVED IN THE SLAVE-TRADE

He stopped: it surely was a groan
That from the hovel came!
He stopped and listened anxiously –
Again it sounds the same.

It surely from the hovel comes!   5
  And now he hastens there,
And thence he hears the name of Christ
  Amidst a broken prayer.

He entered in the hovel now,
  A sailor there he sees,   10
His hands were lifted up to heaven
  And he was on his knees.

Nor did the sailor so intent
  His entering footsteps heed,
But now the Lord's Prayer said, and now   15
  His half-forgotten creed.[1]

And often on his Saviour called
  With many a bitter groan,
In such heart-anguish as could spring
  From deepest guilt alone.   20

He asked the miserable man
  Why he was kneeling there,
And what the crime had been that caused
  The anguish of his prayer.

'Oh I have done a wicked thing!   25
  It haunts me night and day,
And I have sought this lonely place,
  Here undisturbed to pray.

I have no place to pray on board
  So I came here alone,   30
That I might freely kneel and pray
  And call on Christ and groan.

If to the mainmast-head[2] I go,
  The wicked one is there –
From place to place, from rope to rope,   35
  He follows everywhere.

I shut my eyes, it matters not,
  Still still the same I see;
And when I lie me down at night
  'Tis always day with me.   40

THE SAILOR WHO HAD SERVED IN THE SLAVE-TRADE   [2] *mainmast-head* the top of the principal mast of the
[1] *creed* formal statement of beliefs of the Christian   ship.
Church, repeated as a form of devotion.

He follows, follows everywhere
    And every place is hell!
Oh God! – and I must go with him
    In endless fire to dwell.

He follows, follows everywhere,   45
    He's still above, below –
Oh tell me where to fly from him!
    Oh tell me where to go!'

'But tell me', quoth the stranger then,
    'What this thy crime hath been?   50
So haply I may comfort give
    To one that grieves for sin.'

'Oh I have done a cursed deed'
    The wretched man replies,
'And night and day and everywhere   55
    'Tis still before my eyes.

I sailed on board a Guinea-man[3]
    And to the slave-coast went –
Would that the sea had swallowed me
    When I was innocent!   60

And we took in our cargo there,
    Three hundred Negro slaves,
And we sailed homeward merrily
    Over the ocean waves.

But some were sulky of the slaves   65
    And would not touch their meat,
So therefore we were forced by threats
    And blows to make them eat.

One woman sulkier than the rest
    Would still refuse her food –   70
Oh Jesus God! I hear her cries,
    I see her in her blood!

The Captain made me tie her up
    And flog while he stood by,
And then he cursed me if I stayed   75
    My hand to hear her cry.

She groaned, she shrieked – I could not spare,
    For the Captain he stood by –

---

[3] *Guinea-man* ship trading slaves from Guinea.

Dear God! that I might rest one night
  From that poor woman's cry!   80

She twisted from the blows – her blood,
  Her mangled flesh I see;
And still the Captain would not spare –
  Oh, he was worse than me!

She could not be more glad than I   85
  When she was taken down,
A blessed minute – 'twas the last
  That I have ever known!

I did not close my eyes all night,
  Thinking what I had done;   90
I heard her groans and they grew faint
  About the rising sun.

She groaned and groaned, but her groans grew
  Fainter at morning tide,
Fainter and fainter still they came   95
  Till at the noon she died.

They flung her overboard – poor wretch,
  She rested from her pain;
But when, oh Christ! oh blessed God!
  Shall I have rest again?   100

I saw the sea close over her,
  Yet she was still in sight;
I see her twisting everywhere,
  I see her day and night.

Go where I will, do what I can,   105
  The wicked one I see –
Dear Christ, have mercy on my soul,
  Oh God deliver me!

Tomorrow I set sail again
  Not to the Negro shore;   110
Wretch that I am, I will at least
  Commit that sin no more.

Oh give me comfort if you can,
  Oh tell me where to fly –
And bid me hope, if there be hope   115
  For one so lost as I.'

'Poor wretch', the stranger he replied,
  'Put thou thy trust in Heaven,
And call on Him for whose dear sake
  All sins shall be forgiven.   120

This night at least is thine – go thou
  And seek the house of prayer,
There shalt thou hear the word of God
  And he will help thee there!'

From Annual Anthology (1800)

THE BATTLE OF BLENHEIM[1]

I

It was a summer evening,
  Old Kaspar's work was done,
And he before his cottage door
  Was sitting in the sun,
And by him sported on the green   5
His little grandchild Wilhelmine.

II

She saw her brother Peterkin
  Roll something large and round
That he beside the rivulet
  In playing there had found;   10
He came to ask what he had found
That was so large, and smooth, and round.

III

Old Kaspar took it from the boy
  Who stood expectant by,
And then the old man shook his head   15
  And with a natural sigh,
' 'Tis some poor fellow's skull', said he,
'Who fell in the great victory.

THE BATTLE OF BLENHEIM
[1] The battle of Blenheim, 13 Aug. 1704, the most famous victory in the Wars of the Spanish Succession, was credited to John Churchill, 1st Duke of Marlborough, and Prince Eugene of Savoy; the French and Bavarians were defeated.

IV

I find them in the garden for
    There's many here about,
And often when I go to plough
    The ploughshare turns them out –
For many thousand men', said he,
'Were slain in the great victory.'   20

V

'Now tell us what 'twas all about,'   25
    Young Peterkin he cries,
And little Wilhelmine looks up
    With wonder-waiting eyes,
'Now tell us all about the war
And what they killed each other for.'   30

VI

'It was the English', Kaspar cried,
    'That put the French to rout,
But what they killed each other for
    I could not well make out.
But everybody said', quoth he,   35
'That 'twas a famous victory.

VII

My father lived at Blenheim then,
    Yon little stream hard by –
They burnt his dwelling to the ground
    And he was forced to fly;   40
So with his wife and child he fled,
Nor had he where to rest his head.

VIII

With fire and sword the country round
    Was wasted far and wide,
And many a childing mother then   45
    And new-born infant died.
But things like that, you know, must be
At every famous victory.

IX

They say it was a shocking sight
  After the field was won,
For many thousand bodies here
  Lay rotting in the sun –
But things like that you know must be
After a famous victory.

50

X

Great praise the Duke of Marlbro' won,
  And our good Prince Eugene.'
'Why 'twas a very wicked thing!'
  Said little Wilhelmine.
'Nay, nay, my little girl', quoth he,
'It was a famous victory,

55

60

XI

And everybody praised the Duke
  Who such a fight did win.'
'But what good came of it at last?'
  Quoth little Peterkin.
'Why that I cannot tell', said he,
'But 'twas a famous victory.'

65

Charles Lamb   (1775–1834)

Lamb went to Christ's Hospital with Coleridge, and was present at the beginning of the annus *mirabilis, 1797–8 (see pp. 511–13 above), when he first met Wordsworth. He was among the earliest admirers of* Lyrical Ballads, *and (against prevailing opinion) liked* The Excursion. *His best writing can be found in the essays published under the name 'Elia', first in various periodicals (notably the* London Magazine) *and then in book form in 1823 and 1833. Elia's art lay to a large extent in his manner; as Lamb told his publisher, John Taylor, 'The Essays want no Preface: they are all Preface. A Preface is nothing but a talk with the reader; and they do nothing else' (Lucas, ii. 350). Two essays are presented here in full: the first, 'Imperfect Sympathies', may be read as the manifesto for a philosophy applied in the second, 'Witches, and Other Night-Fears'.*

From Letter from Charles Lamb to S. T. Coleridge, 27 September 1796

My dearest friend –

White or some of my friends or the public papers by this time may have informed you of the terrible calamities that have fallen on our family.[1] I will only give you the outlines. My poor dear dearest sister,[2] in a fit of insanity, has been the death of her own mother. I was at hand only time enough to snatch the knife out of her grasp. She is at present in a madhouse from whence I fear she must be moved to an hospital.

God has preserved to me my senses.[3] I eat and drink and sleep, and have my judgement, I believe, very sound. My poor father was slightly wounded, and I am left to take care of him and my aunt. Mr Norris of the Bluecoat school[4] has been very kind to us, and we have no other friend – but, thank God, I am very calm and composed, and able to do the best that remains to do.

From Blank Verse by Charles Lloyd and Charles Lamb (1798)

THE OLD FAMILIAR FACES (COMPOSED JANUARY 1798)

Where are they gone, the old familiar faces?
I had a mother, but she died and left me,
Died prematurely in a day of horrors –
All, all are gone, the old familiar faces.

I have had playmates, I have had companions   5
In my days of childhood, in my joyful schooldays –
All, all are gone, the old familiar faces.

I have been laughing, I have been carousing,
Drinking late, sitting late, with my bosom cronies –
All, all are gone, the old familiar faces.   10

I loved a love once, fairest among women;[1]
Closed are her doors on me, I must not see her –
All, all are gone, the old familiar faces.

I have a friend,[2] a kinder friend has no man;
Like an ingrate, I left my friend abruptly,
Left him, to muse on the old familiar faces.   15

From LETTER FROM CHARLES LAMB TO S. T. COLERIDGE, 27 Sept. 1796
[1] On Thursday 22 Sept. 1796.
[2] Mary Anne Lamb (1764–1847).
[3] Lamb stayed at the Hoxton asylum, Dec. 1795–Jan. 1796.

[4] Christ's Hospital, where Lamb and Coleridge went to school.
THE OLD FAMILIAR FACES
[1] Ann Simmons, Lamb's sweetheart of 1792.
[2] Charles Lloyd.

Ghostlike, I paced round the haunts of my childhood;
Earth seemed a desert I was bound to traverse,
Seeking to find the old familiar faces.

Friend of my bosom, thou more than a brother![3]   20
Why wert not thou born in my father's dwelling,
So might we talk of the old familiar faces?

For some they have died, and some they have left me,
And some are taken from me[4] – all are departed,
All, all are gone, the old familiar faces.   25

From Letter from Charles Lamb to William Wordsworth, 30 January 1801

Separate from the pleasure of your company, I don't much care if I never see a mountain in my life. I have passed all my days in London until I have formed as many and intense local attachments as any of you mountaineers can have done with dead nature.

The lighted shops of the Strand and Fleet Street, the innumerable trades, tradesmen and customers, coaches, wagons, playhouses, all the bustle and wickedness round about Covent Garden, the very women of the town, the watchmen, drunken scenes, rattles; life awake, if you awake, at all hours of the night, the impossibility of being dull in Fleet Street, the crowds, the very dirt and mud, the sun shining upon houses and pavements, the print shops, the old book stalls,[1] parsons cheapening[2] books, coffee-houses, steams of soups from kitchens, the pantomimes – London itself a pantomime and a masquerade: all these things work themselves into my mind and feed me without a power of satiating me.

The wonder of these sights impels me into night-walks about her crowded streets, and I often shed tears in the motley Strand from fullness of joy at so much life. All these emotions must be strange to you; so are your rural emotions to me. But consider, what must I have been doing all my life not to have lent great portions of my heart with usury to such scenes?

My attachments are all local, purely local. I have no passion (or have had none since I was in love – and then it was the spurious engendering of poetry and books) to groves and valleys. The rooms where I was born, the furniture which has been before my eyes all my life, a bookcase which has followed me about like a faithful dog (only exceeding him in knowledge) wherever I have moved, old chairs, old tables, streets, squares where I have sunned myself, my old school – these are my mistresses. Have I not enough, without your mountains? I do not envy you. I should pity you, did I not know that the mind will make friends of anything. Your sun and moon and skies and hills and lakes affect me no more, or scarcely come to me in more venerable characters, than as a gilded room with tapestry and tapers where I might live with handsome visible objects. I consider the clouds above me but as a roof beautifully painted, but

---

[3] Coleridge.
[4] Shortly before this poem was written, Mary Lamb suffered a relapse and was returned to hospital.

From LETTER FROM CHARLES LAMB TO WILLIAM WORDS-WORTH, 30 JANUARY 1801
[1] Stalls selling old books.
[2] *cheapening* bargaining for.

unable to satisfy the mind, and at last, like the pictures of the apartment of a connoisseur, unable to afford him any longer a pleasure.

From Letter from Charles Lamb to Thomas Manning, 22 August 1801

ON MACKINTOSH[1]

Though thou'rt like Judas – an apostate black,
In the resemblance one thing thou dost lack:
When he had gotten his ill-purchased pelf,[2]
He went away and wisely hanged himself.
This thou may do at last – yet much I doubt,
If thou hast any bowels to gush out!

From Letter from Charles Lamb to John Taylor, 30 June 1821

Poor Elia the real (for I am but a counterfeit) is dead. The fact is a person of that name, an Italian, was a fellow-clerk of mine at the South Sea House thirty (not forty) years ago,[1] when the characters I described there existed, but had left it like myself many years – and I having a brother[2] now there, and doubting how he might relish certain descriptions in it, I clapped down the name of Elia to it, which passed off pretty well, for Elia himself added the function of an author to that of a scrivener, like myself.

I went the other day (not having seen him for a year) to laugh over with him at my usurpation of his name, and found him, alas, no more than a name, for he died of consumption eleven months ago, and I knew not of it.

So the name has fairly devolved to me, I think, and 'tis all he has left me.

From Elia (1823)

IMPERFECT SYMPATHIES (FIRST PUBLISHED IN *LONDON MAGAZINE*, AUGUST 1821, ENTITLED 'JEWS, QUAKERS, SCOTCHMEN, AND OTHER IMPERFECT SYMPATHIES')

I am of a constitution so general, that it consorts and sympathizeth with all things; I have no antipathy, or rather idiosyncrasy, in anything. Those national repugnancies do not touch me, nor do I behold with prejudice the French, Italian, Spaniard, or Dutch.
(Sir Thomas Browne, *Religio Medici*)

ON MACKINTOSH
[1] Having defended the French Revolution in *Vindiciae Gallicae* (see pp. 157–8 above), James Mackintosh was persuaded by Burke to repudiate it in *A Discourse on the Study of the Law of Nature and Nations* (1799). Wordsworth and Coleridge also noted Mackintosh's apostasy with disappointment; see *Thirteen-Book Prelude*, ii. 450–6, and *Notebooks*, i. 947.

[2] *pelf* booty, spoil.

FROM LETTER FROM CHARLES LAMB TO JOHN TAYLOR, 30 June 1821
[1] Lamb was a clerk in the Pacific trade office of the South Sea House, 1791–2.
[2] John Lamb the Younger (1763–1821).

That the author of the *Religio Medici*, mounted upon the airy stilts of abstraction, conversant about notional and conjectural essences, in whose categories of being the possible took the upper hand of the actual, should have overlooked the impertinent individualities of such poor concretions as mankind, is not much to be admired. It is rather to be wondered at, that in the genus of animals he should have condescended to distinguish that species at all.

For myself, earthbound and fettered to the scene of my activities, 'Standing on earth, not rapt above the sky',[1] I confess that I do feel the differences of mankind, national or individual, to an unhealthy excess. I can look with no indifferent eye upon things or persons. Whatever is, is to me a matter of taste or distaste, or, when once it becomes indifferent, it begins to be disrelishing. I am, in plainer words, a bundle of prejudices made up of likings and dislikings, the veriest thrall to sympathies, apathies, antipathies.

In a certain sense, I hope it may be said of me that I am a lover of my species. I can feel for all indifferently, but I cannot feel towards all equally. The more purely English word that expresses sympathy will better explain my meaning. I can be a friend to a worthy man who, upon another account, cannot be my mate or *fellow*. I cannot *like* all people alike.[2]

I have been trying all my life to like Scotchmen and am obliged to desist from the experiment in despair. They cannot like me and, in truth, I never knew one of that nation who attempted to do it. There is something more plain and ingenuous in their mode of proceeding. We know one another at first sight. There is an order of imperfect intellects (under which mine must be content to rank) which in its constitution is essentially anti-Caledonian. The owners of the sort of faculties I allude to have minds rather suggestive than comprehensive. They have no pretences to much clearness or precision in their ideas, or in their manner of expressing them. Their intellectual wardrobe (to confess fairly) has few whole pieces in it. They are content with fragments and scattered pieces of Truth; she presents no full front to them – a feature or side-face at the most. Hints and glimpses, germs and crude essays at a system, is the utmost they pretend to. They beat up a little game peradventure, and leave it to knottier heads, more robust constitutions, to run it down. The light that lights them is not steady and polar, but mutable and shifting – waxing, and again waning. Their conversation is accordingly. They will throw out a random word in or out of season, and be content to let it pass for what it is worth. They cannot speak always as if they were upon their oath, but must be understood, speaking or writing, with some abatement. They seldom wait to mature a proposition, but e'en bring it to market in the green ear.[3] They delight to impart their defective discoveries as they arise, without waiting for their full development. They are no systematizers, and would but err more by attempting it. Their minds, as I said before, are suggestive merely.

The brain of a true Caledonian (if I am not mistaken) is constituted upon quite a different plan. His Minerva is born in panoply.[4] You are never admitted to see his ideas in their growth – if indeed they do grow, and are not rather put together upon

---

IMPERFECT SYMPATHIES
[1] *Paradise Lost*, vii. 23.
[2] 'I would be understood as confining myself to the subject of *imperfect sympathies*. To nations or classes of men there can be no direct *antipathy*. There may be individuals born and constellated so opposite to another individual nature, that the same sphere cannot

hold them. I have met with my moral antipodes, and can believe the story of two men meeting (who never saw one another before in their lives) and instantly fighting' (Lamb's note).
[3] *in the green ear* prematurely.
[4] *in panoply* in armour. Minerva was born from the head of Jupiter.

principles of clockwork. You never catch his mind in an undress. He never hints or suggests anything, but unlades his stock of ideas in perfect order and completeness. He brings his total wealth into company, and gravely unpacks it. His riches are always about him. He never stoops to catch a glittering something in your presence to share it with you, before he quite knows whether it be true touch[5] or not. You cannot cry *halves* to anything that he finds – he does not find, but bring. You never witness his first apprehension of a thing. His understanding is always at its meridian; you never see the first dawn, the early streaks. He has no falterings of self-suspicion. Surmises, guesses, misgivings, half-intuitions, semi-consciousnesses, partial illuminations, dim instincts, embryo conceptions, have no place in his brain or vocabulary. The twilight of dubiety never falls upon him. Is he orthodox? He has no doubts. Is he an infidel? He has none either. Between the affirmative and the negative there is no borderland with him. You cannot hover with him upon the confines of truth, or wander in the maze of a probable argument. He always keeps the path. You cannot make excursions with him, for he sets you right. His taste never fluctuates. His morality never abates. He cannot compromise, or understand middle actions. There can be but a right and a wrong. His conversation is as a book. His affirmations have the sanctity of an oath. You must speak upon the square[6] with him. He stops a metaphor like a suspected person in an enemy's country. 'A healthy book!' said one of his countrymen to me, who had ventured to give that appellation to *John Buncle*,[7] 'Did I catch rightly what you said? I have heard of a man in health, and of a healthy state of body, but I do not see how that epithet can be properly applied to a book.'

Above all, you must beware of indirect expressions before a Caledonian. Clap an extinguisher upon your irony if you are unhappily blessed with a vein of it: remember you are upon your oath. I have a print of a graceful female after Leonardo da Vinci,[8] which I was showing off to Mr ****. After he had examined it minutely, I ventured to ask him how he liked 'my beauty' (a foolish name it goes by among my friends), when he very gravely assured me that he had considerable respect for my character and talents (so he was pleased to say) but had not given himself much thought about the degree of my personal pretensions. The misconception staggered me, but did not seem much to disconcert him.

Persons of this nation are particularly fond of affirming a truth which nobody doubts. They do not so properly affirm, as annunciate it. They do indeed appear to have such a love of truth (as if, like virtue, it were valuable for itself) that all truth becomes equally valuable whether the proposition that contains it be new or old, disputed, or such as is impossible to become a subject of disputation. I was present not long since at a party of north Britons where a son of Burns was expected, and happened to drop a silly expression (in my south British way), that I wished it were the father instead of the son – when four of them started up at once to inform me, that 'that was impossible, because he was dead.' An impracticable wish, it seems, was more than they could conceive. Swift has hit off this part of their character (namely their love of truth) in his biting way, but with an illiberality that necessarily confines the passage to the margin.[9]

---

5 *true touch* perfectly true.
6 *upon the square* directly, openly.
7 *The Life and Opinions of John Buncle, Esq.* (1756, 1766), novel by Thomas Amory.

8 The Virgin of the Rocks.
9 Lamb notes a passage from Swift's 'Hints towards an Essay on Conversation': 'There are some people who think they sufficiently acquit themselves, and

The tediousness of these people is certainly provoking. I wonder if they ever tire one another? In my early life I had a passionate fondness for the poetry of Burns. I have sometimes foolishly hoped to ingratiate myself with his countrymen by expressing it. But I have always found that a true Scot resents your admiration of his compatriot even more than he would your contempt of him. The latter he imputes to your 'imperfect acquaintance with many of the words which he uses', and the same objection makes it a presumption in you to suppose that you can admire him. Thomson[10] they seem to have forgotten. Smollett they have neither forgotten nor forgiven for his delineation of Rory and his companion upon their first introduction to our metropolis.[11] Speak of Smollett as a great genius and they will retort upon you Hume's *History* compared with *his* continuation of it.[12] What if the historian had continued *Humphrey Clinker*?[13]

I have, in the abstract, no disrespect for Jews. They are a piece of stubborn antiquity compared with which Stonehenge is in its nonage. They date beyond the pyramids. But I should not care to be in habits of familiar intercourse with any of that nation. I confess that I have not the nerves to enter their synagogues; old prejudices cling about me – I cannot shake off the story of Hugh of Lincoln.[14] Centuries of injury, contempt, and hate, on the one side, of cloaked revenge, dissimulation, and hate, on the other, between our and their fathers, must and ought to affect the blood of the children. I cannot believe it can run clear and kindly yet, or that a few fine words, such as candour, liberality, the light of a nineteenth century, can close up the breaches of so deadly a disunion.

A Hebrew is nowhere congenial to me. He is least distasteful on 'Change,[15] for the mercantile spirit levels all distinctions, as all are beauties in the dark. I boldly confess that I do not relish the approximation of Jew and Christian which has become so fashionable. The reciprocal endearments have, to me, something hypocritical and unnatural in them. I do not like to see the Church and Synagogue kissing and congeeing in awkward postures of an affected civility. If *they* are converted, why do they not come over to us altogether? Why keep up a form of separation when the life of it is fled? If they can sit with us at table, why do they keck[16] at our cookery? I do not understand these half-convertites: Jews christianizing, Christians judaizing – puzzle me. I like fish or flesh. A moderate Jew is a more confounding piece of anomaly than a wet Quaker. The spirit of the synagogue is essentially *separative*.

B—— would have been more in keeping if he had abided by the faith of his forefathers;[17] there is a fine scorn in his face, which nature meant to be of – Christians. The Hebrew spirit is strong in him, in spite of his proselytism. He cannot conquer the

entertain their company, with relating facts of no consequence, not at all out of the road of such common incidents as happen every day. And this I have observed more frequently among the Scots than any other nation, who are very careful not to omit the minutest circumstances of time or place – which kind of discourse, if it were not a little relieved by the uncouth terms and phrases, as well as accent and gesture peculiar to that country, would be hardly tolerable.'

[10] James Thomson (1700–48), author of *The Seasons.*
[11] Rory, the eponymous hero of *Roderick Random* (1748) by Tobias Smollett, arrives in London at ch. 13.

[12] Smollett's *A Complete History of England* (1757–8) was frequently published as a continuation of David Hume's *History of Great Britain* (1754–62).
[13] *The Expedition of Humphry Clinker* (1771), the most accomplished of Smollett's novels.
[14] Ten-year-old boy supposedly crucified and killed by Jews.
[15] *'Change* the Exchange.
[16] *keck* retch.
[17] Judaism. John Braham (1774–1856), renowned tenor of Jewish parentage who converted to Christianity.

620 CHARLES LAMB

shibboleth. How it breaks out when he sings, 'The Children of Israel passed through the Red Sea!' The auditors, for the moment, are as Egyptians to him, and he rides over our necks in triumph. There is no mistaking him. B——— has a strong expression of sense in his countenance, and it is confirmed by his singing. The foundation of his vocal excellence is sense. He sings with understanding, as Kemble[18] delivered dialogue. He would sing the Commandments and give an appropriate character to each prohibition.

His nation, in general, have not over-sensible countenances. How should they? But you seldom see a silly expression among them. Gain, and the pursuit of gain, sharpen a man's visage. I never heard of an idiot being born among them. Some admire the Jewish female physiognomy. I admire it, but with trembling. Jael[19] had those full dark inscrutable eyes.

In the Negro countenance you will often meet with strong traits of benignity. I have felt yearnings of tenderness towards some of these faces, or rather masks, that have looked out kindly upon one in casual encounters in the streets and highways. I love what Fuller[20] beautifully calls these 'images of God cut in ebony'. But I should not like to associate with them, to share my meals and my goodnights with them – because they are black.

I love Quaker ways and Quaker worship. I venerate the Quaker principles. It does me good for the rest of the day when I meet any of their people in my path. When I am ruffled or disturbed by any occurrence, the sight, or quiet voice of a Quaker, acts upon me as a ventilator, lightening the air and taking off a load from the bosom. But I cannot like the Quakers (as Desdemona would say) 'to live with them'.[21] I am all over-sophisticated – with humours, fancies, craving hourly sympathy. I must have books, pictures, theatres, chit-chat, scandal, jokes, ambiguities, and a thousand whim-whams which their simpler taste can do without. I should starve at their primitive banquet. My appetites are too high for the salads which (according to Evelyn[22]) Eve dressed for the angel, my gusto too excited 'To sit a guest with Daniel at his pulse'.[23]

The indirect answers which Quakers are often found to return to a question put to them may be explained, I think, without the vulgar assumption that they are more given to evasion and equivocating than other people. They naturally look to their words more carefully, and are more cautious of committing themselves. They have a peculiar character to keep up on this head. They stand in a manner upon their veracity. A Quaker is by law exempted from taking an oath. The custom of resorting to an oath in extreme cases, sanctified as it is by all religious antiquity, is apt (it must be confessed) to introduce into the laxer sort of minds the notion of two kinds of truth – the one applicable to the solemn affairs of justice, and the other to the common proceedings of daily intercourse. As truth bound upon the conscience by an oath can be but truth, so in the common affirmations of the shop and the marketplace a latitude is expected and conceded upon questions wanting this solemn covenant. Something less than truth satisfies. It is common to hear a person say, 'You do not expect me to speak as if I were upon my oath.' Hence a great deal of incorrectness and inadvertency (short of

[18] John Philip Kemble (1757–1823), greatest trage-dian of his time.
[19] Jael was a murderess, Judges 4: 21.
[20] Thomas Fuller (1608–61) was a favourite author of Lamb's.
[21] *Othello*, I. iii. 248.
[22] John Evelyn, *Acetaria* (1699), learned discourse on salad dressings.
[23] *Paradise Regained*, ii. 278.

falsehood) creeps into ordinary conversation, and a kind of secondary or laic-truth is tolerated, where clergy-truth – oath-truth, by the nature of the circumstances – is not required. A Quaker knows none of this distinction. His simple affirmation being received upon the most sacred occasions, without any further test, stamps a value upon the words which he is to use upon the most indifferent topics of life. He looks to them, naturally, with more severity.

You can have of him no more than his word. He knows, if he is caught tripping in a casual expression, he forfeits, for himself at least, his claim to the invidious exemption. He knows that his syllables are weighed – and how far a consciousness of this particular watchfulness, exerted against a person, has a tendency to produce indirect answers and a diverting of the question by honest means, might be illustrated (and the practice justified) by a more sacred example than is proper to be adduced upon this occasion. The admirable presence of mind, which is notorious in Quakers upon all contingencies, might be traced to this imposed self-watchfulness, if it did not seem rather an humble and secular scion of that old stock of religious constancy which never bent or faltered in the Primitive Friends, or gave way to the winds of persecution, to the violence of judge or accuser, under trials and racking examinations. 'You will never be the wiser, if I sit here answering your questions till midnight,' said one of those upright Justicers to Penn,[24] who had been putting law-cases with a puzzling subtlety. 'Thereafter as the answers may be', retorted the Quaker.

The astonishing composure of this people is sometimes ludicrously displayed in lighter instances. I was travelling in a stagecoach with three male Quakers, buttoned up in the straitest non-conformity of their sect. We stopped to bait at Andover, where a meal (partly tea apparatus, partly supper) was set before us. My friends confined themselves to the tea-table. I in my way took supper. When the landlady brought in the bill, the eldest of my companions discovered that she had charged for both meals. This was resisted. Mine hostess was very clamorous and positive. Some mild arguments were used on the part of the Quakers, for which the heated mind of the good lady seemed by no means a fit recipient. The guard came in with his usual peremptory notice. The Quakers pulled out their money and formally tendered it (so much for tea), I, in humble imitation, tendering mine for the supper which I had taken. She would not relax in her demand. So they all three quietly put up their silver, as did myself, and marched out of the room, the eldest and gravest going first, with myself closing up the rear, who thought I could not do better than follow the example of such grave and warrantable personages. We got in. The steps went up. The coach drove off. The murmurs of mine hostess (not very indistinctly or ambiguously pronounced) became after a time inaudible – and now, my conscience (which the whimsical scene had for a while suspended) beginning to give some twitches, I waited in the hope that some justification would be offered by these serious persons for the seeming injustice of their conduct. To my great surprise not a syllable was dropped on the subject. They sat as mute as at a meeting. At length the eldest of them broke silence, by enquiring of his next neighbour, 'Hast thee heard how indigos go at the India House?' And the question operated as a soporific on my moral feeling as far as Exeter.

---

[24] William Penn (1644–1718), English Quaker.

WITCHES, AND OTHER NIGHT-FEARS (FIRST PUBLISHED IN *LONDON MAGAZINE*, OCTOBER 1821)

We are too hasty when we set down our ancestors in the gross for fools, for the monstrous inconsistencies (as they seem to us) involved in their creed of witchcraft. In the relations of this visible world we find them to have been as rational, and shrewd to detect an historic anomaly, as ourselves. But when once the invisible world was supposed to be opened, and the lawless agency of bad spirits assumed, what measures of probability, of decency, of fitness, or proportion of that which distinguishes the likely from the palpable absurd, could they have to guide them in the rejection or admission of any particular testimony? That maidens pined away, wasting inwardly as their waxen images consumed before a fire; that corn was lodged and cattle lamed; that whirlwinds uptore in diabolic revelry the oaks of the forest; or that spits and kettles only danced a fearful-innocent vagary about some rustic's kitchen when no wind was stirring – were all equally probable where no law of agency was understood. That the Prince of the powers of darkness, passing by the flower and pomp of the earth, should lay preposterous siege to the weak fantasy of indigent eld,[1] has neither likelihood nor unlikelihood *a priori* to us who have no measure to guess at his policy, or standard to estimate what rate those anile[2] souls may fetch in the devil's market. Nor, when the wicked are expressly symbolized by a goat, was it to be wondered at so much, that *he* should come sometimes in that body and assert his metaphor. That the intercourse was opened at all between both worlds was perhaps the mistake – but that once assumed, I see no reason for disbelieving one attested story of this nature more than another on the score of absurdity. There is no law to judge of the lawless, or canon by which a dream may be criticized.

I have sometimes thought that I could not have existed in the days of received witchcraft, that I could not have slept in a village where one of those reputed hags dwelt. Our ancestors were bolder (or more obtuse). Amidst the universal belief that these wretches were in league with the author of all evil, holding hell tributary to their muttering, no simple Justice of the Peace seems to have scrupled issuing, or silly headborough[3] serving, a warrant upon them – as if they should subpoena Satan! Prospero in his boat, with his books and wand about him, suffers himself to be conveyed away at the mercy of his enemies to an unknown island. He might have raised a storm or two, we think, on the passage. His acquiescence is in exact analogy to the non-resistance of witches to the constituted powers. What stops the Fiend in Spenser from tearing Guyon to pieces? Or who had made it a condition of his prey that Guyon must take assay of the glorious bait? We have no guess; we do not know the laws of that country.

From my childhood I was extremely inquisitive about witches and witch-stories. My maid, and more legendary aunt, supplied me with good store.[4] But I shall mention the accident which directed my curiosity originally into this channel. In my father's book-closet, the *History of the Bible* by Stackhouse[5] occupied a distinguished station. The pictures with which it abounds – one of the ark, in particular, and another of Solomon's

---

WITCHES, AND OTHER NIGHT-FEARS
[1] *indigent eld* people in olden times.
[2] *anile* old-womanish.
[3] *headborough* constable.

[4] Coleridge's childhood reading was much the same, see pp. 513–14 above.
[5] Thomas Stackhouse, *New History of the Holy Bible* (1737).

temple, delineated with all the fidelity of ocular admeasurement, as if the artist had been upon the spot – attracted my childish attention. There was a picture, too, of the witch raising up Samuel, which I wish that I had never seen. (We shall come to that hereafter.)

Stackhouse is in two huge tomes, and there was a pleasure in removing folios of that magnitude, which, with infinite straining, was as much as I could manage, from the situation which they occupied upon an upper shelf. I have not met with the work from that time to this, but I remember it consisted of Old Testament stories, orderly set down, with the 'objection' appended to each story, and the 'solution' of the objection regularly tacked to that. The objection was a summary of whatever difficulties had been opposed to the credibility of the history, by the shrewdness of ancient or modern infidelity, drawn up with an almost complimentary excess of candour; the solution was brief, modest, and satisfactory. The bane and antidote were both before you. To doubts so put (and so quashed), there seemed to be an end for ever. The dragon lay dead, for the foot of the veriest babe to trample on.

But (like as was rather feared than realized from that slain monster in Spenser) from the womb of those crushed errors young dragonets would creep, exceeding the prowess of so tender a St George as myself to vanquish. The habit of expecting objections to every passage set me upon starting more objections, for the glory of finding a solution of my own for them. I became staggered and perplexed, a sceptic in long coats. The pretty Bible stories which I had read, or heard read in church, lost their purity and sincerity of impression, and were turned into so many historic or chronologic theses to be defended against whatever impugners. I was not to disbelieve them, but (the next thing to that) I was to be quite sure that someone or other would or had disbelieved them. Next to making a child an infidel is the letting him know that there are infidels at all. Credulity is the man's weakness but the child's strength. Oh, how ugly sound scriptural doubts from the mouth of a babe and a suckling!

I should have lost myself in these mazes and have pined away, I think, with such unfit sustenance as these husks afforded, but for a fortunate piece of ill-fortune, which about this time befell me. Turning over the picture of the ark with too much haste, I unhappily made a breach in its ingenious fabric – driving my inconsiderate fingers right through the two larger quadrupeds (the elephant and the camel) that stare, as well they might, out of the two last windows next the steerage in that unique piece of naval architecture. Stackhouse was henceforth locked up, and became an interdicted treasure. With the book, the objections and solutions gradually cleared out of my head, and have seldom returned since in any force to trouble me. But there was one impression which I had imbibed from Stackhouse which no lock or bar could shut out, and which was destined to try my childish nerves rather more seriously – that detestable picture!

I was dreadfully alive to nervous terrors. The night-time solitude and the dark were my hell. The sufferings I endured in this nature would justify the expression. I never laid my head on my pillow, I suppose, from the fourth to the seventh or eighth year of my life (so far as memory serves in things so long ago), without an assurance, which realized its own prophecy, of seeing some frightful spectre. Be old Stackhouse then acquitted in part, if I say that to his picture of the witch raising up Samuel (oh, that old man covered with a mantle!) I owe not my midnight terrors, the hell of my infancy, but the shape and manner of their visitation. It was he who dressed up for me a hag that nightly sat upon my pillow – a sure bedfellow when my aunt or my maid was far from me. All day long, while the book was permitted me, I dreamed waking over his delineation, and at night (if I may use so bold an expression) awoke into sleep, and found the vision true. I durst not, even in the daylight, once enter the chamber where I slept, without my face turned to the window, aversely from the bed where my witch-ridden pillow was. Parents do not know what they do when they leave tender babes alone to go to sleep in the dark. The feeling about for a friendly arm, the hoping for a familiar voice when they wake screaming and find none to soothe them – what a terrible shaking it is to their poor nerves! The keeping them up till midnight, through candlelight and the unwholesome hours (as they are called), would, I am satisfied, in a medical point of view, prove the better caution. That detestable picture, as I have said, gave the fashion to my dreams – if dreams they were, for the scene of them was invariably the room in which I lay. Had I never met with the picture, the fears would have come self-pictured in some shape or other – 'Headless bear, black man, or ape'[6] – but, as it was, my imaginations took that form.

It is not book, or picture, or the stories of foolish servants which create these terrors in children; they can at most but give them a direction. Dear little T.H.[7] who, of all children, has been brought up with the most scrupulous exclusion of every taint of superstition, who was never allowed to hear of goblin or apparition, or scarcely to be told of bad men, or to read or hear of any distressing story, finds all this world of fear, from which he has been so rigidly excluded *ab extra* in his own 'thick-coming fancies'[8] – and from his little midnight pillow, this nurse-child of optimism will start at shapes unborrowed of tradition, in sweats to which the reveries of the cell-damned murderer are tranquillity.

Gorgons and hydras and chimeras,[9] dire stories of Celaeno and the harpies, may reproduce themselves in the brain of superstition – but they were there before. They are transcripts, types; the archetypes are in us, and eternal.[10] How else should the recital of that which we know in a waking sense to be false come to affect us at all? Or 'Names whose sense we see not, / Fray us with things that be not?'[11] Is it that we naturally conceive terror from such objects, considered in their capacity of being able to inflict upon us bodily injury? Oh, least of all! These terrors are of older standing. They date beyond body – or, without the body, they would have been the same. All the cruel, tormenting, defined devils in Dante – tearing, mangling, choking, stifling, scorching demons – are they one half so fearful to the spirit of a man as the simple idea of a spirit unembodied following him?

> Like one that on a lonesome road
> Doth walk in fear and dread,
> And having once turned round walks on
> And turns no more his head
> Because he knows a frightful fiend
> Doth close behind him tread.
>
> ('The Ancient Mariner', 451–6)

That the kind of fear here treated of is purely spiritual, that it is strong in proportion as it is objectless upon earth, that it predominates in the period of sinless infancy – are

---

[6] From 'The Author's Abstract of Melancholy' prefixed to Robert Burton, *The Anatomy of Melancholy* (1621).

[7] Thornton Leigh Hunt (1810–73), journalist, eldest son of Leigh Hunt.

[8] *Macbeth*, V. iii. 38.

[9] An echo of *Paradise Lost*, ii. 628: 'Gorgons and hydras and chimeras dire.'

[10] Cf. *Thirteen-Book Prelude*, vi. 571: 'the types and symbols of eternity'.

[11] Spenser, *Epithalamion*, 343–4.

difficulties, the solution of which might afford some probable insight into our ante-mundane condition, and a peep at least into the shadowland of pre-existence.

My night-fancies have long ceased to be afflictive. I confess an occasional nightmare, but I do not, as in early youth, keep a stud of them. Fiendish faces, with the extinguished taper, will come and look at me – but I know them for mockeries, even while I cannot elude their presence, and I fight and grapple with them. For the credit of my imagination, I am almost ashamed to say how tame and prosaic my dreams are grown. They are never romantic, seldom even rural. They are of architecture and of buildings – cities abroad, which I have never seen, and hardly have hope to see. I have traversed, for the seeming length of a natural day, Rome, Amsterdam, Paris, Lisbon – their churches, palaces, squares, market-places, shops, suburbs, ruins, with an inexpressible sense of delight, a map-like distinctness of trace, and a daylight vividness of vision, that was all but being awake.

I have formerly travelled among the Westmorland fells (my highest Alps), but they are objects too mighty for the grasp of my dreaming recognition, and I have again and again awoke with ineffectual struggles of the inner eye, to make out a shape, in any way whatever, of Helvellyn. Methought I was in that country, but the mountains were gone. The poverty of my dreams mortifies me. There is Coleridge, at his will can conjure up icy domes and pleasure-houses for Kubla Khan, and Abyssinian maids, and songs of Abara, and caverns 'Where Alph, the sacred river, runs', to solace his night solitudes, when I cannot muster a fiddle. Barry Cornwall has his tritons and his nereids gambolling before him in nocturnal visions, and proclaiming sons born to Neptune, when my stretch of imaginative activity can hardly, in the night season, raise up the ghost of a fishwife. To set my failures in somewhat a mortifying light, it was after reading the noble 'Dream'[12] of this poet that my fancy ran strong upon these marine spectra – and the poor plastic power (such as it is) within me set to work, to humour my folly in a sort of dream that very night. Methought I was upon the ocean billows at some sea nuptials, riding and mounted high, with the customary train sounding their conchs before me (I myself, you may be sure, the leading god), and jollily we went careering over the main, till, just where Ino Leucothea[13] should have greeted me (I think it was Ino) with a white embrace, the billows, gradually subsiding, fell from a sea-roughness to a sea-calm, and thence to a river-motion, and that river (as happens in the familiarization of dreams) was no other than the gentle Thames – which landed me, in the wafture of a placid wave or two, alone, safe and inglorious, somewhere at the foot of Lambeth Palace.

The degree of the soul's creativeness in sleep might furnish no whimsical criterion of the quantum of poetical faculty resident in the same soul waking. An old gentleman, a friend of mine, and a humorist, used to carry this notion so far that when he saw any stripling of his acquaintance ambitious of becoming a poet, his first question would be, 'Young man, what sort of dreams have you?' I have so much faith in my old friend's theory that when I feel that idle vein returning upon me, I presently subside into my proper element of prose, remembering those eluding nereids, and that inauspicious inland landing.

---

[12] Bryan Waller Procter wrote under the name of Barry Cornwall; for 'A Dream', see pp. 709–12.

[13] Girl transformed into a sea-goddess in Homer's *Odyssey*.

Walter Savage Landor   (1775–1864)

The foremost neoclassicist of the time, whose elegiac love-poem 'Rose Aylmer' is here presented in its earliest text. Rose died in 1800 at the age of 20, having been a friend of Landor's at Laugharne. In 'Regeneration' Landor writes on behalf of the Risorgimento, the movement for Italian reunification, while the delicate sensuousness of 'Faesulan Idyll' is a triumph of classical simplicity recalling Coleridge's 'conversation poems'. 'Rose Aylmer' was a favourite poem of Lamb's, and he got on well with its author when they met on 28 September 1832.

From Simonidea (1806)

ROSE AYLMER

Ah what avails the sceptred race,
  Ah what the form divine?
What every virtue, every grace?
  For, Aylmer, all were thine.

Sweet Aylmer, whom these wakeful eyes   5
  May weep, but never see,
A night of sorrows and of sighs
  I consecrate to thee.

From Imaginary Conversations (1824)

REGENERATION

We are what suns and winds and waters make us –
The mountains are our sponsors, and the rills
Fashion and win their nursling with their smiles.
But where the land is dim from tyranny,
There tiny pleasures occupy the place   5
Of glories and of duties, as the feet
Of fabled fairies when the sun goes down
Trip o'er the grass where wrestlers strove by day.
Then Justice (called the Eternal One above)
Is more inconstant than the buoyant form   10
That bursts into existence from the froth
Of ever-varying ocean. What is best
Then becomes worst; what loveliest, most deformed.
The heart is hardest in the softest climes,
The passions flourish, the affections die.   15
    Oh, thou vast tablet of these awful truths
That fillest all the space between the seas,
Spreading from Venice's deserted courts

To the Tarentine and Hydruntine mole,[1]
What lifts thee up? What shakes thee? 'Tis the breath   20
Of God – awake, ye nations, spring to life!
Let the last work of his right hand[2] appear
Fresh with his image – man. Thou recreant slave
That sittest afar off and helpest not,
Oh thou degenerate Albion![3] With what shame   25
Do I survey thee, pushing forth the sponge
At thy spear's length, in mockery at the thirst
Of holy Freedom in his agony,
And prompt and keen to pierce the wounded side![4]

  Must Italy then wholly rot away   30
Amid her slime before she germinate
Into fresh vigour, into form again?
What thunder bursts upon mine ear! Some isle
Hath surely risen from the gulfs profound,
Eager to suck the sunshine from the breast   35
Of beauteous nature, and to catch the gale
From golden Hermus and Melaena's brow.[5]
A greater thing than isle, than continent,
Than earth itself, than ocean circling earth
Hath risen there: regenerate man hath risen.   40
Generous old bard of Chios![6] Not that Jove
Deprived thee in thy latter days of sight
Would I complain, but that no higher theme
Than a disdainful youth, a lawless king,
A pestilence, a pyre,[7] awoke thy song,   45
When on the Chian coast, one javelin's throw
From where thy tombstone, where thy cradle stood,
Twice twenty self-devoted Greeks assailed
The naval host of Asia, at one blow
Scattered it into air – and Greece was free![8]   50
And ere these glories beamed, thy day had closed.
Let all that Elis ever saw, give way,
All that Olympian Jove e'er smiled upon;
The Marathonian columns never told
A tale more glorious, never Salamis,   55
Nor (faithful in the centre of the false)
Plataea, nor Anthela, from whose mount

REGENERATION
[1] Landor laments Italian disunity. Since 1797, from Venice in the north to Taranto and Hydruntum in the south, the country had been carved up first under Napoleon and more recently under Austria.
[2] See Gen. 1: 26–8.
[3] The policy of the British since 1812 had been one of benign neglect.
[4] Landor is recalling John 19: 29–30.

[5] The River Hermus flows into the Aegean behind the promontory of Melaena, which faces the island of Chios.
[6] Birthplace of Homer.
[7] Themes from Homer's *Iliad*; Achilles is the 'disdainful youth', and Agamemnon the 'lawless king'.
[8] Landor alludes to an incident in the Greek War of Independence, Feb. 1822, when the Greeks routed the Turks.

Benignant Ceres wards the blessed laws
And sees the Amphictyon dip his weary foot
In the warm streamlet of the strait below.[9]   60
   Goddess,[10] although thy brow was never reared
Among the powers that guarded or assailed
Perfidious Ilion, parricidal Thebes,[11]
Or other walls whose war-belt e'er enclosed
Man's congregated crimes and vengeful pain,   65
Yet hast thou touched the extremes of grief and joy –
Grief upon Enna's mead and hell's ascent,
A solitary mother;[12] joy beyond,
Far beyond, that thy woe, in this thy fane:
The tears were human, but the bliss divine.   70
   I, in the land of strangers,[13] and depressed
With sad and certain presage for my own,
Exult at hope's fresh dayspring, though afar –
There where my youth was not unexercised
By chiefs in willing war and faithful song;   75
Shades as they were, they were not empty shades
Whose bodies haunt our world and blear our sun,
Obstruction worse than swamp and shapeless sands.
Peace, praise, eternal gladness, to the souls
That, rising from the seas into the heavens,   80
Have ransomed first their country with their blood!
   Oh thou immortal Spartan, at whose name
The marble table sounds beneath my palms –
Leonidas![14] Even thou wilt not disdain
To mingle names august as these with thine;   85
Nor thou, twin-star of glory,[15] thou whose rays
Streamed over Corinth on the double sea,
Achaian and Saronic, whom the sons
Of Syracuse, when death removed thy light,
Wept more than slavery ever made them weep   90
But shed (if gratitude is sweet) sweet tears;
For the hand that then poured ashes o'er their heads
Was loosened from its desperate chain by thee.
   What now can press mankind into one mass,
For Tyranny to tread the more secure?   95

---

[9] The Olympian games were held in Elis; the invading Persians were defeated by the Greeks at Marathon in 490 BC; the Persian fleet was defeated in a strait near Salamis, 480 BC; Plataea was an early ally of the Greeks and the scene of an important Greek victory over the Persians, 479 BC; Anthela, site of the temple of the Greek corn goddess, Demeter (Ceres), where the Amphictony (group of Greek worshippers) met each year.
[10] Goddess Ceres.
[11] Paris, son of the King of Troy (Ilion), abducted Helen; Oedipus killed his father before being made King of Thebes.
[12] Ceres' daughter, Persephone, was taken to Hades while plucking flowers in the vale of Enna.
[13] Landor was living in Florence.
[14] Leonidas, King of Sparta, defended the pass of Thermopylae against the Persians, 480 BC.
[15] Gelon, ruler of Syracuse in Sicily (founded by Corinth), suppressed a revolt against the aristocracy, and made the city a great Hellenic power.

From gold alone is drawn the guilty wire
That adulation trills – she mocks the tone
Of duty, courage, virtue, piety,
And under her sits hope! Oh, how unlike
That graceful form in azure vest arrayed,   100
With brow serene and eyes on heaven alone
In patience fixed, in fondness unobscured!
What monsters coil beneath the spreading tree
Of despotism! What wastes extend around!
What poison floats upon the distant breeze!   105
But who are those that cull and deal its fruit?
Creatures that shun the light and fear the shade,
Bloated and fierce – sleep's mien and famine's cry.
Rise up again, rise in thy dignity,
Dejected man, and scare this brood away!   110

From Gebir, Count Julian, and Other Poems (1831)

FAESULAN IDYLL (COMPOSED BETWEEN 1829 AND 1831)

Here, where precipitate spring with one light bound
Into hot summer's lusty arms expires,
And where go forth at morn, at eve, at night,
Soft airs that want the lute to play with them,
And softer sighs that know not what they want,   5
Under a wall, beneath an orange-tree
Whose tallest flowers could tell the lowlier ones
Of sights in Fiesole right up above[1] –
While I was gazing a few paces off
At what they seemed to show me with their nods,   10
Their frequent whispers and their pointing shoots,
A gentle maid came down the garden steps
And gathered the pure treasure in her lap.
I heard the branches rustle and stepped forth
To drive the ox away, or mule, or goat   15
(Such I believed it must be).
                  For sweet scents
Are the swift vehicles of still sweeter thoughts,
And nurse and pillow the dull memory
That would let drop without them her best stores.
They bring me tales of youth and tones of love,   20
And 'tis and ever was my wish and way
To let all flowers live freely, and all die,
Whene'er their genius bids their souls depart,

FAESULAN IDYLL
[1] From 1829 Landor lived in a villa on a hillside in
Fiesole.

Among their kindred in their native place.
I never pluck the rose; the violet's head   25
Hath shaken with my breath upon its bank
And not reproached me; the ever-sacred cup
Of the pure lily hath between my hands
Felt safe, unsoiled, nor lost one grain of gold.
  I saw the light that made the glossy leaves   30
More glossy; the fair arm, the fairer cheek
Warmed by the eye intent on its pursuit;
I saw the foot that, although half-erect
From its grey slipper, could not lift her up
To what she wanted. I held down a branch   35
And gathered her some blossoms, since their hour
Was come, and bees had wounded them, and flies
Of harder wing were working their way through,
And scattering them in fragments underfoot.
So crisp were some, they rattled unevolved;   40
Others, ere broken off, fell into shells –
For such appear the petals when detached,
Unbending, brittle, lucid, white like snow,
And, like snow, not seen through by eye or sun.
Yet every one her gown received from me   45
Was fairer than the first. I thought not so,
But so she praised them to reward my care.
I said, 'You find the largest.'
                  'This indeed',
Cried she, 'is large and sweet'. She held one forth,
Whether for me to look at or to take   50
She knew not, nor did I. But taking it
Would best have solved (and this she felt) her doubts.
I dared not touch it, for it seemed a part
Of her own self – fresh, full, the most mature
Of blossoms, yet a blossom; with a touch   55
To fall, and yet unfallen. She drew back
The boon she tendered, and then, finding not
The ribbon at her waist to fix it in,
Dropped it, as loath to drop it, on the rest.

From Leigh Hunt's London Journal, no. 63 (13 June 1835) 181

TO THE SISTER OF CHARLES LAMB[1]

Comfort thee, oh thou mourner, yet awhile!
  Again shall Elia's smile

TO THE SISTER OF CHARLES LAMB
[1] Lamb died 27 Dec. 1834, and was buried 3 Jan.
1835.

Refresh thy heart, when heart can ache no more.
    What is it we deplore?
He leaves behind him, freed from griefs and years,   5
    Far worthier things than tears:
The love of friends without a single foe,
    Unequalled lot below!
His gentle soul, his genius, these are thine;
    Shalt thou for those repine?   10
He may have left the lowly walks of men;
    Left them he has – what then?
Are not his footsteps followed by the eyes
    Of all the good and wise?
Though the warm day is over, yet they seek,   15
    Upon the lofty peak
Of his pure mind, the roseate light that glows
    O'er Death's perennial snows.
Behold him! From the spirits of the blessed
    He speaks, he bids thee rest.   20

Charlotte Bury (1775–1861)

Poet and author of 17 novels. 'False and Faithless as Thou Art' is one of her most moving lyrics on a theme much favoured by female writers of the time – the inconstancy of men.

From Poems on Several Occasions (1797)

FALSE AND FAITHLESS AS THOU ART

False and faithless as thou art,
Alas! you still possess my heart;
    Nor e'er can time efface
The thought of joys which now are flown,
Though with them ev'ry hope is gone   5
    Which soothes keen sorrow's trace.

Whate'er appearances may be,
In secret still I sigh for thee
    And mourn that I'm forgot;
Thy fragile vows, to me still dear,   10
Are still remembered with a tear –
    But yet, whate'er my lot.

May all thy life with pleasure teem,
May every sun's revolving beam
    Bring health and joy to thee;   15
And lest remorse thy heart should gain,

> Ah! may you never know the pain
> Which you have caused to me.
>
> Where Happiness (celestial maid!)
> With sprightly Fancy ever swayed   20
>   O'er Sorrow's gloomy power,
> There Melancholy sits, confessed
> Queen of my soul – for now unblessed
>   Is each sad lingering hour.

Charles Lloyd (1775–1839)

In September 1796 he became, first, Coleridge's live-in student, and then his lodger; in 1797 he became a friend of Lamb. 'London' is strongly influenced by Coleridge.

From Blank Verse by Charles Lloyd and Charles Lamb (1798)

LONDON

> *In solitude*
> *What happiness? Who can enjoy alone?*
> *Or, all enjoying, what contentment find?*
>   (*Paradise Lost*, viii. 364–6)

Thou first of human feelings, social love!
I must obey thy powerful sympathies,
E'en though I've often found that those my heart
Most prized were creatures of its warm desires,
Rather than aught which other men (less prone   5
To affections swift, transforming quality)
Might worthy deem or excellent!
                              Thy scenes,
Thy tainted scenes, proud city, now detain
My restless feet. 'Twill soothe a vacant hour
To trace what dim inexplicable links   10
Of hidden nature have inclined my soul
To love what heretofore it most abhorred.
When first, a little one, I marked far off
The wreathed smoke that capped thy palaces,
Oh, what a joyous fluttering of the heart,   15
Oh, what exulting hopes were mine! Methought
Within thy walls there must be somewhat strange,
Surpassing greatly any wondrous dream
Of fairy grandeur which my childhood loved.

And when I heard the busy hum of men   20
And saw the passing crowd in endless ranks,
The many-coloured equipage, and steeds
Gaily caparisoned, it seemed to me
As though all living things were centred here.
But other feelings soon transformed these shows   25
To merest emptiness, e'en till my soul
Would sicken at their presence; for I've sought
To cherish quiet musings, and disdained
The idle forms which play upon the sense,
Yet give the heart no comfortable thoughts.   30
Yes, I have sought the solitary walk
Where I might number every absent friend
And give a tear to each; I've nursed my soul
With strangest contemplation, till it wore
A sad and lonely character, untouched   35
By th' operation of external shapes.
     Yet, London, now thou'rt pleasant – 'tis e'en so!
For I am sick of hopes that stand aloof
From common sympathy; for I am sick
Of pampering delicate exclusive loves,   40
And silly dreams of rapture that would pull
The shrinking hand from every honest grasp,
The shrinking heart from every honest pledge,
Not tricked in gracefulness poetical!
Sometimes, 'tis true, when I have paced the haunts   45
Of crowded occupation, I have felt
A sad repression looking all around,
Nor catching one known face amid the throng
That answered mine with cordial pleasantness.
I've often thought upon some absent friend,   50
E'en till an assured hope that he was nigh
Has made me lift my head and stretch my arm
To gaze upon the form, and grasp the hand
Of him who lived in my wayward dream.[1]
And I have looked, and all has been to me   55
A crowded desolation![2] Not one being
Mid that incessant and perturbed throng
Dreamt of *my* hopes or fears!
                         Then have I paced
With breathless eagerness, and if an eye
Has met my gaze, wherein some trace remote   60
Lived of one on whom my heart has leaned,
A gentle thrilling of awakened love

LONDON
[1] Lines 50–4 look forward to Coleridge's 'Frost at
Midnight', 44–8.

[2] Cf. *Thirteen-Book Prelude*, vii. 594–7.

Has warmed my breast, and haply kindled there
A dream of parted days, that so my feet,
It seemed to me, moved on in solitude.   65
Thus can the heart, by its strange agency,
Extract divine emotion from the scene
Most barren and uncouth, which images
To *him who cannot love*, who never felt
That ever-active warmth commingling still   70
Its own existence with all present things,
Nought beside forms and bodily substances.
    Methinks he acts the purposes of life,
And fills the measure of his destiny
With best-approved wisdom, who retires   75
To some majestic solitude – his mind
Raised by those visions of eternal love,
The rock, the vale, the forest and the lake,
The sky, the sea, and everlasting hills.
He best performs the purposes of life   80
And fills the measure of his destiny
Who holds high converse with the present God[3]
(Not mystically meant), and feels him ever
Made manifest to his transfigured soul.
But few there are who know to prize such bliss,   85
And he who thus would raise his mortal being
Must shake weak nature off, and be content
To live a lonely uncompanioned thing,
Exiled from human loves and sympathies.
Therefore the city must detain *my* feet,   90
For I would sometimes gaze upon a face
That smiles on me, and speaks intelligibly
Of one that answers all my hopes and fears.
    Nor is to me the sentiment of life
Less acceptable, when I contemplate   95
Numberless living and progressive beings
Acting the infinite varieties
Of this miraculous scene. For though the dim
And inharmonious ministrations here
Of heavenly wisdom may confound the sense,   100
The partial sense of man, *my soul* is glad –
Trusting that all, yea, every living thing
Shall understand, in the appointed time,
And praise the inwoven mystery of sin,
Losing each hope and each propellant fear   105
In perfect bliss – and 'God be all in all!'

---

[3] 'The doctrine of Berkeley, of which the author is
a believer, is here alluded to' (Lloyd's note).

John Constable (1776–1837)

The inspiration for many of Constable's greatest paintings came from his memories of the Stour valley on the border of Essex and Suffolk where he grew up. His important letter to John Fisher of 23 October 1821 (despite its wayward grammar) is one of his clearest statements of faith.

From Letter from John Constable to John Fisher, 23 October 1821

How much I can imagine myself with you on your fishing excursion in the New Forest – what river can it be? But the sound of water escaping from mill-dams, so do willows, old rotten banks, slimy posts, and brickwork. I love such things – Shakespeare could make anything poetical. (He mentions poor Tom's haunts among sheep-cots and mills, the water-mist and the hedgepig.) As long as I do paint I shall never cease to paint such places. They have always been my delight. . . .

But I should paint my own places best – painting is but another word for 'feeling'.[1] I associate my 'careless boyhood' to all that lies on the banks of the Stour. They made me a painter, and I am grateful; that is, I had often thought of pictures of them before I had ever touched a pencil, and your picture is one of the strongest instances I can recollect of it. But I will say no more – for I am fond of being an egotist in whatever relates to painting.

Mary Matilda Betham (1776–1852)

Poet, diarist, scholar, and painter, and friend of Mrs Barbauld, Gerge Dyer, Southey, Lamb, and Coleridge (whose portrait she painted in 1808); publications include Biographical Dictionary of the Celebrated Women of every Age and Country *(1804). Though composed c.1798, 'From Matilda Betham's Notes' was not published until 1905. Here, instead of lamenting male inconstancy like other female writers (see, e.g., pp. 631–2, 666–7), Betham reminds her readers of their hold over men.*

From E. Betham, A House of Letters (1905)

FROM MATILDA BETHAM'S NOTES (COMPOSED *C.*1798)

We wish not the mechanic arts to scan,
But leave the slavish work to selfish man;
He claims alone the privilege to war,
But 'tis our smiles that must reward the scar!
We need not these heroic dangers brave   5

From LETTER FROM JOHN CONSTABLE TO JOHN FISHER, 23 October 1821
[1] Cf. Wordsworth's claim that 'poetry is passion', p. 249 above.

Who hold the laurelled conqueror a slave;
We need not search the world for sordid gain,
While we (its proud possessors) can enchain,
When their pursuit is only meant to prove
How much they'd venture to deserve our love.   10
For wealth and honours they can only prize
As making them more worthy in our eyes;
Their insufficiency they would supply,
And to these glittering resources fly!
Let the poor boasters then indulge their pride   15
And think they o'er the universe preside;
Let them recount their numerous triumphs o'er,
And tell the tales so often told before
(Their own much-doubted merit to enhance),
And gain the great reward – a favouring glance!   20
Let them, in bondage, fancy themselves free,
And while fast-fettered vaunt their liberty –
Because they do not massy chains behold,
Suppose that they are monarchs uncontrolled!
How vain to hope 'twould be to them revealed;   25
The flame burns strongest that is most concealed.
   Then with what potent, what resistless art,
Those hidden bonds are twined about the heart,
So that the captive wanders unconfined,
And has no sovereign but o'er his mind.   30
The prize is mutual – either power or fame:
We have the substance, *they* may keep the name.

Sydney Owenson (1776–1859)

Irish nationalist, poet, and novelist, who helped arouse a fashionable interest in romantic Ireland.
Introducing 'The Irish Harp', she noted that it derived from a visit to Ireland in 1805: 'But the
hope I had long cherished of hearing the Irish harp played in perfection was not only far from
being realized, but infinitely disappointed. That encouragement so nutritive to genius, so
indispensably necessary to perseverance, no longer stimulates the Irish bard to excellence, nor
rewards him when it is attained; and the decline of that tender and impressive instrument, once
so dear to Irish enthusiasm, is as visibly rapid, as it is obviously unimpeded by any effort of
national pride or national affection.'

From The Lay of an Irish Harp, or Metrical Fragments (1807)

THE IRISH HARP: FRAGMENT I

'Voice of the days of old, let me hear you. Awake the soul of song.'
(Ossian)

I

Why sleeps the harp of Erin's pride?
Why with'ring droops its shamrock wreath?
Why has that song of sweetness died
Which Erin's harp alone can breathe?

II

Oh 'twas the simplest, wildest thing!   5
The sighs of Eve that faintest flow
O'er airy lyres, did never fling
So sweet, so sad, a song of woe.

III

And yet its sadness seemed to borrow
From love, or joy, a mystic spell;   10
'Twas doubtful still if bliss or sorrow
From its melting lapses fell.

IV

For if amidst its tone's soft languish
A note of love or joy e'er streamed,
'Twas the plaint of lovesick anguish,   15
And still the 'joy of grief' it seemed.

V

'Tis said oppression taught the lay
To him (of all the 'sons of song'
That basked in Erin's brighter day)
The *last* of the inspired throng;   20

VI

That not in sumptuous hall or bow'r,
To victor chiefs on tented plain,
To festive souls, in festal hour,
Did he (sad bard) pour forth the strain.

VII

Oh no! For he, oppressed, pursued,[1]   25
Wild, wand'ring, doubtful of his course,
With tears his silent harp bedewed,
That drew from Erin's woes their source.

VIII

It was beneath th' impervious gloom
Of some dark forest's deepest dell,   30
'Twas at some patriot hero's tomb,
Or on the drear heath where *he* fell.

IX

It was beneath the loneliest cave
That roofs the brow of misery,
Or stems the ocean's wildest wave,   35
Or mocks the sea-blast's keenest sigh.

X

It was through night's most spectral hours,
When reigns the spirit of dismay,
And terror views demoniac pow'rs
Flit ghastly round in dread array.   40

XI

Such was the time, and such the place,
The bard respired *his* song of woe,
To those who had of Erin's race
Survived their freedom's vital blow.

XII

Oh, what a lay the minstrel breathed!   45
How many bleeding hearts around,

THE IRISH HARP: FRAGMENT I
[1] 'The persecution begun by the Danes against the Irish bards finished in almost the total extirpation of that sacred order in the reign of Elizabeth' (Owenson's note).

In suff'ring sympathy enwreathed,
Hung desponding o'er the sound!

XIII

For still his harp's wild plaintive tones
Gave back their sorrows keener still,   50
Breathed sadder sighs, heaved deeper moans,
And wilder waked despair's wild thrill.

XIV

For still he sung the ills that flow
From dire oppression's ruthless fang,
And deepened every patriot woe,   55
And sharpened every patriot pang.

XV

Yet, ere he ceased, a prophet's fire
Sublimed his lay, and louder rung
The deep-toned music of his lyre,
And 'Erin go brach'[2] he boldly sung.   60

Thomas Campbell (1777–1844)

Associate of Byron, and popular poet of the time, known mainly for The Pleasures of Hope
(1799) and Gertrude of Wyoming *(1809). Slavery continued to inspire poets well into the
nineteenth century; Campbell's invective against it portrays 'Congo's chief' as a noble savage.*

From The Pleasures of Hope (1799)

ON SLAVERY

Eternal nature! When thy giant hand
Had heaved the floods and fixed the trembling land,   490
When life sprung startling at thy plastic call
(Endless her forms, and man the lord of all),
Say, was that lordly form inspired by thee
To wear eternal chains and bow the knee?

---

[2] 'Ireland for ever! A national exclamation, and, in
less felicitous times, the rallying point to which many
an Irish heart revolted from the influence of despair'
(Owenson's note).

Was man ordained the slave of man to toil,   495
Yoked with the brutes and fettered to the soil,
Weighed in a tyrant's balance with his gold?
No! Nature stamped us in a heav'nly mould!
She bade no wretch his thankless labour urge
Nor, trembling, take the pittance and the scourge!   500
No homeless Lybian on the stormy deep
To call upon his country's name and weep!
    Lo! Once in triumph, on his boundless plain,
The quivered chief of Congo loved to reign;
With fires proportioned to his native sky,   505
Strength in his arm and lightning in his eye,
Scoured with wild feet his sun-illumined zone,
The spear, the lion and the woods his own;
Or led the combat, bold without a plan –
An artless savage, but a fearless man.   510
    The plunderer came – alas, no glory smiles
For Congo's chief on yonder Indian isles!
Forever fallen, no son of nature now,
With freedom chartered on his manly brow!
Faint, bleeding, bound, he weeps the night away,   515
And, when the sea-wind wafts the dewless day,
Starts, with a bursting heart, for evermore
To curse the sun that lights their guilty shore.
    The shrill horn blew – at that alarum knell
His guardian angel took a last farewell;   520
That funeral dirge to darkness hath resigned
The fiery grandeur of a generous mind.
Poor fettered man! I hear thee whispering low
Unhallowed vows to Guilt, the child of Woe!
Friendless thy heart, and canst thou harbour there   525
A wish but death, a passion but despair?

William Hazlitt (1778–1830)

Although he considered becoming a Unitarian minister (like his father), and was an accomplished painter, Hazlitt (under the strong influence of Coleridge) decided to make his living by writing. Publications include Characters of Shakespeare's Plays *(1817),* The Round Table *(1817, with Leigh Hunt),* Lectures on the English Poets *(1818),* Table Talk *(1821–2);* Liber Amoris *(1823), and* The Spirit of the Age *(1825).*

  'On Gusto' should be read in the light of romantic discussions of the imagination. No writer better evokes what Wordsworth and Coleridge were like during their annus mirabilis *of 1797–8 than Hazlitt in his essay, 'My First Acquaintance with Poets'. Hazlitt's disillusionment is more pronounced in the essay on Coleridge in* The Spirit of the Age *– which reveals much about both subject and author.*

From The Round Table (1817)

ON GUSTO

Gusto in art is power or passion defining any object. It is not so difficult to explain this term in what relates to expression (of which it may be said to be the highest degree), as in what relates to things without expression, to the natural appearances of objects, as mere colour or form. In one sense, however, there is hardly any object entirely devoid of expression, without some character of power belonging to it, some precise association with pleasure or pain. And it is in giving this truth of character from the truth of feeling, whether in the highest or the lowest degree (but always in the highest degree of which the subject is capable), that gusto consists.

There is a gusto in the colouring of Titian.[1] Not only do his heads seem to think, his bodies seem to feel. This is what the Italians mean by the *morbidezza* of his flesh colour. It seems sensitive and alive all over – not merely to have the look and texture of flesh, but the feeling in itself. For example, the limbs of his female figures have a luxurious softness and delicacy, which appears conscious of the pleasure of the beholder. As the objects themselves in nature would produce an impression on the sense – distinct from every other object, and having something divine in it which the heart owns and the imagination consecrates – the objects in the picture preserve the same impression, absolute, unimpaired, stamped with all the truth of passion, the pride of the eye, and the charm of beauty. Rubens makes his flesh colour like flowers; Albani's is like ivory;[2] Titian's is like flesh, and like nothing else. It is as different from that of other painters, as the skin is from a piece of white or red drapery thrown over it. The blood circulates here and there, the blue veins just appear, the rest is distinguished throughout only by that sort of tingling sensation to the eye, which the body feels within itself. This is gusto.

Van Dyck's[3] flesh colour, though it has great truth and purity, wants gusto. It has not the internal character, the living principle in it. It is a smooth surface, not a warm, moving mass. It is painted without passion, with indifference. The hand only has been concerned. The impression slides off from the eye, and does not, like the tones of Titian's pencil, leave a sting behind it in the mind of the spectator. The eye does not acquire a taste or appetite for what it sees. In a word, gusto in painting is where the impression made on one sense excites by affinity those of another.

Michelangelo's[4] forms are full of gusto. They everywhere obtrude the sense of power upon the eye. His limbs convey an idea of muscular strength, of moral grandeur, and even of intellectual dignity; they are firm, commanding, broad and massy, capable of executing with ease the determined purposes of the will. His faces have no other expression than his figures, conscious power and capacity. They appear only to think what they shall do, and to know that they can do it. This is what is meant by saying that his style is hard and masculine; it is the reverse of Correggio's,[5] which is

---

ON GUSTO
[1] Tiziano Vecellio (1490–1576), Venetian painter.
[2] Peter Paul Rubens (1577–1640), great Flemish painter; Francesco Albani (1578–1660), painter of the school of Bologna.
[3] Sir Anthony Van Dyck (1599–1641), Flemish portraitist.
[4] Michelangelo Buonarroti (1475–1564), Italian painter, sculptor, architect.
[5] Antonio Allegri da Correggio (1494–1534), eminent Italian painter.

effeminate. That is, the gusto of Michelangelo consists in expressing energy of will without proportionable sensibility; Correggio's in expressing exquisite sensibility without energy of will. In Correggio's faces as well as figures we see neither bones nor muscles, but then what a soul is there, full of sweetness and of grace – pure, playful, soft, angelical! There is sentiment enough in a hand painted by Correggio to set up a school of history painters. Whenever we look at the hands of Correggio's women, or of Raphael's,[6] we always wish to touch them.

Again, Titian's landscapes have a prodigious gusto, both in the colouring and forms. We shall never forget one that we saw many years ago in the Orleans Gallery of Actaeon hunting.[7] It had a brown, mellow, autumnal look. The sky was of the colour of stone. The winds seemed to sing through the rustling branches of the trees, and already you might hear the twanging of bows resound through the tangled mazes of the wood. (Mr West,[8] we understand, has this landscape; he will know if this description of it is just.)

The landscape background of the St Peter Martyr[9] is another well-known instance of the power of this great painter to give a romantic interest and an appropriate character to the objects of his pencil, where every circumstance adds to the effect of the scene: the bold trunks of the tall forest trees, the trailing ground plants, with that cold convent spire rising in the distance amidst the blue sapphire mountains and the golden sky.

Rubens has a great deal of gusto in his fauns and satyrs and in all that expresses motion, but in nothing else. Rembrandt[10] has it in everything; everything in his pictures has a tangible character. If he puts a diamond in the ear of a burgomaster's wife, it is of the first water – and his furs and stuffs are proof against a Russian winter. Raphael's gusto was only in expression; he had no idea of the character of anything but the human form. The dryness and poverty of his style in other respects is a phenomenon in the art. His trees are like sprigs of grass stuck in a book of botanical specimens. Was it that Raphael never had time to go beyond the walls of Rome, that he was always in the streets, at church, or in the bath? He was not one of the Society of Arcadians.[11]

Claude's[12] landscapes, perfect as they are, want gusto. This is not easy to explain. They are perfect abstractions of the visible images of things; they speak the visible language of nature truly. They resemble a mirror or a microscope. To the eye only they are more perfect than any other landscapes that ever were or will be painted. They give more of nature as cognizable by one sense alone, but they lay an equal stress on all visible impressions; they do not interpret one sense by another; they do not distinguish the character of different objects as we are taught (and can only be taught) to distinguish them by their effect on the different senses. That is, his eye wanted imagination; it did not strongly sympathize with his other faculties. He saw the

---

6   Raffaello Santi (1483–1520), Renaissance artist.
7   In 1798–9, the Duke of Orléans exhibited his collection of old master paintings in London.
8   Benjamin West (1738–1820), historical painter born in America.
9   Hazlitt saw this painting at the Louvre, 1802; it was destroyed by fire in 1867.
10   Rembrandt van Rijn (1606–69), Dutch painter.
11   'Raphael not only could not paint a landscape; he could not paint people in a landscape. He could not have painted the heads or the figures, or even the

dresses of the St Peter Martyr. His figures have always an *indoor* look – that is, a set, determined, voluntary, dramatic character, arising from their own passions, or a watchfulness of those of others, and want that wild uncertainty of expression which is connected with the accidents of nature and the changes of the elements. He has nothing *romantic* about him' (Hazlitt's note).
12   Claude Lorraine (1600–82), French landscape-painter.

atmosphere but he did not feel it. He painted the trunk of a tree or a rock in the foreground as smooth, with as complete an abstraction of the gross, tangible impression, as any other part of the picture; his trees are perfectly beautiful, but quite immovable – they have a look of enchantment. In short, his landscapes are unequalled imitations of nature, released from its subjection to the elements – as if all objects were become a delightful fairy vision, and the eye had rarefied and refined away the other senses.

The gusto in the Greek statues is of a very singular kind. The sense of perfect form nearly occupies the whole mind, and hardly suffers it to dwell on any other feeling. It seems enough for them *to be*, without acting or suffering. Their forms are ideal, spiritual. Their beauty is power. By their beauty they are raised above the frailties of pain or passion; by their beauty they are deified.

The infinite quantity of dramatic invention in Shakespeare takes from his gusto. The power he delights to show is not intense, but discursive. He never insists on anything as much as he might, except a quibble. Milton has great gusto. He repeats his blow twice, grapples with and exhausts his subject. His imagination has a double relish of its objects, an inveterate attachment to the things he describes, and to the words describing them:

> Or where Chineses drive
> With sails and wind their *cany* waggons *light* ...
> Wild above rule or art, *enormous* bliss.
> (*Paradise Lost*, iii. 438–9, v. 297)

There is a gusto in Pope's compliments, in Dryden's satires, and Prior's tales. And among prose writers, Boccaccio and Rabelais had the most of it. We will only mention one other work which appears to us to be full of gusto, and that is *The Beggar's Opera*.[13] If it is not, we are altogether mistaken in our notions on this delicate subject.

From The Liberal, 2 (1823) 23–46

MY FIRST ACQUAINTANCE WITH POETS

My father was a dissenting minister at Wem in Shropshire, and in the year 1798 (the figures that compose that date are to me like the 'dreaded name of Demogorgon'[1]), Mr Coleridge came to Shrewsbury to succeed Mr Rowe in the spiritual charge of a Unitarian congregation there.

He did not come till late on the Saturday afternoon before he was to preach, and Mr Rowe, who himself went down to the coach in a state of anxiety and expectation to look for the arrival of his successor, could find no one at all answering the description but a round-faced man in a short black coat, like a shooting jacket, which hardly seemed to have been made for him, but who seemed to be talking at a great rate to his fellow-passengers. Mr Rowe had scarce returned to give an account of his disappointment, when the round-faced man in black entered, and dissipated all doubts on the subject by beginning to talk. He did not cease while he stayed – nor has he since, that I know of. He held the good town of Shrewsbury in delightful suspense for

---

[13] Popular ballad opera by John Gay (produced 1728).

MY FIRST ACQUAINTANCE WITH POETS
[1] *Paradise Lost*, ii. 964–5.

three weeks that he remained there, 'fluttering the *proud Salopians* like an eagle in a dovecot',[2] and the Welsh mountains that skirt the horizon with their tempestuous confusion agree to have heard no such mystic sounds since the days of 'High-born Hoel's harp or soft Llewellyn's lay!'[3]

As we passed along between Wem and Shrewsbury, and I eyed their blue tops seen through the wintry branches, or the red rustling leaves of the sturdy oak-trees by the roadside, a sound was in my ears as of a siren's song. I was stunned, startled with it, as from deep sleep, but I had no notion then that I should ever be able to express my admiration to others in motley imagery or quaint allusion, till the light of his genius shone into my soul, like the sun's rays glittering in the puddles of the road. I was at that time dumb, inarticulate, helpless, like a worm by the wayside, crushed, bleeding, lifeless – but now, bursting from the deadly bands that 'bound them, / With Styx nine times round them',[4] my ideas float on winged words, and as they expand their plumes, catch the golden light of other years. My soul has indeed remained in its original bondage, dark, obscure, with longings infinite and unsatisfied; my heart, shut up in the prison-house of this rude clay, has never found (nor will it ever find) a heart to speak to – but that my understanding also did not remain dumb and brutish, or at length found a language to express itself, I owe to Coleridge. But this is not to my purpose.

My father lived ten miles from Shrewsbury and was in the habit of exchanging visits with Mr Rowe and with Mr Jenkins of Whitchurch (nine miles farther on), according to the custom of dissenting ministers in each other's neighborhood. A line of communication is thus established, by which the flame of civil and religious liberty is kept alive, and nourishes its smouldering fire unquenchable, like the fires in the *Agamemnon* of Aeschylus, placed at different stations, that waited for ten long years to announce with their blazing pyramids the destruction of Troy.

Coleridge had agreed to come over to see my father, according to the courtesy of the country, as Mr Rowe's probable successor, but in the meantime I had gone to hear him preach the Sunday after his arrival. A poet and a philosopher getting up into a Unitarian pulpit to preach the gospel was a romance in these degenerate days, a sort of revival of the primitive spirit of Christianity, which was not to be resisted.

It was in January 1798 that I rose one morning before daylight, to walk ten miles in the mud, and went to hear this celebrated person preach. Never, the longest day I have to live, shall I have such another walk as this cold, raw, comfortless one in the winter of the year 1798. *Il y a des impressions que ni le tems ni les circonstances peuvent effacer. Dusse-je vivre des siècles entiers, le doux tems de ma jeunesse ne peut renaître pour moi, ni s'effacer jamais dans ma mémoire.*[5]

When I got there the organ was playing the 100th Psalm, and, when it was done, Mr Coleridge rose and gave out his text: 'And he went up into the mountain to pray, HIMSELF, ALONE.'[6] As he gave out this text, his voice 'rose like a steam of rich distilled perfumes',[7] and when he came to the two last words, which he pronounced loud, deep, and distinct, it seemed to me, who was then young, as if the sounds had echoed from

---

[2] Cf. *Coriolanus*, V. vi. 114–15.

[3] Gray, *The Bard*, 28.

[4] Pope, *Ode on St. Cecilia's Day*, 90–1.

[5] 'There are impressions which neither time nor circumstance is able to efface. Were I to live entire centuries, the sweet time of my youth could never be reborn for me - nor could it ever be erased from my memory.' Hazlitt has adapted Rousseau, *Julie, ou la Nouvelle Héloïse* (Amsterdam, 1761), vi. 55–6.

[6] Matt. 14: 23 and John 6: 15.

[7] Milton, *Comus*, 556.

the bottom of the human heart, and as if that prayer might have floated in solemn silence through the universe. The idea of St John came into mind, 'of one crying in the wilderness, who had his loins girt about, and whose food was locusts and wild honey'.[8]

The preacher then launched into his subject like an eagle dallying with the wind. The sermon was upon peace and war, upon church and state (not their alliance, but their separation), on the spirit of the world and the spirit of Christianity – not as the same, but as opposed to one another. He talked of those who had 'inscribed the cross of Christ on banners dripping with human gore'. He made a poetical and pastoral excursion, and, to show the fatal effects of war, drew a striking contrast between the simple shepherd boy driving his team afield, or sitting under the hawthorn piping to his flock 'as though he should never be old', and the same poor country lad, crimped,[9] kidnapped, brought into town, made drunk at an alehouse, turned into a wretched drummer-boy, with his hair sticking on end with powder and pomatum, a long cue at his back, and tricked out in the loathsome finery of the profession of blood – 'Such were the notes our once-loved poet sung.'[10]

And for myself I could not have been more delighted if I had heard the music of the spheres. Poetry and philosophy had met together, truth and genius had embraced under the eye and with the sanction of religion. This was even beyond my hopes. I returned home well-satisfied. The sun that was still labouring pale and wan through the sky, obscured by thick mists, seemed an emblem of the *good cause*, and the cold dank drops of dew that hung half-melted on the beard of the thistle had something genial and refreshing in them – for there was a spirit of hope and youth in all nature, that turned everything into good. The face of nature had not then the brand of *jus divinum*[11] on it, 'Like to that sanguine flower inscribed with woe'.[12]

On the Tuesday following the half-inspired speaker came. I was called down into the room where he was, and went half-hoping, half-afraid. He received me very graciously, and I listened for a long time without uttering a word. I did not suffer in his opinion by my silence. 'For those two hours', he afterwards was pleased to say, 'he was conversing with W.H.'s forehead.' His appearance was different from what I had anticipated from seeing him before. At a distance, and in the dim light of the chapel, there was to me a strange wildness in his aspect, a dusky obscurity, and I thought him pitted with the smallpox. His complexion was at that time clear, and even bright, 'As are the children of yon azure sheen'.[13] His forehead was broad and high; light, as if built of ivory, with large projecting eyebrows, and his eyes rolling beneath them like a sea with darkened lustre. 'A certain tender bloom his face o'erspread,'[14] a purple tinge as we see it in the pale thoughtful complexions of the Spanish portrait-painters, Murillo and Velasquez. His mouth was gross, voluptuous, open, eloquent; his chin good-humoured and round; but his nose, the rudder of the face, the index of the will, was small, feeble, nothing – like what he has done. It might seem that the genius of his face, as from a height, surveyed and projected him (with sufficient capacity and huge aspiration) into the world unknown of thought and imagination, with nothing to support or guide his veering purpose, as if Columbus had launched his adventurous

---

[8] Matt. 3: 3–4 and Mark 1: 3.
[9] *crimped* forced into the army.
[10] Pope, 'Epistle to Robert, Earl of Oxford', 1.
[11] 'The divine right' – i.e. of kings.

[12] *Lycidas*, 106.
[13] Thomson, *The Castle of Indolence*, ii. 295.
[14] Ibid., i. 507: 'A certain tender gloom o'erspread his face.'

course for the New World in a scallop, without oars or compass. So at least I comment on it after the event.

Coleridge in his person was rather above the common size, inclining to the corpulent, or like Lord Hamlet, 'somewhat fat and pursy'.[15] His hair (now, alas, grey) was then black and glossy as the raven's, and fell in smooth masses over his forehead. This long pendulous hair is peculiar to enthusiasts, to those whose minds tend heavenward, and is traditionally inseparable (though of a different colour) from the pictures of Christ. It ought to belong, as a character, to all who preach Christ crucified, and Coleridge was at that time one of those.

It was curious to observe the contrast between him and my father, who was a veteran in the cause, and then declining into the vale of years. He had been a poor Irish lad, carefully brought up by his parents, and sent to the University of Glasgow, where he studied under Adam Smith, to prepare him for his future destination. It was his mother's proudest wish to see her son a dissenting minister. So if we look back to past generations as far as eye can reach, we see the same hopes, fears, wishes, followed by the same disappointments, throbbing in the human heart – and so we may see them, if we look forward, rising up forever, and disappearing, like vapourish bubbles, in the human breast. After being tossed about from congregation to congregation in the heats of the Unitarian controversy and squabbles about the American War, he had been relegated to an obscure village where he was to spend the last thirty years of his life far from the only converse that he loved – the talk about disputed texts of scripture, and the cause of civil and religious liberty. Here he passed his days, repining but resigned, in the study of the Bible and the perusal of the commentators – huge folios not easily got through, one of which would outlast a winter. Why did he pore on these from morn to night (with the exception of a walk in the fields or a turn in the garden to gather broccoli plants or kidney beans of his own rearing, with no small degree of pride and pleasure)? Here were 'no figures nor no fantasies', neither poetry nor philosophy, nothing to dazzle, nothing to excite modern curiosity – but to his lacklustre eyes there appeared, within the pages of the ponderous, unwieldy, neglected tomes, the sacred name of JEHOVAH in Hebrew capitals: pressed down by the weight of the style, worn to the last fading thinness of the understanding, there were glimpses, glimmering notions of the patriarchal wanderings, with palm-trees hovering in the horizon, and processions of camels at the distance of three thousand years; there was Moses with the burning bush, the number of the Twelve Tribes, types, shadows, glosses on the law and the prophets; there were discussions (dull enough) on the age of Methuselah (a mighty speculation!); there were outlines, rude guesses at the shape of Noah's Ark and of the riches of Solomon's Temple; questions as to the date of the creation, predictions of the end of all things; the great lapses of time, the strange mutations of the globe were unfolded with the voluminous leaf, as it turned over; and though the soul might slumber with an hieroglyphic veil of inscrutable mysteries drawn over it, yet it was in a slumber ill-exchanged for all the sharpened realities of sense, wit, fancy, or reason. My father's life was comparatively a dream, but it was a dream of infinity and eternity, of death, the resurrection, and a judgement to come.

No two individuals were ever more unlike than were the host and his guest. A poet was to my father a sort of nondescript, yet whatever added grace to the Unitarian cause

---

[15] *Hamlet*, III. iv. 153.

was to him welcome. He could hardly have been more surprised or pleased if our visitor had worn wings. Indeed, his thoughts had wings, and as the silken sounds rustled round our little wainscoted parlour, my father threw back his spectacles over his forehead, his white hairs mixing with its sanguine hue, and a smile of delight beamed across his rugged cordial face, to think that Truth had found a new ally in Fancy! Besides, Coleridge seemed to take considerable notice of me, and that of itself was enough. He talked very familiarly, but agreeably, and glanced over a variety of subjects.

At dinnertime he grew more animated, and dilated in a very edifying manner on Mary Wollstonecraft and Mackintosh. The last he said he considered (on my father's speaking of his *Vindiciae Gallicae* as a capital performance) as a clever scholastic man, a master of the topics – or as the ready warehouseman of letters, who knew exactly where to lay his hand on what he wanted, though the goods were not his own. He thought him no match for Burke, either in style or matter. Burke was a metaphysician, Mackintosh a mere logician. Burke was an orator (almost a poet) who reasoned in figures because he had an eye for nature; Mackintosh, on the other hand, was a rhetorician who had only an eye to commonplaces. On this I ventured to say that I had always entertained a great opinion of Burke, and that (as far as I could find) the speaking of him with contempt might be made the test of a vulgar democratical mind. This was the first observation I ever made to Coleridge, and he said it was a very just and striking one. I remember the leg of Welsh mutton and the turnips on the table that day had the finest flavour imaginable. Coleridge added that Mackintosh and Tom Wedgwood[16] (of whom, however, he spoke highly) had expressed a very indifferent opinion of his friend Mr Wordsworth, on which he remarked to them: 'He strides on so far before you that he dwindles in the distance!'

Godwin had once boasted to him of having carried on an argument with Mackintosh for three hours with dubious success; Coleridge told him, 'If there had been a man of genius in the room, he would have settled the question in five minutes.' He asked me if I had ever seen Mary Wollstonecraft, and I said I had once for a few moments, and that she seemed to me to turn off Godwin's objections to something she advanced with quite a playful, easy air. He replied that 'This was only one instance of the ascendancy which people of imagination exercised over those of mere intellect'. He did not rate Godwin very high (this was caprice or prejudice, real or affected), but he had a great idea of Mrs Wollstonecraft's powers of conversation, none at all of her talent for book-making. We talked a little about Holcroft.[17] He had been asked if he was not much struck *with* him, and he said he thought himself in more danger of being struck *by* him. I complained that he would not let me get on at all, for he required a definition of every the commonest word, exclaiming, 'What do you mean by a *sensation*, sir? What do you mean by an *idea*?' This, Coleridge said, was barricadoing the road to truth; it was setting up a turnpike-gate at every step we took.

I forget a great number of things (many more than I remember), but the day passed off pleasantly, and the next morning Mr Coleridge was to return to Shrewsbury. When I came down to breakfast I found that he had just received a letter from his friend, T. Wedgwood, making him an offer of £150 a year if he chose to waive his present pursuit and devote himself entirely to the study of poetry and philosophy. Coleridge seemed

---

[16] Thomas Wedgwood (1771–1805), son of Josiah Wedgwood, the famous potter.

[17] Thomas Holcroft (1745–1809), dramatist, novelist, man of letters, noted radical.

to make up his mind to close with this proposal in the act of tying on one of his shoes. It threw an additional damp on his departure. It took the wayward enthusiast quite from us to cast him into Deva's winding vales[18] or by the shores of old romance. Instead of living at ten miles' distance, of being the pastor of a dissenting congregation at Shrewsbury, he was henceforth to inhabit the hill of Parnassus, to be a shepherd on the Delectable Mountains.[19] Alas, I knew not the way thither, and felt very little gratitude for Mr Wedgwood's bounty! I was presently relieved from this dilemma, for Mr Coleridge, asking for a pen and ink, and going to a table to write something on a bit of card, advanced towards me with undulating step and, giving me the precious document, said that that was his address – 'Mr Coleridge, Nether Stowey, Somersetshire' – and that he should be glad to see me there in a few weeks' time, and, if I chose, would come halfway to meet me. I was not less surprised than the shepherd boy (this simile is to be found in *Cassandra*[20]) when he sees a thunderbolt fall close at his feet. I stammered out my acknowledgements and acceptance of this offer (I thought Mr Wedgwood's annuity a trifle to it) as well as I could, and, this mighty business being settled, the poet-preacher took leave, and I accompanied him six miles on the road.

It was a fine morning in the middle of winter, and he talked the whole way. The scholar in Chaucer is described as going 'Sounding on his way';[21] so Coleridge went on his. In digressing, in dilating, in passing from subject to subject, he appeared to me to float in air, to slide on ice. He told me in confidence (going along) that he should have preached two sermons before he accepted the situation at Shrewsbury, one on infant baptism, the other on the Lord's Supper, showing that he could not administer either, which would have effectually disqualified him for the object in view. I observed that he continually crossed me on the way by shifting from one side of the footpath to the other. This struck me as an odd movement, but I did not at that time connect it with any instability of purpose or involuntary change of principle, as I have done since. He seemed unable to keep on in a straight line.

He spoke slightingly of Hume,[22] whose 'Essay on Miracles' he said was stolen from an objection started in one of South's sermons – *Credat Judaeus Apella!*[23] I was not very much pleased at this account of Hume, for I had just been reading, with infinite relish, that completest of all metaphysical *choke-pears*, his *Treatise on Human Nature*, to which the *Essays*, in point of scholastic subtlety and close reasoning, are mere elegant trifling, light summer reading. Coleridge even denied the excellence of Hume's general style, which I think betrayed a want of taste or candour.

He however made me amends by the manner in which he spoke of Berkeley. He dwelt particularly on his *Essay on Vision* as a masterpiece of analytical reasoning – so it undoubtedly is.[24] He was exceedingly angry with Dr Johnson for striking the stone with

---

[18] Cf. *Lycidas*, 55.

[19] In Bunyan's *Pilgrim's Progress* Christian and Hopeful reach the Delectable Mountains after escaping from Doubting Castle and the Giant Despair.

[20] Ten vol. romance by Gauthier de Costes de la Calprenède.

[21] General Prologue to *Canterbury Tales*, 307, where Chaucer remarks of the Clerk, 'Sownynge in moral vertu was his speche'. Hazlitt may also be recalling Wordsworth, *Excursion*, iii. 701, to which Coleridge alludes at the end of *Biographia Literaria*, ch. 5.

[22] David Hume (1711–76), Scottish sceptic and philosopher, whose publications included *Treatise of Human Nature* (1739) and *Essays Moral and Political* (1741–2); Hartley and Berkeley were more to Coleridge's taste.

[23] 'Apella the Jew may believe it' (but I don't): Horace, *Satires*, I. v. 100. Robert South (1634–1716), noted divine and sermonist.

[24] George Berkeley (1685–1753), Bishop of Cloyne, *An Essay Towards a New Theory of Vision* (1709, 1710, 1732).

his foot, in allusion to this author's theory of matter and spirit, and saying, 'Thus I confute him, sir!' Coleridge drew a parallel (I don't know how he brought about the connection) between Bishop Berkeley and Tom Paine. He said the one was an instance of a subtle, the other of an acute mind, than which no two things could be more distinct. The one was a shopboy's quality, the other the characteristic of a philosopher. He considered Bishop Butler[25] as a true philosopher, a profound and conscientious thinker, a genuine reader of nature and of his own mind. He did not speak of his *Analogy* but of his *Sermons at the Rolls Chapel*, of which I had never heard. Coleridge somehow always contrived to prefer the *unknown* to the *known*; in this instance he was right. The *Analogy* is a tissue of sophistry, of wire-drawn, theological special pleading; the *Sermons* (with the Preface to them) are in a fine vein of deep, matured reflection, a candid appeal to our observation of human nature, without pedantry and without bias.

I told Coleridge I had written a few remarks, and was sometimes foolish enough to believe that I had made a discovery on the same subject ('The Natural Disinterestedness of the Human Mind'[26]), and I tried to explain my view of it to Coleridge, who listened with great willingness, but I did not succeed in making myself understood. I sat down to the task shortly afterwards for the twentieth time, got new pens and paper, determined to make clear work of it, wrote a few meagre sentences in the skeleton style of a mathematical demonstration, stopped halfway down the second page, and, after trying in vain to pump up any words, images, notions, apprehensions, facts or observations from that gulf of abstraction in which I had plunged myself for four or five years preceding, gave up the attempt as labour in vain, and shed tears of helpless despondency on the blank unfinished paper. I can write fast enough now. Am I better than I was then? Oh no! One truth discovered, one pang of regret at not being able to express it, is better than all the fluency and flippancy in the world. Would that I could go back to what I then was! Why can we not revive past times as we can revisit old places? If I had the quaint muse of Sir Philip Sidney to assist me, I would write a 'Sonnet to the Road between Wem and Shrewsbury', and immortalize every step of it by some fond enigmatical conceit. I would swear that the very milestones had ears, and that Harmer Hill stooped with all its pines to listen to a poet as he passed!

I remember but one other topic of discourse in this walk. He mentioned Paley,[27] praised the naturalness and clearness of his style, but condemned his sentiments, thought him a mere time-serving casuist, and said that 'the fact of his work on *Moral and Political Philosophy* being made a textbook in our universities was a disgrace to the national character'.

We parted at the six-milestone and I returned homeward, pensive but much pleased. I had met with unexpected notice from a person whom I believed to have been prejudiced against me: 'Kind and affable to me had been his condescension, and should be honoured ever with suitable regard.'[28] He was the first poet I had known, and he certainly answered to that inspired name. I had heard a great deal of his powers of conversation and was not disappointed. In fact, I never met with anything at all like them, either before or since. I could easily credit the accounts which were circulated

[25] Joseph Butler, Bishop of Bristol (1692–1752), whose *Fifteen Sermons* (1726) preached at the Rolls Chapel defines his moral philosophy.

[26] Published as *An Essay on the Principles of Human Action* (1805).

[27] William Paley (1743–1805), theologian and philosopher, whose *Moral and Political Philosophy* (1785) was a university textbook by the time Wordsworth went up to Cambridge in 1787.

[28] *Paradise Lost*, viii. 648–50.

of his holding forth to a large party of ladies and gentlemen, an evening or two, before on the Berkeleian theory, when he made the whole material universe look like a transparency of fine words; and another story (which I believe he has somewhere told himself) of his being asked to a party at Birmingham, of his smoking tobacco and going to sleep after dinner on a sofa, where the company found him to their no small surprise, which was increased to wonder when he started up of a sudden and, rubbing his eyes, looked about him, and launched into a three hours' description of the third heaven, of which he had had a dream, very different from Mr Southey's *Vision of Judgement*, and also from that other *Vision of Judgement* which Mr Murray, the Secretary of the Bridge Street junto,[29] has taken into his especial keeping.[30]

On my way back I had a sound in my ears; it was the voice of fancy – I had a light before me: it was the face of Poetry. The one still lingers there, the other has not quitted my side! Coleridge in truth met me halfway on the ground of philosophy, or I should not have been won over to his imaginative creed. I had an uneasy, pleasurable sensation all the time till I was to visit him. During those months the chill breath of winter gave me a welcoming; the vernal air was balm and inspiration to me. The golden sunsets, the silver star of evening, lighted me on my way to new hopes and prospects. *I was to visit Coleridge in the spring.* This circumstance was never absent from my thoughts, and mingled with all my feelings. I wrote to him at the time proposed and received an answer postponing my intended visit for a week or two, but very cordially urging me to complete my promise then. This delay did not damp, but rather increased my ardour. In the meantime I went to Llangollen Vale by way of initiating myself in the mysteries of natural scenery, and I must say I was enchanted with it. I had been reading Coleridge's description of England in his fine *Ode on the Departing Year*,[31] and I applied it *con amore*[32] to the objects before me. That valley was to me, in a manner, the cradle of a new existence: in the river that winds through it, my spirit was baptized in the waters of Helicon![33]

I returned home and soon after set out on my journey with unworn heart and untried feet. My way lay through Worcester and Gloucester and by Upton – where I thought of Tom Jones and the adventure of the muff.[34] I remember getting completely wet through one day and stopping at an inn (I think it was at Tewkesbury) where I sat up all night to read *Paul and Virginia*.[35] Sweet were the showers in early youth that drenched my body, and sweet the drops of pity that fell upon the books I read! I recollect a remark of Coleridge's upon this very book, that nothing could show the gross indelicacy of French manners and the entire corruption of their imagination more strongly than the behaviour of the heroine in the last fatal scene, who turns away from a person on board the sinking vessel that offers to save her life, because he has thrown off his clothes to assist him in swimming. Was this a time to think of such a circumstance? I once hinted to Wordsworth, as we were sailing in his boat on Grasmere

---

[29] *junto* political clique, cabal.
[30] Southey's *A Vision of Judgement* (1821) describes the reception in heaven of George III; Byron's *The Vision of Judgement* (1822) was a satirical response aimed largely at Southey, though Charles Murray of Bridge Street, an officer of the Constitutional Association, prosecuted the publishers of Byron's poem on the grounds of its libellous attack on George III.
[31] Published in pamphlet form, 1796.

[32] With love.
[33] The River Dee flows through the Vale of Llangollen; the fountains of Aganippe and Hippocrene rose out of Mount Helicon, sacred to the Muses.
[34] Henry Fielding, *Tom Jones* (1749), Book X, ch. 5–7.
[35] Popular novel by Jacques-Henri Bernardin de Saint-Pierre (1737–1814), disciple of Rousseau, published in 1788.

lake, that I thought he had borrowed the idea of his 'Poems on the Naming of Places' from the local inscriptions of the same kind in *Paul and Virginia*. He did not own the obligation, and stated some distinction without a difference in defence of his claim to originality. Any the slightest variation would be sufficient for this purpose in his mind, for whatever *he* added or omitted would inevitably be worth all that anyone else had done, and contain the marrow of the sentiment.

I was still two days before the time fixed for my arrival, for I had taken care to set out early enough. I stopped these two days at Bridgwater, and when I was tired of sauntering on the banks of its muddy river, returned to the inn and read *Camilla*.[36] So have I loitered my life away, reading books, looking at pictures, going to plays, hearing, thinking, writing on what pleased me best. I have wanted only one thing to make me happy – but wanting that, have wanted everything.

I arrived, and was well-received. The country about Nether Stowey is beautiful, green and hilly, and near the seashore. I saw it but the other day after an interval of twenty years from a hill near Taunton. How was the map of my life spread out before me, as the map of the country lay at my feet! In the afternoon, Coleridge took me over to Alfoxden, a romantic old family mansion of the St Aubins, where Wordsworth lived. It was then in the possession of a friend of the poet's who gave him the free use of it.[37] Somehow that period (the time just after the French Revolution) was not a time when nothing was given for nothing. The mind opened, and a softness might be perceived coming over the heart of individuals beneath 'the scales that fence' our self-interest.

Wordsworth himself was from home, but his sister kept house, and set before us a frugal repast – and we had free access to her brother's poems, the *Lyrical Ballads*, which were still in manuscript, or in the form of sibylline leaves. I dipped into a few of these with great satisfaction, and with the faith of a novice. I slept that night in an old room with blue hangings and covered with the round-faced family portraits of the age of George I and II, and from the wooded declivity of the adjoining park that overlooked my window, at the dawn of day, could 'hear the loud stag speak'.[38]

In the outset of life (and particularly at this time I felt it so) our imagination has a body to it. We are in a state between sleeping and waking, and have indistinct but glorious glimpses of strange shapes, and there is always something to come better than what we see. As in our dreams the fullness of the blood gives warmth and reality to the coinage of the brain, so in youth our ideas are clothed and fed and pampered with our good spirits; we breathe thick with thoughtless happiness, the weight of future years presses on the strong pulses of the heart, and we repose with undisturbed faith in truth and good. As we advance, we exhaust our fund of enjoyment and of hope. We are no longer wrapped in lamb's wool, lulled in Elysium. As we taste the pleasures of life, their spirit evaporates, the sense palls, and nothing is left but the phantoms, the lifeless shadows of what *has been*.

That morning, as soon as breakfast was over, we strolled out into the park and, seating ourselves on the trunk of an old ash-tree that stretched along the ground, Coleridge read aloud with a sonorous and musical voice the ballad of Betty Foy.[39] I was not critically or sceptically inclined. I saw touches of truth and nature, and took

---

[36] Popular novel (1796) by Fanny Burney (1752–1840).

[37] Wordsworth paid £23 a year.

[38] Ben Jonson, 'To Sir Robert Wroth', 22.

[39] 'The Idiot Boy'.

the rest for granted. But in 'The Thorn', 'The Mad Mother', and 'The Complaint of a Poor Indian Woman', I felt that deeper power and pathos which have been since acknowledged, 'In spite of pride, in erring reason's spite',[40] as the characteristics of this author; and the sense of a new style and a new spirit in poetry came over me. It had to me something of the effect that arises from the turning up of the fresh soil, or of the first welcome breath of spring 'While yet the trembling year is unconfirmed'.[41]

Coleridge and myself walked back to Stowey that evening, and his voice sounded high

> Of Providence, foreknowledge, will and fate,
> Fixed fate, free will, foreknowledge absolute,
> (*Paradise Lost*, ii. 559–60)

as we passed through echoing grove, by fairy stream or waterfall gleaming in the summer moonlight. He lamented that Wordsworth was not prone enough to belief in the traditional superstitions of the place, and that there was a something corporeal, a matter-of-factness, a clinging to the palpable, or often to the petty, in his poetry, in consequence. His genius was not a spirit that descended to him through the air; it sprung out of the ground like a flower, or unfolded itself from a green spray on which the goldfinch sang. He said, however (if I remember right), that this objection must be confined to his descriptive pieces, that his philosophic poetry had a grand and comprehensive spirit in it, so that his soul seemed to inhabit the universe like a palace, and to discover truth by intuition rather than by deduction.

The next day Wordsworth arrived from Bristol at Coleridge's cottage. I think I see him now. He answered in some degree to his friend's description of him, but was more gaunt and Don Quixote-like. He was quaintly dressed, according to the costume of that unconstrained period, in a brown fustian jacket and striped pantaloons. There was something of a roll, a lounge in his gait, not unlike his own Peter Bell.[42] There was a severe, worn pressure of thought about his temples; a fire in his eye, as if he saw something in objects more than the outward appearance; an intense, high, narrow forehead; a Roman nose; cheeks furrowed by strong purpose and feeling, and a convulsive inclination to laughter about the mouth, a good deal at variance with the solemn, stately expression of the rest of his face. Chantrey's bust[43] wants the marking traits, but he was teased into making it regular and heavy; Haydon's head of him, introduced into the 'Entrance of Christ into Jerusalem',[44] is the most like his drooping weight of thought and expression.

He sat down and talked very naturally and freely, with a mixture of clear gushing accents in his voice, a deep guttural intonation, and a strong tincture of the northern *burr*, like the crust on wine. He instantly began to make havoc of the half of a Cheshire cheese on the table, and said triumphantly that 'his marriage with experience had not been so unproductive as Mr Southey's in teaching him a knowledge of the good things

---

[40] Pope, *An Essay on Man*, i. 293. Hazlitt is presumably thinking of Jeffrey's review of *The Excursion*, pp. 599–601 above.

[41] Thomson, *Spring*, 18.

[42] Wordsworth had completed a version of *Peter Bell* by this time, although the poem was published only in 1819.

[43] Sir Francis Leggatt Chantrey (1781–1841) ex-

hibited his bust of Wordsworth at the Royal Academy in 1821.

[44] Benjamin Robert Haydon (1786–1846), whose 'Christ's Triumphant Entry into Jerusalem' (now at Mount Saint Mary's Seminary, Norwood, Ohio) contains portraits of Wordsworth, Lamb, Keats, and Hazlitt (among others).

of this life'. He had been to see *The Castle Spectre* by Monk Lewis,[45] while at Bristol, and described it very well. He said 'it fitted the taste of the audience like a glove'. This ad captandum[46] merit was however by no means a recommendation of it according to the severe principles of the new school, which reject rather than court popular effect.

Wordsworth, looking out of the low, latticed window, said, 'How beautifully the sun sets on that yellow bank!' I thought within myself, 'With what eyes these poets see nature!' And ever after, when I saw the sunset stream upon the objects facing it, conceived I had made a discovery, or thanked Mr Wordsworth for having made one for me.

We went over to Alfoxden again the day following and Wordsworth read us the story of Peter Bell in the open air, and the comment made upon it by his face and voice was very different from that of some later critics. Whatever might be thought of the poem, 'his face was as a book where men might read strange matters,'[47] and he announced the fate of his hero in prophetic tones. There is a *chaunt* in the recitation both of Coleridge and Wordsworth which acts as a spell upon the hearer, and disarms the judgement. Perhaps they have deceived themselves by making habitual use of this ambiguous accompaniment. Coleridge's manner is more full, animated, and varied; Wordsworth's more equable, sustained, and internal. The one might be termed more dramatic, the other more lyrical. Coleridge has told me that he himself liked to compose in walking over uneven ground, or breaking through the straggling branches of a copsewood, whereas Wordsworth always wrote (if he could) walking up and down a straight gravel-walk, or in some spot where the continuity of his verse met with no collateral interruption.

Returning that same evening, I got into a metaphysical argument with Wordsworth while Coleridge was explaining the different notes of the nightingale to his sister, in which we neither of us succeeded in making ourselves perfectly clear and intelligible.[48] Thus I passed three weeks at Nether Stowey and in the neighbourhood generally devoting the afternoons to a delightful chat in an arbour made of bark by the poet's friend Tom Poole, sitting under two fine elm-trees, and listening to the bees humming round us while we quaffed our flip.[49] It was agreed, among other things, that we should make a jaunt down the Bristol Channel as far as Lynton. We set off together on foot, Coleridge, John Chester and I. This Chester was a native of Nether Stowey, one of those who were attracted to Coleridge's discourse as flies are to honey, or bees in swarming-time to the sound of a brass pan. He 'followed in the chase like a dog who hunts, not like one that made up the cry'.[50] He had on a brown cloth coat, boots, and corduroy breeches, was low in stature, bow-legged, had a drag in his walk like a drover, which he assisted by a hazel switch, and kept on a sort of trot by the side of Coleridge, like a running footman by a state coach, that he might not lose a syllable or sound that fell from Coleridge's lips. He told me his private opinion that Coleridge was a wonderful man. He scarcely opened his lips, much less offered an opinion the whole way – yet, of the three, had I to choose during that journey, I would be John Chester.

[45] Matthew Gregory Lewis (1775–1818), author of a popular novel, *The Monk* (1795), and play, *The Castle Spectre* (1798).

[46] *ad captandum [vulgus]* [designed] to take the fancy of [the crowd].

[47] *Macbeth*, I. v. 62–3.

[48] This argument seems to have inspired 'Expostulation and Reply' and 'The Tables Turned'.

[49] *flip* mixture of hot beer and spirits sweetened with sugar.

[50] *Othello*, II. iii. 363–4.

He afterwards followed Coleridge into Germany, where the Kantean philosophers were puzzled how to bring him under any of their categories. When he sat down at table with his idol, John's felicity was complete; Sir Walter Scott's, or Mr Blackwood's, when they sat down at the same table with the King, was not more so.[51]

We passed Dunster on our right, a small town between the brow of a hill and the sea. I remember eyeing it wistfully as it lay below us; contrasted with the woody scene around, it looked as clear, as pure, as embrowned and ideal as any landscape I have seen since, of Gaspar Poussin's or Domenichino's.[52] We had a long day's march (our feet kept time to the echoes of Coleridge's tongue) through Minehead and by the Blue Anchor and on to Lynton, which we did not reach till near midnight, and where we had some difficulty in making a lodgement. We however knocked the people of the house up at last, and we were repaid for our apprehensions and fatigue by some excellent rashers of fried bacon and eggs. The view in coming along had been splendid. We walked for miles and miles on dark brown heaths overlooking the Channel, with the Welsh hills beyond, and at times descended into little sheltered valleys close by the seaside, with a smuggler's face scowling by us, and then had to ascend conical hills with a path winding up through a coppice to a barren top, like a monk's shaven crown, from one of which I pointed out to Coleridge's notice the bare masts of a vessel on the very edge of the horizon and within the red-orbed disk of the setting sun, like his own spectre-ship in 'The Ancient Mariner'.

At Lynton the character of the sea-coast becomes more marked and rugged. There is a place called the Valley of Rocks (I suspect this was only the poetical name for it) bedded among precipices overhanging the sea, with rocky caverns beneath, into which the waves dash, and where the seagull forever wheels its screaming flight. On the tops of these are huge stones thrown transverse, as if an earthquake had tossed them there, and behind these is a fretwork of perpendicular rocks, something like the Giant's Causeway.

A thunderstorm came on while we were at the inn, and Coleridge was running out bareheaded to enjoy the commotion of the elements in the Valley of Rocks, but, as if in spite, the clouds only muttered a few angry sounds, and let fall a few refreshing drops. Coleridge told me that he and Wordsworth were to have made this place the scene of a prose tale which was to have been in the manner of, but far superior to, *The Death of Abel*,[53] but they had relinquished the design.

In the morning of the second day, we breakfasted luxuriously in an old-fashioned parlour on tea, toast, eggs, and honey, in the very sight of the beehives from which it had been taken, and a garden full of thyme and wild-flowers that had produced it. On this occasion Coleridge spoke of Virgil's *Georgics*, but not well. I do not think he had much feeling for the classical or elegant. It was in this room that we found a little worn-out copy of *The Seasons* lying in a window-seat, on which Coleridge exclaimed, '*That* is true fame!' He said Thomson was a great poet rather than a good one; his style was as meretricious as his thoughts were natural. He spoke of Cowper as the best modern poet. He said the *Lyrical Ballads* were an experiment about to be tried by him and Wordsworth, to see how far the public taste would endure poetry written in a more natural and simple style than had hitherto been attempted – totally discarding the

---

[51] William Blackwood (1776–1834), publisher, and Sir Walter Scott, were Tories; they banqueted with George IV in Edinburgh in 1822.

[52] Gaspar Poussin (1613–75), landscape artist; Domenico Zampieri (1581–1641), Italian artist.

[53] Salomon Gessner, *The Death of Abel* (1758).

artifices of poetical diction, and making use only of such words as had probably been common in the most ordinary language since the days of Henry II.

Some comparison was introduced between Shakespeare and Milton. He said he hardly knew which to prefer. Shakespeare seemed to him a mere stripling in the art; he was as tall and as strong, with infinitely more activity, than Milton, but he never appeared to have come to man's estate – or if he had, he would not have been a man, but a monster. He spoke with contempt of Gray and with intolerance of Pope. He did not like the versification of the latter. He observed that 'the ears of these couplet-writers might be charged with having short memories, that could not retain the harmony of whole passages'. He thought little of Junius[54] as a writer, he had a dislike of Dr Johnson, and a much higher opinion of Burke as an orator and politician, than of Fox or Pitt.[55] He however thought him very inferior in richness of style and imagery to some of our elder prose writers, particularly Jeremy Taylor.[56] He liked Richardson but not Fielding, nor could I get him to enter into the merits of *Caleb Williams*.[57] In short, he was profound and discriminating with respect to those authors whom he liked, and where he gave his judgement fair play; capricious, perverse, and prejudiced in his antipathies and distastes.

We loitered on the 'ribbed sea-sands'[58] in such talk as this a whole morning, and I recollect met with a curious seaweed of which John Chester told us the country name. A fisherman gave Coleridge an account of a boy that had been drowned the day before, and that they had tried to save him at the risk of their own lives. He said he 'did not know how it was that they ventured, but, sir, we have a *nature* towards one another'. This expression, Coleridge remarked to me, was a fine illustration of that theory of disinterestedness which I (in common with Butler) had adopted. I broached to him an argument of mine to prove that *likeness* was not mere association of ideas. I said that the mark in the sand put one in mind of a man's foot not because it was part of a former impression of a man's foot (for it was quite new), but because it was like the shape of a man's foot. He assented to the justness of this distinction (which I have explained at length elsewhere for the benefit of the curious), and John Chester listened not from any interest in the subject, but because he was astonished that I should be able to suggest anything to Coleridge that he did not already know. We returned on the third morning, and Coleridge remarked the silent cottage-smoke curling up the valleys where, a few evenings before, we had seen the lights gleaming through the dark.

In a day or two after we arrived at Stowey, we set out, I on my return home and he for Germany. It was a Sunday morning and he was to preach that day for Dr Toulmin of Taunton. I asked him if he had prepared anything for the occasion. He said he had not even thought of the text, but should as soon as we parted. I did not go to hear him (this was a fault) but we met in the evening at Bridgwater. The next day we had a long day's walk to Bristol, and sat down, I recollect, by a well-side on the road, to cool ourselves and satisfy our thirst, when Coleridge repeated to me some descriptive lines from his tragedy of *Remorse*, which I must say became his mouth and that occasion better than they, some years after, did Mr Elliston's and the Drury Lane boards:

[54] 'Junius' was the pseudonymous author of a series of letters published in the *Public Advertiser*, Jan. 1769–Jan. 1772, attacking Tory worthies.
[55] Charles James Fox (1749–1806), Whig statesman and orator; William Pitt (1759–1806), Prime Minister 1783–1801.
[56] Jeremy Taylor (1613–67), prose stylist famous for *Holy Living* (1650) and *Holy Dying* (1651).
[57] Novel by Godwin (1794).
[58] 'The Ancient Mariner' (1798), 219.

> Oh memory, shield me from the world's poor strife
> And give those scenes thine everlasting life.[59]

I saw no more of him for a year or two, during which period he had been wandering in the Hartz Forest in Germany, and his return was cometary, meteorous (unlike his setting-out). It was not till some time after that I knew his friends Lamb and Southey. The last always appears to me as I first saw him, with a commonplace book under his arm, and the first with a *bon mot* in his mouth. It was at Godwin's that I met him with Holcroft and Coleridge, where they were disputing fiercely which was the best – man as he was, or man as he is to be. 'Give me', says Lamb, 'man as he is *not* to be.' This saying was the beginning of a friendship between us which I believe still continues. Enough of this for the present.

> But there is matter for another rhyme,
> And I to this may add a second tale.
> (Wordsworth, *Hart-Leap Well*, 95–6)

From The Spirit of the Age (1825)

MR COLERIDGE

The present is an age of talkers, and not of doers – and the reason is that the world is growing old. We are so far advanced in the arts and sciences, that we live in retrospect and dote on past achievements. The accumulation of knowledge has been so great that we are lost in wonder at the height it has reached, instead of attempting to climb or add to it; while the variety of objects distracts and dazzles the looker-on.

What niche remains unoccupied? What path untried? What is the use of doing anything unless we could do better than all those who have gone before us? What hope is there of this? We are like those who have been to see some noble monument of art, who are content to admire without thinking of rivalling it – or, like guests after a feast, who praise the hospitality of the donor 'and thank the bounteous Pan',[1] perhaps carrying away some trifling fragments – or, like the spectators of a mighty battle, who still hear its sound afar off, and the clashing of armour and the neighing of the warhorse and the shout of victory is in their ears, like the rushing of innumerable waters!

Mr Coleridge has 'a mind reflecting ages past'.[2] His voice is like the echo of the congregated roar of the 'dark rearward and abyss'[3] of thought. He who has seen a mouldering tower by the side of a crystal lake, hid by the mist but glittering in the wave below, may conceive the dim, gleaming, uncertain intelligence of his eye; he who has marked the evening clouds uprolled (a world of vapours) has seen the picture of his mind – unearthly, unsubstantial, with gorgeous tints and ever-varying forms:

> That which was now a horse, even with a thought
> The rack dislimns, and makes it indistinct
> As water is in water.
> (*Antony and Cleopatra*, IV. xiv. 9–11)

---

[59] Robert William Elliston (1774–1831), famous actor who appeared in *Remorse* when produced at Drury Lane in 1813. The quotation is not to be found in *Remorse* or any other work by Coleridge.

MR COLERIDGE
[1] Milton, *Comus*, 176.
[2] I.M.S., 'On Worthy Master Shakespeare and his Poems', 1, prefixed to the second Folio (1632).
[3] *The Tempest*, I. ii. 50.

Our author's mind is (as he himself might express it) *tangential*. There is no subject on which he has not touched, none on which he has rested. With an understanding fertile, subtle, expansive, 'quick, forgetive, apprehensive'[4] beyond all living precedent, few traces of it will perhaps remain. He lends himself to all impressions alike; he gives up his mind and liberty of thought to none. He is a general lover of art and science, and wedded to no one in particular. He pursues knowledge as a mistress, with outstretched hands and winged speed, but as he is about to embrace her, his Daphne turns – alas, not to a laurel![5] Hardly a speculation has been left on record from the earliest time, but it is loosely folded up in Mr Coleridge's memory, like a rich but somewhat tattered piece of tapestry. We might add (with more seeming than real extravagance) that scarce a thought can pass through the mind of man, but its sound has at some time or other passed over his head with rustling pinions.

On whatever question or author you speak, he is prepared to take up the theme with advantage – from Peter Abelard down to Thomas Moore, from the subtlest metaphysics to the politics of *The Courier*.[6] There is no man of genius in whose praise he descants, but the critic seems to stand above the author, and 'what in him is weak, to strengthen; what is low, to raise and support'.[7] Nor is there any work of genius that does not come out of his hands like an illuminated missal, sparkling even in its defects.

If Mr Coleridge had not been the most impressive talker of his age, he would probably have been the finest writer – but he lays down his pen to make sure of an auditor, and mortgages the admiration of posterity for the stare of an idler. If he had not been a poet, he would have been a powerful logician; if he had not dipped his wing in the Unitarian controversy, he might have soared to the very summit of fancy. But in writing verse, he is trying to subject the muse to *transcendental* theories; in his abstract reasoning, he misses his way by strewing it with flowers. All that he has done of moment, he had done twenty years ago; since then he may be said to have lived on the sounds of his own voice. Mr Coleridge is too rich in intellectual wealth to need to task himself to any drudgery – he has only to draw the sliders of his imagination, and a thousand subjects expand before him, startling him with their brilliancy, or losing themselves in endless obscurity,

> And by the force of blear illusion,
> They draw him on to his confusion.
> (*Macbeth*, III. v. 28–9)

What is the little he could add to the stock, compared with the countless stores that lie about him, that he should stoop to pick up a name, or to polish an idle fancy? He walks abroad in the majesty of an universal understanding, eyeing the 'rich strond', or golden sky above him, and 'goes sounding on his way',[8] in eloquent accents, uncompelled and free!

Persons of the greatest capacity are often those who, for this reason, do the least – for, surveying themselves from the highest point of view amidst the infinite variety of

---

[4] *2 Henry IV*, IV. iii. 99. *forgetive* inventive.

[5] In Greek myth, Daphne was pursued by Apollo; on the point of capture, she was turned by the gods into a laurel-tree.

[6] Peter Abelard (1079–1142), medieval French scholastic. *The Courier* was an evening paper to which

Coleridge contributed; Hazlitt resented Coleridge's involvement with it because of its Tory sympathies.

[7] *Paradise Lost*, i. 22–3.

[8] 'rich strond'; Spenser, *Faerie Queene*, III. iv. 34. 2. 'goes sounding on his way': see p. 648, n. 21.

the universe, their own share in it seems trifling and scarce worth a thought, and they prefer the contemplation of all that is, or has been, or can be, to the making a coil about doing what (when done) is no better than vanity. It is hard to concentrate all our attention and efforts on one pursuit, except from ignorance of others, and, without this concentration of our faculties, no great progress can be made in any one thing. It is not merely that the mind is not capable of the effort; it does not think the effort worth making. Action is one, but thought is manifold. He whose restless eye glances through the wide compass of nature and art will not consent to have 'his own nothings monstered',[9] but he must do this before he can give his whole soul to them. The mind, after 'letting contemplation have its fill',[10] or

> Sailing with supreme dominion
> Through the azure deep of air,
> (Gray, *The Progress of Poesy*, 116–17)

sinks down on the ground, breathless, exhausted, powerless, inactive, or, if it must have some vent to its feelings, seeks the most easy and obvious – is soothed by friendly flattery, lulled by the murmur of immediate applause, thinks as it were aloud, and babbles in its dreams! A scholar (so to speak) is a more disinterested and abstracted character than a mere author: the first looks at the numberless volumes of a library, and says, 'All these are mine'; the other points to a single volume (perhaps it may be an immortal one) and says, 'My name is written on the back of it'. This is a puny and grovelling ambition beneath the lofty amplitude of Mr Coleridge's mind. No, he revolves in his wayward soul, or utters to the passing wind, or discourses to his own shadow things mightier and more various! Let us draw the curtain and unlock the shrine.

Learning rocked him in his cradle, and, while yet a child, 'He lisped in numbers, for the numbers came'.[11] At sixteen he wrote his 'Ode on Chatterton',[12] and he still reverts to that period with delight, not so much as it relates to himself (for that string of his own early promise of fame rather jars than otherwise), but as exemplifying the youth of a poet. Mr Coleridge talks of himself without being an egotist, for in him the individual is always merged in the abstract and general. He distinguished himself at school and at the University by his knowledge of the classics, and gained several prizes for Greek epigrams.[13] (How many men are there – great scholars, celebrated names in literature – who, having done the same thing in their youth, have no other idea all the rest of their lives but of this achievement, of a fellowship and dinner, and who, installed in academic honours, would look down on our author as a mere strolling bard!) At Christ's Hospital where he was brought up, he was the idol of those among his schoolfellows who mingled with their bookish studies the music of thought and of humanity, and he was usually attended round the cloisters by a group of these (inspiring and inspired) whose hearts, even then, burnt within them as he talked, and where the sounds yet linger to mock Elia on his way, still turning pensive to the past![14]

---

[9] *Coriolanus*, II. ii. 77.
[10] John Dyer, *Grongar Hill* (1761), 26.
[11] Pope, *Epistle to Dr Arbuthnot*, 128.
[12] Coleridge's 'Monody on the Death of Chatterton' seems to date from 1790, when he was still at Christ's Hospital.
[13] In 1792 Coleridge was awarded the Browne Medal for Greek verse at Cambridge.
[14] Hazlitt refers to Lamb's essay, 'Christ's Hospital Five and Thirty Years Ago'.

One of the finest and rarest parts of Mr Coleridge's conversation is when he expatiates on the Greek tragedians (not that he is not well-acquainted, when he pleases, with the epic poets, or the philosophers, or orators, or historians of antiquity) – on the subtle reasonings and melting pathos of Euripides; on the harmonious gracefulness of Sophocles, tuning his love-laboured song like sweetest warblings from a sacred grove; on the high-wrought trumpet-tongued eloquence of Aeschylus, whose Prometheus, above all, is like an Ode to Fate and a pleading with Providence, his thoughts being let loose as his body is chained on his solitary rock, and his afflicted will (the emblem of mortality) 'Struggling in vain with ruthless destiny'.[15] As the impassioned critic speaks and rises in his theme, you would think you heard the voice of the man hated by the gods contending with the wild winds as they roar, and his eye glitters with the spirit of antiquity!

Next he was engaged with Hartley's tribes of mind, 'ethereal braid, thought-woven',[16] and he busied himself for a year or two with vibrations and vibratiuncles and the great law of association that binds all things in its mystic chain, and the doctrine of necessity (the mild teacher of charity) and the millennium, anticipative of a life to come;[17] and he plunged deep into the controversy on matter and spirit, and, as an escape from Dr Priestley's materialism[18] (where he felt himself imprisoned by the logician's spell like Ariel in the cloven pine-tree[19]), he became suddenly enamoured of Bishop Berkeley's fairy-world, and used in all companies to build the universe (like a brave poetical fiction) of fine words;[20] and he was deep-read in Malebranche,[21] and in Cudworth's *Intellectual System*[22] (a huge pile of learning – unwieldy, enormous), and in Lord Brook's hieroglyphic theories,[23] and in Bishop Butler's *Sermons*,[24] and in the Duchess of Newcastle's fantastic folios,[25] and in Clarke and South and Tillotson,[26] and all the fine thinkers and masculine reasoners of that age – and Leibniz's *Pre-established Harmony*[27] reared its arch above his head, like the rainbow in the cloud, covenanting with the hopes of man; and then he fell plump ten thousand fathoms down (but his wings saved him harmless) into the *hortus siccus* of dissent,[28] where he pared religion down to the standard of reason and stripped faith of mystery, and preached Christ crucified and the Unity of the Godhead, and so dwelt for a while in the spirit with John Huss and Jerome of Prague and Socinus and old John Zisca,[29] and ran through Neal's *History of*

[15] Wordsworth, *The Excursion*, vi. 557.

[16] Collins, *Ode to Evening*, 7. In *Ode on the Poetical Character*, 47, Collins refers to 'the shad'wy tribes of mind'.

[17] Features of Hartleian philosophy – and, incidentally, of *The Recluse*.

[18] Joseph Priestley, *Disquisitions Relating to Matter and Spirit* (1777).

[19] *The Tempest*, I. ii. 277–9.

[20] For evidence of Coleridge's Berkeleianism, see p. 512 above.

[21] Malebranche (1638–1715), *De la Recherche de la Vérité* (1674).

[22] Ralph Cudworth (1617–88), *True Intellectual System of the Universe* (1678).

[23] Robert Greville, second Baron Brooke (1608–43), *The Nature of Truth, its Union and Unity with the Soul* (1640).

[24] Joseph Butler, Bishop of Bristol (1692–1752), *The Analogy of Religion* (1736).

[25] Margaret Cavendish, Duchess of Newcastle (1624–74) published plays, essays, and poetry in large folio volumes.

[26] Samuel Clarke (1657–1729), metaphysician; Robert South (1634–1716), divine and sermonist; John Tillotson (1630–94), renowned Anglican sermonist.

[27] Gottfried Wilhelm Leibnitz (1646–1716) assumed a 'pre-established harmony' to exist between matter and spirit; see his *Monadology* (1714).

[28] A *hortus siccus* is a collection of dried flowers. This phrase is taken from Burke, *Reflections on the Revolution in France* (1790), p. 15.

[29] John Huss (1369–1415), Bohemian theologian; Jerome of Prague (d. 1416), colleague of Huss; Socinus was the Latinized name of two Italian theologians, Fausto Paolo Sozzini (1539–1604) and Lelio Sozzini (1525–62); John Zisca (d. 1424), Czech soldier and religious leader.

the Puritans, and Calamy's *Non-Conformists' Memorial*[30] (having like thoughts and passions with them); but then Spinoza[31] became his god and he took up the vast chain of being in his hand, and the round world became the centre and the soul of all things in some shadowy sense forlorn of meaning, and around him he beheld the living traces and the sky-pointing proportions of the mighty Pan; but poetry redeemed him from this spectral philosophy, and he bathed his heart in beauty, and gazed at the golden light of heaven, and drank of the spirit of the universe, and wandered at eve by fairy-stream or fountain,

> When he saw nought but beauty,
> When he heard the voice of that Almighty One
> In every breeze that blew, or wave that murmured,
> (Coleridge, *Remorse*, IV. ii. 100–2)

and wedded with truth in Plato's shade, and in the writings of Proclus and Plotinus[32] saw the ideas of things in the eternal mind, and unfolded all mysteries with the Schoolmen, and fathomed the depths of Duns Scotus and Thomas Aquinas, and entered the third heaven with Jacob Behmen, and walked hand in hand with Swedenborg[33] through the pavilions of the New Jerusalem, and sung his faith in the promise and in the word in his *Religious Musings* – and lowering himself from that dizzy height, poised himself on Milton's wings, and spread out his thoughts in charity with the glad prose of Jeremy Taylor,[34] and wept over Bowles' sonnets, and studied Cowper's blank verse, and betook himself to Thomson's *Castle of Indolence*,[35] and sported with the wits of Charles the Second's days and of Queen Anne, and relished Swift's style and that of the *John Bull* (Arbuthnot's we mean – not Mr Croker's),[36] and dallied with the *British Essayists* and *Novelists*,[37] and knew all qualities of more modern writers with a learned spirit, Johnson and Goldsmith and Junius[38] and Burke and Godwin, and the *Sorrows of Werter*,[39] and Jean Jacques Rousseau and Voltaire and Marivaux and Crebillon,[40] and thousands more; now 'laughed with Rabelais in his easy chair'[41] or pointed to Hogarth, or afterwards dwelt on Claude's classic scenes or spoke with rapture of Raphael, and compared the women at Rome to figures that had walked out of his pictures, or visited the Oratory of Pisa, and described the works of Giotto and Ghirlandaio and Massaccio, and gave the moral of the picture of the Triumph of Death (where the beggars and the wretched invoke his dreadful dart but the rich and mighty of the earth quail and shrink before it); and in that land of siren sights and

---

[30]   Daniel Neal, *History of the Puritans* (1732–8); Edmund Calamy, *Non-Conformists' Memorial* (abridged 1775).

[31]   Benedict Spinoza (1632–77), Dutch philosopher.

[32]   Proclus (410–85) and Plotinus (204–70), Platonist philosophers.

[33]   Duns Scotus (1265–1308), Scottish medieval philosopher; Thomas Aquinas (1227–74), medieval theologian; Jacob Behmen (*alias* Boehme) (1575–1624), German mystic; Emanuel Swedenborg (1688–1772), Swedish mystic.

[34]   Jeremy Taylor (1613–67).

[35]   James Thomson, *The Castle of Indolence* (1748).

[36]   *The History of John Bull*, a collection of pamphlets by John Arbuthnot (1667–1735), issued in 1712. *John Bull* was also the name of a Tory newspaper which

began publishing on 17 Dec. 1820, but there is no evidence that John Wilson Croker (1780–1857), Tory politician and man of letters, was involved in its production.

[37]   *British Essayists* (1817), issued in 45 vol.; *British Novelists*, ed. Mrs Barbauld (1810).

[38]   'Junius' authored a series of letters published in the *Public Advertiser* 1769–72, attacking Tory worthies.

[39]   Novel by Goethe (1774).

[40]   Jean Jacques Rousseau (1712–78), French novelist and philosopher; François-Marie Arouet (1694–1778) wrote under the pseudonym of Voltaire; Pierre Carlet de Chamblain de Marivaux (1688–1763), French novelist; Crébillon the Elder (1674–1762), dramatist.

[41]   Pope, *Dunciad*, i. 20.

sounds saw a dance of peasant girls, and was charmed with lutes and gondolas; or wandered into Germany and lost himself in the labyrinths of the Hartz Forest and of the Kantean philosophy, and amongst the cabalistic names of Fichte and Schelling and Lessing[42] and God knows who – this was long after, but all the former while he had nerved his heart and filled his eyes with tears, as he hailed the rising orb of liberty (since quenched in darkness and in blood), and had kindled his affections at the blaze of the French Revolution, and sang for joy when the towers of the Bastille and the proud places of the insolent and the oppressor fell, and would have floated his bark, freighted with fondest fancies, across the Atlantic wave with Southey and others to seek for peace and freedom, 'In Philarmonia's undivided dale!'[43]

Alas! 'Frailty, thy name is *Genius*!'[44] What is become of all this mighty heap of hope, of thought, of learning, and humanity? It has ended in swallowing doses of oblivion and in writing paragraphs in the *Courier*. Such, and so little, is the mind of man!

It was not to be supposed that Mr Coleridge could keep on at the rate he set off; he could not realize all he knew or thought, and less could not fix his desultory ambition. Other stimulants supplied the place, and kept up the intoxicating dream, the fever and the madness of his early impressions. Liberty (the philosopher's and the poet's bride) had fallen a victim, meanwhile, to the murderous practices of the hag Legitimacy. Proscribed by court-hirelings, too romantic for the herd of vulgar politicians, our enthusiast stood at bay, and at last turned on the pivot of a subtle casuistry to the *unclean side* – but his discursive reason would not let him trammel himself into a Poet Laureate or stamp-distributor,[45] and he stopped, ere he had quite passed that well-known 'bourne from whence no traveller returns',[46] and so has sunk into torpid, uneasy repose, tantalized by useless resources, haunted by vain imaginings, his lips idly moving but his heart forever still, or, as the shattered chords vibrate of themselves, making melancholy music to the ear of memory!

Such is the fate of genius in an age when, in the unequal contest with sovereign wrong, every man is ground to powder who is not either a born slave, or who does not willingly and at once offer up the yearnings of humanity and the dictates of reason as a welcome sacrifice to besotted prejudice and loathsome power.

Of all Mr Coleridge's productions, *The Ancient Mariner* is the only one that we could with confidence put into any person's hands, on whom we wished to impress a favourable idea of his extraordinary powers. Let whatever other objections be made to it, it is unquestionably a work of genius – of wild, irregular, overwhelming imagination, and has that rich, varied movement in the verse which gives a distant idea of the lofty or changeful tones of Mr Coleridge's voice. In the *Christabel*, there is one splendid passage on divided friendship. The translation of Schiller's *Wallenstein* is also a masterly production in its kind, faithful and spirited. Among his smaller pieces there are occasional bursts of pathos and fancy equal to what we might expect from him, but these form the exception and not the rule; such, for instance, is his affecting sonnet to the author of *The Robbers*:[47]

---

[42] *cabalistic* esoteric, abstruse. Johann Gottlieb Fichte (1762–1814), Friedrich Wilhelm von Schelling (1775–1854), and Gotthold Ephraim Lessing (1729–81), German philosophers.

[43] Cf. Coleridge's 'Monody on the Death of Chatterton' (1796), 129. 'Philarmonia' means 'love of order'.

[44] Cf. *Hamlet*, I. ii. 146.

[45] Hazlitt swipes at Southey, who became Poet Laureate in 1813, and Wordsworth, Distributor of Stamps for Westmorland, 1813–42.

[46] *Hamlet*, III. i. 78–9.

[47] Johann Christoph Friedrich von Schiller (1759–1805).

Schiller! that hour I would have wished to die,
If through the shudd'ring midnight I had sent
From the dark dungeon of the tower time-rent
That fearful voice, a famished father's cry,
That in no after-moment aught less vast
Might stamp me mortal! A triumphant shout
Black horror screamed, and all her goblin rout
From the more with'ring scene diminished passed.
Ah, bard tremendous in sublimity!
Could I behold thee in thy loftier mood,
Wand'ring at eve, with finely frenzied eye,
Beneath some vast old tempest-swinging wood –
Awhile, with mute awe gazing, I would brood,
Then weep aloud in a wild ecstasy.

His tragedy entitled *Remorse*[48] is full of beautiful and striking passages, but it does not place the author in the first rank of dramatic writers. But if Mr Coleridge's works do not place him in that rank, they injure instead of conveying a just idea of the man, for he himself is certainly in the first class of general intellect.

If our author's poetry is inferior to his conversation, his prose is utterly abortive. Hardly a gleam is to be found in it of the brilliancy and richness of those stores of thought and language that he pours out incessantly, when they are lost like drops of water in the ground. The principal work in which he has attempted to embody his general views of things is *The Friend*,[49] of which, though it contains some noble passages and fine trains of thought, prolixity and obscurity are the most frequent characteristics.

No two persons can be conceived more opposite in character or genius than the subject of the present and of the preceding sketch. Mr Godwin, with less natural capacity and with fewer acquired advantages, by concentrating his mind on some given object and doing what he had to do with all his might, has accomplished much and will leave more than one monument of a powerful intellect behind him; Mr Coleridge, by dissipating his and dallying with every subject by turns, has done little or nothing to justify to the world or to posterity the high opinion which all who have ever heard him converse, or known him intimately, with one accord entertain of him. Mr Godwin's faculties have kept house and plied their task in the workshop of the brain, diligently and effectually; Mr Coleridge's have gossipped away their time and gadded about from house to house, as if life's business were to melt the hours in listless talk. Mr Godwin is intent on a subject only as it concerns himself and his reputation; he works it out as a matter of duty, and discards from his mind whatever does not forward his main object as impertinent and vain. Mr Coleridge, on the other hand, delights in nothing but episodes and digressions, neglects whatever he undertakes to perform, and can act only on spontaneous impulses, without object or method: 'He cannot be constrained by mastery.'[50] While he should be occupied with a given pursuit, he is thinking of a thousand other things; a thousand tastes, a thousand objects tempt him and distract his mind, which keeps open house and entertains all comers and, after being fatigued and amused with morning calls from idle visitors, finds the day

---

[48] Produced at Drury Lane Theatre, 23 Jan. 1813.
[49] Weekly periodical edited by Coleridge, 1808–10.

[50] Chaucer, 'The Franklin's Tale', 764: 'Love wol nat been constreyned by maistrye.'

consumed and its business unconcluded. Mr Godwin, on the contrary, is somewhat exclusive and unsocial in his habits of mind, entertains no company but what he gives his whole time and attention to, and wisely writes over the doors of his understanding, his fancy, and his senses, 'No admittance except on business'. He has none of that fastidious refinement and false delicacy which might lead him to balance between the endless variety of modern attainments. He does not throw away his life (nor a single half-hour of it) in adjusting the claims of different accomplishments, and in choosing between them or making himself master of them all. He sets about his task, whatever it may be, and goes through it with spirit and fortitude. He has the happiness to think an author the greatest character in the world, and himself the greatest author in it. Mr Coleridge, in writing an harmonious stanza, would stop to consider whether there was not more grace and beauty in a *pas de trois*,[51] and would not proceed till he had resolved this question by a chain of metaphysical reasoning without end. Not so Mr Godwin. That is best to him which he can do best. He does not waste himself in vain aspirations and effeminate sympathies. He is blind, deaf, insensible to all but the trump of fame. Plays, operas, painting, music, ballrooms, wealth, fashion, titles, lords, ladies, touch him not: all these are no more to him than to the anchorite in his cell, and he writes on to the end of the chapter through good report and evil report. *Pingo in eternitatem*[52] is his motto. He neither envies nor admires what others are, but is contented to be what he is, and strives to do the utmost he can. Mr Coleridge has flirted with the muses as with a set of mistresses; Mr Godwin has been married twice – to Reason and to Fancy – and has to boast no short-lived progeny by each. So to speak, he has *valves* belonging to his mind to regulate the quantity of gas admitted into it, so that, like the bare, unsightly, but well-compacted steam-vessel, it cuts its liquid way, and arrives at its promised end; while Mr Coleridge's bark, 'taught with the little nautilus to sail',[53] the sport of every breath, dancing to every wave, 'Youth at its prow, and Pleasure at its helm',[54] flutters its gaudy pennons in the air, glitters in the sun, but we wait in vain to hear of its arrival in the destined harbour. Mr Godwin, with less variety and vividness, with less subtlety and susceptibility both of thought and feeling, has had firmer nerves, a more determined purpose, a more comprehensive grasp of his subject, and the results are as we find them. Each has met with his reward – for justice has, after all, been done to the pretensions of each, and we must in all cases use means to ends!

Thomas Moore (1779–1852)

As a poet, Byron told Moore, 'I think no one equal to you' (Marchand, iii. 194). The principal works of the Dublin-born poet and lyrist include The Poetical Works of the Late Thomas Little *(1801),* Irish Melodies *(1808–34),* Lalla Rookh *(1817), and* The Fudge Family in Paris *(1818).*

---

[51] *pas de trois* dance for three people.
[52] 'I delineate for all time.'
[53] Pope, *Essay on Man*, iii. 177.
[54] Gray, *The Bard*, 74.

From The Poetical Works of the Late Thomas Little Esq.
(1801)
LOVE IN A STORM

Loud sung the wind in the ruins above
   Which murmured the warnings of time o'er our head,
While fearless we offered devotions to love,
   The rude rock our pillow, the rushes our bed!

Damp was the chill of the wintery air,   5
   But it made us cling closer, and warmly unite;
Dread was the lightning, and horrid its glare,
   But it showed me my Julia in languid delight.

To my bosom she nestled and felt not a fear
   Though the shower did beat and the tempest did frown;   10
Her sighs were as sweet and her murmurs as dear
   As if she lay lulled on a pillow of down!

From Irish Melodies, 2nd edition (1822)
BELIEVE ME, IF ALL THOSE ENDEARING YOUNG CHARMS

Believe me, if all those endearing young charms,
   Which I gaze on so fondly today,
Were to change by tomorrow, and fleet in my arms,
   Like fairy gifts fading away,
Thou wouldst still be adored, as this moment thou art,   5
   Let thy loveliness fade as it will,
And, around the dear ruin, each wish of my heart
   Would entwine itself verdantly still.

It is not – while beauty and youth are thine own,
   And thy cheeks unprofaned by a tear –   10
That the fervour and faith of a soul can be known,
   To which time will but make thee more dear!
Oh, the heart that has truly loved never forgets,
   But as truly loves on to the close,
As the sunflower turns on her god, when he sets,   15
   The same look which she turned when he rose!

IN THE MORNING OF LIFE

In the morning of life, when its cares are unknown,
   And its pleasures in all their new lustre begin,
When we live in a bright-beaming world of our own,
   And the light that surrounds us is all from within –

Oh it is not, believe me, in that happy time 5
   We can love, as in hours of less transport we may;
Of our smiles, of our hopes, 'tis the gay sunny prime,
   But affection is warmest when these fade away.

When we see the first glory of youth pass us by,
   Like a leaf on the stream that will never return; 10
When our cup, which had sparkled with pleasure so high,
   First tastes of the *other*, the dark flowing urn –
Then, then is the moment affection can sway
   With a depth and a tenderness joy never knew;
Love, nursed among pleasures, is faithless as they, 15
   But the love born of sorrow, like sorrow is true!

In climes full of sunshine, though splendid their dyes,
   Yet faint is the odour the flow'rs shed about;
'Tis the clouds and the mists of our own weeping skies,
   That call the full spirit of fragrancy out. 20
So the wild glow of passion may kindle from mirth,
   But 'tis only in grief true affection appears;
And, ev'n though to smiles it may first owe its birth,
   All the soul of its sweetness is drawn out by tears!

John Taylor (1781–1864)

One of the most important publishers of the early nineteenth century, who in 1806 went into partnership with J. A. Hessey. Together they built up a list that included Keats, Clare, Hazlitt, Lamb, Coleridge, Landor, Darley, De Quincey, Hood, and Carlyle. His elegiac sonnet on Keats's death is one of many contributions to the London Magazine, *which he edited from 1821 to 1825.*

From London Magazine, 3 (1821) 526

SONNET ON THE DEATH OF THE POET J. KEATS (UNSIGNED)

Sic pereunt violae.[1]

And art thou dead? Thou very sweetest bird
   That ever made a moonlight forest ring,
   Its wild unearthly music mellowing;
Shall thy rich notes no more, no more be heard?
Never! Thy beautiful romantic themes 5
   That made it mental heav'n to hear thee sing,

SONNET ON THE DEATH OF THE POET J. KEATS
[1] 'Thus die the violets.'

Lapping th' enchanted soul in golden dreams,
　　Are mute! Ah vainly did Italia fling
　　Her healing ray around thee – blossoming
With flushing flow'rs long wedded to thy verse;　　　　　　10
Those flow'rs, those sunbeams, but adorn thy hearse;
　　And the warm gales that faintly rise and fall
　　In music's clime – themselves so musical –
Shall chaunt the minstrel's dirge far from his father's hall.

Charlotte Dacre (1782–1841)

Writer of sensational novels, best known for the melodramatic Zafloya, or The Moor *(1806),
which strongly influenced Shelley's* Zastrozzi *(1811). Although the poems collected in* Hours of
Solitude *(1805) work through familiar themes of love and betrayal, Dacre's verses are
characterized by a refreshing and lively sharpness of tone.*

From Hours of Solitude (1805)

IL TRIONFO DEL AMOR

So full my thoughts are of thee, that I swear
　　All else is hateful to my troubled soul;
　　How thou hast o'er me gained such vast control,
　　How charmed my stubborn spirit, is most rare!
Sure thou hast mingled philtres[1] in my bowl,　　　　　　5
　　Or what thine high enchantedarts declare
　　Fearless of blame – for truth I will not care
(So charms the witchery), whether fair or foul.
Yet well my lovesick mind thine arts can tell;
　　No magic potions gav'st thou, save what I　　　　　　10
　　Drank from those lustrous eyes when they did dwell
With dying fondness on me – or thy sigh
Which sent its perfumed poison to my brain.
　　Thus known thy spells, thou bland seducer, see –
　　Come practice them again, and oh! again;　　　　　　15
Spellbound I *am*, and spellbound *wish* to be.

TO HIM WHO SAYS HE LOVES

You tell me that you truly love;
　　Ah! know you well what love does mean?
Does neither whim nor fancy move
　　The rapture of your transient dream?

IL TRIONFO DEL AMOR
[1] *philtres* magic potions.

Tell me, when absent do you think   5
  O'er ev'ry look and ev'ry sigh?
Do you in melancholy sink,
  And hope and doubt you know not why?

When present, do you die to say
  How much you love, yet fear to tell?   10
Does her breath melt your soul away?
  A touch, your nerves with transport swell?

Or do you faint with sweet excess
  Of pleasure rising into pain,
When hoping you may e'er possess   15
  The object you aspire to gain?

The charms of every other fair
  With coldness could you learn to view?
Fondly unchanged to her repair,
  With transports ever young and new?   20

Could you for her, fame, wealth despise?
  In poverty and toil feel blessed?
Drink sweet delusion from her eyes
  Or smile at ruin on her breast?

And tell me, at her loss or hate,   25
  Would death your only refuge prove?
Ah! if in aught you hesitate –
  Coward! you dare not say you love.

Leigh Hunt (1784–1859)

*Poet, journalist, and man of letters; friend of Byron, Moore, Lamb, and Keats (among others).
Publications include* The Story of Rimini *(1816),* Foliage *(1818); as editor,* The Examiner
and The Indicator. *'To Hampstead' is one of his most evocative poems, its sentiment given
power by the discipline of its form. For the full context of Hunt's Shelley sonnets, the reader
should consult the latter's assessment of Hunt's deism (Jones, i. 77). 'A Now, Descriptive of a
Hot Day' illustrates Hunt's belief that the essay should entertain. His* Autobiography *recalls
that 'the paper that was most liked by Keats, if I remember, was the one on a hot summer's
day, entitled "A Now". He was with me while I was writing and reading it to him, and
contributed one or two of the passages' (p. 281).*

From The Examiner, no. 385 (14 May 1815) 316

TO HAMPSTEAD (COMPOSED 7 MAY 1815)

As one who after long and far-spent years
  Comes on his mistress in an hour of sleep,
  And half-surprised that he can silence keep
Stands smiling o'er her through a flash of tears,
To see how sweet and self-same she appears;   5
  Till at his touch, with little moving creep
  Of joy, she wakes from out her calmness deep,
And then his heart finds voice, and dances round her ears –
So I, first coming on my haunts again,
  In pause and stillness of the early prime,[1]   10
  Stood thinking of the past and present time
With earnest eyesight, scarcely crossed with pain;
  Till the fresh moving leaves, and startling birds,
  Loosened my long-suspended breath in words.

From Foliage (1818)

TO PERCY SHELLEY, ON THE DEGRADING NOTIONS OF DEITY

What wonder, Percy, that with jealous rage
Men should defame the kindly and the wise,
When in the midst of the all-beauteous skies,
And all this lovely world, that should engage
Their mutual search for the old golden age,   5
They seat a phantom, swelled into grim size
Out of their own passions and bigotries,
And then, for fear, proclaim it meek and sage!
And this they call a light and a revealing!
Wise as the clown,[1] who plodding home at night   10
In autumn, turns at call of fancied elf,
And sees upon the fog, with ghastly feeling,
A giant shadow in its imminent might,
Which his own lanthorn throws up from himself.

TO THE SAME

Yet, Percy, not for this, should he whose eye
Sees loveliness, and the unselfish joy
Of justice, turn him, like a peevish boy,
At hindrances and thwartings, and deny

TO HAMPSTEAD
[1] *prime* about 6 a.m.

TO PERCY SHELLEY, ON THE DEGRADING NOTIONS OF DEITY
[1] *clown* untutored peasant.

Wisdom's divinest privilege, constancy –   5
That which most proves him free from the alloy
Of useless earth, least prone to the decoy
That clamours down weak pinions from the sky.
The Spirit of Beauty,[1] though by solemn quires
Hourly blasphemed, stoops not from its calm end,   10
And forward breathing love, but ever on
Rolls the round day, and calls the starry fires
To their glad watch. Therefore, high-hearted friend,
Be still with thine own task in unison.

TO JOHN KEATS

'Tis well you think me truly one of those
Whose sense discerns the loveliness of things;
For surely as I feel the bird that sings
Behind the leaves, or dawn as it up grows,
Or the rich bee rejoicing as he goes,   5
Or the glad issue of emerging springs,
Or overhead the glide of a dove's wings,
Or turf, or trees, or, midst of all, repose;
And surely as I feel things lovelier still,
The human look, and the harmonious form   10
Containing woman, and the smile in ill,
And such a heart as Charles',[1] wise and warm –
As surely as all this, I see, ev'n now,
Young Keats, a flowering laurel on your brow.

From The Indicator, 1 (1820) 300–2

A NOW, DESCRIPTIVE OF A HOT DAY

Now the rosy- (and lazy-) fingered Aurora, issuing from her saffron house,[1] calls up the moist vapours to surround her, and goes veiled with them as long as she can; till Phoebus, coming forth in his power, looks everything out of the sky, and holds sharp uninterrupted empire from his throne of beams. Now the mower begins to make his sweeping cuts more slowly, and resorts oftener to the beer. Now the carter sleeps atop of his load of hay, or plods with double slouch of shoulder, looking out with eyes winking under his shading hat, and with a hitch upward of one side of his mouth. Now the little girl at her grandmother's cottage-door watches the coaches that go by, with her hand held up over her sunny forehead. Now labourers look well, resting in their white shirts at the doors of rural alehouses. Now an elm is fine there, with a seat under

---

TO THE SAME
[1] An allusion to Shelley's 'Hymn to Intellectual Beauty', 13, published in Hunt's journal, The Examiner.
TO JOHN KEATS
[1] Charles Cowden Clarke (1787–1877), mutual friend of Keats and Hunt.

A NOW, DESCRIPTIVE OF A HOT DAY
[1] The dawn goddess (Aurora) casts an orange-yellow (saffron) light over the world.

it; and horses drink out of the trough, stretching their yearning necks with loosened collars; and the traveller calls for his glass of ale, having been without one for more than ten minutes; and his horse stands wincing at the flies, giving sharp shivers of his skin, and moving to and fro his ineffectual docked tail; and now Miss Betty Wilson, the host's daughter, comes streaming forth in a flowered gown and earrings, carrying with four of her beautiful fingers the foaming glass, for which, after the traveller has drank it, she receives with an indifferent eye, looking another way, the lawful two pence: that is to say, unless the traveller, nodding his ruddy face, pays some gallant compliment to her before he drinks – such as, 'I'd rather kiss you, my dear, than the tumbler', or, 'I'll wait for you, my love, if you'll marry me' – upon which, if the man is good-looking, and the lady in good humour, she smiles and bites her lips, and says, 'Ah, men can talk fast enough', upon which the old stagecoachman, who is buckling something near her before he sets off, says in a hoarse voice, 'So can women too for that matter', and John Boots grins through his ragged red locks, and dotes on the repartee all the day after. Now grasshoppers 'fry', as Dryden says.[2] Now cattle stand in water and ducks are envied. Now boots and shoes and trees by the roadside are thick with dust; and dogs, rolling in it, after issuing out of the water into which they have been thrown to fetch sticks, come scattering horror among the legs of the spectators. Now a fellow who finds he has three miles further to go in a pair of tight shoes is in a pretty situation. Now rooms with the sun upon them become intolerable; and the apothecary's apprentice, with a bitterness beyond aloes, thinks of the pond he used to bathe in at school. Now men with powdered heads (especially if thick) envy those that are unpowdered, and stop to wipe them uphill, with countenances that seem to expostulate with destiny. Now boys assemble round the village pump with a ladle to it, and delight to make a forbidden splash and get wet through the shoes. Now also they make suckers of leather, and bathe all day long in rivers and ponds, and follow the fish into their cool corners, and say millions of 'My eyes!' at tittle-bats.[3] Now the bee, as he hums along, seems to be talking heavily of the heat. Now doors and brick walls are burning to the hand; and a walled lane, with dust and broken bottles in it, near a brick-field,[4] is a thing not to be thought of. Now a green lane, on the contrary, thick-set with hedgerow elms, and having the noise of a brook 'rumbling in pebble-stone',[5] is one of the pleasantest things in the world. Now youths and damsels walk through hayfields by chance; and if the latter say, 'Ha' done then, William', and the overseer in the next field calls out to 'Let thic thear hay thear bide', and the girls persist, merely to plague 'such a frumpish old fellow'.

Now, in town, gossips talk more than ever to one another, in rooms, in doorways, and out of window, always beginning the conversation with saying that the heat is overpowering. Now blinds are let down and doors thrown open and flannel waistcoats left off, and cold meat preferred to hot, and wonder expressed why tea continues so refreshing, and people delight to sliver lettuces into bowls, and apprentices water doorways with tin canisters that lay several atoms of dust. Now the water-cart, jumbling along the middle of the street, and jolting the showers out of its box of water, really does something. Now boys delight to have a water-pipe let out, and see it bubbling away in a tall and frothy volume. Now fruiterers' shops and dairies look pleasant, and

---

[2] Hunt recalls Dryden, *Virgil's Georgics*, iii. 510–11, although the word 'fry' is not used.
[3] *tittlebats* sticklebats.
[4] *brick-field* yard where bricks are made.
[5] Spenser, 'Virgil's Gnat', 163.

ices are the only things to those who can get them. Now ladies loiter in baths; and people make presents of flowers; and wine is put into ice; and the after-dinner lounger recreates[6] his head with applications of perfumed water out of long-necked bottles. Now the lounger, who cannot resist riding his new horse, feels his boots burn him. Now buckskins are not the lawn[7] of Cos. Now jockeys, walking in greatcoats to lose flesh, curse inwardly. Now five fat people in a stagecoach hate the sixth fat one who is coming in, and think he has no right to be so large. Now clerks in offices do nothing but drink soda-water and spruce beer,[8] and read the newspaper. Now the old-clothes-man drops his solitary cry more deeply into the areas on the hot and forsaken side of the street; and bakers look vicious; and cooks are aggravated; and the steam of a tavern-kitchen catches hold of one like the breath of Tartarus. Now delicate skins are beset with gnats; and boys make their sleeping companion start up with playing a burning-glass on his hand; and blacksmiths are super-carbonated; and cobblers in their stalls almost feel a wish to be transplanted; and butter is too easy to spread; and the dragoons wonder whether the Romans liked their helmets; and old ladies, with their lappets unpinned, walk along in a state of dilapidation; and the servant-maids are afraid they look vulgarly hot; and the author, who has a plate of strawberries brought him, finds that he has come to the end of his writing.

From Morning Chronicle, 2 (1838) 436

RONDEAU (COMPOSED 1838)

Nelly kissed me when we met,
    Jumping from the chair she sat in;
Time, you thief, who love to get
    Sweets into your list, put *that* in.
Say I'm jaundiced, say I'm sad,   5
    Say that health and wealth have missed me,
Say I'm growing old, but add,
    Nelly kissed me.

John Wilson ('Christopher North')
(1785–1854)

A prolific contributor to Blackwood's Edinburgh Magazine, *Wilson regarded Wordsworth, Scott, and Byron as the 'three great master-spirits of our day'. The two sonnets presented here give some idea of the power of his verse, with its impressive attempts to capture a Wordsworthian sublimity. He was among the few 'Lake poets' praised by Jeffrey, who commended the poems in* The Isle of Palms *(1812) on the grounds that Wilson 'is scarcely ever guilty of the offence of building them upon a foundation that is ludicrous or purely fantastic' (*Edinburgh Review, *19 (1811–12),*

---

6   *recreates* revives, refreshes.
7   *lawn* fine linen, such as that made on the island of Cos in the Aegean.

8   *spruce beer* beer made from leaves and branches of the spruce fir.

374). The Noctes Ambrosianae *was a popular series of whimsical dialogues which appeared in* Blackwood's, *1822–35, written variously by Wilson, J. G. Lockhart, James Hogg, and William Maginn (1793–1842). In the extract below, by Wilson, the locutors are James Hogg (The Ettrick Shepherd) and Wilson (as Christopher North). Typically for the* Noctes, *it mingles literary satire with discussion of contemporary politics – in this case, the slave-trade. April 1824, the month in which this* Noctes *appeared, was an exciting one for abolitionists: the first parliamentary debate on abolition had taken place on 15 May 1823, and contemporary milestones in the struggle included Wilberforce's speech of 16 March 1824 and Brougham's of 10 June. Slaves were free in British colonies by 1833.*

From The Isle of Palms and Other Poems (1812)

Sonnet III. Written at Midnight, on Helm Crag[1]

Go up among the mountains when the storm
Of midnight howls, but go in that wild mood
When the soul loves tumultuous solitude,
And through the haunted air each giant form
Of swinging pine, black rock, or ghostly cloud   5
That veils some fearful cataract tumbling loud,
Seems to thy breathless heart with life imbued.
Mid those gaunt, shapeless things thou art alone!
The mind exists, thinks, trembles through the ear,
The memory of the human world is gone,   10
And time and space seem living only *here*.
Oh! worship thou the visions then made known,
While sable glooms round Nature's temple roll,
And her dread anthem peals into thy soul.

Sonnet VII. Written on Skiddaw, during a Tempest

It was a dreadful day when late I passed
O'er thy dim vastness, Skiddaw![1] Mist and cloud
Each subject fell[2] obscured, and rushing blast
To thee made darling music, wild and loud,
Thou mountain-monarch! Rain in torrents played   5
As when at sea a wave is borne to heaven –
A watery spire, then on the crew dismayed
Of reeling ship with downward wrath is driven.
I could have thought that every living form
Had fled, or perished in that savage storm,   10
So desolate the day. To me were given
Peace, calmness, joy; then, to myself I said,

Sonnet III. Written at Midnight, on Helm Crag
[1] Helm Crag overlooks Grasmere.

Sonnet VII. Written on Skiddaw, during a Tempest
[1] *Skiddaw* fourth-highest peak in the Lake District (3,053 ft).
[2] *fell* mountain.

Can grief, time, chance, or elements control
Man's chartered pride – the liberty of soul?

From Blackwood's Edinburgh Magazine, 15 (1824) 371–3

NOCTES AMBROSIANAE NO. XIV (extract)

Scene: Sky-blue parlour
Christopher North. How did the Border games go off this spring meeting, Shepherd?
The Ettrick Shepherd. The loupin'[1] was gude, and the rinnin' was better, and the ba' was best. Oh man, that ye had been but there!
North. What were the prizes?
The Shepherd. Bunnets. Blue bunnets – I hae ane o' them in my pouch, that wasna gien awa'. There – try it on.
(The Shepherd puts the blue bonnet on Mr North's head.)
North. I have seen the day, James, when I could have leaped any man in Ettrick.
The Shepherd. A' but ane. The Flying Tailor wad hae been your match ony day. But there's nae denying you used to take awfu' spangs. Gude safe us, on springy meadow grun, rather on the decline, you were a verra grasshopper. But, wae's me – thae crutches! Eheu! fugaces, Posthume, Posthume, labuntur anni![2]
North. Why, even yet, James, if it were not for this infernal gout here, I could leap any man living at hop, step, and jump –
The Shepherd. Hech, sirs! Hech, sirs! But the human mind's a strange thing, after a'! Here's you, Mr North, the cleverest man, I'll say't to your face, noo extant, a scholar and a feelosopher, vauntin' o' your loupin'! That's a great wakeness. You should be thinkin' o' ither things, Mr North. But a' you grit men are perfet fules either in ae thing or anither.
North. Come James, my dear Hogg, draw your chair a little closer. We are a set of strange devils, I acknowledge, we human beings.
The Shepherd. Only luk at the maist celebrated o' us. There's Byron, braggin' o' his soomin', just like yourself o' your loupin'. He informs us that he swom through the streets of Venice, that are a' canals, you ken – nae very decent proceeding – and keepit ploutering on the drumly waves[3] for four hours and a half, like a wild guse, diving too I'se warrant, wi' his tail, and treading water, and lying on the back o' him – wha' the deevil cares?
North. His Lordship was, after all, but a sorry Leander?
The Shepherd. You may say that. To have been like Leander, he should hae swom the Strechts in a storm, and in black midnight, and a' by himself – without boats and gondolas to pick him up gin he tuk the cramp, and had a bonnie lass to dicht him dry – and been drowned at last: but that he'll never be.
North. You are too satirical, Hogg.
The Shepherd. And there's Tammas Mure braggin' after anither fashion o' his exploits amang the lasses. Oh man, dinna you think it rather contemptible, to sit in a cotch wi' a bonnie thochtless lassie, for twa three lang stages, and then publish a sang about it?

NOCTES AMBROSIANAE NO. XIV
[1] *loupin'* leaping, jumping. Wilson was a champion leaper at Oxford, his record being a length of 23 ft.
[2] 'Ah Posthumus, my worthy friend, the years run on apace!' (Horace, *Odes*, II. xiv. 1–2).
[3] *ploutering on the drumly waves* playing idly on the muddy waves.

I ance heard a gran' leddie frae London launching till I thocht she would hae split her sides, at Thomas Little,[4] as she ca'd him. I could scarcely fadom her – but ye ken't by her face what she was thinking – and it was a' quite right – a severe reproof.

North. Mr Coleridge – is he in the habit, Hogg, of making the public the confidants of his personal accomplishments?

The Shepherd. I canna weel tell, for deevil the like o' sic books as his did I ever see wi' my een beneath the blessed licht. I'm no speakin' o' his poems. I'll aye roose[5] them – but *The Freen* and the *Lay Sermons*[6] are aneuch to drive ane to destraction. What's logic?

North. Upon my honour as a gentleman, I do not know; if I did, I would tell you with the greatest pleasure.

The Shepherd. Weel, weel, Coleridge is aye accusing folk o' haeing nae logic. The want o' a' things is owing to the want o' logic, it seems. Noo, Mr North, gin logic be soun reasoning, and I jalouse[7] as much, he has less o't himsel than onybody I ken, for he never sticks to the point twa pages; and to tell you the truth, I aye feel as I were fuddled after perusing Coleridge. Then he's aye speaking o' himsel – but what he says I never can mak out. Let him stick to his poetry, for – oh man! – he's an unyerthly writer, and gies Superstition sae beautifu' a countenance, that she wiles folk on wi' her, like so many bairns, into the flowery but fearfu' wildernesses, where sleeping and wauking seem a' ae thing, and the very soul within us wonders what has become o' the everyday warld, and asks hersel what creation is this that wavers and glimmers, and keeps up a bonnie wild musical sough, like that o' swarming bees, spring-startled birds, and the voice of a hundred streams, some wimpling awa' ower the Elysian meadows, and ithers roaring at a distance frae the clefts o' Mount Abora.[8] But is't true that they hae made him the Bishop of Barbados?

North. No, he is only Dean of Highgate. I long for his 'Wanderings of Cain', about to be published by Taylor and Hessey.[9] That house has given us some excellent things of late. They are spirited publishers. But why did not Coleridge speak to Blackwood? I suppose he could not tell, if he were questioned.

The Shepherd. In my opinion, sir, the bishops o' the Wast Indies should be blacks.

North. Prudence, James, prudence; we are alone to be sure, but the affairs of the West Indies –

The Shepherd. The bishops o' the Wast Indies should be blacks. Naebody'll ever mak me think itherwise. Mr Wilberforce and Mr M'Auley, and Mr Brougham,[10] and a' the ither Saints, have tell't us that blacks are equal to whites; and gin that be true, make bishops o' them. What for no?

North. James, you are a consistent poet, philosopher, and philanthropist. Pray, how would you like to marry a black woman? How would Mr Wilberforce like it?

The Shepherd. I canna answer for Mr Wilberforce, but as for myself, I scunner at the bare idea.

North. Why, a black skin, thick lips, grizzly hair, long heels, and convex shins – what can be more delightful? But to be serious, James, do you think there is no difference between black and white?

---

[4] Thomas Moore published under the name of Thomas Little (see p. 664).
[5] *roose* praise.
[6] Coleridge's *The Friend* was published in a 3-vol. edn in 1818; his *Lay Sermons* in 1817.
[7] *jalouse* suspect.
[8] *Kubla Khan*, 41.
[9] 'The Wanderings of Cain' was published in 1828. For Taylor and Hessey, see p. 665.
[10] Abolitionists: William Wilberforce, Zachary Macaulay (founder of the Society for the Abolition of the Slave-Trade), Henry Brougham.

The Shepherd. You're drawing me into an argument about the Wast Indies, and the neegars. I ken naething about it. I hate slavery as an abstract idea, but it's a necessary evil, and I canna believe a' thae stories about cruelty. There's nae fun or amusement in whipping women to death – and as for a skelp[11] or twa, what's the harm? Hand me ower the rum and sugar, sir.

Thomas De Quincey (1785–1859)

While still a student at Oxford, De Quincey became a correspondent of Wordsworth, whose poetry he deeply admired; he moved into Dove Cottage in October 1809 after the Wordsworths were compelled through lack of space to move to Allan Bank. Through Wordsworth he met Coleridge, who also helped to shape his thinking. The Confessions of an English Opium-Eater *(1822), which was serialized in the* London Magazine *in 1821, is his most important single work. The claims it made for opium were shocking even to the likes of Coleridge, who, in 1833, called the* Confessions *'a wicked book, a monstrous exaggeration' (*Table Talk, i. 581*). De Quincey was one of the earliest readers of the* Thirteen-Book Prelude *(unpublished until 1926), 1810–11, on which he draws heavily both in* Confessions *and its sequel,* Suspiria de Profundis, *which were published in* Blackwood's Edinburgh Magazine, March–July 1845. *In particular, his theory of 'involutes', expounded on p. 689 below, depends on Wordsworth's spots of time (*Prelude, xi. 258ff.*); the idea is taken to an extreme in 'Savannah-la-Mar' and 'The Palimpsest of the Human Brain'.*

From Confessions of an English Opium-Eater (1822)

ANN OF OXFORD STREET (PP. 47–53)

Being myself at that time of necessity a peripatetic (or a walker of the streets), I naturally fell in more frequently with those female peripatetics who are technically called street-walkers. Many of these women had occasionally taken my part against watchmen who wished to drive me off the steps of houses where I was sitting. But one amongst them, the one on whose account I have at all introduced this subject – yet no, let me not class thee, oh noble-minded Ann, with that order of women! Let me find, if it be possible, some gentler name to designate the condition of her to whose bounty and compassion, ministering to my necessities when all the world had forsaken me, I owe it that I am at this time alive.

For many weeks I had walked at nights with this poor friendless girl up and down Oxford Street, or had rested with her on steps and under the shelter of porticos. She could not be so old as myself; she told me, indeed, that she had not completed her sixteenth year. By such questions as my interest about her prompted, I had gradually drawn forth her simple history. Hers was a case of ordinary occurrence (as I have since had reason to think), and one in which, if London beneficence had better adapted its arrangements to meet it, the power of the law might oftener be interposed to protect and to avenge. But the stream of London charity flows in a channel which, though

---

[11] *skelp* slap.

deep and mighty, is yet noiseless and underground, not obvious or readily accessible to poor houseless wanderers – and it cannot be denied that the outside air and framework of London society is harsh, cruel, and repulsive. In any case, however, I saw that part of her injuries might easily have been redressed, and I urged her often and earnestly to lay her complaint before a magistrate; friendless as she was, I assured her that she would meet with immediate attention, and that English justice, which was no respecter of persons, would speedily and amply avenge her on the brutal ruffian who had plundered her little property. She promised me often that she would, but she delayed taking the steps I pointed out from time to time, for she was timid and dejected to a degree which showed how deeply sorrow had taken hold of her young heart, and perhaps she thought justly that the most upright judge and the most righteous tribunals could do nothing to repair her heaviest wrongs. Something, however, would perhaps have been done, for it had been settled between us at length (but unhappily on the very last time but one that I was ever to see her) that in a day or two we should go together before a magistrate, and that I should speak on her behalf. This little service it was destined, however, that I should never realize.

Meantime, that which she rendered to me, and which was greater than I could ever had repaid her, was this. One night, when we were pacing slowly along Oxford Street, and after a day when I had felt more than usually ill and faint, I requested her to turn off with me into Soho Square. Thither we went, and we sat down on the steps of a house which to this hour I never pass without a pang of grief and an inner act of homage to the spirit of that unhappy girl, in memory of the noble action which she there performed. Suddenly, as we sat, I grew much worse: I had been leaning my head against her bosom, and all at once I sank from her arms and fell backwards on the steps. From the sensations I then had, I felt an inner conviction of the liveliest kind that without some powerful and reviving stimulus I should either have died on the spot or should at least have sunk to a point of exhaustion from which all re-ascent under my friendless circumstances would soon have become hopeless.

Then it was, at this crisis of my fate, that my poor orphan companion – who had herself met with little but injuries in this world – stretched out a saving hand to me. Uttering a cry of terror, but without a moment's delay, she ran off into Oxford Street and in less time than could be imagined returned to me with a glass of port wine and spices, that acted upon my empty stomach (which at that time would have rejected all solid food) with an instantaneous power of restoration – and for this glass the generous girl without a murmur paid out of her own humble purse at a time (be it remembered) when she had scarcely wherewithal to purchase the bare necessaries of life, and when she could have no reason to expect that I should ever be able to reimburse her.

Oh youthful benefactress! How often in succeeding years, standing in solitary places and thinking of thee with grief of heart and perfect love – how often have I wished that, as in ancient times the curse of a father was believed to have a supernatural power, and to pursue its object with a fatal necessity of self-fulfilment, even so, the benediction of a heart oppressed with gratitude might have a like prerogative, might have power given to it from above to chase, to haunt, to waylay, to overtake, to pursue thee into the central darkness of a London brothel, or (if it were possible) into the darkness of the grave, there to awaken thee with an authentic message of peace and forgiveness, and of final reconciliation!

I do not often weep, for not only do my thoughts on subjects connected with the chief interests of man daily, nay hourly, descend a thousand fathoms 'too deep for tears';[1] not only does the sternness of my habits of thought present an antagonism to the feelings which prompt tears (wanting of necessity to those who, being protected usually by their levity from any tendency to meditative sorrow, would by that same levity be made incapable of resisting it on any casual access of such feelings) – but also I believe that all minds which have contemplated such objects as deeply as I have done, must for their own protection from utter despondency have early encouraged and cherished some tranquillizing belief as to the future balances and the hieroglyphic meanings of human sufferings. On these accounts, I am cheerful to this hour, and, as I have said, I do not often weep. Yet some feelings, though not deeper or more passionate, are more tender than others, and often, when I walk at this time in Oxford Street by dreamy lamplight, and hear those airs played on a barrel-organ which years ago solaced me and my dear companion (as I must always call her), I shed tears, and muse with myself at the mysterious dispensation which so suddenly and so critically separated us for ever.

THE MALAY (PP. 129–34)

One day a Malay knocked at my door.[1] What business a Malay could have to transact amongst English mountains I cannot conjecture, but possibly he was on his road to a seaport about forty miles distant.

The servant who opened the door to him was a young girl born and bred amongst the mountains, who had never seen an Asiatic dress of any sort – his turban, therefore, confounded her not a little – and as it turned out that his attainments in English were exactly of the same extent as hers in the Malay, there seemed to be an impassable gulf fixed between all communication of ideas (if either party had happened to possess any). In this dilemma, the girl, recollecting the reputed learning of her master (and doubtless giving me credit for a knowledge of all the languages of the earth, besides, perhaps, a few of the lunar ones), came and gave me to understand that there was a sort of demon below, whom she clearly imagined that my art could exorcise from the house.

I did not immediately go down, but when I did, the group which presented itself – arranged as it was by accident, though not very elaborate, took hold of my fancy and my eye in a way that none of the statuesque attitudes exhibited in the ballets at the opera-house, though so ostentatiously complex, had ever done. In a cottage kitchen, but panelled on the wall with dark wood that from age and rubbing resembled oak, and looking more like a rustic hall of entrance than a kitchen, stood the Malay, his turban and loose trousers of dingy white relieved upon the dark panelling. He had placed himself nearer to the girl than she seemed to relish, though her native spirit of mountain intrepidity contended with the feeling of simple awe which her countenance expressed as she gazed upon the tiger-cat before her. And a more striking picture there could not be imagined, than the beautiful English face of the girl, and its exquisite fairness, together with her erect and independent attitude, contrasted with the sallow and bilious skin of the Malay, enamelled or veneered with mahogany, by marine air, his small fierce restless eyes, thin lips, slavish gestures and adorations. Half-hidden by the ferocious-looking Malay was a little child from a neighbouring cottage who had

---

ANN OF OXFORD STREET
[1] Wordsworth, 'Ode', 206.

THE MALAY
[1] De Quincey moved into Dove Cottage, Grasmere, in 1809.

crept in after him and was now in the act of reverting its head, and gazing upwards at the turban and the fiery eyes beneath it, whilst with one hand he caught at the dress of the young woman for protection.

My knowledge of the oriental tongues is not remarkably extensive, being indeed confined to two words: the Arabic word for barley, and the Turkish for opium (madjoon), which I have learnt from *Anastasius*.[2] And as I had neither a Malay dictionary, nor even Adelung's *Mithridates*,[3] which might have helped me to a few words, I addressed him in some lines from the *Iliad*, considering that, of such languages as I possessed, Greek, in point of longitude, came geographically nearest to an oriental one. He worshipped me in a most devout manner, and replied in what I suppose was Malay. In this way I saved my reputation with my neighbours, for the Malay had no means of betraying the secret. He lay down upon the floor for about an hour, and then pursued his journey.

On his departure, I presented him with a piece of opium. To him, as an orientalist, I concluded that opium must be familiar, and the expression of his face convinced me that it was. Nevertheless, I was struck with some little consternation when I saw him suddenly raise his hand to his mouth and (in the schoolboy phrase) bolt the whole, divided into three pieces, at one mouthful. The quantity was enough to kill three dragoons and their horses, and I felt some alarm for the poor creature – but what could be done? I had given him the opium in compassion for his solitary life, on recollecting that, if he had travelled on foot from London, it must be nearly three weeks since he could have exchanged a thought with any human being. I could not think of violating the laws of hospitality by having him seized and drenched with an emetic, and thus frightening him into a notion that we were going to sacrifice him to some English idol. No – there was clearly no help for it. He took his leave, and for some days I felt anxious; but as I never heard of any Malay being found dead, I became convinced that he was used to opium, and that I must have done him the service I designed, by giving him one night of respite from the pains of wandering.

This incident I have digressed to mention because this Malay (partly from the picturesque exhibition he assisted to frame, partly from the anxiety I connected with his image for some days) fastened afterwards upon my dreams, and brought other Malays with him worse than himself, that ran amuck at me, and led me into a world of troubles.

THE PAINS OF OPIUM (PP. 155–60)

I now pass to what is the main subject of these latter confessions – to the history and journal of what took place in my dreams, for these were the immediate and proximate cause of my acutest suffering.

The first notice I had of any important change going on in this part of my physical economy, was from the reawakening of a state of eye generally incident to childhood or exalted states of irritability. I know not whether my reader is aware that many children – perhaps most – have a power of painting, as it were, upon the darkness, all sorts of phantoms. In some, that power is simply a mechanic affection of the eye; others have a voluntary or a semi-voluntary power to dismiss or to summon them – or, as a child once said to me when I questioned him on this matter, 'I can tell them

---

[2] Popular novel (1819) by Thomas Hope (1770–1831), attributed to Byron. [3] Polyglot grammar and dictionary.

to go and they go, but sometimes they come when I don't tell them to come.' Whereupon I told him that he had almost as unlimited a command over apparitions as a Roman centurion over his soldiers.[1]

In the middle of 1817, I think it was, that this faculty became positively distressing to me. At night, when I lay awake in bed, vast processions passed along in mournful pomp, friezes of never-ending stories that to my feelings were as sad and solemn as if they were stories drawn from times before Oedipus or Priam – before Tyre, before Memphis.[2] And at the same time a corresponding change took place in my dreams; a theatre seemed suddenly opened and lighted up within my brain, which presented nightly spectacles of more than earthly splendour. And the four following facts may be mentioned as noticeable at this time:

1. That, as the creative state of the eye increased, a sympathy seemed to arise between the waking and the dreaming states of the brain in one point – that whatsoever I happened to call up and to trace by a voluntary act upon the darkness was very apt to transfer itself to my dreams, so that I feared to exercise this faculty, for, as Midas turned all things to gold that yet baffled his hopes and defrauded his human desires, so whatsoever things capable of being visually represented I did but think of in the darkness, immediately shaped themselves into phantoms of the eye, and, by a process apparently no less inevitable, when thus once traced in faint and visionary colours, like writings in sympathetic ink, they were drawn out by the fierce chemistry of my dreams into insufferable splendour that fretted my heart.

2. For this and all other changes in my dreams were accompanied by deep-seated anxiety and gloomy melancholy, such as are wholly incommunicable by words. I seemed every night to descend – not metaphorically, but literally to descend, into chasms and sunless abysses, depths below depths, from which it seemed hopeless that I could ever re-ascend. Nor did I, by waking, feel that I *had* re-ascended. This I do not dwell upon, because the state of gloom which attended these gorgeous spectacles, amounting at least to utter darkness, as of some suicidal despondency, cannot be approached by words.

3. The sense of space and, in the end, the sense of time, were both powerfully affected. Buildings, landscapes, etc., were exhibited in proportions so vast as the bodily eye is not fitted to receive. Space swelled and was amplified to an extent of unutterable infinity. This however did not disturb me so much as the vast expansion of time: I sometimes seemed to have lived for 70 or 100 years in one night – nay, sometimes had feelings representative of a millennium passed in that time, or, however, of a duration far beyond the limits of any human experience.

4. The minutest incidents of childhood, or forgotten scenes of later years, were often revived. I could not be said to recollect them, for if I had been told of them when waking, I should not have been able to acknowledge them as parts of my past experience. But placed as they were before me, in dreams like intuitions, and clothed in all their evanescent circumstances and accompanying feelings, I *recognized* them instantaneously. I was once told by a near relative of mine[3] that, having in her

---

THE PAINS OF OPIUM

[1] Cf. Matt. 8: 9.

[2] Oedipus and Priam were legendary kings; Tyre was a Phoenician seaport founded in 1400 BC; the Egyptian city of Memphis dates from 3000 BC.

[3] De Quincey's mother, whose story is told in detail on p. 693 below.

childhood fallen into a river, and being on the very verge of death but for the critical assistance which reached her, she saw in a moment her whole life, in its minutest incidents, arrayed before her simultaneously as in a mirror, and she had a faculty developed as suddenly for comprehending the whole and every part. This, from some opium experiences of mine, I can believe; I have indeed seen the same thing asserted twice in modern books, and accompanied by a remark which I am convinced is true – viz. that the dread book of account which the scriptures speak of is, in fact, the mind itself of each individual. Of this at least I feel assured: that there is no such thing as *forgetting* possible to the mind; a thousand accidents may and will interpose a veil between our present consciousness and the secret inscriptions on the mind – accidents of the same sort will also rend away this veil. But alike, whether veiled or unveiled, the inscription remains for ever, just as the stars seem to withdraw before the common light of day, whereas in fact we all know that it is the light which is drawn over them as a veil, and that they are waiting to be revealed when the obscuring daylight shall have withdrawn.

ORIENTAL DREAMS (PP. 167–72)

May 1818

The Malay has been a fearful enemy for months. I have been every night, through his means, transported into Asiatic scenes. I know not whether others share in my feelings on this point, but I have often thought that if I were compelled to forego England and to live in China and among Chinese manners and modes of life and scenery, I should go mad.

The causes of my horror lie deep, and some of them must be common to others. Southern Asia, in general, is the seat of awful images and associations. As the cradle of the human race, it would alone have a dim and reverential feeling connected with it. But there are other reasons. No man can pretend that the wild, barbarous, and capricious superstitions of Africa, or of savage tribes elsewhere, affect him in the way that he is affected by the ancient, monumental, cruel, and elaborate religions of Indostan, etc. The mere antiquity of Asiatic things, of their institutions, histories, modes of faith, etc., is so impressive, that to me the vast age of the race and name overpowers the sense of youth in the individual. A young Chinese seems to me an antediluvian man renewed. Even Englishmen, though not bred in any knowledge of such institutions, cannot but shudder at the mystic sublimity of castes that have flowed apart and refused to mix, through such immemorial tracts of time – nor can any man fail to be awed by the names of the Ganges or the Euphrates.

It contributes much to these feelings that southern Asia is, and has been for thousands of years, the part of the earth most swarming with human life – the great *officina gentium*.[1] Man is a weed in those regions. The vast empires also, into which the enormous population of Asia has always been cast, give a further sublimity to the feelings associated with all oriental names or images. In China, over and above what it has in common with the rest of southern Asia, I am terrified by the modes of life, by the manners, and the barrier of utter abhorrence and want of sympathy placed between us by feelings deeper than I can analyze. I could sooner live with lunatics or brute animals. All this, and much more than I can say or have time to say, the reader must

---

ORIENTAL DREAMS
1   *officina gentium* workshop of peoples.

enter into before he can comprehend the unimaginable horror which these dreams of oriental imagery and mythological tortures impressed upon me.

Under the connecting feeling of tropical heat and vertical sunlights, I brought together all creatures, birds, beasts, reptiles, all trees and plants, usages and appearances that are found in all tropical regions, and assembled them together in China or Indostan. From kindred feelings I soon brought Egypt and all her gods under the same law. I was stared at, hooted at, grinned at, chattered at, by monkeys, by paroquets, by cockatoos. I ran into pagodas and was fixed for centuries at the summit, or in secret rooms. I was the idol, I was the priest, I was worshipped, I was sacrificed. I fled from the wrath of Brama through all the forests of Asia. Vishnu hated me. Seeva laid wait for me. I came suddenly upon Isis and Osiris.[2] I had done a deed, they said, which the ibis[3] and the crocodile trembled at. I was buried for a thousand years in stone coffins, with mummies and sphinxes, in narrow chambers at the heart of eternal pyramids. I was kissed with cancerous kisses by crocodiles, and laid confounded with all unutterable slimy things amongst reeds and Nilotic mud.

I thus give the reader some slight abstraction of my oriental dreams, which always filled me with such amazement at the monstrous scenery, that horror seemed absorbed for a while in sheer astonishment. Sooner or later came a reflux of feeling that swallowed up the astonishment, and left me not so much in terror as in hatred and abomination of what I saw. Over every form, and threat, and punishment, and dim sightless incarceration, brooded a sense of eternity and infinity that drove me into an oppression as of madness. Into these dreams only it was (with one or two slight exceptions) that any circumstances of physical horror entered. All before had been moral and spiritual terrors, but here the main agents were ugly birds, or snakes, or crocodiles – especially the last. The cursed crocodile became to me the object of more horror than almost all the rest. I was compelled to live with him, and (as was always the case almost in my dreams) for centuries. I escaped sometimes, and found myself in Chinese houses with cane tables, etc. All the feet of the tables, sofas, etc., soon became instinct with life. The abominable head of the crocodile, and his leering eyes, looked out at me, multiplied into a thousand repetitions – and I stood loathing and fascinated. And so often did this hideous reptile haunt my dreams, that many times the very same dream was broken up in the very same way: I heard gentle voices speaking to me (I hear everything when I am sleeping), and instantly I awoke.

It was broad noon, and my children were standing, hand in hand, at my bedside, come to show me their coloured shoes or new frocks, or to let me see them dressed for going out. I protest that so awful was the transition from the damned crocodile and the other unutterable monsters and abortions of my dreams to the sight of innocent *human* natures and of infancy, that, in the mighty and sudden revulsion of mind, I wept, and could not forbear it, as I kissed their faces.

EASTER SUNDAY (PP. 173–7)

June 1819

I have had occasion to remark, at various periods of my life, that the deaths of those whom we love – and indeed the contemplation of death generally – is, *caeteris*

---

[2] Brahma, Vishnu and Seeva are Indian deities; Isis and Osiris are Egyptian deities.

[3] *ibis* black and white bird worshipped by ancient Egyptians.

paribus,[1] more affecting in summer than in any other season of the year. And the reasons are these three, I think:

first, that the visible heavens in summer appear far higher, more distant, and (if such a solecism may be excused) more infinite; the clouds, by which chiefly the eye expounds the distance of the blue pavilion stretched over our heads, are in summer more voluminous, massed, and accumulated in far grander and more towering piles;

secondly, the light and the appearances of the declining and the setting sun are much more fitted to be types and characters of the Infinite;[2]

and thirdly (which is the main reason), the exuberant and riotous prodigality of life naturally forces the mind more powerfully upon the antagonist thought of death and the wintry sterility of the grave – for it may be observed generally that wherever two thoughts stand related to each other by a law of antagonism, and exist, as it were, by mutual repulsion, they are apt to suggest each other.

On these accounts it is that I find it impossible to banish the thought of death when I am walking alone in the endless days of summer, and any particular death, if not more affecting, at least haunts my mind more obstinately and besiegingly in that season. Perhaps this cause, and a slight incident which I omit, might have been the immediate occasions of the following dream – to which, however, a predisposition must always have existed in my mind. But having been once roused, it never left me, and split into a thousand fantastic varieties, which often suddenly reunited and composed again the original dream.

I thought that it was a Sunday morning in May, that it was Easter Sunday, and as yet very early in the morning. I was standing, as it seemed to me, at the door of my own cottage. Right before me lay the very scene which could really be commanded from that situation, but exalted (as was usual) and solemnized by the power of dreams. There were the same mountains and the same lovely valley at their feet, but the mountains were raised to more than Alpine height, and there was interspace far larger between them of meadows and forest lawns. The hedges were rich with white roses, and no living creature was to be seen, excepting that in the green churchyard there were cattle tranquilly reposing upon the verdant graves, and particularly round about the grave of a child[3] whom I had tenderly loved, just as I had really beheld them, a little before sunrise in the same summer, when that child died. I gazed upon the well-known scene, and I said aloud (as I thought) to myself, 'It yet wants much of sunrise; and it is Easter Sunday, and that is the day on which they celebrate the first fruits of resurrection. I will walk abroad. Old griefs shall be forgotten today, for the air is cool and still, and the hills are high, and stretch away to heaven, and the forest-glades are as quiet as the churchyard; and, with the dew, I can wash the fever from my forehead, and then I shall be unhappy no longer.'

And I turned as if to open my garden gate – and immediately I saw upon the left a scene far different, but which yet the power of dreams had reconciled into harmony with the other. The scene was an oriental one, and there also it was Easter Sunday and very early in the morning. And at a vast distance were visible, as a stain upon the horizon, the domes and cupolas of a great city – an image or faint abstraction caught

---

Easter Sunday
[1]   all things being equal.
[2]   De Quincey echoes Wordsworth, *Thirteen-Book Prelude*, vi. 571: 'types and symbols of eternity'.

[3]   Catherine Wordsworth (1808–12), the poet's daughter and a favourite of De Quincey.

perhaps in childhood from some picture of Jerusalem. And not a bowshot from me, upon a stone and shaded by Judean palms, there sat a woman – and I looked – and it was – Ann! She fixed her eyes upon me earnestly, and I said to her at length, 'So then I have found you at last.' I waited, but she answered me not a word. Her face was the same as when I saw it last, and yet again how different! Seventeen years ago, when the lamplight fell upon her face, as for the last time I kissed her lips (lips, Ann, that to me were not polluted), her eyes were streaming with tears; the tears were now wiped away. She seemed more beautiful than she was at that time, but in all other points the same, and not older. Her looks were tranquil, but with unusual solemnity of expression, and I now gazed upon her with some awe.

But suddenly her countenance grew dim, and, turning to the mountains, I perceived vapours rolling between us. In a moment all had vanished; thick darkness came on, and, in the twinkling of an eye, I was far away from mountains, and by lamplight in Oxford Street, walking again with Ann – just as we walked seventeen years before when we were both children.

From London Magazine, 8 (1823) 353–6

ON THE KNOCKING AT THE GATE IN MACBETH (FIRST PUBLISHED UNDER THE PSEUDONYM, 'X.Y.Z.')

From my boyish days I had always felt a great perplexity on one point in *Macbeth*. It was this: the knocking at the gate which succeeds to the murder of Duncan[1] produced to my feelings an effect for which I never could account. The effect was that it reflected back upon the murder a peculiar awfulness and a depth of solemnity. Yet however obstinately I endeavoured with my understanding to comprehend this, for many years I never could see *why* it should produce such an effect.

Here I pause for one moment to exhort the reader never to pay any attention to his understanding when it stands in opposition to any other faculty of his mind. The mere understanding, however useful and indispensable, is the meanest faculty in the human mind and the most to be distrusted – and yet the great majority of people trust to nothing else, which may do for ordinary life, but not for philosophic purposes. Of this, out of ten thousand instances that I might produce, I will cite one. Ask of any person whatsoever, who is not previously prepared for the demand by a knowledge of perspective, to draw in the rudest way the commonest appearance which depends upon the laws of that science – as for instance, to represent the effect of two walls standing at right angles to each other, or the appearance of the houses on each side of a street, as seen by a person looking down the street from one extremity. Now in all cases, unless the person has happened to observe in pictures how it is that artists produce these effects, he will be utterly unable to make the smallest approximation to it. Yet why? For he has actually seen the effect every day of his life. The reason is that he allows his understanding to overrule his eyes. His understanding, which includes no intuitive knowledge of the laws of vision, can furnish him with no reason why a line which is known and can be proved to be a horizontal line, should not *appear* a horizontal line; a line that made any angle with the perpendicular less than a right angle

---

ON THE KNOCKING AT THE GATE IN MACBETH
[1] *Macbeth*, II. ii. 54.

would seem to him to indicate that his houses were all tumbling down together. Accordingly he makes the line of his houses a horizontal line and fails of course to produce the effect demanded.

Here then is one instance out of many in which not only the understanding is allowed to overrule the eyes, but where the understanding is positively allowed to obliterate the eyes as it were. For not only does the man believe the evidence of his understanding in opposition to that of his eyes, but (which is monstrous!) the idiot is not aware that his eyes ever gave such evidence. He does not know that he has seen (and therefore *quoad*[2] his consciousness has *not* seen) that which he *has* seen every day of his life.

But to return from this digression. My understanding could furnish no reason why the knocking at the gate in *Macbeth* should produce any effect direct or reflected; in fact, my understanding said positively that it could *not* produce any effect. But I knew better. I felt that it did, and I waited and clung to the problem until further knowledge should enable me to solve it. At length, in 1812, Mr Williams made his début on the stage of Ratcliffe Highway, and executed those unparalleled murders which have procured for him such a brilliant and undying reputation.

On which murders, by the way, I must observe that in one respect they have had an ill effect, by making the connoisseur in murder very fastidious in his taste and dissatisfied with anything that has been since done in that line. All other murders look pale by the deep crimson of his – and as an amateur once said to me in a querulous tone, 'There has been absolutely nothing *doing* since his time, or nothing that's worth speaking of.' But this is wrong, for it is unreasonable to expect all men to be great artists, and born with the genius of Mr Williams.

Now it will be remembered that in the first of these murders (that of the Marrs) the same incident (of a knocking at the door soon after the work of extermination was complete) did actually occur which the genius of Shakespeare had invented[3] – and all good judges and the most eminent dilettanti acknowledged the felicity of Shakespeare's suggestion as soon as it was actually realized. Here then was a fresh proof that I had been right in relying on my own feeling in opposition to my understanding, and again I set myself to study the problem. At length I solved it to my own satisfaction, and my solution is this. Murder in ordinary cases, where the sympathy is wholly directed to the case of the murdered person, is an incident of coarse and vulgar horror, and for this reason – that it flings the interest exclusively upon the natural but ignoble instinct by which we cleave to life (an instinct which, as being indispensable to the primal law of self-preservation, is the same in kind, though different in degree, amongst all living creatures) – this instinct therefore, because it annihilates all distinctions and degrades the greatest of men to the level of 'the poor beetle that we tread on',[4] exhibits human nature in its most abject and humiliating attitude.

Such an attitude would little suit the purposes of the poet. What then must he do? He must throw the interest on the murderer: our sympathy must be with *him* (of course I mean a sympathy of comprehension, a sympathy by which we enter into his feelings and are made to understand them – not a sympathy of pity or approbation). In the

---

[2] *quoad* with respect to.
[3] A servant-girl sent out on an errand returned and knocked at the door while Williams, who had murdered the entire family, was still inside the house.

[4] *Measure for Measure*, III. i. 78.

murdered person all strife of thought, all flux and reflux of passion and of purpose, are crushed by one overwhelming panic: the fear of instant death smites him 'with its petrific mace'.[5] But in the murderer, such a murderer as a poet will condescend to, there must be raging some great storm of passion – jealousy, ambition, vengeance, hatred – which will create a hell within him, and into this hell we are to look. In *Macbeth*, for the sake of gratifying his own enormous and teeming faculty of creation, Shakespeare has introduced two murderers, and as usual in his hands, they are remarkably discriminated. But though in Macbeth the strife of mind is greater than in his wife, the tiger-spirit not so awake, and his feelings caught chiefly by contagion from her – yet, as both were finally involved in the guilt of murder, the murderous mind of necessity is finally to be presumed in both. This was to be expressed; and on its own account, as well as to make it a more proportionable antagonist to the unoffending nature of their victim, 'the gracious Duncan',[6] and adequately to expound 'the deep damnation of his taking off',[7] this was to be expressed with peculiar energy. We were to be made to feel that the human nature (i.e. the divine nature of love and mercy, spread through the hearts of all creatures, and seldom utterly withdrawn from man) was gone, vanished, extinct – and that the fiendish nature had taken its place. And as this effect is marvellously accomplished in the dialogues and soliloquies themselves, so it is finally consummated by the expedient under consideration – and it is to this that I now solicit the reader's attention.

If the reader has ever witnessed a wife, daughter or sister in a fainting fit, he may chance to have observed that the most affecting moment in such a spectacle is that in which a sigh and a stirring announce the recommencement of suspended life. Or if the reader has ever been present in a vast metropolis on the day when some great national idol was carried in funeral pomp to his grave, and chancing to walk near to the course through which it passed, has felt powerfully, in the silence and desertion of the streets and in the stagnation of ordinary business, the deep interest which at that moment was possessing the heart of man; if all at once he should hear the deathlike stillness broken up by the sound of wheels rattling away from the scene, and making known that the transitory vision was dissolved, he will be aware that at no moment was his sense of the complete suspension and pause in ordinary human concerns so full and affecting as at that moment when the suspension ceases, and the goings-on of human life are suddenly resumed. All action in any direction is best expounded, measured, and made apprehensible, by reaction.

Now apply this to the case in *Macbeth*. Here, as I have said, the retiring of the human heart and the entrance of the fiendish heart was to be expressed and made sensible. Another world has stepped in, and the murderers are taken out of the region of human things, human purposes, human desires. They are transfigured: Lady Macbeth is 'unsexed',[8] Macbeth has forgot that he was born of woman, both are conformed to the image of devils, and the world of devils is suddenly revealed. But how shall this be conveyed and made palpable? In order that a new world may step in, this world must for a time disappear. The murderers and the murder must be insulated, cut off by an immeasurable gulf from the ordinary tide and succession of human affairs, locked up and sequestered in some deep recess; we must be made sensible that the world of ordinary life is suddenly arrested, laid asleep, tranced, racked into a dread armistice;

---

[5] *Paradise Lost*, x. 294.
[6] *Macbeth*, III. i. 65.
[7] *Macbeth*, I. vii. 20.
[8] *Macbeth*, I. v. 41.

time must be annihilated, relation to things without abolished, and all must pass self-withdrawn into a deep syncope and suspension of earthly passion.

Hence it is that when the deed is done, when the work of darkness is perfect, then the world of darkness passes away like a pageantry in the clouds. The knocking at the gate is heard, and it makes known audibly that the reaction has commenced – the human has made its reflux upon the fiendish, the pulses of life are beginning to beat again, and the re-establishment of the goings-on of the world in which we live first makes us profoundly sensible of the awful parenthesis that had suspended them.

Oh mighty poet! Thy works are not as those of other men, simply and merely great works of art, but are also like the phenomena of nature, like the sun and the sea, the stars and the flowers, like frost and snow, rain and dew, hailstorm and thunder – which are to be studied with entire submission of our own faculties, and in the perfect faith that in them there can be no too much or too little, nothing useless or inert, but that the further we press in our discoveries, the more we shall see proofs of design and self-supporting arrangement where the careless eye had seen nothing but accident.

N.B. In the above specimen of psychological criticism, I have purposely omitted to notice another use of the knocking at the gate (viz. the opposition and contrast which it produces in the porter's comments to the scenes immediately preceding) because this use is tolerably obvious to all who are accustomed to reflect on what they read. A third use also, subservient to the scenical illusion, has been lately noticed by a critic[9] in the *London Magazine*. I fully agree with him, but it did not fall in my way to insist on this.

From Tait's Edinburgh Magazine, 6 (1839) 94

ON WORDSWORTH'S 'THERE WAS A BOY'

There is amongst the poems of Wordsworth one most ludicrously misconstrued by his critics, which offers a philosophical hint upon this subject, of great instruction. I will preface it with the little incident which first led Wordsworth into a commentary upon his own meaning.

One night, as often enough happened, during the Peninsular war,[1] he and I walked up Dunmail Raise from Grasmere, about midnight, in order to meet the carrier who brought the London newspapers by a circuitous course from Keswick. The case was this. Coleridge, for many years, received a copy of *The Courier*[2] as a mark of esteem, and in acknowledgement of his many contributions to it, from one of the proprietors, Mr Daniel Stuart. This went up in any case, let Coleridge be where he might, to Mrs Coleridge. For a single day it stayed at Keswick for the use of Southey, and on the next it came on to Wordsworth by the slow conveyance of a carrier, plying with a long train of carts between Whitehaven and Kendal. Many a time the force of storms or floods

[9] George Darley (as John Lacy) in his 'Third Letter to the Dramatists of the Day', *London Magazine*, 8 (1823), 275–83, p. 276.

ON WORDSWORTH'S 'THERE WAS A BOY'

[1] *the Peninsular war* war in the Spanish and Portuguese peninsula, 1808–14, between the French

under Napoleon, and the English, Spanish, and Portuguese under Wellington.

[2] Quality evening newspaper during the early nineteenth century, to which Coleridge, Wordsworth, Lamb, and Southey contributed.

would compel the carrier to stop on his route, five miles short of Grasmere at Wythburn, or even eight miles short at Legberthwaite. But as there was always hope until one or two o'clock in the morning, often and often it would happen that, in the deadly impatience for earlier intelligence, Wordsworth and I would walk off to meet him about midnight, to a distance of three or four miles.

Upon one of these occasions, when some great crisis in Spain was daily apprehended, we had waited for an hour or more, sitting upon one of the many huge blocks of stone which lie scattered over that narrow field of battle on the desolate frontier of Cumberland and Westmorland, where King Dunmail with all his peerage fell more than a thousand years ago. The time had arrived, at length, that all hope for that night had left us. No sound came up through the winding valleys that stretched to the north, and the few cottage lights, gleaming at wide distances from recesses amidst the rocky hills, had long been extinct. At intervals, Wordsworth had stretched himself at length on the high road, applying his ear to the ground so as to catch any sound of wheels that might be groaning along at a distance.

Once, when he was slowly rising from this effort, his eye caught a bright star that was glittering between the brow of Seat Sandal and of the mighty Helvellyn. He gazed upon it for a minute or so, and then, upon turning away to descend into Grasmere, he made the following explanation. 'I have remarked from my earliest days that if, under any circumstances, the attention is energetically braced up to an act of steady observation or of steady expectation, then, if this intense condition of vigilance should suddenly relax, at that moment any beautiful, any impressive visual object, or collection of objects, falling upon the eye, is carried to the heart with a power not known under other circumstances. Just now, my ear was placed upon the stretch in order to catch any sound of wheels that might come down upon the lake of Wythburn from the Keswick road; at the very instant when I raised my head from the ground in final abandonment of hope for this night, at the very instant when the organs of attention were all at once relaxing from their tension, the bright star hanging in the air above those outlines of massy blackness fell suddenly upon my eye, and penetrated my capacity of apprehension with a pathos and a sense of the infinite that would not have arrested me under other circumstances.'

He then went on to illustrate the same psychological principle from another instance. It was an instance derived from that exquisite poem[3] in which he describes a mountain boy planting himself at twilight on the margin of some solitary bay of Windermere, and provoking the owls to a contest with himself by 'mimic hootings' blown through his hands – which of itself becomes an impressive scene to anyone able to realize to his fancy the various elements of the solitary woods and waters, the solemn vesper hour, the solitary bird, the solitary boy. Afterwards, the poem goes on to describe the boy as waiting amidst 'the pauses of his skill' for the answers of the birds, waiting with intensity of expectation. And then at length when, after waiting to no purpose, his attention began to relax – that is, in other words, under the giving way of one exclusive direction of his senses, began suddenly to allow an admission to other objects – then, in that instant, the scene actually before him, the visible scene, would enter unawares, 'With all its solemn imagery'. This complex scenery was – what?

---

[3] 'There Was a Boy', published in *Lyrical Ballads* (1800), prior to incorporation in the *Thirteen-Book Prelude*, v. 389–422.

> Was carried *far* into his heart
> With all its pomp, and that uncertain heav'n received
> Into the bosom of the steady lake.
> (*Thirteen-Book Prelude*, v. 408, 411–13)

This very expression, 'far', by which space and its infinities are attributed to the human heart, and to its capacities of re-echoing the sublimities of nature, has always struck me as with a flash of sublime revelation.

From Blackwood's Edinburgh Magazine, 57 (1845) 278–81

SUSPIRIA DE PROFUNDIS: THE AFFLICTION OF CHILDHOOD (EXTRACT)

It was upon a Sunday evening (or so people fancied) that the spark of fatal fire fell upon that train of predispositions to a brain complaint which had hitherto slumbered within her.[1] She had been permitted to drink tea at the house of a labouring man, the father of an old female servant. The sun had set when she returned in the company of this servant through meadows reeking with exhalations after a fervent day. From that time she sickened. Happily a child in such circumstances feels no anxieties. Looking upon medical men as people whose natural commission it is to heal diseases, since it is their natural function to profess it, knowing them only as *ex officio*[2] privileged to make war upon pain and sickness, I never had a misgiving about the result. I grieved indeed that my sister should lie in bed; I grieved still more sometimes to hear her moan. But all this appeared to me no more than a night of trouble on which the dawn would soon arise.

Oh moment of darkness and delirium when a nurse awakened me from that delusion, and launched God's thunderbolt at my heart in the assurance that my sister *must* die! Rightly it is said of utter, utter misery, that it 'cannot be *remembered*';[3] itself, as a remembrable thing, is swallowed up in its own chaos. Mere anarchy and confusion of mind fell upon me. Deaf and blind I was as I reeled under the revelation. I wish not to recall the circumstances of that time, when *my* agony was at its height, and hers in another sense was approaching. Enough to say that all was soon over, and the morning of that day had at last arrived which looked down upon her innocent face, sleeping the sleep from which there is no awaking, and upon me sorrowing the sorrow for which there is no consolation.

On the day after my sister's death, whilst the sweet temple of her brain was yet unviolated by human scrutiny, I formed my own scheme for seeing her once more. Not for the world would I have made this known, nor have suffered a witness to accompany me. I had never heard of feelings that take the name of 'sentimental', nor dreamed of such a possibility. But grief even in a child hates the light, and shrinks from human eyes. The house was large; there were two staircases, and by one of these I knew that about noon, when all would be quiet, I could steal up into her chamber. I imagine that it was exactly high noon when I reached the chamber door. It was locked, but the key was not taken away. Entering, I closed the door so softly that, although it

---

THE AFFLICTION OF CHILDHOOD (extract)
[1] De Quincey's sister Jane, who died in 1790, aged three.

[2] By virtue of their office.
[3] Coleridge, *Osorio*, iv. 411.

opened upon a hall which ascended through all the stories, no echo ran along the silent walls. Then turning round, I sought my sister's face. But the bed had been moved, and the back was now turned. Nothing met my eyes but one large window wide open, through which the sun of midsummer at noonday was showering down torrents of splendour. The weather was dry, the sky was cloudless, the blue depths seemed the express types of infinity,[4] and it was not possible for eye to behold or for heart to conceive any symbols more pathetic of life and the glory of life.

Let me pause for one instant in approaching a remembrance so affecting and revolutionary for my own mind, and one which (if any earthly remembrance) will survive for me in the hour of death, to remind some readers and to inform others that in the original *Opium Confessions* I endeavoured to explain the reason why death, *caeteris paribus*, is more profoundly affecting in summer than in other parts of the year – so far at least as it is liable to any modification at all from accidents of scenery or season. The reason, as I there suggested, lies in the antagonism between the tropical redundancy of life in summer and the dark sterilities of the grave. The summer we see, the grave we haunt with our thoughts; the glory is around us, the darkness is within us. And, the two coming into collision, each exalts the other into stronger relief. But in my case there was even a subtler reason why the summer had this intense power of vivifying[5] the spectacle or the thoughts of death. And, recollecting it, often I have been struck with the important truth that far more of our deepest thoughts and feelings pass to us through perplexed combinations of concrete objects, pass to us as *involutes* (if I may coin that word) in compound experiences incapable of being disentangled, than ever reach us directly, and in their own abstract shapes.

It had happened that amongst our nursery collection of books was the Bible illustrated with many pictures. And in long dark evenings, as my three sisters with myself sat by the firelight round the guard[6] of our nursery, no book was so much in request amongst us. It ruled us and swayed us as mysteriously as music. One young nurse whom we all loved, before any candle was lighted, would often strain her eyes to read it for us – and sometimes, according to her simple powers, would endeavour to explain what we found obscure. We, the children, were all constitutionally touched with pensiveness. The fitful gloom and sudden lambencies of the room by firelight suited our evening state of feelings, and they suited also the divine revelations of power and mysterious beauty which awed us. Above all, the story of a just man – man and yet *not* man, real above all things and yet shadowy above all things, who had suffered the passion of death in Palestine, slept upon our minds like early dawn upon the waters. The nurse knew and explained to us the chief differences in oriental climates, and all these differences (as it happens) express themselves in the great varieties of summer. The cloudless sunlights of Syria – those seemed to argue everlasting summer; the disciples plucking the ears of corn – that *must* be summer; but above all the very name of Palm Sunday (a festival in the English church) troubled me like an anthem. 'Sunday?' What was *that*? That was the day of peace which masked another peace deeper than the heart of man can comprehend. 'Palms?' What were they? *That* was an equivocal word: 'palms' in the sense of 'trophies' expressed the pomps of life; 'palms' as a product of nature expressed the pomps of summer. Yet still even this explanation does

---

[4] Cf. *Thirteen-Book Prelude*, vi. 571: 'types and symbols of eternity'.

[5] *vivifying* As De Quincey was aware, Wordsworth had used this word to describe the spots of time in early versions of The *Prelude*.

[6] *guard* fireguard.

not suffice: it was not merely by the peace and by the summer, by the deep sound of rest below all rest and of ascending glory, that I had been haunted. It was also because Jerusalem stood near to those deep images both in time and in place. The great event of Jerusalem was at hand when Palm Sunday came, and the scene of that Sunday was near in place to Jerusalem. Yet what then was Jerusalem? Did I fancy it to be the *omphalos* (navel) of the earth? That pretension had once been made for Jerusalem, and once for Delphi – and both pretensions had become ridiculous, as the figure of the planet became known. Yes – but if not of the earth, for earth's tenant Jerusalem was the *omphalos* of mortality. Yet how? There on the contrary it was, as we infants understood, that mortality had been trampled underfoot. True, but for that very reason there it was that mortality had opened its very gloomiest crater. There it was indeed that the human had risen on wings from the grave. But for that reason there also it was that the divine had been swallowed up by the abyss; the lesser star could not rise before the greater would submit to eclipse. Summer, therefore, had connected itself with death not merely as a mode of antagonism, but also through intricate relations to scriptural scenery and events.

Out of this digression, which was almost necessary for the purpose of showing how inextricably my feelings and images of death were entangled with those of summer, I return to the bedchamber of my sister. From the gorgeous sunlight I turned round to the corpse. There lay the sweet childish figure, there the angel face – and, as people usually fancy, it was said in the house that no features had suffered any change. Had they not? The forehead indeed, the serene and noble forehead – *that* might be the same. But the frozen eyelids, the darkness that seemed to steal from beneath them, the marble lips, the stiffening hands laid palm to palm as if repeating the supplications of closing anguish – could these be mistaken for life? Had it been so, wherefore did I not spring to those heavenly lips with tears and never-ending kisses? But so it was *not*.

I stood checked for a moment – awe, not fear, fell upon me – and whilst I stood, a solemn wind began to blow, the most mournful that ear ever heard. Mournful! That is saying nothing. It was a wind that had swept the fields of mortality for a hundred centuries. Many times since, upon a summer day, when the sun is about the hottest, I have remarked the same wind arising and uttering the same hollow, solemn, Memnonian, but saintly swell; it is in this world the one sole *audible* symbol of eternity. And three times in my life I have happened to hear the same sound in the same circumstances, viz. when standing between an open window and a dead body on a summer day.

Instantly, when my ear caught this vast Aeolian intonation, when my eye filled with the golden fullness of life, the pomps and glory of the heavens outside, and turning when it settled upon the frost which overspread my sister's face, instantly a trance fell upon me. A vault seemed to open in the zenith of the far blue sky, a shaft which ran up for ever. I in spirit rose as if on billows that also ran up the shaft for ever, and the billows seemed to pursue the throne of God – but that also ran before us and fled away continually. The flight and the pursuit seemed to go on for ever and ever. Frost, gathering frost, some sarsar[7] wind of death, seemed to repel me. I slept, for how long I cannot say; slowly I recovered my self-possession, and found myself standing as before, close to my sister's bed.

---

[7] *sarsar* cold.

Oh flight of the solitary child to the solitary God[8] – flight from the ruined corpse to the throne that could not be ruined! How rich wert thou in truth for after-years! Rapture of grief that, being too mighty for a child to sustain, foundest a happy oblivion in a heaven-born sleep, and within that sleep didst conceal a dream whose meanings in after-years, when slowly I deciphered, suddenly there flashed upon me new light – and even by the grief of a child, as I will show you reader hereafter, were confounded the falsehoods of philosophers.

In the *Opium Confessions* I touched a little upon the extraordinary power connected with opium (after long use) of amplifying the dimensions of time. Space also it amplifies by degrees that are sometimes terrific. But time it is upon which the exalting and multiplying power of opium chiefly spends its operation. Time becomes infinitely elastic, stretching out to such immeasurable and vanishing termini that it seems ridiculous to compute the sense of it on waking by expressions commensurate to human life. As in starry fields one computes by diameters of the earth's orbit, or of Jupiter's, so in valuing the *virtual* time lived during some dreams, the measurement by generations is ridiculous, by millennia is ridiculous – by aeons, I should say (if aeons were more determinate), would be also ridiculous. On this single occasion, however, in my life, the very inverse phenomenon occurred. But why speak of it in connection with opium? Could a child of six years old have been under that influence? No, but simply because it so exactly reversed the operation of opium. Instead of a short interval expanding into a vast one, upon this occasion a long one had contracted into a minute. I have reason to believe that a *very* long one had elapsed during this wandering or suspension of my perfect mind. When I returned to myself, there was a foot (or I fancied so) on the stairs. I was alarmed. For I believed that, if anybody should detect me, means would be taken to prevent my coming again. Hastily, therefore, I kissed the lips that I should kiss no more, and slunk like a guilty thing[9] with stealthy steps from the room. Thus perished the vision, loveliest amongst all the shows which earth has revealed to me; thus mutilated was the parting which should have lasted for ever; thus tainted with fear was the farewell sacred to love and grief, to perfect love and perfect grief.

Oh Ahasuerus,[10] everlasting Jew! Fable or not a fable, thou when first starting on thy endless pilgrimage of woe, thou when first flying through the gates of Jerusalem and vainly yearning to leave the pursuing curse behind thee, couldst not more certainly have read thy doom of sorrow in the misgivings of thy troubled brain than I when passing for ever from my sister's room. The worm was at my heart – and, confining myself to that stage of life, I may say, the worm that could not die. For if, when standing upon the threshold of manhood, I had ceased to feel its perpetual gnawings, that was because a vast expansion of intellect, it was because new hopes, new necessities, and the frenzy of youthful blood, had translated me into a new creature. Man is doubtless *one* by some subtle nexus that we cannot perceive, extending from the new-born infant to the superannuated dotard; but as regards many affections and

---

[8] 'φυγὴ μονου πρὸς μονον. Plotinus' (De Quincey's note). De Quincey quotes the final words of *Ennead*, VI. 9. 11, line 51, in which Plotinus writes of 'deliverance from the things of this world, a life which takes no delight in the things of this world, *escape in solitude to the solitary*'.

[9] *like a guilty thing* cf. *Hamlet*, I. i. 148–9, and Wordsworth, 'Ode', 150.

[10] Because he refused Christ rest on the way to the crucifixion, Ahasuerus was doomed to wander the earth until the Day of Judgement.

passions incident to his nature at different stages, he is *not* one – the unity of man in this respect is coextensive only with the particular stage to which the passion belongs. Some passions, as that of sexual love, are celestial by one half of their origin, animal and earthy by the other half. These will not survive their own appropriate stage. But love which is *altogether* holy, like that between two children, will revisit undoubtedly by glimpses the silence and the darkness of old age – and I repeat my belief that, unless bodily torment should forbid it, that final experience in my sister's bedroom, or some other in which her innocence was concerned, will rise again for me to illuminate the hour of death.

On the day following this which I have recorded, came a body of medical men to examine the brain, and the particular nature of the complaint, for in some of its symptoms it had shown perplexing anomalies. Such is the sanctity of death (and especially of death alighting on an innocent child), that even gossiping people do not gossip on such a subject. Consequently I knew nothing of the purpose which drew together these surgeons, nor suspected anything of the cruel changes which might have been wrought in my sister's head. Long after this I saw a similar case; I surveyed the corpse (it was that of a beautiful boy eighteen years old,[11] who had died of the same complaint) one hour *after* the surgeons had laid the skull in ruins – but the dishonours of this scrutiny were hidden by bandages, and had not disturbed the repose of the countenance. So it might have been here, but if it were *not* so, then I was happy in being spared the shock, from having that marble image of peace, icy and rigid as it was, unsettled by disfiguring images. Some hours after the strangers had withdrawn, I crept again to the room, but the door was now locked, the key was taken away, and I was shut out for ever.

From Blackwood's Edinburgh Magazine, 57 (1845) 742–3

SUSPIRIA DE PROFUNDIS: THE PALIMPSEST (EXTRACT)

What else than a natural and mighty palimpsest is the human brain? Such a palimpsest is my brain; such a palimpsest, oh reader, is yours. Everlasting layers of ideas, images, feelings, have fallen upon your brain softly as light. Each succession has seemed to bury all that went before, and yet in reality not one has been extinguished. And if, in the vellum palimpsest, lying amongst the other *diplomata*[1] of human archives or libraries, there is anything fantastic or which moves to laughter – as oftentimes there is in the grotesque collisions of those successive themes, having no natural connection, which by pure accident have consecutively occupied the roll – yet in our own heaven-created palimpsest, the deep memorial palimpsest of the brain, there are not and cannot be such incoherencies. The fleeting accidents of a man's life and its external shows may indeed be irrelate and incongruous, but the organizing principles which fuse into harmony and gather about fixed predetermined centres, whatever heterogeneous elements life may have accumulated from without, will not permit the grandeur of human unity greatly to be violated, or its ultimate repose to be troubled in the retrospect from dying moments or from other great convulsions.

---

[11] William, De Quincey's son, died 1834. THE PALIMPSEST (EXTRACT)
     [1] *diplomata* historical documents.

Such a convulsion is the struggle of gradual suffocation, as in drowning – and in the original *Opium Confessions* I mentioned a case of that nature communicated to me by a lady from her own childish experience. The lady is still living, though now of unusually great age.[2] And I may mention that amongst her faults never was numbered any levity of principle, or carelessness of the most scrupulous veracity – but, on the contrary, such faults as arise from austerity, too harsh perhaps, and gloomy, indulgent neither to others nor herself. And at the time of relating this incident, when already very old, she had become religious to asceticism.

According to my present belief, she had completed her ninth year when, playing by the side of a solitary brook, she fell into one of its deepest pools. Eventually (but after what lapse of time nobody ever knew) she was saved from death by a farmer who, riding in some distant lane, had seen her rise to the surface – but not until she had descended within the abyss of death, and looked into its secrets as far, perhaps, as ever human eye *can* have looked that had permission to return. At a certain stage of this descent, a blow seemed to strike her, phosphoric radiance sprang forth from her eyeballs, and immediately a mighty theatre expanded within her brain. In a moment, in the twinkling of an eye, every act, every design of her past life lived again – arraying themselves not as a succession but as parts of a coexistence. Such a light fell upon the whole path of her life backwards into the shades of infancy, as the light perhaps which wrapped the destined apostle on his road to Damascus.[3] Yet that light blinded for a season, but hers poured celestial vision upon the brain, so that her consciousness became omnipresent at one moment to every feature in the infinite review.

This anecdote was treated sceptically at the time by some critics. But besides that it has since been confirmed by other experiences essentially the same, reported by other parties in the same circumstances who had never heard of each other. The true point for astonishment is not the *simultaneity* of arrangement under which the past events of life – though in fact successive – had formed their dread line of revelation; this was but a secondary phenomenon. The deeper lay in the resurrection itself, and the possibility of resurrection for what had so long slept in the dust. A pall deep as oblivion had been thrown by life over every trace of these experiences, and yet suddenly, at a silent command, at the signal of a blazing rocket sent up from the brain, the pall draws up and the whole depths of the theatre are exposed. Here was the greater mystery: now this mystery is liable to no doubt, for it is repeated, and ten thousand times repeated by opium, for those who are its martyrs.

Yes, reader, countless are the mysterious handwritings of grief or joy which have inscribed themselves successively upon the palimpsest of your brain – and like the annual leaves of aboriginal forests, or the undissolving snows on the Himalaya, or light falling upon light, the endless strata have covered up each other in forgetfulness. But by the hour of death, but by fever, but by the searchings of opium, all these can revive in strength. They are not dead, but sleeping. In the illustration imagined by myself, from the case of some individual palimpsest, the Grecian tragedy had seemed to be displaced, but was *not* displaced, by the monkish legend – and the monkish legend had seemed to be displaced, but was *not* displaced, by the knightly romance. In some potent convulsion of the system, all wheels back into its earliest elementary stage. The bewildering romance, light tarnished with darkness, the semi-fabulous legend, truth

---

[2] De Quincey's mother, who was over 90.   [3] St Paul; see Acts 22: 6.

celestial mixed with human falsehoods, these fade even of themselves as life advances. The romance has perished that the young man adored. The legend has gone that deluded the boy. But the deep deep tragedies of infancy, as when the child's hands were unlinked for ever from his mother's neck, or his lips for ever from his sister's kisses, these remain lurking below all, and these lurk to the last.

From Blackwood's Edinburgh Magazine, 57 (1845) 750–1

SUSPIRIA DE PROFUNDIS: FINALE TO PART I. SAVANNAH-LA-MAR

God smote Savannah-la-Mar,[1] and in one night, by earthquake, removed her, with all her towers standing and population sleeping, from the steadfast foundations of the shore to the coral floors of ocean. And God said, 'Pompeii did I bury and conceal from men through seventeen centuries: this city I will bury, but not conceal. She shall be a monument to men of my mysterious anger, set in azure light through generations to come – for I will enshrine her in a crystal dome of my tropic seas.'

This city, therefore, like a mighty galleon with all her apparel mounted, streamers flying and tackling perfect, seems floating along the noiseless depths of ocean. And oftentimes in glassy calms, through the translucid atmosphere of water that now stretches like an air-woven awning above the silent encampment, mariners from every clime look down into her courts and terraces, count her gates, and number the spires of her churches. She is one ample cemetery and has been for many a year, but in the mighty calms that brood for weeks over tropic latitudes, she fascinates the eye with a *fata Morgana*[2] revelation, as of human life still subsisting in submarine asylums sacred from the storms that torment our upper air.

Thither lured by the loveliness of cerulean depths, by the peace of human dwellings privileged from molestation, by the gleam of marble altars sleeping in everlasting sanctity, oftentimes in dreams did I and the dark Interpreter cleave the watery veil that divided us from her streets. We looked into the belfries where the pendulous bells were waiting in vain for the summons which should awaken their marriage peals; together we touched the mighty organ keys that sang no *jubilates*[3] for the ear of Heaven, that sang no requiems for the ear of human sorrow; together we searched the silent nurseries where the children were all asleep – and *had* been asleep through five generations.

'They are waiting for the heavenly dawn', whispered the Interpreter to himself, 'and when *that* comes, the bells and the organs will utter a *jubilate* repeated by the echoes of paradise.' Then, turning to me, he said, 'This is sad, this is piteous, but less would not have sufficed for the purposes of God. Look here – put into a Roman clepsydra[4] one hundred drops of water. Let these run out as the sands in an hourglass, every drop measuring the hundredth part of a second, so that each shall represent but the three-hundred-and-sixty-thousandth part of an hour. Now count the drops as they race along, and, when the fiftieth of the hundred is passing, behold! Forty-nine are not because already they have perished, and fifty are not because they are yet to come. You see, therefore, how narrow, how incalculably narrow, is the true and actual present.

SAVANNAH-LA-MAR
[1] Jamaican port destroyed by a tidal wave in 1780.
[2] Mirage seen in the Straits of Messina.

[3] songs of rejoicing; the specific reference is to Psalm 100, beginning (in the Vulgate) 'Jubilate' ('Rejoice').
[4] *clepsydra* water-clock.

Of that time which we call the present, hardly a hundredth part but belongs either to a past which has fled, or to a future which is still on the wing. It has perished, or it is not born. It was, or it is not. Yet even this approximation to the truth is *infinitely* false. For again subdivide that solitary drop which only was found to represent the present into a lower series of similar fractions, and the actual present which you arrest measures now but the thirty-sixth millionth of an hour. And so by infinite declensions the true and very present in which only we live and enjoy, will vanish into a mote of a mote, distinguishable only by a heavenly vision. Therefore the present, which only man possesses, offers less capacity for his footing than the slenderest film that ever spider twisted from her womb. Therefore, also, even this incalculable shadow from the narrowest pencil of moonlight is more transitory than geometry can measure or thought of angel can overtake. The time which *is* contracts into a mathematic point, and even that point perishes a thousand times before we can utter its birth. All is finite in the present, and even that finite is infinite in its velocity of flight towards death. But in God there is nothing finite; but in God there is nothing transitory; but in God there *can* be nothing that tends to death. Therefore it follows that for God there can be no present. The future is the present of God, and to the future it is that he sacrifices the human present. Therefore it is that he works by earthquake. Therefore it is that he works by grief. Oh deep is the ploughing of earthquake! Oh deep' – and his voice swelled like a *sanctus*⁵ rising from the choir of a cathedral – 'Oh deep is the ploughing of grief! But oftentimes less would not suffice for the agriculture of God. Upon a night of earthquake he builds a thousand years of pleasant habitations for man. Upon the sorrow of an infant, he raises oftentimes from human intellects glorious vintages that could not else have been. Less than these fierce ploughshares would not have stirred the stubborn soil. The one is needed for earth, our planet – for earth itself as the dwelling-place of man. But the other is needed yet oftener for God's mightiest intrument; yes', and he looked solemnly at myself, 'is needed for the mysterious children of the earth!'

Lady Caroline Lamb   (1785–1828)

'Then your heart, my poor Caro – what a little volcano that pours lava through your veins!', Byron told Lady Caroline Lamb in 1812 (Marchand, ii. 170). Her passionate nature emerges in the works published posthumously alongside Byron's 'Fugitive Pieces' in 1829. But her most inventive poem is probably her New Canto of Don Juan, written in Byron's persona.

A New Canto (1819)

I

I'm sick of fame – I'm gorged with it, so full
I almost could regret the happier hour

---

⁵ *sanctus* section of the Mass derived from Isa. 6: 3,
'Holy, holy, holy . . .'.

When northern oracles proclaimed me dull,
  Grieving my Lord should so mistake his power[1] –
E'en they who now my consequence would lull,   5
  And vaunt they hailed and nursed the opening flower.
Vile cheats! He knew not, impudent reviewer,
Clear spring of Helicon from common sewer.

II

'Tis said they killed the gentle-souled Montgomery;[2]
  I'll swear they did not shed for him a tear!   10
He had not spirit to revenge their mummery,
  Nor lordly purse to print and persevere.
I measured stings with 'em – a method summary –
  Not that I doubt their penitence sincere;
And I've a fancy running in my head   15
They'll like – or so by some it will be said.

III

When doomsday comes, St Paul's will be on fire
  (I should not wonder if we live to see it);
Of us, proof pickles, Heaven must rather tire
  And want a reckoning – if so, so be it: 20
Only about the cupola, or higher,
  If there's a place unoccupied, give me it –
To catch, before I touch my sinner's salary,
The first grand crackle in the whispering gallery.

IV

The ball comes tumbling with a lively crash,   25
  And splits the pavement up, and shakes the shops,
Teeth chatter, china dances, spreads the flash,
  The omnium[3] falls, the Bank of England stops;
Loyal and radical, discreet and rash,
  Each on his knees in tribulation flops;   30

A NEW CANTO (1819)
[1] Byron's first volume of poems, *Hours of Idleness*
(1807), was greeted with facetious contempt by the
Edinburgh Review. Although the review was actually
written by Henry Brougham, Byron thought that
Francis Jeffrey ('my Lord') was responsible, and took
revenge by making him the chief butt of *English Bards
and Scotch Reviewers*, (1809).
[2] The poet James Montgomery (1771–1854) was

both alive and popular in 1819. Lamb is recalling
Byron's *English Bards and Scotch Reviewers* 419–25, which
laments Montgomery's supposed death on the grounds
of his harsh treatment from the *Edinburgh Review*.
[3] *omnium* at the Stock Exchange, the aggregate
amount of the parcels of different stocks, formerly
offered by government, in raising a loan, for each unit
of capital subscribed.

The Regent raves (Moore[4] chuckling at his pain)
And sends about for ministers in vain.

V

The roaring streamers flap, red flakes are shot
   This way and that, the town is a volcano –
And yells are heard, like those provoked by Lot,   35
   Some of the Smithfield sort, and some *soprano*;
Some holy water seek, the font is hot,
   And fizzing in a tea-kettle *piano*.
Now bring your magistrates, with yeomen backed,
Bawls Belial, and read the riot act!   40

VI

The Peak of Derbyshire goes to and fro;
   Like drunken sot the Monument is reeling;
Now fierce and fiercer comes the furious glow –
   The planets, like a juggler's ball, are wheeling!
I am a graceless poet, as you know,   45
   Yet would not wish to wound a proper feeling,
Nor hint you'd hear, from saints in agitation,
The *lapsus linguae*[5] of an execration.

VII

Mark yon bright beauty in her tragic airs,
   How her clear white the mighty smother tinges!   50
Delicious chaos, that such beauty bares!
   And now those eyes outstretch their silken fringes,
Staring bewildered – and anon she tears
   Her raven tresses ere the wide flame singes –
Oh would she feel as I could do, and cherish   55
One wild forgetful rapture, ere all perish!

VIII

Who would be vain? Fair maids and ugly men
   Together rush, the dainty and the shabby

---

[4] Thomas Moore met Lamb during her affair with Byron, Mar. 1812. He was widely known as the author of a popular lampoon on court life, *The Twopenny Post Bag* (1813).

[5] *lapsus linguae* slip of the tongue.

(No gallantry will soothe ye, ladies, then),
   High dames, the wandering beggar and her *babby*,   60
In motley agony, a desperate train,
   Flocking to holy places like the Abbey,[6]
Till the black volumes, closing o'er them, scowl,
Muffling forever curse, and shriek, and howl.

IX

A woman then may rail, nor would I stint her;   65
   Her griefs, poor soul, are past redress in law –
And if this matter happen in the winter,
   There'll be at Petersburg a sudden thaw,
And Alexander's palace, every splinter
   Burn Christmas-like and merry, though the jaw   70
Of its imperial master[7] take to trembling,
As when the French were quartered in the Kremlin.[8]

X

Rare doings in the north! as trickle down
   Primeval snows, and white bears swash and caper,
And Bernadotte,[9] that swaggerer of renown,   75
   To Bonaparte again might hold a taper,
Aye, truckle[10] to him, cap in hand or crown,
   To save his distance from the sturdy vapour.
Napoleon, too, will he look blank and paly?
He hung the citizens of Moscow gaily;   80

XI

He made a gallant youth[11] his darkling prey,
   Nor e'er would massacre or murder mince;
And yet I fear, on this important day,
   To see the hero pitifully wince!
Go yield him up to Beelzebub, and say,   85
   'Pray treat him like a gentleman and prince.'
I doubt him thoroughbred, he's not a true one,
A bloodhound spaniel-crossed, and no Don Juan.

---

6 Westminster Abbey.
7 *its imperial master* Tsar Alexander I.
8 Napoleon took control of Moscow in Sept. 1812, but retreated a month later.
9 The Frenchman Jean Bernadotte became King of Sweden in May 1811, and joined the allies against Napoleon in 1813.
10 *truckle* kow-tow.
11 Nelson.

XII

Death-watches now, in every baking wall, tick
    Faster and faster, till they tick no more, 90
And Norway's copper-mines about the Baltic
    Swell, heave, and rumble with their boiling ore,
Like some griped giant's motion peristaltic,
    Then burst, and to the sea vast gutters pour;
And as the waters with the fire-stream curl, 95
Zooks! what a whizzing, roaring, sweltering whirl!

XIII

Lo! the great deep laid bare, tremendous yawning,
    Its scalding waves retiring from the shore,
Affrighted whales on dry land sudden spawning,
    And small fish fry where fish ne'er fried before. 100
No Christian eye shall see another dawning –
    The Turkish infidel may now restore
His wives to liberty, and, ere to hell he go,
Roll to the bottom of the Archipelago!

XIV

And now, ye coward sinners (I'm a bold one, 105
    Scorning all here, nor caring for hereafter,
A radical, a stubborn, and an old one),
    Behold! each riding on a burning rafter,
The devils (in my arms I long to fold one)
    Splitting their blue and brazen sides with laughter, 110
Play at snapdragon[12] in their merry fits,
O'er some conventicle for hypocrites.

XV

Aye, serve the skulkers, with their looks so meek,
    As they've, no doubt, served lobsters in their time
(Poor *blacks*! No Wilberforce for them can speak, 115
    Pleading their colour is their only crime);
Trundle them all to bubble and to squeak –
    No doubt they shut their ears against my rhyme,

---

[12] Game in which the players snatch raisins out of
a bowl of burning brandy.

Yet sneak, rank elders, fearful of denials,
To pick Susannahs up in Seven Dials.[13]   120

XVI

Brave fiends! for usurers and misers melt
   And make a hell-broth of their cursed gold!
On all who mock at want they never felt,
   On all whose consciences are bought and sold,
E'en as on me, be stern damnation dealt –   125
   And lawyers, damn them all! The blood runs cold,
That man should deal with misery to mock it,
And filch an only shilling from its pocket.

XVII

Aye, damn them all, a deep damnation wait
   On all such callous, crooked, hopeless souls!   130
Ne'er mince the matter to discriminate,
   But let the devil strike them from the rolls:[14]
'Twill cheer their clients to behold their fate,
   And round their bonfires dance in merry shoals!
Some poor men's tales I've heard upon my journeys   135
Would make a bishop long to roast attorneys!

XVIII

Perhaps the thing may take another turn,
   And one smart shock may split the world in two,
And I in Italy,[15] you soon may learn,
   On t'other half am reeling far from you.   140
No doubt 'twould split where first it ought to burn –
   Across some city that its sins should rue,
Some wicked capital, for instance, Paris,
And stop the melodrames from Mr Harris.[16]

XIX

Save London, none is wickeder or bigger,   145
   An odious place too, in these modern times;

---

[13] Seven Dials, in the Covent Garden area of London, was a notorious red-light district.
[14] *the rolls* official list of those qualified to practise as solicitors.
[15] Byron was indeed in Italy during 1819.
[16] Thomas Harris (died 1820), proprietor and manager of Covent Garden.

Small incomes, runaways, and swindlers eager
    To fleece and dash; and then their quacks and mimes,
Their morals lax, and literary rigour,
    Their prim caesuras, and their gendered rhymes –   150
Mine never could abide their statutes critical,
They'd call them neutral or hermaphroditical.

XX

True, their poor playwrights (truth, I speak with pain)
    Yield ours a picking, and I beg their pardon;
'Tis needless – down must come poor Drury Lane,   155
    And scarcely less poor, down come Covent Garden!
If we must blaze, no squabbles will remain
    That actor's hearts against each other harden –
Committees, creditors, all wrapped in flames,
That leave no joke for Horace Smith or James.[17]   160

XXI

In rebus modus est:[18] whene'er I write
    I mean to rhapsodize, and nothing more;
If some poor nervous souls my muse affright,
    I might a strain of consolation pour,
Talk of the spotless spirits, snowy white,   165
    Which, newly clad, refreshing graves restore,
And silvery wreaths of glory round them curled
Serenely rise above the blazing world.

XXII

Free, bursting from his mound of lively green,
    Winged light as zephyr of the rosy morn,   170
The poor man smiling on the proud is seen,
    With something of a mild, forgiving scorn –
The marbled proud one, haply with the mean,
    Sole on his prayer of intercession borne:
Upward in peal harmonious they move,   175
Soft as the midnight tide of hallowed love.

---

[17] In their *Rejected Addresses*, James and Horace
Smith parodied the styles of authors who submitted
addresses for the opening of Drury Lane Theatre in
1812. 'Cui Bono' was written in the manner of *Childe
Harold*, and was admired by Byron.
[18] 'There is a measure in things.'

XXIII

The rich humane, who with their common clay
   Divided graciously, distinguished few;
Good Christians who had slept their wrongs away,
   In peace with this life, and the next in view;   180
Strugglers with tyrant passion and its prey,
   Love's single-hearted victims, sacred, true,
Who, when dishonour's path alone could save,
Bore a pure pang to an untimely grave –

XXIV

Blessed they, who wear the vital spirit out   185
   Even thus, degrading not the holy fire,
Nor bear a prostituted sense about –
   The misery of never-quenched desire
(Still quenched, still kindling, every thought devout
   Lost in the changeful torment – portion dire!).   190
Return we to our heaven, our fire and smoke,
Though now you may begin to take the joke!

XXV

What joke? My verses – mine, and all beside,
   Wild, foolish tales of Italy and Spain,
The gushing shrieks, the bubbling squeaks, the bride   195
   Of nature, blue-eyed, black-eyed, and her swain,
Kissing in grottos near the moonlit tide,[19]
   Though to all men of commonsense 'tis plain,
Except for rampant and amphibious brute,
Such damp and drizzly places would not suit.   200

XXVI

Mad world! For fame we rant, call names, and fight –
   I scorn it heartily, yet love to dazzle it,
Dark intellects by day, as shops by night,
   All with a bright, new, speculative gas lit,
Wars the blue vapour with the oil-fed light,   205
   Hot sputter Blackwood, Jeffrey, Gifford, Hazlitt[20] –

---

[19] See *Don Juan* ii 1465–88.
[20] William Blackwood (1776–1834), publisher and editor of *Blackwood's Edinburgh Magazine*; William Gifford (1756–1826), editor of the *Quarterly Review*; Jeffrey and Hazlitt were journalists, see pp. 599, 640.

The muse runs madder, and, as mine may tell,
Like a loose comet, mingles heaven and hell.

XXVII

You shall have more of her another time,
   Since gulled you will be with our flights poetic,   210
Our eight, and ten, and twenty feet sublime,
   Our maudlin, hey-down-derrified[21] pathetic;
For my part, though I'm doomed to write in rhyme,
   To read it would be worse than an emetic –
But something must be done to cure the spleen,   215
And keep my name in capitals, like Kean.[22]

From Fugitive Pieces and Reminiscences of Lord Byron with Some Original Poetry, Letters and Recollections of Lady Caroline Lamb, ed. I. Nathan (1829)

MY HEART'S FIT TO BREAK

My heart's fit to break, yet no tear fills my eye,
As I gaze on the moon, and the clouds that flit by;
The moon shines so fair, it reminds me of thee,
But the clouds that obscure it are emblems of me.

They will pass like the dreams of our pleasures and youth,   5
They will pass like the promise of honour and truth,
And bright thou shalt shine when these shadows are gone,
All radiant, serene, unobscured – but alone.

WOULD I HAD SEEN THEE DEAD AND COLD

Would I had seen thee dead and cold
   In thy lone grave asleep,
Than live, thy falsehood to behold,
   And, penitent, to weep;
For better I thy grave could see   5
Than know that thou art false to me!

Or rather, would that I had died
   When happy on thy breast;
My love had then been satisfied,
   And life's last moments blessed –   10
For they taste bliss without alloy
Who die in the sweet dream of joy.

---

[21] 'Hey down derry' is a meaningless refrain in popular ballads.   [22] Byron admired the acting of Edmund Kean.

But no, I feel the fault was mine,
    To think affection's chain
Could thy proud wayward heart confine   15
    When honour's claim was vain:
Who robs the shrine where virtue lies
Will not the stolen relic prize!

Caroline Anne Bowles (1786–1854)

Poet and essayist, established as a poet with the success of Ellen Fitzarthur *(1820). Having been a correspondent of Southey for twenty years, she married him in 1839, shortly before his decline and death in 1843.*

From Ellen Fitzarthur: A Metrical Tale (1820)

STANZAS

She died, she died; yet still to me
She comes, in sad and sober dreaming,
And from her hair a pale light streaming
Shows her as she was wont to be.

She stands in beauty by me still –   5
Alas, that death two hearts should sever
(The father and the child) who ever
Loved, and were so inseparable.

Still are her brow and bosom white,
Her raven hair the one adorning,
And her eyes, sweet as the break of morning,   10
Shine through like stars from the darkest night.

If the quick lustre of her eye
(Can such then sparkle from the grave?)
Be false, may I live still the slave   15
Of this so charming fantasy.

It matters not to me from what
Or whom she gains her beauty now;
I see my child's own sinless brow
And die – if I believe it not.   20

From Blackwood's Edinburgh Magazine, 13 (1823) 275

THERE IS A TONGUE IN EVERY LEAF (SIGNED 'C.')

There is a tongue in every leaf,
  A voice in every rill,
A voice that speaketh everywhere,
In flood and fire, through earth and air,
  A tongue that's never still!   5

'Tis the Great Spirit, wide diffused
  Through everything we see,
That with our spirits communeth
Of things mysterious – life and death,
  Time and eternity.   10

I see Him in the blazing sun
  And in the thunder-cloud;
I hear him in the mighty roar
That rusheth through the forests hoar
  When winds are piping loud.   15

I see Him, hear Him *everywhere*,
  In *all things* – darkness, light,
Silence and sound, but most of all
When slumber's dusky curtains fall
  At the dead hour of night.   20

I *feel* Him in the silent dews
  By grateful earth betrayed,
I *feel* Him in the gentle showers,
The soft south wind, the breath of flowers,
  The sunshine and the shade.   25

And yet, ungrateful that I am,
  I've turned in sullen mood
From all these things whereof He said,
When the great whole was finished,
  That they were 'very good'.   30

My sadness on the loveliest things
  Fell like unwholesome dew;
The darkness that encompassed me,
The gloom I felt so palpably,
  Mine own dark spirit threw.   35

Yet He was patient, slow to wrath,
  Though every day provoked

By selfish, pining discontent,
Acceptance cold or negligent,
    And promises revoked.   40

And still the same rich feast was spread
    For my insensate heart –
Not always so; I woke again
To join creation's rapturous strain,
    'Oh Lord, how good thou art!'   45

The clouds drew up, the shadows fled,
    The glorious sun broke out,
And love, and hope, and gratitude,
Dispelled that miserable mood
    Of darkness and of doubt.   50

Benjamin Robert Haydon (1786–1846)

Artist known for ambitious historical and religious paintings, who quarrelled with most of his patrons, fell into severe debt, and committed suicide; friend of Keats, Wordsworth, Lamb, Hazlitt, Leigh Hunt, and Elizabeth Barrett. He was a copious diarist, and one of his most important entries describes the 'immortal dinner' of 28 December 1817; in few other places are the romantics so vividly brought to life.

The Immortal Dinner

28 December 1817. Wordsworth dined with me; Keats and Lamb with a friend made up the dinner party, and a very pleasant party we had. Wordsworth was in fine and powerful cue. We had a glorious set-to on Homer, Shakespeare, Milton and Virgil. Lamb got excessively merry and witty, and his fun in the intervals of Wordsworth's deep and solemn intonations of oratory was the fun and wit of the fool in the intervals of Lear's passion. Lamb soon gets tipsy, and tipsy he got very shortly, to our infinite amusement.

'Now, you rascally lake poet', said Lamb, 'you call Voltaire a dull fellow.'[1] We all agreed there was a state of mind when he would appear so – and 'Well let us drink his health', said Lamb. 'Here's Voltaire, the Messiah of the French nation, and a very fit one!'

He then attacked me for putting in Newton,[2] 'a fellow who believed nothing unless it was as clear as the three sides of a triangle!' And then he and Keats agreed he had destroyed all the poetry of the rainbow by reducing it to a prism. It was impossible to resist them, and we drank 'Newton's health, and confusion to mathematics!' It was

---

THE IMMORTAL DINNER
[1] A reference to Wordsworth's criticism of *Candide* as the 'dull product of a scoffer's pen' (*Excursion*, ii. 484).

[2] Haydon inserted the face of Newton into the background of his painting 'Christ's Triumphant Entry into Jerusalem'.

delightful to see the good humour of Wordsworth in giving in to all our frolics without affectation and laughing as heartily as the best of us.

By this time other visitors began to drop in, and a Mr Ritchie,[3] who is going to penetrate into the interior of Africa. I introduced him to Wordsworth as such, and the conversation got into a new train. After some time, Lamb, who had seemingly paid no attention to anyone, suddenly opened his eyes and said, alluding to the dangers of penetrating into the interior of Africa, 'And pray, who is the gentleman we are going *to lose?*' Here was a roar of laughter, the victim Ritchie joining with us.

We now retired to tea, and, among other friends, a gentleman who was Comptroller of the Stamp Office came.[4] He had been peculiarly anxious to know and see Wordsworth. The moment he was introduced he let Wordsworth know *who* he officially was. This was an exquisite touch of human nature. Though Wordsworth of course would not have suffered him to speak indecently or impiously without reproof, yet he had a visible effect on Wordsworth. I felt pain at the slavery of office.[5] In command men are despotic, and those who are dependent on others who have despotic control must and do feel affected by their presence. The Comptroller was a very mild and nice fellow, but rather weak and very fond of talking. He got into conversation with Wordsworth on poetry, and just after he had been putting forth some of his silly stuff, Lamb, who had been dozing as usual, suddenly opened his mouth and said, 'What did you say, sir?'

'Why, sir', said the Comptroller, in his milk and water insipidity, 'I was saying . . .', etc. etc. etc.

'Do you say so, sir?' 'Yes sir', was the reply. 'Why then, sir, I say (hiccup) you are – you are a silly fellow!' This operated like thunder. The Comptroller knew nothing of his previous tipsiness and looked at him like a man bewildered. The venerable anxiety of Wordsworth to prevent the Comptroller being angry, and his expostulations with Lamb, who had sunk back again into his doze, as insensible to the confusion he had produced as a being above it; the astonishment of Landseer[6] the engraver, who was totally deaf, and with his hand to his ear and his eye was trying to catch the meaning of the gestures he saw; and the agonizing attempts of Keats, Ritchie, and I to suppress our laughter; and the smiling struggle of the Comptroller to take all in good part without losing his dignity, made up a story of comic expressions totally unrivalled in nature. I felt pain that such a poet as Wordsworth should be under the supervisorship of such a being as this Comptroller. The people of England have a horror of office, an instinct against it. They are right. A man's liberty is gone the moment he becomes official; he is the slave of superiors, and makes others slaves to him. The Comptroller went on making his profound remarks, and when anything very *deep* came forth,[7] Lamb roared out,

> Diddle iddle don
> My son John
> Went to bed with his breeches on,
> One stocking off and one stocking on,
> My son John.

3 Joseph Ritchie (1788–1819), surgeon and African traveller, who died at Murzuk, Libya.
4 John Kingston, Deputy Comptroller of Stamps.
5 Wordsworth was Distributor of Stamps for Westmorland, 1813–42.

6 John Landseer (1769–1852), painter and engraver, father of Edwin Landseer.
7 'Such as "Pray sir, don't you think Milton a very *great genius?*" This I really recollect. 1823' (Haydon's note).

The Comptroller laughed as if he marked it, and went on; every remark Lamb chorused with

> Went to bed with his breeches on
> Diddle iddle on.

There is no describing this scene adequately. There was not the restraint of refined company, nor the vulgar freedom of low, but a frank natural license such as one sees in an act of Shakespeare, every man expressing his natural emotions without fear. Into this company, a little heated with wine, a Comptroller of the Stamp Office walked, frilled, dressed, and official, with a due awe of the powers above him and a due contempt for those beneath him. His astonishment at finding where he was come cannot be conceived, and in the midst of his mild namby-pamby opinions, Lamb's address deadened his views. When they separated, Wordsworth softened his feelings, but Lamb kept saying in the Painting [room], 'Who is that fellow? Let me go and hold the candle once more to his face –

> My son John
> Went to bed with his breeches on!

And these were the last words of C. Lamb. The door was closed upon him. There was something interesting in seeing Wordsworth sitting, and Keats and Lamb, and my picture of Christ's entry towering up behind them, occasionally brightened by the gleams of flame that sparkled from the fire, and hearing the voice of Wordsworth repeating Milton with an intonation like the funeral bell of St Paul's and the music of Handel mingled, and then Lamb's wit came sparkling in between, and Keats' rich fancy of satyrs and fauns and doves and white clouds wound up the stream of conversation. I never passed a more delightful day, and I am convinced that nothing in Boswell is equal to what came out from these poets. Indeed there were no such poets in his time. It was an evening worthy of the Elizabethan age, and will long flash upon 'that inward eye which is the bliss of solitude'.[8] Hail and farewell!

Bryan Waller Procter ('Barry Cornwall')
(1787–1874)

London solicitor, barrister, and man of letters; friend of Leigh Hunt, Lamb, and Dickens. Although Keats and Shelley were hostile to his work, he was the author of some beautiful lyrics. 'A Dream' is a prime example of the poetic reveries made fashionable by the publication of Coleridge's 'Kubla Khan' in 1816; it was one of Lamb's favourites (see p. 625).

---

[8] Wordsworth, *Daffodils*, 15–16.

From Dramatic Scenes and Other Poems (1819)

A DREAM

This is merely the recollection of an actual dream.

The night was gloomy. Through the skies of June
Rolled the eternal moon
Midst dark and heavy clouds that bore
A shadowy likeness to those fabled things
That sprung of old from man's imaginings.   5
Each seemed a fierce reality; some wore
The forms of sphinx and hippogriff, or seemed
Nourished among the wonders of the deep,
And wilder than the poet ever dreamed;
And there were cars – steeds with their proud necks bent;   10
Tower, and temple, and broken continent;
And all, as upon a sea,
In the blue ether floated silently.
I lay upon my bed and sank to sleep;
And then I fancied that I rode upon   15
The waters, and had power to call
Up people who had lived in ages gone,
And scenes and stories half-forgot – and all
That on my young imagination
Had come like fairy visions, and departed.   20
And ever by me a broad current passed
Slowly, from which at times up started
Dim scenes and ill-defined shapes. At last
I bade the billows render up their dead,
And all their wild inhabitants; and I   25
Summoned the spirits who perished,
Or took their stations in the starry sky,
When Jove himself bowed his Saturnian head
Before the One Divinity.

First I saw a landscape fair   30
Towering in the clear blue air,
Like Ida's woody summits, and sweet fields,
Where all that nature yields
Flourishes. Three proud shapes were seen,
Standing upon the green   35
Like Olympian queens descended.
One was unadorned, and one
Wore her golden tresses bound
With simple flowers; the third was crowned,
And from amidst her raven hair,   40
Like stars, imperial jewels shone.

Not one of those figures divine
But might have sat in Juno's chair,
And smiled in great equality
On Jove, though the blue skies were shaken;   45
Or, with superior aspect, taken
From Hebe's hand nectarean wine.
And that Dardanian boy was there
Whom pale Oenone loved;[1] his hair
Was black, and curled his temples round;   50
His limbs were free and his forehead fair,
And, as he stood on a rising ground,
And back his dark locks proudly tossed,
A shepherd youth he looked, but trod
On the green sward like a god —   55
Most like Apollo when he played,
'Fore Midas, in the Phrygian shade,
With Pan, and to the Sylvan lost.[2]

And now from out the watery floor
A city rose (and well she wore   60
Her beauty), and stupendous walls,
And towers that touched the stars, and halls
Pillared with whitest marble, whence
Palace on lofty palace sprung;
And over all rich gardens hung,   65
Where, amongst silver waterfalls,
Cedars and spice-trees and green bowers,
And sweet winds playing with all the flowers
Of Persia and of Araby,
Walked princely shapes; some with an air   70
Like warriors, some like ladies fair
Listening, and, amidst all, the king
Nebuchadnezzar rioting
In supreme magnificence.
This was famous Babylon.   75

That glorious vision passed on.
And then I heard the laurel-branches sigh
That still grow where the bright-eyed muses walked;
And Pelion shook his piny locks, and talked
Mournfully to the fields of Thessaly.[3]   80
And there I saw, piercing the deep blue sky,

A Dream
[1] Paris, who married Oenone, a nymph of Ida, was
a Trojan ('Dardanian').
[2] Midas, King of Phrygia, argued that the music of
Pan (the Sylvan) was better than that of Apollo.
[3] Pelion and Olympus are neighbouring mountains
in Thessaly.

And radiant with his diadem of snow,
Crowned Olympus; and the hills below
Looked like inferior spirits tending round
His pure supremacy; and a sound   85
Went rolling onwards through the sunny calm,
As if immortal voices then had spoken,
And, with rich noises, broken
The silence which that holy place had bred.
I knelt – and as I knelt, haply in token   90
Of thanks, there fell a honeyed shower of balm,
And the imperial mountain bowed his hoary head.
And then came one who on the Nubian sands
Perished for love; and with him the wanton queen
Egyptian in her state was seen;   95
And how she smiled, and kissed his willing hands,
And said she would not love, and swore to die,
And laughed upon the Roman Antony.
Oh matchless Cleopatra! never since
Has one, and never more   100
Shall one like thee tread on the Egypt shore,
Or lavish such royal magnificence;
Never shall one laugh, love or die like thee,
Or own so sweet a witchery;
And, brave Mark Antony, that thou could'st give   105
Half the wide world to live
With that enchantress, did become thee well;
For love is wiser than ambition:
Queen and thou, lofty triumvir, fare ye well.

And then I heard the sullen waters roar,   110
And saw them cast their surf upon the strand,
And then, rebounding toward some far-seen land,
They washed and washed its melancholy shore,
And the terrific spirits, bred
In the sea-caverns, moved by those fierce jars,   115
Rose up like giants from their watery bed,
And shook their silver hair against the stars.
Then bursts like thunder, joyous outcries wild
Sounds as from trumpets, and from drums,
And music, like the lulling noise that comes   120
From nurses when they hush their charge to sleep,
Came in confusion from the deep.
Methought one told me that a child
Was that night unto the great Neptune born;
And then old Triton blew his curled horn,[4]   125

---

[4] Triton raised storms by blowing on a conch-shell
horn.

And the Leviathan lashed the foaming seas,
And the wanton nereides
Came up like phantoms from their coral halls,
And laughed and sung like tipsy Bacchanals,
Till all the fury of the ocean broke   130
Upon my ear. I trembled and awoke.

From English Songs (1832)

A POET'S THOUGHT

Tell me, what is a poet's thought?
    Is it on the sudden born?
    Is it from the starlight caught?
    Is it by the tempest taught?
        Or by whispering morn?   5

Was it cradled in the brain?
    Chained awhile, or nursed in night?
Was it wrought with toil and pain?
Did it bloom and fade again,
    Ere it burst to light?   10

No more question of its birth,
    Rather love its better part!
'Tis a thing of sky and earth,
Gathering all its golden worth
    From the poet's heart.   15

Richard Woodhouse, Jr.   (1788–1834)

Legal advisor to Keats's publishers, Taylor and Hessey, early admirer of Keats's poems, and voracious collector of Keatsiana. The letters presented below are vital to a full understanding of Keats's poetry. The first outlines Keats's concept of the poetical character and negative capability; the second discusses his revision of 'The Eve of St Agnes'.

From Letter from Richard Woodhouse to John Taylor, 27 October 1818

I believe him to be right with regard to his own poetical character, and I perceive clearly the distinction he draws between himself and those of the Wordsworth school.

There are gradations in poetry and in poets. One is purely descriptive, confining himself to external nature and visible objects; another describes, in addition, the effects of the thoughts of which he is conscious, and which others are affected by. Another will soar so far into the regions of imagination as to conceive of beings and substances in situations different from what he has ever seen them, but still such as either have actually occurred or may possibly occur. Another will reason in poetry; another be witty; another will imagine things that never did nor probably ever will occur, or such as cannot in nature occur, and yet he will describe them so that you recognize nothing very unnatural in the descriptions when certain principles or powers or conditions are admitted. Another will throw himself into various characters and make them speak as the passions would naturally incite them to do.

The highest order of poet will not only possess all the above powers but will have as high an imagination that he will be able to throw his own soul into any object he sees or imagines, so as to see, feel, be sensible of, and express all that the object itself would see, feel, be sensible of, or express – and he will speak out of that object, so that his own self will, with the exception of the mechanical part, be 'annihilated'. And it is the excess of this power that I suppose Keats to speak, when he says he has no identity. As a poet, and when the fit is upon him, this is true. And it is a fact that he does by the power of his imagination create ideal personages, substances, and powers – that he lives for a time in their souls or essences or ideas – and that occasionally so intensely as to lose consciousness of what is round him. We all do the same in a degree, when we fall into a reverie.[1]

If, then, his imagination has such power, and he is continually cultivating it and giving it play, it will acquire strength by the indulgence and exercise. This in excess is the case of mad persons. And this may be carried to that extent that he may lose sight of his identity so far as to give him a habit of speaking generally in an assumed character. So that what he says shall be tinged with the sentiments proper to the character which, at the time, has possessed itself of his imagination.

This being his idea of the poetical character, he may well say that a poet has no identity. As a man he must have identity, but as a poet he need not. And in this sense a poet is 'the most unpoetical of God's creatures', for his soul has no distinctive characteristic – it cannot be itself made the subject of poetry that is another person's soul, cannot be thrown into the poet's, for there is no identity (separatedness, distinctiveness) or personal impulse to be acted upon.

Shakespeare was a poet of the kind above mentioned, and he was perhaps the only one besides Keats who possessed this power in an extraordinary degree, so as to be a feature in his works. He gives a description of his idea of a poet:

> The poet's eye, in a fine frenzy rolling,
> Doth glance from heaven to earth, from earth to heaven;
> And as imagination bodies forth
> The forms of things unknown, the poet's pen
> Turns them to shapes, and gives to airy nothing
> A local habitation and a name.
> (*A Midsummer Night's Dream*, V. i. 12–17)

Lord Byron does not come up to this character. He can certainly conceive and describe a dark accomplished villain in love, and a female tender and kind who loves him; or a sated and palled sensualist, misanthrope, and deist – but here his power ends. The true

A LETTER FROM RICHARD WOODHOUSE TO JOHN TAYLOR, 27 October 1818
[1] 'The power of his imagination is apparent in every page of his *Endymion*. And he has affirmed that he can conceive of a billiard-ball – that it may have a sense of delight from its own roundness, smoothness, volubility, and the rapidity of its motion' (Woodhouse's note).

poet cannot only conceive this, but can assume any character, essence, idea, or substance at pleasure. And he has this imaginative faculty not in a limited manner, but in full universality.

Let us pursue speculation on these matters, and we shall soon be brought to believe in the truth of every syllable of Keats' letter, taken as a description of himself and his own ideas and feelings.

From Letter from Richard Woodhouse to John Taylor, 19 September 1819

He had 'The Eve of St Agnes' copied fair.[1] He has made trifling alterations, inserted an additional stanza early in the poem to make the *legend* more intelligible, and correspondent with what afterwards takes place, particularly with respect to the supper and the playing on the lute.[2] He retains the name of Porphyro, has altered the last three lines to leave on the reader a sense of pettish disgust, by bringing Old Angela in (only) dead, stiff and ugly. He says he likes that the poem should leave off with this change of sentiment – it was what he aimed at, and was glad to find from my objections to it that he had succeeded. I apprehend he had a fancy for trying his hand at an attempt to play with his reader, and fling him off at last. I should have thought he affected the 'Don Juan' style of mingling up sentiment and sneering, but that he had before asked Hessey if he could procure him a sight of that work, as he had not met with it – and if 'The Eve of St Agnes' had not, in all probability, been altered before his Lordship had thus flown in the face of the public.[3]

There was another alteration, which I abused for 'a full hour by the Temple clock'.[4] You know, if a thing has a decent side, I generally look no further. As the poem was originally written, *we* innocent ones (ladies and myself) might very well have supposed that Porphyro, when acquainted with Madeline's love for him, and when 'he arose, / Ethereal, flushed'[5] etc. etc. (turn to it), set himself at once to persuade her to go off with him, and succeeded and went over the 'Dartmoor black' (now changed for some other place[6]) to be married, in right honest chaste and sober wise. But as it is now altered, as soon as Madeline has confessed her love, Porphyro winds by degrees his arm round her, presses breast to breast, and acts all the acts of a *bona fide* husband, while she fancies she is only playing the part of a wife in a dream.

This alteration is of about three stanzas, and though there are no improper expressions, but all is left to inference; and though, profanely speaking, the interest on the reader's imagination is greatly heightened – yet I do apprehend it will render the poem unfit for ladies, and indeed scarcely to be mentioned to them among the 'things that are'. He says he does not want ladies to read his poetry; that he writes for men, and that if in the former poem there was an opening for doubt what took place, it was his fault for not writing clearly and comprehensibly; that he should despise a man who

---

From A LETTER FROM RICHARD WOODHOUSE TO JOHN TAYLOR, 19 September 1819
[1] 'The Eve of St Agnes' was composed first 18 Jan.–2 Feb. 1819, and revised the following Sept.
[2] See p. 1041 below. The stanza was dropped from the published text.

[3] *Don Juan*, I–II, had been published in July.
[4] *1 Henry IV*, V. iv. 148: 'fought a long hour by Shrewsbury clock'.
[5] 'Eve of St Agnes', 317–18.
[6] 'the southern moors' (line 351).

would be such an eunuch in sentiment as to leave a maid, with that character about her, in such a situation; and should despise himself to write about it, etc., etc., etc. – and all this sort of Keats-like rhodomontade.

George Gordon Byron, 6th Baron Byron
(1788–1824)

Byron saw himself in a neoclassical tradition running from Pope, through Cowper and Moore, to himself; he was scathing of Wordsworth on the grounds of his metaphysics, and alleged dislike of Popean diction. The Wordsworthian echoes and cadences of Childe Harold's Pilgrimage, *Canto III, extracts from which are presented below, are therefore atypical – and in fact date from a period (summer 1816) when Shelley, as Byron later recalled, 'used to dose me with Wordsworth physic even to nausea' (Medwin, 237).* Manfred *describes the plight of the Byronic overreacher, distinguished from other versions of the Faust character by his defiance of the spirits he invokes and passion for his dead sister, Astarte. Although a drama, Byron claimed to have 'rendered it quite impossible for the stage – for which my intercourse with Drury Lane had given me the greatest contempt' (Marchand, v. 170).* Don Juan *is Byron's masterpiece, of which a complete text of the Dedication and Canto I are presented below. Byron declared, 'I have no plan – I had no plan – but I had or have materials' (ibid., vi. 207), and indeed the manner in which it is written is just as important as the story – as he observed, 'I mean it for a poetical* Tristram Shandy' *(ibid., x. 150).*

From Childe Harold's Pilgrimage: A Romaunt (1812)
WRITTEN BENEATH A PICTURE (COMPOSED C.JANUARY 1812)

I

Dear object of defeated care!
Though now of love and thee bereft,
To reconcile me with despair
Thine image and my tears are left.

2

'Tis said with sorrow time can cope,   5
But this I feel can ne'er be true;
For by the death-blow of my hope
My memory immortal grew.

WRITTEN BENEATH A PICTURE
[1] This poem and 'Stanzas' were inspired by the death of John Edleston, a choirboy at Trinity Chapel to whom Byron was romantically attached, May 1811.

From Childe Harold's Pilgrimage: A Romaunt, 2nd edition, (1812)

STANZAS (COMPOSED *c.*FEBRUARY 1812)

Heu quanto minus est cum reliquis versari quam tui meminisse![1]

1

And thou art dead, as young and fair
   As aught of mortal birth;
And form so soft, and charms so rare,
   Too soon returned to earth!
Though earth received them in her bed,   5
And o'er the spot the crowd may tread
   In carelessness or mirth,
There is an eye which could not brook
A moment on that grave to look.

2

I will not ask where thou liest low,   10
   Nor gaze upon the spot;
There flowers or weeds at will may grow,
   So I behold them not;
It is enough for me to prove
That what I loved and long must love   15
   Like common earth can rot —
To me there needs no stone to tell
'Tis nothing that I loved so well.

3

Yet did I love thee to the last
   As fervently as thou,   20
Who didst not change through all the past,
   And canst not alter now.
The love where death has set his seal
Nor age can chill, nor rival steal,
   Nor falsehood disavow;   25
And, what were worse, thou canst not see
Or wrong, or change, or fault in me.

STANZAS
[1] 'Alas, how much less it is to deal with things left
behind than to remember thee.'

4

The better days of life were ours,
   The worst can be but mine;
The sun that cheers, the storm that lowers,   30
   Shall never more be thine.
The silence of that dreamless sleep
I envy now too much to weep;
   Nor need I to repine
That all those charms have passed away   35
I might have watched through long decay.

5

The flower in ripened bloom unmatched
   Must fall the earliest prey,
Though by no hand untimely snatched,
   The leaves must drop away;   40
And yet it were a greater grief
To watch it withering leaf by leaf
   Than see it plucked today –
Since earthly eye but ill can bear
To trace the change to foul from fair.   45

6

I know not if I could have borne
   To see thy beauties fade;
The night that followed such a morn
   Had worn a deeper shade;
Thy day without a cloud hath passed,   50
And thou wert lovely to the last,
   Extinguished, not decayed –
As stars that shoot along the sky
Shine brightest as they fall from high.

7

As once I wept, if I could weep,   55
   My tears might well be shed,
To think I was not near to keep
   One vigil o'er thy bed,
To gaze, how fondly, on thy face,
To fold thee in a faint embrace,   60
   Uphold thy drooping head;

And show that love, however vain,
Nor thou, nor I, can feel again.

8

Yet how much less it were to gain
    (Though thou hast left me free)   65
The loveliest things that still remain,
    Than thus remember thee!
The all of thine that cannot die
Through dark and dread eternity
    Returns again to me,   70
And more thy buried love endears
Than aught, except its living years.

From Hebrew Melodies (1815)
SHE WALKS IN BEAUTY (COMPOSED *c*.12 JUNE 1814)[1]

I

She walks in beauty like the night
    Of cloudless climes and starry skies,
And all that's best of dark and bright
    Meet in her aspect and her eyes,
Thus mellowed to that tender light   5
    Which heaven to gaudy day denies.

II

One shade the more, one ray the less
    Had half-impaired the nameless grace
Which waves in every raven tress
    Or softly lightens o'er her face –   10
Where thoughts serenely sweet express
    How pure, how dear their dwelling place.

III

And on that cheek and o'er that brow,
    So soft, so calm, yet eloquent,

SHE WALKS IN BEAUTY (composed June 1814)
[1] A MS version of the poem is entitled 'Lines written by Lord Byron after seeing Mrs Wilmot at Lansdowne House'. Byron met Anne Wilmot (1784–1871) on 11 June 1814; she was the wife of his first cousin Robert John Wilmot.

The smiles that win, the tints that glow,   15
But tell of days in goodness spent,
A mind at peace with all below,
A heart whose love is innocent.

From Childe Harold's Pilgrimage *Canto III* (1816; composed 25 April-June 1816)

1

Is thy face like thy mother's, my fair child,
Ada, sole daughter of my house and heart?[1]
When last I saw thy young blue eyes, they smiled;
And then we parted – not as now we part,
But with a hope.
            Awaking with a start,   5
The waters heave around me, and on high
The winds lift up their voices. I depart
Whither I know not, but the hour's gone by
When Albion's lessening shores could grieve or glad mine eye.[2]

2

Once more upon the waters, yet once more![3]   10
And the waves bound beneath me as a steed
That knows his rider – welcome to their roar!
Swift be their guidance, wheresoe'er it lead!
Though the strained mast should quiver as a reed
And the rent canvas fluttering strew the gale,   15
Still must I on – for I am as a weed
Flung from the rock on ocean's foam, to sail
Where'er the surge may sweep, the tempest's breath prevail.

3

In my youth's summer I did sing of one,[4]
The wandering outlaw of his own dark mind;   20
Again I seize the theme then but begun,
And bear it with me as the rushing wind

CHILDE HAROLD'S PILGRIMAGE CANTO III STANZAS 1–7
[1] Byron's only legitimate daughter Augusta Ada, born 10 Dec. 1815. After Lady Byron left him five weeks later, he never saw Ada again.
[2] Byron left England for Belgium, and began writing this canto while at sea, 25 Apr. 1816.
[3] Cf. *Henry V*, III. i. 1.
[4] i.e. Childe Harold. Byron began Canto I on 31 Oct. 1809, when he was 21.

Bears the cloud onwards. In that tale I find
The furrows of long thought, and dried-up tears
Which, ebbing, leave a sterile track behind,   25
O'er which all heavily the journeying years
Plod the last sands of life, where not a flower appears.

4

Since my young days' of passion (joy or pain),
Perchance my heart and harp have lost a string
And both may jar; it may be that in vain   30
I would essay as I have sung to sing.
Yet, though a dreary strain, to this I cling,
So that it wean me from the weary dream
Of selfish grief or gladness; so it fling
Forgetfulness around me. It shall seem   35
To me (though to none else) a not ungrateful theme.

5

He, who grown aged in this world of woe
(In deeds not years), piercing the depths of life
So that no wonder waits him; nor below
Can love or sorrow, fame, ambition, strife,   40
Cut to his heart again with the keen knife
Of silent sharp endurance – he can tell
Why thought seeks refuge in lone caves yet rife
With airy images, and shapes which dwell
Still unimpaired, though old, in the soul's haunted cell.   45

6

'Tis to create, and in creating live
A being more intense, that we endow
With form our fancy, gaining as we give
The life we image – even as I do now.
What am I? Nothing. But not so art thou,   50
Soul of my thought, with whom I traverse earth,
Invisible but gazing, as I glow
Mixed with thy spirit, blended with thy birth,
And feeling still with thee in my crushed feelings' dearth.

---

5 *young days* Byron was 28 at the time of writing.

7

Yet must I think less wildly. I *have* thought   55
Too long and darkly till my brain became,
In its own eddy, boiling and o'erwrought,
A whirling gulf of fantasy and flame;
And thus, untaught in youth my heart to tame,
My springs of life were poisoned. 'Tis too late!   60
Yet am I changed, though still enough the same
In strength to bear what time cannot abate,
And feed on bitter fruits without accusing fate.

. . . .

41

If, like a tower upon a headlong rock,
Thou[1] hadst been made to stand or fall alone,
Such scorn of man had helped to brave the shock;
But men's thoughts were the steps which paved thy throne,
Their admiration thy best weapon shone;   365
The part of Philip's son[2] was thine, not then
(Unless aside thy purple had been thrown)
Like stern Diogenes to mock at men:[3]
For sceptred cynics earth were far too wide a den.

42

But quiet to quick bosoms is a hell,   370
And *there* hath been thy bane: there is a fire
And motion of the soul which will not dwell
In its own narrow being, but aspire
Beyond the fitting medium of desire,
And but once kindled, quenchless evermore,   375
Preys upon high adventure, nor can tire
Of aught but rest – a fever at the core,
Fatal to him who bears, to all who ever bore.

43

This makes the madmen who have made men mad
By their contagion: conquerors and kings,   380

STANZAS 41–5
[1] *Thou* Napoleon, at the time of writing imprisoned on St Helena in the wake of defeat at Waterloo.
[2] *Philip's son* Alexander the Great, son of Philip of Macedonia.
[3] Diogenes, Greek philosopher of fourth century BC, who established the Cynic school, famous for having lived in a tub in rejection of the customs, conventions, and decencies of polite society.

Founders of sects and systems, to whom add
Sophists, bards, statesmen, all unquiet things
Which stir too strongly the soul's secret springs,
And are themselves the fools to those they fool —
Envied, yet how unenviable! What stings   385
Are theirs! One breast laid open were a school
Which would unteach mankind the lust to shine or rule:

44

Their breath is agitation, and their life
A storm whereon they ride, to sink at last;
And yet so nursed and bigoted to strife,   390
That, should their days (surviving perils passed)
Melt to calm twilight, they feel overcast
With sorrow and supineness, and so die;
Even as a flame unfed, which runs to waste
With its own flickering, or a sword laid by   395
Which eats into itself, and rusts ingloriously.

45

He who ascends to mountain-tops shall find
The loftiest peaks most wrapped in clouds and snow;
He who surpasses or subdues mankind
Must look down on the hate of those below.   400
Though high *above* the sun of glory glow
And far *beneath* the earth and ocean spread,
Round him are icy rocks, and loudly blow
Contending tempests on his naked head,
And thus reward the toils which to those summits led.   405

. . . .

68

Lake Leman[1] woos me with its crystal face,
The mirror where the stars and mountains view   645
The stillness of their aspect in each trace
Its clear depth yields of their far height and hue:
There is too much of man here to look through,
With a fit mind, the might which I behold;
But soon in me shall loneliness renew   650

Stanzas 68–98
[1] *Lake Leman* Lake Geneva.

Thoughts hid, but not less cherished than of old,
Ere mingling with the herd had penned me in their fold.

69

To fly from, need not be to hate, mankind;
All are not fit with them to stir and toil,
Nor is it discontent to keep the mind   655
Deep in its fountain, lest it overboil
In the hot throng, where we become the spoil
Of our infection, till too late and long
We may deplore and struggle with the coil[2]
In wretched interchange of wrong for wrong   660
Midst a contentious world, striving where none are strong.

70

There in a moment we may plunge our years
In fatal penitence, and in the blight
Of our own soul turn all our blood to tears,
And colour things to come with hues of night;   665
The race of life becomes a hopeless flight
To those that walk in darkness: on the sea
The boldest steer but where their ports invite,
But there are wanderers o'er eternity
Whose bark drives on and on, and anchored ne'er shall be.   670

71

Is it not better, then, to be alone,
And love earth only for its earthly sake?
By the blue rushing of the arrowy Rhône
Or the pure bosom of its nursing lake,
Which feeds it as a mother who doth make   675
A fair but froward infant her own care,
Kissing its cries away as these awake?
Is it not better thus our lives to wear
Than join the crushing crowd, doomed to inflict or bear?

72

I live not in myself, but I become   680
Portion of that around me; and to me

---

2 coil mortal coil; bustle of life.

High mountains are a feeling, but the hum
Of human cities torture.[3] I can see
Nothing to loathe in nature, save to be
A link reluctant in a fleshly chain,   685
Classed among creatures, when the soul can flee,
And with the sky, the peak, the heaving plain
Of ocean, or the stars, mingle, and not in vain.

73

And thus I am absorbed, and this is life.
I look upon the peopled desert past   690
As on a place of agony and strife
Where for some sin to sorrow I was cast
To act and suffer, but remount at last
With a fresh pinion, which I feel to spring
(Though young, yet waxing vigorous as the blast   695
Which it would cope with) on delighted wing,
Spurning the clay-cold bonds which round our being cling.

74

And when at length the mind shall be all free
From what it hates in this degraded form,
Reft of its carnal life, save what shall be   700
Existent happier in the fly and worm;
When elements to elements conform
And dust is as it should be, shall I not
Feel all I see — less dazzling, but more warm?
The bodiless thought? The spirit of each spot —   705
Of which, even now, I share at times the immortal lot?

75

Are not the mountains, waves and skies a part
Of me and of my soul, as I of them?
Is not the love of these deep in my heart
With a pure passion? Should I not contemn   710
All objects if compared with these, and stem
A tide of suffering, rather than forego
Such feelings for the hard and worldly phlegm
Of those whose eyes are only turned below,
Gazing upon the ground, with thoughts which dare not glow?   715

---

[3] Here and in succeeding lines Byron repeats attitudes he had encountered in 'Tintern Abbey'.

76

But this is not my theme, and I return
To that which is immediate – and require
Those who find contemplation in the urn
To look on one[4] whose dust was once all fire,
A native of the land where I respire   720
The clear air for a while, a passing guest
Where he became a being, whose desire
Was to be glorious ('twas a foolish quest,
The which to gain and keep, he sacrificed all rest).

77

Here the self-torturing sophist, wild Rousseau,   725
The apostle of affliction, he who threw
Enchantment over passion, and from woe
Wrung overwhelming eloquence – first drew
The breath which made him wretched; yet he knew
How to make madness beautiful, and cast   730
O'er erring deeds and thoughts a heavenly hue
Of words like sunbeams, dazzling as they passed
The eyes, which o'er them shed tears feelingly and fast.

78

His love was passion's essence, as a tree
On fire by lightning;[5] with ethereal flame   735
Kindled he was, and blasted – for to be
Thus, and enamoured, were in him the same.
But his was not the love of living dame,
Nor of the dead who rise upon our dreams,
But of ideal beauty, which became   740
In him existence, and o'erflowing teems
Along his burning page, distempered though it seems.

79

This breathed itself to life in Julie,[6] this
Invested her with all that's wild and sweet;
This hallowed, too, the memorable kiss   745
Which every morn his fevered lip would greet

---

[4] *one* Rousseau, born in Geneva, 1712.
[5] An image used also by Shelley and Mary Shelley.

[6] *Julie* heroine of Rousseau's *Julie, ou la Nouvelle Héloïse* (1761), which Shelley and Byron read in 1816.

From hers who, but with friendship, his would meet:[7]
But to that gentle touch, through brain and breast
Flashed the thrilled spirit's love-devouring heat –
In that absorbing sigh, perchance more blessed   750
Than vulgar minds may be with all they seek possessed.

80

His life was one long war with self-sought foes
Or friends by him self-banished, for his mind
Had grown suspicion's sanctuary, and chose,
For its own cruel sacrifice, the kind,   755
'Gainst whom he raged with fury strange and blind.
But he was frenzied – wherefore, who may know,
Since cause might be which skill could never find?
But he was frenzied by disease or woe
To that worst pitch of all, which wears a reasoning show.   760

81

For then he was inspired, and from him came,
As from the Pythian's mystic cave of yore,
Those oracles which set the world in flame,[8]
Nor ceased to burn till kingdoms were no more.
Did he not this for France, which lay before   765
Bowed to the inborn tyranny of years?
Broken and trembling to the yoke she bore,
Till by the voice of him and his compeers
Roused up to too much wrath, which follows o'ergrown fears?

82

They made themselves a fearful monument!   770
The wreck of old opinions, things which grew
Breathed from the birth of time: the veil they rent,
And what behind it lay, all earth shall view.
But good with ill they also overthrew,
Leaving but ruins, wherewith to rebuild   775
Upon the same foundation, and renew
Dungeons[9] and thrones, which the same hour refilled
As heretofore, because ambition was self-willed.[10]

---

[7] Rousseau describes his unrequited love for the Comtesse d'Houdetot in his *Confessions*.
[8] The *Discours* of 1750 and 1753 and *Le Contrat Social* (1762) helped inspire the French Revolution.

[9] *Dungeons* the Bastille was demolished during the Revolution in Paris and not rebuilt.
[10] Ferdinand VII of Spain and Louis XVIII of France were restored to their respective thrones in 1814.

83

But this will not endure, nor be endured!
Mankind have felt their strength and made it felt.   780
They might have used it better, but, allured
By their new vigour, sternly have they dealt
On one another; pity ceased to melt
With her once-natural charities. But they
Who in oppression's darkness caved had dwelt,   785
They were not eagles, nourished with the day;
What marvel then, at times, if they mistook their prey?

84

What deep wounds ever closed without a scar?
The heart's bleed longest, and but heal to wear
That which disfigures it; and they who war   790
With their own hopes, and have been vanquished, bear
Silence but not submission. In his lair
Fixed Passion holds his breath until the hour
Which shall atone for years — none need despair:
It came, it cometh, and will come, the power   795
To punish or forgive; in *one* we shall be slower.

85

Clear placid Leman! thy contrasted lake,
With the wild world I dwelt in, is a thing
Which warns me, with its stillness, to forsake
Earth's troubled waters for a purer spring.   800
This quiet sail is as a noiseless wing
To waft me from distraction; once I loved
Torn ocean's roar, but thy soft murmuring
Sounds sweet as if a sister's voice reproved,
That I with stern delights should e'er have been so moved.   805

86

It is the hush of night, and all between
Thy margin and the mountains, dusk — yet clear,
Mellowed and mingling, yet distinctly seen
(Save darkened Jura, whose capped heights appear
Precipitously steep); and, drawing near,   810
There breathes a living fragrance from the shore
Of flowers yet fresh with childhood; on the ear

Drops the light drip of the suspended oar,
Or chirps the grasshopper one goodnight carol more

87

(He is an evening reveller who makes   815
His life an infancy, and sings his fill);
At intervals, some bird from out the brakes
Starts into voice a moment, then is still.
There seems a floating whisper on the hill,
But that is fancy, for the starlight dews   820
All silently their tears of love instil,
Weeping themselves away, till they infuse
Deep into nature's breast the spirit of her hues.

88

Ye stars which are the poetry of heaven!
If in your bright leaves we would read the fate   825
Of men and empires, 'tis to be forgiven
That in our aspirations to be great,
Our destinies o'erleap their mortal state,
And claim a kindred with you – for ye are
A beauty and a mystery, and create   830
In us such love and reverence from afar
That fortune, fame, power, life, have named themselves a star.

89

All heaven and earth are still – though not in sleep,
But breathless (as we grow when feeling most)
And silent (as we stand in thoughts too deep);[11]   835
All heaven and earth are still: from the high host
Of stars to the lulled lake and mountain-coast,
All is concentred in a life intense
Where not a beam, nor air, nor leaf is lost,
But hath a part of being, and a sense   840
Of that which is of all creator and defence.

90

Then stirs the feeling infinite, so felt
In solitude, where we are least alone –

---

[11] *thoughts too deep* compare 'Thoughts that do often
lie too deep for tears' (Wordsworth, 'Ode', 206).

A truth which through our being then doth melt
And purifies from self; it is a tone,   845
The soul and source of music, which makes known
Eternal harmony, and sheds a charm
Like to the fabled Cytherea's zone,[12]
Binding all things with beauty – 'twould disarm
The spectre death, had he substantial power to harm.   850

91

Not vainly did the early Persian make
His altar the high places and the peak
Of earth-o'ergazing mountains, and thus take
A fit and unwalled temple, there to seek
The spirit in whose honour shrines are weak,   855
Upreared of human hands. Come and compare
Columns and idol-dwellings, Goth or Greek,
With nature's realms of worship, earth and air,
Nor fix on fond abodes to circumscribe thy prayer!

92

The sky is changed, and such a change! Oh night   860
And storm and darkness, ye are wondrous strong,
Yet lovely in your strength, as is the light
Of a dark eye in woman! Far along
From peak to peak, the rattling crags among,
Leaps the live thunder – not from one lone cloud   865
But every mountain now hath found a tongue,
And Jura answers through her misty shroud
Back to the joyous Alps, who call to her aloud![13]

93

And this is in the night – most glorious night,
Thou wert not sent for slumber! Let me be   870
A sharer in thy fierce and far delight,
A portion of the tempest and of thee!
How the lit lake shines, a phosphoric sea,
And the big rain comes dancing to the earth!
And now again 'tis black, and now the glee   875

---

[12] Aphrodite's girdle brought love to those wearing it.

[13] In a note Byron reveals that the storms described here took place at midnight, 13 June 1816.

Of the loud hills shakes with its mountain-mirth,
As if they did rejoice o'er a young earthquake's birth.[14]

94

Now where the swift Rhône cleaves his way between
Heights which appear as lovers who have parted
In hate, whose mining depths so intervene   880
That they can meet no more, though broken-hearted,
Though in their souls (which thus each other thwarted)
Love was the very root of the fond rage
Which blighted their life's bloom, and then departed –
Itself expired, but leaving them an age   885
Of years all winters, war within themselves to wage;

95

Now where the quick Rhône thus hath cleft his way,
The mightiest of the storms hath ta'en his stand:
For here not one but many make their play,
And fling their thunderbolts from hand to hand,   890
Flashing and cast around; of all the band
The brightest through these parted hills hath forked
His lightnings, as if he did understand
That in such gaps as desolation worked,
There the hot shaft should blast whatever therein lurked.   895

96

Sky, mountains, river, winds, lake, lightnings – ye
With night and clouds and thunder, and a soul
To make these felt and feeling, well may be
Things that have made me watchful; the far roll
Of your departing voices is the knoll   900
Of what in me is sleepless – if I rest.
But where of ye, oh tempests, is the goal?
Are ye like those within the human breast?
Or do ye find, at length, like eagles, some high nest?

97

Could I embody and unbosom now   905
That which is most within me! Could I wreak

---

[14] Cf. Shelley, 'Mont Blanc', 72.

My thoughts upon expression, and thus throw
Soul, heart, mind, passions, feelings (strong or weak),
All that I would have sought and all I seek,
Bear, know, feel, and yet breathe – into *one* word,   910
And that one word were lightning, I would speak!
But as it is, I live and die unheard
With a most voiceless thought, sheathing it as a sword.

98

The morn is up again, the dewy morn
With breath all incense, and with cheek all bloom,   915
Laughing the clouds away with playful scorn
And living as if earth contained no tomb,
And glowing into day: we may resume
The march of our existence. And thus I,
Still on thy shores, fair Leman, may find room   920
And food for meditation, nor pass by
Much that may give us pause, if pondered fittingly.

From The Prisoner of Chillon and Other Poems (1816)

PROMETHEUS (COMPOSED JULY OR EARLY AUGUST 1816)

I

Titan! to whose immortal eyes
  The sufferings of mortality
  Seen in their sad reality,
Were not as things that gods despise –
What was thy pity's recompense?   5
A silent suffering, and intense;
The rock, the vulture, and the chain,
All that the proud can feel of pain,
The agony they do not show,
The suffocating sense of woe   10
  Which speaks but in its loneliness,
And then is jealous lest the sky
Should have a listener, nor will sigh
  Until its voice is echoless.

II

Titan! to thee the strife was given   15
  Between the suffering and the will,
  Which torture where they cannot kill;

And the inexorable heaven,
And the deaf tyranny of fate,
The ruling principle of hate   20
Which for its pleasure doth create
The things it may annihilate,
Refused thee even the boon to die:
The wretched gift eternity
Was thine – and thou hast borne it well.   25
All that the thunderer wrung from thee
Was but the menace which flung back
On him the torments of thy rack;
The fate thou didst so well foresee
But would not to appease him tell;   30
And in thy silence was his sentence,
And in his soul a vain repentance,
And evil dread so ill dissembled
That in his hand the lightnings trembled.

III

Thy godlike crime was to be kind,   35
To render with thy precepts less
The sum of human wretchedness,
And strengthen man with his own mind;
But baffled as thou wert from high,
Still in thy patient energy,   40
In the endurance and repulse
Of thine impenetrable spirit,
Which earth and heaven could not convulse,
A mighty lesson we inherit:
Thou art a symbol and a sign   45
To mortals of their fate and force;
Like thee, man is in part divine,
A troubled stream from a pure source;
And man in portions can foresee
His own funereal destiny;   50
His wretchedness and his resistance,
And his sad unallied existence:
To which his spirit may oppose
Itself – an equal to all woes,
And a firm will, and a deep sense,   55
Which even in torture can descry
Its own concentred recompense,
Triumphant where it dares defy,
And making death a victory.

DARKNESS (COMPOSED BETWEEN 21 JULY AND 25 AUGUST 1816)

I had a dream, which was not all a dream.
The bright sun was extinguished, and the stars
Did wander darkling in the eternal space,
Rayless, and pathless, and the icy earth
Swung blind and blackening in the moonless air;   5
Morn came, and went – and came, and brought no day,
And men forgot their passions in the dread
Of this their desolation; and all hearts
Were chilled into a selfish prayer for light:
And they did live by watchfires – and the thrones,   10
The palaces of crowned kings – the huts,
The habitations of all things which dwell,
Were burnt for beacons; cities were consumed,
And men were gathered round their blazing homes
To look once more into each other's face;   15
Happy were those who dwelt within the eye
Of the volcanoes, and their mountain-torch:
A fearful hope was all the world contained;
Forests were set on fire – but hour by hour
They fell and faded – and the crackling trunks   20
Extinguished with a crash – and all was black.
The brows of men by the despairing light
Wore an unearthly aspect, as by fits
The flashes fell upon them; some lay down
And hid their eyes and wept; and some did rest   25
Their chins upon their clenched hands, and smiled;
And others hurried to and fro, and fed
Their funeral piles with fuel, and looked up
With mad disquietude on the dull sky,
The pall of a past world; and then again   30
With curses cast them down upon the dust,
And gnashed their teeth and howled. The wild birds shrieked,
And, terrified, did flutter on the ground,
And flap their useless wings; the wildest brutes
Came tame and tremulous; and vipers crawled   35
And twined themselves among the multitude,
Hissing, but stingless – they were slain for food:
And War, which for a moment was no more,
Did glut himself again; a meal was bought
With blood, and each sat sullenly apart   40
Gorging himself in gloom. No love was left;
All earth was but one thought – and that was death,
Immediate and inglorious; and the pang
Of famine fed upon all entrails – men
Died, and their bones were tombless as their flesh;   45
The meagre by the meagre were devoured,

Even dogs assailed their masters, all save one,
And he was faithful to a corpse, and kept
The birds and beasts and famished men at bay,
Till hunger clung[1] them, or the dropping dead   50
Lured their lank jaws; himself sought out no food,
But with a piteous and perpetual moan
And a quick desolate cry, licking the hand
Which answered not with a caress – he died.
The crowd was famished by degrees, but two   55
Of an enormous city did survive,
And they were enemies; they met beside
The dying embers of an altar-place
Where had been heaped a mass of holy things
For an unholy usage; they raked up,   60
And shivering scraped with their cold skeleton hands
The feeble ashes, and their feeble breath
Blew for a little life, and made a flame
Which was a mockery; then they lifted up
Their eyes as it grew lighter, and beheld   65
Each other's aspects – saw, and shrieked, and died –
Even of their mutual hideousness they died,
Unknowing who he was upon whose brow
Famine had written Fiend. The world was void,
The populous and the powerful – was a lump,   70
Seasonless, herbless, treeless, manless, lifeless –
A lump of death – a chaos of hard clay.
The rivers, lakes, and ocean all stood still,
And nothing stirred within their silent depths;
Ships sailorless lay rotting on the sea,   75
And their masts fell down piecemeal; as they dropped
They slept on the abyss without a surge –
The waves were dead; the tides were in their grave,
The moon their mistress had expired before;
The winds were withered in the stagnant air,   80
And the clouds perished; Darkness had no need
Of aid from them – She was the universe.

Manfred, A Dramatic Poem (composed September 1816–15 February 1817; published 1817)

*There are more things in heaven and earth, Horatio,
Than are dreamt of in your philosophy.*
(*Hamlet*, 1. v. 166–7)

DARKNESS
[1] *clung* shrivelled.

Dramatis Personae
Manfred
Chamois hunter
Abbot of St Maurice
Manuel
Herman
Witch of the Alps
Arimanes
Nemesis
The Destinies
Spirits, etc.

The scene of the drama is amongst the higher Alps – partly in the Castle of Manfred, and partly in the mountains.

ACT I, SCENE I

Manfred alone. Scene: a gothic gallery. Time: midnight.

Manfred The lamp must be replenished, but even then
It will not burn so long as I must watch;
My slumbers (if I slumber) are not sleep
But a continuance of enduring thought,
Which then I can resist not. In my heart   5
There is a vigil, and these eyes but close
To look within – and yet I live, and bear
The aspect and the form of breathing men.
But grief should be the instructor of the wise[1] –
Sorrow is knowledge; they who know the most   10
Must mourn the deepest o'er the fatal truth:
The tree of knowledge is not that of life.
Philosophy and science, and the springs
Of wonder, and the wisdom of the world
I have essayed, and in my mind there is   15
A power to make these subject to itself,
But they avail not. I have done men good,
And I have met with good even among men –
But this availed not. I have had my foes
And none have baffled, many fallen before me –   20
But this availed not. Good or evil, life,
Powers, passions, all I see in other beings
Have been to me as rain unto the sands
Since that all-nameless hour. I have no dread,
And feel the curse to have no natural fear,   25
Nor fluttering throb that beats with hopes or wishes
Or lurking love of something on the earth.
Now to my task.

MANFRED
[1] Eccles. 1: 18.

Mysterious agency!
Ye spirits of the unbounded universe
Whom I have sought in darkness and in light;   30
Ye who do compass earth about, and dwell
In subtler essence; ye to whom the tops
Of mountains inaccessible are haunts,
And earth's and ocean's caves familiar things –
I call upon ye by the written charm   35
Which gives me power upon you: rise, appear! (*a pause*)
They come not yet. Now by the voice of him
Who is the first among you; by this sign
Which makes you tremble; by the claims of him
Who is undying – rise, appear! Appear! (*a pause*)   40
If it be so. Spirits of earth and air,
Ye shall not thus elude me: by a power
Deeper than all yet urged, a tyrant-spell
Which had its birthplace in a star condemned,
The burning wreck of a demolished world,   45
A wandering hell in the eternal space;
By the strong curse which is upon my soul,
The thought which is within me and around me,
I do compel ye to my will. Appear!

A star is seen at the darker end of the gallery. It is stationary, and a voice is heard singing.

First Spirit
Mortal, to thy bidding bowed   50
From my mansion in the cloud
Which the breath of twilight builds
And the summer's sunset gilds
With the azure and vermilion
Which is mixed for my pavilion,   55
Though thy quest may be forbidden,
On a starbeam I have ridden,
To thine adjuration bowed;
Mortal – be thy wish avowed!

Voice of the Second Spirit
Mont Blanc is the monarch of mountains,   60
   They crowned him long ago
On a throne of rocks, in a robe of clouds
   With a diadem of snow.
Around his waist are forests braced,
   The avalanche in his hand;   65
But ere it fall that thundering ball
   Must pause for my command.
The glacier's cold and restless mass
   Moves onward day by day,
But I am he who bids it pass   70

Or with its ice delay.
  I am the spirit of the place
Could make the mountain bow
And quiver to his caverned base –
  And what with me wouldst *thou*?   75

Voice of the Third Spirit
  In the blue depth of the waters
    Where the wave hath no strife,
  Where the wind is a stranger
    And the sea-snake hath life,
  Where the mermaid is decking   80
    Her green hair with shells,
  Like the storm on the surface
    Came the sound of thy spells;
  O'er my calm hall of coral
    The deep echo rolled –   85
  To the spirit of ocean
    Thy wishes unfold!

Fourth Spirit
  Where the slumbering earthquake
    Lies pillowed on fire,
  And the lakes of bitumen   90
    Rise boilingly higher;
  Where the roots of the Andes
    Strike deep in the earth,
  As their summits to heaven
    Shoot soaringly forth;   95
  I have quitted my birthplace,
    Thy bidding to bide –
  Thy spell hath subdued me,
    Thy will be my guide!

Fifth Spirit
  I am the rider of the wind,   100
    The stirrer of the storm;
  The hurricane I left behind
    Is yet with lightning warm;
  To speed to thee, o'er shore and sea
    I swept upon the blast;   105
  The fleet I met sailed well and yet
    'Twill sink ere night be passed.

Sixth Spirit
  My dwelling is the shadow of the night,
  Why doth thy magic torture me with light?

Seventh Spirit
  The star which rules thy destiny   110
  Was ruled, ere earth began, by me;
  It was a world as fresh and fair
  As e'er revolved round sun in air;
  Its course was free and regular,
  Space bosomed not a lovelier star.   115
  The hour arrived, and it became
  A wandering mass of shapeless flame,
  A pathless comet and a curse –
  The menace of the universe.
  Still rolling on with innate force,   120
  Without a sphere, without a course,
  A bright deformity on high,
  The monster of the upper sky!
  And thou beneath its influence born,
  Thou worm whom I obey and scorn!   125
  Forced by a power (which is not thine,
  And lent thee but to make thee mine)
  For this brief moment to descend,
  Where these weak spirits round thee bend
  And parley with a thing like thee –   130
  What wouldst thou, child of clay, with me?

The Seven Spirits
  Earth, ocean, air, night, mountains, winds, thy star,
    Are at thy beck and bidding, child of clay!
  Before thee at thy quest their spirits are –
    What wouldst thou with us, son of mortals? Say!   135

Manfred Forgetfulness –
First Spirit Of what, of whom, and why?
Manfred Of that which is within me; read it there –
  Ye know it, and I cannot utter it.
Spirit We can but give thee that which we possess.
  Ask of us subjects, sovereignty, the power   140
  O'er earth, the whole or portion, or a sign
  Which shall control the elements whereof
  We are the dominators, each and all –
  These shall be thine.
Manfred   Oblivion, self-oblivion –
  Can ye not wring from out the hidden realms   145
  Ye offer so profusely what I ask?
Spirit It is not in our essence, in our skill;
  But – thou mayst die.
Manfred   Will death bestow it on me?
Spirit We are immortal and do not forget;
  We are eternal and to us the past   150

Is, as the future, present. Art thou answered?
Manfred Ye mock me – but the power which brought ye here
   Hath made you mine. Slaves, scoff not at my will!
   The mind, the spirit, the Promethean spark,
   The lightning of my being, is as bright,   155
   Pervading, and far-darting as your own –
   And shall not yield to yours, though cooped in clay!
   Answer, or I will teach ye what I am.
Spirit We answer as we answered; our reply
   Is even in thine own words.
Manfred   Why say ye so?   160
Spirit If, as thou say'st, thine essence be as ours,
   We have replied in telling thee, the thing
   Mortals call death hath nought to do with us.
Manfred I then have called ye from your realms in vain;
   Ye cannot, or ye will not, aid me.
Spirit   Say;   165
   What we possess we offer, it is thine.
   Bethink ere thou dismiss us, ask again;
   Kingdom, and sway, and strength, and length of days –
Manfred Accursed! What have I to do with days?
   They are too long already. Hence! Begone!   170
Spirit Yet pause. Being here, our will would do thee service;
   Bethink thee, is there then no other gift
   Which we can make not worthless in thine eyes?
Manfred No, none – yet stay one moment ere we part,
   I would behold ye face to face. I hear   175
   Your voices, sweet and melancholy sounds,
   As music on the waters, and I see
   The steady aspect of a clear large star –
   But nothing more. Approach me as ye are,
   Or one, or all, in your accustomed forms.   180
Spirit We have no forms beyond the elements
   Of which we are the mind and principle.
   But choose a form – in that we will appear.
Manfred I have no choice; there is no form on earth
   Hideous or beautiful to me. Let him   185
   Who is most powerful of ye, take such aspect
   As unto him may seem most fitting. Come!
Seventh Spirit (*appearing in the shape of a beautiful female figure*).[2]
   Behold!
Manfred   Oh God! If it be thus, and *thou*
   Art not a madness and a mockery,
   I yet might be most happy. I will clasp thee,   190
   And we again will be – (*the figure vanishes*)
                My heart is crushed!

---

[2]   The Spirit appears in the form of Astarte.

Manfred falls senseless. A voice is heard in the incantation which follows.

When the moon is on the wave
  And the glow-worm in the grass,
And the meteor on the grave
  And the wisp on the morass,   195
When the falling stars are shooting
And the answered owls are hooting,
And the silent leaves are still
In the shadow of the hill,
Shall my soul be upon thine   200
With a power and with a sign.

Though thy slumber may be deep
Yet thy spirit shall not sleep;
There are shades which will not vanish,
There are thoughts thou canst not banish;   205
By a power to thee unknown
Thou canst never be alone;
Thou art wrapped as with a shroud,
Thou art gathered in a cloud –
And forever shalt thou dwell   210
In the spirit of this spell.

Though thou seest me not pass by,
Thou shalt feel me with thine eye
As a thing that, though unseen,
Must be near thee, and hath been;   215
And when in that secret dread
Thou hast turned around thy head,
Thou shalt marvel I am not
As thy shadow on the spot,
And the power which thou dost feel   220
Shall be what thou must conceal.

And a magic voice and verse
Hath baptized thee with a curse;
And a spirit of the air
Hath begirt thee with a snare;   225
In the wind there is a voice
Shall forbid thee to rejoice;
And to thee shall night deny
All the quiet of her sky;
And the day shall have a sun   230
Which shall make thee wish it done.

From thy false tears I did distil
An essence which hath strength to kill;
From thy own heart I then did wring

The black mood in its blackest spring;   235
From thy own smile I snatched the snake,
For there it coiled as in a brake;
From thy own lip I drew the charm
Which gave all these their chiefest harm;
In proving every poison known,   240
I found the strongest was thine own.

By thy cold breast and serpent smile,
By thy unfathomed gulfs of guile,
By that most seeming virtuous eye,
By thy shut soul's hypocrisy,   245
By the perfection of thine art
Which passed for human thine own heart,
By thy delight in others' pain,
And by thy brotherhood of Cain,
I call upon thee, and compel   250
Thyself to be thy proper hell!

And on thy head I pour the vial
Which doth devote thee to this trial;
Nor to slumber, nor to die,
Shall be in thy destiny;   255
Though thy death shall still seem near
To thy wish, but as a fear;
Lo! the spell now works around thee
And the clankless chain hath bound thee;
O'er thy heart and brain together   260
Hath the word been passed: now wither!

ACT I, SCENE II

The mountain of the Jungfrau. Time: morning. Manfred alone upon the cliffs.
Manfred The spirits I have raised abandon me,
The spells which I have studied baffle me,
The remedy I recked[3] of tortured me;
I lean no more on superhuman aid,
It hath no power upon the past, and for   5
The future, till the past be gulfed in darkness,
It is not of my search. My mother earth,
And thou fresh-breaking day, and you, ye mountains –
Why are ye beautiful? I cannot love ye.
And thou, the bright eye of the universe   10
That openest over all, and unto all
Art a delight – thou shin'st not on my heart.

---

[3] *recked* thought.

And you, ye crags upon whose extreme edge
I stand, and on the torrent's brink beneath
Behold the tall pines dwindled as to shrubs   15
In dizziness of distance, when a leap,
A stir, a motion, even a breath would bring
My breast upon its rocky bosom's bed
To rest for ever – wherefore do I pause?
I feel the impulse, yet I do not plunge;   20
I see the peril, yet do not recede;
And my brain reels, and yet my foot is firm.
There is a power upon me which withholds
And makes it my fatality to live –
If it be life to wear within myself   25
This barrenness of spirit, and to be
My own soul's sepulchre, for I have ceased
To justify my deeds unto myself
(The last infirmity of evil). (*An eagle passes.*) Aye,
Thou winged and cloud-cleaving minister,   30
Whose happy flight is highest into heaven,
Well may'st thou swoop so near me – I should be
Thy prey, and gorge thine eaglets. Thou art gone
Where the eye cannot follow thee, but thine
Yet pierces downward, onward, or above   35
With a pervading vision. Beautiful!
How beautiful is all this visible world,
How glorious in its action and itself!
But we who name ourselves its sovereigns, we
Half-dust, half-deity, alike unfit   40
To sink or soar, with our mixed essence make
A conflict of its elements, and breathe
The breath of degradation and of pride,
Contending with low wants and lofty will
Till our mortality predominates –   45
And men are what they name not to themselves,
And trust not to each other. (*The shepherd's pipe in the distance is heard.*)
                    Hark! the note,
The natural music of the mountain reed
(For here the patriarchal days are not
A pastoral fable) pipes in the liberal air,   50
Mixed with the sweet bells of the sauntering herd!
My soul would drink those echoes. Oh that I were
The viewless spirit of a lovely sound,
A living voice, a breathing harmony,
A bodiless enjoyment, born and dying   55
With the blessed tone which made me!

Enter from below a Chamois Hunter
Chamois Hunter   Even so

This way the chamois[4] leapt. Her nimble feet
Have baffled me; my gains today will scarce
Repay my breakneck travail. What is here
Who seems not of my trade, and yet hath reached   60
A height which none even of our mountaineers,
Save our best hunters, may attain? His garb
Is goodly, his mien manly, and his air
Proud as a freeborn peasant's, at this distance.
I will approach him nearer.
Manfred (*not perceiving the other*) To be thus;   65
Grey-haired with anguish like these blasted pines,
Wrecks of a single winter, barkless, branchless,
A blighted trunk upon a cursed root,
Which but supplies a feeling to decay —
And to be thus, eternally but thus,   70
Having been otherwise! Now furrowed o'er
With wrinkles; ploughed by moments, not by years;
And hours all tortured into ages — hours
Which I outlive! Ye toppling crags of ice,
Ye avalanches whom a breath draws down   75
In mountainous o'erwhelming, come and crush me!
I hear ye momently above, beneath,
Crash with a frequent conflict, but ye pass
And only fall on things which still would live —
On the young flourishing forest, or the hut   80
And hamlet of the harmless villager.
Chamois Hunter The mists begin to rise from up the valley;
I'll warn him to descend, or he may chance
To lose at once his way and life together.
Manfred The mists boil up around the glaciers; clouds   85
Rise curling fast beneath me, white and sulphury
Like foam from the roused ocean of deep hell
Whose every wave breaks on a living shore,
Heaped with the damned like pebbles. I am giddy.
Chamois Hunter I must approach him cautiously; if near,   90
A sudden step will startle him, and he
Seems tottering already.
Manfred   Mountains have fallen,
Leaving a gap in the clouds, and with the shock
Rocking their Alpine brethren, filling up
The ripe green valleys with destruction's splinters,   95
Damming the rivers with a sudden dash
Which crushed the waters into mist and made
Their fountains find another channel — thus,
Thus in its old age, did Mount Rosenberg;[5]

---

[4] *chamois* antelope found in the highest parts of the Alps.

[5] On 2 Sept. 1806 part of Mt Rossberg fell and buried four villages.

Why stood I not beneath it?
Chamois Hunter   Friend, have a care,   100
  Your next step may be fatal! For the love
  Of him who made you, stand not on that brink!
Manfred (not hearing him) Such would have been for me a fitting tomb;
  My bones had then been quiet in their depth;
  They had not then been strewn upon the rocks   105
  For the wind's pastime, as thus – thus they shall be,
  In this one plunge. Farewell, ye opening heavens!
  Look not upon me thus reproachfully,
  Ye were not meant for me. Earth, take these atoms!
As Manfred is in act to spring from the cliff, the Chamois Hunter seizes and retains him
with a sudden grasp.
Chamois Hunter Hold, madman! Though aweary of thy life,   110
  Stain not our pure vales with thy guilty blood!
  Away with me – I will not quit my hold.
Manfred I am most sick at heart – nay, grasp me not,
  I am all feebleness; the mountains whirl
  Spinning around me – I grow blind. What art thou?   115
Chamois Hunter I'll answer that anon. Away with me;
  The clouds grow thicker – there, now lean on me;
  Place your foot here – here, take this staff, and cling
  A moment to that shrub. Now give me your hand
  And hold fast by my girdle – softly, well.   120
  The chalet will be gained within an hour;
  Come on, we'll quickly find a surer footing
  And something like a pathway, which the torrent
  Hath washed since winter. Come, 'tis bravely done –
  You should have been a hunter! Follow me.   125
As they descend the rocks with difficulty, the scene closes.

ACT II, SCENE I

A cottage amongst the Bernese Alps. Manfred and the Chamois Hunter.
Chamois Hunter No, no – yet pause, thou must not yet go forth;
  Thy mind and body are alike unfit
  To trust each other for some hours, at least.
  When thou art better, I will be thy guide –
  But whither?
Manfred   It imports not. I do know   5
  My route full well, and need no further guidance.
Chamois Hunter Thy garb and gait bespeak thee of high lineage –
  One of the many chiefs, whose castled crags
  Look o'er the lower valleys. Which of these
  May call thee lord? I only know their portals;   10
  My way of life leads me but rarely down
  To bask by the huge hearths of those old halls,
  Carousing with the vassals; but the paths

Which step from out our mountains to their doors
I know from childhood – which of these is thine? 15
Manfred No matter.
Chamois Hunter   Well sir, pardon me the question,
  And be of better cheer. Come taste my wine,
  'Tis of an ancient vintage – many a day
  'T has thawed my veins among our glaciers; now
  Let it do thus for thine. Come, pledge me fairly. 20
Manfred Away, away! There's blood upon the brim!
  Will it then never, never sink in the earth?
Chamois Hunter What dost thou mean? Thy senses wander from thee.
Manfred I say 'tis blood – my blood! The pure warm stream
  Which ran in the veins of my fathers, and in ours 25
  When we were in our youth, and had one heart,
  And loved each other as we should not love,
  And this was shed. But still it rises up,
  Colouring the clouds that shut me out from heaven,
  Where thou art not, and I shall never be. 30
Chamois Hunter Man of strange words and some half-maddening sin
  Which makes thee people vacancy, whate'er
  Thy dread and sufferance be, there's comfort yet –
  The aid of holy men, and heavenly patience –
Manfred Patience and patience hence! That word was made 35
  For brutes of burden, not for birds of prey;
  Preach it to mortals of a dust like thine,
  I am not of thine order.
Chamois Hunter   Thanks to heaven!
  I would not be of thine for the free fame
  Of William Tell! But whatsoe'er thine ill, 40
  It must be borne, and these wild starts are useless.
Manfred Do I not bear it? Look on me – I live.
Chamois Hunter This is convulsion, and no healthful life.
Manfred I tell thee, man! I have lived many years,
  Many long years, but they are nothing now 45
  To those which I must number: ages, ages,
  Space and eternity – and consciousness
  With the fierce thirst of death – and still unslaked!
Chamois Hunter Why, on thy brow the seal of middle age
  Hath scarce been set; I am thine elder far. 50
Manfred Think'st thou existence doth depend on time?
  It doth, but actions are our epochs. Mine
  Have made my days and nights imperishable,
  Endless, and all alike as sands on the shore,
  Innumerable atoms, and one desert, 55
  Barren and cold, on which the wild waves break
  But nothing rests save carcasses and wrecks,
  Rocks, and salt-surf weeds of bitterness.

Chamois Hunter Alas, he's mad — but yet I must not leave him.

Manfred I would I were, for then the things I see   60
  Would be but a distempered dream.

Chamois Hunter   What is it
  That thou dost see, or think thou look'st upon?

Manfred Myself and thee, a peasant of the Alps;
  Thy humble virtues, hospitable home
  And spirit patient, pious, proud and free;   65
  Thy self-respect, grafted on innocent thoughts;
  Thy days of health and nights of sleep; thy toils
  By danger dignified, yet guiltless; hopes
  Of cheerful old age and a quiet grave
  With cross and garland over its green turf,   70
  And thy grandchildren's love for epitaph —
  This do I see, and then I look within —
  It matters not; my soul was scorched already.

Chamois Hunter And would'st thou then exchange thy lot for mine?

Manfred No, friend! I would not wrong thee, nor exchange   75
  My lot with living being. I can bear —
  However wretchedly, 'tis still to bear —
  In life what others could not brook to dream,
  But perish in their slumber.

Chamois Hunter   And with this,
  This cautious feeling for another's pain,   80
  Canst thou be black with evil? Say not so.
  Can one of gentle thoughts have wreaked revenge
  Upon his enemies?

Manfred   Oh no, no, no!
  My injuries came down on those who loved me,
  On those whom I best loved. I never quelled   85
  An enemy, save in my just defence,
  My wrongs were all on those I should have cherished,
  But my embrace was fatal.

Chamois Hunter   Heaven give thee rest,
  And penitence restore thee to thyself;
  My prayers shall be for thee.

Manfred   I need them not,   90
  But can endure thy pity. I depart;
  'Tis time, farewell! Here's gold, and thanks for thee —
  No words, it is thy due. Follow me not.
  I know my path, the mountain peril's past —
  And once again I charge thee, follow not!   95

Exit Manfred.

ACT II, SCENE II

A lower valley in the Alps. A cataract. Enter Manfred.
  It is not noon. The sunbow's rays still arch

The torrent with the many hues of heaven,[6]
And roll the sheeted silver's waving column
O'er the crag's headlong perpendicular,
And fling its lines of foaming light along,   5
And to and fro, like the pale courser's tail,
The giant steed to be bestrode by death,
As told in the Apocalypse.[7] No eyes
But mine now drink this sight of loveliness;
I should be sole in this sweet solitude,   10
And with the spirit of the place divide
The homage of these waters. I will call her.

Manfred takes some of the water into the palm of his hand, and flings it in the air, muttering the adjuration. After a pause, the Witch of the Alps rises beneath the arch of the sunbow of the torrent.

Beautiful spirit, with thy hair of light
And dazzling eyes of glory, in whose form
The charms of earth's least mortal daughters grow   15
To an unearthly stature in an essence
Of purer elements, while the hues of youth –
Carnationed like a sleeping infant's cheek,
Rocked by the beating of her mother's heart,
Or the rose tints, which summer's twilight leaves   20
Upon the lofty glacier's virgin snow,
The blush of earth embracing with her heaven –
Tinge thy celestial aspect, and make tame
The beauties of the sunbow which bends o'er thee;
Beautiful spirit, in thy calm clear brow   25
Wherein is glassed serenity of soul,
Which of itself shows immortality,
I read that thou wilt pardon to a son
Of earth, whom the abstruser powers permit
At times to commune with them, if that he   30
Avail him of his spells, to call thee thus
And gaze on thee a moment.
Witch   Son of earth!
I know thee and the powers which give thee power;
I know thee for a man of many thoughts
And deeds of good and ill (extreme in both),   35
Fatal and fated in thy sufferings.
I have expected this – what wouldst thou with me?
Manfred To look upon thy beauty, nothing further.
The face of the earth hath maddened me, and I
Take refuge in her mysteries, and pierce   40
To the abodes of those who govern her,
But they can nothing aid me. I have sought

---

[6] 'This iris is formed by the rays of the sun over the lower part of the Alpine torrents. It is exactly like a rainbow come down to pay a visit, and so close that you may walk into it. This effect lasts until noon' (Byron's note).
[7] See Rev. 6: 8.

From them what they could not bestow, and now
I search no further.
Witch   What could be the quest
Which is not in the power of the most powerful,   45
The rulers of the invisible?
Manfred   A boon –
But why should I repeat it? 'Twere in vain.
Witch I know not that; let thy lips utter it.
Manfred Well, though it torture me, 'tis but the same;
My pang shall find a voice. From my youth upwards   50
My spirit walked not with the souls of men,
Nor looked upon the earth with human eyes;
The thirst of their ambition was not mine,
The aim of their existence was not mine;
My joys, my griefs, my passions and my powers   55
Made me a stranger; though I wore the form,
I had no sympathy with breathing flesh,
Nor midst the creatures of clay that girded me
Was there but one who – but of her anon.
I said, with men, and with the thoughts of men   60
I held but slight communion, but instead
My joy was in the wilderness – to breathe
The difficult air of the iced mountain's top
Where the birds dare not build, nor insect's wing
Flit o'er the herbless granite; or to plunge   65
Into the torrent, and to roll along
On the swift whirl of the new-breaking wave
Of river-stream or ocean in their flow.
In these my early strength exulted – or
To follow through the night the moving moon,   70
The stars and their development; or catch
The dazzling lightnings till my eyes grew dim;
Or to look, list'ning, on the scattered leaves
While autumn winds were at their evening song.
These were my pastimes, and to be alone;   75
For if the beings of whom I was one
(Hating to be so) crossed me in my path,
I felt myself degraded back to them
And was all clay again. And then I dived
In my lone wanderings to the caves of death,   80
Searching its cause in its effect, and drew
From withered bones and skulls and heaped-up dust
Conclusions most forbidden. Then I passed
The nights of years in sciences untaught,
Save in the old time, and with time and toil   85
And terrible ordeal, and such penance
As in itself hath power upon the air,
And spirits that do compass air and earth,

Space and the peopled infinite, I made
Mine eyes familiar with eternity, 90
Such as, before me, did the Magi[8] and
He[9] who from out their fountain dwellings raised
Eros and Anteros at Gadara,
As I do thee. And with my knowledge grew
The thirst of knowledge, and the power and joy 95
Of this most bright intelligence, until –
Witch Proceed.
Manfred   Oh, I but thus prolonged my words,
Boasting these idle attributes, because,
As I approach the core of my heart's grief –
But to my task. I have not named to thee 100
Father or mother, mistress, friend or being
With whom I wore the chain of human ties;
If I had such, they seemed not such to me.
Yet there was one –
Witch   Spare not thyself; proceed.
Manfred She was like me in lineaments – her eyes, 105
Her hair, her features, all, to the very tone
Even of her voice, they said were like to mine,
But softened all and tempered into beauty.
She had the same lone thoughts and wanderings,
The quest of hidden knowledge, and a mind 110
To comprehend the universe – nor these
Alone, but with them gentler powers than mine:
Pity and smiles and tears (which I had not)
And tenderness (but that I had for her),
Humility (and that I never had). 115
Her faults were mine; her virtues were her own –
I loved her, and destroyed her!
Witch   With thy hand?
Manfred Not with my hand, but heart – which broke her heart:
It gazed on mine and withered. I have shed
Blood, but not hers, and yet her blood was shed – 120
I saw and could not staunch it.
Witch   And for this,
A being of the race thou dost despise,
The order which thine own would rise above,
Mingling with us and ours, thou dost forego
The gifts of our great knowledge, and shrink'st back 125
To recreant mortality? Away!
Manfred Daughter of air, I tell thee, since that hour –
But words are breath; look on me in my sleep
Or watch my watchings – come and sit by me!

---

8   *the Magi* the ancient Persian priestly caste.
9   *He* 'The philosopher Iamblicus. The story of the
raising of Eros and Anteros may be found in his life,
by Eunapius. It is well told' (Byron's note).

My solitude is solitude no more,   130
But peopled with the Furies; I have gnashed
My teeth in darkness till returning morn,
Then cursed myself till sunset; I have prayed
For madness as a blessing – 'tis denied me;
I have affronted death, but in the war   135
Of elements the waters shrunk from me,
And fatal things passed harmless – the cold hand
Of an all-pitiless demon held me back,
Back by a single hair which would not break.
In fantasy, imagination, all   140
The affluence of my soul (which one day was
A Croesus in creation), I plunged deep,
But like an ebbing wave, it dashed me back
Into the gulf of my unfathomed thought.
I plunged amidst mankind; forgetfulness   145
I sought in all save where 'tis to be found,
And that I have to learn; my sciences,
My long-pursued and superhuman art
Is mortal here. I dwell in my despair
And live – and live for ever.   150
Witch   It may be
That I can aid thee.
Manfred   To do this thy power
Must wake the dead, or lay me low with them.
Do so, in any shape, in any hour,
With any torture – so it be the last.
Witch That is not in my province, but if thou   155
Wilt swear obedience to my will and do
My bidding, it may help thee to thy wishes.
Manfred I will not swear! Obey? And whom? The spirits
Whose presence I command – and be the slave
Of those who served me? Never![10]
Witch   Is this all?   160
Hast thou no gentler answer? Yet bethink thee,
And pause ere thou rejectest.
Manfred   I have said it.
Witch Enough! I may retire then – say!
Manfred   Retire!
The Witch disappears.
Manfred (*alone*) We are the fools of time and terror. Days
Steal on us and steal from us, yet we live,   165
Loathing our life, and dreading still to die.
In all the days of this detested yoke

---

[10] Manfred's defiant rejection of the authority of the
spirits is a distinguishing feature of Byron's version of
the Faust legend.

(This heaving burden, this accursed breath,
This vital weight upon the struggling heart
Which sinks with sorrow or beats quick with pain,⠀⠀⠀⠀170
Or joy that ends in agony or faintness);
In all the days of past and future – for
In life there is no present – we can number
How few, how less than few, wherein the soul
Forbears to pant for death and yet draws back⠀⠀⠀⠀175
As from a stream in winter, though the chill
Be but a moment's. I have one resource
Still in my science; I can call the dead
And ask them what it is we dread to be.
The sternest answer can but be the grave,⠀⠀⠀⠀180
And that is nothing; if they answer not . . .
The buried prophet answered to the hag
Of Endor,[11] and the Spartan monarch drew
From the Byzantine maid's unsleeping spirit
An answer and his destiny – he slew⠀⠀⠀⠀185
That which he loved, unknowing what he slew,
And died unpardoned, though he called in aid
The Phyxian Jove, and in Phigalia roused
The Arcadian evocators to compel
The indignant shadow to depose her wrath⠀⠀⠀⠀190
Or fix her term of vengeance; she replied
In words of dubious import, but fulfilled.[12]
⠀If I had never lived, that which I love
Had still been living; had I never loved,
That which I loved would still be beautiful,⠀⠀⠀⠀195
Happy and giving happiness. What is she,
What is she now? A sufferer for my sins,
A thing I dare not think upon – or nothing.
Within few hours I shall not call in vain,
Yet in this hour I dread the thing I dare.⠀⠀⠀⠀200
Until this hour I never shrunk to gaze
On spirit, good or evil; now I tremble
And feel a strange cold thaw upon my heart.
But I can act even what I most abhor
And champion human fears. The night approaches.⠀⠀⠀⠀205
⠀⠀*Exit.*

ACT II, SCENE III

The summit of the Jungfrau mountain. Enter First Destiny.
⠀The moon is rising broad and round and bright,

[11] ⠀1 Sam. 28: 7.
[12] ⠀'The story of Pausanias, King of Sparta (who commanded the Greeks in the Battle of Platea, and afterwards perished for an attempt to betray the Lacedemonians), and Cleonice, is told in Plutarch's life of Cimon, and in the Laconics of Pausanias the Sophist, in his description of Greece' (Byron's note).

And here on snows where never human foot
Of common mortal trod,[13] we nightly tread
And leave no traces. O'er the savage sea,
The glassy ocean of the mountain ice,   5
We skim its rugged breakers, which put on
The aspect of a tumbling tempest's foam,
Frozen in a moment – a dead whirlpool's image;
And this most steep fantastic pinnacle,
The fretwork of some earthquake where the clouds   10
Pause to repose themselves in passing by,
Is sacred to our revels or our vigils.
Here do I wait my sisters, on our way
To the Hall of Arimanes,[14] for tonight
Is our great festival. 'Tis strange they come not.   15

A voice without, singing
    The captive usurper
      Hurled down from the throne,
    Lay buried in torpor,
      Forgotten and lone;
    I broke through his slumbers,   20
      I shivered his chain,
    I leagued him with numbers –
      He's tyrant again![15]
With the blood of a million he'll answer my care,
With a nation's destruction, his flight and despair.   25

Second voice without
    The ship sailed on, the ship sailed fast,
But I left not a sail, and I left not a mast;
There is not a plank of the hull or the deck,
And there is not a wretch to lament o'er his wreck,
Save one whom I held, as he swam, by the hair,   30
And he was a subject well worthy my care –
A traitor on land and a pirate at sea –
But I saved him to wreak further havoc for me!

First Destiny (answering)
    The city lies sleeping;
      The morn, to deplore it,   35
    May dawn on it weeping;
      Sullenly, slowly,
    The black plague flew o'er it –
      Thousands lie lowly;

---

[13] The Jungfrau was first scaled in 1811.
[14] Arimanes derives his name from Ahriman, the principle of darkness and evil in Persian dualism.

[15] The Spirit prophesies the return of Napoleon from St Helena.

Tens of thousands shall perish; 40
   The living shall fly from
The sick they should cherish,
   But nothing can vanquish
The touch that they die from.
     Sorrow and anguish 45
And evil and dread
   Envelop a nation;
The blessed are the dead
   Who see not the sight
Of their own desolation. 50
     This work of a night,
This wreck of a realm, this deed of my doing –
For ages I've done and shall still be renewing!

Enter the Second and Third Destinies.

The Three
   Our hands contain the hearts of men,
     Our footsteps are their graves; 55
   We only give to take again
     The spirits of our slaves!

First Destiny Welcome! Where's Nemesis?
Second Destiny   At some great work,
   But what I know not, for my hands were full.
Third Destiny Behold, she cometh.
Enter Nemesis
First Destiny   Say, where hast thou been? 60
   My sisters and thyself are slow tonight.
Nemesis I was detained repairing shattered thrones,
   Marrying fools, restoring dynasties,
   Avenging men upon their enemies,
   And making them repent their own revenge; 65
   Goading the wise to madness, from the dull
   Shaping out oracles to rule the world
   Afresh – for they were waxing out of date
   And mortals dared to ponder for themselves,
   To weigh kings in the balance, and to speak 70
   Of freedom, the forbidden fruit. Away!
   We have outstayed the hour; mount we our clouds!
Exeunt.

ACT II, SCENE IV

The Hall of Arimanes, Arimanes on his throne, a globe of fire, surrounded by the spirits. Hymn of the Spirits
   Hail to our master, Prince of earth and air!
     Who walks the clouds and waters – in his hand

The sceptre of the elements, which tear
   Themselves to chaos at his high command!
He breatheth, and a tempest shakes the sea;
   He speaketh, and the clouds reply in thunder;   5
He gazeth – from his glance the sunbeams flee;
   He moveth – earthquakes rend the world asunder.
Beneath his footsteps the volcanoes rise;
   His shadow is the pestilence, his path   10
The comets herald through the crackling skies,
   And planets turn to ashes at his wrath.
To him war offers daily sacrifice,
   To him death pays his tribute; life is his,
With all its infinite of agonies,   15
   And his the spirit of whatever is!

Enter the Destinies and Nemesis.
  First Destiny Glory to Arimanes! On the earth
    His power increaseth; both my sisters did
    His bidding, nor did I neglect my duty.
  Second Destiny Glory to Arimanes! We who bow   20
    The necks of men, bow down before his throne.
  Third Destiny Glory to Arimanes! We await
    His nod.
  Nemesis   Sovereign of Sovereigns! We are thine,
    And all that liveth, more or less, is ours,
    And most things wholly so; still to increase   25
    Our power increasing thine, demands our care,
    And we are vigilant. Thy late commands
    Have been fulfilled to the utmost.
Enter Manfred
  A Spirit   What is here?
    A mortal? Thou most rash and fatal wretch,
    Bow down and worship!
  Second Spirit   I do know the man,   30
    A Magian of great power and fearful skill.
  Third Spirit Bow down and worship, slave! What, know'st thou not
    Thine and our sovereign? Tremble, and obey!
  All the Spirits Prostrate thyself and thy condemned clay,
    Child of the earth, or dread the worst!
  Manfred   I know it,   35
    And yet ye see I kneel not.
  Fourth Spirit   'Twill be taught thee.
  Manfred 'Tis taught already; many a night on the earth,
    On the bare ground have I bowed down my face
    And strewed my head with ashes. I have known
    The fullness of humiliation, for   40
    I sunk before my vain despair, and knelt
    To my own desolation.

Fifth Spirit   Dost thou dare
  Refuse to Arimanes on his throne
  What the whole earth accords, beholding not
  The terror of his glory? Crouch, I say!   45
Manfred Bid *him* bow down to that which is above him,
  The overruling Infinite, the Maker
  Who made him not for worship; let him kneel,
  And we will kneel together.
The Spirits   Crush the worm!
  Tear him in pieces!
First Destiny   Hence! Avaunt! He's mine.   50
  Prince of the powers invisible! this man
  Is of no common order, as his port
  And presence here denote. His sufferings
  Have been of an immortal nature like
  Our own; his knowledge and his powers and will,   55
  As far as is compatible with clay
  (Which clogs the ethereal essence), have been such
  As clay hath seldom borne; his aspirations
  Have been beyond the dwellers of the earth,
  And they have only taught him what we know –   60
  That knowledge is not happiness, and science
  But an exchange of ignorance for that
  Which is another kind of ignorance.
  This is not all. The passions, attributes
  Of earth and heaven, from which no power nor being   65
  Nor breath from the worm upwards is exempt,
  Have pierced his heart, and in their consequence
  Made him a thing which I, who pity not,
  Yet pardon those who pity. He is mine,
  And thine, it may be; be it so or not,   70
  No other spirit in this region hath
  A soul like his – or power upon his soul.
Nemesis What doth he here then?
First Destiny   Let *him* answer that.
Manfred Ye know what I have known, and without power
  I could not be amongst ye; but there are   75
  Powers deeper still beyond. I come in quest
  Of such, to answer unto what I seek.
Nemesis What wouldst *thou*?
Manfred   Thou canst not reply to me.
  Call up the dead – my question is for them.
Nemesis Great Arimanes, doth thy will avouch   80
  The wishes of this mortal?
Arimanes   Yea.
Nemesis   Whom would'st thou
  Uncharnel?

Manfred   One without a tomb. Call up
  Astarte.
Nemesis
      Shadow or spirit,
        Whatever thou art,   85
      Which still doth inherit
        The whole or a part
      Of the form of thy birth,
        Of the mould of thy clay
      Which returned to the earth,   90
        Reappear to the day!
      Bear what thou borest,
        The heart and the form,
      And the aspect thou worest
        Redeem from the worm.   95
      Appear! Appear! Appear!
      Who sent thee there requires thee here!

The phantom of Astarte rises and stands in the midst.

Manfred Can this be death? There's bloom upon her cheek,
  But now I see it is no living hue
  But a strange hectic,[16] like the unnatural red   100
  Which autumn plants upon the perished leaf.
  It is the same! Oh God, that I should dread
  To look upon the same – Astarte! No,
  I cannot speak to her; but bid her speak –
  Forgive me or condemn me.   105
Nemesis.
  By the power which hath broken
    The grave which enthralled thee,
  Speak to him who hath spoken,
    Or those who have called thee!
Manfred   She is silent,   110
  And in that silence I am more than answered.
Nemesis. My power extends no further. Prince of air!
  It rests with thee alone; command her voice.
Arimanes Spirit – obey this sceptre!
Nemesis   Silent still!
  She is not of our order, but belongs   115
  To the other powers. Mortal, thy quest is vain,
  And we are baffled also.
Manfred   Hear me, hear me –
  Astarte, my beloved, speak to me!
  I have so much endured, so much endure –
  Look on me! The grave hath not changed thee more 120
  Than I am changed for thee. Thou lovedst me

---

16 *hectic* a flush or heightened colour on the cheek.

Too much, as I loved thee; we were not made
To torture thus each other, though it were
The deadliest sin to love as we have loved.
Say that thou loath'st me not, that I do bear   125
This punishment for both, that thou wilt be
One of the blessed, and that I shall die,
For hitherto all hateful things conspire
To bind me in existence, in a life
Which makes me shrink from immortality –   130
A future like the past. I cannot rest.
I know not what I ask nor what I seek;
I feel but what thou art and what I am,
And I would hear yet once before I perish
The voice which was my music: speak to me!   135
For I have called on thee in the still night,
Startled the slumbering birds from the hushed boughs,
And woke the mountain wolves, and made the caves
Acquainted with thy vainly-echoed name,
Which answered me – many things answered me,   140
Spirits and men, but thou wert silent all.
Yet speak to me! I have outwatched the stars
And gazed o'er heaven in vain in search of thee.
Speak to me! I have wandered o'er the earth
And never found thy likeness – speak to me!   145
Look on the fiends around; they feel for me.
I fear them not, and feel for thee alone –
Speak to me, though it be in wrath, but say –
I reck not what – but let me hear thee once –
This once – once more!
Phantom of Astarte   Manfred!
Manfred   Say on, say on;   150
    I live but in the sound – it is thy voice!
Phantom of Astarte Manfred! Tomorrow ends thine earthly ills.
    Farewell!
Manfred   Yet one word more: am I forgiven?
Phantom of Astarte Farewell!
Manfred   Say, shall we meet again?
Phantom of Astarte   Farewell!
Manfred One word for mercy; say thou lovest me.   155
Phantom of Astarte Manfred!
The spirit of Astarte disappears.
Nemesis   She's gone and will not be recalled;
    Her words will be fulfilled. Return to the earth.
A Spirit He is convulsed; this is to be a mortal
    And seek the things beyond mortality.
Another spirit Yet see, he mastereth himself and makes   160
    His torture tributary to his will;
    Had he been one of us, he would have made

An awful spirit.
Nemesis   Hast thou further question
  Of our great sovereign or his worshippers?
Manfred None.
Nemesis   Then for a time farewell.
Manfred   We meet then –   165
  Where? On the earth?
Nemesis   That will be seen hereafter.
Manfred Even as thou wilt; and for the grace accorded
  I now depart a debtor. Fare ye well!
Exit Manfred

Act III, Scene i

A hall in the castle of Manfred. Manfred and Herman.
Manfred What is the hour?
Herman   It wants but one till sunset,
  And promises a lovely twilight.
Manfred   Say,
  Are all things so disposed of in the tower
  As I directed?
Herman   All, my lord, are ready;
  Here is the key and casket.
Manfred   It is well;   5
  Thou mayst retire.
Exit Herman.
  Manfred (alone)   There is a calm upon me –
  Inexplicable stillness, which till now
  Did not belong to what I knew of life.
  If that I did not know philosophy
  To be of all our vanities the motliest,   10
  The merest word that ever fooled the ear
  From out the schoolman's jargon, I should deem
  The golden secret, the sought kalon,[17] found
  And seated in my soul. It will not last,
  But it is well to have known it, though but once;   15
  It hath enlarged my thoughts with a new sense,
  And I within my tablets would note down
  That there is such a feeling. Who is there?
Re-enter Herman.
Herman My lord, the Abbot of St Maurice craves
  To greet your presence.
Enter the Abbot of St Maurice.
Abbot   Peace be with Count Manfred!   20
Manfred Thanks, holy father; welcome to these walls!
  Thy presence honours them, and blesseth those

---

[17] *kalon* the ideal good, the morally beautiful.

Who dwell within them.
Abbot   Would it were so, Count;
 But I would fain confer with thee alone.
Manfred Herman, retire. (*Exit Herman*) What would my reverend guest? 25
Abbot Thus, without prelude. Age and zeal, my office,
 And good intent, must plead my privilege;
 Our near, though not acquainted neighbourhood
 May also be my herald. Rumours strange
 And of unholy nature are abroad   30
 And busy with thy name – a noble name
 For centuries. May he who bears it now
 Transmit it unimpaired!
Manfred   Proceed, I listen.
Abbot 'Tis said thou holdest converse with the things
 Which are forbidden to the search of man;   35
 That with the dwellers of the dark abodes,
 The many evil and unheavenly spirits
 Which walk the valley of the shade of death,
 Thou communest. I know that with mankind,
 Thy fellows in creation, thou dost rarely   40
 Exchange thy thoughts, and that thy solitude
 Is as an anchorite's, were it but holy.
Manfred And what are they who do avouch these things?
Abbot My pious brethren, the scared peasantry –
 Even thy own vassals, who do look on thee   45
 With most unquiet eyes. Thy life's in peril.
Manfred Take it.
Abbot   I come to save, and not destroy.
 I would not pry into thy secret soul,
 But if these things be sooth, there still is time
 For penitence and pity: reconcile thee   50
 With the true church, and through the church to heaven.
Manfred I hear thee. This is my reply: whate'er
 I may have been, or am, doth rest between
 Heaven and myself. I shall not choose a mortal
 To be my mediator. Have I sinned   55
 Against your ordinances? Prove and punish!
Abbot My son, I did not speak of punishment,
 But penitence and pardon; with thyself
 The choice of such remains. And for the last,
 Our institutions and our strong belief   60
 Have given me power to smooth the path from sin
 To higher hope and better thoughts; the first
 I leave to heaven – 'Vengeance is mine alone!'
 So saith the Lord, and with all humbleness
 His servant echoes back the awful word.   65
Manfred Old man! There is no power in holy men,
 Nor charm in prayer, nor purifying form

Of penitence, nor outward look, nor fast,
Nor agony – nor, greater than all these,
The innate tortures of that deep despair   70
Which is remorse without the fear of hell
But all in all sufficient to itself
Would make a hell of heaven, can exorcise
From out the unbounded spirit the quick sense
Of its own sins, wrongs, sufferance, and revenge   75
Upon itself. There is no future pang
Can deal that justice on the self-condemned
He deals on his own soul.
Abbot   All this is well –
For this will pass away, and be succeeded
By an auspicious hope which shall look up   80
With calm assurance to that blessed place
Which all who seek may win, whatever be
Their earthly errors, so they be atoned;
And the commencement of atonement is
The sense of its necessity. Say on,   85
And all our church can teach thee shall be taught,
And all we can absolve thee shall be pardoned.
Manfred When Rome's sixth Emperor[18] was near his last,
The victim of a self-inflicted wound,
To shun the torments of a public death   90
From senates once his slaves, a certain soldier,
With show of loyal pity, would have staunched
The gushing throat with his officious robe;
The dying Roman thrust him back and said
(Some empire still in his expiring glance),   95
'It is too late – is this fidelity?'
Abbot And what of this?
Manfred   I answer with the Roman,
'It is too late!'
Abbot   It never can be so,
To reconcile thyself with thy own soul,
And thy own soul with heaven. Hast thou no hope?   100
'Tis strange; even those who do despair above
Yet shape themselves some fantasy on earth
To which frail twig they cling like drowning men.
Manfred Ay, father! I have had those earthly visions
And noble aspirations in my youth –   105
To make my own the mind of other men,
The enlightener of nations, and to rise
I knew not whither; it might be to fall,

---

[18]   Byron applies Suetonius's account of the death of
Nero to the suicide of Otho, the sixth Emperor of
Rome.

But fall even as the mountain-cataract
Which, having leaped from its more dazzling height,   110
Even in the foaming strength of its abyss
(Which casts up misty columns that become
Clouds raining from the re-ascended skies)
Lies low but mighty still. But this is passed;
My thoughts mistook themselves.
Abbot   And wherefore so?   115
Manfred I could not tame my nature down; for he
    Must serve who fain would sway, and soothe, and sue,
    And watch all time, and pry into all place –
    And be a living lie, who would become
    A mighty thing amongst the mean (and such   120
    The mass are). I disdained to mingle with
    A herd, though to be leader – and of wolves.
    The lion is alone, and so am I.
Abbot And why not live and act with other men?
Manfred Because my nature was averse from life,   125
    And yet not cruel – for I would not make,
    But find a desolation. Like the wind,
    The red-hot breath of the most lone Simoom,
    Which dwells but in the desert, and sweeps o'er
    The barren sands which bear no shrubs to blast,   130
    And revels o'er their wild and arid waves
    And seeketh not, so that it is not sought,
    But being met is deadly; such hath been
    The course of my existence. But there came
    Things in my path which are no more.
Abbot   Alas,   135
    I 'gin to fear that thou art past all aid
    From me and from my calling; yet so young,
    I still would –
Manfred   Look on me! There is an order
    Of mortals on the earth, who do become
    Old in their youth, and die ere middle age   140
    Without the violence of warlike death –
    Some perishing of pleasure, some of study,
    Some worn with toil, some of mere weariness,
    Some of disease, and some insanity,
    And some of withered or of broken hearts;   145
    For this last is a malady which slays
    More than are numbered in the lists of fate,
    Taking all shapes, and bearing many names.
    Look upon me! For even of all these things
    Have I partaken, and of all these things   150
    One were enough; then wonder not that I
    Am what I am, but that I ever was,
    Or, having been, that I am still on earth.

Abbot Yet hear me still –
Manfred   Old man! I do respect
  Thine order, and revere thine years; I deem   155
  Thy purpose pious, but it is in vain.
  Think me not churlish; I would spare thyself
  Far more than me, in shunning at this time
  All further colloquy – and so farewell.
Exit Manfred
Abbot This should have been a noble creature; he   160
  Hath all the energy which would have made
  A goodly frame of glorious elements,
  Had they been wisely mingled. As it is,
  It is an awful chaos – light and darkness,
  And mind and dust, and passions and pure thoughts,   165
  Mixed and contending without end or order,
  All dormant or destructive: he will perish,
  And yet he must not. I will try once more,
  For such are worth redemption, and my duty
  Is to dare all things for a righteous end.   170
  I'll follow him – but cautiously, though surely.
Exit Abbot

ACT III, SCENE II

Another chamber. Manfred and Herman.
Herman My Lord, you bade me wait on you at sunset:
  He sinks behind the mountain.
Manfred   Doth he so?
  I will look on him.
Manfred advances to the window of the hall.
                      Glorious orb! The idol
  Of early nature, and the vigorous race
  Of undiseased mankind, the giant sons
  Of the embrace of angels, with a sex   5
  More beautiful than they, which did draw down
  The erring spirits who can ne'er return;[19]
  Most glorious orb, that wert a worship ere
  The mystery of thy making was revealed!   10
  Thou earliest minister of the Almighty,
  Which gladdened on their mountain-tops, the hearts
  Of the Chaldean shepherds, till they poured
  Themselves in orisons![20] Thou material God
  And representative of the unknown,   15
  Who chose thee for his shadow! Thou chief star,

[19] See Gen. 6: 1–4.
[20] Cf. *Childe Harold's Pilgrimage*, Canto III, stanza 91,
above. *orisons* prayers.

Centre of many stars, which mak'st our earth
Endurable, and temperest the hues
And hearts of all who walk within thy rays!
Sire of the seasons! Monarch of the climes   20
And those who dwell in them (for near or far,
Our inborn spirits have a tint of thee,
Even as our outward aspects), thou dost rise
And shine and set in glory – fare thee well,
I ne'er shall see thee more! As my first glance   25
Of love and wonder was for thee, then take
My latest look: thou wilt not beam on one
To whom the gifts of life and warmth have been
Of a more fatal nature. He is gone;
I follow.   30

Exit Manfred

ACT III, SCENE III

The mountains. The castle of Manfred at some distance. A terrace before a tower. Time:
twilight. Herman, Manuel, and other dependants of Manfred.

Herman 'Tis strange enough; night after night for years
   He hath pursued long vigils in this tower
   Without a witness. I have been within it –
   So have we all been oft-times; but from it,
   Or its contents, it were impossible   5
   To draw conclusions absolute of aught
   His studies tend to. To be sure, there is
   One chamber where none enter; I would give
   The fee of what I have to come these three years
   To pore upon its mysteries.
Manuel   'Twere dangerous;   10
   Content thyself with what thou knowest already.
Herman Ah, Manuel! Thou art elderly and wise,
   And could'st say much; thou hast dwelt within the castle –
   How many years is't?
Manuel   Ere Count Manfred's birth
   I served his father, whom he nought resembles.   15
Herman There be more sons in like predicament.
   But wherein do they differ?
Manuel   I speak not
   Of features or of form, but mind and habits:
   Count Sigismund was proud, but gay and free,
   A warrior and a reveller; he dwelt not   20
   With books and solitude, nor made the night
   A gloomy vigil, but a festal time,
   Merrier than day; he did not walk the rocks
   And forests like a wolf, nor turn aside
   From men and their delights.

Herman   Beshrew the hour,   25
But those were jocund times! I would that such
Would visit the old walls again; they look
As if they had forgotten them.
Manuel   These walls
Must change their chieftain first – oh, I have seen
Some strange things in them, Herman!
Herman   Come, be friendly,   30
Relate me some to while away our watch;
I've heard thee darkly speak of an event
Which happened hereabouts, by this same tower.
Manuel That was a night indeed. I do remember
'Twas twilight, as it may be now, and such   35
Another evening; yon red cloud, which rests
On Eiger's pinnacle,[21] so rested then,
So like that it might be the same; the wind
Was faint and gusty, and the mountain snows
Began to glitter with the climbing moon.   40
Count Manfred was, as now, within his tower,
How occupied we knew not, but with him
The sole companion of his wanderings
And watchings – her, whom of all earthly things
That lived, the only thing he seemed to love,   45
As he indeed by blood was bound to do,
The lady Astarte, his –
                    Hush! Who comes here?

Enter the Abbot
Abbot Where is your master?
Herman   Yonder, in the tower.
Abbot I must speak with him.
Manuel   'Tis impossible.
He is most private, and must not be thus   50
Intruded on.
Abbot   Upon myself I take
The forfeit of my fault, if fault there be;
But I must see him.
Herman   Thou hast seen him once
This eve already.
Abbot   Sirrah, I command thee
Knock and apprise the Count of my approach!   55
Herman We dare not.
Abbot   Then it seems I must be herald
Of my own purpose.
Manuel   Reverend father, stop,
I pray you pause.

---

[21] The Eiger is a mountain to the east of the Jungfrau.

Abbot	Why so?
Manuel	But step this way,

And I will tell you further.
Exeunt.

ACT III, SCENE IV

Interior of the tower. Manfred alone.

Manfred The stars are forth, the moon above the tops
  Of the snow-shining mountains – beautiful!
  I linger yet with nature, for the night
  Hath been to me a more familiar face
  Than that of man, and in her starry shade   5
  Of dim and solitary loveliness
  I learned the language of another world.
  I do remember me that in my youth
  When I was wandering, upon such a night
  I stood within the Colosseum's wall   10
  Midst the chief relics of almighty Rome;
  The trees which grew along the broken arches
  Waved dark in the blue midnight, and the stars
  Shone through the rents of ruin; from afar
  The watchdog bayed beyond the Tiber, and   15
  More near from out the Caesars' palace came
  The owl's long cry, and, interruptedly,
  Of distant sentinels the fitful song
  Begun and died upon the gentle wind.
  Some cypresses beyond the time-worn breach[22]   20
  Appeared to skirt the horizon, yet they stood
  Within a bowshot, where the Caesars dwelt,
  And dwell the tuneless birds of night; amidst
  A grove which springs through levelled battlements,
  And twines its roots with the imperial hearths,   25
  Ivy usurps the laurel's place of growth;
  But the gladiators' bloody circus[23] stands,
  A noble wreck in ruinous perfection,
  While Caesar's chambers and the Augustan halls
  Grovel on earth in indistinct decay.   30
  And thou didst shine, thou rolling moon, upon
  All this, and cast a wide and tender light
  Which softened down the hoar austerity
  Of rugged desolation, and filled up,
  As 'twere, anew, the gaps of centuries,   35
  Leaving that beautiful which still was so,
  And making that which was not, till the place
  Became religion, and the heart ran o'er

---

[22] *breach* break in the old city walls.   [23] *circus* oval arena.

With silent worship of the great of old –
The dead but sceptred sovereigns who still rule   40
Our spirits from their urns.
                                   'Twas such a night!
'Tis strange that I recall it at this time,
But I have found our thoughts take wildest flight
Even at the moment when they should array
Themselves in pensive order.

Enter the Abbot.

Abbot   My good Lord!   45
I crave a second grace for this approach,
But yet let not my humble zeal offend
By its abruptness; all it hath of ill
Recoils on me. Its good in the effect
May light upon your head – could I say *heart*,   50
Could I touch *that*, with words or prayers, I should
Recall a noble spirit which hath wandered
But is not yet all lost.

Manfred   Thou know'st me not;
My days are numbered and my deeds recorded.
Retire, or 'twill be dangerous – away!   55

Abbot Thou dost not mean to menace me?

Manfred   Not I;
I simply tell thee peril is at hand
And would preserve thee.

Abbot   What dost mean?

Manfred   Look there –
What dost thou see?

Abbot   Nothing.

Manfred   Look there, I say,
And steadfastly; now tell me what thou seest?   60

Abbot That which should shake me, but I fear it not;
I see a dusk and awful figure rise
Like an infernal god from out the earth,
His face wrapped in a mantle, and his form
Robed as with angry clouds. He stands between   65
Thyself and me, but I do fear him not.

Manfred Thou hast no cause; he shall not harm thee, but
His sight may shock thine old limbs into palsy.
I say to thee, retire!

Abbot   And I reply
Never, till I have battled with this fiend.   70
What doth he here?

Manfred   Why, aye, what doth he here?
I did not send for him, he is unbidden.

Abbot Alas, lost mortal! What with guests like these
Hast thou to do? I tremble for thy sake;
Why doth he gaze on thee, and thou on him?   75

Ah! he unveils his aspect: on his brow
The thunder-scars are graven; from his eye
Glares forth the immortality of hell –
Avaunt!
Manfred   Pronounce – what is thy mission?
Spirit   Come!
Abbot What art thou, unknown being? Answer! Speak!   80
Spirit The genius of this mortal. Come, 'tis time!
Manfred I am prepared for all things, but deny
   The power which summons me. Who sent thee here?
Spirit Thou'lt know anon; come, come!
Manfred   I have commanded
   Things of an essence greater far than thine,   85
   And striven with thy masters. Get thee hence!
Spirit Mortal, thine hour is come. Away, I say!
Manfred I knew, and know my hour is come, but not
   To render up my soul to such as thee;
   Away! I'll die as I have lived – alone.   90
Spirit Then I must summon up my brethren. Rise!
Other spirits rise up.
Abbot Avaunt, ye evil ones! Avaunt I say!
   Ye have no power where piety hath power,
   And I do charge ye in the name –
Spirit   Old man!
   We know ourselves, our mission, and thine order;   95
   Waste not thy holy words on idle uses,
   It were in vain – this man is forfeited.
   Once more I summon him: away, away!
Manfred I do defy ye, though I feel my soul
   Is ebbing from me, yet I do defy ye;   100
   Nor will I hence, while I have earthly breath
   To breathe my scorn upon ye, earthly strength
   To wrestle (though with spirits): what ye take
   Shall be ta'en limb by limb.
Spirit   Reluctant mortal!
   Is this the Magian who would so pervade   105
   The world invisible, and make himself
   Almost our equal? Can it be that thou
   Art thus in love with life – the very life
   Which made thee wretched?
Manfred   Thou false fiend, thou liest!
   My life is in its last hour – *that* I know,   110
   Nor would redeem a moment of that hour;
   I do not combat against death, but thee
   And thy surrounding angels; my past power
   Was purchased by no compact with thy crew,
   But by superior science, penance, daring,   115
   And length of watching, strength of mind, and skill

In knowledge of our fathers – when the earth
Saw men and spirits walking side by side,
And gave ye no supremacy. I stand
Upon my strength: I do defy, deny,   120
Spurn back, and scorn ye!
Spirit   But thy many crimes
Have made thee –
Manfred   What are they to such as thee?
Must crimes be punished but by other crimes
And greater criminals? Back to thy hell!
Thou hast no power upon me, *that* I feel;   125
Thou never shalt possess me, *that* I know.
What I have done is done; I bear within
A torture which could nothing gain from thine.
The mind which is immortal makes itself
Requital for its good or evil thoughts,   130
Is its own origin of ill and end,
And its own place and time; its innate sense,
When stripped of this mortality, derives
No colour from the fleeting things without,
But is absorbed in sufferance or in joy,   135
Born from the knowledge of its own desert.
Thou didst not tempt me, and thou couldst not tempt me,
I have not been thy dupe nor am thy prey –
But was my own destroyer, and will be
My own hereafter. Back, ye baffled fiends,   140
The hand of death is on me – but not yours!
The demons disappear
Abbot Alas, how pale thou art! Thy lips are white
And thy breast heaves, and in thy gasping throat
The accents rattle; give thy prayers to heaven;
Pray, albeit but in thought – but die not thus.   145
Manfred 'Tis over; my dull eyes can fix thee not,
But all things swim around me, and the earth
Heaves as it were beneath me. Fare thee well;
Give me thy hand.
Abbot   Cold, cold, even to the heart;
But yet one prayer – alas, how fares it with thee?   150
Manfred Old man! 'Tis not so difficult to die.
Manfred expires.
Abbot He's gone; his soul hath ta'en its earthless flight –
Whither, I dread to think – but he is gone.

From Letter from Lord Byron to Thomas Moore, 28 February 1817 (including 'So We'll Go No More A-roving')

I feel anxious to hear from you, even more than usual, because your last indicated that you were unwell. At present, I am on the invalid regimen myself. The Carnival – that is, the latter part of it – and sitting up late o' nights, had knocked me up a little. But it is over, and it is now Lent, with all its abstinence and Sacred Music.

The mumming closed with a masked ball at the Fenice, where I went, as also to most of the ridottos, etc., etc. And, though I did not dissipate much upon the whole, yet I find 'the sword wearing out the scabbard', though I have but just turned the corner of twenty-nine.

> So we'll go no more a-roving
>   So late into the night,
> Though the heart be still as loving,
>   And the moon be still as bright.
>
> For the sword outwears its sheath,   5
>   And the soul wears out the breast,
> And the heart must pause to breathe,
>   And love itself have rest.
>
> Though the night was made for loving,
>   And the day returns too soon,   10
> Yet we'll go no more a-roving
>   By the light of the moon.

Don Juan (composed 3 July–6 September 1818; first published 1819; edited from MS)

Dedication

I

> Bob Southey! You're a poet – Poet Laureate,[1]
>   And representative of all the race;
> Although 'tis true you turned out a Tory at
>   Last, yours has lately been a common case;
> And now, my epic renegade, what are ye at,   5

DON JUAN
[1] Robert Southey was Poet Laureate 1813–43. Byron's animus towards him derived from the fact that, as he told John Cam Hobhouse on 11 Nov. 1818, 'The son of a bitch, on his return from Switzerland two years ago, said that Shelley and I "had formed a league of incest and practised our precepts with etc." He lied like a rascal, for *they were not sisters* – one being Godwin's daughter by Mary Wollstone-craft, and the other the daughter of the present Mrs Godwin by a *former* husband. The attack contains no allusion to the cause, but some good verses, and all political and poetical. He lied in another sense, for there was no promiscuous intercourse, my commerce being limited to the carnal knowledge of the Miss Clairmont' (Marchand, vi. 76). At hearing Byron read the Dedication, Shelley remarked of Southey that 'The poor wretch will writhe under the lash' (Jones, ii. 42).

With all the Lakers in and out of place?
A nest of tuneful persons, to my eye
Like 'four and twenty blackbirds in a pie,

2

Which pie being opened, they began to sing'
(This old song and new simile holds good),   10
'A dainty dish to set before the King'
Or Regent,[2] who admires such kind of food.
And Coleridge too has lately taken wing,
But like a hawk encumbered with his hood,
Explaining metaphysics to the nation;[3]   15
I wish he would explain his explanation.

3

You, Bob, are rather insolent, you know,
At being disappointed in your wish
To supersede all warblers here below,
And be the only blackbird in the dish;   20
And then you overstrain yourself, or so,
And tumble downward like the flying fish
Gasping on deck, because you soar too high, Bob,
And fall for lack of moisture, quite a dry-bob![4]

4

And Wordsworth, in a rather long *Excursion*   25
(I think the quarto holds five hundred pages),
Has given a sample from the vasty version
Of his new system to perplex the sages;[5]
'Tis poetry (at least by his assertion),
And may appear so when the dog-star rages;[6]   30
And he who understands it would be able
To add a story to the Tower of Babel.

5

You gentlemen, by dint of long seclusion
From better company, have kept your own

---

2 George, Prince of Wales, governed as Prince
Regent 1810–20.
3 Coleridge's recent publications were discursive
prose: *The Stateman's Manual* (1816), *Biographia Literaria*
and *Lay Sermons* (1817), and *The Friend* (1818).

4 *dry-bob* coition without emission.
5 Jeffrey criticized the length of *Excursion* (1814),
p. 600 above.
6 Dogs are supposed to go mad when Sirius (the
dog-star, in the constellation of the Canis Major) rises.

At Keswick, and, through still-continued fusion   35
  Of one another's minds, at last have grown
To deem as a most logical conclusion
  That poesy has wreaths for you alone;
There is a narrowness in such a notion
Which makes me wish you'd change your lakes for ocean.   40

6

I would not imitate the petty thought,
  Nor coin my self-love to so base a vice,
For all the glory your conversion brought,
  Since gold alone should not have been its price.
You have your salary – was't for that you wrought?   45
  And Wordsworth has his place in the Excise.[7]
You're shabby fellows, true – but poets still,
And duly seated on the immortal hill.[8]

7

Your bays may hide the baldness of your brows,
  Perhaps some virtuous blushes (let them go);   50
To you I envy neither fruit nor boughs,
  And for the fame you would engross below
The field is universal, and allows
  Scope to all such as feel the inherent glow –
Scott, Rogers, Campbell, Moore and Crabbe[9] will try   55
'Gainst you the question with posterity.

8

For me who, wandering with pedestrian muses,
  Contend not with you on the winged steed,
I wish your fate may yield ye, when she chooses,
  The fame you envy and the skill you need;   60
And recollect a poet nothing loses
  In giving to his brethren their full meed
Of merit, and complaint of present days
Is not the *certain* path to future praise.

---

7 'Wordsworth's place may be in the Customs; it is, I think, in that of the Excise – besides another at Lord Lonsdale's table, where this poetical charlatan and political parasite picks up the crumbs with a hardened alacrity, the converted Jacobin having long subsided into the clownish sycophant of the worst prejudices of aristocracy' (Byron's note). William Lowther, 1st Earl of Lonsdale, was Wordsworth's patron; he procured Wordsworth's job as Distributor of Stamps, and was the dedicatee of *The Excursion*.

8 Mt Parnassus, sacred to the Muses.

9 Byron saw these poets as working, broadly speaking, within the neoclassical tradition stemming from Pope; to him, they were vastly preferable to the Lake school.

9

He that reserves his laurels for posterity   65
 (Who does not often claim the bright reversion?)
Has generally no great crop to spare it, he
 Being only injured by his own assertion;
And although here and there some glorious rarity
 Arise like Titan from the sea's immersion,   70
The major part of such appellants go
To God knows where – for no one else can know.

10

If, fallen in evil days on evil tongues,[10]
 Milton appealed to the avenger, Time;
If Time, the avenger, execrates his wrongs   75
 And makes the word 'Miltonic' mean 'sublime',
He deigned not to belie his soul in songs,
 Nor turn his very talent to a crime;
He did not loathe the sire to laud the son,[11]
But closed the tyrant-hater he begun.   80

11

Think'st thou, could he, the blind old man, arise
 Like Samuel from the grave,[12] to freeze once more
The blood of monarchs with his prophecies,
 Or be alive again, again all hoar
With time and trials, and those helpless eyes   85
 And heartless daughters, worn and pale and poor –
Would *he* adore a sultan? – *he* obey
The intellectual eunuch Castlereagh?[13]

12

Cold-blooded, smooth-faced, placid miscreant!
 Dabbling its sleek young hands in Erin's gore,   90
And thus for wider carnage taught to pant,
 Transferred to gorge upon a sister-shore;
The vulgarest tool that tyranny could want,
 With just enough of talent, and no more,

[10] *Paradise Lost*, vii. 25–6.
[11] *sire . . . son* Charles I and II.
[12] 1 Sam. 28: 13–14.

[13] Robert Stewart, Viscount Castlereagh (1769–1822), Foreign Secretary 1812–22; he was responsible for imprisoning the leaders of the United Irish rebellion.

To lengthen fetters by another fixed,   95
And offer poison long already mixed.

13

An orator of such set trash of phrase
   Ineffably, legitimately vile,
That even its grossest flatterers dare not praise,
   Nor foes (all nations) condescend to smile;   100
Not even a sprightly blunder's spark can blaze
   From that Ixion grindstone's ceaseless toil,
That turns and turns, to give the world a notion
Of endless torments and perpetual motion.

14

A bungler even in its disgusting trade,   105
   And botching, patching, leaving still behind
Something of which its masters are afraid,
   States to be curbed and thoughts to be confined,
Conspiracy or congress to be made,
   Cobbling at manacles for all mankind –   110
A tinkering slavemaker who mends old chains,
With God and man's abhorrence for its gains.

15

If we may judge of matter by the mind,
   Emasculated to the marrow, *It*
Hath but two objects: how to serve and bind,   115
   Deeming the chain it wears even men may fit;
Eutropius[14] of its many masters – blind
   To worth as freedom, wisdom as to wit –
Fearless, because *no* feeling dwells in ice,
Its very courage stagnates to a vice.   120

16

Where shall I turn me not to view its bonds
   (For I will never feel them)? Italy,
Thy late-reviving Roman soul desponds
   Beneath the lie this state-thing breathed o'er thee;

---

[14] *Eutropius* Roman eunuch raised to high office.

Thy clanking chain and Erin's yet green wounds   125
  Have voices, tongues to cry aloud for me.
Europe has slaves, allies, kings, armies still –
And Southey lives to sing them very ill.

17

Meantime, Sir Laureate, I proceed to dedicate,
  In honest, simple verse, this song to you,   130
And if in flattering strains I do not predicate,
  'Tis that I still retain my 'buff and blue';[15]
My politics, as yet, are all to educate,
  Apostasy's so fashionable too,
To keep *one* creed's a task grown quite herculean –   135
Is it not so, my Tory ultra-Julian?[16]

Canto I

I

I want a hero[17] – an uncommon want
  When every year and month sends forth a new one,
Till after cloying the gazettes with cant,
  The age discovers he is not the true one;
Of such as these I should not care to vaunt,   5
  I'll therefore take our ancient friend Don Juan;
We all have seen him in the pantomime
Sent to the devil, somewhat ere his time.

2

Vernon, the butcher Cumberland, Wolfe, Hawke,
  Prince Ferdinand, Granby, Burgoyne, Keppel, Howe,[18]   10
Evil and good, have had their tithe of talk,
  And filled their signposts then, like Wellesley now;
Each in their turn like Banquo's monarchs stalk,[19]
  Followers of fame, 'nine farrow' of that sow;
France, too, had Buonaparté and Dumourier   15
Recorded in the *Moniteur* and *Courier*.

---

[15] *buff and blue* colours of the Whig Club.
[16] 'I allude not to our friend Landor's hero, the traitor Count Julian, but to Gibbon's hero, vulgarly yclept [called] "The Apostate"' (Byron's note).

[17] A witty variation on the conventional epic opening, 'Of arms and the man I sing . . .'
[18] Celebrated military men.
[19] A reference to *Macbeth*, iv. i. 112–24.

3

Barnave, Brissot, Condorcet, Mirabeau,
    Petion, Clootz, Danton, Marat, La Fayette
Were French, and famous people as we know;
    And there were others, scarce forgotten yet –   20
Joubert, Hoche, Marceau, Lannes, Dessaix, Moreau,[20]
    With many of the military set,
Exceedingly remarkable at times,
But not at all adapted to my rhymes.

4

Nelson was once Britannia's god of war,   25
    And still should be so, but the tide is turned;
There's no more to be said of Trafalgar –
    'Tis with our hero quietly inurned
Because the army's grown more popular,
    At which the naval people are concerned;   30
Besides, the Prince is all for the land-service,
Forgetting Duncan, Nelson, Howe, and Jervis.[21]

5

Brave men were living before Agamemnon
    And since, exceeding valorous and sage –
A good deal like him too, though quite the same none;   35
    But then they shone not on the poet's page,
And so have been forgotten. I condemn none,
    But can't find any in the present age
Fit for my poem (that is, for my new one),
So as I said, I'll take my friend Don Juan.   40

6

Most epic poets plunge *in medias res*
    (Horace makes this the heroic turnpike road),
And then your hero tells, whene'er you please,
    What went before by way of episode,
While seated after dinner at his ease   45
    Beside his mistress in some soft abode –
Palace or garden, paradise or cavern,
Which serves the happy couple for a tavern.

---

[20] All those named in this stanza were French   [21] Distinguished Admirals.
Revolutionaries.

7

That is the usual method, but not mine;
    My way is to begin with the beginning.   50
The regularity of my design
    Forbids all wandering as the worst of sinning,
And therefore I shall open with a line
    (Although it cost me half an hour in spinning)
Narrating somewhat of Don Juan's father   55
And also of his mother, if you'd rather.

8

In Seville was he born, a pleasant city
    Famous for oranges and women; he
Who has not seen it will be much to pity,
    So says the proverb – and I quite agree: 60
Of all the Spanish towns is none more pretty
    (Cadiz perhaps, but that you soon may see).
Don Juan's parents lived beside the river,
A noble stream, and called the Guadalquivir.

9

His father's name was Jóse – Don, of course –   65
    A true Hidalgo, free from every stain
Of Moor or Hebrew blood, he traced his source
    Through the most Gothic gentlemen of Spain;
A better cavalier ne'er mounted horse
    (Or, being mounted, e'er got down again)   70
Than Jóse, who begot our hero, who
Begot – but that's to come. Well, to renew:

10

His mother was a learned lady famed
    For every branch of every science known,
In every Christian language ever named,   75
    With virtues equalled by her wit alone;
She made the cleverest people quite ashamed,
    And even the good with inward envy groan,
Finding themselves so very much exceeded
In their own way by all the things that she did.   80

I I

Her memory was a mine – she knew by heart
    All Calderon and greater part of Lopé,[22]
So that if any actor missed his part
    She could have served him for the prompter's copy;
For her Feinagle's[23] were an useless art,   85
    And he himself obliged to shut up shop – he
Could never make a memory so fine as
That which adorned the brain of Donna Inez.

I 2

Her favourite science was the mathematical,
    Her noblest virtue was her magnanimity,   90
Her wit (she sometimes tried at wit) was Attic all,
    Her serious sayings darkened to sublimity;
In short, in all things she was fairly what I call
    A prodigy – her morning dress was dimity,
Her evening silk or, in the summer, muslin   95
(And other stuffs with which I won't stay puzzling).

I 3

She knew the Latin – that is, the Lord's Prayer,
    And Greek – the alphabet, I'm nearly sure;
She read some French romances here and there,
    Although her mode of speaking was not pure;   100
For native Spanish she had no great care
    (At least her conversation was obscure);
Her thoughts were theorems, her words a problem,
As if she deemed that mystery would ennoble 'em.

I 4

She liked the English and the Hebrew tongue,   105
    And said there was analogy between 'em;
She proved it somehow out of sacred song,
    But I must leave the proofs to those who've seen 'em;
But this I heard her say, and can't be wrong,
    And all may think which way their judgments lean 'em,   110

---

[22] Calderón de la Barca (1600–81) and Lope de Vega (1562–1635), Spanish playwrights.

[23] Gregor von Feinagle (1765–1819) devised a system of mnemonics.

'"Tis strange; the Hebrew noun which means "I am",[24]
The English always use to govern d—n.'

15

Some women use their tongues; she looked a lecture,
 Each eye a sermon, and her brow a homily,
An all-in-all-sufficient self-director   115
 Like the lamented late Sir Samuel Romilly,[25]
The law's expounder and the state's corrector
 Whose suicide was almost an anomaly –
One sad example more that 'All is vanity';[26]
The jury brought their verdict in – 'Insanity'.   120

16

In short, she was a walking calculation,
 Miss Edgeworth's novels stepping from their covers,
Or Mrs Trimmer's books on education,
 Or 'Coeleb's Wife'[27] set out in search of lovers,
Morality's prim personification   125
 In which not envy's self a flaw discovers:
To others' share let 'female errors fall',[28]
For she had not even one – the worst of all.

17

Oh she was perfect past all parallel
 Of any modern female saint's comparison;   130
So far beyond the cunning powers of hell,
 Her guardian angel had given up his garrison;
Even her minutest motions went as well
 As those of the best timepiece made by Harrison;[29]
In virtues nothing earthly could surpass her,   135
Save thine 'incomparable oil', Macassar![30]

---

[24] Yahweh ('I am' in Hebrew) means God, as in 'God damn'.
[25] Romilly (1757–1818) sided with Lady Byron when she separated from her husband, earning Byron's lasting hatred.
[26] See Eccles. 1: 2.
[27] Sarah Trimmer (1741–1810), author of educa-tional manuals, and Hannah More's popular, didactic novel, Coeleb's in Search of a Wife (1808).
[28] Pope, The Rape of the Lock, ii. 17.
[29] John Harrison (1693–1776), horologist.
[30] A brand of hair oil popular during the early nineteenth century.

18

Perfect she was, but as perfection is
   Insipid in this naughty world of ours,
Where our first parents never learned to kiss
   Till they were exiled from their earlier bowers,   140
Where all was peace and innocence and bliss
   (I wonder how they got through the twelve hours) –
Don Jóse, like a lineal son of Eve,
Went plucking various fruit without her leave.

19

He was a mortal of the careless kind   145
   With no great love for learning or the learned,
Who chose to go where'er he had a mind,
   And never dreamed his lady was concerned;
The world, as usual, wickedly inclined
   To see a kingdom or a house o'erturned,   150
Whispered he had a mistress, some said *two* –
But for domestic quarrels *one* will do.

20

Now Donna Inez had, with all her merit,
   A great opinion of her own good qualities;
Neglect, indeed, requires a saint to bear it –   155
   And so indeed, she was in her moralities;
But then she had a devil of a spirit,
   And sometimes mixed up fancies with realities,
And let few opportunities escape
Of getting her liege-lord into a scrape.   160

21

This was an easy matter with a man
   Oft in the wrong and never on his guard;
And even the wisest, do the best they can,
   Have moments, hours, and days, so unprepared
That you might 'brain them with their lady's fan',[31]   165
   And sometimes ladies hit exceeding hard,
And fans turn into falchions in fair hands,
And why and wherefore no one understands.

---

[31] *1 Henry IV*, II. iii. 23.

22

'Tis pity learned virgins ever wed
   With persons of no sort of education,   170
Or gentlemen who, though well-born and bred,
   Grow tired of scientific conversation.
I don't choose to say much upon this head;
   I'm a plain man and in a single station,
But oh, ye lords of ladies intellectual,   175
Inform us truly, have they not hen-pecked you all?

23

Don Jóse and his lady quarrelled – *why*
   Not any of the many could divine,
Though several thousand people chose to try,
   'Twas surely no concern of theirs nor mine;   180
I loathe that low vice curiosity,
   But if there's anything in which I shine,
'Tis in arranging all my friends' affairs
Not having, of my own, domestic cares.

24

And so I interfered, and with the best   185
   Intentions, but their treatment was not kind;
I think the foolish people were possessed,
   For neither of them could I ever find,
Although their porter afterwards confessed –
   But that's no matter, and the worst's behind,   190
For little Juan o'er me threw, downstairs,
A pail of housemaid's water unawares.

25

A little curly-headed, good-for-nothing,
   And mischief-making monkey from his birth;
His parents ne'er agreed except in doting   195
   Upon the most unquiet imp on earth;
Instead of quarrelling, had they been but both in
   Their senses, they'd have sent young master forth
To school, or had him soundly whipped at home
To teach him manners for the time to come.   200

26

Don Jóse and the Donna Inez led
  For some time an unhappy sort of life,
Wishing each other not divorced but dead;
  They lived respectably as man and wife,
Their conduct was exceedingly well-bred,   205
  And gave no outward signs of inward strife –
Until at length the smothered fire broke out,
And put the business past all kind of doubt.

27

For Inez called some druggists and physicians
  And tried to prove her loving lord was mad,   210
But as he had some lucid intermissions,
  She next decided he was only bad;
Yet when they asked her for her depositions,
  No sort of explanation could be had,
Save that her duty both to man and God   215
Required this conduct, which seemed very odd.

28

She kept a journal where his faults were noted
  And opened certain trunks of books and letters –
All which might, if occasion served, be quoted;
  And then she had all Seville for abettors,   220
Besides her good old grandmother (who doted);
  The hearers of her case became repeaters,
Then advocates, inquisitors, and judges –
Some for amusement, others for old grudges.

29

And then this best and meekest woman bore   225
  With such serenity her husband's woes,
Just as the Spartan ladies did of yore
  Who saw their spouses killed, and nobly chose
Never to say a word about them more;
  Calmly she heard each calumny that rose,   230
And saw his agonies with such sublimity
That all the world exclaimed 'What magnanimity!'

30

No doubt this patience, when the world is damning us,
   Is philosophic in our former friends;
'Tis also pleasant to be deemed magnanimous   235
   (The more so in obtaining our own ends);
And what the lawyers call a *malus animus*,[32]
   Conduct like this by no means comprehends:
Revenge in person's certainly no virtue,
But then 'tis not *my* fault, if *others* hurt you.   240

31

And if our quarrels should rip up old stories
   And help them with a lie or two additional,
I'm not to blame, as you well know, no more is
   Anyone else – they were become traditional;
Besides, their resurrection aids our glories   245
   By contrast, which is what we just were wishing all:
And science profits by this resurrection –
Dead scandals form good subjects for dissection.

32

Their friends had tried at reconciliation,
   Then their relations who made matters worse   250
('Twere hard to say upon a like occasion
   To whom it may be best to have recourse;
I can't say much for friend or yet relation);
   The lawyers did their utmost for divorce
But scarce a fee was paid on either side   255
Before, unluckily, Don Jóse died.

33

He died – and most unluckily, because,
   According to all hints I could collect
From counsel learned in those kinds of laws
   (Although their talk's obscure and circumspect),   260
His death contrived to spoil a charming cause:
   A thousand pities also with respect
To public feeling, which on this occasion
Was manifested in a great sensation.

---

[32] *malus animus* bad intent.

34

But ah, he died – and buried with him lay   265
   The public feeling and the lawyers' fees;
His house was sold, his servants sent away,
   A Jew took one of his two mistresses,
A priest the other (at least so they say).
   I asked the doctors after his disease: 270
He died of the slow fever called the tertian
And left his widow to her own aversion.

35

Yes, Jóse was an honourable man –
   That I must say, who knew him very well;
Therefore his frailties I'll no further scan   275
   (Indeed there were not many more to tell),
And if his passions now and then outran
   Discretion, and were not so peaceable
As Numa's (who was also named Pompilius),[33]
He had been ill brought up, and was born bilious.   280

36

Whate'er might be his worthlessness or worth,
   Poor fellow, he had many things to wound him,
Let's own, since it can do no good on earth;
   It was a trying moment that which found him
Standing alone beside his desolate hearth   285
   Where all his household gods lay shivered round him;
No choice was left his feelings or his pride
Save death or Doctors' Commons[34] – so he died.

37

Dying intestate, Juan was sole heir
   To a chancery suit and messuages and lands   290
Which, with a long minority and care,
   Promised to turn out well in proper hands;
Inez became sole guardian (which was fair)
   And answered but to nature's just demands;
An only son left with an only mother   295
Is brought up much more wisely than another.

[33] The reign of Numa, second king of Rome, was   [34] divorce courts.
known for its peaceability.

38

Sagest of women, even of widows, she
   Resolved that Juan should be quite a paragon
And worthy of the noblest pedigree
   (His sire was of Castile, his dam from Aragon).   300
Then for accomplishments of chivalry,
   In case our lord the king should go to war again,
He learned the arts of riding, fencing, gunnery,
And how to scale a fortress – or a nunnery.

39

But that which Donna Inez most desired,   305
   And saw into herself each day before all
The learned tutors whom for him she hired,
   Was that his breeding should be strictly moral;
Much into all his studies she enquired,
   And so they were submitted first to her, all,   310
Arts, sciences – no branch was made a mystery
To Juan's eyes, excepting natural history.

40

The languages (especially the dead),
   The sciences (and most of all the abstruse),
The arts (at least all such as could be said   315
   To be the most remote from common use) –
In all these he was much and deeply read;
   But not a page of anything that's loose
Or hints continuation of the species
Was ever suffered, lest he should grow vicious.   320

41

His classic studies made a little puzzle
   Because of filthy loves of gods and goddesses
Who in the earlier ages made a bustle,
   But never put on pantaloons or bodices;
His reverend tutors had at times a tussle,   325
   And for their *Aeneids*, *Iliad*s, and *Odyssey*s,
Were forced to make an odd sort of apology –
For Donna Inez dreaded the mythology.

42

Ovid's a rake, as half his verses show him,
 Anacreon's morals are a still worse sample,   330
Catullus scarcely has a decent poem,
 I don't think Sappho's 'Ode' a good example,
Although Longinus tells us there is no hymn
 Where the sublime soars forth on wings more ample;
But Virgil's songs are pure, except that horrid one   335
Beginning with *Formosum pastor Corydon*.[35]

43

Lucretius' irreligion is too strong
 For early stomachs, to prove wholesome food;
I can't help thinking Juvenal was wrong
 (Although no doubt his real intent was good)   340
For speaking out so plainly in his song –
 So much indeed as to be downright rude;
And then what proper person can be partial
To all those nauseous epigrams of Martial?

44

Juan was taught from out the best edition,   345
 Expurgated by learned men who place
Judiciously, from out the schoolboy's vision,
 The grosser parts; but fearful to deface
Too much their modest bard by this omission,
 And pitying sore his mutilated case,   350
They only add them all in an appendix[36] –
Which saves, in fact, the trouble of an index;

45

For there we have them all at one fell swoop,
 Instead of being scattered through the pages;
They stand forth marshalled in a handsome troop   355
 To meet the ingenuous youth of future ages,
Till some less rigid editor shall stoop
 To call them back into their separate cages,

---

[35] Erotic poets and poems, including Sappho's 'Ode to Aphrodite' and Virgil's *Eclogue*, ii. (dealing with homoerotic love).

[36] 'Fact. There is, or was, such an edition, with all the obnoxious epigrams of Martial placed by themselves at the end' (Byron's note).

Instead of standing staring altogether
Like garden gods – and not so decent either.   360

46

The missal too (it was the family missal)
   Was ornamented in a sort of way
Which ancient mass-books often are, and this all
   Kinds of grotesques illumined; and how they,
Who saw those figures on the margin kiss all,   365
   Could turn their optics to the text and pray
Is more than I know – but Don Juan's mother
Kept this herself, and gave her son another.

47

Sermons he read and lectures he endured,
   And homilies and lives of all the saints;   370
To Jerome and to Chrysostom[37] inured,
   He did not take such studies for restraints;
But how faith is acquired and then insured,
   So well not one of the aforesaid paints
As St Augustine in his fine *Confessions* –   375
Which make the reader envy his transgressions.

48

This too was a sealed book to little Juan –
   I can't but say that his mamma was right,
If such an education was the true one.
   She scarcely trusted him from out her sight;   380
Her maids were old, and if she took a new one
   You might be sure she was a perfect fright;
She did this during even her husband's life –
I recommend as much to every wife.

49

Young Juan waxed in goodliness and grace;   385
   At six a charming child, and at eleven
With all the promise of as fine a face
   As e'er to man's maturer growth was given.

---

37   Early apologists for Christianity.

He studied steadily and grew apace
   And seemed, at least, in the right road to heaven –   390
For half his days were passed at church, the other
Between his tutors, confessor, and mother.

50

At six, I said, he was a charming child,
   At twelve he was a fine but quiet boy;
Although in infancy a little wild,   395
   They tamed him down amongst them; to destroy
His natural spirit not in vain they toiled
   (At least it seemed so); and his mother's joy
Was to declare how sage and still and steady
Her young philosopher was grown already.   400

51

I had my doubts – perhaps I have them still,
   But what I say is neither here nor there;
I knew his father well, and have some skill
   In character, but it would not be fair
From sire to son to augur good or ill;   405
   He and his wife were an ill-sorted pair –
But scandal's my aversion, I protest
Against all evil speaking, even in jest.

52

For my part I say nothing – nothing – but
   This I will say (my reasons are my own):   410
That if I had an only son to put
   To school (as God be praised that I have none),
'Tis not with Donna Inez I would shut
   Him up to learn his catechism alone –
No, no; I'd send him out betimes to college,   415
For there it was I picked up my own knowledge.

53

For there one learns – 'tis not for me to boast,
   Though I acquired – but I pass over *that*,
As well as all the Greek I since have lost;
   I say that there's the place – but *Verbum sat;*[38]   420

---

[38] *Verbum sat* 'a word [to the wise] is enough'.

I think I picked up too, as well as most,
    Knowledge of matters – but no matter *what* –
I never married – but I think, I know
That sons should not be educated so.

54

Young Juan now was sixteen years of age –   425
    Tall, handsome, slender, but well-knit; he seemed
Active, though not so sprightly, as a page,
    And everybody but his mother deemed
Him almost man. But she flew in a rage
    And bit her lips (for else she might have screamed)   430
If any said so – for to be precocious
Was in her eyes a thing the most atrocious.

55

Amongst her numerous acquaintance, all
    Selected for discretion and devotion,
There was the Donna Julia, whom to call   435
    Pretty were but to give a feeble notion
Of many charms in her as natural
    As sweetness to the flower, or salt to ocean,
Her zone to Venus, or his bow to Cupid
(But this last simile is trite and stupid).   440

56

The darkness of her oriental eye
    Accorded with her Moorish origin
(Her blood was not all Spanish, by the by –
    In Spain, you know, this is a sort of sin);
When proud Granada fell and, forced to fly,   445
    Boabdil wept,[39] of Donna Julia's kin
Some went to Africa, some stayed in Spain;
Her great-great-grandmamma chose to remain.

57

She married (I forget the pedigree)
    With an Hidalgo, who transmitted down   450

---

[39] Boabdil, last king of Granada, wept at its downfall, 1492.

His blood less noble than such blood should be;
    At such alliances his sires would frown,
In that point so precise in each degree
    That they bred *in and in*, as might be shown,
Marrying their cousins – nay, their aunts and nieces,   455
Which always spoils the breed, if it increases.

58

This heathenish cross restored the breed again,
    Ruined its blood, but much improved its flesh;
For from a root the ugliest in old Spain
    Sprung up a branch as beautiful as fresh –   460
The sons no more were short, the daughters plain
    (But there's a rumour which I fain would hush:
'Tis said that Donna Julia's grandmamma
Produced her Don more heirs at love than law).

59

However this might be, the race went on   465
    Improving still through every generation
Until it centred in an only son
    Who left an only daughter; my narration
May have suggested that this single one
    Could be but Julia (whom on this occasion   470
I shall have much to speak about), and she
Was married, charming, chaste, and twenty-three.

60

Her eye (I'm very fond of handsome eyes)
    Was large and dark, suppressing half its fire
Until she spoke, then through its soft disguise   475
    Flashed an expression more of pride than ire,
And love than either; and there would arise
    A something in them which was not desire,
But would have been, perhaps – but for the soul
Which struggled through and chastened down the whole.   480

61

Her glossy hair was clustered o'er a brow
    Bright with intelligence, and fair and smooth;
Her eyebrow's shape was like the aerial bow,

Her cheek all purple with the beam of youth
Mounting, at times, to a transparent glow   485
   As if her veins ran lightning; she, in sooth,
Possessed an air and grace by no means common,
   Her stature tall – I hate a dumpy woman.

62

Wedded she was some years, and to a man
   Of fifty – and such husbands are in plenty;   490
And yet, I think, instead of such a ONE
   'Twere better to have TWO of five and twenty,
Especially in countries near the sun;
   And now I think on't, 'mi vien in mente',[40]
Ladies even of the most uneasy virtue   495
Prefer a spouse whose age is short of thirty.

63

'Tis a sad thing, I cannot choose but say,
   And all the fault of that indecent sun
Who cannot leave alone our helpless clay
   But will keep baking, broiling, burning on,   500
That howsoever people fast and pray
   The flesh is frail, and so the soul undone;
What men call gallantry, and gods adultery,
Is much more common where the climate's sultry.

64

Happy the nations of the moral north!   505
   Where all is virtue, and the winter season
Sends sin, without a rag on, shivering forth
   ('Twas snow that brought St Francis back to reason);
Where juries cast up what a wife is worth
   By laying whate'er sum, in mulct, they please on   510
The lover, who must pay a handsome price,
Because it is a marketable vice.

65

Alfonso was the name of Julia's lord –
   A man well looking for his years and who

---

[40] 'it occurs to me'.

Was neither much beloved nor yet abhorred;   515
   They lived together as most people do,
Suffering each other's foibles by accord,
   And not exactly either *one* or *two*;
Yet he was jealous, though he did not show it,
For jealousy dislikes the world to know it.   520

66

Julia was (yet I never could see why)
   With Donna Inez quite a favourite friend;
Between their tastes there was small sympathy,
   For not a line had Julia ever penned;
Some people whisper (but no doubt they lie,   525
   For malice still imputes some private end)
That Inez had, ere Don Alfonso's marriage,
Forgot with him her very prudent carriage,

67

And that still keeping up the old connection,
   Which time had lately rendered much more chaste,   530
She took his lady also in affection,
   And certainly this course was much the best.
She flattered Julia with her sage protection
   And complimented Don Alfonso's taste,
And if she could not (who can?) silence scandal,   535
At least she left it a more slender handle.

68

I can't tell whether Julia saw the affair
   With other people's eyes, or if her own
Discoveries made, but none could be aware
   Of this; at least no symptom e'er was shown.   540
Perhaps she did not know, or did not care,
   Indifferent from the first, or callous grown;
I'm really puzzled what to think or say –
She kept her counsel in so close a way.

69

Juan she saw and, as a pretty child,   545
   Caressed him often – such a thing might be
Quite innocently done, and harmless styled,

When she had twenty years and thirteen he;
But I am not so sure I should have smiled
    When he was sixteen, Julia twenty-three   550
(These few short years make wondrous alterations,
Particularly amongst sunburnt nations).

70

Whate'er the cause might be, they had become
    Changed; for the dame grew distant, the youth shy,
Their looks cast down, their greetings almost dumb,   555
    And much embarrassment in either eye.
There surely will be little doubt with some
    That Donna Julia knew the reason why;
But as for Juan, he had no more notion
Than he who never saw the sea of ocean.   560

71

Yet Julia's very coldness still was kind,
    And tremulously gentle her small hand
Withdrew itself from his, but left behind
    A little pressure, thrilling, and so bland
And slight, so very slight, that to the mind   565
    'Twas but a doubt – but ne'er magician's wand
Wrought change with all Armida's[41] fairy art
Like what this light touch left on Juan's heart.

72

And if she met him, though she smiled no more,
    She looked a sadness sweeter than her smile,   570
As if her heart had deeper thoughts in store
    She must not own, but cherished more the while,
For that compression in its burning core;
    Even innocence itself has many a wile
And will not dare to trust itself with truth –   575
And love is taught hypocrisy from youth.

73

But passion most dissembles yet betrays
    Even by its darkness; as the blackest sky
Foretells the heaviest tempest, it displays

---

[41] Armida is the sorceress in Tasso, *Jerusalem Delivered*, who ensnares the hero, Rinaldo.

Its workings through the vainly guarded eye,   580
    And in whatever aspect it arrays
        Itself, 'tis still the same hypocrisy;
Coldness or anger, even disdain or hate
Are masks it often wears, and still too late.

74

Then there were sighs, the deeper for suppression,   585
    And stolen glances, sweeter for the theft,
And burning blushes, though for no transgression,
    Tremblings when met, and restlessness when left;
All these are little preludes to possession
    Of which young passion cannot be bereft,   590
And merely tend to show how greatly love is
Embarrassed at first starting with a novice.

75

Poor Julia's heart was in an awkward state –
    She felt it going, and resolved to make
The noblest efforts for herself and mate,   595
    For honour's, pride's, religion's, virtue's sake;
Her resolutions were most truly great
    And almost might have made a Tarquin[42] quake;
She prayed the Virgin Mary for her grace,
As being the best judge of a lady's case.   600

76

She vowed she never would see Juan more
    And next day paid a visit to his mother,
And looked extremely at the opening door
    Which, by the Virgin's grace, let in another;
Grateful she was, and yet a little sore;   605
    Again it opens, it can be no other,
'Tis surely Juan now – no! I'm afraid
That night the Virgin was no further prayed.

77

She now determined that a virtuous woman
    Should rather face and overcome temptation,   610

---

[42] *Tarquin* ancient Roman family known for their cruelty.

That flight was base and dastardly, and no man
  Should ever give her heart the least sensation –
That is to say, a thought beyond the common
  Preference, that we must feel upon occasion
For people who are pleasanter than others,   615
But then they only seem so many brothers.

78

And even if by chance (and who can tell?
  The Devil's so very sly) she should discover
That all within was not so very well,
  And if still free, that such or such a lover   620
Might please perhaps, a virtuous wife can quell
  Such thoughts and be the better when they're over;
And if the man should ask, 'tis but denial –
I recommend young ladies to make trial.

79

And then there are things such as love divine,   625
  Bright and immaculate, unmixed and pure,
Such as the angels think so very fine,
  And matrons who would be no less secure,
Platonic, perfect, 'just such love as mine',
  Thus Julia said, and thought so, to be sure –   630
And so I'd have her think, were I the man
On whom her reveries celestial ran.

80

Such love is innocent, and may exist
  Between young persons without any danger;
A hand may first, and then a lip be kissed –   635
  For my part, to such doings I'm a stranger,
But *hear* these freedoms form the utmost list
  Of all o'er which such love may be a ranger;
If people go beyond, 'tis quite a crime
But not my fault – I tell them all in time.   640

81

Love then, but love within its proper limits
  Was Julia's innocent determination
In young Don Juan's favour, and to him its

Exertion might be useful on occasion;
And lighted at too pure a shrine to dim its   645
    Ethereal lustre, with what sweet persuasion
He might be taught by love and her together –
I really don't know what, nor Julia either.

82

Fraught with this fine intention, and well-fenced
    In mail of proof – her purity of soul,   650
She, for the future of her strength convinced,
    And that her honour was a rock, or mole,
Exceeding sagely from that hour dispensed
    With any kind of troublesome control;
But whether Julia to the task was equal   655
Is that which must be mentioned in the sequel.

83

Her plan she deemed both innocent and feasible,
    And surely with a stripling of sixteen
Not scandal's fangs could fix on much that's seizable,
    Or if they did so, satisfied to mean   660
Nothing but what was good, her breast was peaceable –
    A quiet conscience makes one so serene!
Christians have burnt each other, quite persuaded
That all the Apostles would have done as they did.

84

And if in the meantime her husband died –   665
    But heaven forbid that such a thought should cross
Her brain, though in a dream! And then she sighed;
    Never could she survive that common loss,
But just suppose that moment should betide –
    I only say suppose it, *inter nos*   670
(This should be *entre nous*, for Julia thought
In French, but then the rhyme would go for nought),

85

I only say suppose this supposition:
    Juan being then grown up to man's estate
Would fully suit a widow of condition –   675
    Even seven years hence it would not be too late;

And in the interim (to pursue this vision)
   The mischief, after all, could not be great,
For he would learn the rudiments of love
(I mean the seraph way of those above).   680

86

So much for Julia. Now we'll turn to Juan –
   Poor little fellow, he had no idea
Of his own case, and never hit the true one;
   In feelings quick as Ovid's Miss Medea,
He puzzled over what he found a new one,   685
   But not as yet imagined it could be a
Thing quite in course, and not at all alarming
Which, with a little patience, might grow charming.

87

Silent and pensive, idle, restless, slow,
   His home deserted for the lonely wood,   690
Tormented with a wound he could not know,
   His, like all deep grief, plunged in solitude;
I'm fond myself of solitude or so,
   But then I beg it may be understood –
By solitude I mean a sultan's, not   695
A hermit's, with a harem for a grot.

88

'Oh love, in such a wilderness as this,
   Where transport and security entwine,
Here is the empire of thy perfect bliss,
   And here thou art a god indeed divine!'[43]   700
The bard I quote from does not sing amiss
   With the exception of the second line –
For that same twining 'transport and security'
Are twisted to a phrase of some obscurity.

89

The poet meant, no doubt (and thus appeals   705
   To the good sense and senses of mankind),
The very thing which everybody feels,

---

[43] Campbell, *Gertrude of Wyoming*, iii. 1–4.

As all have found on trial, or may find –
That no one likes to be disturbed at meals
   Or love. I won't say more about 'entwined'   710
Or 'transport', as we knew all that before,
But beg 'security' will bolt the door.

90

Young Juan wandered by the glassy brooks
   Thinking unutterable things; he threw
Himself at length within the leafy nooks   715
   Where the wild branch of the cork forest grew;
There poets find materials for their books,
   And every now and then we read them through
So that their plan and prosody are eligible –
Unless, like Wordsworth, they prove unintelligible.   720

91

He, Juan (and not Wordsworth), so pursued
   His self-communion with his own high soul,
Until his mighty heart in its great mood
   Had mitigated part (though not the whole)
Of its disease; he did the best he could   725
   With things not very subject to control,
And turned, without perceiving his condition,
Like Coleridge, into a metaphysician.

92

He thought about himself, and the whole earth,
   Of man the wonderful, and of the stars,   730
And how the deuce they ever could have birth;
   And then he thought of earthquakes and of wars,
How many miles the moon might have in girth,
   Of air-balloons, and of the many bars
To perfect knowledge of the boundless skies,   735
And then he thought of Donna Julia's eyes.

93

In thoughts like these true wisdom may discern
   Longings sublime and aspirations high,
Which some are born with, but the most part learn
   To plague themselves withal, they know not why;   740

'Twas strange that one so young should thus concern
  His brain about the action of the sky;
If you think 'twas philosophy that this did,
  I can't help thinking puberty assisted.

94

He pored upon the leaves and on the flowers,   745
  And heard a voice in all the winds; and then
He thought of wood-nymphs and immortal bowers,
  And how the goddesses came down to men:
He missed the pathway, he forgot the hours,
  And when he looked upon his watch again,   750
He found how much old Time had been a winner –
He also found that he had lost his dinner.

95

Sometimes he turned to gaze upon his book,
  Boscan or Garcilasso;[44] by the wind
Even as the page is rustled while we look,   755
  So by the poesy of his own mind
Over the mystic leaf his soul was shook,
  As if 'twere one whereon magicians bind
Their spells, and give them to the passing gale,
According to some good old woman's tale.   760

96

Thus would he while his lonely hours away
  Dissatisfied, nor knowing what he wanted;
Nor glowing reverie, nor poet's lay
  Could yield his spirit that for which it panted,
A bosom whereon he his head might lay,   765
  And hear the heart beat with the love it granted,
With – several other things which I forget,
Or which, at least, I need not mention yet.

97

Those lonely walks and lengthening reveries
  Could not escape the gentle Julia's eyes;   770
She saw that Juan was not at his ease;

---
[44] Spanish imitators of Petrarch.

But that which chiefly may, and must surprise
Is that the Donna Inez did not tease
   Her only son with question or surmise –
Whether it was she did not see or would not,   775
Or like all very clever people, could not.

98

This may seem strange, but yet 'tis very common;
   For instance, gentlemen, whose ladies take
Leave to o'erstep the written rights of woman,
   And break the – which commandment is't they break?   780
I have forgot the number, and think no man
   Should rashly quote, for fear of a mistake.
I say, when these same gentlemen are jealous,
They make some blunder which their ladies tell us.

99

A real husband always is suspicious,   785
   But still no less suspects in the wrong place,
Jealous of someone who had no such wishes,
   Or pandering blindly to his own disgrace
By harbouring some dear friend extremely vicious –
   The last indeed's infallibly the case,   790
And when the spouse and friend are gone off wholly,
He wonders at their vice, and not his folly.

100

Thus parents also are at times short-sighted;
   Though watchful as the lynx, they ne'er discover
(The while the wicked world beholds delighted)   795
   Young Hopeful's mistress or Miss Fanny's lover,
Till some confounded escapade has blighted
   The plan of twenty years, and all is over;
And then the mother cries, the father swears,
And wonders why the devil he got heirs.   800

101

But Inez was so anxious and so clear
   Of sight, that I must think on this occasion
She had some other motive much more near
   For leaving Juan to this new temptation;

But what that motive was I shan't say here ––   805
  Perhaps to finish Juan's education,
Perhaps to open Don Alfonso's eyes
In case he thought his wife too great a prize.

102

It was upon a day, a summer's day ––
  Summer's indeed a very dangerous season,   810
And so is spring about the end of May;
  The sun, no doubt, is the prevailing reason;
But whatsoe'er the cause is, one may say
  (And stand convicted of more truth than treason),
That there are months which nature grows more merry in;   815
March has its hares, and May must have its heroine.

103

'Twas on a summer's day, the sixth of June ––
  I like to be particular in dates,
Not only of the age and year, but moon;
  They are a sort of posthouse where the Fates   820
Change horses, making history change its tune,
  Then spur away o'er empires and o'er states,
Leaving at last not much besides chronology,
Excepting the post-obits of theology.

104

'Twas on the sixth of June, about the hour   825
  Of half-past six –– perhaps still nearer seven,
When Julia sat within as pretty a bower
  As e'er held houri in that heathenish heaven
Described by Mahomet and 'Anacreon' Moore[45] ––
  To whom the lyre and laurels have been given   830
With all the trophies of triumphant song;
He won them well, and may he wear them long!

105

She sat, but not alone; I know not well
  How this same interview had taken place,

---

[45] *'Anacreon' Moore* Thomas Moore translated Anacreon's *Odes* (1800).

And even if I knew, I should not tell –   835
   People should hold their tongues in any case;
No matter how or why the thing befell,
   But there were she and Juan, face to face –
When two such faces are so, 'twould be wise
(But very difficult) to shut their eyes.   840

106

How beautiful she looked! Her conscious heart
   Glowed in her cheek, and yet she felt no wrong.
Oh love, how perfect is thy mystic art,
   Strengthening the weak, and trampling on the strong;
How self-deceitful is the sagest part   845
   Of mortals whom thy lure hath led along;
The precipice she stood on was immense –
So was her creed in her own innocence.

107

She thought of her own strength, and Juan's youth,
   And of the folly of all prudish fears,   850
Victorious virtue and domestic truth –
   And then of Don Alfonso's fifty years:
I wish these last had not occurred, in sooth,
   Because that number rarely much endears,
And through all climes, the snowy and the sunny,   855
Sounds ill in love, whate'er it may in money.

108

When people say, 'I've told you *fifty* times',
   They mean to scold, and very often do;
When poets say, 'I've written *fifty* rhymes',
   They make you dread that they'll recite them too;   860
In gangs of *fifty*, thieves commit their crimes;
   At *fifty* love for love is rare, 'tis true –
But then, no doubt, it equally as true is,
A good deal may be bought for *fifty* louis.

109

Julia had honour, virtue, truth and love   865
   For Don Alfonso, and she inly swore
By all the vows below to powers above

She never would disgrace the ring she wore,
Nor leave a wish which wisdom might reprove;
   And while she pondered this, besides much more,   870
One hand on Juan's carelessly was thrown
Quite by mistake — she thought it was her own;

110

Unconsciously she leaned upon the other
   Which played within the tangles of her hair;
And to contend with thoughts she could not smother,   875
   She seemed by the distraction of her air.
'Twas surely very wrong in Juan's mother
   To leave together this imprudent pair,
She who for many years had watched her son so —
I'm very certain *mine* would not have done so.   880

111

The hand which still held Juan's, by degrees
   Gently but palpably confirmed its grasp,
As if it said 'detain me, if you please';
   Yet there's no doubt she only meant to clasp
His fingers with a pure Platonic squeeze;   885
   She would have shrunk as from a toad or asp
Had she imagined such a thing could rouse
A feeling dangerous to a prudent spouse.

112

I cannot know what Juan thought of this,
   But what he did is much what you would do;   890
His young lip thanked it with a grateful kiss,
   And then, abashed at its own joy, withdrew
In deep despair lest he had done amiss —
   Love is so very timid when 'tis new;
She blushed and frowned not, but she strove to speak   895
And held her tongue, her voice was grown so weak.

113

The sun set and uprose the yellow moon —
   The devil's in the moon for mischief; they
Who called her chaste, methinks began too soon
   Their nomenclature; there is not a day,   900

The longest, not the twenty-first of June,
   Sees half the business in a wicked way
On which three single hours of moonshine smile –
And then she looks so modest all the while.

114

There is a dangerous silence in that hour,   905
   A stillness which leaves room for the full soul
To open all itself, without the power
   Of calling wholly back its self-control;
The silver light which, hallowing tree and tower,
   Sheds beauty and deep softness o'er the whole,   910
Breathes also to the heart, and o'er it throws
A loving languor which is not repose.

115

And Julia sat with Juan, half-embraced
   And half-retiring from the glowing arm,
Which trembled like the bosom where 'twas placed;   915
   Yet still she must have thought there was no harm,
Or else 'twere easy to withdraw her waist;
   But then the situation had its charm,
And then – God knows what next – I can't go on;
I'm almost sorry that I e'er begun.   920

116

Oh Plato! Plato! You have paved the way,
   With your confounded fantasies, to more
Immoral conduct by the fancied sway
   Your system feigns o'er the controlless core
Of human hearts, than all the long array   925
   Of poets and romancers – you're a bore,
A charlatan, a coxcomb, and have been
At best no better than a go-between.

117

And Julia's voice was lost except in sighs,
   Until too late for useful conversation;   930
The tears were gushing from her gentle eyes –
   I wish, indeed, they had not had occasion,
But who, alas, can love, and then be wise?

Not that remorse did not oppose temptation,
A little still she strove, and much repented,   935
And whispering 'I will ne'er consent' – consented.

118

'Tis said that Xerxes offered a reward
    To those who could invent him a new pleasure –
Methinks the requisition's rather hard
    And must have cost his majesty a treasure;   940
For my part, I'm a moderate-minded bard,
    Fond of a little love (which I call leisure);
I care not for new pleasures, as the old
Are quite enough for me, so they but hold.

119

Oh pleasure, you're indeed a pleasant thing,   945
    Although one must be damned for you, no doubt;
I make a resolution every spring
    Of reformation, ere the year run out;
But somehow, this my vestal vow takes wing,
    Yet still, I trust, it may be kept throughout: 950
I'm very sorry, very much ashamed,
And mean, next winter, to be quite reclaimed.

120

Here my chaste muse a liberty must take –
    Start not, still chaster reader! She'll be nice hence-
Forward, and there is no great cause to quake;   955
    This liberty is a poetic licence,
Which some irregularity may make
    In the design, and as I have a high sense
Of Aristotle and the rules, 'tis fit
To beg his pardon when I err a bit.   960

121

This licence is to hope the reader will
    Suppose from June the sixth (the fatal day
Without whose epoch my poetic skill
    For want of facts would all be thrown away),
But keeping Julia and Don Juan still   965
    In sight, that several months have passed; we'll say

'Twas in November, but I'm not so sure
About the day – the era's more obscure.

122

We'll talk of that anon. 'Tis sweet to hear
    At midnight on the blue and moonlit deep   970
The song and oar of Adria's[46] gondolier
    By distance mellowed, o'er the waters sweep;
'Tis sweet to see the evening star appear;
    'Tis sweet to listen as the nightwinds creep
From leaf to leaf; 'tis sweet to view on high   975
The rainbow, based on ocean, span the sky;

123

'Tis sweet to hear the watchdog's honest bark
    Bay deep-mouthed welcome as we draw near home;
'Tis sweet to know there is an eye will mark
    Our coming, and look brighter when we come;   980
'Tis sweet to be awakened by the lark
    Or lulled by falling waters; sweet the hum
Of bees, the voice of girls, the song of birds,
The lisp of children and their earliest words;

124

Sweet is the vintage, when the showering grapes   985
    In Bacchanal profusion reel to earth
Purple and gushing; sweet are our escapes
    From civic revelry to rural mirth;
Sweet to the miser are his glittering heaps;
    Sweet to the father is his first-born's birth;   990
Sweet is revenge – especially to women;
Pillage to soldiers, prize-money to seamen;

125

Sweet is a legacy, and passing sweet
    The unexpected death of some old lady
Or gentleman of seventy years complete,   995
    Who've made 'us youth' wait too too long already
For an estate or cash or country-seat,

---

[46] *Adria* Venice.

Still breaking, but with stamina so steady,
That all the Israelites[47] are fit to mob its
Next owner for their double-demand post-obits.   1000

126

'Tis sweet to win (no matter how) one's laurels
  By blood or ink; 'tis sweet to put an end
To strife; 'tis sometimes sweet to have our quarrels,
  Particularly with a tiresome friend;
Sweet is old wine in bottles, ale in barrels;   1005
  Dear is the helpless creature we defend
Against the world; and dear the schoolboy spot
We ne'er forget, though there we are forgot.

127

But sweeter still than this, than these, than all,
  Is first and passionate love – it stands alone   1010
Like Adam's recollection of his fall;
  The tree of knowledge has been plucked, all's known,
And life yields nothing further to recall
  Worthy of this ambrosial sin, so shown
No doubt in fable, as the unforgiven   1015
Fire which Prometheus filched for us from heaven.

128

Man's a strange animal, and makes strange use
  Of his own nature and the various arts,
And likes particularly to produce
  Some new experiment to show his parts;   1020
This is the age of oddities let loose,
  Where different talents find their different marts;
You'd best begin with truth, and when you've lost your
Labour, there's a sure market for imposture.

129

What opposite discoveries we have seen   1025
  (Signs of true genius, and of empty pockets)!
One makes new noses, one a guillotine,
  One breaks your bones, one sets them in their sockets;

---

[47] *Israelites* i.e. money-lenders.

But vaccination certainly has been
   A kind antithesis to Congreve's rockets,   1030
With which the doctor paid off an old pox
   By borrowing a new one from an ox.[48]

130

Bread has been made (indifferent) from potatoes,
   And galvanism has set some corpses grinning,
But has not answered like the apparatus   1035
   Of the Humane Society's beginning,
By which men are unsuffocated gratis;
   What wondrous new machines have late been spinning![49]
I said the smallpox has gone out of late,
Perhaps it may be followed by the great.[50]   1040

131

'Tis said the great came from America,
   Perhaps it may set out on its return;
The population there so spreads, they say,
   'Tis grown high time to thin it in its turn
With war or plague or famine, any way,   1045
   So that civilization they may learn,
And which in ravage the more loathsome evil is:
Their real lues, or our pseudo-syphilis?

132

This is the patent-age of new inventions
   For killing bodies and for saving souls,   1050
All propagated with the best intentions;
   Sir Humphry Davy's lantern,[51] by which coals
Are safely mined for in the mode he mentions,
   Tombuctoo travels, voyages to the Poles
Are ways to benefit mankind, as true,   1055
Perhaps, as shooting them at Waterloo.

---

[48] Benjamin Charles Perkins made new noses; Sir William Congreve (1772–1828) invented an artillery shell; Edward Jenner (1749–1823) first vaccinated against smallpox in 1796.
[49] Luigi Galvani used electricity to attempt to restore corpses to life, as well as for therapeutic purposes (first described 1792); the Humane Society, founded 1774, for the rescue of drowning persons (the 'apparatus' is a resuscitator); the spinning-jenny, patented by James Hargreaves, 1770.
[50] the great syphilis.
[51] Davy (1778–1829), friend of Wordsworth, Coleridge, Scott, and Byron, not only wrote poetry, but invented the miner's safety-lamp, 1815.

133

Man's a phenomenon, one knows not what,
　　And wonderful beyond all wondrous measure;
'Tis pity though, in this sublime world, that
　　Pleasure's a sin, and sometimes sin's a pleasure;　　　　1060
Few mortals know what end they would be at,
　　But whether glory, power, or love or treasure,
The path is through perplexing ways, and when
The goal is gained, we die, you know – and then –

134

What then? I do not know, no more do you –　　　　　　1065
　　And so goodnight. Return we to our story:
'Twas in November when fine days are few,
　　And the far mountains wax a little hoary
And clap a white cape on their mantles blue;
　　And the sea dashes round the promontory,　　　　　　1070
And the loud breaker boils against the rock,
And sober suns must set at five o'clock.

135

'Twas, as the watchmen say, a cloudy night;
　　No moon, no stars, the wind was low or loud
By gusts, and many a sparkling hearth was bright　　　　1075
　　With the piled wood round which the family crowd;
There's something cheerful in that sort of light,
　　Even as a summer sky's without a cloud –
I'm fond of fire and crickets, and all that,
A lobster-salad and champagne and chat.　　　　　　　　1080

136

'Twas midnight; Donna Julia was in bed –
　　Sleeping, most probably – when at her door
Arose a clatter might awake the dead
　　(If they had never been awoke before,
And that they have been so we all have read,　　　　　　1085
　　And are to be so, at the least, once more);
The door was fastened, but with voice and fist
First knocks were heard, then 'Madam, madam – hist!

137

For God's sake, madam – madam, here's my master
   With more than half the city at his back;   1090
Was ever heard of such a cursed disaster!
   'Tis not my fault, I kept good watch – alack!
Do pray undo the bolt a little faster;
   They're on the stair just now, and in a crack
Will all be here – perhaps he yet may fly;   1095
Surely the window's not so *very* high!'

138

By this time Don Alfonso was arrived
   With torches, friends and servants in great number;
The major part of them had long been wived,
   And therefore paused not to disturb the slumber   1100
Of any wicked woman who contrived
   By stealth her husband's temples to encumber;
Examples of this kind are so contagious,
Were *one* not punished, *all* would be outrageous.

139

I can't tell how or why or what suspicion   1105
   Could enter into Don Alfonso's head,
But for a cavalier of his condition
   It surely was exceedingly ill-bred,
Without a word of previous admonition,
   To hold a levee round his lady's bed   1110
And summon lackeys armed with fire and sword,
To prove himself the thing he most abhorred.

140

Poor Donna Julia! Starting as from sleep
   (Mind that I do not say she had not slept)
Began at once to scream and yawn and weep;   1115
   Her maid Antonia, who was an adept,
Contrived to fling the bedclothes in a heap,
   As if she had just now from out them crept –
I can't tell why she should take all this trouble
To prove her mistress had been sleeping double.   1120

141

But Julia mistress, and Antonia maid,
  Appeared like two poor harmless women who
Of goblins, but still more of men afraid,
  Had thought one man might be deterred by two,
And therefore side by side were gently laid   1125
  Until the hours of absence should run through,
And truant husband should return and say,
'My dear, I was the first who came away.'

142

Now Julia found at length a voice, and cried,
  'In heaven's name, Don Alfonso, what d'ye mean?   1130
Has madness seized you? Would that I had died
  Ere such a monster's victim I had been!
What may this midnight violence betide?
  A sudden fit of drunkenness or spleen?
Dare you suspect me, whom the thought would kill?   1135
Search then the room!' Alfonso said, 'I will.'

143

He searched, *they* searched, and rummaged everywhere,
  Closet and clothes-press, chest and window-seat,
And found much linen, lace, and several pair
  Of stockings, slippers, brushes, combs, complete   1140
With other articles of ladies fair,
  To keep them beautiful or leave them neat;
Arras they pricked, and curtains with their swords,
And wounded several shutters and some boards.

144

Under the bed they searched, and there they found –   1145
  No matter what, it was not that they sought;
They opened windows, gazing if the ground
  Had signs or footmarks, but the earth said nought;
And then they stared each others' faces round:
  'Tis odd not one of all these seekers thought   1150
(And seems to me almost a sort of blunder)
Of looking *in* the bed as well as under.

145

During this inquisition Julia's tongue
    Was not asleep: 'Yes, search and search', she cried,
'Insult on insult heap, and wrong on wrong!   1155
    It was for this that I became a bride!
For this in silence I have suffered long
    A husband like Alfonso at my side;
But now I'll bear no more, nor here remain,
If there be law or lawyers in all Spain.   1160

146

Yes, Don Alfonso, husband now no more
    (If ever you indeed deserved the name)!
Is't worthy of your years? You have threescore,
    Fifty or sixty (it is all the same),
Is't wise or fitting causeless to explore   1165
    For facts against a virtuous woman's fame?
Ungrateful, perjured, barbarous Don Alfonso –
How dare you think your lady would go on so?

147

Is it for this I have disdained to hold
    The common privileges of my sex? –   1170
That I have chosen a confessor so old
    And deaf, that any other it would vex,
And never once he has had cause to scold,
    But found my very innocence perplex
So much, he always doubted I was married?   1175
How sorry you will be when I've miscarried!

148

Was it for this that no Cortejo[52] ere
    I yet have chosen from out the youth of Seville?
Is it for this I scarce went anywhere
    Except to bullfights, mass, play, rout and revel?   1180
Is it for this, whate'er my suitors were,
    I favoured none – nay, was almost uncivil?

---

[52] *Cortejo* Spanish cavalier servente.

Is it for this that General Count O'Reilly,
Who took Algiers,[53] declares I used him vilely?

149

Did not the Italian musico Cazzani   1185
  Sing at my heart six months at least in vain?
Did not his countryman, Count Corniani,[54]
  Call me the only virtuous wife in Spain?
Were there not also Russians, English, many?
  The Count Strongstroganoff I put in pain,   1190
And Lord Mount Coffeehouse, the Irish peer,
Who killed himself for love (with wine) last year.

150

Have I not had two bishops at my feet,
  The Duke of Ichar, and Don Fernan Nunez,
And is it thus a faithful wife you treat?   1195
  I wonder in what quarter now the moon is;
I praise your vast forbearance not to beat
  Me also, since the time so opportune is –
Oh valiant man, with sword drawn and cocked trigger,
Now tell me, don't you cut a pretty figure?   1200

151

Was it for this you took your sudden journey
  Under pretence of business indispensable
With that sublime of rascals your attorney,
  Whom I see standing there, and looking sensible
Of having played the fool? Though both I spurn, he   1205
  Deserves the worst, his conduct's less defensible,
Because, no doubt, 'twas for his dirty fee,
And not from any love to you nor me.

152

If he comes here to take a deposition,
  By all means let the gentleman proceed –   1210

---

[53] 'Donna Julia here made a mistake. Count [Alexander] O'Reilly did not take Algiers – but Algiers very nearly took him. He and his army and fleet retreated with great loss, and not much credit, from before that city in the year 1775' (Byron's note).

[54] *musico* musician. Cazzani is an obscene pun on 'cazza' (penis): Corniani derives from 'cornuto' (horned, cuckolded).

You've made the apartment in a fit condition!
 There's pen and ink for you, sir, when you need;
Let everything be noted with precision
 (I would not you for nothing should be feed);
But as my maid's undressed, pray turn your spies out.'   1215
'Oh!' sobbed Antonia, 'I could tear their eyes out!'

153

'There is the closet, there the toilet, there
 The antechamber — search them under, over;
There is the sofa, there the great armchair,
 The chimney (which would really hold a lover).   1220
I wish to sleep, and beg you will take care
 And make no further noise, till you discover
The secret cavern of this lurking treasure —
And when 'tis found, let me, too, have that pleasure.

154

And now, Hidalgo, now that you have thrown   1225
 Doubt upon me, confusion over all,
Pray have the courtesy to make it known
 Who is the man you search for? How d'ye call
Him? What's his lineage? Let him but be shown;
 I hope he's young and handsome — is he tall?   1230
Tell me, and be assured that since you stain
My honour thus, it shall not be in vain.

155

At least, perhaps, he has not sixty years —
 At that age he would be too old for slaughter
Or for so young a husband's jealous fears!   1235
 Antonia, let me have a glass of water;
I am ashamed of having shed these tears,
 They are unworthy of my father's daughter;
My mother dreamed not in my natal hour
That I should fall into a monster's power.   1240

156

Perhaps 'tis of Antonia you are jealous —
 You saw that she was sleeping by my side
When you broke in upon us with your fellows;

Look where you please, we've nothing, sir, to hide;
Only another time, I trust, you'll tell us, 1245
Or for the sake of decency abide
A moment at the door, that we may be
Dressed to receive so much good company.

157

And now, sir, I have done and say no more;
The little I have said may serve to show 1250
The guileless heart in silence may grieve o'er
The wrongs to whose exposure it is slow;
I leave you to your conscience as before –
'Twill one day ask you *why* you used me so?
God grant you feel not then the bitterest grief! 1255
Antonia, where's my pocket-handkerchief?'

158

She ceased, and turned upon her pillow; pale
She lay, her dark eyes flashing through their tears
Like skies that rain and lighten; as a veil,
Waved and o'ershading her wan cheek, appears 1260
Her streaming hair; the black curls strive but fail
To hide the glossy shoulder, which uprears
Its snow through all; her soft lips lie apart,
And louder than her breathing beats her heart.

159

The *señor* Don Alfonso stood confused; 1265
Antonia bustled round the ransacked room
And, turning up her nose, with looks abused
Her master and his myrmidons, of whom
Not one, except the attorney, was amused;
He, like Achates,[55] faithful to the tomb, 1270
So there were quarrels, cared not for the cause,
Knowing they must be settled by the laws.

160

With prying snubnose and small eyes he stood,
Following Antonia's motions here and there
With much suspicion in his attitude; 1275

---

[55] Aeneas's faithful friend in the *Aeneid*.

For reputations he had little care,
So that a suit or action were made good;
  Small pity had he for the young and fair,
And ne'er believed in negatives, till these
Were proved by competent false witnesses.   1280

161

But Don Alfonso stood with downcast looks,
  And truth to say, he made a foolish figure –
When after searching in five hundred nooks,
  And treating a young wife with so much rigour,
He gained no point except some self-rebukes,   1285
  Added to those his lady with such vigour
Had poured upon him for the last half-hour,
Quick, thick, and heavy, as a thunder-shower.

162

At first he tried to hammer an excuse
  To which the sole reply were tears and sobs   1290
And indications of hysterics, whose
  Prologue is always certain throes and throbs,
Gasps and whatever else the owners choose;
  Alfonso saw his wife and thought of Job's;
He saw too, in perspective, her relations,   1295
And then he tried to muster all his patience.

163

He stood in act to speak, or rather stammer,
  But sage Antonia cut him short before
The anvil of his speech received the hammer,
  With, 'Pray sir, leave the room, and say no more,   1300
Or madam dies.' Alfonso muttered, 'D—n her!'
  But nothing else – the time of words was o'er;
He cast a rueful look or two, and did
(He knew not wherefore) that which he was bid.

164

With him retired his *posse comitatus*[56] –   1305
  The attorney last, who lingered near the door

---

[56] *posse comitatus* 'the force of the county'; armed
posse.

Reluctantly, still tarrying there as late as
   Antonia let him, not a little sore
At this most strange and unexplained hiatus
   In Don Alfonso's facts, which just now wore   1310
An awkward look; as he resolved the case
The door was fastened in his legal face.

165

No sooner was it bolted than – oh shame!
   Oh sin! Oh sorrow! And oh womankind!
How can you do such things and keep your fame,   1315
   Unless this world (and t'other too) be blind?
Nothing so dear as an unfilched good name!
   But to proceed, for there is more behind;
With much heartfelt reluctance be it said,
Young Juan slipped, half-smothered, from the bed.   1320

166

He had been hid – I don't pretend to say
   How, nor can I indeed describe the where;
Young, slender, and packed easily, he lay
   No doubt, in little compass, round or square;
But pity him I neither must nor may   1325
   His suffocation by that pretty pair;
'Twere better, sure, to die so, than be shut
With maudlin Clarence in his Malmsey butt.[57]

167

And secondly, I pity not, because
   He had no business to commit a sin   1330
Forbid by heavenly, fined by human laws
   (At least 'twas rather early to begin);
But at sixteen the conscience rarely gnaws
   So much as when we call our old debts in
At sixty years, and draw the accompts of evil,   1335
And find a deuced balance with the Devil.

168

Of his position I can give no notion;
   'Tis written in the Hebrew chronicle[58]

---

[57] See *Richard III*, I. iv. 270.   [58] I Kings I: 1–3.

How the physicians, leaving pill and potion,
   Prescribed by way of blister, a young belle,   1340
When old King David's blood grew dull in motion,
   And that the medicine answered very well;
Perhaps 'twas in a different way applied,
For David lived, but Juan nearly died.

169

What's to be done? Alfonso will be back   1345
   The moment he has sent his fools away.
Antonia's skill was put upon the rack
   But no device could be brought into play –
And how to parry the renewed attack?
   Besides, it wanted but few hours of day;   1350
Antonia puzzled, Julia did not speak
But pressed her bloodless lip to Juan's cheek.

170

He turned his lip to hers, and with his hand
   Called back the tangles of her wandering hair;
Even then their love they could not all command,   1355
   And half forgot their danger and despair.
Antonia's patience now was at a stand –
   'Come, come, 'tis no time now for fooling there',
She whispered in great wrath, 'I must deposit
This pretty gentleman within the closet: 1360

171

Pray keep your nonsense for some luckier night –
   Who can have put my master in this mood?
What will become on't? I'm in such a fright,
   The Devil's in the urchin, and no good –
Is this a time for giggling? this a plight?   1365
   Why, don't you know that it may end in blood?
You'll lose your life, and I shall lose my place,
My mistress, all, for that half-girlish face.

172

Had it but been for a stout cavalier
   Of twenty-five or thirty (come, make haste!) –   1370
But for a child, what piece of work is here!

I really, madam, wonder at your taste –
Come sir, get in; my master must be near.
 There for the present, at the least he's fast,
And if we can but till the morning keep   1375
Our counsel – Juan, mind, you must not sleep!'

173

Now Don Alfonso entering, but alone,
 Closed the oration of the trusty maid;
She loitered, and he told her to be gone –
 An order somewhat sullenly obeyed;   1380
However, present remedy was none,
 And no great good seemed answered if she stayed;
Regarding both with slow and sidelong view,
She snuffed the candle, curtsied and withdrew.

174

Alfonso paused a minute, then begun   1385
 Some strange excuses for his late proceeding;
He would not justify what he had done –
 To say the best, it was extreme ill-breeding;
But there were ample reasons for it, none
 Of which he specified in this his pleading: 1390
His speech was a fine sample, on the whole,
Of rhetoric which the learned call *rigmarole*.

175

Julia said nought, though all the while there rose
 A ready answer – which at once enables
A matron (who her husband's foible knows)
 By a few timely words to turn the tables,   1395
Which, if it does not silence, still must pose,
 Even if it should comprise a pack of fables;
'Tis to retort with firmness, and when he
Suspects with *one*, do you reproach with *three*. 1400

176

Julia in fact had tolerable grounds:
 Alfonso's loves with Inez were well-known;
But whether 'twas that one's own guilt confounds –
 But that can't be, as has been often shown,

A lady with apologies abounds;   1405
   It might be that her silence sprang alone
From delicacy to Don Juan's ear,
To whom she knew his mother's fame was dear.

177

There might be one more motive (which makes two):
   Alfonso ne'er to Juan had alluded –   1410
Mentioned his jealousy, but never who
   Had been the happy lover he concluded
Concealed amongst his premises; 'tis true
   His mind the more o'er this its mystery brooded;
To speak of Inez now were, one may say,   1415
Like throwing Juan in Alfonso's way.

178

A hint, in tender cases, is enough;
   Silence is best – besides there is a *tact*
(That modern phrase appears to me sad stuff,
   But it will serve to keep my verse compact)   1420
Which keeps, when pushed by questions rather rough,
   A lady always distant from the fact –
The charming creatures lie with such a grace,
There's nothing so becoming to the face.

179

They blush, and we believe them – at least I   1425
   Have always done so; 'tis of no great use
In any case attempting a reply,
   For then their eloquence grows quite profuse;
And when at length they're out of breath, they sigh
   And cast their languid eyes down, and let loose   1430
A tear or two, and then we make it up,
And then – and then – and then – sit down and sup.

180

Alfonso closed his speech and begged her pardon,
   Which Julia half-withheld, and then half-granted,
And laid conditions, he thought, very hard on,   1435
   Denying several little things he wanted;

He stood like Adam lingering near his garden,[59]
  With useless penitence perplexed and haunted,
Beseeching she no further would refuse –
  When lo! he stumbled o'er a pair of shoes.   1440

181

A pair of shoes! What then? Not much, if they
  Are such as fit with lady's feet, but these
(No one can tell how much I grieve to say)
  Were masculine: to see them and to seize
Was but a moment's act – ah wel-a-day![60]   1445
  My teeth begin to chatter, my veins freeze;
Alfonso first examined well their fashion,
And then flew out into another passion.

182

He left the room for his relinquished sword
  And Julia instant to the closet flew,   1450
'Fly, Juan, fly! For heaven's sake, not a word –
  The door is open, you may yet slip through
The passage you so often have explored;
  Here is the garden-key – fly – fly – adieu!
Haste, haste! I hear Alfonso's hurrying feet –   1455
  Day has not broke; there's no one in the street.'

183

None can say that this was not good advice,
  The only mischief was it came too late;
Of all experience 'tis the usual price,
  A sort of income tax laid on by fate: 1460
Juan had reached the room-door in a trice
  And might have done so by the garden-gate,
But met Alfonso in his dressing-gown,
Who threatened death – so Juan knocked him down.

184

Dire was the scuffle, and out went the light,   1465
  Antonia cried out 'Rape!' and Julia, 'Fire!'
But not a servant stirred to aid the fight.

[59] *Paradise Lost*, xii. 636.   [60] Cf. Coleridge, 'Christabel', 252.

Alfonso, pommelled to his heart's desire,
Swore lustily he'd be revenged this night;
    And Juan too blasphemed an octave higher,   1470
His blood was up – though young, he was a Tartar,
And not at all disposed to prove a martyr.

185

Alfonso's sword had dropped ere he could draw it,
    And they continued battling hand to hand,
For Juan very luckily ne'er saw it;   1475
    His temper not being under great command,
If at that moment he had chanced to claw it,
    Alfonso's days had not been in the land
Much longer. Think of husbands', lovers' lives,
And how ye may be doubly widows, wives!   1480

186

Alfonso grappled to detain the foe
    And Juan throttled him to get away,
And blood ('twas from the nose) began to flow;
    At last, as they more faintly wrestling lay,
Juan contrived to give an awkward blow,   1485
    And then his only garment quite gave way;
He fled, like Joseph,[61] leaving it – but there,
I doubt, all likeness ends between the pair.

187

Lights came at length, and men and maids who found
    An awkward spectacle their eyes before: 1490
Antonia in hysterics, Julia swooned,
    Alfonso leaning breathless by the door;
Some half-torn drapery scattered on the ground,
    Some blood and several footsteps, but no more –
Juan the gate gained, turned the key about,   1495
And liking not the inside, locked the out.

188

Here ends this canto. Need I sing, or say,
    How Juan, naked, favoured by the night

---

[61] See Gen. 39: 18.

(Who favours what she should not), found his way,
　And reached his home in an unseemly plight?　　　　　　1500
The pleasant scandal which arose next day,
　The nine days' wonder which was brought to light,
And how Alfonso sued for a divorce,
Were in the English newspapers, of course.

189

If you would like to see the whole proceedings,　　　　　1505
　The depositions, and the cause at full,
The names of all the witnesses, the pleadings
　Of counsel to nonsuit or to annul,
There's more than one edition, and the readings
　Are various, but they none of them are dull;　　　　　1510
The best is that in shorthand ta'en by Gurney,[62]
Who to Madrid on purpose made a journey.

190

But Donna Inez, to divert the train
　Of one of the most circulating scandals
That had for centuries been known in Spain　　　　　　1515
　Since Roderic's Goths or older Genseric's Vandals,
First vowed (and never had she vowed in vain)
　To Virgin Mary several pounds of candles;
And then by the advice of some old ladies,
She sent her son to be embarked at Cadiz.　　　　　　1520

191

She had resolved that he should travel through
　All European climes by land or sea
To mend his former morals, or get new,
　Especially in France and Italy –
At least this is the thing most people do.　　　　　　1525
　Julia was sent into a nunnery,
And there perhaps her feelings may be better
Shown in the following copy of her letter:

---

[62] William Gurney (1777–1855), shorthand clerk in
Parliament.

192

'They tell me 'tis decided – you depart.
    'Tis wise, 'tis well, but not the less a pain;   1530
I have no further claim on your young heart –
    Mine was the victim, and would be again;
To love too much has been the only art
    I used; I write in haste, and if a stain
Be on this sheet, 'tis not what it appears –   1535
My eyeballs burn and throb, but have no tears.

193

I loved, I love you, for that love have lost
    State, station, heaven, mankind's, my own esteem,
And yet cannot regret what it hath cost,
    So dear is still the memory of that dream;   1540
Yet if I name my guilt, 'tis not to boast –
    None can deem harshlier of me than I deem:
I trace this scrawl because I cannot rest,
I've nothing to reproach, nor to request.

194

Man's love is of his life a thing apart,   1545
    'Tis woman's whole existence; man may range
The court, camp, church, the vessel and the mart,
    Sword, gown, gain, glory, offer in exchange
Pride, fame, ambition, to fill up his heart,
    And few there are whom these cannot estrange;   1550
Man has all these resources, we but one –
To love again, and be again undone.

195

My breast has been all weakness, is so yet;
    I struggle, but cannot collect my mind;
My blood still rushes where my spirit's set   1555
    As roll the waves before the settled wind;
My brain is feminine, nor can forget –
    To all, except your image, madly blind;
As turns the needle trembling to the pole
It ne'er can reach, so turns to you, my soul.   1560

196

You will proceed in beauty and in pride,
   Beloved and loving many; all is o'er
For me on earth, except some years to hide
   My shame and sorrow deep in my heart's core;
These I could bear, but cannot cast aside   1565
   The passion which still rends it as before,
And so farewell; forgive me, love me – no,
That word is idle now, but let it go.

197

I have no more to say, but linger still,
   And dare not set my seal upon this sheet,   1570
And yet I may as well the task fulfil –
   My misery can scarce be more complete;
I had not lived till now, could sorrow kill;
   Death flies the wretch who fain the blow would meet,
And I must even survive this last adieu,   1575
And bear with life, to love and pray for you!'

198

This note was written upon gilt-edged paper
   With a neat crow-quill – rather hard, but new;
Her small white fingers scarce could reach the taper
   But trembled as magnetic needles do,   1580
And yet she did not let one tear escape her;
   The seal a sunflower, 'Elle vous suit partout'[63]
The motto, cut upon a white cornelian;
The wax was superfine, its hue vermilion.

199

This was Don Juan's earliest scrape – but whether   1585
   I shall proceed with his adventures is
Dependent on the public altogether;
   We'll see, however, what they say to this;
Their favour in an author's cap's a feather,
   And no great mischief's done by their caprice;   1590
And if their approbation we experience,
Perhaps they'll have some more about a year hence.

---

[63] 'She follows you everywhere.'

200

My poem's epic, and is meant to be
   Divided in twelve books, each book containing,
With love and war, a heavy gale at sea,   1595
   A list of ships and captains, and kings reigning,
New characters; the episodes are three:
   A panorama view of hell's in training
After the style of Virgil and of Homer,
So that my name of epic's no misnomer.   1600

201

All these things will be specified in time
   With strict regard to Aristotle's rules,
The vade-mecum of the true sublime
   Which makes so many poets, and some fools;
Prose poets like blank verse, I'm fond of rhyme –   1605
   Good workmen never quarrel with their tools;
I've got new mythological machinery
And very handsome supernatural scenery.

202

There's only one slight difference between
   Me and my epic brethren gone before,   1610
And here the advantage is my own, I ween
   (Not that I have no several merits more,
But this will more peculiarly be seen) –
   They so embellish that 'tis quite a bore
Their labyrinth of fables to thread through,   1615
Whereas this story's actually true.

203

If any person doubt it, I appeal
   To history, tradition, and to facts,
To newspapers (whose truth all know and feel),
   To plays in five, and operas in three acts –   1620
All these confirm my statement a good deal,
   But that which more completely faith exacts
Is that myself, and several now in Seville,
Saw Juan's last elopement with the Devil.

204

If ever I should condescend to prose,   1625
    I'll write poetical commandments which
Shall supersede beyond all doubt all those
    That went before; in these I shall enrich
My text with many things that no one knows,
    And carry precept to the highest pitch: 1630
I'll call the work 'Longinus o'er a bottle,
Or, Every poet his *own* Aristotle'.

205

Thou shalt believe in Milton, Dryden, Pope;
    Thou shalt not set up Wordsworth, Coleridge, Southey,
Because the first is crazed beyond all hope,   1635
    The second drunk, the third so quaint and mouthy;
With Crabbe it may be difficult to cope,
    And Campbell's Hippocrene is somewhat drouthy;
Thou shalt not steal from Samuel Rogers, nor
Commit ... flirtation with the muse of Moore.   1640

206

Thou shalt not covet Mr Sotheby's muse,
    His Pegasus,[64] nor anything that's his;
Thou shalt not bear false witness like the Blues[65]
    (There's one, at least, is very fond of this);
Thou shalt not write, in short, but what I choose: 1645
    This is true criticism, and you may kiss
Exactly as you please, or not, the rod —
But if you don't, I'll lay it on, by G-d!

207

If any person should presume to assert
    This story is not moral, first I pray   1650
That they will not cry out before they're hurt,
    Then that they'll read it o'er again, and say
(But, doubtless, nobody will be so pert)
    That this is not a moral tale, though gay;

---

[64] Pegasus was supposed to carry poets on their   [65] The blue-stockings.
flights of fancy.

Besides, in Canto Twelfth I mean to show 1655
The very place where wicked people go.

208

If, after all, there should be some so blind
  To their own good this warning to despise,
Led by some tortuosity of mind
  Not to believe my verse and their own eyes, 1660
And cry that they 'the moral cannot find',
  I tell him, if a clergyman, he lies;
Should captains the remark or critics make,
They also lie too – under a mistake.

209

The public approbation I expect, 1665
  And beg they'll take my word about the moral,
Which I with their amusement will connect
  (So children cutting teeth receive a coral);
Meantime, they'll doubtless please to recollect
  My epical pretensions to the laurel: 1670
For fear some prudish readers should grow skittish
I've bribed my grandmother's review – the *British*.

210

I sent it in a letter to the editor
  Who thanked me duly by return of post –
I'm for a handsome article his creditor; 1675
  Yet if my gentle muse he please to roast,
And break a promise after having made it her,
  Denying the receipt of what it cost
And smear his page with gall instead of honey,
All I can say is – that he had the money. 1680

211

I think that with this holy new alliance
  I may ensure the public, and defy
All other magazines of art or science –
  Daily or monthly or three-monthly; I
Have not essayed to multiply their clients 1685
  Because they tell me 'twere in vain to try,
And that the *Edinburgh Review* and *Quarterly*
Treat a dissenting author very martyrly.

212

'Non ego hoc ferrem calida juventa
   Consule Planco',[66] Horace said, and so   1690
Say I; by which quotation there is meant a
   Hint that some six or seven good years ago
(Long ere I dreamt of dating from the Brenta[67])
   I was most ready to return a blow,
And would not brook at all this sort of thing   1695
In my hot youth – when George the Third was King.

213

But now at thirty years my hair is gray
   (I wonder what it will be like at forty?
I thought of a peruke the other day),
   My heart is not much greener, and, in short, I   1700
Have squandered my whole summer while 'twas May,
   And feel no more the spirit to retort; I
Have spent my life, both interest and principal,
And deem not what I deemed, my soul invincible.

214

No more, no more – oh never more on me   1705
   The freshness of the heart can fall like dew,
Which out of all the lovely things we see
   Extracts emotions beautiful and new,
Hived in our bosoms like the bag o' the bee:
   Think'st thou the honey with those objects grew?   1710
Alas, 'twas not in them, but in thy power
To double even the sweetness of a flower.

215

No more, no more – oh never more, my heart,
   Canst thou be my sole world, my universe!
Once all in all, but now a thing apart,   1715
   Thou canst not be my blessing or my curse;
The illusion's gone forever, and thou art
   Insensible, I trust, but none the worse,
And in thy stead I've got a deal of judgement –
Though heaven knows how it ever found a lodgement.   1720

---

[66] Horace, *Odes*, III. xiv. 27–8; translated (roughly)   [67] *the Brenta* Venice.
at lines 1695–6.

216

My days of love are over, me no more
   The charms of maid, wife, and still less of widow,
Can make the fool of which they made before;
   In short, I must not lead the life I did do;
The credulous hope of mutual minds is o'er,   1725
   The copious use of claret is forbid too –
So, for a good old gentlemanly vice,
I think I must take up with avarice.

217

Ambition was my idol, which was broken
   Before the shrines of sorrow and of pleasure;   1730
And the two last have left me many a token
   O'er which reflection may be made at leisure;
Now like Friar Bacon's brazen head I've spoken,
   'Time is, time was, time's past';[68] a chemic treasure
Is glittering youth, which I have spent betimes –   1735
My heart in passion, and my head on rhymes.

218

What is the end of fame? 'Tis but to fill
   A certain portion of uncertain paper;
Some liken it to climbing up a hill
   Whose summit, like all hills', is lost in vapour;   1740
For this men write, speak, preach, and heroes kill,
   And bards burn what they call their 'midnight taper' –
To have, when the original is dust,
A name, a wretched picture, and worse bust.

219

What are the hopes of man? Old Egypt's King   1745
   Cheops erected the first pyramid
And largest, thinking it was just the thing
   To keep his memory whole, and mummy hid;
But somebody or other rummaging,
   Burglariously broke his coffin's lid: 1750

---

[68] The words of the brass head, Robert Greene,
Friar Bacon and Friar Bungay (1594), IV. i. 1584, 1595,
1604.

Let not a monument give you or me hopes,
Since not a pinch of dust remains of Cheops.

220

But I, being fond of true philosophy,
   Say very often to myself, 'Alas!
All things that have been born were born to die,   1755
   And flesh (which death mows down to hay) is grass;
You've passed your youth not so unpleasantly,
   And if you had it o'er again, 'twould pass;
So thank your stars that matters are no worse
And read your Bible, sir, and mind your purse.'   1760

221

But for the present, gentle reader and
   Still gentler purchaser, the bard (that's I)
Must with permission shake you by the hand;
   And so your humble servant, and goodbye!
We meet again, if we should understand   1765
   Each other – and if not, I shall not try
Your patience further than by this short sample
('Twere well if others followed my example).

222

'Go, little book, from this my solitude!
   I cast thee on the waters, go thy ways!   1770
And if, as I believe, thy vein be good,
   The world will find thee after many days.'[69]
When Southey's read, and Wordsworth understood,
   I can't help putting in my claim to praise;
The four first rhymes are Southey's every line –   1775
For God's sake, reader, take them not for mine!

To the Po. 2 June 1819 (composed 1 or 2 June 1819; first published 1824; edited from MS)

River that rollest by the ancient walls
   Where dwells the lady of my love,[1] when she

---

[69]   Southey, 'L'Envoy', *The Lay of the Laureate* (1816).
TO THE PO. 2 JUNE 1819
[1]   Contessa Teresa Guiccioli, whose affair with

Byron began Apr. 1819. At the time of writing he
believed her to be with her husband at their estate
Ca'Zen, on the Po.

Walks by thy brink and there perchance recalls
   A faint and fleeting memory of me –
What if thy deep and ample stream should be   5
   A mirror of my heart, where she may read
The thousand thoughts I now betray to thee,
   Wild as thy wave and headlong as thy speed?
What do I say? 'A mirror of my heart'?
   Are not thy waters sweeping, dark and strong?   10
Such as my feelings were and are, thou art,
   And such as thou art were my passions long;
Time may have somewhat tamed them – not forever
   Thou overflow'st thy banks, and not for aye
The bosom overboils, congenial river!   15
   Thy floods subside, and mine have sunk away,
But left long wrecks behind us; yet again
   Borne on our old career unchanged we move,
Thou tendest wildly to the wilder main
   And I to loving one I should not love.   20
The current I behold will sweep beneath
   Her palace walls, and murmur at her feet,
Her eyes will look on thee when she shall breathe
   The twilight air unchained from summer's heat.
She will look on thee; I have looked on thee   25
   Full of that thought, and from this moment ne'er
Thy waters could I name, hear named, or see
   Without the inseparable sigh for her.
Her bright eyes will be imaged in thy stream –
   Yes, they will meet the wave I gaze on now,   30
But mine cannot even witness in a dream
   That happy wave repass me in its flow;
The wave that bears my tear returns no more –
   Will she return by whom that wave shall sweep?
Both tread thy bank, both wander by thy shore,   35
   I near thy source, and she by the blue deep;
But that which keepeth us apart is not
   Distance, nor depth of wave, nor space of earth,
But the distractions of a various lot –
   Ah, various as the climates of our birth!   40
A stranger loves a lady of the land
   Born far beyond the mountains, but his blood
Is all meridian, as if never fanned
   By the bleak wind that chills the polar flood.
My heart is all meridian; were it not,   45
   I had not suffered now, nor should I be,
Despite of tortures ne'er to be forgot,
   The slave again, oh love, at least of thee!
'Tis vain to struggle – I have struggled long
   To love again no more as once I loved.   50

Oh time, why leave this earliest passion strong? –
To tear a heart which pants to be unmoved?

From Letter from Lord Byron to Douglas Kinnaird, 26 October 1819

As to *Don Juan*, confess – confess, you dog (and be candid), that it is the sublime of *that there* sort of writing. It may be bawdy, but is it not good English? It may be profligate, but is it not *life*, is it not *the thing*? Could any man have written it who has not lived in the world? – and tooled in a post-chaise? In a hackney coach? In a gondola? Against a wall? In a court carriage? In a vis-à-vis?[1] On a table – and under it? I have written about a hundred stanzas of a third Canto, but it is damned modest – the outcry has frightened me.[2] I had such projects for the Don, but the *cant* is so much stronger than *cunt* nowadays, that the benefit of experience in a man who had well weighed the worth of both monosyllables must be lost to despairing posterity.[3]

MESSALONGHI, 22 JANUARY 1824. ON THIS DAY I COMPLETE MY THIRTY-SIXTH YEAR (FIRST PUBLISHED 1824; EDITED FROM MS)

1

'Tis time this heart should be unmoved,
    Since others it hath ceased to move;
Yet though I cannot be beloved,
        Still let me love.

2

My days are in the yellow leaf,   5
    The flowers and fruits of love are gone,
The worm, the canker and the grief
        Are mine alone.

3

The fire that on my bosom preys
    Is lone as some volcanic isle,
No torch is kindled at its blaze –   10
        A funeral pile!

From LETTER FROM LORD BYRON TO DOUGLAS KINNAIRD, 26 October 1819

[1] *vis-à-vis* light carriage for two people sitting face to face.

[2] Although *Don Juan*, I–II, received favourable re-

views from some quarters, it was strongly attacked for 'degrading debauchery' and 'shameless indecency'.

[3] All the same, *Don Juan*, III–V, was published in Aug. 1821.

4

The hope, the fear, the jealous care,
    The exalted portion of the pain,
And power of love I cannot share   15
        But wear the chain.

5

But 'tis not thus, and 'tis not here
    Such thoughts should shake my soul, nor now
Where glory decks the hero's bier
        Or binds his brow.   20

6

The sword, the banner, and the field,
    Glory and Greece about us see –
The Spartan borne upon his shield[1]
        Was not more free!

7

Awake (not Greece – she *is* awake),   25
    Awake my spirit – think through whom
Thy life-blood tracks its parent lake
        And then strike home!

8

Tread those reviving passions down,
    Unworthy manhood; unto thee   30
Indifferent should the smile or frown
        Of beauty be.

9

If thou regret'st thy youth, why live?
    The land of honourable death

MESSALONGHI, 22 January 1824 ('On this day I complete my thirty-sixth year')
[1] 'The slain were borne upon their shields' (Byron's
MS note).

Is here: up to the field, and give
Away thy breath!

10

Seek out (less often sought than found)
A soldier's grave, for thee the best,
Then look around and choose thy ground
And take thy rest.

35

Percy Bysshe Shelley (1792-1822)

Shelley's first major poem, Alastor, *explores the dark side of the poetic quest, and can be read in terms of his essays 'On Love' and 'On Life' (though it should be borne in mind that they were composed years later). The journal letter to Peacock of 22 and 25 July 1816 describes the factual background to 'Mont Blanc', and anticipates the poem in a number of ideas and phrases (the landscape it describes also features in Mary Shelley's* Frankenstein*). As in* Alastor, *the author of 'Mont Blanc' and the 'Hymn to Intellectual Beauty' is willing to conceive of a world in which solitude and silence might be vacancy, rather than evidence of a benevolent deity; for this reason 'Mont Blanc' in particular should be read as a response to Coleridge's 'Chamouny; the Hour Before Sunrise. A Hymn' (pp. 558–60). 'Lines Written among the Euganean Hills' seems, at first, to be about the absence of hope, but it contains an important political subtext, and looks forward to a renewed, paradisal 'brotherhood' of man.* Prometheus Unbound, *a complete text of which is presented below, explicates in greater detail the regenerative process for which Shelley hopes, finding it initiated by Prometheus revoking his curse on Jupiter. Shelley called it 'the most perfect of my productions' (Jones, ii. 127); for a detailed account of it, see Mary Shelley's important note, pp. 1085–7.* The Mask of Anarchy, *Shelley's indignant response to the Peterloo Massacre, ought to have been published in 1819. It was sent to Leigh Hunt for* The Examiner, *but Hunt held it back until 1832. If* Adonais, *Shelley's elegy for Keats, is grand in its scale and visionary in its attitude to Keats's death, it evades complacency, finally admitting a sense of despair and uncertainty in its closing stanzas.*

From Alastor; or, The Spirit of Solitude, and Other Poems (1816)

ALASTOR; OR, THE SPIRIT OF SOLITUDE (COMPOSED 10 SEPTEMBER-14 DECEMBER 1815)

Preface

The poem entitled 'Alastor' may be considered as allegorical of one of the most interesting situations of the human mind. It represents a youth of uncorrupted feelings and adventurous genius led forth by an imagination inflamed and purified through familiarity with all that is excellent and majestic, to the contemplation of the universe. He drinks deep of the fountains of knowledge and is still insatiate. The magnificence and beauty of the external world sinks profoundly into the frame of his conceptions, and affords to their modifications a variety not to be exhausted. So long as it is possible for his desires to point towards objects thus infinite and unmeasured, he is joyous and tranquil and self-possessed. But the period arrives when these objects cease to suffice. His mind is at length suddenly awakened and thirsts for intercourse with an intelligence similar to itself. He images to himself the being whom he loves. Conversant with speculations of the sublimest and most perfect natures, the vision in which he embodies his own imaginations unites all of wonderful, or wise, or beautiful, which the poet, the philosopher, or the lover could depicture. The intellectual faculties, the imagination, the functions of sense, have their respective requisitions on the sympathy of corresponding powers in other human beings. The poet is represented as uniting these requisitions, and attaching them to a single image. He seeks in vain for a prototype of his conception.[1] Blasted by his disappointment, he descends to an untimely grave.

The picture is not barren of instruction to actual men. The poet's self-centred seclusion was avenged by the furies of an irresistible passion pursuing him to speedy ruin. But that power which strikes the luminaries of the world with sudden darkness and extinction, by awakening them to too exquisite a perception of its influences, dooms to a slow and poisonous decay those meaner spirits that dare to abjure its dominion. Their destiny is more abject and inglorious as their delinquency is more contemptible and pernicious. They who, deluded by no generous error, instigated by no sacred thirst of doubtful knowledge, duped by no illustrious superstition, loving nothing on this earth, and cherishing no hopes beyond, yet keep aloof from sympathies with their kind, rejoicing neither in human joy nor mourning with human grief; these, and such as they, have their apportioned curse. They languish because none feel with them their common nature. They are morally dead. They are neither friends, nor lovers, nor fathers, nor citizens of the world, nor benefactors of their country. Among those who attempt to exist without human sympathy, the pure and tender-hearted perish through the intensity and passion of their search after its communities, when the vacancy of their spirit suddenly makes itself felt. All else, selfish, blind, and torpid, are those unforeseeing multitudes who constitute, together with their own, the lasting misery and loneliness of the world. Those who love not their fellow-beings live unfruitful lives, and prepare for their old age a miserable grave.

> *The good die first,*
> *And those whose hearts are dry as summer dust,*
> *Burn to the socket!*
> (Wordsworth, *The Excursion*, i. 500-2)
> 14 December 1815

Nondum amabam, et amare amabam, quaerebam quid amarem, amans amare.[2]
(St Augustine, *Confessions*, III. i)

ALASTOR; OR, THE SPIRIT OF SOLITUDE
[1] See Shelley's letter to John Gisborne, 18 June 1822: 'I think one is always in love with something or other; the error (and I confess it is not easy for spirits cased in flesh and blood to avoid it) consists in seeking in a mortal image the likeness of what is perhaps eternal' (Jones, ii. 434). For more on ideal prototypes, see 'On Love', pp. 860–1 below.
[2] 'I was not yet in love, and I loved to be in love, I sought what I might love, in love with loving.'

Earth, ocean, air, beloved brotherhood!
If our great mother[3] has imbued my soul
With aught of natural piety[4] to feel
Your love, and recompense the boon with mine;
If dewy morn, and odorous noon, and even,   5
With sunset and its gorgeous ministers,
And solemn midnight's tingling silentness;
If autumn's hollow sighs in the sere wood,
And winter robing with pure snow and crowns
Of starry ice the grey grass and bare boughs;   10
If spring's voluptuous pantings when she breathes
Her first sweet kisses, have been dear to me;
If no bright bird, insect, or gentle beast
I consciously have injured, but still loved
And cherished these my kindred – then forgive   15
This boast, beloved brethren, and withdraw
No portion of your wonted favour now.
     Mother of this unfathomable world![5]
Favour my solemn song, for I have loved
Thee ever, and thee only; I have watched   20
Thy shadow and the darkness of thy steps,
And my heart ever gazes on the depth
Of thy deep mysteries. I have made my bed
In charnels and on coffins, where black death
Keeps record of the trophies won from thee,   25
Hoping to still these obstinate questionings[6]
Of thee and thine, by forcing some lone ghost,
Thy messenger, to render up the tale
Of what we are. In lone and silent hours,
When night makes a weird sound of its own stillness,   30
Like an inspired and desperate alchemist
Staking his very life on some dark hope,
Have I mixed awful talk and asking looks
With my most innocent love, until strange tears,
Uniting with those breathless kisses, made   35
Such magic as compels the charmed night
To render up thy charge – and though ne'er yet
Thou hast unveiled thy inmost sanctuary,
Enough from incommunicable dream,
And twilight phantasms, and deep noonday thought,   40
Has shone within me, that serenely now
And moveless, as a long-forgotten lyre[7]

[3] *our great mother* Cybele, goddess of the powers of nature.
[4] *natural piety* Wordsworth, 'The Rainbow', 9.
[5] Nature, as well as Necessity; cf. *Queen Mab*, vi. 198: 'Necessity! Thou mother of the world!'
[6] *obstinate questionings* Wordsworth, 'Ode', 144.
[7] An aeolian harp; with lines 42–9 cf. Coleridge, 'Eolian Harp', 36–40.

Suspended in the solitary dome
Of some mysterious and deserted fane,
I wait thy breath, Great Parent, that my strain   45
May modulate with murmurs of the air
And motions of the forests and the sea,
And voice of living beings, and woven hymns
Of night and day, and the deep heart of man.

   There was a poet whose untimely tomb   50
No human hands with pious reverence reared,
But the charmed eddies of autumnal winds
Built o'er his mouldering bones a pyramid
Of mouldering leaves in the waste wilderness;
A lovely youth – no mourning maiden decked   55
With weeping flowers or votive cypress wreath
The lone couch of his everlasting sleep;
Gentle and brave and generous – no lorn bard
Breathed o'er his dark fate one melodious sigh;
He lived, he died, he sung, in solitude.   60
Strangers have wept to hear his passionate notes,
And virgins, as unknown he passed, have pined
And wasted for fond love of his wild eyes.
The fire of those soft orbs has ceased to burn,
And silence, too enamoured of that voice,   65
Locks its mute music in her rugged cell.
   By solemn vision and bright silver dream
His infancy was nurtured; every sight
And sound from the vast earth and ambient air
Sent to his heart its choicest impulses.   70
The fountains of divine philosophy
Fled not his thirsting lips, and all of great
Or good or lovely, which the sacred past
In truth or fable consecrates, he felt
And knew. When early youth had passed, he left   75
His cold fireside and alienated home
To seek strange truths in undiscovered lands:
Many a wide waste and tangled wilderness
Has lured his fearless steps, and he has bought
With his sweet voice and eyes, from savage men,   80
His rest and food. Nature's most secret steps
He like her shadow has pursued, where'er
The red volcano overcanopies
Its fields of snow and pinnacles of ice
With burning smoke, or where bitumen lakes   85
On black bare pointed islets ever beat
With sluggish surge, or where the secret caves
Rugged and dark, winding among the springs
Of fire and poison, inaccessible
To avarice or pride, their starry domes   90

Of diamond and of gold expand above
Numberless and immeasurable halls,
Frequent with crystal column, and clear shrines
Of pearl, and thrones radiant with chrysolite.
Nor had that scene of ampler majesty   95
Than gems or gold, the varying roof of heaven
And the green earth lost in his heart its claims
To love and wonder; he would linger long
In lonesome vales, making the wild his home,
Until the doves and squirrels would partake   100
From his innocuous hand his bloodless food,
Lured by the gentle meaning of his looks,
And the wild antelope that starts whene'er
The dry leaf rustles in the brake, suspend
Her timid steps to gaze upon a form   105
More graceful than her own.
                His wandering step,
Obedient to high thoughts, has visited
The awful ruins of the days of old:
Athens, and Tyre, and Balbec, and the waste
Where stood Jerusalem,[8] the fallen towers   110
Of Babylon, the eternal pyramids,
Memphis and Thebes, and whatsoe'er of strange
Sculptured on alabaster obelisk
Or jasper tomb, or mutilated sphinx,
Dark Ethiopia in her desert hills   115
Conceals. Among the ruined temples there,
Stupendous columns and wild images
Of more than man, where marble daemons watch
The zodiac's brazen mystery[9] and dead men
Hang their mute thoughts on the mute walls around,   120
He lingered, poring on memorials
Of the world's youth, through the long burning day
Gazed on those speechless shapes, nor, when the moon
Filled the mysterious halls with floating shades,
Suspended he that task, but ever gazed   125
And gazed, till meaning on his vacant mind
Flashed like strong inspiration, and he saw
The thrilling secrets of the birth of time.
   Meanwhile an Arab maiden brought his food,
Her daily portion, from her father's tent,   130
And spread her matting for his couch, and stole
From duties and repose to tend his steps –
Enamoured, yet not daring for deep awe
To speak her love – and watched his nightly sleep,

---

[8] Jerusalem was destroyed by the Emperor Titus in AD 70.

[9] Zodiacs were painted on the ceiling of the temple of Isis at Dendera in Egypt.

Sleepless herself, to gaze upon his lips 135
Parted in slumber, whence the regular breath
Of innocent dreams arose. Then when red morn
Made paler the pale moon, to her cold home
Wildered, and wan, and panting, she returned.

    The poet wandering on, through Arabie 140
And Persia and the wild Carmanian waste,
And o'er the aerial mountains which pour down
Indus and Oxus from their icy caves,
In joy and exultation held his way;
Till in the Vale of Kashmir, far within 145
Its loneliest dell, where odorous plants entwine
Beneath the hollow rocks a natural bower,
Beside a sparkling rivulet he stretched
His languid limbs. A vision on his sleep
There came, a dream of hopes that never yet 150
Had flushed his cheek: he dreamed a veiled maid
Sat near him, talking in low solemn tones.
Her voice was like the voice of his own soul
Heard in the calm of thought;[10] its music long,
Like woven sounds of streams and breezes, held 155
His inmost sense suspended in its web
Of many-coloured woof and shifting hues.
Knowledge and truth and virtue were her theme,
And lofty hopes of divine liberty,
Thoughts the most dear to him, and poesy, 160
Herself a poet. Soon the solemn mood
Of her pure mind kindled through all her frame
A permeating fire – wild numbers then
She raised, with voice stifled in tremulous sobs
Subdued by its own pathos; her fair hands 165
Were bare alone, sweeping from some strange harp
Strange symphony, and in their branching veins
The eloquent blood told an ineffable tale.
The beating of her heart was heard to fill
The pauses of her music, and her breath 170
Tumultuously accorded with those fits
Of intermitted song. Sudden she rose,
As if her heart impatiently endured
Its bursting burden: at the sound he turned,
And saw by the warm light of their own life 175
Her glowing limbs beneath the sinuous veil
Of woven wind, her outspread arms now bare,
Her dark locks floating in the breath of night,
Her beamy bending eyes, her parted lips

---

[10] 'His mind ... thirsts for intercourse with an intelligence similar to itself. He images to himself the being whom he loves', p. 835 above; see also 'On Love', pp. 860–1 below.

Outstretched and pale, and quivering eagerly.   180
His strong heart sunk and sickened with excess
Of love. He reared his shuddering limbs and quelled
His gasping breath, and spread his arms to meet
Her panting bosom; she drew back awhile,
Then, yielding to the irresistible joy,   185
With frantic gesture and short breathless cry
Folded his frame in her dissolving arms.
Now blackness veiled his dizzy eyes, and night
Involved and swallowed up the vision; sleep,
Like a dark flood suspended in its course,   190
Rolled back its impulse on his vacant brain.
Roused by the shock he started from his trance –
The cold white light of morning, the blue moon
Low in the west, the clear and garish hills,
The distinct valley and the vacant woods,   195
Spread round him where he stood. Whither have fled
The hues of heaven that canopied his bower
Of yesternight? The sounds that soothed his sleep,
The mystery and the majesty of earth,
The joy, the exultation? His wan eyes   200
Gaze on the empty scene as vacantly
As ocean's moon looks on the moon in heaven.
The spirit of sweet human love has sent
A vision to the sleep of him who spurned
Her choicest gifts. He eagerly pursues   205
Beyond the realms of dream that fleeting shade;
He overleaps the bounds.[11] Alas, alas!
Were limbs and breath and being intertwined
Thus treacherously? Lost, lost, forever lost
In the wide pathless desert of dim sleep,   210
That beautiful shape! Does the dark gate of death
Conduct to thy mysterious paradise,
Oh sleep? Does the bright arch of rainbow clouds
And pendent mountains seen in the calm lake
Lead only to a black and watery depth,   215
While death's blue vault with loathliest vapours hung,
Where every shade which the foul grave exhales
Hides its dead eye from the detested day,
Conduct, oh sleep, to thy delightful realms?
This doubt with sudden tide flowed on his heart;   220
The insatiate hope which it awakened stung
His brain even like despair.
                            While daylight held

---

[11] i.e. between illusion and reality, in trying to
pursue the dream-image into the real world.

The sky, the poet kept mute conference
With his still soul. At night the passion came
Like the fierce fiend of a distempered dream,   225
And shook him from his rest, and led him forth
Into the darkness. As an eagle grasped
In folds of the green serpent, feels her breast
Burn with the poison, and precipitates
Through night and day, tempest and calm and cloud,   230
Frantic with dizzying anguish, her blind flight
O'er the wide airy wilderness; thus driven
By the bright shadow of that lovely dream,
Beneath the cold glare of the desolate night,
Through tangled swamps and deep precipitous dells,   235
Startling with careless step the moonlight snake,
He fled. Red morning dawned upon his flight,
Shedding the mockery of its vital hues
Upon his cheek of death. He wandered on
Till vast Aornos seen from Petra's steep   240
Hung o'er the low horizon like a cloud;
Through Balk and where the desolated tombs
Of Parthian kings scatter to every wind
Their wasting dust, wildly he wandered on
Day after day, a weary waste of hours,   245
Bearing within his life the brooding care
That ever fed on its decaying flame.
And now his limbs were lean: his scattered hair
Sered by the autumn of strange suffering
Sung dirges in the wind; his listless hand   250
Hung like dead bone within its withered skin;
Life, and the lustre that consumed it, shone
As in a furnace burning secretly
From his dark eyes alone. The cottagers,
Who ministered with human charity   255
His human wants, beheld with wondering awe
Their fleeting visitant. The mountaineer,
Encountering on some dizzy precipice
That spectral form, deemed that the spirit of wind
With lightning eyes, and eager breath, and feet   260
Disturbing not the drifted snow, had paused
In its career; the infant would conceal
His troubled visage in his mother's robe
In terror at the glare of those wild eyes,
To remember their strange light in many a dream   265
Of after-times; but youthful maidens, taught
By nature, would interpret half the woe
That wasted him, would call him with false names
Brother and friend, would press his pallid hand
At parting, and watch, dim through tears, the path   270

Of his departure from their father's door.
    At length upon the lone Chorasmian shore
He paused, a wide and melancholy waste
Of putrid marshes. A strong impulse urged
His steps to the seashore; a swan was there,   275
Beside a sluggish stream among the reeds.
It rose as he approached, and with strong wings
Scaling the upward sky, bent its bright course
High over the immeasurable main.
His eyes pursued its flight. 'Thou hast a home,   280
Beautiful bird; thou voyagest to thine home,
Where thy sweet mate will twine her downy neck
With thine, and welcome thy return with eyes
Bright in the lustre of their own fond joy.
And what am I that I should linger here,   285
With voice far sweeter than thy dying notes,
Spirit more vast than thine, frame more attuned
To beauty, wasting these surpassing powers
In the deaf air, to the blind earth, and heaven
That echoes not my thoughts?' A gloomy smile   290
Of desperate hope wrinkled his quivering lips –
For sleep, he knew, kept most relentlessly
Its precious charge, and silent death exposed,
Faithless perhaps as sleep, a shadowy lure,
With doubtful smile mocking its own strange charms.   295
    Startled by his own thoughts he looked around.
There was no fair fiend near him, not a sight
Or sound of awe but in his own deep mind.
A little shallop floating near the shore
Caught the impatient wandering of his gaze.   300
It had been long abandoned, for its sides
Gaped wide with many a rift, and its frail joints
Swayed with the undulations of the tide.
A restless impulse urged him to embark
And meet lone death on the drear ocean's waste,   305
For well he knew that mighty shadow loves
The slimy caverns of the populous deep.
    The day was fair and sunny, sea and sky
Drank its inspiring radiance, and the wind
Swept strongly from the shore, blackening the waves.   310
Following his eager soul, the wanderer
Leaped in the boat, he spread his cloak aloft
On the bare mast and took his lonely seat,
And felt the boat speed o'er the tranquil sea
Like a torn cloud before the hurricane.   315
    As one that in a silver vision floats
Obedient to the sweep of odorous winds
Upon resplendent clouds, so rapidly

Along the dark and ruffled waters fled
The straining boat. A whirlwind swept it on   320
With fierce gusts and precipitating force
Through the white ridges of the chafed sea.
The waves arose; higher and higher still
Their fierce necks writhed beneath the tempest's scourge
Like serpents struggling in a vulture's grasp.   325
Calm and rejoicing in the fearful war
Of wave ruining on wave, and blast on blast
Descending, and black flood on whirlpool driven
With dark obliterating course, he sat:
As if their genii were the ministers   330
Appointed to conduct him to the light
Of those beloved eyes, the poet sat
Holding the steady helm. Evening came on,
The beams of sunset hung their rainbow hues
High mid the shifting domes of sheeted spray   335
That canopied his path o'er the waste deep;
Twilight, ascending slowly from the east,
Entwined in duskier wreaths her braided locks
O'er the fair front and radiant eyes of day;
Night followed, clad with stars. On every side   340
More horribly the multitudinous streams
Of ocean's mountainous waste to mutual war
Rushed in dark tumult thundering, as to mock
The calm and spangled sky. The little boat
Still fled before the storm, still fled like foam   345
Down the steep cataract of a wintry river –
Now pausing on the edge of the riven wave,
Now leaving far behind the bursting mass
That fell, convulsing ocean; safely fled –
As if that frail and wasted human form   350
Had been an elemental god.
                              At midnight
The moon arose – and lo! the ethereal cliffs
Of Caucasus, whose icy summits shone
Among the stars like sunlight, and around
Whose caverned base the whirlpools and the waves,   355
Bursting and eddying irresistibly,
Rage and resound forever. Who shall save?
The boat fled on, the boiling torrent drove,
The crags closed round with black and jagged arms,
The shattered mountain overhung the sea,   360
And faster still, beyond all human speed,
Suspended on the sweep of the smooth wave,
The little boat was driven. A cavern there
Yawned, and amid its slant and winding depths
Engulfed the rushing sea. The boat fled on   365

With unrelaxing speed. 'Vision and love!'
The poet cried aloud, 'I have beheld
The path of thy departure. Sleep and death
Shall not divide us long!'
                    The boat pursued
The windings of the cavern. Daylight shone   370
At length upon that gloomy river's flow;
Now, where the fiercest war among the waves
Is calm, on the unfathomable stream
The boat moved slowly. Where the mountain, riven,
Exposed those black depths to the azure sky,   375
Ere yet the flood's enormous volume fell
Even to the base of Caucasus, with sound
That shook the everlasting rocks, the mass
Filled with one whirlpool all that ample chasm;
Stair above stair the eddying waters rose,   380
Circling immeasurably fast, and laved
With alternating dash the gnarled roots
Of mighty trees that stretched their giant arms
In darkness over it. I' the midst was left,
Reflecting yet distorting every cloud,   385
A pool of treacherous and tremendous calm.
Seized by the sway of the ascending stream,
With dizzy swiftness, round and round and round,
Ridge after ridge the straining boat arose,
Till on the verge of the extremest curve,   390
Where, through an opening of the rocky bank,
The waters overflow, and a smooth spot
Of glassy quiet mid those battling tides
Is left, the boat paused shuddering. Shall it sink
Down the abyss? Shall the reverting stress   395
Of that resistless gulf embosom it?
Now shall it fall? A wandering stream of wind,
Breathed from the west, has caught the expanded sail,
And lo! with gentle motion, between banks
Of mossy slope, and on a placid stream,   400
Beneath a woven grove it sails – and hark!
The ghastly torrent mingles its far roar
With the breeze murmuring in the musical woods.
Where the embowering trees recede, and leave
A little space of green expanse, the cove   405
Is closed by meeting banks, whose yellow flowers
Forever gaze on their own drooping eyes,
Reflected in the crystal calm.[12] The wave
Of the boat's motion marred their pensive task

---

[12] The narcissus, alluding to the Greek youth ob-
sessed with his own image.

Which nought but vagrant bird, or wanton wind,   410
Or falling spear-grass, or their own decay
Had e'er disturbed before. The poet longed
To deck with their bright hues his withered hair,
But on his heart its solitude returned
And he forbore. Not the strong impulse hid   415
In those flushed cheeks, bent eyes, and shadowy frame
Had yet performed its ministry;[13] it hung
Upon his life, as lightning in a cloud
Gleams, hovering ere it vanish, ere the floods
Of night close over it.
                The noonday sun   420
Now shone upon the forest, one vast mass
Of mingling shade whose brown magnificence
A narrow vale embosoms; there huge caves,
Scooped in the dark base of their airy rocks,
Mocking its moans,[14] respond and roar forever.   425
The meeting boughs and implicated leaves
Wove twilight o'er the poet's path as, led
By love, or dream, or god, or mightier death,
He sought in nature's dearest haunt some bank,
Her cradle, and his sepulchre. More dark   430
And dark the shades accumulate. The oak,
Expanding its immense and knotty arms,
Embraces the light beech. The pyramids
Of the tall cedar overarching, frame
Most solemn domes within, and far below,   435
Like clouds suspended in an emerald sky,
The ash and the acacia floating hang
Tremulous and pale. Like restless serpents clothed
In rainbow and in fire, the parasites,
Starred with ten thousand blossoms, flow around   440
The grey trunks, and, as gamesome infants' eyes
With gentle meanings and most innocent wiles
Fold their beams round the hearts of those that love,
These twine their tendrils with the wedded boughs
Uniting their close union; the woven leaves   445
Make network of the dark blue light of day
And the night's noontide clearness, mutable
As shapes in the weird clouds. Soft mossy lawns
Beneath these canopies extend their swells,
Fragrant with perfumed herbs, and eyed with blooms   450
Minute yet beautiful. One darkest glen
Sends from its woods of musk-rose, twined with jasmine,
A soul-dissolving odour, to invite

---

[13] Cf. Coleridge, *Frost at Midnight*, 1: 'The frost performs its secret ministry.'

[14] *Mocking its moans* echoing the moans of the wind in the forest.

To some more lovely mystery. Through the dell,
Silence and twilight here, twin-sisters, keep   455
Their noonday watch, and sail among the shades
Like vaporous shapes half-seen; beyond, a well,
Dark, gleaming, and of most translucent wave,
Images all the woven boughs above,
And each depending leaf, and every speck   460
Of azure sky, darting between their chasms;
Nor aught else in the liquid mirror laves
Its portraiture, but some inconstant star
Between one foliaged lattice twinkling fair,
Or painted bird, sleeping beneath the moon,   465
Or gorgeous insect floating motionless,
Unconscious of the day ere yet his wings
Have spread their glories to the gaze of noon.
   Hither the poet came. His eyes beheld
Their own wan light through the reflected lines   470
Of his thin hair, distinct in the dark depth
Of that still fountain; as the human heart,
Gazing in dreams over the gloomy grave,
Sees its own treacherous likeness there.[15] He heard
The motion of the leaves, the grass that sprung   475
Startled and glanced and trembled even to feel
An unaccustomed presence, and the sound
Of the sweet brook that from the secret springs
Of the dark fountain rose. A spirit[16] seemed
To stand beside him, clothed in no bright robes   480
Of shadowy silver or enshrining light
Borrowed from aught the visible world affords
Of grace, or majesty, or mystery —
But, undulating woods and silent well,
And leaping rivulet and evening gloom   485
Now deepening the dark shades, for speech assuming[17]
Held commune with him, as if he and it
Were all that was — only, when his regard
Was raised by intense pensiveness, two eyes,
Two starry eyes, hung in the gloom of thought   490
And seemed with their serene and azure smiles
To beckon him.
           Obedient to the light
That shone within his soul, he went pursuing
The windings of the dell. The rivulet
Wanton and wild, through many a green ravine   495
Beneath the forest flowed. Sometimes it fell

---

[15] i.e. imagines its continued but uncertain (treacherous) life after death.
[16] Probably nature.

[17] Nature used woods, well, rivulet, and gloom as a
means of speech.

Among the moss with hollow harmony
Dark and profound; now on the polished stones
It danced, like childhood laughing as it went;
Then through the plain in tranquil wanderings crept,   500
Reflecting every herb and drooping bud
That overhung its quietness. 'Oh stream!
Whose source is inaccessibly profound,
Whither do thy mysterious waters tend?
Thou imagest my life: thy darksome stillness,   505
Thy dazzling waves, thy loud and hollow gulfs,
Thy searchless fountain[18] and invisible course
Have each their type in me. And the wide sky
And measureless ocean may declare as soon
What oozy cavern or what wandering cloud   510
Contains thy waters, as the universe
Tell where these living thoughts reside, when stretched
Upon thy flowers my bloodless limbs shall waste
I' the passing wind!'
                            Beside the grassy shore
Of the small stream he went; he did impress   515
On the green moss his tremulous step that caught
Strong shuddering from his burning limbs. As one
Roused by some joyous madness from the couch
Of fever, he did move, yet not like him
Forgetful of the grave, where, when the flame   520
Of his frail exultation shall be spent,
He must descend. With rapid steps he went
Beneath the shade of trees, beside the flow
Of the wild babbling rivulet – and now
The forest's solemn canopies were changed   525
For the uniform and lightsome evening sky.
Grey rocks did peep from the spare moss, and stemmed
The struggling brook; tall spires of windlestrae[19]
Threw their thin shadows down the rugged slope,
And nought but gnarled roots[20] of ancient pines   530
Branchless and blasted, clenched with grasping roots
The unwilling soil. A gradual change was here,
Yet ghastly. For, as fast years flow away,
The smooth brow gathers, and the hair grows thin
And white, and where irradiate dewy eyes   535
Had shone, gleam stony orbs: so from his steps
Bright flowers departed, and the beautiful shade
Of the green groves, with all their odorous winds
And musical motions. Calm, he still pursued

---

[18] *searchless fountain* undiscoverable source.
[19] *windlestrae* dry grass-stalks.

[20] *roots* apparently an error; Shelley may have meant
'trunks' or 'knots'.

The stream, that with a larger volume now   540
Rolled through the labyrinthine dell; and there
Fretted a path through its descending curves
With its wintry speed. On every side now rose
Rocks which, in unimaginable forms,
Lifted their black and barren pinnacles   545
In the light of evening, and, its precipice
Obscuring, the ravine disclosed above,
Mid toppling stones, black gulfs and yawning caves,
Whose windings gave ten thousand various tongues
To the loud stream. Lo! where the pass expands   550
Its stony jaws, the abrupt mountain breaks
And seems, with its accumulated crags,
To overhang the world — for wide expand
Beneath the wan stars and descending moon
Islanded seas, blue mountains, mighty streams,   555
Dim tracts and vast, robed in the lustrous gloom
Of leaden-coloured even, and fiery hills
Mingling their flames with twilight, on the verge
Of the remote horizon. The near scene,
In naked and severe simplicity,   560
Made contrast with the universe. A pine,
Rock-rooted, stretched athwart the vacancy
Its swinging boughs, to each inconstant blast
Yielding one only response, at each pause
In most familiar cadence, with the howl,   565
The thunder and the hiss of homeless streams
Mingling its solemn song, whilst the broad river,
Foaming and hurrying o'er its rugged path,
Fell into that immeasurable void
Scattering its waters to the passing winds.   570
    Yet the grey precipice and solemn pine
And torrent were not all; one silent nook
Was there. Even on the edge of that vast mountain,
Upheld by knotty roots and fallen rocks,
It overlooked in its serenity   575
The dark earth and the bending vault of stars.
It was a tranquil spot that seemed to smile
Even in the lap of horror. Ivy clasped
The fissured stones with its entwining arms,
And did embower with leaves forever green,   580
And berries dark, the smooth and even space
Of its inviolated floor; and here
The children of the autumnal whirlwind bore,
In wanton sport, those bright leaves whose decay,
Red, yellow, or ethereally pale,   585
Rivals the pride of summer. 'Tis the haunt
Of every gentle wind whose breath can teach

The wilds to love tranquillity. One step,[21]
One human step alone, has ever broken
The stillness of its solitude; one voice   590
Alone inspired its echoes – even that voice
Which hither came floating among the winds,
And led the loveliest among human forms
To make their wild haunts the depository
Of all the grace and beauty that endued   595
Its motions, render up its majesty,
Scatter its music on the unfeeling storm,
And to the damp leaves and blue cavern mould,
Nurses of rainbow flowers and branching moss,
Commit the colours of that varying cheek,   600
That snowy breast, those dark and drooping eyes.
   The dim and horned moon hung low, and poured
A sea of lustre on the horizon's verge
That overflowed its mountains. Yellow mist
Filled the unbounded atmosphere, and drank   605
Wan moonlight even to fullness: not a star
Shone, not a sound was heard; the very winds,
Danger's grim playmates, on that precipice
Slept, clasped in his embrace. Oh storm of Death,
Whose sightless speed divides this sullen night,   610
And thou, colossal skeleton,[22] that, still
Guiding its irresistible career
In thy devastating omnipotence,
Art king of this frail world – from the red field
Of slaughter, from the reeking hospital,   615
The patriot's sacred couch, the snowy bed
Of innocence, the scaffold and the throne,
A mighty voice invokes thee: Ruin calls
His brother Death. A rare and regal prey[23]
He hath prepared, prowling around the world –   620
Glutted with which thou mayst repose, and men
Go to their graves like flowers or creeping worms,
Nor ever more offer at thy dark shrine
The unheeded tribute of a broken heart.
   When on the threshold of the green recess   625
The wanderer's footsteps fell, he knew that death
Was on him. Yet a little, ere it fled,
Did he resign his high and holy soul
To images of the majestic past
That paused within his passive[24] being now,   630
Like winds that bear sweet music when they breathe

---

[21] i.e. that of the poet.
[22] i.e. of Death.
[23] i.e. the world's rulers, who will glut Death, so that
their victims may die according to their worth.
[24] *passive* an important detail; cf. 'Mont Blanc', 37–8.

Through some dim latticed chamber. He did place
His pale lean hand upon the rugged trunk
Of the old pine; upon an ivied stone
Reclined his languid head; his limbs did rest,　　　　635
Diffused and motionless, on the smooth brink
Of that obscurest chasm – and thus he lay,
Surrendering to their final impulses
The hovering powers of life. Hope and despair,
The torturers, slept; no mortal pain or fear　　　　640
Marred his repose, the influxes of sense
And his own being unalloyed by pain,
Yet feebler and more feeble, calmly fed
The stream of thought, till he lay breathing there
At peace, and faintly smiling. His last sight　　　　645
Was the great moon, which o'er the western line
Of the wide world her mighty horn suspended,
With those dun beams inwoven darkness seemed
To mingle. Now upon the jagged hills
It rests, and still as the divided frame　　　　650
Of the vast meteor[25] sunk, the poet's blood,
That ever beat in mystic sympathy
With nature's ebb and flow, grew feebler still;
And when two lessening points of light[26] alone
Gleamed through the darkness, the alternate gasp　　　　655
Of his faint respiration scarce did stir
The stagnate night – till the minutest ray
Was quenched, the pulse yet lingered in his heart.
It paused, it fluttered. But when heaven remained
Utterly black, the murky shades involved　　　　660
An image, silent, cold, and motionless,
As their own voiceless earth and vacant air.
Even as a vapour[27] fed with golden beams
That ministered on sunlight ere the west
Eclipses it, was now that wondrous frame –　　　　665
No sense, no motion, no divinity –
A fragile lute on whose harmonious strings
The breath of heaven did wander, a bright stream
Once fed with many-voiced[28] waves, a dream
Of youth, which night and time have quenched for ever –　　　　670
Still, dark, and dry, and unremembered now.
　　Oh for Medea's wondrous alchemy,
Which wheresoe'er it fell made the earth gleam
With bright flowers, and the wintry boughs exhale
From vernal blooms fresh fragrance![29] Oh that God,　　　　675

---

[25] The moon.
[26] From the moon.
[27] *vapour* cloud.

[28] *many-voiced* cf. 'Mont Blanc', 13.
[29] Medea brewed a potion to restore youth; when spilt on the ground, it had the effect described here.

Profuse of poisons, would concede the chalice
Which but one living man[30] has drained – who now,
Vessel of deathless wrath, a slave that feels
No proud exemption in the blighting curse
He bears, over the world wanders for ever,   680
Lone as incarnate death! Oh that the dream
Of dark magician[31] in his visioned cave,
Raking the cinders of a crucible
For life and power, even when his feeble hand
Shakes in its last decay, were the true law   685
Of this so lovely world! But thou art fled
Like some frail exhalation which the dawn
Robes in its golden beams – ah, thou hast fled! –
The brave, the gentle, and the beautiful,
The child of grace and genius. Heartless things   690
Are done and said i' the world, and many worms
And beasts and men live on, and mighty earth
From sea and mountain, city and wilderness,
In vesper low or joyous orison,
Lifts still its solemn voice – but thou art fled;   695
Thou canst no longer know or love the shapes
Of this phantasmal scene, who have to thee
Been purest ministers – who are, alas,
Now thou art not! Upon those pallid lips,
So sweet even in their silence, on those eyes   700
That image sleep in death, upon that form
Yet safe from the worm's outrage, let no tear
Be shed, not even in thought; nor – when those hues
Are gone, and those divinest lineaments
Worn by the senseless wind – shall live alone   705
In the frail pauses of this simple strain.
Let not high verse, mourning the memory
Of that which is no more, or painting's woe
Or sculpture, speak in feeble imagery
Their own cold powers. Art and eloquence   710
And all the shows o' the world are frail and vain
To weep a loss that turns their lights to shade.
It is a woe too 'deep for tears',[32] when all
Is reft at once, when some surpassing spirit,
Whose light adorned the world around it, leaves   715
Those who remain behind not sobs or groans,
The passionate tumult of a clinging hope,
But pale despair and cold tranquillity,

---

[30] *one living man* Ahasuerus, the wandering Jew, doomed to eternal life.
[31] The alchemist aims to find an *elixir vitae* capable of reversing the laws of death and decay.
[32] Wordsworth, 'Ode', 206.

Nature's vast frame, the web of human things,
Birth and the grave, that are not as they were.   720

To Wordsworth (composed probably September–October 1815)

Poet of nature, thou hast wept to know
That things depart which never may return;
Childhood and youth, friendship and love's first glow
Have fled like sweet dreams, leaving thee to mourn.
These common woes I feel. One loss is mine   5
Which thou too feel'st, yet I alone deplore.
Thou wert as a lone star,[1] whose light did shine
On some frail bark in winter's midnight roar;
Thou hast like to a rock-built refuge stood
Above the blind and battling multitude;   10
In honoured poverty thy voice did weave
Songs consecrate to truth and liberty –
Deserting these, thou leavest me to grieve,
Thus having been, that thou shouldst cease to be.[2]

From The Examiner, no. 473 (19 January 1817) 41

Hymn to Intellectual Beauty (composed between 22 June and 29 August 1816; edited from printed text corrected by Shelley)

1

The awful shadow of some unseen Power
Floats though unseen amongst us, visiting
This various world with as inconstant wing
As summer winds that creep from flower to flower;
Like moonbeams that behind some piny mountain shower,   5
It visits with inconstant glance
Each human heart and countenance;
Like hues and harmonies of evening,
Like clouds in starlight widely spread,
Like memory of music fled,   10
Like aught that for its grace may be
Dear, and yet dearer for its mystery.

2

Spirit of Beauty, that doth consecrate
With thine own hues all thou dost shine upon

To Wordsworth
[1] Cf. Wordsworth's praise of Milton, 'London 1802', 9.

[2] Like Byron (see Dedication to *Don Juan*, p. 771 above), Shelley regarded Wordsworth as an apostate to earlier radical views.

Of human thought or form – where art thou gone?   15
Why dost thou pass away and leave our state,
This dim vast vale of tears, vacant and desolate?
    Ask why the sunlight not forever
    Weaves rainbows o'er yon mountain river,
Why aught should fail and fade that once is shown,   20
    Why fear and dream, and death and birth
    Cast on the daylight of this earth
    Such gloom, why man has such a scope
For love and hate, despondency and hope?

3

No voice from some sublimer world hath ever   25
    To sage or poet these responses given;
    Therefore the name of God, and ghosts, and heaven
Remain the records of their vain endeavour,
Frail spells, whose uttered charm might not avail to sever,
    From all we hear and all we see,   30
    Doubt, chance, and mutability.
Thy light alone, like mist o'er mountains driven,
    Or music by the night wind sent
    Through strings of some still instrument,[1]
    Or moonlight on a midnight stream,   35
Gives grace and truth to life's unquiet dream.

4

Love, hope, and self-esteem, like clouds depart
    And come, for some uncertain moments lent.
    Man were immortal and omnipotent,
Didst thou, unknown and awful as thou art,   40
Keep with thy glorious train firm state within his heart.
    Thou messenger of sympathies
    That wax and wane in lovers' eyes;
Thou that to human thought art nourishment,
    Like darkness to a dying flame!   45
    Depart not as thy shadow came,
    Depart not lest the grave should be,
Like life and fear, a dark reality.

HYMN TO INTELLECTUAL BEAUTY
[1] An aeolian harp.

5

While yet a boy I sought for ghosts, and sped
  Through many a listening chamber, cave and ruin   50
  And starlight wood, with fearful steps pursuing
Hopes of high talk with the departed dead.
I called on poisonous names[2] with which our youth is fed –
    I was not heard, I saw them not
    When musing deeply on the lot   55
Of life, at that sweet time when winds are wooing
    All vital things that wake to bring
    News of buds and blossoming.
    Sudden thy shadow fell on me –
I shrieked, and clasped my hands in ecstasy!   60

6

I vowed that I would dedicate my powers
  To thee and thine; have I not kept the vow?
  With beating heart and streaming eyes, even now
I call the phantoms of a thousand hours
Each from his voiceless grave: they have in visioned bowers   65
    Of studious zeal or love's delight
    Outwatched with me the envious night;
They know that never joy illumed my brow
    Unlinked with hope that thou wouldst free
    This world from its dark slavery,   70
    That thou, oh awful loveliness,
Wouldst give whate'er these words cannot express.

7

The day becomes more solemn and serene
  When noon is past; there is a harmony
  In autumn, and a lustre in its sky,   75
Which through the summer is not heard or seen,
As if it could not be, as if it had not been!
    Thus let thy power, which like the truth
    Of nature on my passive youth
Descended, to my onward life supply   80
    Its calm – to one who worships thee,
    And every form containing thee,

---

[2] *poisonous names* presumably those of God and
Christ. In earlier years Shelley did try prayer.

Whom, spirit fair, thy spells did bind
To fear[3] himself, and love all humankind.

From Letter from Percy Bysshe Shelley to Thomas Love Peacock

22 July 1816. From Servox, three leagues remain to Chamounix. Mont Blanc was before us. The Alps with their innumerable glaciers on high, all around, closing in the complicated windings of the single vale; forests inexpressibly beautiful, but majestic in their beauty; interwoven beech and pine and oak overshadowed our road or receded whilst lawns of such verdure as I had never seen before occupied these openings, and, extending gradually, becoming darker into their recesses.

Mont Blanc was before us but was covered with cloud, and its base furrowed with dreadful gaps was seen alone. Pinnacles of snow, intolerably bright, part of the chain connected with Mont Blanc, shone though the clouds at intervals on high. I never knew, I never imagined what mountains were before. The immensity of these aerial summits excited, when they suddenly burst upon the sight, a sentiment of ecstatic wonder not unallied to madness. And remember this was all one scene. It all pressed home to our regard and to our imagination. Though it embraced a great number of miles, the snowy pyramids which shot into the bright blue sky seemed to overhang our path; the ravine, clothed with gigantic pines and black with its depth below (so deep that the very roaring of the untameable Arve which rolled through it could not be heard above), was close to our very footsteps. All was as much our own as if we had been the creators of such impressions in the minds of others, as now occupied our own. Nature was the poet whose harmony held our spirits more breathless than that of the divinest.

25 July 1816. We have returned from visiting this glacier – a scene, in truth, of dizzying wonder. The path that winds to it along the side of a mountain, now clothed with pines, now intersected with snowy hollows, is wide and steep. The cabin of Montanvert is three leagues from Chamounix, half of which distance is performed on mules – not so sure-footed but that, on the first day, the one which I rode fell in what the guides call a 'mauvais pas', so that I narrowly escaped being precipitated down the mountain. The guide continually held that which Mary rode.

We passed over a hollow covered with snow down which vast stones, detached from the rock above, are accustomed to roll. One had fallen the preceding day, a little time after we had returned. The guides desired us to pass quickly, for it is said that sometimes the least sound will accelerate their fall. We arrived at Montanvert, however, safe.

On all sides precipitous mountains, the abodes of unrelenting frost, surround this vale. Their sides are banked up with ice and snow, broken and heaped-up, and exhibiting terrific chasms. The summits are sharp and naked pinnacles whose overhanging steepness will not even permit snow to rest there. They pierce the clouds like things not belonging to this earth. The vale itself is filled with a mass of undulating ice, and has an ascent sufficiently gradual even to the remotest abysses of these horrible deserts.

---

[3] *fear* revere.

It is only half a league (about two miles) in breadth, and seems much less. It exhibits an appearance as if frost had suddenly bound up the waves and whirlpools of a mighty torrent.

We walked to some distance upon its surface. The waves are elevated about 12 or 15 feet from the surface of the mass, which is intersected with long gaps of unfathomable depth, the ice of whose sides is more beautifully azure than the sky. In these regions, everything changes and is in motion. This vast mass of ice has one general progress which ceases neither day nor night. It breaks and rises forever; its undulations sink whilst others rise. From the precipices which surround it, the echo of rocks which fall from their aerial summits, or of the ice and snow, scarcely ceases for one moment. One would think that Mont Blanc was a living being, and that the frozen blood forever circulated slowly through his stony veins.

From History of a Six Weeks' Tour through a Part of France, Switzerland, Germany and Holland, by Percy Bysshe and Mary Shelley (1817)

MONT BLANC. LINES WRITTEN IN THE VALE OF CHAMOUNI (COMPOSED BETWEEN 22 JULY AND 29 AUGUST 1816)

I

The everlasting universe of things
Flows through the mind, and rolls its rapid waves,
Now dark, now glittering, now reflecting gloom,
Now lending splendour, where from secret springs
The source of human thought its tribute brings   5
Of waters, with a sound but half its own,[1]
Such as a feeble brook will oft assume
In the wild woods, among the mountains lone,
Where waterfalls around it leap forever,
Where woods and winds contend, and a vast river   10
Over its rocks ceaselessly bursts and raves.

II

Thus thou, ravine of Arve – dark, deep ravine –
Thou many-coloured, many-voiced vale,
Over whose pines, and crags, and caverns sail
Fast cloud-shadows and sunbeams: awful scene,   15
Where Power in likeness of the Arve comes down
From the ice gulfs that gird his secret throne,
Bursting through these dark mountains like the flame

MONT BLANC. LINES WRITTEN IN THE VALE OF CHAMOUNI
[1] Cf. Wordsworth, 'Tintern Abbey', 107–8.

Of lightning through the tempest; thou dost lie,
Thy giant brood of pines around thee clinging, 20
Children of elder time, in whose devotion
The chainless winds still come and ever came
To drink their odours, and their mighty swinging
To hear — an old and solemn harmony;
Thine earthly rainbows stretched across the sweep 25
Of the ethereal waterfall, whose veil
Robes some unsculptured image; the strange sleep
Which, when the voices of the desert fail,
Wraps all in its own deep eternity;
Thy caverns echoing to the Arve's commotion — 30
A loud, lone sound no other sound can tame;
Thou art pervaded with that ceaseless motion,
Thou art the path of that unresting sound,
Dizzy ravine! — and when I gaze on thee
I seem as in a trance sublime and strange 35
To muse on my own separate fantasy,
My own, my human mind, which passively
Now renders and receives fast influencings,
Holding an unremitting interchange
With the clear universe of things around; 40
One legion of wild thoughts, whose wandering wings
Now float above thy darkness, and now rest
Where that² or thou³ art no unbidden guest,
In the still cave of the witch Poesy,
Seeking among the shadows that pass by,⁴ 45
Ghosts of all things that are, some shade of thee,
Some phantom, some faint image;⁵ till the breast
From which they fled recalls them, thou art there!⁶

III

Some say that gleams of a remoter world
Visit the soul in sleep, that death is slumber, 50
And that its shapes the busy thoughts outnumber
Of those who wake and live.⁷ I look on high;
Has some unknown omnipotence unfurled

---

² *that* the darkness of line 42.
³ *thou* the ravine.
⁴ Cf. Byron, *Childe Harold's Pilgrimage*, iii. 43–5, above.
⁵ Shelley claims that his art bears the same relation to truth as do the shadows, in Plato's allegory of the cave, to a metaphysical reality; see Plato, *Republic*, vii, summarized by Rogers, *Shelley at Work*, pp. 148–7.
⁶ Until Shelley recalls the 'wild thoughts' (line 41) by

coming out of his reverie, the ravine he has been addressing and the mystery that surrounds it are to be found within Poesy's cave (i.e. subject to the imagination and perhaps half-created by it).
⁷ Some say (i) that the soul is visited in sleep by 'gleams' of otherworldly truth; (ii) that death is an extreme form of this visionary sleep, and (iii) that it is more active and imaginative than anything experienced by the living mind.

The veil of life and death? Or do I lie
In dream, and does the mightier world of sleep   55
Spread far around and inaccessibly
Its circles? For the very spirit fails,
Driven like a homeless cloud from steep to steep
That vanishes among the viewless gales!
Far, far above, piercing the infinite sky,   60
Mont Blanc appears, still, snowy, and serene.
Its subject mountains their unearthly forms
Pile around it, ice and rock; broad vales between
Of frozen floods, unfathomable deeps
Blue as the overhanging heaven, that spread   65
And wind among the accumulated steeps;
A desert peopled by the storms alone,
Save when the eagle brings some hunter's bone,
And the wolf tracks her there. How hideously
Its shapes are heaped around! – rude, bare, and high,   70
Ghastly, and scarred, and riven. Is this the scene
Where the old earthquake-daemon taught her young
Ruin? Were these their toys?[8] Or did a sea
Of fire envelop once this silent snow?
None can reply – all seems eternal now.   75
The wilderness has a mysterious tongue
Which teaches awful doubt, or faith so mild,
So solemn, so serene, that man may be
But for such faith with nature reconciled.[9]
Thou hast a voice, great mountain, to repeal   80
Large codes of fraud and woe – not understood
By all, but which the wise, and great, and good
Interpret, or make felt, or deeply feel.[10]

IV

The fields, the lakes, the forests, and the streams,
Ocean, and all the living things that dwell   85
Within the daedal[11] earth; lightning, and rain,
Earthquake, and fiery flood, and hurricane,
The torpor of the year when feeble dreams
Visit the hidden buds, or dreamless sleep
Holds every future leaf and flower; the bound   90
With which from that detested trance they leap;

---

[8] Shelley replaces Christian theology with pagan caprice. With the children of the old earthquake-daemon, cf. Byron, *Childe Harold's Pilgrimage*, iii. 877.
[9] Only by ('But for') a Wordsworthian faith in nature can man be reconciled to the mysterious indifference and violence of nature; otherwise, one must adopt Shelley's respectful open-mindedness ('awful doubt').
[10] Enlightened witnesses to nature's Power will defy the codes of fraud and woe made by Church and State.
[11] *daedal* intricately wrought.

The works and ways of man, their death and birth,
And that of him and all that his may be;
All things that move and breathe with toil and sound
Are born and die;[12] revolve, subside and swell.   95
Power dwells apart in its tranquillity
Remote, serene, and inaccessible:[13]
And *this*, the naked countenance of earth
On which I gaze, even these primeval mountains
Teach the adverting mind. The glaciers creep   100
Like snakes that watch their prey, from their far fountains
Slow rolling on; there, many a precipice,
Frost and the sun in scorn of mortal power
Have piled: dome, pyramid, and pinnacle,
A city of death, distinct with many a tower   105
And wall impregnable of beaming ice.
Yet not a city, but a flood of ruin
Is there, that from the boundaries of the sky
Rolls its perpetual stream; vast pines are strewing
Its destined path, or in the mangled soil   110
Branchless and shattered stand; the rocks, drawn down
From yon remotest waste, have overthrown
The limits of the dead and living world,
Never to be reclaimed. The dwelling-place
Of insects, beasts, and birds, becomes its spoil;   115
Their food and their retreat for ever gone,
So much of life and joy is lost. The race
Of man flies far in dread; his work and dwelling
Vanish like smoke before the tempest's stream,
And their place is not known. Below, vast caves   120
Shine in the rushing torrents' restless gleam,
Which from those secret chasms in tumult welling[14]
Meet in the vale; and one majestic river,
The breath and blood of distant lands, forever
Rolls its loud waters to the ocean waves,   125
Breathes its swift vapours to the circling air.

V

Mont Blanc yet gleams on high: the Power is there,
The still and solemn Power of many sights
And many sounds, and much of life and death.
In the calm darkness of the moonless nights,   130
In the lone glare of day, the snows descend

---

[12] Cf. 'Tintern Abbey', 102–3.   [14] Cf. Coleridge, 'Kubla Khan', 17.
[13] Mont Blanc, the highest mountain in Europe, had
been climbed only three times by 1816.

Upon that mountain; none beholds them there,
Nor when the flakes burn in the sinking sun,
Or the starbeams dart through them; winds contend
Silently there, and heap the snow with breath   135
Rapid and strong, but silently! Its home
The voiceless lightning in these solitudes
Keeps innocently, and like vapour broods
Over the snow. The secret strength of things
Which governs thought, and to the infinite dome   140
Of heaven is as a law, inhabits thee!
And what were thou, and earth, and stars, and sea,
If to the human mind's imaginings
Silence and solitude were vacancy?

From The Examiner, no. 524 (11 January 1818) 24

Ozymandias (composed c.December 1817)

I met a traveller from an antique land
Who said, 'Two vast and trunkless legs of stone
Stand in the desert. Near them, on the sand
Half-sunk, a shattered visage lies, whose frown
And wrinkled lip, and sneer of cold command,   5
Tell that its sculptor well those passions read
Which yet survive, stamped on these lifeless things,
The hand that mocked them, and the heart that fed;
And on the pedestal these words appear:
"My name is Ozymandias,[1] King of Kings,   10
Look on my works, ye mighty, and despair!"
Nothing beside remains. Round the decay
Of that colossal wreck, boundless and bare,
The lone and level sands stretch far away.'

On Love (composed probably 20–5 July 1818; edited from MS)[1]

What is love? Ask him who lives, what is life; ask him who adores, what is God.

I know not the internal constitution of other men, or even of thine whom I now address. I see that in some external attributes they resemble me, but, when misled by that appearance I have thought to appeal to something in common and unburden my inmost soul to them, I have found my language misunderstood like one in a distant and savage land. The more opportunities they have afforded me for experience, the wider has appeared the interval between us, and to a greater distance have the points

---

Ozymandias
[1] Rameses II of Egypt (thirteenth century BC), whose tomb at Thebes was in the shape of a male sphinx.

On Love
[1] This essay, Reiman suggests, is 'Shelley's response to Plato's *Symposium* and may possibly be the false start of an essay introductory to his translation' (*SC*, vi. 639). Shelley translated the *Symposium* 7–20 July 1818.

of sympathy been withdrawn. With a spirit ill-fitted to sustain such proof, trembling and feeble through its tenderness, I have everywhere sought, and have found only repulse and disappointment.

Thou demandest what is love. It is that powerful attraction towards all that we conceive, or fear, or hope beyond ourselves, when we find within our own thoughts the chasm of an insufficient void, and seek to awaken in all things that are, a community with what we experience within ourselves. If we reason, we would be understood; if we imagine, we would that the airy children of our brain were born anew within another's; if we feel, we would that another's nerves should vibrate to our own, that the beams of their eyes should kindle at once and mix and melt into our own, that lips of motionless ice should not reply to lips quivering and burning with the heart's best blood. This is love. This is the bond and the sanction which connects not only man with man, but with everything which exists. We are born into the world and there is something within us which, from the instant that we live and move, thirsts after its likeness; it is probably in correspondence with this law that the infant drains milk from the bosom of its mother. This propensity develops itself with the development of our nature.

We see dimly[2] within our intellectual nature a miniature, as it were, of our entire self, yet deprived of all that we condemn or despise: the ideal prototype of everything excellent or lovely that we are capable of conceiving as belonging to the nature of man – not only the portrait of our external being, but an assemblage of the minutest particulars of which our nature is composed; a mirror whose surface reflects only the forms of purity and brightness; a soul within our soul that describes a circle around its proper paradise which pain and sorrow and evil dare not overleap. To this we eagerly refer all sensations, thirsting that they should resemble or correspond with it.

The discovery of its antitype – the meeting with an understanding capable of clearly estimating the deductions of our own, an imagination which should enter into and seize upon the subtle and delicate peculiarities which we have delighted to cherish and unfold in secret, with a frame whose nerves, like the chords of two exquisite lyres strung to the accompaniment of one delightful voice, vibrate with the vibrations of our own, and of a combination of all these in such proportion as the type within demands: this is the invisible and unattainable point to which love tends, and to attain which it urges forth the powers of man to arrest the faintest shadow of that without the possession of which there is no rest or respite to the heart over which it rules.

Hence in solitude, or in that deserted state when we are surrounded by human beings and yet they sympathize not with us, we love the flowers, the grass, and the waters and the sky. In the motion of the very leaves of spring in the blue air there is then found a secret correspondence with our heart. There is eloquence in the tongueless wind and a melody in the flowing of brooks and the rustling of the reeds beside them, which by their inconceivable relation to something within the soul, awaken the spirits to a dance of breathless rapture, and bring tears of mysterious tenderness to the eyes like the enthusiasm of patriotic success or the voice of one beloved singing to you alone. Sterne says that if he were in a desert he would love some cypress[3] . . . So soon as this want or power is dead, man becomes the living sepulchre of himself, and what yet survives is the mere husk of what once he was.

---

[2] 'These words inefficient and metaphorical. Most words so. No help' (Shelley's note).
[3] 'I declare, said I, clapping my hands cheerily together, that was I in a desert, I would find out wherewith in it to call forth my affections. If I could not do better, I would fasten them upon some sweet myrtle, or seek some melancholy cypress to connect myself to' (Sterne, *A Sentimental Journey*, pp. 115–16).

From Rosalind and Helen (1819)

LINES WRITTEN AMONG THE EUGANEAN HILLS, OCTOBER 1818

Many a green isle needs must be
In the deep wide sea of misery,
Or the mariner, worn and wan,
Never thus could voyage on
Day and night, and night and day,   5
Drifting on his dreary way,
With the solid darkness black
Closing round his vessel's track;
Whilst above, the sunless sky,
Big with clouds, hangs heavily,   10
And behind the tempest fleet
Hurries on with lightning feet,
Riving sail and cord and plank
Till the ship has almost drank
Death from the o'er-brimming deep,   15
And sinks down, down, like that sleep
When the dreamer seems to be
Weltering through eternity;
And the dim low line before
Of a dark and distant shore   20
Still recedes, as ever still
Longing with divided will,
But no power to seek or shun,
He is ever drifted on
O'er the unreposing wave   25
To the haven of the grave.
What if there no friends will greet?
What if there no heart will meet
His with love's impatient beat?
Wander wheresoe'er he may,   30
Can he dream before that day
To find refuge from distress
In friendship's smile, in love's caress?
Then 'twill wreak him little woe
Whether such there be or no: 35
Senseless is the breast, and cold,
Which relenting love would fold;
Bloodless are the veins and chill
Which the pulse of pain did fill;
Every little living nerve   40
That from bitter words did swerve
Round the tortured lips and brow,
Are like sapless leaflets now
Frozen upon December's bough.

On the beach of a northern sea 45
Which tempests shake eternally,
As once the wretch there lay to sleep,
Lies a solitary heap:
One white skull and seven dry bones,
On the margin of the stones 50
Where a few grey rushes stand,
Boundaries of the sea and land.
Nor is heard one voice of wail
But the sea-mews, as they sail
O'er the billows of the gale; 55
Or the whirlwind up and down
Howling like a slaughtered town,
When a king in glory rides
Through the pomp of fratricides.
Those unburied bones around 60
There is many a mournful sound;
There is no lament for him
Like a sunless vapour, dim,
Who once clothed with life and thought
What now moves nor murmurs not. 65

Aye, many flowering islands lie
In the waters of wide agony;
To such a one this morn was led
My bark, by soft winds piloted.
Mid the mountains Euganean 70
I stood listening to the paean
With which the legioned rooks did hail
The sun's uprise majestical;
Gathering round with wings all hoar,
Through the dewy mist they soar 75
Like grey shades, till th' eastern heaven
Bursts, and then, as clouds of even
Flecked with fire and azure lie
In the unfathomable sky,
So their plumes of purple grain, 80
Starred with drops of golden rain,
Gleam above the sunlight woods,
As in silent multitudes
On the morning's fitful gale
Through the broken mist they sail, 85
And the vapours cloven and gleaming
Follow down the dark steep streaming,
Till all is bright and clear and still
Round the solitary hill.

Beneath is spread like a green sea 90
The waveless plain of Lombardy,

Bounded by the vaporous air,
Islanded by cities fair;
Underneath day's azure eyes
Ocean's nursling, Venice, lies,   95
A peopled labyrinth of walls,
Amphitrite's[1] destined halls
Which her hoary sire now paves
With his blue and beaming waves.
Lo! the sun upsprings behind,   100
Broad, red, radiant, half-reclined
On the level quivering line
Of the waters crystalline;
And before that chasm of light,
As within a furnace bright,   105
Column, tower, and dome, and spire,
Shine like obelisks of fire,
Pointing with inconstant motion
From the altar of dark ocean
To the sapphire-tinted skies;   110
As the flames of sacrifice
From the marble shrines did rise,
As to pierce the dome of gold[2]
Where Apollo spoke of old.

Sun-girt city, thou hast been   115
Ocean's child, and then his queen;
Now is come a darker day,
And thou soon must be his prey,
If the power that raised thee here
Hallow so thy watery bier.   120
A less drear ruin then than now,
With thy conquest-branded brow[3]
Stooping to the slave of slaves
From thy throne, among the waves
Wilt thou be, when the sea-mew   125
Flies, as once before it flew,
O'er thine isles depopulate,
And all is in its ancient state,
Save where many a palace gate
With green sea-flowers overgrown   130
Like a rock of ocean's own,
Topples o'er the abandoned sea
As the tides change sullenly.
The fisher on his watery way,

LINES WRITTEN AMONG THE EUGANEAN HILLS
[1] Amphitrite was the daughter of Oceanus (her 'sire', line 98) and the wife of Poseidon.
[2] dome of gold the Delphic oracle.
[3] Venice had recently been conquered by France and Austria.

Wandering at the close of day,   135
Will spread his sail and seize his oar
Till he pass the gloomy shore,
Lest thy dead should, from their sleep
Bursting o'er the starlight deep,
Lead a rapid masque of death   140
O'er the waters of his path.

Those who alone thy towers behold
Quivering through aerial gold,
As I now behold them here,
Would imagine not they were   145
Sepulchres where human forms,
Like pollution-nourished worms,
To the corpse of greatness cling,
Murdered and now mouldering;
But if Freedom should awake   150
In her omnipotence, and shake
From the Celtic Anarch's[4] hold
All the keys of dungeons cold,
Where a hundred cities lie
Chained like thee, ingloriously,   155
Thou and all thy sister band
Might adorn this sunny land,
Twining memories of old time
With new virtues more sublime:
If not, perish thou and they! –   160
Clouds which stain truth's rising day
By her sun consumed away,
Earth can spare ye, while like flowers
In the waste of years and hours,
From your dust new nations spring   165
With more kindly blossoming.

Perish! let there only be
Floating o'er thy hearthless sea,
As the garment of thy sky
Clothes the world immortally,   170
One remembrance more sublime
Than the tattered pall of time,
Which scarce hides thy visage wan –
That a tempest-cleaving swan[5]
Of the songs of Albion,   175
Driven from his ancestral streams
By the might of evil dreams,

---

4 Austrian tyrant, as at line 223.
5 Lord Byron, then living at the Palazzo Mocenigo,

Venice, where Shelley had met him the previous
month.

Found a nest in thee; and Ocean
Welcomed him with such emotion
That its joy grew his, and sprung   180
From his lips like music flung
O'er a mighty thunder-fit,
Chastening terror. What though yet
Poesy's unfailing river,
Which through Albion winds forever,   185
Lashing with melodious wave
Many a sacred poet's grave,
Mourn its latest nursling fled?
What though thou with all thy dead
Scarce can for this fame repay   190
Aught thine own? Oh rather say,
Though thy sins and slaveries foul
Overcloud a sunlike soul?[6]
As the ghost of Homer clings
Round Scamander's[7] wasting springs;   195
As divinest Shakespeare's might
Fills Avon and the world with light,
Like omniscient power which he
Imaged mid mortality;
As the love from Petrarch's urn   200
Yet amid yon hills[8] doth burn,
A quenchless lamp by which the heart
Sees things unearthly – so thou art,
Mighty spirit;[9] so shall be
The city that did refuge thee.   205

Lo, the sun floats up the sky
Like thought-winged liberty,
Till the universal light
Seems to level plain and height;
From the sea a mist has spread,   210
And the beams of morn lie dead
On the towers of Venice now,
Like its glory long ago.
By the skirts of that grey cloud
Many-domed Padua proud   215
Stands, a peopled solitude
Mid the harvest-shining plain,
Where the peasant heaps his grain
In the garner of his foe,
And the milk-white oxen slow   220
With the purple vintage strain,

---

[6] i.e. '[What] Though thy sins ...?'
[7] Scamander, river near Troy.
[8] Petrarch's grave is at Arqua in the Euganean Hills.
[9] Byron.

Heaped upon the creaking wain,
That the brutal Celt may swill
Drunken sleep with savage will;
And the sickle to the sword   225
Lies unchanged, though many a lord,
Like a weed whose shade is poison,
Overgrows this region's foison,
Sheaves of whom are ripe to come
To destruction's harvest home: 230
Men must reap the things they sow,
Force from force must ever flow
Or worse – but 'tis a bitter woe
That love or reason cannot change
The despot's rage, the slave's revenge.   235

Padua, thou within whose walls
Those mute guests at festivals,
Son and mother, Death and Sin,
Played at dice for Ezzelin,[10]
Till Death cried, 'I win, I win!'   240
And Sin cursed to lose the wager,
But Death promised, to assuage her,
That he would petition for
Her to be made Vice-Emperor,
When the destined years were o'er,   245
Over all between the Po
And the eastern Alpine snow,
Under the mighty Austrian.
Sin smiled so as Sin only can,
And since that time, aye, long before,   250
Both have ruled from shore to shore –
That incestuous pair who follow
Tyrants as the sun the swallow,
As repentance follows crime,
And as changes follow time.   255

In thine halls the lamp of learning,
Padua, now no more is burning;[11]
Like a meteor, whose wild way
Is lost over the grave of day,
It gleams betrayed and to betray.   260
Once remotest nations came
To adore that sacred flame,
When it lit not many a hearth
On this cold and gloomy earth;

---

[10]   Ezzelino da Romano, thirteenth-century despot   [11]   Padua University is one of the oldest in Europe.
of Padua. Shelley was in Padua Aug. 1818.

Now new fires from antique light   265
Spring beneath the wide world's might,
But their spark lies dead in thee,
Trampled out by tyranny.
As the Norway woodman quells,
In the depth of piny dells,   270
One light flame among the brakes,
While the boundless forest shakes,
And its mighty trunks are torn
By the fire thus lowly born;
The spark beneath his feet is dead,   275
He starts to see the flames it fed
Howling through the darkened sky
With a myriad tongues victoriously,
And sinks down in fear: so thou,
Oh tyranny, beholdest now   280
Light around thee, and thou hearest
The loud flames ascend, and fearest –
Grovel on the earth! Aye, hide
In the dust thy purple pride!

Noon descends around me now;   285
'Tis the noon of autumn's glow
When a soft and purple mist,
Like a vaporous amethyst,
Or an air-dissolved star
Mingling light and fragrance, far   290
From the curved horizon's bound
To the point of heaven's profound,
Fills the overflowing sky;
And the plains that silent lie
Underneath, the leaves unsodden   295
Where the infant frost has trodden
With his morning-winged feet,
Whose bright print is gleaming yet;
And the red and golden vines,
Piercing with their trellised lines   300
The rough, dark-skirted wilderness;
The dun and bladed grass no less,
Pointing from this hoary tower
In the windless air; the flower
Glimmering at my feet; the line   305
Of the olive-sandalled Apennine
In the south dimly islanded;
And the Alps, whose snows are spread
High between the clouds and sun;
And of living things each one;   310
And my spirit which so long

Darkened this swift stream of song –
Interpenetrated lie
By the glory of the sky:
Be it love, light, harmony,   315
Odour, or the soul of all
Which from heaven like dew doth fall,
Or the mind which feeds this verse
Peopling the lone universe.

Noon descends, and after noon   320
Autumn's evening meets me soon,
Leading the infantine moon
And that one star,[12] which to her
Almost seems to minister
Half the crimson light she brings   325
From the sunset's radiant springs;
And the soft dreams of the morn
(Which like winged winds had borne
To that silent isle, which lies
Mid remembered agonies,   330
The frail bark of this lone being)
Pass, to other sufferers fleeing,
And its ancient pilot, Pain,
Sits beside the helm again.

Other flowering isles must be   335
In the sea of life and agony;
Other spirits float and flee
O'er that gulf – even now, perhaps,
On some rock the wild wave wraps,
With folding wings they waiting sit 340
For my bark, to pilot it
To some calm and blooming cove,
Where for me and those I love,
May a windless bower be built
Far from passion, pain, and guilt, 345
In a dell mid lawny hills
Which the wild sea-murmur fills,
And soft sunshine, and the sound
Of old forests echoing round,
And the light and smell divine   350
Of all flowers that breathe and shine.
We may live so happy there
That the spirits of the air,
Envying us, may even entice

---

[12] Hesper, the Evening Star.

To our healing paradise   355
The polluting multitude;
But their rage would be subdued
By that clime divine and calm,
And the winds whose wings rain balm
On the uplifted soul, and leaves   360
Under which the bright sea heaves;
While each breathless interval
In their whisperings musical
The inspired soul supplies
With its own deep melodies,   365
And the love which heals all strife
Circling like the breath of life,
All things in that sweet abode
With its own mild brotherhood:
They, not it, would change, and soon   370
Every sprite beneath the moon
Would repent its envy vain,
And the earth grow young again.

From Prometheus Unbound (1820)

ODE TO THE WEST WIND (COMPOSED *c.*25 OCTOBER 1819)[1]

I

Oh wild west wind, thou breath of autumn's being;
Thou from whose unseen presence the leaves dead
Are driven, like ghosts from an enchanter fleeing,

Yellow, and black, and pale, and hectic red,
Pestilence-stricken multitudes; oh thou   5
Who chariotest to their dark wintry bed

The winged seeds, where they lie cold and low,
Each like a corpse within its grave, until
Thine azure sister of the spring shall blow

Her clarion o'er the dreaming earth, and fill   10
(Driving sweet buds like flocks to feed in air)
With living hues and odours plain and hill –

ODE TO THE WEST WIND
[1] 'This poem was conceived and chiefly written in a
wood that skirts the Arno, near Florence, and on a
day when that tempestuous wind, whose temperature
is at once mild and animating, was collecting the
vapours which pour down the autumnal rains. They
began, as I foresaw, at sunset, with a violent tempest
of hail and rain, attended by that magnificent thunder
and lightning peculiar to the Cisalpine regions' (Shelley's note).

Wild spirit, which art moving everywhere,
Destroyer and preserver, hear, oh hear!

II

Thou on whose stream, mid the steep sky's commotion,   15
Loose clouds like earth's decaying leaves are shed,
Shook from the tangled boughs of heaven and ocean,

Angels of rain and lightning; there are spread
On the blue surface of thine airy surge,
Like the bright hair uplifted from the head   20

Of some fierce maenad,[2] even from the dim verge
Of the horizon to the zenith's height,
The locks of the approaching storm. Thou dirge

Of the dying year, to which this closing night
Will be the dome of a vast sepulchre,   25
Vaulted with all thy congregated might

Of vapours, from whose solid atmosphere
Black rain, and fire, and hail will burst — oh hear!

III

Thou who didst waken from his summer dreams
The blue Mediterranean, where he lay,   30
Lulled by the coil of his crystalline streams,

Beside a pumice isle in Baiae's bay,
And saw in sleep old palaces and towers
Quivering within the wave's intenser day,[3]

All overgrown with azure moss and flowers   35
So sweet, the sense faints picturing them! Thou
For whose path the Atlantic's level powers

Cleave themselves into chasms, while far below
The sea-blooms and the oozy woods which wear
The sapless foliage of the ocean, know   40

---

[2] *maenad* Bacchante, inspired votary of Bacchus.
[3] In a letter to Peacock of 17 or 18 Dec. 1818, Shelley describes 'passing the Bay of Baiae and ob- serving the ruins of its antique grandeur standing like rocks in the transparent sea under our boat' (Jones, ii. 61).

Thy voice, and suddenly grow grey with fear,
And tremble and despoil themselves[4] – oh hear!

IV

If I were a dead leaf thou mightest bear;
If I were a swift cloud to fly with thee;
A wave to pant beneath thy power, and share   45

The impulse of thy strength, only less free
Than thou, oh uncontrollable! If even
I were as in my boyhood, and could be

The comrade of thy wanderings over heaven,
As then, when to outstrip thy skyey speed   50
Scarce seemed a vision; I would ne'er have striven

As thus with thee in prayer in my sore need.
Oh lift me as a wave, a leaf, a cloud!
I fall upon the thorns of life! I bleed!

A heavy weight of hours has chained and bowed   55
One too like thee – tameless, and swift, and proud.

V

Make me thy lyre, even as the forest is:
What if my leaves are falling like its own?
The tumult of thy mighty harmonies

Will take from both a deep autumnal tone,   60
Sweet though in sadness. Be thou, spirit fierce,
My spirit! Be thou me, impetuous one!

Drive my dead thoughts over the universe
Like withered leaves to quicken a new birth!
And, by the incantation of this verse,   65

Scatter, as from an unextinguished hearth
Ashes and sparks, my words among mankind!
Be through my lips to unawakened earth

---

[4] 'The phenomenon alluded to at the conclusion of the third stanza is well known to naturalists. The vegetation at the bottom of the sea, of rivers, and of lakes, sympathizes with that of the land in the change of seasons, and is consequently influenced by the winds which announce it' (Shelley's note).

The trumpet of a prophecy! Oh wind,
If winter comes, can spring be far behind?   70

From Essays, Letters from Abroad, Translations and Fragments, (1840)

On Life (composed late 1819)

Life and the world, or whatever we call that which we are and feel, is an astonishing thing. The mist of familiarity[1] obscures from us the wonder of our being. We are struck with admiration at some of its transient modifications, but it is itself the great miracle. What are changes of empires, the wreck of dynasties, with the opinions which supported them; what is the birth and the extinction of religious and of political systems, to life? What are the revolutions of the globe which we inhabit, and the operations of the elements of which it is composed, compared with life? What is the universe of stars and suns (of which this inhabited earth is one), and their motions and their destiny, compared with life? Life, the great miracle, we admire not because it is so miraculous. It is well that we are so shielded by the familiarity of what is at once so certain and so unfathomable, from an astonishment which would otherwise absorb and overawe the functions of that which is its object.

If any artist, I do not say had executed, but had merely conceived in his mind the system of the sun, and the stars and planets, they not existing, and had painted to us in words or upon canvas the spectacle now afforded by the nightly cope of heaven, and illustrated it by the wisdom of astronomy, great would be our admiration. Or had he imagined the scenery of this earth, the mountains, the seas and the rivers, the grass and the flowers, and the variety of the forms and masses of the leaves of the woods, and the colours which attend the setting and the rising sun, and the hues of the atmosphere, turbid or serene, these things not before existing, truly we should have been astonished – and it would not have been a vain boast to have said of such a man, 'Non merita nome di creatore, sennon Iddio ed il Poeta'.[2] But now these things are looked on with little wonder, and to be conscious of them with intense delight is esteemed to be the distinguishing mark of a refined and extraordinary person. The multitude of men care not for them; it is thus with life – that which includes all.

What is life? Thoughts and feelings arise, with or without our will, and we employ words to express them. We are born, and our birth is unremembered, and our infancy remembered but in fragments. We live on, and in living we lose the apprehension of life. How vain is it to think that words can penetrate the mystery of our being! Rightly used they may make evident our ignorance to ourselves, and this is much. For what are we? Whence do we come, and whither do we go? Is birth the commencement, is death the conclusion of our being? What is birth and death?

The most refined abstractions of logic conduct to a view of life which, though startling to the apprehension, is in fact that which the habitual sense of its repeated combinations has extinguished in us. It strips, as it were, the painted curtain from this scene of things. I confess that I am one of those who am unable to refuse my assent

---

On Life

[1] *mist of familiarity* cf. Coleridge's 'film of familiarity', *Biographia Literaria*, p. 575 above.

[2] 'None deserves the name of creator except God and the poet'; from Pierantonio Serassi's *Life of Torquato Tasso* (1785).

to the conclusions of those philosophers who assert that nothing exists but as it is perceived.[3]

It is a decision against which all our persuasions struggle, and we must be long convicted before we can be convinced that the solid universe of external things is 'such stuff as dreams are made of'.[4] The shocking absurdities of the popular philosophy of mind and matter, and its fatal consequences in morals, their violent dogmatism concerning the source of all things, had early conducted me to materialism.[5] This materialism is a seducing system to young and superficial minds; it allows its disciples to talk, and dispenses them from thinking. But I was discontented with such a view of things as it afforded; man is a being of high aspirations 'looking both before and after',[6] whose 'thoughts wander through eternity',[7] disclaiming alliance with transience and decay, incapable of imagining to himself annihilation, existing but in the future and the past, being not what he is, but what he has been and shall be. Whatever may be his true and final destination, there is a spirit within him at enmity with nothingness and dissolution. This is the character of all life and being. Each is at once the centre and the circumference, the point to which all things are referred, and the line in which all things are contained. Such contemplations as these, materialism and the popular philosophy of mind and matter alike forbid; they are only consistent with the intellectual system.

It is absurd to enter into a long recapitulation of arguments sufficiently familiar to those enquiring minds whom alone a writer on abstruse subjects can be conceived to address. Perhaps the most clear and vigorous statement of the intellectual system is to be found in Sir William Drummond's *Academical Questions*; after such an exposition it would be idle to translate into other words what could only lose its energy and fitness by the change. Examined point by point and word by word, the most discriminating intellects have been able to discern no train of thoughts in the process of reasoning, which does not conduct inevitably to the conclusion which has been stated.

What follows from the admission? It establishes no new truth, it gives us no additional insight into our hidden nature, neither its action, nor itself. Philosophy, impatient as it may be to build, has much work yet remaining as pioneer for the overgrowth of ages. It makes one step towards this object; it destroys error and the roots of error. It leaves what is too often the duty of the reformer in political and ethical questions to leave – a vacancy. It reduces the mind to that freedom in which it would have acted, but for the misuse of words and signs, the instruments of its own creation. By signs, I would be understood in a wide sense, including what is properly meant by that term, and what I peculiarly mean. In this latter sense, almost all familiar objects are signs, standing not for themselves but for others, in their capacity of suggesting one thought which shall lead to a train of thoughts. Our whole life is thus an education of error.

Let us recollect our sensations as children. What a distinct and intense apprehension had we of the world and of ourselves. Many of the circumstances of social life were then important to us, which are now no longer so. But that is not the point of

---

[3]   The principal tenet of Berkeley's philosophy.
[4]   *The Tempest*, IV. i. 156–7.
[5]   i.e. the philosophy of Locke, Hartley, Priestley, and of the French Enlightenment, particularly Holbach.
[6]   *Hamlet*, IV. iv. 37.
[7]   *Paradise Lost*, ii. 148.

comparison on which I mean to insist. We less habitually distinguished all that we saw and felt from ourselves. They seemed as it were to constitute one mass. There are some persons who in this respect are always children. Those who are subject to the state called reverie feel as if their nature were dissolved into the surrounding universe, or as if the surrounding universe were absorbed into their being.[8] They are conscious of no distinction. And these are states which precede or accompany or follow an unusually intense and vivid apprehension of life. As men grow up, this power commonly decays, and they become mechanical and habitual agents. Thus feelings and then reasonings are the combined result of a multitude of entangled thoughts, and of a series of what are called impressions, planted by reiteration.

The view of life presented by the most refined deductions of the intellectual philosophy, is that of unity. Nothing exists but as it is perceived. The difference is merely nominal between those two classes of thought which are vulgarly distinguished by the names of ideas and of external objects. Pursuing the same thread of reasoning, the existence of distinct individual minds, similar to that which is employed in now questioning its own nature, is likewise found to be a delusion. The words, *I, you, they* are not signs of any actual difference subsisting between the assemblage of thoughts thus indicated, but are merely marks employed to denote the different modifications of the one mind.

Let it not be supposed that this doctrine conducts to the monstrous presumption that I, the person who now write and think, am that one mind. I am but a portion of it. The words *I*, and *you* and *they* are grammatical devices invented simply for arrangement and totally devoid of the intense and exclusive sense usually attached to them. It is difficult to find terms adequate to express so subtle a conception as that to which the intellectual philosophy has conducted us. We are on that verge where words abandon us, and what wonder if we grow dizzy to look down the dark abyss of how little we know!

The relations of *things* remain unchanged by whatever system. By the word *things* is to be understood any object of thought; that is, any thought upon which any other thought is employed, with an apprehension of distinction. The relations of these remain unchanged – and such is the material of our knowledge.

What is the cause of life? That is, how was it produced, or what agencies distinct from life, have acted or act upon life? All recorded generations of mankind have wearily busied themselves in inventing answers to this question. And the result has been religion. Yet that the basis of all things cannot be (as the popular philosophy alleges) mind, is sufficiently evident. Mind (as far as we have any experience of its properties, and, beyond that, experience how vain is argument) cannot create, it can only perceive. It is said also to be the cause; but cause is only a word expressing a certain state of the human mind with regard to the manner in which two thoughts are apprehended to be related to each other. If anyone desires to know how unsatisfactorily the popular philosophy employs itself upon this great question, they need only impartially reflect upon the manner in which thoughts develop themselves in their minds. It is infinitely improbable that the cause of mind – that is, of existence – is similar to mind.

---

[8] Cf. Wordsworth's 'abyss of idealism', p. 481 above. This paragraph is reminiscent of the 'Ode'.

ENGLAND IN 1819 (COMPOSED BY 23 DECEMBER 1819, PUBLISHED 1839, EDITED FROM MS)

An old, mad, blind, despised, and dying king;[1]
Princes, the dregs of their dull race, who flow
Through public scorn – mud from a muddy spring;
Rulers who neither see, nor feel, nor know,
But leech-like to their fainting country cling,   5
Till they drop, blind in blood, without a blow.
A people starved and stabbed in th' untilled field;[2]
An army, which liberticide and prey
Makes as a two-edged sword to all who wield;
Golden and sanguine laws which tempt and slay;   10
Religion Christless, Godless – a book sealed;
A senate, time's worst statute, unrepealed[3] –
Are graves from which a glorious phantom may
Burst, to illumine our tempestuous day.

From Prometheus Unbound (1820)

PROMETHEUS UNBOUND; A LYRICAL DRAMA IN FOUR ACTS (COMPOSED AUGUST 1818–DECEMBER 1819, EDITED FROM PRINTED AND MS SOURCES)

Audisne haec Amphiarae, sub terram abdite?[1]

Preface

The Greek tragic writers, in selecting as their subject any portion of their national history or mythology, employed in their treatment of it a certain arbitrary discretion. They by no means conceived themselves bound to adhere to the common interpretation, or to imitate in story (as in title) their rivals and predecessors. Such a system would have amounted to a resignation of those claims to preference over their competitors which incited the composition: the Agamemnonian story was exhibited on the Athenian theatre with as many variations as dramas.

I have presumed to employ a similar licence. The *Prometheus Unbound* of Aeschylus supposed the reconciliation of Jupiter with his victim as the price of the disclosure of the danger threatened to his empire by the consummation of his marriage with Thetis. Thetis, according to this view of the subject, was given in marriage to Peleus; and Prometheus, by the permission of Jupiter, delivered from his captivity by Hercules. Had I framed my story on this model, I should have done no more than have attempted to restore the lost drama of Aeschylus – an ambition which, if my preference to this mode of treating the subject had incited me to cherish, the recollection of the

---

ENGLAND IN 1819
[1]   George III, on the throne since 1760, was old and ill, and had been insane for years. He died 29 Jan. 1820.
[2]   A reference to the Peterloo Massacre, 16 Aug. 1819.

[3]   An early, deleted version of this line in MS reads: 'A cloak of lies worn on Power's holiday'.
PROMETHEUS UNBOUND; A LYRICAL DRAMA IN FOUR ACTS
[1]   'Do you hear this, Amphiaraus, in your home beneath the earth?' (Cicero, *Tusculan Disputations*, II. xxv. 59).

high comparison such an attempt would challenge might well abate. But in truth, I was averse from a catastrophe so feeble as that of reconciling the champion with the oppressor of mankind. The moral interest of the fable, which is so powerfully sustained by the sufferings and endurance of Prometheus, would be annihilated if we could conceive of him as unsaying his high language and quailing before his successful and perfidious adversary. The only imaginary being resembling in any degree Prometheus, is Satan; and Prometheus is, in my judgement, a more poetical character than Satan, because, in addition to courage and majesty, and firm and patient opposition to omnipotent force, he is susceptible of being described as exempt from the taints of ambition, envy, revenge, and a desire for personal aggrandizement – which, in the hero of *Paradise Lost*, interfere with the interest. The character of Satan engenders in the mind a pernicious casuistry which leads us to weigh his faults with his wrongs, and to excuse the former because the latter exceed all measure. In the minds of those who consider that magnificent fiction with a religious feeling, it engenders something worse. But Prometheus is, as it were, the type of the highest perfection of moral and intellectual nature, impelled by the purest and the truest motives to the best and noblest ends.

This poem was chiefly written upon the mountainous ruins of the Baths of Caracalla,[2] among the flowery glades, and thickets of odoriferous blossoming trees, which are extended in ever-winding labyrinths upon its immense platforms and dizzy arches suspended in the air. The bright blue sky of Rome, and the effect of the vigorous awakening spring in that divinest climate, and the new life with which it drenches the spirits even to intoxication, were the inspiration of this drama.

The imagery which I have employed will be found, in many instances, to have been drawn from the operations of the human mind, or from those external actions by which they are expressed. This is unusual in modern poetry, although Dante and Shakespeare are full of instances of the same kind – Dante indeed more than any other poet, and with greater success. But the Greek poets, as writers to whom no resource of awakening the sympathy of their contemporaries was unknown, were in the habitual use of this power; and it is the study of their works (since a higher merit would probably be denied me) to which I am willing that my readers should impute this singularity.

One word is due in candour to the degree in which the study of contemporary writings may have tinged my composition, for such has been a topic of censure with regard to poems far more popular (and indeed more deservedly popular) than mine. It is impossible that anyone who inhabits the same age with such writers[3] as those who stand in the foremost ranks of our own, can conscientiously assure himself that his language and tone of thought may not have been modified by the study of the productions of those extraordinary intellects. It is true that, not the spirit of their genius, but the forms in which it has manifested itself, are due less to the peculiarities of their own minds than to the peculiarity of the moral and intellectual condition of the minds among which they have been produced. Thus a number of writers possess the form, whilst they want the spirit, of those whom (it is alleged) they imitate; because the former is the endowment of the age in which they live, and the latter must be the uncommunicated lightning of their own mind.

---

[2] Ancient baths in Rome, named after Emperor Caracalla (AD 188–217).

[3] The MS identifies 'such writers' as Wordsworth and Coleridge.

The peculiar style of intense and comprehensive imagery which distinguishes the modern literature of England has not been, as a general power, the product of the imitation of any particular writer. The mass of capabilities remains at every period materially the same; the circumstances which awaken it to action perpetually change. If England were divided into forty republics, each equal in population and extent to Athens, there is no reason to suppose but that, under institutions not more perfect than those of Athens, each would produce philosophers and poets equal to those who (if we except Shakespeare) have never been surpassed. We owe the great writers of the golden age of our literature[4] to that fervid awakening of the public mind which shook to dust the oldest and most oppressive form of the Christian religion. We owe Milton to the progress and development of the same spirit – the sacred Milton was, let it ever be remembered, a republican, and a bold enquirer into morals and religion. The great writers of our own age are, we have reason to suppose, the companions and forerunners of some unimagined change in our social condition, or the opinions which cement it. The cloud of mind is discharging its collected lightning, and the equilibrium between institutions and opinions is now restoring, or is about to be restored.

As to imitation, poetry is a mimetic art. It creates, but it creates by combination and representation. Poetical abstractions are beautiful and new, not because the portions of which they are composed had no previous existence in the mind of man or in nature, but because the whole produced by their combination has some intelligible and beautiful analogy with those sources of emotion and thought, and with the contemporary condition of them. One great poet is a masterpiece of nature which another not only ought to study but must study. He might as wisely and as easily determine that his mind should no longer be the mirror of all that is lovely in the visible universe, as exclude from his contemplation the beautiful which exists in the writings of a great contemporary. The pretence of doing it would be a presumption in any but the greatest; the effect, even in him, would be strained, unnatural, and ineffectual. A poet is the combined product of such internal powers as modify the nature of others, and of such external influences as excite and sustain these powers; he is not one, but both. Every man's mind is, in this respect, modified by all the objects of nature and art; by every word and every suggestion which he ever admitted to act upon his consciousness; it is the mirror upon which all forms are reflected,[5] and in which they compose one form. Poets, not otherwise than philosophers, painters, sculptors and musicians, are in one sense the creators, and in another the creations, of their age. From this subjection the loftiest do not escape. There is a similarity between Homer and Hesiod, between Aeschylus and Euripides, between Virgil and Horace, between Dante and Petrarch, between Shakespeare and Fletcher, between Dryden and Pope: each has a generic resemblance under which their specific distinctions are arranged. If this similarity be the result of imitation, I am willing to confess that I have imitated.

Let this opportunity be conceded to me of acknowledging that I have what a Scotch philosopher characteristically terms, 'a passion for reforming the world'. What passion incited him to write and publish his book, he omits to explain. For my part, I had rather be damned with Plato and Lord Bacon,[6] than go to heaven with Paley and

---

[4] As the MS confirms, Shelley means the Elizabethan age.
[5] Cf. Coleridge's 'convex mirror', p. 505 above.

[6] In the MS, Shelley adds Rousseau and Milton to
this group.

Malthus.[7] But it is a mistake to suppose that I dedicate my poetical compositions solely to the direct enforcement of reform, or that I consider them in any degree as containing a reasoned system on the theory of human life. Didactic poetry is my abhorrence; nothing can be equally well expressed in prose that is not tedious and supererogatory in verse. My purpose has hitherto been simply to familiarize the highly-refined imagination of the more select classes of poetical readers with beautiful idealisms of moral excellence, aware that until the mind can love, and admire, and trust, and hope, and endure, reasoned principles of moral conduct are seeds cast upon the highway of life, which the unconscious passenger tramples into dust although they would bear the harvest of his happiness. Should I live to accomplish what I purpose (that is, produce a systematical history of what appear to me to be the genuine elements of human society), let not the advocates of injustice and superstition flatter themselves that I should take Aeschylus rather than Plato as my model.

The having spoken of myself with unaffected freedom will need little apology with the candid, and let the uncandid consider that they injure me less than their own hearts and minds by misrepresentation. Whatever talents a person may possess to amuse and instruct others (be they ever so inconsiderable), he is yet bound to exert them. If his attempt be ineffectual, let the punishment of an unaccomplished purpose have been sufficient; let none trouble themselves to heap the dust of oblivion upon his efforts. The pile they raise will betray his grave which might otherwise have been unknown.

Dramatis Personae
Prometheus
Demogorgon
Jupiter
The Earth
Ocean
Apollo
Mercury
Hercules
Asia ⎫
Panthea ⎬ Oceanides
Ione ⎭
The Phantasm of Jupiter
The Spirit of the Earth
The Spirit of the Moon
Spirits of the Hours
Echoes
Fauns
Furies
Spirits

---

7 William Paley (1743–1805) argued the usefulness of hell; Thomas Robert Malthus (1776–1834) argued that famine, war, and disease were necessary as means of controlling population growth. Shelley regarded these two men as essentially conservative.

ACT I

Scene: a ravine of icy rocks in the Indian Caucasus. Prometheus is discovered bound to the precipice. Panthea and Ione are seated at his feet. Time: night. During the scene, morning slowly breaks.

Prometheus Monarch of Gods and Daemons, and all spirits
But One, who throng those bright and rolling worlds
Which thou and I alone of living things
Behold with sleepless eyes! Regard this earth
Made multitudinous with thy slaves, whom thou   5
Requitest for knee-worship, prayer, and praise,
And toil, and hecatombs[1] of broken hearts,
With fear and self-contempt and barren hope;
Whilst me, who am thy foe, eyeless in hate,
Hast thou made reign and triumph, to thy scorn,   10
O'er mine own misery and thy vain revenge.
Three thousand years of sleep-unsheltered hours
And moments, aye[2] divided by keen pangs
Till they seemed years, torture and solitude,
Scorn and despair – these are mine empire: 15
More glorious far than that which thou surveyest
From thine unenvied throne, oh mighty God!
Almighty, had I deigned to share the shame
Of thine ill tyranny, and hung not here
Nailed to this wall of eagle-baffling mountain,   20
Black, wintry, dead, unmeasured; without herb,
Insect, or beast, or shape or sound of life –
Ah me, alas! Pain, pain ever, forever!
    No change, no pause, no hope; yet I endure.
I ask the Earth, have not the mountains felt?   25
I ask yon Heaven, the all-beholding Sun,
Has it not seen? The Sea, in storm or calm,
Heaven's ever-changing shadow, spread below,
Have its deaf waves not heard my agony?
Ah me, alas! Pain, pain ever, forever!   30
    The crawling glaciers pierce me with the spears
Of their moon-freezing crystals; the bright chains
Eat with their burning cold into my bones;
Heaven's winged hound,[3] polluting from thy lips
His beak in poison not his own, tears up   35
My heart; and shapeless sights come wandering by,
The ghastly people of the realm of dream,
Mocking me; and the Earthquake-fiends are charged
To wrench the rivets from my quivering wounds
When the rocks split and close again behind;   40
While from their loud abysses howling throng

THE DRAMA   2   *aye* continually.
[1] *hecatombs* numerous sacrifices.   [3] The eagle of Jupiter that tortured Prometheus.

The genii of the storm, urging the rage
Of whirlwind, and afflict me with keen hail.
     And yet to me welcome is Day and Night,
Whether one breaks the hoar-frost of the morn,   45
Or starry, dim, and slow, the other climbs
The leaden-coloured east — for then they lead
The wingless, crawling Hours,[4] one among whom
(As some dark priest hales the reluctant victim)
Shall drag thee, cruel King, to kiss the blood   50
From these pale feet, which then might trample thee
If they disdained not such a prostrate slave.
Disdain? Ah no, I pity thee.[5] What Ruin
Will hunt thee undefended through wide Heaven!
How will thy soul, cloven to its depth with terror,   55
Gape like a hell within! I speak in grief,
Not exultation, for I hate no more
As then, ere misery made me wise. The curse
Once breathed on thee I would recall. Ye Mountains,
Whose many-voiced Echoes, through the mist   60
Of cataracts, flung the thunder of that spell;
Ye icy Springs, stagnant with wrinkling frost,
Which vibrated to hear me, and then crept
Shuddering through India; thou serenest Air,
Through which the Sun walks burning without beams;   65
And ye swift Whirlwinds, who on poised wings
Hung mute and moveless o'er yon hushed abyss,
As thunder, louder than your own, made rock
The orbed world — if then my words had power
(Though I am changed so that aught evil wish   70
Is dead within, although no memory be
Of what is hate), let them not lose it now!
What was that curse, for ye all heard me speak?
First Voice (from the mountains)
Thrice three hundred thousand years
     O'er the Earthquake's couch we stood;   75
Oft, as men convulsed with fears,
     We trembled in our multitude.
Second Voice (from the springs)
Thunderbolts had parched our water,
     We had been stained with bitter blood,
And had run mute, mid shrieks of slaughter,   80
     Through a city and a solitude.
Third Voice (from the air)
I had clothed, since Earth uprose,
     Its wastes in colours not their own,

---

4 *Hours* Latin 'Horae', female divinities supposed to preside over the changing of the seasons.

5 The pivotal statement of the play. Prometheus's Christ-like pity for his torturer is to be his redemption.

And oft had my serene repose
  Been cloven by many a rending groan.   85
Fourth Voice (from the whirlwinds)
We had soared beneath these mountains
  Unresting ages; nor had thunder,
Nor yon volcano's flaming fountains,
  Nor any power above or under
Ever made us mute with wonder.   90
First Voice
  But never bowed our snowy crest
  As at the voice of thine unrest.
Second Voice
  Never such a sound before
  To the Indian waves we bore.
  A pilot asleep on the howling sea   95
  Leaped up from the deck in agony,
  And heard, and cried, 'Ah, woe is me!'
  And died as mad as the wild waves be.
Third Voice
  By such dread words from Earth to Heaven
  My still realm was never riven;   100
  When its wound was closed, there stood
  Darkness o'er the day like blood.
Fourth Voice
  And we shrank back; for dreams of ruin
  To frozen caves our flight pursuing
  Made us keep silence thus, and thus,   105
  Though silence is as hell to us.
The Earth The tongueless caverns of the craggy hills
  Cried, 'Misery!' then; the hollow Heaven replied
  'Misery!' And the Ocean's purple waves,
  Climbing the land, howled to the lashing winds,   110
  And the pale nations heard it, 'Misery!'
Prometheus I heard a sound of voices – not the voice
  Which I gave forth. Mother,[6] thy sons and thou
  Scorn him, without whose all-enduring will
  Beneath the fierce omnipotence of Jove   115
  Both they and thou had vanished, like thin mist
  Unrolled on the morning wind. Know ye not me,
  The Titan? He who made his agony
  The barrier to your else all-conquering foe?
  Oh rock-embosomed lawns and snow-fed streams   120
  Now seen athwart frore[7] vapours, deep below,
  Through whose o'ershadowing woods I wandered once
  With Asia, drinking life from her loved eyes,

---

[6] Earth.   [7] *frore* frosty.

Why scorns the spirit which informs ye, now
To commune with me? Me alone, who checked,   125
As one who checks a fiend-drawn charioteer,
The falsehood and the force of him who reigns
Supreme, and with the groans of pining slaves
Fills your dim glens and liquid wildernesses?
Why answer ye not still, brethren?

The Earth   They dare not.   130

Prometheus Who dares? For I would hear that curse again.
Ha, what an awful whisper rises up!
'Tis scarce like sound; it tingles through the frame
As lightning tingles, hovering ere it strike.
Speak, Spirit! From thine inorganic voice   135
I only know that thou art moving near
And love. How cursed I him?

The Earth   How canst thou hear,
Who knowest not the language of the dead?

Prometheus Thou art a living spirit; speak as they.

The Earth I dare not speak like life, lest Heaven's fell King   140
Should hear, and link me to some wheel of pain
More torturing than the one whereon I roll.
Subtle thou art and good, and though the Gods
Hear not this voice, yet thou art more than God,
Being wise and kind. Earnestly hearken now.   145

Prometheus Obscurely through my brain, like shadows dim,
Sweep awful thoughts, rapid and thick. I feel
Faint, like one mingled in entwining love;
Yet 'tis not pleasure.

The Earth.   No, thou canst not hear;
Thou art immortal, and this tongue is known   150
Only to those who die.

Prometheus   And what art thou,
Oh melancholy Voice?

The Earth.   I am the Earth,
Thy mother; she within whose stony veins,
To the last fibre of the loftiest tree
Whose thin leaves trembled in the frozen air,   155
Joy ran, as blood within a living frame,
When thou didst from her bosom, like a cloud
Of glory,[8] arise – a spirit of keen joy!
And at thy voice her pining sons uplifted
Their prostrate brows from the polluting dust,   160
And our almighty Tyrant with fierce dread
Grew pale, until his thunder chained thee here.
Then – see those million worlds which burn and roll

---

[8]   *a cloud / Of glory* cf. Wordsworth, 'Ode', 64.

Around us; their inhabitants beheld
My sphered light wane in wide heaven; the sea   165
Was lifted by strange tempest, and new fire
From earthquake-rifted mountains of bright snow
Shook its portentous hair beneath Heaven's frown;
Lightning and inundation vexed the plains;
Blue thistles bloomed in cities; foodless toads   170
Within voluptuous chambers panting crawled,
When plague had fallen on man and beast and worm,
And famine and black blight on herb and tree;
And in the corn and vines and meadow-grass
Teemed ineradicable poisonous weeds   175
Draining their growth – for my wan breast was dry
With grief, and the thin air, my breath, was stained
With the contagion of a mother's hate
Breathed on her child's destroyer. Aye, I heard
Thy curse, the which, if thou rememberest not,   180
Yet my innumerable seas and streams,
Mountains, and caves, and winds, and yon wide air,
And the inarticulate people of the dead,
Preserve, a treasured spell. We meditate
In secret joy and hope those dreadful words,   185
But dare not speak them.
  Prometheus   Venerable mother!
All else who live and suffer take from thee
Some comfort: flowers, and fruits, and happy sounds,
And love, though fleeting. These may not be mine;
But mine own words, I pray, deny me not.   190
The Earth. They shall be told. Ere Babylon was dust,
The magus Zoroaster, my dead child,
Met his own image walking in the garden;[9]
That apparition, sole of men, he saw.
For know there are two worlds of life and death;   195
One that which thou beholdest – but the other
Is underneath the grave, where do inhabit
The shadows of all forms that think and live
Till death unite them and they part no more,
Dreams and the light imaginings of men,   200
And all that faith creates or love desires,
Terrible, strange, sublime and beauteous shapes.
There thou art, and dost hang, a writhing shade
Mid whirlwind-peopled mountains; all the gods
Are there, and all the powers of nameless worlds –   205
Vast, sceptred phantoms, heroes, men, and beasts,

---

[9] Zoroaster (sixth or seventh century BC), King of Bactria, founded a religion that remained dominant in Persia for over a thousand years. Shelley may have in mind Zoroaster's formative encounter with the angel Vohu Manah ('good thought'), who introduced him to Ahura-Mazda ('the wise lord'), or God.

And Demogorgon, a tremendous gloom –
And he, the supreme Tyrant,[10] on his throne
Of burning gold. Son, one of these shall utter
The curse which all remember. Call at will   210
Thine own ghost, or the ghost of Jupiter,
Hades or Typhon, or what mightier Gods
From all-prolific Evil since thy ruin
Have sprung and trampled on my prostrate sons.
Ask, and they must reply; so the revenge   215
Of the Supreme may sweep through vacant shades,
As rainy wind through the abandoned gate
Of a fallen palace.
Prometheus   Mother, let not aught
Of that which may be evil pass again
My lips, or those of aught resembling me.   220
Phantasm of Jupiter, arise, appear!
Ione
My wings are folded o'er mine ears;
   My wings are crossed over mine eyes;
Yet through their silver shade appears,
   And through their lulling plumes arise   225
A shape, a throng of sounds:
   May it be no ill to thee
Oh thou of many wounds,
Near whom, for our sweet sister's sake,
Ever thus we watch and wake.   230
Panthea
The sound is of whirlwind underground,
   Earthquake, and fire, and mountains cloven;
The shape is awful like the sound,
   Clothed in dark purple, star-inwoven.
A sceptre of pale gold,   235
   To stay steps proud, o'er the slow cloud
His veined hand doth hold.
Cruel he looks, but calm and strong,
Like one who does, not suffers wrong.
Phantasm of Jupiter. Why have the secret powers of this strange world   240
   Driven me, a frail and empty phantom, hither
   On direst storms? What unaccustomed sounds
   Are hovering on my lips, unlike the voice
   With which our pallid race hold ghastly talk
   In darkness? And, proud sufferer, who art thou?   245
Prometheus Tremendous Image, as thou art must be
   He whom thou shadowest forth. I am his foe,
   The Titan. Speak the words which I would hear

10 Jupiter.

Although no thought inform thine empty voice.

The Earth Listen, and though your echoes must be mute,   250
  Grey mountains, and old woods, and haunted springs,
  Prophetic caves, and isle-surrounding streams,
  Rejoice to hear what yet ye cannot speak.

Phantasm. A spirit seizes me and speaks within:
  It tears me as fire tears a thunder-cloud!   255

Panthea See how he lifts his mighty looks; the heaven
  Darkens above.

Ione   He speaks; oh shelter me!

Prometheus I see the curse on gestures proud and cold,
  And looks of firm defiance and calm hate,
  And such despair as mocks itself with smiles,   260
  Written as on a scroll – yet speak, oh speak!

Phantasm.

  Fiend, I defy thee! With a calm, fixed mind,
    All that thou canst inflict I bid thee do;
  Foul tyrant both of Gods and humankind,
    One only being shalt thou not subdue.   265
  Rain then thy plagues upon me here,
  Ghastly disease, and frenzying fear;
  And let alternate frost and fire
  Eat into me, and be thine ire
Lightning, and cutting hail, and legioned forms   270
Of furies, driving by upon the wounding storms.

  Aye, do thy worst. Thou art omnipotent.
    O'er all things but thyself I gave thee power,
  And my own will. Be thy swift mischiefs sent
    To blast mankind, from yon ethereal tower.   275
  Let thy malignant spirit move
  Its darkness over those I love;
  On me and mine I imprecate
  The utmost torture of thy hate,
And thus devote to sleepless agony   280
This undeclining head, while thou must reign on high.

  But thou, who art the God and Lord – oh thou
    Who fillest with thy soul this world of woe;
  To whom all things of Earth and Heaven do bow
    In fear and worship; all-prevailing foe!   285
  I curse thee! Let a sufferer's curse
  Clasp thee, his torturer, like remorse;
  Till thine infinity shall be
  A robe of envenomed agony,
And thine omnipotence a crown of pain   290
To cling like burning gold round thy dissolving brain.

   Heap on thy soul, by virtue of this curse,
     Ill deeds; then be thou damned, beholding good,
   Both infinite as is the universe,
      And thou, and thy self-torturing solitude.   295
        An awful image of calm power
        Though now thou sittest, let the hour
        Come when thou must appear to be
        That which thou art internally;
      And after many a false and fruitless crime   300
      Scorn track thy lagging fall through boundless space and time.
The Phantasm vanishes.
Prometheus Were these my words, oh Parent?
The Earth   They were thine.
Prometheus It doth repent me; words are quick and vain –
   Grief for awhile is blind, and so was mine.
   I wish no living thing to suffer pain.[11]   305
The Earth
   Misery, oh misery to me,
   That Jove at length should vanquish thee.
   Wail, howl aloud, Land and Sea;
   The Earth's rent heart shall answer ye.
   Howl, spirits of the living and the dead,   310
   Your refuge, your defence lies fallen and vanquished.
First Echo Lies fallen and vanquished?
Second Echo   Fallen and vanquished!
Ione
   Fear not, 'tis but some passing spasm –
     The Titan is unvanquished still.   315
   But see, where through the azure chasm
     Of yon forked and snowy hill,
   Trampling the slant winds on high
     With golden-sandalled feet that glow
   Under plumes of purple dye   320
   Like rose-ensanguined ivory –
     A shape comes now,
   Stretching on high from his right hand
   A serpent-cinctured[12] wand.
Panthea 'Tis Jove's world-wandering herald, Mercury.   325
Ione
   And who are those with hydra tresses[13]
     And iron wings that climb the wind,
   Whom the frowning God represses
     Like vapours steaming up behind,
   Clanging loud, an endless crowd?   330

---

[11] A deleted stage direction in the MS reveals at this point that Prometheus 'bends his head as in pain'.

[12] *cinctured* entwined.

[13] *hydra tresses* hair of snakes.

Panthea
    These are Jove's tempest-walking hounds[14]
    Whom he gluts with groans and blood,
    When charioted on sulphurous cloud
        He bursts Heaven's bounds.

Ione
    Are they now led from the thin dead   335
    On new pangs to be fed?

Panthea The Titan looks as ever — firm, not proud.

First Fury Ha! I scent life!

Second Fury   Let me but look into his eyes.

Third Fury The hope of torturing him smells like a heap
    Of corpses to a death-bird after battle.   340

First Fury Darest thou delay, oh Herald? Take cheer, hounds
    Of hell; what if the Son of Maia[15] soon
    Should make us food and sport? Who can please long
    The Omnipotent?

Mercury   Back to your towers of iron
    And gnash, beside the streams of fire, and wail   345
    Your foodless teeth! Geryon, arise! And Gorgon,
    Chimera, and thou Sphinx,[16] subtlest of fiends,
    Who ministered to Thebes Heaven's poisoned wine:
    Unnatural love and more unnatural hate —
    These shall perform your task.

First Fury   Oh mercy, mercy!   350
    We die with our desire; drive us not back.

Mercury Crouch then in silence.
                  Awful sufferer!
    To thee unwilling, most unwillingly
    I come, by the great Father's will driven down,
    To execute a doom of new revenge.   355
    Alas, I pity thee, and hate myself
    That I can do no more. Aye from thy sight
    Returning, for a season, Heaven seems Hell,
    So thy worn form pursues me night and day,
    Smiling reproach. Wise art thou, firm and good,   360
    But vainly wouldst stand forth alone in strife
    Against the Omnipotent, as yon clear lamps
    That measure and divide the weary years
    From which there is no refuge, long have taught
    And long must teach. Even now thy torturer arms   365
    With the strange might of unimagined pains
    The powers who scheme slow agonies in Hell,
    And my commission is to lead them here,

---

[14] i.e. the Furies.
[15] Mercury.
[16] Geryon, Gorgon, Chimera, and Sphinx are all monsters of classical legend. By solving the riddle of the Sphinx, Oedipus was led to an 'Unnatural love' for his own mother.

Or what more subtle, foul or savage fiends
People the abyss, and leave them to their task.   370
Be it not so! There is a secret known
To thee, and to none else of living things,
Which may transfer the sceptre of wide Heaven,
The fear of which perplexes the Supreme.
Clothe it in words, and bid it clasp his throne   375
In intercession; bend thy soul in prayer,
And like a suppliant in some gorgeous fane
Let the will kneel within thy haughty heart;
For benefits and meek submission tame
The fiercest and the mightiest.

Prometheus   Evil minds   380
Change good to their own nature. I gave all
He has, and in return he chains me here
Years, ages, night and day — whether the sun
Split my parched skin, or in the moony night
The crystal-winged snow cling round my hair —   385
Whilst my beloved race is trampled down
By his thought-executing ministers.
Such is the Tyrant's recompense — 'tis just;
He who is evil can receive no good;
And for a world bestowed, or a friend lost,   390
He can feel hate, fear, shame — not gratitude.
He but requites me for his own misdeed.
Kindness to such is keen reproach, which breaks
With bitter stings the light sleep of Revenge.
Submission, thou dost know I cannot try;   395
For what submission but that fatal word,
The death-seal of mankind's captivity —
Like the Sicilian's hair-suspended sword[17]
Which trembles o'er his crown — would he accept;
Or could I yield? Which yet I will not yield.   400
Let others flatter Crime, where it sits throned
In brief omnipotence; secure are they,
For Justice, when triumphant, will weep down
Pity, not punishment, on her own wrongs,
Too much avenged by those who err. I wait,   405
Enduring thus the retributive hour
Which since we spake is even nearer now.
But hark, the hell-hounds clamour; fear delay!
Behold — Heaven lowers under thy Father's frown!

Mercury. Oh that we might be spared — I to inflict   410
And thou to suffer. Once more answer me:
Thou knowest not the period[18] of Jove's power?

---

[17] Dionysus the Elder, who suspended such a sword   [18] *period* end.
over the flatterer Damocles.

Prometheus I know but this, that it must come.
Mercury   Alas!
  Thou canst not count thy years to come of pain?
Prometheus They last while Jove must reign – nor more nor less   415
  Do I desire or fear.
Mercury   Yet pause, and plunge
  Into eternity, where recorded time,
  Even all that we imagine, age on age,
  Seems but a point, and the reluctant mind
  Flags wearily in its unending flight,   420
  Till it sink, dizzy, blind, lost, shelterless.
  Perchance it has not numbered the slow years
  Which thou must spend in torture, unreprieved.
Prometheus Perchance no thought can count them – yet they pass.
Mercury If thou might'st dwell among the Gods the while,   425
  Lapped in voluptuous joy?
Prometheus   I would not quit
  This bleak ravine, these unrepentant pains.
Mercury Alas! I wonder at, yet pity thee.
Prometheus Pity the self-despising slaves of Heaven –
  Not me, within whose mind sits peace serene   430
  As light in the sun, throned. How vain is talk!
  Call up the fiends.
Ione   Oh sister, look! White fire
  Has cloven to the roots yon huge snow-loaded cedar;
  How fearfully God's thunder howls behind!
Mercury. I must obey his words and thine, alas;   435
  Most heavily remorse hangs at my heart.
Panthea See where the child of Heaven,[19] with winged feet
  Runs down the slanted sunlight of the dawn.
Ione Dear sister, close thy plumes over thine eyes
  Lest thou behold and die; they come – they come   440
  Blackening the birth of day with countless wings,
  And hollow underneath, like death.
First Fury   Prometheus!
Second Fury Immortal Titan!
Third Fury   Champion of Heaven's slaves!
Prometheus He whom some dreadful voice invokes is here –
  Prometheus, the chained Titan. Horrible forms,   445
  What and who are ye? Never yet there came
  Phantasms so foul through monster-teeming Hell
  From the all-miscreative brain of Jove.
  Whilst I behold such execrable shapes,
  Methinks I grow like what I contemplate,   450
  And laugh and stare in loathsome sympathy.

---

[19]   Mercury.

First Fury We are the ministers of pain and fear,
  And disappointment, and mistrust, and hate,
  And clinging crime; and as lean dogs pursue
  Through wood and lake some struck and sobbing fawn,   455
  We track all things that weep and bleed and live,
  When the great King betrays them to our will.[20]
Prometheus Oh many fearful natures in one name,
  I know ye; and these lakes and echoes know
  The darkness and the clangour of your wings.   460
  But why more hideous than your loathed selves
  Gather ye up in legions from the deep?
Second Fury We knew not that; sisters, rejoice, rejoice!
Prometheus Can aught exult in its deformity?
Second Fury The beauty of delight makes lovers glad,   465
  Gazing on one another; so are we.
  As from the rose which the pale priestess kneels
  To gather for her festal crown of flowers
  The aerial crimson falls, flushing her cheek —
  So from our victim's destined agony   470
  The shade which is our form invests us round,
  Else are we shapeless as our mother Night.
Prometheus I laugh your power, and his who sent you here,
  To lowest scorn. Pour forth the cup of pain.
First Fury Thou thinkest we will rend thee bone from bone,   475
  And nerve from nerve, working like fire within?
Prometheus Pain is my element, as hate is thine;
  Ye rend me now — I care not.
Second Fury   Dost imagine
  We will but laugh into thy lidless eyes?
Prometheus I weigh not what ye do, but what ye suffer,   480
  Being evil. Cruel was the Power which called
  You, or aught else so wretched, into light.
Third Fury Thou think'st we will live through thee, one by one,
  Like animal life, and though we can obscure not
  The soul which burns within, that we will dwell   485
  Beside it, like a vain loud multitude
  Vexing the self-content of wisest men;
  That we will be dread thought beneath thy brain,
  And foul desire round thine astonished heart,
  And blood within thy labyrinthine veins   490
  Crawling like agony.
Prometheus   Why, ye are thus now;
  Yet am I king over myself, and rule
  The torturing and conflicting throngs within,
  As Jove rules you when Hell grows mutinous.

---

[20] Besides *Twelfth Night*, I. i. 20–2, Shelley may be
recalling Wordsworth's 'Hart-Leap Well'.

Chorus of Furies

From the ends of the earth, from the ends of the earth,   495
Where the night has its grave and the morning its birth,
    Come, come, come!
Oh ye who shake hills with the scream of your mirth
When cities sink howling in ruin, and ye
Who with wingless footsteps trample the sea,   500
And close upon shipwreck and famine's track
Sit chattering with joy on the foodless wreck –
    Come, come, come!
  Leave the bed, low, cold, and red,
  Strewed beneath a nation dead;   505
  Leave the hatred, as in ashes
    Fire is left for future burning:
  It will burst in bloodier flashes
    When ye stir it, soon returning;
  Leave the self-contempt implanted   510
  In young spirits, sense-enchanted,
    Misery's yet unkindled fuel;
Leave Hell's secrets half unchanted
    To the maniac dreamer – cruel
  More than ye can be with hate,   515
    Is he with fear.
        Come, come, come!
We are steaming up from Hell's wide gate,
  And we burden the blasts of the atmosphere,
  But vainly we toil till ye come here.   520

Ione Sister, I hear the thunder of new wings.
Panthea These solid mountains quiver with the sound
  Even as the tremulous air; their shadows make
  The space within my plumes more black than night.

First Fury

  Your call was as a winged car   525
  Driven on whirlwinds fast and far;
  It rapt us from red gulfs of war;

Second Fury

  From wide cities, famine-wasted;

Third Fury

  Groans half-heard, and blood untasted;

Fourth Fury

  Kingly conclaves stern and cold,   530
  Where blood with gold is bought and sold;

Fifth Fury

  From the furnace, white and hot,
  In which –

A Fury

    Speak not, whisper not!
  I know all that ye would tell,

But to speak might break the spell 535
   Which must bend the Invincible,
      The stern of thought;
   He yet defies the deepest power of Hell.

A Fury
   Tear the veil![21]
Another Fury It is torn!
Chorus
           The pale stars of the morn
Shine on a misery dire to be borne. 540
Dost thou faint, mighty Titan? We laugh thee to scorn.
Dost thou boast the clear knowledge thou wakenedst for man?
Then was kindled within him a thirst which outran
Those perishing waters; a thirst of fierce fever,
Hope, love, doubt, desire – which consume him forever. 545
     One[22] came forth of gentle worth
     Smiling on the sanguine earth;
     His words outlived him, like swift poison
       Withering up truth, peace, and pity.
     Look, where round the wide horizon 550
       Many a million-peopled city
     Vomits smoke in the bright air.
     Hark that outcry of despair!
     'Tis his mild and gentle ghost
       Wailing for the faith he kindled. 555
     Look again, the flames almost
       To a glow-worm's lamp have dwindled;
     The survivors round the embers
       Gather in dread.
         Joy, joy, joy! 560
Past ages crowd on thee, but each one remembers,
And the future is dark, and the present is spread
Like a pillow of thorns for thy slumberless head.

Semichorus I
     Drops of bloody agony flow
     From his white and quivering brow. 565
     Grant a little respite now –
     See, a disenchanted nation[23]
     Springs like day from desolation;
     To Truth its state is dedicate,
     And Freedom leads it forth, her mate; 570
     A legioned band of linked brothers
     Whom Love calls children –

---

[21] A deleted stage direction in the MS reveals that at this point 'The Furies, having mingled in a strange dance, divide, and in the background is seen a plain covered with burning cities'.

[22] *One* Jesus Christ.
[23] France, during the Revolution.

Semichorus II

          'Tis another's:
See how kindred murder kin![24]
'Tis the vintage-time for Death and Sin;
Blood, like new wine, bubbles within,
    Till Despair smothers   575
The struggling world, which slaves and tyrants win.

All the Furies vanish, except one

Ione Hark, sister! What a low yet dreadful groan
  Quite unsuppressed is tearing up the heart
  Of the good Titan, as storms tear the deep,   580
  And beasts hear the sea moan in inland caves.
  Darest thou observe how the fiends torture him?
Panthea Alas, I looked forth twice, but will no more.
Ione What didst thou see?
Panthea   A woeful sight; a youth[25]
  With patient looks nailed to a crucifix.   585
Ione What next?
Panthea   The Heaven around, the earth below
  Was peopled with thick shapes of human death,
  All horrible, and wrought by human hands;
  And some appeared the work of human hearts,
  For men were slowly killed by frowns and smiles. 590
  And other sights too foul to speak and live
  Were wandering by. Let us not tempt worse fear
  By looking forth; those groans are grief enough.
Fury Behold an emblem: those who do endure
  Deep wrongs for man, and scorn, and chains, but heap 595
  Thousandfold torment on themselves and him.
Prometheus Remit the anguish of that lighted stare;
  Close those wan lips; let that thorn-wounded brow
  Stream not with blood – it mingles with thy tears!
  Fix, fix those tortured orbs in peace and death, 600
  So thy sick throes shake not that crucifix,
  So those pale fingers play not with thy gore.
  Oh horrible! Thy name I will not speak –
  It hath become a curse. I see, I see
  The wise, the mild, the lofty, and the just, 605
  Whom thy slaves hate for being like to thee;
  Some hunted by foul lies from their heart's home,
  An early-chosen, late-lamented home,
  As hooded ounces[26] cling to the driven hind;
  Some linked to corpses in unwholesome cells; 610
  Some (hear I not the multitude laugh loud?)
  Impaled in lingering fire. And mighty realms

---

[24] The Reign of Terror.   [26] *ounces* cheetahs.
[25] *a youth* Christ.

Float by my feet, like sea-uprooted isles,
Whose sons are kneaded down in common blood
By the red light of their own burning homes. 615
Fury Blood thou canst see, and fire – and canst hear groans;
Worse things, unheard, unseen, remain behind.
Prometheus Worse?
Fury In each human heart terror survives
The ravin it has gorged; the loftiest fear
All that they would disdain to think were true. 620
Hypocrisy and custom make their minds
The fanes of many a worship, now outworn.
They dare not devise good for man's estate,
And yet they know not that they do not dare.
The good want power, but to weep barren tears; 625
The powerful goodness want – worse need for them;
The wise want love, and those who love want wisdom;
And all best things are thus confused to ill.
Many are strong and rich, and would be just,
But live among their suffering fellow-men 630
As if none felt: they know not what they do.[27]
Prometheus Thy words are like a cloud of winged snakes;
And yet I pity those they torture not.
Fury Thou pitiest them? I speak no more. (*vanishes*)
Prometheus Ah woe!
Ah woe! Alas, pain, pain ever, forever! 635
I close my tearless eyes, but see more clear
Thy works within my woe-illumed mind,
Thou subtle Tyrant! Peace is in the grave.
The grave hides all things beautiful and good:
I am a God and cannot find it there – 640
Nor would I seek it. For, though dread revenge,
This is defeat, fierce King, not victory.
The sights with which thou torturest gird my soul
With new endurance, till the hour arrives
When they shall be no types of things which are. 645
Panthea Alas! What sawest thou more?
Prometheus There are two woes:
To speak, and to behold; thou spare me one.
Names are there, nature's sacred watchwords: they
Were borne aloft in bright emblazonry.
The nations thronged around, and cried aloud 650
As with one voice, 'Truth, Liberty, and Love!'
Suddenly fierce confusion fell from Heaven
Among them – there was strife, deceit, and fear;
Tyrants rushed in, and did divide the spoil.
This was the shadow of the truth I saw. 655

---

[27] Luke 23: 34.

The Earth I felt thy torture, son, with such mixed joy
    As pain and virtue give. To cheer thy state
    I bid ascend those subtle and fair spirits
    Whose homes are the dim caves of human thought,
    And who inhabit, as birds wing the wind,   660
    Its world-surrounding ether; they behold
    Beyond that twilight realm, as in a glass,
    The future: may they speak comfort to thee!
Panthea Look, sister, where a troop of spirits gather,
    Like flocks of clouds in spring's delightful weather,   665
    Thronging in the blue air!
Ione   And see, more come,
    Like fountain-vapours when the winds are dumb,
    That climb up the ravine in scattered lines.
    And hark – is it the music of the pines?
    Is it the lake? Is it the waterfall?   670
Panthea 'Tis something sadder, sweeter far than all.
Chorus of Spirits
      From unremembered ages we
      Gentle guides and guardians be
      Of Heaven-oppressed mortality;
      And we breathe, and sicken not,   675
      The atmosphere of human thought:
      Be it dim, and dank, and grey,
      Like a storm-extinguished day
      Travelled o'er by dying gleams;
        Be it bright as all between   680
      Cloudless skies and windless streams,
        Silent, liquid, and serene;
      As the birds within the wind,
        As the fish within the wave,
      As the thoughts of man's own mind   685
        Float through all above the grave,
      We make there our liquid lair,
      Voyaging cloudlike and unpent
      Through the boundless element:
      Thence we bear the prophecy   690
      Which begins and ends in thee.
Ione More yet come, one by one: the air around them
    Looks radiant as the air around a star.
First Spirit
      On a battle-trumpet's blast
      I fled hither, fast, fast, fast,   695
      Mid the darkness upward cast.
      From the dust of creeds outworn,[28]

---

[28] *creeds outworn* Wordsworth, 'The World is Too Much with Us', 10.

From the tyrant's banner torn,
Gathering round me, onward borne,
There was mingled many a cry –   700
'Freedom! Hope! Death! Victory!'
Till they faded through the sky;
And one sound above, around,
One sound beneath, around, above,
Was moving – 'twas the soul of love;   705
'Twas the hope, the prophecy
Which begins and ends in thee.

Second Spirit

A rainbow's arch stood on the sea,
Which rocked beneath, immovably;
And the triumphant storm did flee,   710
Like a conqueror swift and proud,
Between, with many a captive cloud,
A shapeless, dark and rapid crowd,
Each by lightning riven in half.
I heard the thunder hoarsely laugh.   715
Mighty fleets were strewn like chaff
And spread beneath a hell of death
O'er the white waters. I alit
On a great ship lightning-split,
And speeded hither on the sigh   720
Of one who gave an enemy
His plank, then plunged aside to die.

Third Spirit

I sat beside a sage's bed,
And the lamp was burning red
Near the book where he had fed,   725
When a dream with plumes of flame
To his pillow hovering came,
And I knew it was the same
Which had kindled long ago
Pity, eloquence, and woe;   730
And the world awhile below
Wore the shade its lustre made.
It has borne me here as fleet
As Desire's lightning feet:
I must ride it back ere morrow,   735
Or the sage will wake in sorrow.

Fourth Spirit

On a poet's lips I slept
Dreaming like a love-adept
In the sound his breathing kept;
Nor seeks nor finds he mortal blisses,   740
But feeds on the aerial kisses
Of shapes that haunt thought's wildernesses.

He will watch from dawn to gloom
The lake-reflected sun illume
The yellow bees in the ivy-bloom,   745
Nor heed nor see what things they be;
But from these create he can
Forms more real than living man,
Nurslings of immortality!
One of these awakened me,   750
And I sped to succour thee.

Ione
Behold'st thou not two shapes from the east and west
Come, as two doves to one beloved nest,
Twin nurslings of the all-sustaining air
On swift still wings glide down the atmosphere?   755
And hark, their sweet, sad voices! 'Tis despair
Mingled with love, and then dissolved in sound.

Panthea Canst thou speak, sister? All my words are drowned.

Ione Their beauty gives me voice. See how they float
On their sustaining wings of skyey grain,   760
Orange and azure deepening into gold;
Their soft smiles light the air like a star's fire.

Chorus of Spirits Hast thou beheld the form of Love?

Fifth Spirit
                              As over wide dominions
I sped, like some swift cloud that wings the wide air's wildernesses,
That planet-crested shape swept by on lightning-braided pinions,   765
Scattering the liquid joy of life from his ambrosial tresses:
His footsteps paved the world with light, but as I passed 'twas fading,
And hollow Ruin yawned behind. Great sages bound in madness,
And headless patriots and pale youths who perished, unupbraiding,
Gleamed in the night I wandered o'er; till thou, oh King of sadness, 770
Turned by thy smile the worst I saw to recollected gladness.

Sixth Spirit Ah sister! Desolation is a delicate thing:
It walks not on the earth, it floats not on the air,
But treads with lulling footstep, and fans with silent wing
The tender hopes which in their hearts the best and gentlest bear,   775
Who, soothed to false repose by the fanning plumes above,
And the music-stirring motion of its soft and busy feet,
Dream visions of aerial joy, and call the monster, Love,
And wake, and find the shadow Pain, as he whom now we greet.

Chorus
Though Ruin now Love's shadow be,   780
Following him destroyingly
On Death's white and winged steed,[29]
Which the fleetest cannot flee —

---

[29] Rev. 6: 8.

Trampling down both flower and weed,
Man and beast, and foul and fair,   785
Like a tempest through the air;
Thou shalt quell this horseman grim,
Woundless though in heart or limb.

Prometheus Spirits, how know ye this shall be?

Chorus

In the atmosphere we breathe –   790
As buds grow red when snowstorms flee
    From spring gathering up beneath,
Whose mild winds shake the elder brake,
And the wandering herdsmen know
That the whitethorn²⁹ soon will blow –   795
Wisdom, Justice, Love, and Peace,
When they struggle to increase,
    Are to us as soft winds be
    To shepherd-boys – the prophecy
    Which begins and ends in thee.   800

Ione Where are the spirits fled?

Panthea   Only a sense
Remains of them, like the omnipotence
Of music, when the inspired voice and lute
Languish, ere yet the responses are mute
Which, through the deep and labyrinthine soul,   805
Like echoes through long caverns, wind and roll.

Prometheus How fair these airborne shapes! And yet I feel
Most vain all hope but love – and thou art far,
Asia, who, when my being overflowed,
Wert like a golden chalice to bright wine   810
Which else had sunk into the thirsty dust.
All things are still. Alas, how heavily
This quiet morning weighs upon my heart.
Though I should dream, I could even sleep with grief
If slumber were denied not. I would fain   815
Be what it is my destiny to be,
The saviour and the strength of suffering man,
Or sink into the original gulf of things.
There is no agony and no solace left;
Earth can console, Heaven can torment no more.   820

Panthea Hast thou forgotten one who watches thee
The cold dark night, and never sleeps but when
The shadow of thy spirit falls on her?

Prometheus I said all hope was vain but love; thou lovest.

Panthea Deeply in truth; but the eastern star looks white,   825
And Asia waits in that far Indian vale,

---

³⁰   Hawthorn; cf. Milton, *Lycidas*, 48.

The scene of her sad exile – rugged once,
And desolate and frozen, like this ravine,
But now invested with fair flowers and herbs,
And haunted by sweet airs and sounds, which flow   830
Among the woods and waters, from the ether
Of her transforming presence, which would fade
If it were mingled not with thine. Farewell!

ACT II, SCENE I

Morning. A lovely vale in the Indian Caucasus. Asia alone.
Asia From all the blasts of Heaven thou hast descended –
Yes, like a spirit, like a thought which makes
Unwonted tears throng to the horny eyes,
And beatings haunt the desolated heart
Which should have learnt repose; thou hast descended   5
Cradled in tempests; thou dost wake, oh Spring,
Oh child of many winds! As suddenly
Thou comest as the memory of a dream,
Which now is sad because it hath been sweet;
Like genius, or like joy which riseth up   10
As from the earth, clothing with golden clouds
The desert of our life.
This is the season, this the day, the hour;
At sunrise thou shouldst come, sweet sister mine,
Too long desired, too long delaying, come!   15
How like death-worms the wingless moments crawl!
The point of one white star[31] is quivering still
Deep in the orange light of widening morn
Beyond the purple mountains; through a chasm
Of wind-divided mist the darker lake   20
Reflects it: now it wanes – it gleams again
As the waves fade, and as the burning threads
Of woven cloud unravel in pale air.
'Tis lost! And through yon peaks of cloudlike snow
The roseate sunlight quivers – hear I not   25
The Aeolian music of her[32] sea-green plumes
Winnowing the crimson dawn? (*Panthea enters.*)
                I feel, I see
Those eyes which burn through smiles that fade in tears,
Like stars half-quenched in mists of silver dew.
Beloved and most beautiful, who wearest   30
The shadow of that soul by which I live,
How late thou art! The sphered sun had climbed
The sea, my heart was sick with hope, before
The printless air felt thy belated plumes.

---

[31] Venus, the Morning Star.   [32] i.e. Panthea's.

Panthea Pardon, great sister; but my wings were faint   35
    With the delight of a remembered dream,
    As are the noontide plumes of summer winds
    Satiate with sweet flowers. I was wont to sleep
    Peacefully, and awake refreshed and calm
    Before the sacred Titan's fall and thy   40
    Unhappy love had made, through use and pity,
    Both love and woe familiar to my heart
    As they had grown to thine. Erewhile I slept
    Under the glaucous[33] caverns of old Ocean
    Within dim bowers of green and purple moss,   45
    Our young Ione's soft and milky arms
    Locked then, as now, behind my dark moist hair,
    While my shut eyes and cheek were pressed within
    The folded depth of her life-breathing bosom –
    But not as now, since I am made the wind   50
    Which fails beneath the music that I bear
    Of thy most wordless converse; since dissolved
    Into the sense with which love talks, my rest
    Was troubled and yet sweet, my waking hours
    Too full of care and pain.
Asia   Lift up thine eyes   55
    And let me read thy dream.
Panthea   As I have said,
    With our sea-sister at his feet I slept.
    The mountain mists, condensing at our voice
    Under the moon, had spread their snowy flakes,
    From the keen ice shielding our linked sleep.   60
    Then two dreams came.[34] One I remember not.
    But in the other his pale, wound-worn limbs
    Fell from Prometheus, and the azure night
    Grew radiant with the glory of that form
    Which lives unchanged within, and his voice fell   65
    Like music which makes giddy the dim brain,
    Faint with intoxication of keen joy:
    'Sister of her whose footsteps pave the world
    With loveliness – more fair than aught but her,
    Whose shadow thou art – lift thine eyes on me!'   70
    I lifted them: the overpowering light
    Of that immortal shape was shadowed o'er
    By love, which, from his soft and flowing limbs,
    And passion-parted lips, and keen, faint eyes,
    Steamed forth like vaporous fire – an atmosphere   75
    Which wrapped me in its all-dissolving power

---

[33] *glaucous* pale green.
[34] The relation of the dreams is the main action of
the scene.

As the warm ether of the morning sun
Wraps ere it drinks some cloud of wandering dew.
I saw not, heard not, moved not, only felt
His presence flow and mingle through my blood   80
Till it became his life, and his grew mine,
And I was thus absorbed until it passed,
And like the vapours when the sun sinks down,
Gathering again in drops upon the pines,
And tremulous as they, in the deep night   85
My being was condensed; and as the rays
Of thought were slowly gathered, I could hear
His voice, whose accents lingered ere they died
Like footsteps of far melody. Thy name
Among the many sounds, alone I heard   90
Of what might be articulate; though still
I listened through the night when sound was none.
Ione wakened then, and said to me,
'Canst thou divine what troubles me tonight?
I always knew what I desired before,   95
Nor ever found delight to wish in vain.
But now I cannot tell thee what I seek,
I know not – something sweet, since it is sweet
Even to desire. It is thy sport, false sister;
Thou hast discovered some enchantment old,   100
Whose spells have stolen my spirit as I slept
And mingled it with thine – for when just now
We kissed, I felt within thy parted lips
The sweet air that sustained me, and the warmth
Of the life-blood, for loss of which I faint,   105
Quivered between our intertwining arms.'
I answered not, for the eastern star grew pale,
But fled to thee.
Asia   Thou speakest, but thy words
Are as the air; I feel them not. Oh lift
Thine eyes, that I may read his written soul!   110
Panthea I lift them, though they droop beneath the load
Of that they would express: what canst thou see
But thine own fairest shadow imaged there?
Asia Thine eyes are like the deep, blue, boundless Heaven
Contracted to two circles underneath   115
Their long, fine lashes; dark, far, measureless,
Orb within orb, and line through line inwoven.
Panthea Why lookest thou as if a spirit passed?
Asia There is a change; beyond their inmost depth
I see a shade, a shape – 'tis he, arrayed   120
In the soft light of his own smiles, which spread
Like radiance from the cloud-surrounded moon.
Prometheus, it is thou – depart not yet!

Say not those smiles that we shall meet again
Within that bright pavilion which their beams   125
Shall build o'er the waste world? The dream is told.
What shape is that between us?[35] Its rude hair
Roughens the wind that lifts it, its regard
Is wild and quick, yet 'tis a thing of air —
For through its grey robe gleams the golden dew   130
Whose stars the noon has quenched not.
Dream   Follow, follow!
Panthea It is mine other dream.
Asia   It disappears.
Panthea It passes now into my mind. Methought
   As we sat here, the flower-enfolding buds
   Burst on yon lightning-blasted almond tree,   135
   When swift from the white Scythian wilderness
   A wind swept forth, wrinkling the earth with frost.
   I looked, and all the blossoms were blown down;
   But on each leaf was stamped — as the blue-bells
   Of Hyacinth tell Apollo's written grief[36] —   140
   'Oh follow, follow!'
   Asia   As you speak, your words
   Fill, pause by pause, my own forgotten sleep
   With shapes. Methought among these lawns together
   We wandered, underneath the young grey dawn,
   And multitudes of dense white fleecy clouds   145
   Were wandering in thick flocks along the mountains,
   Shepherded by the slow, unwilling wind;
   And the white dew on the new-bladed grass,
   Just piercing the dark earth, hung silently.
   And there was more which I remember not,   150
   But on the shadows of the morning clouds,
   Athwart the purple mountain slope, was written
   'Follow, oh follow!' as they vanished by;
   And on each herb from which heaven's dew had fallen
   The like was stamped, as with a withering fire.   155
   A wind arose among the pines; it shook
   The clinging music from their boughs, and then
   Low, sweet, faint sounds like the farewell of ghosts,
   Were heard: 'Oh follow, follow, follow me!'
   And then I said, 'Panthea, look on me.'   160
   But in the depth of those beloved eyes
   Still I saw, 'Follow, follow!'
   Echo   Follow, follow!
Panthea The crags, this clear spring morning, mock our voices
   As they were spirit-tongued.

---

[35] It is the second dream.
[36] After Hyacinthus was killed by Zephyrus, Apollo changed his blood into a flower, and wrote his lament, 'Ai', on the petals.

165

Asia   It is some being
Around the crags. What fine clear sounds, oh list!
Echoes (*unseen*)
              Echoes we; listen!
                We cannot stay:
              As dew-stars glisten
                Then fade away,
                  Child of Ocean![37]

170

Asia Hark! Spirits speak! The liquid responses
Of their aerial tongues yet sound.
Panthea   I hear.
Echoes
              Oh follow, follow,
                As our voice recedeth
              Through the caverns hollow
                Where the forest spreadeth; (*more distant*)
              Oh follow, follow,
              Through the caverns hollow;
            As the song floats, thou pursue,
            Where the wild bee never flew,
            Through the noontide darkness deep,
            By the odour-breathing sleep
            Of faint night-flowers, and the waves
            At the fountain-lighted caves,
            While our music, wild and sweet,
            Mocks thy gently-falling feet,
                  Child of Ocean!

175

180

185

Asia Shall we pursue the sound? It grows more faint
  And distant.
Panthea   List, the strain floats nearer now.
Echoes
              In the world unknown
                Sleeps a voice unspoken;
              By thy step alone
                Can its rest be broken,
                  Child of Ocean!

190

Asia How the notes sink upon the ebbing wind!
Echoes
              Oh follow, follow,
              Through the caverns hollow;
            As the song floats thou pursue,
            By the woodland noontide dew,
            By the forest, lakes, and fountains,
            Through the many-folded mountains,
            To the rents, and gulfs, and chasms,

195

200

---

[37] Asia, Panthea, and Ione are daughters of Ocean.

Where the Earth reposed from spasms,
On the day when he and thou
Parted, to commingle now, 205
Child of Ocean!
Asia Come, sweet Panthea, link thy hand in mine,
And follow ere the voices fade away.

ACT II, SCENE II

A forest, intermingled with rocks and caverns. Asia and Panthea pass into it. Two young fauns are sitting on a rock, listening.

Semichorus I of Spirits
The path through which that lovely twain[38]
Have passed, by cedar, pine, and yew,
And each dark tree that ever grew,
Is curtained out from Heaven's wide blue;
Nor sun, nor moon, nor wind, nor rain, 5
Can pierce its interwoven bowers;
Nor aught, save when some cloud of dew,
Drifted along the earth-creeping breeze
Between the trunks of the hoar trees,
Hangs each a pearl in the pale flowers 10
Of the green laurel, blown anew,
And bends, and then fades silently,
One frail and fair anemone;
Or when some star of many a one
That climbs and wanders through steep night, 15
Has found the cleft through which alone
Beams fall from high those depths upon,
Ere it is borne away, away,
By the swift Heavens that cannot stay —
It scatters drops of golden light, 20
Like lines of rain that ne'er unite;
And the gloom divine is all around,
And underneath is the mossy ground.
Semichorus II
There the voluptuous nightingales
Are awake through all the broad noonday. 25
When one with bliss or sadness fails
(And through the windless ivy-boughs,
Sick with sweet love, droops dying away
On its mate's music-panting bosom),
Another from the swinging blossom, 30
Watching to catch the languid close
Of the last strain, then lifts on high
The wings of the weak melody,

---

[38] Asia and Panthea.

Till some new strain of feeling bear
    The song, and all the woods are mute;   35
When there is heard through the dim air
The rush of wings, and rising there
    Like many a lake-surrounded flute,
Sounds overflow the listener's brain
So sweet that joy is almost pain.   40

Semichorus I

There those enchanted eddies play
    Of echoes, music-tongued, which draw,
    By Demogorgon's mighty law,
    With melting rapture or deep awe,
All spirits on that secret way,   45
    As inland boats are driven to ocean
Down streams made strong with mountain-thaw;
      And first there comes a gentle sound
      To those in talk or slumber bound,
    And wakes the destined; soft emotion   50
Attracts, impels them. Those who saw
    Say from the breathing earth behind
    There steams a plume-uplifting wind
Which drives them on their path, while they
    Believe their own swift wings and feet   55
The sweet desires within obey;
And so they float upon their way
Until, still sweet, but loud and strong,
The storm of sound is driven along,
    Sucked up and hurrying – as they fleet   60
    Behind, its gathering billows meet
And to the fatal mountain bear[39]
Like clouds amid the yielding air.

First Faun Canst thou imagine where those spirits live
Which make such delicate music in the woods?   65
We haunt within the least frequented caves
And closest coverts, and we know these wilds,
Yet never meet them, though we hear them oft:
Where may they hide themselves?

Second Faun   'Tis hard to tell.
I have heard those more skilled in spirits say,   70
The bubbles, which the enchantment of the sun
Sucks from the pale faint water-flowers that pave
The oozy bottom of clear lakes and pools,
Are the pavilions where such dwell and float
Under the green and golden atmosphere   75
Which noontide kindles through the woven leaves;

---

[39] The 'destined' spirits are borne by the gathering
'storm of sound' to the fatal mountain.

And when these burst, and the thin fiery air,
The which they breathed within those lucent[40] domes,
Ascends to flow like meteors through the night,
They ride on it, and rein their headlong speed,   80
And bow their burning crests, and glide in fire
Under the waters of the earth again.[41]

First Faun If such live thus, have others other lives,
    Under pink blossoms or within the bells
    Of meadow flowers, or folded violets deep,   85
    Or on their dying odours, when they die,
    Or in the sunlight of the sphered dew?

Second Faun Aye, many more which we may well divine.
    But should we stay to speak, noontide would come,
    And thwart Silenus find his goats undrawn,[42]   90
    And grudge to sing those wise and lovely songs
    Of fate, and chance, and God, and Chaos old,
    And love, and the chained Titan's woeful doom,
    And how he shall be loosed, and make the earth
    One brotherhood: delightful strains which cheer   95
    Our solitary twilights, and which charm
    To silence the unenvying nightingales.

ACT II, SCENE III

A pinnacle of rock among mountains. Asia and Panthea.

Panthea Hither the sound has borne us – to the realm
    Of Demogorgon, and the mighty portal,
    Like a volcano's meteor-breathing chasm,
    Whence the oracular vapour is hurled up
    Which lonely men drink wandering in their youth,   5
    And call truth, virtue, love, genius, or joy;
    That maddening wine of life, whose dregs they drain
    To deep intoxication, and uplift,
    Like maenads[43] who cry loud, 'Evoe! Evoe!' –
    The voice which is contagion to the world.   10

Asia Fit throne for such a Power – magnificent!
    How glorious art thou, Earth! And if thou be
    The shadow of some spirit lovelier still,[44]
    Though evil stain its work, and it should be
    Like its creation, weak yet beautiful,   15
    I could fall down and worship that and thee.
    Even now my heart adoreth – wonderful!
    Look, sister, ere the vapour dim thy brain:

---

[40] *lucent* shining.
[41] Lines 70–82 describe the process by which it was believed swamp gas was produced – giving rise to the *ignis fatuus*, or will-o'-the-wisp.
[42] *undrawn* unmilked; Silenus was a demigod and attendant of Bacchus.
[43] *maenads* drunken female worshippers of Bacchus whose war-cry was 'Evoe'.
[44] Cf. *Paradise Lost*, v. 574–6.

Beneath is a wide plain of billowy mist,
As a lake, paving in the morning sky,
With azure waves which burst in silver light,
Some Indian vale. Behold it, rolling on
Under the curdling winds, and islanding
The peak whereon we stand; midway, around,
Encinctured[45] by the dark and blooming forests,
Dim twilight-lawns, and stream-illumed caves,
And wind-enchanted shapes of wandering mist;
And far on high the keen sky-cleaving mountains
From icy spires of sunlike radiance fling
The dawn, as lifted Ocean's dazzling spray,
From some Atlantic islet scattered up,
Spangles the wind with lamp-like water-drops.
The vale is girdled with their walls; a howl
Of cataracts from their thaw-cloven ravines
Satiates the listening wind, continuous, vast,
Awful as silence. Hark, the rushing snow!
The sun-awakened avalanche! whose mass,
Thrice sifted by the storm, had gathered there
Flake after flake, in Heaven-defying minds
As thought by thought is piled, till some great truth
Is loosened, and the nations echo round,
Shaken to their roots, as do the mountains now.
Panthea Look how the gusty sea of mist is breaking
In crimson foam, even at our feet! It rises
As Ocean at the enchantment of the moon
Round foodless men wrecked on some oozy isle.
Asia The fragments of the cloud are scattered up;
The wind that lifts them disentwines my hair;
Its billows now sweep o'er mine eyes; my brain
Grows dizzy; seest those shapes within the mist?
Panthea A countenance with beckoning smiles: there burns
An azure fire within its golden locks!
Another and another – hark, they speak!
Song of Spirits
To the deep, to the deep,
Down, down!
Through the shade of sleep,
Through the cloudy strife
Of Death and of Life;
Through the veil and the bar
Of things which seem and are,
Even to the steps of the remotest throne,
Down, down!

20
25
30
35
40
45
50
55
60

[45] *Encinctured* surrounded.

While the sound whirls around,
> Down, down!
As the fawn draws the hound,   65
As the lightning the vapour,
As a weak moth the taper;
Death, despair; love, sorrow;
Time both; today, tomorrow;
As steel obeys the spirit of the stone,[46]   70
> Down, down!

Through the grey, void abysm,
> Down, down!
Where the air is no prism,
And the moon and stars are not,   75
And the cavern-crags wear not
The radiance of Heaven,
Nor the gloom to Earth given;
Where there is One pervading, One alone,
> Down, down!   80

In the depth of the deep,
> Down, down!
Like veiled lightning asleep,
Like that spark nursed in embers,
The last look Love remembers,   85
Like a diamond which shines
On the dark wealth of mines,[47]
A spell is treasured but for thee alone.
> Down, down!

We have bound thee, we guide thee   90
> Down, down!
With the bright form beside thee;
Resist not the weakness;
Such strength is in meekness,
That the Eternal, the Immortal,   95
Must unloose through life's portal
The snake-like Doom coiled underneath his throne
> By that alone.

ACT II, SCENE IV

The Cave of Demogorgon. Asia and Panthea.
> *Panthea* What veiled form sits on that ebon throne?
> *Asia* The veil has fallen.

---

[46] A magnet.
[47] Eighteenth-century scientists believed that diamonds glowed in the dark.

Panthea   I see a mighty darkness
 Filling the seat of power, and rays of gloom
 Dart round, as light from the meridian sun,
 Ungazed upon and shapeless; neither limb,   5
 Nor form, nor outline[48] – yet we feel it is
 A living spirit.
Demogorgon   Ask what thou wouldst know.
Asia What canst thou tell?
Demogorgon   All things thou dar'st demand.
Asia Who made the living world?
Demogorgon   God.
Asia   Who made all
 That it contains – thought, passion, reason, will,   10
 Imagination?
Demogorgon God. Almighty God.
Asia Who made that sense which, when the winds of spring
 In rarest visitation, or the voice
 Of one beloved heard in youth alone,
 Fills the faint eyes with falling tears which dim   15
 The radiant looks of unbewailing flowers,
 And leaves this peopled earth a solitude
 When it returns no more?
Demogorgon   Merciful God.
Asia And who made terror, madness, crime, remorse,
 Which from the links of the great chain of things,   20
 To every thought within the mind of man
 Sway and drag heavily, and each one reels
 Under the load towards the pit of death;
 Abandoned hope, and love that turns to hate;
 And self-contempt, bitterer to drink than blood;   25
 Pain, whose unheeded and familiar speech
 Is howling, and keen shrieks, day after day;
 And Hell, or the sharp fear of Hell?
Demogorgon   He reigns.
Asia Utter his name. A world pining in pain
 Asks but his name; curses shall drag him down.   30
Demogorgon He reigns.
Asia   I feel, I know it – who?
Demogorgon   He reigns.
Asia Who reigns? There was the Heaven and Earth at first,
 And Light and Love; then Saturn, from whose throne
 Time fell, an envious shadow; such the state
 Of the earth's primal spirits beneath his sway,   35
 As the calm joy of flowers and living leaves
 Before the wind or sun has withered them,

---

[48] Cf. Milton's description of Death, *Paradise Lost*, ii.
668–9.

And semivital worms; but he refused
The birthright of their being – knowledge, power,
The skill which wields the elements, the thought   40
Which pierces this dim universe like light,
Self-empire and the majesty of love –
For thirst of which they fainted. Then Prometheus
Gave wisdom, which is strength, to Jupiter,
And with this law alone, 'Let man be free',   45
Clothed him with the dominion of wide Heaven.
To know nor faith, nor love, nor law; to be
Omnipotent but friendless is to reign –
And Jove now reigned; for on the race of man
First famine, and then toil, and then disease,   50
Strife, wounds, and ghastly death unseen before,
Fell; and the unseasonable seasons drove,
With alternating shafts of frost and fire,
Their shelterless, pale tribes to mountain caves;
And in their desert hearts fierce wants he sent,   55
And mad disquietudes, and shadows idle
Of unreal good, which levied mutual war,
So ruining the lair wherein they raged.
Prometheus saw, and waked the legioned hopes
Which sleep within folded Elysian flowers,   60
Nepenthe, moly, amaranth,[49] fadeless blooms,
That they might hide with thin and rainbow wings
The shape of Death; and Love he sent to bind
The disunited tendrils of that vine
Which bears the wine of life, the human heart;   65
And he tamed fire which, like some beast of chase
Most terrible, but lovely, played beneath
The frown of man; and tortured to his will
Iron and gold, the slaves and signs of power,
And gems and poisons, and all subtlest forms   70
Hidden beneath the mountains and the waves.
He gave man speech, and speech created thought,
Which is the measure of the universe;
And Science struck the thrones of Earth and Heaven,
Which shook but fell not; and the harmonious mind   75
Poured itself forth in all-prophetic song,
And music lifted up the listening spirit
Until it walked, exempt from mortal care,
Godlike, o'er the clear billows of sweet sound;
And human hands first mimicked and then mocked,   80
With moulded limbs more lovely than its own,
The human form, till marble grew divine,

---

[49] Nepenthe is a grief-banishing drug; moly is a
magic herb; amaranth is an unfading flower.

And mothers, gazing, drank the love men see
Reflected in their race, behold, and perish.
He told the hidden power of herbs and springs,   85
And Disease drank and slept. Death grew like sleep.
He taught the implicated[50] orbits woven
Of the wide-wandering stars, and how the sun
Changes his lair, and by what secret spell
The pale moon is transformed, when her broad eye   90
Gazes not on the interlunar sea.
He taught to rule, as life directs the limbs,
The tempest-winged chariots of the Ocean,[51]
And the Celt knew the Indian. Cities then
Were built, and through their snow-like columns flowed   95
The warm winds, and the azure ether shone,
And the blue sea and shadowy hills were seen.
Such the alleviations of his state
Prometheus gave to man, for which he hangs
Withering in destined pain; but who rains down   100
Evil, the immedicable plague, which, while
Man looks on his creation like a God
And sees that it is glorious, drives him on,
The wreck of his own will, the scorn of earth,
The outcast, the abandoned, the alone?   105
Not Jove; while yet his frown shook Heaven – aye, when
His adversary from adamantine chains
Cursed him – he trembled like a slave. Declare
Who is his master? Is he too a slave?
Demogorgon All spirits are enslaved which serve things evil;   110
Thou knowest if Jupiter be such or no.
Asia Whom calledst thou God?
Demogorgon   I spoke but as ye speak,
For Jove is the supreme of living things.
Asia Who is the master of the slave?
Demogorgon   If the abysm
Could vomit forth its secrets – but a voice   115
Is wanting, the deep truth is imageless;
For what would it avail to bid thee gaze
On the revolving world? What to bid speak
Fate, Time, Occasion, Chance, and Change? To these
All things are subject but eternal Love.   120
Asia So much I asked before, and my heart gave
The response thou hast given; and of such truths
Each to itself must be the oracle.
One more demand; and do thou answer me
As my own soul would answer, did it know   125

---

[50]   *implicated* intertwined.   [51]   *chariots of the Ocean* boats.

That which I ask. Prometheus shall arise
Henceforth the Sun of this rejoicing world:
When shall the destined hour arrive?
Demogorgon   Behold![52]
Asia The rocks are cloven, and through the purple night
    I see cars drawn by rainbow-winged steeds 130
    Which trample the dim winds; in each there stands
    A wild-eyed charioteer urging their flight.
    Some look behind, as fiends pursued them there,
    And yet I see no shapes but the keen stars;
    Others, with burning eyes, lean forth, and drink 135
    With eager lips the wind of their own speed,
    As if the thing they loved fled on before,
    And now, even now, they clasped it. Their bright locks
    Stream like a comet's flashing hair – they all
    Sweep onward.
Demogorgon   These are the immortal Hours, 140
    Of whom thou didst demand. One waits for thee.
Asia A spirit with a dreadful countenance
    Checks its dark chariot by the craggy gulf.
    Unlike thy brethren, ghastly charioteer,
    What art thou? Whither wouldst thou bear me? Speak! 145
Spirit I am the shadow of a destiny
    More dread than is my aspect; ere yon planet
    Has set, the Darkness which ascends with me
    Shall wrap in lasting night Heaven's kingless throne.
Asia What meanest thou?
Panthea   The terrible shadow[53] floats 150
    Up from its throne, as may the lurid smoke
    Of earthquake-ruined cities o'er the sea.
    Lo! it ascends the car; the coursers fly
    Terrified. Watch its path among the stars
    Blackening the night!
Asia   Thus I am answered; strange! 155
Panthea See, near the verge,[54] another chariot stays;
    An ivory shell inlaid with crimson fire
    Which comes and goes within its sculptured rim
    Of delicate strange tracery; the young spirit
    That guides it has the dove-like eyes of hope; 160
    How its soft smiles attract the soul! as light
    Lures winged insects through the lampless air.
Spirit
    My coursers are fed with the lightning,
      They drink of the whirlwind's stream,
    And when the red morning is bright'ning 165

---

[52] *Behold* i.e. the destined hour *has* arrived.   [54] *verge* horizon.
[53] Demogorgon.

They bathe in the fresh sunbeam;
They have strength for their swiftness, I deem –
Then ascend with me, Daughter of Ocean.

I desire – and their speed makes night kindle;
  I fear – they outstrip the typhoon;   170
Ere the cloud piled on Atlas can dwindle
We encircle the earth and the moon;
We shall rest from long labours ere noon –
Then ascend with me, Daughter of Ocean.

ACT II, SCENE V

The car pauses within a cloud on the top of a snowy mountain. Asia, Panthea, and the Spirit of the Hour.

Spirit
          On the brink of the night and the morning
            My coursers are wont to respire;[55]
          But the Earth has just whispered a warning
            That their flight must be swifter than fire –
            They shall drink the hot speed of desire!   5
Asia Thou breathest on their nostrils, but my breath
  Would give them swifter speed.
Spirit   Alas, it could not.
Panthea Oh Spirit, pause and tell whence is the light
  Which fills the cloud? The sun is yet unrisen.
Spirit The sun will rise not until noon. Apollo   10
  Is held in Heaven by wonder; and the light
  Which fills this vapour, as the aerial hue
  Of fountain-gazing roses fills the water,
  Flows from thy mighty sister.
Panthea   Yes, I feel –
Asia What is it with thee, sister? Thou art pale.   15
Panthea How thou art changed! I dare not look on thee;
  I feel, but see thee not. I scarce endure
  The radiance of thy beauty. Some good change
  Is working in the elements, which suffer
  Thy presence thus unveiled. The Nereids[56] tell   20
  That on the day when the clear hyaline[57]
  Was cloven at thine uprise, and thou didst stand
  Within a veined shell, which floated on
  Over the calm floor of the crystal sea,
  Among the Aegean isles, and by the shores   25
  Which bear thy name – love, like the atmosphere
  Of the sun's fire filling the living world,

---

[55] *respire* rest.   [57] *hyaline* glassy, transparent sea.
[56] *Nereids* sea-nymphs, daughters of Nereus.

Burst from thee, and illumined Earth and Heaven
And the deep Ocean and the sunless caves
And all that dwells within them; till grief cast   30
Eclipse upon the soul from which it came:
Such art thou now; nor is it I alone,
Thy sister, thy companion, thine own chosen one,
But the whole world which seeks thy sympathy.
Hearest thou not sounds i' the air which speak the love   35
Of all articulate beings? Feelest thou not
The inanimate winds enamoured of thee? List!

(*Music*)

Asia Thy words are sweeter than aught else but his
    Whose echoes they are – yet all love is sweet,
Given or returned. Common as light is love,   40
And its familiar voice wearies not ever.
Like the wide Heaven, the all-sustaining air,
It makes the reptile equal to the God:
They who inspire it most are fortunate,
As I am now; but those who feel it most   45
Are happier still, after long sufferings,
As I shall soon become.

Panthea   List! Spirits speak.

Voice (*in the air, singing*)
    Life of Life! thy lips enkindle
      With their love the breath between them;
    And thy smiles before they dwindle   50
      Make the cold air fire; then screen them
    In those looks, where whoso gazes
    Faints, entangled in their mazes.

    Child of Light! thy limbs are burning
      Through the vest which seems to hide them,   55
    As the radiant lines of morning
      Through the clouds ere they divide them;
    And this atmosphere divinest
    Shrouds thee wheresoe'er thou shinest.

    Fair are others; none beholds thee,   60
      But thy voice sounds low and tender
    Like the fairest, for it folds thee
      From the sight, that liquid splendour,
    And all feel, yet see thee never,
    As I feel now, lost forever!   65

    Lamp of Earth! where'er thou movest
      Its dim shapes are clad with brightness,
    And the souls of whom thou lovest
      Walk upon the winds with lightness,

Till they fail, as I am failing,   70
Dizzy, lost, yet unbewailing!

Asia
My soul is an enchanted boat,
Which, like a sleeping swan, doth float
Upon the silver waves of thy sweet singing;
And thine doth like an angel sit   75
Beside the helm conducting it,
Whilst all the winds with melody are ringing.
It seems to float ever, forever,
Upon that many-winding river,
Between mountains, woods, abysses,   80
A paradise of wildernesses!
Till, like one in slumber bound,
Borne to the ocean, I float down, around,
Into a sea profound of ever-spreading sound.

Meanwhile thy spirit lifts its pinions   85
In music's most serene dominions,
Catching the winds that fan that happy Heaven.
And we sail on, away, afar,
Without a course, without a star,
But by the instinct of sweet music driven,   90
Till through Elysian garden islets
By thee, most beautiful of pilots,
Where never mortal pinnace glided,
The boat of my desire is guided:
Realms where the air we breathe is love,   95
Which in the winds and on the waves doth move,
Harmonizing this earth with what we feel above.

We have passed Age's icy caves,
And Manhood's dark and tossing waves,
And Youth's smooth ocean, smiling to betray: 100
Beyond the glassy gulfs we flee
Of shadow-peopled Infancy,
Through death and birth to a diviner day –
A paradise of vaulted bowers
Lit by downward-gazing flowers,   105
And watery paths that wind between
Wildernesses calm and green,
Peopled by shapes too bright to see,
And rest, having beheld – somewhat like thee,
Which walk upon the sea and chaunt melodiously!   110

ACT III, SCENE I

Heaven. Jupiter on his throne; Thetis and the other deities assembled.

Jupiter Ye congregated powers of Heaven, who share
 The glory and the strength of him ye serve,
 Rejoice! Henceforth I am omnipotent.
 All else had been subdued to me; alone
 The soul of man, like unextinguished fire,   5
 Yet burns towards Heaven with fierce reproach, and doubt,
 And lamentation, and reluctant prayer —
 Hurling up insurrection, which might make
 Our antique empire insecure, though built
 On eldest faith, and Hell's coeval,[58] fear.   10
 And though my curses through the pendulous air,
 Like snow on herbless peaks, fall flake by flake
 And cling to it;[59] though under my wrath's night
 It climb the crags of life, step after step,
 Which wound it, as ice wounds unsandalled feet,   15
 It yet remains supreme o'er misery,
 Aspiring, unrepressed, yet soon to fall.
 Even now have I begotten a strange wonder,
 That fatal child, the terror of the earth,
 Who waits but till the destined Hour arrive,   20
 Bearing from Demogorgon's vacant throne
 The dreadful might of ever-living limbs
 Which clothed that awful spirit unbeheld,
 To redescend and trample out the spark.
  Pour forth Heaven's wine, Idaean Ganymede,[60]   25
 And let it fill the daedal[61] cups like fire;
 And from the flower-inwoven soil divine
 Ye all-triumphant harmonies arise,
 As dew from earth under the twilight stars.
 Drink! Be the nectar circling through your veins   30
 The soul of joy, ye ever-living Gods,
 Till exultation burst in one wide voice
 Like music from Elysian winds!
        And thou
 Ascend beside me, veiled in the light
 Of the desire which makes thee one with me,   35
 Thetis, bright image of eternity!
 When thou didst cry, 'Insufferable might!
 God! Spare me! I sustain not the quick flames,
 The penetrating presence;[62] all my being

---

58 *coeval* contemporary.
59 *it* the soul of man, as in line 16.
60 A shepherd-boy from Mt Ida, Ganymede was
abducted to satisfy Jupiter's lust.

61 *daedal* beautifully crafted.
62 Semele was consumed by fire when tricked into
lying with Jupiter.

(Like him whom the Numidian seps did thaw   40
Into a dew with poison[63]) is dissolved,
Sinking through its foundations' – even then
Two mighty spirits, mingling, made a third
Mightier than either, which unbodied now
Between us floats, felt although unbeheld,   45
Waiting the incarnation which ascends
(Hear ye the thunder of the fiery wheels
Griding the winds?) from Demogorgon's throne.
Victory! Victory! Feel'st thou not, oh World,
The earthquake of his chariot thundering up   50
Olympus?

(The car of the Hour arrives. Demogorgon descends, and moves towards the throne of Jupiter.)

        Awful shape, what art thou? Speak!
Demogorgon Eternity. Demand no direr name.
Descend, and follow me down the abyss.
I am thy child, as thou wert Saturn's child,
Mightier than thee: and we must dwell together   55
Henceforth in darkness. Lift thy lightnings not.
The tyranny of Heaven none may retain,
Or reassume, or hold, succeeding thee;
Yet if thou wilt (as 'tis the destiny
Of trodden worms to writhe till they are dead),   60
Put forth thy might.
Jupiter   Detested prodigy!
Even thus beneath the deep Titanian prisons
I trample thee! Thou lingerest?
              Mercy! Mercy!
No pity, no release, no respite! Oh,
That thou wouldst make mine enemy my judge,   65
Even where he hangs, seared by my long revenge,
On Caucasus! He would not doom me thus.
Gentle, and just, and dreadless, is he not
The monarch of the world? What then art thou?
No refuge! No appeal!
           Sink with me then;   70
We two will sink on the wide waves of ruin,
Even as a vulture and a snake outspent
Drop, twisted in inextricable fight,
Into a shoreless sea. Let Hell unlock
Its mounded oceans of tempestuous fire,   75
And whelm on them into the bottomless void
The desolated world, and thee, and me,

---

[63] Sabellus dissolved when bitten by a seps (legendary snake) in the Numidian desert.

The conqueror and the conquered, and the wreck
Of that for which they combated.
                    Ai! Ai!
The elements obey me not. I sink   80
Dizzily down – ever, forever, down –
And, like a cloud, mine enemy above
Darkens my fall with victory! Ai! Ai!

ACT III, SCENE II

*The mouth of a great river in the island Atlantis. Ocean is discovered reclining near the shore; Apollo
stands beside him.*

    Ocean He fell, thou sayest, beneath his conqueror's frown?
    Apollo Aye, when the strife was ended which made dim
      The orb I rule, and shook the solid stars.[64]
      The terrors of his eye illumined Heaven
      With sanguine light through the thick ragged skirts   5
      Of the victorious Darkness, as he fell,
      Like the last glare of day's red agony,
      Which from a rent among the fiery clouds
      Burns far along the tempest-wrinkled deep.
    Ocean He sunk to the abyss? To the dark void?   10
    Apollo An eagle so, caught in some bursting cloud
      On Caucasus, his thunder-baffled wings
      Entangled in the whirlwind, and his eyes,
      Which gazed on the undazzling sun, now blinded
      By the white lightning, while the ponderous hail   15
      Beats on his struggling form, which sinks at length
      Prone, and the aerial ice clings over it.
    Ocean Henceforth the fields of Heaven-reflecting sea
      Which are my realm, will heave, unstained with blood,
      Beneath the uplifting winds, like plains of corn   20
      Swayed by the summer air; my streams will flow
      Round many-peopled continents, and round
      Fortunate isles; and from their glassy thrones
      Blue Proteus and his humid nymphs shall mark
      The shadow of fair ships – as mortals see   25
      The floating bark of the light-laden moon
      With that white star,[65] its sightless pilot's crest,
      Borne down the rapid sunset's ebbing sea –
      Tracking their path no more by blood and groans,
      And desolation, and the mingled voice   30
      Of slavery and command, but by the light
      Of wave-reflected flowers, and floating odours,
      And music soft, and mild, free, gentle voices,
      That sweetest music, such as spirits love.

---

[64] *orb* the sun. *solid stars* fixed stars.   [65] Venus, the Morning Star.

Apollo And I shall gaze not on the deeds which make   35
    My mind obscure with sorrow, as eclipse
    Darkens the sphere I guide; but list, I hear
    The small, clear, silver lute of the young spirit
    That sits in the morning star.
Ocean   Thou must away?
    Thy steeds will pause at even, till when farewell.   40
    The loud deep calls me home even now, to feed it
    With azure calm out of the emerald urns
    Which stand forever full beside my throne.
    Behold the Nereids under the green sea –
    Their wavering limbs borne on the wind-like streams,   45
    Their white arms lifted o'er their streaming hair
    With garlands pied and starry sea-flower crowns –
    Hastening to grace their mighty sister's joy. (*A sound of waves is heard.*)
    It is the unpastured sea hungering for calm.
    Peace, monster; I come now. Farewell.
Apollo   Farewell.   50

ACT III, SCENE III

Caucasus. Prometheus, Hercules, Ione, the Earth, Spirits, Asia, and Panthea, borne in the car with the Spirit of the Hour. Hercules unbinds Prometheus, who descends.[66]
Hercules Most glorious among spirits, thus doth strength
    To wisdom, courage, and long-suffering love,
    And thee, who art the form they animate,
    Minister like a slave.
Prometheus   Thy gentle words
    Are sweeter even than freedom long desired   5
    And long delayed.
              Asia, thou light of life,
    Shadow of beauty unbeheld; and ye,
    Fair sister nymphs, who made long years of pain
    Sweet to remember, through your love and care –
    Henceforth we will not part. There is a cave,   10
    All overgrown with trailing odorous plants
    Which curtain out the day with leaves and flowers,
    And paved with veined emerald; and a fountain
    Leaps in the midst with an awakening sound.
    From its curved roof the mountain's frozen tears,   15
    Like snow, or silver, or long diamond spires,
    Hang downward, raining forth a doubtful light;
    And there is heard the ever-moving air
    Whispering without from tree to tree, and birds

---

[66] According to legend, Hercules killed the eagle torturing Prometheus and freed him after Prometheus had made his peace with Jupiter.

And bees; and all around are mossy seats,   20
And the rough walls are clothed with long soft grass –
A simple dwelling which shall be our own,
Where we will sit and talk of time and change
As the world ebbs and flows, ourselves unchanged.
What can hide man from mutability?   25
And if ye sigh, then I will smile; and thou,
Ione, shall chant fragments of sea-music
Until I weep, when ye shall smile away
The tears she brought, which yet were sweet to shed.
We will entangle buds and flowers and beams   30
Which twinkle on the fountain's brim, and make
Strange combinations out of common things,
Like human babes in their brief innocence;
And we will search, with looks and words of love,
For hidden thoughts, each lovelier than the last,   35
Our unexhausted spirits, and, like lutes
Touched by the skill of the enamoured wind,
Weave harmonies divine, yet ever new,
From difference sweet where discord cannot be.
And hither come – sped on the charmed winds   40
Which meet from all the points of Heaven, as bees
From every flower aerial Enna feeds
At their known island-homes in Himera –
The echoes of the human world, which tell
Of the low voice of love, almost unheard,   45
And dove-eyed pity's murmured pain, and music,
Itself the echo of the heart, and all
That tempers or improves man's life, now free.
And lovely apparitions, dim at first,
Then radiant – as the mind, arising bright   50
From the embrace of beauty (whence the forms
Of which these are the phantoms) casts on them
The gathered rays which are reality –
Shall visit us, the progeny immortal
Of Painting, Sculpture, and rapt Poesy,   55
And arts, though unimagined, yet to be.
The wandering voices and the shadows these
Of all that man becomes, the mediators
Of that best worship, Love, by him and us
Given and returned; swift shapes and sounds which grow   60
More fair and soft as man grows wise and kind,
And veil by veil, evil and error fall:
Such virtue has the cave and place around. (*turning to the Spirit of the Hour*)
For thee, fair Spirit, one toil remains. Ione,
Give her that curved shell which Proteus old   65
Made Asia's nuptial boon, breathing within it
A voice to be accomplished, and which thou

Didst hide in grass under the hollow rock.

Ione Thou most desired Hour, more loved and lovely   70
　　Than all thy sisters, this is the mystic shell;
　　See the pale azure fading into silver,
　　Lining it with a soft yet glowing light –
　　Looks it not like lulled music sleeping there?

Spirit It seems in truth the fairest shell of Ocean;
　　Its sound must be at once both sweet and strange.   75

Prometheus Go, borne over the cities of mankind
　　On whirlwind-footed coursers – once again
　　Outspeed the sun around the orbed world;
　　And as thy chariot cleaves the kindling air,
　　Thou breathe into the many-folded shell,   80
　　Loosening its mighty music; it shall be
　　As thunder mingled with clear echoes. Then
　　Return, and thou shalt dwell beside our cave.
　　And thou, oh Mother Earth –

The Earth　　　　　　　　I hear, I feel;
　　Thy lips are on me, and their touch runs down   85
　　Even to the adamantine central gloom
　　Along these marble nerves – 'tis life, 'tis joy,
　　And through my withered, old, and icy frame
　　The warmth of an immortal youth shoots down,
　　Circling. Henceforth the many children fair   90
　　Folded in my sustaining arms – all plants
　　And creeping forms, and insects rainbow-winged,
　　And birds, and beasts, and fish, and human shapes,
　　Which drew disease and pain from my wan bosom,
　　Draining the poison of despair – shall take   95
　　And interchange sweet nutriment; to me
　　Shall they become like sister-antelopes
　　By one fair dam, snow-white and swift as wind,
　　Nursed among lilies near a brimming stream.
　　The dew-mists of my sunless sleep shall float   100
　　Under the stars like balm; night-folded flowers
　　Shall suck unwithering hues in their repose;
　　And men and beasts in happy dreams shall gather
　　Strength for the coming day and all its joy;
　　And death shall be the last embrace of her   105
　　Who takes the life she gave, even as a mother
　　Folding her child, says, 'Leave me not again.'

Asia Oh mother, wherefore speak the name of death?
　　Cease they to love, and move, and breathe, and speak,
　　Who die?

The Earth It would avail not to reply: 110
　　Thou art immortal, and this tongue is known
　　But to the uncommunicating dead.
　　Death is the veil which those who live call life:

They sleep, and it is lifted;[67] and meanwhile
In mild variety the seasons mild –   115
With rainbow-skirted showers, and odorous winds,
And long blue meteors cleansing the dull night,
And the life-kindling shafts of the keen sun's
All-piercing bow, and the dew-mingled rain
Of the calm moonbeams, a soft influence mild –   120
Shall clothe the forests and the fields, aye, even
The crag-built deserts of the barren deep
With ever-living leaves, and fruits, and flowers.
And thou! There is a cavern where my spirit
Was panted forth in anguish whilst thy pain   125
Made my heart mad, and those who did inhale it
Became mad too, and built a temple there,
And spoke, and were oracular, and lured
The erring nations round to mutual war
And faithless faith, such as Jove kept with thee –   130
Which breath now rises, as among tall weeds
A violet's exhalation, and it fills
With a serener light and crimson air
Intense, yet soft, the rocks and woods around;
It feeds the quick growth of the serpent vine,   135
And the dark linked ivy tangling wild,
And budding, blown, or odour-faded blooms
Which star the winds with points of coloured light
As they rain through them, and bright golden globes
Of fruit, suspended in their own green heaven,   140
And, through their veined leaves and amber stems
The flowers whose purple and translucid bowls
Stand ever mantling with aerial dew,
The drink of spirits. And it circles round,
Like the soft waving wings of noonday dreams,   145
Inspiring calm and happy thoughts like mine,
Now thou art thus restored. This cave is thine.
Arise, appear! (*A spirit rises in the likeness of a winged child.*)
          This is my torch-bearer,
Who let his lamp out in old time with gazing
On eyes from which he kindled it anew   150
With love, which is as fire, sweet daughter mine,
For such is that within thine own. Run, wayward!
And guide this company beyond the peak
Of Bacchic Nysa, maenad-haunted mountain,
And beyond Indus and its tribute rivers,   155
Trampling the torrent streams and glassy lakes
With feet unwet, unwearied, undelaying;

---

[67] Cf. 'Mont Blanc', 50: 'death is slumber'.

And up the green ravine, across the vale,
Beside the windless and crystalline pool,
Where ever lies, on unerasing waves,   160
The image of a temple, built above,
Distinct with column, arch, and architrave,
And palm-like capital, and over-wrought,
And populous with most living imagery –
Praxitelean shapes,[68] whose marble smiles   165
Fill the hushed air with everlasting love.
It is deserted now, but once it bore
Thy name, Prometheus; there the emulous youths
Bore to thy honour through the divine gloom
The lamp which was thine emblem – even as those   170
Who bear the untransmitted torch of hope
Into the grave, across the night of life,
As thou hast borne it most triumphantly
To this far goal of time. Depart – farewell.
Beside that temple is the destined cave.   175

ACT III, SCENE IV

A forest. In the background a cave. Prometheus, Asia, Panthea, Ione, and the Spirit of the Earth.

Ione Sister, it is not earthly: how it glides
Under the leaves! How on its head there burns
A light, like a green star whose emerald beams
Are twined with its fair hair! How, as it moves,
The splendour drops in flakes upon the grass!   5
Knowest thou it?

Panthea   It is the delicate spirit
That guides the earth through Heaven. From afar
The populous constellations call that light
The loveliest of the planets; and sometimes
It floats along the spray of the salt sea,   10
Or makes its chariot of a foggy cloud,
Or walks through fields or cities while men sleep,
Or o'er the mountain-tops, or down the rivers,
Or through the green waste wilderness, as now,
Wondering at all it sees. Before Jove reigned   15
It loved our sister Asia, and it came
Each leisure hour to drink the liquid light
Out of her eyes, for which it said it thirsted
As one bit by a dipsas;[69] and with her
It made its childish confidence, and told her   20
All it had known or seen, for it saw much,
Yet idly reasoned what it saw; and called her
(For whence it sprung it knew not, nor do I)

---

[68] Statues carved by Praxiteles.   [69] *dipsas* legendary poisonous snake.

'Mother, dear mother'.

The Spirit of the Earth (running to Asia)
              Mother, dearest mother;
  May I then talk with thee as I was wont?   25
  May I then hide my eyes in thy soft arms
  After thy looks have made them tired of joy?
  May I then play beside thee the long noons
  When work is none in the bright silent air?

Asia I love thee, gentlest being, and henceforth   30
  Can cherish thee unenvied; speak, I pray –
  Thy simple talk once solaced, now delights.

Spirit of the Earth Mother, I am grown wiser, though a child
  Cannot be wise like thee, within this day,
  And happier too – happier and wiser both.   35
  Thou knowest that toads, and snakes, and loathly worms,
  And venomous and malicious beasts, and boughs
  That bore ill berries in the woods, were ever
  An hindrance to my walks o'er the green world;
  And that, among the haunts of humankind,   40
  Hard-featured men, or with proud, angry looks,
  Or cold, staid gait, or false and hollow smiles,
  Or the dull sneer of self-loved ignorance,
  Or other such foul masks, with which ill thoughts
  Hide that fair being whom we spirits call man;   45
  And women too, ugliest of all things evil
  (Though fair, even in a world where thou art fair
  When good and kind, free and sincere like thee),
  When false or frowning made me sick at heart
  To pass them, though they slept, and I unseen.   50
  Well, my path lately lay through a great city
  Into the woody hills surrounding it.
  A sentinel was sleeping at the gate,
  When there was heard a sound so loud, it shook
  The towers amid the moonlight, yet more sweet   55
  Than any voice but thine, sweetest of all;
  A long, long sound, as it would never end –
  And all the inhabitants leapt suddenly
  Out of their rest, and gathered in the streets,
  Looking in wonder up to Heaven, while yet   60
  The music pealed along. I hid myself
  Within a fountain in the public square,
  Where I lay like the reflex[70] of the moon
  Seen in a wave under green leaves – and soon
  Those ugly human shapes and visages   65
  Of which I spoke as having wrought me pain,

---

[70] *reflex* reflection.

Passed floating through the air, and fading still
Into the winds that scattered them; and those
From whom they passed seemed mild and lovely forms
After some foul disguise had fallen, and all   70
Were somewhat changed, and after brief surprise
And greetings of delighted wonder, all
Went to their sleep again; and when the dawn
Came – wouldst thou think that toads, and snakes, and efts,[71]
Could e'er be beautiful? Yet so they were,   75
And that with little change of shape or hue:
All things had put their evil nature off.
I cannot tell my joy, when o'er a lake,
Upon a drooping bough with nightshade twined,
I saw two azure halcyons clinging downward   80
And thinning one bright bunch of amber berries
With quick long beaks,[72] and in the deep there lay
Those lovely forms imaged as in a sky.
So with my thoughts full of these happy changes,
We meet again, the happiest change of all.   85
Asia And never will we part, till thy chaste sister
Who guides the frozen and inconstant moon,
Will look on thy more warm and equal light
Till her heart thaw like flakes of April snow,
And love thee.
Spirit of the Earth What? As Asia loves Prometheus?   90
Asia Peace, wanton! Thou are yet not old enough.
Think ye by gazing on each other's eyes
To multiply your lovely selves, and fill
With sphered fires the interlunar air?
Spirit of the Earth Nay, mother, while my sister trims her lamp   95
'Tis hard I should go darkling.
Asia   Listen, look! (*The Spirit of the Hour enters.*)
Prometheus We feel what thou hast heard and seen – yet speak.
Spirit of the Hour Soon as the sound had ceased whose thunder filled
The abysses of the sky and the wide earth
There was a change: the impalpable thin air   100
And the all-circling sunlight were transformed,
As if the sense of love dissolved in them
Had folded itself round the sphered world.
My vision then grew clear, and I could see
Into the mysteries of the universe: 105
Dizzy as with delight I floated down;
Winnowing the lightsome air with languid plumes
My coursers sought their birthplace in the sun,
Where they henceforth will live exempt from toil,

---

[71] *efts* small lizards.
[72] In the regenerated, purified world, deadly night-shade is no longer poisonous, and kingfishers turn vegetarian.

Pasturing flowers of vegetable fire, 110
And where my moonlike car will stand within
A temple – gazed upon by Phidian forms[73]
Of thee, and Asia, and the Earth, and me,
And you fair nymphs, looking the love we feel,
In memory of the tidings it has borne – 115
Beneath a dome fretted with graven flowers,[74]
Poised on twelve columns of resplendent stone,
And open to the bright and liquid sky.
Yoked to it by an amphisbaenic snake
The likeness of those winged steeds will mock 120
The flight from which they find repose. Alas!
Whither has wandered now my partial tongue
When all remains untold which ye would hear?
As I have said, I floated to the earth:
It was, as it is still, the pain of bliss 125
To move, to breathe, to be; I wandering went
Among the haunts and dwellings of mankind,
And first was disappointed not to see
Such mighty change as I had felt within
Expressed in outward things. But soon I looked, 130
And behold! thrones were kingless, and men walked
One with the other even as spirits do –
None fawned, none trampled; hate, disdain, or fear,
Self-love or self-contempt, on human brows
No more inscribed, as o'er the gate of Hell, 135
'All hope abandon, ye who enter here';[75]
None frowned, none trembled, none with eager fear
Gazed on another's eye of cold command
Until the subject of a tyrant's will
Became, worse fate, the abject of his own, 140
Which spurred him, like an outspent horse, to death;
None wrought his lips in truth-entangling lines
Which smiled the lie his tongue disdained to speak;
None, with firm sneer, trod out in his own heart
The sparks of love and hope, till there remained 145
Those bitter ashes, a soul self-consumed,
And the wretch crept, a vampire among men,
Infecting all with his own hideous ill;
None talked that common, false, cold, hollow talk
Which makes the heart deny the 'yes' it breathes, 150
Yet question that unmeant hypocrisy
Which such a self-mistrust as has no name.

---

[73] Statues carved by Phidias.
[74] The scene described is based on the Pantheon at Rome and the Sala della Biga in the Vatican, both of which Shelley visited. The yoke of the 'biga' (my moonlike car) was a snake with a head at both ends, the amphisbaena.
[75] Dante, *Inferno*, iii. 9.

And women, too – frank, beautiful, and kind
As the free Heaven which rains fresh light and dew
On the wide earth, passed – gentle radiant forms,   155
From custom's evil taint exempt and pure,
Speaking the wisdom once they could not think,
Looking emotions once they feared to feel,
And changed to all which once they dared not be,
Yet being now, made earth like Heaven; nor pride,   160
Nor jealousy, nor envy, nor ill shame,
The bitterest of those drops of treasured gall,
Spoilt the sweet taste of the nepenthe,[76] love.

    Thrones, altars, judgement-seats and prisons (wherein,
And beside which, by wretched men were borne   165
Sceptres, tiaras, swords and chains, and tomes
Of reasoned wrong glozed on[77] by ignorance)
Were like those monstrous and barbaric shapes,
The ghosts of a no more remembered fame
Which, from their unworn obelisks, look forth   170
In triumph o'er the palaces and tombs
Of those who were their conquerors, mouldering round.
These imaged to the pride of kings and priests
A dark yet mighty faith, a power as wide
As is the world it wasted, and are now   175
But an astonishment; even so the tools
And emblems of its last captivity,
Amid the dwellings of the peopled earth,
Stand, not o'erthrown, but unregarded now.
And those foul shapes, abhorred by God and man –   180
Which, under many a name and many a form
Strange, savage, ghastly, dark and execrable,
Were Jupiter, the tyrant of the world;
And which the nations, panic-stricken, served
With blood, and hearts broken by long hope, and love   185
Dragged to his altars soiled and garlandless,
And slain amid men's unreclaiming tears,
Flattering the thing they feared, which fear was hate –
Frown, mouldering fast, o'er their abandoned shrines.
The painted veil, by those who were, called life,   190
Which mimicked, as with colours idly spread,
All men believed and hoped, is torn aside;
The loathsome mask has fallen, the man remains
Sceptreless, free, uncircumscribed – but man:
Equal, unclassed, tribeless, and nationless,   195
Exempt from awe, worship, degree; the king
Over himself; just, gentle, wise – but man.

---

[76] Grief-banishing drink.   [77] *glozed on* explained.

Passionless? No, yet free from guilt or pain,
Which were, for his will made, or suffered them;
Nor yet exempt, though ruling them like slaves,   200
From chance, and death, and mutability,
The clogs of that which else might oversoar
The loftiest star of unascended Heaven,
Pinnacled dim in the intense inane.[78]

ACT IV

Scene: a part of the forest near the Cave of Prometheus. Panthea and Ione are sleeping; they awaken gradually during the first song.

    Voice of unseen Spirits

The pale stars are gone!
For the sun, their swift shepherd,
To their folds them compelling
In the depths of the dawn,
Hastes, in meteor-eclipsing array, and they flee   5
Beyond his blue dwelling,
As fawns flee the leopard.
    But where are ye?

(A train of dark forms and shadows passes by confusedly, singing.)

Here, oh, here;
We bear the bier   10
Of the father of many a cancelled year!
Spectres we
Of the dead Hours be,
We bear Time to his tomb in eternity.

Strew, oh strew   15
Hair, not yew!
Wet the dusty pall with tears, not dew!
Be the faded flowers
Of Death's bare bowers
Spread on the corpse of the King of Hours!   20

Haste, oh haste!
As shades are chased,
Trembling, by day, from heaven's blue waste,
We melt away,
Like dissolving spray,   25
From the children of a diviner day,
With the lullaby
Of winds that die
On the bosom of their own harmony.

Ione What dark forms were they?   30

---

[78] Deep space.

Panthea

The past Hours weak and grey,
With the spoil which their toil
   Raked together
From the conquest but One could foil.

Ione Have they passed?

Panthea   They have passed;   35

They outspeeded the blast,
While 'tis said, they are fled –

Ione Whither, oh whither?

Panthea To the dark, to the past, to the dead.

Voice of unseen Spirits

Bright clouds float in Heaven,   40
Dew-stars gleam on earth,
Waves assemble on ocean –
They are gathered and driven
By the storm of delight, by the panic of glee!
They shake with emotion,   45
They dance in their mirth –
   But where are ye?

The pine boughs are singing
Old songs with new gladness,
The billows and fountains   50
Fresh music are flinging,
Like the notes of a spirit from land and from sea;
The storms mock the mountains
With the thunder of gladness –
   But where are ye?   55

Ione What charioteers are these?

Panthea   Where are their chariots?

Semichorus of Hours I

The voice of the Spirits of Air and of Earth
Has drawn back the figured curtain of sleep
Which covered our being and darkened our birth
In the deep –

A voice   In the deep?

Semichorus II   Oh, below the deep.   60

Semichorus I A hundred ages we had been kept

Cradled in visions of hate and care,
And each one who waked as his brother slept,
Found the truth –

Semichorus II   Worse than his visions were!

Semichorus I We have heard the lute of Hope in sleep;   65

We have known the voice of Love in dreams;
We have felt the wand of Power, and leap –

Semichorus II As the billows leap in the morning beams!

Chorus
  Weave the dance on the floor of the breeze,
    Pierce with song heaven's silent light,   70
  Enchant the Day that too swiftly flees,
    To check its flight ere the cave of Night.

  Once the hungry Hours were hounds
    Which chased the Day like a bleeding deer,
  And it limped and stumbled with many wounds   75
    Through the nightly dells of the desert year.

  But now, oh weave the mystic measure
    Of music and dance and shapes of light;
  Let the Hours, and the spirits of might and pleasure,
    Like the clouds and sunbeams, unite.
A voice   Unite!   80
Panthea See, where the Spirits of the human mind
  Wrapped in sweet sounds, as in bright veils, approach.
Chorus of Spirits
      We join the throng
      Of the dance and the song,
  By the whirlwind of gladness borne along –   85
      As the flying-fish leap
      From the Indian deep,
  And mix with the sea-birds, half asleep.
Chorus of Hours Whence come ye, so wild and so fleet,
  For sandals of lightning are on your feet,   90
  And your wings are soft and swift as thought,
  And your eyes are as love which is veiled not?
Chorus of Spirits
      We come from the mind
      Of humankind,
  Which was late so dusk, and obscene, and blind;   95
      Now 'tis an ocean
      Of clear emotion,
  A Heaven of serene and mighty motion;

      From that deep abyss
      Of wonder and bliss,   100
  Whose caverns are crystal palaces;
      From those skyey towers
      Where Thought's crowned powers
  Sit watching your dance, ye happy Hours;

      From the dim recesses   105
      Of woven caresses,
  Where lovers catch ye by your loose tresses;
      From the azure isles

Where sweet Wisdom smiles,
Delaying your ships with her siren wiles;   110

From the temples high
Of man's ear and eye,
Roofed over Sculpture and Poesy;
From the murmurings
Of the unsealed springs,   115
Where Science bedews her daedal wings.

Years after years,
Through blood and tears
And a thick hell of hatreds, and hopes, and fears,
We waded and flew,   120
And the islets were few
Where the bud-blighted flowers of happiness grew.

Our feet now, every palm,
Are sandalled with calm,
And the dew of our wings is a rain of balm;   125
And beyond our eyes
The human love lies
Which makes all it gazes on paradise.

Chorus of Spirits and Hours
Then weave the web of the mystic measure;
From the depths of the sky and the ends of the earth,   130
Come, swift Spirits of might and of pleasure,
Fill the dance and the music of mirth –
As the waves of a thousand streams rush by
To an ocean of splendour and harmony!

Chorus of Spirits
Our spoil is won,   135
Our task is done,
We are free to dive, or soar, or run
Beyond and around,
Or within the bound
Which clips the world with darkness round.   140

We'll pass the eyes
Of the starry skies
Into the hoar deep to colonize;
Death, Chaos, and Night,
From the sound of our flight   145
Shall flee, like mist from a tempest's might;

And Earth, Air, and Light,
And the Spirit of Might
Which drives round the stars in their fiery flight;

And Love, Thought, and Breath, 150
The powers that quell Death,
Wherever we soar shall assemble beneath;

And our singing shall build,
In the void's loose field,
A world for the Spirit of Wisdom to wield; 155
We will take our plan
From the new world of man,
And our work shall be called the Promethean.

Chorus of Hours Break the dance, and scatter the song;
Let some depart and some remain. 160
Semichorus I We, beyond Heaven, are driven along –
Semichorus II Us the enchantments of earth retain –
Semichorus I Ceaseless, and rapid, and fierce, and free,
With the Spirits which build a new earth and sea,
And a Heaven where yet Heaven could never be – 165
Semichorus II Solemn, and slow, and serene, and bright,
Leading the Day and outspeeding the Night
With the powers of a world of perfect light –
Semichorus I We whirl, singing loud, round the gathering sphere,
Till the trees, and the beasts, and the clouds appear 170
From its chaos made calm by love, not fear –
Semichorus II We encircle the oceans and mountains of earth,
And the happy forms of its death and birth
Change to the music of our sweet mirth.
Chorus of Hours and Spirits
Break the dance, and scatter the song; 175
Let some depart, and some remain;
Wherever we fly we lead along
In leashes, like starbeams, soft yet strong,
The clouds that are heavy with love's sweet rain.
Panthea Ha! They are gone!
Ione   Yet feel you no delight 180
From the past sweetness?
Panthea   As the bare green hill
When some soft cloud vanishes into rain,
Laughs with a thousand drops of sunny water
To the unpavilioned sky!
Ione   Even whilst we speak
New notes arise. What is that awful sound? 185
Panthea 'Tis the deep music of the rolling world,
Kindling within the strings of the waved air
Æolian modulations.
Ione   Listen too,
How every pause is filled with under-notes,
Clear, silver, icy, keen, awakening tones, 190

Which pierce the sense, and live within the soul,
As the sharp stars pierce winter's crystal air
And gaze upon themselves within the sea.
Panthea But see where, through two openings in the forest
Which hanging branches overcanopy,   195
And where two runnels of a rivulet,
Between the close moss, violet-inwoven,
Have made their path of melody – like sisters
Who part with sighs that they may meet in smiles,
Turning their dear disunion to an isle   200
Of lovely grief, a wood of sweet sad thoughts –
Two visions of strange radiance float upon
The ocean-like enchantment of strong sound,
Which flows intenser, keener, deeper yet
Under the ground and through the windless air.   205
Ione I see a chariot – like that thinnest boat
In which the mother of the months[79] is borne
By ebbing light into her western cave
When she upsprings from interlunar dreams –
O'er which is curved an orblike canopy   210
Of gentle darkness, and the hills and woods,
Distinctly seen through that dusk airy veil,
Regard like shapes in an enchanter's glass;
Its wheels are solid clouds, azure and gold,
Such as the genii of the thunderstorm   215
Pile on the floor of the illumined sea
When the sun rushes under it; they roll
And move and grow as with an inward wind.
Within it sits a winged infant: white
Its countenance, like the whiteness of bright snow;   220
Its plumes are as feathers of sunny frost;
Its limbs gleam white through the wind-flowing folds
Of its white robe, woof of ethereal pearl;
Its hair is white – the brightness of white light
Scattered in strings; yet its two eyes are heavens   225
Of liquid darkness, which the Deity
Within seems pouring, as a storm is poured
From jagged clouds, out of their arrowy lashes,
Tempering the cold and radiant air around
With fire that is not brightness; in its hand   230
It sways a quivering moonbeam, from whose point
A guiding power directs the chariot's prow
Over its wheeled clouds, which, as they roll
Over the grass, and flowers, and waves, wake sounds
Sweet as a singing rain of silver dew.   235
Panthea And from the other opening in the wood

---

[79]   The moon.

Rushes, with loud and whirlwind harmony,
A sphere, which is as many thousand spheres,
Solid as crystal, yet through all its mass
Flow, as through empty space, music and light: 240
Ten thousand orbs involving and involved,
Purple and azure, white, and green, and golden,
Sphere within sphere; and every space between
Peopled with unimaginable shapes,
Such as ghosts dream dwell in the lampless deep,   245
Yet each intertranspicuous;[80] and they whirl
Over each other with a thousand motions,
Upon a thousand sightless[81] axles spinning,
And, with the force of self-destroying swiftness,
Intensely, slowly, solemnly roll on,   250
Kindling with mingled sounds, and many tones,
Intelligible words and music wild.
With mighty whirl the multitudinous[82] orb
Grinds the bright brook into an azure mist
Of elemental subtlety, like light;   255
And the wild odour of the forest flowers,
The music of the living grass and air,
The emerald light of leaf-entangled beams
Round its intense yet self-conflicting speed,
Seem kneaded into one aerial mass   260
Which drowns the sense. Within the orb itself,
Pillowed upon its alabaster arms
Like to a child o'erwearied with sweet toil,
On its own folded wings and wavy hair
The Spirit of the Earth is laid asleep,   265
And you can see its little lips are moving
Amid the changing light of their own smiles,
Like one who talks of what he loves in dream –
Ione 'Tis only mocking the orb's harmony.
Panthea And from a star upon its forehead, shoot –   270
Like swords of azure fire, or golden spears
With tyrant-quelling myrtle overtwined,
Embleming Heaven and Earth united now –
Vast beams like spokes of some invisible wheel
Which whirl as the orb whirls, swifter than thought,   275
Filling the abyss with sunlike lightenings;
And perpendicular now, and now transverse,
Pierce the dark soil, and, as they pierce and pass,
Make bare the secrets of the earth's deep heart:
Infinite mines of adamant and gold,   280
Valueless[83] stones, and unimagined gems,

---

[80] They can be seen through or between each other.
[81] *sightless* invisible.
[82] *Multitudinous* thronging.
[83] *Valueless* valuable beyond price.

And caverns on crystalline columns poised
With vegetable silver overspread;
Wells of unfathomed fire, and water-springs
Whence the great sea, even as a child, is fed,   285
Whose vapours clothe earth's monarch mountain-tops
With kingly, ermine snow. The beams flash on
And make appear the melancholy ruins
Of cancelled cycles – anchors, beaks of ships,
Planks turned to marble, quivers, helms, and spears,   290
And gorgon-headed targes, and the wheels
Of scythed chariots, and the emblazonry
Of trophies, standards, and armorial beasts –
Round which Death laughed: sepulchred emblems
Of dead Destruction, ruin within ruin!   295
The wrecks beside of many a city vast,
Whose population which the earth grew over
Was mortal, but not human – see, they lie,
Their monstrous works and uncouth skeletons,
Their statues, homes and fanes; prodigious shapes   300
Huddled in grey annihilation, split,
Jammed in the hard black deep; and over these
The anatomies of unknown winged things,
And fishes which were isles of living scale,
And serpents, bony chains, twisted around   305
The iron crags, or within heaps of dust
To which the tortuous strength of their last pangs
Had crushed the iron crags; and over these
The jagged alligator, and the might
Of earth-convulsing behemoth,[84] which once   310
Were monarch beasts, and on the slimy shores
And weed-overgrown continents of earth
Increased and multiplied like summer worms
On an abandoned corpse, till the blue globe
Wrapped deluge round it like a cloak, and they   315
Yelled, gasped, and were abolished – or some God
Whose throne was in a comet, passed, and cried,
'Be not!' – and like my words they were no more.

The Earth

The joy, the triumph, the delight, the madness!
The boundless, overflowing, bursting gladness!
The vaporous exultation not to be confined!   320
  Ha! Ha! the animation of delight
  Which wraps me, like an atmosphere of light,
And bears me as a cloud is borne by its own wind!

[84] *behemoth* general expression for one of the largest
and strongest animals.

The Moon

   Brother mine, calm wanderer,   325
   Happy globe of land and air,
 Some spirit is darted like a beam from thee,
  Which penetrates my frozen frame,
  And passes with the warmth of flame,
 With love, and odour, and deep melody   330
   Through me, through me!

The Earth

 Ha! Ha! the caverns of my hollow mountains,
 My cloven fire-crags,[85] sound-exulting fountains,
 Laugh with a vast and inextinguishable laughter:
  The oceans, and the deserts, and the abysses   335
  Of the deep air's unmeasured wildernesses,
 Answer from all their clouds and billows, echoing after.

  They cry aloud as I do: 'Sceptred Curse,[86]
  Who all our green and azure universe
 Threatenedst to muffle round with black destruction, sending   340
  A solid cloud to rain hot thunderstones,
  And splinter and knead down my children's bones,
 All I bring forth, to one void mass battering and blending;

  Until each crag-like tower, and storied column,
  Palace, and obelisk, and temple solemn,   345
 My imperial mountains crowned with cloud, and snow, and fire,
  My sea-like forests, every blade and blossom
  Which finds a grave or cradle in my bosom,
 Were stamped by thy strong hate into a lifeless mire:

  How art thou sunk, withdrawn, covered, drunk up   350
  By thirsty nothing, as the brackish cup
 Drained by a desert-troop,a little drop for all;
  And from beneath, around, within, above,
  Filling thy void annihilation, love
 Burst in like light on caves cloven by the thunderball.   355

The Moon

  The snow upon my lifeless mountains
  Is loosened into living fountains,
 My solid oceans flow, and sing, and shine;
  A spirit from my heart bursts forth,
  It clothes with unexpected birth   360
 My cold bare bosom – oh, it must be thine
   On mine, on mine!

  Gazing on thee I feel, I know
  Green stalks burst forth, and bright flowers grow,

---

[85] Volcanoes.   [86] Jupiter.

And living shapes upon my bosom move;   365
   Music is in the sea and air,
   Winged clouds soar here and there,
Dark with the rain new buds are dreaming of –
     'Tis love, all love!

The Earth

   It interpenetrates my granite mass,   370
   Through tangled roots and trodden clay doth pass
Into the utmost leaves and delicatest flowers;
   Upon the winds, among the clouds 'tis spread;
   It wakes a life in the forgotten dead –
They breathe a spirit up from their obscurest bowers –   375

   And like a storm, bursting its cloudy prison
   With thunder and with whirlwind, has arisen
Out of the lampless caves of unimagined being,
   With earthquake shock and swiftness making shiver
   Thought's stagnant chaos, unremoved for ever,   380
Till hate, and fear, and pain, light-vanquished shadows, fleeing,

   Leave Man – who was a many-sided mirror
   Which could distort to many a shape of error
This true fair world of things – a sea reflecting love;
   Which over all his kind, as the sun's Heaven   385
   Gliding o'er ocean, smooth, serene, and even,
Darting from starry depths radiance and life, doth move:

   Leave Man, even as a leprous child is left
   Who follows a sick beast to some warm cleft
Of rocks, through which the might of healing springs is poured;   390
   Then when it wanders home with rosy smile,
   Unconscious, and its mother fears awhile
It is a spirit, then weeps on her child restored:

   Man, oh not men! a chain of linked thought,
   Of love and might to be divided not,   395
Compelling the elements with adamantine stress,
   As the sun rules, even with a tyrant's gaze,
   The unquiet republic of the maze
Of planets, struggling fierce toward Heaven's free wilderness:

   Man, one harmonious soul of many a soul,   400
   Whose nature is its own divine control,
Where all things flow to all, as rivers to the sea;
   Familiar acts are beautiful through love;
   Labour, and Pain, and Grief, in life's green grove
Sport like tame beasts – none knew how gentle they could be!   405

His will – with all mean passions, bad delights,
  And selfish cares, its trembling satellites,
A spirit ill to guide, but mighty to obey –
  Is as a tempest-winged ship, whose helm
  Love rules through waves which dare not overwhelm,   410
Forcing life's wildest shores to own its sovereign sway:

  All things confess his strength. Through the cold mass
  Of marble and of colour his dreams pass –
Bright threads whence mothers weave the robes their children wear;
  Language is a perpetual Orphic song,[87]   415
  Which rules with daedal harmony a throng
Of thoughts and forms, which else senseless and shapeless were:

  The lightning is his slave; Heaven's utmost deep
  Gives up her stars, and like a flock of sheep
They pass before his eye, are numbered, and roll on!   420
  The tempest is his steed, he strides the air;
  And the abyss shouts from her depth laid bare,
'Heaven, hast thou secrets? Man unveils me; I have none.'

The Moon
  The shadow of white Death has passed
  From my path in heaven at last,   425
A clinging shroud of solid frost and sleep;
  And through my newly-woven bowers
  Wander happy paramours
Less mighty, but as mild as those who keep
  Thy vales more deep.   430

The Earth
  As the dissolving warmth of dawn may fold
  A half-unfrozen dew-globe, green and gold
And crystalline, till it becomes a winged mist,
  And wanders up the vault of the blue day,
  Outlives the noon, and on the sun's last ray   435
Hangs o'er the sea, a fleece of fire and amethyst –

The Moon
  Thou art folded, thou art lying
  In the light which is undying
Of thine own joy, and Heaven's smile divine;
  All suns and constellations shower   440
  On thee a light, a life, a power
Which doth array thy sphere; thou pourest thine
  On mine, on mine!

---

[87] i.e. it governs our morals and actions. Orpheus tamed wild beasts, and stopped the tortures of Hades with his music.

The Earth

I spin beneath my pyramid of night,
Which points into the heavens, dreaming delight,   445
Murmuring victorious joy in my enchanted sleep —
As a youth lulled in love-dreams, faintly sighing,
Under the shadow of his beauty lying,[88]
Which round his rest a watch of light and warmth doth keep.

The Moon

As in the soft and sweet eclipse
When soul meets soul on lovers' lips,   450
High hearts are calm, and brightest eyes are dull —
So when thy shadow falls on me,
Then am I mute and still, by thee
Covered; of thy love, Orb most beautiful,   455
Full, oh too full!
Thou art speeding round the sun,
Brightest world of many a one,
Green and azure sphere, which shinest
With a light which is divinest   460
Among all the lamps of Heaven
To whom life and light is given;
I, thy crystal paramour
Borne beside thee by a power
Like the polar paradise,   465
Magnet-like, of lovers' eyes;
I, a most enamoured maiden,
Whose weak brain is overladen
With the pleasure of her love,
Maniac-like around thee move,   470
Gazing, an insatiate bride,
On thy form from every side
Like a mænad round the cup
Which Agave lifted up
In the weird Cadmaean forest.[89]   475
Brother, wheresoe'er thou soarest
I must hurry, whirl and follow
Through the heavens wide and hollow,
Sheltered, by the warm embrace
Of thy soul, from hungry space;   480
Drinking from thy sense and sight
Beauty, majesty, and might,
As a lover or chameleon
Grows like what it looks upon;
As a violet's gentle eye   485
Gazes on the azure sky

---

[88] The youth lies under the halo ('shadow') cast by the light of his beauty into the air above him.

[89] Agave, daughter of Cadmus, became a maenad and killed her own son, Pentheus.

Until its hue grows like what it beholds;
   As a grey and watery mist
   Glows like solid amethyst
Athwart the western mountain it enfolds,   490
   When the sunset sleeps
     Upon its snow –

The Earth
   And the weak day weeps
     That it should be so.
Oh gentle Moon, the voice of thy delight   495
Falls on me like thy clear and tender light
Soothing the seaman, borne the summer night
   Through isles forever calm;
Oh gentle Moon, thy crystal accents pierce
The caverns of my pride's deep universe,   500
Charming the tiger joy, whose tramplings fierce
   Made wounds which need thy balm.

Panthea I rise as from a bath of sparkling water,
   A bath of azure light, among dark rocks,
   Out of the stream of sound.
Ione   Ah me! sweet sister,   505
The stream of sound has ebbed away from us,
And you pretend to rise out of its wave
Because your words fall like the clear soft dew
Shaken from a bathing wood-nymph's limbs and hair.

Panthea Peace, peace! A mighty Power, which is as darkness,   510
   Is rising out of Earth, and from the sky
   Is showered like night, and from within the air
   Bursts, like eclipse which had been gathered up
   Into the pores of sunlight: the bright visions,
   Wherein the singing spirits rode and shone,   515
   Gleam like pale meteors through a watery night.
Ione There is a sense of words upon mine ear –
Panthea A universal sound like words – oh list!

Demogorgon
   Thou Earth, calm empire of a happy soul,
     Sphere of divinest shapes and harmonies;   520
   Beautiful orb! gathering as thou dost roll
     The love which paves thy path along the skies:
The Earth I hear! I am as a drop of dew that dies.

Demogorgon
   Thou Moon, which gazest on the nightly Earth
     With wonder, as it gazes upon thee,   525
   Whilst each to men, and beasts, and the swift birth
     Of birds, is beauty, love, calm, harmony:
The Moon I hear! I am a leaf shaken by thee.

Demogorgon
   Ye kings of suns and stars, Daemons and Gods,

Ethereal Dominations, who possess   530
Elysian, windless, fortunate abodes
Beyond Heaven's constellated wilderness:
A Voice (from above)
Our great Republic hears: we are blessed, and bless.
Demogorgon
Ye happy dead, whom beams of brightest verse
   Are clouds to hide, not colours to portray,   535
Whether your nature is that universe
   Which once ye saw and suffered –
A Voice (from beneath)
                                    Or as they
Whom we have left, we change and pass away.
Demogorgon
Ye elemental Genii, who have homes
   From man's high mind even to the central stone   540
Of sullen lead; from Heaven's star-fretted domes
   To the dull weed some sea-worm battens on:
A confused Voice
We hear: thy words waken Oblivion.
Demogorgon
Spirits, whose homes are flesh; ye beasts and birds;
   Ye worms and fish; ye living leaves and buds;   545
Lightning and wind; and ye untameable herds,
   Meteors and mists, which throng air's solitudes:
A Voice
Thy voice to us is wind among still woods.
Demogorgon
Man, who wert once a despot and a slave;
   A dupe and a deceiver; a decay;   550
A traveller from the cradle to the grave
   Through the dim night of this immortal day:
All Speak: thy strong words may never pass away.
Demogorgon This is the day, which down the void abysm
   At the Earth-born's spell yawns for Heaven's despotism,   555
   And Conquest is dragged captive through the deep:
Love, from its awful throne of patient power
In the wise heart, from the last giddy hour
   Of dread endurance, from the slippery, steep,
And narrow verge of crag-like agony, springs   560
And folds over the world its healing wings.
Gentleness, Virtue, Wisdom, and Endurance:
These are the seals of that most firm assurance
   Which bars the pit over Destruction's strength;
And if, with infirm hand, Eternity,   565
Mother of many acts and hours, should free
   The serpent that would clasp her with his length,

These are the spells by which to reassume
An empire o'er the disentangled Doom.

To suffer woes which Hope thinks infinite;   570
To forgive wrongs darker than death or night;
  To defy Power which seems omnipotent;
To love, and bear; to hope, till Hope creates
From its own wreck the thing it contemplates;
  Neither to change, nor falter, nor repent: 575
This, like thy glory, Titan, is to be
Good, great and joyous, beautiful and free;
This is alone Life, Joy, Empire, and Victory.

The Mask of Anarchy. Written on the Occasion of the Massacre at Manchester[1] (composed 5–23 September 1819; edited from MS)

As I lay asleep in Italy[2]
There came a voice from over the Sea,
And with great power it forth led me
To walk in the visions of Poesy.

I met Murder on the way –   5
He had a mask like Castlereagh[3] –
Very smooth he looked, yet grim;
Seven bloodhounds followed him.[4]

All were fat; and well they might
Be in admirable plight,   10
For one by one, and two by two,
He tossed them human hearts to chew,
Which from his wide cloak he drew.

Next came Fraud, and he had on,
Like Eldon,[5] an ermined gown;   15
His big tears, for he wept well,
Turned to millstones as they fell.

THE MASK OF ANARCHY. WRITTEN ON THE OCCASION OF THE MASSACRE AT MANCHESTER
[1] On 16 Aug. 1819, in St Peter's Field, Manchester, a large public meeting was dispersed by dragoon guards, with a brutality that left six people dead and 80 wounded.
[2] Shelley was in Leghorn when he heard of the Peterloo Massacre, 'and the torrent of my indignation has not yet done boiling in my veins', as he told Charles Ollier on 5 Sept. 1819 (Jones, ii. 117).

[3] Robert Stewart, Viscount Castlereagh, Tory Foreign Secretary.
[4] In 1815, Britain joined an alliance with seven other nations (Austria, France, Russia, Prussia, Portugal, Spain, and Sweden) in an agreement to postpone final abolition of the slave-trade.
[5] John Scott, Baron Eldon, Lord Chancellor, who was responsible for depriving Shelley of access to his children by Harriet Westbrook.

And the little children, who
Round his feet played to and fro,
Thinking every tear a gem,   20
Had their brains knocked out by them.

Clothed with the Bible, as with light,
And the shadows of the night,
Like Sidmouth,[6] next Hypocrisy
On a crocodile rode by.   25

And many more Destructions played
In this ghastly masquerade,
All disguised, even to the eyes,
Like Bishops, lawyers, peers, or spies.

Last came Anarchy: he rode   30
On a white horse, splashed with blood;
He was pale even to the lips,
Like Death in the Apocalypse.

And he wore a kingly crown,
And in his grasp a sceptre shone;   35
On his brow this mark I saw —
'I am God, and King, and Law.'

With a pace stately and fast,
Over English land he passed,
Trampling to a mire of blood   40
The adoring multitude.

And a mighty troop around,
With their trampling shook the ground,
Waving each a blood sword,
For the service of their Lord.   45

And with glorious triumph, they
Rode through England proud and gay,
Drunk as with intoxication
Of the wine of desolation.

O'er fields and towns, from sea to sea,   50
Passed the Pageant swift and free,
Tearing up, and trampling down,
Till they came to London town.

And each dweller, panic-stricken,
Felt his heart with terror sicken   55

Hearing the tempestuous cry
Of the triumph of Anarchy.

For with pomp to meet him came
Clothed in arms like blood and flame,
The hired murderers, who did sing   60
'Thou art God, and Law, and King.

We have waited, weak and lone,
For thy coming, Mighty One!
Our purses are empty, our swords are cold,
Give us glory, and blood, and gold.'   65

Lawyers and priests, a motley crowd,
To the earth their pale brows bowed;
Like a bad prayer, not overloud,
Whispering, 'Thou art Law and God.'

Then all cried with one accord,   70
'Thou art King, and God, and Lord;
Anarchy, to thee we bow,
By thy name made holy now!'

And Anarchy, the Skeleton,
Bowed and grinned to everyone,   75
As well as if his education
Had cost ten millions to the nation.

For he knew the Palaces
Of our Kings were rightly his;
His the sceptre, crown, and globe,   80
And the gold-inwoven robe.

So he sent his slaves before
To seize upon the Bank and Tower,[7]
And was proceeding with intent
To meet his pensioned Parliament;   85

When one fled past, a maniac maid,
And her name was Hope, she said;
But she looked more like Despair,
And she cried out in the air:

'My father Time is weak and grey   90
With waiting for a better day;

---

[7]   The Bank of England and the Tower of London.

See how idiot-like he stands,
Fumbling with his palsied hands!

He has had child after child
And the dust of death is piled
Over everyone but me –   95
Misery, oh, misery!'

Then she lay down in the street,
Right before the horses' feet,
Expecting, with a patient eye,
Murder, Fraud and Anarchy.   100

When between her and her foes
A mist, a light, an image rose,
Small at first, and weak, and frail,
Like the vapour of a vale;   105

Till as clouds grow on the blast,
Like tower-crowned giants striding fast,
And glare with lightnings as they fly,
And speak in thunder to the sky,

It grew – a Shape arrayed in mail   110
Brighter than the viper's scale,
And upborne on wings whose grain
Was as the light of sunny rain.

On its helm, seen far away,
A planet, like the morning's, lay;   115
And those plumes its light rained through
Like a shower of crimson dew.

With step as soft as wind it passed
O'er the heads of men – so fast
That they knew the presence there,   120
And looked – and all was empty air.

As flowers beneath May's footstep waken,
As stars from night's loose hair are shaken,
As waves arise when loud winds call,
Thoughts sprung where'er that step did fall.   125

And the prostrate multitude
Looked – and ankle-deep in blood,
Hope, that maiden most serene,
Was walking with a quiet mien.

And Anarchy, the ghastly birth,   130
Lay dead earth upon the earth;

The Horse of Death, tameless as wind,
Fled, and with his hoofs did grind
To dust the murderers thronged behind.

A rushing light of clouds and splendour,   135
A sense awakening and yet tender,
Was heard and felt – and at its close
These words of joy and fear arose

(As if their own indignant Earth
Which gave the sons of England birth   140
Had felt their blood upon her brow,
And shuddering with a mother's throe

Had turned every drop of blood
By which her face had been bedewed
To an accent unwithstood;   145
As if her heart had cried aloud):

'Men of England, heirs of Glory,
Heroes of unwritten story,
Nurslings of one mighty Mother,
Hopes of her, and one another,   150

Rise like lions after slumber
In unvanquishable number,
Shake your chains to Earth like dew
Which in sleep had fallen on you –
Ye are many; they are few.   155

What is Freedom? Ye can tell
That which slavery is, too well –
For its very name has grown
To an echo of your own.

'Tis to work and have such pay   160
As just keeps life from day to day
In your limbs, as in a cell
For the tyrants' use to dwell.

So that ye for them are made
Loom, and plough, and sword, and spade,   165
With or without your own will bent
To their defence and nourishment.

'Tis to see your children weak
With their mothers pine and peak,[8]

---

[8] *pine and peak* wasting away.

When the winter winds are bleak –   170
They are dying whilst I speak.

'Tis to hunger for such diet
As the rich man in his riot
Casts to the fat dogs that lie
Surfeiting beneath his eye.   175

'Tis to let the Ghost of Gold
Take from toil a thousandfold –
More than ere its substance could
In the tyrannies of old.

Paper coin – that forgery   180
Of the title-deeds, which ye
Hold to something of the worth
Of the inheritance of Earth.

'Tis to be a slave in soul
And to hold no strong control   185
Over your own wills, but be
All that others make of ye.

And at length when ye complain
With a murmur weak and vain,
'Tis to see the Tyrant's crew   190
Ride over your wives and you –
Blood is on the grass like dew.

Then it is to feel revenge
Fiercely thirsting to exchange
Blood for blood and wrong for wrong –   195
Do not thus when ye are strong.

Birds find rest in narrow nest
When weary of their winged quest;
Beasts find fare in woody lair
When storm and snow are in the air.   200

Asses, swine, have litter spread
And with fitting food are fed;
All things have a home but one –
Thou, oh, Englishman, hast none!

This is slavery – savage men   205
Or wild beasts within a den
Would endure not as ye do;
But such ills they never knew.

What art thou Freedom? Oh, could slaves
Answer from their living graves 210
This demand, tyrants would flee
Like a dream's dim imagery.

Thou art not, as impostors say,
A shadow soon to pass away,
A superstition, and a name 215
Echoing from the cave of Fame.

For the labourer thou art bread,
And a comely table spread
From his daily labour come
To a neat and happy home. 220

Thou art clothes, and fire, and food,
For the trampled multitude;
No – in countries that are free
Such starvation cannot be
As in England now we see. 225

To the rich thou art a check,
When his foot is on the neck
Of his victim, thou dost make
That he treads upon a snake.

Thou art Justice; ne'er for gold 230
May thy righteous laws be sold
As laws are in England – thou
Shieldst alike the high and low.

Thou art Wisdom – Freemen never
Dream that God will damn for ever 235
All who think those things untrue
Of which Priests make such ado.

Thou art Peace – never by thee
Would blood and treasure wasted be,
As tyrants wasted them, when all 240
Leagued to quench thy flame in Gaul.[9]

What if English toil and blood
Was poured forth, even as a flood?
It availed, oh Liberty!
To dim, but not extinguish thee. 245

---

9   *Gaul* Revolutionary France.

Thou art Love – the rich have kissed
Thy feet, and like him following Christ,
Give their substance to the free
And through the rough world follow thee;

Or turn their wealth to arms, and make
War for thy beloved sake
On wealth, and war, and fraud – whence they
Drew the power which is their prey.

Science, Poetry, and Thought
Are thy lamps; they make the lot
Of the dwellers in a cot
So serene, they curse it not.

Spirit, Patience, Gentleness,
All that can adorn and bless
Art thou – let deeds, not words, express
Thine exceeding loveliness.

Let a great Assembly be
Of the fearless and the free
On some spot of English ground
Where the plains stretch wide around.

Let the blue sky overhead
The green earth on which ye tread,
All that must eternal be
Witness the solemnity.

From the corners uttermost
Of the bounds of English coast;
From every hut, village and town
Where those who live and suffer moan
For others' misery or their own;

From the workhouse and the prison
Where pale as corpses newly risen,
Women, children, young and old,
Groan for pain, and weep for cold;

From the haunts of daily life
Where is waged the daily strife
With common wants and common cares
Which sows the human heart with tares;

Lastly from the palaces
Where the murmur of distress

Echoes, like the distant sound   285
Of a wind alive around,

Those prison halls of wealth and fashion,
Where some few feel such compassion
For those who groan, and toil, and wail
As must make their brethren pale –   290

Ye who suffer woes untold,
Or to feel, or to behold
Your lost country bought and sold
With a price of blood and gold –

Let a vast Assembly be,   295
And with great solemnity
Declare with measured words that ye
Are, as God has made ye, free.

Be your strong and simple words
Keen to wound as sharpened swords,   300
And wide as targes[10] let them be
With their shade to cover ye.

Let the tyrants pour around
With a quick and startling sound,
Like the loosening of a sea,   305
Troops of armed emblazonry.

Let the charged artillery drive
Till the dead air seems alive
With the clash of clanging wheels,
And the tramp of horses' heels.   310

Let the fixed bayonet
Gleam with sharp desire to wet
Its bright point in English blood,
Looking keen as one for food.

Let the horsemen's scimitars   315
Wheel and flash, like sphereless stars
Thirsting to eclipse their burning
In a sea of death and mourning.

Stand ye calm and resolute,
Like a forest close and mute,   320

---

[10] *targes* shields.

With folded arms and looks which are
Weapons of an unvanquished war;

And let Panic, who outspeeds
The career of armed steeds
Pass, a disregarded shade   325
Through your phalanx undismayed.

Let the laws of your own land,
Good or ill, between ye stand
Hand to hand, and foot to foot,
Arbiters of the dispute,   330

The old laws of England – they
Whose reverend heads with age are grey,
Children of a wiser day;
And whose solemn voice must be
Thine own echo – Liberty!   335

On those who first should violate
Such sacred heralds in their state,
Rest the blood that must ensue,
And it will not rest on you.

And if then the tyrants dare,   340
Let them ride among you there,
Slash, and stab, and maim, and hew –
What they like, that let them do.

With folded arms and steady eyes,
And little fear, and less surprise,   345
Look upon them as they slay,
Till their rage has died away.

Then they will return with shame
To the place from which they came,
And the blood thus shed will speak   350
In hot blushes on their cheek.

Every woman in the land
Will point at them as they stand –
They will hardly dare to greet
Their acquaintance in the Street.   355

And the bold, true warriors
Who have hugged Danger in wars
Will turn to those who would be free,
Ashamed of such base company.

And that slaughter to the nation 360
Shall steam up like inspiration,
Eloquent, oracular –
A volcano heard afar.

And these words shall then become
Like oppression's thundered doom 365
Ringing through each heart and brain,
Heard again – again – again.

Rise like lions after slumber
In unvanquishable number;
Shake your chains to earth like dew 370
Which in sleep had fallen on you –
Ye are many, they are few.'

From Prometheus Unbound (1820)

To a Skylark (composed late June 1820)

Hail to thee, blithe spirit!
  Bird thou never wert –
That from heaven, or near it,
  Pourest thy full heart
In profuse strains of unpremeditated art. 5

Higher still and higher
  From the earth thou springest
Like a cloud of fire;
  The blue deep thou wingest,
And singing still dost soar, and soaring ever singest. 10

In the golden lightning
  Of the sunken sun
O'er which clouds are brightning,
  Thou dost float and run
Like an unbodied joy whose race is just begun. 15

The pale purple even
  Melts around thy flight;
Like a star of heaven
  In the broad daylight
Thou art unseen – but yet I hear thy shrill delight, 20

Keen as are the arrows
  Of that silver sphere,
Whose intense lamp narrows
  In the white dawn clear,
Until we hardly see – we feel that it is there. 25

All the earth and air
   With thy voice is loud,
As when night is bare
   From one lonely cloud
The moon rains out her beams – and heaven is overflowed.   30

   What thou art we know not;
      What is most like thee?
From rainbow clouds there flow not
     Drops so bright to see
As from thy presence showers a rain of melody.   35

   Like a poet hidden
     In the light of thought,
Singing hymns unbidden,
     Till the world is wrought
To sympathy with hopes and fears it heeded not;   40

   Like a high-born maiden
     In a palace-tower,
Soothing her love-laden
     Soul in secret hour,
With music sweet as love, which overflows her bower;   45

   Like a glow-worm golden
     In a dell of dew,
Scattering unbeholden
     Its aerial hue
Among the flowers and grass which screen it from the view;   50

   Like a rose embowered
     In its own green leaves,
By warm winds deflowered
     Till the scent it gives
Makes faint with too much sweet these heavy-winged thieves;   55

   Sound of vernal showers
     On the twinkling grass,
Rain-awakened flowers,
     All that ever was
Joyous and clear and fresh, thy music doth surpass.   60

   Teach us, sprite or bird,
     What sweet thoughts are thine;
I have never heard
     Praise of love or wine
That panted forth a flood of rapture so divine: 65

Chorus Hymeneal[1]
   Or triumphal chaunt
Matched with thine would be all
   But an empty vaunt,
A thing wherein we feel there is some hidden want.   70

What objects are the fountains
   Of thy happy strain?
What fields or waves or mountains?
   What shapes of sky or plain?
What love of thine own kind? What ignorance of pain?   75

With thy clear keen joyance
   Languor cannot be –
Shadow of annoyance
   Never came near thee;
Thou lovest, but ne'er knew love's sad satiety.   80

Waking or asleep,
   Thou of death must deem
Things more true and deep
   Than we mortals dream,
Or how could thy notes flow in such a crystal stream?   85

We look before and after,
   And pine for what is not;
Our sincerest laughter
   With some pain is fraught –
Our sweetest songs are those that tell of saddest thought.   90

Yet if we could scorn
   Hate and pride and fear;
If we were things born
   Not to shed a tear,
I know not how thy joy we ever should come near.   95

Better than all measures
   Of delightful sound;
Better than all treasures
   That in books are found –
Thy skill to poet were, thou scorner of the ground!   100

Teach me half the gladness
   That thy brain must know,
Such harmonious madness

To a Skylark
[1] *Chorus Hymeneal* wedding-song.

From my lips would flow
The world should listen then, as I am listening now.   105

A Defence of Poetry; or, Remarks Suggested by an Essay Entitled 'The Four Ages of Poetry' (extracts) (composed February–March 1821; first published 1840; edited from MS)

According to one mode of regarding those two classes of mental action which are called reason and imagination, the former may be considered as mind contemplating the relations borne by one thought to another, however produced; and the latter, as mind acting upon those thoughts so as to colour them with its own light, and composing from them, as from elements, other thoughts, each containing within itself the principle of its own integrity. The one is the *τὸ ποιεῖν*,[1] or the principle of synthesis, and has for its objects those forms which are common to universal nature and existence itself; the other is the *τὸ λογίζειν*,[2] or principle of analysis, and its action regards the relations of things simply as relations, considering thoughts not in their integral unity but as the algebraical representations which conduct to certain general results. Reason is the enumeration of quantities already known; imagination the perception of the value of those quantities, both separately and as a whole. Reason respects the differences, and imagination the similitudes of things. Reason is to imagination as the instrument to the agent, as the body to the spirit, as the shadow to the substance.

Poetry, in a general sense, may be defined to be 'the expression of the imagination'; and poetry is connate with the origin of man. Man is an instrument over which a series of external and internal impressions are driven, like the alternations of an ever-changing wind over an Aeolian lyre, which move it, by their motion, to ever-changing melody. But there is a principle within the human being (and perhaps within all sentient beings) which acts otherwise than in the lyre, and produces not melody alone, but harmony, by an internal adjustment of the sounds or motions thus excited to the impressions which excite them. It is as if the lyre could accommodate its chords to the motions of that which strikes them, in a determined proportion of sound – even as the musician can accommodate his voice to the sound of the lyre. A child at play by itself will express its delight by its voice and motions, and every inflection of tone and every gesture will bear exact relation to a corresponding antitype in the pleasurable impressions which awakened it. It will be the reflected image of that impression – and as the lyre trembles and sounds after the wind has died away, so the child seeks, by prolonging in its voice and motions the duration of the effect, to prolong also a consciousness of the cause. In relation to the objects which delight a child, these expressions are what poetry is to higher objects.

The savage (for the savage is to ages what the child is to years) expresses the emotions produced in him by surrounding objects in a similar manner – and language and gesture, together with plastic or pictorial imitation, become the image of the combined effect of those objects, and of his apprehension of them. Man in society, with all his passions and his pleasures, next becomes the object of the passions and

---

A DEFENCE OF POETRY
[1] 'making something'.

[2] 'discussing its structure'.

pleasures of man; an additional class of emotions produces an augmented treasure of expressions; and language, gesture, and the imitative arts become at once the representation and the medium, the pencil and the picture, the chisel and the statue, the chord and the harmony. The social sympathies (or those laws from which as from its elements society results) begin to develop themselves from the moment that two human beings coexist; the future is contained within the present as the plant within the seed; and equality, diversity, unity, contrast, mutual dependence, become the principles alone capable of affording the motives according to which the will of a social being is determined to action (inasmuch as he is social), and constitute pleasure in sensation, virtue in sentiment, beauty in art, truth in reasoning, and love in the intercourse of kind. Hence men, even in the infancy of society, observe a certain order in their words and actions distinct from that of the objects and the impressions represented by them, all expression being subject to the laws of that from which it proceeds.

But let us dismiss those more general considerations which might involve an enquiry into the principles of society itself, and restrict our view to the manner in which the imagination is expressed upon its forms.

In the youth of the world, men dance and sing and imitate natural objects, observing in these actions (as in all others) a certain rhythm or order. And although all men observe a similar, they observe not the same order in the motions of the dance, in the melody of the song, in the combinations of language, in the series of their imitations of natural objects. For there is a certain order or rhythm belonging to each of these classes of mimetic representation, from which the hearer and the spectator receive an intenser and a purer pleasure than from any other. The sense of an approximation to this order has been called taste by modern writers. Every man in the infancy of art observes an order which approximates more or less closely to that from which this highest delight results. But the diversity is not sufficiently marked as that its gradations should be sensible, except in those instances where the predominance of this faculty of approximation to the beautiful (for so we may be permitted to name the relation between this highest pleasure and its cause) is very great. Those in whom it exists in excess are poets, in the most universal sense of the word – and the pleasure resulting from the manner in which they express the influence of society or nature upon their own minds, communicates itself to others, and gathers a sort of reduplication from that community. Their language is vitally metaphorical; that is, it marks the before unapprehended relations of things, and perpetuates their apprehension, until the words which represent them become through time signs for portions or classes of thoughts, instead of pictures of integral thoughts; and then if no new poets should arise to create afresh the associations which have been thus disorganized, language will be dead to all the nobler purposes of human intercourse.

These similitudes or relations are finely said by Lord Bacon to be 'the same footsteps of nature impressed upon the various subjects of the world'[3] – and he considers the faculty which perceives them as the storehouse of axioms common to all knowledge. In the infancy of society every author is necessarily a poet, because language itself is poetry; and to be a poet is to apprehend the true and the beautiful, in a word the good which exists in the relation subsisting first between existence and perception, and

---

[3] *Of the Advancement of Learning* (1605), Book III, ch. 1.

secondly between perception and expression. Every original language near to its source is in itself the chaos of a cyclic poem: the copiousness of lexicography and the distinctions of grammar are the works of a later age, and are merely the catalogue and the form of the creations of poetry.

But poets, or those who imagine and express this indestructible order, are not only the authors of language and of music, of the dance and architecture and statuary and painting; they are the institutors of laws, and the founders of civil society, and the inventors of the arts of life, and the teachers who draw into a certain propinquity with the beautiful and the true that partial apprehension of the agencies of the invisible world which is called religion. Hence all original religions are allegorical, or susceptible of allegory, and like Janus have a double face of false and true. Poets, according to the circumstances of the age and nation in which they appeared, were called in the earlier epochs of the world legislators or prophets. A poet essentially comprises and unites both these characters. For he not only beholds intensely the present as it is, and discovers those laws according to which present things ought to be ordered, but he beholds the future in the present, and his thoughts are the germs of the flower and the fruit of latest time. Not that I assert poets to be prophets in the gross sense of the word, or that they can foretell the form as surely as they foreknow the spirit of events – such is the pretence of superstition which would make poetry an attribute of prophecy, rather than prophecy an attribute of poetry.

A poet participates in the eternal, the infinite, and the one; as far as relates to his conceptions, time and place and number are not. The grammatical forms which express the moods of time, and the difference of persons and the distinction of place are convertible with respect to the highest poetry without injuring it as poetry, and the choruses of Aeschylus, and the Book of Job, and Dante's *Paradise* would afford, more than any other writings, examples of this fact, if the limits of this paper did not forbid citation. The creations of sculpture, painting, and music, are illustrations still more decisive.

Language, colour, form, and religious and civil habits of action are all the instruments and the materials of poetry; they may be called poetry by that figure of speech which considers the effect as a synonym of the cause. But poetry in a more restricted sense expresses those arrangements of language, and especially metrical language, which are created by that imperial faculty whose throne is curtained within the invisible nature of man. And this springs from the nature itself of language, which is a more direct representation of the actions and passions of our internal being, and is susceptible of more various and delicate combinations, than colour, form, or motion, and is more plastic and obedient to the control of that faculty of which it is the creation. For language is arbitrarily produced by the imagination and has relation to thoughts alone; but all other materials, instruments and conditions of art, have relations among each other which limit and interpose between conception and expression. The former is as a mirror which reflects, the latter as a cloud which enfeebles, the light of which both are mediums of communication. Hence the fame of sculptors, painters and musicians (although the intrinsic powers of the great masters of these arts may yield in no degree to that of those who have employed language as the hieroglyphic of their thoughts) has never equalled that of poets in the restricted sense of the term, as two performers of equal skill will produce unequal effects from a guitar and a harp. The fame of legislators and founders of religions (so long as their institutions last) alone seems to exceed that of poets in the restricted sense – but it can scarcely be a question whether, if we deduct the celebrity which their flattery of the gross opinions of the vulgar usually conciliates, together with that which belonged to them in their higher character of poets, any excess will remain.

We have thus circumscribed the word 'poetry' within the limits of that art which is the most familiar and the most perfect expression of the faculty itself. It is necessary however to make the circle still narrower, and to determine the distinction between measured and unmeasured language, for the popular division into prose and verse is inadmissible in accurate philosophy.

Sounds as well as thoughts have relation both between each other and towards that which they represent, and a perception of the order of those relations has always been found connected with a perception of the order of the relations of thoughts. Hence the language of poets has ever affected a certain uniform and harmonious recurrence of sound, without which it were not poetry, and which is scarcely less indispensable to the communication of its influence than the words themselves, without reference to that peculiar order. Hence the vanity of translation: it were as wise to cast a violet into a crucible that you might discover the formal principle of its colour and odour, as seek to transfuse from one language into another the creations of a poet. The plant must spring again from its seed or it will bear no flower – and this is the burden of the curse of Babel.

An observation of the regular mode of the recurrence of this harmony in the language of poetical minds, together with its relation to music, produced metre, or a certain system of traditional forms of harmony and language. Yet it is by no means essential that a poet should accommodate his language to this traditional form, so that the harmony which is its spirit be observed. The practice is indeed convenient and popular, and to be preferred, especially in such composition as includes much action: but every great poet must inevitably innovate upon the example of his predecessors in the exact structure of his peculiar versification.

The distinction between poets and prose writers is a vulgar error. The distinction between philosophers and poets has been anticipated. Plato was essentially a poet – the truth and splendour of his imagery and the melody of his language is the most intense that it is possible to conceive. He rejected the measure of the epic, dramatic, and lyrical forms, because he sought to kindle a harmony in thoughts divested of shape and action, and he forbore to invent any regular plan of rhythm which would include, under determinate forms, the varied pauses of his style. Cicero[4] sought to imitate the cadence of his periods but with little success. Lord Bacon was a poet.[5] His language has a sweet and majestic rhythm which satisfies the sense no less than the almost superhuman wisdom of his philosophy satisfies the intellect; it is a strain which distends, and then bursts the circumference of the reader's mind, and pours itself forth together with it into the universal element with which it has perpetual sympathy. All the authors of revolutions in opinion are not only necessarily poets as they are inventors, nor even as their words unveil the permanent analogy of things by images which participate in the life of truth – but as their periods are harmonious and rhythmical and contain in themselves the elements of verse, being the echo of the

---

4   Marcus Tullius Cicero (106–43 BC), Roman statesman and man of letters.
5   'See the Filium Labyrinthi, and the Essay on
Death particularly' (Shelley's note). Francis Bacon

(1561–1626), Lord Chancellor of England, philosopher and essayist.

eternal music. Nor are those supreme poets who have employed traditional forms of rhythm on account of the form and action of their subjects, less capable of perceiving and teaching the truth of things, than those who have omitted that form. Shakespeare, Dante and Milton (to confine ourselves to modern writers) are philosophers of the very loftiest power.

A poem is the very image of life expressed in its eternal truth. There is this difference between a story and a poem: that a story is a catalogue of detached facts which have no other bond of connection than time, place, circumstance, cause and effect; the other is the creation of actions according to the unchangeable forms of human nature, as existing in the mind of the creator, which is itself the image of all other minds. The one is partial, and applies only to a definite period of time, and a certain combination of events which can never again recur; the other is universal, and contains within itself the germ of a relation to whatever motives or actions have place in the possible varieties of human nature. Time, which destroys the beauty and the use of the story of particular facts, stripped of the poetry which should invest them, augments that of poetry, and forever develops new and wonderful applications of the eternal truth which it contains. Hence epitomes have been called the moths of just history;[6] they eat out the poetry of it. The story of particular facts is as a mirror which obscures and distorts that which should be beautiful: poetry is a mirror which makes beautiful that which is distorted.

The parts of a composition may be poetical, without the composition as a whole being a poem. A single sentence may be considered as a whole though it may be found in the midst of a series of unassimilated portions; a single word even may be a spark of inextinguishable thought. And thus all the great historians – Herodotus, Plutarch, Livy[7] – were poets; and although the plan of these writers, especially that of Livy, restrained them from developing this faculty in its highest degree, they make copious and ample amends for their subjection, by filling all the interstices of their subject with living images.

Having determined what is poetry and who are poets, let us proceed to estimate its effects upon society.

Poetry is ever accompanied with pleasure: all spirits on which it falls, open themselves to receive the wisdom which is mingled with its delight. In the infancy of the world, neither poets themselves nor their auditors are fully aware of the excellency of poetry, for it acts in a divine and unapprehended manner, beyond and above consciousness – and it is reserved for future generations to contemplate and measure the mighty cause and effect in all the strength and splendour of their union. Even in modern times, no living poet ever arrived at the fullness of his fame. The jury which sits in judgement upon a poet, belonging as he does to all time, must be composed of his peers; it must be impanelled by Time from the selectest of the wise of many generations. A poet is a nightingale who sits in darkness and sings to cheer its own solitude with sweet sounds; his auditors are as men entranced by the melody of an unseen musician, who feel that they are moved and softened, yet know not whence or why. The poems of Homer and his contemporaries were the delight of infant Greece; they were the elements of that social system which is the column upon which all succeeding civilization has reposed. Homer embodied the ideal perfection of his age in

---

[6] Bacon, *Of the Advancement of Learning*, book II, ch. 2.　　[7] Historians of ancient Greece and Rome.

human character – nor can we doubt that those who read his verses were awakened to an ambition of becoming like to Achilles, Hector and Ulysses. The truth and beauty of friendship, patriotism and persevering devotion to an object, were unveiled to the depths in these immortal creations; the sentiments of the auditors must have been refined and enlarged by a sympathy with such great and lovely impersonations, until from admiring they imitated, and from imitation they identified themselves with the objects of their admiration. Nor let it be objected that these characters are remote from moral perfection, and that they can by no means be considered as edifying patterns for general imitation. Every epoch under names more or less specious has deified its peculiar errors; revenge is the naked idol of the worship of a semi-barbarous age, and self-deceit is the veiled image of unknown evil before which luxury and satiety lie prostrate.

But a poet considers the vices of his contemporaries as the temporary dress in which his creations must be arrayed, and which cover without concealing the eternal proportions of their beauty. An epic or dramatic personage is understood to wear them around his soul, as he may the ancient armour or the modern uniform around his body – whilst it is easy to conceive a dress more graceful than either. The beauty of the internal nature cannot be so far concealed by its accidental vesture, but that the spirit of its form shall communicate itself to the very disguise, and indicate the shape it hides from the manner in which it is worn. A majestic form and graceful motions will express themselves through the most barbarous and tasteless costume. Few poets of the highest class have chosen to exhibit the beauty of their conceptions in its naked truth and splendour, and it is doubtful whether the alloy of costume, habit, etc., be not necessary to temper this planetary music for mortal ears.

The whole objection however of the immorality of poetry rests upon a misconception of the manner in which poetry acts to produce the moral improvement of man. Ethical science arranges the elements which poetry has created, and propounds schemes and proposes examples of civil and domestic life. Nor is it for want of admirable doctrines that men hate, and despise, and censure, and deceive, and subjugate one another. But poetry acts in another and a diviner manner. It awakens and enlarges the mind itself by rendering it the receptacle of a thousand unapprehended combinations of thought. Poetry lifts the veil from the hidden beauty of the world, and makes familiar objects be as if they were not familiar; it re-produces all that it represents, and the impersonations clothed in its Elysian light stand thenceforward in the minds of those who have once contemplated them as memorials of that gentle and exalted content which extends itself over all thoughts and actions with which it coexists. The great secret of morals is love, or a going out of our own nature, and an identification of ourselves with the beautiful which exists in thought, action, or person not our own. A man, to be greatly good, must imagine intensely and comprehensively; he must put himself in the place of another and of many others; the pains and pleasures of his species must become his own. The great instrument of moral good is the imagination – and poetry administers to the effect by acting upon the cause.

Poetry enlarges the circumference of the imagination by replenishing it with thoughts of ever-new delight which have the power of attracting and assimilating to their own nature all other thoughts, and which form new intervals and interstices whose void forever craves fresh food. Poetry strengthens the faculty which is the organ of the moral nature of man, in the same manner as exercise strengthens a limb. A poet therefore would do ill to embody his own conceptions of right and wrong (which are usually those of his place and time) in his poetical creations (which participate in neither). By this assumption of the inferior office of interpreting the effect, in which perhaps after all he might acquit himself but imperfectly, he would resign a glory in a participation in the cause. There was little danger that Homer, or any of the eternal poets, should have so far misunderstood themselves as to have abdicated this throne of their widest dominion. Those in whom the poetical faculty, though great, is less intense (as Euripides, Lucan, Tasso, Spenser) have frequently affected a moral aim, and the effect of their poetry is diminished in exact proportion to the degre in which they compel us to advert to this purpose. . . .

The poetry of Dante may be considered as the bridge thrown over the stream of time, which unites the modern and the ancient world. The distorted notions of invisible things which Dante and his rival Milton have idealized, are merely the mask and the mantle in which these great poets walk through eternity enveloped and disguised. It is a difficult question to determine how far they were conscious of the distinction which must have subsisted in their minds between their own creed and that of the people. Dante at least appears to wish to mark the full extent of it by placing Riphaeus (whom Virgil calls 'justissimus unus'[8]) in Paradise, and observing a most heretical caprice in his distribution of rewards and punishments. And Milton's poem contains within itself a philosophical refutation of that system of which, by a strange but natural antithesis, it has been a chief popular support.

Nothing can exceed the energy and magnificence of the character of Satan as expressed in *Paradise Lost*. It is a mistake to suppose that he could ever have been intended for the popular personification of evil. Implacable hate, patient cunning, and a sleepless refinement of device to inflict the extremest anguish on an enemy – these things are evil; and, although venial in a slave, are not to be forgiven in a tyrant; although redeemed by much that ennobles his defeat in one subdued, are marked by all that dishonours his conquest in the victor. Milton's Devil as a moral being is as far superior to his God as one who perseveres in some purpose which he has conceived to be excellent in spite of adversity and torture, is to one who in the cold security of undoubted triumph inflicts the most horrible revenge upon his enemy, not from any mistaken notion of inducing him to repent of a perseverance in enmity, but with the alleged design of exasperating him to deserve new torments. Milton has so far violated the popular creed (if this shall be judged to be a violation) as to have alleged no superiority of moral virtue to his God over his Devil. And this bold neglect of a direct moral purpose is the most decisive proof of the supremacy of Milton's genius. He mingled, as it were, the elements of human nature as colours upon a single palette, and arranged them into the composition of his great picture according to the laws of epic truth; that is, according to the laws of that principle by which a series of actions of the external universe and of intelligent and ethical beings is calculated to excite the sympathy of succeeding generations of mankind. The *Divina Commedia* and *Paradise Lost* have conferred upon modern mythology a systematic form; and when change and time shall have added one more superstition to the mass of those which have arisen and decayed upon the earth, commentators will be learnedly employed in elucidating the religion of ancestral Europe, only not utterly forgotten because it will have been stamped with the eternity of genius.

[8] 'The one man who was most just' (*Aeneid*, ii. 426).

Homer was the first, and Dante the second epic poet – that is, the second poet the series of whose creations bore a defined and intelligible relation to the knowledge, and sentiment, and religion, and political conditions of the age in which he lived, and of the ages which followed it, developing itself in correspondence with their development. For Lucretius had limed the wings of his swift spirit in the dregs of the sensible world; and Virgil, with a modesty which ill became his genius, had affected the fame of an imitator even whilst he created anew all that he copied; and none among the flock of mock-birds, though their notes were sweet (Apollonius Rhodius, Quintus Calaber, Smyrnaeus, Nonnus, Lucan, Statius, or Claudian[9]), have sought even to fulfil a single condition of epic truth. Milton was the third epic poet. For, if the title of epic in its highest sense is to be refused to the *Aeneid*, still less can it be conceded to the *Orlando Furioso*, the *Gerusalemme Liberata*, *The Lusiad*, or *The Faerie Queene*.[10]

Dante and Milton were both deeply penetrated with the ancient religion of the civilized world – and its spirit exists in their poetry probably in the same proportion as its forms survived in the unreformed worship of modern Europe. The one preceded and the other followed the Reformation at almost equal intervals. Dante was the first religious reformer, and Luther surpassed him rather in the rudeness and acrimony, than in the boldness of his censures of papal usurpation. Dante was the first awakener of entranced Europe; he created a language in itself music and persuasion out of a chaos of inharmonious barbarisms; he was the congregator of those great spirits who presided over the resurrection of learning, the Lucifer of that starry flock which in the thirteenth century shone forth from republican Italy, as from a heaven, into the darkness of the benighted world. His very words are instinct with spirit – each is as a spark, a burning atom of inextinguishable thought, and many yet lie covered in the ashes of their birth, and pregnant with a lightning which has yet found no conductor. All high poetry is infinite; it is as the first acorn, which contained all oaks potentially. Veil after veil may be undrawn, and the inmost naked beauty of the meaning never exposed. A great poem is a fountain forever overflowing with the waters of wisdom and delight – and after one person or one age has exhausted all its divine effluence which its peculiar relations enable them to share, another and yet another succeeds, and new relations are ever developed, the source of an unforeseen and an unconceived delight.

The age immediately succeeding to that of Dante, Petrarch, and Boccaccio, was characterized by a revival of painting, sculpture, music, and architecture. Chaucer caught the sacred inspiration, and the superstructure of English literature is based upon the materials of Italian invention.

But let us not be betrayed from a defence into a critical history of poetry and its influence on society. Be it enough to have pointed out the effects of poetry (in the large and true sense of the word) upon their own and all succeeding times, and to revert to the partial instances cited as illustrations of an opinion the reverse of that attempted to be established by the author of 'The Four Ages of Poetry'.

But poets have been challenged to resign the civic crown to reasoners and mechanists on another plea. It is admitted that the exercise of the imagination is more delightful, but it is alleged that that of the reason is more useful. Let us examine as the grounds of this distinction what is here meant by utility. Pleasure or good in a general

---

[9]   Minor poets of ancient times.
[10] Romance epics by Ariosto, Tasso, Camoens, and Spenser.

sense is that which the consciousness of a sensitive and intelligent being seeks, and in which, when found, it acquiesces. There are two modes or degrees of pleasure – one durable, universal, and permanent; the other transitory and particular. Utility may either express the means of producing the former or the latter. In the former sense, whatever strengthens and purifies the affections, enlarges the imagination, and adds a spirit to sense, is useful. But the meaning in which the author of 'The Four Ages of Poetry' seems to have employed the word utility is the narrower one of banishing the importunity of the wants of our animal nature, the surrounding men with security of life, the dispersing the grosser delusions of superstition, and the conciliating such a degree of mutual forbearance among men as may consist with the motives of personal advantage.

Undoubtedly the promoters of utility in this limited sense have their appointed office in society. They follow the footsteps of poets, and copy the sketches of their creations into the book of common life. They make space, and give time. Their exertions are of the highest value so long as they confine their administration of the concerns of the inferior powers of our nature within the limits of what is due to the superior ones. But whilst the sceptic destroys gross superstitions, let him spare to deface, as some of the French writers have defaced, the eternal truths charactered upon the imaginations of men. Whilst the mechanist abridges, and the political economist combines labour, let them beware that their speculations, for want of a correspondence with those first principles which belong to the imagination, do not tend, as they have in modern England, to exasperate at once the extremes of luxury and want. They have exemplified the saying, 'To him that hath, more shall be given; and from him that hath not, the little that he hath shall be taken away'.[11] The rich have become richer, and the poor have become poorer; and the vessel of the state is driven between the Scylla and Charybdis of anarchy and despotism. Such are the effects which must ever flow from an unmitigated exercise of the calculating faculty.

It is difficult to define pleasure in its highest sense, the definition involving a number of apparent paradoxes. For, from an inexplicable defect of harmony in the constitution of human nature, the pain of the inferior is frequently connected with the pleasure of the superior portions of our being. Sorrow, terror, anguish, despair itself are often the chosen expressions of an approximation to the highest good. Our sympathy in tragic fiction depends on this principle; tragedy delights by affording a shadow of the pleasure which exists in pain. This is the source also of the melancholy which is inseparable from the sweetest melody. The pleasure that is in sorrow is sweeter than the pleasure of pleasure itself – and hence the saying, 'It is better to go to the house of mourning than to the house of mirth'.[12] Not that this highest species of pleasure is necessarily linked with pain. The delight of love and friendship, the ecstasy of the admiration of nature, the joy of the perception and still more of the creation of poetry is often wholly unalloyed.

The production and assurance of pleasure in this highest sense is true utility; those who produce and preserve this pleasure are poets or poetical philosophers.

The exertions of Locke, Hume, Gibbon, Voltaire, Rousseau,[13] and their disciples, in favour of oppressed and deluded humanity, are entitled to the gratitude of mankind. Yet it is easy to calculate the degree of moral and intellectual improvement which the

---

[11] Matt. 25: 29.
[12] Eccles. 7: 2.
[13] 'I follow the classification adopted by the author of "The Four Ages of Poetry", but Rousseau was essentially a poet. The others, even Voltaire, were mere reasoners' (Shelley's note).

world would have exhibited had they never lived. A little more nonsense would have been talked for a century or two, and perhaps a few more men, women and children burnt as heretics. We might not at this moment have been congratulating each other on the abolition of the Inquisition in Spain.[14] But it exceeds all imagination to conceive what would have been the moral condition of the world if neither Dante, Petrarch, Boccaccio, Chaucer, Shakespeare, Calderón, Lord Bacon, nor Milton, had ever existed; if Raphael and Michelangelo had never been born; if the Hebrew poetry had never been translated; if a revival of a study of Greek literature had never taken place; if no monuments of ancient sculpture had been handed down to us; and if the poetry of the religion of the ancient world had been extinguished together with its belief. The human mind could never, except by the intervention of these excitements, have been awakened to the invention of those grosser sciences, and that application of analytical reasoning to the aberrations of society, which it is now attempted to exalt over the direct expression of the inventive and creative faculty itself.

We have more moral, political and historical wisdom than we know how to reduce into practice; we have more scientific and economical knowledge than can be accommodated to the just distribution of the produce which they multiply. The poetry in these systems of thought is concealed by the accumulation of facts and calculating processes. There is no want of knowledge respecting what is wisest and best in morals, government, and political economy – or at least, what is wiser and better than what men now practise and endure. But we let '*I dare not* wait upon *I would*, like the poor cat i' the adage'.[15] We want the creative faculty to imagine that which we know; we want the generous impulse to act that which we imagine; we want the poetry of life – our calculations have outrun conception; we have eaten more than we can digest. The cultivation of those sciences which have enlarged the limits of the empire of man over the external world, has, for want of the poetical faculty, proportionally circumscribed those of the internal world – and man, having enslaved the elements, remains himself a slave. To what but to a cultivation of the mechanical arts in a degree disproportioned to the presence of the creative faculty (which is the basis of all knowledge) is to be attributed the abuse of all inventions for abridging and combining labour, to the exasperation of the inequality of mankind? From what other cause has it arisen that these inventions which should have lightened, have added a weight to the curse imposed on Adam?[16] Thus, poetry, and the principle of self (of which money is the visible incarnation) are the God and the Mammon of the world.

The functions of the poetical faculty are twofold: by one it creates new materials for knowledge and power and pleasure; by the other it engenders in the mind a desire to reproduce and arrange them according to a certain rhythm and order which may be called the beautiful and the good. The cultivation of poetry is never more to be desired than at periods when, from an excess of the selfish and calculating principle, the accumulation of the materials of external life exceed the quantity of the power of assimilating them to the internal laws of human nature. The body has then become too unwieldy for that which animates it.

Poetry is indeed something divine. It is at once the centre and the circumference of knowledge; it is that which comprehends all science, and that to which all science must be referred. It is at the same time the root and the blossom of all other systems of

---

[14] The Spanish Inquisition was suppressed in 1820, restored in 1823, and abolished finally in 1834.

[15] *Macbeth*, I. vii. 44–5.

[16] Gen. 3: 17–19.

thought. It is that from which all spring, and that which adorns all – and that which, if blighted, denies the fruit and the seed, and withholds from the barren world the nourishment and the succession of the scions of the tree of life. It is the perfect and consummate surface and bloom of things; it is as the odour and the colour of the rose to the texture of the elements which compose it, as the form and the splendour of unfaded beauty to the secrets of anatomy and corruption. What were virtue, love, patriotism, friendship etc.; what were the scenery of this beautiful universe which we inhabit; what were our consolations on this side of the grave; and what were our aspirations beyond it – if poetry did not ascend to bring light and fire from those eternal regions where the owl-winged faculty of calculation dare not ever soar? Poetry is not like reasoning, a power to be exerted according to the determination of the will. A man cannot say, 'I will compose poetry'. The greatest poet even cannot say it: for the mind in creation is as a fading coal which some invisible influence, like an inconstant wind, awakens to transitory brightness. This power arises from within, like the colour of a flower which fades and changes as it is developed, and the conscious portions of our natures are unprophetic either of its approach or its departure. Could this influence be durable in its original purity and force, it is impossible to predict the greatness of the results – but when composition begins, inspiration is already on the decline, and the most glorious poetry that has ever been communicated to the world is probably a feeble shadow of the original conception of the poet. I appeal to the greatest poets of the present day, whether it be not an error to assert that the finest passages of poetry are produced by labour and study. The toil and the delay recommended by critics can be justly interpreted to mean no more than a careful observation of the inspired moments, and an artificial connection of the spaces between them by the intertexture of conventional expressions; a necessity only imposed by a limitedness of the poetical faculty itself. For Milton conceived the *Paradise Lost* as a whole before he executed it in portions. We have his own authority also for the muse having 'dictated' to him the 'unpremeditated song',[17] and let this be an answer to those who would allege the fifty-six various readings of the first line of the *Orlando Furioso*. Compositions so produced are to poetry what mosaic is to painting. This instinct and intuition of the poetical faculty is still more observable in the plastic and pictorial arts: a great statue or picture grows under the power of the artist as a child in the mother's womb, and the very mind which directs the hands in formation is incapable of accounting to itself for the origin, the gradations, or the media of the process.

Poetry is the record of the best and happiest moments of the happiest and best minds. We are aware of evanescent visitations of thought and feeling sometimes associated with place or person, sometimes regarding our own mind alone, and always arising unforeseen and departing unbidden, but elevating and delightful beyond all expression – so that even in the desire and the regret they leave, there cannot but be pleasure, participating as it does in the nature of its object. It is, as it were, the interpenetration of a diviner nature through our own, but its footsteps are like those of a wind over a sea, which the coming calm erases, and whose traces remain only as on the wrinkled sand which paves it.

These, and corresponding conditions of being, are experienced principally by those of the most delicate sensibility and the most enlarged imagination – and the state of

---

[17] *Paradise Lost*, ix. 23–4.

mind produced by them is at war with every base desire. The enthusiasm of virtue, love, patriotism and friendship, is essentially linked with these emotions; and whilst they last, self appears as what it is – an atom to a universe. Poets are not only subject to these experiences as spirits of the most refined organization, but they can colour all that they combine with the evanescent hues of this ethereal world; a word or a trait in the representation of a scene or a passion, will touch the enchanted chord, and reanimate, in those who have ever experienced these emotions, the sleeping, the cold, the buried image of the past. Poetry thus makes immortal all that which is best and most beautiful in the world; it arrests the vanishing apparitions which haunt the interlunations of life, and veiling them in language or in form sends them forth among mankind, bearing sweet news of kindred joy to those with whom their sisters abide – abide, because there is no portal of expression from the caverns of the spirit which they inhabit, into the universe of things. Poetry redeems from decay the visitations of the divinity in man.

Poetry turns all things to loveliness: it exalts the beauty of that which is most beautiful, and it adds beauty to that which is most deformed; it marries exultation and horror, grief and pleasure, eternity and change; it subdues to union under its light yoke all irreconcilable things. It transmutes all that it touches, and every form moving within the radiance of its presence is changed by wondrous sympathy to an incarnation of the spirit which it breathes; its secret alchemy turns to potable gold the poisonous waters which flow from death through life; it strips the veil of familiarity from the world, and lays bare the naked and sleeping beauty which is the spirit of its forms.

All things exist as they are perceived, at least in relation to the percipient: 'The mind is its own place, and of itself can make a heaven of hell, a hell of heaven'.[18] But poetry defeats the curse which binds us to be subjected to the accident of surrounding impressions. And whether it spreads its own figured curtain or withdraws life's dark veil from before the scene of things, it equally creates for us a being within our being. It makes us the inhabitants of a world to which the familiar world is a chaos. It reproduces the common universe of which we are portions and percipients, and it purges from our inward sight the film of familiarity which obscures from us the wonder of our being. It compels us to feel that which we perceive, and to imagine that which we know. It creates anew the universe after it has been annihilated in our minds by the recurrence of impressions blunted by reiteration. It justifies that bold and true word of Tasso: 'Non merita nome di creatore, sennon Iddio ed il Poeta'.[19]

A poet, as he is the author to others of the highest wisdom, pleasure, virtue and glory, so he ought personally to be the happiest, the best, the wisest, and the most illustrious of men. As to his glory, let time be challenged to declare whether the fame of any other institutor of human life be comparable to that of a poet. That he is the wisest, the happiest, and the best, inasmuch as he is a poet, is equally incontrovertible: the greatest poets have been men of the most spotless virtue, of the most consummate prudence, and (if we could look into the interior of their lives) the most fortunate of men. And the exceptions, as they regard those who possessed the imaginative faculty in a high yet an inferior degree, will be found on consideration to confirm rather than destroy the rule. Let us for a moment stoop to the arbitration of popular breath, and usurping and uniting in our own persons the incompatible characters of accuser,

---

[18] Ibid., i. 254–5.

[19] 'None deserves the name of creator except God

and the poet', from Pierantonio Serassi's *Life of Torquato Tasso* (1785).

witness, judge and executioner, let us without trial, testimony, or form, determine that certain motives of those who are 'there sitting where we dare not soar'[20] are reprehensible. Let us assume that Homer was a drunkard, that Virgil was a flatterer, that Horace was a coward, that Tasso was a madman, that Lord Bacon was a peculator, that Raphael was a libertine, that Spenser was a Poet Laureate. It is inconsistent with this division of our subject to cite living poets, but posterity has done ample justice to the great names now referred to. Their errors have been weighed and have been found as dust in the balance – if their sins 'were as scarlet, they are now white as snow';[21] they have been washed in the blood[22] of the mediator and the redeemer Time. Observe in what a ludicrous chaos the imputations of real and of fictitious crime have been confused in the contemporary calumnies against poetry and poets; consider how little is as it appears – or appears as it is; look to your own motives, and judge not lest ye be judged.[23]

Poetry, as has been said, in this respect differs from logic: that it is not subject to the control of the active powers of the mind, and that its birth and recurrence has no necessary connection with consciousness or will. It is presumptuous to determine that these are the necessary conditions of all mental causation, when mental effects are experienced insusceptible of being referred to them. The frequent recurrence of the poetical power, it is obvious to suppose, may produce in the mind an habit of order and harmony correlative with its own nature and with its effects upon other minds. But in the intervals of inspiration (and they may be frequent without being durable) a poet becomes a man, and is abandoned to the sudden reflux of the influences under which others habitually live. But as he is more delicately organized than other men, and sensible to pain and pleasure (both his own and that of others) in a degree unknown to them, he will avoid the one and pursue the other with an ardour proportioned to this difference. And he renders himself obnoxious to calumny, when he neglects to observe the circumstances under which these objects of universal pursuit and flight have disguised themselves in one another's garments.

But there is nothing necessarily evil in this error, and thus cruelty, envy, revenge, avarice, and the passions purely evil, have never formed any portion of the popular imputations on the lives of poets.

I have thought it most favourable to the cause of truth to set down these remarks according to the order in which they were suggested to my mind by a consideration of the subject itself, instead of following that of the treatise which excited me to make them public. Thus, although devoid of the formality of a polemical reply, if the views which they contain be just, they will be found to involve a refutation of the doctrines of 'The Four Ages of Poetry', so far at least as regards the first division of the subject. I can readily conjecture what should have moved the gall of the learned and intelligent author of that paper; I confess myself, like him, unwilling to be stunned by the *Theseid*s of the hoarse Codri of the day. Bavius and Maevius[24] undoubtedly are, as they ever were, insufferable persons. But it belongs to a philosophical critic to distinguish rather than confound.

The first part of these remarks has related to poetry in its elements and principles; and it has been shown, as well as the narrow limits assigned them would permit, that

[20] *Paradise Lost*, iv. 829.
[21] Isa. 1: 18.
[22] *washed in the blood* an allusion to Rev. 7: 14.
[23] Matt. 7: 1.
[24] Incompetent ancient poets attacked by Virgil and Horace.

what is called poetry in a restricted sense has a common source with all other forms of order and of beauty according to which the materials of human life are susceptible of being arranged, and which is poetry in an universal sense.

The second part will have for its object an application of these principles to the present state of the cultivation of poetry, and a defence of the attempt to idealize the modern forms of manners and opinion, and compel them into a subordination to the imaginative and creative faculty. For the literature of England, an energetic development of which has ever preceded or accompanied a great and free development of the national will, has arisen, as it were, from a new birth. In spite of the low-thoughted envy which would undervalue contemporary merit, our own will be a memorable age in intellectual achievements, and we live among such philosophers and poets as surpass beyond comparison any who have appeared since the last national struggle for civil and religious liberty. The most unfailing herald, companion, or follower of the awakening of a great people to work a beneficial change in opinion or institution, is poetry. At such periods there is an accumulation of the power of communicating and receiving intense and impassioned conceptions respecting man and nature. The persons in whom this power resides may often (as far as regards many portions of their nature) have little apparent correspondence with that spirit of good of which they are the ministers. But even whilst they deny and abjure, they are yet compelled to serve the power which is seated upon the throne of their own soul. It is impossible to read the compositions of the most celebrated writers of the present day without being startled with the electric life which burns within their words. They measure the circumference and sound the depths of human nature with a comprehensive and all-penetrating spirit, and they are themselves perhaps the most sincerely astonished at its manifestations, for it is less their own spirit than the spirit of the age. Poets are the hierophants of an unapprehended inspiration, the mirrors of the gigantic shadows which futurity casts upon the present, the words which express what they understand not; the trumpets which sing to battle, and feel not what they inspire; the influence which is moved not, but moves. Poets are the unacknowledged legislators of the world.

Adonais: An Elegy on the Death of John Keats, author of Endymion, Hyperion, etc. (1821; composed between 11 April and 8 June 1821)

'Αστὴρ πρὶν μὲν ἔλαμπες ἐνὶ ζωοῖσιν Ἑῷος.
Νῦν δὲ θανών, λάμπεις Ἕσπερος ἐν φθιμένοις.
(Plato)[1]

Preface

Φάρμακον ἦλθε, Βίων, ποτὶ σὸν στόμα, φάρμακον ἦδες—
Τοιούτοις χείλεσσι ποτέδραμε, κοὺκ ἐγλυκάνθη;

ADONAIS: AN ELEGY ON THE DEATH OF JOHN KEATS, AUTHOR OF ENDYMION, HYPERION, ETC. (1821)
[1] Shortly before composing *Adonais*, Shelley translated Plato's 'Epigram on Aster':

Thou wert the morning star among the living,
Ere thy fair light had fled;
Now, having died, thou art as Hesperus, giving
New splendour to the dead.

Τίς δὲ βροτὸς τοσσοῦτον ἀνάμερος, ὡς κεράσαι τοι,
῾Η δοῦναι καλέοντι τὸ φάρμακον; ἔκψυγεν ᾠδά.[2]
(Moschus, *Lament for Bion* 109–12)

It is my intention to subjoin to the London edition of this poem, a criticism upon the claims of its lamented object to be classed among the writers of the highest genius who have adorned our age. My known repugnance to the narrow principles of taste on which several of his earlier compositions were modelled, prove at least that I am an impartial judge. I consider the fragment of *Hyperion* as second to nothing that was ever produced by a writer of the same years.

John Keats died at Rome of a consumption in his twenty-fourth year, on the —— of —— 1821,[3] and was buried in the romantic and lonely cemetery of the Protestants in that city, under the pyramid which is the tomb of Cestius, and the massy walls and towers, now mouldering and desolate, which formed the circuit of ancient Rome. The cemetery is an open space among the ruins covered in winter with violets and daisies. It might make one in love with death[4] to think that one should be buried in so sweet a place.

The genius of the lamented person to whose memory I have dedicated these unworthy verses was not less delicate and fragile than it was beautiful; and where canker-worms abound, what wonder if its young flower was blighted in the bud? The savage criticism on his *Endymion*, which appeared in the *Quarterly Review*, produced the most violent effect on his susceptible mind; the agitation thus originated ended in the rupture of a blood-vessel in the lungs; a rapid consumption ensued, and the succeeding acknowledgements from more candid critics of the true greatness of his powers, were ineffectual to heal the wound thus wantonly inflicted.

It may be well said that these wretched men know not what they do. They scatter their insults and their slanders without heed as to whether the poisoned shaft lights on a heart made callous by many blows, or one like Keats', composed of more penetrable stuff. One of their associates is, to my knowledge, a most base and unprincipled calumniator. As to *Endymion* – was it a poem (whatever might be its defects) to be treated contemptuously by those who had celebrated with various degrees of complacency and panegyric, *Paris*, and *Woman*, and *A Syrian Tale*, and Mrs Lefanu, and Mr Barrett, and Mr Howard Payne,[5] and a long list of the illustrious obscure? Are these the men who, in their venal good nature, presumed to draw a parallel between the Revd. Mr Milman and Lord Byron?[6] What gnat did they strain at here, after having swallowed all those camels?[7] Against what woman taken in adultery, dares the foremost of these literary prostitutes to cast his opprobrious stone?[8] Miserable man! You, one of the meanest, have wantonly defaced one of the noblest specimens of the workman-

---

[2] 'Poison came, Bion, to thy mouth, thou didst know poison. To such lips as thine did it come, and was not sweetened? What mortal was so cruel that could mix poison for thee, or who could give thee the venom that heard thy voice? Surely, he had not music in his soul.'

[3] Keats died 23 Feb. 1821, aged 26.

[4] Cf. Keats, 'Ode to a Nightingale', 52.

[5] Revd George Croly, *Paris in 1815* (1817); Eaton Stannard Barrett, *Woman* (1810); H. Galley Knight,

Ilderim: A Syrian Tale (1816): all these works were reviewed in the *Quarterly*, 1817–20. Mrs Alicia Lefanu (*c.*1795–*c.*1826) was the author of *The Flowers* (1809). John Howard Payne was an American dramatist, whose *Brutus* was reviewed harshly by the *Quarterly*.

[6] Revd Henry Hart Milman's *Saviour, Lord of the Bright City* and *Fall of Jerusalem* were praised by the *Quarterly*, 1818–20.

[7] Matt. 23: 24.

[8] John 8: 7.

ship of God. Nor shall it be your excuse that, murderer as you are, you have spoken daggers but used none.[9]

The circumstances of the closing scene of poor Keats' life were not made known to me until the *Elegy* was ready for the press. I am given to understand that the wound which his sensitive spirit had received from the criticism of *Endymion,* was exasperated by the bitter sense of unrequited benefits; the poor fellow seems to have been hooted from the stage of life, no less by those on whom he had wasted the promise of his genius, than those on whom he had lavished his fortune and his care. He was accompanied to Rome, and attended in his last illness by Mr Severn, a young artist of the highest promise, who, I have been informed, 'almost risked his own life, and sacrificed every prospect to unwearied attendance upon his dying friend'. Had I known these circumstances before the completion of my poem, I should have been tempted to add my feeble tribute of applause to the more solid recompense which the virtuous man finds in the recollection of his own motives. Mr Severn can dispense with a reward from 'such stuff as dreams are made of'.[10] His conduct is a golden augury of the success of his future career; may the unextinguished spirit of his illustrious friend animate the creations of his pencil, and plead against oblivion for his name!

I

I weep for Adonais – he is dead!
Oh weep for Adonais, though our tears
Thaw not the frost which binds so dear a head!
And thou, sad Hour, selected from all years
To mourn our loss, rouse thy obscure compeers,   5
And teach them thine own sorrow, say: 'With me
Died Adonais; till the Future dares
Forget the Past, his fate and fame shall be
An echo and a light unto eternity!'

II

Where wert thou, mighty Mother,[11] when he lay,   10
When thy Son lay, pierced by the shaft which flies
In darkness? Where was lorn Urania
When Adonais died? With veiled eyes,
Mid listening Echoes, in her Paradise
She sat, while one, with soft enamoured breath,   15
Rekindled all the fading melodies,
With which, like flowers that mock the corpse beneath,
He had adorned and hid the coming bulk of death.

---

[9] *Hamlet*, III. ii. 396.
[10] *The Tempest*, IV. i. 156–7.

[11] *mighty Mother* Urania, who Shelley makes the mother of Adonais.

III

Oh weep for Adonais – he is dead!
Wake, melancholy Mother, wake and weep!   20
Yet wherefore? Quench within their burning bed
Thy fiery tears, and let thy loud heart keep,
Like his, a mute and uncomplaining sleep;
For he is gone, where all things wise and fair
Descend. Oh dream not that the amorous Deep   25
Will yet restore him to the vital air –
Death feeds on his mute voice, and laughs at our despair.

IV

Most musical of mourners, weep again!
Lament anew, Urania! He[12] died,
Who was the Sire of an immortal strain,   30
Blind, old, and lonely, when his country's pride,
The priest, the slave, and the liberticide,
Trampled and mocked with many a loathed rite
Of lust and blood;[13] he went, unterrified,
Into the gulf of death, but his clear Sprite   35
Yet reigns o'er earth – the third among the sons of light.

V

Most musical of mourners, weep anew!
Not all to that bright station dared to climb –
And happier they their happiness who knew,
Whose tapers yet burn through that night of time   40
In which suns perished; others more sublime,
Struck by the envious wrath of man or God,
Have sunk, extinct in their refulgent prime;
And some yet live, treading the thorny road
Which leads, through toil and hate, to Fame's serene abode.   45

VI

But now, thy youngest, dearest one, has perished
The nursling of thy widowhood, who grew,
Like a pale flower by some sad maiden cherished,

---

[12] Milton.
[13] When the Stuart monarchy was restored with
Charles II in 1660, those responsible for the execution of Charles I were executed.

And fed with true love tears instead of dew[14] –
Most musical of mourners, weep anew!   50
Thy extreme hope, the loveliest and the last,
The bloom, whose petals nipped before they blew
Died on the promise of the fruit, is waste;
The broken lily lies – the storm is overpast.

VII

To that high Capital,[15] where kingly Death   55
Keeps his pale court in beauty and decay,
He came; and bought, with price of purest breath,
A grave among the eternal. Come away!
Haste, while the vault of blue Italian day
Is yet his fitting charnel-roof! while still   60
He lies, as if in dewy sleep he lay;
Awake him not! surely he takes his fill
Of deep and liquid rest, forgetful of all ill.

VIII

He will awake no more, oh never more!
Within the twilight chamber spreads apace   65
The shadow of white Death, and at the door
Invisible Corruption waits to trace
His extreme way to her dim dwelling-place;
The eternal Hunger sits, but pity and awe
Soothe her pale rage, nor dares she to deface   70
So fair a prey, till darkness, and the law
Of mortal change, shall fill the grave which is her maw.

IX

Oh weep for Adonais! The quick Dreams,[16]
The passion-winged Ministers of thought
Who were his flocks, whom near the living streams   75
Of his young spirit he fed, and whom he taught
The love which was its music, wander not –
Wander no more from kindling brain to brain,
But droop there, whence they sprung; and mourn their lot
Round the cold heart, where, after their sweet pain,   80
They ne'er will gather strength, or find a home again.

---

[14] Lines 48–9 recall Keats's *Isabella*, 424.
[15] *that high Capital* Rome.

[16] *quick Dreams* Keats's poems, which grieve his death.

X

And one with trembling hands clasps his cold head,
And fans him with his moonlight wings, and cries,
'Our love, our hope, our sorrow, is not dead;
See, on the silken fringe of his faint eyes,　　　　　　　　　　85
Like dew upon a sleeping flower, there lies
A tear some Dream has loosened from his brain.'
Lost Angel of a ruined Paradise!
She knew not 'twas her own; as with no stain
She faded, like a cloud which had outwept its rain.　　　　90

XI

One from a lucid urn of starry dew
Washed his light limbs as if embalming them;
Another clipped her profuse locks, and threw
The wreath upon him, like an anadem,[17]
Which frozen tears instead of pearls begem;　　　　　　　　95
Another in her wilful grief would break
Her bow and winged reeds,[18] as if to stem
A greater loss with one which was more weak,
And dull the barbed fire against his frozen cheek.

XII

Another Splendour on his mouth alit –　　　　　　　　　　100
That mouth, whence it was wont to draw the breath
Which gave it strength to pierce the guarded wit,
And pass into the panting heart beneath
With lightning and with music: the damp death
Quenched its caress upon his icy lips,　　　　　　　　　　105
And, as a dying meteor stains a wreath
Of moonlight vapour, which the cold night clips,[19]
It flushed through his pale limbs, and passed to its eclipse.

XIII

And others came – Desires and Adorations,
Winged Persuasions and veiled Destinies,　　　　　　　　　110
Splendours, and Glooms, and glimmering Incarnations
Of hopes and fears, and twilight Fantasies;

---

[17] *anadem* garland of flowers.　　　　　　　[19] *clips* embraces.
[18] *winged reeds* arrows.

And Sorrow, with her family of Sighs,
And Pleasure, blind with tears, led by the gleam
Of her own dying smile instead of eyes,   115
Came in slow pomp – the moving pomp might seem
Like pageantry of mist on an autumnal stream.

XIV

All he had loved, and moulded into thought,
From shape, and hue, and odour, and sweet sound,
Lamented Adonais. Morning sought   120
Her eastern watchtower, and her hair unbound,
Wet with the tears which should adorn the ground,
Dimmed the aerial eyes that kindle day;
Afar the melancholy thunder moaned,
Pale Ocean in unquiet slumber lay,   125
And the wild winds flew round, sobbing in their dismay.

XV

Lost Echo[20] sits amid the voiceless mountains
And feeds her grief with his remembered lay,
And will no more reply to winds or fountains,
Or amorous birds perched on the young green spray,   130
Or herdsman's horn, or bell at closing day;
Since she can mimic not his lips, more dear
Than those for whose disdain she pined away
Into a shadow of all sounds – a drear
Murmur, between their songs, is all the woodmen hear.   135

XVI

Grief made the young Spring wild, and she threw down
Her kindling buds, as if she Autumn were,
Or they dead leaves; since her delight is flown
For whom should she have waked the sullen year?
To Phoebus was not Hyacinth so dear[21]   140
Nor to himself Narcissus, as to both
Thou Adonais: wan they stand and sere
Amid the drooping comrades of their youth,
With dew all turned to tears; odour, to sighing ruth.[22]

---

[20] The nymph Echo faded into an echo of sound when Narcissus rejected her; Narcissus fell in love with his own reflection, and was transformed into a flower.

[21] Hyacinthus, loved by Phoebus Apollo, was killed out of jealousy by Zephyrus, and then turned into a flower by Apollo.
[22] *ruth* pity.

XVII

Thy spirit's sister, the lorn nightingale,   145
Mourns not her mate with such melodious pain;
Not so the eagle, who like thee could scale
Heaven, and could nourish in the sun's domain
Her mighty youth with morning,[23] doth complain,
Soaring and screaming round her empty nest,   150
As Albion wails for thee: the curse of Cain
Light on his head[24] who pierced thy innocent breast,
And scared the angel soul that was its earthly guest!

XVIII

Ah woe is me! Winter is come and gone,
But grief returns with the revolving year;   155
The airs and streams renew their joyous tone;
The ants, the bees, the swallows reappear;
Fresh leaves and flowers deck the dead Seasons' bier;
The amorous birds now pair in every brake,
And build their mossy homes in field and brere;[25]   160
And the green lizard, and the golden snake,
Like unimprisoned flames, out of their trance awake.

XIX

Through wood and stream and field and hill and Ocean
A quickening life from the Earth's heart has burst
As it has ever done, with change and motion,   165
From the great morning of the world when first
God dawned on Chaos; in its steam immersed
The lamps of Heaven flash with a softer light;
All baser things pant with life's sacred thirst,
Diffuse themselves, and spend in love's delight,   170
The beauty and the joy of their renewed might.

XX

The leprous corpse touched by this spirit tender
Exhales itself in flowers of gentle breath;[26]

---

[23] The eagle was believed to be able to replenish its youthful vision by flying into the sun and then diving into a fountain.
[24] *his head* i.e. that of the critic held responsible by Shelley for Keats's death.
[25] *brere* brier.
[26] anemones.

Like incarnations of the stars, when splendour
Is changed to fragrance, they illumine death   175
And mock the merry worm that wakes beneath;
Nought we know, dies. Shall that alone which knows[27]
Be as a sword consumed before the sheath
By sightless lightning? – th' intense atom glows
A moment, then is quenched in a most cold repose.   180

XXI

Alas! that all we loved of him should be,
But for our grief, as if it had not been,
And grief itself be mortal! Woe is me!
Whence are we, and why are we? Of what scene
The actors or spectators? Great and mean   185
Meet massed in death, who lends what life must borrow.
As long as skies are blue, and fields are green,
Evening must usher night, night urge the morrow,
Month follow month with woe, and year wake year to sorrow.

XXII

He will awake no more, oh never more!   190
'Wake thou', cried Misery, 'childless Mother, rise
Out of thy sleep, and slake, in thy heart's core,
A wound more fierce than his with tears and sighs.'
And all the Dreams that watched Urania's eyes,
And all the Echoes whom their sister's song[28]   195
Had held in holy silence, cried: 'Arise!'
Swift as a Thought by the snake Memory stung,
From her ambrosial rest the fading Splendour sprung.

XXIII

She rose like an autumnal Night, that springs
Out of the East, and follows wild and drear   200
The golden Day, which, on eternal wings,
Even as a ghost abandoning a bier,
Had left the Earth a corpse. Sorrow and fear
So struck, so roused, so rapt Urania;
So saddened round her like an atmosphere   205
Of stormy mist; so swept her on her way
Even to the mournful place where Adonais lay.

---

[27] *that alone which knows* the human mind.   [28] Echo repeated Keats's poem at line 15.

XXIV

Out of her secret Paradise she sped,
Through camps and cities rough with stone, and steel,
And human hearts, which to her airy tread   210
Yielding not, wounded the invisible
Palms of her tender feet where'er they fell:
And barbed tongues, and thoughts more sharp than they
Rent the soft Form they never could repel,
Whose sacred blood, like the young tears of May,   215
Paved with eternal flowers that undeserving way.

XXV

In the death-chamber for a moment Death,
Shamed by the presence of that living Might,
Blushed to annihilation, and the breath
Revisited those lips, and life's pale light   220
Flashed through those limbs, so late her dear delight.
'Leave me not wild and drear and comfortless,
As silent lightning leaves the starless night!
Leave me not!' cried Urania. Her distress
Roused Death: Death rose and smiled, and met her vain caress. 225

XXVI

'Stay yet awhile! speak to me once again;
Kiss me, so long but as a kiss may live;
And in my heartless breast and burning brain
That word, that kiss shall all thoughts else survive,
With food of saddest memory kept alive,   230
Now thou art dead, as if it were a part
Of thee, my Adonais! I would give
All that I am to be as thou now art!
But I am chained to Time, and cannot thence depart!

XXVII

Oh gentle child, beautiful as thou wert,   235
Why didst thou leave the trodden paths of men
Too soon, and with weak hands though mighty heart
Dare the unpastured dragon[29] in his den?

---

[29] The critic responsible for Keats's death.

Defenceless as thou wert, oh where was then
Wisdom the mirrored shield,[30] or scorn the spear?   240
Or hadst thou waited the full cycle, when
Thy spirit should have filled its crescent sphere,
The monsters of life's waste had fled from thee like deer.

XXVIII

The herded wolves, bold only to pursue;
The obscene ravens, clamorous o'er the dead;   245
The vultures to the conqueror's banner true
Who feed where Desolation first has fed,
And whose wings rain contagion – how they fled,
When, like Apollo, from his golden bow,
The Pythian of the age one arrow sped   250
And smiled![31] The spoilers tempt no second blow,
They fawn on the proud feet that spurn them as they go.

XXIX

The sun comes forth, and many reptiles spawn;
He sets, and each ephemeral insect then
Is gathered into death without a dawn,   255
And the immortal stars awake again;[32]
So is it in the world of living men:
A godlike mind soars forth, in its delight
Making earth bare and veiling heaven, and when
It sinks, the swarms that dimmed or shared its light   260
Leave to its kindred lamps the spirit's awful night.'

XXX

Thus ceased she: and the mountain shepherds came
Their garlands sere, their magic mantles rent;
The Pilgrim of Eternity[33] (whose fame
Over his living head like Heaven is bent,   265
An early but enduring monument)
Came, veiling all the lightnings of his song
In sorrow; from her wilds Ierne sent
The sweetest lyrist[34] of her saddest wrong,
And love taught grief to fall like music from his tongue.   270

---

[30] Perseus used a mirrored shield to slay the Medusa.
[31] Byron's *English Bards and Scotch Reviewers* attacked those responsible for the harsh review of his *Hours of Idleness*.
[32] The sun is the great poet during his lifetime; the reptiles are the critics; the ephemeral insects imitate the great poet's works; the stars are great poets of the past.
[33] *The Pilgrim of Eternity* Byron.
[34] *sweetest lyrist* Thomas Moore, from Ireland (Ierne).

XXXI

Midst others of less note came one frail Form,[35]
A phantom among men, companionless
As the last cloud of an expiring storm
Whose thunder is its knell. He, as I guess,
Had gazed on Nature's naked loveliness,   275
Actaeon-like,[36] and now he fled astray
With feeble steps o'er the world's wilderness,
And his own thoughts, along that rugged way,
Pursued, like raging hounds, their father and their prey.

XXXII

A pardlike[37] Spirit beautiful and swift,   280
A Love in desolation masked, a Power
Girt round with weakness – it can scarce uplift
The weight of the superincumbent hour:[38]
It is a dying lamp, a falling shower,
A breaking billow; even whilst we speak,   285
Is it not broken? On the withering flower
The killing sun smiles brightly: on a cheek
The life can burn in blood, even while the heart may break.

XXXIII

His head was bound with pansies overblown,
And faded violets, white, and pied, and blue;   290
And a light spear topped with a cypress cone,
Round whose rude shaft dark ivy tresses grew[39]
Yet dripping with the forest's noonday dew,
Vibrated, as the ever-beating heart
Shook the weak hand that grasped it: of that crew   295
He came the last, neglected and apart –
A herd-abandoned deer struck by the hunter's dart.

XXXIV

All stood aloof, and at his partial moan
Smiled through their tears; well knew that gentle band

---

[35]   *one frail Form* Shelley.
[36]   Actaeon, seeing Diana bathing, was turned into a
stag and torn to pieces by his own dogs.
[37]   *pardlike* in an early draft, Shelley has 'Pantherlike'.

[38]   The overhanging ('superincumbent') hour is that
of Adonais' death.
[39]   A spear tipped with a pinecone – a thyrsus.

Who in another's fate now wept his own; 300
As in the accents of an unknown land,
He sung new sorrow; sad Urania scanned
The Stranger's mien, and murmured, 'Who art thou?'
He answered not, but with a sudden hand
Made bare his branded and ensanguined brow, 305
Which was like Cain's or Christ's – oh that it should be so!

XXXV

What softer voice is hushed over the dead?
Athwart what brow is that dark mantle thrown?
What form leans sadly o'er the white deathbed
In mockery of monumental stone, 310
The heavy heart heaving without a moan?
If it be He[40] who, gentlest of the wise,
Taught, soothed, loved, honoured the departed one,
Let me not vex, with inharmonious sighs,
The silence of that heart's accepted sacrifice. 315

XXXVI

Our Adonais has drunk poison – oh
What deaf and viperous murderer could crown
Life's early cup with such a draught of woe?[41]
The nameless worm would now itself disown:
It felt, yet could escape the magic tone 320
Whose prelude held all envy, hate, and wrong,
But what was howling in one breast alone,
Silent with expectation of the song,
Whose master's hand is cold, whose silver lyre unstrung.

XXXVII

Live thou whose infamy is not thy fame! 325
Live! Fear no heavier chastisement from me,
Thou noteless blot on a remembered name!
But be thyself, and know thyself to be!
And ever at thy season be thou free
To spill the venom when thy fangs o'erflow – 330
Remorse and self-contempt shall cling to thee;
Hot Shame shall burn upon thy secret brow,
And like a beaten hound tremble thou shalt – as now.

---

40 *He* Leigh Hunt.
41 Stanzas 36–7 again attack the reviewer responsible for Keats's death. Shelley thought him to be Southey, although the true culprit was John Wilson Croker.

XXXVIII

Nor let us weep that our delight is fled
Far from these carrion kites that scream below –   335
He wakes or sleeps with the enduring dead;
Thou canst not soar where he is sitting now.
Dust to the dust! But the pure spirit shall flow
Back to the burning fountain whence it came,
A portion of the Eternal, which must glow   340
Through time and change, unquenchably the same,
Whilst thy cold embers choke the sordid hearth of shame.

XXXIX

Peace, peace! He is not dead, he doth not sleep –
He hath awakened from the dream of life –
'Tis we who, lost in stormy visions, keep   345
With phantoms an unprofitable strife,
And in mad trance, strike with our spirit's knife
Invulnerable nothings. *We* decay
Like corpses in a charnel; fear and grief
Convulse us and consume us day by day,   350
And cold hopes swarm like worms within our living clay.

XL

He has outsoared the shadow of our night;[42]
Envy and calumny and hate and pain,
And that unrest which men miscall delight,
Can touch him not and torture not again;   355
From the contagion of the world's slow stain
He is secure, and now can never mourn
A heart grown cold, a head grown grey in vain;
Nor, when the spirit's self has ceased to burn,
With sparkless ashes load an unlamented urn.   360

XLI

He lives, he wakes – 'tis Death is dead, not he;
Mourn not for Adonais. Thou young Dawn
Turn all thy dew to splendour, for from thee
The spirit thou lamentest is not gone;

---

[42] The shadow cast by the earth away from the sun.

Ye caverns and ye forests, cease to moan!   365
Cease ye faint flowers and fountains, and thou Air
Which like a mourning veil thy scarf hadst thrown
O'er the abandoned Earth, now leave it bare
Even to the joyous stars which smile on its despair!

XLII

He is made one with Nature: there is heard   370
His voice in all her music, from the moan
Of thunder, to the song of night's sweet bird;
He is a presence to be felt and known
In darkness and in light, from herb and stone,
Spreading itself where'er that Power may move   375
Which has withdrawn his being to its own,
Which wields the world with never-wearied love,
Sustains it from beneath, and kindles it above.

XLIII

He is a portion of the loveliness
Which once he made more lovely: he doth bear   380
His part, while the one Spirit's plastic[43] stress
Sweeps through the dull dense world, compelling there
All new successions to the forms they wear;
Torturing th' unwilling dross that checks its flight
To its own likeness, as each mass may bear;   385
And bursting in its beauty and its might
From trees and beasts and men into the Heaven's light.

XLIV

The splendours[44] of the firmament of time
May be eclipsed, but are extinguished not;
Like stars to their appointed height they climb,   390
And death is a low mist which cannot blot
The brightness it may veil. When lofty thought
Lifts a young heart above its mortal lair,
And love and life contend in it for what
Shall be its earthly doom, the dead live there   395
And move like winds of light on dark and stormy air.[45]

---

[43] *plastic* shaping, moulding.
[44] *splendours* Keats and other poets.

[45] The creative minds of the dead influence the
hearts of the young.

XLV

The inheritors of unfulfilled renown[46]
Rose from their thrones, built beyond mortal thought,
Far in the Unapparent. Chatterton
Rose pale, his solemn agony had not   400
Yet faded from him; Sidney, as he fought
And as he fell and as he lived and loved
Sublimely mild, a Spirit without spot,
Arose; and Lucan, by his death approved:
Oblivion as they rose shrank like a thing reproved.   405

XLVI

And many more whose names on Earth are dark,
But whose transmitted effluence cannot die
So long as fire outlives the parent spark,
Rose, robed in dazzling immortality.
'Thou art become as one of us', they cry,   410
'It was for thee yon kingless sphere has long
Swung blind in unascended majesty,
Silent alone amid an Heaven of song.[47]
Assume thy winged throne, thou Vesper of our throng!'

XLVII

Who mourns for Adonais? Oh come forth   415
Fond[48] wretch, and know thyself and him aright!
Clasp with thy panting soul the pendulous Earth;
As from a centre, dart thy spirit's light
Beyond all worlds, until its spacious might
Satiate the void circumference; then shrink   420
Even to a point within our day and night –
And keep thy heart light lest it make thee sink
When hope has kindled hope, and lured thee to the brink.[49]

---

46 *inheritors of unfulfilled renown* poets who died before they could realize their full potential. Shelley goes on to specify Thomas Chatterton, who committed suicide at the age of 17 in 1770; Sir Philip Sidney, who died in 1586 at the age of 32; and Lucan, who committed suicide in AD 65 at the age of 26.
47 In the Ptolemaic system of astronomy, the songs of concentric whirling spheres around the earth blended into a harmony. Adonais is to be the genius of the third sphere of Venus.
48 *Fond* it is foolish ('Fond') to mourn Adonais.
49 Shelley tells the 'Fond wretch' to keep his heart light so that when death is near, he will not have built too much hope on immortality.

XLVIII

Or go to Rome, which is the sepulchre
Oh not of him, but of our joy: 'tis nought   425
That ages, empires, and religions there
Lie buried in the ravage they have wrought;
For such as he can lend – they borrow not
Glory from those who made the world their prey;[50]
And he is gathered to the kings of thought[51]   430
Who waged contention with their time's decay,
And of the past are all that cannot pass away.

XLIX

Go thou to Rome – at once the Paradise,
The grave, the city, and the wilderness;
And where its wrecks like shattered mountains rise,   435
And flowering weeds, and fragrant copses dress
The bones of Desolation's nakedness,[52]
Pass, till the Spirit of the spot shall lead
Thy footsteps to a slope of green access
Where, like an infant's smile, over the dead,   440
A light of laughing flowers along the grass is spread.[53]

L

And grey walls[54] moulder round, on which dull Time
Feeds, like slow fire upon a hoary brand;
And one keen pyramid with wedge sublime,[55]
Pavilioning the dust of him who planned   445
This refuge for his memory, doth stand
Like flame transformed to marble; and beneath,
A field is spread, on which a newer band
Have pitched in Heaven's smile their camp of death
Welcoming him we lose with scarce extinguished breath.   450

---

[50] Adonais lends his glory to his Roman surroundings; the ruins of empires pass away, while the influence of creative minds endures.
[51] kings of thought including Chatterton, Sidney, and Lucan.
[52] The Protestant cemetery in Rome, where Keats was buried.

[53] Shelley's son William died suddenly at the age of 3 in June 1819.
[54] grey walls of Rome, begun by Aurelian, which bound one side of the cemetery.
[55] The pyramid is a monument to a Roman tribune, Caius Cestius, who died about 30 BC.

LI

Here pause: these graves are all too young as yet
To have outgrown the sorrow which consigned
Its charge to each; and if the seal is set,
Here, on one fountain of a mourning mind,
Break it not thou![56] Too surely shalt thou find   455
Thine own well full, if thou returnest home,
Of tears and gall. From the world's bitter wind
Seek shelter in the shadow of the tomb.
What Adonais is, why fear we to become?

LII

The One remains, the many change and pass;   460
Heaven's light forever shines, Earth's shadows fly;
Life, like a dome of many-coloured glass,
Stains the white radiance of Eternity,
Until Death tramples it to fragments.[57] Die,
If thou wouldst be with that which thou dost seek!   465
Follow where all is fled! Rome's azure sky,
Flowers, ruins, statues, music, words, are weak
The glory they transfuse with fitting truth to speak.

LIII

Why linger, why turn back, why shrink, my Heart?
Thy hopes are gone before: from all things here   470
They have departed – thou shouldst now depart!
A light is passed from the revolving year,
And man, and woman; and what still is dear
Attracts to crush, repels to make thee wither.
The soft sky smiles, the low wind whispers near: 475
'Tis Adonais calls! Oh, hasten thither,
No more let Life divide what Death can join together.

LIV

That Light whose smile kindles the Universe,
That Beauty in which all things work and move,
That Benediction which the eclipsing Curse   480
Of birth can quench not, that sustaining Love

---

[56]   The mourner is told not to break the seal on the fountain of Shelley's grief for William.
[57]   Just as sunlight shining through stained glass separates into different colours, so eternal unity is broken into different people and things on earth.

Which through the web of being blindly wove
By man and beast and earth and air and sea,
Burns bright or dim, as each are mirrors of
The fire for which all thirst – now beams on me,   485
Consuming the last clouds of cold mortality.

LV

The breath whose might I have invoked in song
Descends on me; my spirit's bark is driven
Far from the shore, far from the trembling throng
Whose sails were never to the tempest given;   490
The massy earth and sphered skies are riven!
I am borne darkly, fearfully, afar;
Whilst burning through the inmost veil of Heaven,
The soul of Adonais, like a star,
Beacons from the abode where the Eternal are.   495

Lines to Lord Byron (composed January 1822; edited from MS)

If I esteemed you less, Envy would kill
    Pleasure, and leave to Wonder and Despair
The ministration of the thoughts that fill
    My mind, which, like a worm whose life may share
A portion of the Unapproachable,   5
    Marks your creations rise as fast and fair
As perfect worlds at the creator's will,
    And bows itself before the godhead there.
But such is my regard that, nor your fame
    Cast on the present by the coming hour,   10
Nor your well-won prosperity and power
    Move one regret for his unhonoured name
Who dares these words. The worm beneath the sod
May lift itself in worship to the god.

Felicia Hemans   (1793–1835)

One of the most popular and versatile poets of the period, whose verse ranges from the lyrical to the heroic, exotic, and even violent. If 'Indian Woman's Death Song' recalls 'Complaint of a Forsaken Indian Woman', Hemans's protagonist is, characteristically, more defiant than Wordsworth's. 'The Grave of a Poetess', an elegy to Mary Tighe, alludes to Wordsworth's 'Resolution and Independence', with which it shares a theme – the desire to transcend grief; while 'Nature's Farewell' deals with another Wordsworthian subject, the loss of childhood vision. She herself was mourned in Wordsworth's 'Extempore Effusion' (pp. 479–80).

From Records of Woman (1828)

INDIAN WOMAN'S DEATH SONG

An Indian woman, driven to despair by her husband's desertion of her for another wife, entered a canoe with her children, and rowed it down the Mississippi towards a cataract. Her voice was heard from the shore singing a mournful death-song, until overpowered by the sound of the waters in which she perished. The tale is related in Long's Expedition to the Source of St Peter's River.

Non, je ne puis vivre avec un coeur brisé. Il faut que je retrouve la joie, et que je m'unisse aux esprits libres de l'air.[1]

(*Bride of Messina*, translated by Madame de Staël)

Let not my child be a girl, for very sad is the life of a woman.
(*The Prairie*)

Down a broad river of the western wilds,
Piercing thick forest glooms, a light canoe
Swept with the current: fearful was the speed
Of the frail bark, as by a tempest's wing
Borne leaf-like on to where the mist of spray   5
Rose with the cataract's thunder. Yet within,
Proudly, and dauntlessly, and all alone,
Save that a babe lay sleeping at her breast,
A woman stood. Upon her Indian brow
Sat a strange gladness, and her dark hair waved   10
As if triumphantly. She pressed her child,
In its bright slumber, to her beating heart,
And lifted her sweet voice that rose awhile
Above the sound of waters, high and clear,
Wafting a wild proud strain, her song of death.   15

Roll swiftly to the spirit's land, thou mighty stream and free!
Father of ancient waters, roll, and bear our lives with thee!
The weary bird that storms have tossed would seek the sunshine's calm,
And the deer that hath the arrow's hurt flies to the woods of balm.

Roll on! My warrior's eye hath looked upon another's face,   20
And mine hath faded from his soul, as fades a moonbeam's trace;
My shadow comes not o'er his path, my whisper to his dream,
He flings away the broken reed – roll swifter yet, thou stream!

INDIAN WOMAN'S DEATH SONG
[1] No, I can't live with a broken heart. I must
retrieve my happiness, and be reunited with the spirits
of the air.

The voice that spoke of other days is hushed within *his* breast,
But *mine* its lonely music haunts, and will not let me rest;   25
It sings a low and mournful song of gladness that is gone;
I cannot live without that light – Father of waves, roll on!

Will he not miss the bounding step that met him from the chase?
The heart of love that made his home an ever-sunny place?
The hand that spread the hunter's board, and decked his couch of yore?   30
He will not! – roll, dark foaming stream, on to the better shore!

Some blessed fount amidst the woods of that bright land must flow,
Whose waters from my soul may lave the memory of this woe;
Some gentle wind must whisper there, whose breath may waft away
The burden of the heavy night, the sadness of the day.   35

And thou, my babe! though born, like me, for woman's weary lot,
Smile! – to that wasting of the heart, my own! I leave thee not;
Too bright a thing art *thou* to pine in aching love away,
Thy mother bears thee far, young fawn, from sorrow and decay.

She bears thee to the glorious bowers where none are heard to weep,   40
And where th' unkind one hath no power again to trouble sleep;
And where the soul shall find its youth, as wakening from a dream –
One moment, and that realm is ours: on, on, dark rolling stream!

THE GRAVE OF A POETESS[1]

Ne me plaignez pas – si vous saviez
Combien de peines ce tombeau m'a epargnées![2]

I stood beside thy lowly grave,
    Spring odours breathed around,
And music in the river-wave
    Passed with a lulling sound.

All happy things that love the sun[3]   5
    In the bright air glanced by,
And a glad murmur seemed to run
    Through the soft azure sky.

Fresh leaves were on the ivy-bough
    That fringed the ruins near;   10

THE GRAVE OF A POETESS
[1] 'Extrinsic interest has lately attached to the fine scenery of Woodstock, near Kilkenny, on account of its having been the last residence of the author of *Psyche* [Mary Tighe]. Her grave is one of many in the churchyard of the village. The river runs smoothly by. The ruins of an ancient abbey that have been partially converted into a church reverently throw their mantle of tender shadow over it' (Hemans's note).
[2] Don't pity me; if only you knew how much suffering this tomb has spared me!
[3] Wordsworth, 'Resolution and Independence', 8: 'All things that love the sun are out of doors.'

Young voices were abroad, but thou
    Their sweetness couldst not hear.

And mournful grew my heart for thee,
    Thou in whose woman's mind
The ray that brightens earth and sea,   15
    The light of song was shrined;

Mournful that thou wert slumbering low
    With a dread curtain drawn
Between thee and the golden glow
    Of this world's vernal dawn.   20

Parted from all the song and bloom
    Thou wouldst have loved so well,
To thee the sunshine round thy tomb
    Was but a broken spell.

The bird, the insect on the wing,   25
    In their bright reckless play,
Might feel the flush and life of spring,
    And thou wert passed away!

But then, ev'n then, a nobler thought
    O'er my vain sadness came;   30
Th' immortal spirit woke, and wrought
    Within my thrilling frame.

Surely on lovelier things, I said,
    Thou must have looked ere now,
Than all that round our pathway shed   35
    Odours and hues below,

The shadows of the tomb are here,
    Yet beautiful is earth!
What seest thou then where no dim fear,
    No haunting dream hath birth?   40

Here a vain love to passing flowers
    Thou gav'st, but where thou art
The sway is not with changeful hours –
    There love and death must part.

Thou hast left sorrow in thy song,   45
    A voice not loud, but deep!
The glorious bowers of earth among,
    How often didst thou weep!

Where couldst thou fix on mortal ground
    Thy tender thoughts and high?   50
Now peace the woman's heart hath found,
    And joy the poet's eye.

MOZART'S REQUIEM

These birds of Paradise but long to flee
Back to their native mansion.
        (Byron, 'The Prophecy of Dante', iii. 169–70)

    A Requiem! – and for whom?
    For beauty in its bloom?
For valour fall'n? A broken rose or sword?
    A dirge for king or chief,
    With pomp of stately grief,   5
Banner, and torch, and waving plume deplored?

    Not so, it is not so!
    The warning voice I know,
From other worlds a strange mysterious tone;
    A solemn funeral air   10
    It called me to prepare,
And my heart answered secretly – my own!

    One more then, one more strain
    In links of joy and pain,
Mighty the troubled spirit to enthrall!   15
    And let me breathe my dower
    Of passion and of power
Full into that deep lay – the last of all!

    The last! – and I must go
    From this bright world below,   20
This realm of sunshine, ringing with sweet sound;
    Must leave its festal skies
    With all their melodies
That ever in my breast glad echoes found!

    Yet have I known it long –   25
    Too restless and too strong
Within this clay hath been th' o'ermastering flame;
    Swift thoughts that came and went,
    Like torrents o'er me sent,
Have shaken, as a reed, my thrilling frame.   30

    Like perfumes on the wind
    Which none may stay or bind,
The beautiful comes floating through my soul;

I strive with yearnings vain,
The spirit to detain   35
Of the deep harmonies that past me roll!

Therefore disturbing dreams
Trouble the secret streams
And founts of music that o'erflow my breast;
Something far more divine   40
Than may on earth be mine,
Haunts my worn heart, and will not let me rest.

Shall I then *fear* the tone
That breathes from worlds unknown?
Surely these feverish aspirations *there*   45
Shall grasp their full desire,
And this unsettled fire
Burn calmly, brightly, in immortal air.

One more then, one more strain;
To earthly joy and pain   50
A rich, and deep, and passionate farewell!
I pour each fervent thought
With fear, hope, trembling, fraught,
Into the notes that o'er my dust shall swell.

From Songs of the Affections, with Other Poems (1830)

THE LAND OF DREAMS

And dreams, in their development, have breath
And tears, and tortures, and the touch of joy;
They leave a weight upon our waking thoughts....
They make us what we were not — what they will,
And shake us with the vision that's gone by ...
           (Byron, 'The Dream', 5–7, 15–16)

Oh spirit land, thou land of dreams!
A world thou art of mysterious gleams,
Of startling voices, and sounds at strife –
A world of the dead in the hues of life.

Like a wizard's magic-glass thou art   5
When the wavy shadows float by, and part –
Visions of aspects, now loved, now strange,
Glimmering and mingling in ceaseless change.

Thou art like a city of the past
With its gorgeous halls into fragments cast,   10

Amidst whose ruins there glide and play
Familiar forms of the world's today.

Thou art like the depths where the seas have birth,
Rich with the wealth that is lost from earth –
All the sere flowers of our days gone by,   15
And the buried gems in thy bosom lie.

Yes, thou art like those dim sea-caves,
A realm of treasures, a realm of graves!
And the shapes through thy mysteries that come and go,
Are of beauty and terror, of power and woe.   20

But for *me*, oh thou picture-land of sleep,
Thou art all one world of affections deep –
And wrung from my heart is each flushing dye
That sweeps o'er thy chambers of imagery.

And thy bowers are fair – even as Eden fair;   25
All the beloved of my soul are there!
The forms my spirit most pines to see,
The eyes whose love hath been life to me –

They are there, and each blessed voice I hear,
Kindly, and joyous, and silvery clear;   30
But undertones are in each, that say,
'It is but a dream; it will melt away!'

I walk with sweet friends in the sunset's glow;
I listen to music of long ago;
But one thought, like an omen, breathes faint through the lay –   35
'It is but a dream; it will melt away!'

I sit by the hearth of my early days;
All the home-faces are met by the blaze,
And the eyes of the mother shine soft, yet say,
'It is but a dream; it will melt away!'   40

And away, like a flower's passing breath, 'tis gone,
And I wake more sadly, more deeply lone –
Oh, a haunted heart is a weight to bear!
Bright faces, kind voices, where are ye, where?

Shadow not forth, oh thou land of dreams,   45
The past, as it fled by my own blue streams!
Make not my spirit within me burn
For the scenes and the hours that may ne'er return!

Call out from the *future* thy visions bright,
From the world o'er the grave, take thy solemn light,   50
And oh! with the loved, whom no more I see,
Show me my home as it yet may be!

As it yet may be in some purer sphere –
No cloud, no parting, no sleepless fear;
So my soul may bear on through the long, long day,   55
Till I go where the beautiful melts not away!

Nature's Farewell

The beautiful is vanished, and returns not.
(Coleridge, *The Death of Wallenstein*, V, i. 68)

A youth rode forth from his childhood's home,
Through the crowded paths of the world to roam,
And the green leaves whispered as he passed:
'Wherefore, thou dreamer, away so fast?

Knew'st thou with what thou art parting here,   5
Long wouldst thou linger in doubt and fear;
Thy heart's light laughter, thy sunny hours,
Thou hast left in our shades with the spring's wild-flowers.

Under the arch by our mingling made,
Thou and thy brother have gaily played;   10
Ye may meet again where ye roved of yore,
But as ye *have* met there – oh, never more!'

On rode the youth – and the boughs among,
Thus the free birds o'er his pathway sung:
'Wherefore so fast unto life away?   15
Thou art leaving for ever thy joy in our lay!

Thou mayst come to the summer woods again,
And thy heart have no echo to greet their strain;
Afar from the foliage its love will dwell –
A change must pass o'er thee – farewell, farewell!'   20

On rode the youth, and the founts and streams
Thus mingled a voice with his joyous dreams:
'We have been thy playmates through many a day,
Wherefore thus leave us? Oh yet delay!

Listen but once to the sound of our mirth!   25
For thee 'tis a melody passing from earth.
Never again wilt thou find in its flow
The peace it could once on thy heart bestow.

Thou wilt visit the scenes of thy childhood's glee
With the breath of the world on thy spirit free;　　　　30
Passion and sorrow its depth will have stirred,
And the singing of waters be vainly heard.

Thou wilt bear in our gladsome laugh no part –
What should it do for a burning heart?
Thou wilt bring to the banks of our freshest rill　　　35
Thirst which no fountain on earth may still.

Farewell! When thou comest again to thine own,
Thou wilt miss from our music its loveliest tone;
Mournfully true is the tale we tell –
Yet on, fiery dreamer! Farewell, farewell!'　　　　40

And a something of gloom on his spirit weighed
As he caught the last sounds of his native shade;
But he knew not, till many a bright spell broke,
How deep were the oracles nature spoke!

SECOND SIGHT

Ne'er erred the prophet heart that grief inspired,
Though joy's illusions mock their votarist.
(Charles Robert Maturin)

A mournful gift is mine, oh friends!
　　A mournful gift is mine!
A murmur of the soul which blends
　　With the flow of song and wine.

An eye that through the triumph's hour　　　　5
　　Beholds the coming woe,
And dwells upon the faded flower
　　Midst the rich summer's glow.

Ye smile to view fair faces bloom
　　Where the father's board is spread;　　　　10
I see the stillness and the gloom
　　Of a home whence all are fled.

I see the withered garlands lie
　　Forsaken on the earth,
While the lamps yet burn, and the dancers fly　　　15
　　Through the ringing hall of mirth.

I see the blood-red future stain
　　On the warrior's gorgeous crest;

And the bier amidst the bridal train
  When they come with roses dressed.   20

I hear the still small moan of time
  Through the ivy branches made,
Where the palace, in its glory's prime,
  With the sunshine stands arrayed.

The thunder of the seas I hear,   25
  The shriek along the wave,
When the bark sweeps forth, and song and cheer
  Salute the parting brave.

With every breeze a spirit sends
  To me some warning sign –   30
A mournful gift is mine, oh friends!
  A mournful gift is mine!

Oh prophet heart, thy grief, thy power,
  To all deep souls belong;
The shadow in the sunny hour,   35
  The wail in the mirthful song.

Their sight is all too sadly clear,
  For them a veil is riven;
Their piercing thoughts repose not here,
  Their home is but in heaven.   40

From New Monthly Magazine, 43 (1835) 329

THOUGHTS DURING SICKNESS: II. SICKNESS LIKE NIGHT

Thou art like night, oh sickness, deeply stilling
Within my heart the world's disturbing sound,
And the dim quiet of my chamber filling
With low, sweet voices, by life's tumult drowned.
Thou art like awful night! Thou gatherest round   5
The things that are unseen, though close they lie,
And with a truth, clear, startling, and profound,
Giv'st their dread presence to our mortal eye.
Thou art like starry, spiritual night!
High and immortal thoughts attend thy way,   10
And revelations, which the common light
Brings not, though wakening with its rosy ray
All outward life: be welcome, then, thy rod,
Before whose touch my soul unfolds itself to God!

John Clare (1793–1864)

Like Ann Yearsley and Robert Bloomfield, Clare came from the labouring class; only recently, however, with the publication of his manuscripts, has the full scale of his achievement become known. This selection aims to present some of the best work of one of the foremost poets of the time. Like Bloomfield, Clare was concerned with the increasing separation between landowners and labourers – one of the concerns of 'June' from The Shepherd's Calendar *(compare Bloomfield's 'Summer' from* The Farmer's Boy, pp. 160–1). *Clare was a master not only of descriptive nature poetry, but of the confessional lyric – of which 'First Love', 'I Am', 'O Could I be as I Have Been', and 'Silent Love' are notable examples, each managing to universalize a personal anxiety.*

From London Magazine, 6 (1822) 151

To ELIA (UNSIGNED)

Elia, thy reveries and visioned themes
    To care's lorn heart a luscious pleasure prove,
Wild as the mystery of delightful dreams,
    Soft as the anguish of remembered love;
Like records of past days their memory dances   5
    Mid the cool feelings manhood's reason brings,
As the unearthly visions of romances
    Peopled with sweet and uncreated things;
And yet thy themes thy gentle worth enhances!
    Then wake again thy wild harp's tenderest strings –   10
Sing on, sweet bard, let fairy loves again
    Smile in thy dreams with angel ecstasies;
Bright o'er our souls will break the heavenly strain
    Through the dull gloom of earth's realities.

SONNET (FIRST PUBLISHED *LONDON MAGAZINE* 6 [1822] 272; EDITED FROM MS)

Ere I had known the world and understood
Those many follys wisdom names its own
Distinguishing things evil from things good
The dreads of sin and death ere I had known
Knowledge the root of evil – had I been   5
Left in some lone place where the world is wild
And trace of troubling man was never seen
Brought up by nature as her favour'd child
As born for nought but joy where all rejoice
Emparadised in ignorance of sin   10
Where nature trys with never chiding voice
Like tender nurse nought but our smiles to win
The future dreamless – beautiful would be
The present – foretaste of eternity

From The Shepherd's Calendar (first published 1827; edited from MS)

JANUARY (A COTTAGE EVENING) (EXTRACT)

O spirit of the days gone bye
Sweet childhoods fearful extacy
The witching spells of winter nights   235
Where are they fled wi their delights
When listning on the corner seat
The winter evenings length to cheat
I heard my mothers memory tell
Tales superstition loves so well   240
Things said or sung a thousand times
In simple prose or simpler ryhmes
Ah where is page of poesy
So sweet as theirs was wont to be
The magic wonders that decievd   245
When fictions were as truths believd
The fairey feats that once prevaild
Told to delight and never faild
Where are they now their fears and sighs
And tears from founts of happy eyes   250
Breathless suspense and all their crew
To what wild dwelling have they flew
I read in books but find them not
For poesy hath its youth forgot
I hear them told to childern still   255
But fear ne'er numbs my spirits chill
I still see faces pale wi dread
While mine could laugh at what is said
See tears imagind woes supply
While mine wi real cares are dry   260
Where are they gone the joys and fears
The links the life of other years
I thought they bound around my heart
So close that we coud never part
Till reason like a winters day   265
Nipt childhoods visions all away
Nor left behind one withering flower
To cherish in a lonely hour
Memory may yet the themes repeat
But childhoods heart doth cease to beat   270
At storys reasons sterner lore
Turneth like gossips from her door

June (Extract)

And now when sheering of the flocks are done   105
Some ancient customs mixed wi harmless fun
Crowns the swains merry toils – the timid maid
Pleasd to be praisd and yet of praise affraid
Seeks her best flowers not those of woods and fields
But such as every farmers garden yield   110
Fine cabbage roses painted like her face
And shining pansys trimmd in golden lace
And tall tuft larkheels featherd thick wi flowers
And woodbines climbing oer the door in bowers
And London tufts of many a mottld hue   115
And pale pink pea and monkshood darkly blue
And white and purple jiliflowers that stay
Lingering in blossom summer half away
And single blood walls of a lucious smell
Old fashiond flowers which huswives love so well   120
And columbines stone blue or deep night brown
Their honey-comb-like blossoms hanging down
Each cottage gardens fond adopted child
Tho heaths still claim them where they yet grow wild
Mong their old wild companions summer blooms   125
Furze brake and mozzling ling and golden broom
Snap dragons gaping like to sleeping clowns
And 'clipping pinks' (which maidens sunday gowns
Full often wear catcht at by tozing¹ chaps)
Pink as the ribbons round their snowy caps   130
'Bess in her bravery' too of glowing dyes
As deep as sunsets crimson pillowd skyes
And majoram notts sweet briar and ribbon grass
And lavender the choice of every lass
And sprigs of lads love all familiar names   135
Which every garden thro the village claims
These the maid gathers wi a coy delight
And tyes them up in readiness for night
Giving to every swain tween love and shame
Her 'clipping poseys' as their yearly claim   140
And turning as he claims the custom kiss
Wi stifld smiles half ankering after bliss
She shrinks away and blushing calls it rude
But turns to smile and hopes to be pursued
While one to whom the seeming hint applied   145
Follows to claim it and is not denyd
No doubt a lover for within his coat

June
¹ *tozing* snatching.

His nosegay owns each flower of better sort
And when the envious mutter oer their beer
And nodd the secret to his neighbor near   150
Raising the laugh to make the mutter known
She blushes silent and will not disown
And ale and songs and healths and merry ways
Keeps up a shadow of old farmers days
But the old beachen bowl that once supplyd   155
Its feast of frumity[2] is thrown aside
And the old freedom that was living then
When masters made them merry wi their men
Whose coat was like his neighbors russet brown
And whose rude speech was vulgar as his clown   160
Who in the same horn drank the rest among
And joined the chorus while a labourer sung
All this is past – and soon may pass away
The time torn remnant of the holiday
As proud distinction makes a wider space   165
Between the genteel and the vulgar race
Then must they fade as pride oer custom showers
Its blighting mildew on her feeble flowers

A Vision (composed 2 August 1844; edited from MS)

I

I lost the love, of heaven above;
I spurn'd the lust, of earth below;
I felt the sweets of fancied love, –
And hell itself my only foe.

2

I lost earths joys, but felt the glow,   5
Of heaven's flame abound in me:
'Till loveliness, and I did grow,
The bard of immortality.

3

I loved, but woman fell away;
I hid me, from her faded fame: 10

---

[2] *frumity* a dish of hulled wheat boiled in milk,
seasoned with cinnamon and sugar.

I snatch'd the sun's eternal ray, –
And wrote 'till earth was but a name.

4

In every language upon earth,
On every shore, o'er every sea;
I gave my name immortal birth,   15
And kep't my spirit with the free.

'I Am' (composed by 20 December 1846; edited from MS)

I

I am – yet what I am, none cares or knows;
  My friends forsake me like a memory lost: –
I am the self-consumer of my woes; –
  They rise and vanish in oblivion's host,
Like shadows in love's frenzied stifled throes: –   5
And yet I am, and live – like vapours tost

2

Into the nothingness of scorn and noise, –
  Into the living sea of waking dreams,
Where there is neither sense of life or joys,
  But the vast shipwreck of my lifes esteems;   10
Even the dearest, that I love the best
Are strange – nay, rather stranger than the rest.

3

I long for scenes, where man hath never trod
  A place where woman never smiled or wept
There to abide with my Creator, God;   15
  And sleep as I in childhood, sweetly slept,
Untroubling, and untroubled where I lie,
The grass below – above the vaulted sky.

An Invite to Eternity (composed by July 1847; edited from MS)

I

Wilt thou go with me sweet maid
Say maiden wilt thou go with me

Through the valley depths of shade
Of night and dark obscurity
Where the path hath lost its way   5
Where the sun forgets the day
Where there's nor life nor light to see
Sweet maiden wilt thou go with me

2

Where stones will turn to flooding streams
Where plains will rise like ocean waves   10
Where life will fade like visioned dreams
And mountains darken into caves
Say maiden wilt thou go with me
Through this sad non-identity
Where parents live and are forgot   15
And sisters live and know us not

3

Say maiden wilt thou go with me
In this strange death of life to be
To live in death and be the same
Without this life, or home, or name   20
At once to be, and not to be
That was, and is not – yet to see
Things pass like shadows – and the sky
Above, below, around us lie

4

The land of shadows wilt thou trace   25
And look – nor know each others face
The present mixed with reasons gone
And past, and present all as one
Say maiden can thy life be led
To join the living with the dead   30
Then trace thy footsteps on with me
We're wed to one eternity

Silent Love (composed between 1842 and 1864; edited from MS)

1

The dew it trembles on the thorn
Then vanishes so love is born

Young love that speaks in silent thought
'Till scorned, then withers and is nought

2

The pleasure of a single hour   5
The blooming of a single flower
The glitter of the morning dew
Such is young love when it is new

3

The twitter of the wild birds wing
The murmur of the bees   10
Lays of hay crickets when they sing
Or other things more frail than these

4

Such is young love when silence speaks
Till weary with the joy it seeks
Then fancy shapes supplies   15
'Till sick of its own heart it dies

5

The dew drop falls at mornings hour
When none are standing by
And noiseless fades the broken flower
So lovers in their silence die   20

'O Could I be as I Have Been' (composed between 1842 and 1864; edited from MS)

1

O could I be as I have been
And ne'er can be no more
A harmless thing in meadows green
Or on the wild seashore

2

O could I be what once I was   5
In heaths and valleys green

A dweller in the summer grass
  Green fields and places green

3

A tenant of the happy fields
  By grounds of wheat and beans   10
By gipsey's camps and milking bield[1]
  Where lussious woodbine leans

4

To sit on the deserted plough
  Left when the corn was sown
In corn and wild weeds buried now   15
  In quiet peace unknown

5

The harrows resting by the hedge
  The roll[2] within the Dyke
Hid in the Ariff[3] and the sedge
  Are things I used to like   20

6

I used to tread through fallow lands
  And wade through paths of grain
When wheat ears pattered on the hands
  And headaches[4] left a stain

7

I wish I was what I have been   25
  And what I was could be
As when I roved in shadows green
  And loved my willow tree

8

To gaze upon the starry sky
  And higher fancies build   30

'OH COULD I BE AS I HAVE BEEN'   [3] *ariff* goose-grass.
[1] *bield* shelter.   [4] *headaches* poppies.
[2] *roll* large wooden roller for breaking clods of earth.

And make in solitary joy
Loves temple in the field

First Love (composed between 1842 and 1864; edited from MS)

1

I ne'er was struck before that hour
  With love so sudden and so sweet
Her face it bloomed like a sweet flower
  And stole my heart away complete
My face turned pale a deadly pale   5
  My legs refused to walk away
And when she looked what could I ail
  My life and all seemed turned to clay

2

And then my blood rushed to my face
  And took my eyesight quite away   10
The trees and bushes round the place
  Seemed midnight at noonday
I could not see a single thing
  Words from my eyes did start
They spoke as chords do from the string   15
  And blood burnt round my heart

3

Are flowers the winter's choice
  Is love's bed always snow
She seemed to hear my silent voice
  Not loves appeals to know   20
I never saw so sweet a face
  As that I stood before
My heart has left its dwelling-place
  And can return no more –

John Gibson Lockhart (1794–1854)

Keats's poetry met with widespread criticism when it was first published, one of the leaders of the hunt being Lockhart. His essay on 'The Cockney School of Poetry' in Blackwood's Edinburgh Magazine *brings together many of the arguments against Leigh Hunt and the Cockney school (taken to include Keats). In particular, Lockhart takes exception to Keats's lack of classical learning and his social class. Lockhart nevertheless wrote such lyrics as 'When Youthful Faith has Fled', inspired apparently by grief at the death of Sir Walter Scott, his father-in-law.*

From Blackwood's Edinburgh Magazine, 3 (1818) 519–24

THE COCKNEY SCHOOL OF POETRY, NO. IV (SIGNED 'Z.') (EXTRACTS)

> *Of Keats,*
> *The muses' son of promise, and what feats*
> *He yet may do, etc.*
>
> (Cornelius Webb)[1]

Of all the manias of this mad age, the most incurable, as well as the most common, seems to be no other than the *metromanie*.[2] The just celebrity of Robert Burns and Miss Baillie has had the melancholy effect of turning the heads of we know not how many farm-servants and unmarried ladies; our very footmen compose tragedies, and there is scarcely a superannuated governess in the island that does not leave a roll of lyrics behind her in her bandbox.[3]

To witness the disease of any human understanding, however feeble, is distressing – but the spectacle of an able mind reduced to a state of insanity is of course ten times more afflicting. It is with such sorrow as this that we have contemplated the case of Mr John Keats. This young man appears to have received from nature talents of an excellent, perhaps even of a superior order – talents which, devoted to the purposes of any useful profession, must have rendered him a respectable, if not an eminent citizen. His friends, we understand, destined him to the career of medicine, and he was bound apprentice some years ago to a worthy apothecary in town.

But all has been undone by a sudden attack of the malady to which we have alluded. Whether Mr John had been sent home with a diuretic or composing draught to some patient far gone in the poetical mania, we have not heard. This much is certain: that he has caught the infection, and that thoroughly. For some time we were in hopes that he might get off with a violent fit or two, but of late the symptoms are terrible. The frenzy of the *Poems* was bad enough in its way, but it did not alarm us half so seriously as the calm, settled, imperturbable drivelling idiocy of *Endymion*. We hope, however, that in so young a person, and with a constitution originally so good, even now the disease is not utterly incurable. Time, firm treatment, and rational restraint, do much for many apparently hopeless invalids – and if Mr Keats should happen, at some interval of reason, to cast his eye upon our pages, he may perhaps be convinced of the existence of his malady, which in such cases is often all that is necessary to put the patient in a fair way of being cured....

It is time to pass from the juvenile *Poems* to the mature and elaborate *Endymion: A Poetic Romance*. The old story of the moon falling in love with a shepherd, so prettily told by a Roman classic, and so exquisitely enlarged and adorned by one of the most elegant

---

THE COCKNEY SCHOOL OF POETRY
[1] Apparently from a lost eulogistic poem by Cornelius Francis Webb (?1790–?1848), sometime member of the Hampstead set.

[2] *metromanie* mania for writing poetry.
[3] *bandbox* cardboard box for caps, hats, millinery.

of German poets, has been seized upon by Mr John Keats, to be done with as might seem good unto the sickly fancy of one who never read a single line either of Ovid or of Wieland. If the quantity, not the quality, of the verses dedicated to the story is to be taken into account, there can be no doubt that Mr John Keats may now claim Endymion entirely to himself.

To say the truth, we do not suppose either the Latin or the German poet would be very anxious to dispute about the property of the hero of the 'Poetic Romance'. Mr Keats has thoroughly appropriated the character, if not the name. His Endymion is not a Greek shepherd loved by a Grecian goddess; he is merely a young Cockney rhymester dreaming a fantastic dream at the full of the moon. Costume, were it worthwhile to notice such a trifle, is violated in every page of this goodly octavo. From his prototype Hunt, John Keats has acquired a sort of vague idea that the Greeks were a most tasteful people, and that no mythology can be so finely adapted for the purposes of poetry as theirs. It is amusing to see what a hand the two Cockneys make of this mythology: the one confesses that he never read the Greek tragedians, and the other knows Homer only from Chapman[4] – and both of them write about Apollo, Pan, nymphs, muses and mysteries as might be expected from persons of their education. We shall not, however, enlarge at present upon this subject, as we mean to dedicate an entire paper to the classical attainments and attempts of the Cockney poets.

As for Mr Keats' *Endymion*, it has just as much to do with Greece as it has with 'old Tartary the fierce'. No man whose mind has ever been imbued with the smallest knowledge or feeling of classical poetry or classical history, could have stooped to profane and vulgarize every association in the manner which has been adopted by this 'son of promise'. Before giving any extracts, we must inform our readers that this romance is meant to be written in English heroic rhyme. To those who have read any of Hunt's poems, this hint might indeed be needless; Mr Keats has adopted the loose, nerveless versification and Cockney rhymes of the poet of *Rimini*.[5] But in fairness to that gentleman, we must add that the defects of the system are tenfold more conspicuous in his disciple's work than in his own. Mr Hunt is a small poet, but he is a clever man. Mr Keats is a still smaller poet, and he is only a boy of pretty abilities, which he has done everything in his power to spoil. . . .

We had almost forgot to mention that Keats belongs to the Cockney School of Politics, as well as the Cockney School of Poetry.

It is fit that he who holds *Rimini* to be the first poem should believe *The Examiner* to be the first politician of the day. We admire consistency, even in folly. Hear how their bantling has already learned to lisp sedition. [Quotes *Endymion*, iii. 1–23] And now good morrow to 'the muses' son of promise'; as for 'the feats he yet may do', as we do not pretend to say, like himself, 'Muse of my native land am I inspired',[6] we shall adhere to the safe old rule of *pauca verba*.[7] We venture to make one small prophecy: that his bookseller will not a second time venture £50 upon anything he can write. It is a better and a wiser thing to be a starved apothecary than a starved poet; so back

---

4 A common charge against Keats was that he knew Homer only from the English translation of George Chapman (1614).
5 Leigh Hunt's most important poem, *Rimini*, was published in 1816.

6 *Endymion*, iv. 354. Lockhart deliberately omits the question mark at the end of this line in Keats's text.
7 *pauca verba* few words.

to the shop Mr John, back to 'plasters, pills, and ointment boxes', etc. But for heaven's sake, young Sangrado, be a little more sparing of extenuatives and soporifics in your practice than you have been in your poetry.

From Andrew Lang, The Life and Letters of John Gibson Lockhart (1897)

WHEN YOUTHFUL FAITH HAS FLED (COMPOSED 21 JUNE 1841)

When youthful faith has fled,
   Of loving take thy leave;
Be constant to the dead –
   The dead cannot deceive.

Sweet modest flowers of spring,   5
   How fleet your balmy day!
And man's brief year can bring
   No secondary May.

No earthly burst again
   Of gladness out of gloom;   10
Fond hope and vision vain,
   Ungrateful to the tomb!

But 'tis an old belief,
   That on some solemn shore,
Beyond the sphere of grief,   15
   Dear friends will meet once more.

Beyond the sphere of time,
   And sin, and fate's control,
Serene in changeless prime
   Of body and of soul.   20

That creed I fain would keep,
   That hope I'll not forego;
Eternal be the sleep,
   Unless to waken so.

John Keats (1795–1821)

Keats invested as much energy in his letters as in his poetry. Typically, the important letters presented here mingle localized details of his life in London with important statements about his work; for additional comments on negative capability and the poetical character, see Woodhouse's letters (pp. 712–15). This selection includes both 'Hyperion: A Fragment' and 'The Fall of Hyperion', in which Keats sought, using what he called 'a more naked and Grecian manner' than that of Endymion, *to depict 'the march of passion and endeavour'; Shelley remarked that 'the fragment called "Hyperion" promises for him that he is destined to become one of the first writers of the age' (Jones, ii. 239). The pinnacle of Keats's achievement are the Odes of 1819, which address exclusion, transience, pain, and sickness, in the context of the quest for truth and beauty.*

From Poems (1817)

ON FIRST LOOKING INTO CHAPMAN'S HOMER (COMPOSED OCTOBER 1816)

Much have I travelled in the realms of gold,
    And many goodly states and kingdoms seen;
    Round many western islands have I been
Which bards in fealty to Apollo hold.
Oft of one wide expanse had I been told   5
    That deep-browed Homer ruled as his demesne,
    Yet did I never breathe its pure serene
Till I heard Chapman[1] speak out loud and bold:
Then felt I like some watcher of the skies
    When a new planet swims into his ken;   10
Or like stout Cortez when with eagle eyes
    He stared at the Pacific, and all his men
Looked at each other with a wild surmise –
    Silent, upon a peak in Darien.

ADDRESSED TO HAYDON (COMPOSED 19 OR 20 NOVEMBER 1816)

Great spirits now on earth are sojourning:[1]
    He of the cloud, the cataract, the lake,
    Who on Helvellyn's summit, wide awake,
Catches his freshness from archangel's wing;
He of the rose, the violet, the spring,   5
    The social smile, the chain for freedom's sake;
    And lo! whose steadfastness would never take
A meaner sound than Raphael's whispering.
And other spirits there are standing apart
    Upon the forehead of the age to come;   10
These, these will give the world another heart
    And other pulses: hear ye not the hum
Of mighty workings?[2] –
    Listen awhile ye nations, and be dumb.

ON FIRST LOOKING INTO CHAPMAN'S HOMER
[1] George Chapman (1559–1634) translated *The Whole Works of Homer* (1614).
ADDRESSED TO HAYDON
[1] Keats celebrates the achievement of Wordsworth (lines 2–4), Leigh Hunt (lines 5–6), and Haydon (lines 7–8).
[2] Originally 'Of mighty workings in a distant mart?', but changed at Haydon's suggestion.

From Endymion: A Poetic Romance (1818) (composed April–November 1817), *Book I* (extracts)

A THING OF BEAUTY IS A JOY FOR EVER

A thing of beauty is a joy for ever:
Its loveliness increases; it will never
Pass into nothingness, but still will keep
A bower quiet for us, and a sleep
Full of sweet dreams, and health, and quiet breathing.   5
Therefore, on every morrow, are we wreathing
A flowery band to bind us to the earth,
Spite of despondence, of the inhuman dearth
Of noble natures, of the gloomy days,
Of all the unhealthy and o'er-darkened ways   10
Made for our searching – yes, in spite of all,
Some shape of beauty moves away the pall
From our dark spirits. Such the sun, the moon,
Trees old and young, sprouting a shady boon
For simple sheep; and such are daffodils   15
With the green world they live in; and clear rills
That for themselves a cooling covert make
'Gainst the hot season; the mid-forest brake,
Rich with a sprinkling of fair musk-rose blooms;
And such too is the grandeur of the dooms   20
We have imagined for the mighty dead,
All lovely tales that we have heard or read –
An endless fountain of immortal drink,
Pouring unto us from the heaven's brink.

HYMN TO PAN[1]

Oh thou, whose mighty palace roof doth hang
From jagged trunks, and overshadoweth
Eternal whispers, glooms, the birth, life, death
Of unseen flowers in heavy peacefulness;   235
Who lov'st to see the hamadryads dress
Their ruffled locks where meeting hazels darken,
And through whole solemn hours dost sit, and hearken
The dreary melody of bedded reeds
In desolate places, where dank moisture breeds   240
The pipy hemlock to strange overgrowth;
Bethinking thee, how melancholy loath

HYMN TO PAN
[1] In spite of the fact that Wordsworth disparagingly told Keats that the Hymn to Pan was 'a very pretty piece of paganism', it looks forward to the mature style of the major 1819 odes. Pan is the god of universal nature.

Thou wast to lose fair Syrinx[2] – do thou now,
By thy love's milky brow,
By all the trembling mazes that she ran,   245
Hear us, great Pan!

Oh thou, for whose soul-soothing quiet, turtles[3]
Passion their voices cooingly 'mong myrtles,
What time thou wanderest at eventide
Through sunny meadows that outskirt the side   250
Of thine enmossed realms; oh thou, to whom
Broad-leaved fig trees even now foredoom
Their ripened fruitage, yellow-girted bees
Their golden honeycombs, our village leas
Their fairest-blossomed beans and poppied corn,   255
The chuckling linnet its five young unborn
To sing for thee, low-creeping strawberries
Their summer coolness, pent-up butterflies
Their freckled wings – yea, the fresh-budding year
All its completions; be quickly near,   260
By every wind that nods the mountain pine,
Oh forester divine!

Thou, to whom every faun and satyr flies
For willing service, whether to surprise
The squatted hare while in half-sleeping fit;   265
Or upward ragged precipices flit
To save poor lambkins from the eagle's maw;
Or by mysterious enticement draw
Bewildered shepherds to their path again;
Or to tread breathless round the frothy main,   270
And gather up all fancifullest shells
For thee to tumble into naiads' cells,
And, being hidden, laugh at their out-peeping;
Or to delight thee with fantastic leaping,
The while they pelt each other on the crown   275
With silvery oak-apples, and fir-cones brown –
By all the echoes that about thee ring,
Hear us, oh satyr king!

Oh hearkener to the loud-clapping shears,
While ever and anon to his shorn peers   280
A ram goes bleating; winder of the horn,
When snouted wild-boars routing tender corn
Anger our huntsmen; breather round our farms,
To keep off mildews and all weather harms;

---

[2] When Pan pursued Syrinx, she was changed into a reed.   [3] *turtles* turtle-doves.

Strange ministrant of undescribed sounds,   285
That come a-swooning over hollow grounds
And wither drearily on barren moors;
Dread opener of the mysterious doors
Leading to universal knowledge – see,
Great son of Dryope,   290
The many that are come to pay their vows
With leaves about their brows!

  Be still the unimaginable lodge
For solitary thinkings; such as dodge
Conception to the very bourne⁴ of heaven,   295
Then leave the naked brain; be still the leaven
That spreading in this dull and clodded earth
Gives it a touch ethereal, a new birth;
Be still a symbol of immensity,
A firmament reflected in a sea,   300
An element filling the space between,
An unknown – but no more. We humbly screen
With uplift hands our foreheads, lowly bending,
And giving out a shout most heaven-rending,
Conjure thee to receive our humble paean,   305
Upon thy Mount Lycean!

THE PLEASURE THERMOMETER[1]

Wherein lies happiness? In that which becks
Our ready minds to fellowship divine,
A fellowship with essence, till we shine
Full alchemized, and free of space. Behold   780
The clear religion of heaven! Fold
A rose-leaf round thy finger's taperness
And soothe thy lips; hist, when the airy stress
Of music's kiss impregnates the free winds,
And with a sympathetic touch unbinds   785
Aeolian magic from their lucid wombs;
Then old songs waken from enclouded tombs,
Old ditties sigh above their father's grave,
Ghosts of melodious prophesyings rave
Round every spot where trod Apollo's foot;   790
Bronze clarions awake and faintly bruit
Where long ago a giant battle was;
And from the turf, a lullaby doth pass
In every place where infant Orpheus slept.

---

⁴ *bourne* boundary.
THE PLEASURE THERMOMETER
[1] The 'thermometer' measures happiness by its intensity and selfless involvement; the four 'degrees', in ascending order, are (i) sensual enjoyment of nature (line 782); (ii) music (lines 783–94); (iii) friendship (lines 803–5); (iv) passion (lines 805–42). This passage is spoken by Endymion.

Feel we these things? That moment have we stepped   795
Into a sort of oneness, and our state
Is like a floating spirit's. But there are
Richer entanglements, enthralments far
More self-destroying, leading, by degrees,
To the chief intensity: the crown of these   800
Is made of love and friendship, and sits high
Upon the forehead of humanity.
All its more ponderous and bulky worth
Is friendship, whence there ever issues forth
A steady splendour; but at the tip-top   805
There hangs by unseen film an orbed drop
Of light, and that is love. Its influence,
Thrown in our eyes, genders a novel sense
At which we start and fret; till in the end,
Melting into its radiance, we blend,   810
Mingle, and so become a part of it –
Nor with aught else can our souls interknit
So wingedly. When we combine therewith,
Life's self is nourished by its proper pith,
And we are nurtured like a pelican brood.   815
Aye, so delicious is the unsating food,
That men who might have towered in the van
Of all the congregated world, to fan
And winnow from the coming step of time
All chaff of custom, wipe away all slime   820
Left by men-slugs and human serpentry,
Have been content to let occasion die
Whilst they did sleep in love's Elysium.
And truly, I would rather be struck dumb
Than speak against this ardent listlessness;   825
For I have ever thought that it might bless
The world with benefits unknowingly,
As does the nightingale, up-perched high,
And cloistered among cool and bunched leaves –
She sings but to her love, nor e'er conceives   830
How tiptoe night holds back her dark-grey hood.
Just so may love, although 'tis understood
The mere commingling of passionate breath,
Produce more than our searching witnesseth:
What I know not – but who of men can tell   835
That flowers would bloom, or that green fruit would swell
To melting pulp, that fish would have bright mail,
The earth its dower of river, wood, and vale,
The meadows runnels, runnels pebble-stones,
The seed its harvest, or the lute its tones,   840
Tones ravishment, or ravishment its sweet,
If human souls did never kiss and greet?

From Letter from John Keats to Benjamin Bailey, 22 November 1817

I wish you knew all that I think about genius and the heart – and yet I think you are thoroughly acquainted with my innermost breast in that respect, or you could not have known me even thus long and still hold me worthy to be your dear friend. In passing, however, I must say of one thing that has pressed upon me lately and increased my humility and capability of submission, and that is this truth: men of genius are great as certain ethereal chemicals operating on the mass of neutral intellect – but they have not any individuality, any determined character. I would call the top and head of those who have a proper self, men of power.

But I am running my head into a subject which I am certain I could not do justice to under five years' study and 3 vols. octavo – and moreover long to be talking about the imagination. So, my dear Bailey, do not think of this unpleasant affair if possible – do not – I defy any harm to come of it – I defy – I shall write to Crips this week and request him to tell me all his goings-on from time to time by letter whererever I may be – it will all go on well. So don't, because you have suddenly discovered a coldness in Haydon, suffer yourself to be teased. Do not, my dear fellow.

Oh, I wish I was as certain of the end of all your troubles as that of your momentary start about the authenticity of the imagination. I am certain of nothing but of the holiness of the heart's affections and the truth of imagination. What the imagination seizes as beauty must be truth, whether it existed before or not. For I have the same idea of all our passions as of love: they are all in their sublime, creative of essential beauty. In a word, you may know my favourite speculation by my first book and the little song I sent in my last – which is a representation from the fancy of the probable mode of operating in these matters. The imagination may be compared to Adam's dream:[1] he awoke and found it truth. I am the more zealous in this affair because I have never yet been able to perceive how anything can be known for truth by consequitive reasoning – and yet it must be. Can it be that even the greatest philosopher ever arrived at his goal without putting aside numerous objections? However it may be, oh for a life of sensations rather than of thoughts! It is 'a vision in the form of youth', a shadow of reality to come. And this consideration has further convinced me, for it has come as auxiliary to another favourite speculation of mine – that we shall enjoy ourselves hereafter by having what we called happiness on earth repeated in a finer tone and so repeated. And yet such a fate can only befall those who delight in sensation, rather than hunger as you do after truth; Adam's dream will do here, and seems to be a conviction that imagination and its empyreal reflection is the same as human life and its spiritual repetition. But as I was saying, the simple imaginative mind may have its rewards in the repetition of its own silent working coming continually on the spirit with a fine suddenness. To compare great things with small, have you never, by being surprised with an old melody in a delicious place by a delicious voice, felt over again your very speculations and surmises at the time it first operated on your soul? Do you not remember forming to yourself the singer's face

---

From LETTER FROM JOHN KEATS TO BENJAMIN BAILEY, 22 November 1817
[1] *Paradise Lost*, viii. 452–90.

more beautiful than it was possible, and yet with the elevation of the moment you did not think so? Even then, you were mounted on the wings of imagination so high that the prototype must be hereafter – that delicious face you will see! What a time!

I am continually running away from the subject. Sure this cannot be exactly the case with a complex mind, one that is imaginative and at the same time careful of its fruits, who would exist partly on sensation, partly on thought – to whom it is necessary that years should bring the philosophic mind.[2] Such an one I consider yours and therefore it is necessary to your eternal happiness that you not only drink this old wine of heaven, which I shall call the redigestion of our most ethereal musings on earth, but also increase in knowledge and know all things.

From Letter from John Keats to George and Tom Keats, 21 December 1817

I spent Friday evening with Wells and went the next morning to see 'Death on the Pale Horse'.[1] It is a wonderful picture when West's age is considered, but there is nothing to be intense upon – no women one feels mad to kiss, no face swelling into reality. The excellence of every art is its intensity, capable of making all disagreeables evaporate, from their being in close relationship with beauty and truth. Examine *King Lear* and you will find this exemplified throughout, but in this picture we have unpleasantness without any momentous depth of speculation excited, in which to bury its repulsiveness. The picture is larger than 'Christ Rejected'.

I dined with Haydon the Sunday after you left, and had a very pleasant day. I dined too (for I have been out too much lately) with Horace Smith, and met his two brothers with Hill and Kingston and one Dubois. They only served to convince me how superior humour is to wit in respect to enjoyment. These men say things which make one start without making one feel. They are all alike; their manners are alike; they all know fashionables; they have a mannerism in their very eating and drinking, in their mere handling a decanter. They talked of Kean and his low company. Would I were with that company instead of yours, said I to myself! I know suchlike acquaintance will never do for me, and yet I am going to Reynolds on Wednesday.

Brown and Dilke walked with me and back from the Christmas pantomime. I had not a dispute but a disquisition with Dilke, on various subjects. Several things dovetailed in my mind, and at once it struck me what quality went to form a man of achievement, especially in literature, and which Shakespeare possessed so enormously. I mean *negative capability*; that is, when man is capable of being in uncertainties, mysteries, doubts, without any irritable reaching after fact and reason. Coleridge, for instance, would let go by a fine isolated verisimilitude caught from the penetralium of mystery, from being incapable of remaining content with half-knowledge. This pursued through volumes would perhaps take us no further than this: that with a great poet the sense of beauty overcomes every other consideration, or rather obliterates all consideration.

[2] *the philosophic mind* Wordsworth, 'Ode', 189.

From LETTER FROM JOHN KEATS TO GEORGE AND TOM KEATS, 21 December 1817
[1] Painting by Benjamin West (1738–1820), President of the Royal Academy.

On Sitting Down to Read King Lear Once Again
(composed 22 January 1818; published 1838; edited from MS)

Oh golden-tongued Romance, with serene lute!
Fair plumed siren, queen of far away!
Leave melodizing on this wintry day,
Shut up thine olden pages, and be mute.
Adieu! for, once again, the fierce dispute 5
  Betwixt damnation and impassioned clay
  Must I burn through; once more humbly assay
The bitter-sweet of this Shakespearian fruit.
Chief poet, and ye clouds of Albion,
  Begetters of our deep eternal theme! 10
When through the old oak forest I am gone,
  Let me not wander in a barren dream;
But when I am consumed in the fire,
Give me new phoenix wings to fly at my desire.

SONNET (composed 22–31 January 1818; edited from MS)

When I have fears that I may cease to be
Before my pen has gleaned my teeming brain,
Before high-piled books, in charact'ry,
Hold like rich garners the full-ripened grain;
When I behold, upon the night's starred face, 5
Huge cloudy symbols of a high romance,
And think that I may never live to trace
Their shadows, with the magic hand of chance;
And when I feel, fair creature of an hour,
That I shall never look upon thee more, 10
Never have relish in the fairy power
Of unreflecting love – then on the shore
Of the wide world I stand alone and think,
Till love and fame to nothingness do sink.

From Letter from John Keats to John Hamilton Reynolds,
3 February 1818

It may be said that we ought to read our contemporaries, that Wordsworth etc. should have their due from us. But, for the sake of a few fine imaginative or domestic passages, are we to be bullied into a certain philosophy engendered in the whims of an egotist? Every man has his speculations, but every man does not brood and peacock over them till he makes a false coinage and deceives himself. Many a man can travel to the very bourne of heaven,[1] and yet want confidence to put down his half-seeing.

From LETTER FROM JOHN KEATS TO JOHN HAMILTON REYNOLDS, 3 February 1818

[1] *the very bourne of heaven* Keats alludes to his *Endymion*, i. 295.

Sancho will invent a journey heavenward as well as anybody. We hate poetry that has a palpable design upon us – and if we do not agree, seems to put its hand in its breeches' pocket. Poetry should be great and unobtrusive, a thing which enters into one's soul, and does not startle it or amaze it with itself but with its subject. How beautiful are the retired flowers! How would they lose their beauty were they to throng into the highway crying out, 'Admire me, I am a violet!', 'Dote upon me, I am a primrose!' Modern poets differ from the Elizabethans in this: each of the moderns, like an Elector of Hanover, governs his petty state, and knows how many straws are swept daily from the causeways in all his dominions, and has a continual itching that all the housewives should have their coppers well-scoured. The ancients were emperors of vast provinces – they had only heard of the remote ones and scarcely cared to visit them. I will cut all this – I will have no more of Wordsworth or Hunt in particular. Why should we be of the tribe of Manasseh, when we can wander with Esau?[2] Why should we kick against the pricks, when we can walk on roses? Why should we be owls, when we can be eagles? Why be teased with 'nice-eyed wagtails',[3] when we have in sight 'The cherub Contemplation'?[4] Why with Wordsworth's Matthew, 'with a bough of wilding in his hand',[5] when we can have Jaques 'under an oak',[6] etc.? The secret of the bough of wilding will run through your head faster than I can write it. Old Matthew spoke to him some years ago on some nothing, and because he happens in an evening walk to imagine the figure of the old man, he must stamp it down in black and white, and it is henceforth sacred. I don't mean to deny Wordsworth's grandeur and Hunt's merit, but I mean to say we need not be teased with grandeur and merit, when we can have them uncontaminated and unobtrusive. Let us have the old poets and Robin Hood!

From Letter from John Keats to John Hamilton Reynolds, 3 May 1818

I will return to Wordsworth, whether or no he has an extended vision or a circumscribed grandeur, whether he is an eagle in his nest or on the wing. And to be more explicit and to show you how tall I stand by the giant, I will put down a simile of human life as far as I now perceive it – that is, to the point to which I say we both have arrived at. Well, I compare human life to a large mansion of many apartments, two of which I can only describe, the doors of the rest being as yet shut upon me. The first we step into we call the infant or thoughtless chamber, in which we remain as long as we do not think. We remain there a long while, and, notwithstanding the doors of the second chamber remain wide open, showing a bright appearance, we care not to hasten to it, but are at length imperceptibly impelled by the awakening of the thinking principle within us. We no sooner get into the second chamber, which I shall call the chamber of maiden thought, than we become intoxicated with the light and the atmosphere, we see nothing but pleasant wonders, and think of delaying there

---

[2]   Keats is recalling Gen. and Judges 7: 23.
[3]   little ponds that hold the rains,
      Where the nice-eyed wagtails glance,
      Sipping 'twixt their jerking dance.
      (Leigh Hunt, 'The Nymphs' (1818)

[4]   Milton, 'Il Penseroso', 54.
[5]   Wordsworth, 'The Two April Mornings', 59–60.
[6]   *As You Like It*, II. i. 31.

forever in delight. However, among the effects this breathing is father of, is that tremendous one of sharpening one's vision into the heart and nature of man, of convincing one's nerves that the world is full of misery and heartbreak, pain, sickness, and oppression – whereby this chamber of maiden thought becomes gradually darkened and, at the same time, on all sides of it many doors are set open – but all dark, all leading to dark passages. We see not the balance of good and evil. We are in a mist. *We* are now in that state. We feel the 'burden of the mystery'.[1] To this point was Wordsworth come, as far as I can conceive, when he wrote 'Tintern Abbey', and it seems to me that his genius is explorative of those dark passages. Now if we live, and go on thinking, we too shall explore them. He is a genius and superior to us, insofar as he can, more than we, make discoveries, and shed a light in them. Here I must think Wordsworth is deeper than Milton, though I think it has depended more upon the general and gregarious advance of intellect, than individual greatness of mind. From the *Paradise Lost* and the other works of Milton, I hope it is not too presuming (even between ourselves) to say, his philosophy, human and divine, may be tolerably understood by one not much advanced in years. In his time, Englishmen were just emancipated from a great superstition – and men had got hold of certain points and resting-places in reasoning which were too newly born to be doubted, and too much opposed by the mass of Europe not to be thought ethereal and authentically divine. Who could gainsay his ideas on virtue, vice, and chastity in *Comus*, just at the time of the dismissal of codpieces, and a hundred other disgraces? Who would not rest satisfied with his hintings at good and evil in the *Paradise Lost*, when just free from the inquisition and burning in Smithfield? The Reformation produced such immediate and great benefits, that Protestantism was considered under the immediate eye of heaven, and its own remaining dogmas and superstitions then, as it were, regenerated, constituted those resting-places and seeming sure points of reasoning. From that I have mentioned, Milton, whatever he may have thought in the sequel, appears to have been content with these by his writings. He did not think into the human heart, as Wordsworth has done; yet Milton as a philosopher had sure as great powers as Wordsworth. What is then to be inferred? Oh, many things. It proves there is really a grand march of intellect; it proves that a mighty providence subdues the mightiest minds to the service of the time being, whether it be in human knowledge or religion ...

Letter from John Keats to Richard Woodhouse, 27 October 1818

My dear Woodhouse,

Your letter gave me a great satisfaction, more on account of its friendliness than any relish of that matter in it which is accounted so acceptable in the 'genus irritabile'.[1] The best answer I can give you is, in a clerk-like manner, to make some observations on two principal points, which seem to point like indices into the midst of the whole pro and con, about genius, and views, and achievements, and ambition, etc.

From LETTER FROM JOHN KEATS TO JOHN HAMILTON REYNOLDS, 3 May 1818
[1] Wordsworth, 'Tintern Abbey', 39.

LETTER FROM JOHN KEATS TO RICHARD WOODHOUSE, 27 October 1818
[1] Horace, *Epistles*, II. ii. 102.

First: as to the poetical character itself (I mean that sort of which, if I am anything, I am a member – that sort distinguished from the Wordsworthian or egotistical sublime, which is a thing *per se* and stands alone[2]), it is not itself – it has no self – it is everything and nothing – it has no character – it enjoys light and shade – it lives in gusto, be it foul or fair, high or low, rich or poor, mean or elevated. It has as much delight in conceiving an Iago as an Imogen. What shocks the virtuous philosopher delights the chameleon poet. It does no harm from its relish of the dark side of things, any more than from its taste for the bright one – because they both end in speculation. A poet is the most unpoetical of any thing in existence, because he has no identity, he is continually in for – and filling – some other body. The sun, the moon, the sea, and men and women who are creatures of impulse, are poetical, and have about them an unchangeable attribute; the poet has none, no identity – he is certainly the most unpoetical of all God's creatures. If, then, he has no self, and if I am a poet, where is the wonder that I should say I would write no more? Might I not at that very instant have been cogitating on the characters of Saturn and Ops?[3] It is a wretched thing to confess, but is a very fact that not one word I ever utter can be taken for granted as an opinion growing out of my identical nature – how can it, when I have no nature? When I am in a room with people, if I ever am free from speculating on creations of my own brain, then not myself goes home to myself: but the identity of everyone in the room begins so to press upon me, that I am, in a very little time, annihilated – not only among men; it would be the same in a nursery of children. I know not whether I make myself wholly understood. I hope enough so to let you see that no dependence is to be placed on what I said that day.

In the second place I will speak of my views, and of the life I purpose to myself. I am ambitious of doing the world some good – if I should be spared, that may be the work of maturer years. In the interval I will assay to reach to as high a summit in poetry as the nerve bestowed upon me will suffer. The faint conceptions I have of poems to come brings the blood frequently into my forehead. All I hope is that I may not lose all interest in human affairs, that the solitary indifference I feel for applause, even from the finest spirits, will not blunt any acuteness of vision I may have. I do not think it will – I feel assured I should write from the mere yearning and fondness I have for the beautiful, even if my night's labours should be burnt every morning and no eye ever shine upon them.

But even now I am perhaps not speaking from myself, but from some character in whose soul I now live. I am sure, however, that this next sentence is from myself. I feel your anxiety, good opinion, and friendliness, in the highest degree, and am
Yours most sincerely
John Keats

From Lamia, Isabella, The Eve of St Agnes, and Other Poems (1820)

HYPERION: A FRAGMENT (composed autumn 1818-April 1819)

Book I
Deep in the shady sadness of a vale
Far sunken from the healthy breath of morn,

---

[2] *Troilus and Cressida*, I. ii. 15–16.   [3] Characters in 'Hyperion'.

Far from the fiery noon, and eve's one star,
Sat grey-haired Saturn, quiet as a stone,
Still as the silence round about his lair;   5
Forest on forest hung about his head
Like cloud on cloud. No stir of air was there,
Not so much life as on a summer's day
Robs not one light seed from the feathered grass,
But where the dead leaf fell, there did it rest.   10
A stream went voiceless by, still deadened more
By reason of his fallen divinity
Spreading a shade; the naiad mid her reeds
Pressed her cold finger closer to her lips.

Along the margin-sand large footmarks went,   15
No further than to where his feet had strayed,
And slept there since. Upon the sodden ground
His old right hand lay nerveless, listless, dead,
Unsceptred; and his realmless eyes were closed,
While his bowed head seemed list'ning to the earth,   20
His ancient mother, for some comfort yet.

It seemed no force could wake him from his place;
But there came one who, with a kindred hand
Touched his wide shoulders, after bending low
With reverence, though to one who knew it not.   25
She was a goddess of the infant world;
By her in stature the tall Amazon
Had stood a pigmy's height – she would have ta'en
Achilles by the hair and bent his neck,
Or with a finger stayed Ixion's wheel.   30
Her face was large as that of Memphian sphinx,[1]
Pedestalled haply in a palace court
When sages looked to Egypt for their lore.
But oh, how unlike marble was that face!
How beautiful, if sorrow had not made   35
Sorrow more beautiful than Beauty's self.
There was a listening fear in her regard,
As if calamity had but begun;
As if the vanward clouds of evil days
Had spent their malice, and the sullen rear   40
Was with its stored thunder labouring up.
One hand she pressed upon that aching spot
Where beats the human heart, as if just there,
Though an immortal, she felt cruel pain;
The other upon Saturn's bended neck   45

HYPERION: A FRAGMENT (composed autumn 1818-
April 1819)
[1] Memphis was a city in Egypt. Keats saw a sphinx
in the British Museum, in early 1819.

She laid, and to the level of his ear
Leaning with parted lips, some words she spake
In solemn tenor and deep organ tone,
Some mourning words which in our feeble tongue
Would come in these like accents (oh how frail   50
To that large utterance of the early gods!),
'Saturn, look up! – though wherefore, poor old King?
I have no comfort for thee, no, not one;
I cannot say, "Oh wherefore sleepest thou?"
For heaven is parted from thee, and the earth   55
Knows thee not, thus afflicted, for a god;
And ocean too, with all its solemn noise,
Has from thy sceptre passed, and all the air
Is emptied of thine hoary majesty.
Thy thunder, conscious of the new command,   60
Rumbles reluctant o'er our fallen house,
And thy sharp lightning in unpractised hands
Scorches and burns our once serene domain.
Oh aching time! Oh moments big as years!
All as ye pass swell out the monstrous truth,   65
And press it so upon our weary griefs
That unbelief has not a space to breathe.
Saturn, sleep on! Oh thoughtless, why did I
Thus violate thy slumbrous solitude?
Why should I ope thy melancholy eyes?   70
Saturn, sleep on, while at thy feet I weep!'
    As when, upon a tranced summer night,
Those green-robed senators of mighty woods,
Tall oaks, branch-charmed by the earnest stars,
Dream, and so dream all night without a stir,   75
Save from one gradual solitary gust
Which comes upon the silence, and dies off
As if the ebbing air had but one wave;
So came these words and went, the while in tears
She touched her fair large forehead to the ground,   80
Just where her falling hair might be outspread,
A soft and silken mat for Saturn's feet.
One moon, with alteration slow, had shed
Her silver seasons four upon the night,
And still these two were postured motionless,   85
Like natural sculpture in cathedral cavern –
The frozen god still couchant on the earth,
And the sad goddess weeping at his feet.
Until at length old Saturn lifted up
His faded eyes, and saw his kingdom gone,   90
And all the gloom and sorrow of the place,
And that fair kneeling goddess, and then spake
As with a palsied tongue, and while his beard

Shook horrid with such aspen malady:
'Oh tender spouse of gold Hyperion,
Thea, I feel thee ere I see thy face;
Look up, and let me see our doom in it,
Look up, and tell me if this feeble shape
Is Saturn's; tell me if thou hear'st the voice
Of Saturn; tell me if this wrinkling brow,
Naked and bare of its great diadem,
Peers like the front of Saturn. Who had power
To make me desolate? Whence came the strength?
How was it nurtured to such bursting forth,
While Fate seemed strangled in my nervous grasp?
But it is so, and I am smothered up
And buried from all godlike exercise
Of influence benign on planets pale,
Of admonitions to the winds and seas,
Of peaceful sway above man's harvesting,
And all those acts which deity supreme
Doth ease its heart of love in. I am gone
Away from my own bosom; I have left
My strong identity, my real self,
Somewhere between the throne and where I sit
Here on this spot of earth. Search, Thea, search!
Open thine eyes eterne, and sphere them round
Upon all space – space starred, and lorn of light;
Space regioned with life-air, and barren void;
Spaces of fire, and all the yawn of hell.
Search, Thea, search! And tell me if thou seest
A certain shape or shadow, making way
With wings or chariot fierce to repossess
A heaven he lost erewhile: it must – it must
Be of ripe progress; Saturn must be King.
Yes, there must be a golden victory;
There must be gods thrown down, and trumpets blown
Of triumph calm, and hymns of festival
Upon the gold clouds metropolitan,
Voices of soft proclaim, and silver stir
Of strings in hollow shells; and there shall be
Beautiful things made new, for the surprise
Of the sky-children. I will give command:
Thea! Thea! Thea! Where is Saturn?'
    This passion lifted him upon his feet,
And made his hands to struggle in the air,
His Druid locks[2] to shake and ooze with sweat,
His eyes to fever out, his voice to cease.

95

100

105

110

115

120

125

130

135

[2] i.e. long-haired.

He stood, and heard not Thea's sobbing deep;
A little time, and then again he snatched   140
Utterance thus: 'But cannot I create?
Cannot I form? Cannot I fashion forth
Another world, another universe,
To overbear and crumble this to naught?
Where is another chaos? Where?' That word   145
Found way unto Olympus, and made quake
The rebel three.³ Thea was startled up,
And in her bearing was a sort of hope
As thus she quick-voiced spake, yet full of awe:
'This cheers our fallen house; come to our friends,   150
Oh Saturn, come away and give them heart!
I know the covert, for thence came I hither.'
Thus brief, then with beseeching eyes she went
With backward footing through the shade a space;
He followed, and she turned to lead the way   155
Through aged boughs that yielded like the mist
Which eagles cleave upmounting from their nest.
    Meanwhile in other realms big tears were shed,
More sorrow like to this, and suchlike woe
Too huge for mortal tongue or pen of scribe.   160
The Titans fierce, self-hid, or prison-bound,
Groaned for the old allegiance once more,
And listened in sharp pain for Saturn's voice.
But one of the whole mammoth-brood still kept
His sov'reignty, and rule, and majesty: 165
Blazing Hyperion on his orbed fire
Still sat, still snuffed the incense, teeming up
From man to the sun's god – yet unsecure.
For as among us mortals omens drear
Fright and perplex, so also shuddered he –   170
Not at dog's howl, or gloom-bird's hated screech,
Or the familiar visiting of one
Upon the first toll of his passing-bell,
Or prophesyings of the midnight lamp,
But horrors portioned to a giant nerve   175
Oft made Hyperion ache. His palace bright,
Bastioned with pyramids of glowing gold,
And touched with shade of bronzed obelisks,
Glared a blood-red through all its thousand courts,
Arches, and domes, and fiery galleries;   180
And all its curtains of aurorean clouds
Flushed angerly, while sometimes eagle's wings
(Unseen before by gods or wondering men)

³ Saturn's sons, Jupiter, Neptune, and Pluto.

Darkened the place; and neighing steeds were heard,
Not heard before by gods or wondering men.   185
Also, when he would taste the spicy wreaths
Of incense, breathed aloft from sacred hills,
Instead of sweets, his ample palate took
Savour of poisonous brass and metal sick.
And so, when harboured in the sleepy west   190
After the full completion of fair day,
For rest divine upon exalted couch
And slumber in the arms of melody,
He paced away the pleasant hours of ease
With stride colossal on from hall to hall;   195
While far within each aisle and deep recess
His winged minions in close clusters stood,
Amazed and full of fear, like anxious men
Who on wide plains gather in panting troops
When earthquakes jar their battlements and towers.   200
Even now, while Saturn, roused from icy trance,
Went step for step with Thea through the woods,
Hyperion, leaving twilight in the rear,
Came slope upon the threshold of the west;
Then, as was wont, his palace-door flew ope   205
In smoothest silence, save what solemn tubes
Blown by the serious zephyrs gave of sweet
And wandering sounds, slow-breathed melodies;
And like a rose in vermeil tint and shape,
In fragrance soft, and coolness to the eye,   210
That inlet to severe magnificence
Stood full-blown, for the god to enter in.
   He entered, but he entered full of wrath;
His flaming robes streamed out beyond his heels
And gave a roar as if of earthly fire,   215
That scared away the meek ethereal Hours
And made their dove-wings tremble. On he flared,
From stately nave to nave, from vault to vault,
Through bowers of fragrant and enwreathed light
And diamond-paved lustrous long arcades,   220
Until he reached the great main cupola.
There standing fierce beneath, he stamped his foot,
And from the basements deep to the high towers
Jarred his own golden region; and before
The quavering thunder thereupon had ceased,   225
His voice leaped out, despite of godlike curb,
To this result: 'Oh dreams of day and night!
Oh monstrous forms! Oh effigies of pain!
Oh spectres busy in a cold, cold gloom!
Oh lank-eared phantoms of black-weeded pools!   230
Why do I know ye? Why have I seen ye? Why

Is my eternal essence thus distraught
To see and to behold these horrors new?
Saturn is fallen, am I too to fall?
Am I to leave this haven of my rest,   235
This cradle of my glory, this soft clime,
This calm luxuriance of blissful light,
These crystalline pavilions and pure fanes
Of all my lucent empire? It is left
Deserted, void, nor any haunt of mine.   240
The blaze, the splendour, and the symmetry,
I cannot see – but darkness, death and darkness.
Even here, into my centre of repose,
The shady visions come to domineer,
Insult, and blind, and stifle up my pomp.   245
Fall? No, by Tellus[4] and her briny robes!
Over the fiery frontier of my realms
I will advance a terrible right arm
Shall scare that infant thunderer, rebel Jove,
And bid old Saturn take his throne again.'   250
He spake, and ceased, the while a heavier threat
Held struggle with his throat but came not forth;
For as in theatres of crowded men
Hubbub increases more they call out 'Hush!'
So at Hyperion's words the phantoms pale   255
Bestirred themselves, thrice horrible and cold,
And from the mirrored level where he stood
A mist arose as from a scummy marsh.
At this, through all his bulk an agony
Crept gradual from the feet unto the crown,   260
Like a lithe serpent vast and muscular
Making slow way, with head and neck convulsed
From over-strained might. Released, he fled
To the eastern gates, and full six dewy hours
Before the dawn in season due should blush,   265
He breathed fierce breath against the sleepy portals,
Cleared them of heavy vapours, burst them wide
Suddenly on the ocean's chilly streams.
The planet orb of fire whereon he rode
Each day from east to west the heavens through,   270
Spun round in sable curtaining of clouds;
Not therefore veiled quite, blindfold and hid,
But ever and anon the glancing spheres,
Circles, and arcs, and broad-belting colure,[5]
Glowed through, and wrought upon the muffling dark   275

---

4   *Tellus* the earth.
5   *colure* technical term for 'each of two great circles
which intersect each other at right angles at the poles,
and divide the equinoctial and the ecliptic into four
equal parts' (*OED*).

Sweet-shaped lightnings from the nadir deep
Up to the zenith – hieroglyphics old[6]
Which sages and keen-eyed astrologers
Then living on the earth, with labouring thought
Won from the gaze of many centuries –   280
Now lost, save what we find on remnants huge
Of stone, or marble swart, their import gone,
Their wisdom long since fled. Two wings this orb
Possessed for glory, two fair argent wings
Ever exalted at the god's approach;   285
And now from forth the gloom their plumes immense
Rose one by one, till all outspreaded were,
While still the dazzling globe maintained eclipse,
Awaiting for Hyperion's command.
Fain would he have commanded, fain took throne   290
And bid the day begin, if but for change.
He might not – no, though a primeval god;
The sacred seasons might not be disturbed.
Therefore the operations of the dawn
Stayed in their birth, even as here 'tis told.   295
Those silver wings expanded sisterly,
Eager to sail their orb; the porches wide
Opened upon the dusk demesnes of night;
And the bright Titan, frenzied with new woes,
Unused to bend, by hard compulsion bent   300
His spirit to the sorrow of the time;
And all along a dismal rack of clouds,
Upon the boundaries of day and night,
He stretched himself in grief and radiance faint.
There as he lay, the heaven with its stars   305
Looked down on him with pity, and the voice
Of Coelus, from the universal space,
Thus whispered low and solemn in his ear:
'Oh brightest of my children dear, earth-born
And sky-engendered, son of mysteries   310
All unrevealed even to the powers
Which met at thy creating; at whose joys
And palpitations sweet, and pleasures soft,
I, Coelus, wonder how they came and whence,
And at the fruits thereof what shapes they be,   315
Distinct and visible – symbols divine,
Manifestations of that beauteous life
Diffused unseen throughout eternal space.
Of these new-formed art thou, oh brightest child!
Of these, thy brethren and the goddesses!   320

---

6   Signs of the zodiac.

There is sad feud among ye, and rebellion
Of son against his sire. I saw him fall,
I saw my first-born[7] tumbled from his throne!
To me his arms were spread, to me his voice
Found way from forth the thunders round his head!   325
Pale wox I, and in vapours hid my face.
Art thou, too, near such doom? Vague fear there is,
For I have seen my sons most unlike gods.
Divine ye were created, and divine
In sad demeanour, solemn, undisturbed,   330
Unruffled, like high gods, ye lived and ruled.
Now I behold in you fear, hope, and wrath,
Actions of rage and passion – even as
I see them on the mortal world beneath,
In men who die. This is the grief, oh son;   335
Sad sign of ruin, sudden dismay, and fall!
Yet do thou strive; as thou art capable,
As thou canst move about, an evident god,
And canst oppose to each malignant hour
Ethereal presence. I am but a voice;   340
My life is but the life of winds and tides,
No more than winds and tides can I avail –
But thou canst. Be thou therefore in the van
Of circumstance; yea, seize the arrow's barb
Before the tense string murmur. To the earth!   345
For there thou wilt find Saturn and his woes.
Meantime I will keep watch on thy bright sun,
And of thy seasons be a careful nurse.'
Ere half this region-whisper had come down,
Hyperion arose, and on the stars   350
Lifted his curved lids, and kept them wide
Until it ceased, and still he kept them wide,
And still they were the same bright, patient stars.
Then with a slow incline of his broad breast,
Like to a diver in the pearly seas,   355
Forward he stooped over the airy shore
And plunged all noiseless into the deep night.

Book II

Just at the self-same beat of Time's wide wings
Hyperion slid into the rustled air,
And Saturn gained with Thea that sad place
Where Cybele and the bruised Titans mourned.
It was a den where no insulting light   5
Could glimmer on their tears; where their own groans

---

[7] Saturn.

They felt, but heard not, for the solid roar
Of thunderous waterfalls and torrents hoarse,
Pouring a constant bulk, uncertain where.
Crag jutting forth to crag, and rocks that seemed   10
Ever as if just rising from a sleep,
Forehead to forehead held their monstrous horns;
And thus in thousand hugest fantasies
Made a fit roofing to this nest of woe.
Instead of thrones, hard flint they sat upon,   15
Couches of rugged stone, and slaty ridge
Stubborned with iron. All were not assembled,
Some chained in torture and some wandering.
Coeus, and Gyges, and Briareus,
Typhon, and Dolor, and Porphyrion,[8]   20
With many more, the brawniest in assault,
Were pent in regions of laborious breath,
Dungeoned in opaque element to keep
Their clenched teeth still clenched, and all their limbs
Locked up like veins of metal, cramped and screwed;   25
Without a motion, save of their big hearts
Heaving in pain, and horribly convulsed
With sanguine feverous boiling gurge of pulse.
Mnemosyne was straying in the world;
Far from her moon had Phoebe wandered;   30
And many else were free to roam abroad,
But for the main, here found they covert drear.
Scarce images of life, one here, one there,
Lay vast and edgeways; like a dismal cirque
Of Druid stones upon a forlorn moor,   35
When the chill rain begins at shut of eve
In dull November, and their chancel vault,
The heaven itself, is blinded throughout night.[9]
Each one kept shroud, nor to his neighbour gave
Or word, or look, or action of despair.   40
Creus was one; his ponderous iron mace
Lay by him, and a shattered rib of rock
Told of his rage ere he thus sank and pined.
Iapetus another – in his grasp
A serpent's plashy neck, its barbed tongue   45
Squeezed from the gorge, and all its uncurled length
Dead, and because the creature could not spit
Its poison in the eyes of conquering Jove.
Next Cottus; prone he lay, chin uppermost
As though in pain, for still upon the flint   50

---

[8] The assembly of Titans is influenced by Milton's account of the fallen angels in hell, *Paradise Lost*, i. 376–521.

[9] During his tour of the Lake District in June 1818, Keats visited Castlerigg stone circle near Keswick.

He ground severe his skull, with open mouth
And eyes at horrid working. Nearest him
Asia, born of most enormous Caf,
Who cost her mother Tellus keener pangs,
Though feminine, than any of her sons.   55
More thought than woe was in her dusky face,
For she was prophesying of her glory,
And in her wide imagination stood
Palm-shaded temples and high rival fanes
By Oxus or in Ganges' sacred isles.   60
Even as Hope upon her anchor leans,
So leant she, not so fair, upon a tusk
Shed from the broadest of her elephants.
Above her, on a crag's uneasy shelve,
Upon his elbow raised, all prostrate else,   65
Shadowed Enceladus – once tame and mild
As grazing ox unworried in the meads,
Now tiger-passioned, lion-thoughted, wroth,
He meditated, plotted, and even now
Was hurling mountains in that second war   70
Not long delayed, that scared the younger gods
To hide themselves in forms of beast and bird.
Not far hence Atlas; and beside him prone
Phorcus, the sire of Gorgons. Neighboured close
Oceanus, and Tethys, in whose lap   75
Sobbed Clymene among her tangled hair.
In midst of all lay Themis, at the feet
Of Ops the queen, all clouded round from sight;
No shape distinguishable, more than when
Thick night confounds the pine-tops with the clouds: 80
And many else whose names may not be told.
For when the muse's wings are air-ward spread
Who shall delay her flight? And she must chaunt
Of Saturn and his guide, who now had climbed
With damp and slippery footing from a depth   85
More horrid still. Above a sombre cliff
Their heads appeared, and up their stature grew
Till on the level height their steps found ease;
Then Thea spread abroad her trembling arms
Upon the precincts of this nest of pain,   90
And sidelong fixed her eye on Saturn's face.
There saw she direst strife, the supreme god
At war with all the frailty of grief,
Of rage, of fear, anxiety, revenge,
Remorse, spleen, hope, but most of all despair.   95
Against these plagues he strove in vain, for Fate
Had poured a mortal oil upon his head,
A disanointing poison, so that Thea,

Affrighted, kept her still, and let him pass
First onwards in, among the fallen tribe.   100
    As with us mortal men, the laden heart
Is persecuted more, and fevered more,
When it is nighing to the mournful house
Where other hearts are sick of the same bruise;
So Saturn, as he walked into the midst,   105
Felt faint, and would have sunk among the rest,
But that he met Enceladus' eye,
Whose mightiness and awe of him, at once
Came like an inspiration – and he shouted,
'Titans, behold your god!' At which some groaned,   110
Some started on their feet, some also shouted,
Some wept, some wailed, all bowed with reverence;
And Ops, uplifting her black folded veil,
Showed her pale cheeks and all her forehead wan,
Her eyebrows thin and jet, and hollow eyes.   115
There is a roaring in the bleak-grown pines
When winter lifts his voice; there is a noise
Among immortals when a god gives sign,
With hushing finger, how he means to load
His tongue with the full weight of utterless thought,   120
With thunder, and with music, and with pomp:
Such noise is like the roar of bleak-grown pines,
Which, when it ceases in this mountained world,
No other sound succeeds; but ceasing here,
Among these fallen, Saturn's voice therefrom   125
Grew up like organ, that begins anew
Its strain, when other harmonies, stopped short,
Leave the dinned air vibrating silverly.
Thus grew it up: 'Not in my own sad breast,
Which is its own great judge and searcher-out,   130
Can I find reason why ye should be thus;
Not in the legends of the first of days,
Studied from that old spirit-leaved book
Which starry Uranus with finger bright
Saved from the shores of darkness, when the waves   135
Low-ebbed still hid it up in shallow gloom,
And the which book ye know I ever kept
For my firm-based footstool – ah, infirm!
Not there, nor in sign, symbol, or portent
Of element, earth, water, air, and fire,   140
At war, at peace, or inter-quarrelling
One against one, or two, or three, or all
Each several one against the other three,
As fire with air loud warring when rainfloods
Drown both, and press them both against earth's face,   145
Where, finding sulphur, a quadruple wrath

Unhinges the poor world – not in that strife,
Wherefrom I take strange lore and read it deep,
Can I find reason why ye should be thus.
No, nowhere can unriddle, though I search   150
And pore on nature's universal scroll
Even to swooning, why ye divinities,
The first-born of all shaped and palpable gods,
Should cower beneath what, in comparison,
Is untremendous might. Yet ye are here,   155
O'erwhelmed, and spurned, and battered – ye are here!
Oh Titans, shall I say "Arise"? Ye groan;
Shall I say "Crouch"? Ye groan. What can I then?
Oh heaven wide! Oh unseen parent dear!
What can I? Tell me, all ye brethren gods,   160
How we can war, how engine[10] our great wrath;
Oh speak your counsel now, for Saturn's ear
Is all a-hungered. Thou, Oceanus,
Ponderest high and deep, and in thy face
I see, astonied, that severe content   165
Which comes of thought and musing – give us help!'
    So ended Saturn, and the god of the sea,
Sophist and sage from no Athenian grove,
But cogitation in his watery shades,
Arose, with locks not oozy, and began,   170
In murmurs, which his first-endeavouring tongue
Caught infant-like from the far-foamed sands:
'Oh ye, whom wrath consumes, who, passion-stung,
Writhe at defeat, and nurse your agonies!
Shut up your senses, stifle up your ears,   175
My voice is not a bellows unto ire.
Yet listen, ye who will, whilst I bring proof
How ye, perforce, must be content to stoop;
And in the proof much comfort will I give,
If ye will take that comfort in its truth.   180
We fall by course of nature's law, not force
Of thunder, or of Jove. Great Saturn, thou
Hast sifted well the atom-universe;
But for this reason, that thou art the King,
And only blind from sheer supremacy,   185
One avenue was shaded from thine eyes
Through which I wandered to eternal truth.
And first, as thou wast not the first of powers,
So art thou not the last; it cannot be.
Thou art not the beginning nor the end.   190
From chaos and parental darkness came

---

[10] *engine* activate, turn to the uses of war.

Light, the first fruits of that intestine broil,
That sullen ferment which for wondrous ends
Was ripening in itself. The ripe hour came,
And with it light, and light, engendering   195
Upon its own producer, forthwith touched
The whole enormous matter into life.
Upon that very hour, our parentage,
The heavens and the earth, were manifest;
Then thou first-born, and we the giant-race,   200
Found ourselves ruling new and beauteous realms.
Now comes the pain of truth, to whom 'tis pain;
Oh folly! for to bear all naked truths,
And to envisage circumstance, all calm,
That is the top of sovereignty. Mark well!   205
As heaven and earth are fairer, fairer far
Than chaos and blank darkness, though once chiefs;
And as we show beyond that heaven and earth
In form and shape compact and beautiful,
In will, in action free, companionship,   210
And thousand other signs of purer life –
So on our heels a fresh perfection treads,
A power more strong in beauty, born of us
And fated to excel us, as we pass
In glory that old darkness. Nor are we   215
Thereby more conquered than by us the rule
Of shapeless chaos. Say, doth the dull soil
Quarrel with the proud forests it hath fed,
And feedeth still, more comely than itself?
Can it deny the chiefdom of green groves?   220
Or shall the tree be envious of the dove
Because it cooeth, and hath snowy wings
To wander wherewithal and find its joys?
We are such forest trees, and our fair boughs
Have bred forth not pale solitary doves   225
But eagles golden-feathered, who do tower
Above us in their beauty, and must reign
In right thereof; for 'tis the eternal law
That first in beauty should be first in might –
Yea, by that law another race may drive   230
Our conquerors to mourn as we do now.
Have ye beheld the young god of the seas,[11]
My dispossessor? Have ye seen his face?
Have ye beheld his chariot, foamed along
By noble winged creatures he hath made?   235
I saw him on the calmed waters scud,

---

[11] Neptune.

With such a glow of beauty in his eyes
That it enforced me to bid sad farewell
To all my empire; farewell sad I took,
And hither came to see how dolorous fate   240
Had wrought upon ye, and how I might best
Give consolation in this woe extreme.
Receive the truth, and let it be your balm.'
    Whether through posed conviction, or disdain,
They guarded silence when Oceanus   245
Left murmuring, what deepest thought can tell?
But so it was; none answered for a space,
Save one whom none regarded, Clymene.
And yet she answered not, only complained
With hectic lips, and eyes up-looking mild,   250
Thus wording timidly among the fierce:
'Oh father, I am here the simplest voice,
And all my knowledge is that joy is gone,
And this thing woe crept in among our hearts,
There to remain for ever, as I fear.   255
I would not bode of evil, if I thought
So weak a creature could turn off the help
Which by just right should come of mighty gods;
Yet let me tell my sorrow, let me tell
Of what I heard, and how it made we weep,   260
And know that we had parted from all hope.
I stood upon a shore, a pleasant shore
Where a sweet clime was breathed from a land
Of fragrance, quietness, and trees, and flowers.
Full of calm joy it was, as I of grief,   265
Too full of joy and soft delicious warmth –
So that I felt a movement in my heart
To chide, and to reproach that solitude
With songs of misery, music of our woes;
And sat me down, and took a mouthed shell   270
And murmured into it, and made melody.
Oh melody no more! For while I sang,
And with poor skill let pass into the breeze
The dull shell's echo, from a bowery strand
Just opposite, an island of the sea,   275
There came enchantment with the shifting wind,
That did both drown and keep alive my ears.
I threw my shell away upon the sand
And a wave filled it, as my sense was filled
With that new blissful golden melody.   280
A living death was in each gush of sounds,
Each family of rapturous hurried notes
That fell, one after one, yet all at once,
Like pearl beads dropping sudden from their string;

And then another, then another strain,   285
Each like a dove leaving its olive perch,
With music winged instead of silent plumes,
To hover round my head, and make me sick
Of joy and grief at once. Grief overcame,
And I was stopping up my frantic ears,   290
When, past all hindrance of my trembling hands,
A voice came sweeter, sweeter than all tune,
And still it cried, "Apollo! Young Apollo!
The morning-bright Apollo! Young Apollo!"
I fled, it followed me, and cried "Apollo!"   295
Oh father and oh brethren, had ye felt
Those pains of mine – oh Saturn, hadst thou felt,
Ye would not call this too indulged tongue
Presumptous in thus venturing to be heard.'
   So far her voice flowed on, like timorous brook   300
That, lingering along a pebbled coast,
Doth fear to meet the sea – but sea it met
And shuddered; for the overwhelming voice
Of huge Enceladus swallowed it in wrath –
The ponderous syllables, like sullen waves   305
In the half-glutted hollows of reef-rocks,
Came booming thus, while still upon his arm
He leaned (not rising, from supreme contempt):
'Or shall we listen to the over-wise,
Or to the over-foolish, giant gods?   310
Not thunderbolt on thunderbolt, till all
That rebel Jove's whole armoury were spent,
Not world on world upon these shoulders piled
Could agonize me more than baby-words
In midst of this dethronement horrible.   315
Speak! Roar! Shout! Yell, ye sleepy Titans all!
Do ye forget the blows, the buffets vile?
Are ye not smitten by a youngling arm?
Dost thou forget, sham monarch of the waves,
Thy scalding in the seas? What, have I roused   320
Your spleens with so few simple words as these?
Oh joy, for now I see ye are not lost!
Oh joy, for now I see a thousand eyes
Wide glaring for revenge!' As this he said,
He lifted up his stature vast, and stood,   325
Still without intermission speaking thus:
'Now ye are flames, I'll tell you how to burn
And purge the ether of our enemies;
How to feed fierce the crooked stings of fire
And singe away the swollen clouds of Jove,   330
Stifling that puny essence in its tent.
Oh let him feel the evil he hath done –

For though I scorn Oceanus' lore,
Much pain have I for more than loss of realms.
The days of peace and slumberous calm are fled;   335
Those days, all innocent of scathing war,
When all the fair Existences of heaven
Came open-eyed to guess what we would speak –
That was before our brows were taught to frown,
Before our lips knew else but solemn sounds;   340
That was before we knew the winged thing,
Victory, might be lost, or might be won.
And be ye mindful that Hyperion,
Our brightest brother, still is undisgraced –
Hyperion, lo! His radiance is here!'   345
    All eyes were on Enceladus' face,
And they beheld, while still Hyperion's name
Flew from his lips up to the vaulted rocks,
A pallid gleam across his features stern –
Not savage, for he saw full many a god   350
Wroth as himself. He looked upon them all,
And in each face he saw a gleam of light,
But splendider in Saturn's, whose hoar locks
Shone like the bubbling foam about a keel
When the prow sweeps into a midnight cove.   355
In pale and silver silence they remained,
Till suddenly a splendour, like the morn,
Pervaded all the beetling gloomy steeps,
All the sad spaces of oblivion,
And every gulf, and every chasm old,   360
And every height, and every sullen depth,
Voiceless, or hoarse with loud tormented streams,
And all the everlasting cataracts,
And all the headlong torrents far and near,
Mantled before in darkness and huge shade,   365
Now saw the light and made it terrible.
It was Hyperion: a granite peak
His bright feet touched, and there he stayed to view
The misery his brilliance had betrayed
To the most hateful seeing of itself.   370
Golden his hair of short Numidian curl,
Regal his shape majestic, a vast shade
In midst of his own brightness, like the bulk
Of Memnon's image at the set of sun[12]
To one who travels from the dusking east;   375
Sighs, too, as mournful as that Memnon's harp

---

[12] The statue of Memnon at Thebes in Egypt was
said to give forth a musical sound when touched by
the dawn.

He uttered, while his hands contemplative
He pressed together, and in silence stood.
Despondence seized again the fallen gods
At sight of the dejected King of Day, 380
And many hid their faces from the light.
But fierce Enceladus sent forth his eyes
Among the brotherhood, and at their glare
Uprose Iapetus, and Creus too,
And Phorcus, sea-born, and together strode 385
To where he towered on his eminence.
There those four shouted forth old Saturn's name;
Hyperion from the peak loud answered, 'Saturn!'
Saturn sat near the mother of the gods,
In whose face was no joy, though all the gods 390
Gave from their hollow throats the name of 'Saturn!'

Book III
Thus in alternate uproar and sad peace,
Amazed were those Titans utterly.
Oh leave them, muse! Oh leave them to their woes,
For thou art weak to sing such tumults dire;
A solitary sorrow best befits 5
Thy lips, and antheming a lonely grief.
Leave them, oh muse! For thou anon wilt find
Many a fallen old divinity
Wandering in vain about bewildered shores.
Meantime touch piously the Delphic harp, 10
And not a wind of heaven but will breathe
In aid soft warble from the Dorian flute;
For lo! 'tis for the father of all verse.[13]
Flush everything that hath a vermeil hue,
Let the rose glow intense and warm the air, 15
And let the clouds of even and of morn
Float in voluptuous fleeces o'er the hills;
Let the red wine within the goblet boil,
Cold as a bubbling well; let faint-lipped shells
On sands or in great deeps, vermilion turn 20
Through all their labyrinths; and let the maid
Blush keenly, as with some warm kiss surprised.
Chief isle of the embowered Cyclades,
Rejoice, oh Delos, with thine olives green,
And poplars, and lawn-shading palms, and beech 25
In which the zephyr breathes the loudest song,
And hazels thick, dark-stemmed beneath the shade.
Apollo is once more the golden theme!
Where was he when the giant of the sun[14]

---

[13] Apollo.   [14] Hyperion.

Stood bright amid the sorrow of his peers? 30
Together had he left his mother fair
And his twin-sister[15] sleeping in their bower,
And in the morning twilight wandered forth
Beside the osiers of a rivulet,
Full ankle-deep in lilies of the vale. 35
The nightingale had ceased, and a few stars
Were lingering in the heavens, while the thrush
Began calm-throated. Throughout all the isle
There was no covert, no retired cave
Unhaunted by the murmurous noise of waves, 40
Though scarcely heard in many a green recess.
He listened and he wept, and his bright tears
Went trickling down the golden bow he held.
Thus with half-shut suffused eyes he stood,
While from beneath some cumbrous boughs hard by 45
With solemn step an awful goddess[16] came,
And there was purport in her looks for him,
Which he with eager guess began to read
Perplexed, the while melodiously he said:
'How cam'st thou over the unfooted sea? 50
Or hath that antique mien and robed form
Moved in these vales invisible till now?
Sure I have heard those vestments sweeping o'er
The fallen leaves, when I have sat alone
In cool mid-forest. Surely I have traced 55
The rustle of those ample skirts about
These grassy solitudes, and seen the flowers
Lift up their heads, as still the whisper passed.
Goddess! I have beheld those eyes before,
And their eternal calm, and all that face, 60
Or I have dreamed.' 'Yes', said the supreme shape,
'Thou has dreamed of me; and awaking up
Didst find a lyre all golden by thy side,
Whose strings touched by thy fingers, all the vast
Unwearied ear of the whole universe 65
Listened in pain and pleasure at the birth
Of such new tuneful wonder. Is't not strange
That thou shouldst weep, so gifted? Tell me, youth,
What sorrow thou canst feel – for I am sad
When thou dost shed a tear. Explain thy griefs 70
To one who in this lonely isle hath been
The watcher of thy sleep and hours of life,
From the young day when first thy infant hand
Plucked witless the weak flowers, till thine arm

---

[15] Latona and Diana.   [16] Mnemosyne.

Could bend that bow heroic to all times.   75
Show thy heart's secret to an ancient power
Who hath forsaken old and sacred thrones
For prophecies of thee, and for the sake
Of loveliness new born.' Apollo then,
With sudden scrutiny and gloomless eyes,   80
Thus answered, while his white melodious throat
Throbbed with the syllables: 'Mnemosyne!
Thy name is on my tongue I know not how;
Why should I tell thee what thou so well seest?
Why should I strive to show what from thy lips   85
Would come no mystery? For me, dark, dark
And painful, vile oblivion seals my eyes.
I strive to search wherefore I am so sad
Until a melancholy numbs my limbs;
And then upon the grass I sit and moan   90
Like one who once had wings. Oh why should I
Feel cursed and thwarted, when the liegeless air
Yields to my step aspirant? Why should I
Spurn the green turf as hateful to my feet?
Goddess benign, point forth some unknown thing.   95
Are there not other regions than this isle?
What are the stars? There is the sun, the sun!
And the most patient brilliance of the moon!
And stars by thousands! Point me out the way
To any one particular beauteous star,   100
And I will flit into it with my lyre
And make its silvery splendour pant with bliss.
I have heard the cloudy thunder. Where is power?
Whose hand, whose essence, what divinity
Makes this alarum in the elements   105
While I here idle listen on the shores
In fearless yet in aching ignorance?
Oh tell me, lonely goddess, by thy harp
That waileth every morn and eventide,
Tell me why thus I rave about these groves!   110
Mute thou remainest, mute! Yet I can read
A wondrous lesson in thy silent face:
Knowledge enormous makes a god of me.
Names, deeds, grey legends, dire events, rebellions,
Majesties, sovran voices, agonies,   115
Creations and destroyings, all at once
Pour into the wide hollows of my brain
And deify me, as if some blithe wine
Or bright elixir peerless I had drunk,
And so become immortal.' Thus the god,   120
While his enkindled eyes, with level glance
Beneath his white soft temples, steadfast kept

Trembling with light upon Mnemosyne.
Soon wild commotions shook him, and made flush
All the immortal fairness of his limbs,   125
Most like the struggle at the gate of death;
Or liker still to one who should take leave
Of pale immortal death, and with a pang
As hot as death's is chill, with fierce convulse
Die into life. So young Apollo anguished;   130
His very hair, his golden tresses famed
Kept undulation round his eager neck.
During the pain Mnemosyne upheld
Her arms as one who prophesied. At length
Apollo shrieked – and lo! from all his limbs   135
Celestial[17] . . .

The Eve of St Agnes (composed 18 January–2 February 1819)

I

St Agnes' Eve – ah, bitter chill it was!
The owl, for all his feathers, was a-cold;
The hare limped trembling through the frozen grass,
And silent was the flock in woolly fold.
Numb were the beadsman's fingers, while he told   5
His rosary, and while his frosted breath,
Like pious incense from a censer old,
Seemed taking flight for heaven, without a death,
Past the sweet Virgin's picture, while his prayer he saith.

II

His prayer he saith, this patient, holy man;   10
Then takes his lamp and riseth from his knees,
And back returneth, meagre, barefoot, wan,
Along the chapel aisle by slow degrees.
The sculptured dead on each side seem to freeze,
Imprisoned in black, purgatorial rails;   15
Knights, ladies, praying in dumb orat'ries,
He passeth by; and his weak spirit fails
To think how they may ache in icy hoods and mails.

---

[17] In his annotated copy of *Endymion* (1818), Woodhouse recorded that this poem, 'if completed, would have treated of the dethronement of Hyperion, the former god of the sun, by Apollo (and incidentally of those of Oceanus by Neptune, of Saturn by Jupiter, etc., and of the war of the giants for Saturn's re-establishment), with other events of which we have but very dark hints in the mythological poets of Greece and Rome. In fact, the incidents would have been pure creations of the poet's brain' (p. 426).

III

Northward he turneth through a little door,
And scarce three steps ere music's golden tongue   20
Flattered to tears this aged man and poor;
But no – already had his deathbell rung,
The joys of all his life were said and sung –
His was harsh penance on St Agnes' Eve:
Another way he went, and soon among   25
Rough ashes sat he for his soul's reprieve,
And all night kept awake, for sinners' sake to grieve.

IV

That ancient beadsman heard the prelude soft,
And so it chanced, for many a door was wide
From hurry to and fro. Soon, up aloft,   30
The silver, snarling trumpets 'gan to chide;
The level chambers, ready with their pride,
Were glowing to receive a thousand guests;
The carved angels, ever eager-eyed,
Stared, where upon their heads the cornice rests,   35
With hair blown back, and wings put crosswise on their breasts.

V

At length burst in the argent revelry,
With plume, tiara, and all rich array,
Numerous as shadows haunting fairily
The brain, new stuffed in youth, with triumphs gay   40
Of old romance. These let us wish away,
And turn, sole-thoughted, to one lady there,
Whose heart had brooded all that wintry day
On love, and winged St Agnes' saintly care,
As she had heard old dames full many times declare.   45

VI

They told her how, upon St Agnes' Eve,
Young virgins might have visions of delight,
And soft adorings from their loves receive
Upon the honeyed middle of the night,
If ceremonies due they did aright –   50
As, supperless to bed they must retire,
And couch supine their beauties, lily-white;

Nor look behind, nor sideways, but require
Of heaven with upward eyes for all that they desire.[1]

VII

Full of this whim was thoughtful Madeline.   55
The music, yearning like a god in pain,
She scarcely heard; her maiden eyes divine,
Fixed on the floor, saw many a sweeping train
Pass by – she heeded not at all; in vain
Came many a tiptoe, amorous cavalier,   60
And back retired, not cooled by high disdain,
But she saw not; her heart was otherwhere.
She sighed for Agnes' dreams, the sweetest of the year.

VIII

She danced along with vague, regardless eyes;
Anxious her lips, her breathing quick and short.   65
The hallowed hour was near at hand: she sighs
Amid the timbrels and the thronged resort
Of whisperers in anger, or in sport,
Mid looks of love, defiance, hate, and scorn,
Hoodwinked with fairy fancy – all amort,[2]   70
Save to St Agnes and her lambs unshorn,
And all the bliss to be before tomorrow morn.

IX

So, purposing each moment to retire,
She lingered still. Meantime, across the moors
Had come young Porphyro, with heart on fire   75
For Madeline. Beside the portal doors,
Buttressed from moonlight, stands he, and implores
All saints to give him sight of Madeline
But for one moment in the tedious hours,
That he might gaze and worship all unseen,   80
Perchance speak, kneel, touch, kiss – in sooth such things have been.

THE EVE OF ST AGNES
[1] At this point in a MS version of the poem, Keats
inserted an additional stanza:

'Twas said her future lord would there appear
Offering, as sacrifice (all in the dream),
Delicious food, even to her lips brought near,
Viands, and wine, and fruit, and sugared cream,

To touch her palate with the fine extreme
Of relish; then soft music heard, and then
More pleasures followed in a dizzy stream,
Palpable almost; then to wake again
Warm in the virgin morn, no weeping Magdalen.

[2] *amort* dead.

X

He ventures in – let no buzzed whisper tell;
All eyes be muffled, or a hundred swords
Will storm his heart, love's fev'rous citadel.
For him those chambers held barbarian hordes,   85
Hyena foemen, and hot-blooded lords
Whose very dogs would execrations howl
Against his lineage; not one breast affords
Him any mercy in that mansion foul,
Save one old beldame, weak in body and in soul.   90

XI

Ah, happy chance! The aged creature came,
Shuffling along with ivory-headed wand
To where he stood, hid from the torch's flame
Behind a broad hall-pillar, far beyond
The sound of merriment and chorus bland.   95
He startled her; but soon she knew his face,
And grasped his fingers in her palsied hand,
Saying, 'Mercy, Porphyro! Hie thee from this place;
They are all here tonight, the whole bloodthirsty race!

XII

Get hence! Get hence! There's dwarfish Hildebrand –   100
He had a fever late, and in the fit
He cursed thee and thine, both house and land;
Then there's that old Lord Maurice, not a whit
More tame for his grey hairs. Alas me! Flit,
Flit like a ghost away!' 'Ah, gossip dear,   105
We're safe enough; here in this armchair sit
And tell me how –' 'Good Saints! Not here, not here;
Follow me, child, or else these stones will be thy bier.'

XIII

He followed through a lowly arched way,
Brushing the cobwebs with his lofty plume,   110
And as she muttered, 'Wel-a – wel-a-day!'
He found him in a little moonlight room,
Pale, latticed, chill, and silent as a tomb.
'Now tell me where is Madeline', said he,
'Oh tell me, Angela, by the holy loom   115

Which none but secret sisterhood may see,
When they St Agnes' wool are weaving piously.'

XIV

'St Agnes! Ah! It is St Agnes' Eve –
Yet men will murder upon holy days!
Thou must hold water in a witch's sieve   120
And be liege-lord of all the elves and fays
To venture so; it fills me with amaze
To see thee, Porphyro! St Agnes' Eve!
God's help! My lady fair the conjuror plays
This very night. Good angels her deceive!   125
But let me laugh awhile, I've mickle time to grieve.'

XV

Feebly she laugheth in the languid moon,
While Porphyro upon her face doth look
Like puzzled urchin on an aged crone
Who keepeth closed a wondrous riddle-book,   130
As spectacled she sits in chimney nook.
But soon his eyes grew brilliant, when she told
His lady's purpose; and he scarce could brook
Tears, at the thought of those enchantments cold,
And Madeline asleep in lap of legends old.   135

XVI

Sudden a thought came like a full-blown rose,
Flushing his brow, and in his pained heart
Made purple riot; then doth he propose
A stratagem that makes the beldame start:
'A cruel man and impious thou art –   140
Sweet lady, let her pray, and sleep, and dream
Alone with her good angels, far apart
From wicked men like thee. Go, go! I deem
Thou canst not surely be the same that thou didst seem.'

XVII

'I will not harm her, by all saints I swear',   145
Quoth Porphyro, 'Oh may I ne'er find grace
When my weak voice shall whisper its last prayer,
If one of her soft ringlets I displace,

Or look with ruffian passion in her face;
Good Angela, believe me by these tears,   150
Or I will, even in a moment's space,
Awake, with horrid shout, my foemen's ears,
And beard them, though they be more fanged than wolves and bears.'

XVIII

'Ah, why wilt thou affright a feeble soul?
A poor, weak, palsy-stricken, churchyard thing,   155
Whose passing-bell may ere the midnight toll;
Whose prayers for thee, each morn and evening,
Were never missed!' Thus plaining, doth she bring
A gentler speech from burning Porphyro;
So woeful, and of such deep sorrowing,   160
That Angela gives promise she will do
Whatever he shall wish, betide her weal or woe –

XIX

Which was to lead him, in close secrecy,
Even to Madeline's chamber, and there hide
Him in a closet, of such privacy   165
That he might see her beauty unespied,
And win perhaps that night a peerless bride,
While legioned fairies paced the coverlet
And pale enchantment held her sleepy-eyed.
Never on such a night have lovers met,   170
Since Merlin paid his Demon all the monstrous debt.³

XX

'It shall be as thou wishest', said the Dame,
'All cates⁴ and dainties shall be stored there
Quickly on this feast-night; by the tambour frame⁵
Her own lute thou wilt see. No time to spare,   175
For I am slow and feeble, and scarce dare
On such a catering trust my dizzy head.
Wait here, my child, with patience; kneel in prayer
The while. Ah! Thou must needs the lady wed,
Or may I never leave my grave among the dead.'   180

---

³ Apparently a reference to Merlin's perpetual im-   ⁴ cates delicacies.
prisonment by his mistress, the Lady of the Lake.   ⁵ tambour frame embroidery frame.

XXI

So saying, she hobbled off with busy fear.
The lover's endless minutes slowly passed;
The dame returned, and whispered in his ear
To follow her, with aged eyes aghast
From fright of dim espial. Safe at last,   185
Through many a dusky gallery, they gain
The maiden's chamber, silken, hushed, and chaste,
Where Porphyro took covert, pleased amain.
His poor guide hurried back with agues in her brain.

XXII

Her falt'ring hand upon the balustrade,   190
Old Angela was feeling for the stair,
When Madeline, St Agnes' charmed maid,
Rose, like a missioned spirit, unaware.
With silver taper's light, and pious care,
She turned, and down the aged gossip led   195
To a safe level matting. Now prepare,
Young Porphyro, for gazing on that bed:
She comes, she comes again, like ring-dove frayed and fled.

XXIII

Out went the taper as she hurried in;
Its little smoke, in pallid moonshine, died.   200
She closed the door, she panted, all akin
To spirits of the air, and visions wide —
No uttered syllable, or woe betide!
But to her heart, her heart was voluble,
Paining with eloquence her balmy side,   205
As though a tongueless nightingale should swell
Her throat in vain, and die, heart-stifled, in her dell.

XXIV

A casement high and triple-arched there was,
All garlanded with carven imag'ries
Of fruits, and flowers, and bunches of knot-grass,   210
And diamonded with panes of quaint device,
Innumerable of stains and splendid dyes,
As are the tiger-moth's deep-damasked wings;
And in the midst, 'mong thousand heraldries,

And twilight saints, and dim emblazonings,   215
A shielded scutcheon blushed with blood of queens and kings.

XXV

Full on this casement shone the wintry moon,
And threw warm gules[6] on Madeline's fair breast,
As down she knelt for heaven's grace and boon;
Rose-bloom fell on her hands, together pressed,   220
And on her silver cross soft amethyst,
And on her hair a glory, like a saint:
She seemed a splendid angel, newly dressed,
Save wings, for heaven. Porphyro grew faint;
She knelt, so pure a thing, so free from mortal taint.   225

XXVI

Anon his heart revives; her vespers done,
Of all its wreathed pearls her hair she frees,
Unclasps her warmed jewels one by one,
Loosens her fragrant bodice – by degrees
Her rich attire creeps rustling to her knees.   230
Half-hidden, like a mermaid in seaweed,
Pensive awhile she dreams awake, and sees
In fancy, fair St Agnes in her bed,
But dares not look behind, or all the charm is fled.

XXVII

Soon, trembling in her soft and chilly nest,   235
In sort of wakeful swoon, perplexed she lay,
Until the poppied warmth of sleep oppressed
Her soothed limbs, and soul fatigued away –
Flown like a thought, until the morrow-day,
Blissfully havened both from joy and pain,   240
Clasped like a missal where swart paynims pray;
Blinded alike from sunshine and from rain,
As though a rose should shut, and be a bud again.

XXVIII

Stol'n to this paradise, and so entranced,
Porphyro gazed upon her empty dress,   245

---

[6] *gules* red light.

And listened to her breathing, if it chanced
To wake into a slumberous tenderness;
Which when he heard, that minute did he bless,
And breathed himself, then from the closet crept,
Noiseless as fear in a wide wilderness –   250
And over the hushed carpet, silent stepped
And 'tween the curtains peeped, where lo! – how fast she slept.

XXIX

Then by the bedside, where the faded moon
Made a dim, silver twilight, soft he set
A table, and, half anguished, threw thereon   255
A cloth of woven crimson, gold, and jet.
Oh for some drowsy Morphean amulet![7]
The boisterous, midnight, festive clarion,
The kettle-drum, and far-heard clarionet,
Affray his ears, though but in dying tone;   260
The hall door shuts again, and all the noise is gone.

XXX

And still she slept an azure-lidded sleep
In blanched linen, smooth and lavendered,
While he from forth the closet brought a heap
Of candied apple, quince, and plum, and gourd;   265
With jellies soother than the creamy curd,
And lucent syrups tinct with cinnamon;
Manna and dates, in argosy transferred
From Fez; and spiced dainties, every one
From silken Samarcand to cedared Lebanon.   270

XXXI

These delicates he heaped with glowing hand
On golden dishes and in baskets bright
Of wreathed silver; sumptuous they stand
In the retired quiet of the night,
Filling the chilly room with perfume light.   275
'And now, my love, my seraph fair, awake!
Thou art my heaven, and I thine eremite.
Open thine eyes, for meek St Agnes' sake,
Or I shall drowse beside thee, so my soul doth ache.'

---

[7] *Morphean amulet* sleeping pill.

XXXII

Thus whispering, his warm, unnerved arm   280
Sank in her pillow. Shaded was her dream
By the dusk curtains; 'twas a midnight charm
Impossible to melt as iced stream.
The lustrous salvers in the moonlight gleam,
Broad golden fringe upon the carpet lies;   285
It seemed he never, never could redeem
From such a steadfast spell his lady's eyes;
So mused awhile, entoiled in woofed[8] fantasies.

XXXIII

Awakening up, he took her hollow lute;
Tumultuous, and, in chords that tenderest be,   290
He played an ancient ditty, long since mute,
In Provence called, 'La belle dame sans mercy',
Close to her ear touching the melody –
Wherewith disturbed, she uttered a soft moan.
He ceased – she panted quick – and suddenly   295
Her blue affrayed eyes wide open shone;
Upon his knees he sank, pale as smooth-sculptured stone.

XXXIV

Her eyes were open, but she still beheld,
Now wide awake, the vision of her sleep –
There was a painful change, that nigh expelled   300
The blisses of her dream so pure and deep.
At which fair Madeline began to weep
And moan forth witless words with many a sigh,
While still her gaze on Porphyro would keep;
Who knelt, with joined hands and piteous eye,   305
Fearing to move or speak, she looked so dreamingly.

XXXV

'Ah, Porphyro!' said she, 'but even now
Thy voice was at sweet tremble in mine ear,
Made tuneable with every sweetest vow,
And those sad eyes were spiritual and clear.   310

---

[8] *woofed* woven.

How changed thou art! How pallid, chill, and drear!
Give me that voice again, my Porphyro,
Those looks immortal, those complainings dear!
Oh leave me not in this eternal woe,
For if thou diest, my love, I know not where to go.'   315

XXXVI

Beyond a mortal man impassioned far
At these voluptuous accents, he arose
Ethereal, flushed, and like a throbbing star
Seen mid the sapphire heaven's deep repose;
Into her dream he melted, as the rose   320
Blendeth its odour with the violet –
Solution sweet.[9] Meantime the frost-wind blows
Like love's alarum pattering the sharp sleet
Against the window-panes; St Agnes' moon hath set.

XXXVII

'Tis dark; quick pattereth the flaw-blown sleet.   325
'This is no dream, my bride, my Madeline!'
'Tis dark; the iced gusts still rave and beat.
'No dream, alas! Alas, and woe is mine!
Porphyro will leave me here to fade and pine.
Cruel! What traitor could thee hither bring?   330
I curse not, for my heart is lost in thine,
Though thou forsakest a deceived thing,
A dove forlorn and lost with sick unpruned wing.'`

XXXVIII

'My Madeline! Sweet dreamer! Lovely bride!
Say, may I be for aye thy vassal blessed?   335
Thy beauty's shield, heart-shaped and vermeil dyed?
Ah, silver shrine, here will I take my rest
After so many hours of toil and quest,

---

[9] A MS version of lines 314–22 reads:

See, while she speaks, his arms encroaching
  slow,
Have zoned her, heart to heart – loud, loud
  the dark winds blow!

For on the midnight came a tempest fell;
More sooth, for that his quick rejoinder flows
Into her burning ear – and still the spell

Unbroken guards her in serene repose.
With her wild dream he mingled, as a rose
Marryeth its odour to a violet.
Still, still she dreams; louder the frost-wind
  blows . . .

For Woodhouse's comment on the stanza, see
pp. 714–15 above.

A famished pilgrim, saved by miracle.
　　Though I have found, I will not rob thy nest,　　　　　　340
　　Saving of thy sweet self – if thou think'st well
To trust, fair Madeline, to no rude infidel.

XXXIX

Hark! 'Tis an elfin-storm from fairy land,
　　Of haggard seeming, but a boon indeed.
　　Arise, arise! The morning is at hand;　　　　　　　　345
　　The bloated wassaillers will never heed.
　　Let us away, my love, with happy speed;
　　There are no ears to hear, or eyes to see,
　　Drowned all in Rhenish and the sleepy mead.
　　Awake! Arise, my love, and fearless be,　　　　　　　350
For o'er the southern moors I have a home for thee.'

XL

She hurried at his words, beset with fears,
　　For there were sleeping dragons all around,
　　At glaring watch, perhaps, with ready spears;
　　Down the wide stairs a darkling way they found.　　　355
　　In all the house was heard no human sound;
　　A chain-drooped lamp was flickering by each door;
　　The arras, rich with horseman, hawk, and hound
　　Fluttered in the besieging wind's uproar,
And the long carpets rose along the gusty floor.　　　360

XLI

They glide, like phantoms, into the wide hall;
　　Like phantoms, to the iron porch they glide,
　　Where lay the porter, in uneasy sprawl,
　　With a huge empty flagon by his side;
　　The wakeful bloodhound rose and shook his hide,　　365
　　But his sagacious eye an inmate owns.
　　By one, and one, the bolts full easy slide,
　　The chains lie silent on the footworn stones –
The key turns, and the door upon its hinges groans.

XLII

And they are gone – aye, ages long ago　　　　　　　370
These lovers fled away into the storm.

That night the Baron dreamt of many a woe,
And all his warrior-guests, with shade and form
Of witch and demon, and large coffin-worm,
Were long be-nightmared. Angela the old   375
Died palsy-twitched, with meagre face deform;
The beadsman, after thousand aves told,
For aye unsought for, slept among his ashes cold.

From Letter from John Keats to George and Georgiana Keats, 16 April 1819

Last Sunday I took a walk towards Highgate and, in the lane that winds by the side of Lord Mansfield's park, I met Mr Green, our demonstrator at Guy's, in conversation with Coleridge.[1] I joined them, after enquiring by a look whether it would be agreeable. I walked with him at his alderman-after-dinner pace for near two miles, I suppose. In those two miles he broached a thousand things; let me see if I can give you a list. Nightingales, poetry – on poetical sensation – metaphysics – different genera and species of dreams – nightmare – a dream accompanied by a sense of touch – single and double touch – a dream related – first and second consciousness – the difference explained between will and volition – so many metaphysicians from a want of smoking – the second consciousness – monsters – the kraken – mermaids – Southey believes in them – Southey's belief too much diluted – a ghost story – Good morning – I heard his voice as he came towards me – I heard it as he moved away – I had heard it all the interval (if it may be called so). He was civil enough to ask me to call on him at Highgate goodnight! It looks so much like rain I shall not go to town to day, but put it off till tomorrow.

LA BELLE DAME SANS MERCI: A BALLAD (COMPOSED 21 APRIL 1819; EDITED FROM MS)

I

Oh what can ail thee, knight-at-arms,
Alone and palely loitering?
The sedge has withered from the lake,
And no birds sing.

2

Oh what can ail thee, knight-at-arms,   5
So haggard and so woe-begone?
The squirrel's granary is full,
And the harvest's done.

From LETTER FROM JOHN KEATS TO GEORGE AND GEORGIANA KEATS, 16 APRIL 1819
[1] Coleridge's account of this meeting can be found on p. 596. It took place in the grounds of Kenwood House, seat of William Murray, Lord Mansfield (1705–93). Joseph Henry Green (1791–1863) was Coleridge's literary executor, and had been Keats's demonstrator at Guy's Hospital.

3

I see a lily on thy brow
  With anguish moist and fever dew,   10
And on thy cheeks a fading rose
  Fast withereth too.

4

I met a lady in the meads,
  Full beautiful – a fairy's child;
Her hair was long, her foot was light,   15
  And her eyes were wild.

5

I made a garland for her head,
  And bracelets too, and fragrant zone;
She looked at me as she did love,
  And made sweet moan.   20

6

I set her on my pacing steed,
  And nothing else saw all day long,
For sidelong would she bend, and sing
  A fairy's song.

7

She found me roots of relish sweet,   25
  And honey wild and manna dew,
And sure in language strange she said,
  'I love thee true'.

8

She took me to her elfin grot
  And there she wept, and sighed full sore,   30
And there I shut her wild wild eyes
  With kisses four.

9

And there she lulled me asleep,
  And there I dreamed – ah, woe betide! –
The latest dream I ever dreamed   35
  On the cold hill's side.

10

I saw pale kings and princes too,
  Pale warriors, death-pale were they all;
They cried, 'La belle dame sans merci
  Hath thee in thrall!'   40

11

I saw their starved lips in the gloam
  With horrid warning gaped wide,
And I awoke and found me here
  On the cold hill's side.

12

And this is why I sojourn here,   45
  Alone and palely loitering,
Though the sedge is withered from the lake,
  And no birds sing.

From Letter from John Keats to George and Georgiana Keats, 21 April 1819

Do you not see how necessary a world of pains and troubles is to school an intelligence and make it a soul, a place where the heart must feel and suffer in a thousand diverse ways? Not merely is the heart a hornbook, it is the mind's Bible, it is the mind's experience, it is the teat from which the mind or intelligence sucks its identity. As various as the lives of men are, so various become their souls, and thus does God make individual beings, souls, identical souls of the sparks of his own essence. This appears to me a faint sketch of a system of salvation which does not affront our reason and humanity; I am convinced that many difficulties which Christians labour under would vanish before it.

    There is one which even now strikes me: the salvation of children. In them the spark or intelligence returns to God without any identity, it having had no time to learn of, and be altered by, the heart – or seat of the human passions. It is pretty generally suspected that the Christian scheme has been copied from the ancient Persian and

Greek philosophers. Why may they not have made this simple thing even more simple for common apprehension, by introducing mediators and personages in the same manner as in the heathen mythology abstractions are personified? Seriously, I think it probable that this system of soul-making may have been the parent of all the more palpable and personal schemes of redemption, among the Zoroastrians, the Christians, and the Hindus. For as one part of the human species must have their carved Jupiter, so another part must have the palpable and named mediator and saviour – their Christ, their Oromanes, and their Vishnu.

If what I have said should not be plain enough, as I fear it may not be, I will put you in the place where I began in this series of thoughts. I mean, I began by seeing how man was formed by circumstances – and what are circumstances, but touchstones of his heart? And what are touchstones, but provings of his heart? And what are provings of his heart, but fortifiers or alterers of his nature? And what is his altered nature, but his soul? And what was his soul before it came into the world and had these provings and alterations and perfectionings? An intelligence without identity – and how is this identity to be made? Through the medium of the heart? And how is the heart to become this medium, but in a world of circumstances?

From Lamia, Isabella, The Eve of St Agnes, and Other Poems (1820)

ODE TO PSYCHE (COMPOSED 21–30 APRIL 1819)

Oh goddess! Hear these tuneless numbers, wrung
  By sweet enforcement and remembrance dear,
And pardon that thy secrets should be sung
  Even into thine own soft-conchèd ear.
Surely I dreamt today, or did I see   5
  The wingèd Psyche with awakened eyes?
I wandered in a forest thoughtlessly,
  And, on the sudden, fainting with surprise,
Saw two fair creatures, couched side by side
  In deepest grass, beneath the whisp'ring roof   10
  Of leaves and trembled blossoms, where there ran
      A brooklet, scarce espied.
Mid hushed, cool-rooted flowers, fragrant-eyed,
  Blue, silver-white, and budded Tyrian,
They lay calm-breathing on the bedded grass;   15
  Their arms embraced, and their pinions too;
  Their lips touched not, but had not bade adieu,
As if disjoinèd by soft-handed slumber,
And ready still past kisses to outnumber
    At tender eye-dawn of auroren love.   20
      The wingèd boy[1] I knew;

ODE TO PSYCHE
[1] Cupid.

But who wast thou, oh happy, happy dove?
    His Psyche true!

Oh latest born and loveliest vision far
    Of all Olympus' faded hierarchy!   25
Fairer than Phoebe's sapphire-regioned star,
    Or Vesper, amorous glow-worm of the sky;
Fairer than these, though temple thou hast none,
        Nor altar heaped with flowers;
Nor virgin-choir to make delicious moan   30
        Upon the midnight hours;
No voice, no lute, no pipe, no incense sweet
    From chain-swung censer teeming;
No shrine, no grove, no oracle, no heat
    Of pale-mouthed prophet dreaming.   35

Oh brightest! though too late for antique vows,
    Too, too late for the fond believing lyre,
When holy were the haunted forest boughs,
    Holy the air, the water and the fire;
Yet even in these days so far retired   40
    From happy pieties, thy lucent fans,[2]
    Fluttering among the faint Olympians,
I see, and sing, by my own eyes inspired.
So let me be thy choir, and make a moan
        Upon the midnight hours;   45
Thy voice, thy lute, thy pipe, thy incense sweet
    From swinged censer teeming;
Thy shrine, thy grove, thy oracle, thy heat
    Of pale-mouthed prophet dreaming.

Yes, I will be thy priest, and build a fane   50
    In some untrodden region of my mind,
Where branched thoughts, new grown with pleasant pain,
    Instead of pines shall murmur in the wind;
Far, far around shall those dark-clustered trees
    Fledge the wild-ridged mountains steep by steep;   55
And there by zephyrs, streams, and birds, and bees,
    The moss-lain dryads shall be lulled to sleep;
And in the midst of this wide quietness
A rosy sanctuary will I dress
With the wreathed trellis of a working brain,   60
    With buds, and bells, and stars without a name,
With all the gardener Fancy e'er could feign,[3]
    Who, breeding flowers, will never breed the same:

---

[2] *lucent fans* shining wings.   [3] *feign* invent.

And there shall be for thee all soft delight
  That shadowy thought can win –   65
A bright torch, and a casement ope at night,
  To let the warm love in!

ODE TO A NIGHTINGALE (COMPOSED MAY 1819)

1

My heart aches, and a drowsy numbness pains
  My sense, as though of hemlock I had drunk,
Or emptied some dull opiate to the drains
  One minute past,[1] and Lethe-wards[2] had sunk;
'Tis not through envy of thy happy lot,   5
  But being too happy in thine happiness,
    That thou, light-winged dryad of the trees,
      In some melodious plot
Of beechen green, and shadows numberless,
  Singest of summer in full-throated ease.   10

2

Oh for a draught of vintage! that hath been
  Cooled a long age in the deep-delved earth,
Tasting of flora and the country green,
  Dance, and Provençal song, and sunburnt mirth!
Oh for a beaker full of the warm south,[3]   15
  Full of the true, the blushful Hippocrene,[4]
    With beaded bubbles winking at the brim,
      And purple-stained mouth;
That I might drink, and leave the world unseen,
  And with thee fade away into the forest dim –   20

3

Fade far away, dissolve, and quite forget
  What thou among the leaves hast never known,
The weariness, the fever, and the fret
  Here, where men sit and hear each other groan;
Where palsy shakes a few, sad, last grey hairs,   25
  Where youth grows pale, and spectre-thin, and dies;[5]

ODE TO A NIGHTINGALE
[1] *past* ago.
[2] *Lethe-wards* towards Lethe, river of forgetfulness in Hades.
[3] *warm south* southern wine.

[4] Hippocrene was the spring sacred to the Muses on Mt Helicon.
[5] Perhaps a reference to the death of Tom Keats from consumption, 1 Dec. 1818.

Where but to think is to be full of sorrow
   And leaden-eyed despairs;
Where Beauty cannot keep her lustrous eyes,
   Or new Love pine at them beyond tomorrow.   30

4

Away! Away! For I will fly to thee,
   Not charioted by Bacchus and his pards,
But on the viewless wings of Poesy,
   Though the dull brain perplexes and retards;
Already with thee! Tender is the night,   35
   And haply the Queen Moon is on her throne,
      Clustered around by all her starry fays;
         But here there is no light
Save what from heaven is with the breezes blown
   Through verdurous glooms and winding mossy ways.   40

5

I cannot see what flowers are at my feet,
   Nor what soft incense hangs upon the boughs,
But, in embalmed darkness, guess each sweet
   Wherewith the seasonable month endows
The grass, the thicket, and the fruit-tree wild,   45
   White hawthorn, and the pastoral eglantine,
      Fast-fading violets covered up in leaves,
         And mid-May's eldest child,
The coming musk-rose, full of dewy wine,
   The murmurous haunt of flies on summer eves.   50

6

Darkling I listen; and for many a time
   I have been half in love with easeful Death,
Called him soft names in many a mused rhyme,
   To take into the air my quiet breath;
Now more than ever seems it rich to die,   55
   To cease upon the midnight with no pain,
      While thou art pouring forth thy soul abroad
         In such an ecstasy!
Still wouldst thou sing, and I have ears in vain –
   To thy high requiem become a sod.   60

7

Thou wast not born for death, immortal bird!
 No hungry generations tread thee down;
The voice I hear this passing night was heard
 In ancient days by emperor and clown:
Perhaps the self-same song that found a path 65
 Through the sad heart of Ruth, when, sick for home,
 She stood in tears amid the alien corn;[6]
 The same that oft-times hath
Charmed magic casements, opening on the foam
 Of perilous seas, in fairy lands forlorn. 70

8

Forlorn! The very word is like a bell
 To toll me back from thee to my sole self!
Adieu! The fancy cannot cheat so well
 As she is famed to do, deceiving elf.
Adieu! Adieu! Thy plaintive anthem fades 75
 Past the near meadows, over the still stream,
 Up the hillside, and now 'tis buried deep
 In the next valley-glades:
Was it a vision, or a waking dream?
 Fled is that music — do I wake or sleep? 80

ODE ON A GRECIAN URN (COMPOSED C.MAY 1819)

I

Thou still unravished bride of quietness,
 Thou foster-child of silence and slow time,
Sylvan historian, who canst thus express
 A flowery tale more sweetly than our rhyme —
What leaf-fringed legend haunts about thy shape 5
 Of deities or mortals, or of both,
 In Tempe or the dales of Arcady?[1]
What men or gods are these? What maidens loath?
What mad pursuit? What struggle to escape?
 What pipes and timbrels? What wild ecstasy? 10

---

[6] Ruth was forced, by famine, to leave home and labour in the fields of her kinsman, Boaz (Ruth 2: 1–2).

ODE ON A GRECIAN URN
[1] Tempe and Arcadia, places known in classical times for their beauty and the happiness of their inhabitants.

2

Heard melodies are sweet, but those unheard
   Are sweeter; therefore, ye soft pipes, play on –
Not to the sensual ear, but, more endeared,
   Pipe to the spirit ditties of no tone:
Fair youth, beneath the trees, thou canst not leave   15
   Thy song, nor ever can those trees be bare;
      Bold lover, never, never canst thou kiss,
Though winning near the goal – yet do not grieve;
   She cannot fade, though thou hast not thy bliss,
      For ever wilt thou love, and she be fair!   20

3

Ah, happy, happy boughs! that cannot shed
   Your leaves, nor ever bid the spring adieu;
And, happy melodist, unwearied,
   For ever piping songs for ever new;
More happy love, more happy, happy love!   25
   For ever warm and still to be enjoyed,
      For ever panting and for ever young;
All breathing human passion far above,[2]
   That leaves a heart high-sorrowful and cloyed,
      A burning forehead, and a parching tongue.   30

4

Who are these coming to the sacrifice?
   To what green altar, oh mysterious priest,
Lead'st thou that heifer lowing at the skies,
   And all her silken flanks with garlands dressed?
What little town by river or seashore,   35
   Or mountain-built with peaceful citadel,
      Is emptied of this folk, this pious morn?
And, little town, thy streets for evermore
   Will silent be, and not a soul to tell
      Why thou art desolate, can e'er return.   40

5

Oh Attic[3] shape! Fair attitude! With brede[4]
   Of marble men and maidens overwrought,

---

[2] Compare Hazlitt's remarks on Greek statuary, 'On   [3] *Attic* Grecian.
Gusto', p. 643.   [4] *brede* braid.

With forest branches and the trodden weed;
   Thou, silent form, dost tease us out of thought
As doth eternity. Cold Pastoral!   45
   When old age shall this generation waste,
      Thou shalt remain, in midst of other woe
Than ours, a friend to man, to whom thou say'st,
   'Beauty is truth, truth beauty'; that is all
      Ye know on earth, and all ye need to know.   50

ODE ON MELANCHOLY (COMPOSED *C.*MAY 1819)[1]

1

No, no, go not to Lethe, neither twist
   Wolfsbane,[2] tight-rooted, for its poisonous wine;
Nor suffer thy pale forehead to be kissed
   By nightshade, ruby grape of Proserpine;
Make not your rosary of yew-berries,   5
   Nor let the beetle, nor the death-moth be
      Your mournful Psyche, nor the downy owl
A partner in your sorrow's mysteries;
   For shade to shade will come too drowsily,
      And drown the wakeful anguish of the soul.   10

2

But when the melancholy fit shall fall
   Sudden from heaven like a weeping cloud,
That fosters the droop-headed flowers all,
   And hides the green hill in an April shroud;
Then glut thy sorrow on a morning rose,   15
   Or on the rainbow of the salt sand-wave,
      Or on the wealth of globed peonies;
Or if thy mistress some rich anger shows,
   Imprison her soft hand, and let her rave,
      And feed deep, deep upon her peerless eyes.   20

ODE ON MELANCHOLY
[1] A cancelled opening stanza in MS reads:

Though you should build a bark of dead men's
   bones,
And rear a phantom gibbet for a mast,
Stitch creeds together for a sail, with groans
To fill it out, bloodstained and aghast;

Although your rudder be a dragon's tail,
Long severed, yet still hard with agony,
Your cordage large uprootings from the skull
Of bald Medusa, certes you would fail
To find the Melancholy – whether she
Dreameth in any isle of Lethe dull.

[2] *Wolfsbane* aconite, a poisonous plant.

3

She dwells with Beauty – Beauty that must die;
  And Joy, whose hand is ever at his lips
Bidding adieu; and aching Pleasure nigh,
  Turning to poison while the bee-mouth sips.
Aye, in the very temple of Delight   25
  Veiled Melancholy has her sovran shrine,
    Though seen of none save him whose strenuous tongue
Can burst Joy's grape against his palate fine;
  His soul shall taste the sadness of her might,
    And be among her cloudy trophies hung.   30

Ode on Indolence (composed between 19 March and 9 June 1819; edited from MS)

They toil not, neither do they spin.
(Matthew 6: 28)

1

One morn before me were three figures seen,
  With bowed necks and joined hands, side-faced;
And one behind the other stepped serene,
  In placid sandals and in white robes graced;
They passed, like figures on a marble urn,   5
  When shifted round to see the other side;
    They came again, as when the urn once more
Is shifted round, the first-seen shades return –
  And they were strange to me, as may betide
    With vases, to one deep in Phidian lore.[1]   10

2

How is it, shadows, that I knew ye not?
  How came ye muffled in so hush a masque?
Was it a silent deep-disguised plot
  To steal away, and leave without a task
My idle days? Ripe was the drowsy hour;   15
  The blissful cloud of summer indolence
    Benumbed my eyes; my pulse grew less and less;

ODE ON INDOLENCE
[1] *Phidian lore* sculpture; Phidias sculpted the Elgin
marbles.

Pain had no sting, and pleasure's wreath no flower –
  Oh why did ye not melt, and leave my sense
    Unhaunted quite of all but – nothingness?   20

3

A third time passed they by, and, passing, turned
  Each one the face a moment whiles to me;
Then faded, and to follow them I burned
  And ached for wings, because I knew the three:
The first was a fair maid, and Love her name;   25
  The second was Ambition, pale of cheek
    And ever watchful with fatigued eye;
The last, whom I love more, the more of blame
  Is heaped upon her, maiden most unmeek,
    I knew to be my demon Poesy.   30

4

They faded, and, forsooth, I wanted wings!
  Oh folly! What is love? And where is it?
And, for that poor ambition – it springs
  From a man's little heart's short fever-fit;
For Poesy! No, she has not a joy –   35
  At least for me – so sweet as drowsy noons,
    And evenings steeped in honeyed indolence.
Oh for an age so sheltered from annoy,
  That I may never know how change the moons,
    Or hear the voice of busy common sense!   40

5

A third time came they by – alas, wherefore?
  My sleep had been embroidered with dim dreams;
My soul had been a lawn besprinkled o'er
  With flowers, and stirring shades, and baffled beams;
The morn was clouded, but no shower fell,   45
  Though in her lids hung the sweet tears of May;
    The open casement pressed a new-leaved vine,
  Let in the budding warmth and throstle's lay –
Oh shadows, 'twas a time to bid farewell!
  Upon your skirts had fallen no tears of mine.   50

6

So ye three ghosts, adieu! Ye cannot raise
My head cool-bedded in the flowery grass,
For I would not be dieted with praise –
A pet-lamb in a sentimental farce!
Fade softly from my eyes, and be once more   55
In masque-like figures on the dreamy urn;
Farewell! I yet have visions for the night,
And for the day faint visions there is store.
Vanish, ye phantoms, from my idle sprite,
Into the clouds, and never more return!   60

From Lamia, Isabella, The Eve of St Agnes, and Other Poems (1820)

TO AUTUMN (COMPOSED 19 SEPTEMBER 1819)

1

Season of mists and mellow fruitfulness,
Close bosom-friend of the maturing sun,
Conspiring with him how to load and bless
With fruit the vines that round the thatch-eaves run;
To bend with apples the mossed cottage-trees,   5
And fill all fruit with ripeness to the core;
To swell the gourd, and plump the hazel shells
With a sweet kernel; to set budding more,
And still more, later flowers for the bees,
Until they think warm days will never cease,   10
For summer has o'er-brimmed their clammy cells.

2

Who hath not seen thee oft amid thy store?
Sometimes whoever seeks abroad may find
Thee sitting careless on a granary floor,
Thy hair soft-lifted by the winnowing wind;   15
Or on a half-reaped furrow sound asleep,
Drowsed with the fume of poppies, while thy hook
Spares the next swath and all its twined flowers;
And sometimes like a gleaner thou dost keep
Steady thy laden head across a brook;   20
Or by a cider-press, with patient look,
Thou watchest the last oozings hours by hours.

3

Where are the songs of spring? Aye, where are they?
Think not of them, thou hast thy music too –
While barred clouds bloom the soft-dying day, 25
And touch the stubble-plains with rosy hue;
Then in a wailful choir the small gnats mourn
Among the river sallows,[1] borne aloft
Or sinking as the light wind lives or dies;
And full-grown lambs loud bleat from hilly bourn, 30
Hedge-crickets sing, and now with treble soft
The redbreast whistles from a garden-croft,
And gathering swallows twitter in the skies.

The Fall of Hyperion: A Dream (composed July-September 1819; edited from MS)

Canto I
Fanatics have their dreams, wherewith they weave
A paradise for a sect; the savage too
From forth the loftiest fashion of his sleep
Guesses at heaven; pity these have not
Traced upon vellum or wild Indian leaf 5
The shadows of melodious utterance.
But bare of laurel they live, dream and die;
For Poesy alone can tell her dreams,
With the fine spell of words alone can save
Imagination from the sable charm 10
And dumb enchantment. Who alive can say
'Thou art no poet; may'st not tell thy dreams'?
Since every man whose soul is not a clod
Hath visions, and would speak, if he had loved
And been well nurtured in his mother tongue. 15
Whether the dream now purposed to rehearse
Be poet's or fanatic's will be known
When this warm scribe my hand is in the grave.
    Methought I stood where trees of every clime,
Palm, myrtle, oak, and sycamore, and beech, 20
With plantain, and spice-blossoms, made a screen;
In neighbourhood of fountains, by the noise
Soft-showering in mine ears, and, by the touch
Of scent, not far from roses. Turning round,
I saw an arbour with a drooping roof 25

TO AUTUMN
[1] *sallows* willows.

Of trellis vines, and bells, and larger blooms,
Like floral censers swinging light in air;
Before its wreathed doorway, on a mound
Of moss, was spread a feast of summer fruits,
Which nearer seen, seemed refuse of a meal   30
By angel tasted, or our mother Eve;
For empty shells were scattered on the grass,
And grape-stalks but half bare, and remnants more,
Sweet smelling, whose pure kinds I could not know.
Still was more plenty than the fabled horn[1]   35
Thrice emptied could pour forth, at banqueting
For Proserpine returned to her own fields,
Where the white heifers low. And appetite
More yearning than on earth I ever felt
Growing within, I ate deliciously;   40
And, after not long, thirsted, for thereby
Stood a cool vessel of transparent juice
Sipped by the wandered bee, the which I took,
And, pledging all the mortals of the world,
And all the dead whose names are in our lips,   45
Drank. That full draught is parent of my theme.
No Asian poppy nor elixir fine
Of the soon-fading jealous Caliphat,
No poison gendered in close monkish cell
To thin the scarlet conclave of old men,   50
Could so have rapt unwilling life away.
Among the fragrant husks and berries crushed,
Upon the grass I struggled hard against
The domineering potion, but in vain –
The cloudy swoon came on, and down I sunk   55
Like a Silenus on an antique vase.
How long I slumbered 'tis a chance to guess.
When sense of life returned, I started up
As if with wings; but the fair trees were gone,
The mossy mound and arbour were no more.   60
I looked around upon the carved sides
Of an old sanctuary with roof august,
Builded so high, it seemed that filmed clouds
Might spread beneath, as o'er the stars of heaven.
So old the place was, I remembered none   65
The like upon the earth – what I had seen
Of grey cathedrals, buttressed walls, rent towers,
The superannuations[2] of sunk realms,
Or nature's rocks toiled hard in waves and winds,
Seemed but the faulture[3] of decrepit things   70

THE FALL OF HYPERION: A DREAM
[1]   *the fabled horn* the cornucopia of plenty.

[2]   *superannuations* ruins.
[3]   *faulture* weakness.

To that eternal domed monument.
Upon the marble at my feet there lay
Store of strange vessels, and large draperies
Which needs had been of dyed asbestos wove,
Or in that place the moth could not corrupt,   75
So white the linen; so, in some, distinct
Ran imageries from a sombre loom.
All in a mingled heap confused there lay
Robes, golden tongs, censer and chafing-dish,
Girdles, and chains, and holy jewelleries.   80
    Turning from these with awe, once more I raised
My eyes to fathom the space every way;
The embossed roof, the silent massy range
Of columns north and south, ending in mist
Of nothing; then to eastward, where black gates   85
Were shut against the sunrise evermore.
Then to the west I looked, and saw far off
An image,[4] huge of feature as a cloud,
At level of whose feet an altar slept,
To be approached on either side by steps,   90
And marble balustrade, and patient travail
To count with toil the innumerable degrees.
Towards the altar sober-paced I went,
Repressing haste as too unholy there;
And, coming nearer, saw beside the shrine   95
One minist'ring;[5] and there arose a flame.
When in mid-May the sickening east wind
Shifts sudden to the south, the small warm rain
Melts out the frozen incense from all flowers,
And fills the air with so much pleasant health   100
That even the dying man forgets his shroud;
Even so that lofty sacrificial fire,
Sending forth Maian incense,[6] spread around
Forgetfulness of everything but bliss,
And clouded all the altar with soft smoke,   105
From whose white fragrant curtains thus I heard
Language pronounced: 'If thou canst not ascend
These steps, die on that marble where thou art.
Thy flesh, near cousin to the common dust,
Will parch for lack of nutriment; thy bones   110
Will wither in few years, and vanish so
That not the quickest eye could find a grain
Of what thou now art on that pavement cold.
The sands of thy short life are spent this hour,
And no hand in the universe can turn   115

---

4 *An image* of Saturn.
5 Moneta, the priestess of the temple.
6 *Maian incense* flowery scent.

Thy hourglass, if these gummed leaves be burnt
Ere thou canst mount up these immortal steps.'
    I heard, I looked – two senses both at once,
So fine, so subtle, felt the tyranny
Of that fierce threat and the hard task proposed.   120
Prodigious seemed the toil; the leaves were yet
Burning, when suddenly a palsied chill
Struck from the paved level up my limbs,
And was ascending quick to put cold grasp
Upon those streams that pulse beside the throat.   125
I shrieked, and the sharp anguish of my shriek
Stung my own ears – I strove hard to escape
The numbness, strove to gain the lowest step.
Slow, heavy, deadly was my pace; the cold
Grew stifling, suffocating, at the heart;   130
And when I clasped my hands I felt them not.
One minute before death, my iced foot touched
The lowest stair; and as it touched, life seemed
To pour in at the toes. I mounted up,
As once fair angels on a ladder flew   135
From the green turf to heaven. 'Holy Power',
Cried I, approaching near the horned shrine,
'What am I that should so be saved from death?
What am I, that another death come not
To choke my utterance sacrilegious here?'   140
Then said the veiled shadow: 'Thou hast felt
What 'tis to die and live again before
Thy fated hour. That thou hadst power to do so
Is thy own safety; thou hast dated on
Thy doom.'[7] 'High Prophetess', said I, 'purge off   145
Benign, if so it please thee, my mind's film.'
'None can usurp this height', returned that shade,
'But those to whom the miseries of the world
Are misery, and will not let them rest.
All else who find a haven in the world,   150
Where they may thoughtless sleep away their days,
If by a chance into this fane they come,
Rot on the pavement where thou rotted'st half.'
'Are there not thousands in the world', said I,
Encouraged by the sooth voice of the shade,   155

---

[7] *dated on / Thy doom* postponed your death.

'Who love their fellows even to the death;
Who feel the giant agony of the world;
And more, like slaves to poor humanity,
Labour for mortal good? I sure should see
Other men here – but I am here alone.'   160
'They whom thou spak'st of are no vision'ries',
Rejoined that voice, 'They are no dreamers weak,
They seek no wonder but the human face,
No music but a happy-noted voice,
They come not here, they have no thought to come –   165
And thou art here, for thou art less than they.
What benefit canst thou do, or all thy tribe,
To the great world? Thou art a dreaming thing,
A fever of thyself. Think of the earth;
What bliss even in hope is there for thee?   170
What haven? Every creature hath its home;
Every sole man hath days of joy and pain,
Whether his labours be sublime or low –
The pain alone; the joy alone; distinct.
Only the dreamer venoms all his days,   175
Bearing more woe than all his sins deserve.
Therefore, that happiness be somewhat shared,
Such things as thou art are admitted oft
Into like gardens thou didst pass erewhile,
And suffered in these temples; for that cause   180
Thou standest safe beneath this statue's knees.'
'That I am favoured for unworthiness,
By such propitious parley medicined
In sickness not ignoble, I rejoice –
Aye, and could weep for love of such award.'   185
So answered I, continuing, 'If it please,
Majestic shadow, tell me – sure not all
Those melodies sung into the world's ear
Are useless? Sure a poet is a sage,
A humanist, physician to all men.   190
That I am none I feel, as vultures feel
They are no birds when eagles are abroad.
What am I then? Thou spakest of my tribe –
What tribe?' The tall shade veiled in drooping white
Then spake, so much more earnest, that the breath   195
Moved the thin linen folds that drooping hung
About a golden censer from the hand
Pendent: 'Art thou not of the dreamer tribe?
The poet and the dreamer are distinct,
Diverse, sheer opposite, antipodes.   200
The one pours out a balm upon the world,
The other vexes it.' Then shouted I
Spite of myself, and with a Pythia's spleen:

'Apollo! Faded, far-flown Apollo!
Where is thy misty pestilence to creep   205
Into the dwellings, through the door crannies,
Of all mock lyrists, large self-worshippers,
And careless hectorers in proud bad verse?[8]
Though I breathe death with them it will be life
To see them sprawl before me into graves.   210
Majestic shadow, tell me where I am;
Whose altar this; for whom this incense curls;
What image this, whose face I cannot see,
For the broad marble knees; and who thou art,
Of accent feminine, so courteous.'   215
　　Then the tall shade, in drooping linens veiled,
Spake out, so much more earnest, that her breath
Stirred the thin folds of gauze that drooping hung
About a golden censer from her hand
Pendent – and by her voice I knew she shed   220
Long-treasured tears: 'This temple sad and lone
Is all spared from the thunder of a war[9]
Foughten long since by giant hierarchy
Against rebellion. This old image here,
Whose carved features wrinkled as he fell,   225
Is Saturn's; I, Moneta, left supreme,
Sole priestess of his desolation.'
I had no words to answer, for my tongue,
Useless, could find about its roofed home
No syllable of a fit majesty   230
To make rejoinder to Moneta's mourn.
There was a silence while the altar's blaze
Was fainting for sweet food. I looked thereon,
And on the paved floor, where nigh were piled
Faggots of cinnamon, and many heaps   235
Of other crisped spice-wood – then again
I looked upon the altar, and its horns
Whitened with ashes, and its lang'rous flame,
And then upon the offerings again;
And so by turns, till sad Moneta cried,   240
'The sacrifice is done, but not the less
Will I be kind to thee for thy goodwill.
My power, which to me is still a curse,
Shall be to thee a wonder; for the scenes
Still swooning vivid through my globed brain   245
With an electral changing misery,
Thou shalt with those dull mortal eyes behold,
Free from all pain, if wonder pain thee not.'

---

[8] Suggested candidates include Byron, Wordsworth,　　[9] *war* that of the Titans against the Olympians.
and Moore.

As near as an immortal's sphered words
Could to a mother's soften, were these last.   250
But yet I had a terror of her robes,
And chiefly of the veils, that from her brow
Hung pale, and curtained her in mysteries,
That made my heart too small to hold its blood.
This saw that goddess, and with sacred hand   255
Parted the veils. Then saw I a wan face,
Not pined by human sorrows, but bright-blanched
By an immortal sickness which kills not;
It works a constant change, which happy death
Can put no end to; deathwards progressing   260
To no death was that visage; it had passed
The lily and the snow; and beyond these
I must not think now, though I saw that face –
But for her eyes I should have fled away.
They held me back with a benignant light,   265
Soft-mitigated by divinest lids
Half-closed, and visionless entire they seemed
Of all external things – they saw me not,
But in blank splendour beamed like the mild moon,
Who comforts those she sees not, who knows not   270
What eyes are upward cast. As I had found
A grain of gold upon a mountain's side,
And twinged with avarice strained out my eyes
To search its sullen entrails rich with ore,
So at the view of sad Moneta's brow   275
I ached to see what things the hollow brain
Behind enwombed, what high tragedy
In the dark secret chambers of her skull
Was acting, that could give so dread a stress
To her cold lips, and fill with such a light   280
Her planetary eyes, and touch her voice
With such a sorrow. 'Shade of Memory!'
Cried I, with act adorant at her feet,
'By all the gloom hung round thy fallen house,
By this last temple, by the golden age,   285
By great Apollo, thy dear foster child,
And by thyself, forlorn divinity,
The pale omega of a withered race,
Let me behold, according as thou said'st,
What in thy brain so ferments to and fro.'   290
No sooner had this conjuration passed
My devout lips, than side by side we stood,
Like a stunt bramble by a solemn pine,
Deep in the shady sadness of a vale,
Far sunken from the healthy breath of morn,   295
Far from the fiery noon and eve's one star.

Onward I looked beneath the gloomy boughs,
And saw what first I thought an image huge,
Like to the image pedestalled so high
In Saturn's temple. Then Moneta's voice   300
Came brief upon mine ear: 'So Saturn sat
When he had lost his realms.' Whereon there grew
A power within me of enormous ken
To see as a god sees, and take the depth
Of things as nimbly as the outward eye   305
Can size and shape pervade. The lofty theme
At those few words hung vast before my mind,
With half-unravelled web. I set myself
Upon an eagle's watch, that I might see,
And seeing ne'er forget. No stir of life   310
Was in this shrouded vale, not so much air
As in the zoning of a summer's day
Robs not one light seed from the feathered grass,
But where the dead leaf fell there did it rest.
A stream went voiceless by, still deadened more   315
By reason of the fallen divinity
Spreading more shade; the naiad mid her reeds
Pressed her cold finger closer to her lips.
Along the margin sand large footmarks went
No farther than to where old Saturn's feet   320
Had rested, and there slept – how long a sleep!
Degraded, cold, upon the sodden ground
His old right hand lay nerveless, listless, dead,
Unsceptred; and his realmless eyes were closed,
While his bowed head seemed listening to the earth,   325
His ancient mother, for some comfort yet.
    It seemed no force could wake him from his place;
But there came one who, with a kindred hand
Touched his wide shoulders, after bending low
With reverence, though to one who knew it not.   330
Then came the grieved voice of Mnemosyne,
And grieved I hearkened: 'That divinity
Whom thou saw'st step from yon forlornest wood,
And with slow pace approach our fallen King,
Is Thea, softest-natured of our brood.'   335
I marked the goddess in fair statuary
Surpassing wan Moneta by the head,
And in her sorrow nearer woman's tears.
There was a listening fear in her regard,
As if calamity had but begun;   340
As if the vanward clouds of evil days
Had spent their malice, and the sullen rear
Was with its stored thunder labouring up.
One hand she pressed upon that aching spot

Where beats the human heart, as if just there,   345
Though an immortal, she felt cruel pain;
The other upon Saturn's bended neck
She laid, and to the level of his hollow ear,
Leaning with parted lips, some words she spake
In solemn tenor and deep organ tune –   350
Some mourning words, which in our feeble tongue
Would come in this-like accenting (how frail
To that large utterance of the early gods!):
'Saturn, look up! And for what, poor lost King?
I have no comfort for thee – no, not one;   355
I cannot cry, "Wherefore thus sleepest thou?"
For heaven is parted from thee, and the earth
Knows thee not, so afflicted, for a god;
And ocean too, with all its solemn noise,
Has from thy sceptre passed, and all the air   360
Is emptied of thine hoary majesty.
Thy thunder, captious at the new command,
Rumbles reluctant o'er our fallen house;
And thy sharp lightning in unpractised hands
Scorches and burns our once serene domain.   365
With such remorseless speed still come new woes
That unbelief has not a space to breathe.
Saturn, sleep on. Me thoughtless, why should I
Thus violate thy slumbrous solitude?
Why should I ope thy melancholy eyes?   370
Saturn, sleep on, while at thy feet I weep.'
    As when, upon a tranced summer night,
Forests, branch-charmed by the earnest stars,
Dream, and so dream all night, without a noise,
Save from one gradual solitary gust   375
Swelling upon the silence, dying off,
As if the ebbing air had but one wave;
So came these words, and went, the while in tears
She pressed her fair large forehead to the earth,
Just where her fallen hair might spread in curls,   380
A soft and silken mat for Saturn's feet.
Long, long those two were postured motionless,
Like sculpture builded up upon the grave
Of their own power. A long awful time
I looked upon them; still they were the same,   385
The frozen god still bending to the earth,
And the sad goddess weeping at his feet;
Moneta silent. Without stay or prop
But my own weak mortality, I bore
The load of this eternal quietude,   390
The unchanging gloom, and the three fixed shapes
Ponderous upon my senses a whole moon.

For by my burning brain I measured sure
Her silver seasons shedded on the night,
And every day by day methought I grew   395
More gaunt and ghostly; oftentimes I prayed
Intense, that death would take me from the vale
And all its burdens; gasping with despair
Of change, hour after hour I cursed myself –
Until old Saturn raised his faded eyes,   400
And looked around and saw his kingdom gone,
And all the gloom and sorrow of the place,
And that fair kneeling goddess at his feet.
As the moist scent of flowers, and grass, and leaves
Fills forest dells with a pervading air   405
Known to the woodland nostril, so the words
Of Saturn filled the mossy glooms around,
Even to the hollows of time-eaten oaks,
And to the windings in the foxes' hole,
With sad low tones, while thus he spake, and sent   410
Strange musings to the solitary Pan:
'Moan, brethren, moan, for we are swallowed up
And buried from all godlike exercise
Of influence benign on planets pale,
And peaceful sway above man's harvesting,   415
And all those acts which deity supreme
Doth ease its heart of love in. Moan and wail.
Moan, brethren, moan, for lo! the rebel spheres
Spin round, the stars their ancient courses keep,
Clouds still with shadowy moisture haunt the earth,   420
Still suck their fill of light from sun and moon,
Still buds the tree, and still the seashores murmur.
There is no death in all the universe,
No smell of death – there shall be death. Moan, moan,
Moan, Cybele,[10] moan, for thy pernicious babes   425
Have changed a god into a shaking palsy.
Moan, brethren, moan, for I have no strength left,
Weak as the reed – weak – feeble as my voice –
Oh, oh, the pain, the pain of feebleness.
Moan, moan, for still I thaw – or give me help: 430
Throw down those imps, and give me victory.
Let me hear other groans, and trumpets blown
Of triumph calm, and hymns of festival
From the gold peaks of heaven's high-piled clouds;
Voices of soft proclaim, and silver stir   435
Of strings in hollow shells; and let there be
Beautiful things made new, for the surprise

---

[10] Cybele, mother of the gods.

Of the sky-children.' So he feebly ceased,
With such a poor and sickly sounding pause,
Methought I heard some old man of the earth   440
Bewailing earthly loss; nor could my eyes
And ears act with that pleasant unison of sense
Which marries sweet sound with the grace of form,
And dolorous accent from a tragic harp
With large-limbed visions. More I scrutinized: 445
Still fixed he sat beneath the sable trees,
Whose arms spread straggling in wild serpent forms,
With leaves all hushed; his awful presence there
Now all was silent, gave a deadly lie
To what I erewhile heard – only his lips   450
Trembled amid the white curls of his beard.
They told the truth, though, round the snowy locks
Hung nobly, as upon the face of heaven
A midday fleece of clouds. Thea arose
And stretched her white arm through the hollow dark,   455
Pointing some whither, whereat he too rose
Like a vast giant seen by men at sea
To grow pale from the waves at dull midnight.
They melted from my sight into the woods;
Ere I could turn, Moneta cried, 'These twain   460
Are speeding to the families of grief,
Where roofed in by black rocks they waste in pain
And darkness for no hope.' And she spake on,
As ye may read who can unwearied pass
Onward from the antechamber of this dream,   465
Where even at the open doors awhile
I must delay, and glean my memory
Of her high phrase – perhaps no further dare.

Canto II
'Mortal, that thou may'st understand aright,
I humanize my sayings to thine ear,
Making comparisons of earthly things;
Or thou might'st better listen to the wind,
Whose language is to thee a barren noise,   5
Though it blows legend-laden through the trees.
In melancholy realms big tears are shed,
More sorrow like to this, and suchlike woe
Too huge for mortal tongue, or pen of scribe.
The Titans fierce, self-hid or prison-bound,   10
Groan for the old allegiance once more,
Listening in their doom for Saturn's voice.
But one of our whole eagle-brood still keeps
His sov'reignty, and rule, and majesty;
Blazing Hyperion on his orbed fire   15

Still sits, still snuffs the incense teeming up
From man to the sun's god – yet unsecure.
For as upon the earth dire prodigies
Fright and perplex, so also shudders he;
Nor at dog's howl, or gloom-bird's even screech,   20
Or the familiar visitings of one
Upon the first toll of his passing bell,
But horrors, portioned to a giant nerve,
Make great Hyperion ache. His palace bright,
Bastioned with pyramids of glowing gold,   25
And touched with shade of bronzed obelisks,
Glares a blood-red through all the thousand courts,
Arches, and domes, and fiery galleries;
And all its curtains of aurorean clouds
Flush angerly – when he would taste the wreaths   30
Of incense breathed aloft from sacred hills,
Instead of sweets, his ample palate takes
Savour of poisonous brass and metals sick.
Wherefore, when harboured in the sleepy west,
After the full completion of fair day,   35
For rest divine upon exalted couch
And slumber in the arms of melody,
He paces through the pleasant hours of ease
With strides colossal, on from hall to hall,
While far within each aisle and deep recess   40
His winged minions in close clusters stand
Amazed, and full of fear; like anxious men
Who on a wide plain gather in sad troops
When earthquakes jar their battlements and towers.
Even now, while Saturn, roused from icy trance,   45
Goes step for step with Thea from yon woods,
Hyperion, leaving twilight in the rear,
Is sloping to the threshold of the west.
Thither we tend.' Now in clear light I stood,
Relieved from the dusk vale. Mnemosyne   50
Was sitting on a square-edged polished stone,
That in its lucid depth reflected pure
Her priestess-garments. My quick eyes ran on
From stately nave to nave, from vault to vault,
Through bowers of fragrant and enwreathed light   55
And diamond-paved lustrous long arcades.
Anon rushed by the bright Hyperion;
His flaming robes streamed out beyond his heels,
And gave a roar, as if of earthly fire,
That scared away the meek ethereal hours   60
And made their dove-wings tremble. On he flared . . .

Bright Star, Would I Were Steadfast as Thou Art
(composed 1819; edited from MS)

Bright star, would I were steadfast as thou art –
　Not in lone splendour hung aloft the night
And watching, with eternal lids apart,
　Like nature's patient, sleepless eremite,
The moving waters at their priestlike task　　　　　　　5
　Of pure ablution round earth's human shores,
Or gazing on the new soft-fallen mask
　Of snow upon the mountains and the moors;
No – yet still steadfast, still unchangeable,
　Pillowed upon my fair love's ripening breast,　　　　10
To feel for ever its soft swell and fall,
　Awake for ever in a sweet unrest,
Still, still to hear her tender-taken breath,
And so live ever – or else swoon to death.

George Darley　(1795–1846)

Dublin-born poet, friend of Lamb and Clare, who wrote for The London Magazine; *he was the author of numerous lyrics, including many seventeenth-century pastiches, of which 'A Song' is one of the finest.*

From The Labours of Idleness by Guy Penseval (1826)

MY BOWER IS IN A GREEN DELL

My bower is in a green dell
　Amid the hills so high
That angels, from their huge swell,
　Might step into the sky.

For silence or for sorrow,　　　　　　　　　　　　5
　For meditation made,
Ev'n joy itself must borrow
　A sadness from its shade.

For all adown its steep side
　The antlered oak doth grow,　　　　　　　　　　10
And darkles o'er the dim tide
　That raves and rolls below;

The sable yew, the sear tree
　That loves to sigh alone,

When deep in earth they've left thee   15
   And all thy friends are gone;

The pine wrapped up in grim pall,
   And elm with rooky bow'rs,
Stretching her arms parental
   Over the feeble flowers –   20

These and their leafy peers spread
   Their umbrage o'er the dale,
Lending thee all thy sweet shade,
   My loved, my lonely vale!

But down beside the rude stream   25
   That from the rocks doth pour,
Where Echo with her shrill scream
   Rewordeth back its roar,

My bower blooms, all beauteous
   With buds and blossoms fair,   30
That hang the head, all duteous,
   Whilst I lie dreaming there.

The honeysuckle drooping
   From off her spousal stems,
And o'er her master stooping,   35
   Scatters her purple gems.

Pale lilac bends to kiss me,
   And roses clasp my feet;
Coy violet, but to bless me,
   Peeps from her dim retreat.   40

Upon my lilied pillow
   Thus flow'r-embraced I lie,
And let the hoarse-tongued billow
   Rave my loud lullaby!

Whilst hung amid the bright flowers,   45
   And passioned by their sighs,
About the silent star-hours
   My lyre's wild words arise.

Whether an elve descending
   From out the joyless moon,
And to my bower bending   50
   Sweeps o'er her airy tune,

Or that the vagrant night-breeze
  Poised on its viewless wings
Whispers unto the light trees   55
  Some sweet and amorous things,

I know not – but the words seem
  At times as true and clear,
As to the eye the sunbeam,
  Or thunder to the ear.   60

Sometimes as faint and foundless,
  As perishing and vain,
As senseless, though not soundless,
  As haunt the dreamer's brain.

Perchance they are my wind-lyre's,   65
  Perchance they are my own;
When night puts out the pale fires
  I only know – they're gone!

From Literary Gazette, no.586 (12 April 1828) 236

A SONG

Believed not to be generally known, and written by Thomas Carew, the author of 'He that loves a rosie cheeke'.

It appears (says the correspondent to whom we are indebted for this Song) on the flyleaf of a book once in the possession of the unfortunate Earl of Strafford, when Lord Lieutenant of Ireland, and in that nobleman's writing. The heading is, 'A ryghte pythie Songe by T.C.' – probably the Earl's own opinion, his literary disposition being well known. There is (continues the writer), I believe, however, no other reason, besides the initials, for attributing it to Carew, than its similarity to the above-mentioned lyric in tone and feeling. It might have been the production of Thomas Churchyard, an earlier poet. At all events it is manifestly a very old song. The spelling is a little altered to make it readable.

It is not beautie I demande,
  A christalle browe, the moone's despaire,
Nor the snowe's daughter, a whyte hand,
  Nor mermaide's yellowe pryde of haire.

Tell mee not of youre starrie eies,   5
  Your lips that seeme on roses fedde,
Your breastes where Cupide tombling lyes,
  Nor sleepes for kissing of his bedde.

A bloomie paire of vermeil cheekes
  Like Hebe's in her roddiest houres,   10

A breath that softer musicke speakes
    Than summer windes a-wooing floures.

These are but gawdes: nay, what are lips?
    Corall beneathe the ocean-streame,
Whose brinke when youre adventurer lips,   15
    Full oft hee perisheth on themme.

And what are cheekes but ensignes ofte
    That wave hot youthe to fieldes of bloode?
Did Helene's breaste, though ere' so softe,
    Do Greece or Ilium anie goode?   20

Eies can with balefulle ardoure burne,
    Poison can breath that erste perfumede,
There's manie a whyte hande holdes an urne
    With lovers' hearts to dust consumede.

For christalle browes, there's nought within,   25
    They are but emptie cells for pryde;
Hee who the syrenne's haire woulde winne
    Is mostlie stranglede in the tyde.

Give mee, insteade of beautie's buste,
    A tender heart, a loyale minde,
Which with temptation I coulde truste,   30
    Yet never linkde with erroure finde.

One in whose gentle bosome, I
    Coulde poure mie secrete heart of woes,
Like the care-burthenede honie flie   35
    That hides his murmurrs in the rose.

Mie earthlie comfortoure! whose love
    So indefeisible might bee,
That when mie spirite wonne above,
    Hers could not staye for sympathie.   40

From The Athenaeum, no. 430 (23 January 1836) 67

SERENADE OF A LOYAL MARTYR (SIGNED 'G.D.')

Sweet in her green cell the flower of beauty slumbers,
Lulled by the faint breezes sighing through her hair;

A SONG
[1] ' "Neere" in MS; perhaps meant for "ne'er" ' (Darley's note).

Sleeps she, and hears not the melancholy numbers
Breathed to my sad lute amid the lonely air?

Down from the high cliffs the rivulet is teeming,   5
To wind round the willow banks that lure him from above:
Oh that in tears from my rocky prison streaming,
I too could glide to the bower of my love!

Ah! where the woodbines with sleepy arms have wound her
Opes she her eyelids at the dream of my lay,   10
Listening like the dove, while the fountains echo round her,
To her lost mate's call in the forests far away?

Come then, my bird, for the peace thou ever bearest,
Still heaven's messenger of comfort to me,
Come! this fond bosom, my faithfullest, my fairest!   15
Bleeds with its death-wound, but deeper yet for thee.

Hartley Coleridge   (1796–1849)

In Sonnet IX Hartley Coleridge addresses his mythologized self of 'Frost at Midnight', 'The Nightingale', the conclusion to 'Christabel', and the 'Ode'. There is pathos in the reckoning, more pronounced in 'When I review the course that I have run', published posthumously in 1851. 'To Wordsworth', however, is a moving tribute to the poet who first described him as a 'Seer blessed' ('Ode', 114).

From Poems (1833)

SONNET IX

Long time a child, and still a child, when years
Had painted manhood on my cheek, was I;
For yet I lived like one not born to die;
A thriftless prodigal of smiles and tears,
No hope I needed, and I knew no fears.   5
But sleep, though sweet, is only sleep, and waking,
I waked to sleep no more, at once o'ertaking
The vanguard of my age, with all arrears
Of duty on my back. Nor child, nor man,
Nor youth, nor sage, I find my head is grey,   10
For I have lost the race I never ran,
A rathe December blights my lagging May;
And still I am a child, though I be old –
Time is my debtor for my years untold.

From Essays and Marginalia, ed. Derwent Coleridge (1851)

VII

When I review the course that I have run,
And count the loss of all my wasted days,
I find no argument for joy or praise
In whatsoe'er my soul hath thought or done.
I am a desert, and the kindly sun   5
On me hath vainly spent his fertile rays.
Then wherefore do I tune my idle lays,
Or dream that haply I may be the one
Of the vain thousands, that shall win a place
Among the poets – that a single rhyme   10
Of my poor wit's devising may find grace
To breed high memories in the womb of time?
But to confound the time the muse I woo;
Then 'tis but just that time confound me too.

XV. TO WORDSWORTH

There have been poets that in verse display
The elemental forms of human passions;
Poets have been, to whom the fickle fashions
And all the wilful humours of the day
Have furnished matter for a polished lay;   5
And many are the smooth elaborate tribe
Who, emulous of thee, the shape describe,
And fain would every shifting hue portray
Of restless nature. But, thou mighty seer!
'Tis thine to celebrate the thoughts that make   10
The life of souls, the truths for whose sweet sake
We to ourselves and to our God are dear.
Of nature's inner shrine thou art the priest,
Where most she works when we perceive her least.

Mary Wollstonecraft Shelley (1797–1851)

Daughter of Mary Wollstonecraft and William Godwin, Mary left England with Percy Bysshe Shelley in 1814, and married him two years later. Her most important work is Frankenstein *(1818), which (like Shelley's 'Mont Blanc' and Byron's* Childe Harold's Pilgrimage, Canto III*) has its origins in the summer of 1816, spent with Byron and Shelley at Villa Diodati on Lake Geneva. That earlier period is the subject of the journal entries presented here, inspired first by a re-reading of Byron's poem and then by his death (for Elizabeth Barrett's response to the same event see pp. 1102–3). She was also an accomplished poet, and the three elegies presented here, all inspired by her husband's death, are among her finest verses. One of her most enduring legacies* *is her edition of his poetry; an extract from her valuable note to 'Prometheus Unbound' is also included.*

From Journals (edited from MS)

28 May 1817. I am melancholy with reading the third Canto of *Childe Harold.* Do you not remember, Shelley, when you first read it to me, one evening after returning from Diodati? It was in our little room at Chapuis; the lake was before us and the mighty Jura. That time is past and this will also pass, when I may weep to read these words and again moralize on the flight of time.

Dear Lake! I shall ever love thee. How a powerful mind can sanctify past scenes and recollections! His is a powerful mind, one that fills me with melancholy yet mixed with pleasure, as is always the case when intellectual energy is displayed. To think of our excursions on the Lake; how we saw him when he came down to us or welcomed our arrival with a good-humoured smile. How very vividly does each verse of his poem recall some scene of this kind to my memory. This time will soon also be a recollection. We may see him again and again, enjoy his society, but the time will also arrive when that which is now an anticipation will be only in the memory. Death will at length come and in the last moment all will be a dream.

15 May 1824. This then was the 'coming event' that cast its shadow on my last night's miserable thoughts. Byron has become one of the people of the grave[1] – that innumerable conclave to which the beings I best loved belong. I knew him in the bright days of youth, when neither care or fear had visited me; before death had made me feel my mortality and the earth was the scene of my hopes. Can I forget our evening visits to Diodati, our excursions of the lake when he sang the Tyrolese hymn, and his voice was harmonized with winds and waves? Can I forget his attentions and consolations to me during my deepest misery? Never. Beauty sat on his countenance and power beamed from his eye; his faults being for the most part weaknesses, induced one readily to pardon them. Albe, the dear capricious fascinating Albe has left this desert world.

What do I do here? Why am I doomed to live on seeing all expire before me? God grant I may die young. A new race is springing about me. At the age of twenty-six I am in the condition of an aged person. All my friends are gone; I have no wish to form new. I cling to the few remaining, but they slide away and my heart fails when I think by how few ties I hold to the world. Albe, dearest Albe, was knit by long associations. Each day I repeat with bitterer feelings, 'Life is the desert and the solitude, how populous the grave'[2] – and that region, to the dearer and best beloved beings which it has torn from me, now adds that resplendent spirit, whose departure leaves the dull earth dark as midnight.

From JOURNALS
[1] News of Byron's death on 19 Apr. 1824 at Missolonghi reached England 14 May.

[2] Young, *Night Thoughts,* i. 115–16.

On Reading Wordsworth's Lines on Peele Castle
(composed 8 December 1825; edited from MS)

It is with me, as erst with you,
  Oh poet, nature's chronicler,
The summer seas have lost their hue
  And storm sits brooding everywhere.

The gentlest rustling of the deep   5
  Is but the dirge of him I lost,
And when waves raise their furrows steep,
  And bring foam in which is tossed.

A voice I hear upon the wind
  Which bids me haste to join him there,   10
And woo the tempest's breath unkind
  Which gives to me a kindred bier.

And when all smooth are ocean's plains
  And sails afar are glittering,
The fairest skiff his form contains   15
  To my poor heart's fond picturing.

Then wildly to the beach I rush,
  And fain would seize the frailest boat,
And from dull earth the slight hull push,
  On dancing waves towards him to float.   20

'Nor may I e'er again behold
  The sea, and be as I have been;
My bitter grief will ne'er grow old,
  Nor say I this with mind serene."[1]

For oft I weep in solitude   25
  And shed so many bitter tears,
While on past joys I vainly brood
  And shrink in fear from coming years.

A Dirge (composed November 1827; edited from MS)
TO THE AIR OF 'MY PHILLIDA, ADIEU, LOVE!'

This morn thy gallant bark, love,
  Sailed on a sunny sea;

ON READING WORDSWORTH'S LINES ON PEELE CASTLE
[1] See Wordsworth, 'Elegiac Stanzas Suggested by a
Picture of Peele Castle', 37–40.

'Tis noon, and tempests dark, love,
  Have wrecked it on the lee.
    Ah woe! Ah woe! Ah woe!   5
  By spirits of the deep
  He's cradled on the billow
  To his unwaking sleep.

Thou liest upon the shore, love,
  Beside the knelling surge,   10
But sea-nymphs evermore, love,
  Shall sadly chaunt thy dirge.
    Oh come! Oh come! Oh come!
  Ye spirits of the deep,
  While near his seaweed pillow   15
  My lonely watch I keep.

From far across the sea, love,
  I hear a wild lament,
By Echo's voice for thee, love,
  From ocean's caverns sent: 20
    Oh list! Oh list! Oh list!
  The spirits of the deep —
  Loud sounds their wail of sorrow,
  While I for ever weep.

Oh Listen While I Sing to Thee (composed 12 March 1838; edited from MS)

Oh listen while I sing to thee,
  My song is meant for thee alone;
My thought imparts its melody,
  And gives the soft impassioned tone.

I sing of joy, and see thy smile   5
  That to the swelling note replies;
I sing of love, and feel the while
  The gaze of thy love-beaming eyes.

If thou wert far, my voice would die
  In murmurs faint and sorrowing;   10
If thou wert fake – in agony
  My heart would break, I could not sing.

Then listen while I sing to thee,
  My song is meant for thee alone;
And now that thou art near to me   15
  I pour a full impassioned tone.

From The Poetical Works of Percy Bysshe Shelley, ed.
Mary Shelley (4 vols., 1839)

NOTE ON THE 'PROMETHEUS UNBOUND' (EXTRACTS) (II 132-6, 137-40)

The prominent feature of Shelley's theory of the destiny of the human species was that evil is not inherent in the system of the creation, but an accident that might be expelled. This also forms a portion of Christianity: God made earth and man perfect, till he, by his fall, 'Brought death into the world, and all our woe'.[1] Shelley believed that mankind had only to will that there should be no evil, and there would be none. It is not my part in these notes to notice the arguments that have been urged against this opinion, but to mention the fact that he entertained it, and was indeed attached to it with fervent enthusiasm. That man could be so perfectionized as to be able to expel evil from his own nature and from the greater part of the creation, was the cardinal point of his system. And the subject he loved best to dwell on, was the image of One warring with the Evil Principle, oppressed not only by it, but by all – even the good who were deluded into considering evil a necessary portion of humanity.

A victim full of fortitude and hope, and the spirit of triumph emanating from a reliance in the ultimate omnipotence of good: such he had depicted in his last poem,[2] when he made Laon the enemy and the victim of tyrants. He now took a more idealized image of the same subject. He followed certain classical authorities in figuring Saturn as the good principle, Jupiter the usurping evil one, and Prometheus as the regenerator, who, unable to bring mankind back to primitive innocence, used knowledge as a weapon to defeat evil, by leading mankind beyond the state wherein they are sinless through ignorance, to that in which they are virtuous through wisdom. Jupiter punished the temerity of the Titan by chaining him to a rock of Caucasus, and causing a vulture to devour his still renewed heart. There was a prophecy afloat in heaven portending the fall of Jove, the secret of averting which was known only to Prometheus – and the god offered freedom from torture on condition of its being communicated to him. According to the mythological story, this referred to the offspring of Thetis, who was destined to be greater than his father. Prometheus at last bought pardon for his crime of enriching mankind with his gifts, by revealing the prophecy. Hercules killed the vulture and set him free, and Thetis was married to Peleus, the father of Achilles.

Shelley adapted the catastrophe of this story to his peculiar views. The son, greater than his father, born of the nuptials of Jupiter and Thetis, was to dethrone Evil, and bring back a happier reign than that of Saturn. Prometheus defies the power of his enemy, and endures centuries of torture till the hour arrives when Jove, blind to the real event, but darkly guessing that some great good to himself will flow, espouses Thetis. At the moment, the primal power of the world drives him from his usurped throne, and strength, in the person of Hercules, liberates humanity, typified in Prometheus, from the tortures generated by evil done or suffered. Asia, one of the Oceanides, is the wife of Prometheus (she was, according to other mythological interpretations, the same as Venus and nature). When the benefactor of mankind is liberated, nature resumes the beauty of her prime, and is united to her husband, the

---

EDITOR'S NOTE ON 'PROMETHEUS UNBOUND' (extract)
[1] *Paradise Lost*, i. 3.

[2] *Laon and Cythna*, later retitled *The Revolt of Islam*, composed Mar.–Sept. 1817, published Dec. 1817.

emblem of the human race, in perfect and happy union. In the fourth Act, the poet gives further scope to his imagination and idealizes the forms of creation, such as we know them, instead of such as they appeared to the Greeks. Maternal Earth, the mighty parent, is superseded by the Spirit of the Earth – the guide of our planet through the realms of sky – while his fair and weaker companion and attendant, the Spirit of the Moon, receives bliss from the annihilation of Evil in the superior sphere.

Shelley develops (more particularly in the lyrics of this drama) his abstruse and imaginative theories with regard to the creation. It requires a mind as subtle and penetrating as his own to understand the mystic meanings scattered throughout the poem. They elude the ordinary reader by their abstraction and delicacy of distinction, but they are far from vague. It was his design to write prose metaphysical essays on the nature of man, which would have served to explain much of what is obscure in his poetry; a few scattered fragments of observations and remarks alone remain. He considered these philosophical views of mind and nature to be instinct with the intensest spirit of poetry.

More popular poets clothe the ideal with familiar and sensible imagery. Shelley loved to idealize the real – to gift the mechanism of the material universe with a soul and a voice, and to bestow such also on the most delicate and abstract emotions and thoughts of the mind. Sophocles was his great master in this species of imagery. . . .

In the 'Prometheus Unbound', Shelley fulfils the promise quoted from a letter in the note on *The Revolt of Islam*. The tone of the composition is calmer and more majestic, the poetry more perfect as a whole, and the imagination displayed at once more pleasingly beautiful and more varied and daring. The description of the Hours as they are seen in the cave of Demogorgon, is an instance of this – it fills the mind as the most charming picture; we long to see an artist at work to bring to our view the

> cars drawn by rainbow-winged steeds
> Which trample the dim winds; in each there stands
> A wild-eyed charioteer urging their flight.
> Some look behind, as fiends pursued them there,
> And yet I see no shapes but the keen stars;
> Others, with burning eyes, lean forth, and drink
> With eager lips the wind of their own speed,
> As if the thing they loved fled on before,
> And now, even now, they clasped it. Their bright locks
> Stream like a comet's flashing hair – they all
> Sweep onward.
>
> (*Prometheus Unbound*, II. iv. 130-40)

Through the whole poem there reigns a sort of calm and holy spirit of love; it soothes the tortured, and is hope to the expectant, till the prophecy is fulfilled, and love, untainted by any evil, becomes the law of the world.

England had been rendered a painful residence to Shelley, as much by the sort of persecution with which in those days all men of liberal opinions were visited, and by the injustice he had lately endured in the Court of Chancery, as by the symptoms of disease which made him regard a visit to Italy as necessary to prolong his life. An exile, and strongly impressed with the feeling that the majority of his countrymen regarded him with sentiments of aversion (such as his own heart could experience towards none), he sheltered himself from such disgusting and painful thoughts in the calm retreats of poetry, and built up a world of his own, with the more pleasure, since he hoped to induce some one or two to believe that the earth might become such, did mankind themselves consent. The charm of the Roman climate helped to clothe his thoughts in greater beauty than they had ever worn before. And as he wandered among the ruins, made one with nature in their decay, or gazed on the Praxitelean shapes that throng the Vatican, the Capitol, and the palaces of Rome, his soul imbibed forms of loveliness which became a portion of itself. There are many passages in the 'Prometheus' which show the intense delight he received from such studies, and give back the impression with a beauty of poetical description peculiarly his own. He felt this, as a poet must feel when he satisfies himself by the result of his labours, and he wrote from Rome: 'My "Prometheus Unbound" is just finished, and in a month or two I shall send it. It is a drama, with characters and mechanism of a kind yet unattempted, and I think the execution is better than any of my former attempts.'

Thomas Hood (1799–1845)

Assistant editor of the London Magazine, *friend of Lamb, Hazlitt, and De Quincey. Besides the satires and parodies that made his name, Hood was an able poet, strongly influenced, at least during the early 1820s, by Keats. 'Ode: Autumn' is a tribute to Keats, to whose Odes it alludes.*

From London Magazine 7 (1823) 187-8

ODE: AUTUMN (SIGNED 'H.')

I

I saw old Autumn in the misty morn
  Stand shadowless, like Silence listening
  To silence – for no lonely bird would sing
Into his hollow ear from woods forlorn;
Nor lowly hedge, nor solitary thorn –   5
Shaking his languid locks all dewy bright
With tangled gossamer that fell by night,
  Pearling his coronet of golden corn.
Where are the songs of daylight? In the sun,
  Oping the dusky eyelids of the south,   10
Till shade and silence waken up as one,
  And Morning sings with a warm odorous mouth.
Where are the merry birds? Away, away,
  On panting wings through the inclement skies,
    Lest owls should prey,   15
    Undazzled at noonday,
And tear with horny beak their lustrous eyes.[1]

ODE: AUTUMN
[1] *lustrous eyes* Keats, 'Ode to a Nightingale', 29.

II

Where are the blooms of summer? In the west,
  Blushing their last to the last sunny hours,
When the mild eve by sudden night is pressed,
  Like tearful Proserpine, snatched among flow'rs
    To a most gloomy breast.
Where is the pride of summer, the green prime,
  The many, many leaves wind-wanton? Three
On the mossed elm; three on the naked lime   25
  Trembling – and one upon the old oak tree!
Where is the dryad's immortality?
  Gone into mournful cypress and dark yew,
  Or wearing the long gloomy winter through
In the smooth holly's green eternity.   30

III

The squirrel gloats on his accomplished hoard;
  The ants have brimmed their garners with ripe grain;
    And honey-bees have stored
  The sweets of summer in their luscious cells;[2]
The swallows all have winged across the main;[3]   35
  But here the autumn melancholy dwells,
    And sighs her tearful spells
Amongst the sunless shadows of the plain.
Alone, alone, upon a mossy stone,
  Until her drowsy feet forgotten be,   40
She sits and reckons up the dead and gone,
  With the last leaves for a love-rosary,
  Whilst the all-withered world spreads drearily,
Like a dim picture of the drowned past
  In the hushed mind's mysterious far-away,   45
Doubtful what ghostly thing will steal the last
  Into that distance – grey upon the grey.

IV

Aye, go and sit with her, and be o'ershaded
  Under the languid downfall of her hair;
She wears a coronal of flowers faded
  Upon her forehead, like a constant care;   50
  There is enough of withered everywhere

---

2 Cf. Keats, 'To Autumn', 11.   3 Cf. ibid., 33.

To make her bower, and eternal gloom;
   There is enough of sadness to invite,
If only for the rose that died, whose doom   55
Is Beauty's[4] – she that with the exquisite bloom
   Of conscious cheeks most beautifies the light.
   There is enough of sorrowing, and quite
Enough of bitter fruits this world doth bear;
   Enough of chilly droppings for her bowl,   60
Enough of fear and shadowy despair
   To frame her cloudy prison for the soul.

From London Magazine, 7 (1823) 541

SONNET WRITTEN IN KEATS' ENDYMION (SIGNED 'T.')

I saw pale Dian, sitting by the brink
   Of silver falls, the overflow of fountains
From cloudy steeps; and I grew sad to think
   Endymion's foot was silent on those mountains,
And he but a hushed name that Silence keeps   5
   In dear remembrance – lonely and forlorn,
Singing it to herself until she weeps
   Tears that perchance still glisten in the morn;
And as I mused, in dull imaginings,
   There came a flash of garments, and I knew   10
The awful muse by her harmonious wings
   Charming the air to music as she flew:
Anon there rose an echo through the vale
Gave back Endymion in a dream-like tale.

From The Plea of the Midsummer Fairies (1827)

THE WATER LADY

Alas, the moon should ever beam
To show what man should never see!
I saw a maiden on a stream
And fair was she!

I stayed awhile, to see her throw   5
Her tresses back, that all beset
The fair horizon of her brow
With clouds of jet.

I stayed a little while to view
Her cheek, that wore in place of red   10

---

4 Cf. Keats, 'Ode to a Nightingale', 29.

The bloom of water, tender blue,
Daintily spread.

I stayed to watch, a little space,
Her parted lips if she would sing;
The waters closed above her face   15
With many a ring.

And still I stayed a little more,
Alas! she never comes again;
I throw my flow'rs from the shore,
And watch in vain.   20

I know my life will fade away,
I know that I must vainly pine,
For I am made of mortal clay,
But she's divine!

Louisa Costello (1799–1870)

Painter, poet and novelist; as this selection shows, Costello moves effortlessly from the poetry of betrayed love favoured by female writers of the day, to the more wistful 'fairy' poetry of 'Spirit's Song'.

From Songs of a Stranger (1825)

LINES

If we should ever meet again
    When many tedious years are past;
When time shall have unbound the chain,
    And this sad heart is free at last;
Then shall we meet and look unmoved,   5
As though we ne'er had met – had loved!
And I shall mark without a tear
    How cold and calm thy altered brow;
I shall forget thou once wert dear,
    Rememb'ring but thy broken vow!   10
Rememb'ring that in trusting youth
I loved thee with the purest truth;
That now the fleeting dream is o'er,
And thou canst raise the spell no more!

SPIRIT'S SONG

'Tis thy spirit calls thee – come away!
I have sought thee through the weary day,

I have dived in the glassy stream for thee,
I have gone wherever a spirit might be –

In the earth, where diamonds hide;   5
In the deep, where pearls abide;
In the air, where rainbows, glancing gay,
Smile the tears of the sun away,

I have wandered; mid the starry zone
Through a world by spirits only known,   10
Where 'tis bliss to sail in that balmy air;
But to me 'twas joyless till thou wert there.

I traced the footsteps of the fawn
As it bounded over the dewy lawn;
For the print it left was so light and fair,   15
I deemed thy step had lingered there.

I heard a sound of melody,
Sad and sweet as thy tender sigh;
'Twas the night-bird's tone, but it smote my ear,
For I thought thy own soft voice to hear.   20

I see a form – it is gliding on
Like a cloud that sails in the sky alone,
And the stars gleam through its veil of white –
Oh! can it be aught of earth, so bright?
It beckons me on to my airy home –   25
My own loved spirit! I come! I come!

Letitia Elizabeth Landon   (1802–38)

*Poet and novelist, who lived by her writing from an early age. Like Felicia Hemans, she was
strongly influenced by Wordsworth, as she admits in her tribute, 'On Wordsworth's Cottage,
near Grasmere Lake'. Landon's verse at its best embodies the Wordsworthian virtue of being
able to address deeply felt emotions without the sentimentality favoured by many poets at the end
of the eighteenth century. This is particularly evident in her discussion of the lot of the female
poet in the elegant 'Stanzas on the Death of Mrs Hemans', which provoked a response from the
young Elizabeth Barrett (pp. 1103-5). 'A Poet's Love' laments, among other things, the loss
of imaginative vision; it was published only after her death.*

From The Improvisatrice and Other Poems (1824)

WHEN SHOULD LOVERS BREATHE THEIR VOWS?

When should lovers breathe their vows?
　　When should ladies hear them?
When the dew is on the boughs,
　　When none else are near them;
When the moon shines cold and pale,　　　　　　　　　5
　　When the birds are sleeping,
When no voice is on the gale,
　　When the rose is weeping;
When the stars are bright on high,
　　Like hopes in young love's dreaming,　　　　　　10
And glancing round the light clouds fly,
　　Like soft fears to shade their beaming.
The fairest smiles are those that live
　　On the brow by starlight wreathing;
And the lips their richest incense give　　　　　　　15
　　When the sigh is at midnight breathing.
Oh softest is the cheek's love-ray
　　When seen by moonlight hours,
Other roses seek the day,
　　But blushes are night-flowers.　　　　　　　　　20
Oh when the moon and stars are bright,
　　When the dew-drops glisten,
Then their vows should lovers plight,
　　Then should ladies listen!

From New Monthly Magazine, 44 (1835) 286-8

STANZAS ON THE DEATH OF MRS HEMANS

> *The rose – the glorious rose is gone.*
> (Felicia Hemans, *Lays of Many Lands*)

Bring flowers to crown the cup and lute,
　　Bring flowers, the bride is near;
Bring flowers to soothe the captive's cell,
　　Bring flowers to strew the bier!
Bring flowers! – thus said the lovely song;[1]　　　　5
　　And shall they not be brought
To her who linked the offering
　　With feeling and with thought?

STANZAS ON THE DEATH OF MRS HEMANS
[1] 'Bring Flowers', one of the miscellaneous poems
included in Hemans's *Lays of Many Lands* (1825).

Bring flowers, the perfumed and the pure,
  Those with the morning dew,   10
A sigh in every fragrant leaf,
  A tear on every hue.
So pure, so sweet thy life has been,
  So filling earth and air
With odours and with loveliness   15
  Till common scenes grew fair.

Thy song around our daily path
  Flung beauty born of dreams,
That shadows on the actual world
  The spirit's sunny gleams.   20
Mysterious influence, that to earth
  Brings down the heaven above,
And fills the universal heart
  With universal love.

Such gifts were thine — as from the block,   25
  The unformed and the cold,
The sculptor calls to breathing life
  Some shape of perfect mould;
So thou from common thoughts and things
  Didst call a charmed song,   30
Which on a sweet and swelling tide
  Bore the full soul along.

And thou from far and foreign lands
  Didst bring back many a tone,
And giving such new music still,   35
  A music of thine own.
A lofty strain of generous thoughts,
  And yet subdued and sweet —
An angel's song, who sings of earth,
  Whose cares are at his feet.   40

And yet thy song is sorrowful,
  Its beauty is not bloom;
The hopes of which it breathes are hopes
  That look beyond the tomb.
Thy song is sorrowful as winds   45
  That wander o'er the plain,
And ask for summer's vanished flowers,
  And ask for them in vain.

Ah, dearly purchased is the gift,
  The gift of song like thine;   50
A fated doom is hers who stands

The priestess of the shrine.
The crowd – they only see the crown,
   They only hear the hymn –
They mark not that the cheek is pale,   55
   And that the eye is dim.

Wound to a pitch too exquisite,
   The soul's fine chords are wrung;
With misery and melody
   They are too highly strung.   60
The heart is made too sensitive
   Life's daily pain to bear;
It beats in music, but it beats
   Beneath a deep despair.

It never meets the love it paints,   65
   The love for which it pines;
Too much of heaven is in the faith
   That such a heart enshrines.
The meteor wreath the poet wears
   Must make a lonely lot;   70
It dazzles only to divide
   From those who wear it not.

Didst thou not tremble at thy fame
   And loathe its bitter prize,
While what to others triumph seemed,   75
   To thee was sacrifice?
Oh flower brought from paradise
   To this cold world of ours,
Shadows of beauty such as thine
   Recall thy native bowers.   80

Let others thank thee – 'twas for them
   Thy soft leaves thou didst wreathe;
The red rose wastes itself in sighs
   Whose sweetness others breathe!
And they have thanked thee – many a lip   85
   Has asked of thine for words,
When thoughts, life's finer thoughts, have touched
   The spirit's inmost chords.

How many loved and honoured thee
   Who only knew thy name;   90
Which o'er the weary working world
   Like starry music came!
With what still hours of calm delight
   Thy songs and image blend;

I cannot choose but think thou wert   95
  An old familiar friend.

The charm that dwelt in songs of thine
  My inmost spirit moved;
And yet I feel as thou hadst been
  Not half enough beloved.   100
They say that thou wert faint and worn
  With suffering and with care;
What music must have filled the soul
  That had so much to spare!

Oh weary one! since thou art laid   105
  Within thy mother's breast —
The green, the quiet mother earth —
  Thrice blessed be thy rest!
Thy heart is left within our hearts
  Although life's pang is o'er;   110
But the quick tears are in my eyes,
  And I can write no more.

From The Zenana, and Minor Poems of L.E.L. (1839)

ON WORDSWORTH'S COTTAGE, NEAR GRASMERE LAKE

Not for the glory on their heads
  Those stately hilltops wear,
Although the summer sunset sheds
  Its constant crimson there;
Not for the gleaming lights that break   5
The purple of the twilight lake,
  Half dusky and half fair,
Does that sweet valley seem to be
A sacred place on earth to me.

The influence of a moral spell   10
  Is found around the scene,
Giving new shadows to the dell,
  New verdure to the green.
With every mountain-top is wrought
The presence of associate thought,   15
  A music that has been;
Calling that loveliness to life,
With which the inward world is rife.

His home, our English poet's home,
  Amid these hills is made;
Here with the morning hath he come,   20

There, with the night delayed.
On all things is his memory cast,
For every place wherein he passed
  Is with his mind arrayed –   25
That, wandering in a summer hour,
Asked wisdom of the leaf and flower.

Great poet, if I dare to throw
  My homage at thy feet,
'Tis thankfulness for hours which thou   30
  Hast made serene and sweet;
As wayfarers have incense thrown
Upon some mighty altar-stone
  Unworthy, and yet meet –
The human spirit longs to prove   35
The truth of its uplooking love.

Until thy hand unlocked its store,
  What glorious music slept!
Music that can be hushed no more
  Was from our knowledge kept.   40
But the great Mother[1] gave to thee
The poet's universal key,
  And forth the fountains swept –
A gushing melody for ever,
The witness of thy high endeavour.   45

Rough is the road which we are sent,
  Rough with long toil and pain;
And when upon the steep ascent,
  A little way we gain,
Vexed with our own perpetual care,   50
Little we heed what sweet things are
  Around our pathway blent;
With anxious steps we hurry on,
The very sense of pleasure gone.

But thou dost in this feverish dream   55
  Awake a better mood,
With voices from the mountain stream,
  With voices from the wood.
And with their music dost impart
Their freshness to the world-worn heart,   60
  Whose fever is subdued

ON WORDSWORTH'S COTTAGE, NEAR GRASMERE LAKE
[1] Nature.

By memories sweet with other years,
By gentle hopes, and soothing tears.

A solemn creed is thine, and high,
    Yet simple as a child,   65
Who looketh hopeful to yon sky
    With eyes yet undefiled
By all the glitter and the glare
This life's deceits and follies wear,
    Exalted, and yet mild,   70
Conscious of those diviner powers
Brought from a better world than ours.

Thou hast not chosen to rehearse
    The old heroic themes;
Thou hast not given to thy verse   75
    The heart's impassioned dreams.
Forth flows thy song as waters flow,
So bright above – so calm below,
    Wherein the heaven seems
Eternal as the golden shade   80
Its sunshine on the stream hath laid.

The glory which thy spirit hath
    Is round life's common things,
And flingeth round our common path,
    As from an angel's wings,   85
A light that is not of our sphere,
Yet lovelier for being here,
    Beneath whose presence springs
A beauty never marked before,
Yet once known, vanishing no more.   90

How often with the present sad,
    And weary with the past,
A sunny respite have we had,
    By but a chance look cast
Upon some word of thine that made   95
The sullenness forsake the shade,
    Till shade itself was past:
For hope divine, serene and strong,
Perpetual lives within thy song.

Eternal as the hills thy name,   100
    Eternal as thy strain;
So long as ministers of fame
    Shall love and hope remain.
The crowded city in its streets,

The valley, in its green retreats,   105
    Alike thy words retain.
What need hast thou of sculptured stone?
  Thy temple is thy name alone.

From Life and Literary Remains of L.E.L. (1841)

A POET'S LOVE

Faint and more faint amid the world of dreams,
That which was once my all, thy image, seems
Pale as a star that in the morning gleams.

Long time that sweet face was my guiding star,
Bringing me visions of the fair and far,   5
Remote from this world's toil and this world's jar.

Around it was an atmosphere of light,
Deep with the tranquil loveliness of night,
Subdued and shadowy, yet serenely bright.

Like to a spirit did it dwell apart,   10
Hushed in the sweetest silence of my heart,
Lifting me to the heaven from whence thou art.

Too soon the day broke on that haunted hour,
Loosing its spell, and weakening its power,
All that had been imagination's dower.   15

The noontide quenched that once enchanted ray;
Care, labour, sorrow, gathered on the day –
Toil was upon my steps, dust on my way.

They melted down to earth my upward wings;
I half forgot the higher, better things,   20
The hope which yet again thy image brings.

Would I were worthier of thee? I am fain,
Amid my life of bitterness and pain,
To dream once more my early dreams again.

Thomas Lovell Beddoes   (1803–49)

Although his masterpiece was a play, Death's Jest-Book, *Beddoes is best known today for his short lyrics, which reveal an obsession with the macabre and the supernatural.*

From Poems by the Late Thomas Lovell Beddoes (1851)

DREAM-PEDLARY (COMPOSED BETWEEN 1829 AND 1844)

1

If there were dreams to sell,
　What would you buy?
Some cost a passing bell;
　Some a light sigh
That shakes from life's fresh crown　　　　　　5
Only a roseleaf down.
If there were dreams to sell,
Merry and sad to tell,
And the crier rung the bell,
　What would you buy?　　　　　　　　　　10

2

A cottage lone and still
　With bowers nigh,
Shadowy, my woes to still,
　Until I die.
Such pearl from life's fresh crown　　　　　15
Fain would I shake me down.
Were dreams to have at will,
This would best heal my ill,
　This would I buy.

3

But there were dreams to sell,　　　　　　20
　Ill didst thou buy;
Life is a dream, they tell,
　Waking, to die.
Dreaming a dream to prize,
Is wishing ghosts to rise;　　　　　　　　25
　And if I had the spell
　To call the buried, well,
　　Which one would I?

4

If there are ghosts to raise,
　What shall I call　　　　　　　　　　　30

Out of hell's murky haze,
  Heaven's blue pall?
Raise my loved long-lost boy
To lead me to his joy.
    There are no ghosts to raise;   35
    Out of death lead no ways;
      Vain is the call.

                    5

Know'st thou not ghosts to sue?
  No love thou hast.
Else lie, as I will do,   40
  And breathe thy last.
So out of life's fresh crown
Fall like a rose-leaf down.
    Thus are the ghosts to woo,
    Thus are all dreams made true,   45
      Ever to last!

THE PHANTOM-WOOER (COMPOSED BETWEEN 1843 AND 1848)

                    1

A ghost that loved a lady fair,
Ever in the starry air
  Of midnight at her pillow stood;
And with a sweetness skies above
The luring words of human love,   5
  Her soul the phantom wooed.
Sweet and sweet is their poisoned note,
The little snakes of silver throat
In mossy skulls that nest and lie,
Ever singing 'Die, oh die!'   10

                    2

Young soul, put off your flesh, and come
With me into the quiet tomb,
  Our bed is lovely, dark, and sweet;
The earth will swing us, as she goes,
Beneath our coverlid of snows,   15
  And the warm leaden sheet.
Dear and dear is their poisoned note,
The little snakes of silver throat
In mossy skulls that nest and lie,
Ever singing 'Die, oh die!'   20

From Death's Jest-Book, or The Fool's Tragedy (composed between 1825 and 1848, published 1850)

SONG BY ISBRAND (PP. 86–8)

Squats on a toadstool under a tree
  A bodiless childfull of life in the gloom,
Crying with frog voice, 'What shall I be?
Poor unborn ghost, for my mother killed me
  Scarcely alive in her wicked womb.   5
What shall I be? Shall I creep to the egg
  That's cracking asunder yonder by Nile,
    And with eighteen toes,
    And a snuff-taking nose,
Make an Egyptian crocodile?   10
Sing, "Catch a mummy by the leg
  And crunch him with an upper jaw,
  Wagging tail and clenching claw;
    Take a bill-full from my craw,
    Neighbour raven, caw, oh caw,   15
    Grunt, my crocky, pretty maw!"

Swine, shall I be you? Thou'rt a dear dog;
  But for a smile, and kiss, and pout,
  I much prefer *your* black-lipped snout,
    Little, gruntless, fairy hog,   20
    Godson of the hawthorn hedge.
For, when Ringwood snuffs me out,
  And 'gins my tender paunch to grapple,
Sing, "'Twixt your ankles visage wedge,
  And roll up like an apple."   25

Serpent Lucifer, how do you do?
Of your worms and your snakes I'd be one or two,
  For in this dear planet of wool and of leather
'Tis pleasant to need neither shirt, sleeve nor shoe,
  And have arm, leg, and belly together.   30
  Then aches your head, or are you lazy?
  Sing, "Round your neck your belly wrap,
  Tail-a-top, and make your cap
    Any bee and daisy."

I'll not be a fool, like the nightingale   35
Who sits up all midnight without any ale,
  Making a noise with his nose;
Nor a camel, although 'tis a beautiful back;
Nor a duck, notwithstanding the music of quack
  And the webby, mud-patting toes.   40

I'll be a new bird with the head of an ass,
    Two pigs' feet, two mens' feet, and two of a hen;
Devil-winged; dragon-bellied; grave-jawed, because grass
  Is a beard that's soon shaved, and grows seldom again
    Before it is summer; so cow all the rest;   45
    The new dodo is finished – oh come to my nest!'

Elizabeth Barrett (1806–61)

This brief selection presents some of the most important poems of Barrett's youth and early womanhood, before she composed the poetry for which she is now best known – Sonnets from the Portuguese *(1850),* Casa Guidi Windows *(1851), and* Aurora Leigh *(1856). One of her first idols was Byron, and as a teenager she enjoyed dressing up as his page. Her 'Stanzas on the Death of Lord Byron', among her earliest published poems, shows a deft control of the Spenserian stanza, the essentially slow tempo of which was suited to elegy (more so, perhaps, than to* Childe Harold's Pilgrimage*). Another elegy, 'Stanzas Addressed to Miss Landon', responds to Landon's elegy on Mrs Hemans, advising her to take comfort from Christian consolation. It is underpinned in part by Barrett's reservations about Landon's verse; as she told Lady Margaret Cocks on 9 December 1835, Landon 'is deficient in energy and condensation, as well as in variety. ... There is a vividness and a naturalness, both in the ideas and the expression of them – yes! And a pathos too! She is like a bird of few notes. They are few – but nature gave them!' (*The Brownings' Correspondence, *iii. 159). Barrett's concerns are sharply focused in the elegy she composed a year later for Landon, 'L.E.L.'s Last Question', which deals with Landon's mysterious death, apparently by prussic acid poisoning. Barrett's best work was yet to come, but her originality and unique abilities are evident even in her early work.*

From Globe and Traveller, no. 6733 (30 June 1824)

STANZAS ON THE DEATH OF LORD BYRON (COMPOSED SHORTLY AFTER 14 MAY 1824)

    λέγε πᾶσιν ἀπώλετο.[1]
    (Bion, *Lament for Adonis* 5)

    I am not what I have been.
    (Byron, *Childe Harold's Pilgrimage,* iv. 1662–3)

He *was,* and *is* not! Graecia's trembling shore,
  Sighing through all her palmy groves, shall tell
That Harold's pilgrimage at last is o'er;
    Mute the impassioned tongue, and tuneful shell,
    That erst was wont in noblest strains to swell!   5
  Hushed the proud shouts that rode th' Aegaean wave,

STANZAS ON THE DEATH OF LORD BYRON
[1] 'Tell everyone he is utterly lost.'

For lo! the great deliv'rer breathes farewell!
Gives to the world his mem'ry, and a grave –
And dies amidst the land he lived and fought to save!

Mourn, Hellas, mourn! and o'er thy widowed brow,   10
    For aye the cypress wreath of sorrow twine;
And in thy new-formed beauty, desolate, throw
    The fresh-culled flowers on *his* sepulchral shrine.
    Yes, let that heart, whose fervour was all thine,
In consecrated urn lamented be!   15
    That generous heart whose genius thrilled divine
Hath spent its last most glorious throb for thee –
Then sank amidst the storm that made thy children free.

Britannia's poet, Graecia's hero, sleeps!
    And Freedom, bending o'er the breathless clay,   20
Lifts up her voice, and in her wildness weeps!
    For *us*, a night hath clouded o'er our day
    And hushed the lips that breathed our fairest lay.
Alas! and must the British lyre resound
    A requiem, while the spirit wings away   25
Of *him* who on her strings such music found,
And taught her startling chords to breathe so sweet a sound?

The theme grows sadder – and my soul shall find
    A language in these tears. No more, no more!
Soon, midst the shrieking of the tossing wind,   30
    The 'dark blue depths'[2] he sang of shall have bore
    Our *all* of Byron to his native shore![3]
His grave is thick with voices, murm'ring here
    The awful tale of greatness swiftly o'er;
But mem'ry strives with death and, ling'ring near,   35
Shall consecrate the dust of Harold's lonely bier!

From New Monthly Magazine, 45 (1835) 82

STANZAS ADDRESSED TO MISS LANDON, AND SUGGESTED BY HER
'STANZAS ON THE DEATH OF MRS HEMANS' (SIGNED 'B.')

Thou bay-crowned living one,[1] who o'er
    The bay-crowned dead[2] art bowing,
And o'er the shadeless, moveless brow
    Thy human shadow throwing;

---

[2] Byron, *Manfred*, I. i. 76.
[3] Byron's body arrived in London 5 July 1824.

STANZAS ADDRESSED TO MISS LANDON
[1] Letitia Landon, who nevertheless died in the year
in which this poem was published.
[2] Felicia Hemans.

And o'er the sighless, songless lips   5
    The wail and music wedding,
Dropping o'er the tranquil eyes
    Tears not of *their* shedding³ –

Go take thy music from the dead,
    Whose silentness is sweeter;   10
Reserve thy tears for living brows,
    For whom such tears are meeter;
And leave the violets in the grass
    To brighten where thou treadest –
No flowers for her – oh, bring no flowers,   15
    Albeit 'Bring flowers',⁴ thou saidest.

But bring not near her solemn corse
    A type of human seeming;
Lay only dust's stern verity
    Upon her dust undreaming.   20
And while the calm perpetual stars
    Shall look upon it solely,
Her sphered soul shall look on *them*
    With eyes more bright and holy.

Nor mourn, oh living one, because   25
    Her part in life was mourning:
Would she have lost the poet's flame
    For anguish of the burning?
The minstrel harp, for the strained string?
    The tripod, for th' afflated   30
Woe? Or the vision, for those tears
    Through which it shone dilated?

Perhaps she shuddered while the world's
    Cold hand her brow was wreathing,
But wronged she ne'er that mystic breath   35
    Which breathed in all her breathing;
Which drew from rocky earth and man
    Abstractions high and moving –
Beauty, if not the beautiful,
    And love, if not the loving.   40

Such visionings have paled in sight
    The Saviour she descrieth,
And little recks who wreathed the brow

---

³ See Landon, 'Stanzas on the Death of Mrs He-   ⁴ See ibid., 1–5.
mans', 111.

That on His bosom lieth.
The whiteness of His innocence   45
  O'er all her garments flowing –
There learneth she that sweet 'new song'
  She will not mourn in knowing.

Be blessed, crowned and living one,
  And when thy dust decayeth,   50
May thine own England say for thee
  What now for her it sayeth –
'Albeit softly in our ears
  Her silver song was ringing,
The footsteps of her parting soul   55
  Were softer than her singing.'

From The Athenaeum, no. 587 (26 January 1839) 69

L.E.L.'s Last Question

'Do you think of me as I think of you,
My friends, my friends?'[1] She said it from the sea,
The English minstrel in her minstrelsy,
While under brighter skies than erst she knew[2]
Her heart grew dark, and gropèd as the blind,   5
To touch, across the waves, friends left behind –
'Do you think of me as I think of you?'

It seemed not much to ask – 'as I of you?'
We all do ask the same – no eyelids cover
Within the meekest eyes that question over;   10
And little in this world the loving do
But sit (among the rocks?) and listen for
The echo of their own love evermore;
Do you think of me as I think of you?

Love-learned, she had sung of only love,   15
And as a child asleep (with weary head
Dropped on the fairy book he lately read),
Whatever household noises round him move,
Hears in his dream some elfin turbulence –
Even so, suggestive to her inward sense,   20
All sounds of life assumed one tune of love.

L.E.L.'s Last Question
[1] Barrett's sister, Arabella, explained to Hugh Stuart Boyd on 28 Jan. 1839: 'I daresay you heard of Miss Landon's last letter that she wrote to some friend in England, a day or two before her death.... the question upon which these lines are written were the last words of her letter.'
[2] Landon died on the Gold Coast, where she was staying with her husband, George Maclean, Governor of Cape Coast Castle.

And when the glory of her dream withdrew,
When knightly gestes and courtly pageantries
Were broken in her visionary eyes
By tears, the solemn seas attested true –   25
Forgetting that sweet lute beside her hand,
She asked not, 'Do you praise me, oh my land?'
But 'Think ye of me, friends, as I of you?'

True heart to love, that pourèd many a year
Love's oracles for England, smooth and well –   30
Would God thou hadst an inward oracle
In that lone moment, to confirm thee dear!
For when thy questioned friends in agony
Made passionate response, 'We think of thee',
Thy place was in the dust – too deep to hear!   35

Could she not wait to catch the answering breath?
Was she content with that drear ocean's sound,
Dashing his mocking infinite around
The craver of a little love, beneath
Those stars, content – where last her song had gone?   40
They, mute and cold in radiant life, as soon
Their singer was to be, in darksome death!

Bring your vain answers, cry, 'We think of thee!'
How think ye of her? In the long ago
Delights, or crowned by new bays? Not so;   45
None smile, and none are crowned where lyeth she,
With all her visions unfulfilled – save one,
Her childhood's, of the palm-trees in the sun:
And lo, their shadow on her sepulchre!

Do you think of me as I think of you?   50
Oh friends, oh kindred, oh dear brotherhood
Of the whole world, what are we that we should
For covenants of long affection sue?
Why press so near each other, when the touch
Is barred by graves? Not much, and yet too much,   55
This 'Think upon me as I think of you.'

But while on mortal lips I shape anew
A sigh to mortal issues, verily
Above th' unshaken stars that see us die,
A vocal pathos rolls – and He who drew   60
All life from dust, and *for* all tasted death,
By death, and life, and love appealing, saith,
'Do you think of me as I think of you?'

From The Athenaeum, no. 783 (29 October 1842) 932

SONNET ON MR HAYDON'S PORTRAIT OF MR WORDSWORTH[1]

Wordsworth upon Helvellyn! Let the cloud
Ebb audibly along the mountain wind,
Then break against the rock, and show behind
The lowland valleys floating up to crowd
The sense with beauty. *He* with forehead bowed 5
And humble-lidded eyes, as one inclined
Before the sovran thoughts of his own mind,
And very meek with inspirations proud,
Takes here his rightful place as poet-priest,
By the high altar, singing prayer and prayer 10
To the yet higher heav'ns. A vision free
And noble, Haydon, hath thine art released[2] –
No portrait this, with academic air!
This is the poet and his poetry.

John Stuart Mill   (1806–73)

Philosopher and founder of the Utilitarian Society, 1823–6. In 1828 he suffered a severe depression which led him to reassess his aims and those of his colleagues. A reading of Wordsworth's poetry was instrumental in his recovery, as he revealed in the following passage from his Autobiography.

From Autobiography (1873)

A CRISIS IN MY MENTAL HISTORY (PP. 146–9)

This state of my thoughts and feelings made the fact of my reading Wordsworth for the first time (in the autumn of 1828) an important event in my life. I took up the collection of his poems from curiosity, with no expectation of mental relief from it, though I had before resorted to poetry with that hope. In the worst period of my depression, I had read through the whole of Byron (then new to me), to try whether a poet, whose peculiar department was supposed to be that of the intenser feelings, could rouse any feeling in me. As might be expected, I got no good from this reading, but the reverse. The poet's state of mind was too like my own. His was the lament of a man who had worn out all pleasures, and who seemed to think that life, to all who

---

SONNET ON MR HAYDON'S PORTRAIT OF MR WORD-
SWORTH
[1] Haydon's painting, *Wordsworth on Helvellyn*, was completed in 1842, and is now at the National Gallery, London. It is reproduced by Gill, *William Wordsworth: A Life* (Oxford, 1989), plate 17.

[2] Haydon, a friend of Barrett, forwarded a copy of the sonnet to Wordsworth prior to its publication. In an appreciative letter to her, 26 Oct. 1842, Wordsworth suggested a revision to lines 11–12: 'By a vision free / And noble, Haydon, is thine art released.'

1108 JOHN STUART MILL

possess the good things of it, must necessarily be the vapid, uninteresting thing which I found it. His Harold and Manfred had the same burden on them which I had, and I was not in a frame of mind to desire any comfort from the vehement sensual passion of his Giaours, or the sullenness of his Laras.[1]

But while Byron was exactly what did not suit my condition, Wordsworth was exactly what did. I had looked into *The Excursion* two or three years before, and found little in it, and I should probably have found as little had I read it at this time. But the miscellaneous poems in the two-volume edition of 1815 (to which little of value was added in the latter part of the author's life), proved to be the precise thing for my mental wants at that particular juncture.

In the first place, these poems addressed themselves powerfully to one of the strongest of my pleasurable susceptibilities – the love of rural objects and natural scenery, to which I had been indebted not only for much of the pleasure of my life, but quite recently for relief from one of my longest relapses into depression. In this power of rural beauty over me, there was a foundation laid for taking pleasure in Wordsworth's poetry – the more so, as his scenery lies mostly among mountains, which, owing to my early Pyreneean excursion,[2] were my ideal of natural beauty.

But Wordsworth would never have had any great effect on me, if he had merely placed before me beautiful pictures of natural scenery. Scott does this still better than Wordsworth, and a very second-rate landscape does it more effectually than any poet. What made Wordsworth's poems a medicine for my state of mind was that they expressed not mere outward beauty, but states of feeling, and of thought coloured by feeling, under the excitement of beauty. They seemed to be the very culture of the feelings which I was in quest of. In them I seemed to draw from a source of inward joy, of sympathetic and imaginative pleasure, which could be shared in by all human beings; which had no connection with struggle or imperfection, but would be made richer by every improvement in the physical or social condition of mankind. From them I seemed to learn what would be the perennial sources of happiness, when all the greater evils of life shall have been removed. And I felt myself at once better and happier as I came under their influence. There have certainly been, even in our own age, greater poets than Wordsworth, but poetry of deeper and loftier feeling could not have done for me at that time what his did. I needed to be made to feel that there was real, permanent happiness in tranquil contemplation. Wordsworth taught me this, not only without turning away from, but with a greatly increased interest in the common feelings and common destiny of human beings. And the delight which these poems gave me, proved that with culture of this sort, there was nothing to dread from the most confirmed habit of analysis.

At the conclusion of the *Poems* came the famous 'Ode', falsely called Platonic, 'Intimations of Immortality', in which, along with more than his usual sweetness of melody and rhythm (and along with the two passages of grand imagery but bad philosophy so often quoted), I found that he too had had similar experience to mine – that he also had felt that the first freshness of youthful enjoyment of life was not lasting, but that he had sought for compensation, and found it, in the way in which he was now teaching me to find it. The result was that I gradually, but completely, emerged from my habitual depression, and was never again subject to it. I long continued to value

[1] Byron's *The Giaour* (1813) and *Lara* (1814).

[2] Mill visited the Pyrenees during his stay in France in 1820–1.

Wordsworth less according to his intrinsic merits, than by the measure of what he had done for me. Compared with the greatest poets, he may be said to be the poet of unpoetical natures, possessed of quiet and contemplative tastes. But unpoetical natures are precisely those which require poetic cultivation. This cultivation Wordsworth is much more fitted to give than poets who are intrinsically far more poets than he.

Caroline Norton (1808–77)

One of the most popular poets and novelists of her day. 'My Childhood's Home' is a wistful, moving account of the loss of childhood vision. 'As when from Dreams Awaking' and 'Dreams' display her talent for evoking the borderland between reverie and reality.

From The Undying One (1830)
MY CHILDHOOD'S HOME

I have tasted each varied pleasure,
    And drunk of the cup of delight;
I have danced to the gayest measure
    In the halls of dazzling light.
I have dwelt in a blaze of splendour,   5
    And stood in the courts of kings;
I have snatched at each toy that could render
    More rapid the flight of Time's wings.
But vainly I've sought for joy or peace,
    In that life of light and shade;   10
And I turn with a sigh to my own dear home,
    The home where my childhood played!

When jewels are sparkling round me,
    And dazzling with their rays,
I weep for the ties that bound me   15
    In life's first early days.
I sigh for one of the sunny hours
    Ere day was turned to night,
For one of my nosegays of fresh wild-flowers,
    Instead of those jewels bright.   20
I weep when I gaze on the scentless buds
    Which never can bloom or fade,
And I turn with a sigh to those gay green fields –
    The home where my childhood played.

AS WHEN FROM DREAMS AWAKING

    As when from dreams awaking,
    The dim forms float away

Whose visioned smiles were making
Our darkness bright as day;
We vainly strive, while weeping,   5
From their shining spirit track
(Where they fled while we were sleeping)
To call those dear ones back!

Like the stars, some power divides them
From a world of want and pain;   10
They are there, but daylight hides them,
And we look for them in vain.
For a while we dwell with sadness
On the beauty of that dream,
Then turn, and hail with gladness   15
The light of morning's beam.

So when memory's power is wringing
Our lonely hearts to tears,
Dim forms around us bringing
That brightened former years,   20
Fond looks and low words spoken
Which those dreamy days could boast
Rise; till the spell be broken
We forget that they are lost!

But when the hour of darkness rolls   25
Like heavy night away,
And peace is stealing o'er our souls
Like the dawn of summer day,
The dim sweet forms that used to bless
Seem stealing from us too;   30
We loved them – but joy's sunniness
Hath hid them from our view!

Oh could day beam eternally,
And memory's power cease,
This world a world of light would be,   35
Our hearts were worlds of peace;
But dreams of joy return with night
And dwell upon the past –
And every grief that clouds our light
Reminds us of the last!   40

DREAMS

Surely I heard a voice – surely my name
Was breathed in tones familiar to my heart!
I listened – and the low wind stealing came,
In darkness and in silence to depart.

Surely I saw a form, a proud bright form,   5
Standing beside my couch! I raised mine eyes;
'Twas but a dim cloud, herald of a storm,
That floated through the grey and twilight skies.

Surely the brightness of the summer hour
Hath suddenly burst upon the circling gloom!   10
I dream – 'twas but the perfume of a flower,
Which the breeze wafted through the silent room.

Surely a hand clasped mine with greetings fond!
A name is murmured by my lips with pain;
Woe for that sound, woe for love's broken bond.   15
I start – I wake – I am alone again!

Alfred, Lord Tennyson   (1809–92)

With the publication of Tennyson's Poems, Chiefly Lyrical, *a new chapter in literary history began, just as* Lyrical Ballads *had signalled a similar change 32 years before. And just as Wordsworth and Coleridge referred to the work of Burns and Cowper, so Tennyson was steeped in the influence of the romantics. In the poetry of Shelley, Byron, Keats, Wordsworth, and Coleridge, Tennyson found the inspiration for a poetry of his own. Thus, if 'Mariana' reminds us of 'The Thorn', its tones and cadences are distinctive and new.*

From Poems, Chiefly Lyrical (1830)

MARIANA

Mariana in the moated grange.
(Measure for Measure)

I

With blackest moss the flowerplots
    Were thickly crusted, one and all,
The rusted nails fell from the knots
    That held the peach to the garden wall.
The broken sheds looked sad and strange,   5
    Unlifted was the clinking latch,
    Weeded and worn the ancient thatch
Upon the lonely moated grange.
        She only said, 'My life is dreary,
            He cometh not', she said;   10
        She said, 'I am aweary, aweary –
            I would that I were dead!'

II

Her tears fell with the dews at even,
   Her tears fell ere the dews were dried,
She could not look on the sweet heaven,   15
   Either at morn or eventide.
After the flitting of the bats,
   When thickest dark did trance the sky,
   She drew her casement curtain by,
And glanced athwart the glooming flats.   20
     She only said, 'The night is dreary,
       He cometh not', she said;
     She said, 'I am aweary, aweary –
       I would that I were dead!'

III

Upon the middle of the night,[1]   25
   Waking she heard the nightfowl crow;
The cock sung out an hour ere light;
   From the dark fen the oxen's low
Came to her; without hope of change,
   In sleep she seemed to walk forlorn,   30
   Till cold winds woke the grey-eyed morn[2]
About the lonely moated grange.
     She only said, 'The day is dreary,
       He cometh not', she said;
     She said, 'I am aweary, aweary –   35
       I would that I were dead!'

IV

About a stonecast from the wall
   A sluice with blackened waters slept,
And o'er it many, round and small,
   The clustered marish-mosses[3] crept.   40
Hard by a poplar shook alway,
   All silver-green with gnarled bark,
   For leagues no other tree did dark
The level waste, the rounding grey.
     She only said, 'My life is dreary,   45
       He cometh not', she said;

MARIANA
[1] Cf. Keats, 'Eve of St Agnes', 49.
[2] *Romeo and Juliet*, II. iii. 1.
[3] *marish-mosses* 'the little marsh-moss lumps that float to the surface of water' (Tennyson's note).

She said, 'I am aweary, aweary –
I would that I were dead!'

V

And ever when the moon was low,
    And the shrill winds were up and away,   50
In the white curtain, to and fro,
    She saw the gusty shadow sway.
But when the moon was very low,
    And wild winds bound within their cell,
    The shadow of the poplar fell   55
Upon her bed, across her brow.
    She only said, 'The night is dreary,
      He cometh not', she said;
    She said, 'I am aweary, aweary –
    I would that I were dead!'   60

VI

All day within the dreamy house
    The doors upon their hinges creaked,
The blue fly sung in the pane; the mouse
    Behind the mouldering wainscot shrieked,
Or from the crevice peered about.   65
    Old faces glimmered through the doors,
    Old footsteps trod the upper floors,
Old voices called her from without.
    She only said, 'My life is dreary,
      He cometh not', she said;   70
    She said, 'I am aweary, aweary –
    I would that I were dead!'

VII

The sparrow's chirrup on the roof,
    The slow clock ticking, and the sound
Which to the wooing wind aloof   75
    The poplar made, did all confound
Her sense; but most she loathed the hour
    When the thick-moted sunbeam lay
    Athwart the chambers, and the day
Downsloped was westering in his bower.[4]   80

---

[4] Cf. Milton, *Lycidas*, 31: 'had sloped his westering wheel'.

Then, said she, 'I am very dreary,
    He will not come,' she said;
She wept, 'I am aweary, aweary –
    Oh God, that I were dead!'

Bibliography

This bibliography is restricted chiefly to primary sources and works of reference mentioned in the notes or used in the course of assembling this anthology. It does not repeat details of the books from which the various items have been taken.

Bacon, Francis, *The Works of Francis Bacon*, ed. James Spedding, Robert Leslie Ellis, and Douglas Denon Heath (7 vols, London, 1857–9).

Barker-Benfield, B. C., *Shelley's Guitar* (Oxford: Bodleian Library, 1992).

Barnes, Warner, *A Bibliography of Elizabeth Barrett Browning* (Austin, Tex.: University of Texas and Baylor University, 1967).

Bentley, G. E., Jr., *Blake Books* (Oxford: Clarendon Press, 1977).

Bion, *Bucolici Graeci*, ed. A. S. F. Gow (Oxford: Clarendon Press, 1952).

Blake, William, The Illuminated Books (The William Blake Trust/The Tate Gallery): *Jerusalem*, ed. Morton D. Paley (1991); *Songs of Innocence and Experience*, ed. Andrew Lincoln (1991).

——, *William Blake's Writings*, ed. G. E. Bentley, Jr. (Oxford: Clarendon Press, 1978).

——, *The Complete Poetry and Prose of William Blake*, ed. David V. Erdman, commentary by Harold Bloom (New York: Anchor Books, 1982).

——, *The Letters of William Blake*, ed. Geoffrey Keynes, 3rd edn. (Oxford: Clarendon Press, 1980).

Browning, Elizabeth Barrett, *The Brownings' Correspondence*, ed. Philip Kelley, Ronald Hudson, and Scott Lewis (9 vols, Winfield, Kan.: Wedgestone Press, 1984–91).

Burnet, Thomas, *Archaeologiae Philosophicae* (London, 1692).

Burns, Robert, *The Letters of Robert Burns*, ed. G. Ross Roy (2 vols, Oxford: Clarendon Press, 1985).

Byron, George Gordon, 6th Baron, *The Complete Poetical Works*, ed. Jerome J. McGann and Barry Weller (7 vols., Oxford: Clarendon Press, 1980–93).

——, *Byron's Letters and Journals*, ed. Leslie A. Marchand (12 vols, London: John Murray, 1973–82)

Chaucer, Geoffrey, *Poetical Works*, ed. F. N. Robinson (Oxford: Clarendon Press, 1974).

Cicero, *Laelius, On Friendship and The Dream of Scipio*, ed. J. G. F. Powell (Warminster: Aris and Phillips, 1990).

——, *Tusculan Disputations*, tr. J. E. King (London: Heinemann, 1927).

Clare, John, *The Early Poems of John Clare 1804–1822*, ed. Eric Robinson and David Powell (2 vols, Oxford: Clarendon Press, 1989).

——, *The Later Poems of John Clare 1837–1864*, ed. Eric Robinson and David Powell (2 vols, Oxford: Clarendon Press, 1984).

——, *The Shepherd's Calendar*, ed. Eric Robinson and Geoffrey Summerfield (London: Oxford University Press, 1973).

Coleridge, Samuel Taylor, *The Collected Works of Samuel Taylor Coleridge*, general ed. Kathleen Coburn. Bollingen Series 75 (Princeton, N.J.: Princeton University Press): I. *Lectures 1795 on Politics and Religion*, ed. Lewis Patton and Peter Mann (1971); II. *The Watchman*, ed. Lewis Patton (1970); III. *Essays on his Times*, ed. David V. Erdman (3 vols, 1978); IV. *The Friend*, ed. Barbara Rooke (2 vols, 1969); V. *Lectures 1808–1819 On Literature*, ed. R. A. Foakes (2 vols, 1987); VI. *Lay Sermons*, ed. R. J. White (1972); VII. *Biographia Literaria*, ed. James Engell and W. Jackson Bate (2 vols, 1983); X. *On the Constitution of the Church and State*, ed. John Colmer (1976); XII. *Marginalia*, ed. George Whalley and H. J. Jackson (5 vols, 1980–); XIII. *Logic*, ed. J. R. de J. Jackson (1981); XIV. *Table Talk*, ed. Carl Woodring (2 vols, 1990).

——, *Biographia Literaria, or Biographical Sketches of my Literary Life and Opinions*, ed. Henry Nelson and Sara Coleridge (2 vols, 1847).

——, *Fears in Solitude, France an Ode, and Frost at Midnight* (London, 1798).

——, *Letters*, ed. E. L. Griggs (6 vols, Oxford: Clarendon Press, 1956–71).

——, *Notebooks*, ed. Kathleen Coburn et al. (New York: Pantheon Books, 1957–).

——, *Poetical Works*, ed. E. H. Coleridge (2 vols, Oxford: Clarendon Press, 1912).

——, *Coleridge's Dejection: The Earliest Manuscripts and the Earliest Printings*, ed. Stephen M. Parrish (Ithaca, N.Y.: Cornell University Press, 1988).

——, *Christabel*, ed. E. H. Coleridge (London: Henry Frowde, 1907).

Crabbe, George, *The Complete Poetical Works*, ed. Norma Dalrymple-Champneys and Arthur Pollard (3 vols, Oxford: Clarendon Press, 1988).

De Quincey, Thomas, *Collected Writings*, ed. David Masson (14 vols, Edinburgh: A.& C. Black, 1889–90).

——, *Confessions of an English Opium-Eater and Other Writings*, ed. Grevel Lindop (Oxford: Oxford University Press, 1985).

——, *De Quincey as Critic*, ed. John E. Jordan (London: Routledge, 1973).

Gray, Thomas, *The Poetical Works of Thomas Gray and William Collins*, ed. Roger Lonsdale (Oxford: Oxford University Press, 1977).

Greene, Robert, *The Plays and Poems of Robert Greene*, ed. J. Churton Collins (2 vols, Oxford: Clarendon Press, 1895).

Grylls, R. Glynn, *Mary Shelley* (London: Oxford University Press, 1938).

Haydon, Benjamin Robert, *The Diary of Benjamin Robert Haydon*, ed. Willard Bissell Pope (5 vols, Cambridge, Mass.: Harvard University Press, 1960–3).

Hazlitt, William, *The Round Table* (2 vols, London, 1817).

——, *The Spirit of the Age* (London, 1825).

——, *The Spirit of the Age*, ed. E. D. Mackerness (London: Collins, 1969).

——, *Works* ed. P. P. Howe (21 vols, London: Dent, 1930–4).

Hogg, James, *Selected Poems and Songs*, ed. David Groves (Edinburgh: Scottish Academic Press, 1986).

Horace, *The Odes and Epodes*, tr. C. E. Bennett (Cambridge, Mass.: Harvard University Press, 1936).

——, *Satires, Epistles and Ars Poetica*, tr. H. Rushton Fairclough (Cambridge, Mass.: Harvard University Press, 1942).

Hunt, James Henry Leigh, *Autobiography*, ed. J. E. Morpurgo (London: Cresset Press, 1949).

——, *Foliage* (London, 1818).

Hussey, Cyril C., 'Fresh Light on the Poems of Mary Lamb', *Supplement to C.L.S. Bulletin* no. 213 (Jan. 1972).

Jackson, J. R. de J., *Romantic Poetry by Women: A Bibliography 1770–1835* (Oxford: Clarendon Press, 1993).

Keats, John, *The Letters of John Keats 1814–1821*, ed. Hyder E. Rollins (2 vols, Cambridge, Mass.: Harvard University Press, 1958).

——, *The Poems of John Keats*, ed. Jack Stillinger (Cambridge, Mass.: Harvard University Press, 1978).

——, *The Poems of John Keats*, ed. Miriam Allott (London: Longman, 1970).

——, *The Complete Poems*, ed. John Barnard, 2nd edn. (Harmondsworth: Penguin, 1977).

Lamb, Charles, *The Letters of Charles and Mary Lamb*, ed. E. V. Lucas (3 vols, London: Dent, 1935).

——, *The Letters of Charles and Mary Anne Lamb*, ed. Edwin W. Marrs, Jr. (3 vols, Ithaca, N.Y.: Cornell University Press, 1975–8).

——, *Lamb as Critic*, ed. Roy Park (London: Routledge, 1980).

Landor, Walter Savage, *Landor as Critic*, ed. Charles L. Proudfit (London: Routledge, 1979).

——, *Selected Poetry and Prose*, ed. Keith Hanley (Manchester: Carcanet, 1981).

MacGillivray, J. R., *Keats: A Bibliography and Reference Guide* (Toronto: University of Toronto Press, 1949).

Medwin, Thomas, *Conversations of Lord Byron: Noted during a Residence with his Lordship at Pisa, in the Years 1821 and 1822*, 2nd edn, (London, 1824).

Milton, John, *The Poetical Works of John Milton*, ed. Helen Darbishire (2 vols, Oxford: Clarendon Press, 1952–5).

Moschus, *The Greek Bucolic Poets*, tr. J. M. Edmonds (Cambridge, Mass.: Harvard University Press, 1977).

Plotinus, *Enneads*, tr. A. H. Armstrong (7 vols, London: Heinemann, 1966–88).

Pope, Alexander, *The Twickenham Edition of the Works of Alexander Pope*, general ed. John Butt (London: Methuen and Co. Ltd): I. *Pastoral Poetry and An Essay on Criticism*, ed. E. Audra and Aubrey Williams (1961); II. *The Rape of the Lock*, ed. Geoffrey Tillotson, 3rd edn, (1962); III. i. *An Essay on Man*, ed. Maynard Mack (1950); III. ii. *Epistles to Several Persons*, ed. F. W. Bateson, 2nd edn, (1961); IV. *Imitations of Horace*, ed. John Butt, 2nd edn, (1953); VII-VIII. *The Iliad*, ed. Maynard Mack (1967); IX-X. *The Odyssey*, ed. Maynard Mack (1967); XI. *Index*, ed. Maynard Mack (1969).

Prance, Claude A., *Companion to Charles Lamb* (London: Mansell, 1983)

Roff, Renee, *A Bibliography of the Writings of Charles and Mary Lamb* (New York: Nicholas T. Smith, 1979).

Rogers, Neville, *Shelley at Work*, 2nd edn, (Oxford: Clarendon Press, 1967).

Rousseau, J. J., *Lettres de deux amans, habitans d'une petite ville au pied des Alpes* (6 vols, Amsterdam, 1761).

Shakespeare, William, *The Riverside Shakespeare*, ed. G. Blakemore Evans (Boston: Houghton Mifflin, 1974).

Shelley, Mary, *The Journals of Mary Shelley 1814–1844*, ed. Paula R. Feldman and Diana Scott-Kilvert (2 vols, Oxford: Clarendon Press, 1987).

Shelley, Percy Bysshe, *Shelley's Adonais*, ed. Anthony D. Knerr (New York: Columbia University Press, 1984).

——, *Shelley's Poetry and Prose*, ed. Donald H. Reiman and Sharon B. Powers (New York: W. W. Norton, 1977).

——, *Shelley's Prometheus Unbound: The Text and the Drafts*, ed. Lawrence John Zillman (New Haven, Conn.: Yale University Press, 1968).

——, *Shelley's Prose*, ed. David Lee Clark (London: Fourth Estate, 1988).

——, *The Poems of Shelley*, ed. Geoffrey Matthews and Kelvin Everest (London: Longman, 1989).

——, *The Letters of Percy Bysshe Shelley*, ed. Frederick L. Jones (2 vols, Oxford: Clarendon Press, 1964).

——, *Shelley and his Circle*, ed. K. N. Cameron and Donald H. Reiman (8 vols, Cambridge, Mass.: Harvard University Press, 1961–86).

——, *Posthumous Poems of Shelley*, ed. Irving Massey (Montreal: McGill–Queen's University Press, 1969).

——, *The Complete Poetical Works of Percy Bysshe Shelley*, ed. Neville Rogers (2 vols, Oxford: Clarendon Press, 1972–5).

Sterne, Laurence, *A Sentimental Journey*, ed. Gardner D. Stout, Jr. (Berkeley and Los Angeles: University of California Press, 1967).

Stillinger, Jack, *The Texts of Keats' Poems* (Cambridge, Mass.: Harvard University Press, 1974).

Theocritus, ed. A. S. F. Gow, 2nd edn, (2 vols., Cambridge: Cambridge University Press, 1952).

Thomson, James, *Liberty, The Castle of Indolence, and Other Poems*, ed. James Sambrook (Oxford: Clarendon Press, 1986).

Wollstonecraft, Mary, *A Vindication of the Rights of Woman*, ed. Carol H. Poston (New York: W. W. Norton, 1975).

Woof, Robert, *Shelley: An Ineffectual Angel?* (Grasmere: The Wordsworth Trust, 1992).

——, *Thomas De Quincey 1785–1859* (Grasmere: The Wordsworth Trust, 1985).

——, *Byron: A Dangerous Romantic?* (Grasmere: The Wordsworth Trust, 1989).

Wordsworth, Dorothy, *Journals of Dorothy Wordsworth*, ed. Ernest De Selincourt (2 vols, London: Macmillan & Co. Ltd., 1941).

——, *The Grasmere Journals*, ed. Pamela Woof (Oxford: Clarendon Press, 1991).

Wordsworth, Jonathan, Michael C. Jaye, and Robert Woof, *William Wordsworth and the Age of British Romanticism* (New Brunswick, N.J.: Rutgers University Press, 1987).

Wordsworth, William, *The Cornell Wordsworth*, general ed. Stephen M. Parrish (Ithaca, N.Y.: Cornell University Press): *The Borderers*, ed. Robert Osborn (1982); *Descriptive Sketches*, ed. Eric Birdsall (1984); *An Evening Walk*, ed. James Averill (1984); *The Fourteen-Book Prelude*, ed. W. J. B. Owen (1985); *Home at Grasmere*, ed. Beth Darlington (1977); *Lyrical Ballads, and Other Poems 1797–1800*, ed. James Butler and Karen Green (1992); *Peter Bell*, ed. John Jordan (1985); *Poems in Two Volumes, and Other Poems, 1800–1807*, ed. Jared Curtis (1985); *The Prelude, 1798–1799*, ed. Stephen Parrish (1977); *The Ruined Cottage and The Pedlar*, ed. James Butler (1979); *Shorter Poems, 1807–1820*, ed.

Carl H. Ketcham (1989); *The Thirteen-Book Prelude*, ed. Mark L. Reed (2 vols, 1991); *The White Doe of Rylstone*, ed. Kristine Dugas (1988).

——, *The Letters of William and Dorothy Wordsworth: The Early Years 1787–1805*, ed. Ernest De Selincourt, rev. Chester L. Shaver (Oxford: Clarendon Press, 1967).

——, *The Letters of William and Dorothy Wordsworth: The Middle Years 1806–1820*, ed. Ernest De Selincourt, rev. Mary Moorman and Alan G. Hill (2 vols, Oxford: Clarendon Press, 1969–70).

——, *The Letters of William and Dorothy Wordsworth: The Later Years 1821–1853*, ed. Ernest De Selincourt, rev. Alan G. Hill (4 vols, Oxford: Clarendon Press, 1978–88).

——, *The Letters of William and Dorothy Wordsworth: A Supplement of New Letters*, ed. Alan G. Hill (Oxford: Clarendon Press, 1993).

——, *Correspondence of Henry Crabb Robinson with the Wordsworth Circle 1808–1866*, ed. Edith J. Morley (2 vols, Oxford: Clarendon Press, 1927).

——, *The Poetical Works of William Wordsworth*, ed. Ernest De Selincourt and Helen Darbishire (5 vols, Oxford: Clarendon Press, 1940–9).

——, *The Prose Works of William Wordsworth*, ed. W. J. B. Owen and Jane Worthington Smyser (3 vols, Oxford: Clarendon Press, 1974).

——, *The Prelude: 1799, 1805, 1850*, ed. Jonathan Wordsworth, M. H. Abrams, and Stephen Gill (New York: W. W. Norton, 1979).

——, *The Prelude*, ed. Ernest De Selincourt, rev. Helen Darbishire, 2nd edn, (Oxford: Clarendon Press, 1959).

——, *The Fenwick Notes of William Wordsworth*, ed. Jared Curtis (London: Bristol Classical Press, 1993).

Young, Edward, *Night Thoughts*, ed. Stephen Cornford (Cambridge: Cambridge University Press, 1989).

Index to the Notes

Index of Titles and First Lines